The Good Hotel Guide 1991

The Good Hotel Guide 1991

*Britain and Western Europe
– also Morocco and Turkey*

Editor: Hilary Rubinstein

Managing Editor and Editor for the British Isles:
Caroline Raphael

Continental Editor:
John Ardagh

Contributing Editor:
Susan Gillotti

MACMILLAN
LONDON

Published 1990 by
MACMILLAN LONDON LIMITED
4 Little Essex Street
London WC2R 3LF
and Basingstoke

Associated companies in Auckland, Delhi, Dublin, Gaborone, Hamburg,
Harare, Hong Kong, Johannesburg, Kuala Lumpur, Lagos, Manzini,
Melbourne, Mexico City, Nairobi, New York, Singapore and Tokyo

Editorial assistants: Katinka Ardagh, Frances Bull, Philippa Carlile,
Susan Carlile, Mari Roberts

Illustrations by Tony Matthews
Cover illustration by Garnet Henderson

A CIP catalogue record for this book is available from the British Library

ISBN 0 333 54027 1

Computer typeset by SB Datagraphics Ltd.
Colchester, Essex
Printed in England by Clays Ltd, St Ives plc

Contents

Acknowledgements

The Editor is grateful to Pepita Aris and Alex Liddell for contributing introductions to the Spanish and Portuguese sections. The Appendix "A room with a superfluity" by Miles Kington was first published in *The Independent* on October 23, 1989, © Miles Kington 1989.

A note for new readers

This is an annual guide to hotels, inns and guest houses in the British Isles and the continent of Europe (also Morocco and Turkey) that are of unusual character and quality. The entries are based on reports from readers who write to us when they come across an establishment that has given them out-of-the-ordinary satisfaction, and who also send us their comments, critical or appreciative, when they visit places already included in the Guide. Our task is to collate these reports, check and verify them, making inspections where necessary, and select those which we consider make the grade. No cash changes hands at any point: contributors are not rewarded for writing to us; hotels do not pay for their entries. The editor and his staff accept no free hospitality.

We do not attempt to be comprehensive. There are many blank areas on our maps, including many major cities which lack a single entry. We see no point in lowering our standards in order to recommend an indifferent establishment as "the best available". But of course we are always particularly glad to receive nominations for hotels in a town or a region that is poorly represented.

Most of our entries are small establishments in the hands of resident owners. We don't have any prima-facie objection to large hotels or those run by managers, except that, in our experience, they normally fail to provide the welcome and care for guests' comforts that can be found in the best of the small individually owned hostelries. This failure is particularly evident in the case of hotels owned by chains, which explains why there are few such entries in these pages.

The entries in the book cover a wide range. People want different things from a hotel according to whether they are making a single-night stop or spending a whole holiday in one place, whether they have young children with them, whether they are visiting a city or staying in the remote countryside, and according to their age and means. We make no claims of universal compatibility, but we hope that our descriptions will help you to find hotels that suit your tastes, needs and purse. If an entry has misled you, we beg you to use one of the report forms at the back of the book and tell us, in order that we can do better next time; and we hope that you will also write to us if you have found the Guide useful and a hotel has fulfilled your expectations: endorsement and criticism are both essential if the Guide is to achieve its purpose. Hotels are dropped unless we get positive feedback on them.

Introduction

This 1991 edition marks a new chapter in the history of the Guide. Since 1980, two years after the Guide was founded, we have been published by the Consumers' Association. I was delighted when the CA invited me to join them, and to have the Good Hotel Guide published alongside the Good Food Guide. The GFG has been a model for this Guide. We have in common a determination to describe the shortcomings as well as the virtues of an establishment and to use reports from discriminating readers to provide constant fine-tuning for our entries. And we take identical vows of chastity – no free hospitality, no payment for entries.

Our association with the CA has been a fruitful one, not least for the opportunity we have had to share reports with our older sibling and to enjoy the benefits of their mail-order marketing. Sales of both works have risen steadily during this past decade, and they are now firmly established as leaders in their respective fields. Sadly, this valuable connection has come to an end. A new director at the CA has decreed that the Association must own the copyright in all its publications, and last year required me to sell the copyright if the Guide were to continue under its umbrella. I was invited to continue as editor for the first two years after the sale, on terms to be agreed, but the day-to-day management of the Guide would immediately be transferred to the CA's offices. I did not care for their offer, and, as will be evident, have made other publishing arrangements. But in all respects except the publishing imprint, the 1991 Guide is identical to its predecessors – same principles, same style, same staff.

A change of publisher might seem a purely domestic matter were it not that, within months of my declining their offer to purchase this Guide, the CA announced that they were bringing out their own hotel guide for 1991 – presumably to replace the GHG in the annual mailing offer. A hostile act? At the time of writing, I clearly have no knowledge of the character or policy of this rival publication, to be called the *Which? Hotel Guide*, but am concerned that readers may only too easily confuse the two works. *Caveat emptor* – let the consumer beware!

Perhaps this is an appropriate moment to set out what I consider to be a key characteristic of this Guide – namely, that its entries are based not on any brief single-visit assessment but on the collation of comments from many sorts of readers over many years, and at many times of the year – hotels often wear a different face in the high season. And this steady stream of reports is backed up when necessary by an anonymous inspection – bed and breakfast, and of course dinner if the hotel has a restaurant. We ask our readers to write to us only when they have spent at least one night at a hotel because we know that, however agreeable a room may look when you are being shown round, however attractive the menu, the actual experience of staying can give a very different impression: plumbing, ventilation, insulation, heating, lighting, beds and bedding will only reveal their strengths or weaknesses to the overnight visitor. And how often breakfast the next morning can let the side down – or perhaps redeem a hotel that has served no more than an average meal the night before. Always of key importance is the welcome of the owner or manager sustained over the duration of a visit.

We are far from infallible, but after 13 years we do have a certain confidence in our method of selection and on the judgment of correspondents with whom we have built up a close relationship over more than a decade. And we reckon that we can almost always distinguish between the banal collusive report, inspired (but misguidedly) by the innkeeper, from the genuine comments which provide the backbone of our citations.

Forecasting the nineties

Greenhouse effect or not, the weather is more than usually unpredictable these days – an ultra-hot summer followed by a winter of catastrophic gales and flood. The political barometer, too, is spectacularly volatile – as though a forty-year ice-age has suddenly ended, releasing people power of an unknown strength and direction in many parts of the globe.

Economic forecasting – for the catering trade as much as for any other kind of business – is equally tricky even in the short term. World tourism promises to grow for many years, but last year the number of Britons going abroad exceeded the number of tourists arriving here from foreign parts. Meanwhile, the domestic climate remains unsettled and disheartening: exchange rates are turbulent, inflation shows no sign of easing, mortgages and bank rates have spiralled upwards; the Uniform Business Rate and the poll tax are further causes for anxiety. No wonder British hotels are jittery. They experienced a downturn of trade in 1989 and 1990 promises to be worse – far worse. Small hotels, guest houses and B&Bs are specially disadvantaged: many expect to have to close or else to raise their prices by up to 25 percent because they will be required to pay both the UBR and the poll tax. Already, since the last edition, more Guide hotels than ever before have changed hands or are up for sale – and thus have lost their entries. Among the notable dropouts in the past twelve months are *Hintlesham Hall*, *Homewood Park*, Hinton Charterhouse, *The Draycott*, London (winner of a 1990 César), *The Castle*, Taunton, and *The Feathers*, Woodstock. Other sales of notable hotels are rumoured to be imminent.

We hope that prospects will look less bleak a year hence. In the meantime, however, it could be prudent to check when booking that there has been no change of ownership. There is nothing more depressing than to arrive at a hotel expecting to be welcomed by one *patron* and finding yourself in the hands of another or possibly a manager when you have been expecting a resident proprietor; even worse, a hotel may have closed.

The disparity between the tariffs of British hotels and their continental equivalents has been a sore subject for many years past, and has its roots in a host of unrelated factors: among them the price of land, the cost of loans, and the continental traditions of family ownership of inns through many generations. No one would accuse the majority of owners of the British hotels in this Guide of making an unholy profit. But now, even without the Channel Tunnel and the new faster surface vessels to the European mainland, even without 1992, the lure of "abroad" is bound to grow.

An extra incentive for the individual traveller this year is the opening, for the first time in two generations, of the borders to Eastern Europe. Accommodation may be spartan, but we look forward to the day when we can recommend hotels of character throughout the USSR and the former Soviet bloc, as an alternative to an itinerary of *Holiday Inns* and *Hiltons* or their Eastern European equivalents. We had an appendix on Czech and Bulgarian hotels in 1988, but, not surprisingly, had little or no feedback. If at all possible, we plan to have sections on at least one or two countries which were formerly behind the old Iron Curtain. If you can help, please may we hear from you?

Giving little children a chance

The Guide's chief concern is to assist its readers to find enjoyable lodgings, but inevitably we find ourselves discussing complaints that surface in our correspondence and from time to time we take up the cudgels on certain public matters.

We raised one such issue last year: the large number of British hotels with entries in the Guide that impose restrictions on children. We urged hoteliers who at present impose a ban on children because of the fear that they would drive customers away to try lifting or modifying their restrictions and see what happens. We also urged parents to take *their* responsibilities seriously: to ensure, so far as possible, that their child should not become a nuisance to fellow guests.

We were astonished to find what a storm of controversy was aroused by what we believed to be mild strictures and modest suggestions. A spokesman for the British Hotels, Restaurants and Caterers Association was quoted as saying that he had never heard of hotels placing restrictions on children. Our eyes popped. In 1990 we listed 120 hotels in Britain that imposed restrictions on children – one-third of our British entries. And this is just a trawl of one part of the ocean: the total number of hotels that have, as it were, a sign on the door saying "Room at the Inn, but not for children" must run into thousands.

But it wasn't just the diehards of the hotel industry that took umbrage at our words. Our comments touched a raw nerve with many members of the public. "In our experience, hotels and children don't mix," wrote one correspondent. "If parents were a little more responsible in looking after their children, perhaps I would feel less antagonistic towards their little darlings. I am of the old school who made their children behave. Now my family has grown up, I feel I am entitled to expect peace and quiet on holiday and not to have to forfeit a swim just because the pool is hogged by the children. So hurrah for hotels that say 'Sorry, no children!'" Another writer called children "generally demanding, distracting and disruptive pests". A third invoked lager louts and football hooligans as arguments for keeping children out of their favourite havens of p and q. What dismayed us about some of these letters was the evidence that their writers really did find children abhorrent.

Hotelkeepers took issue with us too – not necessarily because of any child-phobia, but, at least in some cases, because they felt they were offering a public service. "We mainly cater for *tired parents*" wrote Francis Coulson of *Sharrow Bay*. Tricia Howland of *The Steppes*, Ullingswick, told us that we had completely overlooked the views of the public: "We find that in the school holidays our hotel is nearly always full of school teachers. Why? Because we don't take children. It's a heavy plus-factor for many hotels."

We accept that parents – teachers, too – do want to get away from children at times, theirs or anyone else's. And it is of course true that children can misbehave and upset fellow-guests. But so indeed can adults. We find raucous drunken behaviour much more offensive than children's high spirits, even if they occasionally get out of hand. But children do have other drawbacks for the hotelier. They can damage the fabric of rooms – adults can, too, though not usually to the same extent. They may need to be provided with special meals – more work for the staff. Their rooms are often let at a discount, so less profit. And – a woeful shame – they don't contribute to the takings at the bar.

Hoteliers are in the business of making money. We assume that those who impose these restrictions consider it is good for their business but we are far from convinced that they are right. We believe that they are driving potential customers abroad, where hotels really do cherish young children rather than – at best – merely tolerate them, and they are also failing to enfranchise the next generation.

There are hotels in Britain and Ireland that take pride in caring for children as well as adults without either age-group feeling short-changed. But we get to hear of far too few. We would greatly appreciate feedback from parents who have discovered hotels that cater for children's needs but are not exclusively child-oriented and which provide decent cooking at night as well as Marmite and fish fingers at high tea.

All the child-friendly hoteliers we have spoken to are convinced that their policy is rewarding in money as well as in human terms. And we appreciated the remark of Eric Marsh, who has been extending a welcome to children at the *Cavendish*, Baslow (q.v.) for the past 15 years: "It is indeed strange that in Britain one can walk up to the door of many hotels with a child in one hand and a dog in the other, and be obliged to leave the child outside."

We have no wish to see restrictions on children made a statutory offence as in some countries abroad. But we do profoundly hope that the reluctance of many British hotels to give children a chance will change in time. We are delighted to find our views echoed by the distinguished consultant paediatrician, Dr Alan Lucas, of the Medical Research Council's Dunn Nutrition Unit at Cambridge, who has contributed to the appendix on page 801.

Service charges and tipping – a reprise

Another issue, which has been on our agenda for many years past, has been the imposition of service charges and the nudging for tips. We are glad to report that, slowly but inexorably, these regrettable practices are being eroded, and senior members of the catering industry have begun to speak out against them. The 1989 Consumer Protection Act and its recommended Code of Conduct has played a part in changing attitudes. Service charges, the bastard offspring of the mandatory salt-and-pepper charge imposed by Blackpool landladies in the bad old days, are appearing less often though you will still find plenty of establishments that add a "discretionary" 10 percent or 12.5 percent – and still leave the bottom line of the credit voucher open. We are sure such connivances to extract more from the unwary customer will continue for many years yet – but if you choose to show displeasure or disdain for such tactics, they must in time become obsolete. As for tipping, we hope that readers will refrain from slipping something extra into the open palm unless they have received some special service beyond what one has the right to expect of a service industry.

A royal flush of freebies

How can hotels compete more effectively in the face of adverse trade winds? One often-tried recipe is to offer that "little bit extra" – and the 1980s has witnessed an explosion of what Miles Kington in our second Appendix calls Superfluities. We are not so ascetic as to object to a bowl of fruit, a vase of flowers, even a few biscuits or chocolates to welcome us to our room, but we have always been ambivalent about the profusion of "sweeteners" which inevitably have to be paid for by a higher tariff.

At times we have been tempted to feel that the whole freebie business had gone a bit out of hand, but this was before we received a letter from the *Beaufort Hotel*, London. Its owner had had a shockingly simple idea: that what she charged her guests for a night's stay should be genuinely comprehensive – covering everything you can think of except phone calls and personal laundry. Everything? Well, her letter enclosed a list of 36 features of her establishment. It started with complimentary room service (full meals available), complimentary 24-hour bar, free membership of a health club, air-conditioning, remote control TV, video and a video library, Sony Walkman and a cassette library, and ending 20 items or so later with teddy bear, weight scales, free clothes pressing and a jogging map. The rates at *The Beaufort* are on a par with other sophisticated bed-and-breakfasts in this part of London, but its value, if you care to avail yourself of all those free meals and free drinks available on the tariff, is of a different order altogether. We are assured that its prodigious hospitality is rarely abused. And, incidentally, there is no service charge at this hotel and no tipping – a practice which the owner considers degrading.

The Beaufort appears to be ahead of its rivals not by an inch or so but by approximately seven leagues. Will other hotels feel obliged to follow in its footsteps?

It is a sobering thought. Fortunately, this Guide does not cater only for those who can afford to splash out on the Beaufort scale, and we are as intent as ever to propose agreeable accommodation for the mid-price as well as for the budget customer. To help readers in the latter category find more quickly lodgings that will suit their purse, we have this year for the first time indicated with a "Budget" label those hotels, guest houses and inns offering dinner, bed and breakfast at up to about £40 per person (or its foreign currency equivalent), or B&B around £25 and an evening meal around £15. But we would emphasise that these are only rough guides, given inflation, fluctuations of the exchange rate, seasonal changes of tariff, varying prices of rooms in some hotels and so forth, and they do not always apply to single accommodation.

A final word of exhortation

Since it would be foolish to expect that all those readers who have been in the habit of acquiring the Guide from the direct-mail department of Consumers' Association will now buy their copy from a bookshop, we must inevitably expect some fall in total sales. And this in turn will impair the flow of feedback on existing entries and the nomination of new ones. May we therefore implore those of our readers who care about what this Guide stands for to be more generous than ever in supporting the cause. If you have the impulse to tell us about the wonderful or crumby hotel you have just stayed at, do not wait for your emotions to be recollected in tranquillity. Write now!

Bon voyage!

HILARY RUBINSTEIN

The César Awards 1991

In 1984, as a way of demonstrating our appreciation for different kinds of excellence among hotels in Britain and Ireland, we inaugurated annual awards which we called Césars, after the most celebrated of all hoteliers, César Ritz. Hotels of the grandest sort, like the finest restaurants, never lack public attention, but there are many other more modest establishments that are also supremely good in their own way. Their owners are dedicated to their vocation and commonly work from seven in the morning till one in the morning; it was time, we felt, that their contribution to innkeeping should be recognised and honoured along with the professionals at the top of the ladder.

This year, as previously, we have bestowed our accolades on ten hotels, inns and guest houses each of which we consider to be outstanding in its own class. As usual we have given a César for sympathetic eccentricity, but otherwise categories continue to change from year to year. Previous César winners, provided the establishments are still in the same hands and as good as ever, are also indicated.

AWARD	WINNER
The epitome of the grand English country house hotel at its luxurious best	Gravetye Manor East Grinstead, Sussex The serene beauty of an Elizabethan manor house is matched by the grace of William Robinson's natural garden; cuisine and service are of a piece. After 34 years, Peter Herbert's elysium has become a model for all aspiring country hoteliers.
Most auspicious hotel opening in 1990	Llangoed Hall Llyswen, Powys Spectacular restoration of a great country house and its grounds beside the Wye wins *Llangoed Hall* our newcomer of the year award. And *Llangoed* could well become the premier hotel of the Principality.
The embodiment of Scottish hospitality	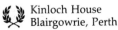 Kinloch House Blairgowrie, Perth Highland cattle roaming the 25-acre estate, a plethora of golf courses nearby, river and loch fishing, game larders, kennels for your gun-dogs – the Shentalls' ivy-creepered country house, with its fine restaurant, offers an enticing taste of Scotland.

Island Hotel of the Year

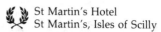 St Martin's Hotel
St Martin's, Isles of Scilly

A warm welcome for this handsome new hotel, the only one permitted on its island, for all its varied attractions – not least for its cosseting of children as well as their parents.

Dedicated hotelmanship

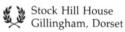 Stock Hill House
Gillingham, Dorset

Peter and Nina Hauser, in their highly personal Victorian country house, are zealous perfectionists in all departments of hotelkeeping. They maintain a fine kitchen and a glorious garden (the kitchen garden is something special too). But it is their total devotion to their guests which wins them this award.

Most audacious city hotel

 The Beaufort
London

This small Knightsbridge hotel could be just another posh bed-and-breakfast. It isn't particularly cheap but (see Introduction) is way ahead of its rivals in what it offers its guests as part of the tariff. Will other hoteliers feel compelled to compete on the *Beaufort* scale?

Best bed-and-breakfast – Irish style

 Bantry House
Bantry, Co Cork

A classical Irish country house overlooking beautiful Bantry Bay, still owned by a direct descendant of the first Earl of Bantry, offers its guests quintessential Irish hospitality.

Preserving traditional virtues of country hospitality

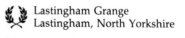 Lastingham Grange
Lastingham, North Yorkshire

There's nothing trendy in the way the Woods treat their guests: the style of the place has changed little in the 45 years of the hotel's lifetime. But visitors to this tranquil corner of the North Moors National Park return year after year and wouldn't have it otherwise.

Best budget hotel of the year

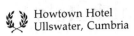 Howtown Hotel
Ullswater, Cumbria

On the unspoilt southern shore of Ullswater, four generations of the Baldry family have been welcoming fell-walkers at their farmhouse hotel. The terms are outstandingly low, but the welcome is as warm as at Sharrow Bay up the road.

Utterly acceptable mild eccentricity

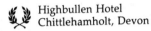 Highbullen Hotel
Chittlehamholt, Devon

Hugh and Pam Neil have been doing things their way for 27 years. Legends abound. Does Hugh still *chambrer* the wine with a hair-drier? An unhotel-like hotel, but for many devotees a home from home.

Special hotels

City hotels with luxury and grandeur

England Connaught, London; Athenaeum, London; Capital, London
Scotland One Devonshire Gardens, Glasgow
Austria Schloss Fuschl, Hof bei Salzburg; Sacher, Vienna
Denmark Angleterre, Copenhagen
France Lancaster, Paris; Cour des Loges, Lyon; Opéra, Toulouse
Norway Continental, Oslo
Spain San Marcos, León; Reyes Católicos, Santiago de Compostela; Alfonzo XIII, Seville
Switzerland L'Arbalète, Geneva

Town hotels of character and/or value

England Priory, Bath; Angel, Bury St Edmunds; Evesham, Evesham; At the Sign of the Angel, Lacock; Lansdowne, Leamington Spa; D'Isney Place, Lincoln; Beaufort, London; Blake's, London; Durrants, London; Hazlitt's, London; L'Hotel, London; Portobello, London; Abbey, Penzance; Jeake's House, Rye; George, Stamford; Mount Royale, York
Scotland Clifton, Nairn; Mansion House, Elgin; White House, Glasgow
Ireland Arbutus Lodge, Cork
Austria Elefant, Salzburg; Amadeus, Vienna; König von Ungarn, Vienna
Belgium Swaene, Bruges; Ter Duinen, Bruges

Denmark 71 Nyhavn, Copenhagen; Weis Stue, Ribe
France Europe, Avignon; Lameloise, Chagny; Angleterre, Chalons-sur-Marne; Diderot, Chinon; Pullman Beauvau, Marseille; La Pérouse, Nice; Vieux Puits, Pont Audemer; Pyrénées, St-Jean-Pied-de-Port
Germany Mönchs Posthotel, Bad Herrenalb; Kleine Prinz, Baden-Baden; Sankt Nepomuk, Bamberg; Westend, Frankfurt-am-Main; Roten Bären, Freiburg; Hanseatic, Hamburg; Bären, Meersburg; Petrisberg, Trier
Italy Umbra, Assisi; Villa Belvedere, Florence; Villa Mozart, Merano; Gregoriana, Rome; Flora, Venice
The Netherlands Ambassade, Amsterdam
Norway Myklebust, Bergen
Portugal Quinta Penha da França, Funchal; Infante de Sagres, Oporto
Spain Parador, Carmona; Hostal América, Granada; Parador, Granada
Sweden Tidbloms, Göteborg
Switzerland Florhof, Zürich
Turkey Kanuni Kervansaray, Çeşme; Yeşil Ev, Istanbul

Rural charm and character in the luxury class

England Elms, Abberley; Hartwell House, Aylesbury; Mallory Court, Bishop's Tachbrook; Buckland Manor, Buckland; Gidleigh Park, Chagford; Maison Talbooth, Dedham; Gravetye Manor, East Grinstead; Manoir aux Quat'Saisons, Great Milton; Hambleton Hall, Hambleton;

Chewton Glen, New Milton;
Gravetye Manor, East Grinstead;
Stapleford Park, Stapleford;
Ston Easton Park, Ston Easton;
Little Thakeham, Storrington;
Cliveden, Taplow; Thornbury
Castle, Thornbury; Sharrow Bay,
Ullswater; Middlethorpe Hall,
York
Wales Bodysgallen, Llandudno;
Llangoed Hall, Llyswen
Scotland Arisaig House, Arisaig;
Inverlochy Castle, Fort William;
Cromlix House, Kinbuck
Channel Islands Longueville
Manor, St Saviour
Ireland Park Hotel Kenmare,
Kenmare
Austria Schloss Dürnstein,
Dürnstein
Belgium Moulin Hideux,
Noirefontaine
Denmark Falsled Kro, Millinge
France Baumanière, Les Baux;
Château de Divonne, Divonne-
les-Bains; Noves, Noves;
Régalido, Fontvieille; Boyer ''les
Crayères'', Reims; Moulin de la
Gorce, La Roche-l'Abeille;
Cantemerle, Vence
Germany Klostergut Jakobsberg,
Boppard; Pflaums, Pegnitz
Greece Villa Argentikon, Chios
Italy Villa Corner, Cavasagra;
Palumbo, Ravello; Condulmer,
Zerman
The Netherlands Kasteel
Wittem, Wittem
Portugal Palácio de Seteais,
Sintra
Spain Residencia, Deyá;
Bobadilla, Loja; El Castell, La
Seu d'Urgell
Yugoslavia Vila Bled, Bled

Rural charm and character at medium price

England Rothay Manor,
Ambleside; Little Barwick
House, Barwick; Cavendish,
Baslow; Netherfield Place,
Battle; Farlam Hall, Brampton;
Collin House, Broadway;
Danescombe Valley, Calstock;
Aynsome Manor, Cartmel;
Grafton Manor, Bromsgrove;
Uplands, Cartmel; Brockencote
Hall, Chaddesley Corbett;
Manor, Chadlington;
Chedington Court, Chedington;
Highbullen, Chittlehamholt;
Summer Lodge, Evershot; Stock
Hill House, Gillingham;
Congham Hall, Grimston; Tarr
Steps, Hawkridge; Field Head
House, Hawkshead; Heddon's
Gate, Heddon's Mouth; Langley
House, Langley Marsh;
Lastingham Grange,
Lastingham; Hope End,
Ledbury; Arundell Arms, Lifton;
Riber Hall, Matlock; Brookdale
House, North Huish;
Whitechapel Manor, South
Molton; Bridgefield House,
Spark Bridge; Plumber Manor,
Sturminster Newton; Calcot
Manor, Tetbury; Priory,
Wareham; Miller Howe,
Windermere; Old Vicarage,
Witherslack
Wales Gliffaes, Crickhowell;
Tyddyn Llan, Llandrillo;
Portmeirion, Portmeirion; Maes-
y-Neuadd, Talsarnau
Scotland Kinloch House,
Blairgowrie; Invery House,
Banchory; Polmaily House,
Drumnadrochit; Factor's House,
Fort William; Dunain Park,
Inverness; Airds, Port Appin;
Tiroran House, Tiroran; Knockie
Lodge, Whitebridge
Ireland Gurthalougha House,
Ballinderry; Rathsallagh House,
Dunlavin; Marlfield House,
Gorey; Assolas, Kanturk;
Roundwood House, Mountrath;
Coopershill, Riverstown;
Ballymaloe, Shanagarry
Austria Gams, Bezau
Belgium 't Convent, Renige
Denmark Steensgaard
Herregårdspension, Faaborg
France Trois Mousquetaires,
Air-sur-la-Lys; Benvengudo,

Les-Baux-de-Provence;
Ombremont, Le Bourget-du-Lac;
Pescalerie, Cabrerets; Marais St-
Jean, Chonas l'Amballan; Poste,
Corps-la-Salette; Cro-Magnon,
Les Eyzies-de-Tayac; Orée du
Bois, Futeau; Relais de la
Magdeleine, Gémenos; Cagnard,
Haut-de-Cagnes; Bon Coin,
Mimizan; Trois Roses, La Petite
Pierre; Hospitaliers, Poët-Laval;
Château de Roussan, St Rémy-
de-Provence; Sept Molles,
Sauveterre-de-Commingues;
Cheval Blanc, Sept-Saulx
Germany Töpferhaus, Alt-
Duvenstedt; Erbguth's
Landhaus, Hagnau; Bergmühle,
Horbruch; Schönberg,
Oberwesel; Wehrle, Triberg
Italy Tenuta di Ricavo,
Castellina in Chianti; Saügo,
Cavalese; Castello, Gargonza;
Sant' Uffizio, Cioccaro;
Norway Utne, Utne
Portugal Abrigo da Montanha,
Monchique; Quinta da Capela,
Sintra
Spain Es Moli, Deyá;
Monasterio de Piedra, Nuévalos;
L'Hermitage, Orient
Sweden Åkerblads, Tällberg
Switzerland Eden, Engelberg;
Rothorn, Schwanden; Soglina,
Soglio

Rural charm, simple style

England Frog Street Farm,
Beercrocombe; Tanyard,
Boughton Monchelsea; Old
Cloth Hall, Cranbrook; Glebe
Farm, Diddlebury; Woodmans
Arms Auberge, Hastingleigh;
Parrock Head, Slaidburn; Manor
Farm Barn, Taynton
Wales Cnapan, Newport
Scotland Riverside, Canonbie;
Glencripesdale House,
Glencripesdale; Argyll, Iona
Ireland Coopershill, Riverstown
France Relais de St-Jacques,
Collonges-la-Rouge; Moulin,
Flagy; Vieux Logis, Lestelle-

Bétharram; Clos Normand,
Martin Église; Équipe, Molines-
en-Queyras; Rostaing,
Passanens; Pins, Sabres;
Pélissaria, St-Cirq-Lapopie; St-
Jean-du-Bruel; Hameau, St-Paul-
de-Vence; Vert, Wierre-Effroy
Germany Lipmann, Beilstein
Portugal Quinta das Torres,
Azeitão; Santa Maria, Marvão
Spain La Posada, Gualchos

Hotels by the sea, luxury style

England Marine, Salcombe
Scotland Knockinaam Lodge,
Portpatrick
France Langoustier, Porque-
rolles; Maquis, Porticcio;
Caribou, Porticciolo; Plage, Ste-
Anne-la-Palud
Greece Akti Myrina, Myrina
Italy Luna Convento, Amalfi;
Pellicano, Porto Ercole
Portugal Reid's, Funchal

Hotels by the sea, medium-priced or simple

England Look Out, Branscombe;
Hell Bay, Bryher; Treglos,
Constantine Bay; Crantock Bay,
Crantock; Whiteleaf, Croyde;
Tregildry, Gillan; Meudon,
Mawnan Smith; St Martin's, St
Martin's; Tides Reach,
Salcombe; Soar Mill Cove, Soar
Mill Cove; Talland Bay, Talland-
by-Looe; New Inn, Tresco
Wales Porth Tocyn, Abersoch;
St Tudno, Llandudno
Scotland Summer Isles,
Achiltibuie; Isle of Colonsay,
Colonsay; Enmore, Dunoon; Isle
of Raasay, Raasay; Kinloch
Castle, Rhum; Isle of Barra,
Tangusdale Beach
Channel Islands White House,
Herm
Denmark Sønderho Kro, Sønderho
France Menez-Frost, Bénodet;
Chez Pierre, Raguenès-Plage;
Ty-Pont, St-Jean-du-Doigt; Ti al-
Lannec, Trebeurden

Italy Casa Albertina, Positano;
Nido di Fiascherino, Tellaro
Spain Aigua Blava, Bagur; Mar I
Vent, Bañalbufar; Parador,
Gomera

Skiing, walking or mountain hotels

England Seatoller, Borrowdale;
Grey Friar Lodge, Brathay;
Lancrigg, Grasmere; Lodore
Swiss, Keswick; Scale Hill,
Loweswater; Mill, Mungrisdale;
Hazel Bank, Rosthwaite;
Howtown, Ullswater; Wasdale
Head, Wasdale Head
Wales Pen-y-Gwryd,
Nantgwynant; Minffordd,
Talyllyn
France Albert Ier, Chamonix-
Mont-Blanc
Germany Unterstmatt,
Schwarzwald-Hochstrasse
Norway Mundal, Fjærland;
Spain Sant Pere, Soldeu,
Andorra
Switzerland Flüela, Davos Dorf;
Chesa Grischuna, Klosters;
Metropol, Zermatt

Small hotels and inns with outstanding cuisine

England Bell, Aston Clinton;
Belle Alliance, Blandford Forum;
Lower Pitt, East Buckland; Stock
Hill House, Gillingham; White
Moss, Grasmere; Dinham Hall,
Ludlow; Brookdale House,
North Huish; Pool Court, Pool-
in-Wharfedale; Well House, St
Keyne; McCoys, Staddlebridge;
Calcot Manor, Tetbury
Wales Plas Bodegroes, Pwllheli;
Crown, Whitebrook
Scotland Farleyer House,
Aberfeldy; Peat Inn, Peat Inn;
Altnaharrie, Ullapool
Belgium Shamrock, Ronse
France de Bricourt, Cancale;
Côte St-Jacques, Joigny; Alain
Chapel, Mionnay; Bretagne,
Questembert; Jean Bardet,

Tours; Pic, Valence; Espérance,
Vézelay; Georges Blanc, Vonnas
The Netherlands De Swaen,
Oisterwijk
Spain Ses Rotges, Cala Ratjada;
Posada, Gualchos
Switzerland Fischerzunft,
Schaffhausen

Friendly informality/hotel run like a private house

England Frog Street Farm,
Beercrocombe; Little Hodgeham,
Bethersden; Appletree Holme
Farm, Blawith; Chilvester Hill
House, Calne; Thornworthy
House, Chagford; Field Head
House, Hawkshead; Walker
Ground, Hawkshead; Huntsham
Court, Huntsham; Fallowfields,
Kingston Bagpuize; Reeds,
Poughill; Howe Villa,
Richmond; Sugarswell Farm,
Shenington; Downhayes,
Spreyton; Old Millfloor,
Trebarwith Strand
Wales Old Rectory,
Llansanffraid Glan Conwy
Scotland Ardfenaig, Bunessan;
Glenfeochan, Kilmore; Ard-na-
Coille, Newtonmore; Baile-na-
Cille, Timsgarry
Austria Erika, Kitzbühel
France Parc des Maréchaux,
Auxerre; Châtenet, Brantôme;
Daille, Florimont-Gaumiers;
Pontot, Vézelay
Greece Ganimede, Galaxidion
Italy San Gregorio, San
Gregorio
Portugal Villa Hostilina,
Lamego; Quinta São Thiago,
Sintra

Hotels in the UK which have good facilities for small children

England Woolley Grange,
Bradford-on-Avon; Bulstone,
Branscombe; Hell Bay, Bryher;
Crantock Bay, Crantock;
Penmere Manor, Falmouth;

Lodore Swiss, Keswick;
Embleton Hall, Longfram-
lington; Linden Hall,
Longhorsley; Polurrian, Mullion;
Dalmeny, St Anne's on Sea;
Seaview, Seaview; Innsacre,
Shipton Gorge; Bridgefield
House, Spark Bridge; Walletts
Court, West Cliffe
Wales Porth Tocyn, Abersoch;
Cnapan, Newport
Scotland Craigendarroch,
Ballater; Isle of Colonsay,
Colonsay; Enmore, Dunoon;
Philipburn House, Selkirk;
Baile-na-Cille, Timsgarry
Channel Islands Sablonnerie,
Sark
Ireland Coopershill,
Riverstown; Sand House,
Rossnowlagh; Ballymaloe,
Shanagarry

Hotels in the UK which welcome families with children

England Cavendish, Baslow;
Eagle House, Bathford;
Evesham, Evesham; Huntsham
Court, Huntsham; Lastingham
Grange, Lastingham; Boscundle
Manor, St Austell; Star Castle,
St Mary's; Bridgefield House,
Spark Bridge; Cliveden, Taplow;

Old Millfloor, Trebarwith
Strand; Higher House, West
Bagborough
Wales Lake Vyrnwy,
Llanwddyn
Scotland Loch Melfort,
Arduaine; Isle of Eriska, Eriska;
Glencripesdale House,
Glencripesdale; Ard-na-Coille,
Newtonmore; Cringletie House,
Peebles
Ireland Coopershill,
Riverstown; Sand House,
Rossknowlagh; Ballymaloe,
Shanagarry

No-smoking hotels in the UK

England Audley House, Bath;
Haydon House, Bath; Holly
Lodge, Bath; Somerset House,
Bath; Sydney Gardens, Bath;
Old Windmill, Bradford-on-
Avon; Woodman's Arms
Auberge, Hastingleigh;
Brandymires, Hawes; Walker
Ground Manor, Hawkshead;
Cotswold House, Oxford;
Nanscawen House, St Blazey;
Sugarswell, Shenington
Wales Old Rectory, Llansaffraid
Glan Conwy
Scotland Altnaharrie, Ullapool

How to read the entries

As in previous editions, entries are in two parts – a citation, usually endorsed by one or several names, followed by relevant information about accommodation, amenities, location and tariffs.

We must emphasise once again that the length or brevity of an entry is not a reflection of the quality of a hotel. The size of an entry is determined in part by what we feel needs to be said to convey a hotel's special flavour and in part by the character and interest of the commendation. In general, country hotels get more space than city hotels because the atmosphere of the hotel matters more with the former and also because it is often helpful, when a hotel is in a relatively remote or little-known area, for the entry to say something about the location.

The names at the end of the citation are of those who have nominated that hotel or endorsed the entry that appeared in a previous edition. Some entries are entirely or largely quoted from one report; if several names follow such an entry, we have distinguished writers of quoted material by putting their names first. We do not give the names of those who have sent us adverse reports – though their contributions are every bit as important as the laudatory ones.

The factual material also varies in length. Some hotels provide a wide variety of facilities, others very few. But the paucity of information provided in some cases may derive from the fact that the hotel has failed to return our detailed questionnaire or send us a brochure. All hotels in the British Isles have completed our form, but the same is not true for continental hotels, even though we send out our questionnaire in five languages and repeat the operation for any recalcitrants a month later. Around a quarter of the hotels in the second half of the book ignore our form or return it months later when the Guide has gone to press. In these instances, we have to rely on the information available from national tourist offices. The fact that no lounge or bar is mentioned in an entry does not mean that a hotel lacks public rooms – only that we can't be sure. The same applies to availability of parking, which we aim to mention in the case of town and city hotels. As to tariffs, in those cases where we have had no communication with a hotel, or where it was unable to give next year's rates, we print the 1990 tariffs, making it clear that these are last year's terms.

Our italicised entries indicate hotels that we feel are worth considering, but which for various reasons – inadequate information, lack of feedback, ambivalent reports – do not at the moment justify a full entry. A hotel whose entry is in italics, with briefer information about its tariffs and facilities, need not be thought of as a half-good establishment, only as one about which we are eager to have more opinions. We hope that, with the help of such feedback, many will rate full entries next year.

There is a limit to the amount of "nuts and bolts" that can be given in any guide book, and we are against providing, as some other guide books do, a lot of potted information in complicated, hard-to-decipher hieroglyphic form. Days and months are abbreviated, but virtually the only other shorthand we use is "B&B" for bed and breakfast and "alc" for à la carte; the "full alc" price is the hotel's estimate per person for a three-course meal and a half-bottle of modest wine, including service and taxes. We try to give as much information as possible (ground-floor rooms, lifts, etc) to enable disabled people to judge whether or not a hotel will be suitable for them. If a hotel tells us it has special facilities for the disabled we give details; if we know it is not suitable we say so. But we do sometimes lack precise information; disabled people should always check with the hotel.

Terms are difficult enough to cope with at the best of times. A few hotels have a standard rate for all rooms regardless of season and length of stay, but most operate a highly complicated system which varies from low season to high (and some have a medium-high season as well), according to length of stay, whether there is a bathroom *en suite* and, in the case of most British hotels, whether a room is in single or double occupancy. And, on top of all that, most British hotels offer breaks of one kind or another, but rarely of the same kind. When we can, we give a room rate rather than a rate per person and hope thereby to give a reliable idea of what people, especially those travelling on their own, can expect to pay. When figures are given without mention of single or double rooms they indicate the range of tariffs per person. Lowest rates are what you pay for the simplest room, or out of season, or both; highest rates are for the "best" rooms – and in high season if the hotel has one. Meal prices are per person, VAT and service are included unless we state otherwise.

There is one crucial point that must be emphasised with regard to the tariffs: their relative unreliability. We ask hotels when they complete our questionnaire in the spring of one year to make an informed guess at their tariffs the following year. There are many reasons why this is a difficult exercise. Please don't rely on the figures printed. You should always check at the time of booking and not blame the hotel or the Guide if the prices are different from those printed.

If you are going for two days or more to a hotel in the British Isles, it will pay you to find out the exact terms of any special offers available. Sometimes these bargain terms are amazing value, and can apply throughout the year, not just in the winter, but they may call for some adjustment in your holiday plans in order to qualify. We also strongly advise you to check whether a hotel is open before making a long detour. We try in all cases to give accurate information, but hotels, particularly small ones, do sometimes close at times when they have told us they expect to be open. And hotels on the Continent often have a weekly closing date, but sometimes fail to make this clear when returning our questionnaire. Finally, they do not always give reliable information about whether or not they take credit cards. If it is vital to you, please check.

We end with our customary exhortation: we implore readers to tell us of any errors of omission or commission in both the descriptive and informative parts of the entries. We make constant efforts to improve our information under "Location", especially with the more out-of-the-way places, but would be very grateful if readers would let us know of any cases where they have found our directions inadequate. We recognise what an imposition it is to be asking readers to write us letters or fill in report forms, but it is essential that people do let us know their views if the Guide is to meet consumer needs as well as it can.

Part one

England
Wales
Scotland
Channel Islands
Northern Ireland
Republic of Ireland

England

Gravetye Manor, East Grinstead

ABBERLEY Hereford and Worcester   Map 2

The Elms Hotel   *Tel* Great Witley (0299) 896666
Stockton Road, Abberley   *Fax* (0299) 896804
Nr Worcester WR6 6AT   *Telex* 337105

For years this exceptionally beautiful and grand Queen Anne mansion
had the first entry in the Guide. It then changed owners and was
dropped. Now, following another change, and though company-owned,
it is readmitted, nominated by faithful regulars. "We like the lovely old
house itself, the well-kept grounds and the beautiful views over
unspoiled countryside. Inside are beautiful, lofty reception rooms with
antique furniture, plenty of flowers, and – *most important* – excellent
lighting. The food is light and delicious, and service, by young and mostly
English staff, quick, friendly and professional. Bedrooms are very
comfortable and well lit, and supplied with the usual extras. At night a
chambermaid comes in specially from a nearby village to turn down beds
and provide yet more fluffy white towels. There's a pleasantly relaxed
and friendly atmosphere, backed up by high standards of housekeeping."

"The new owners have extensively redecorated and the hotel offers the highest standards of comfort, food and service. There's a new manager, the Swedish Cecilia Rydstrom, who is able to combine efficiency with a warm welcome – and to achieve a consistent standard." (*D Whittington, Mr and Mrs JM Pashley*) *The Elms* is fairly formal: jacket and tie for men are required in the restaurant; jeans are out. More reports please.

Open All year.
Rooms 5 suites, 18 double, 2 single – all with bath (23 also have shower), telephone, radio, TV, baby-listening. 9 in Coach House.
Facilities 2 lounges, library, bar, restaurant; conference facilities. 10-acre gardens with tennis, putting, croquet.
Location On A443 between Worcester and Tenbury Wells.
Restrictions Not suitable for &. No dogs.
Credit cards All major cards accepted.
Terms [1990 rates] B&B (English): single £80, double £95–£115, suite £135–£145. Set lunch £13.95, dinner £20; full alc £30. Weekend breaks.
Service/tipping: "Service included but guests may leave a tip if they want."

ALLENDALE Northumberland   Map 4

Bishop Field Country House
Hotel
Allendale, Hexham NE47 9EJ

Tel Hexham (0434) 683248
Fax (0434) 683830

Keith and Kathy Fairless are the third generation of the family to live on this former working farm in a small, attractive town in the moors with excellent walks around – it is alleged to be the geographical centre of Britain. The hotel, in converted cattle byres round a cobbled courtyard, stands in 40-acre grounds. Bedrooms – on the small side – are simple and bright, with plain white walls and cheerful fabrics; all have private facilities. There are comfortable lounges, one for non-smokers, and a full-size snooker table. *Bishop Field* has access to a 6,000-acre estate for shooting, and owns a mile and a half of trout fishing; there are bicycles for hire, and many other sporting activities in the area. The hotel was enthusiastically nominated last year by an American who had stayed for no fewer than 29 days. He was warmly appreciative of the peaceful and beautiful setting, the comfortable accommodation, the reasonable prices, and the "congenial proprietors". A reader this year endorses the nomination: "Good, wholesome yet interesting food, especially the cooked breakfast. The warmth and hospitality of the Fairlesses and their family make the hotel unique." (*Raymond H Neville, E Valerie Warnett*) Vegetarians are catered for. One reader was less enamoured of the fare and thought the decor tacky.

Open All year except 1 week at Christmas.
Rooms 1 suite, 11 double, 1 single – all with bath and/or shower, telephone, radio, TV, tea-making facilities. 2 ground-floor rooms.
Facilities 3 lounges (1 non-smoking), 2 dining rooms. 40-acre grounds; trout fishing. Access to 6,000-acre estate with shooting.
Location 10 m SW of Hexham on B6305. From Allendale take Whitfield road; hotel is on right after 1 m.
Restrictions No children under 7 at dinner. No dogs in public rooms.
Credit cards Access, Visa.
Terms B&B £27–£37; dinner, B&B £40–£50. Set lunch £8, dinner £13. Reduced rates and special meals for children.

AMBLESIDE Cumbria   Map 4

Rothay Manor Hotel   *Tel* Ambleside (053 94) 33605
Rothay Bridge   *Fax* (053 94) 33607
Ambleside LA22 0EH

The Nixon brothers' "welcoming and always comfortable hotel" in a
handsome Georgian house is half a mile from Lake Windermere; it stands
in two acres of garden in a valley surrounded by fine Lakeland mountain
scenery. It is a scheduled building, noted for the grace of its design and
detail, and retains some of the original features. There are comfortable
lounges with antiques and flowers; bedrooms, "bright and clean, with
bathrooms filled with innumerable extras, could not be faulted in any
way". Readers appreciate the "excellent breakfasts" and "scrumptious
teas", and the generous buffet for weekday lunches. The dining room,
decorated in browns and golds with deep pile carpets, velvety curtains,
polished candle-lit tables, heavy glass and tableware and traditionally
clad serving maids in caps and pinnies, overlooks the well-maintained
lawns and gardens. Dinner menus are traditional English, but not
slavishly so; you can choose between five courses at £22 or two at £16.50.
Children and the disabled are welcome at *Rothay Manor*. There can be
disturbance from traffic on a busy one-way system close by; it is worth
asking for a quiet room when booking – rooms are double-glazed. In
winter the Nixons offer music and gourmet weekends, and house parties
for Christmas and the New Year.

Open Early Feb–early Jan.
Rooms 3 suites (1 honeymoon, 2 family) in annexe, 13 double, 2 single – all with
bath, shower, telephone, radio, TV, baby-listening. 1 suite adapted for &.
Facilities 3 lounges (1 with bar), 2 dining rooms. 2-acre garden with croquet.
Near river Rothay and Lake Windermere (¼ m). Sailing, water-skiing, fishing,
riding and golf.
Location On A593 SW of Ambleside towards Coniston. Garden-facing rooms
quietest.
Restrictions No smoking in dining room and 1 lounge. No dogs.
Credit cards All major cards accepted.
Terms (Service at guests' discretion) B&B (English) £44–£63; dinner, B&B
£54–£78. Lunch: weekdays £5–£8, Sun £12. Dinner £16.50 (2-course) and £22
(5-course). Off-season breaks; music courses, French regional dinners. 4-day
Christmas house party, 3-day New Year programme. 2-night min booking at
weekend. Reduced rates for children sharing parents' room; special meals.

Wateredge Hotel   *Tel* Ambleside (053 94) 32332
Borrans Road, Waterhead
Ambleside LA22 0EP

The *Wateredge*, as you might expect, enjoys a choice position at the head
of Windermere looking down the length of the lake with views of
Loughrigg Fells and other landmarks. Owned and run by Mr and Mrs
Cowap, it consists of a pair of 17th-century fisherman's cottages with
some modern additions but still retaining much of the period charm. The
lounges are comfortable and welcoming, with old beams and picture-
windows overlooking the lake. Bedrooms in the original part are also
beamed and have period furniture; the newer ones are larger and
furnished in pine. There are five spacious suites, with patio and balcony,

in an annexe. All have numerous extras – hair-drier, fresh fruit and so on. Meals are served in the two dining rooms in the old part of the building, with low-beamed ceilings and old stone painted walls. There is a choice of starter, followed by soup, then a sorbet, then two alternative main courses, generally a roast and a fish dish, then dessert and cheese. *Wateredge* continues to receive warm endorsements, many from regular visitors: "One of our favourite hotels. We like the choice of lounges – two small, cosy and traditional, one large with picture-windows overlooking the lake. The food is interesting without being pretentious: imaginative soups, good local meat and fish, and a dessert table around which guests gather appreciatively to discuss their extremely difficult decisions. Staff are friendly and cheerful; service is quick." "We had one of the new superior rooms with a balcony and a good lake view. It was one of the best planned and furnished hotel rooms we have stayed in." (*Mrs MH Box, Dr JR Backhurst; also ML Lomax*) The only problem is that it can be noisy from the main road behind; lakeside traffic, heavy at weekends, passes close by the hotel.

Open Early Feb–mid-Dec.
Rooms 5 suites, 15 double, 3 single – all with bath and/or shower, telephone, TV, tea-making facilities. The suites are across a small courtyard.
Facilities 3 lounges, TV room, bar, 2 dining rooms. 1-acre grounds with patio, lake frontage, private jetty, boats available to guests free of charge; fishing, bathing.
Location ½ m S of town; just off A591 at Waterhead on Kendal–Keswick road (rooms on road can be noisy).
Restrictions Not suitable for &. No smoking in dining room. No children under 7. Dogs by prior arrangement, not in suites or public rooms.
Credit cards Access, Amex, Visa.
Terms B&B (English) £34–£62; dinner, B&B £42–£70. Set dinner £20.90. Winter breaks. 1-night bookings sometimes refused, particularly Sat. Reduced rates for children sharing parents' room.
Service/tipping: "No service charge. All tips are distributed equally to all staff."

ARNCLIFFE North Yorkshire   Map 4

Amerdale House Hotel   *Tel* Arncliffe (075 677) 250
Arncliffe, Littondale
Skipton BD23 5QE

Nigel and Paula Crapper have been just over three years at their former Elizabethan manor house with Victorian additions, on the edge of a pretty, unspoilt Dales village in lovely, open country; they have now finished their programme of redecoration and refurbishment. The main house is "solidly Edwardian in style"; bedrooms in the converted stables are "modern, with a Scandinavian feeling, with everything one needs, and a warm, luxurious bathroom". Readers continue to enjoy the peaceful atmosphere and the style of the hotel: "Mr and Mrs Crapper were charming, the staff helpful, and the setting is beautiful, with easy access to lots of interesting places." "It is on a human scale; the rooms pleasant, if not outstanding." "Imaginative menu, fresh ingredients, choice is limited but perfectly adequate – three starters, two main courses, two desserts or cheese." "Satisfying, well-judged portions, perfectly cooked." (*Mrs PM Jones, Joanna L Glover, J Campbell, John Clifford, and others*) Do not expect a telephone, information kits or so on in the bedrooms, nor is there a lift (and three bedrooms are on the second floor). There have been a few murmurs about inadequate heating in very cold weather, and one reader was surprised to have a down duvet on his bed in a heatwave, but even the critics agree: "Prices very reasonable for the quality of the accommodation and the food."

Open Mid-Mar–mid-Nov.
Rooms 2 suites, 10 double – all with bath and/or shower, TV, tea-making facilities. 2 in converted stable block. 1 on ground floor.
Facilities Lounge, bar, restaurant. 2-acre grounds.
Location 17 m N of Skipton; take left fork off B6160 to Arncliffe.
Restrictions No smoking in dining room. No dogs in hotel; kennels available.
Credit cards Access, Visa.
Terms [1990 rates] Dinner, B&B £39–£51. Set dinner £17. 1-night bookings refused for bank holidays and high-season weekends. Reduced rates for children sharing parents' room; special meals.
Service/tipping: "No mention of a service charge is made in our literature, nor are tips expected by staff. If guests wish to give tips they are gratefully received and shared equally."

ASHBOURNE Derbyshire   Map 4

Callow Hall   *Tel* Ashbourne (0335) 43403
Mappleton Road   *Fax* (0335) 43624
Ashbourne DE6 2AA

This impressive 19th-century Derbyshire house "with turrets and twiddles" is approached up a long drive through large grounds with some lovely trees. It is in attractive countryside, quietly located not far from the centre of a small market town, and has recently been extensively renovated, though many of the original features are still intact. *Callow Hall* entered the Guide last year and several visitors, including the original nominators, have written to confirm the entry. Public rooms are spacious and furnished "in a friendly mixture of styles, antique and modern"; most have a fireplace, but some winter visitors have regretted that the drawing room fire was not always lit on cold evenings. Bedrooms in the main house are "beautiful, large and comfortable". Old-fashioned service is appreciated: shoes cleaned, early morning tea brought to the room if preferred – just as well as the tea-making equipment, "while no doubt fool-proof, failed a harder test. It taxed two of the best brains in Europe for several minutes; the tea ended up no more than brown." The friendly and welcoming proprietors, Mr and Mrs Spencer, are now helped in the restaurant by their son, Anthony. The Spencer family have been bakers in Ashbourne for the last five generations and *Callow Hall* has its own bakery and patisserie department. *Patron*/chef David Spencer buys meat by the carcass and all hanging and butchery is done on the premises. The restaurant is popular locally; cooking is "excellent – imaginative, consistent", "superb in quality and presentation", but service can be variable. "Breakfast very good, including fresh orange juice and home-made sausages." (*CG, Dr and Mrs I Sitwell, JEM Ruffer, also Margaret Murray Smith, IC Dewey, and others*) The hotel has private fishing for trout and grayling, with tuition available. A new wing has been built, doubling the number of bedrooms, but the new rooms are said to be small and dark, with no view, and one reader found the last day of an otherwise enjoyable visit spoiled when the hotel was taken over for a local function, not an unusual occurrence. More reports please.

Open All year except 25/26 Dec and possibly 2 weeks Jan or Feb. Restaurant closed to non-residents for lunch except Sun, for dinner Sun.
Rooms 14 double – all with bath, shower, telephone, radio, TV, tea-making facilities, baby-listening.
Facilities Lounge, bar, 2 restaurants; functions/conference facilities. 42-acre grounds with garden, woodland, farmland and stables; fishing (tuition available).
Location ¾ m from Ashbourne; take A515 to Buxton; sharp left at top of first hill by *Bowling Green* pub, first right to Mappleton; cross bridge – drive is on right.
Restrictions Not suitable for &. Dogs by arrangement.
Credit cards All major cards accepted.
Terms (Service at guests' discretion) B&B (English): single occupancy £60–£75, double £80–£110; dinner, B&B: single £80–£95, double £120–£150. Set lunch £12, dinner £21; full alc £25. Weekend and midweek breaks. Reduced rates and special meals for children by arrangement.

ASKRIGG North Yorkshire   Map 4

King's Arms Hotel `BUDGET`   *Tel* Wensleydale (0969) 50258
Market Place, Askrigg
Wensleydale DL8 3HQ

Unassuming, popular 18th-century coaching inn, Grade II listed, in beautiful conservation village at heart of Yorkshire Dales National Park, owned and run by Ray and Liz Hopwood. Some good-sized bedrooms with 4-poster or canopy beds and antique furniture, but top ones are small and low-ceilinged. Reasonably priced meals, "good, straightforward and very filling", served in oak-panelled dining room. Recently much refurbished; new Grill Room. 6 "superior" bedrooms in an adjoining building, and "leisure/fitness facilities" planned for 1991. Cheapest bedrooms, not yet refurbished, are not recommended. 10 doubles, all with bath and/or shower. B&B £20–£27. Set dinner £13.75 [1990]. More reports please.

ASTON CLINTON Buckinghamshire   Map 1

The Bell Inn   *Tel* Aylesbury (0296) 630252
Aston Clinton HP22 5HP   *Fax* (0296) 631250
                                                  Telex 83252

The Bell, at the foot of the Chilterns, on what is still a busy main road, has been an inn since 1650 and was once a staging post for the Duke of Buckingham between his seat at Stowe and his palace on the Mall. But the term "inn" is quite inappropriate to today's sophisticated establishment which has been owned and run, along with a wine business, by the Harris family since 1939; Michael Harris, son of the founding father, and his wife Patsy are much in evidence. It has comfortable bedrooms, some in the original inn with antiques (some have four-posters), and fifteen, spacious and more modern, in converted stables, grouped around a cobblestoned flower-filled courtyard. There's a pavilion across the road for weddings and conferences. But the *raison d'être* of the *Bell* is its popular restaurant with pretty murals where "chef Kevin Cape's menu may look pretentious, but he delivers the goods. The set menu is extremely good value; the à la carte more adventurous." Cooking is "classical French with a modern touch"; there's a continually changing vegetarian menu and a "long and tempting" wine list; "but also a recommended wine which changes weekly – the one on our night was remarkably reasonable''. There are thoughtful touches in the bedrooms, but "it is more a restaurant-with-rooms than a hotel", and "the feeling of a tradition, of the caring of the owner, of keen and cheerful staff, nearly all French, creates a most welcoming impression" (though we do sometimes get reports of linguistic difficulties, mainly at breakfast). (*HR*) In the past we have had complaints about upkeep of the rooms, but there has been some redecoration this year, and a new manager arrived in early 1990. More reports please, particularly on the accommodation side.

Open All year.
Rooms 6 suites, 15 double – all with bath, shower, telephone, radio, TV, baby-listening. 15 in annexe round courtyard.
Facilities Drawing room, smoking room, bar, restaurant. Garden with croquet.
Location On A41, 4 m SE of Aylesbury. Road-facing rooms double-glazed; quieter rooms at rear.
Restrictions No smoking in restaurant. Dogs by arrangement.
Credit cards Access, Visa.
Terms B&B: single £86, double £100–£125, suite £125–£175. Set lunch £15.95, dinner £16.95; full alc £38. Reduced rates for children sharing parents' room; special meals.

ATHERSTONE Warwickshire   Map 1

Chapel House   `BUDGET`   *Tel* Atherstone (0827) 718949
Friar's Gate, Atherstone CV9 1EY

David and Pat Roberts's small guest house, predominantly Georgian, stands in a walled garden just off the square of this old market town which is only two miles from the A5. It had an italicised entry for two years, but *MJ Hill* persuades us to promote it to a full entry: "It is typical of what is best in the GHG – small, personal, individual, welcoming, comfortable, good value, and run with a certain style, and with love. We had a small but comfortable bedroom with lots of thoughtful touches like pot-pourri, dried flowers and shoe-cleaning materials. Downstairs was extremely comfortable and spacious." The restaurant ("charming, if slightly over-decorated") offers residents a menu at 7 pm; but they can take the non-residents' dinner if they prefer. Most readers have enjoyed the food, though one found the dinner "inclined to be pretentious; breakfast, on the other hand, was traditional English, and excellent". A few niggles: "The refusal to confirm our booking in writing was worrying; breakfast finishes very early"; some of the showers have been considered "impractical" or "temperamental", and one visitor in March 1990 had a very hot double room with a small double bed, "and so much furniture we could hardly get to the window to let any air in". *Chapel House* is adjacent to the parish church whose striking clock may disturb light sleepers.

Open All year except Christmas.
Rooms 9 double, 4 single – all with shower (1 also has bath), telephone, radio, TV, baby-listening.
Facilities Lounge, dispense bar, 2 restaurants, conservatory. ¼-acre garden.
Location In market square. Public parking in cul-de-sac in front of hotel.
Restrictions Not suitable for &. No dogs.
Credit cards Access, Diners, Visa.
Terms B&B: single £37.50, double £50. Set dinner £10.50; full alc £27.
Service/tipping: "We do not make a service charge. Tips are optional, and shared among all staff."

AYLESBURY Buckinghamshire   Map 1

Hartwell House   *Tel* Aylesbury (0296) 747444
Oxford Road, Aylesbury   *Fax* (0296) 747450
HP17 8NL   *Telex* 837108

A mellow and serene country seat with Jacobean and Georgian facades, surrounded by some 80 acres of lush parkland designed by a pupil of Capability Brown. The landscaping is a model of its kind; there's a lake, crossed by a bridge taken from the central span of old Kew Bridge, and a fine equestrian statue in the central courtyard. A ruined church and lots of noble statuary are dotted round the grounds. For most of the past 30 years *Hartwell House* was a finishing school for girls but its pedigree dates back to William the Conqueror and the Domesday Book. And Louis XVIII, the exiled King of France, lived here for five years from 1809. The house has been brought to its present luxurious state by Historic House Hotels, an organisation dedicated to the resuscitation of noble British houses which has already done lavish conversions on *Bodysgallen Hall*, Llandudno, and *Middlethorpe Hall*, York (qq.v.).

Visitors to *Hartwell* shortly after its opening in July 1989 reported: "The interior is no less rich in visual pleasure than the grounds; there's an exotic Gothic central staircase, a spectacular 18th-century Great Hall, a fine library, and much else of opulent splendour. One of Britain's best designers, Janey Compton, has given the decor a luxurious but harmonious style. There are fine paintings and antiques. The staff were friendly and relaxed professionals. The restaurant, under Aidan McCormack, offers a long à la carte menu and short set-price ones for every meal. Dinner, however, was the least satisfactory part of the *Hartwell* experience. The menu was ambitious on paper, though somewhat bland on the plate, with the vegetables a little too *al dente*; and there's an extensive wine list, but sadly almost no half-bottles." Bedrooms are spacious – some huge – and well equipped; some have magnificent panelling, original oil paintings and four-posters; extras include current magazines and "real" books. Men are expected to wear jacket and tie for dinner. Future plans include 16 more bedrooms and suites in a stable block, an indoor swimming pool and leisure facilities, and a conference room. (*HR; also Paul Jackson*) More reports please.

Open All year.
Rooms 3 suites, 25 double, 4 single – all with bath, shower, telephone, radio, TV.
Facilities Lift. Great Hall, morning room, drawing room, library, bar, restaurant. 80-acre grounds with trout lake with swimming platform, woodlands, croquet.
Location 2 m S of Aylesbury on the A418 to Thame, outside the village of Stone.
Restrictions No children under 8. No dogs.
Credit cards All major cards accepted.
Terms [Until April 1991] B&B: single £83–£95, double £127–£185, suite £185–£275. Breakfast: continental £6.50, English £9.50. Set lunch £17, dinner £29.50; full alc £38.
Service/tipping: "Service included. Should a guest wish to tip it is up to him or her."

Most hotels have reduced rates out of season and for children, and some British hotels offer "mini-break" rates throughout the year. If you are staying more than one night, it is always worth asking about special terms.

BAKEWELL Derbyshire   Map 4

Milford House Hotel   *Tel* Bakewell (0629) 812130
Mill Street, Bakewell DE4 1DA

"Thank you for your recommendation. I endorse everything you say. I have never stayed in a cleaner, better-kept hotel. Everything was spotless and sparkling. The garden was as well kept as the house." (*Mrs M Mills*)

This unsophisticated hotel is in a charming, quiet part of Bakewell, close to the river Wye, with "nice gentle walks". It has been owned by the Hunt family for over three decades. The decor is simple: "Bedrooms are rather 1950s with comfortable, high beds with good sheets and high-quality blankets; there's a wash basin in the bedroom, a modern shower unit in a shower room, very hot water, good quality towels." The Hunts and their staff are friendly and helpful. A gong announces dinner and breakfast. The latter is English, good and generous. During breakfast you are asked which main course you would like for dinner (which is at 7 pm) – there are three choices, including chicken and a roast. "Excellent value. Nothing at all fancy, just good, plain, traditional English cooking. Everything hot, and nicely presented. Service quick, but not too quick, and friendly." Only quibble: the hotel refrigeration rather too clearly heard in one back room. More reports please.

Open Easter–end Oct.
Rooms 10 double, 2 single – all with bath and/or shower, TV, tea-making facilities.
Facilities Hall with bar, lounge, dining room. 1¼-acre grounds with croquet.
Location 300 yds from town centre; right turn off A6 to Buxton. Parking.
Restrictions Not suitable for &. No children under 10. No dogs.
Credit cards None accepted.
Terms B&B £28–£34; dinner, B&B £40–£46. Set Sun lunch £12, dinner £13. Bar snacks available to residents Mon–Sat; packed lunches on request. Weekly rates.
Service/tipping: "No service charge included. If guests wish to tip they give directly to staff."

BARWICK Somerset   Map 2

Little Barwick House   *Tel* Yeovil (0935) 23902
Barwick, Yeovil BA22 9TD

"One cannot really fault this hotel. We have been visiting it for some years; each time there is an improvement. It is an old house that is being cared for with much love. The friendliness of the Colleys is matched by that of their cats and two Doberman bitches. Lovely breakfasts, especially the continental one. One of our favourite watering holes." "Christopher and Veronica Colley are most pleasant – unassuming but efficient people; we were quickly made to feel at home. Food was of the highest standard, and the girls who served dinner were quick, attentive, smiling and unobtrusive. Everything was sensible and unfussy." "Although it is a restaurant-with-rooms, the bedroom was comfortable, with thoughtful additions – fresh flowers, mineral water, etc. The standard of cooking continues to improve. They cater for the individual without intrusion." "Hospitality marvellous. The Colleys went to endless trouble over our six-year-old grandson's meals and made an almost nominal charge for his bed and board. I cannot speak too highly of their hospitality." The

Colleys' Georgian dower house is in a beautiful garden in a secluded corner of the attractive, minuscule village of Barwick, two miles from Yeovil. It looks out across the valley towards the village with its church and outlying obelisks on the skyline. None of the six bedrooms is particularly large, nor luxuriously furnished, but each is comfortable, with firm beds, very good linen, good lighting, and individually controlled central heating. The restaurant is popular with non-residents; food is "carefully cooked and not too messed about"; game is particularly good, and the desserts varied and not all highly calorific. (*Kenneth E Smith, KGM, Ann Farrow, Mrs JW Gibson, and many others*) One niggle: "Their dogs are allowed in the kitchen."

Open All year except Christmas and New Year.
Rooms 6 double – all with bath and/or shower, radio, TV, tea-making facilities.
Facilities 2 lounges, cellar bar, dining room. 3½-acre garden.
Location Follow signs from Yeovil to Dorchester (A37). Turn left off A37 at the *Red House* pub. Hotel is ¼ m on left.
Restrictions Not suitable for &. Dogs by arrangement only; not in public rooms.
Credit cards All major cards accepted.
Terms B&B: single £46, double £70; dinner, B&B: single £63, double £104.
Vegetarian and special diets catered for. Reductions for 2 nights or more. Winter breaks. 1-night bookings sometimes refused on Sun. Reduced rates for children.
Service/tipping: "Service is included, but any money left is divided among the staff."

BASLOW Derbyshire   Map 4

Cavendish Hotel   *Tel* Baslow (0246) 582311
Baslow DE4 1SP   *Fax* (0246) 582312
                                              Telex 547150

"Very pretty, and beautifully located. Public rooms attractive, well furnished and well decorated, as were our two adjoining bedrooms. Good to see individual furnishing with some nice pieces. A light supper was happily provided in the bedroom for our five-year-old." "I was delighted by my stay, particularly the peace and quiet." "Very courteous staff. Presentation and content of meals excellent. We much appreciated the 'kitchen table' facility with a guided tour of the spotless and extremely efficient kitchen. I do not consider the prices high, bearing in mind the comfort, and the quality of service and meals." The *Cavendish* is one of the few luxurious hotels in the Peak District. It is on the edge of Chatsworth Park, which all the bedrooms overlook. Some of the furnishings come from Chatsworth House. The hotel has been run with style for years by Eric Marsh. Mrs Marsh is responsible for the beautiful flower arrangements in the public rooms. It is worth discussing your accommodation when booking; some bedrooms are "small and unimaginatively decorated", others "generous in size, nicely (not quite beautifully) decorated, with a large bathroom"; all are comfortable and spotless. (*APC, JS Rutter, Ann Saunders; also Peter Rozée, Donald McGavin*) Food is *nouvelle*, with smallish portions; some readers, disagreeing with those quoted above, have found it "overpriced and overdressed". Winter weekend rates are good value: if you book for Friday and Saturday nights you can stay for Sunday night at no extra charge. The *Cavendish* is generally reported to be very warm throughout, but one visitor this year complained of a cold bedroom.

Open All year.
Rooms 1 suite, 23 double – all with bath, shower, telephone, radio, T V, tea-making facilities, mini-bar, baby-listening. 2 ground-floor rooms.
Facilities Hall/reception, lounge, bar, garden room, restaurant; private dining room, conference room. 2-acre grounds with putting green; fishing in rivers Derwent and Wye.
Location On A619 in Chatsworth grounds (leave M1 at exit 29).
Restrictions Not suitable for &. No smoking in restaurant. No dogs.
Credit cards All major cards accepted.
Terms [1990 rates] Rooms: single occupancy £60–£70, double £75–£85. Breakfast from £3.85. Set lunch/dinner £22; full alc £30. Winter bonus weekends. Cots/extra beds available for children (£7.50); special meals by request.
Service/tipping: "No service charge. If a client wishes to leave a tip it is gratefully accepted and shared among all staff."

Fischer's at Baslow Hall
Calver Road, Baslow DE4 1RR

Tel Baslow (0246) 583259

An attractive new entry for Baslow, though its proprietors, Max and Susan Fischer, are well known to gourmets from *Fischer's*, the restaurant they ran in nearby Bakewell. Many of their regulars have followed them to this imposing building which, though built in 1907, looks considerably older. "We arrived hungry after a long drive," writes our inspector, "and were soon enjoying a delicious assortment of sandwiches, beautifully arranged on an oval platter. The Fischers are a charming couple, their staff are without exception well mannered and efficient. Max Fischer is a compulsive collector of antiques and the house is positively crammed with furniture, primarily Victorian and country pine; the walls are bedecked with prints and pictures. The wallpapers and fabrics are at times rather hectic but are of high quality. Fresh flowers, plants, immense bowls of pot-pourri abound. The dining room is light and airy, with well-spaced tables; dinner (four courses with choices for every course) was excellent, everything beautifully presented and uncluttered, properly hot and competently served. The bread rolls were home-baked. There's a separate, welcoming room for breakfast which was probably the nicest I have ever had. Bedrooms, with lots of blue and pink, are up a carved oak staircase. Ours was spacious, dominated by a half-tester bed; it was comfortable and cosy but could have done with a bit less furniture. Bathrooms vary in size and style, some of the loos and showers are almost historic in themselves; there was plenty of hot water at all times. A very promising Guide newcomer." More reports please.

Open All year except Christmas. Restaurant closed to non-residents Sun evening and Mon.
Rooms 1 suite, 4 double, 1 single – all with bath and/or shower, telephone, radio, T V, baby-listening.
Facilities Lounge, 2 restaurants, private dining room. 4½-acre grounds.
Location Take A623 Calver/Stockport through Baslow. Last entrance on right within village boundary.
Restrictions Only restaurant suitable for &. No smoking in restaurant. No children under 10 at dinner. No dogs.
Credit cards Access, Amex, Visa.
Terms (Service at guests' discretion) B&B: single £65, double £80–£100. Alc lunch Tue–Sat £15, set Sun lunch £14.50; set dinner £27.50, full alc dinner £32. Reductions for children's meals.

BASSENTHWAITE LAKE Cumbria   Map 4

The Pheasant Inn   *Tel* Bassenthwaite Lake
Bassenthwaite Lake   (076 87) 76234
Cockermouth CA13 9YE

This popular low, white-washed inn, just out of sight of the lake, has
been run by Mr and Mrs Barrington Wilson for many years. "It nestles at
the bottom of a dip with wooded slopes rising steeply on three sides. The
other side borders the A66 though one cannot see the road, but traffic can
be heard with a north wind. It has a very pretty woodland garden with a
stream frequented by ducks. Inside there are spacious drawing rooms and
lounges, all exquisitely furnished – good rugs on polished oak floors, a
great many easy chairs and sofas, prints and paintings, magazines, and
flower arrangements"; also beamed ceilings, sparkling copper and
brassware, and crackling fires in winter. "The bar," say the owners, "has
not changed character in living memory." Bedrooms vary in style and size
(but none have TV, radio or telephone). One reader this year was pleased
with hers: "Comparatively large, newly decorated and with a reasonably
sized bathroom, plenty of towels, plenty of mirrors in the right places,
plenty of wardrobe space, all done in the palest gold, cream and white.
Our friends, however, had a small, cramped room with small bed and
minute bathroom." Staff are "friendly, if a bit inexperienced". And this
year, as last, the verdict on dinner and breakfast is that they do not come
up to the standards set elsewhere in the inn. Readers in garden-facing
rooms have been bothered by noise from a large extractor fan in the bar;
and one found her room on a summer's night excessively hot.

Open All year except 25 Dec.
Rooms 15 double, 5 single – 19 with bath, 1 with shower. 3 with tea-making
facilities in bungalow annexe.
Facilities 3 lounges (2 for residents), bar, dining room; private party/small
conference facilities. 1½-acre grounds. Sailing, fishing, pony trekking, golf nearby.
Location 7 m NW of Keswick just off A66 (on W side of Bassenthwaite Lake).
Restrictions No smoking in dining room and 1 lounge. No dogs in bedrooms or
public rooms.
Credit cards None accepted.
Terms B&B: single £42, double £70; dinner, B&B (min 3 days): single £58, double
£96. Set Sun lunch £9; set dinner £18. Bar snacks. Weekly rates; winter breaks.
1-night bookings for Sat sometimes refused. Reduced rates for children sharing
parents' room; supper at 6 pm.
*Service/tipping: "A 10% service charge is included in rates and distributed on a point
system to all staff."*

BATH Avon   Map 2

Audley House `BUDGET`   *Tel* Bath (0225) 333110
Park Gardens BA1 2XP

*19th-century house, carefully renovated and decorated, in quiet setting west of
Victoria Park. It has 1¼-acre grounds with lawns and mature trees. Recommended for reasonable rates, large comfortable rooms, generous and delicious
breakfasts and friendly hosts ("and wonderful conversationalists") Gordon and
Sheila Talbot. Ample parking. No smoking. Closed Christmas. 3 double rooms
all with bath and/or shower. B&B double £55. Evening meal by arrangement
£16; bring your own wine. New nomination. More reports please.*

Haydon House   *Tel* Bath (0225) 427351 and
9 Bloomfield Park   444919
Bath BA2 2BY

Magdalene Ashman's sophisticated no-smoking B&B in a spacious
Victorian house a stiff walk up from the centre of Bath has recently been
redecorated "and the cosseting now extends from top (hair-drier) to
bottom (padded loo seats); other extras include carafe of sherry in the
bedroom, *all* the latest mags, *all* the Sunday papers". *Haydon House* is a
great favourite with American visitors to Bath, and the Ashmans are
particularly helpful to their foreign visitors. It has a pretty garden and a
terrace for summer drinks, and a comfortable chintzy lounge, "very *House
and Garden*, with family photos and dried flowers". "We could not fault
the high standards of decor and housekeeping." "Elegant breakfasts,
everything prepared to perfection, included a large bowl of fruit."
(*Patricia Fenn, Joseph and Lola Rhea, and others*) But some readers don't care
for the "compulsorily communal" breakfast.

Open All year.
Rooms 4 double (also let as single) – 1 with bath, 3 with shower, all with
telephone, radio, TV, tea-making facilities.
Facilities Sitting room, breakfast room. ½-acre garden with sun terrace. Sports and
leisure centre nearby.
Location From Bath take A367 (Exeter) up Wells Road about 1 m. Turn right into
shopping area with *Bear* pub on right. At end of short dual carriageway fork right
into Bloomfield Road, then 2nd right turn into Bloomfield Park. Street parking.
Restrictions Not really suitable for &. No smoking. Children "by arrangement".
No dogs.
Credit cards Access, Visa.
Terms B&B (English): single occupancy £30–£35, double £40–£55. Reduced rates
for long stays and Easter breaks. Reduced rates for children sharing parents' room.
(No restaurant.)
*Service/tipping: "No service charge. Since we are effectively welcoming guests into our
home the question of tipping does not arise."*

Holly Lodge   *Tel* Bath (0225) 424042
8 Upper Oldfield Park
Bath BA2 3JZ

Yet again there has been much praise for Carrolle Sellick's small, no-
smoking, B&B hotel. "My fifth visit; the very high standard has been
maintained. The decor of the rooms is charming, breakfast is immaculately served." "Decor co-ordinated, even to cups and saucers. Breakfasts
excellent, with a wide choice, including wonderful croissants." "The
imaginative fruit platter is a welcome innovation for the calorie-
conscious." "Informal yet up to the standards of a small hotel; guests
don't have to mingle, or eat communally." "The new conservatory makes
a charming breakfast room. Our bedroom could not be faulted." "Sets the
standard by which we will judge others." This large Victorian house, with
a half-acre garden, is high up on the slopes opposite the city, of which it
has a magnificent view. Bedrooms are decorated in subtle and restful
colours – book early for those with the view. (*Katharine Wright, EH
Whitaker, Mrs K Kelly, Gordon and Margaret Ward, and many others*) One
reader's mild caveat: "Perhaps a slight weakness for over-decoration."

Open All year.
Rooms 5 double, 1 single – all with bath and/or shower, telephone, radio, TV, tea-making facilities.
Facilities Lounge, breakfast room. ½-acre garden.
Location ½ m SW of city centre, 1st right off Wells Road (A367). Carpark.
Restrictions Not suitable for &. No smoking. No dogs.
Credit cards Access, Visa.
Terms B&B: single £38–£45, double £55–£65. Off-season reductions for 2 nights or more. "Learn to play golf" weeks by arrangement. Reductions for children sharing parents' room. (No restaurant.)
Service/tipping: "Tipping not encouraged. Any contributions shared among staff."

Paradise House Hotel   *Tel* Bath (0225) 317723
86–88 Holloway
Bath BA2 4PX

A civilised B&B run by David and Janet Cutting, seven minutes by foot down to the Roman Baths, the Pump Room and the Abbey (rather longer and a steep uphill slog on the return journey). It is in a quiet cul-de-sac, formerly part of the old Roman Fosse Way. The house itself is c. 1720; it has fine views of the Georgian city, and a well-favoured half-acre walled garden. It has been carefully restored by the Cuttings; decor is in Laura Ashley/Designers Guild style. Readers have enjoyed the thoughtful decor, with period features restored, and the bedrooms (No 1 is "enormous, with brass double bed – really comfortable – and Edwardian bath"), and praised the helpful hosts and the "distinct feeling of generosity about the service". More reports please.

Open All year except 20–31 Dec.
Rooms 9 double – 6 with bath, 1 with shower, all with telephone, radio, TV, tea-making facilities. 1 ground-floor room suitable for &.
Facilities Sitting room, breakfast room. ½-acre garden with patios and croquet.
Location From A4 turn left at first main traffic lights on to A36, A367 Wells and Exeter ring road. At large roundabout (bisected by railway viaduct) take first left (A367 Exeter road). Continue up hill, the Wellsway, about ¾ m; turn left at small shopping area near Dewhurst butcher; continue left down hill into cul-de-sac. Hotel is 200 yds on left. 3 garages (£1 a night) and parking.
Restrictions No children under 3. No dogs.
Credit cards Access, Visa.
Terms B&B: single £33–£53, double £40–£60. Reduced rates for 5 nights or more. 1-night bookings refused for Sat. Children sharing parents' room £10. (No restaurant; dinner reservations made in local restaurants.)

The Priory Hotel   *Tel* Bath (0225) 331922
Weston Road   *Fax* (0225) 448276
Bath BA1 2XT   *Telex* 44612

This large 19th-century neo-Gothic house, two miles from the centre of Bath, is close to the road in front but has two acres of grounds, with a swimming pool, at the back. It's expensive, but it is liked for its tranquillity, the efficient manager, Mr Conboy, and the "attractive, courteous and friendly cosmopolitan staff". It is furnished throughout to a high standard. The drawing room, filled with flowers, books and ornaments, has French windows on to the garden. Bedrooms, which vary in size, are traditional, with fine fabrics and period furniture and efficient bathrooms. In the restaurant, which is in three inter-connecting rooms all different in style and all overlooking the garden, cooking by Michael Collom is sophisticated and reliable. "I have never stayed in a hotel I liked better. Furnishings in excellent taste. Food *very* good. Service friendly and efficient." (*RW Moss, also Jan Morris*) Parking space is limited and can cause congestion.

Open All year.
Rooms 18 double, 3 single – all with bath and/or shower, telephone, radio, TV.
Facilities Drawing room, 2 lounges, restaurant; functions facilities. 2-acre grounds with heated swimming pool and croquet.
Location 1 m W of city centre, just beyond Royal Victoria Park. Limited parking.
Restrictions Only public rooms suitable for &. No smoking in restaurant. No dogs.
Credit cards All major cards accepted.
Terms [1990 rates] B&B (English): single £85, double £120–£170. Set lunch £20, dinner £30; full alc £35.50. 1-night bookings refused for weekends in season. Special meals for children on request.

The Queensberry Hotel   *Tel* Bath (0225) 447928
Russel Street   *Fax* (0225) 446065
Bath BA1 2QF   *Telex* 445628

"Such luxury! A huge, beautiful, antique-furnished room, overlooking the street but quiet. Vast draped bed, immaculate bathroom. Super light breakfast served in our room. Wonderfully central. Parking can be a problem, but the hotel helped with this." "Pleasant, friendly service. The light meals, including a few hot dishes, were ideal after a concert when we didn't want a blow-out." "Nice, fresh, efficient, not the least pompous." Stephen and Penny Ross's upmarket B&B occupies three fine period houses with 18th-century stucco ceilings and cornices, and an attractive drawing room. Some of the rooms at the top are quite small, but are priced accordingly. Hot and cold light meals are now served in the bar at lunchtime and in the evening, there is a 24-hour room service for cold snacks. (*M and M Lawson, RB and ER Fairweather, Paul van Broekhoven; also Vicki Elden*) Only complaints: "Some bottled water would have been welcome in the bedroom." "The guide to Bath restaurants on which they base their recommendations is out of date."

Open All year except 2 weeks over Christmas and New Year.
Rooms 24 double – all with bath, shower, telephone, radio, TV; baby-listening by arrangement.
Facilities Drawing room, bar. Private meeting room. Small patio garden.
Location Off Lansdown Road, above Assembly Rooms.
Restrictions Not suitable for &. No dogs.
Credit cards All major cards accepted.
Terms B&B (continental): single occupancy £65–£110, double £80–£130. 1-night bookings possibly refused at Easter. (No restaurant but 24-hour light-meal service.)
Service/tipping: "Service charge included in room rate but not at a fixed percentage. This is to discourage tipping unless guests wish to give something extra."

Somerset House   *Tel* Bath (0225) 466451
35 Bathwick Hill
Bath BA2 6LD

The Seymours' no-smoking hotel or upmarket guest house, in a handsome Regency mansion a short drive or bus-ride or a stiffish walk uphill from the city centre, has had a Guide entry for many years. As we have said in the past, *Somerset House* is an establishment very much with its own style – wholly congenial to some, irksome to others. Many guests are faithful regulars – "rather serious ABC-types" in the view of a first-timer. It is said to be good for "singles wanting a friendly atmosphere; one feels immediately at home among the books, the grand piano and the family pets". Bedrooms are well maintained, and have private facilities, but no TV. One double, and the single, are said to be very small; some furnishings come in for criticism this year. In the agreeable basement dining room, which also caters for non-residents, meals, cooked by Mrs Seymour, her son and son-in-law, are not gourmet, and are sometimes uneven in execution; but one reader called the food "simple, but beautifully presented, the kind of home-cooking we would like to achieve ourselves, and which does not leave one replete as with restaurant dining". The Seymours grow much of the produce used; and care about the quality of their suppliers. Breakfasts are "particularly good". (*Max and Ruby Milner, and others*) Dinner is served at about 7 pm, though the Seymours say: "We are not inflexible about this, and frequently do a theatre plate at 6.30 or 6.45 by prior arrangement; meals are prepared for service at 7, which seems the most popular time, and that is when they are best eaten!" One reader this year found the lounge somewhat dingy, and preferred the conservatory.

Open All year except 27 Dec–13 Jan. Dining room closed Sun evening.
Rooms 8 double, 1 single – 7 with bath, 2 with shower, all with telephone, radio, tea-making facilities. 1 ground-floor room.
Facilities 2 lounges (1 with bar), TV room, dining room. 1½-acre garden with 7¼-inch gauge model railway. 5 mins from Kennet and Avon canal – angling for temporary members at Bathampton Angling Club; canal boat trips. 15 mins' walk from centre.
Location Junction of Bathwick Hill (which leads to Bath University) and Cleveland Walk. Carpark.
Restrictions Not suitable for &. No smoking. No children under 10. Small dogs only, not in public rooms.
Credit cards Access, Amex, Visa.
Terms B&B £20–£27.50; dinner, B&B £36.55–£44. Set Sun lunch £9.65, dinner £16.50. Vegetarian and simple diets catered for. Midweek breaks; special interest weekends, e.g. Georgian Bath, Roman Bath, Brunel. 5-day Christmas house party by prior arrangement. Reduced rates for children sharing parents' room; special meals.
Service/tipping: "No service charge. If we are forced to take a tip it goes into a tin for the staff."

Sydney Gardens Hotel   *Tel* Bath (0225) 464818 and
Sydney Road   445362
Bath BA2 6NT

Stanley and Diane Smithson's handsome Italianate Victorian villa in a pretty garden is ten minutes from the city centre – just far enough to be peaceful, yet a short walk to Bridge Street. You can park your car in the grounds. It is next to the Kennet and Avon canal; there are good walks along the towpath. The hotel is B&B only, and no-smoking. Visitors appreciate the large, prettily decorated and comfortable bedrooms, and the elegant drawing room with lovely views. "Mr Smithson's paintings and original clocks add interest to the house. A nice touch is that they keep menus from the local restaurants to help guests select an eating place." "The guests' comfort is of paramount importance to the Smithsons. Breakfasts maintain the high standards they set themselves. The garden is a peaceful haven in this busy city." (*Mrs JA Jolly, Jane Dorrell; also Dr RA Mayou, and others*) Only snag – the hotel is close to a railway line which is said to be busy till midnight and after 6 am. One reader found the 9 am end to breakfast and the 10.30 checkout time "a bit early for a leisurely weekend away".

Open All year except Christmas and first 3 weeks Jan.
Rooms 6 double – all with bath, shower, telephone, radio, TV, tea-making facilities.
Facilities Lounge, breakfast room. ½-acre garden; private gateway to park with tennis and walk along adjacent Kennet and Avon canal.
Location From A4 turn left on to A36 ring road towards Exeter and Wells. Cross Avon; gateway to Sydney Gardens is directly ahead. Turn right, pass Holbourne Museum on left, turn left. Hotel is 200 yds up slope on left. From S the approach road (A36) takes you past the hotel. Parking.
Restrictions Not suitable for &. No smoking. No children under 4. Small dogs by arrangement.
Credit cards Access, Visa.
Terms B&B (English): single occupancy £50–£60, double £60–£65. Extra bed £15. Winter midweek breaks. 1-night bookings sometimes refused at weekend. (No restaurant.)
Service/tipping: "As we run the business ourselves, we do not expect tips. If anything is kindly left it is shared among staff."

BATHFORD Avon   Map 2

Eagle House   *Tel* Bath (0225) 859946
Church Street
Bathford BA1 7RS

An imposing listed Georgian building by John Wood the Elder, in a quiet conservation village three miles from Bath. Its young owners, Mr and Mrs Napier, take genuine pride in maintaining the house, set in spacious grounds in a quiet suburban location. All the rooms look out over countryside or the one and a half acres of garden. Readers have praised the Napiers' welcoming, caring approach: "cool entrance hall, large, handsome drawing room with plenty of well-spaced chairs and sofas, tables with magazines and a fine marble fireplace, and generous landing upstairs with sofas, chests of drawers, etc"; and bedrooms are mostly spacious with comfortable beds and scrupulously clean bathroom, though one of the oldest ones has been described to us as "pokey". No dinner is served, but there are plenty of small restaurants and pubs nearby, and in Bath. It's a pleasant alternative to staying in Bath itself; you can avoid the problems of parking in the city if you take a bus. The Napiers write: "*Eagle House* is one of the very small number of establishments in the Bath area which has found it possible to welcome guests who smoke, guests who drink, guests with dogs and guests with children. We are anti-embargo and pro-hospitality." More reports please.

Open 5 Jan–23 Dec.
Rooms 5 double, 1 single – all with bath and/or shower, telephone, TV, tea-making facilities, baby-listening. Also 2 doubles in cottage with bathroom, sitting room, kitchen.
Facilities Drawing room, sitting room, breakfast room. 1½-acre garden with croquet, sandpit.

Location 3 m E of Bath on A363. At roundabout immediately after Batheaston follow sign to Bathford; fork left after railway bridge; after 300 yds take Church Street (first on right). Hotel is 200 yds on right behind high stone wall and wrought-iron gates. Conservation area, so hotel sign not permitted. Ample parking.
Restrictions Not suitable for &. No dogs in public rooms.
Credit cards None accepted.
Terms B&B: single £26–£35, double £37–£53. Winter breaks. 1-night bookings sometimes refused for Sat and bank holidays. Children free in parents' room. (No restaurant.)
Service/tipping: "The only way to end the debate and uncertainty about this is to introduce legislation including a service charge on basic room rates. Tipping should still be permitted."

The Orchard   *Tel* Bath (0225) 858765
80 High Street
Bathford BA1 7TG

John and Olga London's listed Georgian house is "pristine, immaculate and totally tranquil, in attractive countryside set well back from an unbusy road a few miles from Bath" in a one-and-a-half-acre garden – "a picture". It has an elegant sitting room with books, deep, comfortable chairs and antique or period furniture, and attractive bedrooms with pastel decor, deep-pile carpet and large windows overlooking the garden. "All the details exactly right. On arrival we were offered a pot of tea by Mrs London, obviously concerned to do all she could do for guests." Breakfast is "very good", with a choice of local yoghurts and toasted wholemeal bread; it is taken communally at a large table. (*Andrena Woodhams, FW Harris; also Karl Wiegers, and others*)

Open Mar–Oct.
Rooms 4 double, all with bath, shower, TV. 1, with separate entrance, adjoins house.
Facilities Lounge, dining room. 1½-acre grounds.
Location Under railway bridge; first left at *Crown Inn*, up hill; past village store on left. *Orchard* is 100 yds on right.
Restrictions Not suitable for &. No smoking in bedrooms. No children under 11. No dogs.
Credit cards None accepted.
Terms B&B: double £39.50–£57. 1-night bookings sometimes refused for weekend. (No restaurant.)
Service/tipping: "We make it clear that our prices are totally inclusive."

BATTLE East Sussex   **Map 3**

Little Hemingfold Farmhouse   *Tel* Battle (042 46) 4338
    Hotel
Telham, Battle TN33 0TT

Early Victorian farmhouse "higgledy-piggledy" in 40-acre grounds up a bumpy track. Run since 1988 by Paul and Allison Slater. Recommended for good cooking and generous servings at communal dinners at 7.30 (though separate tables can be arranged); set menu with choice of starter and dessert, but alternative main dishes available. Good English breakfasts. Bedrooms vary in size; some quite basic in furnishing, with cramped bathroom, but all have telephone, TV and electric blankets. "What it lacks in luxury it makes up for in hospitality." 13 rooms, 11 with bath and shower. Dinner, B&B £36–£45. Set dinner £16. Was in Guide under earlier owners. More reports please.

Netherfield Place
Battle TN33 9PP

Tel Battle (042 46) 4455
Fax (042 46) 4024
Telex 95284

Michael and Helen Collier's red brick Georgian-style 1920s country house hotel is peacefully situated in large well-kept grounds. The decor is of a high standard, and traditional; the pretty lounge has comfortable chairs and a log fire in winter. Bedrooms, in light colours, vary in size; the doubles on the first floor are said to be particularly attractive. All have flowers, fresh fruit, chocolates and so on, and well-equipped carpeted bathrooms with bathrobes and capacious towels. The panelled restaurant is popular with local people – Sunday lunch is said to be very good value. "It's not the kind of place where you are made to feel one of the family, but more a small and welcoming hotel with an upmarket restaurant – and the residents are at no disadvantage as the table d'hôte menus offer plenty of choice and good value." The food is modern, "not *haute cuisine*, but freshly prepared and cooked, served with style"; there is a vegetarian menu. Many of the vegetables, fruits and herbs are grown in the hotel's kitchen garden. "We returned for our family weekend this October, and everyone insists we go back again next year. The two hard tennis courts are now complete and the hotel willingly supplies equipment. They also have a putting green and croquet." (*Dr and Mrs JEM Whitehead, RCJ Gordon; also WG Solomon, Jean M Willson, and others*)

Open All year except Christmas and New Year.
Rooms 10 double, 4 single – 8 with bath and shower, 6 with bath, all with telephone, radio, TV, baby-listening.
Facilities Lounge, bar, restaurant; conference facilities. 30-acre grounds with gardens, tennis, putting, croquet, clay-pigeon shooting, woodland walks. Golf, fishing, riding nearby.
Location 3 m S of Battle on A2100; turn left towards Netherfield. Hotel is 1½ m on.
Restrictions Bedrooms not suitable for &. No dogs.
Credit cards All major cards accepted.
Terms (Service at guests' discretion) B&B: single £45–£60, double £75–£100. Set lunch £13.50, dinner £14.95; full alc £28. 1-night weekend bookings refused Mar–Oct. Children £5 in parents' room; special meals by arrangement.

BEAMINSTER Dorset   Map 2

The Bridge House Hotel
Prout Bridge
Beaminster DT8 3AY

Tel Beaminster (0308) 862200

Beaminster is an old country town built in mellow stone in the West Dorset hills, in the heart of Hardy country (it is Emminster in *Tess of the D'Urbervilles*). *The Bridge House*, dating probably from the 13th century, stands in a walled garden in the centre of the town. It was taken over in 1987 by Peter Pinkster and extensively refurbished, and is now recommended for reinclusion in the Guide: "Charming welcome, our luxuriously appointed bedroom overlooked the nice garden. Service good, food excellent." "The welcome was warm, the accommodation quiet and very comfortable. Mr Pinkster is also the chef and provided interesting and delicious meals for me despite my severe dietary problems; the normal menu, too, was excellent." There are three or four choices on each course (three plus cheese and coffee) on the dinner menu, and much use of local produce. (*Peter Hall, Alan and Barbara Kenyon*) More reports please.

Open All year.
Rooms 8 double, 1 single – all with bath and/or shower, telephone, radio, TV, tea-making facilities. 5 in coach house. 2 on ground floor.
Facilities Lounge with dispense bar, sitting room, restaurant. ½-acre walled garden.
Location 2 mins' walk from centre. Windows on road double-glazed. Parking.
Restriction No dogs in public rooms.
Credit cards Access, Visa.
Terms B&B £29.50–£45.50; dinner, B&B £45.50–£61.50. Set dinner £18. 1-night bookings sometimes refused over bank holidays.
Service/tipping: "No mention of service charge on bill or menu. If a tip is left it is distributed to staff working at the time – not the proprietor."

BEERCROCOMBE Somerset   Map 1

Frog Street Farm **BUDGET**   *Tel* Hatch Beauchamp
Beercrocombe, Taunton TA3 6AF   (0823) 480430

🏆 *César award in 1988: For outstanding farmhouse hospitality*

"A clean, comfortable home from home and the kindest, most hospitable host and hostess. I didn't know such value for money still existed." "A sumptuous farmhouse, beautifully kept. We enjoyed using the swimming pool at 10 pm, watched by a plump and curious cat." "The bedroom, newly furnished, with a brand new *en suite* bathroom, would have graced a four-star hotel; it had a virtually private sitting room and its own front door." "A happy, tranquil atmosphere." Just a few of this year's tributes to Veronica Cole's large, airy, well-kept and reasonably priced 15th-century farmhouse/guest house on a large working farm, deep in rural Somerset, about 21 miles from the north and south coasts. It has fields and woods on one side, orchards on the other, and a heated pool under the cherry trees. Mrs Cole now lets only three bedrooms, so there are no more than six guests at any time. She is a good straightforward cook; the no-choice menus include roast lamb, roast chicken, pheasant casserole, and "wicked" desserts; most produce used is from the farm. No licence, you bring your own wine. (*Suzanne McKay, DR Shillitoe, the Rev RH Everett, Wendy and Ian Crammond, Mrs EJ Booley, and many others*) This is a working farm; the approach could not be described as *soigné*.

Open Mar–Nov.
Rooms 3 suites – 2 with bath, 1 with shower, all with tea-making facilities.
Facilities 3 sitting rooms (1 with TV), dining room. Garden with heated swimming pool. On 160-acre working farm with trout stream.
Location 7 m SE of Taunton. Leave M5 at exit 25; take A358 to Ilminster, then the turning to Hatch Beauchamp. Turn at *Hatch Inn*, down Station Rd. Then left all way down no-through road. Signposted.
Restrictions Not suitable for ♿. No children under 11. No dogs.
Credit cards None accepted.
Terms B&B £23; dinner, B&B £37 (unlicensed – bring your own wine). Weekly rates.

BETHERSDEN Kent   Map 3

Little Hodgeham   *Tel* High Halden (023 385) 323
Smarden Road, Bethersden   *to change to* (0233) 850323
TN26 3HE

"A unique experience of comfort and pampering." "Faultless and very
good value." "Erica Wallace should be cloned and widely distributed, she
is a national treasure." Australian-born Miss Wallace's 500-year-old half-
timbered Tudor cottage in the tiny village of Bethersden in Kent is
"typical chocolate box", with roses, honeysuckle, ancient beams, antiques, fresh flowers from the garden, log fires in cold weather. It is set in
a flower-filled garden, with a swimming pool, a pond stocked with carp
and tench, and a water garden. There are three double bedrooms with
comfortable beds and lace-trimmed duvets. In the dining room Miss
Wallace presides over "delicious" communally eaten meals elegantly
served with fine bone china and crystal. Guests are consulted in advance
about their likes and dislikes. The private house-party atmosphere of
Little Hodgeham is appreciated by those who enjoy socialising with their
hostess and meeting their fellow guests. Full hotel amenities are not on
offer. (*Bob and Joyce Andrewartha, Clive RS Barter, John and Suzanne Price*)

Open Easter–Sept.
Rooms 1 family, 2 double – all with bath and/or shower, radio, tea-making
facilities, baby-listening.
Facilities Drawing room, TV room, dining room, small conservatory. ½-acre
garden with unheated swimming pool, pond, water garden. Tennis, golf nearby.
Location 10 m W of Ashford. From Bethersden, at *Bull* pub, take Smarden road
for 2 m.
Restrictions Not suitable for &. Children 1–4 by arrangement. Small dogs by
prior arrangement, not in public rooms.
Credit cards None accepted.
Terms [1990 rates] Dinner, B&B £44.50 (£34.50 for stays of 4 nights or more).
Reduced rates for children sharing parents' room, depending on age; special meals
with advance warning.
Service/tipping: "No service charge. Staff is told never to tout for tips."

BIBURY Gloucestershire   Map 2

Bibury Court Hotel   *Tel* Bibury (028 574) 337
Bibury   *Fax* (028 574) 660
Nr Cirencester GL7 5NT

A splendid Tudor mansion, added to and improved in the 1660s, 1750s
and 1920s, with panelled rooms, four-posters and much fine antique
furniture. The Coln river – good fishing for trout – forms the boundary of
the six-acre grounds. The hotel, owned and run "on country house lines"
by Jane Collier with her sister and brother-in-law Anne and Andrew
Johnston, makes a tranquil base for touring the Cotswolds. "The
imposing entrance and elegant facade, particularly when floodlit at night,
make you believe that a formal and expensive hotel exists within. On
closer inspection it is seen to be elegant, but lived in. There are no great
pretensions to being smooth and professional. No uniformed staff, just
friendly people to greet you and show you to your room. The public areas
are well furnished, and the main lounge was a treat in January, with its

huge open fireplace and log fire. In our bedroom the furniture was old rather than antique; the wardrobe door had to be kept shut with a wedge; soft furnishings were of a high quality; bathroom small and plain but adequate." The restaurant, *Collier's*, is in a converted coach house about fifty yards down the drive. There is a new "Antipodean team", Howard Morris and Andrew Seaton, in the kitchen this year. "Pleasant ambience, with subdued lighting and candles and friendly, if somewhat casual, staff. About six choices of each course; cooking a little heavy on butter and cream, but quite imaginative. Wine list extensive and very reasonable, with several half-bottles charged at half the full bottle price." Vegetarians report being well catered for at dinner, "and the bar lunches were just as good". (*BR Coates, Penny Webster, also Margaret Brocato*) "Not immaculate, fairly casual, but charming" is the consensus view, but some readers this year, as previously, have felt the casualness to be excessive.

Open All year except Christmas.
Rooms 1 suite, 14 double, 3 single – all with bath, telephone, TV, baby-listening; radio, tea-making facilities on request.
Facilities Lounge, cocktail bar, breakfast room, dining room, conference room. 6-acre grounds with croquet and fishing. Golf nearby.
Location On edge of village on A433 between Burford and Cirencester.
Restriction Not suitable for severely &.
Credit cards Access, Amex, Visa.
Terms B&B (continental): single £45–£60, double £70–£76, suite £100. Extra bed £15. English breakfast from £3.50. Set lunch £18, dinner £20; full alc lunch £22, dinner £24. 2-day breaks out of season except Cheltenham Gold Cup week. Special meals for children.
Service/tipping: "Our information sheet says we do not charge as we do not pretend to give service. However, the staff pot continues to grow each month, which must mean something."

BISHOP'S TACHBROOK Warwickshire   Map 2

Mallory Court Hotel   *Tel* Leamington Spa (0926) 330214
Harbury Lane   *Fax* (0926) 451714
Bishop's Tachbrook   *Telex* 317294
Leamington Spa CV33 9QB

Jeremy Mort and Allan Holland have been thirteen years at their luxurious country house, built in the 1920s in the Lutyens manner. It enjoys a rural setting, but is only nine miles from Stratford-on-Avon, and a little more from the National Exhibition Centre outside Birmingham. The large grounds with formal gardens, unheated swimming pool, tennis and squash courts, are lovingly maintained. There are several immaculate sitting rooms and a small veranda. Bedrooms, with a floral theme, are comfortable and mostly spacious; all are differently decorated with fine fabrics and period furnishings and are sumptuously equipped. The Blenheim suite, with its spectacular art deco bath and *trompe l'œil* painting on the ceiling, is particularly noteworthy. *Michelin* awards a rosette for the meals served in the oak-panelled dining room (Allan Holland is the chef); there is an extensive wine list. Service is punctilious. The atmosphere is formal – male guests are expected to wear a jacket and tie at dinner. Prices are high – "but it's worth saving up for".

Open All year except Christmas afternoon to New Year.
Rooms 1 suite, 9 double – all with bath, shower, telephone, radio, TV.
Facilities Lounge, drawing room, garden room, dining room. 10-acre gardens
with unheated swimming pool, tennis, squash, croquet. Golf 2 m.
Location 2 m S of Leamington Spa off B4087. Take left turning to Harbury.
Restrictions Not suitable for &. No children under 12. No dogs (kennels nearby).
Credit cards Access, Visa.
Terms B&B (continental): single occupancy £102, double £92–£180, suite £276.
Dinner, B&B £84–£180 per person. English breakfast £9. Set lunch £19.50, dinner
£37.50. Only half-board terms at weekends. Winter breaks.
*Service/tipping: "We actively discourage tipping. It is stated on all our literature that all
prices include VAT and service."*

BISHOPS TAWTON Devon   Map 1

Downrew House   *Tel* Barnstaple (0271) 42497
Bishops Tawton, Barnstaple   *Fax* (0271) 23947
EX32 0DY

*Queen Anne country house in remote rural setting near Barnstaple. 12-acre
grounds with golf course, swimming pool, tennis and croquet. Another change of
ownership in early 1990. First reports speak warmly of friendly and helpful
proprietors, Clive Butler and Bruce Hendricks (new to hotel business),
immaculate bedrooms and good food (plenty of choice – mainly English dishes)
cooked by new chef, Ashley Carkeet. Mealtimes now more flexible. 12 rooms, all
with bath and shower. Dinner, B&B (English) £45.35–£70 [1990]. More reports
please.*

BLAKENEY Norfolk   Map 3

The Blakeney Hotel   *Tel* Blakeney (0263) 740797
The Quay, Blakeney NR25 7NE   *Fax* (0263) 740795

*Overlooking National Trust harbour, with lovely estuary views, quietly situated
family-run hotel with "decent sized" heated indoor swimming pool, saunas,
1-acre grounds. Bedrooms vary in size; most are quite simple. "Well and
comfortably furnished; good food, served by well-trained and exceptionally nice
staff." Children welcome "provided they do not spoil the enjoyment of others";
high teas. 50 rooms, all with bath and/or shower. B&B £39–£53. Set dinner
£15. Was in earlier editions. Recommended for readmission. More reports
please.*

BLANDFORD FORUM Dorset   Map 2

La Belle Alliance   *Tel* Blandford (0258) 452842
Whitecliff Mill Street
Blandford Forum DT11 7BP

This restaurant-with-rooms is run by Lauren and Philip Davison (he is
the chef) in a spacious Victorian house on the quiet outskirts of a pleasant
market-town in the heart of Hardy country. There is an intimate lounge
for aperitifs. Meals, in the quite formal dining room, with lavish fabrics,

are the centre of things. There is a set-price dinner menu, changing almost daily, with five or six choices at each course, much use of local produce, excellent home-made ice-creams, and a wide-ranging wine list. Some overnight visitors in 1989/90 have expressed their entire satisfaction: "It would be difficult for the most fastidious to find anything to complain about in this inviting establishment. A smiling, welcoming hostess, a comfortable room with thoughtful extras, beautifully cooked meals with impeccable service, all make this an island in a sea of mediocrity." "Calm, restful atmosphere, pleasant leisurely gourmet evening." (*I Getley, RC and M Petherick*) However, some winter visitors felt that the decor of the bedrooms was not special, and one couple in a "narrow and cramped" room suffered an excruciatingly uncomfortable bed. The Davidsons tell us that the bedrooms have now been completely redecorated and refurnished, so we'd be glad to hear from recent visitors.

Open All year except Jan. Restaurant closed Sun evening; lunch served Sun, other days by arrangement only.
Rooms 5 double (also available as single) – all with bath, shower, telephone, TV, tea-making facilities, baby-listening.
Facilities Lounge, restaurant. Small garden. Riding stables opposite.
Location Go through town (1-way system); bear left on to Shaftesbury (Warminster) Road; restaurant is 300 yds on right. Parking for 13 cars.
Restrictions Not suitable for &. No smoking in dining room. Children under 7 by arrangement. No dogs in public rooms.
Credit cards Access, Amex, Visa.
Terms B&B (English): single occupancy £45, double £60–£70. Lunch (by arrangement) from £11.50, set dinner £21. Gourmet breaks. Reduced rates and special meals for children by arrangement.
Service/tipping: "We do not expect tips as we believe we pay our staff a fair wage for the good service they offer."

BLAWITH Cumbria   Map 4

Appletree Holme Farm   *Tel* Lowick Bridge (022 985) 618
Blawith, Nr Ulverston
LA12 8EL

"Wonderful in every respect. Non-pretentious pampering from dedicated experts. Fells on the doorstep. One of the most relaxing breaks we have enjoyed." "Lived up to your report in every respect." (*Graham Jones, Mrs David Close*)

Appletree Holme Farm, run by Roy and Shirley Carlsen "as a fine example of living life the way it was meant to be lived", is a secluded old stone farmhouse, with open fires and beamed ceilings, and views of the five acres of carefully tended gardens and orchard with wooded slopes and fells beyond. The four bedrooms are comfortable, clean and well equipped, with lots of hot water. Lounges are welcoming, with open fires, china, furniture, ornaments all chosen with impeccable taste. "We were impressed with the care taken by Roy Carlsen in the cooking: simple fresh ingredients, with imaginative use of fresh herbs." Local game, meats and trout and the Carlsens' own garden vegetables are served in ample helpings; there is a four-course set dinner menu but alternatives are always offered. The extensive breakfast menu includes Cumberland sausages, free-range eggs, oak-smoked kippers and goat's milk yoghurt; orders are taken after dinner. The Carlsens' two border collies and cat are said to be as welcoming as their owners.

Note This is a small establishment, with no reception clerks or porters; the Carlsens say they are not able to receive guests between 2 and 5 pm except by prior arrangement.

Open All year except New Year.
Rooms 2 suites, 2 double – all with bath (2 double, 1 whirlpool), shower, telephone, radio, TV, tea-making facilities. 1 suite adjacent to main building with private entrance and garden.
Facilities Sitting room, library, dining room. 5-acre grounds with gardens, orchards, paddocks. Fishing, shooting, lake bathing nearby.
Location Turn off A5084 up lane opposite Blawith church. After ½ m turn right; after 1 m turn left at farm sign.
Restrictions Not suitable for &. No smoking in dining room and library; discouraged in bedrooms. No children under 10. No dogs in bedrooms or public rooms.
Credit card Amex.
Terms Dinner, B&B £45–£53; single supplement £10. Picnic lunches available. Set dinner £18.50.
Service/tipping: "Tipping does not arise – one does not offer gratuities to one's hosts!"

BLICKLING Norfolk   Map 3

The Buckinghamshire Arms **BUDGET**   *Tel* Aylsham (0263) 732133
Blickling   *Fax* (0263) 734924
Nr Aylsham NR11 6NF

In 1990 the National Trust acquired this 17th-century inn, a popular pub with locals, quietly situated beside – and with fine views of – an NT gem, Blickling Hall. First reports are positive: "Warm, comfortable, welcoming; runs smoothly apart from some minor organisational hitches. No private facilities; deep luxurious Victorian bath, lots of fluffy towels and magazines in the communal bathroom. Standard pub food." Closed Christmas. 3 rooms (with comfortable 4-poster), and TV. B&B: single £38, double £48. Lunch £4.50, dinner £9. More reports please.

BOLTON-BY-BOWLAND Lancashire   Map 4

Harrop Fold Country   *Tel* Bolton-by-Bowland
  Farmhouse Hotel   (020 07) 600
Bolton-by-Bowland
Clitheroe BB7 4PJ

Farm house, "an oasis of tranquillity", in remote location in heart of Pennines, run as a hotel by the "hospitable and delightful" Wood family for 20 years. Recommended for comfortable bedrooms with numerous amenities including TV, and home-cooked meals "with wide variety of interesting choices", served at flexible times. 7 double, all with bath. Dinner, B&B double £88. Was in earlier editions but dropped following criticisms. More reports please.

Do you know of a good hotel or country inn in the United States or Canada? Nominations please to our sibling publication, America's Wonderful Little Hotels and Inns, PO Box 150, Riverside Avenue, Riverside, Conn. 06878, USA.

BORROWDALE Cumbria   Map 4

Seatoller House   `BUDGET`   *Tel* Borrowdale (059 684) 218
Borrowdale, Keswick CA12 5XN   *from mid 1990* Borrowdale
                                                   (076 87) 77218

🍷 *César award in 1984: Most sympathetic guest house*

Seatoller is over 300 years old, and has been run continuously as a guest
house for more than 100 years. It enjoys a "breathtaking setting" at the
head of the Borrowdale valley, near the Honister Pass, close to the
starting point of many spectacular fell walks. Now run by David and Ann
Pepper, it is friendly and remarkably inexpensive, and has long been a
favourite of Guide readers in search of homely comfort, good value and
conviviality, rather than lavish decor, *haute cuisine* and hotel-type
facilities. Meals are communal, served at two large tables – breakfast at
8.30 am and dinner at 7 pm. Bedrooms, some of them quite large, are
"spotless and sympathetically decorated". Two regular visitors report:
"Always remains *marvellous*. All the bedrooms now have a private
bathroom. We were a bit nervous about this, but they are lovely, warm
from the heated towel rail, painted a restful green, and the towels, large
and fluffy, are a vast improvement. The sociable bath queue really isn't
missed at all. They are not all *en suite*, however, so you need a dressing
gown." "The ideal place for a single person as the company is always
very friendly. The food is as good and plentiful as ever." (*Abigail Kirby
Harris, W Ian Stewart*)

Open Mar–Nov. Dining room closed Tue evening.
Rooms 9 double – all with bath and/or shower. 1 in converted bakehouse.
2 ground-floor rooms.
Facilities Lounge, library, dining room, self-service tea-bar; small conference
facilities; drying room. 2-acre grounds.
Location 8 m S of Keswick on B5289. Regular bus service from Keswick.
Restrictions No smoking in dining room and bedrooms. Not suitable for severely
&. No children under 5. No dogs in public rooms.
Credit cards None accepted.
Terms (No service charge) Dinner, B&B £28–£29.50. Packed lunches available.
Weekly rates; special rates for parties of 18 or more. 1-night bookings sometimes
refused. Reduced rates for children sharing parents' room.

BOUGHTON MONCHELSEA Kent   Map 3

Tanyard Hotel   *Tel* Maidstone (0622) 744705
Wierton Hill,
Boughton Monchelsea
Maidstone ME17 4JT

A lovingly restored medieval yeoman's house, later a tannery, now a very
small hotel, "welcoming, comfortable and wonderfully peaceful", owned
and run by Jan Davies. It has an attractive garden with a fishpond, and
enjoys a secluded position on the edge of the Weald of Kent, looking out
over orchards and cottages. Leeds Castle and Sissinghurst, Folkestone,
Dover and Gatwick are all within an hour's drive. There are only five
bedrooms, all heavily beamed, and furnished with good antique pieces. A
magnificent suite with far-reaching views occupies the whole of the top
floor. Readers continue to be warmly appreciative: "Ten out of ten for

preservation of Old English architecture. Brilliant combination of mod cons with the ancient." "Bedrooms individually decorated, with the amenities of home; beds very comfortable and bathrooms state of the art, yet the atmosphere is one of country charm. One of the highlights is the cosy drawing room, with a huge fireplace, that draws the guests together before dinner." "The style could probably be called slightly eccentric in the nicest possible way." There is no choice of the four courses at dinner except for dessert, but guests are asked if they would like alternatives. "Jan Davies' cooking is fine and honest for what it sets out to be – first-rate country fare." (*E and C Vesely, MP Holden, and others*) Most of the niggles arise from the historic nature of the house: "Not for the elderly or disabled; the stairs were a death trap." "The disadvantage of highly polished floors is the creaking, and the patter of feet at night." "The walls are thin, and sensitive noses notice the smells which creep through the cracks." Also: "Though dinner was called for 8, it was not served until 8.30, and one got the feeling they wanted you to have a rather expensive drink first; the wine list is priced with the words 'VAT extra'."

Open Early Mar–mid-Dec. Restaurant closed for lunch.
Rooms 1 suite, 4 double – all with bath and/or shower, telephone, radio, TV, tea-making facilities.
Facilities Hall/reception, lounge, restaurant. 1-acre garden; 9-acre farmland.
Location 5 m S of Maidstone. From B2163 at Boughton, turn down Park Lane opposite *Cock* pub. First right down Wierton Lane. Fork right; *Tanyard* is on left at bottom of hill.
Restrictions Not suitable for &. No children under 6. No dogs.
Credit cards Access, Visa.
Terms B&B (English): single £55.20, double £69, suite (depending on number of occupants) £86.25–£115. Set dinner £18.40. 1-night bookings refused at weekend.
Service/tipping: "Tips are not expected, but if given are distributed to all staff."

BOWNESS-ON-WINDERMERE Cumbria   Map 4

Lindeth Fell Country   *Tel* Windermere (096 62) 3286 and
   House Hotel   4287
Bowness-on-Windermere
LA23 3JP

This solid, well-built Lakeland-stone house stands in extensive grounds with rhododendrons and azaleas, tennis and croquet, and a small tarn with trout. It is owned and run by Pat Kennedy, ex-RAF, and his wife Diana, who does most of the cooking assisted by Sarah Churchward. There are two lounges, one of which has a beautiful Adam-style plaster ceiling and tall, wide windows looking over the treetops to Lake Windermere. There are lots of books which you are encouraged to borrow. Most bedrooms overlook the lake; they are clean and comfortable, with crisply laundered sheets, well-placed lights and lamps, and good towels and even a choice of toilet paper in the bathroom. Food is good traditional English cooking, with at least two choices for each course. The wine list is extensive and reasonably priced. "The outstanding feature here," readers have said in the past, "is the atmosphere, mostly due to the warm, outgoing personalities of the Kennedys – who are a mine of information on local walks, climbs and gardens – and the tranquillity of the house, insulated in its gardens from the bustle and activity of Bowness just down the road." *Andrena Woodhams* agrees: "A find; I felt very much at home. The Kennedys could not have been more welcoming." Some bedrooms have been refurnished this year which may answer earlier criticism that bedroom furniture didn't quite live up to the Edwardian style of the house.

Open 15 Mar–10 Nov.
Rooms 12 double, 2 single – all with bath and/or shower, telephone, radio, TV, tea-making facilities, baby-listening. 1 ground-floor room.
Facilities Ramp. Hall, 2 lounges, dispense bar, dining room. 7-acre grounds with gardens, tennis, croquet, putting, tarn with fishing. Windermere ¾ m.
Location 1 m S of Bowness on A5074.
Restrictions "More suitable for children over 7." Dogs in grounds only.
Credit cards Access, Visa.
Terms [1990 rates] Dinner, B&B: single £40–£46, double £75–£90. Light lunch £5, set dinner £17.50. 1-night bookings sometimes refused Easter and bank holidays. Reduced rates for children sharing parents' room; special meals.
Service/tipping: "I disagree with arbitrary service charges. Here it is optional. I tip for good service, and assume some guests want to do the same."

BRADFORD-ON-AVON Wiltshire　　　　　　　　　　　　Map 2

Bradford Old Windmill　　　　　　　　　　*Tel* Bradford-on-Avon
Masons Lane　　　　　　　　　　　　　　　　　　(022 16) 6842
Bradford-on-Avon BA15 1QN

This converted mill is run by Peter and Priscilla Roberts, founders of the Distinctly Different Association of granaries, chapels, oast houses, railway carriages and the like, turned into inexpensive guest accommodation. It is quietly set in a small garden on a steepish hill overlooking Bradford, and is furnished throughout with old pine and decorated with an eclectic collection of *objets trouvés* acquired during the proprietors' travels round the world. Readers enjoy the "delightful round rooms with magnificent views" (the main bedroom has a round bed as well). And "the no-smoking rule is an added attraction". Priscilla Roberts is a vegetarian and her husband an omnivore, so they compromise in the catering. At breakfast (which is communally taken) there's a wide range of alternatives "to suit carnivores, vegetarians, vegans, healthy and unhealthy eaters". Evening meals are exclusively vegetarian, usually with an international flavour; visitors should check on their availability as Mrs Roberts likes to take the occasional night off. "Our aim," she writes, "is to make our guests feel part of the household – with all the advantages and disadvantages that this entails." More reports please.

Open All year. Dinner sometimes not served (check with owners).
Rooms 3 double, 1 single – 1 with bath, 2 with shower; all with radio, tea-making facilities; TV on request.
Facilities Lounge, dining room. Small garden. River Avon 5 mins' walk.
Location In Bradford on A363 find *Castle* pub. Go down hill towards centre. After 100 yds turn left into private drive immediately before first roadside house.
Restrictions Not suitable for &. No smoking. No children under 8. No dogs.
Credit cards None accepted.
Terms B&B: single £24–£30, double £40–£60. Set dinner £15. Winter breaks, honeymoon packages. 1-night bookings sometimes refused. Reduced rates for children sharing parents' room.
Service/tipping: "Service included in the price. As proprietors we do not expect to be tipped for being nice to our guests. Our payment is in their return visits."

Please make a habit of sending a report if you stay at a Guide hotel.

Woolley Grange Hotel and
Restaurant
Woolley Green
Bradford-on-Avon BA15 1TX

Tel Bradford-on-Avon
(022 16) 4705
Fax (022 16) 4059

This mainly Jacobean manor house opened with a flourish just as we went to press last year, and entered the Guide in italics. It is multi-chimneyed and mullioned-windowed, with an oak-panelled drawing room and a new, bright conservatory, in large grounds with a fishpond, fountain, large walled kitchen garden, swimming pool and grass tennis courts. It has been carefully restored by the Chapman family, with "simple decor and friendly furniture", old beams, brass beds and gas fires in many bedrooms. In the large dining room, meals by Anand Sastry, a graduate of Marco White and Raymond Blanc, are "the best of modern British cookery"; much local produce is used, some of it organic. The hotel's most unusual feature, which we welcome, is that it is very much geared to the needs of families with young children: there is a nursery with a trained nanny and a large playroom in a converted coach house, and nursery tea is served at 5 pm; there's plenty to amuse older children as well. There is no extra charge for these facilities or for cots, "and the children are out of sight in the playroom, so adults can be civilised". Many readers this year have praised the service – "helpful and friendly, if a bit slow at times" and enjoyed the food, but there have also been criticisms: "Service was offhand and dilatory. I asked about the promised baby-listening facility and got a dismissive reply. We felt hungry and dissatisfied after the meal, *nouvelle cuisine* at its most acute, bland and unexceptional; we complained to the owner on several occasions but got no reaction." And there were other comments in a similar vein. Prices are high – perhaps too steep? As we went to press we learned of the appointment of a new chef. More reports badly needed.

Open All year except first week Jan.
Rooms 2 suites, 17 double, 1 single – all with bath and/or shower, telephone, radio, TV, baby-listening. 6 in converted dairy.
Facilities Lounges, conservatory, dining room. 14-acre grounds with gardens, heated swimming pool, tennis and croquet. Boating and fishing in the Avon 1 m.
Location 1 m NE of Bradford-on-Avon; from A363 take B3105 to Trowbridge for 1 m.
Restriction No dogs in restaurant.
Credit cards All major cards accepted.
Terms B&B (continental) double £80–£150 (10% deduction for single occupancy); dinner, B&B £80–£105 per person. Set lunch £16, dinner £26–£32; full alc £35. Off-season packages; Christmas/New Year packages. 1-night bookings at weekends generally refused. Reduced rates for children.
Service/tipping: "We neither make a service charge nor expect tips. Any sums given are distributed to staff by staff."

BRAITHWAITE Cumbria   **Map 4**

Ivy House Hotel
Braithwaite
Keswick CA12 5JY

Tel Braithwaite (059 682) 338

In the centre of a small village two miles from Keswick, this hotel featured in earlier editions of the Guide under different owners. Now it has been bought, extensively redecorated and refurbished by Nick and Wendy

Shill; it has a comfortable lounge with beams, and log fires at each end in winter, a pretty staircase, and well-appointed bedrooms; decor is traditional, with some nice old furniture. The friendly Shills, "very good hosts", run *Ivy House* with a "talented and efficient small staff". "They create a relaxed atmosphere. Dinners, cooked by Mrs Shill and served in a first-floor restaurant, oak-beamed, candle-lit and soothing in character, are very reasonably priced, and first-rate, combining the traditional with the imaginative. There is ample choice on the menu, with vegetarian tastes considered; portions are generous and well presented. Desserts are a delight, and the meal is rounded off with a very good cheeseboard. One is encouraged to dictate the pace of the meal, lingering if so inclined." "Breakfasts are Nick Shill's department, with wide choice and generous portions; toast comes in relays so it does not have time to go floppy. Excellent, unlimited coffee." The hotel has no grounds, but there are good walks from the doorstep – and the Shills keep a walkers' book in which guests enter their planned route in case anyone should get lost. (*Stella M Barratt-Pugh, Mr and Mrs BN Turvey, M and J Mentha*)

Open All year except owners' holiday (not yet fixed).
Rooms 9 double – 7 with bath, 1 with shower, all with telephone, TV, tea-making facilities, baby-listening.
Facilities Lounge, bar, dining room. Lakes, fishing, walking nearby.
Location In centre of village 2 m W of Keswick.
Restrictions Not suitable for &. No smoking in dining room.
Credit cards Access, Visa.
Terms (Service at guests' discretion) Dinner, B&B £39–£45 (£10 supplement for single occupancy). Set dinner £15. Off-season midweek rates. Reductions for children sharing parents' room, depending on age, time of year etc.

BRAMPTON Cumbria   Map 4

Farlam Hall Hotel   *Tel* Hallbankgate (069 76) 234
Brampton CA8 2NG

Readers continue to appreciate the "unaffected and un-snooty welcome extended equally to regulars and casuals" by the Quinion and Stevenson families – parents, son, daughter and son-in-law – and the "total professionalism combined with the desire to give pleasure" which they experience at *Farlam Hall*. The house dates from the 17th century but was considerably enlarged in the 19th. It lies in unspoilt countryside near Hadrian's Wall. The gardens, with mature trees and an ornamental lake, are "especially lovely". Inside it is "visually delightful, with charming *objets d'art*, fine fabrics and paintings everywhere". Bedrooms vary considerably in size and shape; they are individually decorated, "luxurious and comfortable, with 'give-aways' in abundance, and readable bedside books". Dinner is somewhat formal, served punctually at 8 pm, with jacket and tie expected of male diners. The meal, based on local produce, is "excellent, well cooked and presented, and satisfying, and the house wine good value. Breakfast has some interesting non-run-of-the-mill choices." (*IC Dewey, and others*) The restaurant is closed for lunch, but light meals are provided for residents by prior arrangement.

Open All year except Christmas evening–30 Dec and Feb. Restaurant closed for lunch.
Rooms 12 double, 1 single – all with bath and/or shower, telephone, radio, TV. 2 ground-floor rooms.

Facilities 2 lounges, bar, dining room. 5-acre grounds with croquet. Golf nearby.
Location On A689, 2½ m SE of Brampton (*not* in Farlam village).
Restrictions Not suitable for &. No children under 5. Dogs by arrangement only.
Credit cards Access, Visa.
Terms Dinner, B&B £65–£95. Set dinner £24. Winter and spring breaks.
*Service/tipping: "No service charge. Tipping is optional. Guests who wish to thank the
staff should be allowed to do so. Tips are divided among all staff at the end of the season
according to the amount of work done."*

BRANSCOMBE Devon   Map 1

The Bulstone   `BUDGET`   *Tel* Branscombe (029 780) 446
Higher Bulstone
Branscombe EX12 3BL

Peter and Barbara Freeman's small hotel caters specially for families with
small children. It is on the edge of the pretty village of Branscombe which
is scattered along a valley and much of which belongs to the National
Trust. The hotel is warmly nominated by *Jane Curley:* "We demand a
certain standard of accommodation and food, and have a toddler whose
requirements are very different. We like to take frequent holidays so our
budget is fairly limited. *The Bulstone* satisfied us all. We occupied a family
suite. The decor, with brand-new, 'antique-style' pine furniture, Laura
Ashley fabrics, and a plain-coloured, good quality carpet made a welcome
change from the usual assortment of clashing colours and patterns found
in 'family' hotels. The children's rooms have a bunk bed and a cot,
dimmer switches and night-lights. Our daughter's one had a window, but
four of the six suites have internal bedrooms for the children – an
advantage for most mums as the children don't argue about its being light
at bedtime! Everything was provided for children – high chairs, changing
mats, nappy buckets, baby-listening. Children's high tea at 4.45 pm was
plentiful and nutritious, with the accent on additive-free ingredients.
There was an unspoken agreement that parents would endeavour to have
the children in bed by dinner; children were not allowed in the coffee
lounge after dinner. The four-course meal, with locally produced
vegetables and a good range of choices, including a vegetarian dish, was
very good. The hotel has a playroom, a well-equipped outdoor play area,
and a paddock with goats, a pig, a pony and chickens. Children were
encouraged to feed the animals and collect the eggs. It's brilliant! But pity
any unsuspecting guest who arrives without children." More reports
please.

Open Feb–Nov inclusive.
Rooms 10 suites, 2 double – 6 with bath and shower, all with tea-making facilities
and baby-listening. Some on ground floor.
Facilities Lounge, TV lounge, bar, restaurant; mothers' room, playroom, laundry.
3½-acre grounds with children's play area. Near sea and beaches; fishing and
water sports.
Location A3052 from Sidmouth. Take turning on right marked Bulstone ¾. Ignore
all other turnings to Branscombe.
Restriction No smoking in bedrooms, TV lounge, playroom, dining room.
Credit cards None accepted.
Terms B&B £14.50–£22; dinner, B&B £26–£33.50. Packed lunches, snacks
available. Autumn and spring breaks. Reduced rates and high teas for children.
*Service/tipping: Service is included. We do not suggest that tips are given. If customers do
give tips, they are distributed among the staff."*

The Look Out *Tel* Branscombe (029 780) 262
Branscombe EX12 3DP

Last year's italicised entry for Peter and Dodie Leach's small hotel is warmly endorsed this year ("Delightful, comfortable, beautifully situated, peaceful atmosphere"), earning it a full entry. It is a very attractive conversion of coastguard cottages, quietly situated on a cliff on the edge of the village in a pretty garden, with beautiful views over Lyme Bay and easy access to magnificent National Trust cliff walks and Branscombe's vast shingle and sand beach. Inside are flagstones, oak beams, antique and period furniture. The bedrooms, all with sea view, are comfortable and pretty, and some are quite large; all have bath or shower, but they are not all *en suite*. The Austrian chef, Johann Kickinger, offers a menu with four or five choices of each course (it is priced according to the main course, local lobster being the most expensive item). "We were asked to be down at 7.30 to choose our dinner, which was served at 8. Food was good, interesting without being *outrée*, with fresh ingredients, portions not excessive." Service is friendly. (*Renate Wintersteiger, CR, Edward Hibbert*) In reply to last year's criticisms of muzak and kitchen noises, the Leaches tell us that the music system has now been changed and the kitchen door sealed. Only criticisms this year: "Bathroom very small, with irritatingly feeble shower." "Canned orange juice and boring toast at breakfast."

Open All year except Christmas/New Year. Restaurant closed for lunch and on Mon.
Rooms 1 family suite, 5 double – all with bath and/or shower, TV, tea-making facilities, mini-bar; cordless phone available.
Facilities Lounge/bar, dining room. 1-acre garden. Direct access to beach; fishing, golf nearby.
Location ½ m beyond village centre; follow signs to beach.
Restrictions No children under 6. No dogs in public rooms.
Credit cards None accepted.
Terms (Service at guests' discretion) B&B (English): single occupancy £40–£45, double £76–£85. Set dinner £21–£32. Discount on 7-night stays all year and on 2 nights in low season. Reduced rates for children in family suite; special meals on request.

BRATHAY Cumbria Map 4

Grey Friar Lodge BUDGET *Tel* Ambleside (053 94) 33158
Country House Hotel
Brathay, Ambleside LA22 9NE

This small hotel in the heart of the Lake District, once a vicarage, was built in 1869 of green stone and slate. It is on the wooded flanks of Loughrigg Fell and has lovely far-reaching views. Bedrooms are comfortable, clean and well appointed (they vary in size but all have *en suite* facilities). Breakfast is Cumbrian and hearty. "One of the most pleasant small hotels one could wish to visit. On arrival we were greeted by Mr and Mrs Sutton ('Tony and Sheila – we don't stand on ceremony here'). Our luggage was conveyed to our room and I was lent a Hunter Davies guide of the area for the duration of our stay. Our room, overlooking the valley and mountains, was delightful, with comfortable armchairs, good lighting, ample storage space, a full-length mirror, excellent bathroom,

and books and TV to complete our comfort. Downstairs the hotel is
furnished with style and character. The dinners (four courses, no choice,
served at 7.30) were imaginative and hearty. Long may the Suttons
prosper; their terms offer excellent value." *(Joan A Powell; also JT Mills and
RJS Atkinson)*

Open End Mar–end Oct.
Rooms 8 double – all with bath and/or shower, radio, TV, tea-making facilities.
Facilities 2 lounges, dining room. 1-acre garden with patio and sun terrace. River
and fishing ¼ m.
Location 1½ m W of Ambleside on A593.
Restrictions Not suitable for &. No smoking in dining room and bedrooms. No
children under 10. No dogs.
Credit cards None accepted.
Terms Dinner, B&B: £30–£37; single occupancy of small double £6 supplement.
Set dinner £14. Packed lunch on request. Special breaks. 1-night bookings
sometimes refused if made far in advance. Reduced rates for children sharing
parents' room.
*Service/tipping: "Good service is an essential part of our establishment. It should be
natural and automatic. Therefore we neither levy nor expect tips."*

BRIGHTON East Sussex   **Map 3**

The Dove   *Tel* Brighton (0273) 779222
18 Regency Square   *Fax* (0273) 746912
Brighton BN1 2FG

*Small hotel in listed house in seafront Regency Square in heart of Brighton,
"clean, friendly and well run" by Peter and Deborah Kalinke. No lift; rooms
vary in size and position and are priced accordingly. Simple decor with bright
clear colours; "good, fresh breakfast" with plenty of choice. Residential licence;
simple meals provided in consultation with guests. Children welcomed. Closed
18–28 Dec. 8 rooms, all with private facilities. B&B double £48–£78. Meal £9.
New nomination. More reports please.*

Topps Hotel   *Tel* Brighton (0273) 729334
17 Regency Square   *Fax* (0273) 203679
Brighton BN1 2FG

Paul and Pauline Collins' conversion of two terraced houses next door to
The Dove has had a Guide entry for five years. It is "an oasis of
civilisation. Bedrooms warm and cosy, with special touches like fresh
flowers and fully stocked drinks fridge. Bathrooms well appointed, with
lots of huge towels, dressing gowns, loads of toiletries." "Spacious
bedroom, immaculately clean, attractively decorated, with beds as
comfortable as those at home. Excellent breakfasts, with quantities of
grapefruit juice, freshly made bread, smoked haddock. Paul and Pauline
Collins are very friendly and welcoming without being effusive. They
even provided the *New York Herald Tribune* for their American visitors."
"Furnishings eclectic. The public room which acts as reception, library
and meeting place is inhabited by a wonderful, enormous old dresser,
other antiques, and an elderly dog. Reception staff are always helpful.
Paul Collins is a mine of information." In the basement restaurant,
Bottoms, dinners, cooked by Mrs Collins, have been warmly appreciated

too; the wine list includes several good half-bottles. (*Val Ferguson, HM Schottlaender, John Gunson*)

Open All year except Christmas. Restaurant closed Jan, and Sun and Wed.
Rooms 7 double, 5 single – all with bath (9 also have shower), telephone, radio, TV, tea-making facilities.
Facilities Lift. Lounge, bar, restaurant. 200 yds from sea, safe bathing.
Location 200 yds from centre, opposite West Pier, but quietly situated. NCP carpark nearby.
Restrictions Not suitable for &. No dogs.
Credit cards All major cards accepted.
Terms B&B: single £39–£43, double £63–£90. Set dinner £17.95; full alc £22.50. 20% reduction for any two nights Fri/Sat/Sun except public holidays. Reduced rates for children sharing parents' room; special meals.
Service/tipping: "Service is free."

BROADWAY Hereford and Worcester   **Map 2**

Collin House Hotel   *Tel* Broadway (0386) 858354
Collin Lane
Broadway WR12 7PB

This beautiful old Cotswold house stands in large grounds in a lovely location outside Broadway; it is built of golden stone, with mullioned windows and leaded lights. There is a bar with oak beams and a huge inglenook fireplace, and a lounge with a carved stone fireplace. Bedrooms, all different, are furnished "with care and taste. Ours was warm and spacious, with plenty of books, magazines and local information, and a large bathroom, well supplied with toiletries. Beds very comfortable, and the only sound at night was an owl. No TV, telephone or radio in the bedrooms, but this is essentially a quiet country hotel with pleasant staff and proprietors who look after you well. Breakfast was enjoyable, with a good choice. Dinner in the restaurant, beamed, mullion-windowed and candle-lit, was traditional English with old-style puddings." "Exceptionally warm welcome from Mr and Mrs Mills; altogether a very friendly atmosphere." "Winter breaks very good value." (*Joan A Powell, JCT, David and Nancy Zeffman*) John Mills writes: "In addition to the menu we offer extra dishes each day such as fresh fish and local specialities."

Open All year except 5 days from 24 Dec.
Rooms 6 double, 1 single – 5 with bath, 2 with shower, all with tea-making facilities; radio, TV on request.
Facilities Lounge with TV, lounge bar, restaurant. 8-acre grounds with gardens, meadow, unheated swimming pool, croquet, badminton. Horse riding, golf nearby.
Location 1 m W of Broadway on A94. Turn right at Collin Lane (signposted Willersey).
Restrictions Children under 6 accepted subject to discussion with parents. No dogs.
Credit cards Access, Visa.
Terms B&B: single £37.50, double £69–£79; dinner, B&B £42.25–£48.25 per person. Set lunch £13, dinner £15.50–£18; full alc £20. Winter breaks. Reduced rates for children sharing parents' room; special meals.
Service/tipping: "No service charge. If a customer wishes to tip one of my staff I have no objection provided it is not solicited."

We depend on detailed fresh reports to keep our entries up to date.

BROMSGROVE Hereford and Worcester Map 2

Grafton Manor *Tel* Bromsgrove (0527) 579007
Grafton Lane *Fax* (0527) 575221
Bromsgrove B61 7HA

Grafton Manor, owned and run by the Morris family, is an architecturally splendid, early 18th-century mansion built in stone and pink brick, with just nine bedrooms; one is an outsize suite occupying half of one wing on the first floor. Decor varies, but all bedrooms are fitted with appropriate mod cons, including gas coal-fires, and many extras. It is not far from Birmingham, down an isolated lane, but close to the M5. Back rooms which face the motorway have secondary glazing which keeps the traffic out of earshot if not out of sight. If you like to open your window at night make sure you face the other way. The *Manor* has lovely grounds with a lake and water gardens; the modern herb garden, laid out like a chessboard, provides herbs for extensive use in the traditional and modern British dishes served in the magnificent and fairly formal dining room; there is a four-course vegetarian menu as well as the normal table d'hôte. At times the public rooms can be dominated by business visitors, and the cooking, though generally appreciated, can be uneven. Service is generally considered "exceptionally good". More reports please.

Open All year.
Rooms 2 suites (1 on ground floor), 6 double, 1 single – all with bath, shower, telephone, radio, TV, teletext.
Facilities Lounge, lounge/bar, restaurant. 11-acre grounds with gardens, lake, chapel. 2 golf courses nearby.
Location 1½ m S of Bromsgrove off B4091, opposite Stoke turn.
Restrictions Not suitable for &. No children under 7. Dogs in kennels only.
Credit cards All major cards accepted.
Terms (Service at guests' discretion) B&B (English): single £82, double £99, suite £150. Set lunch from £13.50, dinner £25. Christmas package.

BRYHER Isles of Scilly Map 1

Hell Bay Hotel *Tel* Scillonia (0720) 22947
Bryher, Isles of Scilly *Fax* (0720) 23004
Cornwall TR23 0PR

This "excellent hotel", the only one on the tiny island of Bryher (population 66), is owned by Sorrel Atkinson, and stands by Bryher Pool, across the island from the landing point where you can be met by taxi off the boat from Tresco or St Mary's. It is a converted farmhouse in large grounds with accommodation in warm and comfortable apartments built round a courtyard of sub-tropical gardens. They all have a sitting room; a few have cooking facilities and are let on a weekly self-catering basis. The hotel is particularly suitable for and welcoming to children. Readers recommend it for the friendly management and staff, and the high standard of traditional cooking. More reports please.

Open End-Mar–early Oct.
Rooms 14 apartments – 3 with bath and shower, 11 with shower, all with TV, tea-making facilities; portable baby-listening device provided free of charge; some with kitchen.
Facilities Lounge/reception, bar, dining room. 8-acre grounds with pitch and putt golf. Adjacent to sandy beaches.

Location 3 mins by boat from Tresco, 20 mins from St Mary's, then taxi.
Restrictions No smoking in dining room. No children under 5 in dining room in evening.
Credit cards Access, Visa.
Terms [1990 rates] (Service at guests' discretion) Dinner, B&B £32–£55. Bar lunches. Set dinner £16.50. Autumn breaks. Reduced rates for children sharing parents' room; high teas.

BUCKLAND Gloucestershire   Map 2

Buckland Manor   *Tel* Broadway (0386) 852626
Buckland, Nr Broadway
WR12 7LY

A luxurious manor house owned and run by Barry and Adrienne Berman, both very much in evidence, in a harmonious Cotswold hamlet built of mellow honey-coloured stone and, unlike nearby Broadway, an oasis of tranquillity. The ten acres of gardens and grounds are as beautiful as the house; and there is tennis, swimming and croquet. The house is typically Cotswold, much gabled, with mullioned windows. Inside the atmosphere is "stately and traditional with log fires in great old fireplaces, high-backed settees and dark heavy doors and beams. The large public rooms are well furnished with antiques and working fireplaces; there are lovely flower arrangements." Bedrooms are "superbly and very comfortably furnished" with luxurious carpeted bathrooms and many extras. The elegant restaurant, with white-painted panelling, candles, and waitresses in frilly aprons, "must be one of the best in the English countryside". *Michelin* awards a red "M" indicating a carefully prepared meal, not quite up to rosette standards. Chef Martyn Pearn offers "civilised dishes, using excellent raw materials, and vegetables are very good to excellent". The menu is in French with elaborate translations; the wine list concentrates almost exclusively on French and German labels. (*Wayland Kennet*) More reports please.

Open All year except 3½ weeks from mid-Jan.
Rooms 1 suite (2 intercommunicating twin-bedded rooms), 9 double – all with bath and shower, telephone, TV; radio on request. Some ground-floor rooms.
Facilities 3 lounges, dining room. 10-acre grounds with gardens, heated swimming pool, tennis, croquet, putting. Golf, riding nearby.
Location E of B4632, 1½ m SW of Broadway.
Restrictions No children under 12 in hotel, under 8 in restaurant. Dogs by arrangement.
Credit cards Access, Visa.
Terms B&B: single occupancy £125–£200, double £135–£210; suite £205 for 2, £295 for 4. Sun lunch £13.95; full alc £28. Special packages for Christmas, Cheltenham Gold Cup, etc. 1-night bookings refused weekends and bank holidays.
Service/tipping: "No service charge. Tipping entirely at guests' discretion; all gratuities divided among staff."

Hotels often book you into their most expensive rooms or suites unless you specify otherwise. Even if all room prices are the same, hotels may give you a less good room in the hope of selling their better rooms to late customers. It always pays to discuss accommodation in detail when making a reservation.

BUDOCK VEAN Cornwall   Map 1

Budock Vean Golf   *Tel* Falmouth (0326) 250288
** and Country House Hotel**   *Fax* (0326) 250892
Budock Vean, Nr Falmouth
TR11 5LG

A resort-style hotel in fine position in 65-acre grounds with sub-tropical gardens, 9-hole golf-course, 2 all-weather tennis courts, large, covered swimming pool – open in summer, with log fire in winter – and private frontage on the Helford river. New wing has roomy if rather functional bedrooms; those in original building are prettier but smaller. Recommended for well-kept facilities, excellent and varied food, "exceptionally helpful and friendly staff", but can be golf-dominated at times. Children welcomed. Closed during Jan. 59 rooms, all with private facilities. Dinner, B&B double £84–£130 [1990]. More reports please.

BURY ST EDMUNDS Suffolk   Map 3

The Angel Hotel   *Tel* Bury St Edmunds
Angel Hill   (0284) 753926
Bury St Edmunds IP33 1LT   *Fax* (0284) 750092
                                           Telex 81630

💧 *César award in 1985: Best country town hotel*

"I left the *Angel* with a smile – what a pleasurable experience! Rooms are furnished appropriately to the building – chintz and mahogany. Early morning coffee was freshly made with real beans, and there was freshly squeezed orange juice and locally cured bacon, as well as several different sorts of toast. The proprietor, Mary Gough, assisted by her daughter Caroline, was much in evidence and took pleasure from the enjoyment the guests were getting from her hotel." "Service could not have been better. Staff, mostly quite young, were cheerful, polite and attentive. Bedroom small, but quiet, being at the rear. It was newly refurbished, and so clean and bright, with fresh flowers, magazines, books, etc. But only one bedside lamp, which was inconvenient." (*Ion Trewin, RM Booth*)

   The Angel is 15th century in origin with an 18th-century classical facade, now softened by creepers. It is on the main square opposite the great abbey gate, one of Bury's glories, and is very much part of the life of this charming market-town; the comfortable public rooms bustle with activity, particularly on market day (Wednesday). *The Angel*'s teas, sometimes accompanied by harp or piano, are popular. The hotel has two dining rooms; the *Regency Restaurant* is fairly formal, the one in the vaults more modern in style. One reader on a "very reasonable" weekend break found the dinners good, but most are more critical: "nicely served, but bland"; "barely acceptable"; "avoid anything that sounds French". The bedrooms and bathrooms vary greatly in size and shape, as in all old buildings, so it is important to discuss your requirements when booking; front rooms, which overlook the square, can be noisy, but are double-glazed. Those at the back are generally quiet, but one couple in the Charles Dickens room were disturbed by noise from extractor fans and a band playing for a private function, and were not able to turn down the central heating before it went off at midnight. More reports please.

Open All year.
Rooms 1 suite, 27 double, 13 single – 40 with bath, 1 with shower, all with telephone, radio, TV.
Facilities Lounge, bar, 2 restaurants; conference facilities. Parking for 50 cars. Abbey gardens opposite.
Location Central, near Information Centre (front rooms double-glazed). Parking.
Restrictions Not suitable for &. No dogs in restaurants.
Credit cards All major cards accepted.
Terms [1990 rates] Rooms: single £55–£62, double £80–£100, suite £130. Breakfast: continental £4.50, English £6.50. Set lunch £14.50, dinner £25; full alc £30. Weekend rates B&B £39 per person. Christmas programme. Reduced rates and small portions for children.
Service/tipping: "Service included. Tipping not actively encouraged."

CALNE Wiltshire   Map 2

Chilvester Hill House   *Tel* Calne (0249) 813981
Calne SN11 0LP   *Fax* (0249) 814217

"Impossible to disagree with any of the praise in the Guide. The big plus is the quality of the food preparation including careful enquiries into guests' preferences. The unique qualities are Gill Dilley's personality and John Dilley's inexhaustible local knowledge. The imponderable is who you sit with at dinner. We were lucky!" "The Dilleys are not obtrusive; they look after their guests personally and considerately. Pleasantly furnished bedroom; everything works." "Rooms large, comfortable and quiet. Wonderful cooked-to-order breakfast." Three of this year's tributes to this spacious Victorian mansion in seven acres of grounds, with a small, well-cared-for swimming pool. It is close to, but out of earshot of, the A4, set in large grounds with fine views. There are books everywhere "on literally every subject". Guests eat in the family dining room round one "magnificently set" table (couples may find themselves split up). "Good, plain, real food"; vegetables are from the garden. The Dilleys do not have a brochure (though they are now considering having one); enquirers get a personal letter. No choice of menu, but visitors are consulted about their likes and dislikes and Mrs Dilley keeps records of meals served "so that I do not duplicate – or so that I *can* when guests want to eat the same as last time". When not entertaining their guests, Dr Dilley is a consultant occupational physician; Mrs Dilley breeds beef cattle. (*PC Russell, CAW Gibbons, John and Suzanne Price*)

Open All year, except a week off-season (autumn or spring).
Rooms 3 double – all with bath, hand-shower, radio, TV, tea-making facilities.
Facilities Drawing room, sitting room with TV, dining room. 2½-acre grounds with swimming pool; also 5 acres used for cattle; golf and riding locally.
Location ½ m W of Calne; A4 towards Chippenham, after ½ m right turn to Bremhill; immediately turn right into drive with gateposts with stone lions.
Restrictions Not suitable for &. No smoking in dining room. No children under 12. No dogs.
Credit cards All major cards accepted.
Terms B&B: single occupancy £40–£50, double £60–£75. Set dinner £18–£22; packed lunches, pool snacks available. Reductions for stays of a week or more.
Service/tipping: "No service charge. Tips not expected; but if anything is left 'for the girls' it is put in a 'kitty' and shared."

CALSTOCK Cornwall   Map 1

Danescombe Valley Hotel   *Tel* Tavistock (0822) 832414
Lower Kelly
Calstock PL18 9RY

This friendly hotel has a tranquil setting on the steep wooded slopes of the river Tamar, adjoining the grounds of Cotehele House, an exceptionally rewarding National Trust property, 15 minutes' walk away. "The views are lovely; it is such a bonus not having to use the car, and being able to sit for hours on the veranda watching the fast-changing sky and water." Martin Smith and his half-Italian wife, Anna, have extensively renovated the house with Laura Ashley fabrics and antique and traditional furniture. There are deep carpets, well-placed lighting, flowers, plants, magazines and books, and generally a light, airy feeling about the place. Bedrooms are well equipped with pretty duvets and huge pillows. There are big fluffy towels and many extras – including wind-up bath toys – in the bathrooms. *Danescombe Valley* dispenses with many of the things that are expected of hotels these days – no telephones in bedrooms, no TV, no credit cards, for example. Guests are treated more like friends than fee-paying visitors and the Smiths insist on first names all round, which some find off-putting. Dinner is "at 7.30 for 8"; Anna Smith cooks "delicious, well-balanced and very fresh, unfussy" no-choice meals (but you are consulted about likes and dislikes in advance); with "properly cooked vegetables, local cheeses (a special feature), and very good ice-cream". "The wine list is carefully chosen and *very* cheap." (Last year we reported one complaint of a lack of half-bottles. Martin Smith writes: "We have a policy of keeping mark-ups on wine extremely low. This should enable most people not to worry about the cost of a full bottle. In most cases (depending on the wine chosen) I am quite happy to open a full bottle and charge according to the amount consumed.") No cooked breakfasts; but a generous choice including fresh orange juice, poached fruit, yoghurt. (*JA Firth, Mrs NE Guess, and others*)

Open Easter–end Oct. Closed Wed and Thu.
Rooms 5 double – all with bath; tea-making facilities on request.
Facilities Lounge, bar, restaurant. 4 acres of steep woodland; steps down to river Tamar. Fishing, walking, golf and riding nearby.
Location ½ m W of Calstock village; under viaduct, past Methodist church, turn sharp right; follow road parallel to river Tamar for ½ m.
Restrictions Not suitable for &. No smoking in dining room. No children under 12. No dogs in house.
Credit cards None accepted.
Terms Dinner, B&B: double £154, single by arrangement. 1-night bookings sometimes refused Sat.
Service/tipping: "Tips refused unless our refusal gives offence."

CAMPSEA ASHE Suffolk   Map 3

The Old Rectory `BUDGET`   *Tel* Wickham Market
Campsea Ashe, Nr Woodbridge   (0728) 746524
IP3 0PU

"This may not be everyone's cup of tea," writes *Brian Wicks*, commenting on last year's entry, "but it is certainly my glass of wine! It may have a seedy gentry air, the pictures, paintings, prints and photographs may be askew (it is a picture straightener's paradise), and the leg of a table in the dining room was held up by a piece of cardboard to stop it wobbling, but the place has character. My bedroom was quiet, clean, spacious and comfortable; so too was the *en suite* bathroom. It didn't have a radio, TV or phone, but so what? The lounge is large, with a log fire, comfortable armchairs and lots of glossy books. There was no choice of food but it was excellent, and included a superb crème brûlée. The wine list is amazing – one of the best I have seen – and very reasonable, with lots of half-bottles. All this with a full English breakfast for £37 [1990]. Remarkable value." "A fine Georgian rectory, remarkable for the comfort of the bedrooms. Our feeling of being guests at a private house party of the inter-war years was reinforced by the happy trust with which you are asked to note down your drinks in a book. There's a great feeling of tranquillity." (*Gwen and Peter Andrews*) Stewart Bassett's idiosyncratic restaurant-with-rooms is in a spacious Georgian rectory, with high ceilings and grandiose antiques. It enjoys a peaceful setting in a large garden with statuary. (There are jets at a nearby airbase, but they are seldom heard.) Atmosphere and service are laid-back, which won't suit all comers, but it's a wine buff's dream. Regular customers telephone a day or so before to place their order; to many it is a relief not to have to choose the food as well. We said last year that guests share tables for breakfast and dinner. "Never, never!" Mr Bassett writes.

Open All year except Christmas, 3 weeks Feb/Mar, 1 week Nov.
Rooms 6 double, 2 single – all with bath, tea-making facilities, baby-listening.
Facilities Drawing room with TV, honesty bar, conservatory, breakfast room, dining room, private dining room. 4-acre garden with croquet.
Location 1½ m E of A12 on B1078. Next to church.
Restriction No dogs.
Credit cards All major cards accepted.
Terms [1990 rates] B&B (English): single £27, double £43; dinner, B&B: single £40.50, double £70. Set dinner: residents £14.50, non-residents £18.50.
Service/tipping: "No service charge. Tipping must be an entirely voluntary process. Anything given is divided among the staff. No long faces if nothing is given."

CARTMEL Cumbria   Map 4

Aynsome Manor Hotel   *Tel* Cartmel (053 95) 36653
Cartmel, Grange-over-Sands
LA11 6HH

The picturesque village of Cartmel is eight miles south of Windermere and a couple of miles inland of Grange-over-Sands (on the sea, but poor beaches). It is a good base for fell walking (though you need a car). The *Manor*, dating back to the 16th century, is a handsome building with a cobbled courtyard, small garden and lovely views of streams and meadows to the fine 12th-century priory church. It has been restored by the resident proprietors, Tony and Margaret Varley, who run it with their son Christopher and his wife Andrea. There is an oak-panelled dining room with a moulded plaster ceiling, decent paintings, good silver and crystal, and an upstairs lounge of fine proportions with a splendid marble fireplace. Bedrooms are comfortable and traditional; some are in Aynsome Cottage, across the courtyard, which has its own sitting room. Readers this year spent an enjoyable Christmas at the *Manor*, and appreciated the "attractive public rooms, the attentive and courteous service and agreeable atmosphere. It has improved in many respects since our last visit and is even more comfortable and well kept. The five-course dinner is pretty good, with great attention to detail – it would cost considerably more elsewhere. There is an excellent wine list, and the wine is properly served. The young staff are well trained and observant. Whoever complained last year about small portions must have a gargantuan appetite (or the hotel has taken note of the comment).'' (*Mr and Mrs John King-Wilkinson, Elizabeth Sandham*)

Open All year except 2–25 Jan.
Rooms 12 double, 1 single – 11 with bath, 1 with shower, all with telephone, radio, TV, tea-making facilities, baby-listening. 3 in cottage annexe.
Facilities 3 lounges, cocktail bar, dining room. ¾-acre garden. Outdoor swimming pool 2 m, Windermere 7 m.
Location 1 m NE of Cartmel village.
Restrictions Not suitable for &. No smoking in dining room. No children under 6 in dining room for dinner.
Credit cards Access, Amex, Visa.
Terms Dinner, B&B £43–£48. Set lunch £9.50, dinner £17. Winter breaks. Christmas programme. 1-night bookings refused for bank holidays. Reduced rates for children; high tea 5–6 pm.
Service/tipping: "We find guests don't like to be told what to do with their money. We leave the matter optional. The staff do not expect gratuities."

Uplands Tel Cartmel (053 95) 36248
Haggs Lane, Cartmel
Grange-over-Sands LA11 6HD

"We have now stayed half a dozen times and have always been delighted with the food, welcome and generosity of the Peters." "Food really delicious. Mrs Peter and her staff all extremely friendly and helpful." Tom and Diana Peter (he in the kitchen, she front of house) co-own *Uplands* with John Tovey, and the hotel is subtitled "in the *Miller Howe* manner". But it is less theatrical in style, prices are considerably lower and, unlike *Miller Howe*, it offers limited choice on the four-course fixed-price dinner menu, and more flexible mealtimes. The hotel is on a hillside, in two acres of garden, with views over Morecambe Bay, in the uncrowded southern end of the Lake District. It is attractively decorated and furnished; the lounge and dining room are "elegant, in restful pastel greys and pinks", tables in the dining room are well spaced, and service is quiet and efficient. "Individual soup tureen, mini-loaf of home-made granary bread, subsequent dishes never disappointed – flavours are robust and vegetables never boring. Sweets first-class, with judicious use of seasonal and imported fruit." "Excellent, generous breakfasts" – each table has its own toaster with a choice of breads. Bedrooms, though not very spacious, are comfortable and well equipped; two have lovely estuary views. (*Mrs CM Bevan, Mrs E Newall, Francine Walsh, and others*) There is a pained cry from a trained musician this year: "The canned music at dinner is quite awful."

Open 23 Feb–1 Jan. Restaurant closed Mon.
Rooms 5 double – all with bath and/or shower, telephone, TV.
Facilities Lounge, dining room. 2-acre garden. Golf nearby.
Location From Cartmel, with *Pig & Whistle* on right, immediately take left turn; go up Haggs Lane for 1 m; hotel is on left.
Restrictions Not suitable for &. No smoking in dining room. No children under 8. No dogs in public rooms.

Credit cards Access, Amex.
Terms (Excluding 10% service charge) Dinner, B&B: single £55–£65, double £100–£110. Set lunch £12, dinner £20. £10 per night deducted for stays over 2 nights Nov–Mar. Christmas and New Year breaks. 1-night bookings refused for Sat. Reduced rates for children sharing parents' room; special meals on request.
Service/tipping: "As we charge 10% for service we don't accept tips."

CHADDESLEY CORBETT Hereford and Worcester　　　Map 2

Brockencote Hall	*Tel* Kidderminster (056 283) 876
Chaddesley Corbett	*changing in 1990 to* (0562) 777876
Nr Kidderminster DY10 4PY	*Telex* 333431

This turn-of-the century "rich man's domestic pile" in 70-acre grounds not far from Birmingham, with Anglo-French owners, Joseph and Alison Petitjean, "has pale stone walls, and is a little austere from a distance. Inside, however, the over-riding impression is of warm honey-coloured wood, elegant furnishings and a light, cheerful atmosphere." Public rooms are large, light and high-ceilinged, furnishing "agreeable and not too designerish". Bedrooms vary in size. "Our split-level room over-looked the front pastureland. It was quite large, pleasantly furnished in a restrained country house style and well equipped, with plenty of storage space. Furniture was reproduction with much dark wood; carpet and wallpaper were suitably discreet. Food is over-ambitious at times but our main courses on the £30 menu were imaginative and well executed, vegetables were impressive, sweets modern and wittily presented and cheese a marvellously smelly mixture. It was quite expensive, but it is possible to eat here for less; the cheaper three-course meal might have been a better option. And coffee and service are included so no nasty surprises arrive with the bill. Restaurant service is impeccable. Breakfast is reasonable. The owners are charming and professional; the staff particularly well trained and accommodating." A new conservatory-style restaurant was due to open in July 1990. (*DW, also Miles Kington*) One reader's pleasure was spoilt by a noisy wedding party which took over the public rooms.

Open Jan–end Dec. Closed New Year. Restaurant closed for lunch on Sat, for dinner on Sun, also bank holiday Mons.
Rooms 6 double, 2 single – all with bath and/or shower, telephone, radio, TV, baby-listening.
Facilities Bar, lounge, restaurant, 2 functions/conference rooms. 70-acre grounds with lake.
Location On A448 from Kidderminster to Bromsgrove, just S of village.
Restrictions Only restaurant suitable for &. No dogs.
Credit cards All major cards accepted.
Terms B&B (continental): single £57–£88, double £83–£103. Set lunch from £15.50, dinner from £27.50. Weekend breaks.
Service/tipping: "Service included. Tips at customers' discretion."

CHADLINGTON Oxfordshire　　　Map 2

The Manor	*Tel* Chadlington (060 876) 711
Chadlington OX7 3LX	

❦ *César award in 1990: Newcomer of the year, country house division*

David and Chris Grant, who previously owned *Kirkby Fleetham Hall* in Yorkshire, opened *The Manor*, an imposing building in large grounds in a peaceful backwater on the fringe of the Cotswolds, in early 1989, and a glowing reports earned it a *César*. Visitors praised the "genuinely homely country house atmosphere", the "sensitive and tasteful" decor with adventurous colour schemes, and the luxuriously equipped bedrooms, many of them light and large, with lovely views. Mrs Grant's cooking, too, gave pleasure: "Her short menu was interesting – modern English dishes, with simple sauces, and vegetables that were perhaps under-cooked rather than *al dente*. Magnificent wine list ranges the world with very modest mark-up. Breakfast was generous and altogether satisfactory. David Grant is a congenial and loquacious host, and his assistants charming." Autumn visitors endorsed our entry but, regrettably, in early 1990 we received a number of critical reports recording a very cold room on a February night; £22.50 charged for dinner though the hotel's price list quoted £19.50; inattentive service; one CD endlessly repeated at dinner; soggy vegetables. And one honeymoon couple travelled from London to discover that there had been no electricity for several days – the Grants had not warned them in advance. We hope that these were no more than transient lapses from the Manor's usual state of grace.

Open All year. Lunch for residents only.
Rooms 7 double – all with bath and shower, telephone, TV.
Facilities Hall, lounge, library, dining room, 2 private dining rooms. 20-acre grounds.
Location Beside church in village 3 m SE of Chipping Norton. Approach from the A361, S of Chipping Norton.
Restrictions Not suitable for &. Smoking discouraged in dining room. No dogs.
Credit cards Access, Visa.
Terms B&B: single £70–£85, double £105–£130. Set dinner £24.50.
Service/tipping: "Service is included in our prices, as it is at Marks and Spencer or your local garage; you don't enquire about the cost of labour when buying a pair of socks! We pay our staff well, and the cost of this is built into our prices. I am against tipping in any form."

CHAGFORD Devon   **Map 1**

Gidleigh Park Hotel   *Tel* Chagford (0647) 432367
Chagford TQ13 8HH   *Fax* (0647) 432574
                                                        Telex 42643

César award in 1989: Most sumptuous traditional country house hotel

"As always, totally comfortable and luxurious; we never leave feeling less than satisfied with the food and the care we have received."

Gidleigh Park has had a Guide entry since its opening, twelve years ago, as a country house hotel *de grand luxe*. The aim of American owners Paul and Kay Henderson with their managing director and head chef, Shaun Hill, is to provide total comfort in a private house atmosphere for "affluent connoisseurs". The house is set far down a single-track lane in an exceptionally peaceful and beautiful position on the edge of Dartmoor and the banks of the North Teign river. "It is immaculate and the furnishings very sophisticated, but the atmosphere is cosy and welcoming; on each visit one notices improvements and refurbishments." The drawing room is spacious and comfortable, with log fires and a "superb new collection of watercolours"; a bar conservatory overlooks the lovely grounds. There are fourteen bedrooms in the main building, and two in a tiny cottage with a kitchen and breakfast room in the Stockey Furzen woodland across the river; all are luxuriously furnished, with equally luxurious bathrooms, and filled with fresh flowers, fruit, books and many other extras. Prices – inevitably high – are according to the size of the room and its view; courtyard-facing ones are the least expensive.

In 1990 *Michelin* withdrew its rosette after nine years because, it was said, chef Shaun Hill's cooking was "not as sharp as it had been". In the view of one regular visitor: "His cooking gets better and better. He has the happy knack of knowing when to leave well alone with his dishes; there is nothing redundant in the compositions, he combines high technique and good taste; the desserts have improved out of all recognition." (*Padi Howard; also PA Marron, and others*) Croquet is taken seriously here: there are four good quality lawns, and *Gidleigh Park* was the first hotel in Britain to be given the three mallet rating by the Croquet Association.

Open All year.
Rooms 2 suites, 14 double – 14 with bath and shower, 1 with bath, all with telephone, radio, TV. 2 in north wing 75 yds from front door; 2 in cottage 350 yds away.
Facilities Hall, lounge, bar, loggia, 2 dining rooms. 45-acre grounds with gardens, croquet lawns and hard tennis court. Fishing, golf, riding and walking nearby.
Location Approach from Chagford, *not* Gidleigh. From main square, facing Webbers with Lloyds Bank on right, turn right into Mill Street. After 150 yds fork right; go downhill to Factory Crossroad. Go straight across into Holy Street; follow lane 1½ m to end.
Restrictions Not suitable for &. No dogs in public rooms.
Credit cards Access, Visa.
Terms Dinner, B&B (continental): single occupancy £150–£255, double £190–£320. Cooked breakfast £4.50–£9. Set lunch £32, dinner £43. Winter walking holidays. 1-night bookings sometimes refused.
Service/tipping: "We discourage tipping."

Thornworthy House   *Tel* Chagford (0647) 433297
Chagford TQ13 8EY

A rambling Victorian house which, despite its address, is three miles out of Chagford, down twisting lanes to the very edge of Dartmoor – 1,200 feet up, with lovely views, and exceptionally tranquil. It stands in a country garden, with a tennis court. Philip and Vicky Jevons have redecorated and refurbished, giving it "the atmosphere of a comfortable family house", with soft colours, thick carpets, good quality fabrics, pictures and family photographs. There are comfortable reception rooms with log fires; bedrooms are spacious, with lovely views; some have private facilities. The "very nice, hospitable" Jevonses ("who have ten children between them, his, hers and theirs, so they are used to catering for numbers"), run *Thornworthy* as their private home – so do not be surprised if you find toys or children's clothes in your bedroom. Normally there are not more than six or eight guests at one time. Dinners, served at about 8 pm, offer three choices for each course and are generally praised as "good English home-cooking" though one reader says "the food is variable, but when it is good, it is very good". Another adds: "Do not lay down your knife and fork for a rest – the table is likely to be cleared before cutlery hits plate." The wine list is moderately priced and offers a good choice. There are new bedrooms in a converted barn cottage.

Open All year.
Rooms 6 double, 2 single – 6 with bath, 4 with TV. Some in barn and cottage.
Facilities Lounge, TV lounge, dining room. 2½-acre grounds with tennis and clock golf. Riding, golf, fishing, windsurfing nearby.
Location 3 m SW of Chagford. Turn right at top of square. After 150 yds fork left to Fernworthy. At top of hill take second turning on right to Thornworthy. Follow signs to *Thornworthy House.*
Restrictions Not suitable for &. No dogs in public rooms.
Credit cards None accepted.
Terms B&B £32.50; dinner, B&B £50. Set dinner £17.50. Reduced rates and special meals for children.
Service/tipping: "Tips not solicited; if left they go to garden fund."

CHARINGWORTH Gloucestershire   Map 2

Charingworth Manor   *Tel* Paxford (038 678) 555
Charingworth   *Fax* (038 678) 353
Nr Chipping Campden GL55 6NS   *Telex* 333444

Beautiful house up long winding drive in 50-acre grounds with agreeable gardens, lovely views – "just what a Cotswold manor should be" – and antiques, log fires. Best bedrooms in main building; those in stables less liked. "Attentive, friendly and courteous staff, very good modern cooking." Under same ownership as Bishopstrow House, Warminster, and Reids, Madeira (qq.v.). 3 suites, 22 double. B&B double £95–£195. Set lunch £12.50–£15.50, dinner £24.50. New nomination. More reports please.

CHEDINGTON Dorset   Map 2

Chedington Court   *Tel* Corscombe (093 589) 265
Chedington   *from Spring 1991* (0935) 891265
Nr Beaminster DT8 3HY   *Fax* (093 589) 442
                                        from Spring 1991 (0935) 891442

"We revisited after four years and little had changed. . . . Some pleasant redecoration, some extension and development of the gardens, but the superb countryside, the wonderful views, the peace and quiet, the remoteness from the outside world, have all been preserved. Even the prices seem to have increased rather less than those of their competitors."
Chedington Court is a splendid, 1840s country house hotel in the Jacobean style, with curved gables and mullioned windows, in a spectacular position high up in the Dorset hills with panoramic views across Dorset, Devon and Somerset. There are ten acres of parkland that match the grandeur of the building: balustraded and terraced gardens, lots of yews, a croquet lawn and a lake down below. Much of the furniture, in keeping with the building, is solid and understated – some of it came from the state rooms of the liner *Queen Mary.* Public rooms are "well furnished with lovely curtains and masses of books", but not extravagantly decorated. There is a pretty conservatory and a billiard room. The hotel is informally run, with no reception procedure and not

much room service; guests tend to be left to their own devices. Bedrooms are "beautifully furnished with antiques – and everything works. The food is exceptional – most imaginative, altogether delicious, using very good raw materials, with good service." There is limited choice on the five-course dinner menu cooked by Hilary Chapman except for the first course and the "amazing sweet trolley", but "it is a masterpiece in planning with all tastes accounted for and very skilfully served". The wine list is "remarkable for content and value; surely the best selection of half-bottles in England, and at such low prices as to be almost self-defeating". "Mr Chapman's quiet desire for his guests to have everything to their liking is so intense it is almost worrying." Some visitors might find the lack of hotel-style facilities and effusive reception disconcerting, but it has been much to the liking of *Norman Civval, Alison Rossiter, David Morris, and others.*

Open Feb–Dec.
Rooms 10 double – all with bath and/or shower, telephone, radio, TV, tea-making facilities, baby-listening. 1 with 4-poster and double jacuzzi.
Facilities Drawing room, library, billiard room, dining room; conservatory. 10-acre garden with croquet, putting. Golf, fishing nearby; coast 10 m.
Location 4½ m SE of Crewkerne, just off A356 at Winyard's Cap.
Restrictions Only restaurant suitable for &. No dogs.
Credit cards Access, Amex, Visa.
Terms Dinner, B&B: single £80–£90, double £130–£160; B&B only, 20% less. Set dinner £24.50. Reductions for stays of more than 1 night. 1-night bookings refused weekends. Reduced rates for children sharing parents' room; special meals.
Service/tipping: "Service is already paid for so no extra is added or expected."

CHELWOOD Avon   **Map 2**

Chelwood House Hotel   *Tel* Compton Dando (076 18) 730
Chelwood   *Telex* 44830
Nr Bristol BS18 4NH

This dower house, built in 1681, is now a small hotel, run by Jill and Rudolf Birk. It is on the A37 (windows are double-glazed, back rooms are quietest), almost equidistant from Bath, Bristol and Wells, in a small village with lovely views of open countryside. There is angling in Chew Valley Lake nearby, and there are numerous golf courses in the area. Public rooms are well proportioned, with period furniture and fresh flowers. Bedrooms (three have a four-poster) are comfortable, with spacious and well-planned bathrooms. The Birk family are "friendly and professional", and the service "very attentive". "Excellent breakfasts, with first-class croissants, rare enough even in France these days." Readers have in the past praised the "good, straightforward dinners" cooked by Mr Birk, but he is no longer the chef, and one visitor in early 1990 considered the food (and also the decor) "rather fussy". Another disagreed with the pricing policy of the meals: "The price includes main course plus dessert, the starter is extra; I don't like desserts – but was saved by delicious Stilton!" There is now a second conservatory-type dining room. More reports please.

Open All year except last week Dec, first week Jan.
Rooms 8 double, 2 single – all with bath and/or shower, telephone, radio, TV, tea-making facilities.

Facilities 2 lounges, dining room. 1½-acre grounds. Fishing and golf nearby.
Location On A37 8 m S of Bristol.
Restrictions Not suitable for &. No smoking in dining room. No children under 10. No dogs.
Credit cards All major cards accepted.
Terms B&B (English): single £59–£65, double £69–£95. Set lunch £15, dinner from £16.50; full alc £27. Weekend breaks all year except bank holidays.
Service/tipping: "No service charge. We do not encourage tipping but do not discourage guests from showing appreciation if they choose; tips are shared by all staff."

CHIPPING CAMPDEN Gloucestershire   Map 2

Cotswold House Hotel   *Tel* Evesham (0386) 840330
   and Restaurant   *Fax* (0386) 840310
The Square
Chipping Campden GL55 6AN

A fine Regency building in the heart of a small Cotswold town. It has been extensively restored and refurbished by the owners, Robert and Gill Greenstock, and has a particularly noble central staircase. Well-selected antiques sit comfortably next to modern upholstery; "real pictures" hang on the walls; the flower arrangements are "beyond criticism". Comfortable bedrooms, decorated with the same flair, have impeccable bathrooms. The better-proportioned bedrooms face the street and are soundproofed. The quietest ones, at the back, overlook the walled garden, as does the dining room which, with ceiling-high French windows, is an agreeably light, airy place to eat. A resident pianist plays – "from Chopin to Gershwin" – three nights a week. A winter visitor reports: "A very pleasant welcome. Cases carried by proprietor. Room was charming with bowl of fruit etc and well-appointed bathroom. Tea was brought promptly with enormous plate of cinnamon toast. Excellent dinner. Service attentive, cheerful and prompt. Request for vegetables to be well cooked brought them exactly right." Another verdict: "Breakfast was the best meal of the day; second best was the delicious cream teas." (*Bernard Dunstan, Vivian Ellis, and others*) Other comments on the kitchen under Raymond Boreham are mixed: while some visitors have enjoyed "well-prepared, quite imaginative dishes", others report that "the first course soufflé was no soufflé", "some dishes more successful than others", "dull vegetables", "the menu changes only four times a year; after two nights there was nothing else we wanted to try". Service can be "excellent, especially when supervised by the manager, Peter Jordan", but at other times "somewhat irregular". And one guest was disturbed by "loud pop music from the bar, audible until 11 pm in the lounge when the door was open, *and* in our bedroom, which was just over the bar". In addition to the restaurant, there is an "eatery" offering less expensive meals throughout the day. Last year we mentioned that the garden was less manicured than before. The Greenstocks' reply: "The gardener broke his ankle last Easter so a holding operation was carried out by ourselves, hence the comments. We are back to normal now and are even re-laying the garden paths."

Open All year except 25/26 Dec.
Rooms 12 double, 3 single – all with bath and/or shower, telephone, radio, TV; tea-making facilities on request.

Facilities Reception lounge, sitting room, bar, dining room, coffee house; private dining room. Courtyard/patio, 1½-acre grounds with croquet.
Location Central (front rooms sound-proofed). Parking.
Restrictions Not suitable for &. No smoking in restaurants. No children under 8. No dogs.
Credit cards All major cards accepted.
Terms B&B £40–£71; dinner, B&B £62–£93. Set dinner £22. Special breaks all year except bank holidays. 1-night bookings refused at weekends. Special meals for children by arrangement.
Service/tipping: "We are against any form of tipping. But if we have done our job properly our guests will, if they are customary tippers, show appreciation. All tips are given to staff with instructions that everyone receives a share."

CHITTLEHAMHOLT Devon   Map 1

Highbullen Hotel   *Tel* Chittlehamholt (076 94) 561
Chittlehamholt   *Fax* (076 94) 492
Umberleigh EX37 9HD

&♠ *César award: Utterly acceptable mild eccentricity*

This wholly individual un-hotel-like hotel has lovely views across a Devon valley and many facilities for both the sporting and unsporting (listed below) – though the golf course is said to be "good fun, not to be taken too seriously", and the swimming pool is "too small to swim in". Bedrooms in the main house, a Victorian Gothic mansion, are traditional; those in the outbuildings are modern. All are comfortable and well equipped; many are spacious. *Highbullen* has many loyal regulars who enjoy its restfulness and laid-back atmosphere and find it comfortable and friendly. Other visitors, however, may be put off by the lack of formal greeting and the fact that the owners, Hugh and Pam Neil, are not much in evidence. Some find it cliquey: "When the opening gambit at the next table was 'Didn't we meet at Chequers earlier this year?', I felt it wasn't quite me." There is sharp disagreement, too, about the meals, overseen by the Neils' daughter Colette Potter. They are reported by some to be "first-rate" and "very enjoyable, especially the unpretentious yet appetising bar lunches", but others say, "Not a patch on years ago; vegetables soggy and reminiscent of school dinners." There's no criticism, however, of the "seriously good wine list with modest mark-up". Some of the plumbing is reported to be in urgent need of attention, and the supply of hot water not always reliable. But the foibles are easily forgiven by the many addicted Highbullenites, who would hate the golf course to become more professional – or, for that matter, any other part of the *Highbullen* enterprise and there is general agreement that it is good value for money.

Open All year.
Rooms 34 double, 1 single – all with bath and shower, telephone, radio, TV, tea-making facilities. 23 in converted farmhouses and cottages. Some ground-floor rooms.
Facilities Drawing room with conservatory, library, bar with small dance-floor, dining room, cellar restaurant, billiard room; hairdressing and massage facilities; indoor tennis court and swimming pool, sauna, steam room, spa bath, sunbed, exercise room, table-tennis room, squash court. 60-acre grounds with 6-acre garden, 9-hole golf course, tennis, croquet lawn, putting green, outdoor heated swimming pool. Golf and tennis tuition. Fishing in river Mole ½ m.

Location Leave M5 at exit 27; on A361 at South Molton take B3226 for 5.2 m, turn right up hill to Chittlehamholt; go through village ½ m to hotel.
Restrictions Not suitable for &. No smoking in restaurant. No children under 10. No dogs.
Credit cards None accepted.
Terms Dinner, B&B £45–£60. Sunday lunch £12.50, snack lunches. Set dinner £16.50. Midweek breaks Nov–Mar. 1-night bookings may be refused Fri and Sat. Reduced rates for children sharing parents' room.
Service/tipping: "We make it quite clear that service is included and no tips are expected. Some people insist on leaving tips; they are distributed in proportion to individual staff earnings."

CONSTANTINE BAY Cornwall   Map 1

Treglos Hotel   *Tel* Padstow (0841) 520727
Padstow PL28 8JH   *Fax* (0841) 521163

A traditional seaside hotel, excellent for a family holiday, in a choice position overlooking Constantine Bay, 400 yards from a sandy beach with rock pools at low tide. It has a sheltered sunken garden for sunbathing, and an indoor heated pool. The National Trust coastal footpath is nearby; maps of walks are provided by the hotel. *Treglos* has been run for 25 years by Ted and Barbara Barlow; the restaurant manager has been there for 19 years and the chef for 15. Expect old-fashioned courtesies such as cleaning shoes, carrying luggage, room service, tidying rooms during dinner. The hotel has many devoted regular visitors. The disabled and children are welcome. In low season it is a favourite of retired people. Its decor – brick fireplaces, chintzy furniture and patterned carpets – is conventionally English, as is the food. Bedrooms, many with sea views, have light colour-schemes and white fitted furniture; some have a balcony. "What most impressed us was the staff – all excellent, friendly and extremely helpful. Andrew Bridgnorth, the assistant manager, was outstanding. The food was basically very good, with a generous five-course dinner menu, but occasionally the chef got out of his depth. The waiter service at dinner was inconsistent, but we believe this problem will be resolved; at breakfast it was better." (*Clive Burton, and others*) Men are expected to wear a jacket and tie for dinner. "I know," writes Ted Barlow, "that this irritates a minority, but most of our guests prefer it – and meals can be served in the bedroom if required. Our aim is to provide a peaceful and quiet holiday – no canned music, no entertainment, log fires in early and late season." More reports please.

Open 8 Mar–10 Nov.
Rooms Lift, ramps. 4 suites (1 on ground floor), 32 double, 8 single – all with bath, shower, telephone, radio, TV, baby-listening; tea-making facilities on request. 4 self-catering flats in grounds.
Facilities Lift, ramps. 4 lounges, cocktail bar, bridge room, restaurant; children's den, snooker room; indoor heated swimming pool, whirlpool bath. 3-acre grounds. Sandy beach 400 yds. Golf, tennis, riding nearby.
Location Avoid Bodmin and Wadebridge. From crossroads at St Merryn take B3276.
Restrictions No smoking in dining room. No children under 3 in dining room. Dogs at management's discretion; not in public rooms.
Credit cards Access, Visa (restaurant only).
Terms Dinner, B&B £42–£79. Set lunch £9.75, dinner £16.75; full alc £24.75. 1-night bookings sometimes refused.
Service/tipping: "No service charge; tips at guests' discretion."

CRANBROOK Kent   Map 3

The Old Cloth Hall   *Tel* Cranbrook (0580) 712220
Cranbrook TN17 3NR

This Elizabethan house with later extensions enjoys "a lovely setting deep in the country" in large grounds with gardens noted for rhododendrons and azaleas, an unheated swimming pool and tennis court. "Furniture from various periods sits on highly polished floors in the low-ceilinged panelled public rooms. There are books, magazines, flower arrangements everywhere, and a miscellany of relics from a lifetime of journeys sitting next to mellow antiques, family portraits and personal whimsy objects, all reflecting the originality and strong artistic sense of the owner, Katherine Morgan, who emphasises that this is her home, not a hotel." Bedrooms "are scattered among those of herself and absent family"; guests have drinks with her before dinner and dine with her at a large, highly polished table, by candle-light. Many are regulars who enjoy the cooking – "simple dinner party stuff; desserts are the strongest point; second helpings are offered" – and the "lack of the anonymity of an ordinary hotel", and the fact that there are no extras on the bill, but caution that "you might, if unlucky, have to meet bores in the drawing room". There are only three bedrooms; the best one has a "magnificent" four-poster. (*Francine Walsh, Mr and Mrs O'Connor; also A Lasman*)

Open All year except Christmas.
Rooms 3 double – all with bath and/or shower and TV.
Facilities Drawing room, dining room. 13-acre grounds with unheated swimming pool, tennis, croquet.
Location 1 m SE of Cranbrook on the Golford Road to Tenterden.
Restrictions Not suitable for &. No children under 10. No dogs.
Credit cards None accepted.
Terms [1990 rates] B&B: single £45, double £70–£85. Set dinner £20.

CRANTOCK Cornwall   Map 1

Crantock Bay Hotel   `BUDGET`   *Tel* Crantock (0637) 830229
Crantock, Newquay TR8 5SE

This traditional seaside hotel near an old village with an ancient church and thatched cottages has been run for many years by David and Brenda Eyles. It has a stunning and quiet setting facing the Atlantic on the Cornish coast, 200 yards from a sandy beach with rock pools round the edge. Most bedrooms have sea views. It's the sort of friendly place that welcomes your children, their grandparents, and your dogs; bedrooms are geared for families and have an intercom system for baby-listening; plenty of entertainments are organised in season. Food is conventionally English. There are meals for under-fives in the early evening; older children eat with their parents. Many guests have been visiting the hotel regularly for years. Recently a large extension was added, with an indoor swimming pool with spa bath, a toddlers' pool, sauna, exercise room and sun patio. There are six golf courses nearby; Newquay is the nearest big town. One reader felt the facilities for under-fives could have been more imaginative. More reports please.

Open Early Mar–late Nov.
Rooms 27 double, 9 single – all with bath, shower, radio, TV, tea-making facilities, baby-listening.
Facilities 2 lounges, bar lounge, bar, 2 restaurant areas; games room, indoor swimming pool, exercise room; dancing, table-tennis, bar billiards, slide shows, children's parties 2–3 nights a week. 4½-acre grounds with tennis, putting, croquet, children's play area. Sea with sandy beach and safe bathing (lifeguard service) 200 yds; riding, golf nearby.
Location On West Pentire headland, 1 m beyond Crantock; 5 m SW of Newquay. Guests met by arrangement at Newquay and Truro stations.
Restrictions No smoking in dining room and 1 lounge. No dogs in public rooms.
Credit cards All major cards accepted.
Terms Dinner, B&B £30.75–£42.75. Bar lunch from £3.50, set dinner £12.50. 5-day packages; bargain breaks in spring and autumn; half-term rates. Reduced rates and special meals for children.
Service/tipping: "We are against a service charge. However, as visitors do tend to show their 'appreciation', I hold a fund distributed to the staff at the end of the summer. An explanatory note appears in bedrooms."

CROYDE Devon   **Map 1**

The Whiteleaf at Croyde   *Tel* Croyde (0271) 890266
Croyde, Nr Braunton EX33 1PN

"Thank you for including the *Whiteleaf* in the Guide; we would otherwise not have known about it and it certainly deserves an entry. Our room had all we could think of including a well-stocked fridge, and was clean and comfortable, if a fraction small." "Breakfasts were excellent and included fresh orange juice, baked eggs with smoked salmon on top, and vast quantities of toasted home-made bread and marmalade. Lovely warm welcome from Flo Wallington, who takes great pride in her hotel." "Striking value for money."
    Croyde is an attractive seaside village with thatched, colour-washed cottages. The *Whiteleaf* is on the outskirts, in a large garden surrounded by bungalows; the path down to the sweeping sandy beach is through thirties-type wooden chalets. The house itself lacks charm, as does its situation; the decor is not particularly elegant, and the lounge not very large; but readers are rapidly won over by the friendly atmosphere, the comfortable accommodation, and above all by David Wallington's cooking. His British-style menus (plenty of choice) show invention and imagination: "Excellent five-course dinners, including five different vegetables with the main course, all beautifully cooked, every course carefully served by Mrs Wallington." There is a well-chosen, wide-ranging wine list with a good selection of half-bottles. The dining room is large, with well-spaced tables and a view of the garden. The North Devon Coastal Path is easily accessible from the hotel. (*JA Gallimore, Jane Curley, Diane and Brian Smith*) One reader encountered a problem: "Our two-year-old daughter was kindly treated, a cot and a high chair were provided for her, but feeding her in the evening was awkward, as no high tea was available at the *Whiteleaf* and Croyde lacked eating places for young children."

Open All year except early Dec, Jan, 2 weeks May and Aug.
Rooms 5 double – all with bath and/or shower, telephone, radio, TV, tea-making facilities, baby-listening.
Facilities Lounge, bar, dining room. ½-acre grounds. Footpath to Croyde beach with sand, rocks, surfing and bathing (life-guard in season).

Location From Saunton, hotel is on left side before centre of village (400 yds before *Thatched Barn Inn*).
Restrictions Not suitable for &. No dogs in public rooms.
Credit cards Access, Visa.
Terms Dinner, B&B £34–£45. Off-season breaks; 3- and 7-night rates. 1-night bookings occasionally refused. 50% reduction for children sharing parents' room and taking meals.
Service/tipping: "We do not expect or solicit tips. Guests wishing to express appreciation will be so advised, but we will not embarrass them by refusing."

CRUDWELL Wiltshire   Map 2

Crudwell Court Hotel   *Tel* Crudwell (066 67) 355
** and Restaurant**   *Fax* (066 67) 7853
Crudwell, Nr Malmesbury
SN16 9EP

This 17th-century vicarage in a peaceful Wiltshire setting, set in large walled gardens adjoining the church, has been extensively restored by Brian and Susan Howe who bought it in a run-down condition at the beginning of 1987; the result is "a genuine country house atmosphere – restful, calm and unfussy". The 15 bedrooms are individually decorated with pastel colours and Sanderson fabrics; furniture is rather mixed, mostly modern, with some antiques. Rooms on the ground and first floors are large and high-ceilinged, those on the second, up a narrow staircase, are smaller (and cheaper), with lovely views over the surrounding trees and farmland. The Howes have built up a good local restaurant trade thanks to the "very competent and reasonably priced cooking under Paul Lawrence; fresh ingredients cooked with flair without being over-elaborate". There is plenty of choice on the menu; the price of the main course includes a starter and dessert. The wine list is surprisingly long, "and they will provide half of virtually any wine, keeping the other half, no doubt, to prepare some of the very fine food". Other comments: "Welcoming and courteous hosts." "The outdoor heated swimming pool really *is* heated." "Anywhere which accepts dogs deserves an extra mark!" (*William Rankin, Sandra Howard, Isobel MacKenzie, and others*) Responding to last year's comment about "minimal bath towels" the Howes tell us they have now bought new towels for all the bathrooms. A few niggles: "The staircase to the second floor is so narrow it was impossible to take up two cases at once." "Too many sauces cream-based." And an inspector in 1990 reported a rather take-it-or-leave-it attitude towards residents: "We weren't offered help with our suitcases; the towelling bathrobe was damp from a previous user, beds were not turned down at night; and when we asked about borrowing a bathing costume, it was indicated that skinny dipping was the easiest solution – fortunately the pool is secluded!"

Open All year.
Rooms 14 double, 1 single – 14 with bath and shower, 1 with bath, all with telephone, radio, TV, tea-making facilities, baby-listening.
Facilities 2 lounges, dining room. Functions facilities. 3-acre garden with heated swimming pool and croquet. River fishing and lake with water sports nearby.
Location On A429, 3 m N of Malmesbury. Front rooms double-glazed. Hotel is on green opposite *Plough* pub.
Restrictions Not suitable for &. No dogs in public rooms.
Credit cards All major cards accepted.

Terms B&B: single £40–£65, double £75–£100. Set lunch/dinner £17 (snack lunch menu also available). Off-season 2- and 3-day breaks; Christmas and New Year packages. Reduced rates for children sharing parents' room; special meals. *Service/tipping: "No service charge. Tips are gratefully received and shared among all staff according to hours worked."*

DALLINGTON Sussex   Map 3

Little Byres   *Tel* Brightling (042 482) 230
Christmas Farm, Battle Road
Dallington, Heathfield TN21 9LE

"Restaurant-with-chalets" in fairly isolated situation on farm at edge of village in lovely countryside, run by young and "most amiable" Chris and Evelyn Davis. Food – French provincial and modern British – served in "impressively simple" 200-year-old spacious beamed and raftered barn, is "outstanding and beautifully presented". Accommodation in half-timbered and prettily furnished outbuildings fairly basic, but comfortable beds and very good breakfasts. Closed Christmas, 2 weeks Jan. 5 rooms, all with shower. B&B double £35–£45. Set dinner £22.50–£28.50. 2 rather more luxurious rooms planned. Recent nomination. More reports please.

DEDHAM Essex   Map 3

Maison Talbooth   *Tel* Colchester (0206) 322367
Stratford Road, Dedham   *Fax* (0206) 322752
Colchester CO7 6HN   *Telex* 987083

Dedham Vale Hotel   *Tel* Colchester (0206) 322273
Stratford Road, Dedham   *Fax* (0206) 322752
Colchester CO7 6HW   *Telex* 987083

The entrepreneurial Milsom family – Gerald, with sons David and Paul – runs three attractively situated establishments on or near the banks of the river Stour in Dedham, at which they offer a "Mix 'n Match" stay. You can sleep in either *Maison Talbooth* or *Dedham Vale*, but the former serves only breakfast; for other meals, residents have the choice of *Dedham Vale*, half a mile up the road, or another Milsom offspring, *Le Talbooth*, a quarter of a mile further on. *Maison Talbooth* is a luxuriously equipped Victorian house in pretty grounds, with a beautifully proportioned sitting room. Its ten large bedrooms are kitted out with a plethora of pampering extras – tea-making facilities have been added this year – but we have had one complaint about the lack of a writing surface in the bedroom despite its size. The beds are king-sized and the bathrooms are often as opulent as the bedrooms. "It's great! A model of friendly service. So personal that they don't give you a bedroom key – strange but enchanting to a New Yorker." "You can sit in a hot-tub whirlpool, sipping champagne and looking out over exquisite English countryside." *Le Talbooth*'s redesigned dining area has lovely garden and river views; the cooking has been criticised in the past, but under Steven Blake, formerly of the *Meridien*, Piccadilly, in London, it is generally considered to be much improved, though not flawless; there have been mutterings that the table service was not up to the high prices.

Dedham Vale is a less lavish, but fully modernised creeper-covered Victorian mansion in three acres of landscaped garden, close by – but out of earshot of – the A12. The decor is chintzy (in the complimentary sense), and the bedrooms a bit smaller than at *Maison Talbooth* but with almost as many extras (though no showers). Its prices are considerably lower. But we lack feedback on both the *Vale*'s accommodation and on its pretty conservatory-like rôtisserie, the *Terrace Restaurant*. Reports would be welcome.

Note Another Milsom enterprise, *The Pier at Harwich*, receives its first Guide entry this year.

Maison Talbooth
Open All year.
Rooms 5 suites, 5 double – all with bath (2 also with shower), telephone, TV, tea-making facilities, baby-listening. 5 ground-floor rooms.
Facilities Lounge with bar service. Courtesy car to restaurant. Hotel has 2-acre grounds with croquet; restaurant has 3 acres on banks of the Stour; 2 yachts for hire. Fishing, tennis, golf nearby.
Location 6 m NE of Colchester. From A12, about 6 m from Colchester, take Stratford St Mary–Dedham road. After about 1 m take second right-hand turning to Dedham. *Maison Talbooth* is about 1 m down the road on right.
Restriction No dogs.
Credit cards Access, Visa.
Terms (Excluding 10% service charge) B&B (continental): single £80–£105, double £100–£135. English breakfast £5. Set lunch at *Le Talbooth* £16 (packed lunch available); full alc £45. Special breaks. Sailing holidays May–Sept (book a month in advance). 1-night bookings not accepted for weekends Apr–Sept; min 3 nights at Christmas and bank holidays. Reduced rates for children sharing parents' room; room service meals.

Dedham Vale Hotel
Open All year. Restaurant closed Sat lunch, Sun evening.
Rooms 1 suite, 5 double – all with bath, telephone, radio, TV.
Facilities Drawing room, bar, restaurant; function facilities. 3-acre grounds; river 100 yds; fishing and sailing locally.
Location 7 m NE of Colchester off A12.
Restrictions Not suitable for &. No dogs.
Credit cards Access, Visa.
Terms (Excluding 10% service charge) B&B (continental): single £70–£75, double £85–£95. English breakfast £5. Full alc £30. 1-night bookings refused for weekend Mar–Oct. Reduced rates and special meals for children.

DIDDLEBURY Shropshire   **Map 1**

The Glebe Farm   `BUDGET`   *Tel* Munslow (058 476) 221
Diddlebury, Craven Arms
SY7 9DH

Michael and Eileen Wilkes' half-timbered Elizabethan house on a working farm is well endowed with oak beams, flagstones and inglenook fireplaces; they have run it for ten years as a modestly priced guest house. It stands in a garden with a stream, in the centre of a village near the Saxon village church with its fortified tower (and bell which strikes throughout the night!), and is well situated for exploring Housman country and the Welsh Marches. There are only six bedrooms, three of which are in a garden cottage; some have bath or shower fitted into the old structure. Some of the walls are very thin, and the private facilities in the garden cottage are rather cramped. But this does not prevent visitors from writing warmly: "The house is old and delightful, the beds comfortable, and the minute 'facilities' worked well. In the friendly atmosphere we found it easy to get to know our fellow guests." "Delightful house and garden; hosts could not have been more kind and welcoming." A full English breakfast is served between 8.30 and 9 am and "simple but generous" evening meals at 7.45, with a choice of main course, several starters and sweets. (*SM Williams, Prof and Mrs JT Woodward*)

Open Mar–Nov. Closed 10 days in June. Dining room open 4 days a week.
Rooms 5 double, 1 single – 4 with bath and/or shower, all with tea-making facilities, 4 with TV. 3 in cottage in garden.
Facilities Sitting room, bar with TV, dining room. 1-acre garden. Fishing, riding, walking nearby.
Location E of B4368, 4 m NE of Craven Arms.
Restrictions Not suitable for &. No smoking in dining room. No children under 8. No dogs.
Credit cards None accepted.
Terms B&B (English): single occupancy £18–£22, double £40–£52. Set dinner £12. Midweek breaks off-season. Reductions for children.
Service/tipping: "As owners we do not expect a tip. Any gratuities are divided equally among the staff."

DOCKING Norfolk   Map 3

Holland House `BUDGET`
Chequers Street, Docking
Nr King's Lynn PE31 8LH

Tel Docking (048 58) 295
from end 1990/early 1991
(0485) 518295

This friendly and extremely inexpensive B&B in a large Grade II listed Georgian house is in the centre of a Norfolk village – traffic can be heavy during the day, but it is quiet at night, and all the rooms are double-glazed. Mrs Margaret Robinson never accepts more than six people at one time; guests have access to the small walled garden. The house "feels like a home and is filled with solid family furniture; the decor is serviceable rather than elegant. Huge choice of drinks sachets in the bedroom, and a jug of fresh milk." "Warm and immaculate; our double bedroom was spacious, with comfortable bed, small couch and armchair, flowers and ornaments. Bathrooms spotlessly clean, the whole house welcoming and the atmosphere tranquil and relaxing. Very good value indeed." Breakfast, English or continental, is served in the refurbished original kitchen of the house; the cooked variety includes scrambled eggs, bacon, mushrooms, sausages, also kippers. (*Vivienne and David Draper*) More reports please.

Open All year except 2 weeks Christmas/New Year.
Rooms 3 double, 2 single – 1 with shower, all with TV, tea-making facilities.
Facilities Lounge, breakfast room. Small walled garden.
Location In village centre but little traffic at night. House is double-glazed.
Restrictions Not suitable for &. No smoking in breakfast room. No dogs in public rooms.
Credit cards None accepted.
Terms B&B: continental £14, English £16. (No restaurant.)
Service/tipping: "Tips not expected, occasionally offered, and only accepted to avoid giving offence."

DORCHESTER Dorset   Map 2

Casterbridge Hotel   `BUDGET`   *Tel* Dorchester (0305) 264043
49 High East Street
Dorchester DT1 1HU

*Old hotel in Hardy's "Casterbridge"; central, so front rooms can be noisy. Liked
for the friendly welcome from Stuart Turner and his staff and the "excellent and
generous breakfasts". Some bedrooms recently refurbished to a high standard;
they vary in size, and some are said to be too small for comfort, ditto the
bathrooms. No restaurant, but two well-appointed public rooms, and conservatory with fountain. Closed 25/26 Dec. 15 rooms, all with private facilities. B&B
(English): double £40–£50. More reports please.*

DORCHESTER-UPON-THAMES Oxfordshire   Map 2

The George Hotel   *Tel* Oxford (0865) 340404
High Street   *Telex* 83147 attn GEORGE
Dorchester-on-Thames OX10 7HH

An ancient coaching inn with a black-and-white facade in a showplace
village with an enormous abbey, once a 12th-century Augustinian priory,
and also many antique shops. The hotel consists of a number of buildings
lining the drive, some of them half-timbered. Bedrooms vary considerably, from large ones with four-poster, to "cosy" ones under oak beams;
furniture is solid and old-fashioned. "The glory of the interior is the two
dining rooms with heavily beamed and raftered ceiling and brick walls,
stylish in best Olde English tradition." Cooking (despite a rather
pretentious menu) is on the traditional side, especially the Sunday lunch;
it is in keeping with the building. "Not grand gourmet, but very good,"
writes a correspondent who took the whole place for a birthday weekend.
"Everyone praised the food, and when the chef appeared at the end of
our last meal they stood up and applauded him." Service, by local people,
is friendly. (*CKK, Angela Lambert, HR*) There is one thumbs-down from a
reader who got a room inferior to but no cheaper than the one specifically
requested, and was cold because the heating did not come on until 6 pm
on a winter's evening.

Open All year except 1 week over Christmas.
Rooms 14 double, 4 single – all with bath (16 also have shower), telephone, radio,
TV, tea-making facilities, baby-listening. 9 in 2 separate wings. Some on ground
floor.
Facilities Lounge, bar, restaurant. 2-acre grounds.
Location Off A423 Oxford–Reading road. Parking.
Restriction No dogs in public rooms.
Credit cards All major cards accepted.
Terms B&B (English): single £54, double £72–£90. Set lunch £14, dinner £18; full
alc £30. Bargain breaks. Reduced rates and special meals for children.
*Service/tipping: "Service totally at guests' discretion. We wish the industry would adopt
one system of collection and distribution as in Europe."*

Report forms (Freepost in UK) will be found at the end of the Guide.

DORRINGTON Shropshire   Map 4

Country Friends   █BUDGET█   *Tel* Dorrington (074 373) 707
Dorrington SY5 7JD

This long-established restaurant now with three rooms had its first Guide
entry last year, being recommended for "sybaritic short stays at
supermarket prices. Stylish but business-like. Reasonably priced rooms
and generous no-choice breakfast of scrambled eggs and smoked salmon,
brioche and Bucks Fizz." The main building is large, half-timbered, and
dates from the 16th to 19th centuries. The annexe Coach House holds the
three guest bedrooms: they are newly decorated, fresh and bright; one
has a shower *en suite*, two share a stylish bathroom (lots of hot water and
a splendid collection of fluffy towels), all are individually furnished and
of modern design, with wall-to-wall thick carpets and antique furniture.
They are reasonably comfortable. Double-glazing mitigates the sound of
passing traffic. This is an unabashed restaurant-with-rooms. The owners,
Charles and Pauline Whittaker, are both chefs and are not really
interested in people wishing to stay without dining. Top-class restaurant,
with very reasonably priced à la carte and table d'hôte menus. Food is
"modern English and light; portions not large. Ridiculously cheap and
unusually good bar food served at lunch and on quiet evenings. Very nice
owners. But not a house-party hotel, do not expect conviviality." (*CKK, J
and JW*) Dorrington is on a plain but there is glorious walking country all
around in the Shropshire hills.

Open All year except 2 weeks end July, 1 week end Oct. Closed Sun and Mon,
and New Year.
Rooms 3 double – 1 with shower, 2 share bath, all with tea-making facilities. All
in annexe across drive.
Facilities Lounge bar, restaurant. ¼-acre grounds.
Location 6 m S of Shrewsbury. On A49. Rooms double-glazed.
Restrictions Not suitable for &. No smoking in dining room. No dogs.
Credit cards Access, Amex, Visa.
Terms (No service charge) B&B double £36–£38. Set lunch/dinner £14–£15; full
alc £25.

DREWSTEIGNTON Devon   Map 1

Hunts Tor House   █BUDGET█   *Tel* Drewsteignton (0647) 21228
Drewsteignton EX6 6QW

Drewsteignton is a tiny picture-book village below Lutyens's Castle
Drogo, with a Norman church and thatched houses. *Hunts Tor*, which
entered the Guide last year, is extraordinary in that the original building,
dating from about 1640, is enclosed within a large Edwardian house. At
the heart of the building is a small low-ceilinged, heavily beamed room,
wood everywhere, which is one of the two dining rooms; a few steps
away are the lounge and the larger dining room, which belong to the later
part of the house. The four bedrooms, on the first floor, are stylish, but
simple – no telephones, and only the suite has TV – but new, bright and
clean, with an attractive, restrained colour scheme, plenty of storage
space, good lights, and private facilities. The house is full of Victorian and
Edwardian furniture inherited from the previous owners, to which the
present owner, Chris Harrison, who converted *Hunts Tor* into a guest

house, has added Art Deco pottery and other collector's items; the resulting decor is "very turn of the century". The Harrisons do not take more than eight guests at one time, and dinner is for residents only. Guests eat at a communal table in the smaller dining room only if they are very few; there are four tables for separate dining in the other. The four-course, no-choice dinner is at 7.30, cooked by Sue Harrison who trained with Keith Floyd. Her style is "homely, quite modern, with a tendency to the healthy". Guests should warn in advance of any allergies, etc: "When faced with a cauliflower soup and a lamb charlotte oozing with onions," writes Mrs Harrison, "a guest announced that she was allergic to, of course, onions!" Breakfasts are "excellent, including freshly squeezed orange juice and home-made jam and marmalade". (*CKK, GL Collier*)

Open Feb–end Nov. Dining room closed for lunch.
Rooms 1 suite, 3 double – all with bath; TV, tea-making facilities in suite.
Facilities Lounge, bar/dining room, dining room. River Teign nearby, with fishing.
Location In village which is 3 m N of Moretonhampstead.
Restrictions Not suitable for &. No smoking in dining room. No children under 14. No dogs in dining room.
Credit cards None accepted.
Terms [1990 rates] B&B (continental): single £23, double £36, suite £50. English breakfast £3. Set dinner £14. 1-night bookings sometimes refused bank holidays.
Service/tipping: "No tips expected, but we add an optional 15p per person for the Devon Wildlife Trust."

The Old Inn **BUDGET**　　　　　　　*Tel* Drewsteignton (0647) 21276
The Square
Drewsteignton EX6 6QR

A restaurant-with-rooms in a 300-year-old building in the square, owned and run by Rose Chapman with her mother, now "semi-retired". She describes it as "a cross between a cottage and a defrocked pub; an extension of our home". It is friendly, inexpensive and unpretentious. Bedrooms are "basic but comfortable" and not large, none has a bath *en suite* but there are hand-basins with plenty of hot water and the rooms are well lit and have good beds with duvet. There is a menu with a limited choice which changes daily. Rose Chapman explains each dish; you are called to the table when your food is ready. Dinners, served in the "lovely dining room with huge log fire", are "English country-style cooking, with fresh local ingredients, served in generous portions". There are three choices of each course and vegetarians are catered for. Service is "willing, if not always very experienced". "A real walker's breakfast, complete with yoghurt and home-made pork and apple sausages" is served. For some readers the accommodation is altogether too basic, and when the house is full there could be congestion as there is only one bathroom and lavatory. Others consider it "outstanding value; where else at that price would you be offered smoked salmon and scrambled eggs for breakfast? I would commend it to anyone." (*RAL Ogston*) Rose Chapman writes this year that they can no longer offer family accommodation, but "guests will be able to bring their horses as the old stables are being renovated. The riding locally is superb." She emphasises: "We cannot offer hotel service or country house gracious living – it would be an embarrassment to a small ex-pub."

Open All year except Christmas; weekends only in Feb. Restaurant closed for lunch, on Mon, and to non-residents on Sun.
Rooms 3 double, 1 single – all with tea-making facilities.
Facilities Bar, lounge with TV, restaurant. Stabling for visiting horses. Fishing nearby.
Location In village square. Parking.
Restrictions Not suitable for &. No smoking in restaurant. No children under 12. No dogs in public rooms.
Credit card Visa.
Terms [1990 rates] B&B (English) £14. Set dinner £18. 1-night bookings refused for Easter and bank holidays.
Service/tipping: "Service included. I do not like tipping. We pay our workers realistic rates. Some guests try to tip and I explain this is unnecessary. If a tip is left despite this it goes to the staff."

DULVERTON Somerset   **Map 1**

Ashwick Country House   *Tel* Dulverton (0398) 23868
Hotel and Restaurant
Dulverton TA22 9QD

Ashwick House is a small Edwardian country house in a lovely peaceful setting. It is 900 feet up in the Exmoor National Park, set in six-acre grounds with sweeping lawns, mature trees, water-gardens and lily ponds, overlooking the valley of the river Barle. The hall, with long broad gallery and log fire, still has the original William Morris wallpaper; the lounge and library – decorated in purple – are considered by some "particularly stylish", by others gloomy. Bedrooms are "quiet, with lovely views", and attractively decorated, with good lighting and more than the usual extras including TV with in-house films, changed every day, tape recorder, electronic scales "which announce your weight with malicious delight after the *Ashwick* dinner", magazines, mini-bar and fresh flowers. The bedroom called *Ash* is particularly recommended. For years *Ashwick House* was run by Mr and Mrs Sherwood and their son. Sadly, Mr Sherwood senior died at the end of 1988, and his wife in 1989; their son, Richard, is carrying on the business, running the hotel and continuing the *Ashwick* style of English home-cooking: a four-course meal with an emphasis on good local produce. Normally there is no choice of main course, which one visitor bemoans this year – "it is a shame they don't discuss the meal with you at breakfast". However a vegetarian reports: "I always feel very spoiled, with lots of splendid meals cooked just for me. It remains my favourite hotel; difficult to imagine such peace and quiet." (*Tricia Roberts*) Generous breakfasts include freshly squeezed apple juice and good brown toast. Guests are expected to dine in. One reader found his large bedroom seriously underheated – "we obtained 1½ kw by running two hair-driers". More reports please.

Open All year except New Year.
Rooms 6 double – all with bath, shower, radio, TV; telephone on request.
Facilities Hall, lounge, library, bar, dining room. 6-acre grounds with 2 ponds, croquet.
Location 2½ m NW of Dulverton. Take the B3223 Exford–Lynton road. ½ m after cattle grid, hotel signpost directs you left.
Restrictions Not suitable for &. No smoking in dining room. No children under 8. No dogs.
Credit cards None accepted.

Terms Dinner, B&B £48.50–£69.75. Set Sun lunch £10.95, dinner £18.50. Special rates for 2 or 5 nights.
Service/tipping: "No service charge added. Tips are not expected, but if offered are gratefully received by the staff."

EASINGTON Cleveland   Map 4

Grinkle Park Hotel   *Tel* Guisborough (0287) 40515
Easington   *Fax* (0287) 41278
Saltburn-by-the-Sea
TS13 4UB

"Thank you, GHG. Lovely old house, run as a very efficient and welcoming hotel. Most comfortable rooms, interesting menu and sensibly priced wine list. The grounds, with peaceful walks, are a great joy." One of several warm endorsements this year for this fine stone Victorian house in extensive grounds with lawns and a lake, approached by a long drive of rhododendrons. It has been modernised and redecorated by Bass PLC to a high standard. There are comfortable lounges and a fine staircase with a half-landing to a huge stained-glass window. Bedrooms are individually decorated: the most elegant, on the first floor, with four-posters, are named after flowers; those on the second floor are simpler and called after moorland birds. All are well appointed with good bathrooms. The dining room is formal in decor, with fresh posies of flowers, quality china, silver and glass, and tables set well apart. It serves "good sound Yorkshire fare at reasonable prices" with the emphasis on local supplies. Game comes from the estate, fish from the fishing village nearby. Mrs Atkinson, who lives on the estate, makes calorific desserts for the trolley. There is an English cheeseboard, plenty of coffee and an affordable house wine. Service, by local people, is good and friendly. Breakfast is "what you'd expect from a good Northern hotel – huge fry-up if you want it; kippers oak-smoked". (*Paul and Christine Butler, also RI Tulloch, Martyn Smith*) Only qualification: to keep solvent *Grinkle Park* has frequent conferences and functions; holiday guests should discuss accommodation carefully.

Open All year.
Rooms 13 double, 7 single – all with bath and/or shower, telephone, TV, tea-making facilities, baby-listening.
Facilities 2 lounges, bar, billiard room, dining room; conference/functions facilities. 35-acre grounds with lake, tennis, croquet. Sea 4 m with safe bathing; fishing, sailing, climbing, walking, shooting nearby.
Location 2 m E of Loftus. Turn N towards Grinkle off A171 Whitby road.
Restrictions Not suitable for &. No dogs in public rooms.
Credit cards All major cards accepted.
Terms [1990 rates] B&B (English): single £55.50, double £72–£81. Set lunch £9.50, dinner £14.50. Bar meals available. Weekend breaks; 5- and 7-day breaks.
Service/tipping: "Tips at guests' discretion; divided between all staff."

Set dinner refers to a fixed price meal (which may have ample, limited or no choice on the menu). Full alc is the hotel's own estimated price per person of a three-course meal taken à la carte, with a half-bottle of house wine.

EAST BUCKLAND Devon   Map 1

Lower Pitt Restaurant   *Tel* Filleigh (059 86) 243
East Buckland, Barnstaple
EX32 0TD

A 16th-century white-washed stone farmhouse, once two cottages, now
Grade II listed and a popular restaurant-with-rooms, owned and run by
the "helpful and friendly" Suzanne and Jerome Lyons. Tall visitors
should observe the injunction to mind their head when passing through
the doorways, a reminder of *Lower Pitt*'s cottage ancestry. It is in a
peaceful hamlet in the fold of a hillside, surrounded by the walled fields
of South Exmoor – "an ideal spot for walkers". It has a strong following
among local gourmets who appreciate Mrs Lyons's "honest home-
cooking – carefully prepared real food served with style". Residents are
allowed to choose from the à la carte menu for the dinner, B&B rate. The
three small bedrooms are comfortable, with pine furniture, duvets,
electric blankets and "nice touches such as fresh milk in a thermos for the
tea. Mrs Lyons's cooking is better than ever and we thoroughly enjoyed
our dinner and the cooked breakfast." Mrs Lyons writes: "We agree that
our rooms are not luxurious and would point out that this is reflected in
the price; establishments which provide TV, trouser presses and so on in
the room make significantly higher charges to cover these items whether
or not they are used or even required. Our customers generally come for a
quiet retreat and are trying to escape from such modern gadgets." And,
answering comments about lack of a residents' lounge, she says, "We are
adding a new conservatory dining room this year, creating a second
sitting room which will make it more comfortable for residents." Jerome
Lyons has given up his other business interests to join his wife as a full-
time restaurateur. The new A361 North Devon link road has made East
Buckland more easily accessible – only 45 minutes from junction 27 of the
M5. Half-board terms only. More reports please.

Open All year except Jan.
Rooms 3 double – 1 with bath and shower, 2 with shower, all with tea-making
facilities.
Facilities 2 lounges, 2 dining rooms. 2-acre grounds with gardens and terrace.
Sandy beaches and North Devon coast within easy reach.
Location 3 m NW of South Molton. Follow signs to East Buckland from new
North Devon Link Road (A361).
Restrictions Not suitable for &. No smoking in dining rooms. No children under
11. No dogs.
Credit cards Access, Visa.
Terms Dinner, B&B £37.50–£45. Full alc £20. Midweek reductions (3 nights min).
*Service/tipping: "No service charge; tips are at customers' discretion and are divided
equally among all staff. As owners, we do not expect a tip."*

EAST GRINSTEAD West Sussex   Map 3

 **Gravetye Manor**
East Grinstead RH19 4LJ

Tel Sharpthorne (0342) 810567
Fax (0342) 810080
Telex 957239

César award: The epitome of the grand English country house hotel at its luxurious best

An immaculate Elizabethan manor house, with "understated elegance, an exceptional original decor and a cosseting atmosphere". It once belonged to William Robinson, pioneer of the English natural garden, who laid out the beautiful grounds which nowadays are maintained by six gardeners. The house has spacious panelled public rooms with fine paintings and fresh flowers, and a renowned restaurant. Bedrooms, all named after trees, are extremely comfortable, with many extras, including good pictures, and books (one reader was agreeably surprised to find the latest Booker prize-winner in her room – "you don't often find *new* books in hotels"). The bedrooms vary in size; the best are large with panelling, plenty of storage space and garden views. Bathrooms, too, are well equipped. For the past 34 years *Gravetye* has been owned and run by Peter Herbert; there is a new manager, Andrew Russell (Mr Herbert's son Leigh, formerly chef/*patron*, now spends much time in Australia); Mark Raffan is head chef. The kitchen uses fruit, vegetables, herbs, spring water, free-range eggs from the estate, game obtained locally, and salmon, venison and duck breasts all smoked in the hotel's own smoke-house. Food is "excellent", modern French and English, without gimmicks and served in reasonable portions. There is a large staff, efficient and professional, many of them young. Despite its peaceful setting, *Gravetye* is only 20 minutes' drive from Gatwick Airport. (*Heather Sharland, Uwe Kitzinger, and others*)

Open All year. Restaurant closed to non-residents on Christmas evening.
Rooms 12 double, 2 single – 12 with bath and shower, 2 with shower, all with telephone, radio, TV, baby-listening.
Facilities 3 sitting rooms, bar, restaurant; private dining room. 30-acre grounds with gardens, croquet, trout fishing.
Location 5 m SW of East Grinstead off B2110 at West Hoathly sign.
Glyndebourne 40 mins' drive; Gatwick Airport 9 m.
Restrictions Not suitable for &. No smoking in restaurants. No children under 7 except babies. No dogs.
Credit cards None accepted.
Terms (Excluding VAT) B&B: single £87–£93, double £109–£190. Set lunch £19, dinner £22; full alc £35. 1-night bookings refused at weekends Apr–Sept.
Service/tipping: "Prices include service; our staff do not expect tips."

**Woodbury House Hotel
    and Restaurant**
Lewes Road
East Grinstead RH19 3UD

Tel East Grinstead (0342) 313657
Fax (0342) 314801

Michael and Jane Medforth's small hotel on the A22 just south of East Grinstead, recently extended and modernised, convenient for Gatwick and Channel ports, is recommended for spacious, well-furnished and comfortable bedrooms (double-glazed against road noise), professional and quick service. "Excellent breakfast, with nothing pre-packaged." Reasonable three-course daily menu for residents in Garden Room Restaurant; *lighter meals in* Conservatory Bistro. *Restaurant closed Sun evening; bistro closed Sun lunch. 14 rooms, all with bath and/or shower. B&B (English) double £65–£75; dinner, B&B £96.90–£106.90. Set lunch £15.75, dinner £16.75. New nomination. More reports please.*

EASTON GREY Wiltshire   **Map 2**

Whatley Manor   *Tel* Malmesbury (0666) 822888
Easton Grey   *Fax* (0666) 821620
Malmesbury SN16 0RB   *Telex* 449380

Fine country manor house, medium-to-high in price, in 20-acre grounds with swimming pool, tennis, croquet, river with trout fishing. Traditional decor with panelled lounges and library bar, log fires, spacious and comfortable bedrooms. Sauna, solarium, jacuzzi, table tennis. Children and dogs welcomed. 29 rooms (11 rooms in Court House – no room service). B&B double £95–£110. Set lunch £13.50, dinner £26. Dropped from earlier editions following criticisms. Now recommended for unpretentious atmosphere, good food and good value, particularly the Christmas package. More reports please.

EVERSHOT Dorset   **Map 2**

Summer Lodge   *Tel* Evershot (0935) 83424
Evershot DT2 0JR   *Fax* (0935) 83005

🏵 *César award in 1985: Best country house hotel in the medium-price range*

"Wholeheartedly endorse the GHG entry. Our arrival coincided with tea; what a spread! Dinner on both nights was imaginative and very good. Service from the young waitresses friendly without being obtrusive; breakfasts full and very English." "Where else can you still find a real country house hotel in which shoes can be left outside the room to be cleaned at night; your car windows are cleaned every morning; the price really does include everything except drinks; only freshly squeezed orange juice is served; at least one member of staff absolutely refused a tip for carrying heavy cases?" "Food, under the new chef, Roger Jones, [with some choice of most courses, and always a dish suitable for vegetarians] is much improved: *nouvelle* in style, good flavour, with five courses, each small – we never felt too full. The new manager, Mr Ash, is settling in. Rooms in the converted coach house very comfortable. There are constant small but significant improvements." (*Lesley Kay, Edwin Prince, Charles Gorer; also Heather Sharland, and many others*)

Nigel and Margaret Corbett's country house hotel, the Earl of Ilchester's former dower house in a pretty Dorset village, always draws the warmest of compliments, and many visitors are faithful returnees. The comfortable furnishings and attractive decor, Mrs Corbett's beautiful flower arrangements, the remembering of guests' likes and dislikes and the Corbetts' personal farewells to departing guests are all regularly praised. Such is *Summer Lodge's* popularity that at busy times things can be a bit disorganised in the dining room; the coach house rooms sometimes suffer from noise from neighbours; one visitor felt the food now had less of a "home-cooked" feel to it; and some regulars fear that the expansions may lead to a loss of the personal touch; but the consensus remains, as before, strongly favourable.

Open All year, except first 2 weeks Jan.
Rooms 14 double, 3 single – all with bath (6 also have shower), telephone, tea-making facilities; 6 with TV in coach house annexe. 3 ground-floor rooms.
Facilities Drawing room, TV room, bar, dining room. 4-acre garden with heated swimming pool, croquet, tennis. Golf, fishing nearby. Sea 12 m.
Location 10 m S of Yeovil. (*Note* the entrance on village street is for pedestrians only; cars must turn left on reaching village into Summer Lane and then right into drive to house.)
Restrictions No children under 8. No dogs in public rooms.
Credit cards Access, Visa.
Terms B&B (English) £50–£75; dinner, B&B £55–£95. Set lunch £14, dinner £22.50. 3-day breaks in low season; 4-day Christmas break. 1-night bookings sometimes refused for Sat and bank holiday weekends. 40% reduction for children sharing parents' room.
Service/tipping: "Tipping left entirely to our guests' discretion; not necessary as our staff are fully and properly paid."

EVESHAM Hereford and Worcester   **Map 2**

The Evesham Hotel   *Tel* Evesham (0386) 765566
Cooper's Lane   *Fax* (0386) 765443
Evesham WR11 6DA   *Telex* 339342

💧 *César award in 1990: Utterly acceptable mild eccentricity*

An informal, friendly hotel run by the Jenkinson family, with jokey brochure, toy ducks and boats in the baths and resident teddy bears. It enjoys a secluded setting but is only a short walk from the centre of town, and is one of the all too small number of British hotels in the Guide which are genuinely welcoming to children. Bedrooms and bathrooms are well equipped, clean and comfortable. The busy restaurant overlooks the large garden with a huge old cedar of Lebanon; chatty dinner menus offer exotic dishes from around the world as well as plain grills; lunch is a reasonably priced buffet or a choice of hot dishes; the extensive and informative wine list "encompasses Afrikanerdom to Zimbabwe". The Jenkinsons' determinedly jokey attitude may be a bit much for some, and the cooking does not reach any gastronomic heights (desserts, particularly, have disappointed recent reporters), but their attention to detail and their professionalism, and the smiling, helpful staff, keep many visitors happy. (*Michael Schofield, John McCabe*)

Open All year except 25/26 Dec.
Rooms 1 family, 33 double, 6 single – all with bath and/or shower, telephone, radio, TV, tea-making facilities, baby-listening.
Facilities Bar, lounge, restaurant; small indoor swimming pool. 2½-acre grounds.
Location 5 mins' walk from town centre, across river. Parking.
Restrictions Not suitable for ♿. No dogs in public rooms.
Credit cards All major cards accepted.
Terms B&B (English): single £52–£56, double £66–£74, family £84–£90. Buffet lunch £6; full alc dinner £20. Off-season breaks. Reduced rates and special meals for children.
Service/tipping: "Service included. It's my job to pay the staff; the customers pay me."

FALMOUTH Cornwall   Map 1

Penmere Manor Hotel   *Tel* Falmouth (0326) 211411
Mongleath Road   *Fax* (0326) 317588
Falmouth TR11 4PN   *Telex* 45608

An unpretentious and dependable family hotel in a well-bred Georgian house, run "with calm professionalism" by the Pope family for many years. It has plenty of loyal regulars. Sandy beaches are a mile away. The hotel has five acres of sub-tropical gardens and woodland, a large walled garden sheltering a heated swimming pool, snooker and games rooms, and a spotless leisure centre. One of the Popes is always available "which gives the hotel very much the atmosphere of a friend's large house". "Our spacious 'superior' room was in the new wing, added in 1989. It was decorated in pastel colours and furnished with everything one might need including a folding ironing board. Meals were a delight, not *haute cuisine*, but plentiful and well presented, with very fresh fish and an imaginative vegetarian dish. Service throughout was enchanting; the girls were evidently enjoying their work. In a word the place is generous, the product of unstinting care and loving supervision of the charming staff." "Breakfast copious, rooms warm and comfortable." (*C and N Frizzell, Geoff Barratt*) One fly in the ointment: "There was a pianist during dinner, of the dozily and noisily romantic type, but we asked for a table in the far corner of the room and found it bearable."

Open All year except 24–28 Dec.
Rooms 12 superior, 18 double, 9 single – all with bath and/or shower, telephone, radio, T V, tea-making facilities, baby-listening. 13 on ground floor.
Facilities 3 lounges, library, restaurant, games room, snooker room, leisure centre. 5-acre grounds with heated swimming pool, adventure playground. Sandy beach, golf 1 m.
Location 1 m from Falmouth. In Penryn turn right towards Gweek and Constantine. Follow signs to Maenporth. Hotel sign on left into Mongleath road.
Restrictions No smoking in dining room. Dogs by arrangement; not in public rooms.
Credit cards All major cards accepted.
Terms B&B (English): single £45–£50, double £65–£96; dinner, B&B (2 nights min) £44–£53 per person. Set dinner £17.50; full alc £25.60. Winter walking weeks; House & Garden holidays. Reduced rates and special meals for children. *Service/tipping: "We make no service charge; our staff are well remunerated for the services they give willingly. Anything additional left by guests is distributed among all staff including those behind the scenes."*

FOWEY Cornwall   Map 1

Marina Hotel   *Tel* Fowey (0726) 833315
The Esplanade, Fowey PL23 1HY

"A very reasonably priced hotel offering excellent value for money, and caring hospitality in an outstanding setting. The town itself is charming, tumbling down to the water's edge on the Fowey river; it is relatively free of tourist clutter, with minimal traffic as all vehicles must be left in the carparks on the edge of town. You can drive down the 1-in-6 hill to the hotel to unload your luggage but pre-arrival organisation with David Johns, the proprietor, is essential – unloading in front of the hotel blocks the Esplanade. And the altitude problem is not confined to the streets of

Fowey; from the beach at the end of the *Marina*'s small and charming garden to the third and top floor there are 101 steps, of which 60 are inside the hotel from the dining room to the top landing. The listed Georgian building, originally built as the summer retreat of the Bishops of Truro, is more like an elegant and well-maintained home than a hotel. It has a spacious entrance lobby, a curved staircase lit from above by an overhead oval window, and an almost semi-circular first-floor landing. Moulded ceilings and arches add a finishing touch. Some bedrooms overlook the river; four of these have a balcony. Furnishing is simple; our rooms had flowery wallpaper and curtains, individual pictures and decorations, firm beds with good linen; housekeeping is of a very high standard. The dining room has a panoramic view and mealtimes are a picture show of riverscapes and boats. There is plenty of choice on the menu and fresh local fish is normally offered; the cooking is slightly variable but soups are good, and desserts good and abundant. Breakfasts nicely cooked; you get what you ordered." (*David Wallington*) The "skimpy" towels on which a reader commented last year have been replaced by bath sheets; and there is now a summerhouse in the garden where guests can sit sheltered at the water's edge. More reports please.

Open Mar–Oct inclusive.
Rooms 11 double – 9 with bath, 2 with shower, all with telephone, radio, TV, tea-making facilities, baby-listening. 4 with balcony.
Facilities 2 lounges, bar lounge, dining room. Small walled garden with summerhouse, steps to water; moorings available to guests.
Location 1-way circuit, turn right at start of shops.
Restrictions Not suitable for &. No smoking in restaurant. No dogs in public rooms.
Credit cards All major cards accepted.
Terms B&B (English) £22–£37. Single occupancy supplement £6. Bar snacks £2–£3; packed lunches available. Set dinner £14; full alc £20. 2-day and weekly breaks. Reduced rates for children sharing parents' room; high tea.
Service/tipping: "No service charge. Tipping at guests' discretion at end of stay; shared by all staff."

GILLAN Cornwall   **Map 1**

Tregildry Hotel `BUDGET`   *Tel* Manaccan (032 623) 378
Gillan, Manaccan TR12 6HG

"A small, relaxed, unpretentious seaside hotel, well situated with superb views. Rooms are light and comfortable with exceptionally good bathrooms. Bar and lounge attractive and spacious enough to make even a really wet day enjoyable. Food, on a fixed menu (with limited choice), is much better than routine, especially when accompanied by the unusually good, and comparatively cheap, choice of house wines (Mr Norton was in the wine trade for almost 20 years). This hotel is exceptional value." Mr and Mrs Norton's white-painted family-run hotel stands in a tranquil setting in four acres of grounds, with a private footpath to the cove below which is good for fishing, bathing, windsurfing and boating. Most bedrooms have fine views over the bay or creek.

Open Easter–mid-Oct.
Rooms 10 double – all with bath and/or shower, radio, tea-making facilities; TV and baby-listening on request.
Facilities 2 lounges, lounge bar, TV room. 4-acre grounds. Private path to beach – bathing, sailing, fishing, windsurfing.

Location 12 m NE of Helston. From A3083 take B3293. Left at New Town St Martin, follow signs to Manaccan, then Gillan. Hotel sign at T-junction.
Restrictions Not suitable for ♿. No smoking in dining room and bedrooms. No dogs in public rooms.
Credit cards Access, Visa.
Terms B&B £23.50–£27.50; dinner, B&B £34–£40. 30% surcharge for single occupancy. Bar lunch £1.50–£7, set dinner £13. 3-day breaks except in high season. 1-night bookings sometimes refused in high season.
Service/tipping: "Guests may tip if they want to. We hope our staff service is the same whether they do or not."

GILLINGHAM Dorset   Map 2

 **Stock Hill House Hotel**   *Tel* Gillingham (0747) 823626
Wyke, Gillingham SP8 5NR

César award: Dedicated hotelmanship

Peter and Nita Hauser's Victorian manor house is quietly situated in ten acres of parkland, with stream, fountain, lawns, old and rare trees and lots of wildlife. They have spent a lot of time and money refurbishing it since coming here five years ago and the result is "a delight". In the public rooms there are fine rugs, antiques, paintings, mirrors and *objets d'art*. The bedrooms, all differently decorated, vary in size; the large four-poster room with sofa and armchair, huge bathroom, plenty of storage space, and many extras, is particularly commended. Beds, except the four-poster, have duvets, but you can ask for conventional bedding if you prefer it. "Everything is clean and fresh. One is greeted by two statues of Indian horses in the hall, perhaps a reminder that the house adjoins a stud. This is a hotel for those who like to open the window at night and listen to the quiet, who like a walk round the garden, and to sit by a log fire at night." "Everywhere you look there is something unique and dramatic, full of life and colour. Our cases were spirited upstairs when we arrived. Our bedroom was a haven, with huge and comfortable bed, large vase of flowers, gorgeous wallpaper, sumptuous curtains. The Hausers are happy and smiling, the house feels really loved." "Top quality food, and attention to detail from a chef who cares. The day's exertions, be they walking on windy hills or touring the region, are properly balanced by the evening's and night's relaxation. Fresh, perfectly ripe fruit in the bedroom is a splendid touch, as is the music that comes from Austrian-born Peter Hauser's zither once he has prepared the evening meal. The decor, and the embellishments of the food, show that the Hausers share a touch of whimsy; strange, but not tasteless, antiques surround you, and you eat tiny animals, birds and other exotica hand-made from chocolate, puff-pastry or meringue." Peter Hauser's cooking concentrates on fresh, locally produced ingredients and home-grown herbs and vegetables, but a Viennese accent remains. There is plenty of choice on the menu; wines are reasonably priced. Men are expected to wear jacket and tie at dinner. (*David Morris, Ruth West, A Dearing, and others*)

Open All year. Closed Sun evening and Mon except bank holidays.
Rooms 6 double, 2 single – all with bath and/or shower, telephone, radio, TV.
Facilities Foyer with small bar, lounge, breakfast room, restaurant. Indoor swimming pool heated May–Oct. 10½-acre grounds with stream, lake, croquet.

Location On B3081 1½ m from Gillingham, just S of A303.
Restrictions Not suitable for &. No smoking in dining and breakfast rooms. No
children under 7. No dogs.
Credit cards Access, Visa.
Terms Dinner, B&B: single £70–£80, double £150–£160. Set lunch £18, dinner
£26. Midweek reductions in winter. Reduced rates and special meals for
children.
*Service/tipping: "Tipping is between the guest and staff; we are very much against service
charges."*

GOATHLAND North Yorkshire   Map 4

Whitfield House Hotel   `BUDGET`   *Tel* Whitby (0947) 86215
Darnholm, Goathland
Nr Whitby YO22 5LA

*John and Pauline Lusher's old stone farmhouse in beautiful, peaceful setting,
well placed for exploring the North Yorkshire moors, is recommended for good,
simple accommodation and country food (limited choice, using only fresh
ingredients, served in no-smoking dining room), and very reasonable prices.
Closed mid-Dec–mid-Jan. 9 rooms, all with bath and/or shower. Dinner, B&B
£28.50. New nomination. More reports please.*

GRASMERE Cumbria   Map 4

Lancrigg Vegetarian Country   *Tel* Grasmere (096 65) 317
  House Hotel
Easedale, Grasmere LA22 9QN

Our only vegetarian hotel (though also popular with non-vegetarians) is
owned and run by Robert and Janet Whittington. It's a listed building, in
the beautiful and quiet valley of Easedale, just outside Grasmere, and has
large grounds with fine trees, streams and deer, and associations with
Wordsworth, Tennyson and many other writers. There are splendid
walks all around. Last year's nominators, *Lilian and Donald Brown*, wrote:
"At our ages (totalling 140), the comfort and good dinner on return were
extremely welcome. The decor is in reasonable taste, and not fussy. Our
room had a triangular bath big enough for two, a magnificent view of
Silver Howe and Sour Milk Gill, a television and a four-poster. The
lounge has plenty of comfortable furniture and a good fire. The dining
room verges on the elegant; food is good, imaginative, and served in very
generous portions. There is a fair choice of wines, mostly organic.
Breakfasts and packed lunches were also good. The place has a friendly,
cosy air; staff are helpful without being a nuisance." *Gordon Wrigley* adds:
"The Whittingtons have done a wonderful job of the decor. Not all
bedrooms have private facilities but the baths in the shared bathrooms
are from a luxury age long gone. Half the guests, myself included, were
not vegetarian, but enjoyed the food and wine." (Endorsed by *W Welsh,
Eric Norris*) One reader reports persistent cooking smells in the hall.

Open All year except last 2 weeks Jan.
Rooms 11 double, 1 single – 7 with bath and/or shower (some with whirlpool),
all with radio, TV, tea-making facilities, baby-listening. 1 on ground floor.
Telephones to be installed by 1991.

Facilities Lounge, dining room. 27-acre grounds with woodland and streams.
Location ½ m along the Easedale road from Grasmere.
Restrictions No smoking in dining room or lounge. No dogs.
Credit cards None accepted.
Terms [1990 rates] Dinner, B&B £35–£51.50. Set dinner £13.50. Midweek
reductions in low season. 1-night bookings refused for bank holidays. Reduced
rates for children sharing parents' room; special meals.
Service/tipping: "No service charge. Tips optional, shared by all staff at end of season."

White Moss House   *Tel* Grasmere (096 65) 295
Rydal Water, Grasmere LA22 9SE

This small hotel and restaurant, formerly three 18th-century cottages
owned by Wordsworth's family – his descendants lived there until the
1930s – is owned and run by Susan and Peter Dixon. There are five rooms
in the main house on the A591 (heavy lorries banned), and two up a steep
footpath in Brockstone Cottage. They are smallish, with small bathrooms,
but are extensively kitted out with cosseting extras – trouser press, sewing
kit, hair-drier, bath essence, dried *White Moss* lavender, Crabtree and
Evelyn soaps, and so forth. The lounge, too, is small and comfortable, and
conducive to after-dinner fraternisation. Peter Dixon is the chef; dinners,
served at "7.30 for 8", are five-course affairs – good local ingredients,
unpretentiously cooked, with fresh herbs; lots of vegetables; no choice
until dessert; a good selection of English cheeses, and a long and varied
wine list. "Outstanding food, and Muscadet sur lie at £6.50 [1989]
outstanding value. Delightful room in main house." "Elegantly faultless
cooking and service." *(John Ward and Sue Corby, Mrs R Osborne)*
"Children," write the Dixons, "are very welcome provided they can cope
with our dinners which last from 8 to 10; but we have no special facilities
for them."

Open Mar–Nov. Restaurant closed for lunch and on Sun.
Rooms 7 double – all with bath, shower, telephone, radio, TV. 2 in cottage on
hillside (10 mins by car or direct footpath).
Facilities Lounge, bar, dining room. 1-acre garden with terrace. Near Rydal Water
and River Rothay; swimming and fishing.
Location On A591 between Ambleside and Grasmere. Rooms double-glazed;
cottage ones quietest.
Restrictions Not suitable for &. No smoking in dining room. No dogs.
Credit cards None accepted.
Terms Dinner, B&B (English) £55–£70. Set dinner £22. Reduced rates for some
weekends Mar and Nov. 1-night bookings sometimes refused, especially Sat and
bank holidays. 25% reductions in July and Aug for children.
*Service/tipping: "Tipping is not expected. Sometimes guests insist on leaving something,
which we put in a staff box."*

GREAT LANGDALE Cumbria   **Map 4**

Long House   **BUDGET**   *Tel* Langdale (096 67) 222
Great Langdale
Nr Ambleside LA22 9JS

17th-century Lakeland house in 2-acre grounds; low beamed ceilings, open fires.
Excellent base for climbing Langdale Pikes and exploring the valley. Clean,
comfortable, good simple meals: British cooking, using local specialities; bring
your own wine. Unobtrusive but helpful hosts, the Wilkinsons. Recommended

for a relaxed break in beautiful surroundings. Book well ahead. 3 rooms, all with bath. Open Apr–Nov. B&B (English) £19. Set dinner £10. Recent nomination. More reports please.

GREAT LONGSTONE Derbyshire   Map 4

The Croft Country House Hotel   *Tel* Great Longstone (062 987) 278
Great Longstone
Nr Bakewell DE4 1TF

The Croft is a Victorian building with an imposing galleried hall, in four-acre grounds on the edge of a village three miles north of Bakewell, in beautiful walking country. "We warmly recommend the elevation of this unpretentious, family-style country house hotel to a full entry. Genuinely friendly, with efficient service. The set dinner is at 7.30 – guests gather before in the cheerful, flower-filled, galleried hall for drinks – and it is good value; there are choices of first course and dessert, but not of main dish. Limited wine list, reasonably priced. Men wear jacket and tie, women go in for a little gentle dressing up. You sit anywhere in the plain blue dining room and tend to get new neighbours each time. Clive and Rosemary Sheridan are good hosts, with Clive's rather ebullient style gently opening up the shyer guests. Our room had a mix of Victorian and modern pieces and some pleasing prints. We shared a bright, modern bathroom with one other room." "Comfortable bed, attractive building and grounds, nice lounge, small but pleasant bar." (*G & EW, Dr and Mrs James Stewart, William Bentsen*) While most readers have enjoyed their dinners, one is critical: "Can be good, but it's unreliable; and the sorbet course is absurd." Replying to our question about tipping, the Sheridans say, "Tips are not requested or looked for", but a note on the bill reads "Service not included", and "a little sign at reception lets you know that tips will be distributed among the staff". More reports please.

Open 1 Mar–23 Dec.
Rooms 9 rooms – 7 with bath and/or shower. 2 suitable for &.
Facilities Lift. Galleried hall, lounge, TV lounge, restaurant. 4-acre grounds.
Location From Bakewell take A6 to Buxton for 1½ m, turn right on A6020, then left to Great Longstone.
Restrictions No smoking in restaurant. Guide dogs only.
Credit cards Access, Visa.
Terms B&B: single £43–£48, double £54–£70. Set dinner £16.

GREAT MILTON Oxfordshire   Map 1

Le Manoir aux Quat'Saisons   *Tel* Great Milton (0844) 278881
Church Street   *Fax* (0844) 278847
Great Milton OX9 7PD   *Telex* 837552

❧ *César award in 1985: Most brilliant newcomer*

Raymond Blanc's serene country mansion – "a lovely old building, lovingly restored" – with its famous restaurant, double-rosetted in *Michelin*, is 15th and 16th century in origin, and stands in 27 acres of garden and parkland next to the church in a village not far from Oxford. The public rooms are immaculately decorated with fine fabrics, antique and period furniture and fresh flowers, and there are beautiful grounds with a water garden and a well-laid-out vegetable and herb garden. Accommodation is "of the highest quality"; "the bedrooms, with small touches such as a portable radio, a silver hand-mirror and lace-edged sheets and pillow-cases, made us feel that we might be staying with (rich) friends in a private home rather than a hotel; service was exemplary." "Excellent" breakfasts include fresh croissants and rolls, and quality yoghurt, and a recent report praises an "exquisite" picnic lunch. Most readers feel that the quality of food, service and accommodation justifies the "Himalayan" prices, though there are the inevitable critical mutters: "We had expected to be transported with delight by the food, but were not, and how can they charge £21.50 for a starter consisting of four thin slices of scallop and two one-inch pieces of langoustine surrounding a small haystack of green salad?" "£10.50 for the cheese course, £3.50 for after-dinner coffee!" "The whole village felt more like a hideaway for the seriously rich than a genuine community, with the church looking slightly embarrassed in its midst." "No indication on the bath taps as to which was hot and which cold; the jacuzzi did not work; only a young girl was available to carry the bags so we ended up carrying the heavy ones." Considerable changes have taken place at the *Manoir*: there's a new and larger kitchen and a conservatory extension to the restaurant, which is now open seven days a week; nine new bedrooms, all with private terrace, in a converted stable block were due to open in July 1990 as well as a "suite of truly magnificent proportions" in the 16th-century dovecote. We'd be glad for comments on these developments. The off-season special breaks continue to be considered good value. And we welcome the news that the ban on children under 7 has been lifted (see below).

Open All year except Christmas and New Year.
Rooms 5 suites, 14 double – all with bath, shower (some with whirlpool), telephone, radio, TV.
Facilities 2 sitting rooms, restaurant with conservatory; 2 functions rooms. 27 acres landscaped garden and parkland with heated swimming pool, stables.
Location 1 m W of M40/A40, 7 m SE of Oxford. From London take M40: exit 7, 1 mile, 2nd right. From Oxford, take A40, then A329 at Milton Common towards Wallingford, 2nd right.
Restrictions Not suitable for &. No smoking in part of restaurant. Children welcome provided they are kept under control. No dogs in building – free kennel facilities in grounds.
Credit cards All major cards accepted.
Terms [1990 rates] (No single rates) B&B: double £150–£220, suite £300. Set lunch £24.50 (£28 on Sat), dinner £54; full alc £70. Off-season midweek breaks £250 per night for 2 half board (1, 2 or 3 nights). 1-night bookings may be refused for Sat.
Service/tipping: "Service included. Tips are optional and distributed among staff."

The "Budget" label by a hotel's name indicates an establishment where dinner, bed and breakfast is offered at below about £40 per person (or its foreign currency equivalent) or B&B around £25 and an evening meal about £15. These are only rough guides and do not always apply to single accommodation.

GREAT SNORING Norfolk   Map 3

The Old Rectory   *Tel* Fakenham (0328) 820597
Barsham Road, Great Snoring
Fakenham NR21 0HP

The Old Rectory is a listed building tranquilly set in a walled garden in an
unspoilt village, considerably grander than the average country parson-
age. First built in 1500, it is now a mixture of Elizabethan, Georgian and
Victorian Gothic – "an architect's nightmare, but an archaeologist's
dream". Inevitably in such a venerable house the bedrooms vary in size;
some can be cramped, others are "spacious with good antique furniture
and a pleasant view over the garden". Readers have reported "wardrobe
doors with a propensity to come open because of the uneven floor" and a
shortage of hanging space. The rooms are comfortable, rather than
luxurious, with fewer "goodies" than in some country-house establishments. The dining room has mullioned windows, heavy oak beams and
"excellent silver, plate and glass". Food (no choice of main course) is
substantial, "basic and well cooked, plenty of vegetables, nice and crisp,
but not *haute cuisine*. Provided guests realise the limitations of a small
hotel it makes a very pleasant short stay, and is an excellent jumping-off
point for exploring North Norfolk." (*Jane Turner, T and R Rose, and others*)
One reader reports that "the lounge is dimly lit"; another would have
liked some heating in the bathroom. The proprietors, the Scoleses and
Tookes, write: "Our policy of personal service remains unchanged. The
limited menu is appreciated by our guests. We have made a conscious
decision not to change – for the sake of our many return visitors as well as
our new guests."

Open All year except 24–27 Dec. Dining room closed for lunch.
Rooms 6 double, 1 single – all with bath, telephone, TV.
Facilities Sitting room, dining room. 1½-acre walled garden.
Location Behind church on road to Barsham in village 3 m NE of Fakenham off A148.
Restrictions Not suitable for &. No smoking in dining room. Children under
12 not encouraged. No dogs.
Credit cards Amex, Diners.
Terms B&B (English): single £39.50–£52, double £70–£75. Set dinner £16.
*Service/tipping: "No service charge. If a guest wishes to tip this is given to the staff
concerned."*

GRIMSTON Norfolk   Map 3

Congham Hall Country   *Tel* Hillington (0485) 600250
  House Hotel   *Fax* (0485) 601191
Lynn Road, Grimston   *Telex* 81508
King's Lynn PE32 1AH

This elegant Georgian manor house, with 40 acres of velvety lawn,
country garden, paddocks, orchards and parkland, and its own cricket
pitch, is owned and run by "welcoming hosts", Christine and Trevor
Forecast. It has a "large and beautiful drawing room" and a dining room
with a conservatory extension where Clive Jackson cooks "extremely
good" meals – modern cooking with an emphasis on local produce – with
"excellent service". There are two dinner menus: a gourmet "Hobson's
Choice" menu with seven light courses changing twice weekly, and a

four-course menu offering six choices for each course. Bedrooms, including one with a four-poster, are generally well appointed though they vary in size; the suite is "beautiful, with a super-size bed". Visitors appreciate the old-fashioned service; beds are turned down at night and fresh towels provided twice daily. This year, as last, the bedroom lighting is considered inadequate: "60-watt bulbs in the table lamps made it impossible to read in bed." Other niggles: "Early morning tea and newspaper were charged extra, surely they should be included in the high prices?"; there are some criticisms of housekeeping, and "there was no alternative at dinner to the two fixed-price menus, not OK if you are resident and want something light". More reports please.

Open All year.
Rooms 2 suites, 11 double, 1 single – 13 with bath and shower, 1 with shower, all with telephone, radio, TV.
Facilities Hall, lounge, bar, restaurant; boardroom for private parties and meetings. 40-acre grounds with heated swimming pool, jacuzzi, tennis court, cricket pitch, parklands and orchards; stabling for visiting horses. Coast with sandy beaches 10 m; nature and bird sanctuaries, fishing, golf, riding nearby.
Location 6 m NE of King's Lynn. Turn right off A148 to Grimston; *Congham Hall* is 2½ m on left. Do not go to Congham.
Restrictions Not suitable for &. No smoking in restaurant. No children under 12. Dogs in kennels only.
Credit cards All major cards accepted.
Terms B&B (light English): single £70, double £95, suite £145. Full English breakfast £2 added. Set lunch £14.50, 4-course dinner £27.50; "Hobson's Choice" dinner £32. Weekend breaks (Fri–Sun) all year; 3-day Christmas break.
Service/tipping: "All our tariffs carry the statement: 'No service charges are added to your account for any facilities offered in the hotel.' If guests do leave a tip it is passed on to the staff who share it out."

HAMBLETON Leicestershire   **Map 4**

Hambleton Hall   *Tel* Oakham (0572) 756991
Hambleton, Oakham LE15 8TH   *Fax* (0572) 724721
                                             Telex 342888

&? *César award in 1985: Comprehensive excellence in the luxury class*

One of the most luxurious English country house hotels, a stately Victorian mansion in a lovely setting overlooking Rutland Water, on what is almost an island. Its gardens are manicured, with lovely mature trees; the interior has been beautifully decorated by Nina Campbell and is always full of lovely arrangements of fresh flowers. Bedrooms are comfortable and quiet. The restaurant, under chef Brian Baker, continues to elicit superlatives from our readers as well as a *Michelin* rosette; the wine list, largely French, is of a piece with everything else. The owners, Tim and Stefa Hart, are dependably welcoming, and visitors – with occasional gasps at the high prices – continue to express their satisfaction: "Lives up to its high reputation. Food excellent, waiters very attentive." "Quite outstanding." (*Michael Schofield, A and R Payne, Diane and Keith Moss, David Heather, Mrs EH Prodgers*) One reader, in the room called Swallow, was bothered by a noisy kitchen extractor fan.

Open All year.
Rooms 15 double – all with bath, shower, telephone, radio, TV, baby-listening.

Facilities Lift, ramp. Drawing room, bar, dining room; small conference facilities, 2 private dining rooms. 17-acre grounds on lake with trout fishing, windsurfing, sailing; tennis court. Riding, shooting by arrangement.
Location Off A606 Stamford Road 1 m E of Oakham.
Restrictions No children under 9. Dogs by arrangement; not in public rooms, or alone in bedrooms.
Credit cards Access, Visa.
Terms [1990 rates] B&B (continental): single £98, double £98–£200. Set lunch £25, dinner £35; full alc £40. Off-season discounts for stays of 3 nights or more.
1-night bookings generally refused for Sat. Special meals for children on request.
Service/tipping: "No service charge. No additional payment expected."

HARWICH Essex   **Map 3**

The Pier at Harwich   *Tel* Harwich (0255) 241212
The Quay, Harwich CO12 3HH   *Fax* (0206) 322752
                                                          Telex 987083

Long famed for its two restaurants, one – downstairs – cheap and cheerful, the other – upstairs – much smarter, this wing of Gerald Milsom's empire (see also under Dedham) now has six "delightful" bedrooms, modern in style with functional bathroom. Reasonable breakfasts. "Not a place for a lie-in as the pier starts up early, but an excellent overnight stop before the ferry." 6 double rooms, all with bath and shower, with breakfast £55–£65 [1990]. Set meals from £8.50; full alc from £25. 10% service charge added to restaurant bills. New nomination. More reports please.

HASSOP Derbyshire   **Map 4**

Hassop Hall Hotel   *Tel* Great Longstone (062 987) 488
Hassop   *Fax* (062 987) 577
Nr Bakewell DE4 1NS   *Telex* 378485

Historic house north of Bakewell in large grounds with tennis, croquet, helipad. Luxurious interior with impressive public rooms and pianist in the evening. Spacious, elegant country-style bedrooms with fresh fruit, flowers, sumptuous bathrooms. Recommended for welcoming proprietor, Mr Chapman, friendly and professional staff, good food with large choice on menu; vegetarians catered for. 12 rooms, all with bath and shower. Double room £65–£95. Breakfast: continental £5.95, English £8.95. Set dinner £20.95 (£23.50 on Sat) [1990]. Was in earlier editions. Warmly renominated. More reports please.

HASTINGLEIGH Kent   **Map 3**

The Woodmans Arms Auberge   *Tel* Elmsted (023 375) 250
Hassell Street, Hastingleigh
Nr Ashford TN25 5JE

🏵 *César award in 1988: Away-from-it-all delight in the doll's house class*

An inn since the 17th century, the *Woodmans Arms* stands on a small lane leading to nowhere except the Downs, guaranteeing total peace and seclusion. Without the owner's directions it can be difficult to find. It is very small and not at all hotel-like, with only three double rooms. It is attractively furnished, with every detail carefully thought out: "Fresh flowers, mineral water, selection of magazines and books, bathroom with every accessory you could possibly require and lots of hot water, and all extremely clean." The garden room has its own private garden with deck chairs. The *Auberge* has no staff, only the owners Gerald Campion and his wife Susan, and is the kind of place where you are likely to end up on first-name terms with the proprietors. The restaurant can seat no more than ten and "it is of a size that means conversation tends to flow freely among the tables". Dinner, at 7.30, is "outstanding" – "*nouvelle cuisine*-style yet enough for the hearty appetite; excellent fresh ingredients"; "home-cooking at its best; very good breakfast, you can have what you like". The Campions won a César in 1988, and "deserve another, and a kiss on both cheeks; they are warm and charming hosts". "Despite the small size of the hotel, we did not feel we were expected to make conversation with the other guests; but we did because our host's outgoing and amusing personality made it very enjoyable to do so!" "Yes, Gerald Campion is an actor, but he knows his exit lines as well as his entrances." This is a no-smoking establishment; children and dogs are not accommodated. Though the rooms are of a good size, some ceilings are low – tall guests will need to mind their head, and they might find the mirrors a bit low-hung. One cautionary note: "Difficult at a certain age to comply with the request not to use the loo between 11 pm and 7 am but we tried." There is no shortage of showplaces in the neighbourhood: Leeds Castle, Chilham Castle, Dover Castle – and Canterbury is only ten miles away. It is convenient for the Channel ports. (*Caroline Streeter, Mrs M Roberts, Hugo and Veronica Way, Heather Sharland, Rex and Pat Couch, PB Whitehouse, and many others*)

Open All year except 18–24 April, 1 Sept–1 Oct. Restaurant usually closed to non-residents.
Rooms 3 double – all with bath (2 also have shower), telephone, intercom, TV. 1 has private outside entrance and small garden.
Facilities Lounge, dining room. Large grassed garden and paddock. Near sea at Sandgate and Hythe.
Location Off A28 Canterbury road. Hotel will send directions.
Restrictions Not suitable for &. No smoking. No children under 16. No dogs.
Credit cards None accepted.
Terms B&B: single occupancy £60, double £70; dinner, B&B: single £75, double £100. Set dinner £15 (residents), £25 (non-residents). 1-night bookings often refused for Sat.
Service/tipping: "We do not expect tips."

HATCH BEAUCHAMP Somerset   **Map 1**

Farthings Country House Hotel   *Tel* Hatch Beauchamp
Hatch Beauchamp TA3 6SG   (0823) 480664

"I don't often feel sorry to leave a hotel bedroom; here I did. Sandalwood (my room) was delightful; plenty of space to do my exercises, and all the extras I needed but not a lot of unnecessary flummery. Lovely view of the garden. All the staff were most pleasant. I got what I ordered for breakfast – a rare event. When they realised I was a vegetarian a special dinner was cooked for me." (*Mrs EH Prodgers*) George and Claire Cooper's "gem" of a small Georgian house in a secluded garden is in a quiet Somerset village not far from Taunton, and well placed for exploring Somerset, Devon and Dorset. Public rooms are comfortable and welcoming, with plenty of magazines. The bedrooms, all different, all named after trees, are mostly large, light and spacious; one has a spiral staircase leading to a private bathroom. Thoughtful extras include a newspaper brought to the bedroom, milk in a thermos for morning tea and a tin with biscuits. There is an imaginative four-course "English/French" dinner menu with plenty of choice; whenever possible fresh local produce is used. A new cook, Karen Miles, recently arrived and we'd be glad to hear comments on the food.

Open All year except Christmas and part of Jan.
Rooms 5 double, 1 single – all with bath, shower, telephone, radio, TV, tea-making facilities.
Facilities Lounge, lounge bar, 2 dining rooms. 3-acre grounds.
Location In village 6 m SE of Taunton; 4 m from M5, junction 25.
Restrictions Not suitable for &. Dogs by arrangement, not in public rooms.
Credit cards Access, Visa.
Terms B&B: single £65–£90, double £90–£110. Set dinner £22. Special breaks. Reduced rates and special meals for children.
Service/tipping: "No service charge. Gratuities are neither anticipated nor necessary."

HAWES North Yorkshire   Map 4

Brandymires Guest House   **BUDGET**   *Tel* Wensleydale (0969) 667482
Muker Road DL8 3PR

A small, stone, no-smoking guest house just outside the market town, with good views, open fire in lounge and clean, comfortable bedrooms, 2 with 4-poster. Recommended for courteous and helpful proprietors, Gail Ainley and Ann Macdonald, generous breakfasts (at 8.30), good no-choice 4-course dinners (at 7 pm) – "home-style dinner party cooking" – and excellent value for money. Open Apr–Oct. 4 double rooms, all with H&C, sharing 1 bathroom and 1 shower room. B&B £15; dinner, B&B £25. New nomination. More reports please.

Simonstone Hall   *Tel* Wensleydale (0969) 667255
Hawes DL8 3LY

Former home of Earls of Wharncliffe, now a comfortable family-run country house hotel with lovely views of upper Wensleydale. 1½ miles north of Hawes. Panelled drawing rooms with antiques. Sophisticated and imaginative cooking. Local produce (including Wensleydale cheese) served in portrait-hung dining room. 3½-acre grounds. Dogs welcomed. 10 spacious bedrooms, all with bath and shower. Dinner, B&B double £107.25–£117. Recent nomination. More reports please.

Our italicised entries indicate hotels which are worth considering, but which, for various reasons – inadequate information, lack of feedback, ambivalent reports – do not at the moment warrant a full entry. We should particularly welcome comments on these hotels.

HAWKRIDGE Somerset   **Map 1**

Tarr Steps Hotel   *Tel* Winsford (064 385) 293
Hawkridge, Dulverton TA22 9PY

This former Georgian rectory on Exmoor, 12 miles from the coast, is now
a sporting hotel *par excellence*. It is 800 feet above sea level, in eight-acre
grounds with lovely views down the river valley; the famous Tarr Steps
bridge – made from unhewn stone, probably in the Bronze Age – over the
river Barle is 200 yards away. The hotel offers guests three miles of
salmon and trout fly-fishing, stabling for their own horses, rough and
formal shooting, and hunting. Indoors the hotel is "very fishing-y",
relaxed and comfortable, and the guest is made welcome by the affable
proprietor, Desmond Keane, as if to a private house. There is no
television, either in public rooms or bedrooms, no tea- or coffee-making
facilities and only one telephone for guests. In the past some readers have
criticised the cooking, but a new cook arrived at the beginning of the 1989
season, and the food (traditional English, with some choice of each
course) "is very good, well presented but unpretentious, entirely
appropriate to the nature of this delightful country house hotel, and good
value for money. Mr Keane also has some very good wines." (*JL Cubbage*)
The Keanes have recently refurbished many public rooms and bedrooms,
without altering the traditional atmosphere of the hotel, and have worked
very hard in the gardens which have in the past been described as
"slightly wild".

Open Mid-Mar–after Christmas.
Rooms 11 double, 3 single – 11 with bath (1 also has shower). 3 in cottage
annexe. 1 on ground floor with access for &.
Facilities Lounge, bar, dining room. 8-acre grounds with garden; rough and clay-
pigeon shooting, fishing, fox and stag hunting; stables and kennels for guests'
horses and dogs. River bathing 100 yds.
Location Take Hawkridge road from Dulverton. From Hawkridge follow signs to
Tarr Steps and hotel.
Restriction No dogs in public rooms.
Credit cards Access, Visa.
Terms B&B £31. Set Sun lunch £13.50; dinner £17. Bar lunches available.
Midweek breaks. 1-night bookings refused bank holidays and Christmas. Reduced
rates and special meals for children.
*Service/tipping: "No service charge. Anything left goes direct to staff and is shared
equally."*

HAWKSHEAD Cumbria   **Map 4**

Field Head House   *Tel* Hawkshead (096 66) 240
Outgate, Hawkshead LA22 0PY

Hawkshead is a pretty village with small squares linked by flagged or
cobbled alleys and many unusual buildings. *Field Head House*, a mile
away, is owned and run by a Dutch couple, Bob and Eeke van Gulik. It
stands in six acres of woodland, old orchards, rhododendrons and
azaleas, and "has the atmosphere of a good-tempered *pension*". Guests
gather in the drawing room for a drink before dinner "at 7.30 for 8" and
are introduced to each other, though if anyone objects to such contact
there is another lounge to escape to, and you eat at well-spaced separate
tables. There is no choice on the dinner menu until dessert which is

usually "a choice between something substantial for Lake District appetites whetted on the hills, such as marmalade bread pudding, and a lighter alternative". Main courses tend to be locally produced fish or meat – Eskdale trout or Cumbrian ham, for example. There continues to be debate about the portions of food: "not over-large" according to some, "nicely judged so one can manage five courses without feeling over-full" according to others. A reader on her fourth visit comments on some of last year's criticisms: "The decor is very pleasant, and entirely appropriate. There are personal touches, such as pictures and items acquired abroad, which enhance the home-like atmosphere. We feel welcomed as old friends now – yet looked after with the professional touch." "A masterpiece of personal service, cleanliness and, above all, fabulous cooking by Bob van Gulik. Our every request was attended to as if we were the only guests. Great lounges for after-dinner socialising." (*Alison Forrester and David Judson, D and D Hahn; also Jill Schneider, JM Clayton, and others*) Only niggle this year: "Food sometimes not quite hot enough." On the subject of children, Mr van Gulik writes, "Our policy has not changed: we think it unfair to set an age limit, but we are not a family hotel and we try to establish that parents are in full control. In most other West European countries parents are legally responsible for their children's actions until the age of 17 or so; here many judges seem to consider the actions of small children to be acts of God. A consequence of this difference is that parents in Holland, Germany and France tend to take out Third Party Liability insurance for their offspring (and pets)."

Open All year except week before Christmas and last 2 weeks Jan. Lunch by special arrangement only. Restaurant closed Tue (bookings elsewhere made for residents or cold snack provided).
Rooms 7 double – all with bath and/or shower, radio, TV, tea-making facilities.
Facilities 2 lounges (one with dispense bar), dining room. 6-acre grounds with gardens, croquet. Fishing, water sports, walking, golf nearby.
Location From Ambleside take B5286 towards Hawkshead. ½ m past *Outgate Inn* take right turn signposted *Field Head*. From Hawkshead take B5286 towards Ambleside. *Field Head* signposted 1 m N of Hawkshead.
Restrictions Not suitable for &. Smoking in smoking lounge only.
Credit cards None accepted.
Terms B&B £29–£44; dinner, B&B £47.50–£62.50. Set dinner £18.50. £5 surcharge on 1-night stays. 5% discount for regulars. Christmas and New Year breaks. 1-night bookings sometimes refused. Children sharing parents' room £15; special meals (but not outside dinnertime; simple snack can be served in bedroom).
Service/tipping: "Tips are not solicited, but if given are shared by all staff."

Highfield House Hotel BUDGET *Tel* Hawkshead (096 66) 344
Hawkshead Hill
Hawkshead LA22 0PN

Pauline and Jim Bennett's traditional Lakeland stone building, a century old, is just outside Hawkshead on the road to Coniston. It stands on high ground in large gardens with fine trees and shrub; from the public rooms there are lovely views of the valley and peaks. "A splendid spot, properly equipped with daffodils, bluebells, wooden coat-hangers, good linen, inexpensive wine and plenty of good food. There's a warm welcome and a genuinely friendly atmosphere. It seems to have everything one could wish for – at a sensible price." "The Bennetts are excellent hosts; they hit the right balance by being very accommodating and welcoming, but also professional. The rooms are comfortable, warm and well appointed. The food is great! There are two or three choices on the menu for each course; helpings are generous and attractively presented and you are always offered the opportunity of trying a second dessert." There is always a vegetarian dish on the menu. Mrs Bennett tells us: "We have always accepted children of all ages and provide cots, baby seats and high teas, also the use of washing machine and drying facilities." (*David Gadsby, LL Husband, and others*)

Open All year except Christmas and New Year.
Rooms 11 rooms – 8 with bath and/or shower, all with radio, TV, tea-making facilities; baby-listening on request.
Facilities Lounge, dining room; laundry facilities, drying room. 2½-acre garden. Fishing nearby.
Location ¾ m from Hawkshead on road to Coniston and Tarn Hows.
Restrictions Not suitable for &. No smoking in dining room. No dogs in public rooms.
Credit cards None accepted.
Terms [Until March 1991] B&B £18–£24. Set dinner £10.50. Snack and packed lunches available. Reduced rates for children sharing parents' room; special meals by arrangement. Off-season breaks.
Service/tipping: "Service included. Any tips offered are shared among all staff."

Rough Close Country **BUDGET** *Tel* Hawkshead (096 66) 370
House Hotel
Hawkshead LA22 0QF

A small and simple but welcoming hotel is nominated this year, adding to the surprising number of Guide entries for Hawkshead: "*Rough Close*, in beautifully kept gardens, is one mile south of Hawkshead and has lovely views across Esthwaite. It is quiet and peaceful, clean and comfortable. The owners, Mr and Mrs Gibson, are always helpful and charming, and the atmosphere warm and friendly. There is a lounge with TV and a fire in cold weather, a small bar, and only six double rooms (one of which is rather small for two people). The food is very good. Breakfasts [8.45 to 9.15], are of the filling English kind. Dinners (four courses and coffee with no choice except dessert), served punctually at 7, are cooked by the Gibsons; they are extremely good – home-made soups, roast meats, fresh vegetables. Helpings are plentiful; there is nothing elaborate and no ambitious attempts which don't come off. Mr Gibson serves and is the wine waiter." (*Elizabeth Sandham*)

Open Mar–early Nov.
Rooms 6 double – 3 with bath and/or shower, all with tea-making facilities.
Facilities Lounge with TV, bar, dining room. 1-acre grounds. Boating, fishing nearby.
Location 1 m S of Hawkshead on Newby Bridge road.
Restrictions Not suitable for &. No smoking in dining room and bedrooms. No children under 5. No dogs.
Credit cards Access, Visa.
Terms B&B £17–£19; dinner, B&B £26.50–£28.50. Reduced rates for long stays.
Service/tipping: "No service charge. We have a strong aversion to tipping. Clearly proprietors should not be tipped, nor, we believe, should staff who are properly paid for the job they do."

Hotels are dropped if we lack positive feedback. If you can endorse an entry, we urge you to do so.

Walker Ground Manor   *Tel* Hawkshead (096 66) 219
Hawkshead LA22 0PD

"We are not a proper guest house," writes Wendy Chandler. "We practice a much more informal and personal hospitality. The British Travel Authority call this type of accommodation a 'host family'. Our guests are visitors in a much loved private house. They should not expect the amenities of the small hotel or the bottles-on-the-table guest house." "Fantastic welcome, excellent company and superb home-cooking. We were free to use the garden and conservatory. All in all still highly recommended," says the original nominator, on a return visit. Dennis and Wendy Chandler's 16th-century Lakeland house, with original panelling and priest hole, "mostly inexpensive antiques", pictures, ornaments, fine china and crystal stands in large and peaceful grounds with lawns and waterfalls. There are only three guest bedrooms; two have four-poster beds, two have private bathrooms, and there are two other bathrooms in the house. No TV to disturb the peace. Guests dine with the hosts by a log fire in the dining room or in the conservatory by candle-light. Food is "traditional, good and wholesome". The manor is strictly non-smoking; there are cats, but they are not permitted beyond a certain area if guests do not like them. (*Imogen Mottram*) The Chandler's son, Peter, has now joined them, and other members of the family help out from time to time. More reports please.

Open Probably all year.
Rooms 3 double – 1 with bath and shower, 1 with shower, all with tea-making facilities.
Facilities Drawing room, study, dining room, conservatory. 18-acre grounds with 2-acre garden, pasture and woodland. Coniston Water 3 m, Windermere 4 m; river fishing nearby.
Location From B5286 at Hawkshead after about 1 min turn right at garage; through Barnfield estate; sharp right. Do not bear left. House on footpath a few yards ahead.
Restrictions Not suitable for &. No smoking. Teenage children only. No dogs.
Credit cards None accepted.
Terms B&B £20–£35. Set dinner £12. Traditional Christmas and New Year house parties (more expensive).
Service/tipping: "This doesn't apply. We are happy to share our home and entertain our guests. We have no staff."

HAYTOR South Devon   **Map 1**

The Bel Alp House   *Tel* Haytor (036 46) 217
Haytor, Nr Bovey Tracey   *changing end 1990 to* (0364) 661217
TQ13 9XX   *Fax* (036 46) 292
                                       changing end 1990 to (0364) 661292

An Edwardian house, once the home of tobacco millionaire Dame Violet Wills; peacefully set in large grounds on edge of Dartmoor, with lovely views. Carefully restored by "hospitable" owners, Roger and Sarah Curnock. Recommended for personal attention, cleanliness and excellent food; 5-course set dinner (alternatives available) served in no-smoking dining room. Closed Dec, Jan, 1 week July. Traditionally furnished public rooms with bay windows; 9 spacious, light and comfortable bedrooms, all with bath and/or shower. B&B £51–£75. Set dinner £20–£33. Recent nomination. More reports please.

HEDDON'S MOUTH Devon   Map 1

Heddon's Gate Hotel   *Tel* Parracombe (059 83) 313
Heddon's Mouth
Parracombe, Barnstaple EX31 4PZ

💠 *César award in 1990: For sturdy independence in doing their own thing with verve*

A turn-of-the-century Swiss/Victorian lodge with various extensions and steeply terraced gardens, looking over a lovely valley, with views over miles of moorland and wooded hills. The large grounds are surrounded by National Trust and Exmoor National Park land, and several private paths thread through the gardens – one directly on the South West Peninsular coastal path. The hotel has been owned by Robert and Anne De Ville for the past 23 years, and is one to which many guests return frequently. Conflicting opinions have been voiced in the past about the decor, which last year one reader described as "witty and sophisticated, inspired by the *Lucia* stories by EF Benson". "Charming" and "pleasant" are this year's epithets. No one has ever disputed the generosity of the hospitality, the value for money, and the quality of Anne De Ville's dinners, generous in portion, served in the "large, relaxing dining room, with good-sized tables". "Every night we admired her inventive genius and attention to detail and presentation." "The rooms are all individually styled, and those we have seen are delightful. During dinner the beds are turned down and the room tidied; during breakfast the beds are made. The bar and lounges are agreeably furnished, and it is lovely to sit on the terrace overlooking the valley garden, where all you hear is birds and occasional sheep." "Service by a young and well-trained staff was excellent; quiet, courteous and deft. Breakfast very good indeed, with home-made bread, and two eggs always on offer." "The weekly rate was astonishing value." (*JP Berryman, MR Farley, Moira Jarrett, and many others*) The full help-yourself afternoon tea is included in the rates, and the De Villes charge the standard call-box rate for telephone calls made from the bedrooms.

Open Easter–4 Nov, then weekends up to Christmas.
Rooms 4 suites, 9 double, 1 single – all with bath and/or shower, telephone, radio, TV, tea-making facilities. 3 terraced-cottage suites with wheelchair access 70 yds from main building.
Facilities Sitting room, library, bar, card room, dining room. 20-acre grounds with terraced gardens. Access to sea ($\frac{3}{4}$ m) and river ($\frac{1}{4}$ m) by footpaths. Riding, pony trekking, fishing nearby.
Location 6 m W of Lynton; from A39 3 m W of Lynton take Martinhoe–Woody Bay road; turn left towards Hunter's Inn; hotel sign is at next crossroads.
Restrictions No children under 10. Dogs by arrangement, not in dining room.
Credit cards None accepted.
Terms Dinner, B&B £37.70–£55. Set dinner (at 8 pm) £17.50. Reductions for stays of 3 or more days; weekly rates. Christmas and New Year packages. 1-night bookings sometimes refused. 50% reduction for children sharing parents' room.
Service/tipping: "We never make any service charge and staff do not solicit tips; any given are collected, taxed and shared out among staff on basis of hours worked."

> If you have difficulty in finding hotels because our location details are inadequate, please help us to improve directions next year.

HENLEY-IN-ARDEN Warwickshire   Map 2

Ashleigh House   *Tel* Henley-in-Arden (054 62)
Whitley Hill   2315
Henley-in-Arden B95 5DL   *changing in 1990 to* (0564) 792315

A moderately priced B&B in an Edwardian house in quiet, open country,
with one and a half acres of grounds and views over the Warwickshire
countryside towards the Cotswolds. The spacious bedrooms are furnished
almost entirely with Victorian and Edwardian antiques, "ranging from the
exquisite to the kitsch". Many readers find it a welcome alternative to
staying in Stratford-on-Avon, only 15 minutes away by car. "Warm,
welcoming, spotlessly clean; thoughtfully arranged fresh garden flowers
abounding. The breakfast could not be faulted." "Proprietors, Francisco
Garcia and Colin Eades, are wonderful hosts, and very helpful." Light
snacks can be provided, and there are many good restaurants close by.
(*Rosemary Reeves, Susan Gray; also Peter and Sue Godber*)

Open All year.
Rooms 10 double – all with bath and/or shower, telephone, TV, radio and tea-
making facilities. 4 in coach-house annexe.
Facilities Sitting room with TV, reading area, dining room. 1½-acre garden.
Location On B4095 Warwick Road, 1 m from A34 traffic lights in Henley.
Restrictions Not suitable for severely &. No smoking in dining room. Babies not
encouraged. Dogs by arrangement only, not in public rooms.
Credit cards Access, Visa.
Terms B&B: single occupancy £35–£45, double £45–£55. 1-night bookings
sometimes refused. Reduced rates for children sharing parents' room. (No
restaurant; snacks available.)
Service/tipping: "Our staff appreciate tips but they are not expected."

HETHERSETT Norfolk   Map 3

Park Farm Hotel   *Tel* Norwich (0603) 810264
** and Restaurant**   *Fax* (0603) 812104
Hethersett NR9 3DL

*A quite sophisticated family-run and family-welcoming hotel up a tree-lined
drive in landscaped gardens, in agreeable countryside 5 miles south-west of
Norwich. Most bedrooms in garden buildings or purpose-built blocks, some with
4-poster and jacuzzi, some non-smoking. Indoor swimming pool, tennis, putting.
Functions facilities, helipad. Recommended for easy-going atmosphere –
"comfortable but not sloppy", friendly and helpful staff, and excellent dinners:
choice of reasonably priced table d'hôte, changing daily, "menu of the month" in
fractured French with subtitles, changing monthly, and à la carte; but dining
room "slightly cramped". Good breakfast includes fresh fish. Closed 1 week at
Christmas. 35 rooms, all with bath and/or shower, TV etc. B&B double
£62–£105. Set dinner £11; full alc £20–£25. New nomination. More reports
please.*

We asked hotels to estimate their 1991 tariffs some time before
publication so the rates given are often guesswork. Please always
check terms with hotels when making bookings.

HOCKLEY HEATH West Midlands   Map 2

Nuthurst Grange   *Tel* Lapworth (056 43) 3972
Nuthurst Grange Lane   *Fax* (056 43) 3919
Hockley Heath B94 5NL   *Telex* 333485

David and Daryll Randolph's Edwardian house is approached by an
immaculate drive through attractive English parkland. From outside its
architectural merits are undistinguished but it commands superb views
and, though only five miles from Birmingham airport, it is in a quiet
setting. Inside it is elegantly furnished in modern but traditional style,
with plenty of comfortable sofas and stylish flower arrangements in
public rooms. Bedrooms are "delightful", different in colour schemes,
light and spacious, with flowered fabrics, and full of extras. There are two
fairly expensive fixed-price dinner menus; cooking is a blend of classical
and modern; and though in general warmly approved, the feeling is that
it can go over the top at times. More reports please.

Open All year except 1 week over Christmas and New Year.
Rooms 8 double – all with air-spa bath (4 also have shower), telephone, radio,
TV, safe, baby-listening.
Facilities Reception lounge, lounge, restaurant; private dining room. 7½-acre
grounds with croquet, helipad. Riding, hunting, tennis, clay-pigeon shooting, golf,
canal boating nearby.
Location Off A34 between Stratford and Birmingham. Go S through Hockley
Heath, ignore right turn to Redditch. Take next right turn (Nuthurst Grange
Lane).
Restrictions Not suitable for &. Smoking in dining room discouraged. "Children
must be well behaved." No dogs.
Credit cards All major cards accepted.
Terms B&B (continental): single occupancy £85, double £99–£109. Set lunch
£17.50, dinner £27.50 and £32.50. Weekend breaks. Reduced rates and special
meals for children.
*Service/tipping: "We do not encourage tipping. Our employees' wages and pride in their
work are payment in full."*

HOLDENBY Northamptonshire   Map 2

Lynton House   *Tel* Holdenby (0604) 770777
Holdenby NN6 8DJ

A restaurant-with-rooms, new to the Guide this year, in a Victorian
former rectory in open country north of Northampton. The owner, Carlo
Bertozzi, is Italian; his wife Carol does the cooking. Its exterior is red
brick, and there's plenty of red and pink inside. "Tastefully done," writes
our inspector. "The colour scheme works extremely well; there are lots of
pictures and fresh flowers in the entrance hall. We had the best bedroom,
prettily decorated and adequately lit, with a splendid view over a
patchwork of arable fields. Only a shower, as Mr Bertozzi finds his guests,
many of them businessfolk, prefer this, but it worked efficiently. Dinner,
in the attractive dining room with bay window and conservatory
extension, was a delight; there's plenty of choice, and it is not at all run-
of-the mill Italian cooking. Service was excellent throughout. We also
enjoyed the breakfast with perfectly cooked eggs and bacon. We did not
meet Mrs Bertozzi who was in the kitchen; her husband is a charming and
amusing host. Not a place for a holiday, but it has much to recommend it

if you are passing through the area; not really for children though." More reports please.

Open All year except Christmas, 1 week in spring, 2 weeks Aug.
Rooms 3 double, 2 single – all with shower, telephone, radio, TV, tea-making facilities.
Facilities Lounge, cocktail bar, dining room, conservatory; conference/functions facilities. 2½-acre grounds.
Location 6 m NW of Northampton. Leave M1 at exit 18 or 16.
Restrictions Not suitable for ⅙. No children under 6.
Credit cards Access, Visa.
Terms B&B (English): single £60, double £70; dinner, B&B: single £80, double £110. Set lunch £13.75, dinner £20. Weekend rates.
Service/tipping: "No service charge; we discourage tipping."

HOLFORD Somerset   Map 1

Combe House Hotel   *Tel* Holford (027 874) 382
Holford
Nr Bridgwater TA5 1RZ

Richard Bjergfelt's hotel has had something of an in-and-out relationship with the Guide, but enthusiastic regulars ("We keep trying other hotels but return here time after time") have persuaded us to give it another go. It's a 17th-century former tannery, still with a water-wheel, set in a "wonderful, peaceful location" in a wooded combe at the heart of the Quantocks. It has large, well-tended grounds with an indoor swimming pool and sauna, a tennis court, and croquet. Public rooms, with beams and open fires, are not particularly large, and can be crowded in the evening; upstairs is "rather a rabbit warren of passages and corners" and bedrooms are small, but well-appointed and comfortable. Some of the baths are small but there's plenty of hot water. The owner is very much in evidence, the staff friendly and professional; the table d'hôte menu of straightforward dishes, with three or four choices for each course, changes daily. Cooking is "good, if not noteworthy". The tariff is reasonable. There is excellent walking from the front door, and the sea is not far. (*G Latham, and others*) More reports please.

Open Mar–Nov.
Rooms 16 double, 6 single – 16 with bath and/or shower, all with telephone, TV, tea-making facilities; baby-listening on request. 3 in annexe across drive.
Facilities Lounge, smoking room, bar, restaurant. Indoor heated swimming pool, sauna. 3-acre grounds with tennis and croquet. Golf, riding nearby.
Location From A39 turn up lane between garage and *Plough Inn*. Follow signs through village.
Restrictions Not suitable for ⅙. No smoking in main lounge and restaurant. Dogs in some bedrooms only; not in public rooms except bar.
Credit cards Access, Visa.
Terms B&B £26–£37; dinner, B&B £31–£50. Set dinner £12.50. Low season rates. Reduced rates for children sharing parents' room; high tea on request.
Service/tipping: "Service included. If asked, we say there's no need to tip. If a guest insists, then the money is distributed to all staff."

If you have had recent experience of a good hotel that ought to be in the Guide, please write to us at once. Report forms are to be found at the back of the book. Procrastination is the thief of the next edition.

HORTON Dorset   Map 2

Northill House   **BUDGET**   *Tel* Witchampton (0258) 840407
Horton, Wimborne BH21 7HL

Courtney and Joy Garnsworthy's 19th-century former farmhouse stands
in two-acre grounds adjoining a farm in an isolated situation. It continues
to be endorsed by readers: "We were warmly welcomed and quickly
provided with tea and home-made shortbread. Our room was large,
bright, airy and warm, with views of the grounds, including pheasant and
partridge, and fields beyond. The enormous bed was firm and comfortable, with good bedside lights, two hot-water bottles, and fresh milk for
tea- and coffee-making. The *en suite* bathroom was very warm with a
daily change of towels which were quite large enough for us, but perhaps
not for fat folk. Lovely dinners, at 7.30 – simple English cooking with
good vegetables, no choice until the pudding stage but nothing one could
take exception to, and an excellent choice thereafter, the cheeseboard
being exceptional. Breakfasts included freshly squeezed orange juice and
were substantial, especially if one could manage the 'full English'. The log
fires in both bar and lounge were cosy to sit by. Everything was spotless,
with fresh flowers in all rooms. We believe this simple type of country
house hotel is just what ordinary people would love to find in many
locations." "Service charming and helpful in every way." (*Mollie
Farquhar, Mrs J Glover, also RC Brown*) Minor niggles: "No shelf to put the
soap while showering or bathing; and I burned my bottom on the towel
rail, despite the warning notice!" "Garden needs a lot of work."

Open Mid-Feb–20 Dec.
Rooms 9 double – all with bath and/or shower, telephone, radio, TV, tea-making
facilities. 4 in annexe. 1 suitable for &.
Facilities Lounge, bar, dining room, conservatory. 2-acre grounds.
Location 7 m N of Wimborne, ½ m from B3078.
Restrictions No smoking in dining room. No children under 8. No pets.
Credit cards Access, Visa.
Terms B&B (English) £26–£28. Snack lunches. Set dinner £11. 3- and 7-night
breaks.
Service/tipping: "Tips not expected or solicited; but shared among staff if given."

HUNTSHAM Devon   Map 1

Huntsham Court   *Tel* Clayhanger (039 86) 210
Huntsham Valley   *Fax* (039 86) 456
Nr Tiverton EX16 7NA

❀ *César award in 1988: Utterly acceptable mild eccentricity*

This choice example of high Victorian architecture, with huge rooms,
massive fireplaces, impressive panelling and marble pillars, in a secluded
setting in rural Devon roughly halfway between Taunton and Exeter, is
run by Mogens and Andrea Bolwig with the aim of making guests forget
that they are in a hotel at all. There are no locks on bedroom doors, no TV
or telephone. The furniture is eclectic, with Victorian sideboards and
outsize armchairs of the twenties and thirties. The whole place is
dedicated to music: there is a baby grand piano in the hall, uprights in the
drawing room and bar, a pianola in the dining room, and a collection of

over 6,000 records and cassettes, mostly classical with a leaning towards the operatic, which guests are free to play on a hi-fi. The bedrooms are named after composers. Most have a huge bathroom *en suite*. Beethoven has two free-standing old bathtubs with silver claws side by side in the middle of the bathroom, a log fire, a seven-foot-wide bed and a piano. All the bedrooms have a pre-war radio set; two now have an organ. The five-course dinner is eaten communally at a single large table, and there is no menu. Guests help themselves night and day to free tea and coffee in the butler's pantry. The bar can be help-yourself, too, on the honour principle. Breakfast goes on most of the morning. There are a sauna, a mini-gym, tennis, croquet and lots of bicycles ("but they don't have good brakes"). *Huntsham* is often taken over by professional groups during the week, and private parties at weekends. Some visitors this year have considered the "eccentricity" far from mild, the standards of decor, upkeep and cleanliness unacceptable, and the atmosphere altogether too laid-back. Others have found *Huntsham* much to their taste: "Staff couldn't have been more attentive or pleasant; high quality and well-balanced home-cooking." "Good beds, hot water, excellent music." "A truly unique experience; I still smile when I remember it." (*Peter Carson, Richard Townend, Judith Malinowski*)

Open All year. Lunch by arrangement only.
Rooms 5 suites, 11 double – all with bath and pre-war wireless; baby-listening possible.
Facilities Hall, drawing room, library with snooker table, music room, bar, dining room; sauna, mini-gym, table-tennis room. 8-acre garden with croquet, bicycles, tennis courts, barbecue. Trout-fishing in private lake, riding, golf, shooting nearby.
Location M5 to Taunton, then A361 towards Bampton; turn left to Huntsham when signposted. Or take exit 27 off M5, turn sharp right on bridge in Sampford Peverell and continue for 4 m.
Restrictions Not suitable for &. No dogs (kennels 2 m away).
Credit cards All major cards accepted.
Terms [1990 rates] B&B: single occupancy £60 and £75, double £79–£89, suite £99. Set dinner £22.50. House parties; midweek and weekend breaks; occasional jazz, opera and special weekends; Christmas and New Year programmes. 1-night bookings sometimes refused for weekend. Reduced rates for children sharing parents' room.
Service/tipping: "Although we do not expect tips, when a guest is happy with service and staff we accept a tip in the spirit in which it has been given. Not to do so would offend."

HURSTBOURNE TARRANT Hampshire   Map 2

Esseborne Manor   *Tel* Hurstbourne Tarrant
Hurstbourne Tarrant   (0264) 76444
Nr Andover SP11 0ER   Fax (0264) 76473

Small late Victorian manor with new extension in "reasonably pretty" countryside between Newbury and Andover, well set back from A343. 2-acre garden with tennis. Owned since 1988 by Michael and Frieda Yeo, formerly of the much larger and grander Ardanaiseig, Kilchrenan, Scotland (q.v.), and managed by their son Simon. Recommended for pleasant welcome, good food, simply and carefully cooked but vegetables a bit crisp for some, friendly dining room service. 12 comfortable, well-equipped bedrooms, some with quite modern decor. Dinner, B&B double £141–£168. Was in Guide under previous owners. More reports please.

JERVAULX North Yorkshire   **Map 4**

Jervaulx Hall   *Tel* Bedale (0677) 60235
Jervaulx, Masham   *Fax* (0969) 23206
Ripon HG4 4PH

Useful base for touring or walking holiday in Yorkshire Dales, an early Victorian mansion in 8-acre grounds on edge of ruins of Jervaulx Abbey. Has been in Guide for many years, appreciated for its dependable comforts of furnishings and fittings. But hotel seems to have hit a bad patch recently. Much criticism of room maintenance, service, cooking. Not all reports adverse; we hope for better news next year. Open Mid-Mar–mid-Nov. 10 double rooms, all with bath. Dinner, B&B: single £75, double £85–£110.

The Old Hall   *Tel* Bedale (0677) 60313
Jervaulx Abbey
Jervaulx, Masham
Ripon HG4 4PH

Last year's italicised entry for Ian and Angela Close's home, formerly the servant's quarters of Jervaulx Hall, has had a warm endorsement and promotion to a full entry. "We've been here several times; it has a private party atmosphere – sherry in the lounge before dinner so that guests can be introduced, dinner with the hosts at a single large oak table, and conversation continuing over coffee in the lounge. Ian Close really knows the area and makes tourism much more than just a quick look round. His wife, Angela, is an excellent cook; food is mainly good roasts with all the trimmings, very well done and beautifully presented in a room full of antiques. Water comes from a private spring and tastes delicious. Bedrooms are particularly attractive – we have stayed in most of them; they all have good firm beds, well-equipped bathrooms, and some fine pieces of antique furniture. It is not a place for people who want a private weekend, but an excellent country house where conversation, good food and drink and lovely surroundings create a special atmosphere." (*Robert Swift*)

Open All year.
Rooms 3 double – all with bath, shower, tea-making facilities. 2 self-catering cottages
Facilities Drawing room, dining room. 4-acre grounds with access to Abbey grounds.
Location On A6108, 12 m N of Ripon, next to Jervaulx Abbey.
Restrictions Not suitable for &. No dogs in public rooms.
Credit cards None accepted.
Terms B&B £28; set dinner £16.
Service/tipping: "Service included. Tipping shouldn't be necessary. We pay staff properly."

This year we have introduced "Budget" labels indicating hotels offering accommodation at around £40 (or its foreign currency equivalent) for dinner, bed and breakfast or £25 for B&B and £15 for an evening meal. But we would emphasise that this is a rough guide only, and does not always apply to single rooms.

KESWICK Cumbria   Map 4

Lodore Swiss Hotel   *Tel* Borrowdale (059 684) 285
Keswick CA12 5UX   *Fax* (059 684) 343
                                                      Telex 64305

This large (for the Guide) hotel just south of Keswick enjoys a splendid
position in 40-acre grounds, which include the Lodore Falls, on Derwent
Water, which many rooms overlook. Outwardly it is a stern Victorian
Cumbrian pile, inside are large and comfortable public rooms, equally
comfortable bedrooms of varying sizes, and many facilities for indoor and
outdoor entertainment (see below). It had a Guide entry for many years
when it was owned and run by the Swiss family England. It is now
owned by one of the major hotel chains, Stakis PLC, and after a few early
hiccups re-enters, warmly recommended. "If anything, it gets better.
Most of the staff we met under the previous owners seem to be there still.
Discreet improvements have been made. The restaurant is more inventive
but its prices remain reasonable and its standards are still very high."
"First-class management, excellent food and service. The lounge and
bedrooms have been completely refurbished with delightful results. And,
unique in my experience, the bill can be read and understood immediately." (*Gareth and Rosalind Gunning, Paul Barraclough; also HM Schottlaender*)
The hotel welcomes children and has a nursery run by trained nannies
which is open from 8 am to 6 pm.

Open All year except 3 Jan–14 Feb.
Rooms 2 suites, 59 double, 9 single – 68 with bath and shower, 2 with shower, all
with telephone, radio, TV, tea-making facilities, baby-listening.
Facilities Lift, ramp. Lounge, bar, restaurant, private dining room, functions
room. Music on Sat. Indoor swimming pool, gym, squash court, games room,
saunas, beauty salon, hairdresser, nursery for children under 6 (8 am–6 pm).
40-acre grounds with swimming pool, tennis, children's play area.
Location 3 m S of Keswick, on B5284 to Borrowdale.
Restrictions No smoking in restaurant. No dogs.
Credit cards All major cards accepted.
Terms (Service at guests' discretion) B&B from £55; dinner, B&B from £60. Light
lunches; set Sun lunch £12, set dinner £23; full alc £37. Christmas and New Year
packages. Reduced rates and special meals for children.

****
* **Traveller's tale** *We did not mind the kitsch – including photographs of* *
* *plastic flowers in ornate gilded frames – as much as the many layers of* *
* *filth embellishing the kitsch. The sheets had human hairs on them. The* *
* *basin, loo, TV, four-poster, nick-nacks, above all the cot, were covered in* *
* *dirt. When we politely suggested clean sheets, a bare-footed sullen girl* *
* *changed the sheets for equally dingy and repellent ones. And when we* *
* *gave them £5 and said we were sorry but the room was not quite up to* *
* *the standard we wanted, we were first given excuses (the sheet-* *
* *washing apparatus was "down") and then accused, rudely, of being* *
* *"vegetarians". I assume "vegetarians" is the landlord's euphemism* *
* *for people who want clean sheets and un-stained cots for their baby.* *
****

KILVE Somerset   **Map 1**

Meadow House   *Tel* Holford (027 874) 546
Sea Lane, Kilve TA5 1EG

*Former rectory in truly rural setting in Quantocks foothills, a short walk from
unspoilt beach. Run as small hotel by Alec and Tina Samson who write, "It is
also our home; all downstairs rooms, even the kitchen, are open to guests."
Recommended for large, comfortable bedrooms, "excellent cooking" (English
with French additions, with limited choice), "no fuss, no pretensions". 8 rooms,
4 in cottage suites, all with bath and/or shower. Half board rates only: double
room £100–£120. Was in Guide under previous owners. More reports please.*

KING'S LYNN Norfolk   **Map 3**

The Tudor Rose   `BUDGET`   *Tel* King's Lynn (0553) 762824
St Nicholas Street   *Fax* (0553) 764894
King's Lynn PE30 1LR

*In town centre, "equally successful as pub, restaurant and hotel", part-medieval
building carefully restored by Ian and Chris Carter. Recommended for
"attentive and courteous" owners, "very adequate" bedrooms, good food in bars
and restaurant; extensive vegetarian menu. Closed Christmas. 9 double, 5 single
rooms, 13 with bath and/or shower. B&B double £45. Set dinner £8.50; full alc
£20 [1990]. New nomination. More reports please.*

KINGSTON BAGPUIZE Oxfordshire   **Map 2**

Fallowfields   *Tel* Oxford (0865) 820416
Southmoor, Kingston Bagpuize   *Fax* (0865) 820629
Nr Abingdon OX13 5BH   *Telex* 83388 attn FALLOWFIELDS

Once the home of the Begum Aga Khan, now a "private house taking in
paying guests", and Guide readers appreciate the "personal and kindly
welcome" of its owner, Alison Crowther. It is full of good Victorian
pictures, decent china and glass, and books. There is an immaculate
garden with a small swimming pool and a hard tennis court. The spacious
bedrooms have good lighting, expensive chintzes, drapes and frills, deep-
pile fitted carpets, and furniture is a mixture of antique and repro.
Bathrooms are large, with instant hot water, masses of towels, and lots of
extras. Some of the paintings are by Mrs Crowther (who also illustrates
the dinner menus), others were collected by her late husband. Dinner, by
candle-light, is at 8 pm; you are asked to choose from the menu by 6.30.
The four courses are "plentiful and excellent", with lots of good
vegetables grown on the premises, and a sweet trolley laden with high-
cholesterol goodies. "The staff were exceptionally helpful without being
obtrusive." (*RD and SA Mackay*) Direct-dial telephones have now been
added in the bedrooms.

> Don't trust out-of-date editions. Many hotels are dropped and new
> ones added every year.

Open 1 Apr–30 Sep. Winter-weekend house parties for min 4 people – advance booking only. Dinner not served Wed.
Rooms 4 double – all with bath and/or shower, telephone, radio, TV, tea-making facilities.
Facilities Lounge, TV lounge, dining room. 2-acre garden, 10-acre paddock; tennis, table-tennis, croquet, heated swimming pool. Riding, golf, river and lake fishing, windsurfing and water-skiing at Stanton Harcourt Leisure Centre nearby.
Location On A420 8 m SW of Oxford, 6 m from Abingdon. Light sleepers may be disturbed by traffic on A420, in 1 north room.
Restrictions Not suitable for &. Smoking discouraged in dining room. No children under 10. Dogs at management's discretion, not in public rooms.
Credit cards Access, Visa.
Terms B&B £28–£35. Set dinner £16.50. 5% discount to regular visitors who have stayed 14 days or more.
Service/tipping: "We do not make a service charge, a fact made clear to clients. If they regard service as exceptional they may hand contributions to the proprietor for distribution to the staff."

KIRKBY FLEETHAM North Yorkshire   Map 4

Kirkby Fleetham Hall Hotel   *Tel* Northallerton (0609) 748711
Kirkby Fleetham   *Fax* (0609) 748747
Northallerton DL7 0SU

This fine house, Elizabethan in parts but substantially remodelled 200 years ago to give it its present Georgian appearance, stands in large grounds outside a secluded village, with a 12th-century Knights Templar church adjoining, but is only two miles from the A1. It had an entry in earlier editions of the Guide under the ownership of the Grants who have now moved to *The Manor*, Chadlington (q.v.). It is now owned by Roderick Richman, who is not always in residence; a new manager, Stephen Mannock, arrived in November 1989. The decor is elegant country house in style; bedrooms, named after birds, are all different, with lovely views, "spacious and very comfortable". "Utter peace and tranquillity; don't come here if you enjoy a hive of activity. Staff are cheerful, helpful and courteous, without being in any way obsequious." The English breakfast is said to be very good, and dinner, "*nouvelle* in style but not in portion, was wonderful". The wine list is "extensive with some interesting and unusual wines. The hotel is relatively expensive, but, I believe, worth it." (*Brian Wicks, also His Hon Judge Bernard Marder QC, Dick and Sue Lee, and others*) Some niggles: "At this price why not provide proper-sized bath soap?"; one room is said to suffer noise from the kitchen fans; and a visitor in 1989 bemoaned the lack of garden chairs and had an uncomfortable bed. More reports please.

Open All year.
Rooms 22 double – all with bath and/or shower, telephone, radio, TV, baby-listening.
Facilities 2 lounges, bar, restaurant. 30-acre grounds with walled garden, lake with fishing, clay-pigeon shooting.
Location 1 m N of Kirkby Fleetham; follow signs to Kirkby Hall and church.
Restrictions Not suitable for &. Dogs in ground-floor bedrooms only; not in public rooms.
Credit cards All major cards accepted.
Terms B&B (English): single occupancy £75, double £102–175. Set lunch £16, dinner £28. Reduced rates for children in family room; special meals.
Service/tipping: "No service charge. We do not encourage or expect tips."

KIRKOSWALD Cumbria   Map 4

Prospect Hill Hotel   **BUDGET**   *Tel* Lazonby (076 883) 500
Kirkoswald, by Penrith
CA10 1ER

This unsophisticated small hotel, owned by John and Isa Henderson, is a conversion of 18th-century farm buildings on a remote road in the Eden Valley, an untrippery area north of Penrith, easily reached from the M6. It has old beams and open fires, and "a mixture of good old furniture and interesting junk". Bedrooms (not all *en suite*) vary in size, several have brass beds. Inexpensive à la carte dinners are served in a fine old barn, and there's a vegetarian menu. "Very pleasant meal, obviously freshly cooked as we had a long wait!" reports one visitor; others too have enjoyed the food. Generous breakfasts feature locally baked bread, "real" honey and marmalade. "Friendly owners, clean and comfortable place." "Good value for money." (*Mrs K Kelly, Charles M Ross, Dr FM Halle*) More reports please.

Open All year except Feb and Christmas Day.
Rooms 7 double, 3 single – 5 with bath and/or shower, all with tea-making facilities.
Facilities TV lounge, reading room, bar lounge, bar, breakfast room, dining room. 1-acre grounds with croquet. Fishing nearby.
Location 1 m N of Kirkoswald on B6413. First building on left at top of hill.
Restrictions Not suitable for &. No dogs.
Credit cards All major cards accepted.
Terms [1990 rates] B&B £18–£35. Packed lunches. Full alc dinner £15.20.
Surcharge made for 1-night bookings over bank holiday weekends. Discounts for long stays and group bookings. Reduced rates for children sharing parents' room; special meals.
Service/tipping: "No service charge. No strict policy about tipping. Many guests want to thank the staff; rather silly to refuse! Staff decide how it is distributed. We prefer cash to a sum added to a credit card."

LACOCK Wiltshire   Map 2

At The Sign of the Angel   *Tel* Lacock (024 973) 230
Church Street, Lacock
Chippenham SN15 2LA

César award in 1989: Inn of the year

This 14th-century half-timbered inn at the heart of the ancient wool village of Lacock, now preserved by the National Trust, has been run by the Levis family for 37 years. It is quintessentially English with low doorways, oak panelling, polished brass and silverware, antique furniture, open fires, and comfortable sofas and easy chairs in the lounge; the atmosphere is "domestic and intimate". Food in the candle-lit dining room is "archetypal good honest English cooking"; much of the produce comes from local suppliers. The pricing of the dinner menu has been altered so that guests now pay according to whether they take one, two or

Don't keep your favourite hotel to yourself. The Guide supports: it doesn't spoil.

three courses in addition to the main one (invariably a roast, with a fish or vegetarian alternative); there are several choices of starter and dessert. Breakfasts include home-made bread and thick-cut marmalade. "There was a period when it seemed to be resting on its laurels, but the service is very amiable *and* efficient now. What is particularly pleasant – and very evident at breakfast – is the range of quality and produce they have available. Guests need not fear the 'cold' Sunday supper (residents only). There is hot soup, bubble and squeak(!), a roaring fire in winter and virtually total privacy." (*Mr and Mrs RE Osborne; also Eugene Hilman, William A Grant*) One plaint: "In midsummer to have tourists peering through the dining room is a bit off-putting."

Open All year except 22 Dec–6 Jan. Restaurant closed for Sat lunch; also Sun dinner to non-residents.
Rooms 8 double – all with bath, telephone, TV, tea-making facilities; 2 in cottage across garden. 1 ground-floor room.
Facilities Lounge, 2 dining rooms. 1-acre garden with stream.
Location 7 m S of M4 (exit 17); E of A350 between Chippenham and Melksham. Limited off-street parking.
Restrictions Not suitable for &. No children under 8. No dogs in public rooms.
Credit cards Access, Amex, Visa.
Terms (Service at guests' discretion) B&B £45–£65; dinner, B&B £65–£92. Set lunch £16–£20, dinner £20–£25; full alc £26. Winter breaks, midweek summer breaks.

LANGHO Lancashire   Map 4

Northcote Manor   *Tel* Blackburn (0254) 240555
Northcote Road, Langho   *Fax* (0254) 246568
Nr Blackburn BB6 8BE

A restaurant-with-rooms in a Victorian manor house with later additions, set in pretty countryside on the edge of the Ribble Valley, with its back to the A59, 15 minutes from the M6. It is "all olde worlde atmosphere" with beams, oak panelling, roaring fires, handsome staircase and Victorian furniture. The six bedrooms, recently refurbished, vary in size. The manor is owned by Craig Bancroft and Nigel Haworth; Nigel is also the chef. Some criticisms last year of housekeeping and breakfast, but a 1990 inspection reports: "Breakfast was more than adequate, including freshly squeezed fruit juice, and newspapers free of charge. Dinner was ambitious modern cooking, most of it successful, but with occasional coarseness or clumsiness in execution. The sitting room, unfortunately, is crowded and often smokey, and the dining room has too many tables. But service is all one could hope for – well trained, friendly and confident. *Northcote Manor* knows what it is about, delivers with style and attention and quality, and the owners and staff are exceedingly pleasant and unpretentious."
Note Although the owners in the 1990 Guide said tipping was unnecessary, service is now "at guests' discretion" – and (we are told) expected.

Open All year except Christmas and New Year.
Rooms 6 double – all with bath and/or shower, telephone, radio, TV, tea-making facilities, baby-listening.
Facilities Bar, lounge, restaurant; private dining room. 2-acre grounds.
Location From M6, junction 31, take A59 towards Whalley. Hotel is on left at sign for Old Langho.
Restrictions Not suitable for &. No dogs in public rooms.

Credit cards Access, Visa.
Terms B&B (English): single occupancy £60, double £70. Set lunch £12, full alc lunch £25, dinner £32. Weekend rates. ½-price meals for children.
Service/tipping: "Service at guests' discretion. Tips evenly distributed among all staff."

LANGLEY MARSH Somerset   Map 1

Langley House Hotel
and Restaurant
Langley Marsh
Wiveliscombe TA4 2UF

Tel Wiveliscombe (0984) 23318
Fax (0984) 23442

Peter and Anne Wilson's 16th-century house with 18th-century additions and alterations stands in three acres of landscaped gardens in a quiet rural corner of Somerset. It was omitted from last year's Guide as they had put it on the market; now they have decided to stay on and its entry returns: "Beautifully decorated and immaculately clean." "Bedrooms attractive, of medium size, with some nice touches" (though one had no dressing table). It has an "elegant, well-proportioned drawing room" with fresh flowers and an open fire, and a small, slightly crowded dining room, recently redecorated – the effect is "charming and unusual". Peter Wilson's dinners are generally praised: "Cooking is on the *nouvelle* side, though portions are more generous, but far from huge." "At last vegetables that taste of vegetables; at last a chef who doesn't overcook everything!" There are four courses on weekdays, and five at weekends, with no choice until dessert or cheese. Service "friendly, but a little uncoordinated. Breakfast very well cooked and presented. Toast particularly good." One reader felt the extras on the bill were expensive.

Open All year except Feb.
Rooms 1 family, 6 double, 1 single – all with bath and/or shower, telephone, radio, TV, baby-listening.
Facilities 2 drawing rooms, bar, restaurant. 3-acre garden with croquet.
Location ½ m N of Wiveliscombe. Turn right at town centre.
Restrictions Not suitable for &. No smoking in restaurant. Children under 7 by arrangement. No dogs in public rooms.
Credit cards Access, Amex, Visa.
Terms [1990 rates] B&B (English): single £52.50–£57.50, double £75–£93, suite £125; dinner, B&B: single £72.25–£77.25, double £114.50–£140, suite £164.50–£172. Set dinner £19.75 and £23.50. 2-day breaks all year. 1-night bookings sometimes refused at weekends and bank holidays.

LASTINGHAM North Yorkshire   Map 4

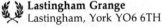 **Lastingham Grange**
Lastingham, York YO6 6TH

Tel Lastingham (075 15) 345

César award: For preserving traditional virtues of country hospitality

"Hear hear!" is the most recent – and most brief – endorsement we've received in 1989/90 of this Guide favourite. Other reports also echo last year's praise: "Hotel superbly run." "Owner and staff very helpful and friendly." Bedrooms are "comfortable and clean", breakfasts "large and delicious", dinners (four courses with a reasonable amount of choice) "always good and sometimes very good". *Lastingham Grange* is a modest country hotel, thoroughly traditional in both decor and style of cooking, which has appeared in the Guide since the first edition. It was opened as a hotel in 1946 by the father of the present proprietor, Dennis Wood, and is an old stone creeper-covered house with a courtyard and large grounds with a carefully tended garden, fine old trees and fields, in a particularly tranquil setting in the heart of the North Moors National Park. (*Dr RM Williamson; also Don and Denise Hahn, Richard H Lamb*) Newspapers, morning coffee and afternoon tea are included in the rates; shoes are cleaned if left outside the bedroom at night.

Open Mar–Dec.
Rooms 10 double, 2 single – 10 with bath (2 also have shower), all with telephone, radio, TV, tea-making facilities, baby-listening.
Facilities Hall, lounge, dining room; laundry facilities. 10-acre grounds with garden, croquet, swings, slides, adventure playground. In National Park, near moors and dales; riding, golf, swimming nearby.
Location Off A170, 5 m N of Kirkbymoorside. Turn N towards Appleton-le-Moor 2 m E of Kirkbymoorside.
Restrictions Not suitable for &. No smoking in dining room. Dogs by arrangement only, not in public rooms.
Credit cards Amex, Diners.
Terms [1990 rates] B&B (English): single £45.50, double £84.50; dinner, B&B: single £55–£59, double £102–£107. Set lunch £10.75, dinner £17.25. Light and picnic lunches available. Reduced rates for long stays and winter breaks. Children under 12 sharing parents' room free; special meals.
Service/tipping: "No service charge. Tipping is discouraged."

LAVENHAM Suffolk   Map 3

The Great House Hotel   *Tel* Lavenham (0787) 247431
and Restaurant
Market Place, Lavenham
CO10 9QZ

"A delightful find. Truly Gallic. Rooms enormous and very comfortable. A typical French restaurant-with-rooms," writes a correspondent of this rather improbably American-owned, French-run establishment in a lovely, quintessentially English old market-town. Another praises the "polite and unobtrusive concern of the staff and their ability to turn an ordinary visit into an occasion". *The Great House* is a well-preserved medieval building with a Georgian facade. The poet Stephen Spender lived here in the 1950s, and one of the suites is named for him. There are only four bedrooms, all spacious, all with a sitting room or sitting area, bathroom (quite small), gas fire, TV and antiques. They are attractively decorated, though – as you might expect in a building of this age – some windows are on the small side and some do not shut properly. Squeaking floorboards are another period feature. In the oak-beamed, candle-lit dining room with its original inglenook fireplace Régis Crépy produces "imaginative, beautifully presented" meals which he describes as "rural French and English"; the set menus are particularly good value. In summer meals can be served in the paved, flowery courtyard. We are pleased to learn that children are welcome at *The Great House*. (*Gwen and Peter Andrews; also G Sampson, and others*) A few niggles this year: "Not all the staff have adequate English." "Could do with a good spring-clean." And whereas one reader finds the breakfast "excellent" another considers it "only adequate". More reports please.

Open All year. Restaurant closed Sun night and Mon in winter.
Rooms 3 suites, 1 double – all with bath and/or shower, telephone, radio, TV, tea-making facilities, baby-listening.
Facilities Bar/lounge, restaurant; patio. ½-acre grounds with swings.
Location Behind Market Cross. From High Street take Market Lane to Guildhall. Parking.
Restrictions Not suitable for &. No dogs in public rooms.
Credit cards Access, Visa.
Terms: [1990 rates] B&B (English): single occupancy £50–£68, double £66–£78; dinner, B&B: single £61.95, double £93.90. Set lunch £8–£14, dinner £14; full alc £20–£30. Reduced rates for children sharing parents' room. 2- and 3-night breaks.
Service/tipping: "No service charge. Tips at guests' discretion, shared among staff."

LEAMINGTON SPA Warwickshire   Map 2

The Lansdowne Hotel   *Tel* Leamington Spa (0926) 450505
Clarendon Street   *Telex* 337556
Leamington Spa CV32 4PF

🏵 *César award in 1989: Best town house hotel*

David and Gillian Allen's elegant Regency town house is near the centre of this once fashionable and still delightful watering place, convenient for Warwick Castle, the National Exhibition Centre (25 minutes by car) and the National Agricultural Centre (10 minutes). Public rooms are not large, and some bedrooms are very small, but they are "carefully furnished for all one's needs, spotless, cosy and attractive, with firm beds, though storage space can be limited if you are on a protracted visit. Breakfasts are good, dinner beautifully done – home-cooking in the best sense, with vegetables varied and interestingly cooked. Wines are good value for money. The Allens try to ensure that you feel at home. They have a nice staff too; we thoroughly enjoyed our visit." (*RI Johnson, Mrs RB Richards*) Last year we recorded a reader's complaint that light meals were not available in the evening as an alternative to the four-course meal. The hotel now tells us that snacks may be ordered in the lounge – a victory for the modest consumer.

Open All year. Limited food service 24 Dec–7 Jan.
Rooms 10 double, 5 single – 5 with bath, shower, 7 with shower, all with telephone, radio, double glazing; TV, baby-listening by arrangement. 2 on ground floor.
Facilities Residents' lounge with TV, bar, restaurant. Small garden. Discounts for guests for local attractions such as Ragley Hall, Warwick Castle, Coventry Cathedral crypt.
Location Central, on A425 (rooms are double-glazed). Private carpark.
Restrictions No smoking in dining room. No children under 5. No dogs.
Credit cards Access, Visa.
Terms B&B £19.65–£38.95; dinner, B&B £33.95–£51.90. Set lunch £12.95, dinner £13.95; full alc £17.85. 2-night packages. Reduced rates for children sharing parents' room; special meals by arrangement.
Service/tipping: "We have always felt this to be an unnecessary impost. However, if guests ask to recognise a particular service we try to get the member of staff together with the guest for a few personal words."

> Please write and confirm an entry when it is deserved. If you think that a hotel is not as good as we say, write and tell us.

LEDBURY Hereford and Worcester   Map 2

Hope End Country House Hotel   *Tel* Ledbury (0531) 3613
Hope End, Ledbury HR8 1JQ

Hope End celebrated its eleventh anniversary as a hotel in 1990. It is all
that remains of Elizabeth Barrett Browning's childhood home. Once a
Moorish fantasy, most of the original was pulled down by later owners,
leaving one lone minaret and huge stable gates. It is in a beautiful hidden
valley, a place of great serenity. The hard-working owners tend a vast
walled organic vegetable and fruit garden. The unpretentious bedrooms,
mostly pine-clad, are pleasantly furnished, with woven covers on the
beds. "'Those it pleases, are mightily pleased,' says the Guide. We were
among the mightily pleased. The quality of silence here is unusual; it lies
in a hollow, surrounded by high trees. No sound of traffic of course, but
also no sound of wind. The interior is full of beautiful bare wood and
autumn colours. Furniture includes some antique pieces, but is mostly
plain and of the Scandinavian type. Fabrics are often woven wool.
Everywhere there are paintings and drawings. The entire five-course
menu changes daily; there are two choices of starter and three of dessert.
The style is Patricia Hegarty's own: modern British that has taken on
board eclectic influences. Meals are healthy, avoiding salt and cholesterol
where possible, and rely heavily on fresh produce, organically grown by
the Hegartys. The style is simple, almost purist." (*CKK, Karen Trinder, and
others*)

As we have said in the past, the Hegartys' "un-unctuous" approach is
inhibiting to some visitors; they offer none of the trappings of a luxury
hotel and only the minimum of formalities. Some visitors this year have
been put off by the emphasis on healthy eating, the very limited choice
on the menu (particularly the "indifferent cheeses"), the absence of a bar,
the lack of a shower and the minimal soaps in the bathroom, and have
felt that the prices are high for what is offered.
Note Patricia Hegarty's recently published *An English Flavour* contains 130
Hope End recipes.

Open Last week Feb–last week Nov inclusive. Closed Mon and Tue nights.
Restaurant closed for lunch.
Rooms 1 suite, 8 double – all with bath, telephone, tea-making facilities; 1 in
cottage 200 yds from main house, 1 in minaret.
Facilities 3 sitting rooms, dining room. Walled garden; 40 acres of parkland.
Location 2 m N of Ledbury, just beyond Wellington Heath. *Hope End* is
signposted.
Restrictions Not suitable for &. No smoking in dining room. No children
under 14. No pets.
Credit cards Access, Visa.
Terms B&B (English): single occupancy £78–£122, double £88–£132. Set dinner
£27. Reduced rates for 2 or more nights; special breaks Mar and Nov. Advance
bookings only for weekends.
Service/tipping: "Our prices are fully inclusive. No tipping expected."

****
* **Traveller's tale** *The bathroom wall sloped. It was impossible to stand* *
* *under the shower; the only way was to kneel.* *
****

LEONARD STANLEY Gloucestershire   Map 2

The Grey Cottage   **BUDGET**   *Tel* Stonehouse (0453) 822515
Leonard Stanley
Stonehouse GL10 3LU

The omission of *The Grey Cottage* from last year's Guide provoked
outbursts from several readers: "We have recently revisited; the welcome
was just as warm, and the facilities just as good. In every room there are
hair-driers, tea-making facilities, fruit, biscuits, flowers, mineral water,
high-quality shampoo and bath gel – and Alka Seltzer. All three
bedrooms have private facilities [but they are not all *en suite*]. Breakfast
was a joy; those who still enjoy a good old-fashioned English breakfast
are catered for just as well as are vegetarians and health-food fanatics.
Excellent value for the price." "Beautiful well-kept house and grounds;
extremely friendly hosts." "Comfortable, caring atmosphere." And – a
reference to our comments in 1988/9 – "the Reeveses do smoke, but so
do we, and they never lit up until we made the first move". The Reeveses,
moreover, have now banned smoking in the guest bedrooms. Their grey-
stone Cotswold house is spotlessly clean, with beams and log fires, and
fresh flowers and books everywhere. Advance booking is essential.
Dinner is sometimes available by prior arrangement, and priced accordingly – "ours was excellent; superbly served, and the table set with the
best crockery and cutlery"; and there are plenty of good local restaurants.
(*Pamela E Anderson, Mr and Mrs Michael Sciortino, Barry Cottam*)

Open All year except New Year.
Rooms 2 double, 1 single – all with bath and/or shower, radio, TV, tea-making
facilities; telephone, baby-sitting available.
Facilities Lounge with TV, sun lounge, dining room. ½-acre garden with patio.
Location 3 m from M5 junction 13, between villages of Leonard Stanley and King
Stanley.
Restrictions No smoking in bedrooms. No dogs in bedrooms.
Credit None accepted.
Terms (Not VAT-rated) B&B: single £28, double £48. Meals according to guests'
requirements; max £20. Reductions for 4 nights or more. 1-night bookings
sometimes refused at weekends.
Service/tipping: "No service charge. And we have no 'great expectations' of tips."

LEW Oxfordshire   Map 2

The Farmhouse Hotel   **BUDGET**   *Tel* Bampton Castle (0993) 850297
  and Restaurant   *Telex* 83242
University Farm
Lew, Nr Bampton OX8 2AU

*Modernised but unpretentious farmhouse with popular restaurant, 3 m SW of
Witney, well set back from the road and attached to a 216-acre working farm in
a tiny village with fewer than 60 inhabitants. Run by the Rouse family.
Bedrooms characterful, comfortable and well equipped; one adapted for &.
Atmosphere too informal for some; others find it friendly and welcoming, and
praise the food and service. Near Brize Norton airfield, but quiet at night.
Closed Christmas, New Year. 6 double rooms, all with bath and/or shower. B&B
from £20. Set dinner £14 [1990]. Was in earlier editions. Recommended for reinclusion – "but probably not for your more upmarket readers". More reports
please.*

LEWDOWN Devon   Map 1

Lewtrenchard Manor   *Tel* Lewdown (056 683) 256
Lewtrenchard   *Fax* (056 683) 332
Nr Okehampton EX20 4PN

This splendid manor in a peaceful Devon valley eight miles from
Tavistock is Elizabethan in origin, E-shaped with mullioned windows; the
interior is a mixture of styles, owing to Victorian embellishments and
alterations. Public rooms have decorated plaster ceilings and dark oak
panelling, with ornate fireplaces in the lounge and drawing room; the
small dining room is hung with oil paintings and family portraits; there is
a grand staircase, and a long gallery. Bedrooms are of a good size and
traditionally decorated, with useful extras. The manor stands in 11-acre
grounds with impressive formal gardens, a dovecote, and a private lake
with fishing. The proprietors, James and Sue Murray, are "charming,
convivial and civilised" hosts. The "excellent" chef, David Shepherd,
cooks meals which are "ornate, in keeping with the manor, sophisticated
and very professional, though portions can be a bit over-generous". More
reports please.

Open All year except 3 weeks in Jan. Lunch by arrangement (except Sun).
Rooms 1 suite, 7 double – all with bath, shower, telephone, radio, TV.
Facilities 2 lounges, bar lounge, 2 dining rooms. 11-acre grounds with fishing
lake, croquet lawn.
Location 8 m N of Tavistock. Just S of A30 at Lewdown.
Restrictions Not suitable for &. No children under 8. No unattended dogs in
bedrooms, no dogs in public rooms.
Credit cards All major cards accepted.
Terms B&B (English): single from £65, double from £90, suite £110–£130. Set Sun
lunch £16, dinner £27; full alc £35. Discounts for long stays and in low season.
Special meals for children on request.
Service/tipping: "We feel the guests should decide if a tip is warranted or not."

LICHFIELD Staffordshire   Map 4

Oakleigh House Hotel   `BUDGET`   *Tel* Lichfield (0543) 262688
25 St Chad's Road
Lichfield WS13 7LZ

*Small hotel quietly situated 10 mins' walk from centre of city of Dr Johnson's
birth, near Stowe Pool. Recommended for "charmingly furnished rooms with
thoughtful touches, delightfully appointed conservatory restaurant with
straightforward, well-cooked food (plenty of choice) and unpretentious wine list;
friendly and welcoming owners". Popular with business travellers seeking non-
standardised accommodation. ½-acre garden. Restaurant closed 26 Dec to early
Jan, 2 weeks about July. 10 rooms (5 in converted stable block), 8 with bath.
B&B double £44–£48. Residents' set dinner at 7 pm £9; full alc £19.75. Recent
nomination, endorsed in the main, though a non-smoker was bothered by
smokey atmosphere. More reports please.*

> We asked hotels to quote 1991 prices. Not all were able to predict
> them in the late spring of 1990. Some of our terms will be inaccurate.
> Do check latest tariffs at the time of booking.

LIFTON Devon   **Map 1**

The Arundell Arms   *Tel* Lifton (0566) 84666
Lifton PL16 0AA   *Fax* (0566) 84494

This creeper-covered stone building, on the A30 (front rooms are sound-proofed and ventilated), formerly a coaching inn, has been owned by Ann Voss-Bark for over a quarter of a century and has had a Guide entry for many years. It is very much a sportsperson's hotel "with the camaraderie that exists when people with a common interest are together", and is particularly popular with people who fish: it has 20 miles of salmon, trout and sea-trout fishing on the river Tamar and its tributaries, a three-acre stocked lake, and offers fishing courses of all kinds; there are two full-time fishing instructors. In winter there are shooting packages, and also bridge and golfing holidays, cookery courses and gourmet weekends; meetings and conferences, too, are catered for. Reports in 1989/90 are all strongly favourable, and not only from the sporting community: "No finer base in England to fish. The public rooms are not at all slick but rather manage to look a bit shabby (in a very positive 'English' way) even with new curtain fabrics and extreme cleanliness. There is wonderful bar food; dinners, especially fish, are simple, unfussy and excellent; the same with breakfasts, especially if you have your own fresh trout to be steamed and served with bacon on toast. The rooms are simple, clean and adequate. Being here makes you want to forswear forever all those over-fussy hotels with choreographed dinners." "Outstanding in every way. A week of their dinners was a memorable plus to our very successful Devon holiday. Wines also excellent – a wide selection at reasonable prices." "Nice, welcoming staff, happy to have our two young children; they gave us a separate bedroom for them at a nominal rate." (*Mrs AM Bennett, Prof LJ Herrmann, DJ Fisher, also DW Mullock*) Only niggle: "Strangely, for such a hotel, no porridge for breakfast."

Open All year except 4 days over Christmas.
Rooms 19 double, 10 single – all with bath and/or shower, telephone, TV, tea-making facilities; baby-listening in main building. 5 rooms in annexe.
Facilities Lounge, cocktail bar, 2 restaurants; 3 conference rooms.
Location 3 m E of Launceston on A30 (front rooms sound-proofed).
Restrictions Not suitable for &. No smoking, no dogs in restaurant.
Credit cards All major cards accepted.
Terms [1990 rates] B&B £37–£50. Set lunch £13, dinner £22. Fishing holidays all year; shooting, bridge, bird-watching, cookery holidays, gourmet weekends in off-season. Children under 16 free in parents' room; special meals on request.
Service/tipping: "No charge is made for service, nor are tips expected. I feel strongly that this is a service industry and there should be no obligation either mandatory or morally on guests to tip. Any gratuities given are pooled and distributed monthly and equally to all staff."

LINCOLN Lincolnshire   **Map 3**

D'Isney Place Hotel   *Tel* Lincoln (0522) 538881
Eastgate, Lincoln LN2 4AA   *Fax* (0522) 511321

A Georgian B&B hotel with a garden, with some bedrooms overlooking the nearby cathedral. Back rooms are peaceful, those on the street side get some traffic noise, particularly on weekdays (but the windows are double-glazed). It has neither reception nor breakfast room; breakfast, continental or English, is served in the bedrooms which vary in size and style from quite simple singles to honeymoon suites with whirlpool bath. "Very comfortable, convenient and quiet though in the heart of Lincoln. Our room had a view of a paddock with horses, and a large bathroom. Delicious breakfast served in the bedroom with a newspaper." (*Ann Baxter*) Bathrobes are provided, and fresh milk for the tea and coffee-making facilities. Last year we reported a niggle about a mattress; the Paynes tell us that beds have now been replaced and they add: "We like to know when visitors have cause for complaint; we can usually do something about it and it certainly brings about quicker improvement than if they write to you."

Open All year.
Rooms 1 suite, 14 double, 2 single – all with bath and/or shower, 2 with jacuzzi, all with telephone, radio, TV, tea-making facilities. Also 3 cottages, 100 yds away, each with 2 double bedrooms, lounge, dining room, kitchen.
Facilities No public rooms. 1-acre garden.
Location By cathedral. Rooms double-glazed. Carpark.
Restrictions Not suitable for &. No smoking in 2 bedrooms.
Credit cards All major cards accepted.
Terms B&B: single £37–£49, double £57–£65. Weekend breaks. No charge for children in parents' room. (No restaurant.)
Service/tipping: "No service charge. No tipping; but guests do leave gifts for staff."

LITTLE SINGLETON Lancashire   Map 4

Mains Hall Hotel   *Tel* Poulton-le-Fylde
86 Mains Lane, Little Singleton   (0253) 885130
Nr Poulton-le-Fylde FY6 7LE   *Fax* (0253) 894132

Small old manor house 7 miles from Blackpool in pastoral setting, with pleasant 4-acre grounds with river frontage; oak panelling, log fires, some 4-posters. New owners, Roger and Pamela Yeomans, arrived in early 1990; first reports speak warmly of welcome, comfortable bedrooms, and food – straightforward cooking on limited menu. "Breakfasts need some improving, as does the wine list." 9 double rooms, all with bath and/or shower; with breakfast £55–£95. Set dinner £16.50. More reports please.

LONDON   Map 3

The Abbey Court   *Tel* (071) 221 7518
20 Pembridge Gardens, W2 4DU   *Fax* (071) 792 0858
                                                  Telex 262167

A small, expensive, luxuriously equipped B&B in a relatively quiet street near Notting Hill Gate, convenient for transport to the West End and the City. Outside are window-boxes, bay trees and carriage lamps; inside are magnificent flower arrangements in the hall and reception, and antique and period furniture. Bedrooms are mostly medium in size, though at least one single is extremely small. They vary in style; some have grand four-posters, others are more cottagey. All have a marble bathroom with a whirlpool bath. The decor is pretty, and not over-lavish. Breakfast is generous, with freshly squeezed orange juice, home-made muesli, croissants and brioches. There is no restaurant, but light meals and tea are available, served in the bedroom. Not for the infirm, as the hotel is on five storeys and has no lift.

Open All year.
Rooms 16 double, 6 single – all with bath and/or shower, telephone, radio, TV. 3 on ground floor.
Facilities Reception lounge. Small garden.
Location Central, near Notting Hill Gate tube station. Meter parking.
Restrictions Not suitable for &. No children under 12. No dogs.
Credit cards All major cards accepted.
Terms Rooms: single £75, double £120–£160. Continental breakfast £6. (No restaurant, but light alc meals and teas served.)
Service/tipping: "We make no charge for service. This is a choice we leave to our guests."

Athenaeum Hotel *Tel* (071) 499 3464
116 Piccadilly, W1V 0BJ *Fax* (071) 493 1860
Telex 261589

The *Athenaeum* is the flagship hotel of the Rank chain and has been completely refurbished in the past three years. It has an enviable position overlooking Green Park (jogging maps and suits available for the energetic), and all the trimmings that one would expect from a deluxe West End hotel. There are two floors of no-smoking bedrooms, and all are double-glazed; the quietest ones are on the side, but they lack the view of the park. The large lounge is attractive in a "country house style", the cocktail bar is mahogany-panelled. Food in the restaurant, with soft colours and alcoves, is excellent, if expensive; the menu is French. Parking, shared with the adjacent hotel, costs £20.50 a day. For those who prefer to self-cater, the hotel rents apartments in an adjacent building on a quiet side street. (*Mrs MW Atkinson, also David Lodge*)

Open All year.
Rooms 22 suites, 79 double, 11 single – all with bath, shower, telephone, radio, TV; free in-house films; double-glazing, air-conditioning; 24-hour room service. 33 1- and 2-bedroom apartments in adjacent building.
Facilities Lifts. Lounge, cocktail bar, restaurant; conference and function facilities.
Location Central; valet parking (£20.50 per day). (Underground Green Park.)
Restrictions No smoking in some bedrooms. Guide dogs only.
Credit cards All major cards accepted.
Terms [1990 rates] Rooms: single £160, double £173–£188, suite £230–£270. Breakfast: continental £8, English £11. Set lunch £19.50, dinner £24; full alc £30. Special meals for children on request.
Service/tipping: "No service charge. Tips not expected."

Basil Street Hotel *Tel* (071) 581 3311
8 Basil Street *Fax* (071) 581 3693
Knightsbridge, SW3 1AH *Telex* 28379

Privately owned by the third generation of the family who founded it 80 years ago, *The Basil* "offers modern comfort in an elegant old atmosphere". It is in a small but busy road leading off Sloane Street (convenient for Hyde Park and Harrods); it's an Edwardian building, furnished with antiques, mirrors and paintings, and has numerous public rooms, including a panelled restaurant serving French-oriented food, a coffee shop, a cellar wine bar and a ladies' club. The impressive room on the left of the entrance was once a booking hall for the London Underground. The 94 bedrooms include family rooms; most have a private bathroom. They vary greatly in size, style and position and include a "magnificent" suite; some of them can be surprisingly quiet for central London. Comments this year: "Room service much better; improvement of rooms continues. Food very acceptable." "Attractive decor, service charming and prompt." (*Richard Creed, Susan E Rayner*) Only criticism: "They are let down by the dining room staff from time to time." The hotel has introduced a "Basilite" scheme whereby visitors who have stayed at least five times enjoy discounted tariffs and weekend concessions.

Open All year.
Rooms 1 suite, 44 double, 48 single – 72 with bath and shower, all with telephone, radio, TV; baby-sitting.
Facilities Lounge bar, ladies' lounge, coffee shop, wine bar, dining room; facilities for conferences, functions, private meals.
Location Central; public carpark nearby. (Underground Knightsbridge.)
Restrictions Not suitable for &. No dogs in public rooms.
Credit cards All major cards accepted.
Terms [1990 rates] (Service at guests' discretion) Rooms: single £49.50–£93.50, double £76–£121, family £170.50, suite £188. Breakfast: continental £4.50, English from £8. Set lunch £13.75; full alc dinner £22. No charge for children under 12 sharing parents' room; special meals.

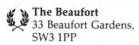

The Beaufort   *Tel* (071) 584 5252
33 Beaufort Gardens,   *Fax* (071) 589 2834
SW3 1PP   *Telex* 929200

César award: Most audacious city hotel

Diana Wallis, a former television producer, opened this small, pricey hotel in 1986 with the aim of providing "an English country-house atmosphere in the heart of London". It has an excellent position, on a quiet square just round the corner from Harrods. Much thought has been given to making the guest feel at home. On arrival you are given a front-door key, bedrooms are stocked (but not cluttered) with numerous extras – flasks of brandy, chocolates, biscuits and bathroom goodies. Most unusual is the pricing structure. "My policy," writes Ms Wallis, "is that you charge for a room and that covers everything except phone calls and personal laundry. Our price includes breakfast, full meals served in the bedroom (Roux brothers' *sous vide*), drinks from the 24-hour bar, membership of a nearby health club, transistors, videos – and much else besides. I hate tipping, which is degrading; we pay our staff 50–100 per cent more than the top London hotel payer." Apart from two porters all the staff are female, and women travelling on their own find this a particularly sympathetic place to stay. The decor is pretty, with pale colours, fresh flowers everywhere, original watercolours, and comfortable sofas and chairs. The staff are friendly and helpful, and once a month there is a champagne party for guests. *The Beaufort* is air-conditioned throughout. As is usual in buildings of this kind, some of the top rooms are quite small.

Open 2 Jan–22 Dec.
Rooms 7 suites, 18 double, 3 single – all with bath and/or shower, telephone, radio, TV/video; tea-making facilities available. Some ground-floor rooms.

Facilities Lift. Lounge with honour bar. Free membership of nearby health club.
Location Central, near Harrods. Meter parking; public carpark nearby.
(Underground Knightsbridge.)
Restrictions No children under 10 except for babies. Dogs by arrangement only.
Credit cards All major cards accepted.
Terms B&B (continental): single £150–£250, double £160–£250, suite £250. No
charge for extra bed in suite. (No restaurant but light meals served in bedrooms
7–9 pm.)
*Service/tipping: "We do not encourage tipping as the tariff is all-inclusive. We pay above
average wages and a 10% service charge is included in the tariffs."*

Blakes Hotel   *Tel* (071) 370 6701
33 Roland Gardens, SW7 3PF   *Telex* 8813500

Blakes' dark green exterior contrasts strikingly with its red-brick Victorian
neighbours in a residential street a few minutes' walk from South
Kensington Underground. And there's plenty of black in its decor,
theatrically stylish with a pronounced Oriental accent, designed by the
proprietor, Anouska Hempel, who is constantly refurbishing. One four-
postered bedroom is black and red with a black bathroom; one is all pink
silk with a large sitting room. Antiques, original paintings and rare silks
abound. All the bedrooms are different; some are opulent, with heavy
drapes and dark colours, others are plainer and lighter but equally
stunning. It is best to discuss the style of room you prefer when booking;
none is particularly large. Some have tape deck and stereo among the
extras. Reception is laid-back which won't suit all comers. In the darkly
mirrored dining room in the basement, where tables have alternate black
and white cloths, David Wilson's menus are cosmopolitan and pricey; his
cooking is "of a high standard", and the service "outstanding". Breakfasts
are said to be "delicious, with carrot juice, good croissants and decent
thick brown toast". The clientele is international and trendy, but not
everyone considers that *Blakes* quite lives up to the prices charged. More
reports please.

Open All year. Restaurant closed 25/26 Dec.
Rooms 12 suites, 30 double, 10 single – all with bath and/or shower, telephone,
TV, baby-listening; 12 with radio.
Facilities Lift. "Chinese Room" (lounge – light refreshments served), bar,
restaurant.
Location Central; meter parking. (Underground South Kensington or Gloucester
Road.)
Restrictions Not suitable for &. No dogs.
Credit cards All major cards accepted.
Terms Rooms: single £130–£150, double £180–£300, suite £215–£600. Breakfast:
continental £7.50, English £14. Full alc from £60. Special meals for children on
request.
*Service/tipping: "We do not levy a service charge on accommodation; tips are at guests'
discretion. We add a 15% charge to restaurant and room-service bills which is included in
the waiting staff's wages."*

Capital Hotel   *Tel* (071) 589 5171
22–24 Basil Street, SW3 1AT   *Fax* (071) 225 0011
                                                                       Telex 919042

A smallish, sophisticated hotel, with a *fin de siècle* decor, owned by David
Levin who also owns *L'Hotel* (below). It is in a narrow but busy side street

near Harrods – parking is not easy, but the hotel has a small garage. The bedrooms, designed by Mrs Levin, have fabrics by the American designer, Ralph Lauren; they are double-glazed, air-conditioned and elegant in a country house sort of way, though with many urban extras, including full sound and vision service. Some are quite small; they may be dark with patterned wallpaper and heavy drapes, though other rooms are lighter in style. Bathrooms are lavishly marbled, and comprehensively equipped, including "wonderfully fluffy towels". The *Capital's* restaurant, with its "gentle Nina Campbell interior" and imposing chandeliers, has long been a mecca for London gourmets; under chef Philip Britten, it regained its *Michelin* rosette in 1990 for its fine French cooking. "Very courteous and efficient service," reports a recent diner. "Superb fish mousse with excellent sauce. Good main course except for the ludicrous absence of potatoes. Very expensive wine list." More reports please.

Rooms 8 suites, 28 double, 12 single – all with bath, shower, telephone, radio, TV; 24-hour room service.
Facilities Lift. Lounge, bar, restaurant; 2 private dining rooms. Business facilities.
Location Central. Rooms double-glazed; rear rooms quietest. Garage for 12 cars (£8 per night). (Underground Knightsbridge.)
Restriction Dogs at management's discretion, not in public rooms.
Credit cards All major cards accepted.
Terms Rooms: single £150, double £175, suite £265. Breakfast: continental £7.50, English £10.50. Set lunch £18.50, dinner £38; full alc £40. Cot £10, extra bed £30, special meals for children.
Service/tipping: "Service included. No tipping expected."

Colonnade Hotel
2 Warrington Crescent, W9 1ER

Tel (071) 286 1052
Fax (071) 286 1057
Telex 298930

A family-run hotel in a rambling Grade II Victorian listed building in a quiet residential area, but only fifteen minutes by bus or underground (Warwick Avenue station) to centre. Recommended for agreeable location, clean, well thought-out bedrooms (they vary in size and style), and reasonable rates. Light meals or à la carte in restaurant with waterfall. 49 rooms, all with private facilities (some spa baths). B&B (English) double £77–£88. Set dinner £12.50. Recent nomination. More reports please.

The Connaught
Carlos Place, W1Y 6AL

Tel (071) 499 7070

"On a chart of one to ten, I rate *The Connaught* as a ten." "Maintains its superior style." "Service almost beyond compare and the value surprisingly good when you consider the prices charged in fairly mediocre London hotels for an overnight stay." Typical comments on one of London's most exclusive hotels; it has no brochure, rates are "on application", guests' privacy is jealously guarded, the bedrooms are usually booked months in advance. It is in the heart of Mayfair, in a relatively unbusy street. The decor is sophisticated, with comfortable furniture, antiques and luxurious fabrics; flowers abound. The restaurant, under *maître* chef Michel Bourdin, is *Michelin*-rosetted and formal, with gleaming panels, arched windows and glittering chandeliers, and staff in tailcoats or long white aprons; exquisite French dishes rub shoulders with steak and kidney pie and bread and butter pudding. Jacket and tie are *de rigueur*, jeans are out. One reader this year laments the "very inadequate possibility for payment" (only Access is accepted).

Open All year.
Rooms 24 suites, 60 double, 30 single – all with bath, shower, telephone, TV; baby-sitting, 24-hour room service.
Facilities Lounge, cocktail bar, grill room, restaurant.
Location Central. No private parking. (Underground Bond Street.)
Restrictions Not suitable for severely &. No dogs.
Credit card Access.
Terms On application.
Service/tipping: "15% added; shared among staff on 'points' basis."

Durrants Hotel	*Tel* (071) 935 8131
George Street, W1H 6BJ	*Fax* (071) 487 3510
	Telex 894919

A traditional, well-bred and relatively inexpensive hotel encased in a late 18th-century shell; it has been added to during the years, creating a quaint, rambling effect. In summer flowery window-boxes stretch the width of its facade. Formerly a coaching inn, it is one of the oldest privately owned hotels in London. It is convenient for Oxford Street, Harley Street, Marylebone Road and the Wallace Collection. Bedrooms are individually decorated and well equipped; most are quiet, especially those in the rear. "Exceptionally good value considering London's usually exorbitant prices. Our room, although small, was pleasantly decorated and equipped with all modern conveniences. The bathroom, too, was modern. The hotel is slightly run-down in parts (there was chipped and peeling paint on some walls), but such minor damage only reminds one of the building's age; overall it is charming. The staff and owner were extremely pleasant and helpful. Breakfast was plentiful, though not of exceptional quality. Despite its central location, it was extremely quiet at night. Overall *Durrants* perfectly fitted our requirements for mid-city accommodation." (*Cathryn Bryck*) The panelled dining room is an agreeable place to eat, but it is not inexpensive, nor is the food particularly distinguished; there are plenty of good restaurants in the area.

Open All year. Restaurant closed 25/26 Dec.
Rooms 3 suites, 73 double, 20 single – 86 with bath and/or shower, all with telephone, radio, TV. Some ground-floor rooms.
Facilities 2 lifts. 3 residents' lounges, bar, snug room, restaurant, breakfast room, tea room; conference facilities.
Location Central (some front rooms could be noisy). Public carpark 5 mins' walk. (Underground Marble Arch.)
Restriction No dogs.
Credit cards Access, Amex, Visa.
Terms Rooms: single £55–£75, double £85–£100, suite £135–£200. Breakfast: continental £5.25, English £8. Set lunch £22, dinner £34. Full alc £35.
Service/tipping: "Service is included in all bills apart from the restaurant where an optional service charge of 12½% is added."

We are particularly keen to have reports on italicised entries.

Ebury Court   *Tel* (071) 730 8147
26 Ebury Street, SW1W 0LU

*This friendly, old-fashioned and reasonably priced hostelry in five adjoining
houses conveniently near Victoria Station was run for over half a century by
Diana and Romer Topham and was something of a Guide institution. In July
1989 the Tophams retired, to be succeeded by their daughter and son-in-law,
Marianne and Nicholas Kingsford. Considerable changes are in hand: refurbishment of public rooms and bedrooms; bathrooms and showers added where
possible, tea- and coffee-making facilities and hair-driers installed. The
restaurant, formerly in the basement, will be brought up to the ground floor;
already there is a new kitchen team. By 1991 these improvements should be
bearing fruit, but for the moment the entry must continue to be in italics. Prices
have risen somewhat. Closed Christmas/New Year. 43 rooms, 19 with private
facilities. B&B (English) double £95. Set lunch £15, dinner £20. Reports on the
new set-up badly needed.*

The Fenja   *Tel* (071) 589 7333
69 Cadogan Gardens, SW3 2RB   *Fax* (071) 581 4958
                                                  Telex 934272

This discreet and elegant small hotel in a residential street near Sloane
Square, with some rooms overlooking Cadogan Gardens (to which guests
have access), enters the Guide this year, warmly recommended: "We
could not have been more delighted. The house is beautifully proportioned, and carefully decorated in Edwardian style, filled with antique
and period furniture, original pictures and marble busts." Bedrooms, all
different, are named after English artists and writers. Turner, a "superior
double", is "remarkably quiet and impressively decorated in pale shades,
with a magnificent four-poster, beautiful hexagonal table and Chippen-
dale-style chairs"; Jane Austen is more feminine, with flowery fabrics.
The bedrooms have fresh flowers and fruit; instead of a mini-bar there is
a drinks tray with cut-glass decanters; you are charged for what you
consume. "Excellent and very generous English breakfast – it cost only £3
more than the continental, and set us up for the entire day." *The Fenja*
goes in for cosseting service – cases carried, shoes polished, "they even
fed the parking meter for us". (*Francine and Ian Walsh*) There's no
restaurant, but light meals can be served in the bedrooms.

Open All year.
Rooms 12 double, 1 single – all with bath and/or shower, telephone, radio, TV.
1 ground-floor room.
Facilities Lift. Drawing room; conference room. Access to Cadogan Gardens.
Location Central, near Sloane Square (Underground Sloane Square). Meter
parking.
Restrictions Not suitable for &. No dogs.
Credit cards Access, Visa.
Terms Rooms: single £90, double £120–£180. Breakfast: continental £6, English
£9. (No restaurant, but light meals available.)

If you think we have over-praised a hotel or done it an injustice,
please let us know.

The Goring Hotel   *Tel* (071) 834 8211
15 Beeston Place, SW1W 0JW   *Fax* (071) 834 4393
                                                  Telex 919166

A dependably comfortable hotel in a useful location near Victoria, Buckingham Palace and Westminster. It was built in 1910 by the present Mr Goring's grandfather, and claims to have been the first hotel in the world to have a bathroom and central heating in every bedroom. The atmosphere and decor are English traditional; bedrooms, in pastel colours, have good quality furniture. Many guests are regulars. "Public rooms superb; the cleanest and best-kept hotel I have visited. Staff friendly and very helpful." There is a large relaxing bar overlooking an inner courtyard garden and lawn (not, however, accessible to guests). The restaurant offers quiet and professional service, traditional dishes, and a good choice for vegetarians. (*AD Stokes, Sarah F Baird, Alfred E Knopf, Mrs Don Simecheck*) In the past we have said that Goring the Third sleeps in each room looking for weak spots; this year one reader says: "He seemed to have missed my bed which had a slightly lop-sided mattress", and another: "He had not tried the shower in my small (and not very well-equipped) single room – the only way to use it was by kneeling."

Open All year.
Rooms 6 suites, 41 double, 39 single – all with bath, shower, telephone, radio, TV; some with air-conditioning. 24-hour room service.
Facilities Lift. Lounge, bar, restaurant; 5 function rooms. 1-acre garden (no access for guests).
Location Central, near Buckingham Palace (front rooms are double-glazed). Garage and mews parking. (Underground Victoria.)
Restrictions Not suitable for &. No dogs.
Credit cards All major cards accepted.
Terms Rooms: single £115, double £170, suite £210. Breakfast: continental from £6, English from £9. Set lunch £19.50, dinner £25; full alc £36. Special meals for children on request.
Service/tipping: "No service charge for hotel but 10% added to restaurant bills. Guests are informed that tipping is not necessary or expected."

Hazlitt's   *Tel* (071) 434 1771
6 Frith Street, W1V 5TZ   *Fax* (071) 439 1524

A "delightful small hotel" in the heart of Soho, well situated for West End theatres and restaurants. Formerly a nurses' home, it was created from three terrace houses built in 1718. It takes its name from the essayist, who died in one of the houses a century later; the 23 bedrooms are named after famous residents and visitors to the house. Rooms are light and airy; at the top of the house they are quite small, lower down they have high ceilings; all have agreeable prints and plants, firm beds (though the doubles are on the small side), and decent linen. Some of the bathrooms have a "glorious free-standing bath, with brass taps, wooden towel rail and wooden loo seat – so refreshing *not* to have a tiled bathroom for once". The hotel is furnished throughout with mahogany, oak and pine. An "excellent" continental breakfast – fresh orange juice, "real" coffee, fresh rolls and croissants – is served in the bedrooms (there's no breakfast room); light refreshments and cream teas are available in a sitting room. "Staff conscientious and helpful, and they were wonderful to our young daughter; the hotel is immaculately clean." "Our spacious and comfortable front room gave us a good view of Soho action; next time we may ask for one at the back which might be less interesting, but more quiet." Not suitable for the infirm as there's no lift. (*Dr PH Tattersall, Diana Cooper, H Richard Lamb*)

Open All year except 21–26 Dec.
Rooms 1 suite, 17 double, 5 single – 22 with bath (20 have hand shower), 1 with shower, all with telephone, TV. 3 on ground floor.
Facility Lounge.
Location Central. NCP nearby. (Underground Tottenham Court Road.)
Restriction No dogs.
Credit cards All major cards accepted.
Terms [1990 rates] (excluding VAT) Rooms: single £77, double £86, suite £132. Continental breakfast £4.85. (No restaurant, but teas and light refreshments available.)
Service/tipping: "We do not charge for service. Tips are pooled and distributed equally among staff."

Knightsbridge Green Hotel   *Tel* (071) 584 6274
159 Knightsbridge, SW1X 7PD   *Fax* (071) 225 1635

This small family-owned hotel on Knightsbridge, close to Harrods and Hyde Park, is unusual in having mostly suites, each with a double room, reception room and bathroom; they are simply and attractively decorated, well lit, and have good bathrooms; there are also double and single rooms. It does not offer the trappings of a luxurious hotel – there's no doorman or porter, and the only public room is the Club Room on the first floor where free tea and coffee are available all day. Continental or English breakfast is delivered to the room. Front rooms are double-glazed to keep out traffic noise; those at the back are quietest. Visitors, many of them regulars, appreciate "peace in the centre of a city", helpful staff, comfortable and spacious rooms, "spotless housekeeping", and good value for money. (*Colin and Anna MacKenzie, Isobel Mackenzie, and others*)

Open All year, except 4 days at Christmas.
Rooms 14 suites, 6 double, 4 single – all with bath, shower, telephone, TV, tea-making facilities; baby-listening by arrangement.
Facilities Lift. Club Room on first floor with complimentary coffee and tea.
Location Central (bedrooms overlooking Knightsbridge double-glazed). NCP in Pavilion Road nearby. (Underground Knightsbridge.)
Restrictions Not suitable for severely &. No dogs.
Credit cards Access, Amex, Visa.
Terms [1990 rates] Rooms: single £75, double £90, suite £105. Breakfast: continental £6, English £8. (No restaurant.)
Service/tipping: "Our rates include a service charge; guests are discouraged from further tipping by a notice in the bedroom."

L'Hotel   *Tel* (071) 589 6286
28 Basil Street, SW3 1AT   *Fax* (071) 225 0011
                                              Telex 919042 attn L'HOTEL

A centrally located B&B in the upper-price bracket, owned by the Levins who also own the neighbouring *Capital* (q.v.). Rooms are decorated in French country style. *L'Hotel* dispenses with such extras as porterage, hair-driers, and bathroom accessories to maintain prices at a reasonable level for central London. Rooms are all different, but each has fabric-lined walls, window blinds and curtains, a tiny but well-thought-out bathroom, pine chairs, chests and cupboards, efficient heating, attractive lighting, lots of hot water at all times and a mini-bar. The staff are relaxed and pleasant, and there is a choice of eating arrangements for those not wishing to eat out – the admirable restaurant of the *Capital Hotel* next door or the good-value food in the *Metro*, the busy wine bar in the basement. Breakfasts, also served in the *Metro*, include fresh orange juice, good croissants and coffee. You need to book well ahead to have a choice of rooms: some are smaller than others and lack the cosy benefit of a gas coal-fire; rooms above the wine bar can be noisy until late into the night; the suite at the top is quietest. Parking is not easy. Visitors in early 1990 felt that some refurbishment was due, and that the *Metro* meals were not quite as good as previously. Another reader commented, "Breakfast was OK but the *Metro* was smokey from the night before, and I disliked the 'white tea' and 'lemon tea mix' packages on the tray; tea bags would be infinitely preferable."

Open All year. Wine bar closed Sat evening, Sun and some public holidays, except for residents' breakfasts.
Rooms 1 suite, 11 double – all with bath, shower, telephone, radio, TV, tea-making facilities, mini-bar. 1 ground-floor room. (*Note:* no room service.)
Facilities Lift. Wine bar/brasserie.
Location Central. Rear bedrooms quietest. NCP opposite. (Underground Knightsbridge.)
Restriction Dogs at management's discretion.
Credit cards Access, Amex, Visa.
Terms B&B (double or single occupancy) £110, suite £145. Extra bed in room £20. Alc meal in wine bar about £15.
Service/tipping: "Service included. Tipping at guests' discretion."

Number Sixteen   *Tel* (071) 589 5232
16 Sumner Place, SW7 3EG   *Fax* (071) 584 8615
                                                 Telex 266638

A conversion of four attractive late Victorian townhouses in a fairly quiet street only minutes from South Kensington tube station. The decor throughout is attractive, with antique and period furniture and an interesting selection of paintings and prints. There is a comfortable lounge and bar, and a conservatory looking on to a pretty garden. Bedrooms vary in size and price; quietest ones overlook the garden. Many were redecorated in 1989, the rest are being done in 1990. More reports please.

Open All year.
Rooms 26 double, 10 single – all with bath and/or shower, telephone, TV; radio on request.
Facilities Lift. Reception, drawing room, bar, conservatory. Garden.
Location Central. Garden-facing rooms quietest. Parking 5 mins walk. (Underground South Kensington.)
Restrictions Not suitable for &. No children under 12. No dogs.
Credit cards All major cards accepted.
Terms [Until 1 Apr 1991] B&B: single £40–£95, double £70–£155.
Service/tipping: "No service charge. No stated policy about tips, but staff are adequately paid; any tips given are shared equally."

Please make a habit of sending in a report as soon as possible after a visit when details are still fresh in your mind.

The Pelham Hotel   *Tel* (071) 589 8288
15 Cromwell Place, SW7 2LA   *Fax* (071) 584 8444
                                              Telex 8814714

This lush hotel, owned by Kit and Tim Kemp, opened in 1989 in a busy
road near South Kensington tube station (front bedrooms are double-
glazed). "It's captivating, inviting one to sink into luxury and forget
forever the rest of the world." The public rooms are beautifully decorated
with antiques, fine fabrics, paintings and flowers. All the bedrooms are
different, varying from large suites with chandeliers, moulded rococo
ceilings and lavish drapes to small double rooms with queen- or king-size
beds; all have well-stocked mini bars, and opulent bathrooms with
generous extras. There is a small and pretty restaurant in the semi-
basement. The cooking is French, and promises well. The set lunch at
£12.50 [1990] for three-courses is "amazing value"; the wine list is on the
expensive side, and the background music sometimes intrusive. The staff
are "friendly and genuinely interested in pleasing the guests". *The
Pelham*'s manager is Sally Bulloch who has moved from *The Draycott*
which won a César last year but has now changed hands. (*SG; SAF*) More
reports please.

Open All year.
Rooms 2 suites, 35 double – all with bath, shower, telephone, radio, TV, baby-
listening. 24-hour room service.
Facilities Lounge, bar, restaurant.
Location By South Kensington tube station. Front rooms double-glazed.
Restrictions Not suitable for &. Dogs at management's discretion.
Credit cards Access, Amex, Visa.
Terms Rooms: single or double occupancy £130 and £155, suite £250. Breakfast:
continental £7.50, English £10.50. Set lunch £12.50; full alc £28. Special meals for
children by arrangement.
Service/tipping: "'No charge is made for service' is written on the menu."

The Portobello Hotel   *Tel* (071) 727 2777
22 Stanley Gardens, W11 2NG   *Fax* (071) 792 9641
                                              Telex 268349

The *Portobello* is a six-floor Victorian terrace house, in a good location on
a quiet residential street within strolling distance of the Portobello Road
market and not far from Kensington Gardens. The design, by Julie
Hodges, is an eclectic mix of styles, Victorian to Gothic, with gilt mirrors,
marble fireplaces, four-posters, palms, Edwardiana, cane and wicker
furniture. Some of the rooms, called cabins, are poky, even if they have
essential elements of life-support such as colour TV, tiny fridge and
micro-bathroom. But there are also, as you work downwards, normal-
sized rooms and ritzy suites – the Bath Room has mirrors above the bed
and painted clouds on the ceiling, the Round Room has a round bed and
free-standing Edwardian bath. There is a tiny lift. The *Portobello* is
"relaxed and discreet"; "eccentric and pleasantly surprising"; "staff most
friendly and helpful". (*John D Jones*) There is porterage and room service
between 8 am and 4 pm, but reception are on duty day and night. For the
benefit of international travellers, there is 24-hour bar and restaurant
service in the garden-style basement, but gastronomy has never been the
hotel's strong point. The continental breakfast, which comes with the tea-

and coffee-making facilities in the bedroom, is "packaged and disappointing", but a full English breakfast is served in the restaurant. More reports please.

Open 2 Jan–24 Dec.
Rooms 7 suites, 9 double, 9 single – 4 with bath and shower, 21 with shower, all with telephone, radio, TV, tea-making facilities, fridge.
Facilities Small lift. Lounge, bar, restaurant (open 24 hours a day to residents).
Location Central. Meter parking. (Underground Notting Hill Gate.)
Restrictions Not suitable for &. No dogs in public rooms.
Credit cards All major cards accepted.
Terms [1990 rates] (Service not included) B&B (continental): single £59.80–£63.25, double £94.88–£151.16. English breakfast £8. Full alc £20–£25. Special meals for children.

Swiss Cottage Hotel　　　　　　　　　*Tel* (071) 722 2281
4 Adamson Road, NW3 3HP　　　　　　　*Fax* (071) 483 4588
　　　　　　　　　　　　　　　　　　　　Telex 297232

Conversion of Victorian terraced house in quiet residential street in north-west London, conveniently placed for transport to centre. Filled with attractive antiques and paintings; delightful Tea House suite in cottage in garden. Recommended for comfortable bedrooms, good bathrooms, friendly and helpful service. 80 rooms – 17 new ones in adjacent building – most with private facilities. B&B (continental) double £68–£120. Set dinner £17.50 [1990]. More reports please.

LONG MELFORD Suffolk　　　　　　　　　　　　Map 3

Countrymen Restaurant　　　　　　　　*Tel* Sudbury (0787) 312356
　at the Black Lion Hotel　　　　　　　*Fax* (0787) 74557
The Green
Long Melford, CO10 9DN

This old coaching inn overlooking the green in a picture-book village (with many antique shops) had an entry in earlier Guide editions under previous owners. In 1989 it was taken over by the Erringtons who moved their *Countrymen Restaurant*, which they had run in Long Melford for six years, into the hotel. Stephen Errington, *Dorchester* trained, is chef and his wife Janet is front of house. They have redecorated and refurbished the public rooms, and first reports are favourable: "Not luxurious, but extremely comfortable. Pleasantly decorated and modernised with no loss of period character. Our bedroom was large, with pine antiques including a four-poster bed; the bathroom was modern and filled with bath foam, hand lotion etc. Meal excellent, if somewhat pricey; staff friendly and efficient." "It is a truly family business: Stephen cooks (and it is first-class), Janet runs things extremely efficiently, her father acts as host behind the bar, and her mother covers the reception desk. Breakfast as good as dinner." (*Cathryn Bryck, Patricia Pells*) There are two informal lounges with books and games. Bedrooms have views of the village; one is a family suite "where well-behaved children are welcome and catered for".

Open All year except Christmas. Restaurant closed Sun night and New Year.
Rooms 1 suite, 8 double – all with bath, shower, telephone, radio, TV, tea-making facilities, baby-listening.
Facilities Lounge, bar, restaurant. Small walled garden.
Location On green of village 2 m N of Sudbury. Traffic might disturb light sleepers.
Restrictions Not suitable for &. "Well-behaved children welcome." No dogs in public rooms.
Credit cards Access, Visa.
Terms B&B: single £45–£55, double £60–£70, suite £75–£80; dinner, B&B: single £60–£70, double £90–£100, suite £105–£110. Set lunch £12, dinner £20. Reduced rates for children; special meals on request.
Service/tipping: "No service charge. Tipping discretionary but not encouraged. Tips distributed among staff."

LONGFRAMLINGTON Northumberland   Map 4

Embleton Hall   *Tel* Longframlington (066 570) 249
Longframlington
Nr Morpeth NE65 8DT

A small family-run country hotel in an early 18th-century stone building with Victorian additions. Only 30 minutes from Newcastle; also "an excellent base from which to explore this magnificent coastal stretch of Northumbria". Public rooms and bedrooms attractively furnished in traditional style. Recommended for courteous, friendly atmosphere, excellent and carefully served food. Children welcome. 5-acre grounds with walled garden, rare breeds of poultry, and resident goat, also tennis and croquet. 10 bedrooms, all with private facilities. B&B double £55. Set lunch £9.50, dinner £17. New entry in 1990. More reports please.

LONGHORSLEY Northumberland   Map 4

Linden Hall Hotel   *Tel* Morpeth (0670) 516611
Longhorsley   *Fax* (0670) 88544
Morpeth NE65 8XF   *Telex* 538224

Only 30 minutes' drive from Newcastle is this ivy-clad mansion of considerable grandeur, built in 1812 in the classical style, and set in 300-acre grounds with many sporting facilities (see below). It is not privately owned but the manager, Jon Moore, and his staff, many of whom have been there for several years, are "conspicuously friendly and helpful"; old-fashioned service – beds turned down at night, for example – is the order of the day. And, unusually for a luxury hotel, *Linden Hall* welcomes and caters for children. There had been suggestions that the decor was a bit tired; but recently the public rooms and 20 bedrooms were refurbished and redecorated. Bedrooms are well appointed, though one visitor in the side building found his "compact"; those in the main building are larger. Keith Marshall took over as chef in March 1989 and the general feeling is that the restaurant falls short of "the impeccable standards of the rest of this beautiful hotel", perhaps because it caters extensively for conferences, banquets and so on; but the much less expensive *Linden Pub* is "really rather good". One niggle: "Why, if there is a fridge in the bedroom, do they not provide fresh milk?"

Open All year.
Rooms 2 suites, 41 double, 2 single – all with bath, shower, telephone, radio, TV, tea-making facilities, baby-listening. 10 ground-floor rooms, 2 suitable for &.
Facilities Lift, ramps. 2 lounges, 2 bars, conservatory, TV room, pub, restaurant; children's playroom; functions/conference facilities; billiards, table-tennis, sauna, solarium. 300-acre grounds with tennis, jogging trail, putting, croquet, clay-pigeon shooting, children's playground.
Location 4 m N of Morpeth; 1 m N of Longhorsley off A697.
Restriction Dogs in some bedrooms only (£5); not in public rooms.
Credit cards All major cards accepted.
Terms B&B (English): single £90, double £105, suite £175. Set lunch £15.95, dinner £19.50; full alc £30; 3-course meal in pub £5–£6. Special breaks throughout year (Fri–Mon only Mar–Oct); theme weekends, sporting holidays in low season. Reduced rates and special meals for children.
Service/tipping: "Tipping is up to the customer."

LOWER BRAILES Oxfordshire   Map 2

Feldon House   *Tel* Brailes (060 885) 580
Lower Brailes
Nr Banbury OX15 5HW

"Our third visit. We stayed in one of the two new rooms in the converted outbuildings. Everything, as usual, was perfect. The room was superb, the food wonderful, the Withericks their usual charming selves. *Feldon House* is an oasis for us." "Food and attention to detail first-class. But not for anyone who dislikes church bells – the tower is right next door!" "Very reasonably priced. Books everywhere; relaxed, family atmosphere. Service attentive, if slightly rushed at times." (*DF Swift, PH Hill, Barbara Nicoll*)

Maggie and Allan Witherick's small early 19th-century house is in a walled garden in the heart of a village on the Shipston-on-Stour–Banbury road. It makes a good base for touring the Cotswolds and is convenient for Stratford-on-Avon. *Feldon House* is quiet and welcoming, and furnished with taste and style. There is a drawing room and two dining rooms – one in a conservatory. The four bedrooms are well appointed and warm; all have private bathrooms, but those in the main house are not *en suite*, so a dressing gown might be worth packing. Allan Witherick cooks "very English meals, with good bespoke ingredients and no fancy tricks"; lots of fresh vegetables, very generous portions; no choice (likes and dislikes can be discussed in advance) – three courses for lunch, four for dinner. Breakfast, a cooked, help-yourself affair, is served round a large Victorian table – "books are provided for the anti-social and the hung-over". More reports please.

Open All year. Restaurant closed Sun evening.
Rooms 4 double – all with bath, shower, telephone; some with TV and tea-making facilities. 2 in converted coach house.
Facilities 2 lounges, TV room, dining room, conservatory dining room. Terrace. ⅔-acre garden with croquet.
Location In middle of village on B4035 between Shipston and Banbury. Near church. Parking.
Restrictions Not suitable for &. No dogs.
Credit cards Access, Visa.
Terms B&B (English) £19–£42, dinner, B&B £38.50–£61.50. Set lunch £16, dinner £19.50. 3-day bargain breaks.
Service/tipping: "Tips not solicited. If anything left it is distributed among all staff."

LOWER SWELL Gloucestershire   Map 2

Old Farmhouse Hotel   *Tel* Cotswold (0451) 30232
Lower Swell, Stow-on-the-Wold
Cheltenham GL54 1LF

There's been another change of ownership at this 16th-century stone
farmhouse in secluded walled garden in an unspoiled Cotswold village
near Stow-on-the-Wold. A young Dutchman, Erik Burger, who is also
part owner, is now the resident manager, with Chris Rayner as chef.
"This small hotel certainly deserves a Guide entry; very friendly,
attentive service, relaxed atmosphere. The small dining room and bar are
attractively decorated. Our large family room was comfortable, well
appointed and light. The food, though not outstanding, was good value
and unpretentious (excellent treacle tart; very good coffee)." (*Ann and
David Williams*) Bedrooms are clean, comfortable, and individually
decorated; the smaller ones are in the main building; larger ones, more
modern in style, are in a converted stable block. There is a table d'hôte
menu with choices for each course, and also an à la carte menu. Erik
Burger writes: "We welcome babies and small children; they are not
excluded from the bar or dining room." A few niggles: one reader
experienced poor bedroom lighting; and "the dress of the staff, including
the manager, was perhaps a little too informal".

Open All year. Restaurant closed Mon lunchtime to non-residents.
Rooms 1 suite, 14 double – 12 with bath and shower, 1 with bath, all with
telephone, radio, TV, tea-making facilities. 7 in converted stables. 3 on ground
floor. 1 self-catering flat.
Facilities Lounge, bar, 2 restaurants; conference facilities. 2-acre garden.
Location 1 m W of Stow-on-the-Wold by B4068.
Restrictions Not suitable for &. No smoking in restaurants. Dogs at
management's discretion; not in public rooms.
Credit cards Access, Visa.
Terms B&B: single £19.75, double £39.50–£71, suite £92.50; dinner, B&B: single
£32, double £64–£94, suite £116. Snack lunch approx £8, set dinner £12.25; full
alc £19. Discounts for long stays. Christmas, New Year, Easter packages. 1-night
bookings refused Sat and bank holidays.
Service/tipping: "Service included. When guests tip staff share it."

LOWESWATER Cumbria   Map 4

Scale Hill Hotel   *Tel* Lorton (090 085) 232
Loweswater
Nr Cockermouth, CA13 9UX

"Firmly retains its high standards. One of the nicest hotels I know." "A
blissful hotel. Lovely atmosphere of trust and peace. Large, light rooms –
no key unless required. No demand for large deposit on booking. Tea laid
out in the sitting room for anyone to partake of, and in generous
quantities. Excellent value." (*David Gilchrist, Diana Ross*) Continued warm
praise for this 17th-century coaching inn which has been owned by the
Thompson family for several generations; currently it is run by Michael
Thompson, his wife Sheila and daughter Heather – the latter two being

---

All inspections are carried out anonymously.

responsible for the cooking. It is in a secluded position between Crummock and Loweswater, in one of the least trippery parts of the Lake District, and has spectacular views of the hills to the north-west. The National Trust land at Crummock Water is half a mile through the woods. Earlier comments, endorsed this year: "A self-confident establishment, run with a slightly military efficiency and bonhomie." "Clever flower arrangements, Mr Thompson very hospitable. More like a private house in the country than a hotel. The cats are quite a feature of the place." Rooms vary in size and style, some are spacious; they are "well furnished with much-appreciated extras – nail-brush and hair-drier in bathroom, electric blankets. No telephones or radios in the bedroom, no television anywhere – just peace, comfort and beautiful scenery." Food is generally enjoyed: "On the plain side, vegetables imaginative and well cooked; good packed lunches." Sunday night supper is a cold meal apart from soup; breakfast is from 9 am. More reports please.

Open Mar–Nov.
Rooms 12 double, 5 single – all with bath and/or shower. 2 doubles in annexe 16 yds from hotel. 2 ground-floor rooms.
Facilities 4 lounges (1 non-smoking), bar, dining room; laundry, drying room. 1-acre grounds. Walking and climbing, golf, pony trekking nearby, also 3 lakes with boating, fishing, swimming.
Location 12 m W of Keswick, just off B5289.
Restriction No dogs in public rooms.
Credit cards None accepted.
Terms Dinner, B&B £39–£62. Bar lunches, packed lunches. Set dinner £16. Christmas and New Year packages. 1-night advance bookings refused. Reduced rates for children sharing parents' room; high tea provided.
Service/tipping: "Service is included in the rate; we do not expect anything extra."

LUDLOW Shropshire   Map 2

Dinham Hall   *Tel* Ludlow (0584) 876464
Ludlow SY8 1EJ   *Fax* (0584) 876019

Paul and Marian Johnson's hotel in a former school, an 18th-century listed building near the castle, opened in late 1988, and Chris Galvin's ambitious modern cooking – "amazing to find in the middle of Shropshire" – promptly won recognition in national competitions. Early reports to the Guide, too, were enthusiastic: "It aims at the highest standards and triumphantly succeeds. We had a charming and extremely comfortable room and a meal that would have been exceptional anywhere. It does not smother you in unwanted luxuries or impress with astronomical prices. It is too sophisticated for that. What it does give you are *real* luxuries like a huge jug of freshly squeezed orange juice at breakfast." "Comfortable beds, well-stocked mini-bar, fresh milk for morning tea, bowl of exotic fruit. Spotless and well-equipped bathroom. Much attention to detail. The house is warm, the staff young and willing. Pretty dining room with lots of fresh flowers." (*Diana Rothenstein, EB*) In early 1990, however, there were reports of "chaos", perhaps in the owner's absence, "mitigated only by the friendly staff. There were delays at dinner and in settling the bill; no one was sure how to work the computer." And one reader felt the decor was too florid, and the food over-elaborate. For those in need of exercise the hotel has a gym; it can arrange clay-pigeon shooting, fishing, gliding, riding and hot-air ballooning for guests, "and we have strong links with some of the best game shooting in the UK". More reports please.

Open All year.
Rooms 11 double, 3 single – all with bath and/or shower, telephone, radio, TV, mini-bar, tea-making facilities. 1 on ground floor.
Facilities 2 lounges, lounge bar, restaurant, private dining room; gym, sauna. ¾-acre garden with terrace. Shooting, clay-pigeon shooting, fishing, riding, gliding, hot-air ballooning nearby.
Location Near castle. Parking.
Restrictions No children under 6. No dogs in building; kennelling facility.
Credit cards Access, Amex, Visa.
Terms [1990 rates] B&B (English): single £50–£55, double £70–£115; dinner, B&B: single £70–£75, double £110–£155. Full alc £28.50. Off-season theme breaks. Reduced rates for children in family room; special meals.
Service/tipping: "No service charge. Tipping at guests' discretion, not encouraged by staff."

The Feathers   *Tel* Ludlow (0584) 875261
Bull Ring, Ludlow SY8 1AA   *Fax* (0584) 876030
                                                     Telex 35637

The Feathers has been an inn since the 17th century. It has a spectacular half-timbered front elevation, carved mantelpieces and elaborately ornamented plaster ceilings, panelling and original fireplaces. Bedrooms are traditionally furnished but thoroughly modern in the comforts they offer; most are of a good size, and all have private bathrooms; some suites have fires and four-posters. Service is friendly and efficient, with helpful porterage. The food is well served, and generally considered to be "of high quality" – particularly the "crisp roast duck and properly under-cooked vegetables", though one reader found the desserts and cheeses "unimpressive". (*Sarah Baird, RO Marshall, ML Borish*) *The Feathers* is Ludlow's premier hotel, as well as a showpiece in its own right – be prepared for lots of passing trade, and conferences, banquets and coach parties. It is not ideal for the disabled – because of its venerable age, there are lots of steps. There is no garden, but a "very nice patio" off the dining room and a new billiard room.

Open All year.
Rooms 6 suites, 24 double, 10 single – all with bath, shower, telephone, radio, TV, tea-making facilities and baby-listening.
Facilities Lift. Lounges, 2 bars, restaurant; billiard room. Conference/banqueting facilities.
Location In town centre. Carpark.
Restrictions Not suitable for severely &. No smoking in restaurant and some bedrooms. No dogs in bedrooms.
Credit cards All major cards accepted.
Terms B&B (English): single £60–£65, double £86–£95, suite £102–£112. Set lunch £12.50; full alc dinner £22. 2-night breaks. Christmas programme. Reduced rates and special meals for children.
Service/tipping: "No service charge. Tipping is a matter between staff and customer. It is not essential and service will not be affected."

> The length of an entry need not reflect the merit of a hotel. The more interesting the report or the more unusual or controversial the hotel, the longer the entry.

LYNMOUTH Devon

Map 1

Tors Hotel
Lynmouth EX35 6NA

Tel Lynton (0598) 53236

Set on a hill in 5-acre grounds with woodland and shrubs and fine views of Lynmouth and Bristol Channel. "Relaxed and comfortable", run "in ebullient style" by manager Gary Hayward. Rooms vary in size and position; priced accordingly – best ones have sea view. Food "good and plentiful"; excellent cream teas. Games room, outdoor swimming pool. Children welcome. Open Mar–early Jan. 34 double rooms, all with bath (4 also have shower). B&B £27– £34.50; dinner, B&B £37–£44.50 [1990]. Weekly rates. Warmly nominated by a regular visitor. More reports please.

LYTHAM ST ANNE'S see ST ANNE'S-ON-SEA

Map 4

The Dalmeny Hotel

MAIDEN NEWTON Dorset

Map 2

Maiden Newton House
Maiden Newton
Nr Dorchester DT2 0AA

Tel Maiden Newton (0300) 20336

The heart of Hardy country – Maiden Newton is the Chalk Newton of *Tess of the D'Urbervilles* – and there is good walking in the area. *Maiden Newton House* is a honey-coloured antique-filled 15th-century Tudor mansion (rebuilt in the early 19th century) with mullioned windows, beautiful chimneys, high-ceilinged hall, elegant lounge and individually styled bedrooms. It is set in 11 acres of secluded parkland and gardens overlooking the river Frome, and is part hotel, part private house taking guests – log fires, warm bedrooms in winter, agreeable colour schemes, books and maps, dogs and cats, all adding to the home-like atmosphere. Bryan and Elizabeth Ferriss, "warm and generous hosts", introduce guests to each other in the lounge, then sit down to dinner with them, one at each end of the table, an arrangement people find either fun or tiresome. No choice on the four-course dinner menu but you are given notice in case a dish is not to your liking, and special diets are happily catered for. It is "all real food, fresh vegetables and much variety and ingenuity"; fish dishes are a speciality. "Bryan Ferriss is particularly to be commended for offering a glass of wine with each course from a carefully chosen selection of wines. The house-party style works very well – we played impromptu parlour games until 1.30 am with our fellow guests, none of whom we had ever met before." (*ST Pankhurst*) "The owners rose to new heights of care for their guests on our last visit when they tactfully gave my loudly snoring husband a bedroom to himself at no extra charge," adds a reader who had better remain anonymous.

Open Feb–Dec.
Rooms 5 double, 1 single – 5 with bath and shower, 1 with shower, all with TV.

Facilities Drawing room/bar, library/TV room, dining room; functions facilities. 11-acre grounds with stabling for visiting horses, croquet, ¾ m trout-fishing on river Frome. Golf, sailing, riding, hunting, walking nearby.
Location From A356 in centre of village take road signposted Yeovil. Entrance gates 200 yds on left near church.
Restrictions Not suitable for ⅙. No smoking in dining room and 2 bedrooms. No children under 12 in dining room at night (suppers by arrangement). Small dogs only; not in public rooms.
Credit cards Access, Visa.
Terms B&B: single £70–£90, double £88–£125. Set dinner £26. Lunches and packed lunches on request. 1-night bookings for weekends sometimes refused if made too far in advance. Weekly half-board rates; house-party rates.
Service/tipping: "We discourage tipping."

MALVERN WELLS Hereford and Worcester   Map 2

The Old Vicarage ▐BUDGET▌   *Tel* Malvern (0684) 572585
Hanley Road
Malvern Wells WR14 4PH

This former Victorian vicarage, in a lawned garden on the slopes of the Malvern Hills overlooking the Severn Vale, is essentially a B&B, though dinners can be served by arrangement. The owner, Michael Gorvin, is knowledgeable about local eating places – and the *Michelin*-rosetted *Croque-en-Bouche* restaurant is just up the road. Most visitors enjoy the friendly welcome, the "atmosphere of a well-loved home, with a collection of much-read books", the comfortable and clean accommodation – "large, light bedrooms, full of period character, with lots of stripped pine" – and the good breakfasts. (*Mr and Mrs LK Cook, D and E Holt*) But some of the bathrooms are separated from the bedroom only by a curtain or a louvred door which doesn't suit everyone; bathroom lighting could be improved; and one visitor in early 1990 found the public rooms draughty. More reports please.

Open All year except Christmas.
Rooms 1 family, 5 double – 3 with bath, 3 with shower, all with TV, tea-making facilities; baby-listening by arrangement. 1 ground-floor room.
Facilities Lounge, dining room. ¾-acre garden.
Location From Malvern take A449 Wells Road; turn left down B4209 Hanley Road – *Old Vicarage* on the right just before Green Lane turn-off.
Restrictions No smoking in dining room. Dogs by arrangement only, not in public rooms.
Credit cards None accepted.
Terms B&B (English): single occupancy £28–£30, double £38–£46. Reduced rates for children. (No restaurant.)

MANCHESTER   Map 4

Etrop Grange   *Tel* Manchester (061) 437 3594
Bailey Lane, Etrop Green   *Fax* (061) 499 0790
Manchester Airport M22 5NR

Our only Manchester entry, a small Georgian Grade II listed country house down a leafy lane, 12 minutes' drive from the city centre and half a mile from the airport, run by John and Susan Roebuck. "Welcome extremely friendly and helpful. Lots of help with finding our way round Manchester. Lovely garden, all in blossom; nice to be in such a countrified place after a day in the city. Bedroom clean, frills and bows everywhere and the ubiquitous festoon blinds; nice bathroom. Dinner *very* good; everything prettily decorated, lots of cut glass, waitresses in demure print frocks, all making a Victorian atmosphere." Cooking is "essentially British with modern refinements". Most visitors have found the bedrooms attractive and well furnished but an artist visitor thought them excessively fussy. Proximity to the airport does make the rooms slightly noisy, but there is secondary glazing. Because of its proximity to the airport, *Etrop Grange* is popular with businessfolk and honeymooners. A 1990 visitor considered the breakfasts, charged extra, rather expensive, "and predictable, but good", and the charges for telephone calls excessively high. We'd welcome more reports.

Open All year.
Rooms 1 suite, 6 double, 1 single – 7 with bath and shower, 1 with shower, all with telephone, radio, TV, tea-making facilities, baby-listening.
Facilities Lounge, drawing room, conservatory, dining room; small conference room. 1-acre garden. Courtesy airport car.
Location 12 minutes' drive S of city centre. Leave M56 motorway at junction 5 to airport.
Restrictions Not suitable for &. No dogs in public rooms.
Credit cards Access, Amex, Visa.
Terms [1990 rates] Rooms: single from £68, double from £78. Breakfast: continental £4.95, English £6.95. Set lunch £12.50, dinner £21.95. Weekend reductions. Honeymoon breaks. Reduced rates for children; special meals if advance warning is given.
Service/tipping: "We do not encourage guests to leave tips as good levels of service should not be specially rewarded."

MATLOCK Derbyshire   **Map 4**

Riber Hall   *Tel* Matlock (0629) 582795
Matlock DE4 5JU   *Fax* (0629) 580475

A partly Elizabethan country manor high above the town in a peaceful setting, yet easily reached from the M1. It has heavy oak beams, thick stone walls and public rooms full of period furniture in the main building. The bedrooms are across a steep gravelled courtyard (not recommended for the disabled); many have four-poster beds and genuine antiques, as well as "books and magazines, complimentary sherry and chocolates – almost too many goodies. Super bathroom with whirlpool bath and bidet." Dinner is served either in the main dining room or in the smaller rooms upstairs (the former is considered the more relaxing); the atmosphere is formal. Views on the food continue to differ, from "most enjoyable and exquisitely served" to "at best a misunderstanding of *nouvelle cuisine*, the chef seeming to believe that presentation was more important than content. The desserts were particularly out of control." But there's "a very good wine list with a whole page of half-bottles". On the staff, too, there is dissent: "some a bit frosty"; "attentive, friendly and courteous" are two views. But there is unanimity about the accommodation: "excellent, almost perfect". (*P Honney*) One correspondent, however, found the food unexceptional, and conversation in the sitting room difficult because of the close proximity of others; and another reader called the atmosphere "less than sympathetic". More reports please.

Open All year.

Rooms 11 double – all with bath and shower (5 have whirlpool bath), telephone, radio, TV, tea-making facilities, mini-bar. All rooms round courtyard.

Facilities Lounge, 2 dining rooms; conference/functions facilities. 4½-acre grounds with tennis; clay-pigeon shooting. Fishing, golf nearby.

Location W of M1, exit 28. 1 m off A615; turn S at Tansley.

Restrictions Not suitable for &. No children under 10. No dogs.

Credit cards All major cards accepted.

Terms [1990 rates] B&B (continental): single £59–£75, double £78–£120. Set lunch £12.50; full alc dinner £25. Hideaway breaks in low season.

Service/tipping: "No service charge. Tipping is discretionary and not expected; distributed to all staff at end of month."

MAWNAN SMITH Cornwall   Map 1

Meudon Hotel   *Tel* Falmouth (0326) 250541
Nr Falmouth TR11 5HT   *Fax* (0326) 250543
                                              Telex 45478

An old Cornish mansion: a mellow stone building with massive granite pillars and mullioned windows on to which has been grafted a modern bedroom wing. Its chief glories are its location and its garden. Its location is 200 acres of protected Cornish coastline between the Fal and Helford rivers, at the head of a lovely valley leading down to its own private beach. Its garden – eight and a half acres of sub-tropical, rare flowering shrubs and plants – was laid out in the 18th century by Capability Brown, and is still carefully maintained. The hotel has been run for many years by Harry Pilgrim and his family and offers old-fashioned service – beds turned down at night, shoes cleaned, early morning tea brought to the room (though there are tea-making facilities for those who prefer them) – of a kind which has long since disappeared from many pricier establishments. After an absence of a few years the hotel was readmitted to the Guide last year and, with one exception, reports have continued to be favourable, like this one: "Good-size bedrooms, nicely furnished, with ample space to stow luggage; lounge and bar comfortable and elegant, the dining room incorporates a large and airy conservatory and provides a delightful garden-like setting for the excellent meals served by a pleasant and professional staff." The five-course dinner menu changes daily, with the emphasis on traditional dishes. (*HM Schottlaender, Roy and Mary Bromell*) Poor insulation between some rooms was a complaint in the past; Harry Pilgrim tells us that this is now more or less remedied; "and" (answering a criticism last year) "all our bread is from our excellent local baker, it is *not* pre-sliced". This year's niggle is one we have heard before: "There are always two or three items on the menu for which a large supplement has to be paid." More reports please.

Open Feb–Dec.

Rooms 4 suites, 24 double, 4 single – all with bath, shower, telephone, radio, TV, tea-making facilities. 18 on ground floor.

Facilities 3 lounges, bar, sun loggia, restaurant; laundry, hairdressing salon. 8½-acre grounds leading to private beach. Free golf at Falmouth Golf Club.

Location 4 m S of Falmouth. From Truro take A39 for 7 m, follow signs for Mabe and Mawnan Smith. Bear left at *Red Lion*. Meudon is on right after 1 m.

Restrictions No children under 5. Dogs by arrangement.

Credit cards Access, Diners, Visa.

Terms [1990 rates] B&B (English) £50–£70; dinner, B&B £60–£85. Set lunch £12.50, dinner £22.50; full alc £33. Reductions for long stays. 3-day spring and autumn breaks. Reduced rates for children; high teas.
Service/tipping: "No service charge; guests are not made to feel obliged to tip. Anything left is distributed evenly among all staff."

MIDDLECOMBE Somerset   Map 2

Periton Park Hotel   *Tel* Minehead (0643) 706885
Middlecombe   *Fax* (0643) 702698
Nr Minehead TA24 8SW   *Telex* 42513

Victorian country house, with large, attractive, comfortable lounge and original Victorian billiard room with full-size table. In "wonderfully quiet and peaceful" setting in 30-acre grounds just outside Minehead, on edge of Exmoor National Park. Recommended for "attentive, friendly, but not overbearing owners" Ian and Christine Dodd, spacious bedrooms and "excellent modern cooking" by Clive Arthur, though some readers would welcome a few simpler dishes as well. Breakfast, served in the bedroom, "not very satisfactory if you don't eat a cooked one", and "though the tariff says service is at guests' discretion, 10% was added to our bill". 7 rooms, all with bath and/or shower. B&B £40–£55. Set dinner £17.50. Was in Guide under previous owners. More reports please.

MIDDLETON-IN-TEESDALE County Durham   Map 4

The Teesdale Hotel   *Tel* Teesdale (0833) 40264
Middleton-in-Teesdale
Nr Barnard Castle DL12 0QG

A modernised Grade II listed coaching inn, family run, in the market square of a village in the heart of the High Pennines. Comfortable public rooms; bedrooms (best ones in front) recently refurbished. Pretty dining room serving good traditional food; high standard of service. 13 bedrooms, 10 with private facilities. Also 4 self-catering cottages. Dinner, B&B double £83.50. Set dinner £14.25. Recent nomination. More reports please.

MINCHINHAMPTON Gloucestershire   Map 2

Burleigh Court Hotel   *Tel* Brimscombe (0453) 883804
Minchinhampton, Nr Stroud   *Fax* (0453) 886870
GL5 2PF

This 18th-century Pevsner-listed Cotswold house, owned and run by the Benson family, stands in a specially attractive five-acre garden designed by Clough Williams-Ellis on an extremely steep hillside; from the front there are magnificent views across the Stroud valley. The interior is "pleasant and comfortable, rather than stylish, and very English"; "public rooms bright, clean and tidy, comfortable chairs, brightly burning fires, cheery staff". Dinners, served in the light dining room with French windows overlooking the grounds, offer "very good choice on the set menu", with "standard English hotel dishes offered alongside classic French provincial, modern British and vegetarian, as well as a 'health menu'". They are generally considered "excellent, with fresh and plentiful vegetables", though one reader found some dishes a little heavy on the sauces. Debate continues about the "much-advertised dessert trolley" – "exquisite," says one reader, "good, but not *that* brilliant," says another. Breakfasts are praised. Two readers this year report the friendly welcome accorded to small children. The bedrooms are all different, and while some are described to us as "attractively decorated and spacious", "impeccable", and "charming", we still get the odd complaint of a "substandard room, not very clean". But this is generally forgiven, and last year's verdict still holds good: "Not for those in search of a luxury weekend with luggage-toting porters and 24-hour room service, but highly recommended for a restful and good-natured weekend." (*Mr and Mrs Gordon Turner, Brenda J Kelly; also Patricia Higgins, Helen and Charles Priday, and others*)

Open All year except 24 Dec–4 Jan.
Rooms 1 suite, 16 double – all with bath and/or shower, telephone, radio, TV, tea-making facilities, baby-listening. 6 ground-floor rooms in stable block adjoining main building.
Facilities 2 lounges, bar lounge, restaurant; private dining/conference room. 5-acre grounds with terrace, heated Victorian plunge pool, putting green. Golf, riding nearby.
Location ½ m S of A419 at Brimscombe; follow signs for Minchinhampton and *Burleigh Court.*
Restrictions No smoking in dining room. No dogs.
Credit cards All major cards accepted.
Terms [1990 rates] B&B (English): single occupancy £54–£59, double £70–£80. Alc lunch £14 (bar lunches available Mon–Fri), dinner £21; on Sun set lunch £10.50; buffet supper from £10.95. 1-night bookings sometimes refused. Reduced rates for children sharing parents' room; special meals.
Service/tipping: "Tips not expected. There is, however, a box and money given is shared between the staff."

MITHIAN Cornwall   Map 1

Rose-in-Vale Country   **BUDGET**   *Tel* St Agnes (087 255) 2202
House Hotel
Mithian, St Agnes TR5 0QD

Small Georgian manor house with modern additions in peaceful setting in a wooded valley. 11-acre grounds with gardens, swimming pool, woodland, pasture, stream; sandy beach 2 m. Recommended for friendly proprietors and staff, welcoming attitude to children, good cooking using local ingredients (table d'hôte and à la carte menus; bar meals and packed lunches). Open Mar–Oct inclusive. 17 rooms all with bath and/or shower. Dinner, B&B (English) double £59.90. New nomination. More reports please.

MORETON-IN-MARSH Gloucestershire   Map 2

Manor House Hotel   *Tel* Moreton-in-Marsh
Moreton-in-Marsh GL56 0LJ   (0608) 50501
                                                    Fax (0608) 51481
                                                    Telex 837151

Mellow Cotswold manor of varying dates, popular with weekenders; some rooms traditional, and said to be in need of modernising, while modern ones in new block are "on the small side". Recommended by one regular visitor "with a soft spot for it", for warmth and comfort, excellent service; there are porters ("an endangered species these days") and beds are turned down at night. "Lovely" indoor swimming pool, sauna, spa bath; food "improved beyond recognition – good, plain cooking with excellent raw materials, good choice and lots of fish each day". Tranquil 2-acre garden with al fresco meals in fine weather, tennis. 38 rooms, all with bath or shower. B&B double £63–£70. Set dinner £18.50. New nomination. More reports please.

MORSTON Norfolk   **Map 3**

Morston Hall   *Tel* Cley (0263) 741041
Morston, Holt NR25 7AA   *Fax* (0263) 741034

Dennis and Jill Heaton's Georgian house, recently opened as a small hotel, quietly set in a village west of Blakeney, in "delightful" wooded garden. Warmly recommended for friendly welcome, agreeable atmosphere and comfort. Attractive, thoughtfully equipped bedrooms. Good dinners, using fresh produce, generally served communally. Open Jan–Nov. Restaurant closed Thurs. 4 rooms, all with bath and shower. Dinner, B&B £40–£56. New nomination. More reports please.

MOULSFORD-ON-THAMES Oxfordshire   **Map 2**

The Beetle and Wedge Hotel   *Tel* Cholsey (0491) 651381
Moulsford-on-Thames OX10 9JF

An old hotel on an attractive stretch of the Thames, with a riverside terrace, which made its Guide debut last year, the *Beetle and Wedge* is celebrated in *Three Men in a Boat* and HG Wells's *Mr Polly*. It was bought in 1988 by Richard and Kate Smith of the *Royal Oak*, Yattendon (q.v.); they divide their time between the two, and are continuing to make improvements. In summer it does a busy bar trade and can be crowded at times. The restaurant, overlooking the river, with polished mahogany tables "sparkling with candles, fresh flowers and bowls of fruit", serves unpretentious food, with set price and à la carte menus changing every day. Vegetables are plentiful and good; desserts, particularly hot ones, are praised, but the cooking is said to be heavy on cream. Most of the restaurant dishes are also available as bar food. Bedrooms are plain but well appointed, with comfortable beds, though a recent visitor noted a chest of drawers "with half the pulls missing"; baths are mostly small. Breakfasts are "first rate", with fresh orange juice, fresh fruit, warm rolls and the choice of hot dishes. Service may be shambolic at times. A reporter in spring 1990 found the decor of the public rooms somewhat dark; another visitor complained of poor housekeeping. More reports please.

Open All year.
Rooms 9 double, 4 single – all with bath and/or shower, telephone, radio, TV, tea-making facilities; baby-listening on request.
Facilities Lounge, 2 bars, 2 restaurants; conference facilities. ⅓-acre grounds. Boating, fishing.
Location On river, on edge of village 8 m NW of Reading.

Restrictions Not suitable for &. Dogs by arrangement, not in restaurant.
Credit cards Access, Amex, Visa.
Terms B&B (English): single from £70, double from £80. Bar meals. Set lunch/dinner £20–£25; full alc £20. Weekend breaks. Reduced rates for children sharing parents' room; special meals on request.
Service/tipping: "No service charge. We leave tips to guests' discretion. They are distributed evenly among staff after deduction of tax."

MULLION Cornwall   Map 1

Polurrian Hotel   *Tel* Mullion (0326) 240421
Mullion TR12 7EN   *Fax* (0326) 240083

"I spent holidays with my parents here when I was young, and was not disappointed when I returned recently. It retains the same happy and informal atmosphere. All the communal rooms are welcoming to all ages. During the day the lounge is the heart of the hotel, with parents and children in and out in swimming gear, surfboards under arm, bags and baggage trailing behind. Hotel visitors with young children often dread suppertime; here high tea is served in the small dining room between 5.30 and 6.30, and there is a daily choice of fresh foods as well as the ubiquitous hamburgers and sausages. In the evening the place is transformed. The lounge is filled with chinking glasses, the dining room is gently lit. Everyone dresses for dinner, ties for the men, elegance for the women. Teenagers, too, are catered for – the sports complex is open in the evening, and there is a room for them with electronic games, pool table and music centre."

The *Polurrian* is one of the few hotels we know that is really welcoming to and geared for children as well as their parents, with many facilities, both indoors and out (see below), for their entertainment. It is in a stunning position on cliffs on the Lizard Peninsula, overlooking Polurrian Cove. The National Trust owns most of the surrounding land and there are marvellous walks in both directions; even in August it is relatively quiet. There are lovely views over Mounts Bay towards Land's End. Bedrooms are mostly quite simply furnished but they are comfortable, and for regulars what counts most is "the friendliness of the staff plus Robert Francis's imaginative vision and ability to concern himself with every detail of the running of this family hotel". The food is generally liked – "of a good standard, with fresh fish predominating". (*Sue Payne, Gwen and Peter Andrews; also Anthony S Bowell*)

Note Mr Francis last year opened the only hotel permitted on St Martin's in the Scillies; it has its first Guide entry this year, and wins a César.

Open Easter–Dec.
Rooms 4 suites, 33 double, 3 single – all with bath, shower, telephone, radio, TV, baby-listening, 24-hour room service. Some ground-floor rooms. Also self-catering apartments and bungalows.
Facilities 4 lounges (1 non-smoking), 4 bars, 2 restaurants; toddlers' playroom, laundry facilities. 12-acre grounds with outdoor swimming pool, tennis, croquet, toddlers' playground; Indoor Leisure Club with swimming pool, squash, sauna, solarium, snooker room, teenage centre (small charges made for some facilities). Beach at cliff bottom. Windsurfing, golf nearby.
Location ¼ m from Mullion village; go towards harbour, pass cricket field on left; turn for hotel is on right.
Restriction No dogs in public rooms; must be on lead in grounds (£4 a day plus £1 for meals).

Credit cards All major cards accepted.
Terms [1990 rates] (Service at guests' discretion) B&B £33–£71.50; dinner, B&B £47–£78. Set dinner £14.50; full alc £12–£15. Children under 6 free of charge in parents' room.

MUNGRISDALE Cumbria   Map 4

The Mill Hotel   `BUDGET`   *Tel* Threlkeld (076 87) 79659
Mungrisdale, Penrith CA11 0XR

Mungrisdale is only a dozen miles from the Penrith exit of the M6, but well away from the tourist pack, and at the foot of the fells. *The Mill*, a simple but civilised cottage dating from the 17th century, has been owned and run by Richard and Eleanor Quinlan for the last eight years. It has a lovely setting in two acres of grounds with a millrace, waterfall and trout stream, and offers attractive accommodation, warmth, friendly service and imaginative cooking using fresh local produce; bread is baked daily. Dinner is a set menu with some choice, served at 7 pm; there is a small, carefully selected wine list. Guests, many of them regulars, continue to praise the relaxed atmosphere, the "cosy, well-equipped bedrooms, with *fresh* flowers", the "personal, attentive but unobtrusive service, and carefully balanced home-cooking of a high standard. The owners work hard to give their guests pleasure. The furnishings are not lush; the style suits the surroundings and atmosphere." This is not a hotel for misanthropes; public rooms are small, and can be crowded at busy times – "old-fashioned conversation after dinner with fellow guests" is one of the pleasures here. (*PE Carter, Mrs JE Hart; also J Mandelstam, and others*) *Note* Not to be confused with a nearby pub with rooms, *The Mill Inn* at Mungrisdale, though this might be a useful standby if *The Mill* is full.

Open Feb–Nov.
Rooms 9 double – 5 with bath and/or shower, all with tea-making facilities; 5 with TV; radio on request.
Facilities Lounge, TV lounge, sun lounge, dining room; games room; drying room. 2-acre grounds with millrace, waterfall and trout stream. Ullswater 5 m with fishing, sailing etc; hang-gliding, golf nearby.
Location 2 m N of A66. Leave M6 at Penrith (exit 40); turn off midway between Penrith and Keswick.
Restrictions Not suitable for &. No smoking in restaurant. Dogs at owners' discretion, not in public rooms.
Credit cards None accepted.
Terms B&B: single £29.50–£34, double £44–£59; dinner, B&B: single £35.50–£45, double £61–£79. Set dinner £14.50. Weekly rates. Reduced rates for children sharing parents' room; special meals.
Service/tipping: "No service charge. Tipping not required or looked for."

NEW MILTON Hampshire   Map 2

Chewton Glen Hotel   *Tel* Highcliffe (0425) 275341
Christchurch Road   *Fax* (0425) 272310
New Milton BH25 6QS   *Telex* 41456

Once the home of the writer, Captain Marryat, author of *The Children of the New Forest*, for whom its restaurant is named, *Chewton Glen* is a sumptuous country hotel with an international clientele on the southern fringe of the New Forest. It has long been one of the most expensive country house hotels in Britain. Decor is luxurious, with antiques and fine fabrics as well as modern comforts. The hotel has huge grounds with gardens, walking and jogging trails, a nine-hole golf course, swimming pool, tennis, croquet; in 1990 a health club with indoor swimming pool, saunas, gymnasium and hairdressing salon was opened, as well as 12 new bedrooms; two indoor tennis courts are under construction. The hotel has been run for 24 years by Martin Skan with an unusually large staff. Food, "modern French", under Pierre Chevillard, has earned the restaurant a *Michelin* rosette. There is a vegetarian menu.

This year, as last, *Chewton Glen* has a mixed bag of reports from readers. There are the lyrical: "Absolutely divine"; "Enchanting welcome from reception"; "Faultless. Worth every penny"; "Restaurant service consistently good, staff training must be terrific; they manage to retain an individual note in spite of being so many (and so many guests). Food sophisticated and occasionally brilliant." (*Rex and Pat Couch, JS Rutter, Dr CS Shaw, CKK*) But other reports indicate that the consistently flawless performance to be expected of the prices charged is not always delivered. The restaurant is criticised by readers who have had disappointing food and slow service; there are again reports of poor housekeeping. One reader found that the final bill "was about four times the room rate because nothing was included in the price", and a couple who had made a booking for July only discovered afterwards that they should have been given a 10 percent discount for a three-night stay. "Eventually we got a refund, but this is hardly the sign of an efficient hotel." More reports please.

Open All year.
Rooms 13 suites, 49 double – all with bath, shower, telephone, radio, TV. 1 suite in coach house. 6 ground-floor rooms.
Facilities Lounge, sun lounge, tearoom, bar, restaurant, 5 conference/banqueting rooms; pianist in lounge most evenings, snooker room; fitness centre with indoor swimming pool, gymnasium, hairdressing salon. 70-acre grounds with lake, tennis, croquet lawn, putting, jogging course, heated swimming pool, helipad. 2–3 m walk through grounds to shingle beach; fishing, riding, sailing, golf nearby; chauffeur service.
Location Do not follow New Milton signs. From A35, take turning to Walkford and Highcliffe; go through Walkford, then left down Chewton Farm road. Entrance on right.
Restrictions Only restaurant suitable for &. No children under 7. No dogs; kennel facilities nearby.
Credit cards All major cards accepted.
Terms Rooms (no single rate): double from £140, suite from £290. Breakfast: continental £9, English £13. Set lunch £22, dinner £42; full alc from £47. Off-season rates 1 Nov–31 Mar; Christmas and Easter 4-day packages. 1-night bookings usually refused for Sat.
Service/tipping: "Our prices are fully inclusive; all our guests are made aware of this."

NORTH HUISH Devon   **Map 1**

Brookdale House   *Tel* Gara Bridge (054 882) 402
North Huish
South Brent TQ10 9NR

Charles and Carol Trevor-Roper's Victorian Gothic rectory of "irreproachably faded gentility" at the head of a wooded valley (floodlit after dark) is Grade II listed, with fine moulded ceilings and marble fireplaces. Though not far from the Plymouth to Exeter road (A38), *Brookdale House* is in a secluded situation, in large wooded grounds with a waterfall. The bedrooms, sympathetically converted, vary considerably, and are priced according to size and position. Some are "large, well proportioned, thoughtfully equipped, with *en suite* bathroom positively stuffed with goodies", and even the smaller ones meet with almost unqualified approval. The dining room, "repro-Regency with extravagant displays of real and artificial flowers" is in the hands of Terry Rich who trained at *Gravetye Manor* (q.v.), *Paris House* and *Le Gavroche*. He provides "very good food, varied and imaginative, in a light style, with much emphasis on the organic nature of the ingredients"; there's plenty of choice on the frequently changing set-price dinner menu, and an "outstandingly interesting wine list". The rates include a generous English breakfast. (*Richard D Creed, PA Marron, and others*) Mr Trevor-Roper writes: "We offer a friendly yet professional service; we do have some quirks – creaky floorboards, antiquated plumbing and a slightly faded decor – but the lack of glossy magazine perfection adds to our guests' ability to relax." Regarding the "raffish music" emanating from his office, which has been commented on in the past, he says, "My much maligned 25-year-old record player has suffered a terminal breakdown. However, I reassure you and your readers that it will soon be replaced and normal service resumed."

Open All year except 3 weeks in Jan.
Rooms 8 double – all with bath, telephone, radio, TV, tea-making facilities. 2 (cheaper) rooms in cottage 25 yds from main building.
Facilities Lounge, bar, dining room. 4½-acre grounds with garden, stream, waterfall. Dartmoor 10 mins' drive, beaches 15 mins.
Location 7 m SW of Totnes. Off A38 take Avonwick, South Brent exit. In Avonwick turn right opposite *Avon Inn*, then first left to North Huish. Go up lane to top of hill, turn right, signposted *Brookdale House*; at bottom of hill turn right, hotel is first on left.
Restrictions Not suitable for &. No smoking in dining room. No children under 10. No dogs.
Credit cards Access, Visa.
Terms B&B (English): single occupancy £70, double £75–£95; dinner, B&B £60–£87.50 per person. Set dinner £25. Bar lunches. Christmas, New Year and winter breaks. 1-night bookings sometimes refused at busy weekends.
Service/tipping: "No service charge added to bills, but if tips are offered they are not refused. We assume our customers are intelligent enough to decide whether to leave tips for staff. If they have made this decision it would be churlish to refuse."

NUNNINGTON North Yorkshire   Map 4

Ryedale Lodge   *Tel* Nunnington (043 95) 246
Nunnington
Nr Helmsley, York YO6 5XB

Once Nunnington railway station, *Ryedale Lodge* is now a welcoming hotel – or restaurant-with-rooms – run by Jon and Janet Laird. The setting is peaceful, with no other houses visible across the rolling farmland; there is an agreeable half-mile walk along the defunct railway track to the river Rye. Bedrooms are "all different, comfortable and nicely decorated", with fresh fruit, sweets, television and good bathrooms, though not a great deal of storage space for luggage. The dining room, with conservatory extension, does a busy non-resident trade and the cooking is mostly praised this year, though a slight problem for residents could be that the menu does not change often "and, for example, a dessert that on one night was delicious was a bit dried out at the next meal". A few niggles: "'Baby-listening' consisted of the owner listening at the bottom of the stairs." "Bedroom not all that well maintained." "Service, particularly at breakfast, is leisurely, which might irritate those in a hurry." More reports please.

Open All year except Jan. Restaurant closed for lunch.
Rooms 1 suite, 6 double – all with bath (1 also has shower), telephone, radio, TV, tea-making facilities.
Facilities Lounges with bar service, restaurant, conservatory. 4-acre grounds. River Rye 10 mins' walk; trout fishing.
Location 1 m due W of Nunnington towards Oswaldkirk. Pass Nunnington Hall on left; after 400 yds turn right at crossroads. Pass church on right; hotel is 1 m further on right.
Restrictions No smoking in the dining room. No dogs.
Credit cards Access, Visa.
Terms [1990 rates] B&B (English) £32.50–£46.75; dinner, B&B £54–£70.25. Set dinner £23.50; full alc £30. 2-day breaks; weekly rates. Christmas and New Year packages. Reduced rates and special meals for children.
Service/tipping: "No service charge. Tips at guests' discretion, shared equally between all staff."

OTLEY Suffolk   Map 3

Otley House `BUDGET`   *Tel* Helmingham (0473) 890253
Otley, Ipswich IP6 9NR

"Your high praise justified in every respect." "Exactly as described in the guide. We enjoyed our three-day stay very much." (*RW Baldwin, MW Atkinson*) *Otley House*, owned and run by Mike Hilton and his Danish wife Lise, belongs to the Wolsey Lodge group of guest-taking private houses. It is a "fine, plain, square country house" in rural Suffolk, Grade II listed, with a Grade I staircase, in three acres of mature peaceful grounds with a small lake. Tea is served in the billiard room – there is an "excellent" billiard table – and guests gather for coffee and conversation in a Regency drawing room after dinner. The four-course dinners, taken communally with silver and crystal on the tables, are "delicious, varied, and well presented and served". There is no choice of menu; the owners like to be warned in advance of special diets or preferences; and Mrs Hilton is delighted to cook Scandinavian dishes for those who ask. The large light bedrooms, furnished with antiques, are "comfortable and sparkling clean with small extras such as pot-pourri, tissues, and a hair-drier. Regarding last year's niggle, that bedrooms can be on the cold side in winter, Mrs Hilton writes: "We have put an extra radiator in our one 'chilly' bedroom and now guests complain it is too warm! We are not open in the colder part of the year, but we do run the central heating full time, with individually controlled thermostats."

Open 1 Mar–31 Oct. Dining room closed for lunch and on Sun.
Rooms 4 double – all with bath (3 also with shower), radio, TV.
Facilities Hall, drawing room, TV/billiard room, dining room; tea terrace. 3-acre grounds with small lake, croquet. Golf, fishing, riding nearby.
Location In Otley village, 7 miles N of Ipswich, on B1079; opposite small road to Swilland.

Restrictions Not suitable for ♿. Smoking in billiard room only. No children under 12. No dogs.
Credit cards None accepted.
Terms B&B (English): single occupancy £32–£34, double £40–£46. Set dinner £14; vegetarian meals by arrangement. 1-night bookings sometimes refused for Sat.
Service/tipping: "Service included; any tips are given to the staff to share."

OXFORD Oxfordshire   Map 2

Bath Place Hotel   *Tel* Oxford (0865) 791812
4 and 5 Bath Place OX1 3SU   *Fax* (0865) 791834

Restaurant-with-rooms, a tasteful renovation of a group of 17th-century cottages with narrow staircases, sloping floors, exposed beams and lots of character, in a small alleyway off Holywell Street; no vehicle access, some reserved parking places quite close by – reserve in advance. Inspectors in 1990 liked the decor and some of the cooking – "good ingredients, main course of Michelin rosette standard" – but found bedroom and restaurant at breakfast-time cold, service pleasant but amateurish, and prices high for what is offered, "but most of the ingredients for a good hotel are there". 8 double rooms, 5 with bath, 3 with shower, with breakfast £80–£95 [1990]. Set lunch £12–£15, dinner £20–£25. More reports please.

Cotswold House   `BUDGET`   *Tel* Oxford (0865) 310558
363 Banbury Road
Oxford OX2 7PL

Jim and Anne O'Kane's no-smoking B&B had its first Guide entry last year and two correspondents write to confirm: "Immaculate and attractive bedroom, warm and well lit. Adequate in size, with excellent shower room. Thoughtful touches such as wine glasses, electric kettle, refrigerator. The owners are delightful and most welcoming. Breakfast was excellent, with fresh fruit on the table." "Would there were something similar in Cambridge!" (*PM Spence, Jean Carolin*) *Cotswold House* has a small garden; it is two miles north of the city centre, with frequent buses. Vegetarian breakfasts available; plenty of pubs and restaurants nearby.

Open All year except Christmas.
Rooms 5 double, 2 single – all with shower, TV, tea-making facilities.
Facilities Small lounge, dining room. Small garden.
Location Just off ring road on Oxford side of A423. Parking.
Restrictions Not suitable for ♿. No smoking. No dogs.
Credit cards None accepted.
Terms B&B: single £20–£25, double £40–£47. Reduced rates for children sharing parents' room. (No restaurant.)

```
************************************************************
*                                                          *
*  Perennial Plaint As a priest, I must perforce occupy a single room when  *
*  on holiday. Having paid a hefty single-room supplement, why should I     *
*  be expected to occupy a room little bigger than a broom cupboard for the *
*  privilege?                                               *
*                                                          *
************************************************************
```

PAULERSPURY Northamptonshire   Map 3

Vine House Hotel   *Tel* Paulerspury (032 733) 267
and Restaurant
Paulerspury
Nr Towcester NN12 7NA

*Karen and Christine Snowdon's restaurant with 6 compact, well-maintained
bedrooms in adjoining residence, in small village just off A5, is recommended
for restful atmosphere, excellent "modern English" cooking by Jonathan
Stanbury, light and airy decor and "delicious, ample breakfasts". 1-acre garden.
Closed 2 weeks end Mar, and Sun to non-residents. 5 double rooms, 1 single –
1 with bath and shower, 5 with shower. B&B double £65. Set lunch/dinner £16
and £23. New nomination. More reports please.*

PENCRAIG Hereford and Worcester   Map 2

Pencraig Court Hotel   **BUDGET**   *Tel* Ross-on-Wye (098 984) 306
Pencraig, Nr Ross-on-Wye
HR9 6HR

This unassuming, friendly Georgian country house, comfortably modernised, entered the Guide last year, nominated by a regular correspondent:
"The site is lovely, overlooking the Wye just downstream from Ross – a
pleasant sloping garden with benches and tables and fine copper beeches.
The room we had was one of the most comfortable we have ever enjoyed,
with a double and a single bed, sofa and two armchairs, more than
adequate hanging and drawer space, and well-equipped bathroom.
Breakfast was excellent, with a large selection of cereals and home-made
porridge. The owners, Mr and Mrs Sykes, are friendly and welcoming.
The hotel is on the A40, but our room overlooked the garden so it was
quiet." There are two pleasant sitting rooms and a comfortable dining
room. The menu offers English cooking, with some choice. (*Mrs RB
Richards*) More reports please.

Open Apr–Oct inclusive.
Rooms 2 suites, 7 double, 2 single – all with bath, TV.
Facilities 2 lounges, bar, restaurant. 4-acre grounds.
Location 3 m SW of Ross-on-Wye, on the A40.
Restrictions Not suitable for &. No dogs except guide dogs.
Credit cards All major cards accepted.
Terms [1990 rates] B&B (English) £18–£35; dinner, B&B £29–£46. Bar lunches, set
dinner £12.50. Special breaks. Reduced rates and special meals for children.
Service/tipping: "Our prices include tax and service. Gratuities not expected by our staff."

PENZANCE Cornwall   Map 1

The Abbey Hotel   *Tel* Penzance (0736) 66906
Abbey Street
Penzance TR18 4AR

🏵 *César award in 1985: Utterly acceptable mild eccentricity*

"Why is *The Abbey* my favourite of all the Guide hotels I have visited? The
answer is an indefinable something – atmosphere, style, call it what you

will. You say: 'Some people might not like the laid-back style'; it is not unknown for Mrs Cox to throw out people she feels don't fit in! It is *not* for everyone, but it is the only place I regularly visit where I look forward with such keen anticipation to sitting in the drawing room having tea, and to eating in the panelled dining room. I doubt that anyone would have mixed feelings; you fall in love with it, or it leaves you cold." "Our bedroom had a gas log-fire in the large marble fireplace, kilims on the floor, two huge, squidgy armchairs, fresh garden roses. Excellent food, starting at breakfast with good marmalade, crunchy toast, large dollops of butter unencumbered by wrappings, through to the sticky rich petits pots de chocolat at the end of dinner, not forgetting the good meat and fish, fresh veg, and fresh herbs on nearly everything. And not fussily *nouvelle*, I'm glad to say."

The Coxes 17th-century house is in one of the narrow streets that run down from the centre of Penzance towards the harbour. There are magnificent views across Penzance Bay from the front; rear rooms look out over an attractive walled garden. It is filled with flowers, magazines, books, curios, paintings and photographs. There are open fires in the public rooms. Bedrooms, some large, have patchwork quilts, floral canopies and sprigged wallpaper. (*Christopher Walls, Diana Ross; also Brian and Patricia Roberts, Nicholas Bratza, and others*) Most readers are enthusiastic about the food, though one comments: "It's OK, not great but better than most places in Cornwall", and one reader who had asked for a bath was given "a shower and loo in a built-in wardrobe – a bit small for comfort".

Open All year.
Rooms 1 2-bedroomed apartment, 6 double – 1 with bath and shower, 3 with bath, 3 with shower, all with TV, tea-making facilities. Apartment on first floor in adjoining building.
Facilities Drawing room, dining room. Small rear garden.
Location Take road for sea front; after 300 yds, just before bridge, turn right, after 10 yds turn left. Hotel is at top of slipway. Courtyard parking for 4 cars.
Restrictions Not suitable for &. No children under 5. No dogs in public rooms.
Credit cards Access, Amex, Visa.
Terms (No service charge) B&B (English): single £45–£55, double £65–£95; apartment £90–£110. Set dinner £18.50; full alc £21.50. Winter breaks Nov–Mar; 3-day Christmas package. Reduced rates for children sharing parents' room; special meals.

POOL-IN-WHARFEDALE West Yorkshire   Map 4

Pool Court Restaurant with Rooms
Pool-in-Wharfedale
Otley LS21 1EH

Tel Leeds (0532) 842288
Fax (0532) 843115

Michael Gill's restaurant-with-rooms is a fine Georgian mansion, though in a not particularly attractive setting as new houses and a busy trunk road impinge; but this does not deter the visitors, both first-timers and regulars, who write to praise its "splendid interior, attractively decorated throughout" and the "excellent French food" cooked by David Watson and served in the "elegant soft grey dining room, sparkling with candle-light and beautiful crystal". In addition to the main menu, four courses priced according to the main one, a no-choice three-course dinner is offered for £10–£12.50. Vegetarians are also catered for. There are no public rooms apart from the bar and the coffee lounge, which is used by diners in the evening. The six bedrooms are comfortable and equipped with a mass of extras – fresh flowers, a fridge with wines and soft drinks, a tray with fruit, dates, raisins and nuts, books, even a little safe behind a picture on the wall. "Excellent attention to detail; it is a pleasure to have a good-sized bathroom" – and beds are turned down at night, a rarity in many full-blown hotels these days. Staff are "courteous, efficient and friendly". The continental breakfasts are "generous and delicious". (*Nicholas Crawley, NM Tapley, John E Parsons*) One niggle: "Is it really necessary to have those silly computerised push-buttons to get into one's bedroom?" And one reader found the public rooms crowded at the weekend and the overall atmosphere "pretentious".

Open All year except 25 Dec–9 Jan, 2 weeks July/Aug. Closed Sun and Mon. Lunch served only to pre-arranged parties of 10 or more.
Rooms 5 double, 1 single – all with bath, shower, telephone, radio/alarm, TV, bar, fridge, wall-safe, double-glazing; baby-listening by prior arrangement.
Facilities Bar, coffee lounge, restaurant; private dining room. ½-acre grounds.
Location 3 m N of Leeds airport on A658. Equidistant (9 m) from Leeds, Bradford and Harrogate.
Restrictions Not really suitable for ๒. No dogs; kennel facilities available.
Credit cards All major cards accepted.
Terms B&B (continental): single from £70, double £95–£120. Set dinner (3 courses, no choice) £10–£12.50; main menu c. £29.50. Weekend rates. Cookery courses. 1-night bookings sometimes refused. Reduced rates and special meals for children by arrangement.
Service/tipping: "10% service charge added to bills for large private parties. Apart from that we feel that tipping is entirely up to the guest. We don't ask for or expect it, but if a guest wishes to give something it is gratefully received."

POOLE Dorset   **Map 2**

The Mansion House Hotel   *Tel* Poole (0202) 685666
Thames Street, Poole BH15 1JN   *Fax* (0202) 665709
                                                  Telex 41495 SELECT

A well-run hotel in a handsome Georgian townhouse in a quiet cul-de-sac near the old parish church and Poole's bustling quay. It has a grand sweeping staircase leading up from the hall to a comfortable and stylish residents' lounge and well-equipped bedrooms with many extras – books, magazines, sherry and so on. The panelled restaurant is also a fashionable dining club, with lower prices for members; hotel residents are automatically made temporary members. Chef Tony Parsons offers a long, traditional menu. Experiences of meals can be variable; the restaurant is often very busy. A recent view of dinner: "The service was effervescent, the cooking and the helpings copious; wine list somewhat higgledy-piggledy." Meals are also available in the grill bar, and there is a limited room service for meals. More reports please.

Open All year except 26 Dec–7 Jan.
Rooms 1 suite, 19 double, 9 single – all with bath, shower, telephone, radio, TV; baby-listening by telephone.
Facilities Lounge, bar, breakfast room, restaurant, grill bar; private dining room. Poole Quay 100 yds; fishing, boating, sailing.

Location Follow signs for Poole Quay. Thames St is off quay, between Fisheries Office and Maritime Museum – signposted to the parish church. 2 private carparks either side of hotel.
Restrictions Not suitable for &. Dogs at proprietors' discretion.
Credit cards All major cards accepted.
Terms (Excluding 10% service charge) B&B: single £69, double £91–£104, suite £137. Set lunch £12.50, dinner £17.50; full alc £25. Weekend rates. Reduced rates and special meals for children. *Service/tipping: "10% is added to bill and shared among all staff at end of month."*

PORT GAVERNE Cornwall   Map 1

Port Gaverne Hotel   *Tel* Bodmin (0208) 880244
Port Gaverne   *Fax* (0208) 880151
Nr Port Isaac PL29 3SQ

This unpretentious 17th-century coastal inn enjoys a splendid position in a sheltered cove in an isolated village not far from Port Isaac. Just a small road separates it from a safe bay with sand, shingle and rock; there are good walks along the coast. Some rooms are in an annexe and some in cottages which are also let on a self-catering basis. It has been run by Frederick Ross and his wife for over twenty years and "manages to combine the atmosphere of an ancient inn with that of a comfortable small hotel". It is welcoming to families, many of whom have been visiting it for years. They praise it for the "courteous reception, friendly and prompt service at all times", and the well-appointed bedrooms (even the singles) with "comfortable beds, plenty of hanging space and an air of generosity – boiling hot water at all times, and lots of extras in the bathroom". Dinner is "good value" with three courses, each with three or four choices. The English breakfast is generous and good. Don't expect five-star facilities. "Our aim," says Frederick Ross, "is to be the best of what we are, an elderly Cornish coastal inn, in a particularly beautiful and rugged location, providing pleasant, comfortable accommodation, well above average food and a happy, relaxing atmosphere." (*William Ritchie, Dr and Mrs B Fleshler*)

Open All year except 8 Jan–16 Feb.
Rooms 7 suites, 16 double, 3 single – 13 with bath and shower, 6 with bath, all with telephone, TV, baby-listening. 3 in annexe, 15 in 7 cottages which are also let on a self-catering basis.
Facilities Residents' lounge, TV lounge, 4 bars, dining room. Cottages have a garden courtyard, annexe has a garden.
Location Take B3314 from Delabole or Wadebridge, then B3267.
Restrictions Children under 7 who dine with parents served at 7 pm only. No dogs in dining room.
Credit cards All major cards accepted.
Terms B&B (English) £37–£41; dinner, B&B (min 2 nights) £44.50–£89. Snack lunches, bar suppers; alc dinner £17. Weekly rates; Christmas and New Year packages. Reduced rates and special meals for children.
Service/tipping: "Service charge now eliminated. Gratuities will be invested in a building society interest-bearing account and distributed to staff at Christmas and Easter."

> Important reminder: terms printed must be regarded as a rough guide only to the size of the bill to be expected at the end of your stay. For latest tariffs, check when booking.

PORTLOE Cornwall   Map 1

The Lugger Hotel   *Tel* Truro (0872) 501322
Portloe TR2 5RD   *Fax* (0872) 501691

Seaside hotel run for three generations by the Powell family, recently totally redecorated and refurnished. Recommended for lovely situation on water's edge, good food – traditional English, including very fresh fish; vegetarians catered for – smooth and efficient service. No children under 12. No dogs. 19 rooms (most spacious ones in annexe), all with bath and/or shower. Dinner, B&B £44–£49. Set lunch £8.50, dinner £13.50. Was in earlier edition of Guide; now renominated. More reports please.

POSTBRIDGE Devon   Map 1

Lydgate House Hotel   **BUDGET**   *Tel* Tavistock (0822) 88209
Postbridge
Yelverton PL20 6TJ

Small hotel in lovely setting in centre of Dartmoor; River Dart, with bathing and fishing, runs through its 37-acre grounds. Recommended for clean, bright, welcoming but not effusive atmosphere. Food, with very limited choice, "good, simple but unusual", using local produce and home-reared meat; vegetarian dishes offered. 9 rooms, 2 with bath, 3 with shower, all with TV. *B&B £20–£22. Set dinner £10.50. Was in 1989 Guide under previous owners. Warmly recommended for re-admission. More reports please.*

POUGHILL Cornwall   Map 1

Reeds   *Tel* Bude (0288) 352841
Poughill, Bude EX23 9ELL

❧ *César award in 1990: Most cosseting guest house*

"Delighted that Margaret Jackson has won a César; she deserves it for maintaining a consistently high standard in every department." "We think of *Reeds* not as a hotel, but rather as an elegant house where we go to stay with a charming, warm-hearted friend." Two regulars this year endorse Margaret Jackson's "oasis of relaxation for the weary traveller". *Reeds* is a turn-of-the-century house quietly situated in a large garden in a little village (its name is pronounced poffil) close to the dramatic north Cornish coast. The National Trust owns much of the coastline and there are many fine walks in the area. The house is large, attractive and spotless, in a lovely garden. Bedrooms are spacious and restful, decorated in soft pastel colours, with lots of storage space, hair-driers, shampoos, magazines, fruit, biscuits, and fresh milk in a little thermos for early morning tea. "Beds are extremely comfortable, and there are *proper*, i.e. enamelled cast-iron, baths." No bedroom television (but there is one downstairs). Dinner at 8 is in private-household dinner-party style, with elegant linen, silver and candles. There are no choices, but the menu is always displayed early in the day so that dissenters can ask for an alternative; and you are asked your culinary preferences on booking. (*Jean Willson, RE Carter; also Padi Howard, Ruth West, and others*) There are no hidden extras. Coffee or tea is available at any time for no charge. Visitors have complete freedom to use all the house.

Open All year Fri pm–Tues am. Closed Christmas.
Rooms 3 double – all with bath, shower, tea-making facilities; radio on request.
Facilities Drawing room, hall with bar facilities, TV room. 4-acre grounds. Sea 1 m – sandy beaches and coastal walks. Fishing, golf nearby.
Location Take Poughill Road from Bude. Turn left at Post Office towards Northcott Mount. *Reeds* is about 400 yds on left beyond garden centre.
Restrictions Not suitable for &. No smoking in dining room; smoking not encouraged in bedrooms. No children under 16. No pets.
Credit cards None accepted.
Terms B&B £32.50–£37.50. Light lunch (cheese and fruit) on request £3. Set dinner £19.50.
Service/tipping: "I am totally opposed to the idea of tipping and actively (and, I hope, politely) discourage it."

POWBURN Northumberland   Map 4

Breamish House Hotel   *Tel* Powburn (066 578) 266
Powburn, Alnwick NE66 4LL   *Fax* (066 578) 500

This unpretentious Georgian-style house, "furnished like a house, not a hotel", in a peaceful setting up a winding drive at the foot of the Cheviot hills, had an entry in earlier editions. Now, under new owners, Alan and Doreen Johnson, both fresh to the hotel trade, it is readmitted: "We have only the highest praise. A lovely room, very spacious, with nice little touches – bowl of sweets, fresh fruit, mineral water, fresh milk in a vacuum container." "Good British country food, with excellent ingredients." "Comfortable and relaxing. Cleanliness is absolute. Everything is done to ensure your comfort; staff are friendly and helpful." "We and our dog were welcomed and looked after with great attention to detail; many of the old members of staff are still there." (*F Brian Perring, Mrs VM Williamson, Rev and Mrs K Habershon, also Sydney Downs*) Not all bedrooms are large, however; one reader bemoaned the lack of local information; another disliked the muzak in the dining room, and a visitor who arrived late having been delayed by a bad storm was made to feel distinctly unwelcome. More reports please.

Open Feb–Dec.
Rooms 10 double, 1 single – all with bath and/or shower, telephone, radio, TV, tea-making facilities, baby-listening.
Facilities 2 drawing rooms, dining room. 5½-acre grounds with woodland and stream.
Location In centre of village on A697, 22 m N of Morpeth.
Restrictions Only restaurant suitable for &. No smoking in dining room. Limited facilities for very young children. Dogs by arrangement; not in public rooms.
Credit cards None accepted.
Terms Dinner, B&B £44–£65. Special rates for long stays. Off-season breaks.
Service/tipping: "We are against mandatory service charges. If guests insist on recognising exceptional service tips are distributed among all staff according to hours worked."

Always let a hotel know if you have to cancel a booking, whether you have paid a deposit or not. Hotels lose thousands of pounds and dollars from "no-shows".

RASKELF North Yorkshire   Map 4

Old Farmhouse Country   **BUDGET**   *Tel* Easingwold (0347) 21971
Hotel and Restaurant
Raskelf YO6 3LF

*18th-century farmhouse off A19 NW of York, conveniently situated for touring
in North Yorkshire. Run by the Frost family, and warmly recommended for
comfortable bedrooms, with good storage space and modern bathrooms, and for
particularly good home cooking – 4-course dinners with plenty of choice;
generous Yorkshire breakfasts. Emphasis on personal service rather than do-it-
yourself. Open Feb–22 Dec. 10 double rooms, 6 with bath, 4 with shower.
Dinner, B&B double £56–£68. New nomination. More reports please.*

RICHMOND North Yorkshire   Map 4

Howe Villa   **BUDGET**   *Tel* Richmond (0748) 850055
Whitcliffe Mill
Richmond DL10 4TJ

César award in 1989: Perfection in the guest house division

"An establishment with style, good taste, very pleasant, friendly
atmosphere, no rules and regulations. One is made to feel like an
honoured guest at a friend's home." "Our third visit, everything as good
as ever. Of all the smaller, personally run places in the Guide this is our
favourite. Not only is Anita Berry a delightful, welcoming hostess, she is
also a marvellous cook; the dining room has been enlarged and there is a
lovely feel of spaciousness throughout the house with its mainly white
walls and paintwork." "Bedrooms immaculate and well equipped,
including umbrella, bowl of fruit; wonderfully spacious bathroom. The
lounge where dinner is ordered is a delight, beautifully proportioned and
decorated, with attractive upholstery, lots of good magazines and a lovely
view of the river Swale. Breakfasts include a huge choice of cereals,
muesli, yoghurt etc, no less than fourteen preserves, and eggs done any
way you want, freshly cooked and delicious." "The atmosphere is rare
indeed. We normally shy away from 'house party' hotels, but our fellow
guests were interesting and friendly." Again readers write in warm
appreciation of this reasonably priced Georgian house with only four
bedrooms in a large garden, bounded by trees on one side and, on the
other, a glorious stretch of the river Swale. The approach to *Howe Villa* is
not particularly salubrious, but the house has large, elegantly proportioned rooms, and has been restored with taste and charm. The four-
course menu offers a choice of starters, desserts and cheeses, and a
substantial main course – "English cooking at its very best, beautifully
presented". There is small selection of wines. (*Moira Jarrett, Heather Kirk,
RI Johnson, Mrs D Williamson; also Sir Brian and Lady Rix, BN Turvey, and
many others*)

Open Mar–end Nov.
Rooms 4 double – all with bath and/or shower, radio, TV, tea-making facilities.
Facilities Large drawing room, dining room. ½-acre garden on river Swale.

Location ½ m from centre of Richmond – take A6108 signposted Leyburn and Reeth; at the ATS Tyre service station turn left, keep left, following signs to *Howe Villa*.
Restrictions Not suitable for severely ♿. No children under 12. No dogs.
Credit cards None accepted.
Terms Dinner, B&B £33–£38. Set dinner £15. Reduction for 3 days or more.
Service/tipping: "Guests do like to say thank you, perhaps with a small gift. I accept, enjoying the pleasure it gives them, but do not like service charges."

ROMALDKIRK Durham   Map 4

The Rose and Crown   *Tel* Teesdale (0833) 50213
Romaldkirk
Nr Barnard Castle DL12 9EB

This old inn on the village green of a picturesque Dales village, near High Force Waterfall and the rewarding Bowes Museum at Barnard Castle, and well situated for country sports, was taken over in 1989 by Christopher and Alison Davy whose *Black Swan* at Ravenstonedale had an entry in previous Guide editions. Since their arrival they have been busy renovating and redecorating the *Rose and Crown* which "is bigger, and more suited to their talents and standards". "There is still much to do, but the ground floor has been refurbished very tastefully; it is warm and welcoming, with obliging staff." The bedrooms, all with *en suite* bathrooms, are "well equipped and comfortable". Meals in the oak-panelled dining room are "as good as those the Davys served at Ravenstonedale"; "you need to do some energetic walking to work off the large portions". "The bar food is of a high standard." One reader reported a rather small duvet, and sloping oak beams in the private sitting room – "don't stand up too suddenly!" (*Gordon W Provis, Susan Philips, Mrs E Stewart, Stephanie Sowerby, and others*) More reports please.

Open All year except Christmas.
Rooms 2 suites, 8 double, 1 single – all with bath and/or shower, telephone, radio, TV, tea-making facilities, baby-listening. 5 courtyard rooms. 1 on ground floor.
Facilities Lounge, lounge bar, Crown Room for bar meals, restaurant. River Tees ½ m; reservoir fishing nearby.
Location On village green. Parking.
Restriction No dogs in restaurant.
Credit cards Access, Visa.
Terms B&B: single £45, double £55, suite £70. Set lunch £9, dinner £15. Winter breaks, midweek rates, New Year house parties. Reduced rates for children on application; special meals.
Service/tipping: "We make no service charge. The staff are well paid so tipping is not encouraged."

ROSTHWAITE Cumbria   Map 4

Hazel Bank Hotel   `BUDGET`   *Tel* Borrowdale (059 684) 248
Rosthwaite   *from mid-1990* (076 87) 77248
Nr Keswick CA12 5XB

"I have just returned from my 24th week's holiday at *Hazel Bank*," writes *Dennis Dent*, "and, if my mathematics are not at fault, I have enjoyed 144 wonderful evening meals, every one of which has seemed like a special occasion. It has never ceased to amaze me how John Nuttall, who does all the cooking, gets everything just right. And the atmosphere is wonderful. Nothing is impersonal. When all are gathered for dinner, and in the bar and lounge afterwards, it is like a house party. Although I stay there on my own I have never felt lonely or left out. The rooms enjoy fine views of the highest mountains in England; they are attractively decorated and impeccably maintained." Other visitors, too, have appreciated the "friendly and helpful staff", and the "very happy atmosphere" generated by Gwen and John Nuttall who have carefully restored and modernised their 125-year-old house while preserving its Victorian atmosphere. It is quietly situated in large, beautifully landscaped grounds; each bedroom is named for the Fell it dramatically overlooks. The dining room is light and airy; meals, served at set times, are wholesome and straightforward, with plenty of fresh vegetables; no choice except dessert. (*Dr Anne Szarewski, A Greasley; also Dr and Mrs Burcombe*) Many visitors to *Hazel Bank House* are returnees; it is generally booked up months ahead. The Nuttalls cater for a large proportion of walkers, ramblers, etc; there is a drying room, and packed lunches are provided.

Open Mid-Feb–mid-Dec.
Rooms 8 double, 1 single – 3 with bath, 5 with shower, 4 with TV, all with tea-making facilities. 2 ground-floor rooms.
Facilities Residents' lounge, bar lounge, dining room; drying room. 4-acre grounds. Derwentwater 4 m.
Location 7 m S of Keswick on B5289. Turn left up drive just before village.
Restrictions Not suitable for ė. No smoking in dining room. No children under 6. Dogs by prior arrangement only (80p); not in public rooms.
Credit cards None accepted.
Terms Dinner, B&B £30–£32. Weekly rates. Reduced rates for children sharing parents' room. 1-night bookings refused if requested far in advance.
Service/tipping: "Tipping is not expected; regulars know this but some people like to show their appreciation. Tips are distributed to all staff."

RYE East Sussex   Map 3

Jeake's House   `BUDGET`   *Tel* Rye (0797) 222828
Mermaid Street TN31 7ET   *Fax* (0797) 225758

"A beautiful house; we were made to feel most welcome on arrival. Atmosphere and interior decorations excellent and everything so clean! The view from our bedroom was outstanding. Breakfast in the old chapel was delicious. The other guests looked just as happy." *Jeake's House*, named after the Jeake family who built it – a later occupant was the American writer, Conrad Aiken – is a beautiful old listed building on one of Rye's cobbled streets and is now a very reasonably priced B&B owned by Francis and Jenny Hadfield. It has a Victorian parlour with upright piano, sheet music of the period and armchairs with antimacassars; there are shelves of old-fashioned books for guests to borrow. Bedrooms, some with brass or mahogany bedsteads, look over the old rooftops of Rye or face south across the marsh to the sea; most have private bath or shower. "One of the most comfortable beds I have ever slept in, with *proper* sheets; excellent bathroom, with lots of hot water. The whole house is charmingly arranged." Breakfast is served in the adjoining former Quaker meeting house, "a large, galleried, white-painted room with high windows and some good paintings; a welcoming fire, books, plants, small pieces of china, some very good; separate tables with white laundered linen and napkins". Parking is a slight problem, but there is a carpark at the end of the road. (*Heather Conolly, Claire Jacquier*) Vegetarian as well as traditional breakfasts are on offer; the Hadfields keep a stock of menus from local restaurants and help guests make dinner reservations.

Open All year.
Rooms 1 suite, 9 double, 1 single – 7 with bath, 2 with shower, all with radio, TV, tea-making facilities.
Facilities Sitting room, dining room. Payphone in hall. Beaches nearby.
Location In centre of Rye; carpark nearby.
Restrictions Not suitable for ⅍. No dogs in public rooms.
Credit cards Access, Visa.
Terms B&B: single £20, double £36–£48, suite £60. 1-night bookings sometimes refused for Sat in high season. Reductions for stays of 4 or more days. Reduced rates for children sharing parents' room. (No restaurant.)
Service/tipping: "We neither expect nor encourage tipping, but any gratuities are shared among staff."

The Old Vicarage **BUDGET**   *Tel* Rye (0797) 222119
Guest House
66 Church Square
Rye TN31 7HF

A B&B which featured for years in the Guide is warmly recommended for re-admission under new owners, Paul and Julia Masters: "I can't imagine a better location in Rye. This cosy pink vicarage near the church is approached along a footpath which leads between the church and a few cottages on either side. From the windows you can see the church tower (and hear the bell on the quarter hour, which I find very comforting). Beyond the church, in the distance, you can see the river which leads out to sea. If you put a head out of the window and look left you can see the rooftops of Rye, sloping gently downhill. The atmosphere is friendly and relaxing – and they even gave us a double room at single price to accommodate a third person in our party. The new owners have kept the standards high, and have gone about tackling the endless tasks of running a B&B with enthusiasm. We were given complimentary newspapers, a garage space for the car (which in Rye is an advantage), a map with crosses marking the best restaurants and pubs in town and an enormous breakfast." The guests' lounge and breakfast room overlook the small walled garden. Bedrooms, with Laura Ashley fabrics and wallpapers, have drinks tray, TV, hair-drier, magazines etc; four have private facilities. "The owners have the magic quality of appearing when needed and staying invisible the rest of the time." (*Andrena Woodhams, Gary Arbour*)
Note Not to be confused with *The Old Vicarage Hotel*, a small hotel in East Street.

Open All year except Christmas.
Rooms 1 suite, 4 double – 1 with bath, 3 with shower, all with radio, TV, tea-making facilities.
Facilities Lounge, dining room. Walled garden.
Location Through Lanogate Arch to High Street, first left East Street, left again to Church Square. Parking nearby.
Restrictions Not suitable for ⅍. No smoking in bedrooms. No children under 12. No dogs.
Credit cards None accepted.

Terms B&B (English) £17–£40. Winter breaks Nov–Mar. 1-night bookings sometimes refused for Sat Apr–Oct. (No restaurant.)
Service/tipping: "No service charge. No tips expected – we enjoy what we do."

ST ANNE'S-ON-SEA Lancashire   Map 4

The Dalmeny Hotel	*Tel* St Anne's (0253) 712236
19–33 South Promenade	*Fax* (0253) 724447
St Anne's-on-Sea FY8 1LX	

Run by the energetic and enterprising Webb family, this is one of the all too few seaside hotels recommendable for parents with young families. It is a cheerful, bustling establishment on the seafront, well endowed with sporting facilities, and offers plenty of entertainment in season (see below). There are three restaurants, "all to be recommended": *The Barbecue*, offering an à la carte menu which changes daily, *The Carvery*, open for breakfasts (substantial English) and lunch (joints and salads), and *C'est La Vie*, serving lunch and dinner (adults only in the evening), where food is French in style, "of a very high standard, cooked to perfection and beautifully presented in delightful surroundings; relaxed and friendly atmosphere, professional staff". There is also the *Buttery Bar* for sandwiches, salads, coffees and teas. The Webbs, who have owned the hotel since 1945, claim that the *Dalmeny* is unique in its flexible approach to the needs of families: their tariff is for rooms only so that families can choose their own "package" from any of the restaurants or use the small kitchens in the suites specially designed for families with babies or small children. Visitors appreciate the facilities, the good value for money and the efficient and friendly staff at the *Dalmeny*, but point out that rooms vary considerably in size, and that noise can be a problem, from traffic, ballrooms and kitchen. The hotel also caters for conferences and meetings. More reports please.

Open All year except 24–26 Dec.
Rooms 20 suites, 84 double and family – all with bath (7 also have shower), telephone, radio, TV, tea-making facilities, baby-listening; some with balcony; suites have kitchenette. 6 ground-floor rooms.
Facilities Lifts, ramp. Lounge bar, 2 lounges, TV room, ballroom with bar, Buttery Bar, 3 restaurants; indoor heated swimming pool, solarium, squash court, games room; organised crèche and family entertainments in holiday periods, live music, discos; children's outdoor play area. 4 championship golf courses nearby.
Location On seafront, 200 yds S of pier; 300 yds from town centre. Carparks and garages.
Restriction No smoking in *C'est la Vie* restaurant and 1 lounge. No dogs.
Credit cards Access, Visa.
Terms (Service at guests' discretion) [1990 rates] Rooms: single occupancy £25–£50, double £36–£58, suite £43–£86. Breakfast £4.75 (£2 for children). Light lunch from £3.20, set lunch £11.50, dinner £9.75 and £18.50; full alc (*Barbecue*) £16.75. Special breaks; weekly rates. 1-night bookings refused in high season. Reduced rates and special menus for children.

```
*****************************************************
*                                                   *
*  Traveller's tale The room was mock antique. The bed looked as though  *
*  Garibaldi's mother had honeymooned in it. In fact, like all the rest of the  *
*  furniture, it was as antique as a Big Mac.       *
*                                                   *
*****************************************************
```

ST AUSTELL Cornwall   Map 1

Boscundle Manor   *Tel* Par (072 681) 3557
Tregrehan   *Fax* (072 681) 4997
St Austell PL25 3RL

This rambling old manor, part medieval with thick walls and beams but
mainly 18th-century, lies in a bosky setting about a mile from the sea at
Carlyon Bay. It is furnished with a variety of assorted objects, some good
antiques, some comfortable chairs, "but in no way *arranged* or set out to
impress". Public rooms "are not opulent but have a country charm.
Bedrooms, with good bathrooms, are informal and comfortable, every
piece of furniture and print chosen with loving care" – but some are
small. The conservatory is bright and inviting for breakfast. The
restaurant is awarded two red crossed knives and forks by *Michelin*,
indicating an agreeable place to eat; food is "presented with style and
flair, using fresh and well-chosen ingredients, handled with respect and
perfectly served". The owners, Andrew and Mary Flint, have spent much
time making improvements in the grounds; there is a particularly
attractive garden with a heated pool, and a golf practice area is now in
operation. *Boscundle Manor* has "mildly eccentric" characteristics, as we
have said in the past; its informality is not universally approved, but
those in favour appreciate "the combination of easy cordiality and
comfort with understated luxury". More reports please.

Open Easter and mid-Apr–mid-Oct. Restaurant closed for lunch, and Sun evening
to non-residents.
Rooms 1 suite, 8 double, 2 single – all with bath and/or shower (5 with spa bath),
telephone, radio, TV, some with tea-making facilities. 3 in cottage in garden.
Facilities Sitting room, cocktail bar, dining room, private dining room,
conservatory, games room. 9-acre grounds with 2-acre gardens, croquet, golf
practice area, heated swimming pool, lake, ponds, woodlands. Beaches 1 m and
6 m; riding, coastal walks, fishing nearby.
Location 2 m E of St Austell, 100 yds off A390 on road signposted Tregrehan.
Restrictions Not suitable for &. Dogs by arrangement; not in public rooms.
Credit cards Access, Visa.
Terms B&B (English): single £52.50, double £80–£95, suite £140. Set dinner £20.
Special meals for children by arrangement.
*Service/tipping: "All rates include service. We actively discourage anyone from leaving
extra money."*

ST BLAZEY Cornwall   Map 4

Nanscawen House   `BUDGET`   *Tel* Par (072 681) 4488
Prideaux Road, St Blazey
Par PL24 2SR

A new recommendation from *Carrolle Sellick*, proprietor of *Holly Lodge*
(q.v.): "A fine old country house in a secluded location in five-acre
grounds with a heated swimming pool. It is convenient for touring in
Cornwall, being only five miles from Fowey. Guests have their own entry
and a comfortable sitting room. There are log fires in winter. There are
only three bedrooms, beautifully decorated, all with private facilities
including a spa bath. One has a four-poster. The proprietors, Janet and
Keith Martin, are kind and considerate at all times. Janet provides superb
meals (four courses, no choice) using home-grown produce from Keith's

extensive garden." Like *Holly Lodge* this is a no-smoking hotel. Not licensed; bring your own wine.

Open All year except Christmas and New Year.
Rooms 3 – all with bath and shower, telephone, radio, TV, tea-making facilities.
Facilities Drawing room, dining room. 5-acre garden with swimming pool (heated until Sep). Golf, riding, beaches, sea- and river-fishing nearby.
Location After level-crossing in St Blazey, from Lostwithiel (A390), turn right opposite Texaco garage into Prideaux Road. *Nanscawen* is ¾ m on right.
Restrictions Not suitable for &. No smoking. No children under 12. No dogs.
Credit cards Access, Visa.
Terms B&B double £55–£60. Set dinner £15.
Service/tipping: "We do not expect tips."

ST IVES Cornwall   Map 1

The Garrack Hotel   *Tel* St Ives (0736) 796199
Burthallan Lane, Higher Ayr   *Fax* (0736) 798955
St Ives TR26 3AA

A traditional seaside hotel that "caters admirably for children but is run so that *all* the guests enjoy themselves". It is owned and managed by the Kilby family and stands in two-acre grounds overlooking St Ives' spectacular surfing Porthmeor Beach, well away from the hubbub of the town. Some of the rooms are in the creeper-covered older building, other more spacious ones are in a modern wing; the latter all enjoy a fine view over the bay. The hotel has a leisure centre with a swimming pool; books and games in the sitting room give it a lived-in feeling. It was dropped from the Guide following criticisms of the food and the decor of some of the rooms. Now the former chef Graham Jones has returned and "the table d'hôte menu was on the whole excellent. It was a joy to be served a perfectly grilled Dover sole unspoiled by a superfluous sauce. Cooked breakfasts were superb, and there was a large array of cereals and preserves." And an inspector reports: "The restaurant attracts outside diners and has a conservatory extension. We ate well at both meals. Our room in the extension was a fair size, simple and traditional in style with a well-appointed bathroom. There is a relaxed family feel about the place. Many of the staff have been here for some time and are loyal, attentive and willing." (*J and Bruce Lee, and others*) We do still get complaints about bedroom decor and the limited amount of choice on the menu, and service can be disorganised at busy times. More reports please.

Open All year.
Rooms 2 suites, 15 double, 4 single – 14 with bath and shower, 2 with shower, all with telephone, radio, TV, baby-listening.
Facilities Residents' lounge, TV lounge, bar lounge, dining room. Leisure centre with swimming pool, sauna, whirlpool, solarium and coffee shop. 2-acre grounds.
Location ½ m from centre. From Penzance on B3311 turn right on B3306 towards St Ives. Hotel is off this, to left.
Restrictions Not suitable for &. Dogs by prior arrangement; in some rooms only.
Credit cards All major cards accepted.
Terms B&B: single £23.50–£28.50, double £56–£80.50; dinner, B&B: single £35.50–£40.50, double £80.50–£105.00. Set lunch £7, dinner £13.50; full alc £16.
Service/tipping: "We think the idea that a charge for service should be added to the bill is too ridiculous for words. But we have no objection if guests wish to show appreciation and our staff undoubtedly appreciate the gesture. But we prefer the hotel not to be involved."

ST KEYNE Cornwall Map 1

The Well House
St Keyne
Liskeard PL14 4RN

Tel Liskeard (0579) 42001

"A gem. Hidden down a narrow Cornish lane, five miles from the coast, a comfortable grey-stone house subtly and tastefully converted by Nicholas Wainford into a delightful small hotel. It is personally run with the help of a team of enthusiastic, caring and well-trained staff. Old-fashioned service, rare these days." "A most peaceful house, skilfully adapted without spoiling the sense of light and space. Bedroom exquisitely clean with fine beds, good sheets and lighting, and fresh flowers. The decor was entirely black, white and cream, a bit clinical for me. Mr Wainwright was a helpful and perceptive host. Two dignified King Charles spaniels added to our sense of welcome."

Since its first appearance in the Guide in 1989, this Victorian country house has been drawing enthusiastic reviews. It enjoys a secluded setting in three and a half acres of grounds in a pretty, unspoilt spot in the Looe valley. The bedrooms, most of a good size, have gleaming, well-appointed *en suite* bathrooms. Public rooms, decorated in cool colours, have "a twenties/thirties atmosphere". There is a cosy panelled bar, and a lounge with log fire; the dining room is hung with pictures of food; its bay windows overlook the garden and swimming pool the well-spaced tables are impeccably set. The cooking, by David Pope, a graduate of the *Capital*, London, and *Gidleigh Park*, Chagford (qq.v.), is "modern, delicious, imaginative, fresh; there's an excellent cheeseboard". "Wine list carefully selected, and wide ranging in price." "Excellent breakfast, with exotic fruit salad, freshly baked croissants and brioches and home-made marmalade." Nicholas Wainford is "a very earnest man"; the atmosphere is courteous rather than easily convivial – and the prices are less high than those of many prestigious country house hotels. (*Jill Leuw, JM Chandler, Veronica Greig, and others*)

Open All year. Restaurant closed Mon to non-residents.
Rooms 8 double – all with bath, shower, telephone, radio, TV.
Facilities Sitting room, bar, restaurant. 3½-acre grounds with tennis, croquet and heated swimming pool. Walking, fishing, riding, golf nearby.
Location 3 m S of Liskeard on B3254. Don't go to St Keyne station; at church take left fork to St Keyne Well; *Well House* is ½ m on left.
Restrictions Not suitable for &. No children under 8 in dining room at night. Dogs by arrangement.
Credit cards Access, Amex, Visa.
Terms B&B (continental): single occupancy £57.50–£65, double £90–£110. Cooked breakfast £6.50 extra. Set lunch £21, dinner £30; full alc £33.50. Bargain breaks Nov–Mar excluding Christmas. 1-night bookings sometimes refused.
Service/tipping: "No service charge. Tips are entirely at clients' discretion."

ST MARTIN'S Isles of Scilly Map 1

St Martin's Hotel
St Martin's, Isles of Scilly
Cornwall TR25 0QW

Tel Scillonia (0720) 22092
Fax (0720) 22298
Telex 94015906

César award: Island Hotel of the Year

"Absolutely the best hotel in which I've ever stayed," was the accolade of one of our regular correspondents, much travelled in the realms of good hotels. Tucked into a hillside looking across a sandy beach towards Tresco, this is the only hotel permitted on St Martin's, the third largest of the Scilly Islands (population 84). It opened last year, to a design approved by the Duke of Cornwall (a.k.a. the Prince of Wales). Its owner is Robert Francis whose *Polurrian Hotel* at Mullion has had a Guide entry for some years. Mr Francis now divides his time between the two. Many readers have written to us this year about the new hotel's "idyllic setting, its cottage design blending into the coastline. There is a feeling of unusual warmth and friendliness, and the use of stone and the light and airy interior with Laura Ashley-type fabrics create an atmosphere of quiet luxury devoid of pretentiousness." The *Polurrian* has always been known for its welcoming attitude to children and this is also a feature of the new hotel; accommodation and breakfast are free for under-16s sharing their parents' room, and there are high teas at 5.30. "It is perfect for children, being next to a sandy but never crowded beach. Guests not beach-minded can relax in the gardens or the swimming pool pavilion." Most readers have found the staff helpful and willing; the food, with "the attractions of *nouvelle cuisine*, but more robust though not excessive portions", has been praised by some, but found variable by others, and there have been other minor teething problems. But on balance the verdict is highly favourable.

Open All year.
Rooms 2 suites, 22 double – all with bath, shower, telephone, radio, TV, baby-listening.
Facilities 2 lounges (main one with bar), restaurant; snooker room. 2½-acre grounds with indoor heated swimming pool. Sandy beaches 50 yds.
Location Only hotel on St Martin's. Helicopter from Penzance to Tresco, boat to St Martin's. Hotel will make transport arrangements.
Restrictions Not suitable for &. No smoking in main lounge and some bedrooms. Dogs in certain bedrooms only, not in public rooms.
Credit cards All major cards accepted.
Terms [1990 rates] B&B £31.50–£87.50; dinner, B&B £49–£105. Set lunch £6.50–£10.50, dinner £17.50. Single occupancy by arrangement. Winter theme breaks (murder mystery, etc). Free accommodation for children under 16 in parents' room; special meals.
Service/tipping: "Service included. We discourage tipping."

ST MARY'S Isles of Scilly
Map 1

Star Castle Hotel
St Mary's, Isles of Scilly
Cornwall TR21 0JA
Tel Scillonia (0720) 22317

St Mary's is easily reached by boat or helicopter from the mainland and is an excellent base for an island-hopping Scillonian holiday. The *Star Castle* is a modest but welcoming hotel, originally an Elizabethan fortress, with a dry moat and 18-foot-wide ramparts, in a spectacular position overlooking the town, harbour and neighbouring islands. It has extensive grounds, with lawns enclosed by tall hedges forming welcoming suntraps. There is a covered heated swimming pool and a grass tennis court. Some of the bedrooms ("comfortable and well appointed") are in the old building; two singles, with shower, are in guardhouses on the ramparts. Other larger ones, in two modern annexes in the garden, are recommended for families, though not well insulated. Mr and Mrs

Reynolds, the resident owners, are "always in evidence; they and their staff were extremely friendly and helpful". There is a dungeon bar where snack lunches are served, and the dining room is the former officers' mess. Straightforward cooking on a set menu with three choices of each course; but a summer visitor was critical of the food, complained of portion control, and found the restaurant "all hustle and bustle" and the public rooms crowded.

Open Mar–Oct.
Rooms 22 double, 2 single – all bath and/or shower, telephone, radio, TV, tea-making facilities. 16, with baby-listening, in 2 blocks in garden.
Facilities 2 lounges, games room, bar, restaurant. 4½-acre grounds with tennis, covered heated swimming pool. Sandy beaches, safe bathing and fishing nearby.
Location Central, overlooking town and harbour, but in large grounds so not noisy. Regular boats and helicopter flights to Scilly Islands from Penzance.
Restrictions Not suitable for &. Dogs in garden rooms only (£1.25 per day).
Credit cards None accepted.
Terms Dinner, B&B £40–£60. Set dinner £13.50. Packed and bar lunches available; vegetarian meals on request. Reduced rates for children sharing parents' room; high tea.
Service/tipping: "No service charge. Tips are not expected – but gratefully received if given!"

SALCOMBE Devon   **Map 1**

Marine Hotel   *Tel* Salcombe (054 884) 2251
Cliff Road   *Fax* (054 884) 3109
Salcombe TQ8 8JH   *Telex* 42513

A sophisticated, extensively modernised hotel perched above Salcombe's lovely estuary. There are beautiful views from the open-plan public rooms and most of the bedrooms. The *Marine* had an entry in earlier editions of the Guide but was omitted last year when we received critical reports following a change of management. Now, after yet another change, readers recommend its reinstatement: "In spite of the odd hiccup, it is the perfect place for a weekend break. Its position is ideal; it is almost like being at sea. The newer bedrooms on the lower level are very attractively decorated, with extra-large beds and balcony. Early morning tea and a newspaper, brought to the bedroom, are included in the rates." "A most civilised hotel. Bedroom not large but comfortable and well planned, with excellent storage and good lighting. The pink and green decor throughout the hotel is restful and charming." On the food there is dissent: "Much improved"; "Very good, with a touch of *nouvelle cuisine*, so attractively presented"; "Present obsession with sauces unsatisfactory". The new managers and the junior staff are all said to be "helpful and skilled". (*Mrs PM Jones; also Cdr RM Douglas, and others*) In late 1989 we had several reports of surliness in the dining room but this now seems to have been sorted out. The sporting facilities are shared by the time-share apartments in the garden, so could be crowded at peak times. There is live music in the public rooms at dinner and Sunday lunch. One reader was surprised to be asked to pay a deposit of £50 per person for a party of six half a year in advance. More reports please.

Open All year.
Rooms 1 suite, 42 double, 9 single – all with bath, shower, telephone, radio, TV, baby-listening.

Facilities Lounge, library, bar, restaurant, dinner-dance on Sat; indoor swimming pool, jacuzzi, sauna, solarium, gym, beauty salon. $\frac{1}{4}$-acre grounds with swimming pool, moorings, fishing.
Location 300 yds from centre. Parking.
Credit cards All major cards accepted.
Terms [1990 rates] Dinner, B&B: single £44.50–£77, double £89–£154, suite £134–£174. Set lunch £9.50, dinner £20; full alc £25. Reduced rates and special meals for children.
Service/tipping: "Service included. We do not solicit gratuities, but any tips left are equally distributed among all staff except manager."

Tides Reach Hotel   *Tel* Salcombe (054 884) 3466
South Sands, Salcombe TQ8 8LJ   *Fax* (054 884) 3954

A cheerful, modern, efficient family-run hotel, with a huge range of activities available for sporting folk, both outdoors and in the hotel's own leisure complex (see below). It has a choice location: South Sands is a mile to the south of Salcombe itself, well away from the crowded summer scene, facing across the estuary and surrounded by National Trust land. "This is how a family hotel should be run. Young energetic staff, well-maintained public areas. Rooms well equipped and brightly decorated." Visitors regularly commend the friendly attentive staff, the bright attractive bedrooms (many with balcony), lounges and restaurant – though, bad news for some, the public rooms have muzak, and there are no non-smoking areas. Debate continues about the dinners: "very good" is one view; "too ambitious" another. (*T Hodge, also Miss M Nelson, CR*) One reader in room 4 suffered a continuous banging noise from the kitchen doors underneath.

Open Mar–Nov.
Rooms 3 suites, 35 double, 3 single – all with bath and/or shower, telephone, radio, TV; some with sea view and balcony.
Facilities Lift, ramp to entrance. Lounge, sun lounge, reading lounge, cocktail bar, pool bar, restaurant; health and beauty salon, hairdressing salon, sauna, whirlpool bath, gym, games room, squash court with spectator lounge, snooker; heated swimming pool with sliding doors to make it open in summer. 2-acre grounds with garden, pond, tea lawn. 10 yds from beach with safe bathing, windsurfing school, sea fishing, sailing.
Location 1 mile S of Salcombe; follow signs to Bolt Head and South Sands.
Restrictions Access to some facilities and movement outside hotel may be difficult for &. No children under 8. No dogs in public rooms.
Credit cards All major cards accepted.
Terms Dinner, B&B (English): single £49–£79, double £98–£110, suite £128–£180. Light and packed lunches. Set dinner £21.75; full alc £32. Bargain breaks, off-season breaks. Reduced rates for children.
Service/tipping: "Service included. Tipping at the discretion of the customer, should he or she wish to show appreciation."

SALTFORD Avon   **Map 2**

Brunel's Tunnel House   *Tel* Saltford (0225) 873873
High Street, Saltford
Nr Bristol BS18 3BQ

A guest house in a Grade II listed Georgian building in a conservation village between Bristol and Bath, one of three tunnel houses in Britain. It was bought by the famous 19th-century engineer, Isambard Kingdom

Brunel, so that the Great Western Railway line which he designed could be excavated underneath. Trains still use the tunnel: "There is a slight rumble when a train passes but it does not impinge on conversation or sleep." The resident "very welcoming" owner Muriel Mitchell, helped by her "friendly and helpful" daughter Sarah, is assembling a collection of Brunel memorabilia. "It is a much cared for village house," she writes, "and we aim to keep its honest, unprissy period appeal." An inspector occupied a "prettily decorated" bedroom; good hanging space, but only one "miniscule" bedside table. "Dinner (no choice) was acceptable, if not frightfully imaginative, with well-cooked vegetables. There's an attractive sheltered garden. It makes a good overnight stop, but would not be ideal for a holiday base as the immediate surroundings lack appeal. Many guests were regulars, on business." "Rooms bright, clean and comfortable," adds *Frances Ward*, "and delicious toast for breakfast."

Open All year except Christmas. Dining room closed for lunch.
Rooms 7 doubles – 1 with bath and shower, 6 with shower, all with telephone, radio, TV, tea-making facilities.
Facilities Lounge/bar, dining room. ½-acre garden. River Avon with marina 15 mins' walk; golf nearby.
Location Midway between Bath (5½ m) and Bristol (6½ m). At Saltford Motor Services turn up Beech Road off A4; hotel is at bottom of Beech Road.
Restrictions Not suitable for &. No smoking in dining room. Dogs by prior arrangement only; not in public rooms.
Credit cards Access, Amex, Visa.
Terms B&B: single £38–£44, double £46–£54; dinner, B&B: single £50.50–£56.50, double £71–£79. Set dinner £12.50. Reduced rates for children sharing parents' room; special meals by arrangement.
Service/tipping: "No service charge since courteous service is implicit in the way we work. Tipping left to the discretion of customers – it is neither expected nor encouraged, but if offered is not refused."

SANDY PARK Devon   Map 1

Mill End Hotel   *Tel* Chagford (0647) 432282
Sandy Park, Chagford TQ13 8JN   *Fax* (0647) 433106

This converted mill, whose wheel still turns in its quiet courtyard, stands in two-acre grounds in the Teign valley on the edge of Dartmoor. It has 12 miles of fishing on the river Teign; a ghillie is available by prior arrangement, and during one weekend in July free fishing tuition is offered to guests. There are good walks from the gates of the hotel, which entered the 1990 edition of the Guide in italics. *Adrian Scott* writes to confirm: "Superb, well-run country hotel; log fires, well-equipped bedrooms and excellent food. Owner Nicholas Craddock is a commanding presence." "Superb wine list, good food and service, comfortable lounges, luxurious bedrooms (only mildly haunted); delicious croissants," reports *CM Begg*. The decor is homely rather than elegant; some bedrooms are modern, some old and chintzy. There is plenty of choice (of traditional English cooking) on the menu.

Open All year except 12–22 Dec, 10–18 Jan.
Rooms 15 double, 2 single – 14 with bath and shower, 3 with bath, all with telephone, radio, TV, tea-making facilities, baby-listening. Some on ground floor.
Facilities 3 lounges (1 with TV), bar, restaurant. 2-acre grounds. River frontage with fishing.
Location Near A382 between Whiddon Down and Moreton Hampstead.

Restrictions No smoking in dining room. No dogs in public rooms.
Credit cards All major cards accepted.
Terms Rooms: single £26.50–£50, double £40–£66. Breakfast £4.50–£7.50. Dinner, B&B: single £50–£78, double £95–£130. Set lunch £20, dinner £25. 2-day breaks, off-season breaks. Fishing weekend; wine and food weekends. Reduced rates and special meals for children sharing parents' room. 1-night bookings refused at Christmas, Easter and special weekends.
Service/tipping: "Generally speaking we discourage tipping. But some people like to leave quite large sums of money and it seems churlish to prevent them. Hotel staff are not highly paid and some of our visitors can and do afford it. What is received is distributed by a committee on a pro rata basis."

SCALBY North Yorkshire   Map 4

Wrea Head Country Hotel   *Tel* Scarborough (0723) 378211
Scalby   *Fax* (0723) 363457
Nr Scarborough YO13 0PB

Personally run, friendly hotel in 19th-century building in quiet situation three miles north-west of Scarborough on edge of North Yorkshire National Park. "Expensively furnished in good taste", warm and comfortable. Bedrooms and bathrooms vary in size; some are large, with lovely views. 14-acre wooded and landscaped grounds. Good service. Breakfasts recommended, but dinner severely criticised this year. A drawback could be the hotel's reliance on group trade. 21 rooms, all with bath and/or shower. B&B double £70–£110. Set dinner £17.50. More reports please.

SEAHOUSES Northumberland   Map 4

Beach House Hotel   `BUDGET`   *Tel* Seahouses (0665) 720337
Seahouses NE68 7SR

Mr and Mrs Craigs's quiet hotel on the edge of town, with good views of Farne Island, is recommended for "excellent rooms, friendly service, high quality cooking" of 6-course dinner, with limited choice and much use of local produce, and good choice of inexpensive wines. "Breakfast just as good, including locally smoked kippers." Small garden; sandy beach 500 yds. 14 rooms all with bath and/or shower. Closed early Nov–Mar. Dinner, B&B double £35–£42. New nomination. More reports please.

SEAVIEW Isle of Wight   Map 1

Seaview Hotel   *Tel* Seaview (0983) 612711
High Street, Seaview PO34 5EX   *Fax* (0983) 613729

Nicholas and Nicola Hayward's seaside hotel is an unassuming three-storey bay-windowed Edwardian house with a symmetrical facade, at the foot of the High Street and near a beach in an old-fashioned and picturesque sailing village. The village is normally a peaceful place, but buzzes with activity in July and August. The house "has something of the atmosphere of a maritime museum, with fine paintings and artefacts of ships everywhere". Bedrooms vary in size; front rooms have a view of the sea and coast. Some readers have been entirely satisfied this year: "Just how a seaside hotel should be. Comfortable if plain twin bedroom with a 1920s mahogany wardrobe, large dressing table and tallboy. Food served in the very pretty dining room was seasonable and fresh." "The cooking is both imaginative and unpretentious. As a near non-carnivore I particularly appreciated the generous helpings of fresh vegetables." "Excellent kippers for breakfast." Children are welcome, though the very young are not allowed in the restaurant after 7.30 pm; a "very good" high tea is served for them at 5.45 pm or they are served in a special room if dining later. The dining room can get very busy; at certain times of year there are two sittings. (*Minda Alexander, also Raymond Harris, Philip Norman, and others*) This year there are criticisms as well as compliments: one guest found his bedroom, just above the kitchen, noisy until late, and hot, and was disappointed with the limited choice of main dish on the half-pension menu. A Christmas visitor found the place under-staffed. A guest on a special break was surprised at the number of extras on her bill. She also found the service at dinner notably less friendly than at breakfast. And though the hotel tells us it makes no service charge and expects no tip, one visitor was peeved to be presented with a credit card voucher with the bottom line left blank.

Open All year.
Rooms 2 suites, 14 double – 14 with bath, 2 with shower, all with telephone, radio, TV, baby-listening. 2 with patio on ground floor.
Facilities 2 lounges, cocktail bar, public bar, restaurant. Patio and courtyard. Sea and sandy beaches nearby with sailing, fishing, windsurfing, etc.
Location In centre of village, near sea. Follow signs for seafront.
Restrictions Not suitable for &. No smoking in 1 lounge; smoking discouraged in dining room. No small children in dining room after 7.30 pm. No dogs in public rooms.
Credit cards Access, Amex, Visa.
Terms B&B: single £36–£54, double £62–£70; dinner, B&B: single £46–£50, double £86–£100. Full alc £17. Breakaway, weekend, weekly tariffs. Reduced rates and special meals for children.
Service/tipping: "We do not make a service charge, or expect tips."

SHENINGTON Oxfordshire   **Map 2**

Sugarswell Farm   `BUDGET`   *Tel* Tysoe (029 588) 512
Shenington, Nr Banbury
OX15 6HW

"It's all you say," writes *MRJ Holmes*, endorsing last year's nomination for this working dairy farm in rural Oxfordshire. "The house is quite new, built of stones from a demolished cottage, and Rosemary Nunneley is a delightful host. There are only three bedrooms. Ours had two armchairs *and* a sofa, and spectacular views across fields and hills. We watched a hundred cows passing our window morning and evening. Comfortable beds, ample drawer space, large and well-equipped bathroom. Visitors (never more than six) eat round a large table. This worked well during our stay; all our fellow guests were compatible. Food is excellent; good coffee too. No choice, but vegetables etc are served in individual tureens. *Sugarswell* is an ideal holiday centre: Stratford, Warwick and the Cotswold villages are in easy reach." (*Heather Kirk*) This is a mostly no-smoking establishment, but there is one room where the desperate can go for a puff. No licence; bring your own wine. One snag (except for theatre goers): "Dinner is at 6.30."

Open All year.
Rooms 3 double – all with bath, TV, tea-making facilities.
Facilities Drawing room, dining room. 360-acre farm.
Location 2¼ m NW of Banbury on Edge Hill road, W of A422.
Restrictions Almost entirely non-smoking. No children under 15. No pets.
Credit cards None accepted.
Terms B&B: single £26–£28, double £37–£43; dinner, B&B: single £40–£42, double £65–£71. Set dinner £15. Unlicensed. Bring your own wine.
Service/tipping: "No service charge. Tips at guests' discretion; shared among staff."

SHEPTON MALLET Somerset   Map 2

Bowlish House Restaurant   *Tel* Shepton Mallet (0749) 342022
Wells Road
Shepton Mallet BA4 5JD

This restaurant with only four bedrooms in a beautiful Palladian house, scheduled Grade II, in a National Conservancy area, had an entry in earlier editions of the Guide but was dropped when it changed hands. Many readers have written this year to recommend the hospitality and good food offered by the new owners, Linda and Bob Morley: "A delightful house, lovely antique furniture, a cosy bar. We felt like personal guests because (a) there were never more than three other couples staying, (b) the extraordinary personal attention of Mr Morley and (c) the 'home' rather than 'restaurant' cooking of Mrs Morley who is self-taught. The cuisine is not unsophisticated, just not over-elaborate. The wine list is extensive and pretty reasonable. Our seven-year-old daughter was always accommodated by adaptations of the main menu – at appropriate prices." "Not grand, but elegant and comfortable. The food is *excellent*, with a reasonably priced menu (choice of six dishes for each course, including a vegetarian main course), all carefully cooked for each diner. A very good place to stay if sightseeing in Bath, Wells, Glastonbury, Stourhead." "Comfortable bedroom with nice personal touches, not the usual commercial guest packs." There is an agreeable conservatory for after-dinner coffee; public rooms are on an intimate scale. (*D and K Vargas, MV Beaumont, Mrs SJ Durke, and others*) Only niggles: "The bed was such that we tended to be thrown into the middle"; "There can be slight traffic noise from the nearby road".

Open All year except 25–27 Dec.
Rooms 4 double – all with bath, radio, TV, tea-making facilities.
Facilities Lounge, bar, dining room, conservatory. ¼-acre garden.
Location ¼ m outside Shepton Mallet, on A371 to Wells.
Restrictions No smoking in dining room while other guests are eating. No dogs in public rooms.
Credit cards Access, Visa.
Terms (No service charge) B&B (continental) double £46. English breakfast £4. Set dinner £18.50; full alc £22.

Deadlines: nominations for the 1992 edition should reach us not later than 1 June 1991. Latest date for comments on existing entries: 10 June 1991.

SHIPTON GORGE Dorset   **Map 2**

Innsacre Farmhouse Hotel   *Tel* Bridport (0308) 56137
Shipton Gorge
Nr Bridport DT6 4LJ

Innsacre is a 17th-century farmhouse with a beamed lounge complete with log fire, books and games for the whole family ("pets are also welcome", says the brochure). It lies in the hollow of ancient hills a couple of miles back from the beach. It has the air of an old-fashioned French auberge; cobbles up the drive, lots of flowers round the terrace, flower-pots bedecking an outside flight of stairs. Piglets roaming the garden remind visitors that it was not long ago a working farm. Readers frequently comment on the happy atmosphere, created by the Smith family, and three this year write of the particularly kind treatment accorded to their young children: "They were treated with affectionate and conspiratorial indulgence. We were even given the run of the kitchen during the night in case we needed anything for them." Bedrooms vary in size; nothing fancy in the decor, but they are comfortable, with crisp cotton bed-linen, fresh flowers and a bowl of fruit." "*Innsacre* is probably best described as a restaurant-with-rooms," writes another correspondent, "and one could call the bedrooms 'idiosyncratic', but they are much preferable to the faceless comfort of those in a chain hotel." The restaurant, in the former barn, has stone walls and quaint windows. There is a new chef, Simon Mazzei-Sgaglione, and recent comments on the food are enthusiastic: "Daytime menus exceptionally good, with delicious hot game pie and crisp salads; irresistible puddings." "We don't agree that portions are too big – they are sensible, like everything else in this nice place. The cooking was of a high standard and completely lacked the assertive pretentiousness you find everywhere now – not that it lacked sophistication and ambition, but there was no 'side'. Breakfast was the usual country house hotel blow-out. Service straightforward, friendly, utterly un-servile." (*HR, SC Robinson, J Campbell, Spencer and Lucy de Grey, Julia Holman*)

Open All year.
Rooms 7 double – all with bath, TV, tea-making facilities, baby-listening.
Facilities Wheelchair access; chair lift. Lounge, bar, restaurant; snooker room. 10-acre grounds with orchard and gardens. 2 m from Chesil Beach with pebble beach, fishing, safe bathing.
Location 2 m E of Bridport; second turning to Shipton Gorge off A35 Dorchester–Bridport.
Restriction No dogs in restaurant.
Credit cards All major cards accepted.
Terms [1990 rates] B&B (English): single £16–£32, double £28–£56; dinner, B&B: single £34.50–£50.50, double £65–£93. Set lunch £12.50, dinner £19.50. Off-season rates. Reduced rates for children sharing parents' room; special meals.
Service/tipping: "No service charge. We discourage tipping."

****

 Traveller's tale *The place is a dictionary definition of frills and furbelows. The beswagged and beribboned tented dining room reminded me of the chorus line at the* Folies Bergère.

****

SIMONSBATH Somerset   Map 1

Simonsbath House Hotel   *Tel* Exford (064 383) 259
Simonsbath
Nr Minehead TA24 7SH

Mike and Sue Burns's 17th-century hunting lodge stands in two-acre
grounds in the heart of Exmoor National Park. Most rooms have lovely
views over the river Barle. The half-panelled lounge and library bar have
comfortable seating; log fires burn in cold weather. Bedrooms, all
individually designed, have period furniture and smallish bathrooms.
You choose your dinner from a menu which changes daily, and wait
about 30 minutes while it is prepared. Readers this year comment on the
"beautiful setting, the enthusiasm and friendliness of the caring hosts",
the good and well-served dinners, but one found the dark decor of some
of the rooms a trifle claustrophobic. The hotel's brochure, rather coyly
called An Invitation, declares its aim: "The atmosphere of a home with
welcoming owners and a caring staff to relax and pamper you with good
old-fashioned hospitality." More reports please.

Open 1 Feb–end Nov.
Rooms 7 double – all with bath and/or shower, telephone, radio, TV, tea-making
facilities.
Facilities Lounge, library, dining room. 2-acre grounds. Coast 8 m, river fishing
nearby.
Location 7 m SE of Lynton.
Restrictions Not suitable for &. No smoking in dining room. No children under
10. No dogs.
Credit cards All major cards accepted.
Terms (Service at guests' discretion) B&B £34.50–£43; dinner, B&B £49.50–£58.
Set dinner £15 (£17.50 to non-residents).

SLAIDBURN Lancashire   Map 4

Parrock Head Hotel   *Tel* Slaidburn (020 06) 614
Slaidburn, Clitheroe BB7 3AH

"A delight. Richard and Vicky Umbers are friendly and welcoming in the
nicest possible way, without being pushy. Mrs Umbers is an accomplished host and is as bright, cheerful and beautifully dressed at breakfast
as she is throughout the day." The Umbers' former farmhouse has a
remote and beautiful location at the foot of Bowland Fells, on the
Lancashire–Yorkshire border, with dales on one side, majestic moorland
on the other. Three bedrooms, "spacious and comfortable", are in the
main building, six are in two blocks of garden cottages. *Parrock Head* is
"spotlessly clean", and warm and comfortable, even in the depths of
winter; there are log fires in the large sitting room on the first floor and a
library filled with books and magazines, maps and tourist information.
Guests are introduced to each other before dinner, which encourages a
relaxed, friendly atmosphere. In the spacious dining room, which also
caters to non-residents, the Umbers offer a reasonably priced à la carte
menu, cooked by young chefs, with four choices of starter and main
course and three of dessert. There's a new head chef this year, and a
recent visitor reports: "Food is good, well prepared and interesting (but
not a lot of it). Good wine list." Breakfasts are "king-size"; packed

lunches "of a high standard". (*Mrs RS Reston, DJ Logan, J Dudley, and others*) Rooms in the annexe – jokingly called The Shed – may be quieter than those in the main house which are directly off the bar and lounge.

Open All year except Christmas week. Limited opening of restaurant in Jan.
Rooms 2 suites, 8 double – all with bath, shower, telephone, TV, tea-making facilities, baby-listening. 7 in 2 blocks of garden cottages. 3 ground-floor rooms.
Facilities Reception lounge, residents'/diners' lounge, library, bar, restaurant. 1½-acre grounds; reservoir fishing 2 m; bird watching.
Location 9 m N of Clitheroe. Take B6478 to Slaidburn; hotel is 1 m NW up unmarked road.
Restrictions No smoking in dining room. Dogs in garden cottages only.
Credit cards Access, Amex, Visa.
Terms Dinner, B&B: single £46–£50, double £75–£85. Full alc £18–£20. Light lunches on request; packed lunches available. 3-night midweek breaks. 1-night bookings refused for Sat if the reservation does not include dinner. Reduced rates for children sharing parents' room; special meals.
Service/tipping: "No service charge. Tips not requested but accepted if offered and distributed monthly to all staff."

SOAR MILL COVE Devon   **Map 1**

Soar Mill Cove Hotel   *Tel* Kingsbridge (0548) 561566
Soar Mill Cove   *Fax* (0548) 561223
Nr Salcombe TQ7 3DS

This small hotel, owned and run by Norma and Keith Makepeace and their son, also Keith, new to the Guide this year, is "beautifully situated at the head of an isolated cove, surrounded by National Trust land, with splendid cliff walks starting from its grounds. Our bedroom was comfortable and well furnished, with a large sitting area and a patio. The proprietors and staff are friendly and helpful." "About half the rooms have wonderful sea views, the others overlook a sheltered garden; it has five-acre grounds with putting green, grass tennis court and indoor and outdoor swimming pools. The hotel is ideal for a holiday with young children. Ours were made very welcome right from the beginning. Plus points are the lack of steps (it is all on ground level); the fact that you can listen in to the children after their bedtime on a telephone handset; the very good laundry facilities, and the freshly cooked food for their supper at 5:30. It was such a relief to know that here was a hotel that wasn't going to serve a fortnight's supply of beefburgers, fish fingers, chips and ice-cream." Adult meals too, with plenty of choice including fresh local fish, lobster, meat and garden produce, come in for praise, with special mention of the sweet trolley. The dining room and lounge have large windows overlooking the bay. Some of the bedrooms are vibrantly floral in decor. (*Mrs MH Box, Mrs Elizabeth Cousins; also PJ Arnsby-Wilson*)

Open 11 Feb–29 Dec.
Rooms 1 suite, 11 double, 2 single – all with bath, telephone, radio, TV, tea-making facilities, baby-listening.
Facilities Lounge, bar, restaurant. 5-acre grounds with indoor and outdoor swimming pools, tennis, table-tennis, donkeys. Sandy bay across meadow.
Location Approx 5 m SW of Kingsbridge by A381. Turn sharp right at Malborough; follow signs for Soar.
Restrictions Suitable for only partially &. No smoking in restaurant. Dogs by arrangement.
Credit cards Access, Visa.

Terms B&B (English): single £50–£68, double £90–£120, suite £160–£240; dinner, B&B: single £60–£85, double £100–£155, suite £200–£300. Set lunch £15, dinner £27–£33. Christmas house-party. Reduced rates and special meals for children.
Service/tipping: "No service charge. Tipping entirely at guests' discretion."

SOURTON Devon   Map 1

Collaven Manor Hotel   *Tel* Bridestowe (083 786) 522
Sourton, Nr Okehampton   *Fax* (083 786) 570
EX20 4HH

"A small 15th-century manor, not very grand, a mini-fortress of rough grey stone, hairy with ivy, in five-acre grounds with a rocky garden and secluded croquet lawn. All around are great open Dartmoor spaces." The interior, all beams, inglenook fireplaces and stone walls with fresh flowers, shiny copper and fine old china plates, is "remarkably spick and span". Bedrooms are "pretty and beautifully equipped but not luxurious", with extras such as a decanter of sherry, iced water, fresh milk and good toiletries. One has a four-poster. Beds are turned down during dinner. Many readers have written of the kindness of the owners, Mr and Mrs Buckley; and service is willing and helpful. Guests dine in one of two restaurants; the *Hamilton* is considerably pricier than the *Inglenook*. The menus, regularly changed, with a surprising amount of choice, range from quite simple dishes in the *Inglenook* to highly ambitious ones in the *Hamilton*. Most readers have appreciated their dinner, though there is one report of overcooked vegetables, and one reader, while praising the quality and freshness of the ingredients, felt that some of the more daring combinations did not quite come off – "but it is never boring!" The English breakfast, including "delicious freshly smoked haddock and four types of home-made jams and marmalade, served in pretty little bowls", continues to be praised. (*Caroline Spencer, Mrs J Wise, Mr and Mrs Froggatt, and others*)

Open All year except 2 weeks in Jan.
Rooms 7 double, 2 single – all with bath and/or shower, telephone, radio, TV, tea-making facilities. 1 with 4-poster.
Facilities Lounge, lounge bar, 2 restaurants. 5-acre grounds with pitch and putt golf, bowls, croquet, clay-pigeon shooting.
Location 8 m S of Okehampton on A386 to Tavistock.
Restrictions Not suitable for &. No children under 12. No dogs.
Credit cards Access, Visa.
Terms B&B (English): single £50, double £77–£95. Set lunch £13.95 (packed lunch available). Dinner £13.95 in *Inglenook*, £19.95 in *Hamilton*. Special breaks; Christmas and New Year packages.
Service/tipping: "Guests should not be obliged to tip; it is left entirely to their discretion."

SOUTH MOLTON Devon   Map 1

Whitechapel Manor   *Tel* South Molton (076 95) 3377
South Molton EX36 3EG   *Fax* (076 95) 3797

"We have rarely received such a warm welcome without feeling in any way pressured. John and Patricia Shapland and their staff went to endless trouble to ensure that we were comfortable, and were happy to give us dinner in our room when our three-month-old baby was being troublesome." (*Ben and Juliet Browne*) Other readers, too, endorse last year's praise for the Shaplands' fine Grade I listed Elizabethan manor which they have been running as an upmarket country house hotel since 1987 and are still continuing to improve. It is in large grounds in an isolated setting near the Exmoor National Park. The interior is "substantial, graceful and restful; it has been brought gently into the 20th century without losing its original charm. The entrance hall is dominated by a magnificent carved oak Jacobean screen. The rooms have high ceilings, some with intricate plaster carvings and mouldings, and deep recessed windows. Furnishings and fabrics throughout are of the highest quality. It is totally quiet – the walls are so thick that you cannot hear a sound from either side or above." The talented young chef, Thierry Lepretre-Granet, has this year earned a *Michelin* rosette for his "modern, sophisticated" cooking on a four-course menu, though portions were too *nouvelle* for one reader, who "had to order potatoes for every meal". Bedrooms, in various shapes and sizes, "have all the essentials"; bathrooms are "adequate" or large, "with constantly replenished large towels". "The service is totally personal – the Shaplands do almost everything themselves." A few niggles: little change on the menu during a three-day visit; "atmosphere is delightfully relaxed and informal, but perhaps slightly lacking in professionalism bearing in mind the high prices"; the room named Peverel is said to be poorly insulated.

Open All year.
Rooms 1 suite, 7 double, 2 single – all with bath, shower, telephone, radio, TV, baby-listening; tea-making facilities on request.
Facilities Bar, 2 lounges, restaurant. 15-acre grounds with garden, croquet. Fishing, golf, riding nearby. Exmoor 2 m. Sea 18 m.
Location Leaving M5 motorway at junction 27, follow signs to Barnstaple and South Molton. At South Molton roundabout turn right.
Restrictions Not suitable for &. No smoking in dining room. Dogs by arrangement; not in hotel.
Credit cards Access, Visa.
Terms B&B (English): single £50–£120, double £80–£140, suite £157.50–£175. Set lunch £22.50, dinner £28 and £37.50. Packed lunch available. Winter rates. 1-night bookings refused for bank holidays. Special meals for children.
Service/tipping: "No service charge made. Nor is tipping encouraged."

SOUTHWOLD Suffolk — Map 3

The Swan Hotel *Tel* Southwold (0502) 722186
Market Place *Fax* (0502) 724800
Southwold IP18 6EG *Telex* 97223

Most of the hotels in this unspoilt town are owned by Adnams, the brewer and wine merchant. Their latest showpiece, *The Swan* is warmly nominated this year: "It has been restored at great expense and reorganised, and is now a hotel of fine standing with an authentic ambience and few fripperies. I have stayed seven times in the last nine months. Staff are welcoming and anxious to please. Reception rooms are spacious, full of light and comfortably furnished. Bedrooms vary considerably; those in the main building have a view over the little town square, the new ones in the back garden do not have quite the same feeling. But the dining room exudes quality – white linen, sparkling glasses, lots of space. Three menus are proposed; they are inventive, with fresh produce, and are well cooked, presented and – generally – well served. The wine list is comprehensive. Breakfast is of the 'improved' English genre – good, freshly brewed coffee, wholemeal toast. The icing on the cake? Rise at the not-too-early hour of 7 and you will see the dray horses led clattering under the archway entrance from their stables in the town to be hitched to their drays in the brewery just behind the hotel – fine sight, fine sound, and a fine smell of horse, leather strapping and brewing." (*William A Howard; also MP Holden*) Only niggle: "No bathroom shelf."

Open All year.
Rooms 2 suites, 38 double, 5 singles – 43 with bath and shower, 2 with shower, all with telephone, radio, TV; baby-listening if requested in advance. 18 in garden. Some on ground floor.
Facilities Lift, ramps, wheelchair etc for &. Drawing room, reading room, bar, dining room. Garden. Sea 150 yds.
Location Central, on market square, by town hall.
Restrictions No smoking in dining room. Dogs in garden rooms only.
Credit cards Access, Amex, Visa.
Terms B&B (English): single £36–£46, double £72–£86, suite £110. Bar lunch from £2, set lunch £12–£18, dinner £15.50–£22.50. Midweek winter breaks. Reduced rates for children sharing parents' room; high teas 5.30–6 pm.
Service/tipping: "No service charge. Gratuities at customers' discretion."

SPARK BRIDGE Cumbria   Map 4

Bridgefield House   *Tel* Lowick Bridge (022 985) 239
Spark Bridge   *Fax* (022 985) 379
Nr Ulverston LA12 8DA

Spark Bridge is on the banks of the river Crake, a short drive to the fells and the lakes themselves; the scenery is beautiful if less dramatic than further north, and it is well away from the tourist hordes. *Bridgefield House*, David and Rosemary Glister's late 19th-century gentleman's residence on a quiet country lane, is "bright, welcoming and charmingly furnished and decorated", and warm throughout in cold weather, with fires in drawing room and dining room and individually controlled radiators in bedrooms. "Our large room was well furnished with antiques and had generous cupboard and drawer space. Mr Glister is a delightful host, both when you arrive and at mealtimes." "He is always on the lookout for anything he can do to please. Mrs Glister is much less in evidence, as she is tied to the kitchen, but is always delightful when she comes out to greet one or to say goodbye." Dinner, at 7.30 for 8 sharp, is the high point of a visit to *Bridgefield House*. While having a drink guests choose from three starters and three desserts. There is only one main course, accompanied by interesting vegetables, followed by a sorbet, then sweet and savoury. "Mrs Glister's cooking continues to be superb, the main course is always unusual and delicious. Mr Glister had remembered the wine we liked on our last visit and made sure it was available." "We never felt too full; excellent wines, with lots of half-bottles. Tea was brought to our bedroom every morning at 8, even when there was a power cut." The Glisters' generosity and ungrasping attitude towards people who often get second-class-citizen treatment in hotels also deserve a mention: they make no supplementary charges for single people nor for one-night stays, practices which they regard as unfair. Children are welcome – there's no charge for high-chairs, cots and high teas or the laundering of babies' clothes; there is no service charge (see below). The hard-working Glisters are constantly making improvements to their home and garden and trying new enterprises; this year David Glister "has started bee-keeping, and samples of honey at breakfast had a distinctive taste and aroma; we are hoping for a good yield in 1990!" (*Michael and Betty Appleby, Moira Jarrett, Clarissa Cave, PE Carter*)

Open All year, but for lunch only on Christmas Day.
Rooms 5 double – all with bath, shower, telephone, radio, baby-listening; tea-making facilities on request.
Facilities Drawing room, bar, dining room. 3-acre garden with swings and see-saw. Sea bathing 3 m; fishing, walking nearby.
Location Off A5092 on back road from Spark Bridge to Lowick Bridge.
Restrictions Not suitable for &. No smoking in dining room. "Well-disciplined dogs only", not in public rooms.
Credit cards Access, Visa.
Terms [1990 rates] B&B £33. Packed lunches on request; set dinner £17 (£20 to non-residents). Spring and autumn breaks. Children 3 and under free, under 12 50% reduction; high teas; free laundry service for babies' clothes.
Service/tipping: "The inclusion of a service charge is iniquitous and should be banned by law. Let's face it, it is only an extra increase in the tariff."

SPREYTON Devon   **Map 1**

Downhayes   `BUDGET`   *Tel* Bow (0363) 82378
Spreyton, Crediton EX17 5AR

This traditional Devon farmhouse dating from the 16th century stands in its own 15 acres in deep countryside high in the mid-Devon hills, 20 miles west of Exeter – a car is essential. *Downhayes* belongs to Wolsey Lodges, a group dedicated to "making the visitor feel like a guest in a private house", and readers continue to confirm how successfully Prue Hines achieves this objective. "A lovely welcome, hot tea and chocolate cake by the fire in the pretty sitting room while Mrs Hines consulted us about dinner. We were the only guests. Our bedroom, off the sitting room, had a French window looking on to the garden, and the bathroom was pretty, with lots of towels. Decor was in soft pastel shades and the beds were warm and comfortable (during dinner Mrs Hines turned on the electric blanket). Dinner was delicious, including excellent fresh vegetables, and we spent the rest of the evening in front of the sitting room fire. Breakfast was of the same high standard, with home-made jam and marmalade. The personal touch is everywhere; Mrs Hines works very hard to make sure you have a good time; nothing is left to chance. You couldn't find anywhere better for a holiday on Dartmoor." (*Ruth West; also Theo Schofield*) No more than six guests can be accommodated at any time; they have their own lounge with log fire, books, parlour games and TV. Dinner, by candle-light, is served punctually at 8 pm (four courses, with two choices of starter and dessert, ending with cheese and coffee). No licence but guests' wine is decanted for them. There is a large barn with a games area and studio. In answer to last year's only criticism, Mrs Hines tells us that the breakfast orange juice is now fresh. She is not planning to increase her rates in 1991. Only one fly in the ointment: "There is a slurry pit behind the house; the smell could be unpleasant if the wind were in the wrong direction."

Open 1 Jan–20 Dec; also New Year.
Rooms 3 double – 2 with bath. 1 ground-floor room.
Facilities Lounge with TV, dining room. 15-acre grounds with games room and studio, garden and pasture.
Location 9 m SW of Crediton. Leave A30 at Whiddon Down (Merrymeet roundabout), follow signs to Spreyton. *Downhayes* is on left 1½ m N of Spreyton on Bow Road.
Restrictions Not suitable for wheelchairs. No smoking in bedrooms. No children under 12. No pets.
Credit cards None accepted.
Terms (Not VAT-rated) B&B £18.50–£32. Light lunch on request £6. Set dinner £12.50. Weekly half-board rate. 5-day embroidery course in June and Sept. Unlicensed – bring your own drink.
Service/tipping: "We do not impose a service charge, nor do we expect tips."

STADDLEBRIDGE North Yorkshire   Map 4

McCoy's at the Tontine   *Tel* East Harlsey (060 982) 671
Staddlebridge
Nr Northallerton DL6 3JB

⊞ *César award in 1989: Utterly acceptable mild eccentricity*

"Confirm all the enthusiastic reports; we really enjoyed *McCoy's* (at a price). We arrived cross and exhausted after a journey of solid roadworks, but everyone was so friendly and the decor such a successful mixture of comfort and flamboyance that we were soon soothed and able to enjoy a delicious meal in the bistro. More formal dinner in the restaurant on Saturday night – absolutely first-class food. Slight hiccup over the cheese which I wanted to see before choosing (this seemed to be quite a novel idea). After a bit of whispering I was led downstairs through the kitchen (very clean and full of friendly faces) into a cold room where I was ungrudgingly shown many, many cheeses by the person who knew all about them. I ended up with five. Grand piano in the breakfast room – and ghostly strains of piano playing at 3 am – but somehow this was entirely in keeping and pleasurable. We were particularly enchanted to hear the gurgling internal water pipes mentioned in the '89 GHG." (*Charles and Annabel Rathbone*) *McCoys* is a stone Victorian house on a busy main road, with effective double-glazing. It has no grounds to speak of, but good views. Bedrooms have bright wallpapers and curtains and comfortable beds; there are bold flowered fabrics and large squashy sofas in the lounges; furniture is "a mix of antiques, bamboo and junk". It's run by the three McCoy brothers. Peter is in charge of the accommodation. Tom is the chef in the restaurant, which "is small, and furnished with giant parasols, odd chairs, 1930s lamps and 1920s net curtains, with 1940s music tinkling in the background". His cooking is much praised: "delicious", "eclectic", "confident", "occasionally reckless". Eugene cooks "straightforward but stylish meals" in the busy bistro downstairs; it is more simply furnished and cheaper, with close-packed tables, blackboard menus and loud rock music. Breakfast is served until lunchtime and it is "a long, leisurely meal including exotic fruits, excellent coffee, and newspapers". One dissident view: "The 'charm' of the surroundings was deeply lost on me; the awfulness of the stairs, corridors and entrances is beyond a joke."

Open All year except 25/26 Dec. Restaurant closed Mon.
Rooms 6 double – all with bath, shower, telephone, radio, TV.

Facilities 2 lounges, breakfast room, bistro with bar, restaurant.
Location Junction of A19/A172 (rooms double-glazed). 6 m NE of Northallerton.
Restriction Not suitable for &.
Credit cards All major cards accepted.
Terms (Service at guests' discretion) B&B (English): single £69, double £89. Full
alc in bistro £18, in restaurant £35–£40.

STAMFORD Lincolnshire   Map 3

The George of Stamford   *Tel* Stamford (0780) 55171
71 St Martin's   *Fax* (0780) 57070
Stamford PE9 2LB   *Telex* 32578

🏆 *César award in 1986: Finest old coaching inn*

Stamford is a remarkably unspoilt medieval town, and *The George* is its
historic coaching inn, preserving plenty of innish features such as a
flower-tubbed cobbled courtyard but neither prettified nor self-conscious.
Bedrooms, some with antique furniture, are "beautifully decorated" and
comfortable with well-appointed bathrooms and towels that are changed
daily; even the smaller rooms are approved. Comfortable sofas abound in
the public rooms, and the oak-panelled dining room is "very fine"; it
offers traditional roasts as well as more modern cooking, and again
pleases most readers. In the garden lounge cheaper and simpler food is
available. In the past we have had reports of poor and often unfriendly
service, but this year it is "welcoming and friendly; and we enjoyed the
atmosphere at lunchtime on Monday when the York Bar was full of local
farmers". "As a lone woman traveller I found reception staff and porter
soothing and reassuring. No single was available, but I was offered a
double at the single rate. Morning pot of coffee and newspaper were
delivered on the dot of requested time." (*Mary Fagan, Jane Kaminski*)

Open All year.
Rooms 1 suite, 34 double, 12 single – all with bath and/or shower, telephone,
radio, TV, baby-listening; 24-hour room service.
Facilities Lounge, 2 bars, 3 restaurants; 4 private dining rooms, business centre.
1-acre grounds with patio and monastery garden. Golf ½ m; fly fishing and sailing
at Rutland Water 5 m.
Location In town centre (front rooms double-glazed; rooms overlooking courtyard
are quietest). Parking for 190 cars.
Restrictions Only restaurant suitable for &. No dogs in restaurant.
Credit cards All major cards accepted.
Terms B&B: single £64–£85, double £90–£140, suite £110–£140. Light lunches;
full alc £24. Christmas package; weekend breaks. Reduced rates for children
sharing parents' room; special meals.
*Service/tipping: "Service included. Gratuities are at guests' discretion and distributed
between all staff on a points basis."*

STANTON WICK Avon   Map 2

Carpenters Arms `BUDGET`   *Tel* Compton Dando (076 18) 202
Stanton Wick, Pensford   *Fax* (076 18) 763
Bristol BS18 4BX

This small inn, originally a row of miners' cottages, in a hamlet
overlooking the Chew valley, had an italicised entry in two editions of the

Guide but was then dropped for lack of feedback, so we were glad to be told: "The picture in our mind's eye conjured up by your entry came true the moment we saw this charming inn, tucked away in the beautiful rural countryside on the north side of the Mendip Hills. We were given a warm and friendly welcome and were so pleased that we immediately booked for a second night. This meant that we occupied two bedrooms; both were tastefully decorated, appropriately for the rustic ambience, but with all modern facilities. All the bedrooms are above the bars and restaurant but the floors were well sound-proofed and only a faint murmur was heard in our bedroom immediately above the bar. According to appetite and budget, you can eat in the restaurant or you can eat buffet-style in the *Coopers Parlour* with its cheerful piano. The food is varied and of a high standard. The charm of the place is enhanced by the attentive and cheerful team headed by Nigel Pushman. We found the atmosphere a delight." "Manages to serve both locals and visitors and provide all modern comforts without losing its character as an ancient inn." (*John Gillett, William Ritchie*)

Open All year except Christmas Day.
Rooms 9 double – all with bath, shower, telephone, radio, TV, tea-making facilities, baby-listening.
Facilities Cocktail lounge, 2 bars, main restaurant, Coopers Parlour.
Location On A37, 10 m W of Bath.
Restrictions Not suitable for &. No children under 10. No dogs in bedrooms.
Credit cards All major cards accepted.
Terms (Service at guests' discretion) B&B: single occupancy £39.50, double £46.50. Set Sun lunch £10. Full alc: Coopers Parlour from £10, restaurant £17. Reduced rates for children sharing parents' room. Winter and spring weekend breaks.

STAPLEFORD Leicestershire   **Map 4**

Stapleford Park   *Tel* Wymondham (057 284) 522
Stapleford, Melton Mowbray   *Fax* (057 284) 651
LE14 2EF   *Telex* 342319

🏆 *César award in 1989: Most exciting newcomer of the year*

Stapleford Park was opened in 1988 by Bob and Wendy Payton. It is a luxurious country house combined with elements of an American resort hotel. Its full title is *Stapleford Park Country House Hotel and Sporting Estate*, and there are many outdoor pursuits on offer in the 500 acres of woods and parkland, including basketball, a jogging track, and an equestrian centre in an impressive stable block half a mile from the house. The house is a Grade I listed building, a mixture of periods and styles saved from Disney eclecticism by the beauty of the ivory-coloured stone and the gentleness of the lakeside setting. Inside are stone arches, lots of dark mahogany, magnificent wood carvings attributed to Grinling Gibbons in the dining room, a "clubby" library, and a 19th-century Elizabethan-style wing. Breakfast, with fresh orange juice, home-made bread, blueberry muffins and good coffee, is served on Peter Rabbit china in the vaulted 16th-century refectory. The "signature bedrooms" have each been designed by a "famous name" – Lady Jane Churchill, Lindka Cierach, Liberty, Tiffany, etc. Turnbull and Asser has men's shirting fabric on the wall, tweed-covered chairs, framed bow-ties, and pictures hung by braces; Crabtree and Evelyn has hundreds of pictures of wild flowers and herbs; Max Pike has a free-standing bath in front of the window in the bedroom.

"The scale of the house and the quality of the furnishings make all other country house hotels seem modest by comparison," a reader commented last year. "One quickly establishes a relationship with the staff that is unlike anything previously experienced in a hotel. They are told to make you feel as if you were guests at their dinner party, and they do. Bob Payton's casual bonhomie belies a highly professional attention to detail." A 1990 comment: "We were slightly disconcerted by the off-beat jokiness of the brochure, but reserved judgement – fortunately. The welcome by Bob Payton and his entire staff is warm, friendly and relaxed. Our room was very attractive and comfortable, with lovely views. Perhaps lighting a little too subdued everywhere? And butter just a little too cold. Otherwise full marks." (*Joy and Raymond Golding*) There is also, however, an opposing view: "It's stuffy, pretentious and very expensive, and though the staff were helpful and pleasant, the attitude of Mr and Mrs Payton was cold." The restaurant has had several identity crises in its first two years. In early 1990 the kitchens were taken over by an American husband and wife team, Rick Tramonto and Gale Gand, who summarise their American new-wave style of cooking, with unusual combinations and informal presentation, as "fresh tastes and fun". At the time of going to press we have not had reports on this new regime; we would welcome them.

Open All year.
Rooms 4 suites, 31 double – all with bath, shower, telephone, radio, satellite TV, baby-listening.
Facilities Lift, ramp. Drawing room, salon, 3 sitting rooms, library, dining room, breakfast room, banqueting suite. 500-acre parkland with church, lake with fishing, tennis, mini-golf, basketball, croquet, clay-pigeon shooting, jogging track, equestrian centre.
Location 4 m E of Melton Mowbray. From A1 turn off at Colsterworth; take B676 for 9 m, turn to Stapleford.
Restrictions No smoking in dining room. Children under 10 by prior arrangement only.
Credit cards All major cards accepted.
Terms [1990 rates] (Service at guests' discretion) B&B (continental): single occupancy or double £105–£185, suite £200–£275. English breakfast £8. Full alc £30. 2 night min stay at weekends. Christmas programme. Special meals for children on request.

STON EASTON Somerset   Map 2

Ston Easton Park   *Tel* Chewton Mendip
Ston Easton, Nr Bath BA3 4DF   (076 121) 631
                                                Fax (076 121) 377

🎉 *César award in 1987: Comprehensive excellence in a luxury country house hotel*

Peter and Christine Smedley's grand, immaculately restored Palladian house stands in 26 acres of parkland with gardens designed by Humphry Repton in the 18th century; the river Norr, which runs through the grounds, still flows over Repton's flight of shallow cascades, and the gardens are now being restored on the lines of Repton's plan. The public rooms are high-ceilinged and imposing, with many distinctive architectural features, but are also welcoming with log fires and spectacular flower arrangements. Bedrooms, individually designed by Jean Monro, an expert on 18th-century decoration, are elegant in different ways. Those on the first floor have the huge windows and fine proportions of the original master bedrooms, those on the floor above are smaller. *Ston Easton* is a decorous place: jacket and tie *de rigueur* at dinner, no children under 12. But the open friendliness of the owners and their staff help to dispel any tendency towards the stuffiness so often found in the grander sort of hotel. Visitors have again written enthusiastically of the warm welcome, the impressive decor, and the practice of upgrading visitors' accommodation at no extra cost when the rooms are available. "We felt totally mollycoddled. Our shoes were cleaned, our cars were valeted. Even our bedroom clocks were put forward with an accompanying note as our stay coincided with the arrival of British Summer Time. We ate in the hotel every day. The food, while not of the highest level, lived up to all expectations." (*GN Levy; also Paul Jackson, Sharon Gutman*) Other readers, too, have praised the food, but in the absence of the chef, Mark Harrington, it does not always come up to scratch. *Ston Easton*'s tariff is naturally high, but there is no stinting on service or appointments. Two luxury suites have been created in the gardener's cottage on the banks of the river.

Open All year.
Rooms 2 suites 19 double – all with bath, shower, telephone, radio, TV; tea-making facilities in suites.
Facilities Drawing room, salon, library, 2 restaurants; private dining room; billiard room, servants' room for chauffeurs etc. Terrace. 26-acre grounds with river; fishing.
Location On A37 from Bristol to Shepton Mallet.
Restrictions Only restaurant suitable for &. No children under 12. No dogs in building (kennels on premises).
Credit cards All major cards accepted.
Terms [1990 rates] B&B (continental): double £115–£285, suite £220–£240. English breakfast £7. Set lunch £21.50, dinner £32. Vegetarian and low-fat meals on request. 4-day Christmas programme; winter breaks. 1-night bookings refused for bank holidays.
Service/tipping: "No service charge is included or gratuity expected."

STORRINGTON West Sussex   Map 3

Abingworth Hall   *Tel* West Chiltington
Thakeham Road   (0798) 813636
Storrington RH20 3EF   *Fax* (0798) 813914
                                                     Telex 877835

This solid, virtuous Edwardian country house hotel, once the home of Sir Oswald Mosley, stands in large grounds with a well-tended ornamental lake; it is well placed for touring the South Downs and only 28 miles from Gatwick Airport. Though the decor is not particularly ambitious, it has large public rooms including a no-smoking conservatory and a handsome and fairly formal dining room (jacket and tie required for men). There is a mixed bag of reports for *Abingworth Hall* this year, ranging from a guest at the Christmas house party who has nothing but praise: "No extra charges – even for wine in unlimited quantities. Mrs Bulman created a relaxed and happy atmosphere, and I cannot endorse last year's comment that Mr

Bulman lacks bonhomie." Other encomia: "Bulmans most hospitable; staff helpful and friendly." "Food – internationally prepared fare with beautifully light sauces – so good that despite two full meals a day I never suffered." (*Katie Plowden; also Richard Creed, and others*) On the negative side, however, there is a report of a very small double room with a dangerously low sloping beam and inadequate water pressure in the windowless bathroom, "and breakfast was a traditional English affair, with stone cold toast". "Portions of food ridiculously small." "Heavy background muzak." Commenting on one of last year's criticisms Mrs Bulman writes: "Our table d'hôte menu changes daily and the à la carte menu changes once a week on Friday."

Open All year except first 2 weeks Jan.
Rooms 1 suite, 18 double (1 non-smoking), 2 single – all with bath and/or shower, telephone, radio, TV. Some on ground floor.
Facilities Drawing room, cocktail bar, conservatory, restaurant; functions room. 8-acre grounds with heated swimming pool, putting green, croquet, tennis, lake, 2 helipads.
Location On B2139, 2 m N of Storrington.
Restrictions Not suitable for &. No smoking in conservatory. No children under 10. No dogs.
Credit cards All major cards accepted.
Terms [Until May 1991] B&B (English): single £58, double £80, suite £135; dinner, B&B £60–£86 per person. Set lunch £16, dinner £27; full alc £35. Special breaks. Christmas house party. 1-night bookings sometimes refused for Sat in summer.
Service/tipping: "No service charge; our staff are instructed not to solicit for tips. But we do not actively discourage tipping – our staff receive substantial gratuities which are paid out to them twice a year after deduction of tax and though we pay well over the average rate for the job we could not afford to increase the wages bill to the level reached with the help of the tip fund."

Little Thakeham Hotel   *Tel* Storrington (0903) 744416
Merrywood Lane   *Fax* (0903) 745022
Storrington RH20 3HE

This "outstandingly beautiful" Lutyens manor house, with gardens designed by the great Gertrude Jekyll (the heated swimming pool, grass tennis court and croquet lawn are tucked away so as not to diminish their natural beauty), "nestles happily in the South Downs, commanding superb views across the surrounding countryside". It is run as a luxurious country house hotel by Tim and Pauline Ractliff, and had entries in earlier editions of the Guide but was dropped because of an accumulation of criticisms including inadequate heating in cold weather. The house may still be difficult to heat in winter owing to the large rooms and high ceilings, but our inspector in the warm spring of 1990 had nothing but praise for the "charming and efficient reception". "The carpet," she writes, referring to one of the earlier complaints, "could indeed have done with a good clean in places, but a little faded charm fits a house like this. As we were almost the only residents we were upgraded to an executive suite at no extra cost." The bedroom was large, "with vast, much-bedecked bed, elaborate drapes, an equally large sitting room, and a bathroom quite startlingly modern in contrast, with deep sunken bath, lots of toiletries, thick and numerous towels (replaced during dinner). Our friends, in a similar suite, had two smallish baths, which they found a bit awkward." In the elegant dining room, food was "good, if not great, everything freshly cooked and properly hot". Desserts were the least satisfying part of the meal; service was "attentive and helpful". Breakfast was "good apart from commercial jams, a limited choice of cereals and slightly slow service". But all in all, her verdict was highly favourable. More reports please.

Open All year except 23 Dec–5 Jan.
Rooms 2 suites, 7 double – all with bath, shower, telephone, radio, TV. 1 on ground floor.
Facilities Lounge, bar, restaurant. 6-acre grounds with heated swimming pool, tennis, croquet.
Location 1½ m N of Storrington; right turn off B2139.
Restriction No dogs.
Credit cards All major cards accepted.
Terms (Service at guests' discretion) B&B (English): single occupancy £70–£110, double £140–£160, suite £175–£200; dinner, B&B: single £97.50–£137.59, double £195–£215, suite £230–£255. Set lunch £18.50, dinner £27.50.

STRATFORD-ON-AVON Warwickshire   Map 2

Stratford House Hotel   *Tel* Stratford-on-Avon
Sheep Street   (0789) 68288
Stratford-on-Avon CV37 6EF   *Fax* (0789) 295580

This small Georgian house had an entry in earlier editions of the Guide as a B&B; later a restaurant, *Shepherd's*, was added. Under new owner, Sylvia Adcock, with chef Jonathan George, it is readmitted following an inspector's report: "The house is ancient, and in one of the town's prettiest old streets, very near the theatre. You enter through a paved passage/patio – very pretty with exuberant plants, hanging baskets, stoneware and statues. Inside it is pleasant understated English, with rosy Sanderson's soft furnishings and moss-green carpets. Our smallish bedroom, overlooking the courtyard, was clean and well lit, with nice, quiet, modern furniture and a good bathroom. The restaurant, also open to non-residents, is beautifully thought out, with splendid well-framed prints and attractive tableware; half of it is a large conservatory jutting out into the patio; service was very attentive. Food was beautifully presented and delicious apart from some slightly heavy pasta. Breakfast was good too. Quite expensive, but good value, with a relaxed, unfussy atmosphere." More reports please.

Open All year.
Rooms 1 family, 9 double – all with bath (3 also have shower), telephone, radio, TV, tea-making facilities; baby-sitting on request.
Facilities Lounge, bar, restaurant. Patio.
Location Central. 100 yds from theatre. Hotel has parking arrangements.
Restrictions Not suitable for &. No dogs.
Credit cards All major cards accepted.
Terms (Service at guests' discretion) B&B: single £50–£60, double £54–£80, family £85–£98. Full alc £20.

****
*   *
* **Traveller's tale** *The plates for the steak were cold. On being told this,* *
* *the waitress (one of the owners) said: "Chefs simply won't heat plates* *
* *these days."*   *
*   *
****

STRETTON Leicestershire   Map 4

Ram Jam Inn
Great North Road
Stretton LE15 7QX

Tel Castle Bytham (0780) 410776
Fax (0780) 724721
Telex 342888

This old coaching inn on the Great North Road was converted a few years ago into a motel with a difference by the owners of *Hambleton Hall* (q.v.). Not long after its opening it suffered a serious fire; last year it reopened totally refurbished. This year both manageress and chef are new. The *Ram Jam* is an open-plan pub with a snack bar, salad bar and restaurant, and a small but comfortable sitting area. The bedrooms are large, with large bathrooms, and face away from the A1. "Just as pleasant as it was before the fire. The rooms are prettily decorated to high standards and have comfortable beds, but there are few extras in the bathroom. Our double bed was huge. Unfortunately the restaurant menu now has only one vegetarian dish, but the staff were pleased to help and service was excellent." (*E Blakely; also M and B Appleby*) In deference to the drink-driving laws, the *Ram Jam* offers all-day tea and coffee and has a breath-tester at the door.

Open All year except Christmas Day.
Rooms 7 double, 1 single – all with bath, shower, telephone, radio, TV, tea-making facilities.
Facilities 2 bars, restaurant, grill, snack bar. 2-acre grounds.
Location On W side of A1, 9 m N of Stamford. Travelling S take B668 exit for Oakham; travelling N turn off through garage just past B668 turnoff.
Restriction Only restaurant suitable for &.
Credit cards Access, Amex, Visa.
Terms [1990 rates] (Service at guests' discretion) Rooms: single occupancy £35, double £45. Breakfast: continental from £1.50, English from £3.25. Full alc £15.

STURMINSTER NEWTON Dorset   Map 2

Plumber Manor
Sturminster Newton DT10 2AF

Tel Sturminster Newton
(0258) 72507
Fax (0258) 73370

🏆 *César award in 1987: Sustained excellence in a middle-price country hotel*

This handsome Jacobean house in the heart of Hardy countryside has been the home of the Prideaux-Brunes since the early 17th century and for the past 18 years has been run as a restaurant-with-rooms by brothers Richard and Brian Prideaux-Brune. The atmosphere is very much a family one; dogs lie around on the lawn and in front of the fire, and accompany you when you go for a walk, and it's the sort of place which will lend you tennis gear if you did not bring your own. The jovial Richard is much in evidence and "somehow manages to give every guest his personal attention" – he waits and does reception and bar. There are six bedrooms in the house, opening off a gallery hung with family portraits, and ten (four new ones this year) in a converted stable block 50 yards away; the latter are particularly well appointed and have been highly praised; and this year a reader staying in the main house reported: "Very comfortable room, spacious, with nice old bits of furniture, but uncluttered. Like the rest of the house, it was refreshingly un-designerish, and felt like houses in the country one actually does stay in rather than a 'country house hotel'. Despite the casual air, everything had been carefully thought out. The food, cooked by Brian P-B, served in the spacious dining room, was all of a piece with the house, not wildly exciting, but carefully prepared, using good ingredients, portions not too large, served at a decent pace. There is a moderate wine list, with a reasonable number of half-bottles.'' There are two set menus – the more expensive one has more choice. *Plumber Manor* styles itself as a restaurant-with-rooms; those in search of comprehensive cosseting would probably be happier elsewhere. But the consistency of its standards and the comfort of the bedrooms makes it a far more attractive hotel than many that boast that name. ''Conservative'' is one reader's epithet this year. ''Terribly, terribly British,'' comments a visitor from America.

Open 1 Mar–end Jan. Restaurant closed for lunch.
Rooms 16 double – all with bath, shower, telephone, TV, tea-making facilities. 10 (6 on ground floor) in stable block 50 yds from main building.
Facilities Lounge, bar, gallery, restaurant in main house; sitting/meeting room in converted barn. 4-acre gardens with tennis, croquet, trout stream.
Location 2 m SW of Sturminster Newton; on A357 to Haselbury Bryan.
Restrictions No smoking in dining room. No children under 12. No dogs.
Credit cards Access, Visa.
Terms [1990 rates] Dinner, B&B (English) £50–£70. Set dinner £18 and £22. Winter bargain breaks.

TALLAND-BY-LOOE Cornwall   Map 1

Talland Bay Hotel   *Tel* Polperro (0503) 72667
Talland-by-Looe PL13 2JB   *Fax* (0503) 72940

''A very good hotel for a family summer holiday.'' ''We were entirely delighted. The setting is an oasis of peace on the coastal walk, far from crowds and traffic. We had a beautiful room with a large balcony overlooking the impeccably maintained swimming pool. Service was fast, unobtrusive and friendly. Six dinners were excellent by any standards, one was average (Sunday, presumably chef's night off). There was an enterprising wine list and a selection of about 15 well-chosen malts. Most of our fellow guests had been to *Talland* several times before; we will certainly return.'' (*W Rankin, PS Linklater; also Prof Sir Alan and Lady Cook, Wilson G Francis*)

This 16th-century Cornish country house, with an unpretentious decor, in two and a half acres of carefully tended sub-tropical gardens, overlooks an unspoilt bay. Bedrooms are agreeably furnished in traditional style; some are small – best discuss your requirements on booking. Breakfast is a generous affair starting with a buffet of cereal, muesli etc; the cooked dishes are carefully prepared and generous. A buffet lunch is offered by the pool in summer. The hotel has no lack of aficionados, but other visitors have been more critical, one disagreeing about the food, another finding the decor lacking in style and the bar cramped, a third considering the prices high for what is on offer. Service is said to be willing but inexperienced and overstretched at times. Out of season the owners, Major and Mrs Mayman, fill the hotel with bridge, bird-watching, painting, archaeology, geology and yoga holidays. More reports please.

Open Mid-Feb–end Dec, Christmas and New Year.

Rooms 1 suite, 17 double, 5 single – all with bath and/or shower, telephone, radio, TV, baby-listening. 2 in hotel grounds, 2 across lane. 2 ground-floor rooms specially adapted for &.
Facilities Lounge, no-smoking lounge, bar, dining room. 2½-acre grounds with swimming pool, putting and croquet. 5 mins' walk to beach with safe swimming.
Location 2¼ m SW of Looe, turn left at hotel sign on Looe–Polperro road.
Restrictions No children under 5 in dining room at night. Dogs in certain rooms only; not in public rooms.
Credit cards All major cards accepted.
Terms Dinner, B&B £40–£72. Set lunch £8, dinner £16; full alc £28. 1-night bookings refused in high season. Bridge, bird-watching, painting, archaeology, geology, yoga, honeymoon, Christmas and New Year packages. Reduced rates for children sharing parents' room; high teas.
Service/tipping: "No service charge. We do not encourage tipping; it is left entirely to guests' discretion."

TAPLOW Berkshire   Map 2

Cliveden   *Tel* Burnham (0628) 668561
Taplow SL6 0JF   *Fax* (0628) 661837
                                                        Telex 846562

This magnificent Grade I listed stately home, meticulously restored and elegantly furnished, in large and lovely National Trust grounds on the Thames, went through teething troubles in its early days but now offers "a delightful escape from reality where you can enjoy being cosseted with old-world charm". It is warmly nominated by the author of our appendix on hotels' attitudes towards children, *Dr Alan Lucas*: "Certainly one of the best hotels we have stayed at in Britain. What is extraordinary is that in such grand surroundings there is real human warmth. There is little to criticise. The care is what one would expect: everything from offering to unpack to unflinchingly catering for the personal – sometimes eccentric – whims of the customers. The public rooms are spectacular, with breathtaking views. The bedrooms are all quite different; those I have seen are marvellous; the ones on the second floor have the best views. The dining room must be one of the finest in Britain; food is serious and interesting and there is an extraordinary wine list for customers with deep pockets; the communal breakfast is friendly and unstuffy. The hotel manager is there on weekdays, and there are two assistant managers whose personal qualities and ability are of the highest order. *Cliveden* accepts children, and the baby-sitting is the best and most professional we have ever had. The facilities are marvellous [see below], and are growing; the new pavilion with heated swimming pool, jacuzzi, gymnasium etc is a lovely place to relax, and its staff are welcoming, intelligent and delightful. The only possible disadvantage is that at weekends the grounds are full of National Trust visitors, but even then it is possible to escape to the pavilion area which is totally private. *Cliveden* is, of course, very expensive but to my mind offers good value for money."

Open All year.
Rooms 8 suites, 20 double, 3 single – 30 with bath and shower, 1 with shower, all with telephone, radio, TV; baby-listening on request. 9 on ground floor.
Facilities Lift. 4 sitting rooms, 2 dining rooms, bar, grill room, billiards room, conference room. 375-acre grounds. Indoor and outdoor swimming pools and tennis courts, squash, horses, practice golf, jogging routes, fishing, boating.
Location 10 m NW of Windsor. Exit 7 from M4.
Credit cards Access, Diners, Visa.

Terms B&B: single £150, double £185–£265, suite £310–£450. Set lunch £26, dinner £39; full alc £40. 1-night bookings sometimes refused for weekends. Special meals for children on request.
Service/tipping: "No service charge. Tips not expected. This is stated on the menu."

TAYNTON Oxfordshire   Map 2

Manor Farm Barn   BUDGET   *Tel* Burford (099 382) 2069
Taynton, Burford OX8 4UH

💧 *César award in 1987: Best rural B&B*

"Our fourth visit. I can't praise it highly enough – summer or winter. Lovely location. The attention to detail in the bedrooms is a tremendous plus. The enormous breakfasts are outstanding, both because of their size and because they are beautifully prepared. Even fish is available, given a day's notice." Mr and Mrs Florey's welcoming, comfortably modernised Cotswold stone farmhouse enjoys a rural setting in an unspoilt hamlet near Burford, which has a lovely old church, but no shop, pub or post office. Tranquillity is guaranteed by the extensive grounds and adjoining pastures down to the river Windrush. It has only three bedrooms, all with beamed ceiling and private bathroom. Breakfast – the only meal served – is taken communally at an elegant mahogany table. It's an excellent base for touring the Cotswolds, but you will need a car. (*LF Stuckey*)

Open Feb–Dec except Christmas, New Year and owners' holiday in winter.
Rooms 3 double – all with bath, shower, radio, TV, tea-making facilities.
Facilities 2 lounges, dining room. 8-acre grounds with garden and paddocks.
Location 1½ m NW of Burford; from Burford, take A361 towards Stow-on-the-Wold; turn left towards Taynton at roundabout, then left by church.
Restrictions Not suitable for &. No smoking in dining room. No children under 10. No dogs.
Credit cards None accepted.
Terms B&B double from £45. 1-night bookings refused Sat. (No restaurant.)
Service/tipping: "Service included. Tips not required or looked for."

TEIGNMOUTH Devon   Map 1

Thomas Luny House   BUDGET   *Tel* Teignmouth (0626) 772976
Teign Street
Teignmouth TQ14 8EG

This beautifully proportioned Georgian house, near the fish quay in the old quarter of Teignmouth, was built by the marine artist Thomas Luny, and has recently been turned into an informal, very small, reasonably priced hotel by John and Alison Allan, who previously ran a well-liked Guide hotel, *Woodhayes* at Whimple (now back in the Guide under new owners). You approach through an archway into a courtyard where there is ample parking. The lounge and dining room, both with open fires, lead through French windows into a walled garden. The three bedrooms, all different, "are generous in size, with bath or shower, Malvern water, books and magazines. Excellent three-course (no choice) dinners, with plenty of fresh produce; the wine list is small, well chosen and sensibly priced. Breakfasts are substantial, continental or English, with home-made preserves." "The Allans give it the feeling of a home, with every consideration for the guests' comfort." (*SEC Dean, John Knapman, and others*)

Open Mid-Jan–mid-Dec.
Rooms 4 double – all with bath and/or shower, telephone, radio, TV.
Facilities 2 lounges, dining room. Walled garden. 5 mins' walk to sea with sandy beach.
Location Follow signs to quay, then Teign Street. Courtyard parking.
Restrictions Not suitable for &. No smoking in the dining room. No children under 12.
Credit cards None accepted.
Terms B&B £27.50; dinner, B&B £41. Set dinner £13.50.
Service/tipping: "No service charge levied, nor tips expected."

TETBURY Gloucestershire   Map 2

Calcot Manor   *Tel* Leighterton (066 689) 391
Beverstone   *Fax* (066 689) 394
Tetbury GL8 8YJ

Last year there were a few niggles about *Calcot Manor*; this year there's nothing but praise: "A very well-managed hotel with a professional team keeping an eye on the smallest detail and showering unobtrusive attention on visitors. The main building provides comfortable lounges with log fires and a most attractive dining room. Our bedroom with six-foot bed gave us the best night's sleep away from home that we can remember." "The weekend was everything we hoped for. Very comfortable 'standard' room in courtyard, morning tea brought to us, superb food and splendid service, always vigilant and willing but not obtrusive." The manor, owned and run by Brian and Barbara Ball, with son Richard, is a timeless mellow Cotswold house with a range of venerable outbuildings, including a fine 14th-century tithe barn. There is also a heated outdoor pool. Bedrooms, which vary in size, have been cleverly fitted into the old building and there are some newer ones in a converted stable block. Some have a large and luxurious bathroom (four have a whirlpool bath). No errors of taste; decor is restrained rather than adventurous. The "peach-coloured restaurant", with innovative modern cooking by the young chef Ramon Farthing, boasts a *Michelin* rosette. There are two set menus – three or six courses – but no à la carte. The wine list is catholic, and well described, with an unusually modest mark-up. (*Paul and Christine Butler, James and Mary Gibson*)

Open All year except 2–11 Jan. Restaurant closed to non-residents Sun night.
Rooms 13 double – all with bath, shower (4 have whirlpool bath), telephone, radio, TV. 5 ground-floor rooms in courtyard.
Facilities Lounge with dispense bar, drawing room, dining room (pianist on Sat night); private dining room, conference facilities. 4-acre grounds with croquet lawn, outdoor swimming pool (heated May–Sep). Fishing, golf and riding nearby.
Location 3 m W of Tetbury on A4135. Parking.
Restrictions No smoking in dining room. No children under 12. No dogs.
Credit cards All major cards accepted.
Terms B&B (English): single occupancy from £80, double £100–£130; dinner, B&B: single from £110, double £165–£195. Set lunch £16 and £25, dinner £27.50 and £35. Weekend or midweek breaks; Christmas package; gourmet and wine weekends in Autumn. 1-night bookings refused during Badminton, Gold Cup week, Gatcombe horse trials, some bank holidays.
Service/tipping: "We do not make a service charge and tips are not expected."

THORNBURY Avon   Map 2

Thornbury Castle   *Tel* Thornbury (0454) 418511
Thornbury   *Fax* (0454) 416188
Bristol BS12 1HH   *Telex* 449986

"An imposing building on the edge of an attractive and well-heeled village, peacefully set in vast grounds with well-tended gardens and a vineyard." The castle was never finished, but the remains, mostly dating from the early 16th century, have been luxuriously renovated and make an impressive hotel. Baronial public rooms have huge fireplaces, mullioned windows, antique furniture and tapestries. Bedrooms vary considerably in size; all have a well-appointed bathroom and the extras to be expected of this class of hotel. "Ours, approached up a spiral staircase, occupied the full width of one wing. It was immense, with stone walls, an old four-poster, ornate plasterwork ceiling, two huge fireplaces, each with a gas coal-fire, neutral carpet with oriental rugs, tapestry curtains and matching bedcover. Tapestries hung over each fireplace, and there were some splendid pieces of antique furniture. Although on an operatic scale, the room was warm and comfortable, with sympathetic lighting. It would, perhaps, have benefited from a few personal touches such as flowers, magazines, books and local information. Breakfast, served in the bedroom, was first-class." The restaurant in two dining rooms ("sombre, and either magnificently baronial or gloomy according to taste") is popular locally, but the direction of the kitchens underwent some vicissitudes in 1989/90, and current feeling is that, though the service is very good, the cooking is "not quite up to the standard of the rest of the operation". There is an extensive wine list including good-value wines from all over the world and a vegetarian dish on the menu each day. Though some readers have commented on the slightly impersonal, international feeling of the castle, the general verdict is, "You pay for luxury, and you get it." (*David Morris, David and Kate Wooff; also Mr and Mrs T Hodge, and others*) The proprietor, Maurice CR Taylor, writes: "I would like to make a small correction to your 1990 entry. I am not American, though I lived in Canada for 18 years and in California for ten. Were I American I would be proud of it, but I am English, and proud of that."

Open All year except 2–12 Jan.
Rooms 1 suite, 15 double, 2 single – all with bath, shower, telephone, radio, TV; tea-making facilities on request. 5 rooms across small courtyard.
Facilities 2 lounges, 2 dining rooms. 12-acre grounds with walled garden, vineyard and farm. Clay-pigeon shooting. Fishing, indoor heated swimming pool nearby.
Location 12 m N of Bristol, at N edge of Thornbury, just off B4061; lodge gate beside St Mary's parish church.
Restrictions Not suitable for &. No smoking in dining rooms. No children under 12. No dogs.
Credit cards All major cards accepted.
Terms B&B (continental): single £68–£75, double £85–£180, suite £155–£180. Set lunch £16.50, dinner £26.50. Winter breaks. Christmas programme. 2-night stay min for Sat.
Service/tipping: "We feel our customers are entitled to good service. Gratuities are not expected."

TREBARWITH STRAND Cornwall   Map 1

The Old Millfloor **BUDGET**   *Tel* Camelford (0840) 770234
Trebarwith Strand
Tintagel PL34 0HA

A small secluded guest house set in a fern-filled glen by a mill-stream, with old beams, gleaming wood, fresh flowers, clever use of fabrics, light and colour. Not for the disabled or infirm, since there is a steep path down from the road (best to take the minimum of luggage), but perfect for families: lots of pets, ten acres of grounds and the beach ten minutes' walk away; and the prices are ridiculously modest. "I cannot speak highly enough of *The Old Millfloor*. Our room had an old-fashioned feel, with white walls, pure white linen, lots of lace, big feather pillows. Both evenings our dinner (by candle-light in the small beamed dining room with different crystal each night) was excellent. Janice Waddon-Martyn puts together her menus with sensitivity and an emphasis on flavour not richness." Dinner (7.30 to 9) offers one choice of first course and dessert; menus tend to feature home-made soups and ice-creams, fresh vegetables, lashings of clotted cream. No licence, bring your own wine. "The atmosphere is quiet and relaxing." "No TV, radio or papers (except Sunday). Cats and books available by the fire for wetter days." (*Deborah Loveluck-Newman*) In the past the plumbing has been said to be "unpredictable". More reports welcome.

Open Easter–Nov.
Rooms 3 doubles with H&C and TV.
Facilities Restaurant with lounge. 10-acre grounds with garden, orchard, paddocks and stream. Beach 10 mins' walk. Riding centre 2½ m.
Location 2 m S of Tintagel.
Restrictions Not suitable for &. No dogs.
Credit cards None accepted.
Terms (No VAT) B&B £15. Dinner £10.50 (unlicensed – bring your own wine). 1 child sharing parents' room free; special meals.
Service/tipping: "No service charge. Tips not expected."

TRESCO Isles of Scilly   Map 1

The Island Hotel   *Tel* Scillonia (0720) 22883
Tresco, Isles of Scilly   *Fax* (0720) 23008
Cornwall TR24 0PU

Tresco is a private island, two miles by one, renowned for the Abbey Gardens, with exotic plants from all over the world. No cars are allowed – there are bicycles for hire, and guests of *The Island Hotel* are met on arrival (by boat or helicopter) by a tractor and trailer – so Tresco (day trippers apart) is exceptionally peaceful. The hotel is a modern building with five acres of grounds beside the sea, and a private beach. It enjoys dramatic views of the rocky coast and other islands, and a peaceful and beautiful setting. There have recently been some changes: reception enlarged, public areas recarpeted in pale green, three bedrooms, all with balcony, added. In the winter of 1990 the dining room, lounge and garden terrace will be extended, nine more bedrooms added, and three small doubles converted into singles. The hotel has many regular visitors who find it "comfortable, relaxed in the right way, with good and appropriate food, acceptable wine list". "Our hosts, John and Wendy Pyatt, welcomed us personally; transport in tractors is available free round the island. Succulent dinners. Breakfast not quite as good." "Expensive but worth it." The extensive dinner menu always features one low-fat dish as well as a vegetarian one, but is sometimes criticised by readers who would prefer fewer dishes and simpler presentation. On Sunday evenings there is a lavish buffet; snack lunches are served in the garden. (*Richard Creed, Rev IA Watson, and others*) Rooms vary in size, style and position, and are charged accordingly; some have thin walls. The hotel is not really suitable for young children; some visitors find the hotel "cliquey", and feel there is an excessive emphasis on time-keeping at meals. More reports please.

Open Mar–end Oct.
Rooms 1 suite, 27 double, 2 single – all with bath, shower, telephone, radio, TV, baby-listening; 7 with tea-making facilities. 2 ground-floor rooms.
Facilities Lounge, bar lounge, bar, TV room, dining room, adults' games room, children's playroom; laundry facilities. 5-acre grounds with terrace, heated swimming pool, bowls, croquet, badminton; private beach with safe bathing. Boats, sailing dinghies for hire.
Location Scheduled helicopter flight (British International Helicopters Ltd – approx 20 minutes) or boat (approx 2½ hours) from Penzance; not Sun. Advance booking essential.
Restrictions Island not suitable for &. No dogs allowed on Tresco.
Credit cards None accepted.
Terms Dinner, B&B £62–£110. Set lunch £10, bar lunches available, dinner £22. Discounts for pre-booked stays of over 5 nights; Tresco gardeners' 7-day spring/autumn holiday. Reduced rates for children in bunk beds or cots; 6 pm high tea.
Service/tipping: "No service charge made or tips expected. If guests wish to reward courtesy and good service or a particular person for some extra service it is entirely up to them."

The New Inn　　　　　　　　　　　　　　　*Tel* Scillonia (0720) 22844
Tresco, Isles of Scilly
Cornwall TR24 0QQ

A much cheaper alternative to *The Island Hotel* and more like a country pub, *The New Inn*, run by Chris and Lesley Hopkins, offers friendly hospitality and good food, with simple but adequate accommodation. The only public rooms are the bars and a lounge. Bedrooms are fairly small but have a pretty floral decor and good lighting; many have lovely sea views; all now have telephone and TV. The bathrooms have good fluffy towels but lack "freebies". There is a small garden and a swimming pool. The food, on a simple but imaginative set menu with plenty of choice, is "of a high standard, combining fresh ingredients, skilful cooking and excellent presentation; fish dishes are particularly good. The staff are friendly and helpful." Good breakfasts and bar lunches. "Better value for money you will not find." (*Abigail Kirby Harris, Ken and Mildred Evans*)

Open All year.
Rooms 10 double, 2 single – all with bath, shower, telephone, radio, TV, tea-making facilities, baby-listening.
Facilities Lounge, lounge bar, public bar, restaurant. Garden with swimming pool. Sandy beaches with safe bathing and fishing.
Location As for the *Island* above. Hotel will make travel arrangements.
Restrictions Not suitable for &. No dogs allowed on Tresco.
Credit cards None accepted.

Terms Dinner, B&B (English) £30–£49. Bar lunches. Set dinner £14.50. Special breaks. Christmas and New Year packages. Reduced rates and special meals for children.

Service/tipping: "It is time to face up to the truth. Pay and conditions in the industry are not as good as employers make out so tips are a necessary evil. I have yet to visit an average hotel or restaurant in any country that was pompous enough to say they didn't accept gratuities, so why should British hotels be expected to refuse what is often one of the best reflections of the standards offered by a hotel? My staff do very well for tips which are pooled and shared equally between them."

TROUTBECK Cumbria   Map 4

Mortal Man Hotel `BUDGET`   *Tel* Ambleside (053 94) 33193
Troutbeck, Nr Windermere
LA23 1PL

Annette and Christopher Poulsom's modest Lakeland inn peacefully set on a hilltop above the Troutbeck Valley celebrated its tricentenary in 1989 and made its Guide debut in 1990. It is warmly endorsed: "Atmosphere delightful, pre-dinner drinks in cosy bar lounge; two large, friendly dogs with a liking for after-dinner mints. Rooms a little small but spotless and warm with lovely views. Food outstanding in choice, quality and quantity. Different menu daily." "Breakfast scheduled for 9 am but we needed to leave earlier. Christopher Poulsom was only too happy to oblige – and with one of the best English breakfasts I have eaten for some while. What a pity other hoteliers can't give the same value for money." "Atmosphere friendly, welcoming and relaxed. Good packed lunches." The oak-beamed residents' lounge has an open fire in winter; there are old hunting prints on the walls, comfortable easy chairs, gleaming brass-topped tables. In the welcoming public bar, also beamed, good bar food is served from a separate kitchen. (*DJ Logan, IC Dewey, Martin Bailey, and others*)

Open Mid-Feb–mid-Nov.
Rooms 10 double, 2 single – all with bath, shower, telephone, radio, TV, tea-making facilities.
Facilities Lounge, lounge bar, public bar, restaurant. ½-acre grounds.
Location 3 m N of Windermere.
Restrictions Not suitable for &. No children under 5.
Credit cards None accepted.
Terms Dinner, B&B £35–£40. Set lunch £10, dinner £16.50. Reductions for longer stays.
Service/tipping: "Service included. The rates quoted above are what I like to get – no more, no less."

TROWBRIDGE Wiltshire   Map 2

The Old Manor Hotel `BUDGET`   *Tel* Trowbridge (0225) 777393
Trowle, Trowbridge BA14 9BL   *Telex* (0225) 765443

Fine listed house, part medieval with Queen Anne alterations, in 4-acre grounds near the handsome market town of Trowbridge. Bedrooms, varying in size, in recently converted barns and cowsheds. Nothing special about the decor, but recommended for comfortable, well-equipped bedrooms, furnished in pine, and good plain cooking by Diane Humphreys using fresh ingredients, with limited choice. Meals for residents only. No hidden charges. Closed 2 weeks in winter. 14 rooms, all with private facilities. B&B double £48–£54; full alc £20. New nomination. More reports please.

TRURO Cornwall   Map 1

Alverton Manor   *Tel* Truro (0872) 76633
Tregolls Road, Truro TR1 1XQ   *Fax* (0872) 222989

A splendid Grade II listed sandstone building, once a convent, in an attractive hillside setting in walking distance of town centre. Recently extensively refurbished, but original features retained; heavy hangings, period furniture, sumptuous flower arrangements in public rooms. Large, comfortable bedrooms. Food – nouvelle in style, using Cornish ingredients – inventive and sophisticated. Slightly impersonal, perhaps business-oriented atmosphere. 25 rooms, all with bath and/or shower. B&B double £90–£125. Alc dinner (excluding wine) £30. New hotel, recently nominated. More reports please.

ULLINGSWICK Hereford and Worcester   Map 2

The Steppes Country House   *Tel* Hereford (0432) 820424
    Hotel
Ullingswick
Nr Hereford HR1 3JG

Ullingswick is a tiny Domesday-old hamlet quietly situated in the Wye valley, well situated for exploring the County of Hereford and the Welsh Marches. The *Steppes* is a Grade II listed 17th-century country house, rich in exposed beams, inglenook fireplaces and other period features, and furnished with antiques; there is a cellar bar, with flagged floor and rough stone walls; two bedrooms are in converted stables, with vaulted ceilings. It is a highly personal guest house which does not suit those in search of hotel-type service, but many regular visitors write to us in praise of the comfortable and spacious bedrooms, with good beds and reading lights and large bathrooms, and the "delicious and imaginative meals". The four-course dinners, no choice except by prior arrangement, are served at 7.30 pm by candle-light with classical music. (There is also an à la carte menu offering "less adventurous" food, and vegetarian dishes, but you must order from this by 10 am.) Continental breakfast can be served in the bedroom. English, in the dining room, must be ordered the night before. (*Heather Kirk, Moira Jarrett, AG Saunders*) Concerning earlier comments about high-cholesterol cooking, Tricia Howland writes: "Only polyunsaturated fats are used in the preparation of meals, and only the finest lean cuts of meat. Margarine is always available; all cream used is fat-reduced. One guest carried out a cholesterol check after her week's stay and found her count had dropped from 5.2 to 4.3!" Two niggles this year: "The cooked breakfast isn't served until 9 am, and everyone is served at once so one cannot hope to leave until 10 am." (But continental breakfast is served from 8 to 10.) "We hate canned music and it was very loud at our table next to the speaker. We even had it at breakfast!"

Open All year except 2 weeks before Christmas and 2 weeks after New Year.
Rooms 5 double – all with bath and/or shower, telephone, radio, TV, mini-bar, tea-making facilities. 1 on ground floor.
Facilities Lounge, cellar bar, dining room. 1½-acre garden with duck pond, sheep, rabbits and chickens; riding and fishing nearby.
Location 7 m NE of Hereford off A417 Gloucester to Leominster road.
Restrictions No smoking in bar and dining room. No children under 12. No dogs in public rooms.
Credit cards Some may be accepted in 1990/91.
Terms Dinner, B&B £35–£44. Bargain breaks all year; Christmas and New Year 3-day house parties.
Service/tipping: "Service included. We do not ask for or expect any form of gratuity."

ULLSWATER Cumbria   Map 4

 Howtown Hotel `BUDGET`   *Tel* Pooley Bridge (076 84) 86514
Ullswater, Penrith CA10 2ND

César award: Best budget hotel of the year

"Our first visit; a unique and worthwhile experience. Atmosphere extremely sympathetic. Spotlessly clean, and a rare example of a family-run country hotel untouched by changing times and mores. We were the only newcomers; everyone else had been returning for years." "Wonderful position, a marvellous place to stay; good home-cooked food; it is a pleasure to have the bed turned down during dinner, and early morning tea brought to the room rather than to have to make it yourself." This comfortable farmhouse on the unspoilt southern shore of Ullswater has long been a favourite of Guide readers, particularly walkers and climbers, and is run by Jacquie Baldry and her son David – the fourth generation of the family to be involved. It is in complete contrast to the luxurious and sophisticated *Sharrow Bay* (below) two miles away. *Howtown* is a long low building set 100 yards back from the road. Few of the bedrooms have private facilities and furnishings are comfortable and homely rather than elegant. The food is generous rather than sophisticated – dinner, with limited choice, is at 7 pm; cold and packed lunches are available. The atmosphere is relaxed and the tariff astoundingly low. The hotel has its own private foreshore on Ullswater. (*Sally Saysell, Mrs C Moncreiffe*) *Howtown* is not easy to get into, due to the very high return rate.

Open End Mar–1 Nov.
Rooms 13 double, 3 single – 3 with bath, 1 with shower, 4 in 2 annexes in grounds. 4 self-catering cottages.
Facilities 4 lounges, 2 bars, TV room, dining room. 2-acre grounds. 300 yds from lake with private foreshore; walking, climbing, riding, golf nearby.
Location On E shore of lake 4 m S of Pooley Bridge.
Restrictions Not suitable for &. No children under 7. Dogs at management's discretion (£1 a day); not in public rooms.
Credit cards None accepted.
Terms [1990 rates] Dinner, B&B £25. Lunch: cold on weekdays from £5.50, table d'hôte on Sun from £6.50; set dinner £9. Reductions for 4-night stays. 1-night bookings sometimes refused. Reduced rates for children sharing parents' room.
Service/tipping: "No service charge. Any gratuities offered are distributed equally among the staff."

Sharrow Bay Country House   *Tel* Pooley Bridge (076 84) 86301
   Hotel   *Fax* (076 84) 86349
Ullswater, Penrith CA10 2LZ

💧 *César award in 1985: For distinguished long service*

Brian Sack and Francis Coulson have run their celebrated country house
hotel on the beautiful, less-crowded eastern shore of Ullswater for forty-
one years. They are still very much in evidence, "smiling down at you in
a kind, avuncular manner over the top of their spectacles". *Sharrow Bay*
is renowned for the prodigal generosity of the meals (breakfasts and
afternoon teas being of the same scale and quality as lunches and dinners)
and a similar prodigality in the furnishings in the bedrooms, filled with
innumerable cosseting extras. Throughout the house, too, there is a
profusion of *objets d'art*, collected over the years. Some of the bedrooms,
particularly those in the main house, are small; those in the annexe, Bank
House, a mile away, are larger. An unusually large staff copes with the
residents and the casual diners. Public rooms can get crowded when the
restaurant is busy. As usual most readers are full of praise: "Bedroom
small and filled with every kind of everything, but very comfortable, view
breathtaking. Food probably the best we've ever eaten. Service and
attitude absolute perfection; everyone you meet is helpful beyond the
bounds of duty – and would they accept any kind of tip? No chance: 'You
have already paid for service, sir.'" "Total relaxation and well-being; a
unique experience. The hospitality dispensed belongs to a bygone age.
The staff are wonderful, and the manager, Nigel Lawrence, is charming
and really wants to make your stay a happy one." "It oozes service. The
waiters in blazers and flannels are a lovely touch." (*Minda Alexander,
Richard Gollin, Mrs JJ Jackson, ML Dodd, and many others*) A few criticisms,
mostly from visitors in peak season: "Too many people in too little space.
Not relaxed but regimented; everyone goes in to dinner at the same time
so you have to queue." "Service slow when it was packed to capacity."
"Breakfast beginning at 9 am is too late." "It would be convenient if they
accepted credit cards, even if this meant raising the tariff a little." But the
ayes still have it by a large majority.

Open Mar–Nov inclusive.
Rooms 6 suites, 17 double, 7 single – 26 with bath and/or shower, all with
telephone, radio, TV; some with tea-making facilities. 17 in cottages, Lodge
annexe and Bank House, at varying distances from main building. 5 ground-floor
rooms.
Facilities 4 lounges, conservatory, breakfast room, 2 dining rooms. 12-acre
grounds at Sharrow, 5 acres at Bank House; garden, woodlands; $\frac{1}{2}$ m of lake shore
with safe bathing, private jetty and boathouse; fishing, boating, walking, climbing.
Location On E shore of Ullswater, 2 m S of Pooley Bridge. Turn by small church
in Pooley Bridge and take Howtown Lane. (M6 exit 40.)
Restrictions No smoking in dining room. No children under 13. No dogs.
Credit cards None accepted.
Terms Dinner, B&B single £65–£115. Set lunch from £19 (light lunches also
available weekdays), dinner from £35. 10% midweek reductions Mar, Nov.
1-night bookings sometimes refused, especially weekends.
*Service/tipping: "No service charge. We and our staff give our services freely and do not
expect to be rewarded by clients directly. If a particularly persistent client wishes to
impose his will upon us we say (we hope without causing offence) that tipping is a feudal
system and degrades both giver and receiver."*

UPPINGHAM Leicestershire   Map 1

The Lake Isle Restaurant   *Tel* (0572) 822951
and Town House Hotel   *Fax* (0572) 822951
16 High Street East
Uppingham, Rutland LE15 9PZ

Claire and David Whitfield's "Restaurant and Town House Hotel" in an 18th-century building in main street (entrance in an alley at the side) of attractive small market-town. Bedrooms, in building at rear and adjacent cottage, vary in size and character. Restaurant, with country-style decor, offers French cooking with limited choice; meals priced according to the number of courses taken. Some readers this year are enthusiastic about the rooms – "attractive and comfortable", and the cooking – "simple; good quality in all aspects". But there are criticisms of some bedrooms, and of the welcome. Hence these italics. Closed bank holiday Mon, restaurant closed Sun evening (light meal available to residents) and Mon lunch. 11 rooms, all with bath and/or shower. B&B (English): single £36–£42, double £54–£70. Set lunch £11.50, dinner £17–£20. More reports please.

UPTON SNODSBURY Hereford and Worcester   Map 2

Upton House   *Tel* Upton Snodsbury
Upton Snodsbury   (090 560) 226
Nr Worcester WR7 4NR

A Grade II listed house, "black and white and beautifully decorated", set in large gardens next to the Norman church in a village six miles from Worcester. "Accommodation in three very pretty double bedrooms, with chintzes, floral prints, towelling robes and all the extras one could want. Bathrooms excellent. Comfortable sitting and dining room, both with antiques, log fires, beams and magazines. Dinner at a large table – guests dine together. Delicious food, well cooked and imaginative. Four courses plus cheese. We were made very welcome by the owners, Angela and Hugh Jefferson. A thoroughly delightful place to spend a few days." *Upton House*, which had its first Guide entry last year, recommended "to anyone looking for a traditional English country home with good food", belongs to the Wolsey Lodge consortium of private houses offering accommodation. No choice of meals; you advise your hosts of likes and dislikes when booking, and there is no obligation to dine in; the Jeffersons are happy to advise you about the good restaurants in the area. No licence; bring your own wine. (*Brenda Michelson, SL Dance*) More reports please.

Open All year except Christmas, New Year. Dining room closed for lunch.
Rooms 3 – all with private bathroom (2 *en suite*), telephone, radio, TV, tea-making facilities, baby-listening.
Facilities Lounge, dining room. 2-acre grounds.
Location 6 m E of Worcester on A422. In village turn towards Pershore. House is 150 yds on right.
Restrictions Not suitable for &. Smoking in bedrooms discouraged. No children under 14. Dogs in car or kennel only.
Credit cards None accepted.

Terms Double room: B&B £30; dinner, B&B £95. £10 surcharge for single occupancy. Set dinner £17.50. 1-night bookings sometimes refused for weekends. Bring your own wine.
Service/tipping: "This is run as a home; there is very little tipping."

VERYAN Cornwall   Map 1

The Nare Hotel   *Tel* Truro (0872) 501279
Carne Beach, Veryan TR2 5PF   *Fax* (0872) 501856

Seaside hotel in particularly agreeable situation on Roseland Peninsula, surrounded by National Trust land. 4-acre grounds, with secluded gardens, outdoor swimming pool, tennis; safe, sandy beach. Extensively and attractively refurbished by new owners, Mr and Mrs Gray, whose aim is "to provide comfort and old-fashioned service in a tranquil setting". Recommended for comfortable accommodation (many spacious bedrooms, but some quite small), and excellent breakfasts. Lots of choice on dinner menu; cooking "somewhat variable". 40 rooms, all with bath and/or shower. B&B £35–£77. Dinner, B&B £45–£87 (min 3 days). Set dinner £17.50 [1990]. Was in earlier editions under previous owners. More reports please.

WALKINGTON Humberside   Map 4

The Manor House   *Tel* Hull (0482) 881645
Northlands, Walkington   *Fax* (0482) 866501
Hull HU17 8RT

"We stayed here on Christmas Eve and were very impressed by the friendly welcome and the insistence that staying the night was no problem even though we would be the only guests as they close on Christmas Day. Our room was large and very comfortable with huge windows overlooking the gardens and plenty of sitting and storage space; furniture was smart, of the gilt-knobs-with-everything style. The bathroom was equally large and comfortable. A pianist played in the drawing room before dinner; the dining room was busy; everything was very much of 'an occasion'. Breakfast, on Christmas morning, was wheeled in on a trolley by the proprietors, Derek and Lee Baugh, and no corners had been cut – freshly squeezed orange juice, hot toast and rolls, boiled eggs, ample coffee, plus floral decoration."

This imposing, luxuriously appointed yellow-brick 19th-century manor house with mock-Tudor black and white gabling is quietly situated in three-acre grounds with mature trees, manicured lawns and rolling fields beyond, but is not far from Kingston-upon-Hull. Public rooms are large and comfortable. In the blue dining room with a conservatory extension, the menu (French with English subtitles) is extremely flowery. Chef/*patron* Derek Baugh's "fairly flamboyant style of cooking – *nouvelle* in Yorkshire-sized portions" is in character with everything else. Service is "helpful and willing". (*Pat and Jeremy Temple, RA Humphries*)

Open All year except 25/26 Dec and New Year's Day. Restaurant closed lunchtime and bank holidays.
Rooms 5 double – all with bath, telephone, radio, TV, tea-making facilities.
Facilities Drawing room, restaurant, conservatory. 3-acre grounds.

Location 3 m SW of Beverley. Take Newbald Road off Beverley Westwood York Road.
Restrictions Not suitable for &. No children under 12.
Credit card Access.
Terms B&B: single £61.50, double £88. Set dinner £23.50. 2-night half-board package.
Service/tipping: "No service charge. Service at guests' discretion, shared among staff on basis of hours worked."

WAREHAM Dorset   **Map 2**

Priory Hotel   *Tel* Wareham (0929) 551666
Church Green   *Fax* (0929) 554519
Wareham BH20 4ND   *Telex* 41143

Enthusiastic reports on the former Priory of Lady St Mary, now an "English Country Manor Hotel", bring it back to the Guide after an absence of some years: "A medieval cluster of buildings sandwiched between the river Frome and the town church in an unspoilt Dorset town, close to the last outpost of Royalist resistance to Cromwell, Corfe Castle. The transformation from priory to hotel has been handled with taste and care by the owners, Mr and Mrs John Turner, right down to the extensive gardens which provide a glorious frame for the beauty of the buildings. Every room is furnished and decorated individually and includes the best available towels and bathrobes, an extensive mini-bar and practically every convenience you could wish for. The staff are professional and cheerful. Food was terrific; dinner on Saturday night, in the newly converted abbot's cellar, was of a high standard, English in style, four delicious courses; a full breakfast is served until 10.30 am in the bedrooms or dining room. There are two beautifully furnished lounges. Thank God there is no piped music; the Turners obviously prefer the real thing, and a wonderful pianist entertained us on Saturday evening; loudspeakers in the restaurant enabled diners to enjoy the performance." "In August the place was awash with colour and fragrance; courtyards filled with flowers, fountains in secluded alcoves. Our suite in a restored outbuilding had French windows which opened on to the river." *(John Bennett, Debby Jellett, and others)*

Open All year.
Rooms 2 suites, 14 double, 3 single – all with bath, shower, radio, TV, tea-making facilities on request. 2 suites, 2 double in riverside boathouse. Some ground-floor rooms.
Facilities 2 lounges, bar, restaurant; pianist on Sat night. 4½-acre grounds with river frontage; mooring, fishing.
Location By town church and river.
Restriction No dogs.
Credit cards All major cards accepted.
Terms (Service at guests' discretion) [1990 rates] B&B (English): £60–£85, double £70–£150, suite £160. Set Sun lunch £13.95, dinner £19.50 (£22.50 on Sat); full alc from £28. Off-season rates.

Our italicised entries indicate hotels which are worth considering, but which, for various reasons – inadequate information, lack of feedback, ambivalent reports – do not at the moment warrant a full entry. We should particularly welcome comments on these hotels.

WARMINSTER Wiltshire   Map 2

Bishopstrow House   *Tel* Warminster (0985) 212312
Warminster BA12 9HH   *Fax* (0985) 216769
                                                      Telex 444829

Late Georgian country house in 27 acres bordering river Wylye. Luxurious furnishings. Indoor and outdoor tennis court and swimming pools; fishing, shooting, golf available. Was in earlier editions; now owned by Blandy brothers who also own Reids, Madeira (q.v.). A new manager, David Dowden, arrived in Jan 1990. "Expensive, but memorable for courtesy and friendliness of staff, comfortable rooms; civilised and peaceful." 32 rooms, all with bath, shower. Children welcome. B&B (continental) double £98–£150. Set lunch £14, dinner £25 [1990]. Many enthusiastic renominations, but some criticisms of Chris Suter's cooking. More reports please.

WASDALE HEAD Cumbria   Map 4

Wasdale Head Inn   `BUDGET`   *Tel* Wasdale (094 67) 26229
Wasdale Head, Nr Gosforth
CA20 1EX

This unsophisticated but efficiently run inn, in an isolated and magnificent setting not far from Wastwater, is famous in the annals of British mountaineering, and popular among walkers and climbers. It has a panelled and comfortably old-fashioned residents' bar and lounge. The main bar is named after the inn's first landlord, Will Ritson, reputed to be the world's biggest liar; in his memory liar competitions are held once a year. The pine-panelled bedrooms are simple and not large, but clean, comfortable and well lit, all with private facilities, plenty of hot water and lovely views. "Telephone, but no TV, praise be!" There is a jolly snug bar serving "good home-made food" and "a splendid selection of beers". Visitors enjoy the warm welcome, the substantial breakfast, announced by a gong at 8 am, and the "interesting" packed lunches. The five-course dinners served "on the dot at 7.30", in the dining room with its authentic old furnishings, have limited choice, and are "mostly very good, and adequate in quantity. Puddings very 'moreish'." The atmosphere is relaxed; there are no dress rules because the clientele are on the whole genuine walkers and climbers. There is a large drying room and a simple laundry service. (*H Way, DA Cash*)

Open Open mid-Mar–mid-Nov, 28 Dec–13 Jan.
Rooms 9 double, 2 single – all with bath and/or shower, telephone, tea-making facilities, baby-listening. Self-catering units and apartments nearby.
Facilities Residents' lounge, residents' bar, public bar, restaurant; drying room. ½-acre grounds.
Location Follow signs for Wasdale Head from Gosforth or Santon Bridge.
Restrictions Not suitable for ♿. No children under 7 in dining room at night (high tea available). No dogs in public rooms.
Credit cards Access, Visa.
Terms [1990 rates] Dinner, B&B (English): single £42, double £80. Bar lunches. Set dinner £15. Reductions for stays of 4 nights or more.
Service/tipping: "No service charge. We do not accept tips."

WATERHOUSES Staffordshire   Map 4

The Old Beams Restaurant   *Tel* Waterhouses (0538) 308254
  with Rooms
Waterhouses
Staffs ST10 3HW

"Excellence without pretension; no hushed tones, no unnecessary fussiness; good service without servility. The standard of cooking and accommodation was perfect. Beautifully appointed bedroom in the main house; the bed was one of the most comfortable I have slept in for ages. Faultless dinner. Breakfast, too, was a model." A warm endorsement for last year's nomination of Nigel and Ann Wallis's small, 18th-century, heavily beamed (as its name implies) house, on the edge of the Peak District National Park on the Ashbourne to Leek road (all rooms are double-glazed). It is a restaurant, with rooms of varying sizes. Five are in the annexe opposite: "They are very comfortable, and immaculately kept. Furnishings and fabrics are top quality; we had magazines, sewing kit, and delicious chocolate truffles. Very good bathroom with good lighting, potted plants and plastic duck as well as the usual oils, shampoos, etc." Dinner, in the beamed restaurant with a conservatory, where a grand piano is sometimes played, is "excellent", "*nouvelle*-ish, but with generous portions, and carefully cooked by Nigel Wallis. His wife, Ann, efficiently and exuberantly looks after front of house and makes the desserts. Very good house wines. There is a lovely garden, floodlit at night. The atmosphere is relaxed and welcoming." (*John Edington, Pat and Jeremy Temple*) *Michelin* awards the restaurant a red "M", halfway to a rosette.

Open All year. Restaurant closed Mon, Sat lunch, Sun evening.
Rooms 6, all with bath, telephone, radio, TV. 5 in annexe opposite. 3 on ground floor.
Facilities Lounge, bar, restaurant, conservatory/restaurant, private dining room. ½-acre garden.
Location On A532 between Ashbourne and Leek. All rooms double-glazed.
Restrictions Smoking discouraged in bedrooms. No children under 4. No dogs.
Credit cards All major cards accepted.
Terms [1990 rates] B&B: single occupancy £50–£70, double £65–£85. Set lunch £12.65, dinner £20; full alc £30.
Service/tipping: "No service charge. Tips at guests' discretion; staff divide the pool among themselves."

WATERMILLOCK Cumbria   Map 4

Leeming House Hotel   *Tel* Pooley Bridge (076 84) 86622
Watermillock   *Fax* (076 84) 86443
Penrith CA11 0JJ   *Telex* 64111

The only Guide hotel belonging to the Trusthouse Forte chain. It is an early Victorian house in magnificent, well-kept grounds with mature trees, running down to Ullswater. The views, particularly from the first-floor bedrooms, are superb. It has warm comfortable lounges and a cosy panelled bar. Readers last year were enthusiastic about the upkeep of the grounds, the standard of housekeeping, and the professionalism of the manager, Christopher Curry, and staff. "It is warm and welcoming in winter. Beds are turned down and bathroom cleaned during dinner and breakfast. No rigid mealtimes, no house-party atmosphere." The restaurant, with garden views, is quite formal (jacket and tie *de rigueur* for men), and "maintains a very high standard". "Bedrooms, though not large, are tastefully decorated. Bathrooms have thick towels and generous allocations of soaps and shampoos which are replenished daily." "Outstanding breakfasts with home-made jams and honey." A new wing is due to open in September 1990, bringing the number of bedrooms up to 40. A visitor in early 1990 found the service "helpful, and the atmosphere calm and relaxed though dignified", but was miffed at being charged the full rate for an "ordinary" room in the cottage annexe which will be phased out with the opening of the new wing. We'd be glad of more reports please, particularly on the new accommodation.

Open All year.
Rooms 39 double, 1 single – all with bath and/or shower, telephone, radio, TV. 10 ground-floor rooms.
Facilities Drawing room, sitting room, library, cocktail bar, dining room; conference facilities. 20-acre grounds with lake frontage (fishing, sailing, etc), arboretum and helipad. Pony trekking, golf, shooting.
Location On west shore of Ullswater on A592.
Restrictions No smoking in dining room and 11 bedrooms. No dogs in public rooms.
Credit cards All major cards accepted.
Terms Rooms: single £70–£100, double £100–£125. Breakfast: continental £5.75, English £8.25. Set lunch £15, dinner £29.50. 2-day breaks all year. Christmas and New Year packages. Winter pheasant shooting parties for groups of 8 or more. 1-night bookings sometimes refused for weekends and bank holidays. Reduced rates for children sharing parents' room; special meals by arrangement.
Service/tipping: "All prices include service; any gratuities are collected and distributed to all staff."

The Old Church Hotel   *Tel* Pooley Bridge (076 84) 86204
Watermillock   *Fax* (076 84) 86368
Penrith CA11 0JN

A small hotel, owned and run by Kevin and Maureen Whitemore, in a "stunning" lakeside position, catering "for those who want a get-away-from-it-all break" – no radio or TV in the bedrooms (but there is a TV lounge). It is an 18th-century house built on the site of a 12th-century church, reached by a long private drive off the A592. The gardens go down to the water and there are fine views. The comfortable lounges are decorated in soft colours and there is plenty of evidence throughout of Mrs Whitemore's flair for soft furnishings – she runs upholstery courses in the hotel twice a year in low season. Guests gather in the bar at 7.30 for the 8 pm dinner – English cooking with plenty of choice, served in a pretty dining room with old wooden tables and fresh flowers; teas are also a feature of *The Old Church*. The cheerfulness and efficiency of the staff and the friendliness of the owners have been commented on in the past, and this is endorsed by honeymooners in 1989: "We had just the right amount of attention, and a luxurious room with stunning views of the lakes and fells." (*RG Hepburn*) Rooms vary in size and style, so it is worth discussing the accommodation you want when booking. The Whitemores write: "We have five children of our own and welcome other people's children, and provide cots, high-chairs etc; but we are sometimes dismayed at the lack of control exercised by parents over their children."

Open Mar–Nov inclusive.
Rooms 10 double – all with bath, telephone, baby-listening.
Facilities Hall, lounge, TV lounge, bar, dining room. 4-acre grounds on lake with mooring and fishing; windsurfers and rowing boat available.
Location 3 m S of Pooley Bridge; 5 m from junction 40 on the M6.
Restrictions Not suitable for &. No smoking in dining room. No dogs.
Credit cards Access, Visa.
Terms [1990 rates] Dinner, B&B £68–£88. Alc lunch from £4; set dinner £23.50. Weekly rates. 1-night bookings sometimes refused for bank holidays. Soft furnishing courses Mar and Nov. Special meals for children.
Service/tipping: "We hope service charge and tipping will disappear. We normally suggest that money offered should be spent on the guests' next visit."

WATERROW Somerset   Map 1

Hurstone Farmhouse Hotel   *Tel* Wiveliscombe (0984) 23441
Waterrow, Wiveliscombe TA4 2AT

"Excellent value, and so very friendly. We were greeted by staff as our car stopped, and offered tea. It's a delightful, peaceful place. Rooms are charming. Food well prepared; enormous helpings, often interesting dishes." "Unpretentious, quiet and relaxing. Our bedroom was small but neat; the bed, with duvet, was comfortable. Good choice of food, decent wine list, friendly and efficient service." "Wonderful value for money." Satisfied visitors in 1989/90 to this far-off-the-beaten-track Georgian farmhouse with fine views down the combe and up the far hillside. It is owned by John Bone, who is much in evidence, and run with the help of manager/chef Denis Moylan. There are four or five choices of each course on the menu; milk, butter, cream and cheese are produced on the farm as well as cider from its organic orchard. (*Mike and Pam Ive, MF Mulcahy, H Robinson, Jane Shelton*) One complaint: inadequate heating in room, inadequate hot water in bathroom.

Open All year.
Rooms 1 family suite (1 double, 1 single), 4 double – all with bath, shower, telephone, TV, tea-making facilities, baby-listening.
Facilities Lounge, TV lounge, dining room. Terrace and gardens; 65-acre farmland with small trout river. Riding, tennis, golf nearby.
Location ¼ m off B3227 at Waterrow (signposted); 3 m SW of Wiveliscombe.
Restrictions Not suitable for &. Dogs by arrangement only.
Credit cards Access, Amex, Visa.
Terms (No service charge) B&B: single £43–£48.50, double £66–£75, suite £86–£105; dinner, B&B: single £57.50–£63, double £95–£105, suite £120–£140. Full alc £19.50. Weekend and midweek breaks all year except public holidays; 5% discount for stays of 7 nights or more; Christmas and New Year programmes. Reduced rates and special meals for children.

WELLAND Hereford and Worcester   Map 2

Holdfast Cottage Hotel   *Tel* Hanley Swan (0684) 310288
Welland, Nr Malvern WR13 6NA

Small hotel, 17th century at heart, in large garden in quiet situation, 4 m SE of Malvern, facing Little Malvern Priory and Malvern Hills on one side and Bredon Hill and the Cotswolds on the other. Agreeable terrace for sitting in warm weather. Rooms quite small; bedrooms simple but comfortable. 8 rooms, all with bath and/or shower. B&B double £60–£64. Set dinner £14–£16.50. Recent change of management – now run again by owners, Dennis and Diana Beetlestone; could we have reports please?

WEST BAGBOROUGH Somerset   Map 1

Higher House   `BUDGET`   *Tel* Bishops Lydeard
West Bagborough   (0823) 432996
Taunton TA4 3EF

William and Jo Beaumont's country house stands in three acres of garden and paddocks on the south side of the Quantocks, and looks over the Vale of Taunton towards the Brendon Hills and Exmoor; excellent walks from the village lead up to the hills. *Higher House* is a 17th-century farmhouse with later additions, built round two courtyards, one of which now contains a heated swimming pool, the other a herb garden. Readers continue to appreciate the "home-like atmosphere", the two comfortable lounges, almost always with a fire, the spacious and well-maintained bedrooms and the "excellent and abundant" evening meals, eaten communally – with no choice except of "scrumptious" desserts. Breakfasts, served between 8 and 10 am, offer a wide choice and are considered "especially good". "A very enjoyable stay. William Beaumont is a perfect host. Guests receive a warm welcome, and you are given tea and cake as soon as you arrive. Our bedroom had a four-poster and the most wonderful views." (*S Saysell*) Those not caring to eat communally can dine in the morning room. Cots, high chairs and special meals are available for children. More reports please.

Open All year except Christmas and possibly other times so owners can rest or decorate.
Rooms 1 family suite, 5 double – 4 with bath and/or shower, all with telephone, TV, tea-making facilities, baby-listening.
Facilities Hall with bar, drawing room with snooker table, TV lounge, dining room. 3-acre grounds with heated swimming pool and paddock.
Location Take A358 from Taunton to Minehead. After about 8 m take road on right signposted West Bagborough; *Higher House* is at end of village.
Restrictions Not suitable for &. No smoking or dogs in dining room.
Credit cards Access, Visa.
Terms B&B: single occupancy £25–£30, double £35–£50. Set dinner £12.50. Packed lunches on request. Discounts for 2 or more nights. Weekly rates.
Service/tipping: "Any tips left are divided between our part-time cleaners. We have no other staff. We do have a garden fund!"

WEST CLIFFE Kent   Map 3

Wallett's Court   *Tel* Dover (0304) 852424
  Country House Hotel
West Cliffe, Dover CT15 6EW

A "glorious white-washed old building with beautiful dining room and lounge full of lovely furniture and antiques. Particularly lovely fireplace in the lounge, with exposed brickwork and black wood-burning stove. Very friendly proprietors. Meals astonishingly good value – interesting, well cooked and very reasonably priced. Bedrooms in the annexe are functional; those in the main building, mostly quite large, are the best in their price category that I have every stayed in. Very good breakfast. I have used this as a stop-over before crossing the Channel on numerous occasions and never been disappointed." "A delight; no fussiness or pretension; a most relaxing hotel." Other visitors, too, enthuse about Lea and Chris Oakley's manor house (at least the main building, parts of which date back to Domesday), set in rural surroundings on the white cliffs of Dover, a mile from St Margaret's Bay. On weekdays there is a three-course dinner at £12.50, and on Saturday a more expensive gourmet meal – with a small amount of choice on each menu. (*John Moseley, Mrs A Duncan, PJ Guy, and others*) There continue to be complaints of poor insulation in the annexe – no joke if your neighbour has to rise before dawn for the Channel crossing; of limited service during the day; and when the owners are away the food and welcome seem to suffer a bit.

Open All year except 2 weeks Nov, 4 days over Christmas. Restaurant closed for lunch and on Sun.
Rooms 2 family suites, 5 double – all with bath, shower, radio, TV, tea-making facilities. 4 in converted barn.
Facilities Lounge, bar, dining room, functions room; games room. 3-acre grounds. 1 m from St Margaret's Bay with bathing, windsurfing, tennis club.
Location 3 m N of Dover, 1 m down B2058 off A258 Dover–Deal road. Hotel is on right opposite church.
Restrictions Not suitable for &. No dogs.
Credit cards Access, Visa.
Terms [1990 rates] B&B: single occupancy £32–£42, double £40–£55. Set dinner on weekdays £16; gourmet dinner on Sat £22. Reduced rates for children sharing parents' room; special meals.

WHIMPLE Devon   Map 1

Woodhayes Hotel   *Tel* Whimple (0404) 822237
Whimple, Nr Exeter EX5 2TD

This large white Georgian country house in a peaceful apple-orchard village off the A30 had a Guide entry for many years under the ownership of John and Alison Allan. They have moved to *Thomas Luny House*, Teignmouth, which enters the Guide this year, and *Woodhayes*, now owned and run by Frank and Katherine Rendle, is warmly recommended for reinstatement. "They have redecorated and refurbished the ground floor and the result is a delight – bright, colourful and welcoming; pastel shades and floral prints abound. Deep comfy armchairs and settees in the lounges. Bedroom first-class – crisp sheets, fluffy towels in the bathroom which were changed as if by magic as soon as one's back was turned. Charmingly decorated dining room with fresh table linen and napkins. A nice touch was the personal menu." "Dinner is at about 8. Mrs Rendle is a self-taught chef, and the cooking and presentation are quite exceptional. There is a sorbet between the fish and meat courses. Mr Rendle is barman, wine waiter and waiter." "Breakfast, served by the host, just as good as dinner." (*WR Duckers, Dr EJ Wood, also K and H Bender*) Mrs Rendle writes: "There are very few extras as the rates include a newspaper, early morning and afternoon tea, and tea or coffee at other times. We tell our visitors that they have only to pick up the phone if they want anything at *any* time. We get quite a few elderly people, and they find this reassuring, particularly at night. Our set menu looks rather long but we serve quite small portions and guests can pick and choose; and we can always offer alternatives."

Open All year.
Rooms 6 double – all with bath with shower attachment, telephone, radio, TV.
Facilities 2 lounges, bar, restaurant. 4-acre grounds with tennis and croquet.
Location 8 m E of Exeter, ¾ m off A30; on right just before Whimple village.
Restrictions Not suitable for &. No smoking in dining room. No children under 12. No dogs.
Credit cards All major cards accepted.
Terms B&B: single £50–£55, double £70–£75; dinner, B&B: single £63–£68, double £93–£98. Set lunch £14, dinner £19. Reduced rates for children sharing parents' room; special meals on request.
Service/tipping: "Service is included. We actively discourage tipping."

WHITEWELL Lancashire   Map 4

The Inn at Whitewell   *Tel* Dunsop Bridge (020 08) 222
Whitewell, Nr Clitheroe BB7 3AT

A long low stone house by a church, surrounded by rolling hills, with lawns down to the river Hodder (the inn has six miles of fishing rights). Inside, the atmosphere is more that of a country house than a pub, with sonorous clocks, heavy curtains on sturdy wooden rails, antique settles, oak gate-leg tables, old cricketing and sporting prints and log fires. The inn was new to the Guide last year, recommended by *Anne Laurence* as "slightly scruffy in a very soothing way with the most wonderful views over the river and the foothills of the Pennines; service friendly and the food good. I had a bar meal for dinner and an excellent breakfast with good coffee and, most unusually for a hotel, good sausages." Since then considerable refurbishment of the bedrooms has taken place, with a predictable rise in prices. "Our newly refurbished room was rather less of a success than the older ones. There was a vast four-poster bed with one of those convex mattresses you have to cling to, and a splendidly kitted out Victorian bathroom in which nothing worked very well. But it was warm and comfortable, and we had an excellent dinner." The inn also houses an art gallery and wine merchant; an unusually good range of wines is available with meals. More reports please.

Open All year.
Rooms 10 double – all with bath (4 also have shower), 9 with telephone, 6 with radio and TV. 2 more rooms in nearby farmhouse can be taken as family accommodation.
Facilities Hall/coffee room, residents' lounge with TV, 2 bars, restaurant. 3-acre grounds; 6 m fishing rights on river Hodder.
Location 6 m NW of Clitheroe. Take B6246 from Whalley or road through Dunsop Bridge from B6478.
Restrictions Bedrooms not suitable for &. No Alsatians, Rottweilers etc in public rooms.
Credit cards All major cards accepted.
Terms B&B (English): single £30–£38, double £45–£53; dinner, B&B: single £36–£59, double £59–£92. Bar lunches. Set dinner £20; full alc £25. Reduced rates and special meals for children.
Service/tipping: "Service included. Our policy is to deter politely and with humour any form of tipping."

WICKHAM Hampshire   Map 2

The Old House Hotel   *Tel* Wickham (0329) 833049
The Square, Wickham PO17 5JG   *Fax* (0329) 833672

Creepered early-Georgian Grade II listed house with attractive garden in picturesque, part-medieval, part-Georgian village square. Now a small hotel run by Richard Skipwith and his French-born wife Annie, with unpretentious restaurant, specialising in regional French cooking, in former outhouse and stables. Panelled and beamed rooms, furniture antique or period. Bedrooms (3 in annexe) vary in size. Some criticisms this year – noise both inside (plumbing and early morning cleaning) and out (traffic); service in general pleasant and polite, but some lapses. Hence these italics. Closed 2 weeks Christmas, 2 weeks Easter, 2 weeks July or Aug; hotel closed bank holidays, Sat and Sun; restaurant closed all day Sun, also Mon and Sat lunchtime. 12 rooms, all with bath and shower. B&B double £85–£95. Full alc £33. More reports please.

WILLITON Somerset   Map 1

Curdon Mill   `BUDGET`   *Tel* Stogumber (0984) 56522
Lower Vellow
Williton TA4 4LS

Attractively converted water-mill on Richard and Daphne Criddle's 200-acre working farm at foot of Quantocks. The water wheel still works; the mill shaft hangs across the dining room ceiling. Simple English cooking; generous helpings with lots of fresh vegetables. Large English breakfast. Accommodation "imaginatively and tastefully created". Dining room and lounge comfortably furnished. Garden well laid out with a swimming pool. Recent reports praise food but criticise bedroom upkeep and breakfast. 6 double rooms, 1 with bath and shower, 5 with shower. B&B £18.50–£25. Set dinner £15. More reports please.

The White House Hotel   *Tel* Williton (0984) 32306
  and Restaurant
Williton TA4 4QW

🏆 *César award in 1988: For combining the best of two worlds – French flair with English dependability*

An aficionado writes: "A symmetrical white house with louvred shutters on the main road running through the small town, separated from the road by a semi-circle of lawn with a couple of tall palms. The Smiths can't resist nice things, and the lounge is now graced by a restored, elegant little Georgian piano which visitors may play. The whole building is full of good paintings and prints; it oozes artistic good taste. The hotel is personally run, and the owners very much in evidence; the atmosphere is relaxed, friendly and civilised. The strength of the Smiths' cooking lies in perpetuating the great Elizabeth David French Provincial cooking tradition, though there is the occasional modern or traditional English dish on the menu. There are few restaurants in England where one gets vegetables of such high quality." (CKK)

Dick and Kay Smith have been the proprietors of *The White House* for over 22 years and have had an entry in the Guide almost continually since our first edition in 1978. The hotel is also liked by the food guides – *Michelin* awards it a red "M" for the quality of its cooking. It is well placed for exploring Somerset, particularly the Quantocks. It does not offer a house-party atmosphere or sybaritic luxury, and last year's entry voiced criticisms from some readers, but the Smiths tell us that the entrance hall and staircase area have been redecorated, the hotel has been recarpeted and telephones have been installed in the bedrooms. And a reader joins in the defence: "Everything of a very high standard. Though the food is the focus of the hotel the accommodation was perfectly satisfactory. My room was on the road but I was not bothered by traffic. Public rooms and areas were peaceful and well kept. I thoroughly enjoyed my visit." Responding to a comment about long delays at times in the dining room, Dick Smith writes: "Most of the dishes are cooked to order; much preparation each day goes to ensure that the delay is minimal." *En suite* facilities are planned for the two rooms that do not have them at present. Breakfasts are said to be "as good as dinner".

Open Mid-May–Nov. Restaurant closed for lunch.
Rooms 1 family suite, 11 double, 1 single – 10 with private facilities (1 not *en suite*), all with telephone, radio, TV; tea-making facilities on request, baby-listening possible. 4 rooms in courtyard annexe, some on ground floor. All will have private facilities by Spring 1991.
Facilities Lounge, bar, dining room. 2 m from coast; shingle beach 2 m, sandy beach 8 m.
Location On A39 in centre of village; courtyard rooms quietest. Parking.
Restrictions No smoking in dining room. Dogs by arrangement, not in public rooms.
Credit cards None accepted.
Terms B&B: single £28–£41, double £50–£66, suite £76; dinner, B&B: single £48–£63, double £90–£110, suite £132. Set 5-course dinner £24. 3- and 4-day breaks; weekly terms. Reduced rates for children.
Service/tipping: "We do not make a service charge. If guests add anything to the bill it is given to the staff involved."

WINDERMERE Cumbria   Map 4

Miller Howe   *Tel* Windermere (096 62) 2536
Rayrigg Road   *Fax* (096 62) 5664
Windermere LA23 1EY

💡 *César award in 1986: For theatrical brilliance and imaginative largesse*

For some years the postbag for John Tovey's celebrated hotel has been mixed, and 1989/90 is no exception. There is no dispute about the setting, perched above Windermere with a magnificent view to the great peaks across the water. And we continue to get reports extolling the "excellent food and beautiful accommodation", the staff – "not really like staff; there when you need them, they disappear when you don't", and the ambience: "magic". "It is probably one of the best hotels in England." Dinners at *Miller Howe* are theatrical occasions (with two sittings at busy times); prompt starting time for everyone, dimmed lights, the joint solemnly carried round the tables, no choice. This is enjoyed by some, but others react against the "mass dining experience"; and whereas some of the dishes are considered "interesting and flavourful" or "of bizarre genius", the orchestration of ingredients, "flavour piled upon flavour, colour upon colour" is too much for some. The bedroom decor, too, gets varied reviews: "Ours was comfortable in a homely way; the bathroom had a dated but lived-in feel." "Weird, with plastic ducks in the bathtub and gadgets strewn around." The service charge of 12½ percent is another cause for complaint. At busy times, particularly the weekend, things can become rushed and impersonal; and there have been reports of some failings when John Tovey is away. (*Irene F Holland, Mrs R Osborne, Pandora Sarson*) John Tovey tells us that he has built a conservatory which eases some of the lounge congestion, totally refurbished six bedrooms, and refurnished the dining room.

Open Mid-Mar–early Dec.
Rooms 11 double, 2 single – 11 with bath, 2 with shower, all with radio, telephone; TV on request.
Facilities 3 lounges, conservatory, 2 dining rooms; terrace. 4-acre grounds with landscaped garden. Walking, climbing, tennis, sailing, fishing, water sports nearby.
Location On A592 N of Bowness. Lake-facing rooms quietest.
Restrictions Not suitable for ♿. No smoking in dining room. No children under 12. No dogs in public rooms.
Credit cards All major cards accepted.
Terms (Excluding 12½% service charge) Dinner, B&B £67–£110. Set dinner £28. Packed lunches £10. Off-season breaks, residential cookery courses Mar and Nov. 1-night bookings sometimes refused on Sat.
Service/tipping: "A surcharge of 12½% is added to all final accounts in lieu of gratuities."

WINTERINGHAM South Humberside   Map 4

Winteringham Fields   *Tel* Scunthorpe (0724) 733096
Winteringham DN15 9PF

Germain and Annie Schwab's part 16th-century manor house in a cluster of buildings round a courtyard and garden is in a "quite pretty" old village, dating back to Roman times, on the south bank of the Humber estuary. It's a restaurant with only six bedrooms, all called after dignitaries in the area's history. It enters the Guide following an inspector's report: "Our room, overlooking the quiet village street, had original beams and was attractively if rather fussily decorated, à la Laura Ashley. The dressing table was on a slope because of the uneven floor; charming, but also irritating when things fell off, and it was impossible to get the mirror to stay in one position. Lighting was poor. Beds (turned down while we dined) were very comfortable. Bathroom with rather small bath; good sized towels and nice extras. The building is quiet but dark, with narrow corridors and staircase and heavy Victorian furniture. Comfortable lounges, with interesting *objets d'art*, mostly Victorian; small dining room, attractively done up. Swiss-born Germain Schwab is chef. Dinner was a gastronomic event which lasted three hours: all dishes were presented beautifully on exceedingly large white plates; minute portions of numerous vegetables – different for each main course; cheese trolley with huge choice. There's a large staff for the size of the place; we were impressed by their efficiency, attentiveness and good timing. Wonderful continental breakfast, served until late in the morning, with plentiful freshly squeezed orange juice. We thoroughly enjoyed our stay, despite the unprepossessing Humberside location. Not cheap, but worth every penny." More reports please.

Open All year except first 2 weeks Mar, first week Aug, Christmas, New Year. Restaurant closed bank holidays.
Rooms 1 suite, 5 double – all with bath and/or shower, telephone, TV. 2 in courtyard. 2 on ground floor.
Facilities Lounge, bar, restaurant, private dining room, conservatory. ½-acre grounds.
Location In centre of village, 4 m from Humber Bridge.
Restrictions No smoking in restaurant. No children under 12. No dogs.
Credit cards Access, Visa.
Terms B&B (continental): single £55, double £70–£75, suite £85. Set lunch £13.50, full alc dinner £30.

WITHERSLACK Cumbria   Map 4

The Old Vicarage   *Tel* Witherslack (044 852) 381
Witherslack   *Fax* (044 852) 373
Grange-over-Sands LA11 6RS

🏆 *César award in 1990: Outstanding hospitality – Lakeland style*

This small Georgian hotel is in the less dramatic but still attractive walking country south of Lake Windermere, and though only 15 minutes from the M6, it is quiet and secluded, away from the heart of the village. It is run by Roger and Jill Burrington-Brown and Stanley and Irene Reeve. There are William Morris curtains, Heal's lampshades, lots of pine and cane in the bedrooms, ample reading lights. Duvets on the beds, but you can ask for traditional bedding. The five-course set dinner (served "at 7.30 for 8") offers no choice except for hot or cold desserts, and you are warmly encouraged to have both. Cooking is English; portions very generous. Breakfasts are "excellent, everything freshly cooked – delicious home-made brioche, toast made from home-made bread". This year there are five new double rooms all with a sitting area and *en suite* facilities. They are in a new annexe in traditional Lakes style, built round a courtyard in an orchard in adjoining grounds. "Absolutely lovely; bathroom enormous, one of the best I have ever seen." There's also a new all-weather tennis court. "There is nothing solemn or flash or unctuous about *The Old Vicarage*'s style of hospitality," we said last year, "but it offers an unaffected warmth of welcome which most of us yearn for on our travels, and find less often than we would like." And visitors this year warmly endorse these sentiments. (*F Brian Perring, JE Borron, Mr and Mrs BF Green, and many others*) "Some of the rooms in the main house are, quirky from the point of view of bathrooms," adds a correspondent. "One double room had the bath and basin *in* the room, screened off by a designer curtain; another had an 'armchair' continental-type bath. But everything well kept, clean and comfortable."

Open All year except Christmas. Restaurant closed for lunch.
Rooms 12 double, 1 single – all with bath and/or shower, telephone, radio, TV, tea-making facilities. 5 in orchard annexe, 1 designed for &.
Facilities 2 lounges, bar lounge, restaurant, private dining room. 5-acre grounds with tennis, lawns and woodlands. Sea 3 m, Lake Windermere 8 m, river fishing 5 m. Fell walking.

Location From M6 take exit 36; follow route to Barrow-in-Furness. Turn off A590 signposted Witherslack and take first turn left past phone-box. Hotel is ½ m along this lane on left.
Restrictions No smoking in restaurant. Children by arrangement only. Dogs by arrangement only; not in public rooms.
Credit cards All major cards accepted.
Terms [1990 rates] B&B £35–£55; dinner, B&B £56.50–£76.50. Set dinner £21.50. 3-day breaks all year except bank holidays. Reduced rates for children; special meals.
Service/tipping: "Service included. We do not imply that tips are required, but naturally are pleased and grateful if guests choose to show that they are perhaps more than satisfied. Tips are shared among staff twice yearly."

YATTENDON Berkshire   Map 2

The Royal Oak Hotel   *Tel* Hermitage (0635) 200440
The Square
Yattendon, Nr Newbury
RG16 0UF

A picturesque creeper-covered old building in a pretty village, cosy, laid back, but also sophisticated, with young owners, Kate and Richard Smith, who also own – and reside at – the *Beetle and Wedge* at Moulsford (q.v.). It comprises a pub, a restaurant and five smart bedrooms. No formal reception; staff can be hard to find at times, and are a bit casual for some tastes. The lounge has comfortable sofas, a log fire and magazines; the restaurant is small – only eight tables – but discreetly elegant, with polished wood tables, thick curtains and stencilled walls. The cooking is Anglo-French, ambitious and interesting, not too fussy. Desserts can be very rich. The kitchens also serve the pub – "spruce and inviting with newspapers hanging on sticks" – which offers similar meals or snacks at lower prices than in the restaurant. Bedrooms are light, spacious and smart with antique furniture and well-equipped bathrooms, "but lights are a bit dim". Some bedrooms look on to the walled rose-garden at the back; those above the pub can be noisy until late at night. Lavish breakfasts are cooked to order. (*AP Collett, David Thibodeau*) More reports please.

Open All year.
Rooms 5 double – all with bath (1 also has shower), telephone, radio, TV; baby-listening on request.
Facilities Lounge, bar, 2 restaurants. ½-acre garden.
Location Just N of M4 between exits 12 and 13.
Restrictions Only restaurant and bar suitable for &. Dogs by arrangement only.
Credit cards Access, Amex, Visa.
Terms (Service at guests' discretion) B&B: single from £70, double from £80. Full alc £25 in bar, £35 in restaurant. Weekend breaks except Christmas and New Year. Reduced rates for children sharing parents' room; special meals on request.

****
Perennial Plaint *We live in Switzerland and like to eat English-style when in England. Why is it so hard to find "traditional English cooking" and why is one so often offered an aping of French cuisine, with sorbets before the main course and other fatuous examples of contemporary fads?*
****

YORK North Yorkshire   **Map 4**

The Grange Hotel   *Tel* York (0904) 644744
Clifton, York YO3 6AA   *Fax* (0904) 612453
                                                   Telex 57210

Sophisticated new hotel, Regency in style, on a busy road 5 minutes' walk from
Minster; front rooms double-glazed, spacious carpark at rear. Pedigree owners,
*Gordon Campbell-Grey, ex-*Feathers, Woodstock, *and Douglas Barrington, ex-*
Lygon Arms, Broadway. *Recommended for attractive decor of public rooms,*
well-equipped bedrooms (though limited storage space). Comfortable bar,
brasserie offering reasonably priced food, tranquil restaurant with striking decor
but cooking not quite up to expectations. Not owner-managed, but staff
attentive and friendly. 29 rooms, all with bath and/or shower; 2 with facilities
for &. *B&B (English): single £78, double £95. Set lunch £13, dinner £21.*

Hobbits   `BUDGET`   *Tel* York (0904) 624538
9 St Peter's Grove
Clifton, York YO3 6AQ

"Thoroughly agree with your recommendation of this small, comfortable
and friendly hotel in a leafy street of Victorian houses. Rosemary Miller
couldn't have been more friendly. Communal breakfast included excellent home-made stewed gooseberries with yoghurt – delicious with
muesli. The house is full of jugs, which Mrs Miller collects." "*Hobbits* has
winding stairways that lead to the attic rooms. Ours was large, with
comfortable beds, large writing desk and chairs, small bathroom and
shower. Coming down to breakfast was an adventure; the long dining
room table was elegant with its white table-cloth and shining silver."
Rosemary Miller's five-roomed, reasonably priced B&B in a quiet suburb
is a good ten minutes' walk or an easy bus ride from the centre of York.
Decor and furnishing are stylish and attractive. *Hobbits* is Mrs Miller's
family home; it includes two children, a cat, a dog and canaries. Guests
normally share a table at breakfast, but there is a separate small table for
those wanting more privacy. (*Caroline Currie, Joseph and Lola Rhea*)

Open All year except 3 days over Christmas.
Rooms 4 double, 1 single – all with shower (1 also with bath), radio, TV, tea-
making facilities, fridge, baby-listening.
Facilities Lounge, TV lounge, dining room. Small garden with patio. River Ouse
5 minutes with fishing and boating.
Location Just off A19 from N. Private parking.
Restrictions Not suitable for &. No smoking in 2 bedrooms. No dogs in public
rooms.
Credit card Visa.
Terms B&B: single £20–£25, double £40–£45. Reduced rates for children. (No
restaurant.)
Service/tipping: "No service charge. We don't expect tips but if guests kindly leave
something it is given to the member of staff who has looked after them."

We invite British hotels to tell us of their policy on service charges
and tipping. Some hotels ignore this request. Replies, when given,
are printed at the end of an entry.

Middlethorpe Hall   *Tel* York (0904) 641241
Bishopthorpe Road   *Fax* (0904) 620176
York YO2 1QB   *Telex* 57802

"First-class in every respect. Friendly and attentive service, comfortable
and roomy accommodation, beautiful grounds and gardens. Expensive,
but worth every penny." One of many similar comments in 1989/90 on
this noble house with imposing facades in large grounds near York
racecourse. It was rescued from decay by Historic House Hotels Ltd, who
also restored *Bodysgallen Hall*, Llandudno and, more recently, *Hartwell
House* at Aylesbury (qq.v.). Built in the reign of William III and
subsequently the home of the diarist Lady Mary Wortley Montagu,
Middlethorpe Hall is a pedigree mansion with gardens and parkland
appropriate to its grandeur. It has been immaculately restored in keeping
with its period; the interior decoration is "in excellent taste; public and
private rooms comfortable and quiet" (but a few bedrooms are small and
one, in the stables, adjacent to the maids' closet, is not recommended).
Last year several readers felt that the food let the place down. Complaints
continue, but some disagree vehemently: "I have visited eleven times
in the past 18 months. The standard of cooking and presentation is
excellent, even when the head chef is not on duty, and there's plenty of
choice." "Excellent food, well prepared, beautifully served, and tasting of
the ingredients." (*JR Hamilton, Martin Craven, Sue Braithwaite*). We should
be glad of further contributions to this culinary debate.

Open All year.
Rooms 6 suites, 20 double, 4 single – all with bath, shower, telephone, radio, TV;
2 suites in cottages; 18 courtyard rooms.
Facilities Lift. Drawing rooms, library, bar, 2 restaurants; private dining facilities.
26-acre grounds with croquet, walled garden and lake. Racecourse, golf nearby.
Location 1½ m S of city, by racecourse.
Restrictions Not suitable for &. No children under 8. No dogs.
Credit cards All major cards accepted.
Terms [1990 rates] Rooms: single £80–£93, double £108–£145, suite £160–£185.
Breakfast: continental £6, English £9. Set lunch max £15.90, dinner £25.90; full alc
£34.50. Champagne breaks Nov–Apr; 4-day Christmas package.

Mount Royale Hotel   *Tel* York (0904) 628856
The Mount, York YO2 2DA   *Fax* (0904) 611171

Richard and Christine Oxtoby's long-established hotel, Gothic in appearance, William IV in the main though with modern extensions, is near the
racecourse, a few minutes' walk from Micklegate Bar and three-quarters
of a mile from the Minster. Front rooms get traffic noise though this is
mitigated by double-glazing; back ones overlook the attractive garden
with a swimming pool and are quiet; the spacious new ones in the garden
annexe, connected to the main building by a covered walkway, are
warmly recommended. Readers generally appreciate the un-hotel-like
atmosphere, with long-serving friendly staff – and the dogs and cats.
Breakfast and dinner are substantial, and generally considered to be of a
high standard, though there are occasional murmurs about the vegetables. During 1989 we heard that some rooms were in need of
refurbishment; the Oxtobys tell us that most rooms were refurbished and
redecorated during the winter of 1989, with bathrooms being modernised, and separate shower cubicles added where possible. Regarding our

comment that the meals are too substantial for some they say: "If people
have smaller than average appetites we willingly reduce the portion size;
and if they do not want to go through the whole menu we arrange the
price accordingly."

Open All year except 7 days at Christmas.
Rooms 2 suites, 19 double, 2 single – all with bath, shower, telephone, radio, TV,
tea-making facilities and baby-listening. 4 in garden annexe with covered
walkway to main building. Some ground-floor rooms.
Facilities 2 lounges, bar, dining room with conservatory. 1½-acre grounds with
swimming pool heated May–Oct.
Location On A64 from Tadcaster (front rooms have secondary glazing). Hotel is
on right just before traffic lights at junction with Albemarle Road opposite sign to
Harrogate (A59). Parking for 24 cars.
Restrictions Not suitable for ⅛. Dogs by arrangement; not in public rooms.
Credit cards All major cards accepted.
Terms B&B (English): single £70–£80, double £75–£95, suite £85–£110. Light
lunches available; set dinner £19.50. 2-day breaks (excluding bank holidays).
1-night bookings refused over some bank holiday periods. Reduced rates for
children sharing parents' room; special meals by arrangement.
*Service/tipping: "Very few staff anywhere seem to be embarrassed by being tipped. What
our staff collect themselves is their affair, and anything added by credit cards etc is
divided and added to their wages weekly."*

****

Traveller's tale *Clearly the place had some pretensions to style. Well-
warmed plates for our main course were deftly placed, held between
spoon and fork with a "no touch" technique that would have done credit
to an operating theatre. There appeared to be only one set of serving
implements and I was wondering how the waiter was proposing to serve
my wife's poached salmon after my steak. However, more thought had
gone into the operation than I had imagined, as he dived into his trouser
pocket and triumphantly brought forth another spoon and fork.*

****

Wales

Llangoed Hall, Llyswen

ABERSOCH Gwynedd

Map 4

Porth Tocyn Hotel
Abersoch LL53 7BU

Tel Abersoch (075 881) 3303
Fax (075 881) 3538

⊞ *César award in 1984: Best family hotel*

A long-time favourite of Guide readers, and a particularly good hotel for a holiday with children – though it's not exclusively a family hotel – the *Porth Tocyn* stands in a choice position on a headland overlooking Cardigan Bay and Snowdonia. "A really excellent hotel, well run, with most comfortable bedrooms, helpful and extremely willing service, and plenty of room (not just one lounge, but several, all well appointed and with lovely views). Food most enjoyable. Any small complaints (a broken bedside light, a jammed wardrobe) were dealt with *at once*. One of the nicest hotels I've ever stayed in." Readers in the past have praised the two-course dinner (including coffee and petits fours) offered as an alternative to those unable to cope with five courses, the impressive Welsh cheeseboard, the "old-fashioned 'nursery' puds", the lack of music in the dining room, the imaginative self-service buffet lunch on Sunday, and "fresh flowers everywhere; the atmosphere of a family home but a professional standard of service". "The location is superb and if you are blessed with a few good days, weather-wise, this hotel must rank as one of the best for families in the whole UK." (*EAO Whiteman, S Parsons, and others*)

Open Week before Easter–mid-Nov.
Rooms 14 double, 3 single – all with bath, shower, telephone, TV; radio and tea-making facilities on request; some baby-listening facilities. 3 ground-floor rooms.
Facilities 6 sitting rooms, restaurant, bar, TV room. Garden with tennis court, swimming pool (heated May–end Sep). Set in hotel's 25-acre farm; sea a few mins' walk, safe bathing. Heritage coastal walk, water sports, fishing, golf, riding nearby.
Location 2½ m S of Abersoch, through hamlets of Sarn Bach and Bwlchtocyn; follow signs marked Gwesty/Hotel.
Restrictions No children under 7 in dining room at night (high teas available until 6.15 pm). Dogs in bedrooms only – bring dog basket.
Credit card Access.
Terms B&B £28.50–£46. Buffet lunch Sun £12.50; set dinner £14.50 (2 courses), £22 (5 courses). Bargain breaks out of season. 1-night bookings sometimes refused. Reduced rates and special meals for children.
Service/tipping: "No service charge. Tipping is fast dying out here. It is irrelevant to a proper modern hotel bill. We do not promote tipping, but if someone wants to leave something by way of appreciation that is fine."

CAPEL GARMON Gwynedd   Map 4

Tan-y-Foel   *Tel* Betws-y-Coed (069 02) 507
Capel Garmon
Nr Betws-y-Coed LL26 0RE

Two years ago Barrie Michael, a professional photographer, and his wife, Hazel, opened a small guest house in Llanfachreth, *Ty Isaf*, recommended by many readers. Now they have moved to larger premises, a late 16th-century grey-stone farmhouse set into the hillside high above the Conwy Valley. There are 88 acres of farmland for walking, a private stream for trout fishing, and bird-watching nearby. In close proximity to the house is their "menagerie of dogs, cats, horses, geese, hens . . . even bees!" *Tan-y-Foel* is recommended for "magnificent views, comfortable and spacious accommodation, fresh flowers, small house-party atmosphere, relaxed informality". Mrs Michael cooks with flair; dinner is communal from a set menu, but preferences are discussed beforehand. Sherry is served in the drawing room "and it didn't appear on the bill (nice touch that), and an excellent dinner follows, beautifully cooked and presented". "A sense of fun abounds in this very peaceful place. No traffic. No television. No newspapers." For photographers, Barrie Michael offers the use of his darkroom, and courses during the low season. (*Mr and Mrs EL Compton, Len and Iris Parker, and others*)

Open Mid-Feb–mid-Jan. Dining room closed 1 night per week by arrangement with guests.
Rooms 1 suite, 5 double – all with bath and/or shower, telephone, radio, tea-making facilities, baby-listening.
Facilities Lounge, library, dining room, billiard room, darkroom.
Covered heated swimming pool (enclosed in productive orangery). 3-acre formal garden in 88 acres farmland; private trout fishing.

Location From A470 take turning to Capel Garmon (midway between Llanrwst and Betws-y-Coed). *Tan-y-Foel* is exactly 1.2 m on left.
Restrictions Smoking permitted only in library. No children under 14. Dogs by arrangement, not in public rooms.
Credit cards None accepted.
Terms B&B £28–£36; dinner, B&B £42.50–£50. Set dinner £17.50–£18.50. 1-night bookings sometimes refused for Easter, other public holidays, Aug.
Service/tipping: "No service charge. Tips never solicited or accepted. We hope guests feel sufficiently at home not to consider it."

CRICKHOWELL Powys   Map 1

Gliffaes Country House Hotel   *Tel* Bwlch (0874) 730371
Crickhowell NP8 1RH   *Fax* (0874) 730463

"There is nowhere quite like it. In perfect weather its remoteness makes it a wonderful source of refreshment. In the evening, all one can hear is the song of birds and the sound of the river. The hotel is as hotels were fifty years ago. Guests are looked after but not pandered to. No one hopes you will enjoy your meal or have a good day." Another reader, concerned that escalating costs are making most agreeable hotels unaffordable, thinks *Gliffaes* the most desirable hotel in the Guide. Bouquets and brickbats fly around the *campaniles* of this imposing Italianate mansion with its magnificent gardens in the valley of the Usk, midway between the Brecon Beacons and the Black Mountains. It's an unashamedly traditional country hotel, run for more than 40 years by the Brabner family. Lots of fishing tackle everywhere – the hotel has two stretches on the Usk and there are eight fishable reservoirs in the vicinity – and lots of polished Victorian furniture which "is heavy and old and the hotel gives the impression of being a bit run-down and dilapidated". Criticisms are often delivered in good spirit: "The service at mealtimes was haphazard and unprofessional, but willing." "The staff, mostly young Australians, are pretty casual. It is unusual perhaps, on choosing a Burgundy, to be told 'that will put some colour in your cheeks'. However, I would return as often as I could." "Beds were untidy, and towels ghastly colours. But this delightful hotel feels like home." A big plus for guests is the elastic mealtimes: dinner is served between 7.30 and 9.30 (last orders 9.15 – the table d'hôte menu can be ordered directly in the dining room, while à la carte orders are taken in the bar). (*RAL Ogston, Robert Vigars, and others*) Last year a reader criticised an unacceptable Beaujolais vintage. Mr Brabner rejoins: "The remark was inaccurate, misleading and born of ignorance. We offered 56 wines from 15 areas, and none from the year reported."

Open Mid-Mar–end Dec.
Rooms 22 double (6 can be let as singles) – 17 with bath, 5 with shower, all with telephone, radio, tea-making facilities, baby-listening. 3 (with TV) in annexe.
Facilities 2 sitting rooms, bar, billiards room, conservatory, dining room. 29-acre grounds with 6-acre gardens, croquet lawn, putting green. Brown trout and salmon fishing in river Usk.
Location 2½ m W of Crickhowell. Turn left off the A40 at Gliffaes sign; 1 m to hotel's gates.
Restrictions Not suitable for &. No smoking in dining room. No dogs in hotel (kennels available).
Credit cards All major cards accepted.

Terms [1990 rates] B&B £25.50–£34.50; dinner, B&B £39.40–£48.40; full board £45–£55. Set lunch £8.90 (£12.90 on Sun), dinner £13.90. Reduced rates and special meals for children by arrangement.
Service/tipping: "No service charge. Service is an integral part of the rates. We have adjusted our wages accordingly. If a guest insists on leaving a gratuity, it is accepted gracefully."

CWMYSTWYTH Dyfed   Map 1

Hafod Lodge   `BUDGET`   *Tel* Pontrhydygroes (097 422) 247
Cwymystwyth
Aberystwyth SY23 4AD

Small welcoming guest house in quiet setting in some of Wales' most wild and remote country. Recommended for comprehensive comforts and hospitality of owners, Colin and Jenny Beard. "Family antiques mix with furnishings of more recent acquisition." Picnic hampers and candle-lit dinners, featuring seasonal, regional and "imaginative" ingredients. 3 rooms – all with bath or shower. B&B £24–£32, dinner, B&B £36–£44. Set dinner for non-residents (by reservation only) £19. New nomination. More reports please.

EGLWYSFACH Powys   Map 1

Ynyshir Hall   *Tel* Glandyfi (065 474) 209
Eglwysfach
Machynlleth SY20 8TA

Pink-washed 16th-century manor house, backed by Ynyshir bird resserve, in idyllic wooded setting on southern shore of Dovey estuary, owned by artist Rob Reen and wife Jean. Decor is handsome mix of Victorian furniture, contemporary paintings, oriental rugs; atmosphere light, airy. Restaurant uses fresh ingredients, many from walled garden. "Artists Valley" nearby, painting courses available. Recommended for "excellent food, charming service, reasonable prices". Open all year except possibly part of January. 10 rooms – all with bath and/or shower. B&B £28–£60; dinner, B&B £43–£75. Set lunch/dinner £17 [1990]. Dropped last year because of new ownership, now re-nominated. More reports please.

LLANBERIS see NANTGWYNANT   Map 4

Pen-y-Gwryd Hotel

LLANDRILLO Clwyd   Map 4

Tyddyn Llan Country House   *Tel* Llandrillo (049 084) 264
  Hotel and Restaurant   *Fax* (049 084) 264
Llandrillo, Nr Corwen LL21 0ST

💧 *César award in 1989: Welsh hotel of the year*

Readers continue to praise Peter and Bridget Kindred's lovingly restored 18th-century, grey-stone country house hotel. Standing in tranquil countryside in the Vale of Edeyrnion, it offers restful views of the surrounding Berwyn Mountains. Guests can enjoy fishing on the hotel's private one-and-a-half-mile beat; guides are available for walking through the local forests and along old droving roads. "Thoroughly endorse your entry – sheer bliss. The house attractive, clean and inviting, our dinner one of the best in Wales. Peter Kindred is a friendly and amusing host and his wife maintains very high standards for the restaurant." Last winter an extension was built to the restaurant and sitting room; French windows lead on to a pillared veranda where guests can enjoy afternoon tea and watch croquet. "We stayed at the top of the house – it was wonderfully cosy and our greatest disturbance, which was no disturbance at all, was from the house martins nesting in the eaves above our bedroom window. The comfortable room and good food made *Tyddyn Llan* a terrific place to return to after long and strenuous walks in the mountains." The restaurant uses fresh local ingredients and herbs from the garden, and all dishes are cooked to order. David Barratt is the chef. (*Pat and Jeremy Temple; John Edington, Peter and Ann Brown, and others*)

Open All year.
Rooms 10 double – all with bath and/or shower, telephone, radio, tea-making facilities, baby-listening.
Facilities Sitting room with TV, dining room; drying room. Occasional musical and gourmet evenings. 3-acre grounds with water garden, croquet. Private fishing in river Dee behind hotel, ghillie available; guided walks.
Location Through Corwen on A5 take B4401 to Llandrillo.
Restrictions Not suitable for &. Dogs by arrangement, not in public rooms.
Credit cards Access, Visa.
Terms [1990 rates] B&B: single £37–£40.50, double £60–£67; dinner, B&B: single £51–£56.50, double £92–£99. Set dinner £18. Special interest weekends; mini-breaks (2 or more nights); Christmas and New Year house parties. Reduced rates and early suppers for children.
Service/tipping: "No service charge. If a guest wishes to offer a tip, it is divided among staff."

LLANDUDNO Gwynedd   Map 4

Bodysgallen Hall   *Tel* Deganwy (0492) 584466
Llandudno LL30 1RS   *Fax* (0492) 582519
                                                     Telex 617163

💧 *César award in 1988: For a notable contribution to architectural conservation and first-rate hotel management*

A Grade I listed house standing in its own parkland on a hillside about a mile away from the Victorian seaside resort of Llandudno. The house is mainly 17th-century with skilful later additions, including nine cottages grouped around a secluded courtyard bright with flowers. Among its delights are a 17th-century knot garden and an 18th-century walled rose garden; the "peacefulness and beauty of the gardens" are a draw for many readers. Two of its finest rooms are the large entrance hall and first-floor drawing room, both with oak panelling, splendid fireplaces and stone-mullioned windows. The bedrooms ("ours, No 1, with four-poster, was super romantic") are spacious and elegantly furnished, with many extras such as bottled Welsh spring water and home-made biscuits;

bathrooms are Edwardian-style with handsome fittings. The hotel is run by a private company, Historic House Hotels (see also *Middlethorpe Hall*, York, and *Hartwell House*, Aylesbury, in England), dedicated to restoring and bringing to life buildings of architectural merit. The food, under the direction of chef Martin James – modern in style with impeccable ingredients – pleases readers once again. (*RO Marshall, Ed Hobson and Judy Seabridge*) One reader, while intending to return, found the staff "a bit brusque" and lamented her expensive continental breakfast: "An orange juice, a pot of coffee and four slices of *cold* brown toast between us." Another echoed an earlier criticism: the absence of "a host figure".

Open All year.
Rooms 9 cottage suites, 18 double, 1 single – all with bath and/or shower, telephone, radio, TV; tea-making facilities in cottages. 1 cottage with ramps for &.
Facilities Hall, drawing room, cocktail bar, library, dining room; conference centre. 247-acre parkland with gardens, tennis and croquet. Sandy beaches 2 m. Riding, shooting, fishing nearby.
Location SE of Llandudno on A470; 1 m on right.
Restrictions No children under 8. Guests requested not to smoke in dining room. Dogs in cottages and grounds only.
Credit cards All major cards accepted.
Terms Rooms: single £78–£108, double £103–£135, suite £148–£160. Breakfast: continental £5.50, Welsh £8.25. Set lunch £14.50, dinner £25. Off-season winter and spring champagne breaks.
Service/tipping: "Our prices include a mandatory service charge. It is given to all staff at the end of each month according to length of service, tax being deducted at source."

The St Tudno Hotel   *Tel* Llandudno (0492) 874411
North Parade, Llandudno   ·   *Fax* (0492) 860407
LL30 2LP   *Telex* 61400

💧 *César award in 1987: Best seaside resort hotel*

An enterprising, stylishly decorated hotel on the seafront of this Victorian seaside resort, run by Martin and Janette Bland. It has had much praise in the past for its friendly welcome, accommodation (though some rooms are small) and food – "a real find", "a little gem", etc. The pretty decor of the dining room has been appreciated: "Its green and white trellis wallpaper and its plants make you feel you are eating in a garden." The hotel went through an uneven patch last year with suggestions that it was resting on its laurels. Although there are still occasional murmurs of discontent, 1990 appears to herald a change: "Nice to see standards being maintained. Very good food, outstanding wine list." "A superb welcome, room tastefully done up (a little twee), highly recommended." "Top-class restaurant, a great weekend – surpasses any other hotel we have tried in the Guide." (*Richard O Whiting, AJ Garrett, Barbara and William Mason, Mr and Mrs FPA Wood, and others*)

Open Mid-Jan–26 Dec.
Rooms 20 double, 1 single – all with bath and/or shower, telephone, radio, TV, tea-making facilities and fridge, baby-listening. 1 ground-floor double with shower.
Facilities Lift. Non-smoking residents' lounge, coffee lounge, lounge bar, restaurant; indoor heated swimming pool; small front patio. Safe sandy beaches, pier, boat rides, fishing, sailing, windsurfing; 3 golf courses close by.

Location Central, opposite pier. Limited free promenade parking and very small carpark at rear of hotel (£5 per night).
Restrictions Not suitable for &. No smoking in sitting room or dining room. No children under 5 at dinner. No dogs.
Credit cards Access, Amex, Visa.
Terms B&B: single £42.50–£62.50, double £64–£108; dinner, B&B: single £63.50–£83.50, double £106–£150. Bar lunches. Set Sun lunch £11.95, dinner £20.95. Full alc £24–£26. 2-night breaks all year; winter weekend breaks. 1-night bookings often refused for bank holidays; sometimes for Sat in winter. Reductions according to age for children sharing parents' room; high tea.
Service/tipping: "If customers enjoy personalised service and feel inclined to tip they should be allowed to do so. As hoteliers, we would never dream of adding a service charge automatically."

LLANGAMMARCH WELLS Powys   Map 1

The Lake Country House Hotel   *Tel* Llangammarch Wells
Llangammarch Wells LD4 4BS   (059 12) 202

A half-timbered Welsh manor house in 50 acres of woodland bordered by the river Irfon, with a well-stocked lake; "an excellent hotel in a beautiful area devoid of good hotels". It enters the Guide this year warmly recommended: "Jean-Pierre Mifsud and his wife are extremely friendly hosts and their staff provide a relaxed, courteous and helpful service. The bedrooms are large, comfortable and well equipped, as are the bathrooms; a number of them are in fact suites. The reception rooms are impressive, and the airy dining room is a delight. Dinners are good (the presentation occasionally over-elaborate), there's a splendid cheeseboard, and the breakfasts are excellent. Prices extremely reasonable." The wine list is praised – it has around 300 offerings, including 50 clarets. (*Amy and Stephen Pratt, also Mrs KJ Milligan, and others*) More reports please.

Open All year except Jan.
Rooms 9 suites, 8 double, 2 single – all with bath and/or shower, telephone, TV. 2 on ground floor.
Facilities 3 lounges, billiard room, dining room. 50-acre grounds with lake, small golf course, tennis court. 4½ m river fishing (tuition available).
Location A40 to Abergavenny; follow signs to Builth Wells. A483 to Garth; follow signs to hotel.
Restrictions No smoking in dining room, 1 lounge, some bedrooms. Children under 8 by arrangement. Dogs in some bedrooms, not in public rooms.
Credit cards Access, Amex, Visa.
Terms [1990 rates] B&B: single £65, double £80, suite £95–£120. Set lunch £12.50, dinner £19.50. 2-night breaks. Reduced rates for children; special meals on request.
Service/tipping: "Prices fully inclusive. Tips not expected. If guests insist, money is shared equally among staff."

LLANRUG Gwynedd   Map 4

The Seiont Manor Hotel   *Tel* Caernarfon (0286) 76887
Llanrug, Caernarfon LL55 2AQ   *Fax* (0286) 2840

An architecturally distinctive hotel, new to the Guide, well situated for exploring the Snowdonia National Park and Anglesey, created from a series of small interconnected barns. The reception rooms have fine Chinese carpets on highly polished parquet, antiques, attractive botanical prints and dried flower arrangements. Vivaldi is played in every room (and after numerous repetitions can be tedious). The bedrooms are light, airy, painted in simple but sophisticated pastel shades, well lit, attractively furnished. The main dining room, reserved for non-smokers, is spectacular, under a glass roof with reproduction trees and bamboo furniture. With white napery and fresh flower arrangements, it is attractive both night and day. The chef has worked under Raymond Blanc at the *Manoir aux Quat'Saisons* (q.v.), but our inspectors were lukewarm about the dinners, and about the wine list. In other respects, the hotel gave satisfaction and promises well as a tranquil rural retreat. There are plans, however, for a conference centre. More reports welcome.

Open All year.
Rooms 4 studios, 24 double – all with bath, shower, telephone, radio, TV, tea-making facilities, baby-listening.
Facilities Library, lounge, 2 bars, 3 dining rooms. Indoor swimming pool, sauna and gym. 150-acre grounds with river, salmon fishing, jogging track. Sea 4 m.
Location 2½ m W of Caernarfon. A4086 towards Llanberis; hotel is on left ½ m before Llanrug.
Restrictions Not suitable for &. No smoking in main dining room. No dogs.
Credit cards All major cards accepted.
Terms (Service at guests' discretion) B&B: single £60, double £80, suite £125. Set lunch £9.95, dinner £14.95; full alc £25. Special breaks and theme weekends. Reduced rates for children; special meals.

LLANRWST Gwynedd   Map 4

Meadowsweet Hotel   *Tel* Llanrwst (0492) 640732
Station Road, Llanrwst LL26 0DS

John and Joy Evans are the owners of this agreeable Victorian restaurant with rooms on the outskirts of a tiny market town. The river Conwy is 200 yards away, and Snowdonia a few miles up the road. Rooms at the front overlook a large field filled with sheep (and also the road). "The service was friendly and unpretentious, just as one would expect in a Welsh rural market town. The bedrooms are well furnished with nice touches and the two public bathrooms are like mini-chemist shops with selections of shampoo and other necessary toiletries." The restaurant offers a four-course menu at £19.50, "excellent cooking with plenty of choice, high quality ingredients and inventive dishes". There is a fine wine list with "no fewer than 70 half-bottles". (*Gwenda Griffith; H Richard Lamb, Chris and John Gunson*) Criticism of the decor and service resulted in an italicised entry in 1990, but there has been much redecoration and refurbishment, and reports this year have encouraged us to reinstate the former full entry. But complaints still surface; we'd welcome more reports.

Open All year.
Rooms 10 double – all with shower, telephone, TV, baby-listening.
Facilities Bar lounge, residents' lounge, dining room. Salmon/trout fishing, horse riding, golf within easy reach; sea 10 m.
Location ¼ m N of town centre on A470. (Back rooms quietest.)
Restrictions Not suitable for &. No smoking in dining room. No dogs in dining room (guide dogs excepted).
Credit cards Access, Visa.
Terms B&B £25–£45; dinner, B&B (min 2 nights winter, 3 nights summer) £40–£60. Set lunch £11, dinner £19.50; full alc (summer only) £28. Reduced rates for

children sharing parents' room; special meals.
Service/tipping: "No service charge. Should a guest wish to add anything for exceptional service, the management will share this amount among all the staff, but gratuities are not expected."

LLANSANFFRAID GLAN CONWY Gwynedd   Map 4

The Old Rectory   *Tel* Glan Conwy (0492) 580611
Llanrwst Road   *Fax* (0492) 584555
Llansanffraid Glan Conwy
LL28 5LF

Georgian in origin, *The Old Rectory* stands in secluded grounds up a steep drive, with views over the river Conwy estuary to Conwy Castle and Snowdonia. The owners, Wendy and Michael Vaughan, have furnished it "with masses of delightful pictures and beautiful flowers", "*objets d'art*, framed family photos, and pot-pourri everywhere – all chosen with comfort and relaxation in mind". "The warmth and friendliness of the Vaughans' welcome made us feel immediately at home, and our delightful room was as well furnished and equipped as a country-house bedroom should be. Plenty of hot water, gloriously comfortable (and dramatic-looking) bed, two armchairs set to look out over the small garden to the estuary and mountains in the distance: what more could one want? Dinner is, in effect, a dinner party, with guests introduced to each other over cocktails before sitting down together at a large table in the dining room. Michael Vaughan serves unobtrusively and Wendy's food is outstanding: there is a fixed starter, a choice of main course (organised earlier in the day), and a choice of puddings or Welsh cheeses. Our companions were very good company and no one went to bed before midnight." The village is a convenient stop on the way to the Holyhead crossing to Ireland; and for a longer stay, this part of North Wales offers a lovely landscape for walking, historic castles, and the beautiful north-west coast. The Vaughans know the area well and are happy to suggest places to visit. *The Old Rectory* is a non-smoking establishment. (*Anne Bagamery, Mary Anne Evans, Janet M Kruse*)

Open 1 Feb–7 Dec. Dining room closed for lunch and occasionally for dinner (guests warned when booking).
Rooms 4 double – all with bath and/or shower, telephone point, radio, TV.
Facilities Drawing room, dining room, morning room. 2-acre grounds. Sea with safe bathing 3 m; fishing, golf, riding, sailing nearby.
Location On A470, ½ m S of A55.
Restrictions Not suitable for &. No smoking. No children under 12. No dogs.
Credit cards Access, Visa.
Terms (No service charge) Dinner, B&B: single occupancy £69.50–double £99.50–£119.50. 50% reduction for children sharing parents' room. 1-night bookings refused bank holidays.

```
************************************************
*                                              *
* Traveller's tale The rooms have barely enough room for two normally *
* sized adults with luggage. We had to pass around the bed to the window *
* and back to the wardrobe and bathroom in shifts.                     *
*                                              *
************************************************
```

LLANWDDYN Powys

Map 4

Lake Vyrnwy Hotel
Llanwddyn
Montgomeryshire SY10 0LY

Tel Llanwddyn (069 173) 692
Fax (069 173) 259

A substantial turn-of-the century Tudor mansion standing 150 feet above the lake with a notable view down its four-and-a-half-mile length, and set in 24,000 acres of meadows and forest. Under previous owners it won a César in 1986 "for preserving traditional values in a sporting hotel". Sporting activities, especially fishing, are still a major draw, but the deliberately cultivated old-fashioned air has vanished. An inspector reports: "The public rooms are elegant in a club-like way: really comfortable leather chairs, fishing and sporting prints, and a gun book. The drawing room is pale yellow and blue with window-seats along a wall and a wonderful view. There are masses of beautifully upholstered chairs, and a log fire in the early evening. Our bedroom had some of the prettiest curtains I have seen. Service in the main dining room is by nice Welsh ladies and lasses. Children are welcome – there is masses of room for them to run, and things to climb on. But there are some caveats: it is important to book a room overlooking the lake, as the ones at the rear have a scruffy view. If tranquillity is what you are seeking, avoid bank holiday weekends and the summer holidays. And if you have sophisticated tastes in food, prepare for disappointment. Breakfasts are excellent: perfectly presented and generous but dinners are no more than so-so. The menu tends towards standard starters and roasts. The terrine was without any flavour, the mackerel the size of a sardine, the lamb and beef overcooked and served with the same gravy, the potatoes badly roasted. But by the fire later, other guests told us they thought it good." More reports welcome.

Open All year.
Rooms 2 suites, 24 double, 3 single – all with bath and/or shower, telephone, radio, TV, baby-listening.
Facilities Drawing room, cocktail bar, public bar, restaurant. 33-acre grounds; sporting rights on 24,000 acres meadow, moorland and forest, 1,100-acre lake for fishing, sailing.
Location At SE corner Lake Vyrnwy, well signed from Shrewsbury, Chester and Welshpool.
Restrictions Only restaurant suitable for &. No dogs in public rooms, kennels available.
Credit cards All major cards accepted.
Terms [1990 rates] B&B: single £39.75, double £45.50–£54.50, suite £95.50. Dinner, B&B (2 day min): single £49.50, double £72.50–£97.50, suite £119. Set lunch £10.75, dinner £17.75. 1-night bookings refused peak weekends.
Service/tipping: "Entirely at guest's discretion. Collected in tronc and distributed to all."

LLYSWEN Powys

Map 1

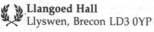 **Llangoed Hall**
Llyswen, Brecon LD3 0YP

Tel Llyswen (0874) 754525
Fax (0874) 754545

César award: Most auspicious newcomer of 1990

One of the finest country houses in Wales, built by Clough Williams-Ellis (of *Portmeirion* fame – q.v.), opened its doors as a luxury hotel in May

1990. Here is our first report, from a connoisseur of hotel excellence: *"Llangoed Hall* has the instant making of a very splendid country hotel. The building itself might have been *designed* for conversion with fine big public rooms overlooking a croquet lawn and tennis court, and a meadow running down to the Wye, while its bedrooms are cheerful and airy and have been turned into delightful *en suite* bedrooms and suites – furnished half in antiques (I think) and half in Laura Ashley, whose widower Sir Bernard is the financial angel behind it all. The setting is perfectly lovely – wooded hills behind, river-meadowed in front, and a brilliant young gardener, Chris Frank, is bringing the formal and vegetable gardens of the old house back to glory (and has added a maze): indeed part of the pleasure of the place is the experience of seeing a great country house brought to life more or less from scratch, the hall having been uninhabited for years, and sadly neglected for longer still. As for the service, though it was a bit rough, perhaps, during the night I was there, it shows signs of being very professional. Breakfast included Welsh exotica like laver bread and grilled smoked salmon with poached eggs, while on the dinner menu there was red mullet with pea and coriander mousse, breast of chicken filled with wild mushrooms, poached fruits served with prune and armagnac ice cream. I thought (as a sneerer at excessively grand hotels) that *Llangoed* had got just about the right balance between poshness and informality, and my only criticism, in these very early days, is that in a hotel that consciously sets out to make the most of its Welsh setting, no Welsh voice is there to greet you when you arrive. If all goes well, *Llangoed* will almost certainly become the No 1 hotel in Wales. Expensive, but worth it as an extremely comfortable base in the middle of an exquisite and mercifully little-developed countryside." (*Jan Morris*)

Open All year except 3–26 Jan.
Rooms 5 suites, 17 double, 1 single – all with bath, shower, telephone, radio, TV.
Facilities 2 drawing rooms, library, 2 dining rooms. 10 acre grounds with tennis court, croquet. Salmon and trout fishing and riding nearby.
Location 11 m SE of Builth Wells and 11 m NE of Brecon on A470.
Restrictions No smoking in dining room. No children under 8. Dogs in kennels in grounds only.
Credit cards All major cards accepted.
Terms (Service at guests' discretion) B&B: single £65–£85, double £75–£165, suite £165–£195. Set lunch £17.50, dinner £32.50. Reduced rates for children; special meals.

NANTGWYNANT Gwynedd   Map 4

Pen-y-Gwryd Hotel   **BUDGET**   *Tel* Llanberis (0286) 870211
Nantgwynant, Llanberis
LL55 4NT

An inn since the early 1800s and well known to mountain climbers, *Pen-y-Gwryd* is run by Mr and Mrs Chris Briggs with their daughter Jane and her husband, Brian Pullee. It stands in the middle of the Snowdonia National Park, and in 1953 was used as a training base for the successful Everest team. "What the P-y-G has to offer," wrote *James Seely* last year, "is solid comfort, a well-stocked bar and cellar, plentiful and appetising nursery cooking and, above all else, old-fashioned hospitality and good fellowship. Charles Kingsley – of *Water Babies* fame – called this mountain inn 'the divinest pigsty under the canopy'. The act has been cleaned up since then, but it is good to think of our Victorian forebears enjoying the same relaxed conviviality that exists here today. It's a perfect centre for walking and climbing, and for exploring some of the most lovely countryside in the British Isles." Other readers echo this praise: "We found the food most satisfactory. The staff were young, enthusiastic, and *helpful*." "Non-climbers are made to feel as welcome as climbers." "If the visitor appreciates hot baths in Victorian tubs the size of swimming pools, the dinner gong at 7.30 followed by an excellent five-course meal, and lively, often intellectual, conversation, this is the place." "The beds are big and solid and very comfortable. The furniture in the games room has been left as it was, adding to its character and charm – where else could you find a proper (i.e. non-electronic) games room these days?" (*SJ Curtis, Gwen and Peter Andrews, and others*)

Open Mar–Nov, New Year, weekends only Jan and Feb.
Rooms 22 rooms – 1 with TV. 1 with bath, on ground floor across courtyard.
Facilities Lounge, 3 public rooms, residents' bar, games room, restaurant. 1-acre grounds; natural swimming pool. River fishing nearby.
Location From Nantgwynant signposted Pen-y-Gwryd.
Credit cards None accepted.
Terms [1990 rates] B&B £16–£20. Bar and packed lunches £2–£3, set dinner £10. Reduced rates and special meals for children.
Service/tipping: "No service charge, but there is a staff gratuity box available for guests who wish to contribute. They usually do!"

NEWPORT Dyfed   Map 1

Cnapan BUDGET   *Tel* Newport (0239) 820575
East Street, Newport
Pembrokeshire SA42 0WF

"A charming little guest house" (in previous editions we have described *Cnapan* as "more than a guest house, less than a hotel") in an attractive small town (a good bookshop, a couple of art galleries, and nice little houses on hilly streets). "We were welcomed by all four owners, given a delicious sandwich lunch, and helped with advice on places to visit. Our rooms were full of useful guidebooks, other interesting books and magazines, and beautiful decorations." "The drawing room and 'bar' were lovely and well supplied with board games and such trivial pursuits to make any guest feel completely relaxed and happy." "Excellent food, and huge portions – even for those hungry after walking all day!" *Cnapan* is run by John and Eluned Lloyd and their daughter and son-in-law, Judith and Michael Cooper. Mother and daughter cook the meals: there is lots of choice, including vegetarian dishes. Breakfasts are serve-yourself-as-much-as-you-like, with home-made bread. Much entices near the village as well: you can be exploring the rock pools on Parrog beach after a ten-minute walk, or picking up the spectacular coastal path towards Cwm-yr-Eglwys in fifteen. (*Mirit and Michael Ehrenstein; and others*)

Note There is another Newport, in Gwent; do not go there for *Cnapan*.

Open All year except 25/26 Dec and Feb. Restaurant closed Tue Apr–Oct; open to non-residents at weekends Nov–Jan.
Rooms 5 double – all with shower, radio, TV, tea-making facilities, baby-listening.
Facilities Lounge, bar, restaurant. Small garden. 10 mins' walk to estuary and sea; fishing, bird-watching, pony-trekking, golf, boating nearby.

Location In centre of small town (but quiet at night). Parking.
Restrictions Not suitable for &. Smoking banned in dining room; discouraged elsewhere. No dogs.
Credit cards Access, Visa.
Terms B&B £20; dinner, B&B £32. Full alc £18.50. 1-night bookings refused for bank holiday and high season weekends. Reduced rates for children under 12; nursery teas.
Service/tipping: "We dislike service charges and equally the idea of 'building them in'. However, if customers wish to show extra appreciation, we accept the tips which we then distribute among the staff."

PORTHKERRY South Glamorgan   Map 1

Egerton Grey   *Tel* Rhoose (0446) 711666
  Country House Hotel
Porthkerry, Nr Cardiff CF6 9BZ

19th-century former rectory 10 miles from Cardiff, close to Cardiff airport (occasional noise), now very comfortable country house hotel with 7-acre garden and sea views. Peaceful setting, croquet, tennis. Bedrooms "range from grand four-poster to small nursery at top, furnished with style and taste. Huge Victorian baths." Present owners, the Pitkins, arrived July 1989. Recommended for friendly atmosphere, correct service, serious cuisine. 10 rooms – all with bath and/or shower. B&B £32.50–£65. Set dinner £15, full alc £27.50. New nomination. More reports please.

PORTMEIRION Gwynedd   Map 4

The Hotel Portmeirion   *Tel* Penrhyndeudraeth
Portmeirion LL48 4ER   (0766) 770228
                        Fax (0766) 771331
                        Telex 61540

❦ *César award in 1990: Brilliant restoration of a great hotel to former glory*

Re-established, after a seven-year closure following a fire. The *Portmeirion* stands on the edge of an estuary in Cardigan Bay, surrounded by a spectacular Italianate village complete with piazza, campanile, pavilions and colonnade. "A perfect 'fantasy escape'", "great fun", are two readers' comments this year. In summer as many as 3,000 visitors a day may come to the village, but the hotel itself is protected against this invasion. Surrounding the village are acres of woodland and miles of sandy beaches. Our inspector's description after the re-opening still holds: "This is the folly–village built by the late Sir Clough Williams-Ellis on a private wooded peninsula above Tremadog Bay. Cottages in the village can be rented separately; but the hotel itself is a new persona of truly phoenix-like burnish. The exterior remains that of a comfortable and unpretentious early Victorian Welsh *plas*; the interior has been refurbished in an exuberant mixture of oriental dazzle and overblown *World of Interiors*. No expense has been spared – even the fire doors are elegant – and there is any amount of ruching and draping and gilding and silking. Set against the heightened exotica of Portmeirion village, and contrasted with its incomparable setting above a wide sandy estuary, where herons stalk and cormorants dive immediately outside the hotel windows, the building triumphantly brings off its decor. While some clients may find its taste suspect, others will enjoy it for its very extravagance." This year's postbag has included praise for the "attractively furnished village rooms", "not too elaborate food", "cheerful and pleasant staff". (*S and W Beresford, Dr Ian Anderson*) Several complaints – we hope no more than teething problems: the lack of a manager in the bar and dining room, long delays in the dining room, and poor food: "Lobster thermidor done with a sheet of singed plastic cheese on top, scrambled eggs similar to a curdled custard." Breakfasts, too, except for the coffee, have been called "a real let-down". More reports please.

Open All year, except 14 Jan–8 Feb. Restaurant closed for lunch Mondays except bank holidays.
Rooms 1 suite, 13 double in hotel; 5 suites, 15 double in village – all with bath, shower, telephone, radio, TV; tea-making facilities in village rooms; baby-sitting by arrangement.
Facilities 2 lounges, 2 bars (harpist or pianist most nights), dining room; functions room. 5-acre garden with swimming pool (heated end May–mid-Sep), tennis; free golf at Porthmadog Golf Club. Sandy beaches.
Location SW of Penrhyndeudraeth, SE of Porthmadog, off A487 at Minffordd.
Restrictions Not suitable for &. (but 3 village rooms have no steps and are accessible by car). No smoking in dining room and lounges. No children under 7 in main hotel dining room in evening; main hotel bedrooms unsuitable for cots. No dogs.
Credit cards All major cards accepted.
Terms Rooms: double £50–£85, suite £60–£125 (single: deduction of £10 from relevant room rate). Breakfast £7.50, set lunch £11.50 (£13.50 on Sun), dinner £21.50. Half portions for children. Christmas, New Year and off-season breaks. Min 2-night bookings at weekend in high season.
Service/tipping: "A service charge is not included in our tariff and tipping is neither encouraged nor expected. If guests decide to leave tips they are banked and shared equally among staff involved."

PWLLHELI Gwynedd   Map 4

Plas Bodegroes   *Tel* Pwllheli (0758) 612363
Nefyn Road, Pwllheli LL53 5TH   *Fax* (0758) 701247

This grade II listed Georgian manor house in a peaceful setting in the Lleyn Peninsula entered our pages in 1989 and has won many plaudits for its restaurant. It was converted by Welsh-born Chris Chown and his Faroese wife Gunna á Trødni into a comfortable restaurant-with-rooms. "It's amazing," wrote our inspector, "to find cooking of this calibre in such an out-of-the-way spot. The house is stylish without being grand, soothing in layout and well proportioned; with pleasing views of lawns and beeches, and utter silence except for rookery noises and other more melodious birdsong." The style of cooking is *nouvelle* with inspired sauces and the flavour of real food; only the best local produce is used. Though Chris Chown calls this a restaurant-with-rooms, bedrooms are well equipped and clean (front ones are the larger, with four-posters and the best views). Our inspector took breakfast in a small, east-facing room in the sunshine – "freshly squeezed orange juice, real porridge, perfectly poached eggs. Worth a long detour from anywhere". Pwllheli is a quiet seaside resort; there is golf nearby, and lots of interesting sightseeing. Few recent reports; more, please.

Open Mar–31 Dec. Restaurant closed Tue.
Rooms 1 suite, 4 double – all with bath, shower, telephone, radio, TV, baby-listening; 2 with mini-bar, 1 with jacuzzi.
Facilities Bar, lounge, 2 dining rooms, breakfast room. 6½-acre grounds. Safe, sandy beach 1 m. Golf nearby.
Location On left on Nefyn road (A497) 1 m W of Pwllheli.
Restrictions Only restaurant suitable for &. No smoking in main dining room and 1 bedroom. Dogs by arrangement; not in public rooms.
Credit cards Access, Visa.
Terms B&B £25–£45; dinner, B&B £45–£65. Set dinner £23. 1-night bookings refused bank holidays and Sat in season.
Service/tipping: "Service, VAT, heat and light, ingredients and poll tax included. Tips not expected, but accepted. Any received are split according to hours worked, irrespective of seniority."

TALSARNAU Gwynedd   **Map 4**

Hotel Maes-y-Neuadd   *Tel* Harlech (0766) 780200
Talsarnau LL47 6YA   *Fax* (0766) 780211

Maes-y-Neuadd (pronounced Mice-er-Nayeth, meaning the mansion in the meadow) is tucked into a wooded hillside smothered in rhododendrons, looking out across Snowdonia National Park and reached by a narrow lane which climbs a one-in-five hill. Dating originally from the 14th century, it was enlarged in the 16th and 17th; there are oak beams, decorated plasterwork and an inglenook fireplace. Eight acres of lawns, orchards and paddocks surround it; the renowned Royal St David's golf course is only three miles away, and Portmeirion and Harlech castle are nearby. The two couples who own it, the Horsfalls and the Slatters, have completely restored this attractive, grey, granite and slate mansion, furnishing it with good antique and modern furniture; plain clear colour-washed walls show the pretty patterned chintzes to advantage. This year a conservatory lounge has been added, and three new bedrooms in the coach house, designed by architect co-owner Michael Slatter. "It is as comfortable, warm and welcoming as ever," wrote a returning visitor, confirming earlier praise. "The service is always so pleasant and friendly." But reports on a new chef, who arrived in October 1989, have been mixed. "Pretentious in style, but short on quantity" was one comment. Another reader found the food over-rich and longed for simpler dishes. Breakfasts have had the thumbs down too. More reports please.

Open All year except 10 days early Dec. Lunch by reservation only Mon–Sat.
Rooms 2 suites, 13 double, 1 single – all with bath and/or shower, telephone, TV. 4 rooms in coach house 10 yds from main building. 3 ground-floor rooms suitable for &.
Facilities 2 lounges, bar, 2 dining rooms; small conference room/private dining room. 8-acre grounds with sun terraces, croquet, orchard and paddock. Sea, golf, riding, sailing, fishing, climbing nearby.
Location Off B4573, 3 m NE of Harlech. Hotel sign at junction.
Restrictions No smoking in dining rooms. Children under 7 at management's discretion, not in dining room for dinner. No dogs.
Credit cards All major cards accepted.
Terms B&B: single £35–£38.50, double £80–£116, suite £90–£130; dinner, B&B (2 nights min): single £52–£57.50, double £115–£160, suite £125–£160. Set lunch £13.75, dinner £23.50; full alc £30. 1 night bookings refused Easter, Christmas,

Bank Holidays. 3-day Christmas house party. Reduced rates for children sharing parents' room; high tea at 6 pm.
Service/tipping: "No service charge. Tips not solicited in any way. If a guest adds a gratuity it is divided among restaurant and kitchen staff."

TALYLLYN Gwynedd   Map 4

Minffordd Hotel   *Tel* Corris (0654) 761665
Talyllyn, Tywyn LL36 9AJ

🏆 *César award in 1985: Outstanding value in a country hotel*

"A real jewel." "It fully lives up to all the praise in the Guide." The *Minffordd Hotel* is an exemplary small family hotel in the medium-price range, at the head of one of the most peaceful and little known valleys in Wales, the Dysynni Valley. The footpath to the top of Cader Idris starts by the front gate, Talyllyn lake is half a mile away, and some of Wales's most beautiful scenery lies all round this former coaching inn (its name means "roadside"). Mr and Mrs Bernard Pickles have owned the hotel for 13 years, and their son Jonathan is the excellent chef. They have preserved the old-world atmosphere of the rambling building while comfortably modernising it. Everything is spick and span. It is not a hotel for the misanthrope: guests are introduced to each other and the smallness of the public rooms makes socialising inevitable, though tables in the dining room are well spaced. Visitors this year have been pleased: "Excellent packed lunches, a table where children could play draughts and backgammon, splendid food." "Peace, tranquillity and unobtrusive personal service, bedrooms of the highest standard." Another enthusiast wrote: "Can I add anything to all the gentle praises that have appeared in the Guide? Only this: when you go, stay at least three days. Any shorter stay would be cheating yourself." Bernard Pickles discourages bed-and-breakfast guests and now offers *demi-pension* only. "Bed-and-breakfast guests," he says, "are as ships that pass in the night, never to enjoy what we have to offer them." (*Mrs M Green, Mrs Lesley Brown, MH Williams, and others*)

Open Mar–Dec, weekends only Nov–Dec, 3 days at Christmas. Restaurant closed lunchtime, and to non-residents Sun and Mon.
Rooms 7 double – all with bath and/or shower, telephone, radio, tea-making facilities. 3 ground-floor rooms.
Facilities Sun room, lounge bar, parlour, dining room; laundry facilities. 3-acre garden; paddock and river. Talyllyn lake ½ m – fishing by arrangement.
Location 8 m SW Dolgellau. At junction of A487 and B4405.
Restrictions Not suitable for severely &. No smoking in dining room. No children under 3. No dogs.
Credit cards Access, Diners, Visa.
Terms Dinner, B&B: single £49–£56, double £78–£92. Set dinner £14.75; packed lunches on request. Off-season breaks; reductions for long stays; Christmas package. 1-night bookings refused at peak times. Reduced rates and special meals for children.
Service/tipping: "Service is free and part of the caring family-run atmosphere. Tips are not part of our arrangements."

When hotels have failed to return their questionnaire, we have quoted 1990 prices, with a note to that effect.

THREE COCKS Powys   **Map 1**

Three Cocks Hotel   **BUDGET**   *Tel* Glasbury (049 74) 215
and Restaurant
Three Cocks, Nr Brecon LD3 0SL

"A welcoming haven amid spectacular countryside" begins a recent
report on this 15th-century inn with a cobbled forecourt, ivy-clad walls,
worn steps, and great oak beams. It stands in grounds of one and a half
acres in the Brecon Beacons National Park, half a mile from the river Wye.
"Two fires blazing in the hall; a well-furnished bedroom, and an excellent
restaurant." It is owned by Mr and Mrs Winstone; she is Belgian, he is the
chef, and the cooking has French and Belgian overtones. "The owners are
delightful, friendly but professional in their relationship with their guests.
The food is extremely good, vegetarians are well catered for if their
requirements are made known in advance, and the wine selection is
worth drinking. There's a lovely wood-panelled lounge." Breakfasts are
also praised. (*Dr and Mrs RJ Davies, and others*) Two readers commented
unfavourably on net curtains that separate some bathrooms and
bedrooms, causing light to disturb sleeping partners; one regretted no
heating or light in two lounges during a late autumn visit. Front rooms
can be noisy. Towels can be flimsy. More reports please.

Open Mid-Feb–end Nov. Restaurant closed Sun lunch, Tue.
Rooms 7 double – all with bath and/or shower; radio and baby-listening on
request.
Facilities Reception lounge, lounge, TV lounge, bar/breakfast room, dining room.
¼-acre lawn.
Location 5 m from Hay-on-Wye on A438 Brecon–Hereford road. Rear rooms
quietest. Parking.
Restriction No dogs.
Credit cards Access, Visa.
Terms [1990 rates] B&B: single £30–£48, double £48; dinner, B&B double (min
2 nights) £72. Set lunch £10, dinner £18; full alc £23. Reduced rates and special
meals for children.
*Service/tipping: "Service included; tips at customers' discretion. Shared between
restaurant and kitchen staff."*

TREFRIW Gwynedd   **Map 4**

Hafod House Hotel   **BUDGET**   *Tel* Llanrwst (0492) 640029
Trefriw, Gwynedd LL27 0RQ   *Fax* (0492) 641351

*On bank of Conwy valley, overlooking Denbigh moors, well placed for touring
North Wales; golf, climbing, pony trekking, lake and river fishing nearby.
Converted 17th-century farmhouse with barn restaurant with exposed beams
and original open hearth fireplace, 1-acre garden. 6 well-appointed bedrooms,
all with bath and/or shower and balcony; two have 4-poster and jacuzzi.
Dinner, B&B: £38–£43.50. New nomination. More reports please.*

There are many expensive hotels in the Guide. We are keen to
increase our coverage at the other end of the scale. If you know of a
simple place giving simple satisfaction, please write and tell us.

WHITEBROOK Gwent   Map 2

The Crown at Whitebrook   *Tel* Monmouth (0600) 860254
Whitebrook, Nr Monmouth   *Fax* (0600) 860607
NP5 4TX

In a steeply wooded valley a mile from the river Wye, a cosy 17th-century
inn, now extended and modernised, offering excellent food and attractive
accommodation. It returns to a full entry after many reports praising the
new owners, Sandra and Roger Bates. "A restaurant-with-rooms," writes
one reader, "like the *Riverside* at Canonbie (q.v.). Strongly recommended
for food, drink, service, peace and quiet." Rooms are small but well
equipped, with plenty of wardrobe space. "The highlight is dinner,
including mallard, local salmon, and Welsh lamb. The style is French, but
not too *nouvelle*. The service is truly excellent and overall there's a very
informal and friendly atmosphere." "At night there was only the
susurration of the breeze in the trees and the softly running Wye. In the
morning we woke to the sound of robins and more wrens than I've seen
in years." (*ECM Begg, John Gillett, G and EW Waldron, Mr and Mrs BJ Steptoe,
RC Petherick, Jill Marshall, and others*)

Open All year except 2 weeks Jan and Christmas. Restaurant closed for lunch
Mon.
Rooms 12 double – all with bath, shower, telephone, radio, TV, tea-making
facilities. 1 ground-floor room.
Facilities Lounge with small bar, restaurant, breakfast room. 3-acre garden with
terrace.
Location 5 m S of Monmouth; W of A466 at Bigsweir Bridge, 2 m up narrow lane.
Restrictions Suitable for partially & only. No smoking in restaurant. No dogs in
public rooms.
Credit cards All major cards accepted.
Terms B&B £32–£42; dinner, B&B £49.50–£59.50. Set lunch £11.95, dinner
£19.95. Children free if sharing adults' room.
Service/tipping: "We believe everyone should expect good service without tipping."

Scotland

Kinloch House Hotel, Blairgowrie

ABERFELDY Tayside   **Map 5**

Farleyer House Hotel   *Tel* Aberfeldy (0887) 20332
Aberfeldy, Perthshire   *Fax* (0887) 29430
PH15 2JE

Frances Atkins, chef/*patronne*, and her husband Bill have moved from
their celebrated inn-cum-restaurant, *The Old Plow* at Speen in Buckinghamshire, to the peaceful countryside of Perthshire, where they
have bought the white-washed former dower house of Castle Menzies.
Nestling on a hillside overlooking the Tay valley, the hotel is an hour or
so's drive from Edinburgh or Glasgow. Decorated in a welcoming
country-house style, *Farleyer House* is praised for its solid comfort:
"Reception rooms very good indeed, service most adequate, tea
excellent, the sheets divine – only our bedroom and sitting room a trifle
cold." (*Tom Jaine*) Other writers, while appreciating the cooking, have
been less enthusiastic about the accommodation. Dinner is a four-
course affair featuring local produce and ambitious combinations of

flavours. The Atkins are planning a series of "theme breaks" related to the hotel and the area; also cookery courses out of season. New to the Guide this year, more reports please.

Open All year.
Rooms 2 suites, 8 double, 1 single – all with bath, shower, telephone, radio, TV.
Facilities Drawing room, 2 libraries (1 with drinks dispensary). 70-acre grounds with garden and croquet, golf, woods and parkland. River Tay with salmon/trout fishing ½ m; water sports 3 m; shooting, riding, golf arranged.
Location In Aberfeldy take B846 across Wade Bridge to Kinloch Rannoch.
Restrictions No smoking in dining room. No children under 10. Dogs by prior arrangement; not in bedrooms or public rooms.
Credit cards Access, Amex, Visa.
Terms Dinner, B&B £65–£100. Full alc £40.
Service/tipping: "Our staff do not expect tips but will accept if a guest offers one."

ACHILTIBUIE Highland   Map 5

Summer Isles Hotel   *Tel* Achiltibuie (085 482) 282
Achiltibuie, by Ullapool
Ross and Cromarty IV26 2YG

In a remote and beautiful setting north-west of Ullapool, reached by a 15-mile single-track road, the *Summer Isles* is a splendid base for bird-watchers, walkers and fishermen (it holds fishing rights in the area), and has spectacular views over the sea and a great scattering of little islands. The owners, Mark and Geraldine Irvine, advise guests to bring welling-tons, binoculars, paint-boxes, comfortable old clothes – their dogs if they like (though not children under eight). Most guests change for dinner, served promptly at 8. It is a sophisticated five-course meal: a recent menu included chilled avocado soup with chervil, home-made buckwheat and caraway loaf, hot mousse of fresh local scallops, haunch of Sika venison with bacon and juniper, a choice of five puddings, and Scottish cheeses. Our postbag has been full of praise for the cooking: "The most satisfying food that we have encountered in 30 years of travelling." "Superb and very well balanced." Bedrooms are comfortable though not lavishly appointed; some are quite small. The Loghouse Suite is recommended for families – "fresh milk in the fridge and top-ups of fruit during the week". (*J and M Cole, Barbara Wooldridge, Roger Bland, Virginia and Charles Day, and others*) Two readers hold strong views on the recently built hydroponi-cum, source of much fresh produce on the table: "a monstrous building", "vast and ugly". Two correspondents complained about the crowded lounge before dinner; one was forced to take sherry in the hall.

Open Easter–mid-Oct.
Rooms 2-roomed suite (sleeps 2–5; available for self-catering Oct–May), 10 double – all with bath and/or shower. Suite and 7 rooms in Loghouse annexe 3 yds from main building. Some ground-floor rooms.
Facilities Lounge with TV, cocktail bar, public bar, dining room, café for teas and light lunches. Sea and beaches nearby; fishing, walking, bird-watching.
Location 10 m N of Ullapool; take twisting single-track road skirting Lochs Lurgain, Badagyle and Oscaig for 15 m. Hotel is just past post office.
Restrictions Not suitable for &. No smoking in dining room. No children under 8. No dogs in public rooms.
Credit cards None accepted.
Terms [1990 rates] B&B (Scottish): single occupancy £34–£47, double £50–£72, suite £85 (for 2). Packed lunch £5.50. Set dinner £25. Spring breaks.

Service/tipping: "Service included in all prices; we do not expect our customers to tip. If guests insist on showing special appreciation, the money is divided evenly among all staff."

ARDUAINE Strathclyde   **Map 5**

Loch Melfort Hotel   *Tel* Kilmelford (085 22) 233
Arduaine, by Oban   *Fax* (085 22) 214
Argyll PA34 4XG

Readers for many years have enjoyed the spectacular setting of this hotel. "The situation must afford one of the most superb views from any hotel, not just in Scotland, but in the entire world." A characteristic loch-side house converted into a small modern hotel with a motel-like extension, it lies on the coast road between Oban and Crinan, with views towards the islands of Jura and Scarba. All rooms have large picture-windows facing the sea. This year it has new owners, Philip and Rosalind Lewis, fresh to the hotel business – he a refugee from the motor trade, she from publishing. Visitors during the early months of their regime were mostly delighted: "The Lewises gave a very warm welcome to everyone." "It is a very relaxed place where you may sit and read, or be convivial." "The Lewises were marvellous, neither looming over us nor abandoning us." Children are warmly welcomed, and one reader told us of an incident where Rosalind Lewis had been particularly helpful to parents with a fractious child. (*Anne Laurence, and others*) Not all *Loch Melfort* prospects please, however; one visitor considered the accommodation somewhat spartan and was critical of cooking and service. More reports please, especially on the food.

Open Early Mar–3 Jan.
Rooms 25 double, 1 single – all with bath and/or shower, telephone, TV, tea-making facilities, baby-listening. 20, with balcony/patio, in separate wing. 10 ground-floor rooms.
Facilities Portable ramp. 2 lounges, library, bar, restaurant. 30-acre grounds; on loch; safe bathing (cold), windsurfing, fishing, etc.
Location 19 m S of Oban on A816.
Restrictions No smoking in dining room. No dogs in main house.
Credit cards Access, Visa.
Terms B&B £42–£55. Bar meals; picnic lunches. Set dinner £18.50–£22. Reduced rates for children sharing parents' room; special meals on request.
Service/tipping: "No service charge. Tipping at guests' discretion. Tips distributed among all staff."

ARDVASAR Skye, Highland   **Map 5**

Ardvasar Hotel   **BUDGET**   *Tel* Ardvasar (047 14) 223
Ardvasar, Sleat, Isle of Skye
Inverness-shire IV45 8RS

A white-washed stone former coaching inn, a mile from the Armadale Ferry, the *Ardvasar Hotel* was built as a hostelry in the 18th century and still serves the needs of visitors from over the water as well as locals. It is an unassuming place, "friendly and hospitable", "spotlessly clean". "Accommodation, though simple, was comfortable, and our spacious room had a wonderful view across the Sound of Sleat." Bill and Gretta Fowler's aim is an informal atmosphere; there is nothing special about the decor, but visitors continue to appreciate the hotel's hospitality, especially the cooking. "Beautiful fresh-caught lobsters." "Excellent cheeseboard – all local cheeses with home-made oatcakes. Good breakfast with proper butter in a dish." The four-course menu changes daily and offers a good choice. (*Mrs M Wall; and others*) Only complaint: the wine list could have been longer.

Open Mar–Nov.
Rooms 9 doubles, 1 single – all with bath and/or shower, tea-making facilities; 4 with TV; baby-listening on request.
Facilities Lounge, TV lounge, cocktail bar, public bar, dining room. Small garden. Safe but rocky bathing ½ m.
Location In tiny village. 2 ferries to island, Kyle of Lochalsh–Kyleakin and Mallaig–Armadale, operate all year round but latter will not take vehicles in winter. Also car ferry Glenelg–Kylerhea in summer.
Restrictions Not suitable for &. Dogs at management's discretion.
Credit card Access.
Terms B&B: single, £20–£25, double £45–£55; dinner, B&B: single £35–£40, double £62–£80. Set dinner £16; picnic lunches and bar meals available. Children sharing parents' room charged for meals only; special meals on request.
Service/tipping: "No service charge. Tipping not expected but if anyone is pleased enough to want to tip, we are pleased to thank them personally!"

ARISAIG Highland   Map 5

The Arisaig Hotel   *Tel* Arisaig (068 75) 210
Arisaig, Inverness-shire
PH39 4NH

A welcoming old-fashioned inn, on the seashore at Arisaig village, on the Road to the Isles. The immediate surroundings are "tatty" (an understatement according to some), with a boatyard just across the road, but you have only to raise your eyes to enjoy the distant views of Skye, Eigg, Muck and Rhum, and the hotel hopes to have the eyesore removed before 1990 is out. Do not confuse *The Arisaig Hotel* with *Arisaig House*, below. It is a small family enterprise, with George and Janice Stewart ("a really splendid couple with lots of humour and bags of resilience") and their son Gordon sharing nearly all the work; the tariff is accordingly modest. Some bedrooms are quite small and basic and not all have private facilities, but they are spotlessly clean and there is plenty of hot water. The decor is functional, and weak on pictures or ornaments, but the restaurant offers good, honest cooking, with the freshly caught fish specially recommended. There is a respectable wine list, reasonably priced. (*AW and DC Murdoch, P Macaulay and A Rodger, John Gillett, and others*)

Open All year.
Rooms 13 double, 2 single – 6 with bath, all with telephone, radio, tea-making facilities, baby-listening.
Facilities Residents' lounge, TV lounge, lounge bar, public bar, dining room. ½-acre garden. Rocky and tidal beach by hotel; sandy beaches 5 mins' drive away, with safe bathing, yachting. Fishing permits arranged.
Location Take A830 for Mallaig, which is off A82 just N of Fort William. Hotel is on edge of village.
Restrictions Not suitable for severely &. No smoking in dining room. No dogs in public rooms.
Credit cards None accepted.

Terms B&B £22–£31; dinner, B&B £28–£62. Bar lunches, packed lunches; full alc £24. 5% reduction for stays of a week or more. Reduced rates for children under 14; special meals.
Service/tipping: "*No service charge. If a guest wishes to tip, we request that it be given to reception so that it can be shared by all.*"

Arisaig House   *Tel* Arisaig (068 75) 622
Beasdale, Arisaig   *Fax* (068 75) 626
Inverness-shire PH39 4NR   *Telex* 777279

An imposing grey granite Victorian country house with lovely views of the water and islands, Ruth and John Smither's *Arisaig House* is in complete contrast to the *Arisaig Hotel*, above. It stands in large grounds with walks to the beach where Prince Charlie (the Bonnie one) is said to have hidden; the gardens are a particular delight. The interior is a perfect thirties period piece. The dining room has panelled walls and sparkling crystal on polished wood tables – "A spacious room, but a little distracting; 1930s cherrywood panelling and Deco lights, but Chippendale furniture." Readers this year praise the immaculate housekeeping, elegantly arranged fresh flowers, friendly service, and comfortable bedrooms, "not overdone". Breakfasts are said to be *vastly* improved, following earlier criticism. But there have been reports of food not quite *comme il faut*, and wines poured without opportunities for tasting. A new chef, Matthew Burns, was appointed in March 1990. More reports please, especially on the restaurant.

Open Easter–mid-Nov.
Rooms 13 double, 2 single – all with bath and hand shower (13 *en suite*), telephone, TV.
Facilities Reception, 2 lounges, lounge bar, restaurant. 20-acre grounds with gardens, terraces, croquet lawn, woodland, clay-pigeon shooting. Helipad. Sea 10 mins' walk with rock and sandy beach; loch, sea and river fishing.
Location On A830 3 m S of Arisaig.
Restrictions Not suitable for &. No smoking in dining room. No children under 10. No dogs.
Credit cards Access, Visa.
Terms Dinner, B&B (Scottish): single £77–£82.50, double £187–£242. Bar lunches; set dinner £33. 10% reduction for 5-day or longer bookings made direct and settled by cash or cheque (except Aug/Sep).
Service/tipping: "*No charge is made for service and our staff do not expect gratuities.*"

AUCHENCAIRN Dumfries and Galloway   Map 5

Balcary Bay Hotel   *Tel* Auchencairn (055 664) 217
Auchencairn, Nr Castle Douglas
DG7 1QZ

A modernised 17th-century smuggler's inn on the edge of Balcary Bay, retaining much of its old character and atmosphere. Unpretentious and reasonably priced, it is owned and run by Ron and Joan Lamb and their son Graeme, and is quietly situated on the shore road just outside the village of Auchencairn. Warm recommendations brought it back to the Guide last year, and a 1990 visitor is rhapsodic in her praise: "We are totally under the spell of this charming hotel in its idyllic setting." (*Penny Spokes*) Earlier views: "All accommodation is of a high order; central heating throughout, well-appointed, light and airy bedrooms, most with bathroom *en suite*, comfortable public rooms. Service throughout is highly attentive but unobtrusive. The hotel stands in well-tended mature gardens and has extensive views; sporting interests – golf, fishing, riding – are well catered for in the area, and there are numerous good walks." "Charming flower arrangements and attractive colour schemes throughout. Dogs are welcome (under control). Very friendly atmosphere." There is a limited-choice set menu using local produce, and an extensive à la carte menu and wine list.

Open Early Mar–early Nov.
Rooms 11 double, 2 single – 12 with bath and shower, all with telephone, radio, TV, tea-making facilities.
Facilities 2 lounges, 2 bars, restaurant. 3½-acre grounds on bay with sand/rock beach; safe bathing, fishing.
Location Off A711 Dumfries/Kircudbright road, 2 m S of Auchencairn on shore road.
Restrictions Not suitable for &. No dogs in public rooms.
Credit cards Access, Visa.
Terms B&B £28–£38. Dinner, B&B £42–£53. Set dinner £15; full alc £20. Bar meals available. Early and late season rates; reductions for 3- and 7-night stays. Half-price for children sharing parents' room; special meals.
Service/tipping: "Payment for service is not expected or encouraged. Gratuities are shared among all staff."

BALLATER Grampian   Map 5

Craigendarroch Hotel and   *Tel* Ballater (033 97) 55858
   Country Club   *Fax* (033 97) 55447
Braemar Road, Ballater   *Telex* 739952
Aberdeenshire AB3 5XA

A sophisticated establishment with a difference, *Craigendarroch* is a Scottish baronial hotel-cum-elaborate sports complex, part of an ambitious time-sharing enterprise in Royal Deeside. The residents of the hotel and the occupants of the lodges surrounding it have the run of the extensive facilities – swimming pools, squash and snooker, curling and a ski-slope. The hotel's *soigné* restaurant, *The Oaks Room*, under Bill Gibb, provides sophisticated food, *nouvelle cuisine* in style, in elegant surroundings (reservation essential); the recently opened *Lochnagar* "has a lovely view and good meals at a reasonable price", and the *Café Jardin* shares the chef and kitchens and provides simpler meals at much lower prices, popular with children. Visitors this year write: "Fresh flowers in our room, a glass of sherry, a bowl of fruit, a porter who refused to accept a tip." "Delightful atmosphere, excellent breakfast, excellent club facilities." "The staff are very friendly, hardworking and full of goodwill." Children are welcome, and there is a crèche. (*Mr and Mrs GG Thomas, Dr FM Halle, G Brafman, Mr and Mrs C Moncreiffe*) A word or two of caution: "there may be some pressure to purchase a 'time-share' lodge"; "light sleepers might be disturbed by the continuous low-pitched noise of the machinery at the country club".

Open All year.
Rooms 2 suites, 48 double (including 3 family) – all with bath, shower, telephone, radio, TV, tea-making facilities; baby-sitting service.

Facilities Lift, ramps, wc for &. 2 lounges, 2 bars, 3 restaurants; live music/disco 3 times a week. Club facilities include swimming pool, squash, snooker, children's room with games and pool table, health and beauty salon, sauna, solarium. 29-acre grounds with tennis courts, curling, putting green and dry-ski slope. Golf, fishing, and winter sports nearby.
Location On A93 ½ m W of Ballater.
Restrictions No smoking in *Oaks* restaurant and some bedrooms. No dogs.
Credit cards All major cards accepted.
Terms B&B: single £79.50–£85, double £105–£115, suite £150–£270. Full alc dinner from £25. Reduced rates for children sharing parents' room; special meals. *Service/tipping: "Service included. No gratuities accepted."*

Darroch Learg Hotel **BUDGET**   *Tel* Ballater (033 97) 55443
Ballater, Aberdeenshire AB3 5UX

In 5-acre grounds on the side of a wooded mountain, a 10-minute walk from Ballater, the Darroch Learg, *in two pink-and-grey granite houses, offers a quiet setting and lovely scenery. Spacious public rooms, traditionally furnished, comfortable bedrooms. Food is "plain, rather old-fashioned, but freshly cooked and plentiful, and the staff, all wearing tartan, friendly and pleasant". Open Feb–Nov. 19 double rooms, 4 single, 20 with bath or shower, 1 suitable for &. B&B £23–£32. Set dinner £14. New to the Guide last year. More reports please.*

BALQUHIDDER Tayside   Map 5

Kings House Hotel **BUDGET**   *Tel* Strathyre (087 74) 646
Balquhidder
Perthshire FK19 8NY

Attractive roadside inn, family run, well situated for visiting Trossachs, offering bright and cheerful accommodation, good food in dining room with log fire. 9 bedrooms (none en suite, all with H&C), small but well appointed; lots of chintz. Recommended for "well-cooked, dinner-party style food based on steaks, salmon, venison" and "real porridge". Lovely views, peacocks in garden, no noise despite being on road. Fishing permits available, stalking and shooting arranged. B&B: single £18, double £35. Bar lunches. Set dinner £13.50, full alc £20 [1990]. New nomination. More reports please.

BANCHORY Grampian   Map 5

Banchory Lodge Hotel   *Tel* Banchory (033 02) 2625
Banchory, Kincardineshire   *Fax* (033 02) 5019
AB3 3HS

On the banks of the river Dee, superbly positioned for salmon and trout fishing, a white-painted Georgian building, filled with Victorian and Edwardian furniture and bric-à-brac lovingly collected over the years by the resident owners Mr and Mrs Jaffray who this year celebrate their 25th anniversary here. The hotel has many loyal returnees – not just fishing folk but also golfers (there are three courses close by). "The outstanding quality of the service," runs one report, "and the majestic location are a complete recipe for a relaxing and stimulating holiday." (*Gerald Howarth MP, JD Spencely, ML Smith, and others*) As usual complaints focus on the restaurant, mostly about the cooking, though poor service in the dining room and "paltry helpings" are also mentioned.

Open 30 Jan–12 Dec.
Rooms 10 suites, 12 double, 1 single – 21 with bath or shower, all with telephone, radio, TV, tea-making facilities, baby-listening.
Facilities 2 lounges, cocktail bar, dining room, private dining room. 12-acre grounds with salmon and trout fishing (book well in advance).
Location 5 mins' walk from centre.
Restriction Not suitable for &.
Credit cards All major cards accepted.
Terms [1990 rates] (Excluding VAT) B&B: single £55, double £80–£90; dinner, B&B: single £70, double £112–£122. Set lunch £10, dinner £20. Reduced rates for children; special meals.
Service/tipping: "Service included. Central pool in office for tips."

Invery House	*Tel* Banchory (033 02) 4782
Bridge of Feugh, Banchory	*Fax* (033 02) 4712
Kincardineshire AB3 3NJ	*Telex* 73737

"A truly superb hotel, outstanding in every way. Beautiful bedrooms and bathrooms. Impeccable service. Incredible setting." So began a report last year on this pale pink mansion, purchased in 1985 by Stewart and Sheila Spence and carefully transformed into a highly sophisticated country house hotel. "As you approach from the south you pass over the rushing river Feugh. White boulders guide you to the house. The flagstoned porch is liberally filled with antiques, flowers and stuffed birds, as is the main hall, which is warm underfoot, mostly peach with green velvet, and has dark Edwardian furniture. Our bedroom, Rokeby (all the bedrooms are called after novels by Sir Walter Scott who is said to have visited the house) was a riot of designer chintz. The bathroom had everything, even a telephone (though the bath was awkward to use, approached up two steps, and with the taps in the middle). Drinks were served in the drawing room where we chose our dinner and consulted the vast wine list. In the sage-green dining room we sat in huge upholstered armchairs, so enormous we were miles away from each other across the table." (*Jane Kaminski, Lt Col SJ Furness, and others*) The food is "excellent", though "the superb wine list has horrid prices". "A designer hotel for designer people?" was one comment from a reader who had difficulty accommodating his shoulders in the huge kidney-shaped bath. There has been a change of manager and chef this year. More reports please.

Open All year except Jan.
Rooms 2 suites, 9 double, 3 single – all with bath, shower, telephone, radio, TV.
Facilities Bar, 2 lounges, dining room; 2 private dining/conference rooms. 47-acre grounds with 1 mile private fishing, croquet, putting, helipad. Chauffeur-driven car available for guests' use. Golf nearby.
Location 18 m W of Aberdeen. Take A93 to Banchory then A974 S to Fettercairn for 1 m. Look for sign.
Restrictions Only restaurant suitable for & (ramp). No children under 8. Dogs in kennels only.
Credit cards All major cards accepted.
Terms (Service at guests' discretion) B&B: single £75–£125, double £85–£155, suite £165–£225. Set lunch £16.50, dinner £31.50. Autumn, winter and spring breaks. Special meals for children on request.

BEATTOCK Dumfries and Galloway

Map 5

Auchen Castle Hotel
Beattock, Moffat
Dumfriesshire DG10 9SH

Tel Beattock (068 33) 407
Fax (068 33) 667
Telex 777205 attn AUCHEN

Just north of Beattock village, in the Scottish borders, this grey sandstone mid-19th century mansion, former home of the William Younger family, sits imposingly in a 50-acre woodland garden complete with trout lake. The hotel, traditional in style, is run by Hazel and Robert Beckh. A reader travelling on his own writes: "It's excellent for an overnight stop. Staff extremely friendly, room rather small but with a particularly comfy bed." Another adds: "The hotel deserves glowing tributes. We were greeted by the owner who had no difficulty with our late arrival for dinner. The standard of furnishings was exceptional and dinner a masterpiece of achievement. The atmosphere at the 'disco dinner' on Saturday was so relaxing that no one in the restaurant could resist becoming involved." "Lovely setting, nice rooms, good food, first class." (*RP Williams; W Long, David Turner*) Some correspondents have been less complimentary. "The dining room lacks atmosphere." "Lovely grounds, but no hospitality, rooms basic, dinner average, poor breakfast."

Open All year except 3 weeks over Christmas and New Year.
Rooms 22 double, 3 single – 13 with bath, 12 with shower, all with telephone, radio, TV, tea-making facilities, baby-listening. 10 in Cedar Lodge annexe.
Facilities Lounge, bar, dining room; 2 conference rooms. Sat dinner-dance mid-Oct–end Mar. 50-acre grounds with trout loch; boat. Fishing on river Annan; golf, riding, tennis, sailing nearby.
Location 1 m N of Beattock village with signed access from A74.
Restrictions Not suitable for &. No dogs in dining room.
Credit cards Access, Amex, Diners.
Terms B&B: single £39–£42, double £48–£64; dinner, B&B: single £53–£57, double £67–£94. Bar lunches. Set dinner £15. Special breaks; golf holidays. Reduced rates and special meals for children on request.
Service/tipping: "Service included. Tips not expected, but any received are distributed to staff in full."

BLAIRGOWRIE Tayside

Map 5

Kinloch House Hotel
By Blairgowrie
Perthshire PH10 6SG

Tel Essendy (025 084) 237
Fax (025 084) 333

César award: The embodiment of Scottish hospitality

"Superb." "Without a doubt one of the best hotels we have stayed in." "An ideal retreat." Accolades again for David and Sarah Shentall's ivy-covered country house hotel with an oak-panelled hall and bar, and a magnificent gallery, in a 25-acre estate complete with Highland cattle. It is popular with shooting parties, having a game larder, drying facilities and kennels for the gun-dogs, and also with fishermen and golfers (there are 40 golf courses within an hour's drive). It has one of the best restaurants in the area (on the formal side, jackets and ties expected). "A country house hotel of real warmth and character where one immediately feels welcome and relaxed. The presence of family portraits, *objets d'art*, fresh flowers and books adds to the impression of staying in a very

comfortable home rather than a hotel. Housekeeping standards are high."
There is also praise for the views from the bedrooms, and for the peaceful
setting – "often the only sounds to be heard are the cries of wild geese
and ducks". The bedrooms are well appointed; several small double
rooms have recently been converted to single, answering criticism that
some rooms were cramped. David Shentall "is a charming, courteous
man, informative about his food, a superb host" and "a restaurateur who
knows his business". "The restaurant was a delight, the service first-class,
the food beyond criticism, reasonably priced." (*Major and Mrs WF Garnett,
Paul and Christine Butler, RG Tricker, Mrs L Morley, G Anderson*)

Open All year. Closed Christmas.
Rooms 2 suites, 14 double, 5 single – all with bath and/or shower, telephone,
radio, TV, tea-making facilities, baby-listening. 4 ground-floor rooms.
Facilities Ramp. Lounge, TV lounge, cocktail bar, conservatory, dining room.
25-acre grounds with highland cattle and croquet lawn. River and loch fishing,
shooting, stalking, golf nearby.
Location 3½ m W of Blairgowrie on A923 Dunkeld road.
Restrictions No smoking in dining room. Dogs only in certain bedrooms, not in
public rooms.
Credit cards All major cards accepted.
Terms Dinner, B&B £57.50–£72.50. Bar lunches. Set lunch £12.50, dinner £18.50.
Reductions for stays of 3 or more nights. 1-night bookings occasionally refused in
peak season. Reduced rates and special meals for children by arrangement.
*Service/tipping: "Tipping not encouraged. If people insist the money is distributed among
staff."*

BRIDGE OF MARNOCH Grampian   Map 5

The Old Manse of Marnoch
Bridge of Marnoch
Huntly, Aberdeenshire AB5 5RS

Tel Aberchirder (046 65) 873
from Dec 1990 (0466) 780873

On the banks of the river Deveron, this is a 19th-century guest house new
to the Guide last year, warmly recommended for its friendly welcome,
good food, immaculate bedrooms, and reasonable price. It is much used
by fishermen, and shooting and stalking can also be arranged. There are
wooded walks down to the river, and five-acre grounds with old-
fashioned roses, a formal herb parterre, and a walled kitchen garden. The
decor reflects the many years the proprietors, Patrick and Keren Carter,
spent in the Middle East. Bold colours predominate in the public rooms;
the dining room, where dinner is served communally, is dark red with
nautical prints. Our inspector reported, "*The Old Manse* lifts itself
effortlessly from the 'guest house B&B level' by virtue of its food. It's a
well-run and friendly small hotel in an interesting part of Scotland."
More reports welcome.

Open All year except occasional weekends Nov–Feb.
Rooms 4 double – 1 with bath, 1 with shower, 2 sharing 1 bathroom, all with
radio and tea-making facilities.
Facilities Lounge, dining room. Garden with stream and walks to river. Fishing,
stalking and shooting arranged. Cookery workshops in off-season.
Location On B9117 less than 1 m W of A97 Huntly–Banff route.
Restrictions Not suitable for &. No smoking or dogs in dining room.
Credit cards None accepted.
Terms B&B £15–£33. Set lunch £5, dinner £10. Reduced rates for children sharing
parents' room; special meals on request.
Service/tipping: "No service charge. Guests are not expected to tip their hosts."

BUNCHREW Highland   Map 5

Bunchrew House   *Tel* Inverness (0463) 234917
Bunchrew, by Inverness IV3 6TA

Recently bought by Alan and Patsy Wilson, and in italics last year,
Bunchrew House graduates to a full entry in 1991 as the result of
favourable reports. The house is a pink sandstone Scottish baronial
concoction set around a 15th-century tower; it stands in 18 acres of
wooded grounds on the shores of Beauly Firth. Close enough to Inverness
for convenience, yet distant enough for peace and tranquillity, its major
attraction may be the beautiful glens that stretch to the south – Affric,
Strathglass and Strathconon. Inside, there is dark panelling, thick carpets,
and open fires. The dining room has a view of the water. A visitor last
year praised the "superb meals" and called it "the highlight of two weeks
in Britain". Two readers this year have been equally pleased: "Very
comfortable rooms, warm and interesting atmosphere, good food and
unpretentious and genuine service." "The place became home within
hours. When we arrived, tea and shortbread appeared by magic. It's one
of the few hotels that still bring you early morning tea and turn down
beds. And the redoubtable head waiter even donned waders to help me
out of the hotel's boat after a late-night sail in search of seals." (*P and S
Hawkins, Mrs Rita D Darwin*)

Open All year.
Rooms 6 double – all with bath and shower, telephone, radio, TV, baby-listening.
Facilities Drawing room, cocktail bar, 2 restaurants. Rolls Royce with chauffeur,
helicopter available for sightseeing.
Location 3 m from centre of Inverness on A862 towards Beauly.
Restrictions Not suitable for &. No smoking in restaurants. Dogs by prior
arrangement only.
Credit cards Access, Amex, Visa.
Terms B&B single occupancy £50–£72, double £65–£95. Set lunch £9.50, dinner
£19.50. 3-day breaks. Reduced rates and special meals for children.
Service/tipping: "Totally at guests' discretion for exceptional service."

BUNESSAN Mull, Strathclyde   Map 5

Ardfenaig House   *Tel* Fionnphort (068 17) 210
Bunessan, Isle of Mull
Argyllshire PA67 6DX

Standing at the head of a small loch where only the sounds of sheep,
curlews and sea birds disturb the silence, the hotel has grounds that give
directly on to the moor and there are many pleasant walks for bird-
watchers and sketchers. Built in the 1700s and formerly belonging to the
Duke of Argyll, it is full of books (owner Ian Bowles was formerly a
librarian at Oxford), as well as antiques. It has a real country atmosphere,
with pink clematis smothering the porch, wellington boots by the door,
portraits on the stairs, and no fewer than three grand pianos; also a
friendly Cavalier King Charles spaniel. There are only five rooms for
guests; they share three bathrooms – "very near the bedrooms, and much
nicer, in an old-fashioned way, than most *en suite* bathrooms". There is a
house-party atmosphere at dinner (four courses, no choice, with wines
that are "excellent and not overpriced"). Reports continue to be

warmly enthusiastic about the welcome given by Ian Bowles, his helpful advice about places to visit, and the relaxed but attentive service at all times. (*Gillian Smith, D Barr*)

Open Mid-May–end Sep. Restaurant closed for lunch, and to non-residents on Sun.
Rooms 4 double, 1 single – all with tea-making facilities. Maximum 6 guests at a time.
Facilities Lounge, bar, music room, sun room, dining room. 18-acre grounds sloping down to loch with shingle beach (plenty of sandy beaches nearby). Fishing, safe bathing.
Location 3½ m W of Bunessan on Iona ferry road. Hotel's long drive is on right.
Restrictions Not suitable for &. No smoking in dining room. No children under 12. No dogs in public rooms.
Credit cards None accepted.
Terms Dinner, B&B £70. Set dinner £20. Discount for 3 or more nights' stay.
Service/tipping: "Our prices are structured to include a service charge which is distributed each week to the staff."

BUSTA Shetland   Map 5

Busta House Hotel   *Tel* Brae (080 622) 506
Busta, Brae   *Fax* (080 622) 588
Shetland ZE2 9QN   *Telex* 9312100218

On Busta Voe with own small harbour, and claiming to be oldest continuously inhabited building in Shetland, Busta House re-enters Guide with new owners Peter and Judith Jones. Initial reports favourable: "peat fires in large drawing room; well-stocked library"; "cooking skilled, outcome delicious"; "good service, friendly staff, range of 120 malt whiskies". 20th-century conveniences in bedrooms (TV, hair-drier, etc); same-day laundry. 30 miles north of Lerwick. Open 3 Jan–22 Dec. 20 rooms – all with bath and/or shower. B&B £32.50–£50. Set dinner £18.20. More reports please.

CANONBIE Dumfries and Galloway   Map 5

Riverside Inn   *Tel* Canonbie (038 73) 71512
Canonbie
Dumfriesshire DG14 0UX

🏆 *César award in 1985: Best inn of the year*

This 17th-century fisherman's retreat on the banks of the Esk – "much more comfortable than the word 'inn' would suggest" – is a perennial favourite of readers. "Can't speak too highly of it." "Delightful bedroom, comfortable public rooms, jolly good food." "I don't think I've eaten better anywhere." "Excellent, good value for money." Robert and Susan Phillips' small inn or restaurant-with-rooms is well placed for touring Hadrian's Wall and the Solway coast, and as a staging post on long-haul journeys. There are six pleasantly decorated bedrooms, two in a garden cottage overlooking the river. Readers find them well equipped and well priced, but it is the bar meals and dinners that receive even higher praise. There are four or five choices for each course (e.g. wild mushroom and smoked bacon soup, fresh crayfish tails in garlic butter, casserole of

Angus beef in real ale, whisky and ginger syllabub). Breakfasts are impressive too; a reader who travels often writes, "The menu is more comprehensive than anywhere I know; one can have absolutely anything one wants and several things one wouldn't think of having." Rooms vary in size (it is wise to discuss your requirements on booking) and have "everything that a good hostess would put there from fruit to needle and thread, and books". (*Christopher and Alison Davy, T Wade-Evans, R Berry, Stephanie Sowerby, also Heather Sharland, John Gillett, Michael Owens, Dr and Mrs Mathewson, William A Grant, ECM Begg, and others*)

Open All year except 25/26 Dec, 1/2 Jan, 2 weeks Feb, 2 weeks Nov. Restaurant closed for lunch and Sun night (bar meals available).
Rooms 6 double – 4 with bath, 2 with shower, all with radio, TV, tea-making facilities. 2 in cottage in garden. 1 ground-floor room.
Facilities Reception/coffee lounge, lounge bar, residents' lounge, dining room. Small garden. Park opposite with children's play area. River Esk 100 yds; salmon and sea-trout fishing (permits from hotel).
Location M6 exit 44. 14 m N on A7; turn off A7 into Canonbie. Inn is at bottom of hill by river Esk bridge.
Restrictions No smoking in dining room. No children under 10. No dogs.
Credit cards Access, Visa.
Terms B&B: single from £30, double £60–£62. Set dinner £18. Bar lunches. 2-day breaks Nov–Apr. Weekly rates.
Service/tipping: "No service charge. Tipping is discouraged. If guests insist, staff share it among themselves."

COLONSAY Strathclyde · Map 5

Isle of Colonsay Hotel　　　　　*Tel* Colonsay (095 12) 316
Argyllshire PA61 7YP　　　　　　　*Fax* (095 12) 353

💫 *César award in 1988: Island hotel in a class of its own*

Visitors come to Colonsay to enjoy its remote setting and its golden beaches. There are dramatic rocky cliffs, woods, heathland and lochs, and good terrain for cycling. At the centre of its life is the *Isle of Colonsay Hotel*, overlooking Scalasaig harbour and run by Kevin Byrne, a man of formidable energy, and his wife Christa. The inn is more than 250 years old and caters hospitably to locals and visitors alike. This year it has opened its own bookshop specialising in "the rather arcane subject of Colonsay and Oransay". Infrequent ferry schedules will maroon visitors on the island for at least two days, but many choose to stay longer. The recently introduced Seafood Bar (seasonal) has proved popular, and guests who want a trip offshore can go out with a naturalist on the hotel's 28-foot launch *Wild Life*. Bedrooms vary in size, are conventional in decor and some have views; all have central heating and electric blankets. Readers continue to be enthusiastic: "A long-standing ambition fulfilled, and neither the hotel nor the island disappointed. Kevin Byrne is a lively and helpful host, full of information about the island, how to get over to sea-bound Oransay, where to see birds, wild flowers, and iron-age forts. No choice of courses at dinner, but we found them all good and enjoyable. An isolated and delightful place to stay, and very good value." (*Dr RL Holmes and Dr MW Atkinson*)

Open 1 Mar–5 Nov and 2 weeks New Year.
Rooms 8 double with shower, 3 single – all with radio and tea-making facilities; TV, telephone and baby-listening on request. 1 garden bungalow with shower for family accommodation.
Facilities Residents' lounge, sun room, cocktail bar, public bar, Seafood Bar (May–Sep), restaurant. 1-acre grounds with garden, burn, sandpit, vegetable gardens. ½ m to sandy beach and lochs.
Location 400 yds W of harbour. Car/passenger ferry from Oban Mon, Wed, Fri (37 m crossing, 2¼ hours); additional ferries in high season; hotel courtesy car to/from all sailings.
Restrictions "Disabled guests welcome but facilities not perfect." No smoking in dining room. No dogs in public rooms.
Credit cards All major cards accepted.
Terms Dinner, B&B £42–£51. Set dinner £15. Reductions for long stays; special rates off season. Children sharing parents' room charged only for meals, except in high season.
Service/tipping: "No service charge; our staff are properly paid. Gratuities are shared by our domestic staff among themselves."

DRUMNADROCHIT Highland   Map 5

Polmaily House Hotel   *Tel* Drumnadrochit (045 62) 343
Drumnadrochit
Inverness-shire IV3 6XT

Wonderfully positioned for visiting the dramatic scenery of the glens nearby, this rambling Edwardian mansion in 18-acre grounds is a few miles to the west of Loch Ness. It has pleased readers for many years, offering a tranquil rural setting and with an ambience more like a private house than a hotel. The bedrooms are individually decorated and furnished; "comfortable beds and carpets that were ecstasy to the feet, the bathroom well equipped". "A relaxed atmosphere, not at all stuffy. We had a small sofa and window seat, so it was a nice place to sit and read. The food was excellent, the packed lunches outstanding in quantity and quality." Alison Parsons's menus combine enterprising starters (cream of prawn, sweet pepper and ginger soup, savoury walnut roulade with asparagus and quail's eggs) with more traditional local fare (wild salmon with sorrel sauce, fillet of Aberdeen Angus beef). "Mrs Parsons's exquisite cooking puts the hotel in a class of its own." (*Edith and David Holt, J Coats, and others*) But one reader this year was critical of the hotel's attitude towards children and reported no choice of food and an "unwelcome feeling" in the lounge.

Open Easter–late Oct.
Rooms 7 double, 2 single – doubles with bath, all with radio; baby-listening on request.
Facilities Drawing room, bar, reading room with TV (residents only), restaurant. 18-acre grounds with tennis, croquet, unheated swimming pool; fishing, shooting, stalking, pony trekking nearby.
Location 2 m W of Drumnadrochit on A831 Cannich road.
Restrictions Not suitable for &. No smoking in dining room and bar area. No dogs in hotel.
Credit cards Access, Visa.
Terms B&B (Scottish) £40–£45. Set dinner £17.50. Discounts for long stays. Reduced rates for children sharing parents' room; high teas at 6 pm on request.
Service/tipping: "No service charge. Tips are not solicited."

DUNOON Strathclyde

Map 5

Enmore Hotel
Marine Parade, Kirn
Dunoon, Argyllshire PA23 8HH

Tel Dunoon (0369) 2230

David and Angela Wilson have successfully transformed what was once a rather ordinary Victorian villa, into a small, quite luxurious hotel. Dunoon, a popular seaside resort a century ago, makes a convenient base for exploring the Isles of Arran and Bute and the Mull of Kintyre. The *Enmore* overlooks the Clyde estuary a mile out of town. The bedrooms are filled with creature comforts: bowls of fruit, well-chosen books, electric blankets; many have views of the sea, garden, or mountains in the distance. The Wilsons are keen on beds – there are five four-posters and a water-bed, and two bathrooms have a jacuzzi. Luxury breaks are popular and include flowers, champagne, even a heart-shaped box of chocolates and breakfast in bed. But the hotel also gets high marks for its restaurant: "Each meal was a joy – fresh vegetables, fresh local salmon, shellfish, venison." "Good, nicely balanced starters and main courses and interesting soups." The staff are unruffled by children. "Scrupulously clean and well-appointed, relaxed and cheerful service, varied and flavoursome food, reasonable cost. What a joy it was to come away feeling proud to be British and not ashamed of what we used to offer." *(JH Whitehead, also Dr R and Mrs A Littlewood, A Taylor, and others)*

Open Mid-Jan–mid-Dec.
Rooms 1 suite, 8 double, 3 single – all with bath and/or shower, telephone, radio, TV, baby-listening; 1 with water-bed, 2 with whirlpool bath; tea-making facilities on request. 2 ground-floor rooms.
Facilities 2 lounges, games room, cocktail bar, dining room; 2 squash courts. 1-acre grounds with private shingle beach across road; safe but cold bathing, boating. Golf, swimming pool, tennis and pony trekking nearby.
Location On Marine Parade between 2 ferries, 1 m N of Dunoon.
Restrictions Not suitable for &. No smoking in dining room. Children under 7 not encouraged at dinner.
Credit cards Access, Visa.
Terms B&B: single £38, double £74, suite £106; dinner, B&B: single £46–£56, double £88–£110, suite £122–£142. Set dinner £18. Special breaks. Reduced rates and special meals for children.
Service/tipping: "If tips are offered they are distributed among staff."

EDINBURGH Lothian

Map 5

The Howard Hotel
36 Great King Street
Edinburgh EH3 6QH

Tel (031) 557 3500
Fax (031) 557 6515
Telex 727887

Returning to Guide after change of ownership, with plans to be "the most luxurious townhouse in Edinburgh", a welcoming small hotel in handsome Georgian area north of Princes Street, 5–10 mins' walk from city centre. £1.4 million refurbishment; new chef. Prices naturally jacked up. 16 rooms – all with bath and shower. B&B: single £95, double £145–£185, suite £250. Set lunch £15, dinner £30 [1990]. More reports please.

Sibbet House   *Tel* (031) 556 1078
26 Northumberland Street   *Fax* (031) 557 4365
Edinburgh EH3 6LS   *Telex 727972*

*Elegant Georgian stone-built family home in New Town, 10-minute walk from
city centre. Bedrooms sympathetically furnished with antiques as well as 20th-
century conveniences: central heating, electric blankets, colour TV, tea- and
coffee-making facilities, hair-driers. Recommended for spotlessly clean rooms,
copious breakfast, and friendly but not overpowering hosts, the Sibbets.
Bagpipe-loving owner will play on request. Many restaurants, pubs nearby.
Open May–Sep. 3 double rooms, all with bath and/or shower. B&B £20–£35.
New nomination, more reports please.*

ELGIN Grampian   **Map 5**

The Mansion House Hotel   *Tel* Elgin (0343) 548811
The Haugh, Elgin   *Fax* (0343) 547916
Moray IV30 1AW

An imposing 19th-century Scots baronial mansion, complete with
castellated tower and stair turret, standing in five acres of grounds with
many fine trees, overlooking the river Lossie, a quarter of a mile from the
town centre. It is owned and run by Fernando Oliveira, who comes from
Portugal, and his Scottish wife. In 1989 it acquired an indoor pool
complete with jacuzzi, sauna, Turkish bath and "comprehensive gymnasium". Our inspector recently gave the hotel a general seal of approval:
she noted the warm reception, her comfortable room ("a symphony of
blue and white"), the dining room softened by pretty pink table-cloths
and tulip-shaped wine glasses, and the fairly priced set-menu dinner. The
wine list, with nearly 100 wines, included many bottles under £10, and
20 half-bottles. A reader this year cites the "varied and delicious table
d'hôte menus, beautifully presented". Another found the atmosphere
"relaxed and friendly" throughout his stay, and "the breakfast delicious:
porridge and cream, Arbroath smokies and fresh rolls". The hotel is
popular with visitors on business and "discerning fishing and shooting
parties". (*Mrs JG Mathieson, David Lea-Wilson*)

Open All year.
Rooms 18 double – all with bath, shower, telephone, radio, TV, tea-making
facilities, baby-listening.
Facilities Residents' lounge, bar, bistro, dining room; function room. Heated
indoor pool. 5-acre grounds with children's play area. River with fishing nearby.
Location Coming E from Inverness or W from Aberdeen on A96 turn off Elgin
High St into Alexandra Rd; take turning into Haugh Rd, then first turning on left.
Parking.
Restrictions Not suitable for &. No dogs.
Credit cards All major cards accepted.
Terms B&B: single £49–£60, double £75–£95; dinner, B&B: single £60–£80,
double £95–£130. Set lunch £10, dinner £20. Reduced rates for children; special
meals.
Service/tipping: "Service included. Tipping not expected."

More nominations for good Edinburgh hotels would be welcome.

ERISKA Strathclyde
Map 5

Isle of Eriska Hotel
Eriska, Ledaig, by Oban
Argyllshire PA37 1SD

Tel Ledaig (0631) 72371
Fax (0631) 72531
Telex 777040

An imposing Victorian mansion on a small private island off the west coast, one mile wide and a mile and a half long, linked by a bridge to the mainland. There are magnificent views down the Lynn of Lorne to Mull, and the island is rich in flora and fauna. The hotel is owned by Robin Buchanan-Smith, a minister of the Church of Scotland, and his wife Sheena, and run on country-house lines. For many years the hotel has had a devoted following of those who love its old-fashioned, fairly formal (jacket and tie at dinner) style of hospitality. Readers this year have praised the well-appointed bedrooms and public rooms, personal and friendly service, attention paid to the needs of small children, and "generally satisfactory" food. The hotel has tennis, croquet and ponies. (*MGB Scott, CJ Uncles*) One criticism of the serve-yourself breakfast: "Scrambles around the buffet are perhaps not the most civilised way to dine in the morning; lids thoughtfully replaced on the serving dishes put paid to any semblance of crispy bacon."

Open Mar–Nov.
Rooms 1 suite, 15 double – all with bath, shower, telephone, radio, TV, tea-making facilities, baby-listening. 2 ground-floor rooms with access for &.
Facilities Ramp. 2 halls, drawing room, library, dining room. 320-acre grounds with tennis, croquet, putting green, water sports, ponies. Loch 5 mins.
Location 12 m N of Oban. 4 m W of A828.
Restrictions No children under 10 in dining room at night (high tea at 6 pm). No dogs in dining room.
Credit cards Access, Amex, Visa.
Terms [1990 rates] B&B: single £65–£98, double £112–£126, suite on application. Set lunch £8, dinner £33. Off-season rates. Reduced rates for children sharing parents' room; high teas.
Service/tipping: "No service charge. No tipping."

FORSS Highland
Map 5

Forss House Hotel
Forss, by Thurso
Caithness KW14 7XY

Tel Forss (084 786) 201

A small hotel in an under-represented corner of Scotland, converted from listed Victorian home, in attractive 20-acre wooded setting with salmon stream. Abundant wildlife including herons, owls and often otters. Recommended for tasteful furnishings, comfortable beds, undisturbed quiet. Good dinner and wine list, outstanding breakfast ("crispy bacon with soft and creamy scrambled eggs"). 7 double rooms, all with private facilities (2 in sportsman's lodge overlooking river). B&B (Scottish) single £30–£40, double £55–£70. Set lunch £8.50, dinner £14.50. New nomination. More reports please.

If you are nominating a hotel, please do make sure that you tell us enough to convey its character and quality. We can't make good bricks without plenty of straw.

FORT WILLIAM Highland   Map 5

The Factor's House   *Tel* Fort William (0397) 5767
Torlundy, Fort William   *Fax* (0397) 2953
Inverness-shire PH33 6SN   *Telex* 776229 attn F H

Built in the early part of the century for the factor (estate manager) of
what is now *Inverlochy Castle* (see below), *The Factor's House* is owned
and run by Peter Hobbs, son of *Inverlochy's* owner, Grete Hobbs, as an
entirely independent enterprise and at half the prices of the *Castle*. The
house is modern and has a fresh, light, airy feeling. Bedrooms are
furnished in white-painted bamboo with cool Designers Guild wallpaper,
but are on the small side and somewhat austere. The lounges, too, are
small which makes private conversation difficult. However, the simplicity
of the decor has not diminished readers' praise for the hotel, "Your entry
is accurate in all respects. A nice experience." "Full marks, quite the most
friendly hotel I have stayed at. Every single member of the staff seemed
genuinely interested in the guests." The chef, Steven Doole, continues to
preside and his cooking is again rated "excellent". *The Factor's House* falls
somewhere between hotel and restaurant-with-rooms, with the special
attraction of being at the foot of Ben Nevis in some of Scotland's best
walking country. (*JRR, RAL Ogston, Joseph and Lola Rhea, William A Grant*)

Open Mid-Jan–mid-Dec. Closed Sun Nov–Mar.
Rooms 7 double – all with bath and/or shower, telephone, T V. 1 on ground floor.
Facilities 2 lounges, dining room. Small garden but guests have access to
Inverlochy's 500-acre grounds and tennis court. Sailing, fishing, pony trekking,
golf, clay-pigeon shooting available.
Location 3 m NE of Fort William on A82, just after turn-off to *Inverlochy Castle*.
Restrictions Not suitable for &. No children under 6. No dogs.
Credit cards All major cards accepted.
Terms [1990 rates] B&B: single occupancy £46–£75, double £69–£80. Set lunch
(residents only) £7.50, dinner from £20. Special meals for children on request.
*Service/tipping: "We do not expect tips but if given they are gratefully received and
distributed equally amongst staff. We do not leave the bottom of credit card vouchers
blank."*

Inverlochy Castle   *Tel* Fort William (0397) 2177
Torlundy, Fort William   *Fax* (0397) 2953
Inverness-shire PH33 6SN   *Telex* 776229

&❀ *César award in 1984: For incomparable grandeur*

This spectacular Scottish baronial house stands in 500 acres of grounds,
rich in rhododendrons, on the lower slopes of Ben Nevis in the heart of
the West Highlands. It won its César in our first year of those awards. Its
fame and impressive advance booking owe much to its châtelaine, Grete
Hobbs, who decided 22 years ago to turn her husband's family home into
a platonic idea of a country house hotel. "Spacious accommodation,
wonderful views, service and food," writes a reader this year. "We had
the most beautifully decorated room, with fresh flowers everywhere." It
is in a class of its own, not so much for its 'incomparable grandeur' as for
its exceedingly high standards and the remarkable friendliness of those
who run it. The vast inner hall and the drawing room are both warm with
blazing fires and have comfortable sofas and armchairs." "Room service

and service at dinner were smooth, swift and courteous. The key to the hotel's success is its manager, Michael Leonard; he has been there many years yet his perfectionist eye and his enthusiasm are as keen as ever." "After dinner our first night, we had a game of chess. The next night, we left the dining room and were delighted to find coffee, delicious petits fours and the chess set ready and waiting for us by the fire." (*John E Parsons, Mrs D Simecheck, S Pankhurst, and others*) The hotel's restaurant, *Michelin*-rosetted for many years, is to have a new chef appointed in the winter of 1990/91. It is possible that the hotel will be put on the market shortly.

Open Mid-Mar–mid-Nov.
Rooms 1 suite, 14 double, 1 single – all with bath, shower, telephone, radio, TV, baby-listening; 24-hour room service.
Facilities Great hall, drawing room, 2 dining rooms, billiard room; facilities for small conferences out of season. 500-acre grounds with gardens; all-weather tennis court; trout fishing on nearby private loch. Several golf courses within easy driving distance; pony trekking. Chauffeur-driven limousines for hire.
Location Take turning to NW off A82, 3 m N of Fort William just past golf club. Guests met by arrangement at station or airports.
Restrictions Not suitable for &. Guests requested not to smoke in dining room. Children under 12 accepted only if sharing parents' room. No dogs in hotel (kennels available).
Credit cards Access, Visa.
Terms B&B: single £110–£121, double £150–£180, suite £185–£220. Set lunch £23, dinner £38. Reduced rates for children sharing parents' room; special meals.
Service/tipping: "There is no service charge and tipping is not expected."

GLASGOW Strathclyde

Map 5

One Devonshire Gardens
1 Devonshire Gardens G12 0UX

Tel Glasgow (041) 339 2001 and
334 9494
Fax (041) 337 1663

A trendy, opulent hotel, "furnished with magisterial confidence", in the fashionable West End suburb a short distance from the city centre. "You ring the bell each time to enter what looks like a very elegant private house." Last year a reader reported: "We had the most amazing room, huge and in a decadent/Victorian style which managed to remain completely tasteful and unintimidating. Fresh fruit and magazines, numerous pillows on the vast four-poster, a bath in which a six-foot rugby player could lie flat out, and many big towels, all combined to make an extremely comfortable, nay, sensuous, place to stay." Another reader called the hotel "sumptuous and stunning". The restaurant, oppressively grand to some ("black 'fleurs du mal' wallpaper"), achieves high scores, "first rate and not overpriced considering its excellence". (*JRR; also Uwe Kitzinger, and others*) But a few niggles continue: front rooms suffer from road noise, and the "lighting in the bedrooms is designed as a spectacle rather than for spectacles". There are 19 additional bedrooms this year, two of which are mews suites. More reports, please.

Open All year except Christmas Day. Lunch not served Sat.
Rooms 2 suites, 25 double – 24 with bath and shower, 3 with shower, all with telephone, radio, TV, baby-listening.
Facilities 2 drawing rooms, study, clubroom/bar, restaurant. Boardroom and private dining room.

Location 2 m from city centre at intersection of Great Western and Hyndland Roads.
Restrictions Not suitable for &. Dogs by prior arrangement, not in public rooms.
Credit cards All major cards accepted.
Terms B&B (continental): single occupancy £100–£113, double £130–£145, suite £165. Scottish breakfast £5. Alc lunch £20, set dinner £30. No charge for children sharing parents' room; special meals by arrangement.
Service/tipping: "Tipping is entirely up to guests. All tips are divided amongst the staff."

The White House   *Tel* Glasgow (041) 339 9375
11–13 Cleveden Crescent   *Fax* (041) 337 1430
G12 0PA   *Telex* 777582

🥂 *César award in 1988: For enterprise and innovation in a city hotel*

Our postbag has mostly been full of favourable reports this year on this handsome townhouse hotel-without-restaurant in the centre of a classical Georgian crescent not far from the city centre. It is a series of three adjoining terrace houses comprising 32 suites and rooms, and its prices compare favourably with the city's conventional five-star establishments. The decor is "a curious mix of the grandiose and the utilitarian" – all rooms have a fully fitted kitchenette and mini-bar; the hotel also offers full room service for meals, and has a tie-in with three downtown restaurants; guests can charge the bill to their hotel account and a courtesy Mercedes is provided for travel to and from the restaurant. Most rooms are large and high-ceilinged, with a dining table and chairs as well as easy chairs and sofas; the bathrooms have all the essentials for comfort. Readers continue to praise the fine service and helpful staff, but have mixed views on using the room service for meals. "Breakfasts poor", writes one. "Breakfasts and sandwiches with huge salads were good, but our main course of salmon was tiny, hard and dry." It is probably better to eat out. (*James Gibson, John D Spencely, Gillian Smith, and others*)

Open All year.
Rooms 12 suites, 13 double, 7 single – all with bath, shower, telephone, radio, TV, kitchenette (some are in mews cottages). 3 ground-floor rooms.
Facilities Room service for meals; conference/private dining room. Small garden belonging to Crescent.
Location 1 m W of Glasgow town centre, off Great Western Road (A82). Private parking. Courtesy car to town centre at 8.15 am Mon–Fri and to associated restaurants in evening.
Restrictions Not suitable for &. No dogs.
Credit cards All major cards accepted.
Terms Rooms: single £70, double £82, suite £82–£123. Room service meals: breakfast from £5, full alc dinner £20. (No restaurant; room service available for meals.)
Service/tipping: "No service charge. Tipping at guests' discretion."

GLEN CANNICH Highland   Map 5

Cozac Lodge   *Tel* Cannich (045 65) 263
Glen Cannich by Beauly
Inverness-shire IV4 7LX

Returning to the Guide under new owners Brian and Enid Butler, an attractive 1912 hunting lodge in scenic, remote setting overlooking loch, near Inverness.

Mahogany panelled hall, large dining room, smaller breakfast room, sitting room with comfortable chairs. Recommended by two readers: "Spacious bedroom, roomy bathroom, boiling hot water always available. Great value for money." "A haven of hospitality. A delight to come down each evening for a drink next to the log fire, with a view of the loch and hills. Delicious 5-course fixed-menu dinner; overall atmosphere friendly, relaxed." But one reader, in a cool August, complained of lack of heating, and also of small food portions. Open Easter–Oct. 7 rooms, all with bath or shower. B&B £24–£32, dinner, B&B £41–£49. More reports please.

GLENCRIPESDALE Highland   Map 5

Glencripesdale House   *Tel* Salen (096 785) 263
Glencripesdale, Loch Sunart
Acharacle, Argyllshire PH36 4JH

💧 *César award in 1989:* Non-pareil *hotel for those who want to get even further away from it all*

Bill and Susan Hemmings's civilised guest house is one of the most remote hostelries in Britain. It stands on the south side of Loch Sunart and at the end of an eight-mile rough forestry track that takes an hour to drive. Guests arriving by train will be met by Bill Hemmings at Fort William, the railhead. Deer graze on the front lawn. There's excellent beachcombing: "Great varieties of shells from across the Atlantic and amazing examples of stones positively riddled with quartz and other bright metals, dazzling in the sunshine." *Glencripesdale* is a modernised 18th-century farmhouse; bedrooms are caringly furnished and comfortable. The book-lined sitting room is equally welcoming. In such a remote setting, guests tend to get to know each other quickly; during the day, however, readers report walking for hours without encountering another soul. "A trip in the boat with Dr Hemmings, seeing seals, otters etc, is a must, and a delight." "Mrs Hemmings's meals are delicious, imaginative, and never repetitive – a miracle here." A warning about the terrain: "nearly all walking from the house involves an initial hike through dense woods, and when you do get out into the open, the going can be *exceedingly* rough if there has been much rain"; and "low ground clearance makes the track unsuitable for certain cars". (*Alan Greenwood, JMT Ford, AG Saunders, G Frew, and others*)

Important note Acharacle is only a postal address; it is a two-hour drive from the house. If you arrive by car, the Hemmings appreciate an offer to pick up supplies on the way.

Open Mar–end Oct. Christmas and New Year.
Rooms 4 double – 2 with bath, 2 with shower. 1 self-catering unit.
Facilities Library/lounge, dining room, children's playroom. 2-acre grounds; nature reserve ¼ m; rock and shingle beaches, fishing nearby; windsurfer and inflatable boat with outboard motor for hire.
Location *Do not* go to Acharacle. Hotel is on S side of Loch Sunart. Take A861 towards Strontian; fork left on A884. *Glencripesdale* is through Laudale estate. (Hotel will send detailed directions.)
Restrictions Not suitable for &. No smoking in dining room. Dogs by arrangement, not in public rooms or bedrooms.
Credit cards None accepted.

Terms [1990 rates] Dinner, B&B (including packed lunch) £51–£57. 1-night bookings Mon–Thurs only. Reduced rates for children; special meals on request. *Service/tipping: "Tips not sought. Our policy of donations to Cancer Research Campaign continues, unless guests leave something special for our helper; if so, it goes directly to him/her."*

GLENLIVET Grampian   Map 5

Minmore House Hotel <kbd>BUDGET</kbd>   *Tel* Glenlivet (080 73) 378
Glenlivet
Banffshire AB3 9DB

A newly refurbished Victorian country house in the heart of the whisky country, and formerly the home of George Smith, founder of Glenlivet, whose distillery is just next door. It stands in four acres of secluded garden above the river Livet on which it has fishing rights, and fishing is also available on the Avon and Spey. The area, beautiful and untouristy, has lots of good walks around. The hotel is owned and run by Belinda Luxmoore, who a decade or so ago was known to readers of the Guide as owner of *Foxdown Manor* in Bideford, assisted by daughter Jessica and son-in-law Nick Holmes. It was nominated last year by an alumna of *Foxdown*: "Warmest of welcomes, huge bedroom, many charming touches – vases of flowers, pot-pourri, fresh fruit . . . Quite wonderful five-course dinner. Breakfast a splendour of delicious things. Marvellous value." We sent along an inspector who endorsed these commendations. We look forward to more reports.

Open Apr–31 Oct.
Rooms 1 suite, 7 double, 2 single – all with bath, radio, tea-making facilities.
Facilities Hall, drawing room, bar, dining room. 4-acre grounds with terraced garden, croquet, tennis, unheated swimming pool. Fishing rights on the Livet, and by arrangement on the Avon and Spey.
Location From Grantown on Spey take A95 to Ballindalloch and turn right on to B9008. Follow signs to Glenlivet.
Restrictions Only restaurant suitable for &. No smoking in dining room. No dogs in public rooms.
Credit cards Access, Visa.
Terms Dinner, B&B £40. Set lunch £5, dinner £16; full alc £20. Weekly rates. 1-night bookings may be refused if made far in advance. Reduced rates for children; special meals.
Service/tipping: "Service included. All tips go to staff."

HARRAY LOCH Orkney   Map 5

Merkister Hotel <kbd>BUDGET</kbd>   *Tel* Harray (085 677) 366
Harray Loch, Dounby
Orkney KW17 2LF

In own grounds on edge of Loch Harray, considered by many the best trout-fishing loch in Orkney, modest hotel owned and run by keen fisherman Angus MacDonald and his family. Open Apr–Oct. 15 rooms – 1 with bath and shower, 10 with shower. B&B: single £25.50, double £49.50. Bar meals £5. Set dinner £10.50; full alc £20. New nomination. More reports please.

INVERNESS Highland   **Map 5**

Dunain Park Hotel   *Tel* Inverness (0463) 230512
Inverness
Inverness-shire IV3 6JN

"A modest house, glittering with friendship and, in all things, perfection." Rave reviews this year, as last, on this Italianate early 19th-century country house near Inverness, owned by Ann and Edward Nicoll. The hotel now has fourteen bedrooms (six suites added to the main house this year, and two in a garden cottage), individually decorated "in the most delightful fashion". There are books everywhere, also stereo and tapes. The lounges have log fires and there are pleasing views from the windows; the hotel sits in six acres of gardens and woodlands overlooking the Caledonian Canal. "There was complete peace and no traffic noise." "Our room was large and airy, with superb views. Every comfort was provided, from bath gels and flannels to recent issues of Scottish magazines, and the staff were all friendly and helpful." "There were fresh flowers everywhere and everything was spotless." Reports on Ann Nicoll's cooking are no less enthusiastic: "Her four-course dinners send even middle-aged stomachs happily to sleep. The self-service pudding table was clearly heaven for a young male guest – he made four visits." There is a heated indoor pool and sauna where guests can work off the splendid food (though it is not large enough to satisfy really athletic swimmers). We appreciate a note on *Dunain Park's* menus: "Guests are asked not to smoke in the dining room. If you wish to withdraw to a lounge, please let us know and we will be happy to delay your next course." (*JF Holman, Louise Lamb, Anna Kaposi and Gary Bullock, JD Spencely, and many others*)

Open All year. Restricted meal service during owners' holidays – probably 2 weeks Feb, 2 weeks Nov.
Rooms 8 suites, 6 double – all with bath (8 also have shower), telephone, radio, TV; tea-making facilities by arrangement. 2 suites, both with kitchenette, in converted coach house, 100 yds from hotel. Some suites at ground level.
Facilities 3 lounges, dining room. Indoor heated swimming pool, sauna. 6-acre grounds with garden, badminton, croquet. Fishing, shooting, golf, tennis nearby.
Location 2½ m S of centre of Inverness, off A82 to Fort William. Turn left shortly after Craig Dunain hospital which is on right.
Restrictions No smoking in dining room. "Not suitable for children, unless well behaved." No dogs in public rooms.
Credit cards All major cards accepted.
Terms [1990 rates] B&B £39–£57.50. Set lunch £14.50, dinner £22.50. Reduced rates 3- and 7-day stays. Reduced rates for children sharing with two adults; special meals on request.
Service/tipping: "Service at guests' discretion. Any tips received are shared equally among all staff."

The 1992 Guide will appear in the autumn of 1991. Reports are particularly useful in the spring, and they need to reach us by June 1991 if they are to help the 1992 edition.

IONA Strathclyde   Map 5

Argyll Hotel   **BUDGET**   *Tel* Iona (068 17) 334
Isle of Iona
Argyllshire PA76 6SJ

On the tiny pilgrim island of Iona (three and a half miles long and one and a half wide), reached by a five-minute ferry journey from the Isle of Mull, Mrs Fiona Menzies's hotel stands in the village street facing the sea, with its front lawn running down to the shore; it is just a few minutes' walk from the ferry landing. An earlier visitor described "the drawbridge-up pleasure of seeing the last ferry leave in the evening bearing the day's visitors away", and the sound of the sea, lulling her to sleep at night. The bedrooms are smallish and cottagey; it's worth asking for one with a sea view, rather than one in the annexe at the back. There are two sitting rooms with open fires (and no TV), full of local history and bird books, and a built-on sun lounge with creaking wicker chairs. Beds are said to creak, too. A more recent correspondent adds: "Wonderful food – they bake their own bread, grow their own vegetables, make their own yoghurt and use local salmon and venison. Dinner ridiculously cheap. A vegetarian alternative main course is always provided though the menus are otherwise 'no choice'. A great place for getting away from it all – or most of it anyway." (Endorsed this year by *JMT Ford*)

Open Easter–mid-Oct.
Rooms 10 double, 9 single – 2 with bath and shower, 7 with bath, all with tea-making facilities; baby-listening available.
Facilities 2 lounges, sun lounge, dining room. ½-acre grounds on seashore with rocks, sand, safe bathing; sea and loch fishing.
Location In village, near jetty. Iona reached by direct steamer from Oban in summer or by car or bus across Mull to Fionnphort, then passenger ferry. No cars on Iona. Carparks at Oban and Fionnphort.
Restrictions Not suitable for &. No smoking in dining room and 1 lounge. No dogs in dining room.
Credit cards Access, Visa.
Terms (No service charge) B&B £20–£27.50; dinner, B&B £32–£39.60. Set dinner £12; snacks and light lunches from £2.50. 1-night bookings occasionally refused weekends. Reduced rates and special meals for children.

KENMORE Tayside   Map 5

Kenmore Hotel   *Tel* Kenmore (088 73) 205
The Square, Kenmore   *Fax* (088 73) 262
Perthshire PH15 2NU

In one of Scotland's prettiest villages, overlooking the River Tay, 16th-century hotel in two buildings on opposite sides of the square. Recommended for friendly, helpful staff, good restaurant, comfortable lounge/bar with blazing log fire, relaxed atmosphere. Excellent base for walks by river or in surrounding mountains. Own golf course; river and loch fishing for salmon and trout, boats available. 38 rooms – all with bath and/or shower. B&B: single £25–£40, double £45–£70. Set lunch £6.75–£9, dinner £17.50. New nomination. More reports please.

> If you are recommending a bed-and-breakfast hotel and know of a good restaurant nearby, do mention it in your report.

KENTALLEN Highland

Map 5

Holly Tree Hotel
Kentallen, Appin
Argyllshire PA38 4BY

Tel Duror (063 174) 292
Fax (063 174) 345

Kentallen's former railway station, right on the shore of Loch Linnhe, has been enlarged and extensively renovated, and is now the welcoming *Holly Tree Hotel*. "It still retains Edwardian features – the Glasgow Art Nouveau ticket office is intact; the Railway Bar was formerly the station's tearoom. But the bedrooms are distinctly of the eighties, spacious and delightfully furnished in a combination of traditional (lots of pine) and modish (peach chintz etc), with expensive, specially designed carpets throughout." There are extensive views over the loch, and additional tables with water views in the dining room this year; the hotel has a mile of private waterside grounds. A reader last year wrote: "You will not get the grandeur or the superior deference of *Claridge's*, but you will get charming, efficient service, and delightful food from extensive five-course menus." Readers this year have noted the relaxed attitude towards children: "The Robertsons' young daughter served part of our breakfast, which gave the place an air of informality we liked very much." "They took our children out in their fishing boat in the morning, not charging for their accommodation or meals despite our protests." (*MGB Scott, C and M Carus-Rattle, John E Borron; and others*) But informality in the dining room went too far for some: "friendly but harassed service"; "service was amateur, with waiters very audibly calling out orders".

Open Mar–end Oct, Christmas and New Year.
Rooms 12 double – all with bath and/or shower, telephone, TV, tea-making facilities. 2 ground-floor rooms.
Facilities Residents' lounge, lounge bar, restaurant. 5-acre grounds with slipway, boats for residents' use, fishing, safe bathing in loch. Riding, windsurfing, skiing nearby.
Location On A828, 3 m S of Ballachulish Bridge.
Restriction No smoking in dining room.
Credit cards Access, Amex, Visa.
Terms [1990 rates] Dinner, B&B: single £44–£63, double £88–£118. Set dinner £25. Autumn/winter breaks; Christmas and New Year packages. Reduced rates for children; special meals.
Service/tipping: "No service charge. Tipping left to customer's discretion."

KILCHRENAN Strathclyde

Map 5

Ardanaiseig Hotel
Kilchrenan, by Taynuilt
Argyllshire PA35 1HE

Tel Kilchrenan (086 63) 333
Fax (086 63) 222

On a wooded promontory beside Loch Awe, in the heartland of Clan Campbell, a handsome, large, grey stone Scottish baronial mansion with a celebrated woodland garden. It has a comfortable and prettily decorated drawing room, welcoming library, beautifully appointed dining room, and 14 bedrooms, varying in decor. Jonathan Brown, whose family home this has been since 1964, personally assumed management of the hotel a year or so ago. "A delightful place to stay, remote and peaceful, surrounded by fine gardens and splendid views across Loch Awe. Well-furnished spacious rooms, and friendly, helpful staff, especially the

Browns." "My wife and I have stayed at many of the leading British country house hotels in the Guide. *Ardanaiseig* is the finest, pound for pound. Beautiful house, lovely grounds, absolute quiet, friendly but unobtrusive staff, absolutely attentive when required. And finally – some of the finest cooking, simple, fresh, absolutely delicious." (*Dr RL Holmes and Dr MW Atkinson, Robert Freidus*) In April 1990, Martin Vincent, a graduate of *Inverlochy Castle, Gravetye Manor* (qq.v.) and the *Dorchester*, took over in the kitchen. We'd be pleased to have more reports.

Open Apr–early Nov.
Rooms 12 double, 2 single – all with bath (10 also with shower), telephone, radio, TV.
Facilities Library/bar, drawing room, dining room. 100-acre grounds on Loch Awe, trout and salmon fishing.
Location Off A85 Glasgow–Oban road at Taynuilt on to B845 signposted Kilchrenan. Turn left at village pub up 3½ m single-track road.
Restrictions Not suitable for &. No children under 8. No dogs in public rooms.
Credit cards All major cards accepted.
Terms [1990 rates] Dinner, B&B: single £88, double £136–£192. Reductions for 2-night stays. Reduced rates for children sharing parents' room.

Taychreggan Hotel   *Tel* Kilchrenan (086 63) 211
Kilchrenan, by Taynuilt
Argyllshire PA35 1HQ

Admirably converted old fishing inn, on Loch Awe, 19 miles from Oban, long a favourite with Guide readers under previous regime, recently acquired by John and Monika Tyrrell. Idyllic setting on shore, at end of 7-mile single track road; popular for fishing, boats available. In italics because of mixed reports on reception and service, with some of last year's teething troubles persisting. Readers mention comfortable Laura Ashley-esque bedrooms, impeccable bathrooms, delightful dining room overlooking water. Gail Struthers remains as chef; her cooking continues to please. Open 25 Mar–27 Oct. 15 rooms – all with bath and/or shower. Dinner, B&B £35–£45. Bar lunches. More reports please.

KILDRUMMY Grampian   Map 5

Kildrummy Castle Hotel   *Tel* Kildrummy (097 55) 71288
Kildrummy, by Alford   *Fax* (097 55) 71345
Aberdeenshire AB3 8RA   *Telex* 94012529

One of those great Scottish baronial houses built around the turn of the century, *Kildrummy Castle* has been a hotel for the past 26 years. It is in the heart of the Donside, about an hour's drive from Aberdeen in 15 acres of fine gardens overlooking the ruins of a 13th-century castle. There have been many appreciative correspondents. The appeal for anglers is its 3½-mile private stretch of the Don for trout and salmon fishing. Further attraction for some is the library, "a fascinating fabric-covered room full of character, with a crackling log fire". Lunch and dinner menus offer more than a dozen choices including hearty Scottish soups, North Sea prawns, venison and pheasant, as well as lighter dishes – "nothing too extravagant, but good-sized portions and well cooked". Readers praise the unobtrusive, "courteous and friendly" service, and the "well-equipped bedrooms (hair-drier, electric blankets, TV, radio) *and early* morning tea". In response to criticism in the past of tobacco smells, there is now a policy of no smoking in the dining room. (*D and N Mulliken, Mr and Mrs W Saynor, and others*)

Open All year.
Rooms 15 double, 1 single – all with bath and/or shower, telephone, radio, TV, tea-making facilities, baby-listening.
Facilities Drawing room, library, lounge bar, dining room, snooker room. 15-acre garden; 3½ m private fishing on river Don. Golf nearby.
Location NE of Ballater on A97 Ballater–Huntley road.
Restrictions Not suitable for &. No smoking in dining room. No dogs in public rooms.
Credit cards Access, Amex, Visa.
Terms B&B £41–£48; dinner, B&B £45–£67.50. Set lunch £12, dinner £19.50; full alc £29. Children free if sharing with 2 adults; special meals.
Service/tipping: "Tipping at guests' discretion. No service charge."

KILFINAN Strathclyde   Map 5

Kilfinan Hotel   *Tel* Kilfinan (070 082) 201
Kilfinan, Nr Tighnabruaich
Argyllshire PA21 2AP

"A splendid recommendation – truly remote setting, with only a handful of houses, including this pub – and food worthy of a *Michelin* star." So began a recent report on this century-old black-and-white coaching inn in the tiny clachan of Kilfinan. "The welcome was as warm as the log fire, and the service was excellent." Kilted Tony Wignell runs the hotel with his wife Gina. The bedrooms are large and bright, the bathrooms well stocked with extras. "So peaceful we can't wait to return. Spotlessly clean, very friendly, warm cosy bar. Well worth the 16 miles of single-track road." Dinner – "exceptionally good, four courses with choices at each course except for soup" – is served in two dining rooms with rich burgundy wall-coverings, immaculate napery and fresh flowers. The hotel is popular as a base for hunting, shooting and fishing, but has also been recommended as "a most restful place to spend a few days, and ideal for bird-watchers, painters, photographers and walkers". (*Gillian Cave, Letitia Sinker, Prof IB Houston, and others*)

Open All year.
Rooms 1 suite, 10 double – 10 with bath, 1 with shower, all with telephone, radio, TV, baby-listening.
Facilities Public bar, bar lounge, 2 dining rooms; functions room. 1-acre grounds. Private sandy beach on Loch Fyne 1 m. Fishing on Kilfinan Burn; sea angling, golf, deer stalking, clay-pigeon shooting nearby.
Location In tiny village, next to church. On B8000 9 m NW of Tighnabruaich.
Restrictions Not suitable for &. No smoking in dining room. No dogs.
Credit cards Access, Amex, Visa.
Terms (Service at guests' discretion) B&B: single £37–£42, double £54–£72; dinner, B&B: single £57–£62, double £94–£112. Full alc dinner £27.50. Reduced rates for children sharing parents' room; special meals.

****
Traveller's tale *Our bedroom was high, wide and handsome, but blessed with two-tone singing in the pipes. Although the tenor subsided, the soprano was not giving up, even for the duty manager.*
****

KILLIECRANKIE Tayside   Map 5

Killiecrankie Hotel   *Tel* Pitlochry (0796) 3220
Pass of Killiecrankie   *Fax* (0796) 2451
By Pitlochry
Perthshire PH16 5LG

At the northern entrance to the pass of Killiecrankie, three miles from
Pitlochry, is this pleasant small hotel in a beautiful wooded setting,
overlooking the river Garry. The bedrooms are individually decorated
using furniture in natural pine made by local craftsmen. Under the new
ownership of Colin and Carole Anderson, it re-enters the Guide this year
with many favourable reports. "The Andersons are a wonderful couple
who immediately make you feel at home." "Staff and owners friendly
and helpful; everywhere spotlessly clean", "very comfortable beds",
"good house wine", "food better than before", "astoundingly imaginative, beautifully cooked". There are four acres of grounds, with putting
and croquet; golf, fishing and hill walking are nearby. (*David Thibodeau;
Mrs SE Fry, Mrs MH Box, and others*) More reports please.

Open Late Feb–early Nov.
Rooms 10 double, 2 single – 8 with bath and/or shower, all with radio; tea-
making facilities available. 4 ground-floor rooms.
Facilities Lounge with TV, bar, dining room. 4-acre grounds with putting,
croquet. Killiecrankie RSPB reserve just across river.
Location 3 m N of Pitlochry, just off A9, signposted Killiecrankie.
Restrictions No smoking, children under 5, or dogs in dining room.
Credit cards Access, Visa.
Terms B&B £33.80–£34.80; dinner, B&B £50.85–£52. 1-night bookings sometimes
refused. Spring, autumn breaks.
*Service/tipping: "No service charge; tipping neither encouraged nor discouraged. It acts
as a great incentive for the front and back of house staff."*

KILMORE Strathclyde   Map 5

Glenfeochan House   *Tel* Kilmore (063 177) 273
Kilmore, by Oban
Argyllshire PA34 4QR

A turreted Victorian building, former baronial home of the Clan
Campbell, standing at the head of Loch Feochan in a 350-acre estate
which includes a six-acre garden, one of the Great Gardens of the Scottish
Highlands. It is run as a highly select guest house by Patricia Baber, a
former Cordon Bleu teacher, her husband, David, and her son, James
Petley. There are only three bedrooms; meals (taken communally) are for
residents only – guests are consulted about the menu in the morning, and
much of the food is produced by the estate. Its original nominator waxed
lyrical: "The soft warm lighting of the entrance hall and the magnificent
staircase with its beautifully pargeted canopy tell you at once that you've
made the right choice. A most excellent dinner in the elegant dining
room, cooked by our hostess, followed by coffee in an equally elegant
drawing room. The setting is splendid: trees, loch and mountain changing
all the time as sun and cloud chase over the landscape. At the right time
of year you will be stunned by the colour – great carpets of daffodils and
snowdrops so thick you cannot see the grass, and mountainous masses of
rhododendrons, many species not to be seen elsewhere in Britain." Other

readers join in the praise: "an exquisite private home", "your bedroom has fresh flowers and fruit every day", "we were treated as though our every whim was important." (*Diana Birchall, John and Shirley Kitchen, and others*) Two readers lament the communal dining: "At these prices we would have preferred separate tables." "General conversation at dinner continues afterwards in the beautiful, but not cosy, drawing room. Not the place to go if you have a lot to say to each other."

Open 1 Mar–31 Oct.
Rooms 3 double – all with bath, radio, T V, tea-making facilities. 3-bedroom cottage for letting.
Facilities Drawing room, dining room. 350-acre estate with 6-acre garden and 1½-acre walled garden, open to public; croquet, boules. Salmon and sea-trout fishing free to guests, clay-pigeon shooting, hill walking, loch bathing.
Location 5 m S of Oban on A816 at head of Loch Feochan.
Restrictions Not suitable for &. No smoking in dining room; preferred no smoking in bedrooms. No children under 10. Dogs by arrangement only; not in bedrooms or public rooms.
Credit cards None accepted.
Terms B&B double £95–£112. Packed lunch £5, set dinner £25.
Service/tipping: "Service included. Tipping not encouraged; any money left is distributed between all staff."

KINBUCK Central   Map 5

Cromlix House	*Tel* Dunblane (0786) 822125
Kinbuck, Dunblane	*Fax* (0786) 825450
Perthshire KK15 9JT	*Telex* 779959

It is now nine years since the Hon Ronald Eden, whose family have owned the 5,000 acres of *Cromlix* for four centuries, turned his massive Victorian house into a luxury hotel. There is one fishing loch within strolling distance – and others nearby – plus a grouse moor and lovely wooded grounds where deer, sheep, pheasants, wild duck and rabbits abound. The house itself is grand in a formal way: there is a Victorian conservatory, a good library, and a chapel; the large entrance hall is panelled, the morning room has comfortable chintz chairs and a giant log basket beside the elegant fireplace, the dining room is candle-lit at night, with stiffly starched white table-cloths. "A lovely elegant hotel, but comfortable as well," wrote a reader this year. "They employ charming young people who are pleasant, willing and helpful." There are large bedrooms with even larger bathrooms – "marvellous" – though one reader recently missed not having fresh flowers, writing paper and adequate soap. Dinners (a six-course fixed menu, but with alternatives offered) have been highly praised for quality and the "international scope of the provisions". (*Heather Sharland, Anna Kaposi and Gary Bullock, WH Davidson*) A new chef, Simon Burns, formerly at the *Isle of Eriska* (q.v.) arrived in early 1990. More reports please.

Open All year.
Rooms 8 suites, 6 double – all with bath, shower, telephone, radio, T V; baby-listening available.
Facilities 2 lounges, 3 dining rooms, conservatory. 5,000-acre grounds with croquet, clay-pigeon shooting, trout fishing, tennis, riding and shooting (advance booking advisable).
Location ¼ m N of Kinbuck, 4 m S of Braco. Take A9 out of Dunblane; turn left on to B8033; go through Kinbuck village, take second left after a small bridge.

Restrictions Not suitable for &. No smoking in dining rooms.
Credit cards All major cards accepted.
Terms [1990 rates] B&B: single occupancy £85–£120, double from £120, suite £155–£190. Set lunch £22, dinner £35. Winter breaks. 4-day Christmas and New Year packages. Reduced rates for children sharing parents' room; special meals.
Service/tipping: "Our staff do not expect to be tipped. We don't feel a service charge should be added or tipping encouraged."

KINGUSSIE Highland   Map 5

The Osprey Hotel   *Tel* Kingussie (0540) 661510
Kingussie
Inverness-shire PH21 1EN

Readers continue to appreciate *The Osprey* – rather more of a guest house than a hotel despite its name – for its reasonable tariff, warm welcome, and good food. "Although tiny and – at a glance – unremarkable as a place to stay, it aspires to a country house atmosphere and, through the efforts of Duncan and Pauline Reeves, achieves that goal." The public rooms are small, and guests may be asked to share tables at dinner, "but the delicacy with which two very different couples were seated together – two academics (us) plus a City couple up to display their dogs at a field trial – was delightful and successful". Pauline Reeves's cooking always receives warm praise. The food is generous and robust (avocado roulade, pheasant soufflé, venison casserole), and vegetarians are happily catered for. "An excellent meal, and Duncan Reeves an ideal host." The wine list is extensive: the brochure promises over 250 bottles; but one correspondent this year found it "pretentious – much was out of stock". Bedrooms are clean, comfortable, "warm and welcoming", and "bathrooms modern with lots of large, fluffy towels". The owners bring you a portable phone if you get a call. Traffic noise used to be a problem but has been reduced this year with the abolition of a nearby lorry park. *The Osprey* is well placed in the heart of the Spey Valley for all the leisure activities of the region – walking, fishing, golf, riding, skiing. Aviemore is 12 miles off, the Cairngorms 30 minutes by car. (*R Berry, Mrs M Wall, NJ Ferguson; and others*)

Open 1 Jan–31 Oct.
Rooms 7 double, 1 single – 1 with bath and shower, 4 with shower.
Facilities Lounge, TV room, dining room. Small garden. Golf, fishing, gliding, sailing, canoeing, windsurfing nearby; sports facilities at the Aviemore Centre.
Location Near A9, about 12 m SW of Aviemore. 200 yds from village centre; parking for 10 cars.
Restrictions Not suitable for &. No smoking in dining room. No dogs in public rooms.
Credit cards All major cards accepted.
Terms Dinner, B&B £35–£50. Set dinner £18.50, full alc £23. Reduced rates for children.
Service/tipping: "No service charge. If people wish to tip – and some definitely do – the gratuity is accepted with thanks and given to staff as a bonus at Christmas."

Please don't be shy of writing again about old favourites. Too many people feel that if they have written once, years ago, there is no need to report on a revisit.

KNIPOCH Strathclyde

Map 5

Knipoch Hotel
Knipoch, by Oban
Argyllshire PA34 4QT

Tel Kilninver (085 26) 251
Fax (085 26) 249

A smart, pricey, fairly formal country house hotel in a tranquil setting beside Loch Feochan, an arm of the sea stretching four miles inland just south of Oban. The original house was first mentioned in 16th-century records of feuds and rivalry between Scottish clans; it now belongs to the Craig family, who personally run the hotel. Inside are welcoming log fires, attractive flower arrangements, lots of highly polished wood surfaces, Persian rugs on stripped pine floors, deep leather armchairs. "We were welcomed by the owner in a hall with a real log fire, brought tea, and our sons fed promptly and efficiently. Our rooms were comfortable. Quality does not come cheap, but it was worth it." "We liked the no-choice menu and it was unusually good – tasty smoked salmon, succulent lamb." "If one is eating grandly for six nights, there has to be a lightness of touch – and there is." (*Prof DV Lindley, David Lea-Wilson*) But there have been grumbles about some of the rooms: "Very small with a tiny bath, much like a motel in the US." "A view of the loch, yes, but across a noisy parking area." And one reader complained about the background music in the bar: "Either too loud or inaudible, and we were tired of Sibelius after a few days."

Open Mid-Feb–mid-Nov and New Year. Lunch by arrangement only.
Rooms 18 double – all with bath, shower, telephone, radio, TV, baby-listening. Tea-making facilities on request.
Facilities Reception hall, lounge, bar, 3 dining rooms. 3-acre grounds. On sea loch; fishing, sailing, golf, tennis, hill walking, pony trekking nearby.
Location 6 m S of Oban on A816.
Restrictions Not really suitable for &. No smoking in dining room. No young children in dining room. No dogs.
Credit cards All major cards accepted.
Terms [1990 rates] B&B £49.50; dinner, B&B £79. Set dinner £29.50. Children under 5 half price; special meals.
Service/tipping: "No service charge. If tips are offered they are accepted, since to refuse can offend some guests. They are never solicited."

MOFFAT Dumfries and Galloway

Map 5

**Beechwood Country House
  Hotel**
Harthope Place, Moffat
Dumfriesshire DG10 9RS

Tel Moffat (0683) 20210

"A small friendly hotel with particularly good food," writes our inspector of this grey stone Victorian house, once a girls' school, standing in a 12-acre beech wood just outside Moffat, re-entering our pages this year with new owners Lynda and Jeffrey Rogers. "The decor is pastel, with pale chintz, somewhat unexciting – but it is immaculate and comfortable, and Mr and Mrs Rogers fall over themselves to give a warm welcome. The bedrooms have everything you could need: books, magazines (all the latest), toiletries, hair-drier. The dinner menu comprises six or seven starters and main courses and changes monthly; the cooking approaches *nouvelle* in taste and presentation, but the portions are generous. The wine list was good, the coffee good and strong. A very comfortable bed and an OK breakfast, so-so toast, good Loch Fyne kipper." *Beechwood* is about three-quarters of an hour north of Carlisle, an hour or so from Glasgow and Edinburgh – a useful stop on the way north or south. More reports please.

Open Feb–Dec.
Rooms 7 double – all with bath and/or shower, telephone, radio, TV, tea-making facilities, baby-listening.
Facilities Lounge, cocktail bar and library, restaurant, conservatory. Small garden.
Location Proceed along High Street. Turn into Harthope Place between church and school.
Restrictions Only restaurant suitable for &. No smoking, no dogs in restaurant.
Credit cards Access, Amex, Visa.
Terms B&B £27–£43.75; dinner, B&B £39.80–£55.25. Set lunch £10.75, dinner £16.20. Reduced rates for children; special meals.
Service/tipping: "At discretion of customer. Distributed among all staff."

MUIR OF ORD Highland   Map 5

The Dower House   *Tel* Inverness (0463) 870090
Highfield, Muir of Ord
Ross-shire IV6 7XN

A slightly Gothic one-storey series of linked 19th-century cottages, originally built for the dowager of the MacKenzie-Gillander family, now in its third year as a welcoming small country hotel owned by Robyn and Mena Aitchison. They formerly ran a restaurant, *Le Chardon*, in nearby Cromarty, but decided to expand so that their family could have more space. We sent an inspector along and here is her report: "The furnishings are a mixture of Victorian, pine and loose-covered comfortable chairs and sofas. We loved the decor – a riot of patterns, borders and bows done with huge flair and a vibrant colour sense. But it is very feminine and very much to the taste of American travellers, on whose itinerary the hotel already is. The lounge is small, with a bar; the dining room warm and welcoming with polished tables, chairs upholstered in green, likewise green napkins tied with green tartan ribbons. Dinner was very good: marinaded fish salad, chicory soup, hare with juniper berries, butterscotch pudding with rum sauce, Scottish cheeses, then good coffee by the fire with home-made truffles. We slept well in utter peace and quiet. We thought it all very good value with only one caveat: there were no locks on the bedroom doors." More reports please.

Open All year except 1 week Oct, 2 weeks Mar. Group booking only New Year.
Rooms 1 suite, 4 double – all with bath or shower, telephone, radio. TV and tea-making facilities on request.
Facilities Lounge, dining room. 2½-acre grounds with trees and lawn, small formal garden, swings and tree house.
Location 11 m NW of Inverness. 1 m N of Muir of Ord, at double bend, signal left; proceed through green and white lodge gates. Follow private drive 300 yds.
Restrictions No smoking in dining room. Dogs by prior arrangement only, not in public rooms.
Credit cards Access, Amex, Visa.
Terms (No service charge) B&B £40–£65; dinner, B&B £62–£87. Set lunch £12.50, dinner £22. Reduced rates for children sharing parents' room; special meals.

NAIRN Highland

Map 5

Clifton House
Viewfield Street, Nairn
Nairnshire IV12 4HW

Tel Nairn (0667) 53119
Fax (0667) 52836

🏅 *César award in 1987: Utterly acceptable mild eccentricity*

High praise this year for Gordon Macintyre's extraordinary old family hotel looking over the Moray Firth and stuffed with paintings, sculptures, bas-reliefs, *objets trouvés* and books galore, "the indifferent nestling happily against the tasteful, the tasteless complementing the outrageous". "I think this is one of the best hotels in Scotland for atmosphere, friendliness and value for money," wrote one reader. "We were quite enraptured," said another. Last year a reader found "the clutter on every available surface neither fascinating nor interesting, just plain irritating, everything contrived for effect". Mr Macintyre has risen to the defence: "Of course it's done for effect!! Masses of flowers, all over the place, are put there for effect; the curtains are lined and interlined for effect, the linen table napkins are starched for effect; the pictures are hung for effect. In the winter, when we have recitals, we have musicians who play for effect; and I love it. It is, in effect, my life." There have been no detractors this year: "The food was good – not outstanding – roast guinea fowl with herbs, excellent Scottish cheese." "The wine list is very comprehensive (many wines under £10, and no pressure to pay if the taste of the wine you ordered was incompatible with the food)." The hotel uses its own hens, ducks and geese, the fish is fresh and the salmon wild, and the bread, oatcakes, muesli, marmalade and jams are all made in the kitchen. Breakfast is served from 8 am onwards, without time limit, and the hotel is happy to provide picnic lunches "from the simplest sandwich to an elegant hamper with plates, glasses and linen". (*Lt Col SJ Furness, Dr JB Wylie*)

Open March–end Oct.
Rooms 9 double, 7 single – 15 with bath, 1 with shower; beds have continental quilts, but conventional bedding available on request.
Facilities Drawing room, sitting room, T V room, 2 restaurants. 1-acre grounds. Fishing, shooting, riding, beach, tennis courts, swimming pool, golf nearby. Plays, concerts, recitals Mar–Apr.
Location 500 yds from town centre; coming from Inverness turn left at roundabout on A96. Parking for 20 cars.
Restrictions Not suitable for &. No dogs in dining room.
Credit cards All major cards accepted.
Terms [1990 rates] B&B: single £40–£48, double £75–£85. Set lunch £15, dinner £21; full alc £26.
Service/tipping: "A service charge is not imposed; nor are tips expected."

NEWTON STEWART Dumfries and Galloway

Map 5

Creebridge House Hotel
Minnigaff, Newton Stewart
Wigtownshire DG8 6NP

Tel Newton Stewart (0671) 2121

Attractive grey stone Scottish country house, once owned by Earls of Galloway, in 3 acres of garden and woodland a short walk from town centre. Comfortable drawing room, informal bar featuring 30 malt whiskies and selection of real ales, dining room with menu based on fresh, local produce. Cooking, by chef and co-owner Chris Walker, specially recommended. Croquet; fishing arranged on rivers Cree and Bladnoch. 17 rooms – all with private bathrooms (one on ground floor with ramp). B&B: single £15–£32.50, double £30–£65. Set dinner £15, full alc £17.95. New nomination. More reports please.

NEWTONMORE Highland   Map 5

Ard-Na-Coille Hotel   *Tel* Newtonmore (054 03) 214
Kingussie Road, Newtonmore
Inverness-shire PH20 1AY

We continue to receive encouraging reports on this small Edwardian shooting lodge set high above the road in two acres of pine trees, with magnificent views over Strathspey towards the Cairngorms. A three-year programme of upgrading is now complete, and readers praise the owners, Nancy Ferrier and Barry Cottam, for their welcome and their evident desire to please. New beds and newly-decorated bedrooms and bathrooms have all been appreciated – and so has the ambitious cooking and the "first rate wine list at bargain-basement prices". A representative verdict: "The food and service were outstandingly good and the terms very reasonable." (*Gerald L Fox, G Brafman, M Paterson, and others*)

Open 29 Dec–mid-Nov.
Rooms 6 double, 1 single – all with bath and/or shower, radio, baby-listening.
Facilities Lounge, TV lounge, dining room; drying room; terrace. 2-acre grounds. Fishing, golf, riding, shooting, hill walking nearby; skiing at Aviemore 15 m.
Location Leave A9 at Newtonmore/Kingussie signs. Hotel is at northernmost edge of Newtonmore, just outside speed restriction signs.
Restrictions Not suitable for &. Dogs in certain bedrooms only, never in public rooms.
Credit cards None accepted.
Terms B&B £30–£35; dinner, B&B £49.50–£55. Set dinner £19.50. Special breaks. Reduced rates for children sharing parents' room; high teas. 1-night bookings possibly refused Bank Holidays.
Service/tipping: "Service charges should be abolished by law. Tipping is an iniquitous anachronism. We do not expect gratuities from our customers, but if any are left staff receive an equal share and the remainder is used to support a community charity."

ONICH Highland   Map 5

Allt-nan-Ros Hotel   *Tel* Onich (085 53) 210
Onich, by Fort William   *Fax* (085 53) 462
Inverness-shire PH33 6RY

The name of this hotel is Gaelic for burn of the roses. It is on the north shore of Loch Linnhe, on the Fort William to Glasgow road, and enjoys panoramic views of the surrounding mountains and lochs. Originally built as a Victorian shooting lodge, it has been attractively converted by its owners, Lachlan, Fiona and James MacLeod. Most recent correspondents have liked the friendly staff and warm welcome on arrival by the young kilted James MacLeod. "It is a warm-hearted, very Scottish house/hotel, where excellent food and service is offered. All rooms are spotless and comfortable. There's a country house atmosphere (definitely *no* TV in the lounge!) with friendly chat in the evening." (*John and Ann Holt, and others*) Warning: the hotel is close to the busy A82.

Open Mar–Nov.
Rooms 18 double with bath and shower, 3 single with shower, all with telephone, radio, TV, tea-making facilities, baby-listening. 2 in converted stable. 6 ground-floor rooms.
Facilities Ramps, WC for &. Hall, lounge, lounge bar, dining room. Terraced lawn overlooking road and loch. Fishing from shoreline, shingle beach, boat available.
Location On A82 10 m SW of Fort William.
Restriction No smoking in dining room.
Credit cards All major cards accepted.
Terms [1990 rates] B&B £28.50–£37.50; dinner, B&B £42.50–£52.50. Alc lunch. Set dinner £17.50. 3-, 5- and 7-day breaks. Reduced rates and special meals for children.
Service/tipping: "If people do tip, we distribute it equally among all staff."

PEAT INN Fife   **Map 5**

The Peat Inn   *Tel* Peat Inn (033 484) 206
Peat Inn, By Cupar
Fifeshire KY15 5LH

🎖 *César award in 1990: Newcomer of the year, restaurant-with-rooms division*

The Residence is a recently built annexe to David and Patricia Wilson's long-renowned *Peat Inn*. Set at a country crossroads six miles from St Andrews, the inn offers some of the finest food in Scotland and, since 1987, eight luxurious mini-suites in the new block adjoining the restaurant, sympathetically built to blend with the environment. "The view from the bedroom window is of Fife fields," wrote a recent visitor. "Open the window and the smell of peat smoke drifts by." The bedrooms have been individually decorated, some in bold patterns, and are as luxurious as they come: a separate sitting area, marble bathrooms, TV with teletext, a desk, slippers and bathrobes ("changed along with the towels when we went to dinner!"); even Scrabble and playing cards. "It was pure Hollywood. We really enjoyed it." But the real reason one comes here is the restaurant, one of only three Scottish establishments to win a *Michelin* rosette in 1990. David Wilson's cooking has earned him many awards; there is also an outstanding wine list. "Breakfast of fresh orange juice and fruit, wonderful coffee, fresh croissants and masses of wonderful toast, butter and preserve." (*H Sharland*) One reader, however, visiting for four nights, complained of inadequate service outside restaurant hours. But the *Peat Inn* makes no claim to be considered a hotel. It dubs itself a Restaurant with Residence – and is a fine example of that species.

Open *Residence* open all year, except 2 weeks Nov, 2 weeks Jan. Restaurant closed Sun and Mon.
Rooms 8 suites – all with bath, shower, telephone, radio, TV. 1 suitable for &.
Facilities Ramp. 2 lounges (1 in *Residence*), restaurant. ¾-acre grounds.
Location At junction of B940/B941 6 miles south of St Andrews.
Restrictions No smoking in restaurant. No children under 10. No dogs.

Credit cards All major cards accepted.
Terms B&B (continental): £98–£112 per suite. Set lunch £15.50, dinner £27; full alc £36.
Service/tipping: "We add nothing to the bill and staff do not expect extras."

PEEBLES Borders   Map 5

Cringletie House Hotel   *Tel* Eddleston (072 13) 233
Peebles, Peeblesshire EH45 8PL   *Fax* (072 13) 244

In a magnificent setting, right out in the country with extensive views over the surrounding hills, a pink stone mansion built in the Scottish baronial manner with turrets and dormers, surrounded by garden, woodland and a 28-acre estate. It is possible to go for extensive walks without leaving the grounds. Stanley and Aileen Maguire, the resident owners, celebrate their 20th year here in 1991. Readers appreciate the Maguires' traditional, slightly formal style of hospitality, the pleasant decor, Aileen Maguire's cooking and, not least, the reasonable tariff. "It's the sort of place where you felt comfortable spending all day just relaxing in the gardens and playing tennis or croquet. And we loved the wonderful teas in the garden and in the lounge." "The service is beyond reproach." The two-acre "superb" walled garden produces many of the vegetables that find their way to the table; dinners are liked as much as ever – "The salmon with spinach sauce was so good we had it on three nights; the best dessert trolley we have ever seen." Many of the bedrooms have high ceilings; they are prettily furnished, with an absence of fussiness; eight were redecorated this year. Breakfast times, once felt by readers to be too limited, have been extended to 8.15–9.15 am. (*John Freebairn, Mrs KJ Milligan, Prof DV Lindley, David Angwin, and others*)

Open 9 Mar–2 Jan.
Rooms 12 double, 1 single – all with bath, shower, telephone, radio, TV, baby-listening.
Facilities Bar lounge, 2 lounges (1 non-smoking), dining room. 28-acre grounds with tennis, 9-hole putting green, croquet, children's play area, 2-acre kitchen garden. Golf, fishing nearby.
Location 2½ m N of Peebles on A703.
Restrictions Not suitable for &. 1 no-smoking lounge; smoking discouraged in dining room. No dogs in public rooms.
Credit cards Access, Visa.
Terms (Service at guests' discretion) B&B: single £39–£50, double £72. Lunch from £5 (Sun £12.50), set dinner £20. Off-season rates. Reduced rates for children; high teas.

PLOCKTON Highland   Map 5

The Haven Hotel   `BUDGET`   *Tel* Plockton (059 984) 223
Innes Street, Plockton
Ross and Cromarty IV52 8TW

Converted merchant's house 50 yards from sea-front in delightful West Highland village with white-washed cottages along the shore road. Recommended for "excellent value for money". "Cosy, books in most spare spaces, welcoming reception, staff friendly and efficient, wholesome food, good choice of wine." Small bar, 3 sitting rooms (2 non-smoking), restaurant. Bedrooms well equipped. Easy access for boats; good sailing, trout-fishing nearby. Open

1 Feb–20 Dec. 13 rooms – all with bath or shower. B&B £25–£28; dinner, B&B £32–£40. Set dinner £17. New nomination, more reports please.

PORT APPIN Strathclyde   Map 5

The Airds Hotel   *Tel* Appin (063 173) 236
Port Appin, Appin   *Fax* (063 173) 535
Argyllshire PA38 4DF

Plenty of enthusiasm as previously for the hospitality and high standards of hotel-keeping offered by Eric and Betty Allen at this early 18th-century ferry inn. It looks across a small road towards Loch Linnhe, the islands of Lismore and the mountains of Morvern. A fine prospect, and on the opposite side of the road is a lawn where you can take tea or drinks and admire the view. "At first the hotel is disconcertingly ordinary, but when you go inside, you find the staff are very welcoming." "The young waitresses have quiet lilting West Coast voices, and wear attractive long tartan skirts – the whole atmosphere exudes peace and quiet." The drawing room has deep, softly cushioned sofas and chairs. Flower arrangements abound. The corridors leading to the bedrooms have warm red carpets; stuffed squirrels and birds and stags' heads dot the way. Bedrooms are stylish and comfortable; fluffy thick white towels are changed twice a day." The dining room is elegant, and Betty Allen's cooking is a major draw. (*Alicia Gregg Phillips, Mrs P Carr, Robert Ribeiro, PL Aston, Mrs CM Bevan, PA Morgan, W Ian Stewart, and others*) As previously there are also dissenters: small rooms, mean helpings, some maintenance faults and the price of children's high tea were among this year's complaints.

Open Early Mar–early Jan.
Rooms 1 suite, 12 double, 1 single – all with bath and/or shower, telephone, radio, TV, baby-listening. 2 in garden annexe.
Facilities 2 lounges, small residents' bar, dining room. Small garden; near loch with shingle beach, bathing, fishing, boating; pony trekking, forest walks.
Location 2 m off A828, 25 m from Fort William and Oban. Parking for 30 cars.
Restrictions Not suitable for &. Guests requested not to smoke in dining room. No children under 5. No dogs.
Credit cards None accepted.
Terms B&B £43–£76. Set dinner £32. Christmas/New Year breaks. Reductions for children sharing parents' room; special meals.
Service/tipping: "No service charge and we do not expect tips. When guests insist, the money is distributed to all members of staff."

PORTPATRICK Dumfries and Galloway   Map 5

Knockinaam Lodge Hotel   *Tel* Portpatrick (077 681) 471
Portpatrick, Wigtownshire
DG9 9AD

Nestling in a wooded glen with steep cliffs which shelter it on three sides, on the fourth it faces the sea, looking towards the coast of Ireland. There are superb cliff walks and, in spring, carpets of bluebells and primroses in the woods. There is a beach, sandy at low tide, but this is no bucket-and-spade place – it is an exclusive small hotel with imaginative, sophisticated cooking. It is run by the young French owner Marcel Frichot and his English wife, Corinna. The five-course menus change daily; readers have sometimes found the portions small – "a bit of something delicious sitting in a puddle of sauce, not that we were ever hungry" – or if you find the dishes too adventurous something simpler will be served on request. Lots of country-house-type extras in the rooms: sewing kit, pot-pourri, bath oil in a bottle, travelling robes and fresh flowers. Beds are turned down during dinner. "At times all one can hear is the sea interrupted by the delicate chimes of the antique clocks dotted around the hall and on the landings; somehow they do not intrude into the night," a visitor wrote recently. "It is impossible to fault," wrote another this year. (*E Newall, April Young*)

Open 15 Mar–4 Jan.
Rooms 9 double, 1 single – all with bath and shower, telephone, radio, TV. Baby-listening by arrangement.
Facilities Lounge, residents' lounge, bar, restaurant. 30-acre grounds, with garden and croquet. Private beach 100 yds, swimming "for the brave"; sea fishing. Wildlife, walks, golf nearby.
Location 9 m SW of Stranraer. 3 m before Portpatrick on the A77 there is a left turn, well signposted.
Restrictions Bedrooms not suitable for &. No smoking in restaurant. Dogs by arrangement only; not in public rooms.
Credit cards All major cards accepted.
Terms [1990 rates] Dinner, B&B single £85, double £140–£170. Bar lunches £4–£12. Set dinner £28. Reduced rates for children under 12 sharing parents' room; high teas.
Service/tipping: "Tipping not encouraged; any money left is distributed among all staff."

PORTREE Skye, Highland   **Map 5**

Viewfield House   BUDGET   *Tel* Portree (0478) 2217
Portree, Isle of Skye
IV51 9EU

"Our first visit and very much enjoyed. Exceptional cuisine, each mealtime a delight. Service warm and friendly. The house itself, set in beautiful grounds, is quite unlike any hotel I have stayed in – full of history." "I intended staying only one night, and ended up staying four. A real find." *Viewfield House* entered the Guide two years ago, nominated for its "lack of commercial imperatives: it was the home for many years of Colonel 'Jock' Macdonald and his wife Evelyn, who ran the place as an extended house party; passing tourists found themselves swept into a life-style almost Victorian in its prodigality. Crammed with china and *objets impériaux, Viewfield* is time-capsulated and unique." Bedrooms have no *en suite* bathrooms, no telephones, no TV; they do have hand basins and electric fires. Family traditions are now maintained by Colonel Jock's grandson Hugh and his wife Linda, and guests are still expected to contribute to the enhancement of life after dinner. "All cooking is home cooking, no packets or cardboard gateaux!" says Hugh Macdonald. (*Nancy and Denis Elliott; AM Henley*)

Open May–mid-Oct.
Rooms 9 double, 5 single – all with H&C and tea-making facilities; baby-listening available.
Facilities Drawing room, TV room, dining room. 20-acre grounds with croquet, swings, woodland walks (and midges).

Location On S side of Portree, 10 minutes' walk from centre; driving towards Broadford turn right just after BP petrol station on left.
Restrictions Not suitable for &. Smoking during meals not popular. No dogs in public rooms.
Credit cards None accepted.
Terms B&B £16–£18. Packed lunch £2.50, set dinner £12. Reduced rates for children; special meals, given advance notice.
Service/tipping: "No stated policy. We just don't expect people to tip unless they want to because they feel they have received outstanding service."

QUOTHQUAN Strathclyde   Map 5

Shieldhill Country House Hotel   *Tel* Biggar (0899) 20035
Quothquan, Biggar   *Fax* (0899) 21092
Lanarkshire ML12 6NA   *Telex* 777308

An elegantly refurbished grey stone manor house, with parts dating from the 13th century, in the rolling hills of Lanarkshire, overlooking the river Clyde. Owned by two Californians, Christine Dunstan and Jack Greenwald (she is originally from Cheshire), it has an oak-panelled lounge, formal drawing room, library and welcoming bar. The bedrooms have been done in their entirety by Laura Ashley; each is different – some have fireplaces, four-poster beds, jacuzzi. *Shieldhill* opened in 1988. There may still be some teething troubles, but here are two favourable reports: "A house of great character decorated with no expense spared. Everything is new and clean." "The very comfortable decor makes you feel you are staying in someone's country house. The service was excellent, the staff cared, the cooking was good." (*JM Mackay, Dr S Cantor, David Donald*) We'd welcome more reports.

Open All year.
Rooms 1 suite, 10 double – all with bath and/or shower, telephone, radio, TV, baby-listening; tea-making facilities on request.
Facilities 2 lounges, bar, library. 7-acre grounds, croquet. River fishing 10 mins' walk.
Location 5 m from Biggar, off B7016, signposted.
Restrictions Not suitable for &. No smoking in dining room or bedrooms. No dogs.
Credit cards All major cards accepted.
Terms (Service at guests' discretion) [1990 rates] B&B: single £76–£120, double £86–£130. Full alc dinner £26. Off-season breaks. Reduced rates for children; special meals.

RAASAY Skye, Highland   Map 5

Isle of Raasay Hotel   **BUDGET**   *Tel* Raasay (047 862) 222
Isle of Raasay
by Kyle of Lochalsh, Skye
Inverness-shire IV40 8PB

"A remote and beautiful spot and a good hotel. An unusual combination which we can recommend," wrote a correspondent last year of this small hotel on a tiny island (four miles by fifteen) reached by a 15-minute ferry journey from Skye. It sits 300 yards from the water and is run by Mrs Nicolson, whose husband is the ferry master, assisted by able local staff. "The residents' lounge and dining rooms have magnificent views; the bar is open to the public most evenings, and some 15 or 20 local people drop in, providing company if one fancies a change." Raasay itself is "one of the Inner Hebrides' most enchanting islands – a world apart from the increasingly crowded roads of Skye. The hotel's situation is superb and the island excellent for wildlife, walking, peace and quiet." Visitors are advised to bring weather-proof shoes or boots for straying anywhere off the (very few) stretches of road, and also to fill up their tanks and get other requirements before leaving Skye since there is no petrol on the island and the village shop is sparsely stocked. Readers are divided about the food: "simple and well cooked, with fresh ingredients," according to some; but others have been more critical, with complaints of inadequate helpings. More reports please.

Open Early Apr–end Sep.
Rooms 11 double, 1 single – all with bath, radio, TV, tea-making facilities. 6 ground-floor rooms, 1 specifically designed for &.
Facilities Lounge, TV lounge, lounge bar, dining room. 2-acre grounds. Good walking and bird watching country; trout fishing in lochs; 5 mins from sea.
Location Travel to Kyle and take ferry to Kyleakin. Proceed to Sconser village on Loch Sligachan; there are three 6-car ferries daily (except Sun) to Raasay, taking about 15 mins. Hotel is signposted from ferry terminal.
Restrictions No smoking in dining room. No dogs in public rooms.
Credit cards None accepted.
Terms B&B from £26; dinner, B&B from £40. Bar and packed lunches available. Set dinner from £14.50. 50% reduction for children under 10; special meals on request.
Service/tipping: "No service charge. Tips at guests' discretion and shared by all members of staff."

RHUM Highland   **Map 5**

Kinloch Castle   *Tel* Mallaig (0687) 2037
Isle of Rhum
Inverness-shire PH43 4RR

Where can you experience an Edwardian bath with seven controls ranging from shower through wave, douche, spray, plunge and sitz to startling jet? On the Isle of Rhum (an hour by ferry from Mallaig) at the exotic *Kinloch Castle*, a pink sandstone shooting lodge built in 1901 for the millionaire textile magnate Sir George Bullough, now a small hotel and self-catering hostel for visitors to this wildlife reserve. Two nominators describe its wonders. "Early in the last century the hardy Hebrideans abandoned their attempts to tame Rhum for crofting and emigrated to America. Now most of the population is furred or feathered: red deer, which are studied by resident naturalists, and eagles may be the most striking. Sir George found this wilderness of rock and loch, heather, scree and waterfalls so romantic that he built a holiday home there; today *Kinloch Castle* is a monument to Edwardian self-indulgence, where guests can recover from hill walking in exotic bathrooms, enter the dining room to the Grand March from *Aida* performed by his mechanical organ, and play billiards in a room from which the cigar-smoke is sucked by his prototype air-conditioner." (*Tom Pocock*) "The castle is unchanged since 1901. Visitors can use all rooms. The bathrooms (none *en suite*) are original and amazing, the forerunners of today's whirlpool/spa baths. Not exactly comfortable bedrooms (though some are better than others), because, again, everything is original and a bit past its prime. It really is like staying in a museum. Dinner and breakfast are taken at the vast dining table overlooking the bay; the food is okay, trying hard, not special; the whole experience of staying in the hotel makes up for inadequacies. It's probably best not to stay too long – four days would be the maximum." (*L Highton*) We look forward to more reports.

Open Mar–Oct.
Rooms 9 rooms in castle, 13 in hostel in former servants' quarters (blankets, pillows and pillowslips provided).
Facilities Great hall, drawing room, smoking/billiard room, library, ballroom. Nightly dinner parties, occasional ceilidhs. 26,000-acre nature reserve; trout fishing (sea and loch).
Location Off coast opposite Mallaig (West Highland rail terminus for trains from Glasgow). No cars allowed. Take Caledonian MacBrayne ferry (Mallaig 0687 2403) or arrange charter with Bruce Watt Cruises (Mallaig 0687 2320) or Murdo Grant (Arisaig 068 75 224). Journey approx 1 hr.
Restrictions No children under 7 in the castle. No pets.
Credit cards None accepted.
Terms (Service at guests' discretion) Dinner, B&B £52.50; self-catering in hostel £7. Packed lunches. Set dinner £18.50. Reduced rates for children.

ROCKCLIFFE Dumfries and Galloway   Map 4

Baron's Craig Hotel   *Tel* Rockcliffe (055 663) 225
Rockcliffe, by Dalbeattie
Kircudbrightshire DG5 4QF

In "relatively unfrequented and very beautiful part of Galloway", Victorian Scottish baronial hotel in wooded setting overlooking heather hills and Solway Firth. Recommended for "masses of comfortable lounges, lovely terrace for sundowners, good views, perfectly adequate food and drink (though dining room service a bit rough and ready)". Sandy beach, safe bathing. Windsurfing, sailing, golf nearby. Open 29 Mar–17 Oct. 26 rooms, 20 with bath. B&B double £57–£87. Set lunch £11.50, dinner £16.50 [1990 rates]. New nomination. More reports please.

ST OLA Orkney   Map 5

Foveran Hotel   `BUDGET`   *Tel* Kirkwall (0856) 2389
St Ola, Nr Kirkwall
Orkney KW15 1SF

A Scandinavian-style, architect-designed small hotel, well located for island hopping, bird watching and excursions to Orkney's wealth of Neolithic and Viking remains. Some 1990 tributes: "Norma Gerrard runs the hotel on informal but professional lines; it has a very friendly atmosphere. We particularly appreciated the evening meals, which often featured locally caught fish and Orkney beef and cheese." "The hotel, croft-like in appearance outside, is most comfortable and relaxing, with splendid views from the dining room across Scapa Flow. A car (or bike) is essential, but the location is ideal." "Breakfasts excellent: apart from the usual grill we had kedgeree, kippers, haddock and home-made fish cakes. Dinner almost always good, small but well-chosen wine list, and reasonably priced." (*DA and PM Hawkins, Mr and Mrs JRS Homan, RAL Ogston*)

Open Apr–Oct. Restaurant closed to non-residents on Sun.
Rooms 1 family, 4 double, 3 single – all with bath and/or shower, radio, tea-making facilities. All on ground floor.
Facilities Ramps. Sitting room, TV/games room, dining room. 20-acre grounds with rugged beach, cold sea. Sandy beaches nearby.
Location 2¼ m from Kirkwall on A964 Orphir Road.
Restriction No dogs in public rooms.
Credit cards Access, Visa.
Terms [1990 rates] B&B: single £26, double £42. Full alc dinner £16. Reduced rates for children; special meals.
Service/tipping: "Optional. Distributed to staff on pro-rata basis for hours worked."

SELKIRK Borders Map 5

Philipburn House Hotel *Tel* Selkirk (0750) 20747
Selkirk TD7 5LS *Fax* (0750) 21690

Last appearing in the Guide in 1987, *Philipburn House* returns with high praise for its combination of sophisticated meals for parents and supervised activities for children. Now in its 18th year under the ownership of Anne and Jim Hill, it stands in a wooded setting in Border country where there is splendid walking and fishing. The hotel dates from 1751, but has been much extended over the years; the decor is Scandinavian-style with chintz fabrics and pine furniture. "Our children were in heaven from the moment we arrived. They were able to fish, horseback ride, and play in the hotel grounds under the supervision of the staff, completely independent of us. We were able to walk with the local guide who had wonderful stories of the history of the area." "They are adept at making the adults feel special too, which is refreshing for a mother of small children. It is a lovely place to relax, and enjoy excellent food and wine." The menu, changing daily, offers three or four starters and main courses (many suitable for vegetarians), and puddings such as "sticky toffee pudding with custard, farmhouse black cherry pie warm from the stove, spotted dick with rum and cream, chocolate Calvados crunch". (*N and D Mulliken, Alison Masson*)

Open All year.
Rooms 2 suites, 14 double – all with bath and/or shower, telephone, radio, TV, tea-making facilities, baby-listening. 2 cottages, 2 poolside apartments, lodge separate from main building. 1 ground-floor bedroom.
Facilities Ramps. Residents' lounge, bar, coffee room, 2 restaurants; conference facilities, games room; laundry. Dancing in poolside restaurant Sat after dinner. 5-acre grounds with heated swimming pool, children's play area. Riding, golf, hill walking, fishing nearby.
Location ¾ m W of Selkirk.
Restrictions If smokers disturb other guests they will be asked to desist (restaurant and lounge). No children under 5 in restaurant. Dogs by arrangement only, not in public rooms.
Credit cards All major cards accepted.
Terms B&B £44–£48. Set lunch £8.50, dinner £20; full alc £25. Reduced rates for children; high tea 5 pm.
Service/tipping: "No service charge. We discourage tipping but it still goes on."

SHIELDAIG Highland   Map 5

Tigh An Eilean Hotel [BUDGET]   *Tel* Shieldaig (052 05) 251
Shieldaig, Strathcarron
Ross-shire IV54 8XN

Attractively decorated small hotel on edge of sea in unspoilt fishing village overlooking National Trust Isle of Pines. Recommended for beautiful position on loch, excellent food, small but good wine list, pleasant proprietor and staff. Sitting room, TV room, residents' bar, public bar. Private fishing (salmon, sea and brown trout) on river Balgy, Loch Damh. Drying room. Open Easter–late Oct. 12 rooms – 5 with bath and shower. B&B £23–£24.75; dinner, B&B £35.75–£37.50. Set dinner £13.75 [1990]. New nomination. More reports please.

STEWARTON Strathclyde   Map 5

Chapeltoun House Hotel   *Tel* Stewarton (0560) 82696
Off Irvine Road (B769)   *Fax* (0560) 85100
Stewarton, Ayrshire KA3 3ED

A substantial Edwardian house 20 miles south of Glasgow, built by a wealthy industrialist as a private residence; it has oak-panelled public rooms with log fires, well-equipped, individually decorated bedrooms, and large grounds with mature gardens. It is conveniently situated for visits to Culzean Castle and Glasgow, there is excellent golfing in the area, and Prestwick Airport is nearby. Owned by Colin and Graeme McKenzie, it has been praised in the past as "comfortable in every way". "We were given a very large room with a king-sized bed and a round bay window that overlooked fields. There was a bowl of fresh fruit and two glasses of sherry waiting for us. Tea followed, with a roaring fire in the large lounge. It seemed as though we had found our own castle." Another visitor enjoyed "the kitchen garden full of herbs and vegetables". But two readers found shortcomings: "Beds turned down but no fresh towels and rubbish not removed, no information on breakfast the night before, breakfast not generous and poorly presented, some shabby furniture." "The McKenzies made us very welcome but we felt they could lead from the front a bit more in eliminating the 'tatty'." More reports please.

Open All year except 1 Jan.
Rooms 8 double – 6 with bath, 2 with shower, all with telephone, radio, TV.
Facilities Foyer, lounge, cocktail bar, 2 dining rooms. 20-acre grounds with river and mature gardens. Golf, fishing, riding nearby. Sea 6 m.
Location 2 m SW of Stewarton, towards Irvine on B769.
Restrictions Only restaurant suitable for &. No smoking in dining room. No children under 12. Dogs by arrangement, not in public rooms.
Credit cards Access, Amex, Visa.
Terms B&B: single occupancy £65–£79, double £89–£124. Set lunch £17, dinner £25.50.
Service/tipping: "Any tips offered are gratefully received and placed in a tronc and distributed to all members of staff."

STRATHTUMMEL Tayside   Map 5

Port-an-Eilean Hotel   **BUDGET**   *Tel* Tummel Bridge (088 24) 233
Strathtummel, by Pitlochry
Perthshire PH16 5RU

*1865 sporting lodge beside Loch Tummel; glorious Highland scenery all around.
Steep, spectacular drive through 21 acres of rhododendrons and silver birches to
loch shore. Mr and Mrs Gordon Hallewell are "welcoming and friendly" hosts.
Public rooms have lofty ceilings and works by modern Scottish artists: prints,
oils, tapestries, collages. Bedrooms, "with good beds", vary greatly in size; most
overlook loch. "Dinners good, breakfasts bountiful." Changes taking place this
year: number of bedrooms reduced, formal bar converted to "serve yourself",
larger public areas available as result. Open May–Sep. 5 rooms – all with bath.
B&B £24–£28. Set dinner £13.50 [1990]. In italics because of transitions. More
reports please.*

STRONTIAN Highland   Map 5

Kilcamb Lodge Hotel   *Tel* Strontian (0967) 2257
Strontian, Argyllshire
PH36 4HY

*Small, secluded hospitable hostelry in 30-acre grounds, a haven for wildlife, on
lovely Loch Sunart, with half a mile of private shoreline; boats and fishing
arranged. Small bar, large lounge, attractive dining room. Readers appreciate
Suzanne Bradbury's cooking, traditional Scottish fare, well prepared. But some
criticisms of guest-housey elements and room maintenance. Open Easter–20
Oct. 9 rooms – all with bath and/or shower. B&B £30; dinner, B&B £46. Set
dinner £17.50. More reports please.*

TANGUSDALE BEACH Barra, Outer Hebrides   Map 5

Isle of Barra Hotel   **BUDGET**   *Tel* Castlebay (087 14) 383
Tangusdale Beach, Castlebay   *Fax* (087 14) 385
Isle of Barra PA80 5XW

A modern hotel, particularly suitable for children, on the smallest of the
inhabited Western Isles, owned by George and Maureen Macleod. "It is
well sited right on the beach, and has a spectacular outlook over the bay
with its frequent beautiful Atlantic sunsets. The building itself has little
character, but it has been well finished and has all the facilities one could
want. There are one or two extremely safe beaches where children may
be let loose without concern, and places where seals and otters can be
seen without lengthy or difficult walks. The cooking is good; we
produced a lobster one morning and told them exactly how we wanted it
for dinner that evening, and they made an excellent job of it." (*RS
McNeill*) There's good beachcombing, bird watching and hill walking.
There is a five-hour ferry four times a week from Oban, and a daily flight
from Glasgow. Watching the scheduled air service landing on the
enormous cockle-shell beach is "unfailing entertainment".

Open Apr–Oct.
Rooms 35 double – all with bath and shower, radio, TV, tea-making facilities, baby-listening.
Facilities Cocktail bar, lounge. Weekly ceilidhs. Beach nearby.
Location 2 m W of Castlebay. From ferry turn left; keep on main road. If without car, advise hotel; they will meet you.
Restrictions Not suitable for &. No dogs in public rooms.
Credit cards Access, Visa.
Terms B&B: single £35, double £55. Set dinner £15, full alc £20. Reductions for 4 days or more. Reduced rates for children sharing parents' room; special meals. *Service/tipping: "No service charge. Tips are distributed to staff."*

TIMSGARRY Lewis, Outer Hebrides   Map 5

Baile-na-Cille   *Tel* Timsgarry (085 175) 242
Timsgarry, Uig
Isle of Lewis PA86 9JD

🄫 *César award in 1990: Shangri-La of the Outer Hebrides*

"We welcome dogs, children, grannies and even fishermen," writes Joanna Gollin of the 18th-century manse on the wild west coast of Lewis that she and her husband, Richard, have converted into a welcoming hotel. It sits on the edge of a sandy bay "at the end of a 15-mile single-track road across a soggy landscape of peat interspersed with tiny lochs. When you reach Timsgarry, however, the scenery changes to soft, springy turf, hazy blue hills, and long white sands." "Why is this our favourite place? It could be the miles of deserted sandy beaches, the marvellous collection of tapes, records and books (for rainy days!), the comfortable furnishings . . . but more important than all this is the 'atmosphere'. The owners *genuinely* enjoy having guests, and Joanna is a lovely cook." Most rooms have sea views; some are a little small (three-quarters are in converted stables and cowsheds). A few readers mention "limited" cupboard and drawer space. Eating is communal ("an abundance of fresh local produce"). Richard Gollin travels almost daily to Stornaway to collect supplies, and guests without transport can be deposited at various points for walking and climbing. It is a wonderful area for naturalists. "This remote area would not suit people looking for sophisticated five-star treatment, but for anyone wanting to get away from it all it is an ideal hideaway." (*S Pankhurst, and others*) One dissenter complained of over-leisurely meals: "It took over half an hour to get toast at breakfast. All meals tended to be drawn out, which with good companions can lead to excellent discussion but which can sometimes be a strain."

Open Apr–mid-Oct.
Rooms 2 family suites, 8 double, 2 single – 6 with bath, all with tea-making facilities, baby-listening. 9 in 3 converted stable blocks by main entrance. Some ground-floor rooms.
Facilities 3 lounges (1 with TV, 1 with music), dining room; drying room. 3-acre grounds with walled garden, children's play area, cricket pitch, direct access to beach (dinghy, windsurfer and fishing rods available). Near 7 sandy beaches with safe bathing; fishing, sailing.
Location 34 m W of Stornoway. Take A858 from Stornoway or Tarbert to Garynahine, B8011 towards Uig; at Timsgarry shop turn right down to shore. *Note* All road signs are now in Gaelic only.
Restrictions Not really suitable for &. No smoking in dining room; preferably no smoking in bedrooms. Dogs by arrangement.

Credit cards None accepted.
Terms B&B £16.50–£28; dinner, B&B £32.50–£44. Set dinner £16 (lobster dinner extra); packed lunches. Weekly packages for walkers, bird-watchers, fishermen. Reduced rates and special meals for children.
Service/tipping: "We are 100% against tipping, but if people insist the money goes straight to the staff. We have a lot fewer problems and embarrassment with tipping than with smokers! We say 'no smoking' in the dining room but some still try to light up between courses. Mrs G goes in with the fire extinguisher."

TIRORAN Mull, Strathclyde   Map 5

Tiroran House   *Tel* Tiroran (068 15) 232
Tiroran, Isle of Mull
Argyllshire PA69 6ES

Readers continue to enthuse about this well-bred, very cosseting former shooting lodge owned by Robin and Sue Blockey. It sits above Loch Scridain, with 15 acres of gardens and woodland sweeping down to the water, and is well situated for visiting all parts of Mull. The drive from the ferry is forested, barren, mountainous, gently undulating and coastal in turn; much of it is along a single track. *Tiroran* by contrast is an oasis of sophistication and civilisation. The two drawing rooms are decorated in pretty fabrics and have many antiques. Small arrangements of flowers are everywhere. The larger bedrooms are just as thoughtfully furnished, with comfortable beds, small sofas, "bath towels so big they can wrap round you twice". Some rooms are quite small. One of the two dining rooms is a flower-filled conservatory with a view of the water, the other a warm soft red room with bookcases, a fireplace, and oak tables. The table settings are "a delight". Dinners, served at 7.45 at separate tables, feature three starters and a single main course, Scottish cheese, and three puddings, at least one of which is hot. The packed lunches are "marvellous: capacious wicker baskets, different sandwiches every day, hot soup, delicious cakes, fresh fruit, and little jugs and jars with condiments". Guests are expected to be walking or touring during the day. Most enjoy having a drink together before dinner to share their sightseeing experiences. "For a few the service may seem slow," one correspondent told us, "but that is an expected drawback when all the guests are being served like friends at a private dinner." "A gem," wrote another reader this year. "I doubt, after years of using the Guide, that I have ever stayed anywhere that I enjoyed so much," wrote a third. "The Blockeys clearly live up to the motto 'service before self'." (*April Young, Dr E Gerver, Paul and Christine Butler, Gillian Smith*)

Open 1 June–6 Oct. Lunch for residents only, by prior arrangement.
Rooms 8 double, 1 single – all with bath, shower, radio, tea-making facilities. 3 in cottage 40 yds from hotel.
Facilities 2 drawing rooms, dining room. 15-acre grounds with woodland, lawn and stream; croquet. On sea loch safe for bathing, sailing, canoeing.
Location Oban–Craignure ferry (45 mins) bookable with Caledonian McBrayne, The Pier, Gourock PA19 1QP. (Lochaline–Fishnish ferry, not bookable, but much cheaper, necessitates a longish but superb drive through Morvern.) From Craignure take A849 to Fionnphort. At head of Loch Scridain (17 m) turn right on to B8035; after 5 m turn left to Tiroran (1 m). Entrance through stone gate marked Tiroran and Bungalow.
Restrictions Not suitable for &. No smoking in dining room. No children under 10. Dogs by arrangement, not in public rooms.
Credit cards None accepted.

Terms Dinner, B&B £77–£96. Packed lunches. Set dinner £25. Reductions for stays of 3 nights or more; 5- and 7-day holidays include car ferry reimbursement. *Service/tipping: "There is no service charge and no gratuities are expected."*

TOBERMORY Mull, Strathclyde   Map 5

The Tobermory Hotel **BUDGET**   *Tel* Tobermory (0688) 2091
53 Main Street
Tobermory, Isle of Mull
Argyllshire PA75 6NT

Attractive conversion of old colour-washed fisherman's cottages overlooking harbour, returning to Guide under new ownership. Small and picturesque yachting centre, Tobermory overlooks Sound of Mull; hotel can arrange excursions by motor yacht on request. Readers praise "warm and comfortable rooms" in winter and welcome from friendly staff – but there's been criticism of food ("it always sounded better than it actually was"). 15 rooms – 8 with bath or shower. B&B £19–£25; dinner, B&B £30–£37. Set dinner £13. More reports please.

ULLAPOOL Highland   Map 5

Altnaharrie Inn   *Tel* Dundonnell (085 483) 230
Ullapool, Wester Ross IV26 2SS

✿ *César award in 1987: Away-from-it-all delight in the featherweight class*

In an idyllic setting on the shore of Loch Broom, this "treasure among hotels", a former drover's inn, now firmly established as one of Britain's finest restaurants-with-rooms, is one of only three restaurants in Scotland to earn a *Michelin* rosette. "Every serious patron of unique hotels should visit it once in a lifetime so as to set a standard against which to judge all the others." It is owned by Fred Brown and his Norwegian wife Gunn Eriksen (she is the cook), and its decor is described as "Scottish-Scandinavian". "The whole thing is a bit precious but not pretentious, and its achievement in such a remote spot must have required great logistic planning." Guests are fetched by ferry from Ullapool harbour for the ten-minute ride. It helps if you enjoy your fellow guests: "One is obliged to be in close contact with others, both pre- and post-prandially, because only one small lounge is available – but this is not offered as a criticism." "It could be hard for keen hill-walkers to climb An Teallach or other temptingly close peaks within the constraints of the daily ferry timetable. But the food was superb in every detail: wonderful nettle-and-brie soup, pigeon, cloudberry ice-cream." There are selections of cheese from France and Norway as well as Ireland, Scotland and England – and three desserts every night. As a reader said last year: "You must try them all, or Gunn will be upset!" (*David N Ing, W Ian Stewart, Rev AG Mursell; also Mrs M Wall, Marjory and Michael Thrusfield, Dr James Mair*) Altnaharrie is a non-smoking hotel.

Open Easter–late Oct, probably Christmas and New Year. Occasional closures in summer; please telephone.
Rooms 7 double – all with bath and/or shower. 2 in separate buildings.

Facilities Hall, 2 lounges, dining room. 15-acre grounds with gardens, on loch; pebbled beach, safe (but cold) bathing; trout and salmon fishing by arrangement; hill walking.
Location On south shore of Loch Broom. Access by launch from Ullapool harbour (normal collection times 2.45, 4.45, 6 pm). Private parking in Ullapool. Guests requested to telephone on arrival in Ullapool.
Restrictions Not suitable for &. No smoking. Children "only if old enough to enjoy our dinner which usually lasts over 2 hours". Dogs by arrangement, not in public rooms.
Credit cards None accepted.
Terms [1990 rates] Dinner, B&B double £82–£89. 1 night bookings occasionally refused. Reduced rates for children sharing parents' room.
Service/tipping: "No service charge. We try to discourage tipping. The staff try to refuse politely any that are offered."

The Ceilidh Place　　　　　　　　　　　　　　　*Tel* Ullapool (0854) 2103
14 West Argyle Street
Ullapool, Wester Ross IV26 2TY

  César award in 1986: Utterly acceptable mild eccentricity

Mellowed a bit from earlier years when readers cited "the ageing hippy atmosphere", but continuing to attract both superlatives ("Absolutely super"; "So good its reputation should almost be passed only by word of mouth") and the faintest of faint praise ("Oh dear, I can say that it is an interesting place . . .") – but the ayes have it. This hotel – also clubhouse, restaurant, coffee shop, bookshop – near the centre of Ullapool is run by Jean and Robert Urquhart (he a TV actor when not a hotelier) as a new-world establishment with genuine verve. Its attractions are the reasonably priced accommodation and the myriad activities: sea angling, water skiing, loch fishing and pony trekking, as well as more leisurely pursuits such as listening to music. The lounge is "very pleasant". Younger guests "may lie on the floor or walk about barefoot, and the wine service is a matter of choosing your own from a forest of bottles on a dresser at the end of the room". The place can be very busy at times; service is enthusiastic and helpful, "if a bit scatty" or "a farce". "The place is well designed and has a pleasant atmosphere, though the annexe bedrooms are a mixed lot." Reports on the food are mixed, too, ranging from "the worst meal we have eaten in ages" to "absolutely excellent". (*RAL Ogston, Robin C Smith, Dr James Mair, RLA Gollin, David Thibodeau*)

Open All year except 2 weeks mid-Jan.
Rooms 12 double, 3 single – 8 with bath, all with telephone. Guest's pantry for tea-making. 11 extra rooms (simpler, with bunk beds, etc.) in Clubhouse annexe.
Facilities Lounge, Clubhouse bar with live music, coffee shop, games room, dining room; ceilidhs, jazz, classical and folk music evenings once a week winter, 3–4 nights summer. Rocky beach.
Location First right after pier at W end of Main Street. Large carpark.
Restrictions Not suitable for &. No dogs in public rooms.
Credit cards All major cards accepted.
Terms B&B £20–£40; bed in Clubhouse £8.50–£10. Packed lunches available. Full alc dinner £20. Special rates for 6 days or more; occasional courses; activity holidays. Reduced rates for children sharing parents' room; special meals.
Service/tipping: "We do not look for tips. Wages should be paid to allow people to live on them and prices charged must cover this. However, some people do still leave tips and they are shared equally by everyone."

WALLS Shetland Islands   Map 5

Burrastow House   *Tel* Walls (059 571) 307
Walls, Shetland ZE2 9PB

On the remote west side of Shetland in a peaceful setting where you may
see otters and seals, a "fine, small Georgian house, 'Scottish-plain'", with
views across to the island of Vaila. Inside, it is "warm, comfortable and
furnished with good pictures and *objets d'art*"; there are peat fires, a cosy
library, and a dining room where guests can enjoy excellent food. In
earlier editions of the Guide under previous owners, it returns with warm
praise for the new ones, Bo Simmons and Ann Prior, who are
knowledgeable about Shetland and genuinely welcoming of children and
pets. "The house is decorated in a very sympathetic and relaxing way.
The furniture is a well-worn miscellany picked up from local sales, which
gives the hotel a very lived-in appearance. It is like staying in a house
rather than a hotel as both the owners are so welcoming. The style may
not suit everyone, but if you do not mind occasional pop music is charming." "Dinner has a nice balance of local and more exotic dishes. Fish,
soups, puddings – even scrambled eggs – particularly recommended.
Good (organic) house wines and a nice and catholic collection of other
wine at welcoming modest prices." (*RT Clement, S Stanley*)

Open Mar–end Sep. Mid-Nov–mid-Dec.
Rooms 3 – all with bath, tea-making facilities; TV on request.
Facilities Sitting room, dining room, library with TV/video. 2-acre grounds. Own
pier and boat for residents; safe swimming.
Location 27 m W of Lerwick, 2 m SW of Walls. From Lerwick to Walls, up hill; on
brow turn left, proceed 2 m to dead end.
Restrictions Not suitable for ♿. No smoking in dining room. No dogs in dining
room.
Credit cards None accepted.
Terms B&B: single £41, double £70; dinner, B&B: single £50, double £90. Packed
lunches; alc lunch £15, set dinner £17.50. Special breaks 1 Oct–31 Mar.
*Service/tipping: "Tips accepted in the spirit in which they are given but we don't openly
encourage."*

WEST LINTON Borders   Map 5

Medwyn House   *Tel* West Linton (0968) 60542
Medwyn Road, West Linton
Peeblesshire EH46 7HB

A former coaching inn, 18 miles south of Edinburgh, converted to a
Victorian country house in 1864, now a small hotel, with a panelled hall
with open fire, large drawing room, comfortably appointed bedrooms and
30-acre grounds with gardens and woodland. Owned by Anne and Mike
Waterston, and italicised last year, it now earns a full entry for its
"civilised and friendly welcome, fine food, warm hospitality, and five-star
treatment with no formality". A recent visitor writes: "A super quiet place
to stay if you want to explore Edinburgh or the surrounding countryside;
the whole place is very welcoming." There is an elegant dining room and
warm praise for Anne Waterston's cooking; preferences are ascertained
on arrival. No licence – bring your own drink (no corkage). (*Sue
Hemmings, Angela Jacques, and others*) More reports welcome.

Open All year.
Rooms 3 rooms – all with bath, radio, tea-making facilities; TV on request.
3-bedroomed cottage sometimes available.
Facilities Lounge/hall, drawing room, dining room. 30-acre grounds; 18-hole golf course next door (50% reduction on greens fees).
Location Off A702 on Baddinsgill, signposted Medwyn Road/Golf Course.
Restrictions Not suitable for &. No smoking in dining room or bedrooms. No children under 10 unless by special arrangement. No dogs in public rooms.
Credit cards None accepted.
Terms (No service charge) B&B £27–£37; dinner, B&B £42–£52. Reduced rates for children by arrangement.

WHITEBRIDGE Highland   Map 5

Knockie Lodge   *Tel* Gorthleck (045 63) 276
Whitebridge
Inverness-shire IV1 2UP

"This is a country house hotel which really *is* in the country – wild and beautiful to the east of Loch Ness (which cannot be seen as it lies over the hills). What *can* be seen from the hotel are local lochs and vast vistas of Highland scenery with not another dwelling in sight." Ian and Brenda Milward's 200-year-old hotel, formerly a hunting lodge for the Chief of Clan Fraser, enjoys a beautiful position in lightly wooded countryside that offers many opportunities for photography, bird watching, sailing, climbing and pony trekking, as well as fishing and deer stalking. The lodge has a comfortable sitting room, with books and magazines, and a billiard room with a full-size table. The dining room is inviting, with silver and candle-light, five-course menus (no choice until dessert) and a "wide-ranging wine list". Bedrooms are unfussy and snug, with fitted carpets, good hanging space, fresh flowers, and immaculate modern bathrooms – although one writer recently warned that at least two have baths so small that "one needs to be a contortionist". The absence of radio and TV adds to the country-house atmosphere, and another visitor has commented on the pleasing contrast between daytime and evening pursuits: "The breakfast and dinners are delicious and elegant – and since one is rather 'outdoorsy' during the day, it is pleasant to dress for dinner, and spend a delightful evening with the hosts and fellow guests." (*WI Stewart, R Berry, and others*)

Open 28 Apr–27 Oct.
Rooms 8 double, 2 single – all with bath and/or shower, telephone; tea-making facilities on request.
Facilities Drawing room with self-service bar, sitting room, dining room, billiard room. 10-acre grounds. 4 lochs within easy walking distance, sailing; deer stalking, pony trekking, golf nearby.
Location 2 m down single-track private road W off B862, 8 m N of Fort Augustus.
Restrictions Not suitable for &. No smoking in dining room. No children under 10. Dogs by prior arrangement; not in public rooms.
Credit cards All major cards accepted.
Terms Dinner, B&B £55–£80. Set dinner £20.
Service/tipping: "No service charge, but if guests particularly want to leave something it is given in its entirety to staff."

Please never tell a hotel you intend to send a report to the Guide. Anonymity is essential for objectivity.

Channel Islands

Château La Chaire, Rozel Bay, Jersey

HERM Map 1

The White House Hotel *Tel* Guernsey (0481) 22159
Herm, via Guernsey *Fax* (0481) 710066

⊞ *César award in 1987: Best family hotel away from it all*

Herm, three miles from Guernsey, is one and a half miles long and one
mile wide, with one church, one pub – and one hotel, *The White House*.
It has a population of approximately 40 including children (though it has
to meet an invasion of 1,000 or more day-visitors from Guernsey in the
summer). It is also a unique fief, run by the Tenants of Herm, Peter and
Jenny Wood. The official brochure dubs it "heaven on earth". A reader
adds, "The hotel offers peace and tranquillity in a fantastic setting." There
are no TV sets or telephones in the rooms, just "glorious views over the
sea to Guernsey". It is praised for its good value, "very good" food (not
overly ambitious, menus changed daily), spotlessly clean rooms, and
newly heated swimming pool. There are isolated beaches within a few
minutes' stroll; day trippers have their own restaurant and rarely

intrude. Residents change for dinner, but the *White House* "caters equally well for children (baby-listening, high teas at 5 pm, lots of board games and jigsaws for rainy days), managing at the same time to keep civilised standards – a rare combination." (*Mr and Mrs J Antell, IG Tew; and others*) The only niggles have been about the bedroom furniture ("MFI type"), the hot-water system ("not very hot at 7 am"), and breakfast ("staff training and *fresh* orange juice are needed").

Open Mar–Oct.
Rooms 30 double, 2 single – all with bath, shower, radio, tea-making facilities, baby-listening. 22 in 3 cottages in grounds. 7 ground-floor rooms.
Facilities 2 lounges, 3 bars, 2 restaurants. 3-acre garden with solar-heated swimming pool, tennis court. Sandy beaches with safe bathing; private harbour and mooring facilities; fishing.
Location 3 m from Guernsey via hourly ferry service from St Peter Port (15–20 minutes). Hotel meets guests at airport or ferry. (No cars on Herm.)
Restrictions Herm not really suitable for ⅄ (those wishing to visit must land at high tide). No smoking in 1 restaurant. No dogs.
Credit cards Access, Visa.
Terms Dinner, B&B £33–£44. Set lunch £9, dinner £15. Reduced rates for children, special meals.
Service/tipping: "Gratuities are not expected but when given are shared out equally among the staff."

ROZEL BAY Jersey   Map 1

Château La Chaire   *Tel* Jersey (0534) 63354
Rozel Bay, St Martins   *Fax* (0534) 65137
                                               Telex 437334

A small luxury hotel nestled on the slope of the Rozel Valley on the north-eastern tip of Jersey, six miles from St Helier. Built in 1843, it has panelled public rooms, handsomely decorated bedrooms, and a restaurant featuring seafood (a smaller selection of dishes is offered "for the more traditional palate"). The hotel is surrounded by a terraced garden and there is a sandy beach with safe swimming nearby. *Château La Chaire* entered our pages as a new nomination last year. A reader in 1990 reports: "The hotel is off the beaten track even by Jersey standards; it's halfway up a steep hill. The public rooms are lovely. Our large and well decorated room had a jacuzzi and a nice balcony. The staff were pleasant and knowledgeable without being pretentious. The restaurant was good – sometimes very good; we felt the best dishes were non-fish ones such as medallions of Scottish beef, and chicken liver and blackcurrant pâté. The wine list covered a wide range and was reasonable by London standards. The drawback is that the grounds should be tackled only by the reasonably fit." (*Dr P Silverstone, and others*) A new chef arrived in January and early reports are warm in his praise.

Open All year.
Rooms 13 double – all with bath, shower, telephone, radio, TV.
Facilities Lounge, bar, restaurant/conservatory. 7 acre garden with rare shrubs and trees. Sandy beach nearby, safe for swimming. Harbour short walk, fishing from pier head.
Location 6 m from St Helier. From parish of St Martins, follow signs for Rozel. In village take 1st turning on left; hotel car park 200 yds on left.
Restrictions Not suitable for ⅄. No children under 7. No dogs.
Credit cards All major cards accepted.

Terms (10% service charge added to non-residents' dinner) B&B: single £48–£100, double £70–£105; dinner, B&B: single £62–£115, double £98–£135. Set lunch £9.95, dinner £16; full alc £24. Reduced rates for children sharing parents' room. Winter and Christmas breaks.
Service/tipping: "Any tips received by staff are pooled."

ST PETER PORT Guernsey   Map 1

La Frégate Hotel   *Tel* Guernsey (0481) 24624
Les Cotils   *Fax* (0481) 20443

Once an 18th-century manor house, though the facade has been much altered since, *La Frégate* has a fine location in its own terraced garden high on a hill above St Peter Port's bustling harbour, about five minutes' walk from the old markets with their striped awnings and locally caught seafood. Some rooms have double-glazed patio windows leading on to a private balcony, most enjoy splendid south-westerly views over the town and neighbouring islands; they are spacious, and well furnished in a functional but comfortable style. A bonus is *La Frégate's* esteemed restaurant, fairly formal – tie and jacket *de rigueur* – and with a busy local following attracted by the ambitious and comprehensive menu (French with a good selection of seafood). The table d'hôte menu (for residents only) is served between 7 and 7.30 pm, full à la carte from 7 to 9.30. "We were there a week. The residents' dinner was excellent and although we had to order by 7.30, there was no attempt made to rush us through our meal. The only thing wrong was the weather which was dreadful, but if one has to endure cold, mist and rain, *La Frégate* is the place to do it." (*Dr J Backhurst*)

Open All year.
Rooms 9 double, 4 single – all with bath, shower, telephone, TV, tea-making facilities; 6 with balcony.
Facilities Residents' lounge, lounge bar, restaurant. 2-acre grounds with terraced gardens. 5 mins' walk to harbour with fishing, 10 mins to indoor leisure centre; beaches nearby.
Location Near Candie Gardens. 5 mins' walk from town centre. Difficult to find: request map in advance, or telephone for directions on arrival on the island. Private carpark.
Restrictions Not suitable for &. No children under 14 in hotel, under 9 in restaurant. No dogs.
Credit cards All major cards accepted.
Terms (Service at guest's discretion) B&B: single £54.50, double £103. Set lunch £10.50, dinner (residents only) £15.50; full alc £25–£30. 1-night bookings refused Apr–Oct.

Midhurst House   `BUDGET`   *Tel* Guernsey (0481) 24391
Candie Road, St Peter Port

Readers of the Guide continue to praise Brian and Jan Goodenough's "modest but immaculate hotel" in an elegant Regency townhouse quietly located ten minutes' walk up from the harbour. Prices are very reasonable. "Our bedroom had been decorated since our visit the year before, not because it needed doing but because Jan and Brian are forward-looking in all they do to make *Midhurst* the best." "Jan is an efficient and unobtrusive host and Brian's cooking is first-class. Drinks in the sitting room at 6.30 pm help to create a friendly atmosphere." There is a four-course dinner (two choices per course) made from fresh ingredients bought daily at the market. A drawback for some is the early dinnertime but for others, Jan Goodenough explains, it is an attraction: the majority of guests are "over 50s" who enjoy a gentle stroll after dinner while it is still light; and many guests attend concerts, theatres, and so on starting at 8 pm, and this way they are not rushed. (*FM Rothwell; B and E Hoyle, Georgina Woolley; and others*) Only criticisms: space limited in the rooms in the cottage-style annexe; and "tables in the dining room a shade too close together, so conversation is inhibited".

Open Apr–mid-Oct.
Rooms 8 double – 2 with bath, 6 with shower, all with radio, TV, tea-making facilities. 3 in cottage annexe. 4 ground-floor rooms.
Facilities Lounge, dining room. Small garden. Sea 10 mins' walk.
Location 5 mins' walk from town centre, near Candie Museum and Cambridge Park. Limited free lock-up garaging for guests; free public parking nearby.
Restrictions Not suitable for &. No smoking in dining room. No children under 8. No dogs.
Credit cards None accepted.
Terms B&B £20–£25; dinner, B&B £27–£32. Set lunch £7, dinner £7.50. Reduced rates for children. Doubles let as singles low season only.
Service/tipping: "No service charge. Tipping is not expected. If guests insist this is distributed between staff in proportion to hours worked."

ST SAVIOUR Guernsey   Map 1

La Hougue Fouque Farm   `BUDGET`   *Tel* Guernsey (0481) 64181
Route du Bas Courtil

Readers have been quick to endorse last year's nomination of this comfortable family hotel converted from a farmhouse in the centre of Guernsey. Quiet and secluded, surrounded mainly by green fields, it is liked for its spacious grounds, mostly open lawn, well-maintained pool (sometimes spoiled by too many outsiders), friendly service, and good value. There are tubs of flowers, poolside tables with umbrellas, and outdoor barbecues, weather permitting. "We had a relatively small room, but it led on to an attractive communal balcony." "The food was good, and there was plenty of it on the table d'hôte menu. The lunches in the bar are *very* good. Even in the depth of winter the restaurant was full on Friday and Saturday evenings, mainly with locals." (*Helen and Charles Priday, IG Tew*)

Open All year.
Rooms 7 triple, 2 suites, 4 double – all with bath, telephone, radio, TV, tea-making facilities, baby-listening. 2 on ground floor.
Facilities 2 lounges, 1 bar, 2 restaurants. Pianist Fri and Sat. Large grounds with garden and solar-heated pool.
Location In countryside, near airport, but not in flight path. Transport from airport or harbour can be arranged.
Restriction No dogs.
Credit cards Access, Visa.
Terms (No service charge) B&B £20–£34; dinner, B&B £26–£40. Single supplement £10. Set lunch £7.95, dinner £10.95; full alc £20. Reduced rates for children; special meals.

Please make a habit of sending a report if you stay at a Guide hotel.

ST SAVIOUR Jersey   Map 1

Longueville Manor Hotel

Tel Jersey (0534) 25501
Fax (0534) 31613
Telex 4192306

❦ *César award in 1986: The pearl in the Jersey oyster*

Standing in large grounds at the foot of its own private wooded valley, one and a half miles inland from Jersey's capital, St Helier, *Longueville Manor* has long been a mecca among country house hotels in the Channel Islands. It is well away from the tourist hubbub, and – a plus for golfers – only two and a half miles from the Royal Jersey Golf Club. The setting is sophisticated. The hotel has comfortable sitting-around places including a small, well-chosen library; outside there is a large heated swimming pool where lunch may be taken in fine weather. The bedrooms, individually decorated, are "lovely" and "lavish and comfortable". The hotel has been run by the Lewis and Dufty families for the past forty years. Its restaurant has recently enjoyed wide acclaim, and the wine waiters have been praised for being "exceptionally helpful without the snobbery so many seem to affect". A new chef, Andy Baird, late of *Hambleton Hall* (q.v.), arrived in April. First reports are enthusiastic.

Open All year.
Rooms 2 suites, 30 double, 1 single – all with bath (7 also have shower), telephone, radio, TV. 8 ground-floor rooms.
Facilities Lift. Bar/lounge, drawing room, library, dining room; conference facilities. 15-acre grounds with swimming pool (heated in season) and putting green. Golf, bowls, squash, tennis within easy reach. 1½ m from sea with sandy beaches.
Location 1½ m E of St Helier; bus stops near main hotel gates. From airport, take main road to St Helier; near harbour follow sign A17 to Georgetown. Take A3 for 1 m; hotel is on left.
Restrictions No children under 7. No smoking in part of dining room. No dogs in public rooms.
Credit cards All major cards accepted.
Terms B&B: single £67–£80, double £103–£166, suite £200–£236; dinner, B&B £22 extra per person. Set lunch £17, dinner £25; full alc £35. Winter weekend breaks; Christmas/New Year package. Reductions for children sharing parents' room.
Service/tipping: "No stated policy – tipping is at customers' discretion."

SARK   Map 1

Hotel Petit Champ   **BUDGET**   *Tel* Sark (0481) 832046
Sark, via Guernsey

Sark, only three and a half miles long but with nearly 40 miles of coastline, is the smallest of the four main Channel Islands. There are no cars, but all parts of the coast are easily reached on foot or by bicycle. The *Petit Champ*, owned by Mr and Mrs Terry Scott, is a pleasant, late 19th-century granite building in a secluded part of the island, well away from the day trippers' tracks. Most of its rooms ("comfortable without being luxurious") have views of the sea and neighbouring islands, and all are centrally heated. There are no radios or television. The hotel has a well-tended, sheltered garden and a solar-heated swimming pool built into a disused quarry – a fine sun-trap out of the wind. It will take you ten minutes to walk down to a secluded bay with sand at low tide – but allow half an hour for the climb back. Guests are advised to bring suitable shoes for rock scrambling, a torch for exploring caves, and binoculars for bird watching. In the evening, smart attire is preferred, "as befits dinner by candle-light". Roy Bettencourt, the chef, has been at the hotel for four years, and a reader describes his dinners as "excellent, well balanced and interesting". Sark lobster is featured. (*J and V Stuart; also Miranda Mackintosh*)

Open Mid-Apr–early Oct.
Rooms 2 family suites (doubles with adjoining singles), 11 double, 3 single – all with bath and/or shower. Some on ground floor.
Facilities 3 sun lounges, lounge/library, TV lounge, bar, 3 dining rooms. 1-acre garden with heated swimming pool. Steep walk to sandy beach, safe bathing.
Location By road, follow lane towards sea by Methodist Chapel, or head for Beau Regard and turn right along field path just before duck pond.
Restrictions Sark not suitable for seriously &. No smoking in dining room, lounge/library. Children must be old enough to sit with parents at dinner. No dogs.
Credit cards All major cards accepted.
Terms Dinner, B&B £37–£40. Set lunch from £10 (or snacks), dinner from £14. ⅓ reduction for children sharing parents' room; special meals on request.
Service/tipping: "We abandoned a service charge several years ago but some guests still insist on leaving gratuities. When it is impossible to refuse tips without causing offence, the tips are pooled and shared out at the end of the season (with interest added)."

La Sablonnerie   *Tel* Sark (0481) 832061
Sark, via Guernsey

An off-the-beaten-track hotel (really a restaurant-with-rooms) in Little Sark, the southern peninsula of the island. The rooms – "simple and charming" – are sprinkled about the tiny hamlet; there has been some redecoration this year. "Our room was tiny but beds were made during breakfast, sheets turned back during dinner, towels changed regularly. Everyone, without exception, was extremely friendly. Mealtimes are fixed fairly rigidly, but this was no hardship as the food was well worth sitting down for. The lounge and dining room are small so one gets to know people very quickly; single people and couples may be asked to share a table." The hotel is surrounded by its own working farm, interesting walks and striking scenery. Possible drawbacks: not many rooms have private facilities; some might find the situation rather cut off owing to the absence of cars on Sark. Few recent reports; more please.

Open Easter–Oct.
Rooms 1 suite, 14 double, 6 single – 6 with bath and shower, 6 with shower only. Many in cottages in courtyard and garden.
Facilities 2 lounges, sun lounge, 2 bars, 2 restaurants, conservatory. 5-acre grounds with gardens and croquet lawn, surrounded by hotel's 100-acre farmland. Small coves and pebble beaches suitable for bathing nearby; sandy bay 15 mins' walk. Hotel boat for trips round island; fishing.
Location At southern tip of island. Guests are met by tractor or horse and carriage.
Restrictions Sark not suitable for severely &. No children under 8. No dogs.
Credit cards Access, Amex, Visa.
Terms (Excluding 10% service charge) B&B £19.50–£29; dinner, B&B £33–£44; full board £35–£46; supplement for private bathroom. Set lunch £12, dinner £16. Reduced rates and high tea for children.

Northern Ireland

Blackheath House, Coleraine

Glassdrumman House   *Tel* Annalong (039 67) 68585
   and Lodge   *Fax* (039 67) 68451
85 Mill Road   *Telex* 747717
Annalong BT34 4QN

A 19th-century house in a pastoral setting with mountain views, offering very comfortable accommodation and splendid food. In the early 1980s the owners, Graeme and Joan Hall, moved from Belfast and started a farm. They learned to cook and bake and tend their herd of Aberdeen Angus cattle. A surplus of produce led eventually to three restaurants: one for quick lunches and afternoon tea, the *Kitchen Garden* for more upmarket lunches and dinner, and the *Memories* restaurant which, except by special arrangement, is open only on Saturday night and serves a formidable six-course meal – "medieval in quantity", according to a recent report. These are in *Glassdrumman House*. Later the *Lodge* was added, a rather plain converted farmhouse a mile and a half down the road, providing accommodation. It nestles in the shadow of Slieve Binian, one of the most spectacular peaks in the Mountains of Mourne – magnificent walking terrain. Bedrooms vary in size, but all are attractively decorated and have good views of mountains or sea. There is a library with hundreds of books. A set dinner is served at the *Lodge* from Monday to Friday; there are patios for outdoor dining in summer. Transport is provided if you want to dine at *Glassdrumman House*. No recent reports. More please.

Open All year. Restaurant closed Tue in winter; *Memories* Restaurant open Sat evening, other days by arrangement.
Rooms 8 double – all with bath, shower, telephone, T V; nanny available.
Facilities Drawing room, library, breakfast room; 3 restaurants in separate building 1½ m away. Conference and office facilities. 8-acre gardens, 35-acre farm, duck pond, tennis court. Rocky beach 1 m, safe bathing, sandy beach 8 m.
Location Off A2, 6 m S of Newcastle, 1 m N of Annalong.
Restrictions Not suitable for &. Preferably no children under 12. No dogs in bedrooms or public rooms (in barns only).
Credit cards Access, Visa.
Terms (Service at guests' discretion) B&B: single £50, double £65–£75. Set lunch £10, dinner £17.50; Sat dinner in *Memories* £25.

COLERAINE Co Londonderry   Map 6

Blackheath House   *Tel* Aghadowey (0265) 868433
112 Killeague Road
Blackhill, Coleraine BT51 4HH

A listed former rectory set in two acres of landscaped gardens in the midst of a prosperous farming area, *Blackheath House*, owned and run by Joe and Margaret Erwin, started life as *Macduff's* restaurant, which continues to have a strong local following. The building stands four-square and solid, in a large mature garden with a lily pond. The interior is comfortably cluttered with old furniture. Last year we said that some of the modern furniture in the bedrooms slightly jarred with the general ambience of restfulness and old-world gentility; the Erwins tell us that the bedrooms have been refurbished and some of the modern furniture replaced by antiques. Dinner is à la carte with plenty of choice and considered excellent value for money. Breakfast is a hearty affair; those not worried about cholesterol can indulge in a monster Ulster Fry. The Causeway Coast is just ten miles away (beaches and cliff walks), and there are eight 18-hole and two 9-hole golf courses within twenty minutes' drive. No recent feedback. More reports welcome.

Open All year except Christmas, New Year. Restaurant closed Sun and Mon.
Rooms 6 double – 2 with bath and shower, 4 with shower, all with telephone, radio, T V, tea-making facilities.
Facilities Residents' lounge and dining room, restaurant with lounge. Indoor swimming pool (heated May–Sep). 2-acre garden. Fishing, shooting, riding, golf nearby; sea 11 m.
Location 4 m N of Garvagh on A29 Killeague road, signposted to left.
Restrictions Not suitable for &. No children under 12. No dogs.
Credit cards Access, Visa.
Terms B&B: single occupancy £25–£30, double £45–£50. Full alc dinner £18–£20.
Service/tipping: "We believe tips should not be expected; it is left entirely to the customer. If anyone does tip the money is divided between those who have contributed to the service of that customer."

Republic of Ireland

Bantry House, Bantry

ADARE Co Limerick   **Map 6**

Dunraven Arms Hotel   *Tel* Limerick (061) 396209
Main Street   *Fax* (061) 396541
                                                        Telex 70202

In picture-postcard village on main west coast route, 10 miles from Limerick, picturesque old inn with new wing and good rooms. Lots of outdoor pursuits nearby, particularly golf and equestrian activities. Recommended for "real professionalism", and "admirable restaurant – half the price of others, and twice the fun". Bar popular (and noisy) at weekends. Bedrooms traditionally decorated, well equipped. Closed Good Friday. 47 rooms, all with bath and/or shower. B&B: single IR£35–IR£50, double IR£50–IR£75. Set lunch IR£9.50, dinner IR£19.50 [1990] (excluding 12½% service charge). Recent nomination. More reports please.

> Don't trust out-of-date editions. Many hotels are dropped and new
> ones added every year.

AGLISH Co Tipperary   Map 6

Ballycornac House **BUDGET**   *Tel* Nenagh (067) 21129
Aglish, Nr Borrisokane   *Fax* (0509) 20043 attn PAXMAN
                                     Telex 39603 attn PAXMAN

A 300-year-old farmhouse surrounded by gardens and paddocks in peaceful countryside 4 miles from Lough Derg. New to the Guide *Ballycornac* might be described as a country cottage hotel. It has a small living room, prettily furnished bedrooms that are "comfortably big by contrast", and welcoming open turf fires (also central heating). There is sailing and fishing on the Lough, but the hotel will appeal especially to readers who enjoy riding: the owners, John and Rosetta-Anne Paxman, specialise in half-bred Irish hunting horses and will arrange morning rides or, in the summer, Lough Derg "gourmet rides" – 150 miles on horseback with a mini-bus return to the hotel each evening. A "very good tea is served each afternoon. At 8 pm the guests reassemble for drinks in the same room; they dine together with the hosts at 8.30. The food is cordon bleu, the bread and cakes home-made." In winter, guests come for fox hunting and rough shooting; except for private parties, the hotel is closed February and March. "The cost is reasonable, the service good provided guests don't expect it all hours of the day." More reports please.

Open All year except Feb, Mar. Dining room closed for lunch.
Rooms 1 suite, 3 double, 1 single – all with bath.
Facilities Sitting room, dining room. Garden, paddocks. Sailing, boating, fishing, bird watching nearby; hunting and shooting in winter.
Location From Borrisokane take Portumna Road; take first right after Borrisokane; after 3 m turn left into Aglish village.
Restrictions Not suitable for &. Smoking forbidden in bedrooms, discouraged in public rooms. Dogs by arrangement.
Credit cards Amex, Visa.
Terms [1990 rates] B&B IR£18–IR£22; dinner, B&B IR£32–IR£37. Set dinner IR£16. 50% reduction for children under 12; special meals.
Service/tipping: "Tipping at guests' discretion."

BALLINA Co Mayo   Map 6

Mount Falcon Castle   *Tel* Ballina (096) 21172
Ballina   *Fax* (096) 21172
                                            Telex 40899

"I loved its uniqueness. I wasn't asked to sign in. I didn't get a room key. The delightfully furnished room was the size of a small bungalow. Everything was home-produced, including butter, jam and marmalade. Cora, the wolfhound, takes a little getting used to, but once she has her chair by the fire in the lounge she is very relaxed. Anytime I am in the area, I will stay again." This grey stone mansion, dating from 1876, lies just south of Ballina in the beautiful wild countryside of County Mayo. It is excellent for fishing, being set in a large estate on the banks of the River Moy, on which it has eight miles of rights. The castle was bought in 1932 by Constance Aldridge and her husband, Major Robert, to entertain their fishing friends and has been run ever since as a country house hotel, grand yet informal. Log fires and fresh flowers greet you in the reception rooms; bedrooms are large and comfortable. In country house style, dinner is at a fixed time; guests are seated at the long mahogany table with the hostess, now in her eighties, at its head. Menus make use of the best local produce, straightforwardly cooked; there's plenty of local salmon (*Mount Falcon* produces its own excellent gravad lax), local meat and game and vegetables grown on the estate farm. (*Michael Kenefick*)

Open 1 Apr–31 Jan. Closed Christmas.
Rooms 9 double, 1 single – all with bath and shower.
Facilities Drawing room, sitting room, dining room. 100-acre grounds with tennis court, woodland, pasture, river frontage with fishing; shooting in winter. Riding nearby; golf 10 m.
Location 4 m S of Ballina on Foxford road.
Restrictions Not suitable for &. No smoking in dining room.
Credit cards All major cards accepted.
Terms (Excluding 10% service charge) B&B IR£40; half board IR£52.50; full board IR£60. Set lunch IR£7.50 (by arrangement), dinner IR£16.50. Weekly rates; special rates for family holidays. 1-night bookings sometimes refused at height of fishing season. Reduced rates for children; special meals.

BALLINDERRY Co Tipperary   Map 6

Gurthalougha House   *Tel* Borrisokane (067) 22080
Ballinderry, Nenagh

"It's a little scruffy at the edges, but the owners were friendly and the food was excellent," writes a visitor this year to this 19th-century house set on the shores of Lough Derg at the end of an avenue which winds for a mile through 150 acres of forest. In the grounds are woodland walks with a great variety of wildlife – squirrels, badgers, otters, hawks, jays and kingfishers. In the distance are lovely views to the mountains of Clare and Galway. The gentle informality of Michael and Bessie Wilkinson (he the cook, she front of house) has appealed to many readers. Dinners are entirely by candle-light, served in a room furnished in the simple elegance of a by-gone age. There is a small, daily changing menu. Bedrooms have been described as the sort Lord Peter Wimsey might easily have occupied – "The bathroom (and bath) were easily the largest we've seen anywhere." "It's a bit cold in winter," writes another visitor this year, "but worth its place in the Guide." (*S and W Beresford, Esler Crawford, and others*) One dissenter appreciated the dinner, thought the dining room and lounge attractive, but hated the many clashing colours in her bedroom.

Open All year except Christmas, 1 week in June. Restaurant closed for lunch; snacks by arrangement.
Rooms 8 double – 6 with bath, 2 with shower, all with telephone.
Facilities Sitting room, library, TV room, dining room. 150-acre grounds with forest walks, gardens; ½ m lake shore with private quay, safe bathing, boats, ghillie available; windsurfing, pony trekking.
Location On shores of Lough Derg, W of Ballinderry village, which is 16 m N of Nenagh. (Signposted from Borrisokane.)
Restrictions Not suitable for &. No small children or dogs in dining room.
Credit cards Access, Amex, Visa.
Terms B&B IR£27–IR£35. Set dinner IR£19.50. Weekend breaks. 33% reduction for children under 10; high teas.
Service/tipping: "Tipping at guests' discretion."

Please write and confirm an entry when it is deserved. If you think that a hotel is not as good as we say, write and tell us.

BALLYLICKEY Co Cork   Map 6

Sea View House Hotel   *Tel* Bantry (027) 50073
Ballylickey, Bantry   *Fax* (027) 51555

A friendly, unpretentious, comfortable hotel set in five-acre grounds three miles north of Bantry, with good views over Bantry Bay and distant mountains. It is run by Kathleen O'Sullivan with "an unbeatable combination of integrity, thoughtfulness for her guests, good house-keeping and a real talent for cooking". Initial impressions disappoint (Ballylickey lacks character), but readers warm to *Sea View*'s welcome and service. "The food was consistently very good, and the breakfasts outstanding. The atmosphere of the place was simply great fun." "The whole range of seafood (scallops, seafood crêpes, prawns, the 'bouquet of seafood', superb pink river-trout, fish mousses) was particularly worthy of note. Good sound wine list, reasonably priced. Wide variety of Irish dishes." Packed lunches are available, and tea and cakes in the afternoon. Nine large bedrooms were added last year, and all rooms redecorated. Little recent feedback. More reports welcome.

Open 15 Mar–31 Oct.
Rooms 9 suites, 8 double – 12 with bath, 3 with shower, all with telephone. 2 in cottages in garden. 1 ground-floor room with shower for ♿.
Facilities Lounge, TV room, cocktail bar, 2 dining rooms. 5-acre grounds. Game fishing, sea fishing, pony trekking, boating, beaches and golf nearby.
Location 3 m N of Bantry towards Glengarriff, 70 yds off main road.
Restriction No dogs in public rooms.
Credit cards Access, Amex, Visa.
Terms (Including 10% service charge) [1990 rates] B&B: single IR£27.50–IR£32.50, double IR£45–IR£64, suite IR£55–IR£70. Set dinner IR£17.50. Midweek and weekend breaks. Reduced rates and special meals for children.
Service/tipping: "10% service charge shared equally among all staff."

BALLYMOTE Co Sligo   Map 6

Temple House   **BUDGET**   *Tel* Sligo (071) 83329
Ballymote

A Georgian mansion in 1,000 acres of farmland and woods enters our pages this year. It overlooks Temple House Lake (excellent for coarse fishing) and the ruins of the castle built by the Knights of Templar in 1200 AD; it has been the home of the Percevals for more than three centuries. There are two sitting rooms with open fires; and five bedrooms, all with central heating and electric blankets. "The bedrooms and public rooms are magnificent – far better than any top London hotel; but don't expect London service. Mrs Perceval cooks and serves the food. Only 12 persons can stay at one time, and everyone sits around one large dining table. It was like being invited to a dinner party each night, never knowing who the other guests would be. Boats on the lake are free and fishing rods may be borrowed. It remained light until 11 pm, so fishing was possible after dinner – a wonderful way to relax. The most beautiful place I have stayed at for years." (*ML Dodd*) The farm is run organically with particular attention to conservation; on Tuesdays there are "special treats for serious music lovers". More reports welcome.

Open Easter–30 Nov.
Rooms 2 suites, 2 double, 1 single – 1 with bath, 2 with shower.

Facilities 2 sitting rooms, dining room. Formal terraced garden. 1,000-acre farm and woodlands, lake; coarse fishing, boating.
Location 14 m S of Sligo on N17, signposted from Dublin. Ask for directions in Ballymote at Esso Garage.
Restrictions Not suitable for &. No dogs.
Credit cards Amex, Visa.
Terms B&B IR£25–IR£28; dinner, B&B IR£40–IR£43. Midweek breaks. Reductions for long stays. Reduced rates for children; special meals if required.
Service/tipping: "Service charge not added. Tips not expected, but occasionally offered, and much appreciated."

BALLYVAUGHAN Co Clare   Map 6

Gregans Castle Hotel
Tel Ennis (065) 77005
Fax (065) 77111

"Tremendous value, peaceful setting. Full marks for comfort and welcome." "Staff particularly friendly and helpful." Peter and Moira Haden's country house hotel is in the heart of the Burren, an area roughly halfway between Galway and Shannon airport, full of rare flowers and plants (alpine and arctic), a paradise for botanists and ornithologists. It is also rich in historic and prehistoric remains, and Yeats and Lady Gregory lived nearby. The Hadens have invested much thought and money in the interior and the gardens. Readers continue to appreciate the "large, tastefully furnished rooms" with no telephone or TV – the upper ones have particularly beautiful views over Galway Bay – and the suites, some with patio. The beds are firm, the bathrooms spotless, and the bar, library and lounges relaxing. "And the croquet was the best of all the hotels we visited." In the past we have reported criticisms of the food, both its quality and its quantity, but almost everyone has been satisfied this year: "The menu is well balanced and generous and we were pressed to try extra items." "Food beautifully cooked and presented." (*Michael Wace, Amanda Stuart, Mrs L Hill, and others*) But one reader felt service in the dining room was a little brisk.

Open Easter–late Oct.
Rooms 6 suites, 9 double, 1 single – all with bath and shower. 3 on ground floor.
Facilities Hall, lounge with TV, library, bar, dining room. 12-acre grounds with parkland, gardens, croquet. Safe, sandy beach 4½ m; harbour with swimming and boating 3½ m.
Location On N67 between Ballyvaughan and Lisdoonvarna, 3½ m SW of village, at foot of Corkscrew Hill.
Restriction No dogs.
Credit cards Access, Visa.
Terms (Excluding 12½% service charge) B&B: single IR£58, double IR£76. Set dinner IR£20; alc lunch available. Half-board rates for 3 or more nights. Reduced rates for children; special meals.

BANTRY Co Cork   Map 6

Bantry House
Bantry
Tel (027) 50047

César award: Best bed-and-breakfast – Irish style

In a spectacular setting overlooking Bantry Bay and the Caha mountains is a grand classical Irish country house, open to the public but offering accommodation in two newly decorated wings. It is owned by Mr and Mrs Shelswell-White; he is a direct descendant of Richard White, first Earl of Bantry. It enters our pages with an inspector's high praise: "The house is magnificently situated overlooking the water. Dark green gates set into a high stone wall flanked by lodges are all that can be seen from the road. When one arrives there is not a great deal of available service or 'human contact', but one is constantly aware of the thought and care behind the operation." *Bantry House* guests have the use of a separate sitting room, billiard room, dining room and television room. "The bedrooms are pretty, warm and comfortable. Fresh milk, home-made biscuits, tea- and coffee-making facilities are on the landing, and requests are dealt with promptly and kindly. There's a lovely new breakfast room". The countryside surrounding Bantry is delightful, and nearby are small cheese-makers, good little restaurants, and the studios and workshops of artists and potters. It is a great area for sailing and water sports, "a trifle more chilly than the Mediterranean, but much cleaner". In 1990, *Bantry House* began providing dinners to residents by arrangement on weekdays in the summer months. We would welcome reports on these. Meanwhile *O'Connor's Seafood Restaurant* in Bantry is recommended.

Open All year.
Rooms 1 suite, 7 double – all with bath and shower, telephone.
Facilities Sitting room, billiard room, dining room, TV room. Occasional concerts in library. 20-acre grounds, near sea. Sandy beach $\frac{1}{4}$ m.
Location On outskirts of Bantry, via gate lodge and private avenue.
Restrictions Not suitable for &. Dogs in grounds only.
Credit cards Access, Amex, Visa.
Terms (Service included) [1990 rates] B&B IR£35–IR£40. Set dinner IR£18. Wine licence only. Reduced rates for children; special meals.

BLESSINGTON Co Wicklow   Map 6

Tulfarris Hotel and   *Tel* Naas (045) 64574
   Country Club   *Fax* (045) 64423
                                                  Telex 60915

A new recommendation, Maureen and Barry Pocock's "country house par excellence, in a delightful setting by a lake, the main building dating from 1760, with a new courtyard complex sympathetically added. The food is superb. Service was friendly and efficient and the owner took time to talk to his guests. The lounge has a fireplace of unusual design and the fire was lit even on an August evening. Our bedroom was huge, as was our double bed, with all facilities and a lovely bathroom. It's on the edge of the beautiful Wicklow mountains and very tranquil, yet only 25 miles from Dublin." (*Mrs A Fletcher*) There are two restaurants, the *Tulach Fearghuis* room for gourmet dining and the cheaper *Courtyard Bistro*. The hotel has a health and fitness centre with a swimming pool, is surrounded by its own nine-hole golf course and has two floodlit tennis courts and direct access to Blessington Lakes with fishing, sailing and windsurfing. More reports please.

Open All year.
Rooms 4 suites, 16 double, 1 single – all with bath, shower, telephone, radio, TV. Some, on ground floor, suitable for &.

Facilities Ramps. 2 lounges, 2 bars, 2 restaurants. Conference facilities. Health centre with indoor swimming pool. 50-acre grounds with 9-hole golf course, tennis, lake with fishing, sailing, windsurfing.
Location 6 m S of Blessington off N81. Turn left at Poulaphouca.
Restriction No dogs in public rooms.
Credit cards All major cards accepted.
Terms (Service at guests' discretion) [1990 rates] B&B (Irish): single IR£57.50–IR£82.50, double IR£75–IR£115. Set meals: bistro IR£20, restaurant IR£29. Weekend rates. Reduced rates for children sharing parents' room; special meals on request.

CASHEL BAY Co Galway   Map 6

Cashel House Hotel
Tel Clifden (095) 31001
Fax (095) 31077
Telex 50812

Well-established manor house hotel, an oasis in the rugged wilderness of Connemara, at the head of Cashel Bay in 50-acre estate with prize-winning garden and woodland walks, hard tennis court, tiny private beach, ponies and horses for trekking. "Most delightful hotel I've visited for many years'," writes one enthusiast, but in italics as others criticise upkeep, service, decor and cooking. We hope just a temporary bad patch. Open 10 Feb–5 Jan, possibly closed Nov. 32 rooms – all with bath and shower. B&B IR£44–IR£64; set dinner IR£23.50 (excluding 12½% service charge). More reports please.

CASTLEBALDWIN Co Sligo   Map 6

Cromleach Lodge Country House
Castlebaldwin, Nr Boyle
Tel Sligo (071) 65155
Fax (071) 65455

Admired for its superb setting on a hillside above lovely Lough Arrow, *Cromleach Lodge* offers spreading vistas with hardly a house in sight – rural Ireland at its best. Here an ambitious local couple, Christy and Moira Tighe, have enlarged their own home into a sophisticated guest house – nine more rooms with bath have been added since last year. The cooking is serious and professional. Breakfast, served on unusual Rosenthal china, includes good home-made wheaten bread and preserves. (*Rosemary Reeves*) Some find the decor in the bar/lounge and bedrooms over-ornate, and the piped mealtime music irritating.

Open All year except 22–31 Dec. Restaurant closed for lunch and on Sun.
Rooms 12 double, 2 single – all with bath and/or shower, telephone, radio, TV, tea-making facilities.
Facilities Lounge, 2 dining rooms, private dining room. 1-acre garden in 30-acre farm. Private access to Lough Arrow; boating, surfing. Hotel can arrange fishing, walking, hill climbing and archaeology trips.
Location 10 m N of Boyle, off N4 Dublin–Sligo road. Turn E at Castlebaldwin.
Restrictions Not suitable for &. No smoking in dining room, 1 lounge, some bedrooms. No dogs.
Credit cards Access, Amex, Visa.
Terms B&B single IR£18–IR£48, double IR£96. Set dinner IR£22. 30% reduction for children sharing parents' room; special meals (before 7 pm).
Service/tipping: "Optional" 10% service charge added to bills. Shared among staff.

CASTLEHILL Co Mayo   Map 6

Enniscoe House   *Tel* Crossmolina (096) 31112
Castlehill   *Fax* (096) 31112
Nr Crossmolina, Ballina   *Telex* 40855

Fine Georgian country house on shores of Lough Conn in attractive setting of 150-acre grounds with gardens, woodland and working farm. Antiques, family portraits, open fires; bedrooms with canopied and 4-poster beds, views of parkland and lake. Relaxed, comfortable atmosphere, "sympathetic traditional hospitality". Private landing stage, boats and ghillies available for fishing; riding arranged. Closed Jan. 7 double rooms, all with private facilities. B&B IR£35–IR£45. Set dinner IR£16. Recent nomination. More reports please.

CORK Co Cork   Map 6

Arbutus Lodge Hotel   *Tel* Cork (021) 501237
Montenotte   *Fax* (021) 502893
                                                   Telex 75079

"We have never eaten in a better restaurant – anywhere. We were sorry we could stay only one night," wrote a reader last year. "A lovely house with beautiful views, a wonderful restaurant, and the true hospitality of a warm Irish family," wrote another more recently. *Arbutus Lodge*, once the home of the Lord Mayor of Cork, is run by the Ryan family, father, mother, two sons and their wives. It is named for the arbutus tree in its prize-winning garden, which has many rare trees and shrubs. The house is in the posh suburb of Montenotte, fifteen minutes' walk or five minutes' drive from the centre of town. It was built about 1800, a master cooper's house, and some rooms still reflect the solid virtues of its origins. Others, in the modern extension grafted on either side of the main building, are "more functional than beautiful", and there has been criticism this past year both of decor and room maintenance. The candle-lit restaurant is spacious, with starched white table-cloths and fresh flowers; it has a large bay window giving a view of the city and river below. Michael Ryan serves fine Irish meat and seafood, and offers a "tasting menu" (six courses *plus* sorbet and coffee) as well. (*Mrs JC Smye, HF King, Cathryn Bryck, and others*) There is a good wine list, though one reader felt IR£18 [1990] a high price to pay for one of the least expensive bottles. The work of contemporary Irish artists is shown in the public rooms.

Open All year, except 24–30 Dec. Restaurant closed Sun (bar meals available).
Rooms 8 double, 12 single – all with bath and/or shower, telephone, radio, TV, baby-listening.
Facilities Lounge, bar, 2 dining rooms. 1-acre garden with patio and croquet.
Location 1½ m up hill from town centre. Parking.
Restrictions Not suitable for &. No dogs.
Credit cards All major cards accepted.
Terms B&B: single IR£30–IR£75, double IR£60–IR£98. Set lunch IR£15.25, dinner IR£19.25; full alc IR£27. Weekend rates; gourmet weekends. Reduced rates and special meals for children.
Service/tipping: "No service charge. Guests should tip only if they receive exceptional service."

DUNLAVIN Co Wicklow   Map 6

Rathsallagh House   *Tel* Naas (045) 53112
                                                Fax (045) 53343

Kay and Joe O'Flynn's "very grand" country house in huge grounds
35 miles from Dublin had its first Guide entry last year. "It's a long block
of converted Queen Anne stable buildings surrounded by untold acres of
lawns, croquet, golf, a gurgling brook somewhere nearby, and sheep and
horses everywhere, close enough to see, far enough not to disturb. Kay
O'Flynn cooks, wonderfully, he runs the large farm and co-hosts at
night." There are ten guest rooms, "warm and of extreme luxury", each
with a "generous bathroom with a huge tub and bath sheets rather than
towels; cupboards galore, tea trays, bookshelves – with the right books.
Dinner, after pour-yourself drinks in the drawing room, was four courses
of delicate joy. At night the beds were made ready and, as we seemed in
need of coddling, hot-water bottles inserted to help us sleep. In the
morning, after a dip in the indoor solar-heated swimming pool, an Irish
breakfast awaits – freshly baked breads, rolls, toast, home-made jams,
eggs, black pudding, sausages and perfect bacon. The atmosphere is said
to be welcoming and "tranquil except perhaps on the nights of the local
hunt meeting" – *Rathsallagh* is a good base for hunting with some of
Ireland's leading packs, and horses may be hired. (*Gitta Sereny, Neil
O'Kennedy*)

Open All year except 18 Dec–2 Jan.
Rooms 10 double – all with bath (most also have shower), telephone, tea-making
facilities. 2 in courtyard.
Facilities Drawing room, sitting room, dining room, conference room; billiard
room, indoor heated swimming pool. 500-acre grounds with tennis, croquet, golf
academy, pheasant shooting, hunting.
Location 2 m SW of Dunlavin.
Restrictions Preferably no smoking in dining room and sitting room. No children
under 12.
Credit cards Access, Diners, Visa.
Terms [1990 rates] B&B IR£50. Set Sun lunch (winter only at 2.30 pm) IR£19.50,
dinner IR£21.50.
Service/tipping: "If guests feel service is especially helpful, tipping is acceptable."

GOREY Co Wexford   Map 6

Marlfield House   *Tel* Gorey (055) 21124
Courtown Road   *Fax* (055) 21572
                                                Telex 80757

The former dower house of the Courtown estate, a noble three-storey
Regency house in large grounds with a lovely garden, tennis and croquet,
is now Ray and Mary Bowe's sophisticated country house hotel, with
stylish, "if sometimes over the top" decor, lots of pictures and "lovely"
furniture, much of it antique. There's a "very grand" reception lounge
with Doric pillars, marble floor and 18th-century marble mantelpiece.
The bedrooms are immaculate and "luxurious in a private house way.
Bathrooms very well lit, with jacuzzi and everything you could possibly
want including an enormous bath sheet." Six sumptuous suites, each
decorated with a different "theme" – Irish, Georgian, French, etc – each

with a marble fireplace and large marble bathroom, are in a new wing. Breakfasts are "excellent", and *Michelin* awards a red "M" for the quality of the "modern French" cooking, using local produce and home-grown vegetables and herbs, served in the dining conservatory which is "pure fantasy, full of greenery and mirrors, with enormous hanging baskets of geraniums". Staff are "welcoming and highly competent". And *Marlfield House* is in a choice position, a mile from the sea with sandy beaches, close to a golf course, and with plenty of the beauty spots of Co Wicklow at hand. More reports please.

Open All year except Dec.
Rooms 7 suites, 12 double – all with bath, shower, telephone, TV; tea-making facilities, radio and baby-listening on request. Some on ground floor.
Facilities Reception drawing room, library, lounge bar, gallery, restaurant, conservatory. 36-acre grounds with tennis and croquet. Sea with sandy beaches and safe bathing 1 m.
Location 1 m from Gorey on the Courtown road.
Restrictions No smoking in dining room. No dogs.
Credit cards All major cards accepted.
Terms (Service at guests' discretion) [1990 rates] B&B: single IR£60–IR£75, double IR£110–IR£132, suite IR£176–IR£395. Set lunch IR£18, dinner IR£28. Weekend and midweek reductions in off season. High teas for children on request.

KANTURK Co Cork   Map 6

Assolas Country House and Restaurant

Tel Kanturk (029) 50015
Fax (029) 50795

"One of the most beautiful settings we have ever seen," wrote a reader recently. An elegant 17th-century manor house set in beautiful grounds beside a river, this has been the home of the Bourke family for more than 70 years. Everything denotes care and good housekeeping – the gravel *outside* the gate is raked, and the grass verges and hedges are neat and trimmed along the driveway. The lawns and tennis court slope away down to the river which comes complete with wooden bridge, weir, small boat and swans. The house, with white paint and green creepers, is well proportioned and the public rooms attractive: polished furniture, lovely ornaments, lots of books and candles, flowers, sparkling glass and damask napkins in the dining room. Readers endorse *Assolas* again this year: "It couldn't have been more charming," says one, but another found the food only average, and her bedroom, "though big enough to hold a dance in, was rather poorly furnished".

Open Mid-Mar–1 Nov.
Rooms 9 double – all with bath, shower (3 have whirlpool), telephone. 3 in courtyard building.
Facilities 2 lounges, restaurant; private dining room. 7-acre grounds with gardens, tennis, croquet, river with boating and trout fishing. Salmon fishing and golf nearby.
Location 3½ m NE of Kanturk; turn off road towards Buttevant.
Restrictions Not suitable for &. No babies. No dogs.
Credit cards All major cards accepted.
Terms B&B: single occupancy IR£48–IR£55, double IR£80–IR£145. Set dinner IR£25. 1-night bookings refused if for more than 1 month ahead. Reduced rates for children sharing parents' room.
Service/tipping: "Our prices are fully inclusive. Tipping is actively discouraged; if guests still tip in appreciation the money is pooled and shared by all staff."

KENMARE Co Kerry   **Map 6**

Hawthorn House   `BUDGET`   *Tel* Killarney (064) 41035
Shelbourne Street

A reasonably priced bed and breakfast (the restaurant has been closed) in
a town with a wide choice of places to eat. "The decor is very frilly, but
that is the end of my grouse," writes a visitor this year. "It is run superbly.
Enormous thought has gone into the rooms. Fruit and chocolate biscuits
await you; there are nice magazines, paperbacks and books on the birds
and flora of Ireland. We had drinks in the little sitting room where
everyone was introduced. A party of young Dutchmen were directed to a
good 'singing pub'; others went to a restaurant. I'm glad we chose the
small breakfast plate: a regular one consisted of six rashers of bacon, three
sausages, and an egg, all of good quality and perfectly cooked. It is a
wonderful base in a charming little town, with magnificent scenery all
around." More reports welcome.

Open All year except 2 weeks midwinter and 3 days Christmas.
Rooms 6 double, 2 single – all with bath or shower; TV in 3 rooms.
Facilities Lounge, breakfast room.
Location In centre of town, but quiet. Parking.
Restrictions Not suitable for &. No dogs.
Credit cards None accepted.
Terms (No service charge) [1990 rates] B&B (Irish): single from IR£18, double
IR£30–IR£36. (No restaurant.)

Park Hotel Kenmare   *Tel* Killarney (064) 41200
                                                  Fax (064) 41402
                                                  Telex 73905

"A grand hotel in the old sense, a little stuffy, but with outstanding food."
"Superb grounds, comfortable public rooms, courteous and helpful staff."
"Surroundings delightful, dinner and breakfast faultless." "Extremely
well run. Not cheap, but well worth it." Continuing praise for this
substantial grey mansion built at the turn of the century as a railway hotel
and set in a park with beautiful views of the Kenmare estuary and the
mountains of west Cork. The decor is impressive – a magnificent oak
staircase, antiques and good paintings in the public rooms. Bedrooms, for
the most part, are spacious. The restaurant, under Matt Darcy, offers
French style cooking with Irish ingredients; it is one of only two
establishments in the Republic to earn a *Michelin* rosette. There is a long
and varied wine list. (*Dr R Wise, Mrs JC Smye, G Berneck and Dr C
Herxheimer, and others*) One reader found the combination of pianist,
harpist and muzak (albeit at different times) too intrusive; another
complained of the price charged for a small room. Francis Brennan, the
owner, tells us 31 rooms have been completely renovated this year,
giving the hotel "some of the biggest bedrooms in its grade in the
country". More reports please.

Open 23 Dec–2 Jan, Easter–mid-Nov.
Rooms 9 suites, 37 double, 3 single – all with bath and/or shower, telephone,
radio, TV, baby-listening. Ground-floor rooms.
Facilities Ramps, lift. Drawing room, cocktail lounge, TV/games room,
restaurant. 11-acre grounds, with tennis, golf and croquet. Rock beach, safe
bathing, fishing 5 mins' walk.

Location 60 m west of Cork, adjacent to village. Signposted.
Restriction No dogs.
Credit cards Access, Visa.
Terms Dinner, B&B: single IR£115–IR£128, double IR£224–IR£264, suite IR£334–IR£396. Set lunch IR£16.50, dinner IR£36; full alc IR£55. Christmas and New Year programmes. Reduced rates for children sharing parents' room; special meals.
Service/tipping: "Service included. Tips at guests' discretion."

LETTERFRACK Co Galway   Map 6

Rosleague Manor Hotel   *Tel* Letterfrack (095) 41101
Letterfrack, Connemara   *Fax* (095) 41168

A Regency house in twenty-acre grounds seven miles north of Clifden, overlooking a sheltered bay surrounded by mountains and forests. "A five-star recommendation: I came for three days away from urban, pre-packaged supermarket living. It could not have answered the demand better – about the only thing that comes from a package here is cornflakes. The food is virtually one hundred percent home-grown or locally caught, with fish at the top of the bill. The wines are notably cheaper than in other Irish hotels of this standard. But the real quality of *Rosleague* lies in the atmosphere. The first thing you notice is that there is not a TV to be seen; the second is that there is not a clock in sight: no one is reminded of the passing of time, the Marschallin in *Rosenkavalier* would have loved it. She might even have gone into the bar and met the locals." Well situated for walks in Connemara National Park, the hotel is also recommended for the view: "I could see eleven mountains from my bedroom without craning my neck." Patrick and Anne Foyle, brother and sister, are warm and welcoming hosts: "They welcomed my 70-year-old parents, who had arrived chilled to the bone and luggage-less from a delayed flight. Patrick turned up the heat in the room with the canopied bed, offered whiskies, and laid on sandwiches next to the fire in the lounge an hour later – smoked salmon and smoked chicken. A beautiful 'old house' feel about the place." (*John Higgins, M M Marlowe, and others*)

Open Easter–Nov.
Rooms 21 rooms – all with bath and/or shower, telephone. 2 ground-floor rooms.
Facilities Drawing room, sitting room, conservatory cocktail bar, billiard room, dining room. 20-acre grounds, tennis court, path to water's edge.
Location 7 m Clifden, 1 m Letterfrack, on the road to Leenane/Westport.
Restrictions No smoking in dining room. Dogs by arrangement in bedrooms, not in public rooms.
Credit cards Access, Visa.
Terms (Service at guests' discretion) B&B single IR£40–IR£55, double IR£60–IR£100, suite IR£90–IR£120. Set dinner IR£21.

MALLOW Co Cork   Map 6

Longueville House and   *Tel* Mallow (022) 47156
   Presidents' Restaurant   *Fax* (022) 47459

A noble Georgian mansion set in a 500-acre wooded estate above the Blackwater river, sometimes called the Irish Rhine. It belongs to Michael and Jane O'Callaghan whose family owned the land centuries ago, until Cromwell confiscated it and demolished their castle. The public rooms are stylishly decorated and there are family portraits and antiques. One of the glories of the house is its Victorian conservatory, full of graceful ironwork. "The kitchen is now the heart of *Longueville*," write the O'Callaghans, whose son, William, is chef. He spent a year with Raymond Blanc and cooks with flair. An inspector this year, while appreciating an excellent dinner, had some reservations: "No one greeted us on arrival (an inner office door was shut on us!), we were given a smallish room on the top floor even though the place wasn't full, the bed linen wasn't good – pillow cases off-white and badly ironed – and breakfast wasn't up to the standard usual in country house hotels: unfresh orange juice, very poor scrambled egg (which tasted smoky). Good bread, weak tea. This is an elegant mansion, closer in style to a hotel than a country house, with, regrettably, a 'take it or leave it' attitude." More reports please.

Open 1 Mar–20 Dec.
Rooms 13 double, 3 single – all with bath and/or shower, telephone, radio, TV.
Facilities Drawing room, cocktail bar, restaurant, small conference room. 500-acre estate with gardens, croquet, 2 m fishing on River Blackwater.
Location 4 m W of Mallow on Killarney road.
Restrictions Only restaurant suitable for &. No smoking in dining room (if absolutely necessary, small second dining room available). No children under 10. No dogs in house.
Credit cards All major cards accepted.
Terms B&B: single IR£50–IR£55, double IR£90–IR£130. Set lunch IR£16, dinner IR£20–IR£28.
Service/tipping: "No service charge. Tipping not encouraged, but if guests insist money is distributed evenly every month."

MOUNTRATH Co Laois   **Map 6**

Roundwood House   *Tel* Portlaoise (0502) 32120

💱 *César award in 1990: Outstanding Irish hospitality*

"The house is pure Palladian, somewhat plain, set in pleasant parkland with some huge sweet chestnut trees and a couple of donkeys as well as two thoroughbred fillies grazing underneath. The library, drawing room and dining room are beautifully proportioned, comfortable and well-furnished; central heating kept the place warm and there were open fires as well." "Dinner is served around a large table for all guests. The food was excellent, with perfectly cooked vegetables and as much as was requested." "The host and hostess are charming and children are welcomed. Good wines, good everything. Dying to go again!" Three happy readers praise the traditional Irish hospitality at *Roundwood House*, owned by Frank and Rosemarie Kennan. It lies in large grounds in the shadow of the unspoilt and beautiful Slieve Bloom Mountains. For children there are games to play, woods to explore, animals to feed. The parkland may be a bit neglected in places, the house rather ramshackle, but correspondents continue to endorse an earlier report extolling the purism of this "architectural gem". The writer of that report had a room with authentic 18th-century furniture and Georgian colours. No curtains on the window, only shutters. The carpet was quite threadbare, but accurately chosen, she felt, for the old-world look. The service was faultless, prices very reasonable. Verdicts: "Highly recommended for anyone passing through the middle of Ireland." "I was bowled over. A great sense of effortless hospitality overwhelms you as soon as you set foot in it." (*Martin L Dodd, JR Bennett, Eithne Scallan*)

Open All year except Christmas Day.
Rooms 6 double – all with bath.
Facilities Drawing room, library, dining room. 18-acre grounds with croquet, swings, stables. Golf, river fishing nearby.
Location N7 from Dublin to Limerick. At Mountrath turn right at T-junction, then left on to Kinnitty Rd. Proceed 3 m exactly.
Restrictions Not suitable for &. No dogs in bedrooms or public rooms.
Credit cards All major cards accepted.
Terms B&B: single occupancy IR£32, double IR£52. Set lunch IR£10, dinner IR£17. Reduced rates for children sharing parents' room; special meals.
Service/tipping: "No service charge. Full profit-sharing system in operation so no tipping necessary. The result is that staff don't care who tips and who doesn't."

MOYARD Co Galway   Map 6

Crocnaraw Country House   *Tel* Clifden (095) 41068
Moyard, Connemara

Lucy Fretwell's Georgian country house on the shores of Ballinakill Bay, set in twenty acres of prize-winning gardens and fields with fine views, "is not a hotel in the accepted sense. It is slightly frayed around the edges, and full of character, all odd shapes, nooks and crannies. The decor is quite idiosyncratic, a mixture of furniture styles with a variety of rugs scattered randomly; the effect is a kind of charming rusticity. There are two lounges, one small, almost monastic in style, with comfortable, but not 'easy chair' seating, mainly used by non-resident diners, the other large, with vast couches and chairs into which you sink almost without trace. Nothing matched, and there was a variety of artefacts around; the whole effect was pleasing and comfortable. Most bedrooms overlook the garden and the mountains beyond. Ours was large and light, with a bay window and an equally spacious bathroom with a large window. Food was good though with little or no choice (the brochure is slightly misleading as it says dinner is à la carte). Perhaps this was because it was very quiet when we were there. Our dog was welcomed too, and there is a house dog, small, elderly and friendly." (*Mrs S Tennent*) Seafood is a speciality of the restaurant when the weather allows. Good fishing, golf and beaches nearby. Only niggles: "The house is in need of some maintenance, and our bedroom might have been a little cleaner. But it certainly passed the 'would you return?' test."

Open May–Oct.
Rooms 7 double, 2 single – all with bath (2 also have shower) 1 on ground floor.
Facilities Drawing room, sitting room, dining room. 20-acre grounds with gardens, lake and woodland; croquet, donkeys and ponies. Golf, fishing, sandy beaches nearby.
Location 6 m N of Clifden on road to Westport.
Restrictions No dogs in public rooms. No children under 10.
Credit cards Amex, Visa.
Terms (Service at guests' discretion) [1990 rates] B&B: single IR£25–IR£30, double IR£50–IR£56; dinner, B&B: single IR£48, double IR£86–IR£92. Set alc lunch IR£10, dinner IR£18. 25% reduction for children; special meals if required.

OUGHTERARD Co Galway   Map 6

Currarevagh House   *Tel* Galway (091) 82312

Retaining the atmosphere of a bygone age with an emphasis on old-fashioned hospitality, this mid-Victorian country house is in a "blissfully quiet setting" in huge grounds on the banks of Lough Corrib and offers some of the best scenery and fishing in Ireland. Readers have praised the capacious beds, splendid bathroom fittings, Edwardian furniture and good home cooking, including a lavish help-yourself breakfast laid out on the dining room sideboard each morning. *Currarevagh* (pronounced curra-reeva) has been in the Hodgson family for five generations; it is now run by Harry Hodgson and his wife, June, "who are friendly and helpful, and a mine of information about the locality," writes a regular. "Because it lacks formal elegance and designer stylishness, it is comfortable and relaxing. The country house style food may disappoint some, but for us not to have to make decisions except about wine, and to know what to expect on a Friday, is a relief. Dinner is generally a roast with all the trimmings and second helpings are always available. Gradually over the years the meat has got rarer (when appropriate) and the vegetables crisper and more imaginative. The starters and desserts are light in touch." Another reader felt the dinners (with no-choice menu) were slightly uninteresting "but this was forgiven as the breakfasts and afternoon teas were *so* good; we had a super few days and were made to feel very welcome." (*Valerie Watson, Sara A Price; also HF King, Clare Fletcher*) The owners' young dog is said to be "fairly over-exuberant".

Open Apr–Oct. By arrangement other times for parties of 8 or more (except Christmas and New Year). Lunch by arrangement, for residents only.
Rooms 13 double, 2 single – 13 with bath, 2 with shower. 3 ground-floor rooms in mews.
Facilities Drawing room, sitting room, TV room, bar, dining room. 150-acre grounds with lakeshore fishing (ghillie available), boating, swimming, tennis, croquet. Golf, riding nearby.
Location 4 m NW of Oughterard on Lakeshore road.
Restrictions Not ideal for &. No smoking in dining room. Children under 12 by arrangement. Dogs by arrangement, only on lead in public rooms.
Credit cards None accepted.
Terms B&B: single IR£35–IR£45, double IR£70. Set dinner IR£16. Weekly rates. 1-night bookings sometimes refused for high season if booked too far ahead. Reduced rates for children sharing parents' room.
Service/tipping: "10% added for service and divided among all staff. Our problem used to be that front staff received tips (some quite large) and kitchen staff received nothing. Guests are asked not to tip individual members of staff."

PROSPEROUS Co Kildare   Map 6

Curryhills House Hotel   *Tel* Naas (045) 68150
Prosperous, Nr Naas   *Fax* (045) 68805

A large Irish farmhouse converted into a small family hotel, 'found' by inspectors last year: "West of Dublin, between the Kildare horse-breeding country (hence the horsey chatter of some guests) and the black peat-bogs (hence the fuel for the fire in the big salon/bar). Not a promising setting – but it's a pleasant Georgian farmhouse with modern additions, amid a garden newly landscaped by owners Billy and Bridie Travers, both much in evidence. An unpretentious country hotel with a wayward charm, its public rooms typically Irish-shabby, its bedrooms large, modern and comfortable. The basement dining room, a bit enclosed, serves goodish unsophisticated country food: the garlicky mushrooms come from a giant mushroom factory down the road. There's Irish traditional music and singalongs on Fridays and Saturdays in the bar, always filled with chatty local people. And why the name Prosperous? – in the 18th century this village was a wealthy textile-making centre." More reports welcome.

Open All year except Christmas week. Restaurant closed Sun, Mon, Good Friday.
Rooms 10 – all with double and single bed, bath, shower, telephone, tea-making facilities, baby-listening; TV on request. Ground-floor rooms.
Facilities Ramps. Lounge/bar, TV room, restaurant. Traditional Irish singing Fri and Sat. Award-winning gardens. Horse riding and racing, fishing, golfing nearby.
Location 30 km W of Dublin, 11 km NW of Naas. From N7 turn to Sallins, then straight road to Clane. Turn left at Jet station and proceed 2 m.
Restriction No dogs in public rooms.
Credit cards All major cards accepted.
Terms (Excluding 10% service charge) B&B: single IR£36, double IR£56. Set lunch IR£10.50, dinner IR£14.50; full alc IR£18. Children under 12 sharing parents' room charged for meals only.
Service/tipping: "At guest's discretion."

RATHNEW Co Wicklow   Map 6

Hunter's Hotel   **BUDGET**   *Tel* Wicklow (0404) 40106
Newrathbridge

One of Ireland's oldest coaching inns, which has been in the Gelletlie family for generations and is now owned and run by Mrs Maeve Gelletlie. It had an entry in earlier editions of the Guide and is now brought back by enthusiastic reports from several readers: "It's that rarity now in Ireland, the small family-owned and family-run hotel. Little has changed in the last quarter century except that a few more of the rooms have 'facilities' and the window frames rattle less than they did. Outside is a rambling garden with appropriately rambling roses, running down to a stream. Tea and whiskey are served throughout the day, usually jointly. A coal fire always burns in the diminutive bar. Food is copious – no hint of the *nouvelle* here – and fish is especially good. Don't expect a key to your bedroom. The old, honest style rules here." "Exquisite simplicity." "Excellent; polite staff, perfect food and service, very clean." (*John Higgins, Jan Morris, Andrew Reeves*)

Open All year. House guests only over Christmas/New Year.
Rooms 13 double, 4 single – 10 with bath and shower, all with telephone, tea-making facilities.
Facilities Lounge, TV room, bar, dining room. 5-acre gardens by river; fishing. Golf, tennis, riding, sea fishing nearby.
Location 28 m S of Dublin. Turn off N11 Dublin–Wexford at Ashford.
Credit cards All major cards accepted.
Terms B&B IR£27.50. Set lunch IR£11, dinner IR£16.

If you have had recent experience of a good hotel that ought to be in the Guide, please write to us at once. Report forms are to be found at the back of the book. Procrastination is the thief of the next edition.

Tinakilly House Hotel   *Tel* Wicklow (0404) 69274
                                                  Fax (0404) 67806

A grey stone mansion of monumental splendour, with views to the sea a
quarter-mile away, offering old-fashioned opulence – golden chandeliers
and sconces, polished dark wood, rococo fireplaces, softly upholstered
formal sofas and chairs, red carpets, potted plants, and a magpie
miscellany of glittering bric-à-brac. The rooms, including the 14 bedrooms, six of which have four-poster beds of imperial dimensions, are
large and high-ceilinged with tall windows. The splendour originated
with Captain Robert Halpin, one-time commander of Brunel's *Great
Eastern* who, in his retirement, constructed this remarkable building and
its bosky pleasure gardens. The present owner, William Power, is a
knowledgeable hotelier and many reports praise the friendly service and
also the food: "positively symphonic", "quite superb", "lightly cooked
and attractively presented". One reader demurred, "We wished the food
had reached the same heights as the hotel, and that the service in the
delightful dining rooms had been less casual." More reports please.

Open All year.
Rooms 1 suite, 13 double – all with bath and/or shower (4 also have whirlpool
bath), telephone, TV, tea-making facilities.
Facilities Hall, bar, residents' lounge, 3 dining rooms; conference facilities. 7-acre
grounds, tennis court. Golf nearby.
Location From Dublin on N11, go through Rathnew village on R750. House
signposted on left after about ¼ m.
Restrictions Not suitable for &. No children under 7. No dogs.
Credit cards Access, Visa.
Terms [1990 rates] B&B: single IR£60–IR£75, double IR£70–IR£100. Set lunch
IR£15, dinner IR£25. Discounts for stays of 3 nights or more. 1-night bookings
refused Christmas, New Year, Easter.
*Service/tipping: "We include a mandatory 10% service charge which is part of staff
remuneration. This saves clients embarrassment."*

RIVERSTOWN Co Sligo   Map 6

Coopershill   *Tel* Sligo (071) 65108
Riverstown   *Fax* (071) 65466
                                  Telex 40301 ATTN COOPERSHILL

💧 *César award in 1987: Outstanding Irish hospitality*

"As close to perfection as I have found", "The house is beautiful and
unspoilt, the hosts charming and attentive, the food delicious. I hope it
stays exactly as it is – any change would be for the worse" – two reports
this year on this grey-stone family mansion in the heart of Yeats country.
It stands in a spectacular position, with the Bricklieve mountains and vast
peat bogs to the south, and the town of Sligo and the sea to the north.
Many readers have endorsed an earlier report: "One of the grand houses
built by the landed Anglo-Irish families in the 18th century. It is situated
in a huge estate and in complete silence. The rooms are tall and gracious
and the furniture old-fashioned (five bedrooms have four-poster or
canopied beds). Do not expect a smart hotel – this is the home of an old
Irish family in which you are a welcome guest." Brian and Lindy O'Hara,
who own *Coopershill*, "are unobtrusive yet totally attentive to everyone's
needs". "Their hospitality was just right, and I wish we had stayed

longer." For those who do, there are many delightful walks and wildlife is abundant. (*Ann Duncan, GT Williams, Lise Chase*)

Open Mid-Mar–31 Oct. Out-of-season house parties by arrangement.
Rooms 6 double – all with bath and/or shower, tea-making facilities.
Facilities Halls, drawing room with TV and piano, dining room; table-tennis room. 500 acres woods and farmland with wildlife, large garden, river with coarse fishing. Trout fishing, sandy beach, championship golf course nearby.
Location At Drumfin crossroads, 11 m from Sligo–Dublin road (N4), turn to Riverstown. *Coopershill* signposted from Drumfin.
Restrictions Not suitable for &. Smoking in drawing room only. Dogs allowed, but not in house.
Credit cards Access, Amex, Visa.
Terms B&B IR£35–IR£43.50. Light lunch IR£5; packed lunches on request; set dinner IR£17.50. Reductions for stays of 3 nights or more. 50–75% reduction for children under 12 sharing parents' room; special meals on request.
Service/tipping: "Guests not expected to tip. But if they wish to money is distributed among the staff."

ROSEMOUNT Co Westmeath   Map 6

Coolatore House   **BUDGET**   *Tel* Athlone (0902) 36102
Rosemount, Moate

On the slopes of Knockastia – reputed centre of Ireland – rambling Victorian house in 12-acre "tree garden". Drawing room and library with antiques and family heirlooms; four guest bedrooms (one en suite, others with bathrooms nearby). Recommended for beautiful furnishings, "simple but decent dinner" (no choice, taken with other guests), modest terms. Fox hunting and lake fishing (coarse and game) arranged. Open all year, advance bookings appreciated. 4 rooms – 1 with bath. B&B: single IR£25, double IR£40–IR£50. Set dinner IR£15. (No lunch.) New nomination. More reports please.

ROSSNOWLAGH Co Donegal   Map 6

The Sand House Hotel   *Tel* Newport (072) 51777
                                              Fax (072) 52100
                                              Telex 40460

Named for the two-mile stretch of sandy beach at its doorstep, a welcoming purpose-built hotel owned and run by Mary and Vin Britton and their sons Conor and David. Guests come to *Sand House* to enjoy the views of Donegal Bay, the variety of water sports, and the riding, fishing and golf available nearby. Recent visitors have praised the delightful staff and the feeling of a caring family ownership, including "faultless service in the dining room". One especially appreciated the luxury of having the bedspread turned down, night-clothes laid out, and a hot-water bottle in the bed. Fish is a speciality (the hotel farms its own Donegal Bay clams, oysters and fresh mussels), and the cooking gets high marks. There is piped music in the dining room. However, not all care for the decor: "excruciating colour scheme", "claustrophobically patterned suites". More reports please.

Open 1 May–early Oct.
Rooms 2 suites, 32 double, 6 single – all with bath and/or shower, telephone, baby-listening. TV on request.
Facilities 4 lounges, TV lounge, lounge bar, residents' cocktail bar, restaurant, games room. Folk music Fri and Sat in high season. 2-acre grounds with tennis, miniature golf, croquet and paddock; on 2-mile safe sandy beach with swimming, canoeing, windsurfing (boards and canoes available at hotel). Fishing, golf, riding nearby.
Location On Donegal Bay 10 m S of Donegal Town. At Ballyshannon branch on to coast road and follow yellow signs.
Restrictions Not suitable for &. Some no-smoking areas. Dogs by arrangement, not in public rooms.
Credit cards All major cards accepted.
Terms B&B: single IR£30–IR£37.50, double IR£60–IR£80. Set lunch IR£9.50, dinner IR£17.50. Special breaks (3 or more days); golf and fishing holidays. Reduced rates for children sharing parents' room; children's dinner 6–7 pm.
Service/tipping: "10% added to room rates which is distributed to all staff. Restaurant service charge optional."

SHANAGARRY Co Cork   Map 6

Ballymaloe House   *Tel* Cork (021) 652531
Shanagarry, Nr Midleton   *Fax* (021) 652021
                                              Telex 75208

🐛 *César award in 1984: For generating house-party conviviality*

The usual crop of accolades for *Ballymaloe's* hospitality: the comfortable rooms, occasionally a bit shabby, the "admirable amalgam of friendliness and formality", the wonderful meals – "the selection of hors d'oeuvre such as I have never seen before, and the most perfect ice-cream I have ever eaten", "the very distinguished wine list", etc, etc. Myrtle and Ivan Allen's addictive hotel is a gracious rambling house, more Georgian than anything else though somehow also ageless, with a Norman keep on one side and relatively modern pink-washed cottages on the other. Decor is restrained and unfrilly, but the walls are full of Ivan Allen's exciting and varied picture collection. The bedrooms vary in size; most are quite large. "My room was more a suite than a bedroom: large bathroom with fresh large warm towels each day, six-foot bed large enough for three and supplied in expectation with six pillows, large sofa, ample drawer and cupboard space." Close to the house lies a 400-acre farm; and three miles beyond is the charming little fishing port of Ballycotton. Virtually everything you eat, apart from the fish, is home-grown or raised on the Allens' farm. "The grounds are delightful, complete with small lake and canoe, and flower-bordered stream with bridges crossing it which are perfect for playing 'Pooh sticks'. Children of all ages seem to pop up everywhere from nowhere." *Ballymaloe* is an exceptionally convivial house, with nearly all the extended Allen family contributing to the special quality of its hospitality. (*John Higgins, Mrs JC Smye, IT Glendinning, and others*) Only breakfasts disappointed: "Less good than anywhere else we stayed; we objected to paying *extra* for the smallest glass of orange juice."

Open All year except 23–26 Dec.
Rooms 28 double, 2 single – all with bath and/or shower, telephone, baby-listening. 12 in courtyard, 4 on ground floor suitable for &.

Facilities 3 sitting rooms, 5 inter-connecting dining rooms, TV room. 400-acre farm and grounds with tennis court, heated swimming pool, 5-hole golf course, croquet, children's play area; craft shop. Ballymaloe Cookery School and herb garden nearby. Sea 3 m, with safe sand and rock beaches; fishing, riding by arrangement.

Location 20 m E of Cork; 2 m E of Cloyne on Ballycotton road, L35.

Restrictions 1 dining room for non-smokers. No dogs in bedrooms or public rooms.

Credit cards All major cards accepted.

Terms (Excluding 10% service charge) B&B (continental) IR£41.25–IR£64. Dinner, B&B IR£66.50–IR£90. Set lunch IR£13, dinner IR£26.50. Winter bargain breaks. Special meals for children.

Service/tipping: "10% mandatory charge used for annual bonuses and weekly extras in pay packets. Customers and staff seem to like this arrangement as it is quite clear."

****

Traveller's tale *On the floor of our room was an aerosol with pictures of cockroaches on it. The room had not been cleaned. I don't mean it was not clean – it was dirty. You could take the dirt off the furniture with your finger and the bathroom had not been cleaned at all. One could – and did – write one's name in the dirt. I went down to the desk and asked the clerk what the aerosol was for. "Flies," he said. "Funny flies," I said, pointing to the graphic pictures of cockroaches milling over the can in droves. He shrugged, gallicly. "The room is filthy," I said. "Je me désole," he replied. "When will someone come to clean it?" "The daughter of the proprietor comes at five." She came, but not up. I went down. I told her of the state of the room, in English this time, which she spoke well. She came up and viewed dispassionately the filthy bath, and agreed that all was not as it should be. She didn't actually say so, but she may have grieved a bit. "Well, are you going to clean it?" I asked. She said she had a problem with her back – also with letting this room. "Particularly to me," I told her, and we left.*

****

Part two

Austria
Belgium
Denmark
France
Germany
Greece
Italy
Luxembourg
Malta
including Gozo
Morocco
The Netherlands
Norway
Portugal
including the Azores and Madeira
Spain
*including Andorra, the Balearics,
the Canaries and Gibraltar*
Sweden
Switzerland
including Liechtenstein
Turkey
Yugoslavia

Austria

Weinhaus Happ, Innsbruck

ALPBACH 6236 Tyrol   **Map 15**

Hotel Alpbacherhof   *Tel (05336) 5237*
                                                    Fax (05336) 5016

Set in a very pretty Tyrolean village where the skiing is good and the air
superbly clear, this pleasant family-run chalet-style hotel has an indoor
pool, a terrace and a garden, and it serves dinners by candle-light; most
rooms have a balcony with a view. "A real winner, in an idyllic spot,"
writes an enthusiast this year. "Herr Bischofer is a welcoming proprietor
and his staff are very friendly. Our bedroom and bathroom were both
massive." Others this year have concurred: "We were awakened by the
tinkling of cowbells." "You are constantly waited on hand and foot."
"They will even look after an aged parent for you." All agree about the
excellent service, and most reports praise the food, though one reader
warns that the à la carte meals are far better than the *en pension* ones
served in a room catering for package tours. The smaller and darker
rooms facing the road do not have a balcony. (*John Moseley, Thelma
Abbotson, Mrs Don Simecheck, and others*)

Open 16 Dec–30 Mar, 15 May–30 Sep.
Rooms 2 suites, 48 double, 5 single – all with bath and/or shower, telephone, radio, TV.
Facilities Lift. Bar, 2 lounges, TV room, restaurant; conference facilities. Indoor heated swimming pool. Terrace (for meals in fine weather); garden.
Location Alpbach is in a valley S of Innsbruck–Kufstein main road. Hotel is central. Parking.
Restriction Not suitable for &.
Credit card Visa.
Terms B&B 680–900 Sch; dinner, B&B 880–1,100 Sch; full board 150 Sch added. Set lunch 200 Sch, dinner 295 Sch. Reduced rates and special meals for children.

ANIF 5081 Salzburg   Map 15

Hotel Friesacher
Tel (06246) 2075
Fax (06246) 2075-49
Telex 632943

Anif is an attractive village and all-season resort just south of Salzburg, amid woods and mountains. The *Friesacher*, newly fitted out with solarium and fitness centre, is a sizeable modern chalet-style hotel with large neo-rustic bedrooms and scenic balconies overlooking meadows and hills. It continues to be liked, for its cooking, comfort, and friendly service. "Waitresses in pretty national costume serve good basic food either in the rather airless restaurant or in the garden." One annexe, five minutes' walk away, is near to a house where Herbert von Karajan once lived. The Friesacher family also own two cheaper restaurants close by which serve buffet-style meals. A recent visitor enjoyed eating outdoors and listening to accordion music at one of these. (*Richard Osborne, AJ Ormerod*) Another reader reports less attractive noises: traffic from the nearby main road, aircraft buzz from the airport.

Open All year except 2–17 Jan. Restaurant closed Wed.
Rooms 3 suites, 44 double, 7 single – 49 with bath, 5 with shower, all with telephone, radio, TV; many with balcony. 18 in annexe. Some ground-floor rooms.
Facilities Lift. Lounge, bar, dining room; conference facilities. Sauna, solarium and fitness room. Garden with café.
Location 4 km S of Salzburg. Leave *Autobahn* at Salzburg, turn right at Anif (1 km) and turn ½ km on road to Hellbrunn. Parking.
Restriction Not suitable for &.
Credit cards Access, Diners, Visa.
Terms B&B: single 580–780 Sch, double 880–1,180 Sch, suite 1,280–1,380 Sch. Set lunch 130 Sch, dinner 210 Sch; full alc 290 Sch. Reduced rates and special meals for children.

BERWANG 6622 Tyrol   Map 15

Sporthotel Singer   **BUDGET**
Tel (05674) 8181
Fax (05674) 8181-83

Berwang is a busy summer and skiing resort a few miles west of the towering Zugspitze, just off the Innsbruck–Stuttgart main road; here the Singer family's chalet-hotel, sizeable and fairly smart, stands on a pine-studded hillside. The owners' personal touch, the efficient and courteous staff, the good food and the spacious rooms with balconies have all been praised by recent visitors. "The facilities of bathing, sauna, massage, jacuzzi did not impinge on those looking merely to enjoy strolling in the countryside." One reader, visiting out of season, was dismayed to find an old people's bingo session in progress. But another "found it hard to manufacture even the smallest complaint". (*RS McNeill*) A new lounge and reception in Tyrolean style are being installed.

Open 19 Dec–7 Apr, 9 May–6 Oct.
Rooms 25 suites, 35 double, 10 single – 58 with bath and/or shower, all with telephone, radio; many with balcony; T V in suites and some double rooms.
Facilities Lift. Lounge, *Stüberl*, 2 bars, 2 restaurants; children's playroom. Dancing, Tyrolean evenings; fitness/sports centre with whirlpool, sauna and massage. Small garden with terraces.
Location 80 km NW of Innsbruck. Garages and open parking.
Credit cards Diners, Visa.
Terms B&B: single 510–980 Sch, double 860–1,720 Sch, suite 1,220–2,120 Sch. Set lunch 105–250 Sch, dinner 150–500 Sch; full alc 250–550 Sch. Reduced rates and special meals for children.

BEZAU 6870 Vorarlberg	**Map 15**

Gasthof Gams	*Tel* (05514) 2220
	Fax (05514) 2220-24
	Telex 59144

Renewed enthusiasm for the Nenning family's *gemütlich* and very personal hotel, a converted 17th-century coaching inn, with modernised bedrooms and public rooms decked out in traditional Austrian style. It adjoins green fields and wooded hills, on the edge of a quiet town beside the Bregenz forest. Two reports this year: "It combines many of the facilities of a much more upmarket hotel (jacuzzi, heated outdoor pool, etc) with the intimacy and unpretentiousness of a smaller one. Service is first rate, and the food freshly cooked and attractively prepared, with sensible use of local products such as Pfifferlinge and blueberries. The pool is kept scrupulously clean by Herr Nenning himself. The terraces were pleasant for meals in hot weather, and the views to the mountains are inviting. All very good value." "A charming place, with good food and a real welcome for children. The warmth of the welcome is genuine and the 'typical Austrian' atmosphere is unselfconsciously achieved. There are no group tours at this hotel." (*Alan Blyth, Melissa Maier, and others*) Rooms do vary in size.

Open All year except 1–18 Dec.
Rooms 6 suites, 18 double, 10 single – all with bath and/or shower, telephone, T V; baby-listening on request; some with balcony. Some ground-floor rooms.
Facilities Lift. Lounge, bar, 4 dining rooms; conference/functions rooms; games room, sauna, solarium, hot whirlpool; terraces. Large garden with swimming pool (heated May–Oct) and 3 tennis courts.
Location 30 km SE of Bregenz, 37 km NW of Lech. Central. Parking.
Credit card Access.
Terms B&B: single 430–580 Sch, double 780–820 Sch, suite 1,080–1,160 Sch; dinner, B&B: single 590–740 Sch, double 1,100–1,140 Sch, suite 1,400–1,440 Sch. Set lunch/dinner 160–400 Sch; full alc 320 Sch. Reduced rates and special meals for children.

If you are nominating a hotel, please err on the side of saying too much. Many suggestions have to be rejected only because they are too brief.

DÜRNSTEIN 3601 Niederösterreich   Map 15

Hotel Schloss Dürnstein   *Tel* (02711) 212
                                                              Fax (02711) 351
                                                                Telex 71147

"One of the world's most beautiful hotels"; "a warm welcome from Frau
and Herr Thiery, and breakfast a gastronomic experience"; "excellent
food on a spacious terrace overlooking the Danube" – three tributes this
year and last to this always-admired *Schloss*, which stands inside a lovely
old village (Richard Cœur de Lion was imprisoned here in 1192). It is
perched above the Danube, with spectacular views of the winding river
from most bedrooms. Built in 1630, it was owned by the Princes
Starhemberg for centuries, and was used as a refuge by the Emperor
Leopold I when he was fleeing from the Turks. Some 50 years ago it was
restored by the Thiery family, who still own and run it. Rather a formal
place, it has beautiful antique furniture both in the public rooms and in
the bedrooms. Recent views: "Breakfast on the terrace, with the birds
singing, is sheer perfection. Our comfortable room was both homely and
grand." "Our room the size of a tennis court was filled with antiques. You
live with the family as in a stately home, with no choice for dinner."
"Breakfast arrived on two huge trays and was placed on a genuine 16th-
century table in our room. Go there just for the history and romance."
(*M and D Chambers, Ruth H and Robert D Todd, Peter Brown*)

Open 22 Mar–8 Nov.
Rooms 2 suites, 31 double, 4 single – all with bath, shower, telephone, radio, TV;
baby-listening on request. Some ground-floor rooms.
Facilities Lift. Lounge, TV room, bar, restaurant, grill room with dance floor;
private dining room. Indoor and outdoor swimming pool; fitness centre. Terrace
overlooking Danube; fishing and boating.
Location At end of main street in village. Parking.
Credit cards All major cards accepted.
Terms B&B: single 950 Sch, double 1,450 Sch, suite 2,800 Sch; dinner, B&B: single
1,250 Sch, double 2,050 Sch, suite 3,500 Sch. Set lunch 280 Sch, dinner 350 Sch;
full alc 450 Sch. No charge for children under 6 sharing parents' room; special
meals.

EFERDING 4070 Oberösterreich   Map 15

Gasthof-Pension Dieplinger   **BUDGET**   *Tel* (07272) 3111
Brandstatt 4   *Fax* (07272) 3111-53

"Brandstatt is a tiny village on the Danube some 30 km west of Linz,"
writes our nominator this year. "The Dieplinger family have run the
Gasthof (restaurant) here for many years, right by the little port, and the
food is excellent, especially the fish. The *pension*, also right by the river, is
200 metres away. The two are very much run together by the family. The
rooms were excellent: those newly converted on the second floor are very
comfortable and tastefully furnished. Service can be a bit erratic, but is
always friendly and helpful. Wonderful bicycling along the river." (*Diana
Holmes*)

Open 1 May–31 Oct. Closed Thu.
Rooms 16 double, 4 single – all with shower, telephone; 3 with TV. All rooms in
annexe 150 metres from restaurant. Ground-floor room.
Facilities TV room, restaurant, conference facilities; terrace. Table-tennis room.

Location 3 km from Eferding on Passau–Leinz road. Parking.
Credit cards None accepted.
Terms B&B: single 330 Sch, double 620 Sch.

FILZMOOS 5532 Salzburg   Map 15

Hotel Hanneshof   `BUDGET`   *Tel* (06453) 275
Fax (06453) 574-21

In a skiing and summer resort at the foot of the Dachstein, about an hour by
road from Salzburg, the Mayr family runs this friendly and efficient chalet-style
hotel, spruce and modern, next to their butcher's shop. Indoor swimming pool,
good Austrian cooking, children welcomed. Closed November. 43 rooms, 20
apartments, all with bath or shower. B&B 340–670 Sch. Half board 420–790 Sch.
Recent nomination. More reports welcome.

FREISTADT 4240 Oberösterreich   Map 15

Gasthof Deim   `BUDGET`   *Tel* (07942) 2111
zum Goldenen Hirschen
Böhmergasse 8

Set on a wild granite plateau between Linz and the Czech frontier,
Freistadt is a handsome old town with towers, gateways and traces of
ramparts. Within these is the *Deim*, a genuine and remarkable old inn
with a pretty garden. A few years ago it inspired one reader to wax lyrical
(he wrote of "ancient walls, arched roofs, canopied beds, foaming beer
pots, antique furniture, happy laughing waitresses in local costume . . ."),
and this year too it has proved seductive: "A charming place that retains a
Leigh-Fermor feel of a *Mitteleuropa* adventure. The people are courteous
in a grave rather than effusive way, which is pleasant. Everything is
scrupulously, almost fanatically, clean. I enjoyed breakfast in an
atmospheric room, and dinner was approved too." "Beautiful and
charming, with flowers everywhere and the best goulash in Austria or
Hungary." "All modern conveniences and luxuries combined with old-
world charm" (but a few rooms may be somewhat basic). (*D Barr, C and
M Hédoin*)

Open All year.
Rooms 17 double, 6 single – 19 with bath and/or shower, all with telephone,
radio, TV.
Facilities Lounge, TV room, 3 restaurants. Garden.
Restriction Not suitable for &.
Location Central. Parking. Town is 40 km NE of Linz.
Credit card Diners.
Terms B&B: single 300 Sch, double 560 Sch; dinner, B&B: single 400 Sch, double
720 Sch. Set lunch/dinner 70–160 Sch; full alc 170 Sch. Reduced rates and special
meals for children.

> We quote either prices per room, or else the range of prices per
> person – the lowest is likely to be for one person sharing a double
> room out of season, the highest for a single room in the high season.

GARGELLEN 6787 Vorarlberg   Map 15

Hotel Madrisa   *Tel* (05557) 6331
Montafon   *Fax* (05557) 6331-82

A friendly family-run ski hotel ("a great place for children"), traditional in
style but well modernised: it stands next to nursery slopes in the lovely
Montafon valley, and would be good for summer as well as winter
holidays. "Simply wonderful," runs one recent report. "We had a large
airy room in the new wing, with a balcony facing the village church and
mountains beyond. The food was scrumptious, and the service very
friendly, with the Rhomberg family, the owners, much involved." Earlier
views: "The breakfasts were a wonderful array, and the evening meals
were imaginative." "The Rhomberg family carried our bags and gave us
extra bedding. The hotel exuded warmth, and generous amounts of food
appeared regularly. The value for money makes me blink when I think of
other ski resorts." The rooms in the older part have been called "ample,
warm and rustic", but unlike the newer ones they do not have a balcony.
(*I Fishman, and others*) One reader felt that the hotel's popularity and
increase in size was harming its personal touch.

Open 15 Dec–20 Apr, 20 June–29 Sep.
Rooms 5 suites, 48 double, 12 single – 54 with bath and/or shower, 49 with
telephone, 37 with radio; TV and baby-listening on request.
Facilities Lift. Hall, lounge, reading room, games room, *Stüberl*, dining room;
children's playroom (with children's films); disco; indoor swimming pool, sauna.
Large grounds with terrace, lawn, ski-lift.
Location 28 km S of Bludenz. In centre of Gargellen. Parking.
Credit cards Access, Amex, Diners (for extras only).
Terms Dinner, B&B 800–1,400 Sch in winter, 570–820 Sch in summer. Set meals
300 Sch; full alc 350 Sch. In skiing season bookings are normally for 1 week (Sat–
Sat). Weekly and Christmas packages. Reductions for children sharing parents'
room; special meals on request.

GRAZ 8010 Styria   Map 15

Schlossberg Hotel   *Tel* (0316) 80700
Kaiser Franz Josef-Kai 30   *Fax* (0316) 8070-160

A 400-year-old inn, newly renovated and enlarged, in a quiet but central
side street of Austria's second city. It has beamed ceilings and rambling
corridors, but a modern lift. "The staff are delightful," says a report this
year. "The hotel has been renovated to a high standard, with lovely
antiques and pale blue bedroom carpets. Excellent buffet breakfast served
in an attractive room." Roof garden with swimming pool; solarium and
fitness room. Back rooms quietest. (*Mrs Hilary Croft, K and S Bishop*)

Open All year except 22 Dec–2 Jan.
Rooms 5 suites, 16 double, 33 single – all with bath or shower, telephone, radio,
TV.
Facilities Lift. Bar, TV room; conference facilities. Roof garden with swimming
pool; solarium and fitness room.
Location Close to town centre. Parking.
Credit cards All major cards accepted.
Terms B&B: single 1,100–1,400 Sch, double 1,600–2,000 Sch, suite 1,300–
2,600 Sch. (No restaurant.)

HOF BEI SALZBURG 5322 Salzburg   Map 15

Hotel Schloss Fuschl   *Tel* (06229) 22530
                                                  Fax (06229) 2253-531
                                                  Telex 633454

The former hunting lodge of the prince-archbishops of Salzburg is today a most luxurious hotel – "truly elegant" says an admirer this year. It overlooks Lake Fuschl with the mountains as backdrop, 20 kilometres from Salzburg: you can lunch or dine overlooking the lake, where the sunsets can be spectacular. "A dream! Sparkling lake and lilac-lined gardens. Very good food, but tiny portions." Earlier accounts: "It retains much of its castle/hunting lodge atmosphere, despite addition of marble swimming pool and jacuzzi. *Nouvelle cuisine* very, very good, but also happy to serve us a lunch of pumpkin soup and smoked ham." (The food has also been described as "Austrian international".) "The staff were outstandingly welcoming and helpful." Rooms facing the roadway can be a bit noisy, owing to the influx of visitors: best are those facing the lake, or the chalets in the garden. Swimming both in an indoor pool and in the lake. (*Marie and Hans Haenlein, Mrs Don Simecheck*)

Open All year.
Rooms 23 suites, 56 double, 5 single – all with bath and/or shower, telephone, radio, TV. 61 in buildings in the garden. Some ground-floor rooms.
Facilities Salons, bar, 2 restaurants, conservatory; conference facilities. Indoor heated swimming pool, sauna, whirlpool. Large park with terrace for outdoor meals. Private beach and swimming area on lake, boat rental, surfing, sailing, tennis court and 9-hole golf course.
Location 20 km E of Salzburg; take road 158 to St Gilden; turn left 1 m after village of Hof.
Restriction Not suitable for &.
Credit cards All major cards accepted.
Terms B&B: single 1,050–1,950 Sch, double 1,900–3,500 Sch, suite 2,800–6,000 Sch. Set lunch 420 Sch, dinner 440 Sch. Children under 12 sharing parents' room free of charge; special meals on request.

****
Traveller's tale *The best of the house rules was the one pinned up in the bathroom. To avoid unnecessary noise – remember that "unnecessary noise" – we were instructed to fill the bath* slowly *and – wait for it – finish filling the bath using the shower-head, not the taps! Have you ever tried to do this? Do you know how long it takes? The explanation for this piece of high comedy was that the "architectural constraints" on the building made the plumbing rather noisy. The plumbing* was *noisy; it wasn't nightingales that kept us awake, but the sound of loos flushing, and basins swishing. Breakfast is syncopated by a relay of flushing lavatories.*
****

INNSBRUCK 6020 Tyrol   Map 15

Weinhaus Happ   `BUDGET`   *Tel* (0512) 582980
Herzog-Friedrich Strasse 14   *Fax* (0512) 86803
                                                          Telex 533511

"Right in the centre of the action", a small *Weinhaus*-cum-hotel in an old
street flanked with arcades that leads directly to the 15th-century
Goldenes Dächl (golden roof). Latest reports: "Clean, large rooms,
wonderful food." "A narrow winding staircase leads up to the reception
where Madame's welcome was warm; another two floors up, our large,
rather bare room had a small balcony overlooking the street." (*Sheryl
Thomsen, Angela and David Stewart, and others*) Some rooms are larger and
better furnished than others. The food has been found "very good and
copious" by some (notably the game in autumn), only adequate by
others, who suggest the *Weisses Kreuz* down the street as an alternative.

Open All year. Restaurant closed Sun.
Rooms 1 suite (for 4), 11 double, 5 single – 9 with bath and/or shower, all with
telephone, radio, TV.
Facilities Lift. 3 restaurants; conference facilities. Garden.
Location Central, in pedestrian zone. Garage 3 mins' walk.
Credit cards All major cards accepted.
Terms B&B: single 480–520 Sch, double 800–860 Sch, suite 1,200–1,300 Sch. Set
lunch/dinner 75–120 Sch. Reduced rates and special meals for children.

Gasthof Weisses Rössl   `BUDGET`   *Tel* (0512) 583057
Kiebachgasse 8

*Attractive, unassuming hotel in pedestrian zone in old part of town, owned and
run by the enterprising Plank family; commended for comfort, charm, good
breakfasts and dinners (Tyrolean dishes), fair prices. 14 rooms all with bath and
shower. B&B: single 600–780 Sch, double 900-1,080 Sch. Set menus 70–170 Sch.
Recent nomination. More reports please.*

KITZBÜHEL 6370 Tyrol   Map 15

Familien-Hotel Erika   *Tel* (05356) 4885
                                                          Fax (05356) 467413
                                                          Telex 51264

"The hiking and adventure hotel *Erika*" (as its brochure calls it), where
there's never a dull moment and you all join in the fun, might not seem
quite our sort of place. It's a large red mansion with a modern annexe,
beside a busy road junction at the edge of Kitzbühel. One visitor who had
completed her *forty-fifth* holiday there told us, "Uschi and Benedikt
Schorer work hard to please. One wet and cold day they produced paints
and sheets of glass and we were all put to painting on glass. On other
days, Mrs Schorer would take us up the mountains, or inflict an
adventurous bicycle ride on us, or Mr Schorer would take guests for a day
on the golf course. At the start of each walk or other fiendish activity, we
would all join hands in a circle, announce our name, profession and
where we came from. Drinks are served in the large garden, and light
classical concerts are held in the swimming pool area. Food is ample and

enjoyable." An informative orange leaflet, with the programme for the day, is handed out at breakfast – e.g. "Good morning, dear *Erika*-guest! This afternoon at 5 pm we will do some ARCHERY! Tomorrow we will organise a funny ERIKA–BICYCLE–TOUR!"

Two other recent visitors, admittedly Club Med freaks, have also succumbed: "The deft professionalism and the Austrian charm simply disarm criticism. The Schorers (their family have owned the *Erika* since 1920) are totally dedicated. The hotel has been sprucely modernised; bedrooms, most with balcony, are all comfy and homely. In summer, 80 per cent of guests are English. We were awestruck by the overall good humour and incredible value." (*JA and KA*)

Open All year except Oct–15 Dec and 10 Apr–15 May.
Rooms 36 double – all with bath, telephone, radio; baby-sitter on request.
Facilities 3 lounges, bar, restaurant. Indoor swimming pool, sauna, solarium and steam-bath. Garden with children's playground.
Location 3 mins' walk from town centre. Parking.
Restriction Not suitable for &.
Credit cards Amex, Diners, Visa.
Terms Dinner, B&B 550–620 Sch; full board 750–1,020 Sch. Reduced rates and special meals for children.

LANS 6072 Tyrol   **Map 15**

Gasthof "Zur Traube" Isserwirt   `BUDGET`   *Tel* (0512) 77261
Lans, Nr Innsbruck

In a pretty village above Innsbruck, with fine mountain views, Zur Traube *is a typical Tyrolean inn with flowered balconies. It has been run by the friendly Raitmayr family for 15 generations. The welcome, comfort and cooking are all admired. Closed 17 Oct–10 Nov. 24 rooms, all with bath and/or shower. B&B double 740–780 Sch. Set menus 140–150 Sch. Endorsed this year, but further reports welcome.*

LECH AM ARLBERG 6764 Vorarlberg   **Map 15**

Hotel Alexandra   *Tel* (05583) 2848
                                                              Fax (05583) 3150
                                                                 Telex 52550

A very friendly family-run chalet-hotel beside fields and hills, furnished in local style, with excellent cooking (notably the weekly buffet of "farmer's food"). Closed 16 Apr–22 June, 17 Sep–8 Dec. 19 rooms, all with bath and/or shower. Half board: summer 410–450 Sch, winter 780–1,140 Sch. Recent nomination. More reports welcome.

Hotels often book you into their most expensive rooms or suites unless you specify otherwise. Even if all room prices are the same, hotels may give you a less good room in the hope of selling their better rooms to late customers. It always pays to discuss accommodation in detail when making a reservation.

LIENZ 9900 Tyrol   Map 15

Hotel Tristachersee   *Tel* (04852) 67666
                                                                Fax (04852) 67699

Lienz, in the shadow of the Dolomites and not far from Italy, is the capital
of eastern Tyrol and "a delightful town". Just to its east, set amid
woodlands beside a small lake, is this attractive modernised hotel; the
dining terrace and the flowery bedroom balconies face over the water.
Two reports bring it into the Guide this year: "Run by the delightful
young Keuzers, who know their business. The surroundings are idyllic,
the rooms superb, the house wines very good." "Josef Keuzer has
renovated this beautiful old building and brought in an extremely able
chef. Austrian *nouvelle cuisine* is excellent. Medaillons of veal in a
chestnut sauce were the highlight of my holiday." (*AD Button, ML Dodd*)
But drinks prices are said to be high. More reports welcome.

Open All year except Nov.
Rooms 32 double, 12 single – all with bath, shower, telephone, radio, TV, baby-
listening.
Facilities Lobby, 2 restaurants, covered dining terrace. Indoor swimming pool.
Park with children's play area, bathing, fishing.
Location 5 km E of Lienz.
Restriction Not suitable for &.
Credit cards None accepted.
Terms B&B 450–690 Sch, suite 590–690 Sch; dinner, B&B 110 Sch added per
person. Set lunch/dinner 140–180 Sch; full alc 300 Sch. Reduced rates and special
meals for children.

MÖSERN BEI SEEFELD 6100 Tyrol   Map 15

Hotel Lärchenhof   `BUDGET`   *Tel* (05212) 8167

Recently modernised, the Holzer family's seductive, small chalet-style hotel,
6 km SW of the big resort of Seefeld, has panoramic views of the Inn valley and
makes a good centre for skiing and summer walking. Welcoming ambience; log
fire in the lounge, chaises-longues on the terrace. Good breakfasts; good value
overall. Light evening meals available. Open May–November, 15 Dec–5 Apr.
24 rooms, all with bath or shower. B&B 240–460 Sch [1990]. Recent nomination.
More reports please.

MUTTERS 6162 Tyrol   Map 15

Hotel Restaurant Muttererhof   `BUDGET`   *Tel* (0512) 587491
Nattererstrasse 20   *Fax* (0512) 587491-5
Mutters, bei Innsbruck

Mutters and Natters are two pretty villages just south of Innsbruck. This
year there's been more debate among Guide readers as to the merits and
defects of the neat flower-girt *Muttererhof*, run by twin sisters, and facing
a "breathtaking" landscape. On the whole, the ayes again have it, as
witness this American's report: "A dream come true! Our three-day stay
was perfection. Our room was large, furnished very nicely, with a view of
the Alps and the tiny village of Natters looking like a toy. The staff were
always scrubbing and polishing. The kitchen is in full view of the guests

and it sparkles. Of the few small dining rooms, we were shown into the loveliest, a small panelled room. The food was well prepared and generous. There was an aura of gaiety; Frau Stark-Egger, the manager, joined us, and we felt like guests in a friend's home. Breakfasts were the best of our trip." Another report concurs: "A home from home." But a third speaks of uninspiring decor, lack of lounge, and dour staff. And not all rooms are large or have a sunny balcony. The big heated swimming pool is commended. (*Norma Kessler, Ian Harris*)

Open 22 Dec–6 Apr, 10 May–20 Oct.
Rooms 1 suite, 18 double, 1 single – all with bath and/or shower, telephone; many with balcony.
Facilities Hall, bar, *Stüberl*, restaurant; functions room. Indoor swimming pool, sauna and solarium. Garden.
Location 6 km SSW of Innsbruck, S of Natters, E of Gotzens.
Restriction Not suitable for &.
Credit cards Access, Amex, Visa.
Terms B&B 330–440 Sch; half board 400–540 Sch; full board 490–600 Sch. Set dinner 130 Sch; full alc 220–250 Sch. Reduced rates and special meals for children.

ST NIKOLA 4381 Oberösterreich   Map 15

Donau-Hof **BUDGET**   *Tel* (07268) 8107

In a small village on a scenic stretch of the Danube known as Strudengau, east of Grein. Smilingly friendly Frau Aigner's hotel has a young, willing staff, very good food at fair prices, fine river views from room balconies. Patio where meals can be taken. Sauna, fitness room; outdoor pool close by. 18 rooms, all with bath or shower. Dinner, B&B single 390–420 Sch [1990]. New nomination. More reports please.

SALZBURG 5020   Map 15

Hotel Elefant   *Tel* (0662) 843397
Sigmund-Haffnergasse 4   *Fax* (0662) 840109
                                                   Telex 632725

Tall, narrow and medieval, this typical Salzburg townhouse stands on a quiet street right in the city's historic heart; it has been an inn for 400 years. The area is pedestrian: you can drive your car up to load or unload, but the police may ask questions. The hotel has been renovated, and recent visitors have been mainly satisfied. Most bedrooms are said to be pleasant and comfortable, though some may be rather dull and functional. The renovated restaurant has been judged attractive, and its cooking reasonable if unremarkable. "We had a top-floor double room, quiet and pretty, not at all small, with a fine view of the cathedral. Helpful front desk, and delicious buffet breakfasts." "A delightful hotel and an interesting meal." (*Patrick Barclay, RAL Ogston, Liz and Tom Piatt*) A serious criticism this year of a firm booking not honoured, and failure to apologise.

Open All year.
Rooms 1 suite, 26 double, 10 single – all with bath and/or shower, telephone, radio, TV. Ground-floor rooms.

Facilities Lift. Lounge, bar, TV room, breakfast room, dining room; conference facilities.
Location Central. Municipal parking 5 mins' walk away.
Credit cards All major cards accepted.
Terms [1990 rates] B&B 450–600 Sch; dinner, B&B 600–750 Sch. Reduced rates and special meals for children.

Pension Nonntal   *Tel* (0662) 841427
Pfadfinderweg 6–8   *Fax* (0662) 8467006

Otto and Anna Huemer run a small and homely *pension* with a pretty garden in quiet residential south-east Salzburg, with a spectacular view of the Hohensalzburg fortress, and only ten minutes' walk from the centre. Readers this year and last have written of the Huemers' kindness to their guests, of the "warm family atmosphere", "excellent breakfasts" and comfortable rooms with antiques. "Our room was quiet and romantic, overlooking floral gardens, and Herr Otto was an outstanding host," write Americans. "A warm welcome, and home-cooked Austrian dishes in a cosy restaurant." (*Diana Holmes, Dave and Gaye Yerrick, and others*) However, some visitors have been critical of the food, or have found some rooms shabby. Those in the main building are judged better than those in the annexe.

Open All year except 1–28 Nov. Restaurant closed Sun.
Rooms 4 suites, 10 double, 4 single – all with bath or shower, telephone. 10 with TV. 8 in annexe. 2 ground-floor rooms.
Facilities Salon/breakfast room, restaurant with bar; functions room. Garden with terrace and lawns. Bicycles available.
Location In SE suburbs. Leave *Autobahn* at Salzburg-Süd, take Friedensstrasse, Hellbrunnerstrasse, Hofhaymer-Allee, Nonntaler Hauptstrasse. Frequent buses to city centre. Free transport by hotel's bus from station or airport.
Restriction No smoking in breakfast room.
Credit cards Access, Amex, Visa.
Terms B&B: single 650–700 Sch, double 850–1,100 Sch; dinner, B&B: single 850 Sch, double 1,200–1,500 Sch. Set dinner 245–450 Sch. Children under 6 free of charge. Special winter/weekend arrangements.

Hotel Schloss Mönchstein   *Tel* (0662) 8485550
Mönchsberg Park 26   *Fax* (0662) 848559
                                                       Telex 632080

Once the guest house of an archbishop, now an expensive hotel, this dun-coloured, creeper-covered *Schloss* stands high on the Mönchsberg just above central Salzburg, but is easy of access: a lift service, running till 2 am, whisks you up in 30 seconds from the tourist hurly-burly below. A large and pleasant garden, antiques in the halls and dining room, spacious rooms, and breakfast on a flowery terrace are among the assets – but oddly there is no lounge. "Friendly welcome, excellent service, a lovely room and very good food: worth every schilling," writes one recent visitor. (*C and M Hédoin*) 1990 visitors were equally enchanted: "Really special. A delightful suite overlooking a charming garden. Dinner *nouvelle cuisine*, but enjoyed without reservation." (*Sqn Ldr and Mrs RGW Adams*)

Open All year.
Rooms 6 suites, 11 double – all with bath and/or shower, telephone, radio, TV, mini-bar; baby-listening on request; 24-hour room service. Ground-floor rooms.

Facilities Lift. Bar, café, restaurant; terrace. Chapel for weddings. Weekly concerts. Large garden with tennis court.
Location Above Salzburg on Mönchsberg – hotel is signposted. 3 mins by car from city centre, 7 mins by the Mönchsberg lift. Parking and garages.
Credit cards All major cards accepted.
Terms B&B: single 1,400–2,000 Sch, double 2,300–4,900 Sch, suite 4,100–6,200 Sch. Set lunch 350–750 Sch, dinner 550–1,200 Sch; full alc 570 Sch. Reduced rates for children; special meals on request.

Hotel Zistelalm `BUDGET`   *Tel* (0662) 20104
Auf dem Gaisberg   *Fax* (0662) 20104-200

Situated 1,000 metres up on the Gaisberg just east of the city, this gemütlich *chalet-style mountain* Gasthaus, *owned by the Hauser family, caters for skiers in winter, walkers in summer. Good food and beer, swimming pool in a meadow, rustic decor. Closed 21 Oct–21 Dec. 26 rooms, 15 with bath and shower. B&B 250–490 Sch. Set lunch from 135 Sch, dinner from 250 Sch. Recent nomination. More reports please.*

SCHLOSS ROSENAU 3924 Niederösterreich   **Map 15**

Museumsverein `BUDGET`   *Tel* (02822) 8221
 Schloss Rosenau   *Fax* (02822) 8221-8

The village of Schloss Rosenau, not far from the Czech border, lies amid quiet rolling countryside, good for walking and cross-country skiing. The yellow-fronted *Schloss* from which it gets its name is now partly a remarkable 18th-century Masonic museum and partly a hotel – outwardly grand-looking but with fairly simple bedrooms. "Mainly it's an excellent restaurant, with Czech-influenced cuisine – best calf's liver I've ever eaten," runs a recent report. "Bedrooms plain but acceptable, owner accommodating." Others agree about the good wines and food – tasty, plentiful and imaginative. "Rooms nicely heated. Host most attentive, carried my luggage to the room himself. Heated pool, delightful walks, lots of cross-country skiing." (*Mary Clark*)

   Note The *Schloss* has close links with the *Pension Weissenhofer* next door, and guests who book may find themselves sleeping at the *Pension*, unless they specify.

Open All year except 25 Jan–28 Feb.
Rooms 1 suite, 17 double – all with shower, TV, baby-listening.
Facilities Lift. Dining room, 2 *Stüberl*. conference and banqueting rooms; sun terrace. Masonic museum and baroque church. Park with covered heated swimming pool, sauna, 2 tennis courts and miniature golf.
Location 8 km SW of Zwettl.
Credit cards All major cards accepted.
Terms B&B 320–400 Sch; half board 410–490 Sch. Set lunch/dinner 120–150 Sch; full alc 200–400 Sch. Reduced rates and special meals for children.

Please don't be shy of writing again about old favourites. Too many people feel that if they have written once, years ago, there is no need to report on a revisit.

SCHRUNS 6780 Vorarlberg   Map 15

Hotel Krone `BUDGET`   *Tel* (05556) 2255
Fax (05556) 4879

Schruns is a pleasant market town in the Montafon valley, and near its
centre is this small hotel, all wood panelling, chintzy curtains and cosy
Gemütlichkeit – "A gem," says a recent visitor. The Mayer family have run
it for four generations, and readers continue to enjoy their hospitality, and
the food, service and comfort. "The Mayers maintain a keen interest in
the running of their hotel and the behaviour of the staff reflects their
simple kindness. Our meals were beautifully planned, delightfully
cooked and served with great charm." (*BJ Walter*) More reports welcome.

Open 20 Dec–7 Apr, mid-May–end Oct. Restaurant closed Thu.
Rooms 8 double, 1 single – all with bath, shower, telephone, radio; TV for hire.
Facilities Lounge, bar, 2 restaurants. Garden terrace; river frontage with trout
fishing.
Location 12 km SE of Bludenz. Central, near the Kronen bridge. Parking.
Restriction Not suitable for &.
Credit card Diners.
Terms B&B 310–420 Sch; dinner, B&B 450–550 Sch; full board 550–660 Sch. Set
lunch 140–160 Sch, dinner 160–190 Sch; full alc 210 Sch. Reduced rates and
special meals for children.

SEEHAM 5164 Salzburg   Map 15

Hotel Walkner   *Tel* (06217) 550

*Endorsed this year by returning regulars, this friendly modern family-run hotel
is in a rural setting near a lake, amid flattish but attractive scenery 20 km north
of Salzburg, near Mattsee. Lovely gardens with pool, wide stone-flagged terrace
with views where meals are served when fine. Goodish Austrian food, with
help-yourself salads. Airy bedrooms. Open 23 Mar–30 Oct. 24 rooms, most with
private facilities. B&B: single 400–700 Sch, double 700–1,240 Sch. Set meals
180–240 Sch. Fuller reports welcome.*

VIENNA   Map 15

Hotel Amadeus   *Tel* (01) 638738
Wildpretmarkt 5   *Telex* 111102
Vienna 1010

Praise enough to make any Salieri jealous has been heaped by readers
on this *Amadeus*, a modern hotel in a small street near St Stephan's
Cathedral. "Tasteful and comfortable rooms, quiet at night." "Flowers
everywhere, fine prints on the walls, staff all very pleasant. The
bedrooms and public rooms are decorated in red and white like the
Austrian flag; the hotel is fully carpeted with rich red rugs; there are
crystal chandeliers throughout." Visitors have especially enjoyed the
buffet breakfast, and one thought the atmosphere "pure Maria Theresa
and delightful". (*Roger Diamond*)

Open All year except over Christmas.
Rooms 18 double, 12 single – all with bath and/or shower, telephone, radio; 22 with TV.
Facilities Breakfast room.
Location Central, down a small turning off Tuchlauben.
Restriction Not suitable for &.
Credit cards All major cards accepted.
Terms B&B: single 1,210–1,385 Sch, double 1,555–1,780 Sch. (No restaurant.)

Hotel Kaiserin Elisabeth
Weihburggasse 3
Vienna 1010

Tel (01) 515260
Fax (01) 515267
Telex 112422

In an historic building down a side street near St Stephan's, a demure traditional hotel where Liszt and Wagner were once guests. This year, a guest enjoyed the enthusiastic welcome and varied buffet breakfast (it includes porridge). "Charming, efficient staff and a delightful room with wooden beds." Rooms are mostly quiet, but front ones may have some traffic noise. (*Mrs Hilary Croft, Paul Palmer*) No restaurant, but snacks are available all day.

Open All year.
Rooms 3 suites, 46 double, 14 single – all with bath and/or shower, telephone, radio, TV.
Facilities 2 lifts. Lobby with bar, lounge.
Location Central, in pedestrian zone near cathedral. Parking arrangement with nearby garage.
Credit cards All major cards accepted.
Terms B&B: single 800–1,150 Sch, double 1,400–1,700 Sch, suite 1,950 Sch. Extra bed 260 Sch. (No restaurant.)

König von Ungarn
Schulerstrasse 10, Vienna 1010

Tel (01) 5265200
Fax (01) 515848
Telex 116240

Few citizens of newly democratic Hungary look back with much love to their old monarchy, but this "King of Hungary" continues to rule over the affections of its Guide visitors. Honeymooners in 1990 found the food delicious and the staff friendly. Others have written: "A very romantic art-nouveau-decorated hotel in the heart of old Vienna. Excellent courteous service." It's a finely restored 16th-century building close to St Stephan's, its glass-domed courtyard now an attractive lounge "where an inspired variety of cocktails is served". Everyone praises the "warm and helpful" staff, also the buffet breakfasts and the rooms (those at the back are quietest). "When you go through the fine bevelled-glass doors you have the feeling of entering an exclusive club." The elegant and fashionable restaurant, under separate ownership, is good but very expensive. One pleasant touch is that the hotel provides its guests with daily reports, in three languages, on places to visit and other suggestions for the day. (*Jeannette and Guy Hubbard, Ruth H and Robert D Todd, Julia and Nigel Rhodes*)

Open All year.
Rooms 70 beds – 28 rooms with bath, 4 with shower, all with telephone.
Facilities Lift. Lounge, bar, TV room, children's room, restaurant (under separate ownership).

Location Central, near St Stephan's Cathedral, but in a maze of one-way streets.
Parking.
Terms B&B: single 1,500–1,800 Sch, double 1,750–2,000 Sch.

Pension Nossek   *Tel* (01) 5337041
Graben 17   *Telex* 113113
Vienna 1010

Dr Renato Cremona's high-ceilinged old-world *pension* was founded by
his grandmother before 1914, and now he runs it together with two
sisters, who are judged "very friendly and helpful". It occupies the top
floors of a stately office building, in the fashionable Graben, a traffic-free
street in the heart of town. And it has again won a lot of praise this year:
"We had a charming suite, staff were delightful, breakfast was good."
"Atmosphere friendly; constant boiling-hot water; generous breakfasts."
Most rooms are large, clean and airy, but not all have yet been renovated,
prompting the comment this year: "Furnishings are strictly Salvation
Army, but it made little difference considering the fantastic location, fair
price and warm hospitality." (*C and M Hédoin, Darrell R Lund, WG Francis,
and others*)

Open All year.
Rooms 3 suites, 16 double, 8 single – 18 with bath, 6 with shower (but no wc), all
with telephone.
Facilities Lift. Reading room, breakfast room.
Location On corner with Habsburgergasse. Central, but quiet. Underground
carpark 1 min's walk.
Restriction Not suitable for &.
Credit cards None accepted.
Terms B&B: single 300–700 Sch, double 800–900 Sch, suite 1,100 Sch. (No
restaurant.)

Hotel im Palais Schwarzenberg   *Tel* (01) 784515
3 Rennweg 2   *Fax* (01) 784714
Vienna 1030   *Telex* 136124

*The stately home of the von Schwarzenberg family since the 18th century, now a
sophisticated hotel with fine restaurant; the present Prince still owns it. Bombed
during the war, but faithfully reconstructed. Only 15 minutes' walk from the
Opera, but in its own big park. Guests stay in the former stables and servants'
quarters. Praised this year for its food, lovely dining room and bedrooms, but
some bedrooms are small, and "petty meanness" and muddles have been
criticised in past. 38 rooms, all with bath. B&B 1,500–2,250 Sch [1990]. Re-
nominated this year. More reports welcome.*

Hotel Römischer Kaiser   *Tel* (01) 5127751
Annagasse 16   *Fax* (01) 5127751-13
Vienna 1010   *Telex* 113696

Built in 1684 as the private palace of the Imperial Chancellor, and today a
small, very personal and fairly luxurious hotel, with period furnishings
and plenty of chandeliers. It is very central, just off the Kärntnerstrasse,
but in a traffic-free road. A very personal slant this year: "I had been

warned that the Viennese notion of modernism got stuck in the 1950s, and so it was here – room largely panelled in pleasant wood, wallpaper a sort of Jugenstil pattern. I thought the furniture unprepossessing, an echo of the *Zweites Rokoko* that Franz Josef was so fond of. But the staff were friendly, and the room well looked after. My main complaint is the noise – late revellers leaving nearby discos, then the bells of the Annakirche ringing from 6.15 am." (*David Wurtzel*) No restaurant: lots nearby. More reports welcome.

Open All year.
Rooms 23 double – all with bath, shower, telephone, radio, T V, air-conditioning.
Facilities Lobby with bar, breakfast room.
Location Central, near opera house and cathedral.
Restriction Not suitable for &.
Credit cards All major cards accepted.
Terms B&B: single 1,300–1,600 Sch, double 1,700–2,400 Sch. (No restaurant.)

Hotel Sacher
Philharmonikerstrasse 4
Vienna 1015

Tel (01) 51456
Fax (01) 51457-810
Telex 112520

Heaven knows what Hapsburg ghosts are hiding behind the red velvet drapes of this famous old Viennese institution, founded in 1876. Nowadays it has slipped out of the limelight but we've had two favourable reports recently, one from a reader who has made over 20 visits in as many years: "Family owned and run, its Grand Hotel atmosphere is mitigated by quite a personal touch. Maybe it trades too much on its role in past Viennese history, but it has now been modernised, for example, the hall has air-conditioning in summer. The restaurant is a bit too selfconsciously Viennese, but it is good – though the much-hyped Sachertorte is actually better in other pastry shops. Decor is traditional Austrian with many original paintings. One upstairs bit of the restaurant has zither music at times, played perhaps by a distinguished professional musician on his day off. The place is expensive, but one is not rooked" – "Luxury, courtesy and a romantic atmosphere. We had dinner in the Red Salon, so evocative that I expected Crown Prince Rudolph to walk in at any moment." (*FM Steiner, M and D Chambers*)

Open All year.
Rooms 4 suites, 86 double, 37 single – all with bath and/or shower, telephone, radio, T V.
Facilities Lift. Bar, 3 restaurants, 2 cafés.
Location Central, near the Opera. Garage opposite.
Credit cards All major cards accepted.
Terms [Until April 1991] B&B: single 1,450–3,200 Sch, double 2,950–4,400 Sch, suite 8,800–13,200 Sch. Children under 12 free of charge.

Pension Suzanne
Walfischgasse 4
Vienna 1010

Tel (01) 5132507

This pension *close to the Opera House has its entrance next to a sex shop, but is comfortable and quiet (double-glazing) and has pleasant Viennese furnishings (handsome beds and tables, fine mirrors, decent pictures). Staff a bit scatty but pleasant and helpful. 34 beds, most rooms with bath or shower. B&B 380–445 Sch [1990 rates]. Few recent reports; more welcome.*

VILLACH 9500 Carinthia   Map 15

Romantikhotel Post   *Tel* (04242) 261010
Hauptplatz 26   *Fax* (04242) 26101420
                                               Telex 45723

In a town on the old Vienna–Venice road, a former 16th-century palace which has been a hotel for 250 years (Empress Marie Thérèse stayed here). Bedrooms combine character with modern comforts; friendly service; excellent breakfast buffet and main meals, which you can eat in the pretty garden. 80 rooms, all with bath and/or shower. B&B: single 450–700 Sch, double from 880 Sch. Set meals 200–300 Sch. Recently endorsed. More reports please.

WAGRAIN 5602 Salzburg   Map 15

Hotel-Gasthof Moawirt   **BUDGET**   *Tel* (06413) 8818
Schwaighof 123

Wagrain is an all-year resort backed by forested hills south of Salzburg, just off the *Autobahn* to Villach. Outside it stands this spruce modern flower-decked chalet, commended again recently: "Quiet, comfortable and spacious. We were the only guests and did not arrive till 8.15 pm, but they opened up the kitchen for us: splendid trout and wines." "Charming owners, the Maurers; a large spotless room with balcony, and good dinners and breakfasts." The attractive countryside is perfect for summer walking and winter skiing (a chair-lift is opposite the hotel). Traffic can be audible from front rooms. More reports please.

Open All year.
Rooms 23 double, 4 single – all with bath or shower, telephone, radio, TV, baby-listening; many with balcony.
Facilities Lift. Lounge/bar, TV room, breakfast room, dining room; folk music once a week. Sun terrace and garden. Bathing in private lake.
Location About 75 km S of Salzburg, just off Salzburg–Villach *Autobahn*.
Credit cards Access, Amex, Diners.
Terms [1990 rates] B&B 250–470 Sch; dinner, B&B 360–630 Sch. Reduced rates and special meals for children.

WEIZ 8160 Styria   Map 15

Romantikhotel Modersnhof   *Tel* (03172) 3747
Büchl 32   *Fax* (03172) 3747-2

Outside a pleasant town amid lovely wooded hill-country north-east of Graz, here's quite an elegant modern hotel – a low white building with balconies beside a swimming pool. Dropped from last year's Guide through lack of feedback, it is now brought back by two reports: "Clean and pretty; excellent dinner, delightful owner." "Attractive, quiet setting beside apple orchards. The Maier family are warm and friendly. Delightful to sit on the terrace. Restaurant a bit lacking in character, but food was well cooked and imaginative." (*C and M Hédoin, Roger Diamond*)

Open 1 Apr–10 Jan.
Rooms 7 double – all with bath, shower, telephone, radio, TV.
Facilities Lounge, breakfast room, bar, restaurant; terrace. Garden with swimming pool and tennis court.
Location 3 km SE of Weiz which is 25 km NE of Graz.
Restriction Not suitable for &.
Credit cards All major cards accepted.
Terms B&B: single 850 Sch, double 1,250 Sch; dinner, B&B: single 1,300 Sch, double 2,150 Sch. Set lunch 350 Sch, dinner 450 Sch; full alc 425 Sch. Reduced rates and special meals for children.

****

Traveller's tale *Service throughout was appalling: incompetent, slow, and graceless. The final straw was approaching the c. 12-foot-long reception desk and (politely) asking the sulky-looking receptionist for the bill. Without looking up she gestured "Over there" towards a colleague. On my stupefied "What did you say?" she repeated irritably "Over there" and returned, presumably, to contemplation of the disasters of her love life. The other one took about half an hour to make the usual mess of coping with the minicomputer's presentation of the bill and dealing with the credit card.*

****

****

Traveller's tale *We were told that the dining room was open at 7.30. It was – but not for dinner! The waitress would take no orders other than for aperitifs until, at 8, "himself" entered and made a somewhat prima donna-ish tour of the tables. He took our order at 8.15. We were tired and not pleased – and said so. He superciliously told himself off for being un mauvais garçon. Thereafter our service was of such rapidity as to be positively unpleasant – with seconds between courses.*

****

Belgium

Hôtel Les Ramiers, Crupet

AARTSELAAR 2630 Antwerpen　　　　　　　　　　　　**Map 9**

Hostellerie Kasteelhoeve　　　　　　　　　　*Tel* (03) 457.95.86
Groeninghe　　　　　　　　　　　　　　　　*Fax* (03) 458.13.68
Kontichsesteenweg 78

A 17th-century manor just south of Antwerp, stylishly transformed into a
restaurant-with-rooms, in pleasing open-plan design. This is its Guide
debut: "This collection of old Flemish buildings makes a perfect
alternative to the banal modern hotels of the city. The cooking is superb
(*Gault Millau toque*) and well presented; breakfasts are first-rate, including
freshly squeezed orange juice. Rooms are comfortable and fully equipped.
The staff are helpful and charming. Beyond the courtyard is a well-
designed garden, newly planted, with arbours covered in honeysuckle."
(*RS More*) More reports welcome.

Open All year except 5–20 Aug and 20 Dec–5 Jan.
Rooms 1 suite, 6 double, 1 single – all with bath, shower, telephone, radio, TV,
baby-listening.
Facilities Ramps. 2 lounges, bar, restaurant.

Location In N outskirts of Aartselaar, which is 8 km S of Antwerp.
Credit cards All major cards accepted.
Terms Rooms: single 3,000 Bfrs, double 4,250 Bfrs. Breakfast 500 Bfrs. Set lunch 1,750 Bfrs, dinner 2,400–3,000 Bfrs; full alc 2,400–3,000 Bfrs.

BRUGES West-Vlaanderen   Map 9

Hotel Adornes   *Tel* (050) 34.13.36
St Annarei 26   *Fax* (050) 34.20.85
Bruges 8000

Run by a pleasant young couple, this B&B hotel beside a canal is in a 17th-century house, well modernised without loss of its character (polished wood floors and exposed beams). It continues to be warmly endorsed: "Wonderful location: our room had a view over two canals from its three large windows. It was agreeably furnished with an excellent bathroom. Good breakfast in a bright, beamed room with candles, flowers and a fire in the hearth." "Cleanliness and character. Fresh flowers in the room. Interesting cellar lounge." All admire the "copious" breakfasts. (*Mark Pemberton and Claire Wrathall, JC Ford, Dr FP Woodford*) But thin party walls and assertive plumbing can produce noise. Gourmets are advised not to miss the two-rosetted *Karmeliet*, 20 metres up the street.

Open All year except 2 Jan–13 Feb.
Rooms 20 double (also let as single) – all with bath, shower, telephone, radio, TV. 2 on ground floor.
Facilities Lift, ramps. 2 lounges, breakfast room.
Location Central. Go from Markt to theatre; hotel is signposted. Parking.
Credit cards Access, Amex, Visa.
Terms B&B: single 2,100–3,000 Bfrs, double 2,300–3,200 Bfrs. (No restaurant.)

Hotel Anselmus   *Tel* (050) 34.13.74
Riddersstraat 15
Bruges 8000

The Dutoit-Schoores' friendly B&B, in a quiet street near the central market, is again popular this year. It is an attractive old Flemish-style gabled house with a massive wooden door, and takes its name from an eminent humanist of Bruges who lived here and was possibly a contemporary of Erasmus. The interior has been skilfully and beautifully converted. "Very comfortable, clean and quiet; generous breakfasts." "Rooms small but warmly furnished." (*Moira and John Cole, Braham Murray*)

Open All year.
Rooms 1 suite, 8 double, 1 single – all with bath, shower, telephone, radio, TV, baby-listening. 2 ground-floor rooms.
Facilities Hall, lounges, breakfast room.
Location 5 mins' walk from the market square. 1 garage; street parking.
Credit cards Access, Amex, Visa.
Terms B&B: single 2,000 Bfrs, double 2,300 Bfrs, suite 3,500 Bfrs. (No restaurant.)

> Don't keep your favourite hotel to yourself. The Guide supports: it doesn't spoil.

Hotel Aragon   *Tel* (050) 33.35.33
Naaldenstraat 24   *Fax* (050) 34.28.05
Bruges 8000   *Telex* 81593

Central, in a quiet street near the Markt, a small, spruce B&B hotel with
"delightful" owners, "magnificent" breakfasts. Closed 6 Jan–15 Feb. 20 rooms,
all with bath and/or shower. B&B: single 1,950–2,650 Bfrs, double 2,500–
3,250 Bfrs. Enthusiastic new nomination. More reports welcome.

Hotel Bryghia   *Tel* (050) 33.80.59
Oosterlingenplein 4   *Fax* (050) 34.14.30
Bruges 8000

"This charming family hotel in a quiet part of Bruges is set in a former
15th-century merchant's house. Some rooms overlook a quiet square,
others a quiet canal. Ours was beautifully furnished. An interesting
breakfast served in a pleasant beamed room" – one of five plaudits this
year and last. Another mentions the friendly owner, Herman Cools.
(*Brian and Elisabeth Hoyle, David H Clark and others*)

Open All year.
Rooms 18 double – 15 with bath and shower, 3 with shower, all with telephone,
radio, TV, tea- and coffee-making facilities.
Facilities Lounge, TV room, breakfast room.
Location Central. Parking.
Restriction Not suitable for &.
Credit cards All major cards accepted.
Terms B&B: single 2,600 Bfrs, double 2,950–3,200 Bfrs. Reduced rates for children
sharing parents' room. (No restaurant.)

Hotel de Orangerie   *Tel* (050) 34.16.49
Kartuizerinnenstraat 10   *Fax* (050) 33.30.16
Bruges 8000   *Telex* 82443

A creeper-covered 16th-century house in the heart of Bruges beside the
quiet Dijver canal, now an unusually stylish hotel, praised again in
1989/90: "The most attractive features of the old building have been
preserved or restored. The superb public rooms are full of colourful rugs,
lush fresh plants, spectacular flower displays, and an astounding
collection of Delvaux originals (a painter who loves to put naked ladies in
railway stations). A canary chirrups cheekily by the front door. Bedrooms
frame a lovely central garden. Ours, with a lot of cane furniture and an
incongruous mini-bar, was not ideally designed and I thought it a bit
over-priced. But we much enjoyed breakfast, a lavish display including
beautifully smoked ham and gigantic kiwis, served in a glorious room
with large fireplace and chandelier. Pity there's no restaurant." Others
have approved the pleasant staff, "simple, spacious bedrooms", and the
bar with open fireplace and period furniture. (*Francine and Ian Walsh; also*
Caroline Streeter, Rebecca More) In summer breakfast and drinks are served
on a terrace by the canal. The hotel now has an annexe opposite, *De*
Tuilerieën, with indoor pool, sauna and solarium: but a visitor there this
year was put off by the piped music, lack of hot water and unresponsive
staff.

Open All year.
Rooms 5 suites, 14 double – all with bath, shower, telephone, radio, TV, mini-bar, baby-listening. Some ground-floor rooms. 25 rooms in annexe, *De Tuilerieën*, opposite.
Facilities Lift. Bar, TV room, breakfast room; conference facilities. Garden and canalside terrace. Swimming pool, jacuzzi, sauna, solarium in annexe.
Location Central, near Markt. Private parking 5 mins' walk.
Credit cards All major cards accepted.
Terms [1990 rates] B&B: single 4,250 Bfrs, double 5,250–5,950 Bfrs, suite 7,500 Bfrs. Reduced rates for children on request. (No restaurant.)

Die Swaene
Steenhouwersdijk 1, 8000

Tel (050) 34.27.98
Fax (050) 33.66.74
Telex 82446

This "charming hotel" is set in a 15th-century house on a quiet canal. As a B&B it has long been liked for its "comfortable family atmosphere", and it has a restaurant which was recently enlarged, specialising in fish. More enthusiasm this year: "I really do love this place. It is full of gilt, red velvet and dark colours, fake flowers and copies of great masters. But somehow it all works together to create an impression of Flemish elegance. Our spacious and prettily decorated room overlooked the canal. Service remains excellent." Rooms vary in size: "Ours was beautiful, service very welcoming, breakfast consistently superb. Excellent dinner from the set menu, but this did not change during our visit." Others have also extolled the food (including "lavish" breakfasts), the friendly service, the pretty garden, and the "splendid lounge with a piano which guests may play". The lounge, with its open fire and fine painted ceiling, is the restored meeting room of the Guild of Taylors, dating from 1779; free coffee and tea are still served here every afternoon from two till four. (*Lynne and David Allen, Donald and Joan Tranter, Norma and Bob Simon, and others*)

Open All year. Restaurant closed Wed.
Rooms 2 suites, 19 double, 3 single – all with bath, shower, telephone, radio, TV, baby-listening. 4 ground-floor rooms.
Facilities 2 lifts. Lobby, lounge, bar, breakfast room, restaurant. Terrace, garden.
Location Central (but quiet); signposts from the market square. Garage.
Credit cards All major cards accepted.
Terms B&B: single 3,000 Bfrs, double 3,700–4,950 Bfrs, suite 6,800–7,950 Bfrs. Set lunch 1,700 Bfrs, dinner 2,250 Bfrs; full alc 3,000 Bfrs. Special meals for children.

Hotel Ter Duinen
Langerei 52
Bruges 8000

Tel (050) 33.04.37
Fax (050) 34.42.16

A dedicated and very friendly young couple, the Bossu-Van den Heuvel, run this inexpensive canalside hotel, about 800 metres from the centre. In 1989/90, some ten reports have again sung its praises – notably for its "delicious" and lavish breakfasts, attractive newly renovated rooms and warm ambience. "Tiny and adorable. Our lovely room, one flight up, faced the canal; excellent lighting, and a modern bathroom with all amenities. Delicious coffee." "The enthusiastic young owners are very much in love with their hotel, and their love for their guests is enormous. The rooms are beautiful and cosy and the view is breathtaking. The breakfast is royal." "Baskets of flowers hang everywhere. Our attractively furnished room had a balcony with canal view." "Beds the most comfortable we have ever slept in." "I took a party of seven very fussy German ladies, all pleasantly surprised." "The rooms are furnished with subtle printed fabrics and period furniture. We enjoyed moonlight over the canals." Some have found the rooms facing the canal noisy, others not; some back rooms are rather small. (*Norma Kessler, RSOB and ML Evans, Marion and Peter Marsh, and many others*) A connoisseur from New England adds: "Belgian wcs are the best in Europe."

Open All year.
Rooms 18 – all with bath and/or shower, telephone, TV; baby-listening on request.
Facilities Lift. Lounge/bar with TV.
Location On canal 10–15 mins' walk from centre. Street parking in front of hotel; garage available (100 Bfrs 1st night, 50 Bfrs thereafter). Windows double-glazed.
Restriction Not suitable for &.
Credit cards All major cards accepted.
Terms B&B: single 2,000–2,200 Bfrs, double 2,300–3,200 Bfrs. Reduced rates for children. (No restaurant.)

Hotel Wilgenhof   *Tel* (050) 36.27.44
Polderstraat 151, Sint-Kruis   *Fax* (050) 36.28.21
Bruges 8310

A tastefully converted farmhouse in the quiet polder two miles NE of Bruges. Bright, nicely decorated, comfortable rooms with large modern bathrooms; fresh flowers everywhere. Good buffet breakfasts, served in the garden when fine, off Limoges china. No other meals. 6 rooms, all with bath and shower. B&B: single 2,400 Bfrs, double 2,800–4,000 Bfrs [1990]. Endorsed this year but further reports welcome.

BRUSSELS   **Map 9**

Hôtel Agenda   *Tel* (02) 539.00.31
6–8 rue de Florence   *Fax* (02) 539.00.63
Brussels 1050   *Telex* 63947

Very fairly priced by expensive Brussels standards, this small modern hotel off the Avenue Louise has again been liked this year. Bedrooms are spacious, comfortable and quiet. "A genuinely warm greeting. Our room had big windows, lots of cupboards, soft chairs, and a kitchenette. Breakfast was delicious, served in a small pretty room." There are no other public rooms, and no restaurant, but *Les Cadets de Gascogne* down the block is recommended. (*Norma and Bob Simon, RAL Ogston*)

Open All year.
Rooms 3 suites, 26 double, 9 single – all with bath, shower, telephone, TV, kitchenette. 2 ground-floor rooms.
Facilities Lounge, breakfast room. Small garden.
Location In side street off Avenue Louise, 700 metres S of Place Louise. Garage.
Restriction Not suitable for &.
Credit cards All major cards accepted.
Terms B&B: single 3,000 Bfrs, double 3,550 Bfrs, suite 4,050 Bfrs. Reduced rates for children. (No restaurant.)

CRUPET 5332 Namur   Map 9

Hôtel Les Ramiers   *Tel* (083) 69.90.70
32 rue Basse   *Fax* (083) 69.98.68

A delectable little restaurant-with-rooms in a rural setting by a stream, on
the edge of an out-of-the-way Ardennes village between Namur and
Dinant. "Charming, flower-decked, with an outside terrace for drinks.
Bedrooms are in the annexe, a functional building 15 minutes' walk away,
but the room was satisfactory. The restaurant, small and elegant, bore
accolades on its walls that seemed richly deserved judging by my warm
chicken liver salad with poached quail's eggs. Breakfast was above
average, too." (*Gault Millau toque* for such dishes as lobster in truffle
butter.) (*Bettye Chambers*)

Open All year except 2–19 Dec, 16–29 Mar and 5 days in Sep. Closed Mon and
Tue.
Rooms 6 double – all with bath and/or shower, radio, TV. Rooms are in annexe
800 metres from restaurant.
Facilities Lounge, bar, 2 restaurants. Garden; terrace for lunch in fine weather.
Location Crupet is 20 km S of Namur, reached from N47 or N49.
Restriction Not suitable for &.
Credit cards All major cards accepted.
Terms B&B: single 1,850 Bfrs, double 2,150 Bfrs. Set lunch/dinner 1,300–
2,250 Bfrs; full alc 2,500 Bfrs. Reduced rates for children sharing parents' room.

DURBUY 5480 Luxembourg Belge   Map 9

Le Sanglier des Ardennes   *Tel* (086) 21.10.88
Rue Comte Théodule d'Ursel 99   *Fax* (086) 21.24.65
                                                   Telex 42240

Durbuy is a pretty but touristy village amid lovely woodlands in the
valley of the river Ourthe. Here three small hotels, the *Sanglier, Cardinal*
and *Vieux Durbuy*, are under the same ownership (Maurice Caerdinael)
and are run jointly, with the *Sanglier* serving as the restaurant for all three.
Its expensive sophisticated cooking wins a *Gault Millau toque*, and readers
this year who dined on a terrace by the river much enjoyed their
asparagus sorbet and fish ravioli. Also admired are the truite amoureuse,
sole poached in vermouth and tournedos of doe (should that be
"tournedoe"?). Visitors have liked the spacious bedrooms with pleasant
fabrics, in all three hotels, and the views of the river and medieval castle.
(*Prof and Mrs JF Woodward, Dr A Robertson*) But one this year found not all
of the staff charming, and felt he was over-charged.

Open All year except Jan. Restaurant closed Thu.
Rooms 6 suites, 39 double – all with bath and TV; 26 with telephone. Suites have
radio and kitchenette. Some ground-floor rooms.
Facilities Lounge, bar, 3 dining rooms; banqueting room, conference facilities;
terrace. The *Cardinal* has a large garden.
Location 45 km S of Liège. Hotels are central; the *Cardinal* has private parking.
Credit cards All major cards accepted.
Terms Rooms 2,200–2,850 Bfrs, suite 3,750–4,750 Bfrs. Breakfast 295 Bfrs. Set
meals 1,200–1,750 Bfrs; full alc 1,875 Bfrs.

We depend on detailed fresh reports to keep our entries up to date.

GENT 9000 Oost-Vlaanderen   Map 9

Hotel St Jorishof   *Tel* (091) 24.24.24
Botermarkt 2   *Fax* (091) 24.26.40
                                             Telex 12738

Also known as the Cour St-Georges, *this venerable pile in the heart of the old town dates from the 13th century (Charles V, Napoleon stayed there). Fine old public rooms, including Gothic hall. Staff friendly, food mostly excellent: but rooms in new annexe are somewhat small and simple. Closed 3 weeks July, 3 weeks Christmas. 37 rooms, all with bath and shower. B&B: single 1,825–3,500 Bfrs, double 2,350–3,500 Bfrs. Set meals 1,050–1,550 Bfrs [1990]. Recent criticisms: more reports welcome.*

HAMOIS-EN-CONDROZ 5360 Namur   Map 9

Château de Pickeim   *Tel* (083) 61.12.74
136 route Ciney-Liège   *Fax* (083) 61.13.51

A turreted neo-Gothic mansion amid rolling pastoral country 22 km east of Dinant, just off N97 to Liège. Family-run and friendly, it offers good honest cooking (trout, venison, frog's legs, etc); gastronomic weekends are held. Many rooms have views. Closed Jan. 23 rooms, 20 with bath and shower. B&B: single 1,200 Bfrs, double 1,650–2,050 Bfrs. Set meals 675–1,375 Bfrs. New nomination. More reports welcome.

HERBEUMONT 6803 Luxembourg Belge   Map 9

Hostellerie du Prieuré de   *Tel* (061) 41.14.17
  Conques   *Fax* (061) 41.27.03
Route de Florenville 176

A stylishly converted 18th-century priory, long, low and white, surrounded by neat gardens, and standing by the banks of the river Semois in the heart of the Ardennes forest. Long lawns set with apple trees run down to the curving river. And most recent reporters have found the hotel as charming as its setting: "Madame was pleasant and chatty, the owner is fatherly and friendly, and service is carried out by efficient country women. Furniture is either genuine rustic or good repro, and the beamed second-floor rooms ooze atmosphere (bedrooms vary in size and style). I enjoyed the food tremendously – fantastic home-smoked salmon, hot lobster salad, sensitively cooked foie de veau, good cheeses. Public rooms are comfortable and smartly furnished with antiques, and a profusion of gorgeous old ornaments and lovely old paintings. We enjoyed our stay." The elegance, good cooking and general professionalism have been admired too (*Ian and Francine Walsh, William A Grant*), though some have noted poor housekeeping, and a surly welcome if you don't speak French. A new annexe, *La Résidence*, has six suites.

Open 1 Mar–13 Nov and 24 Nov–1 Dec. Restaurant closed Tue.
Rooms 6 suites in annexe, 9 double, 2 single – all with bath, shower, telephone, TV.

Facilities 2 salons, bar, 2 restaurants. Garden on river; boating, fishing.
Location 3 km SE of Herbeumont.
Restriction Not suitable for ♿.
Credit cards All major cards accepted.
Terms B&B: single 2,700–3,900 Bfrs, double 3,200–3,500 Bfrs, suite 4,800 Bfrs. Set lunch/dinner 950–2,200 Bfrs; full alc 2,000 Bfrs. 1-night bookings refused for Sat. Reduced rates and special meals for children.

KEMMELBERG 8948 West-Vlaanderen   Map 9

Hostellerie du Mont Kemmel   *Tel* (057) 44.41.45
Berg 4   *Fax* (057) 44.40.89

Mont Kemmel, one of the low hills that break the dead flat Flanders plain, is just south of Ypres: here thousands died on 1914/18 battlefields where now deer graze, birds sing, and gastronomes frequent this restaurant-with-rooms (Gault Millau toque) *built in heavy local style. Much comfort; wide views over the plain. Closed 16 Jan–28 Feb. 14 rooms, all with bath and shower. B&B: single 2,000 Bfrs, double 3,000 Bfrs. Full alc 2,500–2,750 Bfrs. New nomination. More reports welcome.*

LISOGNE 5501 Namur   Map 9

Hôtel du Moulin de Lisogne   *Tel* (082) 22.63.80
                                                   Fax (082) 22.21.47

On the edge of a village north-east of Dinant, this *Relais du Silence* is a tactfully converted watermill in a pastoral setting beside a stream. It is run by a young couple, the Blondiaux, who put the accent very much on food rather than bedrooms, as reports this year again stress: "The food is truly magnificent – mussels in a cream sauce served with pre-dinner drinks, then quail mousse, poached salmon with a delicious sauce, pear sorbet, saddle of lamb. Service of a high standard, and dining room a pleasure. Our room was large, clean and adequate, despite poor lighting and cramped bathroom." Others, while also loving the food and "imposing" rooms, have spoken harshly of poor bedroom maintenance. Recommended for "young romantics who put a higher premium on atmosphere than a plastic liner in the wastepaper bin". (*Nancie Hewly, Colin and Pam Murray*)

Open 10 Feb–10 Dec.
Rooms 9 double – all with bath, shower, telephone; 2 in annexe.
Facilities 2 salons, bar; conference room. Garden with tennis court.
Location Lisogne is 7 km NE of Dinant, off N 936 to Liège.
Restriction Not suitable for ♿.
Credit cards All major cards accepted.
Terms B&B: single 1,600 Bfrs, double 2,100 Bfrs. Set lunch/dinner 1,300–1,750 Bfrs; full alc 2,500 Bfrs. Reduced rates and special meals for children.

> If you are nominating a hotel, please do make sure that you tell us enough to convey its character and quality. We can't make good bricks without plenty of straw.

MALMÉDY 4890 Liège

Hostellerie Trôs Marets	*Tel* (080) 33.79.17
et Résidence	*Fax* (080) 33.79.10

route des Trôs Marets

Map 9

In lovely rolling wooded country north-east of Malmédy, near the German frontier, this sleek modern hostelry has a neat garden set amid thick trees. Public rooms and bedrooms are furnished in heavy Belgian country style, which can create a gloomy initial impression, but readers continue to be pleased by the welcome, the comfort, the peace and quiet, and the food – including the "delightful" breakfasts with Ardennes ham and home-made jam. "Food excellent and beautifully served, fresh flowers and a bowl of fruit in our room," said one report this year. Another commends the swimming pool: "Beautifully clean, set off by a tiled scenic end wall, and glass sliding doors to a terrace with sunbeds and parasols." "In the beautiful dining room we had imaginative, light courses – cubes of warm goose liver, turbot lasagne, quail with wild mushrooms." (*John W Behle, Nancy Hewly, MB Jackson*) One reader found the tall trees around the main building a bit oppressive; the annexe on a hillside close by has better views and more feeling of space.

Open All year except 12 Nov–20 Dec.
Rooms 4 suites, 7 double – all with bath and/or shower, telephone, radio, TV; baby-sitting. Suites in garden annexe.
Facilities Lounge, bar, restaurant; conference room; indoor swimming pool and solarium. Garden, terrace.
Location At Mont, 5 km NE of Malmédy on N28 to Eupen. Parking.
Restriction Not suitable for &.
Credit cards All major cards accepted.
Terms B&B: single 3,000–3,250 Bfrs, double 4,300–6,500 Bfrs, suite 7,500–15,000 Bfrs. Set lunch/dinner 1,375–2,100 Bfrs; full alc 2,100 Bfrs.

NEERIJSE 3055 Brabant

Map 9

Kasteel van Neerijse	*Tel* (016) 47.28.50
Lindenhoflaan 1	*Fax* (016) 47.23.80
	Telex 20519

South-west of the university town of Leuven (where the Flemish-Walloon conflict has been at its most destructive), this red-brick 18th-century mansion stands in its own lovely park, with a pond and old mill nearby. It is now a four-star hotel, and has been much liked this year: "Peaceful friendly atmosphere, charming trendy-looking staff, relaxed courtesy. Our comfortable room, bright and airy, faced the park; mixed furnishings sort of great-grandmother style; the stairway decor leaves room for improvement. But the large dining room, with its candelabra and antique chairs, has the elegance of an old manor house. Breakfast very good." (*GB and CH*) Reports on the gourmet restaurant would be welcome.

Open All year.
Rooms 30 – all with bath, telephone, TV.
Facilities Lift. Lounge, bar, restaurant; conference facilities. Park with tennis court.
Location 10 km SW of Leuven towards Overisje by N263.
Credit cards All major cards accepted.
Terms [1990 rates] B&B double 3,000–3,500 Bfrs. Alc meals 1,300 Bfrs.

NOIREFONTAINE 6831 Luxembourg Belge   Map 9

Auberge du Moulin Hideux   *Tel* (061) 46.70.15
Route de Dohan 1   *Fax* (061) 46.72.81
                                                Telex 41989

An enchanting country hotel with glorious food: but does it quite justify
its very high prices? And are not the staff a shade pretentious? That's the
general verdict this year on the famous and luxurious *Moulin*, secluded in
a wooded valley in the Ardennes near the French border. "Excellent as
always"; "It is certainly paradise; the rooms were exquisite and the
bathrooms sumptuous"; "A perfect little hotel, with the best food of any
small hostelry in Europe" – these are comments this year, but along with
some notes of doubt. It's a big converted millhouse by a pond, and is
owned and run by Charles and Martine Lahire who are steeped in the
traditions of good hotelkeeping. Not only do they provide distinguished
cooking (*Michelin* rosette, two *Gault Millau toques*) and bedrooms with
supreme comforts, they also know how to welcome and cosset their
guests, and make them feel like well-remembered friends. "When we
wrote to book a return visit after two years," says a recent visitor, "the
Lahires sent us a note to say that the family of owls that had nested
outside our bedroom last time had all survived." "To have breakfast on
the terrace on a beautiful morning is probably the nearest we shall ever
get to heaven." (*M and D Chambers, D and L Allen, Norma Kessler, the Rt
Hon William Rodgers, Padi and John Howard, and others*). However, the wine
mark-ups are steep; and while everyone admires the welcome and the
kindness of the Lahires themselves, some readers this year have found
their staff "snooty". One new visitor said he was made to feel guilty
because he did not order champagne as an aperitif; another agreed that
the *sommelier* was officious.

Open Mid-Mar–mid-Nov. Restaurant closed Wed Mar–June.
Rooms 3 suites, 10 double – all with bath and/or shower, telephone, radio, TV.
Facilities Sitting room, loggia, restaurant. Garden with tennis court.
Location 3 km S of E411; take exit 25.
Restriction Not suitable for &.
Credit cards All major cards accepted.
Terms B&B: double 5,200–6,000 Bfrs, suite 7,500 Bfrs. Set meals 2,200 Bfrs; full
alc 2,500 Bfrs.

DE PANNE 8470 West-Vlaanderen   Map 9

Hostellerie Le Fox   *Tel* (058) 41.28.55
Walckiersstraat 2   *Fax* (058) 41.58.79

This family-run restaurant-with-rooms, in a popular coastal resort near
Ostend, is much reputed for its fish and local dishes (*Michelin* rosette, two
red *Gault Millau toques*), and has been admired this year: "Food brilliant,
rooms excellent: modern, clean and quiet." "*Very* Belgian: spotlessly
clean, soulless rooms, ponderous decor in dining room, professional
service. One chap describes the dishes as though discussing a rare work
of art. The *menu gastronomique* brought some very good food, notably the

---

·All inspections are carried out anonymously.

mussels, scallops, turbot, lobster, and a brilliant smoked salmon pancake dish that was totally over the top but it worked. A lovely end to the holiday." (*R Boven, and others*) The brochure makes the decor look artily unponderous; your views, please.

Open All year except Oct and 1–15 Jan. Restaurant closed Tue, also Mon evening in low season.
Rooms 14 double – all with bath, shower, telephone, radio, TV, baby-listening.
Facilities Salon, bar, restaurant.
Location Central. Garage. Town is 31 km W of Ostend.
Restriction Not suitable for &.
Credit cards All major cards accepted.
Terms B&B: single 1,650 Bfrs, double 2,300–2,600 BFrs. Set lunch/dinner 1,500, 1,950 and 2,850 Bfrs; full alc 2,300–2,500 Bfrs. Special meals for children.

RENINGE 8981 West-Vlaanderen   Map 9

't Convent   *Tel* (057) 40.07.71
Halve Reningestraat 1   *Fax* (057) 40.11.27

A short drive inland from either Ostend or Dunkerque, this idiosyncratic hotel, "really a medieval barn in a field", and not easy to find, has bedrooms ranging in style from Louis XVI to Provençal, some with four-poster beds. "Ours was small but beautiful, with wood panelling and velvet drapes," runs a recent account. "We were welcomed warmly, and food and service were brilliant during one of their 'gastronomic weekends' – seafood, foie gras, salmon mousse, pigeon, presented with style." (*Sandra E Garrick*) Others have written: "We had most unusual rooms, outrageously decorated but great fun. Ours looked on to a pasture with cows whose heavy breathing woke me in the night. The loft bar for drinks is charming, and the meal was a delight, served efficiently." "Some rooms are fairly small, but others are bigger and retain a convent flavour: canopied painted bed, stone floor, icons and other such medieval trinkets, and a bathroom like a private chapel with the basin in an arched alcove." (Endorsed this year by *Anne Rapley*)

Open All year except Feb, last week of Aug. Closed Tue evening and Wed.
Rooms 10 double – all with bath and/or shower (3 with whirlpool), telephone, radio, TV. All in annexe 50 metres from restaurant. Some ground-floor rooms. 1 equipped for &.
Facilities Bar, restaurant; conference facilities. Terrace.
Location On edge of village, 15 km NW of Ieper (turn off N65 at Oostvleteren).
Credit cards All major cards accepted.
Terms Rooms: single 1,800–2,500 Bfrs, double 2,500–4,500 Bfrs. Breakfast 300 Bfrs. Reduced rates and special meals for children.

RONSE 9681 Oost-Vlaanderen   Map 9

Hostellerie Shamrock   *Tel* (055) 21.55.29
Ommegangstraat 148   *Fax* (055) 21.56.83
Maarkedal, Ronse   *Telex* 86165

Set amid rolling wooded country just north-east of Ronse, a textile town between Brussels and Lille, is this smart and stylish restaurant-with-rooms. You go up a long drive in a well-kept garden to what seems to be a private house in mock-Tudor style. Recent visitors thought it "one of the

very best hotel/restaurants in Belgium" (*Michelin* rosette and two re
Gault Millau toques for its modern French cooking). "A comfortable
welcoming and relaxed atmosphere, with expert and charming service
The rooms have recently been refurbished and are now brighter an
lighter, with sumptuous bathrooms. The food we found better than ever."
The main staircase with carved wooden balcony descends directly into
the elegant dining room, giving residents the opportunity for spectacula
entry. (*Pat and Jeremy Temple*) Wine prices have been called "fiendishly"
high.

Open All year except 15–31 July. Closed Sun evening and Mon except public
holidays.
Rooms 1 suite, 5 double – all with bath, shower, telephone, TV.
Facilities Salon, bar, restaurant; small conference room. Garden.
Location 5 km NE of Ronse, off N62, near Louise-Marie.
Restriction Not suitable for &.
Credit cards All major cards accepted.
Terms [1990 rates] B&B: single 4,800 Bfrs, double 5,700 Bfrs, suite 6,500 Bfrs;
dinner, B&B: single 6,900 Bfrs, double 9,900 Bfrs, suite 10,700 Bfrs. Set meals
1,500–2,700 Bfrs; full alc 3,225 Bfrs.

SAINTE-CÉCILE 6819 Luxembourg Belge   Map !

Hostellerie Sainte-Cécile   *Tel* (061) 31.31.6?
Rue Neuve 81   *Fax* (061) 31.50.04

In a village in a forest by the winding river Semois, close to the French frontie
east of Sedan, this charming hostelry has a waterside garden and elegan
restaurant with good food (some local Ardennes dishes). Good bedrooms, too
Go-ahead young owners. Closed mid-Jan–mid-Feb. 16 rooms, with private
facilities. Half board obligatory; 2,400 Bfrs [1990]. New nomination. More
reports please.

SPA 4880 Liège   Map 9

Hôtel La Heid des Pairs   *Tel* (087) 87.73.46
Avenue du Prof Henrijean 143   *Fax* (087) 77.06.44

On the western outskirts of the town that gave its name to all spas, a delightful,
elegantly furnished villa in a big garden. Friendly patron, well-equipped rooms,
stylish breakfasts. No restaurant: lots in town. Outdoor unheated swimming
pool. Closed 2 weeks Feb. 11 rooms, all with bath and/or shower; B&B 2,500–
4,600 Bfrs [1990]. New nomination. More reports welcome.

TILFF-SUR-OURTHE 4040 Liège   Map 9

Hôtel du Casino   *Tel* (041) 88.10.15
3 place du Roi Albert   *Fax* (041) 88.33.16

In the winding valley of the Ourthe, just south of the Liège industrial
conurbation, a small family-run restaurant-with-rooms, reasonably
priced, and endorsed this year for its comfort and "delicious" food. Last
year's view: "The building, a former brasserie dating from 1622, has been

lovingly restored by the owners, the Claes. Our good-sized room was tastefully decorated in French country style, with beamed ceiling, silk-covered walls, and windows overlooking the river. The food was delicious – terrine of rabbit, lobster mousse, breast of wild pigeon. Breakfast, too, was excellent, including cheese and baked apples." (*John and Connie Partridge; RSOB and ML Evans*) But poor reading lights, all agree.

Open All year except 15 Dec–15 Jan. Restaurant closed Mon.
Rooms 6 double – 5 with bath, all with telephone.
Facilities Salon, bar, 2 restaurants.
Location 11 km S of Liège.
Restriction Not suitable for &.
Credit cards None accepted.
Terms B&B: single 1,400 Bfrs, double 1,900 Bfrs. Set lunch/dinner 1,800 Bfrs; full alc 2,000–2,500 Bfrs. Special meals for children on request.

****

Traveller's tale *We arrived by night at a splendid modern resthouse in this far corner of Cappadocia. We negotiated dinner without difficulty from the voluble maître d' who had worked for some years in a Wimpy bar in South London. Getting a room proved more difficult; it depended how the owner felt, and making him feel good proved to be our evening's chore. We were alone in the restaurant listening to Turkish music when the owner came out of his office, somewhat drunk, and sat hunched over a raki. The maître d' whispered that we might get a room if we acted jolly and suggested that we danced. So we got up and did a Turkish dance suitably instructed and led by the maître d'. Then we had to take photographs of the depressed owner and even kiss him on the cheeks. Only sheer exhaustion and the prospect of a night sleeping in the car prompted us to do this, but we managed. Finally, the maître d' whispered that we had the room. No palace this: thin mattress, few blankets, lumpy pillows, and the bathroom (the staff washroom it transpired) stank. We stayed two days. The area was magical – a piece of the Garden of Eden – the resthouse was in its way restful, if bizarrely managed, the food was good, and the owner's manic depression did not dampen the maître d's antics.*

****

Denmark

Hotel d'Angleterre, Copenhagen

ANS BY 8643 Kjellerup   Map 7

Kongensbro Kro
                                                    Tel 86.87.01.77
                                                    Fax 86.87.92.17

Pleasant modernised inn with a garden beside a quiet river, between Viborg and Silkeborg. Informal ambience, much comfort, good service and food, notably local river fish. Lounge with open fire. Closed Christmas, 31 Dec–7 Jan. 15 rooms, all with shower. B&B double 535–675 Dkr. Set meals 90–185 Dkr. New nomination. More reports please.

The 1992 Guide will appear in the autumn of 1991. Reports are particularly useful in the spring, and they need to reach us by June 1991 if they are to help the 1992 edition.

COPENHAGEN   Map 7

Hotel d'Angleterre   *Tel* 33.12.00.95
Kongens Nytorv 34   *Fax* 33.12.11.18
1050 Copenhagen K   *Telex* 15877

This epitome of a grand hotel, founded in 1755, has been compared to the
Connaught in London, and is likewise something of a national institution.
It is close to the harbour and the royal palace, and has a fine restaurant
(speciality: canard à la presse) and a brasserie with the longest bar in
Copenhagen. "Imagine a room that has been furnished with a mixture of
first-class repro and genuine antiques, a large bathroom where all the
fittings are luxurious antique reproductions (allied with a telephone) and
you have the ultimate in comfort and efficiency – with personal service to
match. Scandinavian breakfast (do they eat the rest of the day?) arrived
on a trolley delivered by a woman looking like a cross between Ursula
Andress and Marilyn Monroe, who apologised for waking me up! The
brasserie claims 'reasonable prices' but you won't get out for under £20 a
head, and more with wine, though the food is good." (*Braham Murray*)
The hotel has just been acquired by the 121-strong Nikko hotel chain of
Japan – can it still remain a *Connaught*-like Danish institution? Please send
us news.

Open All year. Brasserie closed Christmas and New Year.
Rooms 28 suites, 81 double, 21 single – all with bath, shower, telephone, TV.
Facilities Lifts. Lobby, bar, 2 restaurants.
Location Central, opposite the Royal Theatre.
Credit cards Probably all major cards accepted.
Terms Rooms: single 1,650–1,900 Dkr, double 1,800–2,200 Dkr. Set lunch/dinner
199 Dkr; full alc 200–330 Dkr. Weekend reductions; off-season rates. Children
under 12 sharing parents' room free; special meals on request.

Hotel Ascot   *Tel* 33.12.60.00
Studiestræde 57   *Fax* 33.14.60.40
1554 Copenhagen V   *Telex* 15730

*On a quiet, pleasant street close to Tivoli and Strøget, Copenhagen's famous
pedestrian area. 18th-century facade, old-fashioned red-carpeted winding
stairway. Contemporary colour schemes in bedrooms: some of these are small,
others are in suites with kitchenette, terrace, sitting room. The quietest face
inner courtyards. Good breakfasts in an attractive room, no restaurant. 123
rooms and suites, all with bath or shower. B&B: single 590–750 Dkr, double
790–1,090 Dkr [1990]. Recently renominated. More reports please.*

---

71 Nyhavn Hotel   *Tel* 33.11.85.85
Nyhavn 71   *Fax* 33.93.15.85
1051 Copenhagen   *Telex* 27558

Restored some 20 years ago as a smart and expensive hotel, this 19th-
century warehouse stands on the *Nyhavn* (New Harbour) in the heart of
the old city; Hans Andersen lived next door. Readers especially enjoy the
"lively bustle" (but there's no traffic noise) and the adjacent canal with its
restaurants and bars. "Comfortable rooms and friendly service," runs a

report this year. "The usual excellent open Danish sandwiches for lunch, but the fish at dinner was spoilt by the *nouvelle cuisine* treatment." Others have much enjoyed the smorgasbord in this *Pakhuskælderen* restaurant. The cheapest bedrooms are very small (thick walls and low beams have imposed restraints on room space); the dearer ones have a view over the canal. "A charming conversion with comfortable rooms, friendly service and a good breakfast." (*D Graham-Hodgson, and others*)

Open All year. Restaurant closed 24–26 Dec.
Rooms 6 suites, 39 double, 37 single – all with bath and/or shower, telephone, radio, TV; baby-listening on request.
Facilities Lift. Lounge, bar, restaurant; 2 conference/functions rooms.
Location In town centre, near Royal Opera and Royal Castle, facing Nyhavn canal and harbour. Parking for 8 cars.
Restriction Not suitable for &.
Credit cards All major cards accepted.
Terms Rooms: single 980–1,380 Dkr, double 1,280–1,680 Dkr, suite 2,280 Dkr. Breakfast 85 Dkr. Set lunch 170 Dkr, dinner 300 Dkr. Weekend reductions 1 Oct–30 Apr, Easter and Christmas holidays. Children under 12 sharing parents' room free; special meals on request.

Hotel Vestersøhus
Vestersøgade 58
1601 Copenhagen V

Tel 33.11.38.70
Fax 33.11.00.90
Telex 15708

Ten minutes' walk from the centre of the old town. Recent reports: "First-rate, with modest but well-furnished rooms and extremely pleasant staff." "I had a spacious sixth-floor room overlooking the canal, and kitchen/dining area with balcony overlooking the other side – well equipped and clean. Good to be able to cook where dinner can be very expensive." There's traffic noise during the day, but rooms are double-glazed; those at the back are very quiet but have no view. (*Robert W Phillips, Mary E Hanson*) One 1990 visitor thought the furnishings shabby and the plumbing archaic, and was disappointed not to find a decent restaurant nearby. More reports please.

Open All year.
Rooms 4 suites, 23 double, 6 single – all with bath and/or shower, telephone, TV.
Facilities Lift. Lounge, breakfast room; roof garden.
Location 10 mins' walk from centre, on W edge of old town. Parking.
Restriction Not suitable for &.
Credit cards All major cards accepted.
Terms [1990 rates] B&B: single 750–950 Dkr, double 860–1,050 Dkr, suite 1,150–1,265 Dkr. (No restaurant.)

FAABORG 5600 Funen

Map 7

Steensgaard Herregårdspension
Steensgård 4, Millinge

Tel 62.61.94.90
Fax 62.61.78.61

"Would appeal to those in search of the genuine country house atmosphere," writes a recent visitor to this beautiful half-timbered 14th-century manor house on the island of Funen. The countryside here is among the prettiest in Denmark – hills and fields dotted with long low farmhouses. The hotel is set in one of three buildings round a cobbled courtyard; on one side is a working farm and on the other a tennis court and an enclosure with deer and wild boar. The rooms are furnished with many antiques – Louis XIV, Italian rococo and English. There are spacious lounges, a library lined with leather-bound volumes, and a grand hall decorated with hunting trophies. "A very beautiful place, with a feeling of space and privacy. We thought the food was good – wholesome and not too rich." Endorsed in 1990: "Top marks for food, service and lodging." Dinner (three courses) is served in the candle-lit dining room promptly at 7 o'clock. (*C de Koning, JD Monteith, BJ Walter*) *Warning*: the stable clock chimes every half-hour.

Open All year except Feb.
Rooms 3 suites, 10 double, 2 single – 13 with bath and/or shower, all with telephone, mini-bar. 5 in annexe.
Facilities Hall, 5 salons, library, dining room; billiards, piano, chess. Large park with deer and wild boar; lake (fishing), tennis and riding. Rocky beach 2 km.
Location NW of Millinge, a village NW of Faaborg.
Restriction Not suitable for &.
Credit cards All major cards accepted.
Terms [1990 rates] B&B double 590–950 Dkr. Set lunch 145 Dkr, dinner 250 Dkr. Reduced rates for children under 12; special meals on request. Guests are expected to have dinner.

MILLINGE 5642 Funen   **Map 7**

Falsled Kro   *Tel* 62.68.11.11
Assensvej 513   *Fax* 62.68.11.62

Jean-Louis Lieffroy must certainly be the greatest French chef at work in Denmark since Blixen's fictional Babette! The main differences are that *his* "feast" is prepared nightly, his chic clientele is anything but poor and puritan, and instead of those cailles en sarcophages that made cinema history he serves, for example, langoustines in a cream sauce, monkfish au beurre blanc, moist breast of guinea fowl. Even breakfasts might include "crème fraîche with honey, freshly squeezed orange juice, quail's eggs served on bacon and endless excellent coffee". This "utterly charming" hotel on the central island of Funen was a smuggler's inn during the 15th century; it is now a cluster of old thatched buildings round a small cobbled courtyard with a fountain. The "enchanting" bedrooms – some with Spanish floor tiles, and some with four-poster beds – are in outbuildings and cottages across the road. The garden runs down to the sea and the yacht harbour. "A really terrific place," writes an expert American traveller this year. "The service, breakfasts and main meals were all superb, using vegetables and herbs from the gardens. Rooms in the main building are a bit cramped: but the suites in the annexe, a former barn, are delightful." In short: very expensive but worth it. (*Alfred Knopf Jr*)

Open All year except Jan, Feb, Christmas and New Year. Restaurant closed Mon in low season.
Rooms 3 suites, 9 double, 2 single – 11 with bath, 2 with shower, all with telephone, 10 with TV. Suites, with lounge and mini-bar, are in *Ryttergården* farmhouse opposite the hotel. Some ground-floor rooms.
Facilities Lounge, bar, café, restaurant. Garden. Sea 100 metres.
Location 10 km NW of Millinge; S of Odense on Faaborg–Assens road.
Restriction Not suitable for &.
Credit cards All major cards accepted.
Terms Rooms: single 650 Dkr, double 1,250 Dkr, suite 1,700 Dkr. Breakfast 112 Dkr. Set lunch 220 Dkr, dinner 300–690 Dkr. Special meals for children.

NYBORG 5800 Funen   Map 7

Hotel Hesselet   *Tel 65.31.30.29*
Christianslundsvej 119   *Fax 65.31.29.58*
                                                   Telex 9 297122

A low-built modern hotel east of Odense, with views of the nearby sea. Architecture Japanese-influenced; hotel looks nicer inside than outside. Helpful staff, good food (international/French), attractive swimming pool, free bicycle hire, Japanese garden. Hotel does substantial conference business. Closed 2 weeks Christmas/New Year. 46 rooms, all with bath and shower. B&B: single 765 Dkr, double 1,200 Dkr. Set meals 180–305 Dkr. Recent nomination. More reports please.

RIBE 6760 Jutland   Map 7

Hotel Dagmar   *Tel 75.42.00.33*
Torvet 1   *Fax 75.42.36.52*

Ribe, with its 800-year-old cathedral, nesting storks (back this year after a sabbatical) and narrow cobbled streets, is an old town of great charm on the flat windy west coast of Jutland. The characterful *Dagmar*, built in 1581, looks across the main square to the cathedral. The ground-floor rooms are hung with splendid paintings, and filled with antique and repro furniture. Front bedrooms have tiny windows overlooking the church; some others lack a view, but most have lovely paintings and are quiet. One recent visitor praised the "attentive staff" and "elegant" food: "We chose to eat in the more casual cellar restaurant and were surprised by the quality and quantity. Breakfast was 'serve yourself' and copious." Others have enjoyed the candle-lit restaurant (but one this year found the *cuisine* too *nouvelle* for his taste). In summer a night watchman arrives, "dressed in black, carrying a lantern and singing his watchman's song": guests are invited to join him on his nightly rounds. (*D Graham-Hodgson, William A Grant*)

Open All year, except Christmas and New Year.
Rooms 47 double, 1 single – 20 with bath, 28 with shower, all with telephone, radio, TV, mini-bar.
Facilities Lounge, bar, 2 restaurants; conference facilities; music and dancing on Fri and Sat except July.
Location Central; Ribe is 34 km SE of Esbjerg.
Restriction Not suitable for &.
Credit cards All major credit cards accepted.
Terms [1990 rates] B&B: single 480–580 Dkr, double 680–780 Dkr; dinner, B&B: single 630–730 Dkr, double 980–1,080 Dkr. Set menu 105–276 Dkr, full alc dinner 370 Dkr. Reduced rates and special meals for children.

Hotel Restaurant Weis Stue   **BUDGET**   *Tel 75.42.07.00*
Torvet

A tiny inn, also in the medieval town centre, eagerly commended as a cheaper alternative to the *Dagmar*: "Denmark is the best-kept holiday secret of Europe, Ribe of Denmark, and the *Weis Stue* of Ribe. It is perhaps the finest of Ribe's old buildings, and its early 18th-century interior contains some notable furniture. Our room, the Panel Room, is the showpiece, its two longer walls covered in magnificent medieval panelling. The windows, with tiny ancient panes, looked out on to the cathedral. The twin beds were comfortable. We managed to get into this room by bending low and almost crawling, with our heads bowed beneath innumerable beams (if you were Falstaff, they would hoist you in through the window). There is no lounge, but three dining rooms each stuffed with antiques, plus a courtyard and banqueting hall. The food was superb, our best meal in Denmark, though breakfast was modest by Danish standards. Service was efficient, but a little impersonal." Endorsed by a reader this year, with the caveats that (a) mopeds can be noisy at night, (b) the restaurant, very popular, needs to be booked well ahead, and (c) the owners are not always gracious. (*Rev Michael Bourdeaux, D Graham-Hodgson*)

Open All year except 24/25 Dec.
Rooms 4 double, 1 single.
Facilities Restaurant, banqueting hall; small courtyard. 200 metres from river.
Location Central, in old town.
Restriction Not suitable for &.
Credit cards None accepted.
Terms B&B: single 200 Dkr, double 400 Dkr. Full alc 200 Dkr. Special meals for children.

SØNDERHO 6720 Fanø   Map 7

Sønderho Kro   *Tel* 75.16.40.09
Kropladsen 11

"Certainly the most exciting thing on the island of Fanø, which is really only a long sand dune." The inn is at one end, in the picturesque old fishing village of Sønderho; it is one of the oldest inns in Denmark, dating from 1772, and has been owned by the same family for three generations. "The Sorensens are lovely people and aim to please," runs a 1990 report. "The rooms we had were spare but clean, and the bathrooms modern and fine. But the food is nothing to write home about. The real joy is the location, with its fantastic ten-mile beach of hard sand." Others call the hotel "quaint and charming". The entrance hall has a roaring fire in cold weather; antiques and modern paintings abound. "My husband was most taken with the waitresses, all blonde bombshells, very helpful and friendly. The food was delicious and the service fast and efficient. The puddings were decorated imaginatively with all manner of exotic fruits, most of which I couldn't name. Breakfasts, too, were superb, with an excellent selection of home-made jam." The innkeepers tell us: "Our cooking is 100% *ecological* (without poison)." (*Alfred A Knopf Jr, Liz King, JD Monteith*)

Open All year except 8 Jan–10 Feb. Possibly closed Christmas.
Rooms 7 double – all with bath and/or shower. 5 ground-floor rooms.
Facilities Hall, salons, restaurant. Garden. By sea with sandy beach and safe bathing; golf and tennis nearby.
Location 20 mins by ferry from Esbjerg, then a 20-min drive. In SE part of Sønderho, on left by church.
Credit cards Access, Diners, Visa.
Terms [1990 rates] B&B double 560–810 Dkr. Reduced rates for children; special meals.

France

Hôtel le Cep, Beaune

Our French entries are so numerous that readers might find it useful to have a brief note on the different kinds of hotel to be found in France and on their classification in the main French guides.

The generally efficient but impersonal hotels of the big chains (Concorde, Méridien, Pullman and Sofitel at the upper end of the market; Altéa, Mercure and Novotel in the middle range; Campanile, Ibis and Fimotel in the cheaper bracket) do not, with one exception, feature in this book. The smaller hotels of character that we prefer are almost all individually owned and run; but many of them do group together for the purposes of joint marketing and promotion. Of these associations, the most superior and expensive is *Relais et Châteaux*, many of whose members are converted châteaux or luxury inns; some are excellent, but our readers sometimes find them pretentious or overpriced. A rival grouping is that of the *Châteaux et Demeures de Tradition*, mostly middle-priced and often very attractive. The *Logis de France* is a huge fraternity of some 4,500 family-owned small-town hotels or rural auberges, identifiable by their bright green and yellow signboards; usually they are quite simple but well-run places, offering value for money. *Châteaux Accueil* is a newly formed association of châteaux with just a few bedrooms, converted into guest houses, offering bed and breakfast, and sometimes an evening meal. They are generally run by their original family owners. The *Relais du Silence* are specially quiet hotels, often in isolated settings. These are the kinds of places to which *Michelin* may give a red rocking chair for being "very quiet and secluded". *Michelin* also bestows a red-print classification on a hotel whose looks or ambience it finds especially pleasant.

As for food, so important in France, we make a point in these pages of stating whenever a hotel has won an award for its cuisine from *Michelin* or its rival the *Gault Millau* guide. Even one rosette in *Michelin* indicates cooking of a high standard; its top rating is three rosettes, given to only 19 establishments in France in 1990. *Gault Millau* awards *toques* (chefs' hats), its top grade being four of them; it also differentiates between black-print *toques* for traditional cooking and red-print ones for the *cuisine inventive* that this controversial guide blatantly prefers. We ourselves do not necessarily share *Gault Millau*'s tastes; nor will many of our readers, who may consider that this red-*toqued nouvelle cuisine*, with its generally high prices and small portions is less delectable than more classic French fare. For them a useful indicator could be the red "R" that *Michelin* awards for "good food at moderate prices" (also quoted in our text).

We also mention the *Michelin* awards in other countries in this book that are served by its red guides (Benelux, Germany, Italy, Spain/Portugal); and in the case of Benelux we quote *Gault Millau* too.

The often tricky subject of service is simple in France: by law 15% is added to hotel and restaurant bills. You need leave nothing extra.

AGDE 34300 Hérault

Map 10

La Tamarissière
21 quai Théophile-Cornu

Tel 67.94.20.87
Fax 67.21.38.40
Telex 490225

The old fishing port of Agde, with its fortified ex-cathedral made from the tufa-ash of a nearby extinct volcano, lies just inland from the new resort of Cap d'Agde, built in the style of a Provençal fishing village; close by is Europe's largest nudist holiday town. *La Tamarissière* competes with these exotica by being a fishermen's *buvette* or snackbar transformed into a chic and stylish waterside inn, at the mouth of the Hérault, with three red *Gault Millau toques* for its *nouvelle cuisine* based on Languedoc dishes. It was dropped from the Guide for lack of news, but is re-nominated this year: "Luxurious, with a pretty garden and good swimming pool. Food stylish, over-elaborate in presentation, but service excellent. Dining terrace facing the river (and road). Front rooms have river-facing balconies: they can be noisy (pop music), but the delight of lying in bed watching the yachts and fishing boats makes up for this." (*MA Godfrey*) Another 1990 report criticised the sound-proofing and lukewarm water.

Open 15 Mar–15 Nov. Restaurant closed Sun evening and Mon in low season.
Rooms 29 – 28 with bath, 1 with shower, all with telephone, radio, TV.
Facilities 3 lounges, TV room, restaurant; terrace. Garden with swimming pool.
Location 4 km SW of Agde by D32.
Restriction Not suitable for &.
Credit cards All major cards accepted.

Terms Rooms 400–840 frs. Breakfast 60 frs. Dinner, B&B 510–705 frs per person; full board 620–845 frs. Set lunch/dinner 130, 205 and 305 frs; full alc 400 frs. Children under 5 sharing parents' room free of charge.

AIRE-SUR-LA-LYS 62120 Pas-de-Calais   Map 9

Hostellerie des Trois   *Tel* 21.39.01.11
  Mousquetaires   *Fax* 21.39.50.10
Château du Fort de la Redoute

The Venet family run a very popular *hostellerie* where you need to book. It's a small, late 19th-century château in a garden beside a pond, 40 miles from Calais and with easy access to the motorway. Although it gets full of the British, the ambience and the excellent cooking remain essentially French. Lots more praise this year: "The building oozes atmosphere, accentuated by the bustling friendliness of the staff." "A larger-than-life place, all hustle and bustle. Madame greeted us like family. Our rooms were spacious. Dinner was huge portions, and imaginative blending of flavours and colours. Service very efficient." "Madame a charming and welcoming host, meals unfailingly delicious, every bedroom tasteful, individual and immaculate." Rooms in the new wing are especially enjoyed (one is "furnished in the Japanese style with maize-coloured grass wallpaper and antiques"). "We enjoyed our truite aux baies sauvages, jugged pork and the farandole of desserts." A reader who stayed on till lunch the next day found that all his fellow-countrymen had gone: "We were surrounded by French families enjoying a relaxed Sunday lunch. It was one of the best meals we've ever had in France." (*Barbara A Barratt, Dr M Ingram, C Turner, Philippa Herbert, and others*) Service can be slow when they are busy. One report this year of a booking not honoured.

Open 15 Jan–15 Dec. Closed Sun evening and Mon.
Rooms 1 suite, 25 double – all with bath and/or shower, telephone, TV. 3 in pavilion in park.
Facilities 2 salons, 3 restaurants; conference room. Garden with golf putting.
Location On N43 between St-Omer and Lillers, 2 km from centre of Aire on Arras side. Private parking.
Restriction Not suitable for &.
Credit cards All major cards accepted.
Terms Rooms 200–400 frs. Breakfast 36 frs. Set lunch/dinner 83, 130 and 195 frs; full alc 280 frs. Reduced rates and special meals for children.

AIX-EN-PROVENCE 13100 Bouches-du-Rhône   Map 11

Hôtel Le Mozart   **BUDGET**   *Tel* 42.21.62.86
49 cours Gambetta

A modern, well-designed B&B hotel, on a boulevard close to the city centre, but quiet. "We found it cheerful and spacious, with pleasant staff," say readers this year. The breakfast room is dull; but most bedrooms have a balcony with views. It has a lift and an underground garage. (*HC Hart, Charles P Cords*)

Open All year.
Rooms 40 double, 8 single – all with bath and/or shower, telephone, TV.
Facilities Lift. Breakfast room; small terrace.

Location 500 metres SE of town centre (cours Mirabeau). Garage.
Credit cards Access, Visa.
Terms [1990 rates] B&B: single 240–260 frs, double 270–300 frs. (No restaurant.)

AJACCIO 2A Corse-du-Sud, Corsica   Map 11

Hôtel Costa   *Tel* 95.21.43.02
2 boulevard Colomba   *Telex* 468080

In a relatively quiet part of Corsica's torrid, dusty capital, 200 metres from the sea: a well-run modern-ish B&B hotel with large rooms, good coffee, sixties decor – and a garage. Useful. Warning: the Maison Bonaparte, *where he was born, is a bore. 53 rooms, all with private facilities, 288–441 frs. Breakfast 32 frs [1990]. New nomination. More reports please.*

Eden Roc   *Tel* 95.52.01.47
Route des Iles Sanguinaires   *Fax* 95.52.05.03
                                                           Telex 460486

This fairly smart, family-run hotel above the sea, beside the coast road west of Ajaccio, continues to be much admired: "Smart, efficient and comfortable, with large rooms and a luxurious restaurant, and full of gymnasiums, massage rooms, etc." "A delightful choice for our two weeks' holiday. The hotel is set into the hillside, and from our balcony (all rooms face seaward) there was a magnificent view of the bay. Meals (food was excellent) are taken on a beautiful terrace above a lovely garden where there is a swimming pool. Staff were most courteous and helpful, the ambience was relaxed, and breakfast included marvellous coffee. Just across the quiet road is a small sandy rock-girt cove from which one can swim in the clear, clean blue water." (*AF Thomas, Diane and Keith Moss*)

Open All year.
Rooms 5 suites, 35 double – all with bath, telephone, TV, balcony, air-conditioning.
Facilities Lift. Bar, TV room, billiard room, restaurant; thalassotherapy centre, terrace. Garden with heated swimming pool; private beach.
Location 8 km W of Ajaccio. Parking.
Credit cards All major cards accepted.
Terms [1990 rates] Rooms: single 300–920 frs, double 500–1,360 frs, suite 900–2,040 frs. Breakfast 60 frs. Set lunch/dinner 220 frs; full alc 460 frs. Special meals for children on request.

ALBERTVILLE 73200 Savoie   Map 10

Hôtel Million   *Tel* 79.32.25.15
8 place de la Liberté   *Fax* 79.32.25.36
                                                           Telex 306022

As this dullish sub-Alpine town gets ready to host the 1992 Winter Olympics, so Philippe Million prepares to lavish his renowned cuisine, among the best in Savoy (two *Michelin* rosettes, two *Gault Millau toques*), on the visiting celebrities and expense-account reporters who will crowd out his sumptuous hostelry, bringing him many a million francs in custom. Our own reporters continue to extol his "original cooking in the modern style": "Amazingly rich local variations, glorious desserts," runs one letter this year. "Plentiful breakfasts, and a good wine list with delicious local Savoy wines at low prices." The waiters are friendly, while the bedrooms, large, clean and modern, are adequate if unexciting: most are in a modern extension at the back. There is a comfortable lounge and bar, and in summer you can dine in elegance on a flowery terrace facing the small and pretty garden. New apartment blocks near the hotel obscure the outlook. But 20 minutes' walk up the hill is the medieval walled hill-village of Conflans, where the views are superb. (*Dr and Mrs A Winterbourne, Dave Watts*)

Open All year except 22 Apr–8 May, 16 Sep–1 Oct.
Rooms 26 double, 2 single – 26 with bath, shower, TV, all with telephone, 12 with air-conditioning.
Facilities Lift. 3 lounges, bar, breakfast room, dining room. Small garden, terrace for dining.
Location Central. Parking. Albertville is 45 km SE of Annecy.
Credit cards Amex, Diners, Visa.
Terms Rooms: single 400 frs, double 600 frs. Breakfast 60 frs. Set lunch/dinner 170, 270, 370 and 470 frs. Special meals for children.

ALBI 81000 Tarn   **Map 10**

Hostellerie St-Antoine   *Tel* 63.54.04.04
17 rue St-Antoine   *Fax* 63.47.10.47

The Rieux family have run an inn since 1734 at this old house in the town centre, now rebuilt in a dull modern style: but it still has old furniture, and spaciousness, and a garden at the back with big trees. The garden-facing rooms are quiet. The cooking wins a *Gault Millau toque*, though our readers tend to find it not remarkable enough for the high prices asked. "Staff welcoming, head waiter with a sense of humour," says a visitor this year, "modern bedroom vast and well furnished. Table d'hôte dinner very good; breakfast in room or on terrace, more than one could want. Reception staff first-class." (*Dr W Leggat Smith, Ralph Dubery, and others*)

Open All year. Restaurant closed Sat lunch, and Sun evening Nov–Mar.
Rooms 8 suites, 34 double, 8 single – all with bath, shower, telephone, TV. 30 with air-conditioning. 4 in annexe.
Facilities Lift. 3 lounges, bar, restaurant; conference facilities. Garden. Guests have access to swimming pool and tennis court at *La Réserve* (under same management) 3 km away.
Location Central. Parking.
Credit cards All major cards accepted.
Terms B&B: single 370–530 frs, double 520–850 frs, suite 900–1,000 frs. Set meals 150–200 frs. Reduced rates and special meals for children.

St-Clair   **BUDGET**   *Tel* 63.54.25.66
Rue St-Clair

In the pedestrian quarter of the old town, near the cathedral, here is a cheaper but still comfortable alternative to our other Albi entry. Most rooms face a courtyard and are quiet. No bar or lounge, but adequate breakfasts, including some fresh fruit. Open Easter–Oct. 12 rooms, all with bath and shower, 180–280 frs. Breakfast 28 frs [1990]. No restaurant, lots nearby. New reports welcome.

AMBOISE 37400 Indre-et-Loire   Map 8

Hotel Restaurant La Brèche   **BUDGET**   *Tel* 47.57.00.79
26 rue Jules Ferry

This family-run *Logis de France*, new to the Guide this year, stands in a quiet street just across the broad Loire from picturesque Amboise and its noble château, which François I turned into a centre of junketings, masquerades and fights between wild animals. *La Brèche's* delights are less exotic, but real: "We dined in the old garden to the sound of the fountain and the song of a frog. Meals were inexpensive and very good, cooked with typical French finesse and served promptly and deftly by the co-owner. The restaurant was well patronised by locals. The hotel, a former villa, very clean and comfortable, is managed by a friendly young couple." (*Christine Lawrie and Dr John Coker*)

Open All year except over Christmas, New Year and Jan. Restaurant closed Sun evening and Mon 1 Oct–Easter.
Rooms 12 double – 4 with bath, 6 with shower, all with telephone.
Facilities Lounge with TV, bar, dining room. Garden.
Location On N bank of Loire, 1.5 km from centre of Amboise. Parking.
Restriction Not suitable for &.
Credit cards Access, Visa.
Terms [1990 rates] B&B: single 140–240 frs, double 175–295 frs; dinner, B&B; 144–286 frs per person. Set lunch/dinner 68, 99 and 145 frs; full alc 300 frs. Special meals for children.

LES ANDELYS 27700 Eure   Map 9

Hostellerie de la Chaîne d'Or   *Tel* 32.54.00.31
27 rue Grande

This 18th-century auberge with a flowery courtyard, on the main square of the old town, enjoys a spectacular position on a loop of the Seine above Rouen; most rooms overlook the shimmering river and the island opposite. At night it is quiet save for passing barges, but they don't operate very late. A visitor reports this year: "Dinner was delicious, served with just the right blend of formality and cheerful spirits, in a dining room facing that heart-lifting view. Our room was one of the few without that view of the wide and wonderful river. It faced the garden and was large, clean and quiet, with its own bathroom: but it was basically furnished and lacked character." Some rooms are better furnished, and most are large, but bathrooms are not the hotel's strong point. However, dinner in the beautiful beamed dining room, with tables well spaced, fresh flowers, candles and exemplary service, "had exciting new tastes and could not be faulted", according to another admirer. The old part of Les Andelys is a picturesque village, dominated by the ruins of Richard Cœur de Lion's Château Gaillard; it is only 15 minutes by car from Giverny, with Monet's lovely garden. (*HR, M Fanthorpe, and others*)

Open All year except 1 Jan–2 Feb. Closed Sun evening and Mon.
Rooms 11 double, 1 single – 5 with bath, 2 with shower, all with telephone.
Facilities Dining room, breakfast room, functions room. Courtyard.
Location In Petit Andelys, on the river. Parking. (Village is 39 km SE of Rouen.)
Restriction Not suitable for &.
Credit cards Access, Visa.

Terms [1990 rates] Rooms 140–390 frs. Breakfast 45 frs. Set lunch 120 frs, dinner 320 frs.

ANGERS 49100 Maine-et-Loire   Map 8

Hôtel du Mail   **BUDGET**   *Tel* 41.88.56.22
8 rue des Ursules   *Telex* 720930

Our first entry for Anjou's historic castle-crowned capital: central but quiet, it's an 18th-century mansion built round a courtyard. Bedrooms with antiques; good breakfasts; car lock-up. No restaurant: but L'Amandier, close by and medium-priced, is recommended. 27 rooms, most with bath and/or shower. B&B: single 149–234 frs, double 193–268 frs. New nomination. More reports welcome.

ANTIBES 06600 Alpes-Maritimes   Map 11

Hôtel le Mas Djoliba   *Tel* 93.34.02.48
29 avenue de Provence   *Fax* 93.34.05.81

A villa in a lovely garden, with a little of the air of a private house, but not smart; it is in a quiet residential street, some 600 metres from the beach, and has been much liked again in 1989/90: "A family-run hotel of character (charming and attentive owners), with a tranquil atmosphere. Our large room with small balcony was simply but pleasantly furnished. We enjoyed our week enormously." "Food such as you'd get in a French household, not gourmet but good. Small but pretty swimming pool. Staff all very friendly and accommodating, including the poodle, Plato." Meals served in vine-arbour when fine. (*HM and Jean Levy, Amanda Garrett*)

Open All year.
Rooms 1 suite, 4 triple, 9 double, 1 single – all with bath and/or shower, telephone, TV. 2 with terrace in annexe.
Facilities Lounge with bar and TV, dining room. Garden with swimming pool.
Location 1.5 km S of town centre off Boulevard Wilson. Parking.
Credit cards All major cards accepted.
Terms [1990 rates] B&B: single 320–390 frs, double 440–590 frs, suite 760–970 frs; dinner, B&B: single 460–530 frs, double 720–870 frs, suite 1,320–1,530 frs. Set lunch/dinner 140 frs. Reduced rates for children; special meals on request.

ARDRES 62610 Pas-de-Calais   Map 9

Grand Hôtel Clément   *Tel* 21.82.25.25
91 esplanade du Maréchal Leclerc   *Fax* 21.82.98.92
                                                  Telex 130886

On the edge of a small town near Calais, a family-run hotel much frequented by the British. Garden with swings, log fire in bar in winter. Beautiful well-known restaurant, with nouvelle-*ish cooking* (Gault Millau *red* toque) *done by the son of the house, François Coolen. Some bedrooms are attractive, but many others tend to be substandard: small, dingy, fusty, unkempt. Closed 15 Jan–15 Feb and Mon. 17 rooms, 16 with bath or shower, 180–280 frs. Breakfast 35 frs. Set meals 100–300 frs. Continued criticism of bedrooms, but restaurant admired by readers. Back rooms are quietest. More reports needed.*

ARLES 13200 Bouches-du-Rhône   Map 11

Hôtel d'Arlatan   *Tel* 90.93.56.66
26 rue du Sauvage   *Telex* 441203

Former home of the Counts of Arlatan, this lovely 15th-century building with its pleasant garden is down a quiet side street in the heart of old Arles. Provençal antiques and fabrics in the rooms. But service, though friendly, tends to be disorganised; and many rooms are small, need refurbishing, and are overpriced. A potentially lovely hotel resting on its laurels. 42 rooms, all with bath and/or shower, 298–598 frs. Breakfast 42 frs [1990]. No restaurant. Criticisms this year. More reports please.

Hôtel Calendal   **BUDGET**   *Tel* 90.96.11.89
22 place Pomme

Mistral's epic poem about fishermen has given its name to this modest but pleasant B&B hotel near the Roman theatre and arena. Rooms simply but well furnished; lovely shady garden where drinks and breakfast are served. Closed 16 Nov–31 Jan. 27 rooms, 23 with bath and shower, 160–280 frs. Breakfast 26 frs. No restaurant; Hostellerie des Arènes and Le Grillon are good inexpensive restaurants nearby. Recently endorsed nomination. More reports please.

Grand Hôtel Nord-Pinus   *Tel* 90.93.44.44
Place du Forum   *Fax* 90.93.34.00

A most intriguing nomination this year. Classified *monument historique*, this venerable hotel stands in the heart of old Arles, facing Mistral's statue. It has some fine Provençal furniture, and remarkable bullfight posters; visiting matadors and opera singers have often stayed here. It had long let itself run to seed, but has now been remodelled and reopened: "All the rooms we saw at this lovely old hotel were charming. Ours had tasteful salmon-coloured decor, wrought-iron and glass night-tables, and a huge bathroom with fabulous big thick towels. The staff were all friendly." (*M and J Vella*) The restaurant, suitably named *La Corrida*, has just been entrusted to a young chef, Anne-Sophie Caen, who trained *chez* Bocuse, Vergé, etc, and is offering such dishes as foie gras of duck with figs and marinated tunny-fish with guacamole. On her cooking, and on this reborn hotel, we await your reports with bated breath.

Open All year. Restaurant closed Sun and Mon midday.
Rooms 2 suites, 24 double – all with bath and/or shower, telephone, TV; 6 with air-conditioning.
Facilities Lift. Restaurant; conference facilities.
Location Central. Hotel has parking service.
Credit cards Amex, Diners, Visa (restaurant only).
Terms [1990 rates] Rooms 500–850 frs, suite 950–1,100 frs. Dinner, B&B 700–1,350 frs per person.

ARNAY-LE-DUC 21230 Côte-d'Or   **Map 10**

Chez Camille   *Tel* 80.90.01.38
1 place Edouard-Herriot   *Fax* 80.90.04.64

A converted 16th-century posthouse in a small Burgundy town, now a
soigné hotel, much liked again in 1989/90 for its "welcoming owners,
charming rooms and excellent food" (owner/chef Armand Poinsot wins a
Michelin rosette and two *Gault Millau toques* for dishes such as cream of
frog's legs with Japanese pearls). "The second best meal of my whole
life," said another reader this year, "we thought we'd died and gone to
heaven. Sweet bedrooms, beautifully furnished public rooms with
subdued lighting and restful decor." "The restaurant is pretty, in a glassed
courtyard, where one has full view of the kitchen. Madame presides over
a fleet of well-trained waiting staff." Outdoor summer dining under
parasols or by torch-light. Vegetarians well catered for. (*Alison Patey, AP
Collett, and others*)

Open All year except Christmas Eve.
Rooms 3 suites, 11 double – all with bath, telephone, TV; baby-listening possible.
3 doubles in house 6 km away.
Facilities 2 lounges, dining room; sauna.
Location Central. Town is on N6, 28 km SE of Saulieu.
Restriction Not suitable for &.
Credit cards All major cards accepted.
Terms [1990 rates] Rooms: double 385 frs, suite 550–750 frs. Breakfast 45 frs.
Dinner, B&B 470 frs per person. Set lunch/dinner 130–240 frs; full alc 300 frs.
Reduced rates and special meals for children.

ARPAILLARGUES 30700 Gard   **Map 11**

Hôtel Marie d'Agoult   *Tel* 66.22.14.48
  Château d'Arpaillargues   *Fax* 66.22.56.10
Uzès   *Telex* 490415

Four kilometres west of fascinating Uzès (q.v.), on the edge of the village
of Arpaillargues, stands this 18th-century château, formerly the home of
the d'Agoult family (Marie d'Agoult was Liszt's mistress, and their
daughter Cosima married Richard Wagner). It is now a stylish and well-
run country hotel, "luxurious and restful", with a library, park, and views
over the rolling hills. Readers this year have preferred the "large, light
and airy" rooms in the château itself to those in the annexe. "The pool
and tennis facilities were excellent, the dining in the garden delightful
and the service friendly." (*AJ Collins, Anne and Jonathan Sofer*) Visitors
have praised the lunchtime restaurant by the pool, and some think the
cooking very good (e.g. terrine de rascasse and magret de canard); but one
report judges it "too adventurous for the chef's abilities" – and the French
guides do not rave either.

Open 15 Mar–15 Nov. Restaurant closed Wed in low season.
Rooms 2 suites, 25 double – all with bath, shower, telephone. 5 ground-floor
rooms.
Facilities 2 salons, bar, 4 restaurants; conference facilities; courtyard. Large
grounds with tennis courts and swimming pool.
Location 4 km W of Uzès.

Credit cards All major cards accepted.
Terms Rooms: double 400–500 frs, suite 820–980 frs. Breakfast 50 frs. Half board 500–650 frs per person. Set lunch/dinner 130–195 frs; full alc 255 frs. Special meals for children on request.

AUDIERNE 29113 Finistère   **Map 8**

Le Goyen   *Tel* 98.70.08.88
                                                          Telex 940422

Audierne is a pleasant harbour town in the far south-west of Brittany, near the rocky, storm-lashed Pointe du Raz, France's Land's End. Here this very spruce modern hotel, famous for its fish cooking (*Michelin* rosette, three red *Gault Millau toques*), is enthusiastically restored to the Guide this year by an inspector: "A natural for the GHG. It oozes efficiency and stylishness in a non-oppressive way. A warm welcome from a well-trained staff; Madame obviously a dynamic force. Our room was pretty, with new pine furniture and modern bathroom; the tiny balcony overlooked the bay, all quiet at night. The glassed-in section of the dining room, wonderfully light and spacious, faced the evening sun over the port; the main room behind looked darkish, dullish. We had the 200 fr menu [1990]: smoked salmon, six special oysters, chunks of daily market fish in a well-judged saffron sauce, duck more *nouvelle* in concept, glorious butter, wines expensive. All excellent. Clientele mainly French, mostly quite young and expensively casual."

Open All year except mid-Nov–mid-Dec, mid-Jan–early Feb. Restaurant closed Mon in low season, except public holidays.
Rooms 9 suites, 20 double – all with bath and/or shower, telephone, TV.
Facilities Lift. Salon, bar, dining room; conference facilities. Terrace.
Location Central, near harbour. Audierne is 35 km W of Quimper.
Credit cards Access, Visa.
Terms [1990 rates] Rooms 250–380 frs, suite 495 frs. Breakfast 40 frs. Dinner, B&B 320–420 frs per person. Set lunch/dinner 160–380 frs. Special meals for children.

AUDINGHEN 62179 Pas-de-Calais   **Map 9**

La Maison de la Houve `BUDGET`   *Tel* 21.32.97.06
Audinghen, Nr Wissant

Another boon as a first or last stop for ferry-goers: an old modernised farmhouse in a rural setting north of Boulogne, near Cap Gris Nez, owned and run by an elegant and friendly Parisienne. Characterful rooms, good breakfasts; no restaurant but several nearby. 8 rooms, 5 with bath or shower. B&B: single 80–130 frs, double 100–150 frs – a snip. New nomination. More reports welcome.

```
***************************************************
*                                                 *
* Traveller's tale The staff were of the fawning "I nice to you, you give *
* me nice tip" brigade that leaves me cold. The sincerity dripped like *
* honey from a cobra.                             *
*                                                 *
***************************************************
```

AUVILLERS-LES-FORGES 08260 Ardennes   Map 9

Hostellerie Lenoir   *Tel* 24.54.30.11

Jean Lenoir's comfortable restaurant-with-rooms, in a village near the
Belgian frontier, is reputed to be one of the best in the Ardennes, but
expensive (*Michelin* rosette, two *Gault Millau toques*, for such dishes as
mousse of pigeon with foie gras). It used to be a modest café run by M
Lenoir's parents, in the pre-war days when he was born in a room above
the bar. Now it is "exquisitely furnished" and has some pretensions – as
one recent visitor reports: "Each course is accompanied by a different
bunch of flowers, varying with the colour of your car: ours was a red
Mercedes, so we were welcomed by red roses, served on a silver tray. It's
a charming little hotel, with attentive service, nice decor, and a fountain
next door." A reader this year noted the framed congratulatory telegram
from Paul Bocuse on one wall, and thought it well merited: "The sole en
croûte was deliciously creamy. Our bedroom, in a functional-looking
block, had pale green and pink fabric-covered walls." (*Diana Cooper,
EM Jacob*)

Open All year except Jan, Feb, and Fri.
Rooms 3 suites, 15 double, 3 single – all with bath and/or shower, telephone;
18 with radio, 3 with TV. All in separate building in the garden. Some ground-
floor rooms.
Facilities Lift. 2 lounges, bar, 2 dining rooms; functions room. Terrace, garden.
Location 14 km SW of Rocroi, on D877 to Laon.
Credit cards All major cards accepted.
Terms Rooms 145–300 frs, suite 390 frs. Breakfast 32 frs. Dinner, B&B 265–420 frs
per person. Set lunch/dinner 200–410 frs; full alc 350–400 frs. Reduced rates and
special meals for children on request.

AUXERRE 89000 Yonne   Map 10

Le Parc des Maréchaux   *Tel* 86.51.43.77
6 avenue Foch   *Fax* 86.51.31.72
                                                   Telex 800997

A visitor this year enjoyed breakfasting under the lime trees in the garden
of this "idiosyncratic bed-and-breakfast hotel" in a quiet part of an old
cathedral city. Staffed "by people who seem to enjoy working in a hotel",
it's an appealing and unusual place, run in a very personal way by its
patronne, Espérance Hervé, a doctor's wife. "The genteel 1856 mansion is
set in its own big garden amid lovely and unusual trees. This was
formerly known as the Parc des Maréchaux, so the comfortable bedrooms
are now named after French marshals such as Lyautey (but not Pétain).
The American bar, all plush red velvet, is called L'Araucaria, after the
100-year-old Chilean monkey-puzzle tree in the garden. These may be
gimmicks, but there is nothing forced about the private house atmosphere, especially in the comfortable sitting room where under chandeliers
I took a pleasant breakfast to the strains of Chopin." Visitors arriving late
were offered a cold supper in their room – pretty good, for a B&B hotel.
(*Mrs MB Richards, MR Freeman*)

Open All year.
Rooms 24 double, 1 single – all with bath, shower, telephone, TV, baby-listening.
Ground-floor rooms.

Facilities Lift, ramps. Lounge, bar, tearoom; conference room. Garden.
Location 500 metres W of town centre. Private parking.
Credit cards Access, Amex, Visa.
Terms Rooms: single 230–275 frs, double 300–350 frs. Breakfast 33 frs. No charge for children under 7. (No restaurant.)

AVALLON 89200 Yonne   Map 10

Le Moulin des Templiers   *Tel* 86.34.10.80
Vallée du Cousin

"Utterly charming, full of character and very French," says a visitor this year to this old Guide favourite – an idyllically situated old watermill, attractively converted into a small bed-and-breakfast hotel, beside the quiet-flowing Cousin in a pastoral valley outside Avallon. "Wonderfully warm and welcoming" is another view this year. "A very pretty building, with a delightful garden along the river where breakfast is served in fine weather. And breakfast is excellent, with eggs from Madame's hens and perfect coffee. Our room was comfortable and prettily decorated, but too small for a long stay." Another comment: "The Paisley pattern fabrics used to decorate every inch of wall and ceiling make them a shade claustrophobic." (*A Liddell, Kate and Jeremy Cross*)

Open 15 Mar–30 Oct.
Rooms 12 double, 2 single – all with bath and/or shower, telephone.
Facilities Breakfast terrace. Garden with *boules*, riverside terrace.
Location 3 km W of Avallon in direction of Vézelay. Parking.
Credit cards None accepted.
Terms Rooms 210–300 frs. Breakfast 30 frs. (No restaurant.)

AVIGNON 84000 Vaucluse   Map 11

Hotel d'Angleterre   **BUDGET**   *Tel* 90.86.34.31
29 boulevard Raspail

On a quiet street within the ramparts. A cut above the average small town-centre hotel, and cheap; rooms simple but clean, newly redecorated. Breakfasts so-so. Connection with Angleterre unknown. Closed 16 Dec–21 Jan. 40 rooms, most with bath or shower, 160–325 frs. Breakfast 28 frs. No restaurant: try Fourchette or Férigoulo, both cheapish. Re-nominated this year. More reports welcome.

Hôtel d'Europe   *Tel* 90.82.66.92
12 place Crillon   *Fax* 90.85.43.66
                                                          Telex 431965

This former 16th-century aristocrat's house stands in a small square near the Papal Palace. It was already an inn when Napoleon stayed here in 1799; and with its elegant furnishings and cool grace it has far more character than the average modern Avignon hotel. This year, all six reports have been favourable – on the attentive old-style service, the air-conditioned bedrooms, the breakfasts, and dining in the small charming courtyard. An earlier view: "The courtyard and public rooms, filled with flowers and antiques, are a feast to the eye and spirit." Provençal cuisine in the hotel's *Vieille Fontaine* restaurant is admired. You can eat in a rather formal dining room or, preferably, under the plane trees beside a fountain in the courtyard – "a magical experience". Just a few gripes: a few of the rooms are "pokey", and some at the back can suffer from traffic noise. And: "The piped music seems a strange error of taste in an otherwise well-run hotel. We had a delicious meal and listened to Glen Miller and Danny Boy five times." (*Marilyn Frampton, Dr RL Holmes and DR MW Atkinson, Simon Small and others*) A new chef this year, and new rooms added.

Open All year.
Rooms 10 suites, 36 double, 1 single – all with bath, telephone, radio, TV, air-conditioning.
Facilities Lift. 2 salons, bar, TV room, restaurant; conference facilities. Courtyard. 5 mins' walk from Papal Palace.
Location By Porte de l'Oulle on W side of city. Private garage (40 frs).
Restriction Not suitable for &.
Credit cards All major cards accepted.
Terms Rooms 435 frs, suite 1,500 frs. Breakfast 60 frs. Set lunch 155 frs, dinner 200 frs; full alc from 300 frs. Special meals for children on request.

BARBIZON 77630 Seine-et-Marne   Map 9

Hôtellerie du Bas-Bréau   *Tel* 60.66.40.05
22 rue Grande   *Fax* 60.69.22.89
                                                     Telex 690953

A well-known traditional auberge, very luxurious, frequented by rich Parisians, in a village near Fontainebleau that once had an important artists' colony. Commended for its charming peaceful atmosphere, beautiful garden, tennis court, and excellent food (Michelin rosette, two Gault Millau toques). Closed Jan. 20 rooms, all with bath and shower. B&B single 1,050 frs, double 1,450–1,550 frs. Set meals 290 and 340 frs. Recent nomination. More reports needed.

LE BARROUX 84330 Vaucluse   Map 11

Hôtel Les Géraniums   `BUDGET`   *Tel* 90.62.41.08
Place de la Croix   *Fax* 90.62.56.48

"Le Barroux is an out-of-the-way hill-village, topped by an old castle, amid glorious country up near Mont Ventoux. This old stone building, pleasantly converted but still quite simple, is the kind of authentic local auberge that is becoming harder to find in touristy Provence: you need to go right up into the wilder hinterland, as here. The charming young *patronne* supervises the meals, served in a beamed *salle* or out on the terrace, facing the view. Good local cuisine: tripes provençales, fresh apple pie; local wine a bit rough. The best bedrooms, with modern bathrooms, are in the new annexe." (*JA*)

Open All year except Jan.
Rooms 22 double – all with bath or shower, telephone. 9 in nearby annexe.
Facilities Salon with TV, bar, restaurant; 2 terraces. Garden. Solarium, table-tennis.
Location Le Barroux is 10 km N of Carpentras. Parking.

Restriction Not suitable for &.
Credit cards All major cards accepted.
Terms Rooms 170–210 frs. Breakfast 25 frs. Dinner, B&B 180–260 frs per person.
Set meals 70, 120 and 150 frs; full alc 140 frs. Reduced rates and special meals for
children.

BAUDUEN 83630 Var   **Map 11**

Auberge du Lac   *Tel 94.70.08.04*

*In upper Provence, just west of the mighty Gorges du Verdon, three old houses
in the village have been joined into one to form this pleasant unassuming
auberge, overlooking the large lake of Ste-Croix (bathing, sailing, fishing).
Comfortable rooms with old furniture, good classic cooking, friendly service by
the owner, M Bagarre. Open 15 Mar–15 Nov. 10 rooms, all with bath and
shower. B&B double 350–420 frs. Set menus 110–260 frs. Recent nomination.
More reports please.*

LES BAUX-DE-PROVENCE 13520 Bouches-du-Rhône   **Map 11**

Le Mas d'Aigret   *Tel 90.54.33.54*
                                                                      Fax 90.54.41.37

This ruined hill-village-cum-castle, on a rocky spur of the Alpilles, is one
of the showplaces of Provence. In the Middle Ages it was the seat of a
great feudal family and a leading "court of love" where troubadours
played. Then it came under the rule of a sadistic viscount who would
kidnap his neighbours and laugh as he forced them to jump to their
deaths from the clifftop. In 1632 Richelieu had the castle demolished.
Today it is a ghost realm, where coach parties daily pick their way across
the jagged rocks of bauxite (from which Les Baux takes its name) and
through the spooky remains of medieval grandeur. It is best visited by
moonlight.

An Englishman, Pip Phillips, and his French wife have just taken over
this converted stone *mas* below the village: its restaurant is built into the
natural rock but, as our nominator reports this year, "In fine weather all
meals are served on the large tree-shaded terrace with a fine view over
the valley, and at night with the fabulous backdrop of the floodlit castle.
The young chef's cuisine is innovative and enjoyable; service very
pleasant, but a bit slow. Bedrooms are small but have every facility, and
most have terrace or balcony. Green lawns, brilliant flower beds and a
large swimming pool." (*Max and Ruby Milner*) Mr Phillips writes: "We are
eliminating all aspects denoting 'hotel': this is our home where we
welcome our friends and guests" (but preferably no children under ten).
Your views, please.

Open 1 Mar–4 Jan. Restaurant closed Wed lunch.
Rooms 1 suite, 14 double – all with bath, shower, telephone, TV; many with
balcony or terrace.
Facilities Salon, bar, restaurant. Garden; terrace. Outdoor swimming pool.
Location 400 metres E of village on D27 A. 19 km NE of Arles.
Restriction Not suitable for &. Prefers no children under 10.
Credit cards All major cards accepted.

Terms Rooms: double 400–520 frs, suite 750 frs. Breakfast 50 frs. Dinner, B&B: 465–640 frs per person. Set lunch 120 frs, dinner 150, 230 and 290 frs; full alc 320 frs. Gourmet golf holidays. Reduced rates and special meals for children.

Oustaù de Baumanière

Tel 90.54.33.07
Fax 90.54.40.46
Telex 420203

This renowned hotel/restaurant, in the valley below the old village, is owned by that doyen of great French chefs, 93-year-old Raymond Thuilier, and is run by his grandson, with Alain Burnel as chef. This year, *Michelin* has dropped its third rosette but even two rosettes can still signify great cooking, and our readers have again found it superb: "The chocolate soufflé is unbelievable," says one reader, adding, "We have never felt so coddled in luxury. The perfect hotel in the most idyllic setting. The swimming pool and grounds are beautifully maintained." Others have been impressed alike by the luxurious bedrooms, the splendid breakfasts and the very real beauty of the place. "At night, the crescent moon, starlight and floodlit château, the eerie white rocks, the discreetly lit pool . . ." (*Marie and Dominic Chambers*) However, some reports this year and last have found the service aloof, even rude; one visitor was put without warning in a small, ugly room in an annexe 800 metres away, and judged that management is not leading its staff properly. At such high prices, this is hardly excusable. More reports please.

Open All year except 20 Jan–4 Mar. Closed Wed and Thu midday 1 Nov–31 Mar.
Rooms 12 suites, 13 double – all with bath, telephone, TV, air-conditioning. 14 in 3 annexes. 8 ground-floor rooms.
Facilities Salon, restaurant. Garden, swimming pool, tennis courts, riding stables.
Location 19 km NE of Arles; 86 km NW of Marseilles.
Credit cards All major cards accepted.
Terms [1990 rates] Rooms 750–875 frs, suite 1,200 frs. Breakfast 80 frs. Dinner, B&B 1,100–1,250 frs per person. Set lunch/dinner 500–600 frs.

La Benvengudo

Tel 90.54.32.54

The great white rocky crags of the Alpilles rise above the garden of this creeper-covered farmhouse, in the valley south-west of Les Baux. It is far cheaper than the *Baumanière*, but quite glamorous in its own way: dinners are served in a cosy room with antiques or on a floodlit patio, and there is a large and lovely swimming pool in the big garden. "The gardens are beautifully kept," says a visitor this year. "Walnut trees, apricots, lavender, roses. The pool was very clean and clear, and our rooms were spacious, with old furniture, even a four-poster bed in one. Each room had a private terrace. The staff were at all times charming, and dinner was very good." An earlier view: "Cooking is very fresh and individual, e.g. a delicious combination of moules and escargots. We liked Madame, especially when she padded round gardening in bare feet." Others have found the place "very comfortable and friendly", "peaceful and civilised". But the service can be slow; and some readers consider the food "not above average". (*Simon Small, N D'Emden and H Osman, G Evans*)

Open 1 Feb–10 Nov. Restaurant closed lunchtime and Sun evening.
Rooms 3 suites, 17 double – all with bath or shower, telephone; suites have kitchenette. 10 (with terrace and TV) in annexe. Ground-floor rooms.
Facilities Salon, TV room, restaurant. Garden with terrace, swimming pool and tennis court.
Location 2 km SW of Les Baux, off D78. Parking.
Credit cards Access, Visa.
Terms [1990 rates] Rooms 365–480 frs, suite 750 frs. Breakfast 45 frs. Dinner, B&B 415–470 frs per person. Set lunch/dinner 190–230 frs.

La Cabro d'Oro   *Tel* 90.54.33.21
                                                       Telex 401810

Also owned by Raymond Thuilier (see above), this 'Golden Goat' is a spacious and sophisticated modern hotel in *mas* style, with bungalows spread around a big ornate garden. It is more informal than the *Oustaù* and less highly priced, and is preferred by its nominators this year: "The best hotel we have enjoyed in France for some years. The restaurant was superb (*Michelin* rosette), with a friendly giant of a Provençal head waiter." "Friendly and helpful staff, delightful pool." The accent is on sport: tennis, riding, etc. (*Denis E O'Mulloy, Donald Williams*)

Open All year except 12 Nov–21 Dec. Closed Mon, and Tue midday 31 Oct–31 Mar.
Rooms 22 – all with bath and/or shower, telephone, TV, air-conditioning. Ground-floor rooms suitable for &.
Facilities Restaurant; functions room. Terrace. Outdoor swimming pool, tennis court; riding.
Location Close to the *Oustaù*, just west of village.
Credit cards All major cards accepted.
Terms [1990 rates] Rooms: single 450 frs, double 700 frs. Breakfast 55 frs. Dinner, B&B 480–625 frs per person. Set lunch/dinner 245–320 frs.

BAYEUX 14400 Calvados   **Map 8**

Hôtel d'Argouges   *Tel* 31.92.88.86
21 rue St-Patrice   *Fax* 31.92.69.16
                                                       Telex 772402

"Very pretty, very French, charming atmosphere." "Exactly as provincial France should be – owners delightful." So run reports this year and last on this 18th-century, private townhouse, now converted into an elegant, family-run B&B hotel, warm and welcoming, with beamed bedrooms, low ceilings, an attractive lounge and a small garden. It is also quiet (especially the annexe rooms), being set back from the street behind a courtyard, opposite the market square, and has private parking. The cathedral and that tapestry are 600 metres away. (*Alan and Beth Horsley, Peter Hill, and others*)

Open All year.
Rooms 2 suites, 20 double, 3 single – all with bath and/or shower, telephone, radio; 10 with TV; baby-listening on request. 12 in building in garden.
Facilities Salon, breakfast room; courtyard. Garden.
Location Central. Parking.
Restriction Not suitable for &.
Credit cards All major cards accepted.
Terms B&B: single 199–369 frs, double 219–369 frs, suite 390–559 frs. Reduced rates for children. (No restaurant.)

BEAULIEU 06310 Alpes-Maritimes   Map 11

La Réserve   *Tel* 93.01.00.01
Boulevard Maréchal Leclerc   *Fax* 93.01.28.99
                                                  Telex 470301

This famous pink palace beside the rocky shore was one of the most
fashionable venues of pre-war Riviera society. Greta Garbo, Virginia
Woolf and of course Scottie all stayed or dined here; today regular guests
include Robert Maxwell. In the past two years it has acquired a new
manager and a new chef, Joël Garault, but our 1990 reports suggest that
it's as good as ever and deserves its two *Gault Millau toques* (for e.g.
poissons crus marinés, carré d'agneau aux aromates and hot lemon
soufflé). You can dine on the terrace by the sea, or in an elegant paved
patio. Period furniture and a tinkling piano recall the old days. The
swimming pool is heated in winter, or you can bathe from the rocks. Most
rooms, suitably luxurious, face the sea. "Our room was very elegant, and
the balcony perfect. The *sommelier* was happy to discuss the merits of
Australian and New Zealand wine without a trace of chauvinism." "The
rooms facing the sea are fantastic." (*Shellard Campbell, Alfred A Knopf Jr,
JA*)

Open All year except mid-Nov–mid-Dec.
Rooms 3 suites, 50 double – all with bath, shower, telephone, radio, TV.
Facilities Lift. Salon, bars, restaurant; terrace. Garden with swimming pool.
Sauna, solarium.
Location On seafront. Parking.
Restrictions Not suitable for &. No children under 10 in July and Aug.
Credit cards Amex, Diners, Visa.
Terms B&B: single 790–1,640 frs, double 1,090–2,490 frs, suite 2,590–4,690 frs.
Set lunch/dinner: 340–430 frs in winter, 370–470 frs in summer; full alc 590 frs.

BEAUMONT 24440 Dordogne   Map 10

Hôtel des Voyageurs   `BUDGET`   *Tel* 53.22.30.11

Meals of outstandingly good value (Michelin *red R*), *especially the lavish help-
yourself hors d'oeuvre buffet, are offered at this simple but friendly restaurant-
with-rooms in a village on the river Dordogne. Rustic dining room; summer
dining in garden. Good breakfasts, too. Rooms adequate. Closed Oct–Feb, Mon
except July/Aug. 10 rooms, some with bath or shower, 90–200 frs. Set meals 70–
400 frs. New nomination. More reports please.*

BEAUNE 21200 Côte-d'Or   Map 10

Hôtel le Cep   *Tel* 80.22.35.48
27 rue Maufoux   *Fax* 80.22.76.80
                                                  Telex 351256

In the centre of Burgundy's wine capital, a beautiful 17th-century house
with antique furnishings, but newly modernised. One recent visitor
enjoyed breakfast in the garden courtyard with its elegant tables and
chairs, and thought the staff "exceptionally kind". An earlier view: "A
charming little hotel. Dinner was very good in the lovely restaurant next

door." (This bears the name of its chef, Bernard Morillon, and wins a *Michelin* rosette and *Gault Millau toque*.) (*Deborah F Reese, Joe Van der Sneppen*) Each bedroom is named after a *Grand Cru* wine of the Côte d'Or vineyards; the modern ones, though nice, have less character than the old rooms; front rooms can be noisy.

Open All year. Restaurant closed Feb, Mon, and Tue lunch.
Rooms 49 – all with bath and/or shower, telephone, TV. 5 suites in courtyard annexe. 1 room suitable for &.
Facilities Lift. Lounge, bar, restaurant; functions facilities; courtyard. Garden.
Location Central, near Hôtel-Dieu. Garage parking.
Credit cards All major cards accepted.
Terms Rooms: single 450 frs, double 550–850 frs. Breakfast 55 frs. Set lunch/dinner 160–320 frs. Special meals for children.

Hôtel La Closerie　　　　　　　　　　*Tel* 80.22.15.07
61 route de Pommard　　　　　　　　　*Fax* 80.24.16.22
　　　　　　　　　　　　　　　　　　Telex 351213

A modern purpose-built hotel in the quiet southern outskirts, just off the N74 to Chalon. Spacious foyer, modern bedrooms, and plenty of creature comforts, including large shady garden and pleasant swimming pool, enlarged this year. Excellent breakfasts. Closed 24 and 31 Dec. 46 rooms, some new this year, all with bath and shower. B&B: single 372–452 frs, double 434–514 frs. No restaurant, but you can order meals by phone from a traiteur. Warmly endorsed this year, but fuller reports welcome.

BEAUREPAIRE 38270 Isère　　　　　　　　　　**Map 10**

Hôtel-Restaurant Fiard　　　　　　　　　*Tel* 74.84.62.02
Avenue des Terreaux

In a small town SE of Vienne, off the Rhône valley, a quite smart, newly refurbished restaurant-with-rooms: gracious hostess, attractive modern furniture, excellent classic cooking and Côte-du-Rhône wines. Closed Jan. 15 rooms, all with bath and shower, single 220 frs, double 300–350 frs. Set menus 110–380 frs. Recent nomination. More reports please.

LE BEC-HELLOUIN 27800 Eure　　　　　　　　　　**Map 8**

Auberge de l'Abbaye　　　　　　　　　*Tel* 32.44.86.02

Much liked again in 1989/90 for its "good fresh food and warm welcome", this "deceptively simple" 18th-century half-timbered Norman auberge stands on the green of a picturesque village. Rooms, some furnished with antiques, are thought "very pretty", while the dining room with its low-beamed ceiling offers "dinners of a high standard", according to one report this year. *Le Bec-Hellouin* was the home of one of Europe's great Benedictine monasteries, and three archbishops of Canterbury came from here in medieval times. The monastery, formerly a ruin, has now been restored and once again houses a religious community. The Gregorian chant in its abbey is worth hearing, and a reader this year was delighted by the tawny owls that call all night –

"sheer bliss". (*William A Howard, AJ Jeffs, MVG Masefield, and others*) Note that there is a third kind of local noise, the abbey bells that also sound all night. "A wondrous peel," say some. Some comments in 1990 suggest a fall in standards.

Open 23 Feb–7 Jan.
Rooms 1 suite, 7 double – all with bath, shower, telephone.
Facilities TV lounge, 3 dining rooms; courtyard.
Location 5 km from Brionne; SW of Rouen, W of N138. Parking.
Restriction Not suitable for &.
Credit cards Access, Visa.
Terms Rooms 300–450 frs. Breakfast 32 frs. Set lunch 120 frs, dinner 260 frs. Reduced rates and special meals for children.

BELLEGARDE-SUR-VALSÉRINE 01200 Ain   Map 10

Hôtel Le Fartoret   *Tel* 50.48.07.18
Éloise   *Fax* 50.48.23.85

Set amid fine scenery on a hillside near the Swiss frontier, this old country auberge has recently expanded and become grander, losing some of its former simple charm. But it is still run in jovial style by the bulky, bearded Robert Gassilloud and his family; and it offers the pleasures of a sheltered swimming pool ("a sun-trap"), small but pretty and comfortable rooms with nice views, and Savoyard furnishings and cuisine. Food and service were criticised last year, but not this: "Dinner was superb, served by pleasant staff in a palatial dining room." Some rooms may be "rather basic"; best are front ones in the new wing. (*R and W Bowden, Liz King and B Schenk, Ivana Copelli*)

Open All year.
Rooms 2 suites, 33 double, 5 single – all with bath and/or shower, telephone; 11 with TV. Some in garden annexe. Ground-floor rooms.
Facilities 2 lifts. Lounge, bar, 3 dining rooms; conference facilities. Garden with tennis court and swimming pool.
Location Éloise is 5 km SE of Bellegarde, off N508 to Annecy.
Credit cards All major cards accepted.
Terms [1990 rates] Rooms: single 190 frs, double 210–320 frs. Breakfast 38 frs. Dinner, B&B 290–357 frs per person; full board 350–417 frs. Set lunch/dinner 140–250 frs; full alc 325 frs. Reduced rates and special meals for children.

BÉNODET 29118 Finistère   Map 8

Hôtel Ménez-Frost   *Tel* 98.57.03.09
4 rue J Charcot

Bénodet is a very pleasant resort in south-west Brittany, at the mouth of the quiet river Odet studded with pleasure-boats. It is busy with French families in August, but the season ends in early September when many amenities close, even if the hotels stay open longer. This one, just right for a family holiday, has again been admired this year. "It has so many facilities," explains one devotee, "heated outdoor swimming pool, tennis, ping pong, and it's near good beaches. Our bedroom had dull decor but a balcony overlooking the pool; in our building the rooms were grouped in pairs, useful for a family. Breakfast was very good, apart from the packaged butter and jams. The manager was wonderful, keeping an eye on everything in a charming fashion." Many rooms face the pool, but are not noisy. No restaurant, which some families might find a handicap: but there are good eating places nearby, such as the *Poste*, across the road. (*RM Flaherty*)

Open Easter–30 Sep; self-catering suites open all year.
Rooms 6 suites, 30 double, 23 single – all with bath, shower, telephone, baby-listening; some with balcony. 12 ground-floor rooms. 3 self-catering apartments.
Facilities Salon, bar, TV room, reading room; conference facilities. Garden with heated swimming pool; solarium, sauna, tennis, table-tennis.
Location Central, near post office, port and ferry. Parking.
Credit cards Access, Visa.
Terms Rooms: single 280–365 frs, double 300–405 frs, suite 490–700 frs. Breakfast 35 frs. Children under 3 free of charge. (No restaurant.)

BEUZEVILLE 27210 Eure   **Map 8**

Auberge du Cochon d'Or   `BUDGET`   *Tel* 32.57.70.46
and Le Petit Castel
Place du Général-de-Gaulle

This spruce old Norman auberge and adjacent modern hotel, in a small town near Honfleur, are both owned and run by the Folleau family. Most guests sleep at the *Castel*, a *Logis de France*, recently renovated and still well liked; recent visitors had a pleasant room facing the quiet walled garden (those at the front, by the main road, might be noisier). The welcome is friendly. As for the *Cochon d'Or*, where you eat, readers feel that it well deserves its *Michelin* red "R" for good value (one couple enjoyed truite farcie and tripes au calvados). "Normandy cooking at its best." "An enjoyable meal in a relaxing atmosphere – guinea-fowl in a grapefruit and orange sauce." One reader who liked the food thought the hotel itself a bit ordinary. More reports please.

Open 15 Jan–15 Dec. Restaurant closed Mon.
Rooms 21 double – 17 with bath, 4 with shower; 16 with telephone; 12 with TV. 16 at *Le Castel*.
Facilities 2 lounges (1 at *Le Castel*), TV room, restaurant; 2 conference rooms. Garden.
Location In centre. Quietest rooms in *Petit Castel*. Beuzeville is 15 km SE of Honfleur, just N of Paris–Caen motorway. Parking.
Credit cards Access, Visa.
Terms B&B: single occupancy 200 frs, double 340 frs. Set meals 70, 100, 140 and 195 frs; full alc 200 frs.

BEYNAC 24220 Dordogne   **Map 10**

Hôtel Bonnet   `BUDGET`   *Tel* 53.29.50.01

Owned and run by the "always cheerful" Renée Bonnet, this charming and unpretentious hotel, with its flowery creeper-covered terrace, stands in a village above a curve in the Dordogne where four medieval castles are in view. Liked again this year: "Friendly, and professionally run, with good food and service." "We stayed in the beautifully converted barns at the back, with views over the pretty garden and stream. Rooms in the main hotel are pleasant, too, but not such a treat." The hotel is on a main road, making some front rooms noisy. (*Dr ME Boxer, Mrs CS Robinson, Fred Sweet, and Mary Connolly*)

Open 18 Apr–15 Oct.
Rooms 21 double, 1 single – all with bath and/or shower, telephone. Some rooms in annexe.
Facilities Salon, restaurant, terrace. Garden; river with fishing, swimming.
Location 10 km W of Sarlat.
Credit cards Access, Visa.
Terms Rooms: single 130–190 frs, double 195–260 frs. Breakfast 26 frs. Dinner, B&B 260–285 frs per person. Set lunch/dinner 110, 170 and 210 frs; full alc 280 frs. Reduced rates for children under 7; special meals.

BIOT 06410 Alpes-Maritimes   **Map 11**

Hôtel-Restaurant Galerie des   *Tel* 93.65.01.04
  Arcades
16 place des Arcades

An idiosyncratic 15th-century inn/café/bistro/art gallery in the arcaded main square of a picturesque hill-village behind Antibes. Engagingly Bohemian *patron*, André Brothier, has lined the dining room with Braques and Miros, and he attracts a lively clientele of local fellow-Bohemians. Bedrooms are olde worlde, but the plumbing is not. The inn's hyper-relaxed atmosphere may not suit all tastes: pop music may resound from the café while you eat your aioli or sardines farcies. "Typically and rustically French. The rooms were perfectly acceptable, but as we all know the French see food as more important. On our visit, my charcuterie and soup could have fed the whole restaurant, and standards were superb. Madame was charming." (*David Lees, JA*)

Open All year. Restaurant closed 11 Nov–10 Dec.
Rooms 12 double – all with bath and/or shower, telephone, TV. 2 in annexe.
Facilities Bar, TV room, 2 restaurants. Patio.
Location Central, some garages. Biot is 8 km NW of Antibes.
Restriction Not suitable for &.
Credit cards None accepted.
Terms Rooms 200–400 frs. Breakfast 30 frs. Set lunch/dinner 140–150 frs; full alc 180 frs. Reduced rates and special meals for children.

LE BLANC 36300 Indre   **Map 10**

La Domaine de l'Étape   **BUDGET**   *Tel* 54.37.18.02
Route de Belâbre

An appealing rural find by two reporters this year, in quiet, unspoilt countryside east of Poitiers. Secluded down a country lane, in its own big park, it's a sturdy *fin-de-siècle* mansion, outwardly no beauty, but with other joys: "Paddocks full of wild flowers, with donkeys, two mares and their foals. Most guests took their aperitifs on the lawn, enchanted by the antics of the foals. Now and then Madame would whizz by on her bicycle. Parking? – you just find a spot under the trees. All very relaxed and great fun. The restaurant was efficiently run by two delightful women, and the food was good, cheap and well presented. Bedrooms are in the house and in two separate buildings, one purpose-built and rather unattractive, the other an old farm outbuilding, where we had a spacious room." "Mme Seiller was most welcoming. A simple 100-franc meal, perfect in both quantity and quality, is served to residents in the evening: the soup tureen, pâté terrine and cheeseboard are all left on the table for you to help yourself as often as you wish. The best of French home-cooking – a verdict endorsed by a crowded room of enthusiastic French guests." (*C and M Hédoin, Colin Pilkington*) A new annexe with suites has just been added. The hotel has its own lake for fishing and boating, its own stables for riding, and there's an aerodrome nearby for gliding and parachuting.

Open All year. Restaurant closed for lunch.
Rooms 30 double – all with bath and/or shower, telephone, TV. 16 in 2 annexes.
Facilities Lounge with TV, 2 dining rooms. Large grounds with garden, lake, fishing, riding.
Location 6 km SE of Le Blanc (which is 60 km E of Poitiers), off D10 to Belâbre; hotel poorly signposted.
Restriction Not suitable for &.
Credit cards Access, Diners, Visa.
Terms Rooms 180–330 frs. Breakfast 36 frs. Set dinner 100 frs; full alc 120 frs.

BLOIS 41000 Loir-et-Cher   Map 8

Anne de Bretagne   *Tel* 54.78.05.38
31 avenue Jean-Laigret

Useful for a Loire valley stopover: a clean and friendly hotel in the upper town, near the castle, well above the river. Pleasant bar, and patio for drinks and breakfast. Closed 18 Feb–18 Mar. 29 rooms, most with bath and/or shower. B&B double 210–355 frs. No restaurant: plenty in town. Endorsed this year, but fuller reports requested.

BONNEVAUX-LE-PRIEURÉ 25620 Saône   Map 10

Le Moulin du Prieuré   *Tel* 81.59.21.47

The glorious Brême valley is a green winding cleft in the Jura, near picturesque Ornans where Courbet was born and where he painted (museum). "The scenery is grandiose and the silence complete. The hotel is a converted watermill and parts of its mechanism can still be seen; the bedrooms are in separate modern chalets. Guests prepare their own breakfast in their rooms, a system developed with fishermen and walkers in mind who want to start at crack of dawn. Monsieur deals mostly with the fishing (season begins in May), while Madame looks after the restaurant in regal manner. Innovative dishes of high quality, with menus changing seasonally." *Gault Millau toque*. Public rooms are gracefully furnished in local style. (*AF Thomas*)

Open 15 Mar–15 Nov. Closed Sun evening and Mon in low season.
Rooms 8 double – all with bath/shower, telephone, TV. 1 in annexe.
Facilities Lounge, restaurant. Garden. Fishing.
Location 8 km NE of Ornans by D67 and D280.
Credit cards All major cards accepted.
Terms Rooms 300–330 frs. Breakfast 25 frs. Set menu 320 frs; full alc 300 frs.

BORDEAUX 33000 Gironde   Map 10

Hotel Burdigala   *Tel* 56.90.16.16
115 rue Georges-Bonnac   *Fax* 56.93.15.06
                                                          Telex 572981

Our first-ever entry for this large and graceful city, making its Guide
debut with this inspector's 1990 report: "Ten minutes' walk from the
centre, a new medium-sized purpose-built hotel, four-star and fairly
glossy, but below luxury prices. The large marble-floored open-plan foyer
was too coolly formal for my taste, but service was courteous and rooms
comfortable (water could have been hotter). A fountain plashes in the
small, chic restaurant where the *nouvelle*-ish cuisine (salade de cailles,
raviolis de langouste, etc) is OK but unexciting. Many better and cheaper
eating places can be found in the *vieille ville* where Mauriac's ghost still
hovers." More reports please.

Open All year.
Rooms 7 suites, 64 double – all with bath, shower, telephone, radio, TV, air-
conditioning.
Facilities Lift, ramps. 3 salons, bar, restaurant; conference facilities.
Location Ten mins' walk from centre. Underground garage.
Credit cards All major cards accepted.
Terms Rooms: single 600 frs, double 650 frs, suite 1,000 frs. Breakfast 58 frs. Set
lunch 200 frs, dinner 250 frs; full alc 300 frs. Children under 4 free; special meals
on request.

LA BOUILLE 76530 Seine-Maritime   Map 8

Hôtel Saint-Pierre   *Tel* 35.18.01.01

Set in a pretty hamlet on the Seine near Rouen, this friendly restaurant-
with-rooms offers good river views and fine food. It is restored to the
Guide this year by five commendations. "A lovely room overlooking the
Seine and breakfast on the terrace. The menu was wonderful." "The
overall menu did not alter, but the food was excellent, housekeeping
meticulous, and Mme Huet friendly." There's a colourful bar, and meals
can be taken on the terrace. (*Bruce Wass, P Gill, Mr and Mrs PS Wood and
others*) Wines are thought too pricey.

Open All year. Closed Tue evening and Wed 1 Nov–31 Mar.
Rooms 7 double – all with bath and/or shower, telephone; 3 with TV.
Facilities Restaurant. Terrace.
Location 20 km SW of Rouen: take Maison Brûlée turning off Paris–Le Havre
autoroute.
Credit card Visa.
Terms Rooms: single 300 frs, double 400 frs. Breakfast 40 frs. Set lunch/dinner
160–240 frs; full alc 250–350 frs. Off-season reductions. Reduced rates for children
sharing parents' room; special meals.

BOURBON-L'ARCHAMBAULT 03160 Allier   Map 10

Hôtel des Thermes   *Tel* 70.67.00.15
Avenue Charles Louis Philippe

"The rooms are most comfortable, and an exquisite dinner was served in
an atmosphere of old-fashioned courtesy and cherishing. The brothers

Barichard deserve highest praise for civility of the gravest kind," says a recent report. Indeed the brothers have already won First Prize for Welcome and Friendliness in the Allier *département* for their sedate and spruce hotel: it is set in a spa town of northern Auvergne where Talleyrand used to take a cure for rheumatism. Here Guy Barichard wins a *Michelin* rosette for his foie gras poêlé aux morilles, but he is also expert at the simpler dishes, such as omelettes and sole, that most *curistes* prefer. Our own readers remain enthusiastic this year: "The food was French cooking at its best and the service first-class." "Possibly the best bedroom we have had in French hotels." The hotel has a garden-terrace facing the cure centre and a private lake for fishing, five kilometres away. (*AG Catchpole, M Neale, Christine Lawrie and Dr John Coker, Brig Laurence and Fran Fowler*) Front rooms can be noisy, for they face a main road; main house rooms are said to be better than annexe ones.

Open 22 Mar–31 Oct.
Rooms 1 suite, 17 double, 4 single – 10 with bath, 6 with shower, all with telephone. 4 in annexe.
Facilities Salon, TV room, dining room. Large grounds with terrace, garden and private lake; fishing.
Location 200 metres from town centre. Town is 23 km W of Moulins. Garage.
Restriction Not suitable for &.
Credit cards Access, Visa.
Terms Rooms: single 125 frs, double 280 frs, suite 300 frs. Breakfast 29 frs. Full board: single 270 frs, double 580–660 frs, suite 705 frs. Set lunch/dinner 86, 155, 200 and 295 frs. Special meals for children.

LE BOURGET-DU-LAC 73370 Savoie   Map 10

Hôtel Ombremont   *Tel* 79.25.00.23
                                                            Fax 79.25.25.77
                                                            Telex 980832

The large Lac du Bourget is Lamartine's *Le Lac* where he mourned his lost love. Here, secluded in its big garden by the lake, just outside the smart resort of Le Bourget, is this handsome gabled country house, whose sympathetic young owners, the Carlos, have again this year won readers' hearts: "A delightful hotel with food to match; the tone is set by the Carlos." "The Carlos do all they can to make one's stay enjoyable." The cooking (*Michelin* rosette, *Gault Millau toque*) is judged "very distinguished" by a cookery writer, who adds: "I ate magret stuffed with foie gras, a very intelligent combination, and a very pretty fruit salad served on attractive plates. From the water this hotel appears to be hung on a series of ledges, on the rock face, with a dark mass of conifers behind. The terraces with their green and white umbrellas look infinitely inviting. Black merlins skim over the water." Bedrooms are "elegantly furnished"; views from the dining room's open balcony are superb. But the stairs are numerous and the swimming pool is not easy of access. (*Pepita Aris, AJ Collins, Donald B Williams, and others*)

Open All year except 2 Jan–5 Feb. Restaurant closed Sat midday in low season.
Rooms 2 suites, 16 double – all with bath, shower, telephone, radio, baby-listening; some with TV. 2 in chalet in park.
Facilities Salon, bar, billiard room, gym, restaurant; conference facilities; terrace. Garden, with swimming pool, leading down to lake; rocky beach with lifeguard.
Location 2 km N of Le Bourget, on N504.
Restriction Not suitable for &.

Credit cards Access, Visa.
Terms [1990 rates] Rooms 550–750 frs, suite from 1,300 frs. Set meals 195–450 frs. Reduced rates and special meals for children.

BOURROUILLAN 32370 Gers   Map 10

Hôtel-Restaurant Le Moulin   *Tel* 62.09.06.72
   du Comte
Manciet

In the depths of rural Gascony, a new entry proposed by a reader with a Tati-esque relish for the quirks of French holiday-making: "It's a watermill amid fields, with not another building in sight. We did a happy zombie-like triangle between our room, the restaurant and the pool, which the children loved. The set menus worked up in quality towards the weekend, starting with the more obscure parts of animals, and becoming superb by Thursday. For breakfast (lots of toast and home-made jam), we sat at a big table in the family sitting room, where my children giggled at a large Monegasque gentleman in vividly striped pyjamas. The lighting in our room was the usual French semi-gloom; I read by the light of the loo. They had a disco which mercifully was closed. The lounge was rather gloomy but the sunsets were beautiful – and we all want to go again next year." (*EL*) Genuine rustic decor (beamed ceilings, etc). More reports clearly needed.

Open 1 Mar–31 Dec. Closed Christmas.
Rooms 10 – all with bath, telephone; 7 with TV. 4 ground-floor rooms.
Facilities Salon with TV, restaurant; night club, functions facilities. Garden with swimming pool.
Location Bourrouillan is 9 km NW of Manciet, off N124 Condom–Aire-sur-Adour.
Credit cards Amex, Visa.
Terms Rooms 230–300 frs. Breakfast 25 frs. Dinner, B&B 220–280 frs per person; full board 280–320 frs. Set lunch/dinner 80, 115 and 200 frs; full alc 235 frs. Reduced rates and special meals for children on request.

BRANTÔME 24310 Dordogne   Map 10

Le Châtenet   *Tel* 53.05.81.08
                                                       Fax 53.05.85.52

Brantôme, on the river Dronne north of Périgueux, is a beautiful but trippery small town. Just outside it, away from the crowds and by the river, stands this delightful 17th-century ranch-like manor, all mellow brown stone, with creepers and outdoor galleries. It was converted by its English-speaking owners, the Laxtons (he was educated in England and is now the mayor of Brantôme), whom readers again this year have found utterly charming. "This lovely comfortable hotel feels like a home. Bedrooms are spacious: most overlook the garden." Breakfasts including eggs, served on Limoges china, have been judged delicious. There's a beautifully kept garden, smallish but welcome pool, and a clubhouse bar where you write down what you take. Two grievances: "Breakfast came 20 minutes late, coffee was cool and – horrors! – a flag was put on our table, not even a Union Jack (we are British) but Stars and Stripes. And why, when the garden was full of fresh flowers, did our room only have dried ones?" Bed-and-breakfast only, but there are no fewer than three

Michelin-rosetted restaurants nearby (see Champagnac-de-Belair), while the Laxtons will recommend good cheaper places too. (*HR, C and M Hédoin, Eileen Broadbent, and others*)

Open All year, except possibly a short while in low season (1 Nov–1 Apr).
Rooms 2 suites, 8 double – all with bath, shower, telephone, TV, baby-listening. 1 ground-floor room equipped for &. with electrically manned bed and special fittings (20% reduction for &.). 2 rooms in cottage with lounge and kitchenette.
Facilities Lounge; clubhouse with bar; terrace. 18-acre grounds with swimming pool, tennis court, children's playground; river frontage, fishing, canoeing.
Location 1/2 m W of Brantôme, off D78.
Credit cards Access, Visa.
Terms Rooms 300–450 frs, suite 650 frs. Breakfast 45 frs. (No restaurant.)

BRIOUDE 43100 Haute-Loire   Map 10

Hôtel de la Poste et Champanne   `BUDGET`   *Tel* 71.50.14.62
1 boulevard Docteur Devins

A delightfully down-to-earth and very traditional hotel in the main street, in between a lace-making museum and a salmon museum – fancy that. It is run "with verve and atmosphere" by the octogenarian Albertine Barge and her family, including granddaughters whose panache is much admired by readers this year. Latest reports: "Delicious food but far too much!" "We loved it. The help-yourself breakfast was the best we had in France." "A smiling welcome, a decent modern bedroom and balcony, a good dinner and breakfast." "Mme Barge is a wonderful character. Good plain peasant-style cooking, in contrast to the mouth-watering and beautifully presented sweets." "The menu of regional dishes was a delight." (*BW Ribbons, Gillian van Gelder*) *Michelin* and *Gault Millau* concur, by awarding their "good value" red print for the cheaper set menus (local dishes such as potée de lentilles and tourte aux choux). Some recent modernisation, but bedrooms can still be "a bit basic", even in the new annexe.

Open All year except 1–20 Jan and Sun evening Oct–May.
Rooms 2 for 4 people, 18 double – 10 with bath and shower, 4 with shower, all with telephone and TV. 14 with balcony, in garden annexe.
Facilities Reading room, TV room, bar with terrace, 4 dining rooms; functions room. Small garden.
Location Central; annexe has parking.
Credit card Visa.
Terms Rooms 100–240 frs. Breakfast 22 frs. Half board 180 frs per person; full board 230 frs. Set lunch/dinner 60, 88 and 150 frs. Reduced rates for children; special meals on request.

CABASSON 83230 Var   Map 11

Hôtel-Restaurant Les Palmiers   *Tel* 94.64.81.94
Chemin des Palmiers   *Telex* 400233

West of Le Lavandou, secluded in woodland yet near to sandy beaches – not an easy combination on this crowded coast. A cheerful, well-modernised hotel in local style, fairly smart yet not pretentious, run elegantly by the Guinets (he reserved, she charming). Bedrooms and cooking both approved. 29 rooms, all with bath and/or shower, 360–700 frs. Breakfast 50 frs. Set menus 135–190 frs. Recently re-nominated. More reports welcome.

CABOURG 14390 Calvados   **Map 8**

Pullman Grand Hôtel   *Tel* 31.91.01.79
Promenade Marcel Proust   *Fax* 31.24.03.20
                                                     Telex 171364

In a once-so-fashionable and still popular Normandy resort, this is the grand hotel where Proust often stayed, the model for the seaside hotel in his fictional Balbec. Well restored, it still has marble pillars and chandeliers. Modern comforts (ask for the chambre Marcel Proust); *goodish food in* Le Balbec *restaurant; madeleines served with breakfast in the big* belle époque *dining room that he called the Aquarium. 70 rooms, all with bath, double 460– 1,200 frs. Full alc 220 frs. Few recent reports. More welcome.*

CABRERETS 46330 Lot   **Map 10**

La Pescalerie   *Tel* 65.31.22.55

This 18th-century Quercy rural mansion, restored and decorated in exquisite taste (many bedrooms have antiques), stands alone at the foot of a rocky hill, just outside the village. A large semi-formal garden stretches away to the wooded banks of the Célé where you can swim if you wish and where jays call and kingfishers arrow through the shadows. The hotel is run in country house style by Hélène Combette and her surgeon husband, and again this year has won rave notices: "Lovely! The rooms were delightful, the food a revelation (everything fresh), the service attentive, the setting wonderful." "The jewel in the crown. It's not just the atmosphere (exquisite), the warm welcome, the luxurious comfort, the beauty, the food, the garden; it's the feeling of hard-working professional determination to keep a well-oiled machine rolling smoothly, yet make it appear that it happens by happy accident. Les Combettes, we salute you!" One reader had a small room with a large marble bathroom; others have enjoyed breakfast (honey in the comb) on the terrace under a magnolia tree, and the playful house dog Micki. (*Dr and Mrs A Winterbourne, RGL Pugh, NM Mackintosh, and others*)

Open 1 Apr–1 Nov.
Rooms 10 double – all with bath, shower, telephone, TV.
Facilities Lounge with TV, bar, dining room; breakfast terrace. Garden leading to river with swimming, fishing, boating.
Location At La Fontaine de la Pescalerie, 2.5 km NE of Cabrerets on D41 to Figeac.
Restriction Not suitable for &.
Credit cards All major cards accepted.
Terms [1990 rates] Rooms 450–620 frs. Breakfast 50 frs. Set lunch/dinner 195–240 frs.

Please never tell a hotel you intend to send a report to the Guide. Anonymity is essential for objectivity.

CAEN 14000 Calvados   Map 8

Le Dauphin   *Tel* 31.86.22.26
29 rue Gémare   *Telex* 171707

Robert Chabredier's restaurant-with-rooms forms part of an ancient
priory, in a corner of Caen near the castle which somehow escaped the
1944 devastation. Bedrooms are nothing special, but the cooking (*Gault
Millau toque*), notably fish, has again won raves this year: "The restaurant
is a bright airy room. There stands M Chabredier like a cardboard cut-out,
his whites so white and crisply starched that one wonders which is the
greater, his laundry or his cream bill. Highlights of his very good food
were oysters stuffed with leeks, monkfish with a crab coulis, and apple
and mirabelle tarts. Vegetables were sadly overcooked. And the menu
does not change, so there are no surprises. Children are welcome."
Others have admired the panaché de poissons, "really gamey game
terrine", partridge in cider sauce, the Normandy cheeseboard, and the
breakfasts "with home-made breads, stewed and fresh fruit", served in a
light room with tapestry-covered walls and timber beams. (*Diana Cooper,
JE Fisher, M and JS*) But bedrooms have been found rather airless and the
double-glazing not totally effective.

Open All year except 17 July–8 Aug and Christmas Eve. Restaurant closed Sat.
Rooms 22 double – all with bath and shower, telephone, T V. 7 in annexe next door.
Facilities Lift in annexe. Bar, 3 dining rooms.
Location Central; signposted from château. Rooms in main building are quiet, the
others are sound-proofed. Private parking; garage nearby.
Restriction Not suitable for &.
Credit cards All major cards accepted.
Terms Rooms: single 260–340 frs, double 280–360 frs. Breakfast 40 frs. Set meals
85, 150, 210 and 320 frs; full alc 250 frs. Reduced rates for children sharing
parents' room; special meals on request.

CALVI 2B Haute-Corse, Corsica   Map 11

Les Aloës ▆BUDGET▆   *Tel* 95.65.01.46
Quartier Donatéo
Calvi, 20260

The old fortified port of Calvi, now Corsica's largest summer resort, has a
delightful setting on a wide bay with a superb sandy beach, a Venetian
citadel looming above, and mountains in the background. An ideal spot
for viewing all this is the peace and cool of the *Aloës*, an unpretentious
modern B&B hotel above the town and away from the noise. "Rooms are
small, but all are quiet and some have a superb view of the bay," says a
recent visitor. "We took breakfast on our own small terrace" (rooms at the
back are especially quiet). Others have referred to the "helpful management", but one visitor thought the plumbing "bizarre". Of the many
restaurants down by the port, try the inexpensive *San Carlù*. (*Christian
Draz*)

Open May–Oct.
Rooms 26 – all with bath and/or shower, telephone. 5 with terrace in annexe.
Facilities Salon, bar, T V room, library. Terrace and garden. Beach 1 km.
Location 1 km SW of town centre: take route d'Ajaccio or route de l'Usine
Électrique. Parking.
Credit cards All major cards accepted.

Terms Rooms: single 190 frs, double 280–460 frs. Breakfast 26 frs. 1-night bookings sometimes refused in high season. (No restaurant.)

CAMBRAI 59400 Nord   Map 9

Hôtel Beatus **BUDGET**   *Tel 27.81.45.70*
718 avenue de Paris   *Telex 820597*

A "very pretty" low white building, set back from the road, a mile out of town. It has an elegant bar, quiet and comfortable rooms furnished in Louis XV/XVI styles, and has been liked again this year. "A charming quiet garden; Madame very chatty and helpful, quite a character." "Two ghost-like elderly ladies, and a young country girl, gave us a gracious welcome. Rooms were stylishly furnished, with lovely views of flower-beds. Pretty white lanterns along the well-trimmed lawn, where we had a nice breakfast." Another reader pulled out all the stops, dubbing the *Beatus* "the friendliest hotel we have ever visited". (*C Bagshawe, Alan Butterworth, A and C Herxheimer*).

Open All year.
Rooms 26 double – all with bath, shower, radio, TV, baby-listening. 12 ground-floor rooms.
Facilities Salon, bar, breakfast room. Garden.
Location 15 km SW of town centre on N44 to St-Quentin. Garage, private parking.
Credit cards All major cards accepted.
Terms Rooms 270–290 frs. Breakfast 35 frs. Reduced rates for children sharing parents' room. (No restaurant.)

CANCALE 35260 Côtes-du-Nord   Map 8

Restaurant et Hôtel de Bricourt   *Tel 99.89.64.76*
1 rue Duguesclin (restaurant)

Just about Brittany's finest modern cooking (two *Michelin* rosettes, four red *Gault Millau toques*) is to be found at *patron*/chef Olivier Roellinger's *very* chic restaurant-with-six-rooms-five-minutes'-drive-away, in this delightful if ultra-touristy fishing port. The restaurant is down town; the hotel part is up on the cliff, facing the fabulous view across the bay that Colette describes in *Le Blé en Herbe* (here in Cancale she wrote this novel of first love in 1923). Our nominator reports: "The hotel, a handsome villa, is run by a delightful and considerate lady who arranged for her daughter to baby-sit and brought us a first-class breakfast. Rooms are well furnished, with marble bathrooms; there's no lounge, but a small garden leading to the clifftop for sitting out when fine. The outstanding view over the oyster-beds extends across the bay to Mont St-Michel. The restaurant is equally outstanding. Oysters of course were superb, as were other fish dishes. The striking feature of M Roellinger's cooking is his very effective use of spices – the hotel bedrooms are named after them." (*Helen and Charles Priday*)

Open Mar–Dec. Restaurant closed Tue, and Wed except July and Aug.
Rooms 6 – all with bath and/or shower, telephone.
Facilities Restaurant. Garden.

Location Restaurant central; bedrooms 1 km NE of centre. Parking. Cancale is 14 km E of St-Malo.
Restriction Not suitable for &.
Credit cards In restaurant all major cards accepted.
Terms [1990 rates] Rooms 500 frs. Breakfast 50 frs. Alc meals (excluding wine) 250–340 frs. Special meals for children.

CANNES 06400 Alpes-Maritimes   Map 11

Chalet de l'Isère   `BUDGET`   *Tel* 93.38.50.80
42 avenue de Grasse

A striking contrast to the swanky palace-hotels down along La Croisette, this small and personal *pension* stands on a hillside in the suburbs, within ten minutes' walk of the front. It was dropped from the Guide in 1986, but is now in new hands and is re-nominated by 1990 visitors: "The rooms are plain but neat and charming. There's a garden courtyard where we took our meals – family-style affairs, always delicious. The owner is a former French legionnaire." (*Jennifer Mills*) The house once belonged to Guy de Maupassant, and from here he would gaze out at the sea and the rocky Esterel coast. More reports please.

Open All year except Jan, Christmas/New Year.
Rooms 2 triple, 5 double, 1 single – 7 with shower, all with telephone.
Facilities Bar, restaurant. Garden where meals are served.
Location 700 metres from town centre. Parking.
Restriction Not suitable for &.
Credit cards Access, Visa.
Terms Rooms 165–180 frs, triple 240–260 frs. Breakfast 20 frs. Dinner, B&B double 335–360 frs; full board double 465–500 frs. Set lunch/dinner 75 frs. Reduced rates and special meals for children.

CARCASSONNE Aude   Map 10

Domaine d'Auriac   *Tel* 68.25.72.22
Route de St-Hilaire, 11009   *Fax* 68.47.35.54
                                                          Telex 500385

An imposing creeper-covered 19th-century mansion, lying peacefully amid its own woodlands two miles outside Carcassonne, and just across the motorway (out of earshot) from the medieval hilltop fortress. An elegant dining room with a blazing fire in winter; terrace for al fresco meals in summer; cooking (Michelin rosette) much admired by readers this year. Most bedrooms pleasant and spacious, some a bit run down. Closed Sun evening and Mon midday Oct–Easter. 23 rooms, all with bath and shower. Rooms 600–1,100 frs. Set menus 200–380 frs. Some recent criticisms. More reports please.

Hôtel du Donjon   *Tel* 68.71.08.80
2 rue du Comte-Roger   *Fax* 68.25.06.60
La Cité, 11000   *Telex* 505012

Within the walled medieval fortress, this fairly smart Logis de France *is in a beautifully converted ancient building with red tiled floors and rough stone walls but all mod cons. There's a charming rear garden where you can escape*

from the tourist mob, and eat out in summer. Affable welcome, good local dishes
such as cassoulet. Some bedrooms small. Restaurant closed Sun. 36 rooms, all
with bath and shower, 10 air-conditioned. B&B: single 390–430 frs, double 520–
590 frs. Set meal 120 frs. Endorsed this year, but fuller reports welcome.

Hôtel des Remparts   *Tel* 68.71.27.72
3 place du Grand Puits, La Cité, 11000

In a relatively secluded part of the much-visited medieval Cité, an old house
with friendly owners and a fine 14th-century spiral staircase; but the bedrooms
are modern. 18 rooms, all with bath and shower. B&B: single 300 frs, double
330–360 frs. No restaurant, but try the Donjon, above. Recent nomination.
More reports please.

CARSAC-AILLAC 24200 Dordogne   **Map 10**

Le Relais du Touron   *Tel* 53.28.16.70

Plenty of unaffected Dordogne rural charm is to be found at this 19th-
century *gentilhommière*, in deep wooded countryside outside a small
village east of Sarlat. It consists of two buildings, one with two bedrooms
and a salon, the other with ten bedrooms and the restaurant, and has
been tastefully converted and recently opened as a hotel by its Belgian
owner, Claudine Carlier. New to the Guide last year, it has won plenty
more praise in 1989/90 – for the peace and quiet, the pretty and well-
equipped rooms, and the "delightful" Madame Carlier "who has a
passion for baroque music". The cooking, with lots of regional specialities, is judged "imaginative and beautifully presented", though one
reader felt that a less extensive menu ("it cannot possibly all be fresh")
would achieve even better results. "Swimming pool a joy." (*C and M*
Hédoin, John and Jean Bush, Roy and Olwyn Wadlow)

Open 15 Mar–15 Nov. Restaurant closed for lunch and Fri evening out of season.
Rooms 12 double – all with bath and/or shower, telephone. 2 ground-floor
rooms.
Facilities Salon/bar with TV, restaurant. Garden; terrace. Indoor swimming pool.
Location Outside Touron, 8 km E of Sarlat. Parking.
Credit cards All major cards accepted.
Terms [1990 rates] Double room 262–388 frs; dinner, B&B 432–544 frs. Set
lunch/dinner 78, 110 and 215 frs; full alc 190 frs. Reduced rates and special meals
for children.

CARTERET 50270 Manche   **Map 8**

Hôtel de la Marine   *Tel* 33.53.83.31
11 rue de Paris   *Fax* 33.53.39.60

This small fishing port south-west of Cherbourg is now a busy summer
resort, with a fine sandy beach. It was the setting for *Une vieille maîtresse*,
a stark tale of passion by Barbey d'Aurevilly, a powerfully flamboyant
Norman writer too little known in Britain. His is not the fate of the

Marine, besieged by Brits off the ferries. But this sturdy family-run seaside hotel keeps up its standards (*Michelin* rosette, two *Gault Millau toques*), and it won much praise from several visitors this year: "Friendly welcome, pleasant rooms, excellent food and service – the best of the ten hotels we stayed at in northern France, all taken from the Guide." "A delicious vegetarian meal", but the local fish dishes are even better ("I can still smell that fish soup"). Friendly and efficient staff, a patio for drinks, and sea views from some rooms. (*BW Ribbons, A and B Horsley, Mrs EH Prodgers, Joyce Blick*)

Open 1 Feb–11 Nov. Restaurant closed Sun evening and Mon in low season.
Rooms 3 suites, 27 double, 1 single – all with bath, shower, telephone, TV. 3 suites in annexe.
Facilities Salon, bar, 2 restaurants; terrace. Beach 300 metres.
Location In village of Carteret, which is part of Barneville-Carteret; 37 km S of Cherbourg.
Restriction Not suitable for &.
Credit cards Access, Diners, Visa.
Terms [1990 rates] Rooms: single 250 frs, double 320–420 frs. Breakfast 35 frs. Dinner, B&B 305–400 frs per person; full board 335–485 frs. Set lunch/dinner 99, 175, 240 and 350 frs; full alc 350–400 frs. Reduced rates for children; special meals on request.

CASSIS 13260 Bouches-du-Rhône   **Map 11**

Hotel de la Plage du Bestouan   *Tel* 42.01.05.70
Plage du Bestouan   *Fax* 42.01.34.82
                                                          Telex 441287

A breezy modern hotel right by the beach, at the western end of a very picturesque if rather overvisited fishing port-turned-resort. Family owned, impeccably run; very good food and service. Most rooms have sea-facing balcony. Open end Mar–Nov. 29 rooms, all with bath and/or shower. B&B: single 292 frs, double 404–474 frs. Half board 310–400 frs per person. New nomination; more reports welcome.

CENTURI PORT 2B Haute-Corse, Corsica   **Map 11**

Le Vieux Moulin `BUDGET`   *Tel* 95.35.60.15
Centuri Port 20238   *Fax* 95.35.60.24

"Near the northern tip of scenic Cap Corse is this crumbly, untarted-up, utterly Corsican fishing village," writes a reporter this year, restoring to the Guide this equally untarted-up auberge. "Some readers might find it too basic and inefficient, but we succumbed to its wayward Corsican charm. Good fresh fish is served, rather slowly, on an idyllic wide terrace facing the port and sea. The Gauguinesque paintings on the walls are the *patron*'s own work. His staff are somewhat haywire, but amiable; the bedrooms are defiantly unmodernised but somehow cosy, and extremely cheap. OK for a night or two, maybe not longer. It's an informal, old-fashioned place, set in a pre-war time warp – but much of Corsica is like that, that's part of its appeal. They are planning a smart modern extension, but I rather hope that the FLNC bomb-squads will deter them, as they usually do in Corsica." (*JA and KA*) A visiting hotelière from Italy this year gave a strong thumbs-down to service, comfort and maintenance, and found the set menus unchanging (best eat à la carte). We'd welcome more news.

Open 1 Apr–30 Sep.
Rooms 14 double – all with bath or shower, telephone; 8 with TV.
Facilities Salon, TV room, bar, restaurant; disco in July/Aug. Terrace. Solarium. Sea 15 km.
Location Centuri Port is 59 km NW of Bastia.
Restriction Not suitable for &.
Credit cards All major cards accepted.
Terms Rooms 195 frs. Breakfast 20 frs. Dinner, B&B 360 frs per person. Set lunch/dinner 120, 215 and 245 frs; full alc 200 frs. Reduced rates and special meals for children on request.

CÉRET 66400 Pyrénées-Orientales   **Map 10**

La Terrasse au Soleil   *Tel* 68.87.01.94
Route de Fontfrède   *Fax* 68.87.39.24

Splendidly situated in the Pyrenean foothills south of Perpignan, this small modern hotel built in local Catalan style has fine views of the mountains and distant sea. Bedrooms are large, modern and comfortable, notably those in the new annexe. "The staff of the house were friendly, and we had a fine view from our balcony," says a recent visitor, "but the food was nothing special and service was slow." Another thought the hotel "wonderful", with *nouvelle*-ish food generously served. (*Dr W Leggat Smith, Dave Watts*) But the table d'hôte is much less interesting than the *carte*, and the welcome can be offhand.

Open 3 Mar–6 Jan.
Rooms 1 suite, 25 double – all with bath or shower, telephone, TV, baby-listening. 14 in 2 annexes. Ground-floor rooms.
Facilities 4 salons, bar, 2 restaurants; conference room; terrace where meals are served. Garden with swimming pool, tennis court and golf practice.
Location Céret is 31 km SW of Perpignan.
Credit cards Access, Visa.
Terms Rooms 440–950 frs. Breakfast 60 frs. Dinner, B&B: single 670–1,090 frs, double 900–1,320 frs. Set lunch/dinner 140, 190 and 320 frs; full alc 250 frs. Special meals for children.

CHABLIS 89800 Yonne   **Map 9**

Hostellerie des Clos   *Tel* 86.42.10.63
Rue Jules Rathier   *Fax* 86.42.17.11
            Telex 351752

Patron/chef Michel Vignaud's elegant and select hotel/restaurant, a converted almshouse in a well-known wine town, is one of the best in North Burgundy, winning a *Michelin* rosette and two red *Gault Millau toques* for what a reader has called "light creative cookery, perfectly complementing the great wines of Chablis" (e.g. kidneys and grapes cooked in Chablis). The decor is modern and stylish, and the accent is firmly on the restaurant: but the modernised bedrooms are serviceable, most readers this year agree. "A lovely hotel in a charming old town. Dinner delicious; our bedroom was adequate without being luxurious." "The public rooms were light and beautifully furnished. Madame

Vignaud ran the restaurant charmingly, the food was excellent." "The cuisine was light and refined, beautifully if rather ostentatiously presented." "Breakfast included anything from poached pears to home-made fruit loaf. Our spacious room had a view over the flower-filled courtyard." "They are restaurateurs, not hoteliers, and it does show: our pretty room had no mirrors or dressing table." (*CM Jones, PJ Guy, Harriet and Tony Jones, and many others*) One reader reported chaotic service at breakfast.

Open All year except 12 Dec–9 Jan. Restaurant closed Wed, Thu midday except 1 June–30 Sep.
Rooms 26 double – all with bath, shower, telephone, radio, TV. 2 suitable for ঙ.
Facilities Lift. Salon, bar, restaurant; conference room; terrace and garden.
Location Central, parking. Chablis is 19 km E of Auxerre.
Credit cards Access, Visa.
Terms Rooms: single occupancy 200–455 frs, double 230–520 frs. Breakfast 45 frs. Dinner, B&B 495–620 frs per person. Set lunch/dinner 150, 255 and 370 frs; full alc 350 frs. Special meals for children.

CHAGNY 71150 Saône-et-Loire   **Map 10**

Hostellerie du Château de   *Tel* 85.87.13.86
  Bellecroix   *Fax* 85.91.28.62
                                   Telex 283155

A creeper-covered and turreted castle of medieval origin, set in its own park just south of Chagny in the heart of Burgundy. It has a heated pool, charmingly furnished bedrooms, tables under the trees for drinks, and excellent regional cooking (black *Gault Millau toque*). This year, readers on their honeymoon were delighted: "A beautiful place, with everything of high quality. We had an amazing room in an annexe, with four-poster bed, draped tapestries and luxurious bathroom. Food was the best ever and service impeccable." (*Susan and Gordon Marshall*) Further reports welcome.

Open 1 Feb–20 Dec. Closed Wed.
Rooms 19 double – all with bath and/or shower, telephone, TV. 6 in annexe. Ground-floor rooms.
Facilities Salon, bar, 2 dining rooms. Garden with heated swimming pool.
Location 2 km S of Chagny, off N6.
Credit cards All major cards accepted.
Terms Rooms 480–850 frs. Breakfast 45 frs. Dinner, B&B 480–680 frs per person; full board 680–880 frs. Set lunch/dinner 95, 195 and 295 frs; full alc 300 frs.

Hôtel Lameloise   *Tel* 85.87.08.85
36 place d'Armes   *Fax* 85.87.03.57
                                   Telex 801086

Possibly the best cuisine in Burgundy (three *Michelin* rosettes, three red *Gault Millau toques*) is provided by Jacques Lameloise at his elegantly converted 15th-century mansion in the main street of a dullish little town amid woods and vineyards. "Absolute perfection: wonderful food and wine, marvellous service, lovely bedroom and bathroom," runs one report this year. Most other recent visitors have been equally bowled over: "As good as ever: cuisine superb, staff splendid, bedrooms luxurious"; "the best cuisine we've had in France"; "elegant rooms with

ntiques, beamed ceilings and fireplaces"; "a quietly luxurious atmosphere, attentive and courteous service"; and so on. Terrine de foie gras
aux artichaux and a warm apple tart with sharp sorbet have been singled
out. The bedrooms, recently renovated, have superb bathrooms. (*Harriet
and Tony Jones, Kate and Steve Murray-Sykes, Rosamund Hebdon, Alan F
Thomas, and others*)

Open All year except 18 Dec–23 Jan and 1 May. Closed Wed, and Thu midday.
Rooms 1 suite, 20 double – all with bath and/or shower, telephone, radio, TV.
Facilities Lift. Salon, bar, restaurant.
Location Central. Garage parking.
Credit cards Access, Visa.
Terms Rooms 320–1,000 frs. Breakfast 70 frs. Alc meals (excluding wine) 310–
460 frs.

CHÂLONS-SUR-MARNE 51000 Marne   Map 9

Hôtel d'Angleterre et Restaurant   *Tel* 26.68.21.51
Jacky Michel   *Telex* 842078
19 place Monseigneur Tissier

This traditional hotel in the town centre, small but very *soigné* and newly
modernised, is praised for its excellent, friendly service and for owner
Jacky Michel's innovative cooking (*Michelin* rosette, *Gault Millau toque*). A
1990 report runs: "Wonderful ambience in the dining room, food
superbly cooked and presented. The receptionist even persisted in
telephoning about 16 hotels in Paris to find us a room there – 'All part of
the service!' we were told with a smile." Other readers found it
'exceptional value for very high quality. The welcome was smiling and
friendly, the furnishings and decor attractive, and the bathrooms super.
The cooking is superb, especially the 160-franc set menu available on
weekdays. The wine list includes 12 pages of champagnes alone." You
can take drinks on a pretty terrace. And it's worth visiting the big nearby
lake of Chantecoq, "where cranes stay for a large part of the year on their
migration from Siberia. In the evening some three to four thousand return
from the fields in huge formations, calling to each other – a wonderful
sight and sound at dusk." (*Mrs JA Hayward; Pat and Jeremy Temple*)

Open 8 Jan–30 June and 23 July–20 Dec. Closed Sun; restaurant also closed Sat
lunch.
Rooms 18 double – all with bath and/or shower, telephone, TV.
Facilities Lounge with TV, bar, restaurant. Small terrace where meals are served
in summer.
Location Central; near Notre Dame en Vaux. Parking.
Credit cards All major cards accepted.
Terms Rooms 370–500 frs. Breakfast 40 frs. Set meals 160–400 frs; full alc 300 frs.
Special meals for children.

CHALON-SUR-SAÔNE 71100 Saône-et-Loire   Map 10

Hôtel St-Georges   *Tel* 85.48.27.05
32 avenue Jean-Jaurès   *Fax* 85.93.23.88
                                                         Telex 800330

A commercial hotel next to the station in a biggish town: that might spell
mediocrity in Britain or the US, but this is France. And again in 1989/90

visitors have admired the "friendly welcome, excellent reception" and
Michelin-rosetted cooking of young Yves Choux – but not so much the
bedrooms. "Food good and not *nouvelle* – large portions of well-flavoured
dishes such as wild boar with cherries and fillet of hare. Public rooms
quite smart, and bathrooms fairly modern, but bedrooms could do with
updating." "Our room was comfortable but dark and dull. Food
delicious." (*Kate and Steve Murray-Sykes, Mrs J Thomas, Mary Hanson*) One
reader failed to get the special vegetarian meal he had ordered, and did
not relish being rung by front desk at 8 am to be wished *"une excellente
journée"*.

Open All year except Christmas Eve.
Rooms 46 double, 2 single – all with bath or shower, telephone, radio, TV, mini-
bar, air-conditioning.
Facilities Lift. Bar with TV, restaurant; conference facilities.
Location Central, near railway station. Garage.
Credit cards All major cards accepted.
Terms Rooms: single 250–300 frs, double 300–360 frs. Breakfast 40 frs. Set
lunch/dinner 135, 200 and 350 frs; full alc 350 frs. Reduced rates for children
sharing parents' room; special meals.

CHAMONIX-MONT-BLANC 74400 Haute-Savoie   Map 1●

Hôtel Albert 1er   *Tel* 50.53.05.0●
119 impasse du Montenvers   *Fax* 50.55.94.4●
                                                         Telex 38077●

Admired again by several readers in 1989/90, this sizeable chalet-type
ski-hotel stands in its own big garden near the middle of the resort; many
rooms have a balcony and views of Mont Blanc. "Comfortable and
efficient: we enjoyed the excellent dinner, swimming pool and fantastic
views." "Our impeccably clean room had lovely furnishings. The dining
room with fresh flowers and beautiful china was the perfect setting for
the superb meal" (owner/chef Pierre Carrier's cooking wins a *Michelin*
rosette and two red *Gault Millau toques*). Others have praised the
ambience and professionalism and have enjoyed using the pool, jacuzzi
and sauna. "A roomy and comfortable hotel, full of well-heeled skiers
enjoying their *après-ski*. Log fire and piano in the salon." When fine, it's
well worth taking the *téléphérique* (the world's highest, they claim) to a
point just below the summit of Mont Blanc. (*Mrs RB Richards, AJ Collins,
Paul Jackson, Harriet and Tom Jones*)

Open All year except 13–31 May, 21 Oct–5 Dec. Restaurant closed Wed midday.
Rooms 9 suites, 20 double, 3 single – all with bath, shower, telephone, radio, TV,
mini-bar.
Facilities Lift. Bar, lounge, 3 dining rooms, table-tennis room; sauna, whirlpool,
solarium. Large garden with tennis court, swimming pool (heated in summer),
children's play area.
Location In side road, 150 metres from station; 500 metres from town centre.
Parking and garages.
Credit cards All major cards accepted.
Terms B&B: single 450–600 frs, double 550–700 frs, suite 810–965 frs. Dinner,
B&B 405–730 frs per person; full board 505–830 frs. Set meals 165–390 frs.
Reduced rates and special meals for children.

We are particularly keen to have reports on italicised entries.

Auberge du Bois Prin   Tel 50.53.33.51
Les Moussoux   Fax 50.53.48.75
                                                  Telex 319259

Also owned by the Carrier family (see above), a sleek and elegant chalet-style hotel outside the town centre, with fine views of Mont Blanc from front rooms. Good food, a garden, and a beautiful terrace for breakfast. Open 1 June–15 Oct, 13 Dec–20 May. 11 rooms, all with bath and shower. B&B: single 575–730 frs, double 740–945 frs. Set meals 160–350 frs. Re-nominated this year after earlier criticisms (of pretentiousness). More reports please.

CHAMPAGNAC-DE-BELAIR 24530 Dordogne   Map 10

Hostellerie le Moulin du Roc   Tel 53.54.80.36
                                                  Fax 53.54.21.31
                                                  Telex 571555

A gracefully converted 17th-century walnut mill, set quietly by a stream in a village near Brantôme. Lots of flowers and antiques; rooms small but pretty. Swimming pool. This idyllic setting, and the renowned cooking of Solange Gardillou, the owner's wife, have prompted many glossy articles and a chic moneyed international clientele. But some readers this year (and the French guides support them) feel that the cuisine is losing its sparkle and that the Moulin is coasting on its reputation. Closed 15 Nov–15 Dec, 15 Jan–15 Feb; restaurant closed all Tue, Wed lunch. 14 rooms, all with bath, 380–680 frs. Set meals 200–350 frs [1990]. More reports, please.

CHÂTEAU-ARNOUX 04160 Alpes-de-Haute-Provence   Map 11

La Bonne Étape   Tel 92.64.00.09
Chemin du Lac   Fax 92.64.37.36
                                                  Telex 430605

Some of the best cooking in Provence (two *Michelin* rosettes, three red *Gault Millau toques*) is provided by the anglophile Gleize family (father created the restaurant at the *Capital* in London, son worked at the *Connaught*) at their elegantly converted and fairly expensive 17th-century coaching inn. The setting is a bit cramped, on the main Grenoble–Marseille highway, in a small town in a dull part of the Durance valley; but there are open fields at the back and some rooms have a balcony facing these, over the swimming pool. Front rooms can be noisy. Reports this year and last: "Beautiful rooms, outstanding food." "A wonderful place, with charming rooms. We enjoyed roast pigeon, wild boar with raisins and pignon nuts, and stuffed courgette flowers." Try also the local herb-fed lamb. (*Alan F Thomas, Lynne and David Allen*)

Open 12 Feb–2 Dec, 11 Dec–5 Jan. Closed Sun evening and Mon out of season. Restaurant closed 24 Dec.
Rooms 7 suites, 11 double – all with bath, shower, telephone, radio, TV; air-conditioning.
Facilities Salon, bar, 2 dining rooms; small conference room. Garden with heated swimming pool and patio.

Location Near town centre, which is 14 km S of Sisteron. Parking.
Restriction Not suitable for &.
Credit cards All major cards accepted.
Terms Rooms: double 400–800 frs, suite 950 frs. Breakfast 70 frs. Dinner, B&B
800–950 frs per person. Set lunch/dinner 190, 320, 370 and 420 frs; full alc
390 frs. Special meals for children on request.

CHÂTEAU-GONTIER 53200 Mayenne　　　　　　　　　　　　Map 8

Le Jardin des Arts　　　　　　　　　　　　　　　　　*Tel* 43.70.12.12
5 rue Abel Cahour　　　　　　　　　　　　　　　　　*Fax* 43.70.12.07

*A lovely name for an attractive hotel, newly converted from an old mansion
close to the river Mayenne, in a small town north of Angers. Spiral staircases,
well-furnished bedrooms, fine views across big tiered gardens to the river. Good
food. 20 rooms, all with bath and shower. B&B: single 285–385 frs, double 315–
410 frs. Set meals 70–220 frs. Enthusiastic new nomination. More reports
welcome.*

CHÂTILLON-SUR-SEINE 21400 Côte-d'Or　　　　　　　　　　Map 9

Hotel de la Côte d'Or　　　　　　　　　　　　　　　*Tel* 80.91.13.29
Rue Charles Ronot

Châtillon is a small town on the upper Seine between Troyes and Dijon,
noted for its museum of antiquities which include gold and silver Grecian
artefacts of the 6th century BC, found in 1953 at nearby Vix, in the tomb
of a Gallic princess. Not quite in that class of distinction, but very pretty
and charming, is the ivy-covered *Côte d'Or*, a *Logis de France*: "A favourite
stop-over point for me. Dinner – ah, dinner! – is served out in the
courtyard (when fine), under vast rustling chestnut and sycamore trees,
filled with cooing doves. A fountain plays gently, lights in the trees come
on as the afterglow fades from the skies, the service is friendly and
prompt but not hurried. The *menu régional* was excellent value: the vast
array of cheeses went well with the delicious walnut brown bread. My
little room had a comfortable bed, two elegant chairs, a tiny antique desk,
fresh flowers." (*Hilary Swenson*) Some redecoration is planned for the end
of 1990. More reports would be welcome.

Open All year except mid-Dec–23 Jan. Closed Sun evening and Mon except
public holidays, July and Aug.
Rooms 10 double – 7 with bath and shower, 2 with shower, all with telephone,
TV.
Facilities Salon, bar, restaurant. Garden.
Location Central, near river. Parking. Town is 64 km SE of Troyes.
Restriction Not suitable for &.
Credit cards All major cards accepted.
Terms [1990 rates] Rooms: single 180 frs, double 270–480 frs. Breakfast 35 frs. Set
meals 85–340 frs; full alc 290 frs. Special meals for children on request.

If you are nominating a hotel, please err on the side of saying too
much. Many suggestions have to be rejected only because they are
too brief.

CHAVOIRES 74290 Haute-Savoie

Map 10

Pavillon de l'Ermitage

Tel 50.60.11.09

The Tuccinardi family's white villa beside the lovely lake of Annecy is a formally elegant restaurant whose Bressane cooking is generally felt to deserve its *Michelin* rosette. "Yes, the cuisine is indeed distinguished, with portions dauntingly large," runs one recent report, "but the bedrooms with their faded decor are serviceable rather than attractive." Curiously, a reader this year felt the opposite: disappointing food, huge excellent room. Another visitor had "a lovely room with a view over the lake, and a palatial pink marble bathroom". Back rooms with balconies facing the lake are best: front ones face the main road. In summer you can dine by the water's edge on a smart terrace under the trees. (*Alex Liddell, PJ Forrest, Peter and Ann Jones*)

Open Mar–end Oct.
Rooms 2 suites, 8 double – all with bath and telephone.
Facilities Lounge, bar, restaurant. Terrace and lakeside garden.
Location 3 km E of Annecy on Lake Annecy.
Restriction Not suitable for &.
Credit cards All major cards accepted.
Terms [1990 rates] Rooms 350–460 frs. Breakfast 40 frs. Dinner, B&B 350–520 frs per person. Set lunch/dinner 190, 250 and 380 frs.

CHEFFES 49125 Maine-et-Loire

Map 10

Château de Teildras

Tel 41.42.61.08
Telex 722268

"Excellent food, friendly owners, and a relaxing rural setting," say visitors this year to this elegant 16th-century château on the edge of a quiet village beside the pretty river Sarthe, north of Angers. It is the family home of the Comte de Bernard du Breil, who in order to preserve his estate has turned it tastefully into a hotel. He is helped by his wife and two daughters, one of them married to an American writer. You can ride, fish or go for walks in the large park. "We sipped tea in the rose garden and enjoyed an elegant room with high beamed ceiling and royal blue floral wallpaper. It had a view across the fields. Dinner was expensive but well prepared." "Magnificent atmosphere, delicious food." "The public rooms are beautifully decorated with tapestries, paintings and plants, and the lighting is subdued. Our bedroom had antiques, and its windows looked on to the park with its lovely trees and three cows munching in the sunlight." (*Mrs P Carr, Nancy P Barker, and others*) However, one visitor thought the grounds poorly maintained, and another found the family ambience a bit too intrusive.

Open 1 Mar–30 Nov, Christmas and New Year's Eve.
Rooms 11 double – all with bath, shower, telephone, TV.
Facilities 2 salons, bar, 2 dining rooms. Wooded park. Golf, country club nearby.
Location 19 km N of Angers. Turn out of Cheffes towards Juvardeil; château is signposted.
Credit cards All major cards accepted.
Terms B&B: single 484–789 frs, double 835–1,010 frs; dinner, B&B: single 625–905 frs, double 985–1,319 frs. Set lunch/dinner 195–260 frs; full alc 300 frs. Children under 12 sharing parents' room free; special meals.

CHÊNEHUTTE-LES-TUFFEAUX 49350 Maine-et-Loire   Map 10

Hostellerie du Prieuré   *Tel* 41.67.90.14
                                                             Fax 41.67.92.24
                                                             Telex 720379

"Airy and exhilarating, with a wonderful view down over the Loire", this smart and well-known hostelry, converted from a medieval priory, stands on a bluff above the river, amid 60 acres of private wooded park. Two reports this year were enthusiastic: "There's a nice lived-in feel about the place, not at all starchy. While bedrooms in the main building are elegant and spacious, with canopied beds and antiques, they do get noise from the Loire below; those in the bungalows amid oak and pine woods are less luxurious, but cosy and quiet, and each has its own private garden. Food rates highly, with dishes more copious than usual: excellent foie gras, lobster terrine, veal sweetbreads, poulette. A good selection of prime local wines, and breakfast generous by French standards. The waiting staff are young and friendly, the chambermaids adept at quick Molière style repartee. Amazingly friendly owners. Only hazard: squirrels dropped 'visiting-cards' on our car." "Spacious main rooms, enjoyable dinner, impeccable service, nicely landscaped pool. An elegantly furnished bedroom: but the bath was mean, narrow and plastic." "The terraces and flower gardens are wonderful." (*F and IW, HR, and others*) Visit the nearby caves in the tufa cliffs: some are used for mushroom growing, some have ancient sculptures, some are still lived in by troglodytes.

Open All year except 5 Jan–5 Mar.
Rooms 2 suites, 33 double – 32 with bath, 2 with shower, all with telephone, TV. 15 in pavilion in park. Ground-floor rooms.
Facilities Lounge, bar with TV, restaurant. Large grounds with mini-golf, tennis court, heated swimming pool; fishing in the Loire.
Location 7 km NW of Saumur off D751.
Credit cards Access, Amex, Visa.
Terms [1990 rates] Rooms: single 500–950 frs, double 650–1,250 frs, suite 1,000–1,450 frs. Breakfast 60 frs. Set lunch/dinner 280, 340 and 390 frs; full alc 405 frs. Reduced rates and special meals for children.

CHINON 37500 Indre-et-Loire   Map 10

Hôtel Diderot   **BUDGET**   *Tel* 47.93.18.8
4 rue Buffon

Rabelais spent his boyhood, and Joan of Arc first met the Dauphin, in this fine old town on the Cher with a half-ruined hilltop castle. Here this modest B&B, liked as much as ever this year, is run by a friendly Cypriot Theodore Kazamias: "He's such a jolly fellow. We had a superb large room with nice new bathroom." "The welcome was warm and genuine, the jams delicious. M Kazamias is always around to chat." The house is attractive, built of pale stone, much of it covered by a vine, with a wrought-iron balcony on the second floor, reached by a spiral staircase. Inside are exposed beams, and a welcoming salon. Breakfasts, taken communally, include a huge choice of home-made preserves. A great bonus is the courtyard, closed at night, where cars can be safely parked. Some rooms are spacious, others quite small; courtyard-facing ones are the quietest. Foam pillows have been criticised. (*Andrew Davis, RM Flaherty, J and A Larken, Nikki D'Emden and Harry Onsman, and others*)

Open All year.
Rooms 24 double – all with bath or shower, telephone; TV on request. 4 in courtyard, 3 in nearby annexe. Ground-floor rooms.
Facilities Lounge, bar with TV, breakfast room; courtyard.
Location Near place Jeanne d'Arc; hotel is well signposted. Parking in courtyard.
Credit cards All major cards accepted.
Terms B&B: single 200–280 frs, double 270–380 frs. (No restaurant.)

Château de Marçay

Tel 47.93.03.47
Fax 47.93.45.33
Telex 751475

A stone 15th-century château with pepperpot towers and formal garden, set in open country south of Chinon, and now a smart and stylish hotel. Readers still like it a lot: "It is reached down a chestnut-tree-lined gravel drive. Our vast room occupied an entire floor in one of the towers, and had a splendid old fireplace, antique prints and period furniture. The elegant reception rooms have spectacular flower arrangements. The open-air swimming pool was bliss. Dinner on the terrace, watching the swallows race across the sky, was near perfect – the food leans towards *nouvelle* with very few vegetables (*Michelin* rosette, two red *Gault Millau toques*). Both the *maitre d'* and the *sommelier* were young women, smart and charming; prompt yet unhurried service by local waitresses. Breakfast about adequate though 25 frs extra for orange juice seemed extortionate." Rooms in the pavilion annexe are also pleasant, and cheaper than those in the château. (*Ian and Francine Walsh, and others*)

Open All year except 6 Jan–23 Feb.
Rooms 3 suites, 35 double – 27 with bath and shower, 11 with shower, all with telephone; 27 with TV. 11 in pavilion annexe.
Facilities Lift. 2 salons, TV room, bar, restaurant; conference/functions facilities; 2 terraces. Gardens with tennis court, heated swimming pool and children's playground.
Location 7 km S of Chinon by D116.
Credit cards All major cards accepted.
Terms Rooms 520–1,255 frs. Breakfast 60 frs. Dinner, B&B: single 890 frs, double 1,290 frs. Set lunch/dinner 230 and 360 frs. Special meals for children.

CHISSAY-EN-TOURAINE 41400 Loir-et-Cher   Map 8

Château de Chissay

Tel 54.32.32.01
Fax 54.32.43.80
Telex 750393

General de Gaulle stayed here briefly in June 1940, before leaving for England. Near the banks of the Cher east of Tours, it is a typical turreted Loire Valley château, dating in parts from the 13th century, formerly inhabited by two French kings and now refurbished as a fairly luxurious hotel, new to the Guide this year: "A delightful experience. The grounds and gardens, including a lovely swimming pool, are extensive. Service was outstanding, and our room exquisitely furnished with antiques. Food is exceptional, in a lovely dining room where classical music plays softly. Lounges are comfortable." (*Carol Callahan*) More reports please.

Open Mar–Dec. Restaurant closed 24 Dec.
Rooms 9 suites, 16 double, 4 single – all with bath, 28 with telephone. 1 in annexe. 1 on ground floor.
Facilities Lift. 2 salons, TV room, restaurant; banqueting room. Terrace; garden with swimming pool.
Location Outside Chissay village, 3 km W of Montrichard.
Restriction Not suitable for &.
Credit cards All major cards accepted.
Terms [1990 rates] Rooms: single 450 frs, double 500–1,000 frs, suite 920–1,400 frs. Breakfast 50 frs. Dinner, B&B 580–930 frs per person; full board 760–1,110 frs. Set lunch/dinner 160–280 frs; full alc 300–350 frs. Reduced rates for children sharing parents' room.

CHONAS L'AMBALLAN 38121 Isère	Map 10

Domaine de Clairefontaine   *Tel* 74.58.81.52
                                                 Fax 74.58.84.18
                                                 Telex 308132

"A worthwhile stop-over: excellent food, served by an earnest waitress in a beautiful dining room" – a report this year on this converted 18th-century mansion on the edge of the village, in a lovely rural setting. It makes a cheaper alternative to the *Marais St-Jean* (see below). An inspector's earlier view: "The nicest kind of unpretentious French country hotel, family run, slightly down-at-heel, reasonably priced. We had breakfast on the terrace amid birdsong, facing vistas of meadows and rolling hills. A big garden and lovely lawn, a pond, a farm-like feeling – idyllic. The house, which once belonged to the bishops of nearby Vienne, is now run by charming, petite Madame Girardon and her two sons, who trained *chez* Outhier at *La Napoule*. Their cooking is not in that class, but it is good (poulet à l'ail, truite au fenouil); menus have limited choice and change little, so a short stay might be best. Friendly if amateurish service." (*Liz King and Bridget Schenk, Dr Margaret Curtis, and others*) Some rooms are in the main building, others in a converted outhouse: they are quite simple, and one visitor thought they lacked comfort. Another found the *cuisine* too *nouvelle* for his tastes and appetite.

Open All year except Dec and Jan. Restaurant closed Mon midday.
Rooms 18 double – 12 with bath and/or shower; 16 with telephone. 6 in annexe next to main building. 4 ground-floor rooms.
Facilities Salon, 2 dining rooms; terrace. Garden, tennis court.
Location Turn off A7 motorway at Vienne Sud; village, well-signposted, lies to W of N7, 9 km S of Vienne. Parking
Credit card Visa.
Terms [1990 rates] Rooms 150–400 frs. Breakfast 32 frs. Dinner, B&B 280–350 frs per person. Set lunch 130 frs, dinner 300 frs. Special meals for children.

Hostellerie le Marais St-Jean   *Tel* 74.58.83.28
                                                 Fax 74.58.81.90

"Delightful," says a returning devotee this year. "Christian and Suzette Heugas were as friendly as ever." They own and run a very stylish modern hotel, in a big pink converted farmhouse set amid pretty country near the Rhône, south of Vienne. Earlier praise: "Attractive pieces of old France everywhere, beautiful flowers and lovely antiques. The bedrooms were spacious and comfortable, the view from our room like a postcard

Dinner was the best meal I have had in France, beautifully presented, and breakfast was special too, with bowls of home-made jams. M and Mme Heugas are that lovely combination of dedicated, enthusiastic and modest." Others, too, have much enjoyed the food (*Gault Millau toques*), such as duck in a sharp fruit sauce and "real country soups", and have appreciated the beamed ceiling and tiled floor of the cool and sober dining room, and the luxurious bedrooms. "Our children had great fun with the owners' dogs." (*Ray Everett*)

Open All year except 11–30 Nov, Feb, Tue evening and Wed.
Rooms 10 double – all with bath, shower, telephone, TV. 1 ground-floor room with easy access for &.
Facilities 3 lounges, bar, restaurant; conference room. Garden with terrace for al fresco meals.
Location Turn off A7 motorway at Vienne Sud; village, well-signposted, lies to W of N7, 9 km S of Vienne.
Credit cards All major cards accepted.
Terms Rooms: single 480 frs, double 520 frs. Breakfast 50 frs. Set lunch/dinner 150, 270 and 320 frs; full alc 280 frs. Reduced rates and special meals for children.

CLUNY 71250 Saône-et-Loire	**Map 10**

Hôtel-Restaurant de	*Tel* 85.59.00.58
Bourgogne	*Fax* 85.59.03.73
Place de l'Abbaye	

A rambling but dignified old hotel in the main square of this picturesque medieval town, facing what remains of the mighty Romanesque abbey that in the Middle Ages was one of Europe's leading religious, artistic and intellectual centres. The well-kept *Bourgogne* has been an inn since the 18th century (Lamartine often stayed here and guests can still sleep in his bed). Most of its bedrooms look out on to green hills or to the towers of the abbey. A 1990 account: "A tourist hotel in a tourist centre, yet it has an old-fashioned French style and atmosphere, both in its decor and the homely service. The dining room is more formally elegant: here the food just about deserves its *Michelin* rosette." Rooms vary in size. The Gosse family owners are judged "most cordial". (*Kate and Steve Murray-Sykes, Mrs MD Prodgers*)

Open 10 Feb–20 Dec. Closed Tue except high season; restaurant also closed Wed midday.
Rooms 3 suites, 12 double – 8 with bath, 4 with shower, all with telephone, 4 with TV.
Facilities Ramps. Salon, bar, restaurant. Small courtyard where drinks and breakfasts are served in fine weather. Films, concerts.
Location On N79, 25 km NW of Mâcon. Hotel is opposite the abbey (back rooms quietest). Garage parking.
Credit cards All major cards accepted.
Terms Rooms 390–450 frs, suite 800–900 frs. Breakfast 40 frs. Dinner, B&B double 830–1,380 frs. Set lunch/dinner 110–200 frs; full alc 300 frs. Reduced rates and special meals for children.

We asked hotels to quote 1991 prices. Not all were able to predict them in the late spring of 1990. Some of our terms will be inaccurate. Do check latest tariffs at the time of booking.

COLLIOURE 66190 Pyrénées-Orientales   Map 10

Hôtel Madeloc   *Tel* 68.82.07.56
Rue Romain-Rolland

"Madame was delightfully friendly, breakfast was good, the decor pleasant, and our balcony had table, chairs and parasol" – a report this year on this modern B&B hotel, cool and efficient, with a spacious foyer. It is ten minutes' walk up a steepish hill from the quayside of a picturesque and popular fishing-port-cum-trendy-resort, south-east of Perpignan. It has a garden, and upper rooms have views over the hills. (*Brian and Rosalind Keen, D and J Smith*)

Open Easter–15 Oct.
Rooms 21 suites – all with bath and/or shower, telephone.
Facilities Salon, T V room; terrace. Garden. Beach 600 metres.
Location 10 mins' walk from centre, towards station; parking.
Restriction Not suitable for &.
Credit cards Access, Diners, Visa.
Terms Rooms 220–320 frs. Breakfast 32 frs. (No restaurant.)

COLLONGES-LA-ROUGE 19500 Corrèze   Map 10

Relais de St-Jacques **BUDGET**   *Tel* 55.25.41.02
de Compostelle   *Telex* 283155

Collonges is a handsome 16th-century village built of local purple-red stone, carefully restored and set in lush green valleys a few miles north of the Dordogne. Its fine buildings include a 12th-century church; the ruined château of the Vicomte de Turenne, former lord of the region, stands just to the west. The *Relais*, again popular in 1989/90, offers clean, inexpensive, very simple bedrooms; it also has friendly owners, the Castéras, whose cooking earns a *Michelin* red "R" for good value. "Sheer delight," says a reader in 1990. "Interesting village, charming staff, simple but adequate rooms with piping hot water. And a splendid menu (trout with almonds memorable); the excellent wine list includes some cheap half-bottles. Fresh flowers everywhere, and a large breakfast." Other recent accounts: "Charming old inn, funky bedrooms, welcoming hosts, good hearty food. Watching the sun set over the red village is not to be missed." "The restaurant's ambience is one of rural sophistication, with expert service. The food is among the best we have had anywhere – tremendous platters of hors d'oeuvre, massive helpings of stuffed lamb, superb goat's cheeses." "Madame is slightly disorganised but very welcoming. A very cosy salon and a marvellous dinner." "M Castéra loves to chat with his guests after dinner, even if their French is poor." (*Dr AF and Mrs M Polmear, Lynne and David Allen*) But be warned that annexe rooms are especially basic. And there can be muddles over bookings.

Open 1 Feb–30 Nov. Closed Tue evening and Wed in low season.
Rooms 11 double, 1 single – 5 with bath and shower, 2 with shower, all with telephone. 9 in annexe.
Facilities Salon, bar, 2 dining rooms, dining terrace.
Location 21 km SE of Brive; follow signs to Meyssac. Hotel is central. Parking.
Restriction Not suitable for &.
Credit cards All major cards accepted.

Terms Rooms 110–260 frs. Breakfast 35 frs. Dinner, B&B 200–270 frs per person. Set lunch/dinner 120–240 frs; full alc 300 frs. Reduced rates and special meals for children.

COLY 24120 Dordogne   Map 10

Manoir d'Hautegente   *Tel* 53.51.68.03

Set amid deep country near Terrasson, some 20 kilometres north of Sarlat, this fine creeper-covered mansion has been owned by the Hamelin family for 300 years; now Madame Hamelin and her son Paul (both of whom speak excellent English) have tastefully converted it into a delightful small hotel. "The house is beautiful, amid water gardens, streams, fields and woods, and the interior has been furnished and decorated with imagination. The bedrooms are all different and all lovely, with antiques and big, comfortable beds. In the salon, a log fire blazes when the evenings get cool. Dinner, a five-course set meal, is cooked by Madame Hamelin, using her own foie gras, confit de canard, cèpes – and it is excellent. It has a strong regional bias, but there are some lighter, more innovative dishes too. Breakfasts are a delight. A peaceful place and the family are charming, though never intrusive." Endorsed this year: "We sipped our kir royal in the garden by the millstream. Then, in the finely appointed dining room, we enjoyed the owners' own terrine de foie gras (outstanding), pigeon, generous cheeses, raspberry tart. More like really good home-cooking than restaurant food, but no less delicious for that. Wine mark-ups ridiculously modest. Breakfast in the garden was equally perfect. A few years' back the Hamelins went into the foie gras business seriously, the hotel side came later. Only slight drawback: the hotel stands against a high hillside, with no views on that side." (*Jennifer Harte, HR*) A swimming pool has just been built, and there's talk of more bedrooms.

Open Easter–1 Nov.
Rooms 10 double – all with bath, telephone, baby-listening. 1 ground-floor room.
Facilities Lounge, library, restaurant. Garden with swimming pool; river with private fishing.
Location 19 km N of Sarlat. Parking.
Credit cards Access, Visa.
Terms Rooms 450–620 frs. Breakfast 50 frs. Dinner, B&B 460–540 frs per person. Set dinner 200 frs; full alc 250 frs. Reduced rates and special meals for children.

COMBLOUX 74920 Haute-Savoie   Map 10

Aux Ducs de Savoie   *Tel* 50.58.61.43
Le Bouchet   *Telex* 319244

This big modern chalet, where most rooms have a balcony facing Mont Blanc, is the leading hotel of a sizeable skiing and summer resort near Megève. Warm, friendly and well run, with large bedrooms; food good, but choice limited. Open-air pool, heated in summer. Open 8 June–30 Sep, 18 Dec–22 Apr. 50 rooms, all with bath. B&B: single 388–498 frs, double 426–536 frs. Set menus 130–150 frs. Recent nomination. More reports please.

Report forms (Freepost in UK) will be found at the end of the Guide.

COMPIÈGNE 60200 Oise   Map 9

Hostellerie du Royal-Lieu   *Tel* 44.20.10.24
9 rue de Senlis

Joan the Maid was captured and sold to the English in this historic town
with its huge royal palace; then the Germans in 1918, and later the
French in 1940, signed ignominious armistices in a clearing in the nearby
forest. In today's happier age, British, French and German tourists rub
shoulders in this "excellent" restaurant-with-rooms just outside the town.
It is on a dull main road, but overlooks quiet greenery at the back. An
inspector reports in 1990: "A thoroughly recommendable one-night stop.
The chef/*patron* Angelo Bonechi is a sociable fellow who gave us
comfortable rooms in a modern annexe at the back, overlooking the
garden." Another recent view: "It makes a great first night in France
because it reminds you of all the things the French do better than us in
hotels – delicious food, making their guests feel looked after in an
unservile way, and an unfussed view of children in public places. We had
a superb meal. The rooms are small and cluttered with heavy repro
furniture, but all look out on to greenery and a little flock of doves."
Others have agreed, though one or two have thought the food
pretentious and over-priced (certainly it's not cheap) and one criticised
the service. There's a useful lock-up courtyard for cars. (*HR, SR Bateman,
and others*)

Open All year.
Rooms 3 suites, 15 double – all with bath and/or shower, telephone, TV. Ground-
floor rooms.
Facilities Salon, bar, restaurant; terrace for meals in fine weather. Garden.
Location 3 km SW of town, on Senlis road (D932A).
Credit cards All major cards accepted.
Terms Rooms 345 frs, suites 450 frs. Breakfast 30 frs. Set lunch/dinner 150, 190
and 300 frs; full alc 350 frs. Special meals for children.

CONDRIEU 69420 Rhône   Map 10

Hôtellerie Beau Rivage   *Tel* 74.59.52.24
                                                 Fax 74.59.59.36
                                                 Telex 308946

An old creeper-covered hotel beside the *beau rivage* of the Rhône, in Côte
du Rhône vineyard country. Many recent visitors have spoken well of
its owners, the Humann family, and of its *Michelin*-rosetted food. In
summer you can take drinks under white parasols on the "wonderful"
terrace right by the river, or dine out on the stone-flagged patio. "We had
a splendid room with fabric-covered walls and fine furniture. The public
areas are spacious and the gardens lovely. The service had a flourish, and
the dinners were among the best of our holiday." "We were delighted at
the standards of cuisine, welcome and service – we found the porter
polishing all the guests' cars' windscreens, quite unasked." "A typically
French hotel with slightly higgledy-piggledy room arrangements."
(*Stephan and Kate Murray-Sykes, and others*) There's a petro-chemical works
half a mile away, whose low throbbing can be heard at night.

Open All year except 5 Jan–15 Feb.
Rooms 2 suites, 22 double – all with bath, shower, telephone, radio, TV, baby-listening.
Facilities Salon, bar, 2 restaurants. Terrace restaurant overlooking the Rhône. Garden, fishing.
Location 40 km S of Lyon, on N86. Leave A7 at Condrieu exit (coming from N), or Chanas exit (from S).
Restriction Not suitable for &.
Credit cards All major cards accepted.
Terms [1990 rates] Rooms 500–720 frs. Breakfast 57 frs. Set meals 260–385 frs.

CONQUES 12320 Aveyron   Map 10

Hôtel Sainte-Foy
Tel 65.69.84.03
Fax 65.72.81.04

This famous old village between Figeac and Rodez was a leading staging-post on the pilgrimage to Santiago. It straggles along a steep wooded hillside above a gorge, and its slate-roofed houses and cobbled streets surround a massive abbey church, renowned for the Romanesque stone carving on the west doorway and for its rich gold and silver treasure. The *Sainte-Foy* is named after the martyred girl whose weird gold relic is still to be seen in the abbey museum. It's a fine medieval house facing the abbey, with handsome old furniture in the public rooms. Cars can get up to the hotel to unload baggage, but must then park below the village. "The location was perfect, staff were friendly, we liked the food and atmosphere," says a reader this year. Dining in the leafy, gently floodlit courtyard is a special delight: the food is traditional and regional, and very well cooked ("delicious tripoux"). The staff, all female, are helpful and charming. (*Mary E Hanson, D and L Allen, and others*) Since last year, the hotel has added ten more rooms and conference facilities.

Open Mar–1 Nov.
Rooms 1 suite, 28 double, 6 single – all with bath and/or shower, telephone.
Facilities 2 lifts. Lounges, TV room, bar, dining room; conference facilities; interior patio. Indoor swimming pool and fitness room planned.
Location Off D601 and not far from N662 between Figeac (54 km) and Rodez (37 km). Hotel is central, opposite cathedral. Garage and carpark.
Restriction Not suitable for &.
Credit cards Access, Amex, Visa.
Terms Rooms 220–400 frs, suite 500–650 frs. Breakfast 35 frs. Dinner, B&B 300–400 frs per person. Set lunch/dinner 90–230 frs. Special meals for children.

CORDES 81170 Tarn   Map 10

Hôtel Le Grand Écuyer
Rue Voltaire
Tel 63.56.01.03
Fax 63.56.16.99
Telex 530955

This former hunting lodge of the Counts of Toulouse is a select place with fine antiques and spacious rooms. It stands inside a famous old ramparted hilltop village, whose streets today are lined with boutiques and craft shops. It was built by the Counts in the 13th century as a defence against Simon de Montfort and his cruel anti-Cathar crusaders. "A wonderful way to bid farewell to the Cathars," writes one north-bound visitor. "A bedroom with a comfortable four-poster, pleasant carpets, a high timbered ceiling, and the best-appointed bathroom I've met outside Paris.

A good, relaxed meal, capped by the virtuoso dessert production"
(*Michelin* rosette and two red *Gault Millau toques*). Others this year and
last have praised in the highest terms the rooms, bathrooms, service and
food (especially *patron*/chef Yves Thuriès's desserts): "When I die, dear
Lord, please send me to *Le Grand Écuyer*. I have such a poignant memory
of rising in the morning and opening the shutters to find myself floating
on a sea of mist sunk in the valley while the sun sparkled on the green
hills above." (*Stephen and Ali Warshaw, Lynne and David Allen*) This year,
however, more than one reader was disappointed by this much-starred
cuisine. An inspector thought the place was straining pretentiously after
effect – "all that raising of dish-covers at the same time".

Open Mar–Oct.
Rooms 1 suite, 12 double – all with bath, shower, telephone, radio, TV.
Facilities Lounge, bar, TV room, 3 dining rooms. Terrace.
Location In centre of village which is 25 km NW of Albi. Public parking down the
hill, crowded in high season.
Restriction Not suitable for &.
Credit cards All major cards accepted.
Terms Rooms 540–790 frs, suite 1,000–1,300 frs. Breakfast 50 frs. Set
lunch/dinner 180, 250, 320 and 360 frs. Special meals for children on request.

Hostellerie du Vieux Cordes   **BUDGET**   *Tel* 63.56.00.12
Rue St-Michel   *Telex* 530955

Again warmly admired, this stylish but not expensive *Logis de France*,
newly redecorated, stands next to a medieval church: you can dine on the
terrace, or in a delightful courtyard under a huge ancient wistaria. A 1990
saga: "Five of us and a baby turned up looking a scruffy lot; but though
they were full and busy they couldn't have been more helpful and
friendly (even when Daisy aged two upset a glass of wine) – a
demonstration of French hospitality at its awesome best. And our 70-
franc menus, including one vegetarian alternative, were delicious." "A
friendly welcome, and a lovely view of the valley from our room.
Breakfast was the best of our trip." (*HR, CR; John and Rita Newnham*)

Open All year except Jan.
Rooms 21 double – all with bath and/or shower, telephone, TV.
Facilities Lounge with TV, bar, restaurant. Small garden, courtyard.
Location Central; parking nearby.
Restriction Not suitable for &.
Credit cards Access, Diners, Visa.
Terms Rooms: single 265–375 frs, double 300–400 frs. Breakfast 35 frs. Dinner,
B&B: single 370 frs, double 550 frs. Set meals 75–250 frs; full alc 250 frs. Special
meals for children on request.

CORPS-LA-SALETTE 38970 Isère   **Map 10**

Hôtel de la Poste   **BUDGET**   *Tel* 76.30.00.03
Route Napoléon 85

"Une bonne étape", "a fabulous meal for 80 francs" (*Michelin* red "R") –
two 1990 plaudits for the highly traditional *Poste*, "a busy and bustling
hotel, always full". It is in a scenic village along the Route Napoléon, high
up on the winding Grenoble to Provence highway (N85) in the Dauphiné
Alps; Bonaparte rested here on his way from Elba to Paris. "No *nouvelle*

cuisine here – vast helpings, a very pleasant dining room, and the best breakfast we had in France. Our room was Victorian (apart from the bathroom) but comfortable." Another recent visitor also found the food enjoyable and copious, but noted a shortage of hot water. Of the two annexes across the road, one is "rather basic" while the other has smartly decorated rooms giving on to a private courtyard with tables and chairs. One reader had a room with walls "covered in gold silk damask and the shower room was all new in lilac pink with gold taps". (*Mrs K Cowherd, I Ziar, Philippa and Peter Herbert*)

Open End Jan–end Nov.
Rooms 30 double – 19 with bath or shower, 20 with telephone, T V. 10 in annexe opposite. 1 ground-floor room suitable for &.
Facilities Salon, T V room, tearoom, 3 dining rooms; terrace. Lake with sailing and fishing 500 metres.
Location In centre of village. Garage parking.
Credit cards Access, Visa.
Terms B&B: single 210–230 frs, double 260–440 frs; dinner, B&B 200–320 frs per person. Set meals 85, 125 and 240 frs; full alc 160 frs. Reduced rates and special meals for children.

COTIGNAC 83850 Var   **Map 11**

Hostellerie Lou Calen **BUDGET**   *Tel* 94.04.60.40
1 cours Gambetta   *Telex* 400287

This much-visited village in the hilly Var hinterland is oddly situated at the foot of a brown cliff holed with caves, some of them once inhabited. The small, family-run *Lou Calen* (Provençal for "the place of the oil-lamp") has been enjoyed this year and last by readers who liked dining on the terrace with its wide view, and thought the food well cooked and generously served. Rooms are very simple, furnished in local country style, but have modern plumbing (some front ones suffer from traffic noise). One previous visitor enthused over the "fantastic array of help-yourself hors d'œuvre with delicious dressings", another over the "pieds et paquets and sinful great hunks of tarte aux fraises" on the cheaper menu. (*MD Abrahams, Philippa Herbert, Dave Watts, and others*) The large swimming pool, not always perfectly tended and sometimes crowded, is reached through a small garden. A reader this year found the service lacking in warmth and the *demi-pension* menu too unvaried.

Open Early Apr–1 Jan. Restaurant closed Wed except July/Aug.
Rooms 8 suites, 8 double – all with bath and/or shower, telephone, T V. 2 suites in garden annexe. 2 ground-floor rooms.
Facilities Salon with T V, bar, breakfast room, restaurants. Garden with terrace and swimming pool.
Location On Route des Gorges du Verdon. For Cotignac take exit Brignoles or Le Luc-Toulon off N7. Central (3 rooms might have traffic noise). Parking.
Credit cards All major cards accepted.
Terms Rooms 232–418 frs. Breakfast 40 frs. Dinner, B&B: 277–370 frs per person. Set lunch/dinner 120, 190 and 240 frs; full alc 250 frs. Reduced rates and special meals for children.

We get less feedback from smaller and more remote hotels. But we need feedback on all hotels: big and small, far and near, famous and first-timers.

COULANDON 03000 Allier   Map 10

Le Chalet   **BUDGET**   *Tel* 70.44.50.08
                                              Fax 70.44.07.09

Halfway between the market town of Moulins and the village of
Souvigny (fine priory church), this former hunting lodge stands in its own
spacious park with a small lake full of fish. It has been judged "an oasis of
rural calm, with charm, comfort and good simple food", in "a lush
pastoral setting with nightingales". Its owner is a Monsieur Hulot, more
adroit at providing holidays than his namesake was at taking them – and
our readers have again enjoyed taking them *chez lui* this year. They like
the setting, and the clean and pretty bedrooms (especially those in the
annexe), though the cooking may be variable and the service slow. Some
rooms have exposed beams, and there's even a comfortable library. "The
amazing Gallic chinoiserie wallpapers are all Sandersons." The hotel is a
Relais du Silence, but one reader was disturbed by traffic noise from the
main road and recommends the annexe rooms as quieter. (*C and M
Hédoin, RCJ Gordon*)

Open 1 Feb–31 Oct. Restaurant closed midday.
Rooms 25 double – all with bath and/or shower, telephone; 18 with TV. Some in
annexe.
Facilities Lounge, dining room with terrace, library. Large park with pond.
Location 6 km W of Moulins, down side-road just off D945 towards Souvigny.
Restriction Not suitable for &.
Credit cards All major cards accepted.
Terms B&B: single 209–296 frs, double 282–412 frs; dinner, B&B 208–360 frs per
person. Set lunch/dinner 70 and 115 frs; full alc 180 frs. Special meals for
children.

CRÈCHES-SUR-SAÔNE 71680 Saône-et-Loire   Map 10

Hostellerie du Château   *Tel* 85.37.12.04
  de la Barge

Admired again in 1989/90, this handsome creeper-covered 17th-century
manor near Mâcon has been tactfully converted into a pleasant country
hotel; graceful but informal, and slightly old-fashioned, it exudes
Burgundian well-being. "An excellent, vibrant country hotel," runs a
report this year, "well patronised by the well-heeled local bourgeoisie."
The two salons have comfortable period furnishings; some bedrooms are
large, also in period style, others are smaller but good value. In the large
lovely dining room, a log fire burns in winter and big windows look on to
the garden; drinks, breakfast and lunch can be served out on its terrace in
summer. The cooking, mainly Burgundian but with some inventive
touches, is judged excellent: e.g. terrine de brochet in a rich tarragon
sauce, confits de canard, and "a delicious vacherin full of raisins on the
heavily laden sweet-trolley". Service is mostly very good. The hotel's
setting is unpromising, on the edge of a dull village. But it would make a
good base for touring south Burgundy and the Beaujolais – including the
village of Vaux that was the original for Chevalier's *Clochemerle*. (*William
Davis, Dr BS Hoyle, MH Knight*)

Open All year except 26 Oct–5 Nov, 20 Dec–8 Jan. Closed Sat, Sun in low season.
Rooms 2 suites, 22 double – 17 with bath, 5 with shower, all with telephone, air-conditioning. 2 ground-floor rooms.
Facilities Lift. Salon, TV room, restaurant. Garden with children's playground.
Location Leave A6 at Mâcon Sud exit; follow signposts for Gare TGV.
Credit cards All major cards accepted.
Terms B&B: single 155 fr, double 233 frs. Set lunch/dinner 75, 129 and 165 frs; full alc 145 frs. Reduced rates and special meals for children.

LES DEUX-ALPES 38860 Isère   Map 10

Hôtel La Bérangère   *Tel* 76.79.24.11
BP 32   *Fax* 76.79.55.08
                                                 Telex 320878

Les Deux Alpes, south-east of Grenoble, is a large, popular, not very smart ski-resort; but this well-run, well-equipped hotel *is* quite smart and has above-average food for its species (*Gault Millau toque*). It is thrice nominated this year: "Manages to retain *Relais et Châteaux* standards without the atmosphere of snobbery you sometimes find. Its location right next to one of the ski-runs is perfect. The decor of the rooms was a bit heavy and dark for my taste, but the housekeeping was faultless. In the warm and cosy restaurant, the staff were courteous and the food interesting and delicious. Nice south-facing terrace." "Good hotels in ski-resorts at fair prices are rare. This one excels in comfort and food." "Staff perfectly charming to everyone; marvellous atmosphere, fantastic food." (*Mary Hanson, PA Marron, Mrs P Carr*)

Open 15 Dec–12 May and 30 June–1 Sep.
Rooms 59 double – all with bath, shower, telephone, TV.
Facilities Lift. 2 lounges, bar, games room, restaurant; terrace where lunch is served in fine weather. Outdoor and indoor swimming pool; sauna.
Location Resort is 74 km SE of Grenoble.
Restriction Not suitable for &.
Credit cards Access, Amex, Visa.
Terms Rooms: single 400–500 frs, double 420–620 frs. Breakfast 45 frs. Dinner, B&B 405–870 frs per person. Full board 455–940 frs. Set lunch/dinner 190–275 frs; full alc 330 frs. Reduced rates for children; special meals on request.

DIJON 21000 Côte-d'Or   Map 10

Hôtel La Cloche   *Tel* 80.30.12.32
  Restaurant Jean-Pierre Billoux   *Fax* 80.30.04.15
14 place Darcy   *Telex* 350498

A large, imposing hotel, traditional but well modernised, and centrally located on a big square. "Rooms are all double-glazed, so there is no noise. There is a garage, a quiet garden, a cosy bar, and a lounge which has changing art exhibitions. Our split-level room was large, with good views; lighting could have been better, but the bathroom was huge. The main attraction is the magnificent restaurant in the old cellars (two *Michelin* rosettes, three red *Gault Millau toques*) which Jean-Pierre Billoux, one of Burgundy's best young chefs, rents from the hotel: cooking is traditional Burgundian with modern overtones and wines are of course superb. Lunch is also served in a small conservatory. Very good service." (*P and JT*) More reports welcome.

Open All year.
Rooms 4 suites, 73 double, 3 single – all with bath, shower, telephone, radio, TV, air-conditioning. Ground-floor rooms.
Facilities Lifts. Lounge, bar, restaurant; conference facilities. Garden.
Location Central (rooms are double-glazed). Garage.
Credit cards All major cards accepted.
Terms [1990 rates] Rooms: single 360–550 frs, double 480–550 frs, suite 1,050–1,150 frs. Breakfast 50 frs. Alc meals in *Restaurant Jean-Pierre Billoux* 320–465 frs (excluding wine). Reduced rates for children.

Hotel Wilson   *Tel* 80.66.82.50
1 rue de Longvic

Fairly central, on a main square, a nicely converted 17th-century posthouse. Large, individually furnished rooms with modern rustic-style furnishings; some exposed beams; public rooms with high-timbered ceilings. Lock-up courtyard carpark. Average breakfast; no restaurant, but the neighbouring Thibert (*three* Gault Millau toques) *is recommended. 27 rooms, all with bath or shower 300–400 frs. Breakfast 40 frs. New nomination. More reports welcome.*

DINAN 22100 Côtes-du-Nord   **Map 8**

Hôtel d'Avaugour   *Tel* 96.39.07.49
1 place du Champs-Clos

An old Breton mansion, spacious, comfortable and characterful, with a striking position on top of the ramparts of a handsome medieval hilltop town. Front rooms can be noisy: rear ones are quieter and look over the lovely garden. Several reports this year, as in the past, stress the superb situation, good food (Gault Millau toque), but shabby rooms. Service and welcome, however, have improved. 27 rooms, all with bath and shower, 260–380 frs. Breakfast 37 frs. Set meals with wine 120–200 frs [1990]. Renominated by several readers, with reservations. More reports please.

DIVONNE-LES-BAINS 01220 Ain   **Map 10**

Château de Divonne   *Tel* 50.20.00.32
Route de Gex   *Fax* 50.20.03.73
                                                    Telex 309033

Being only 12 miles from wealthy cosmopolitan Geneva, this fashionable spa resort has a casino with a bigger turnover than any other in France (Monaco is another country). It also has this "excellent 19th-century reproduction of a Loire Valley *château*", whose owner/chef this year won a second *Michelin* rosette and retained his two red *Gault Millau toques* – deservedly, writes one of our own gastronomic pundits: "Guy Martin's old-fashioned sausage with lentils is excellent, and his pièce de résistance, three ravioli of foie gras with a light truffle juice, is not to be missed. Upper-class French hotels are usually appalling: this is one of the few whose furnishings show real style and talent." It's a handsome white building amid farmland, on a hill above the town, with its own helipad by the gate. Its marble foyer has magnificent modern sculptures; public rooms are smartly furnished in period style.

"On a summer evening," ran an earlier report, "dinner on the terrace was pure ecstasy: the pale yellow stone facade floodlit, tables lit by oil-lamps, and Mont-Blanc 80 kilometres away glowing pink in the sunset. Breakfast on the sunlit terrace was also splendid, with delicious goat's cheese. The hotel's young and enthusiastic owners have the knack of choosing caring, charming and very hardworking staff, and the ambience is warm and individual; nor is the place over-expensive – by Geneva standards. Bedrooms are spacious and characterful, with genuine antiques; ours had the same superb view as from the terrace." (*Pepita Aris, Neil and Jacqueline Britton*)

Open Early Mar–early Jan. Restaurant closed Tue, and Wed midday 4 Sep–19 June.
Rooms 5 suites, 15 double, 7 single – all with bath or shower, telephone, TV. 3 ground-floor rooms.
Facilities Lift, ramps. Salon, bar, 2 restaurants; conference facilities. Park with terrace, tennis, table-tennis and helipad.
Location On road to Gex, on W side of Divonne, which is 19 km N of Geneva (leave Lausanne motorway at Divonne-Coppet).
Credit card Visa.
Terms [1990 rates] Rooms: single 475 frs, double 970 frs, suite 1,500 frs. Breakfast 65 frs. Dinner, B&B 695–1,090 frs per person. Set lunch/dinner 220–410 frs. Reduced rates and special meals for children.

DOMME 24250 Dordogne   Map 10

Hôtel de l'Esplanade   *Tel* 53.28.31.41

This well-known showpiece village on a cliff above the Dordogne has been tastefully restored in the tradition of Viollet-le-Duc, and is full of expensive antique shops and foie gras. In the daytime in summer it is horribly crowded, but when the trippers have gone it quietens down and "magic is in the air". The *Esplanade*, a medium-priced *Logis de France*, is worthy of this setting, and is run with style by *patron*/chef René Gillard and his friendly wife. Five reports this year all sing its praises: "Very pretty blue and yellow dining room, service delightful, food delicious" (*Michelin* rosette, *Gault Millau toque*). "Our cottage annexe on three levels had handsome antiques but one shower worked poorly. In the main building, a very pretty lounge, panoramic views and wonderful food (regional dishes)." "*Patronne* friendly, helpful and unbossy." Bedrooms are decorated in a variety of floral wallpapers; some have a balcony with views of the valley. (*Prof and Mrs JF Woodward, Mary Hanson, Derek and Julia Smith, and others*)

Open 15 Feb–15 Nov. Closed Sun evening and Mon in low season.
Rooms 2 suites, 16 double – all with bath and/or shower, telephone; some with balcony. 5 in annexes.
Facilities Salon with TV, bar, restaurant; terraces.
Location 13 km S of Sarlat.
Restriction Not suitable for &.
Credit cards Access, Amex, Visa.
Terms [1990 rates] Dinner, B&B 292–410 frs; full board 402–520 frs. Set meals 130–300 frs. Special meals for children on request.

DUCEY 50220 Manche   Map 8

Auberge de la Sélune   `BUDGET`   *Tel* 33.48.53.62
2 rue St-Germain

The Girres family runs a neat little hotel with garden and terrace above
the river, in a dullish Norman village not far from Mont-St-Michel.
Bedrooms are said to be clean and pretty; the best are those at the back,
facing garden and river. Readers again this year have enjoyed dishes such
as crab pie and truite duceyne, and have spoken well of the comfort and
the charming garden. "It is difficult to find fault with this pleasant hotel;
breakfast was first-class." As last year, however, there are suggestions
that the service lacks professionalism and that the welcome is bland
rather than warm. (*BW Ribbons, Lynne M Allen, Dr and Mrs BS Hoyle, and
others*)

Open All year except Feb. Closed on Mon 1 Oct–1 Mar.
Rooms 19 double, 1 single – 19 with bath and shower, all with telephone. 3 in
garden pavilion.
Facilities Lounge, bar, 2 restaurants; 2 seminar rooms. Garden with terrace.
Location On N176, 11 km SE of Avranches (garden rooms quietest). Carpark.
Restriction Not suitable for &.
Credit cards Access, Diners, Visa.
Terms Rooms 210–230 frs. Breakfast 28 frs. Set lunch/dinner 68, 95 and 120 frs;
full alc 100 frs.

DURAVEL 46700 Lot   Map 10

Auberge du Baran   `BUDGET`   *Tel* 65.24.60.34
                                                         Fax 65.24.60.68

*Simple inn, popular with locals, with nice view of Romanesque church in
village in lovely Lot valley, 12 km east of Fumel. Run by "friendly and pleasant"
Roger and Letitia Washbourne, from Bath, so not very French in atmosphere.
Good food served in pretty dining room, or, in summer, on a "delightful terrace
covered in wistaria and tobacco plants". But accommodation basic and hot
water said to be unreliable. Restaurant closed mid-Jan–early Mar and end Nov–
early Dec. 7 double rooms, all with bath. Dinner, B&B 200 frs; full board 260 frs.
More reports please.*

****
Traveller's tale *The maître d' was a dead ringer for Basil Fawlty's
Manuel. We arrived overfed from our previous hotel and had no desire to
agonise through the country house hotel ritual of sitting in a smoke-filled
lounge perusing a French-language menu sipping an unwanted aperitif
waiting for Manuel to condescend to take our order and, at his pleasure,
call us to a table. We wanted a minimum of fuss, simple food, no wine.
When we refused the lounge and asked to be seated directly, Manuel
punished us by placing us at the rear of the dining room, by the kitchen,
as far away from the empty window tables as possible.*
****

L'ÉPINE 51460 Marne   **Map 9**

Aux Armes de Champagne   *Tel* 26.66.96.79
                                                              Fax 26.66.92.31
                                                              Telex 830998

An old coaching inn, restored and modernised, in the square of a village
east of Châlons-sur-Marne. The dining room and most bedrooms face the
huge, floodlit basilica of Notre Dame, a place of pilgrimage in the Middle
Ages. Today's pilgrims to the hotel come above all for its cooking
(*Michelin* rosette) which remains excellent under a talented new chef,
Patrick Michelon, according to this year's reports: "The food was again
exquisite and the rooms welcoming – an outstanding hotel." "The meal
was superb, with amuse-gueules and exquisitely filled pastry; breakfast
was first class, the welcome warm and the garden beautiful." Others have
praised the "friendly greeting, flowers everywhere, and well-groomed
small garden", where drinks can be taken. Noisy lorries sometimes pass
the dining room, but bedrooms are quiet, especially those at the back and
in the new annexe. They are also larger than in the main building. Jean-
Paul Perardel remains the hotel's owner, but no longer does the cooking
himself. He has his own champagne vineyard, and the long wine list is
devoted mainly to bubbly. (*Thelma Nichols, M Firth, Dr Peter Woodford, and
others*)

Open All year except 8 Jan–11 Feb. Closed Sun evening and Mon Nov–Mar.
Rooms 39 double – all with bath and/or shower, telephone; 12 with TV. 16 in
2 annexes 150 metres from main building. Some ground-floor rooms.
Facilities Bar, TV room, 2 restaurants; functions facilities; concerts in summer.
Small garden with mini-golf.
Location Central; village is 8.5 km E of Châlons, on N3. Parking.
Credit cards Access, Visa.
Terms Rooms 500–650 frs. Breakfast 50 frs. Set lunch/dinner 100, 195 and
425 frs. Special meals for children.

ÉTRETAT 76790 Seine-Maritime   **Map 8**

Le Donjon   *Tel* 35.27.08.23
Chemin de St-Clair

New to the Guide this year: a much creeper-clad mansion (not as old as it
looks) on the edge of an old-fashioned Norman bathing resort where
Maupassant spent many years; its dining room overlooks the famous
arched cliffs that Monet loved to paint. "Our 'koala room' was a suite
occupying one wing of this unusual building; our own outdoor stairway
led to the gorgeous swimming pool. Each room is decorated in individual
fashion – Chinese, rustic, etc. Personalised attention from Madame Abo
Dib and her charming staff. Delicious food, varying nightly" (braised
oysters with chicory, salmon with leeks, etc). (*Tom Cunningham*) More
reports welcome.

Open All year.
Rooms 8 double – all with bath, telephone, TV.
Facilities Bar, lounge, restaurant; banqueting facility.

Location Fairly central, parking.
Restriction Not suitable for &.
Credit cards Amex, Diners, Visa.
Terms Rooms: double 600 frs. Set lunch/dinner 110–260 frs; full alc 250 frs.
Reduced rates and special meals for children. Half board obligatory.

EYNE 66800 Pyrénées-Orientales   Map 10

Auberge d'Eyne   `BUDGET`   *Tel* 68.04.71.12

Eyne is an unspoilt village up on the glorious Cerdagne plateau near
Saillagouse (q.v.). Here this attractive old rural auberge, described as
"upmarket rustic", with bedrooms in period style, has been liked again
this year: "A very old solid stone building, once a farm, and quite simple.
We had a small but pretty bedroom done in good taste. Dinner was not
outstanding but OK – lamb casserole, salmon in a Pernod sauce on the
99-franc menu. Service not effusive but polite. A large lounge with huge
chimney-piece; games such as Scrabble lie around. Very quiet at night.
Good walks all around." (*C and AR*)

Open All year.
Rooms 11 double – all with bath/shower, telephone. Ground-floor rooms.
Facilities Lounge, bar, 2 dining rooms, brasserie. Garden.
Location 6 km E of Saillagouse, 75 km W of Perpignan.
Credit cards All major cards accepted.
Terms Rooms 375 frs. Breakfast 35 frs. Set lunch/dinner 99 frs; full alc 120 frs.
Reduced rates and special meals for children.

LES EYZIES-DE-TAYAC 24620 Dordogne   Map 10

Hôtel Cro-Magnon   *Tel* 53.06.97.06
                                                        Telex 570637

Les Eyzies, France's leading "centre of prehistory", is dominated by steep
cliffs riddled with palaeolithic caves. It is bedlam at the height of the
tourist season, though it quietens down in the evening. In its outskirts is
this handsome creeper-covered old hotel, a traditional family-run place
with plenty of atmosphere. Its chief drawback is proximity to the railway
and main road: quietest rooms are those in the pleasant annexe, set in a
large garden with a swimming pool on the other side of the railway. The
demi-pension meals are described as "good but not inspirational" (the
inspiration is perhaps reserved for *à la carte* dishes such as salade
périgourdine which earn the *Michelin* rosette). This earlier description
remains valid: "The entrance hall has an English coaching inn feel, with
wood-panelled walls, pretty flowers, brasses polished daily; there is a
delightful and quiet residents' lounge upstairs. Our room was a fair size,
spotless, furnished and wallpapered in rustic style; plumbing noises were
the only snag. The hotel's family owners, Jacques and Christiane
Leyssales, chat warmly with their guests. The ambience is friendly and
personal." (Endorsed this year by *M and J Vella*)

Open End Apr–mid-Oct. Restaurant closed Wed lunch except public holidays.
Rooms 4 suites, 20 double – all with bath and/or shower, telephone; 10 with TV.
8 in annexe by swimming pool.
Facilities 2 lounges, 2 dining rooms. Garden restaurant. 5 acres of parkland with
heated swimming pool and river.

Location 800 metres W of town centre. Parking.
Restriction Not suitable for &.
Credit cards All major cards accepted.
Terms B&B: double 434–504 frs, suite 634–784 frs; dinner, B&B 350–620 frs per person. Set lunch/dinner 120–320 frs. Special meals for children on request.

Les Glycines　　　　　　　　　　　　　　　　　　*Tel* 53.06.97.07

The creeper-covered *Glycines*, by a river about ten minutes' walk from the village, is regarded by some readers as a better bet than the *Cro-Magnon*, above, partly because it is further from the railway. Plaudits this year and last: "The garden is an informal heaven – chairs and loungers under a willow or by the pool, or on lush grass, with farmland beyond. Chic, blonde Madame smiles, the staff are most helpful. Meals were very good – small and delicious helpings, with all vegetables crisp and fresh. The baby deer was pink and juicy – a shame when we'd seen them in the woods that day." "Superb comfortable rooms with lovely views, outstanding cuisine, and a large new swimming pool." "Food very good, though tending towards *nouvelle cuisine* with rather small portions; enormous choice of delicious desserts." You can take drinks on a vine-shaded terrace. "Our room in the new annexe was quiet but small, with doors opening on to our own table and chairs in the sunny courtyard." Some rooms in the main building are also small. (*Jack and Sandra Clarfelt, Mr and Mrs Wilmot-Allistone, Mr and Mrs R Porter*)

Open Mid-Apr–1 Nov.
Rooms 25 – all with bath and telephone; 6 with TV. 2 rooms accommodating 4 in separate building in garden. 5 ground-floor rooms.
Facilities 2 salons, bar, restaurant; terrace for al fresco meals. Large garden with swimming pool.
Location On road to Périgueux, by the river. Parking.
Credit cards Access, Amex, Visa.
Terms Rooms 263–340 frs. Breakfast 41 frs. Dinner, B&B 330–427 frs per person; full board 405–490 frs. Set lunch/dinner 115–330 frs; full alc 300 frs. Special meals for children on request.

ÈZE-BORD-DE-MER 06360 Alpes-Maritimes　　　　　**Map 11**

Le Cap Estel　　　　　　　　　　　　　　　　　*Tel* 93.01.50.44
　　　　　　　　　　　　　　　　　　　　　　　　　Fax 93.01.55.20
　　　　　　　　　　　　　　　　　　　　　　　　Telex 470305

An Italianate villa on a headland between Monaco and Beaulieu, now an elegant family-run luxury hotel with a quiet, sedate clientele. Regular devotees have long praised the bedrooms, all with terrace or loggia and air-conditioning, the comfortable public lounge and poolside bar, the buffet lunches, and the dinners. This year and last, others have written of the "wonderful greeting", the "beautifully maintained pool", and: "A magnificent position, excellent food and brilliant service by a young highly trained team who would do credit to the Brigade of Guards. The lad looking after the open-air swimming pool had your mattress and towels spread out when he saw you coming. A lovely building in a lovely setting." (*Tom and Rosemary Rose, George Pick, Gerald M Newton, Alan F Thomas*) However, one visitor this year was sharply critical of plumbing, room upkeep, "ordinary" cooking and "surly, slow and disorganised staff"; and even regulars admit that the hotel "may not be as spruce as it was". We'd be glad of more comments on these highly conflicting reports.

Open Mid-Mar–31 Oct.
Rooms 8 suites, 35 double – all with bath, shower, telephone, terrace or loggia, air-conditioning. 6 in two bungalows.
Facilities Lift. Bar/salon, restaurant, grill room. Garden with terrace; al fresco meals in summer. Indoor and outdoor swimming pool.
Location 10 km E of Nice on Moyen Corniche road.
Credit cards Access, Amex, Visa.
Terms Dinner, B&B double 1,900–2,850 frs. Set lunch/dinner 380 frs; full alc 500 frs. Special meals for children on request.

LA FAVÈDE 30110 Gard   Map 10

À l'Auberge Cévenole   *Tel* 66.34.12.13
                                                          Telex 490925

A hamlet just off the N106, in the attractive southern foothills of the Cévennes (but be warned that the approach up the industrial valley from Alès, to the south, is not so attractive). Here the *Cévenole*, much frequented by the British (be warned of that, too), is a neat, white-walled, red-roofed building in local style, sprucely and prettily decorated. It wins *Michelin*'s red rocking chair and two red gables for secluded tranquillity and pleasant charm, and from one reader the comment: "Charming and peaceful, with a lovely and very clean pool. The staff were attentive, the setting elegant and traditional, but the food on the set menu did not quite live up to its promise." Others continue to praise the well-kept garden, the well-furnished rooms, and Madame's friendly attentiveness. They have enjoyed the food, too: but charges for extras are said to be very high. (*Liz King, Bridget Schenk, and others*)

Open 1 Mar–30 Nov. Possibly Christmas and New Year.
Rooms 3 suites, 17 double – all with bath or shower and telephone; TV on request. 8 in bungalows with ground-floor rooms.
Facilities Salon, TV room, dining room. Terrace where meals are served. Garden with swimming pool, mini-tennis.
Location 3 km W of La Grand-Combe, on D283.
Credit cards Access, Visa.
Terms [1990 rates] Rooms 160–260 frs. Breakfast 48 frs. Dinner, B&B 310–450 frs per person. Special meals for children.

FÈRE-EN-TARDENOIS 02130 Aisne   Map 9

Hostellerie du Château   *Tel* 23.82.21.13
                                                          Fax 23.82.37.81
                                                          Telex 145526

A luxurious manor house, part Renaissance, part 19th century, standing in its own sizeable park within a forest, 45 kilometres west of Reims. New owners, the Fremiots, took over in 1989, but a 1990 visitor found the place still well run, and the food still deserving its *Michelin* rosette and two red *Gault Millau toques*: "Service was excellent, and our room with marble bathroom was luxurious and well decorated. Dinner, in one of three rooms, included very good jellied lobster, sliced pigeon with cabbage, and fresh strawberry and raspberry pastry. Breakfast excellent too, with very strong coffee." Rooms are said to vary greatly: older ones in the main house have more personality, but attic ones are small; newer ones in the modern annexe are plainer but larger, with superior bathrooms (some suites have a jacuzzi). "Very peaceful and relaxing." (J Gazdak)

Open All year.
Rooms 9 suites, 14 double – all with bath, shower, telephone, T V. Ground-floor rooms. 1 specially adapted for &.
Facilities Salon, bar, 3 restaurants; conference facilities. Large grounds with golf and tennis.
Location 3 km N of Fère-en-Tardenois, on road to Fismes.
Credit cards All major cards accepted.
Terms [1990 rates] Rooms 600–970 frs, suite 1,100–1,600 frs. Breakfast 65 frs. Dinner, B&B 795–1,305 frs per person. Set meals 290–430 frs.

FLAGY 77940 Seine-et-Marne   Map 9

Hostellerie du Moulin   *Tel* (1) 60.96.67.89
2 rue du Moulin

This idyllic haunt, an old Guide favourite, has won little but praise in 1989/90. It's a 13th-century millhouse, beautifully converted into a rustic-style restaurant-with-rooms, in a pretty village south-east of Fontainebleau. There's a pleasant lounge with some of the old mill-wheels and pulleys, and in summer you can eat out under weeping willows beside a stream, with the murmur of rushing water close by. "A lovely room up a spiral staircase, deep sleep by grace of the running water, delicious food - bliss!" "Delightful and welcoming, food excellent, room small but comfortable." "The owner, Claude Scheidecker, is a most urbane and courteous man, and his taste must account for the meticulous attention to detail in the pretty little bedrooms and the romantic dining room by the river." (*Braham Murray, Sue Cohen, RCJ Gordon and others*) The food seems to have improved since last year, when it was much criticised.

Open 22 Jan–15 Sep, 27 Sep–20 Dec. Closed Sun evening and Mon (Mon evening and Tue at Easter, Whitsun, and 11 Nov).
Rooms 3 triple, 7 double – all with bath, shower, telephone; 3 with T V.
Facilities Lounge, bar, restaurant. Garden on river; fishing (permit obtainable in village).
Location 23 km S of Fontainebleau by N6 (18 km); turn right on to D403, and immediately left on to D120.
Restriction Not suitable for &.
Credit cards All major cards accepted.
Terms Rooms: single 180 frs, double 225–270 frs, triple 390 frs. Breakfast 35 frs. Dinner, B&B: 270–341 frs per person; full board 410–481 frs (minimum 4 days). Set lunch/dinner 140 frs; full alc 240 frs. Reduced rates and special meals for children.

LA FLÈCHE 72200 Sarthe   Map 8

Le Vert Galant   `BUDGET`   *Tel* 43.94.00.51
70 Grande Rue

La Flèche, between Angers and Le Mans, is a pleasant town on the Loir (not the Loire) with a famous military college where Descartes was a pupil. Severe Cartesian logic does not seem to loom too large at this amiably shambolic and very pleasing centrally located restaurant-with-rooms (*Michelin* red "R"), discovered for us this year. "A lovely stretch of river where one can wander under the trees, feeding wild ducks and looking across to a floodlit château. The hotel, a short walk away, gave us a warm welcome and a quiet, comfortable room of style and elegance. The hotel's ambience is charmingly pre-war, old-fashioned and unpretentious; the entrance/bar/reception gets chaotic at busy times, with no room for anyone's feet. But dinner was good, served efficiently in a room with bold decor. During our meal, the chandelier in our room dropped on to our bed, reminding us of the saying, '*Sans quelque chose d'imprévu, quelles vacances?*', though we might have been less amused had it happened a few hours later." (*Maureen and Don Montague*)

Open All year except 20 Dec–10 Jan. Restaurant closed Thu.
Rooms 10 – 7 with bath and/or shower, all with telephone, TV.
Facilities Bars, restaurant. Garden.
Location Central. Town is 42 km SW of Le Mans.
Restriction Not suitable for &.
Credit cards Access, Visa.
Terms Rooms 155–191 frs. Breakfast 20 frs. Set meals 67–145 frs.

FLORIMONT-GAUMIERS 24250 Dordogne   Map 10

La Daille   *Tel* 53.28.40.71
Florimont-Gaumiers, Domme

Again in 1989/90, nothing but praise for this secluded farmhouse south of Domme, run in personal style by Derek and Barbara Brown as a four-bedroom guest house/restaurant – a stirring example of the British love-affair with the Dordogne. Set in the hills above the Céou valley, the house is built in local stone with an external stone staircase and pigeon tower, but internally it has been sensitively modernised, with new bathrooms; rooms enjoy fine views across the valley. The Browns are said to "strike just the right balance of friendliness and professionalism". Raptures this year: "The dinners were marvellous: Barbara was treasurer for years of the British Epicure Society." "Dinners were beautifully cooked using home-grown vegetables and fruit." "How pleasant to sit under the walnut tree looking at the garden. Then there is the evening gathering in the courtyard to meet one's fellow guests." "Breakfast on our little terrace was a delight." (*Jean and Frank Tovey, KJ Smart, Michael and Julie Potter, HC, and others*) One possible snag: no sitting room. No lunches, but you can buy your own snacks and enjoy them in the garden.

Open 1 May–1 Nov. Restaurant closed for lunch.
Rooms 3 double, 1 single – all with bath or shower. Single room in annexe.
Facilities Restaurant. Garden, terrace.
Location *La Daille* is signposted from Gaumiers village, which is just W of the D46, 13 km S of Domme and 5 km NW of Salviac.
Restrictions Not suitable for &. No children under 7.
Credit cards None accepted.
Terms Dinner, B&B (min 3 days) 330–370 frs. Set dinner (by reservation only) 130 frs.

If you think we have over-praised a hotel or done it an injustice, please let us know.

FONDETTES 37230 Indre-et-Loire   Map 8

Manoir du Grand Martigny   *Tel 47.42.29.87*

Just west of Tours, a 16th-century manor in a big park, now a friendly, sophisticated guest house run by M and Mme Desmarais who speak excellent English. Handsome decor throughout. Warm, relaxed atmosphere, good breakfasts, good facilities for families. Open 15 Mar–15 Nov. 7 rooms, all with bath and shower. B&B double 400–600 frs. No restaurant, several near by. Recent nomination endorsed this year but more reports welcome.

FONTAINEBLEAU 77300 Seine-et-Marne   Map 9

Hôtel de l'Aigle Noir   *Tel* (1) 64.22.32.65
27 place Napoléon Bonaparte   *Fax* (1) 64.22.17.33
    Telex 694080

Facing the gardens of Napoleon's favourite palace, Fontainebleau's grandest hotel has Louis XVI and Empire decor, and bedrooms varying from Victorian plush to modern plain. Upkeep and cooking have sometimes been criticised in the past, but this year all reports are glowing: "Our room had plushy fabrics, and a balcony overlooking the town. Service was second to none. The restaurant provided some of the best cuisine I've had for a long time (*Michelin* rosette), à la carte and table d'hôte alike, and the piano bar is an ideal place to relax to live music. The swimming pool looked inviting." "Comfortable, with good meals, breakfast and service." "Superbly modernised. Most rooms quiet." The lock-up garage is a boon. (*Richard Taylor, Isabel and John Brasier*)

Open All year. Restaurant closed Christmas Eve.
Rooms 6 suites, 49 double, 2 single – all with bath and/or shower, telephone, radio, TV. 2 equipped for &.
Facilities Lift. Salons, bar, restaurant; conference facilities. 2 patios. Indoor swimming pool.
Location Central. Garage.
Credit cards All major cards accepted.
Terms Rooms 800 frs, suite 1,200–2,000 frs. Breakfast 75 frs. Set lunch/dinner 200–290 frs; full alc 400 frs. Children under 12 free in parents' room; special meals.

FONTGOMBAULT 36220 Indre   Map 10

Auberge de l'Abbaye   *Tel 54.37.10.82*

Exuding authentic rural Frenchness, this "delightful small inn" (a comment this year) stands in a village of the Creuse valley between Poitiers and Châteauroux: "Five 16th-century cottages grouped round a shady courtyard (where you take breakfast) have been sympathetically converted into a small comfortable hotel. The *patron* is a man of talents who even mends cameras. The food was delicious, served in the stone-flagged entrance hall. The monastery up the road does a nice Gregorian chant. Front bedrooms suffer from early traffic noise." Madame writes to us: "C'est moi qui fait la cuisine, plûtot du type traditionnel, et nous fabriquons nous-mêmes charcuterie, sauces, pâtisseries. Nous aimons les clients qui aiment la maison et qui apprécient les petits coins tranquilles de campagne. L'été, nous servons le repas le plus souvent sur la terrasse, à l'ombre d'un gros tilleul. À 50 mètres coule une belle rivière. Nous pouvons louer des bicyclettes pour visiter la région." (*Ann Mary Bishop, Roger Hornby*) Encore des rapports, SVP.

Open All year.
Rooms 5 double, 1 single – 4 with shower (2 have wc).
Facilities Bar, dining room; terrace where meals are served. River 50 metres.
Location 8 km NW of Le Blanc towards Chattelerault.
Restriction Not suitable for &.
Credit card Visa.
Terms [1990 rates] Rooms 95–180 frs. Breakfast 22 frs. Set meals 85 frs. Reduced rates for children sharing parents' room.

FONTVIEILLE 13990 Bouches-du-Rhône   Map 11

Auberge La Régalido   *Tel* 90.54.60.22
Rue Frédéric-Mistral   *Fax* 90.54.64.29
                                                    Telex 441150

Daudet's windmill (not the real one actually, but that's another story) stands on a hill outside this tiny town in the foothills of the Alpilles, near Arles. Down a side street is this former oil-mill, now a most welcoming auberge, luxurious yet unpretentious. Run with flair and enthusiasm by the Michel family, it has a flowery garden where meals are served on fine days, and its cooking earns a *Michelin* rosette – deservedly, says this year's latest of many admiring reports: "The hall is in sober Provençal country style, with antique furniture and much dark wood. Our room up in the eaves was a total contrast – bright modern bamboo furniture, flowery light fabrics, a vase of roses, a sloping beamed ceiling, a smart modern bathroom with white and green tiles, and best of all a roof-terrace with loungers. Jean-Pierre Michel couldn't be more pleasant and helpful, and service is exemplary. The cooking is old-fashioned Provençal of a serious standard: portions are large and the cream sauces alarmingly copious. Breakfast was the best we had in France." Many others have written in similar vein: "wonderful place", "friendly and welcoming", "a superb lunch" etc. (*David Wooff, Mrs JB Priestley, and others*)

Open 26 Jan–30 Nov. Restaurant closed Mon, also Tue lunch.
Rooms 14 double – 12 with bath, 2 with shower, all with telephone, TV, air-conditioning. 1 on ground-floor.
Facilities 3 lounges (1 with TV), bar, restaurant; functions room. Garden, terrace.
Location 5 km NE of Arles. Leave *autoroute* A7 at Cavaillon, direction St-Rémy-de-Provence, or at Nîmes, direction Arles. Parking.
Credit cards All major cards accepted.
Terms [1990 rates] Rooms: single 390–520 frs, double 520–940 frs, suite 1,200 frs. Breakfast 68 frs. Dinner, B&B: single 730–870 frs, double 1,250–1,900 frs. Set lunch/dinner 210–380 frs; full alc 350–400 frs. Special menu for children 110 frs.

Set dinner refers to a fixed price meal (which may have ample, limited or no choice on the menu). Full alc is the hotel's own estimated price per person of a three-course meal taken à la carte, with a half-bottle of house wine.

FOUGÈRES 35300 Ille-et-Vilaine   Map 8

Balzac Hôtel   `BUDGET`   *Tel 99.99.42.46*
15 rue Nationale

A pleasant traditional B&B hotel, in the traffic-free heart of an old Breton town where Balzac (hence the name) set his stirring saga of Royalist rebellion, Les Chouans. Jovial, helpful owners; comfortable, chintzy rooms and foyer/lounge. Open all year. 20 rooms, some with private facilities. Single 139 frs, double 149– 219 frs. Breakfast 20 frs [1990]. New nomination. More reports please.

FOX-AMPHOUX 83670 Var   Map 11

Auberge du Vieux Fox   `BUDGET`   *Tel 94.80.71.69*

In a remote hill-village of Upper Provence, with glorious wide views on all sides, this seductive auberge is housed in a 16th-century presbytery and schoolhouse (one bedroom has an old school-desk). Old beams, and an air of civilised simplicity: music room, library, outdoor dining terrace. Patron-chef Jean-Charles Martha's cooking is admired. Closed 20 Dec–20 Jan. 10 rooms, all with bath or shower. B&B double from 245 frs. Set menus 115–235 frs. Re- nominated after change of ownership. More reports eagerly awaited.

FROENINGEN 68720 Haut-Rhin   Map 9

Auberge de Froeningen   *Tel 89.25.48.48*
2 route d'Illfurth

In a village 7 km SW of Mulhouse, an elegant restaurant-with-rooms (oriental carpets in the red-walled dining room), in a spruce modern house built in local style with flower-decked balconies. Cosy bedrooms, convivial ambience, excellent food. Large grounds. 7 rooms, all with bath and shower, 260–320 frs. Breakfast 32 frs. Set menus 100–320 frs. Recent nomination. More reports please.

FUTEAU 55120 Meuse   Map 9

A l'Orée du Bois   *Tel 29.88.28.41*
                                                     Fax 29.88.24.52

Several readers this year have joined in the eulogies for this unusually seductive hotel, owned and run by a charming young couple, Paul and Roselyne Aguesse. It is an attractive white-washed old building, set on a wooded hillside in the pretty Argonne countryside where Lorraine meets Champagne. Bedrooms, spacious, light and freshly decorated, are in a new annexe. The large dining room includes a new glass extension with "glorious views over the countryside", and here M Aguesse's cooking (*Gault Millau toque*) has been again much enjoyed by returning devotees: "On each table, fresh flowers and candles. The menu is sophisticated, all cooked to order and all excellent – mosaique de saumon, foie chaud de canard, boned pigeon served rosy pink, poached figs and sorbets. The home-made bread is delicious, the butter is Echiré, and breakfasts are superb, with fresh fruit and home-made jams. A log fire in the cosy rustic-style bar with its beamed ceiling. All delightful on a summer evening". The bedrooms are "not luxurious but good value for money". "M Aguesse is a warm and friendly host. Extremely quiet rural location." "All the meals were good, and service pleasant." (*Padi and John Howard, John Moseley, Peter and Hendrika Dale, and others*)

Open All year except Jan. Closed Sun evening and Tue.
Rooms 7 – all with bath, telephone, TV.
Facilities Lounge, bar, TV room, restaurant. Terrace, garden.
Location 1 km S of Futeau, which is 13 km E of Ste-Ménehould (turn S off N3 at Les Islettes).
Credit cards Access, Visa.
Terms Rooms: single 245 frs, double 320 frs. Breakfast 36 frs. Set lunch/dinner 105–300 frs; full alc 340 frs. Reduced rates for children sharing parents' room; special meals.

GÉMENOS 13420 Bouches-du-Rhône   Map 11

Relais de la Magdeleine   *Tel* 42.82.20.05
                                                     Fax 42.32.02.26

Perhaps the most highly admired of all our French rural entries. Peaceful, happy and cultured, yet smart and elegant, it is a 17th-century *bastide* in a large walled garden with a lovely bathing pool, on the outskirts of a small town within easy reach of the coast at Cassis, and of the wild, strange massif of La Sainte Baume. One of this year's eulogies: "It is immensely sophisticated, yet relaxed. The owners, the Marignanes, are civilised and welcoming hosts. The strains of Schubert and Mozart predominate in the evening. Drinks are served on the terrace before dinner, whose five-course menu changed daily. The portions were just right, the contrasts of flavours a real pleasure; desserts showed off the chef's skill. The tables, spread under towering plane trees, were prettily laid. Breakfasts included four kinds of bread and four conserves. At the weekend, the quiet, adult mood of the place changed with the arrival of families with young children, all well behaved, but they did manage to take over the pool. Our bedroom had Provençal antiques, a good firm bed and superb reading lights. At night the only noise was the hee-hawing of Carole, the resident donkey. By day, the sound of cicadas fills the air; white chaises-longues with striped mattresses lie by the large sparkling pool."

Some other recent tributes: "The proprietor is charming and has a superb collection of paintings and tapestries." "M Marignane is always about and has a nice sense of humour." "The service was faultless, and the food was delicious." "The dining rooms were cool and spacious. There was an aura of peace, especially on the terrace in the early evening when drinks were served under floodlit plane trees." (*Susan Gilotti; Dr and Mrs Ali Alibhai, Barbara and Bruce Fireman, Anthony and Laura Gilbert, and others*)

Open 1 Mar–10 Nov.
Rooms 4 suites, 16 double – all with bath and/or shower, telephone, TV.
Facilities 2 salons, 2 restaurants. Garden with swimming pool.
Location On outskirts of Gémenos, which is 23 km E of Marseilles. Exit Pont de l'Étoile from Aix–Toulon motorway.

Restriction Not suitable for &.
Credit cards Access, Visa.
Terms B&B: single 420–455 frs, double 515–740 frs, suite 740–1,020 frs. Dinner,
B&B 420–710 frs per person; full board 600–890 frs. Set lunch/dinner 180 frs; full
alc 260 frs. Reduced rates and special meals for children.

GÉRARDMER 88400 Vosges   Map 9

Grand Hôtel Bragard   *Tel* 29.63.06.31
Place du Tilleul   *Fax* 29.60.90.58

*Within 500 metres of the lovely lake in this big, popular Vosges resort, an old-
fashioned hotel newly renovated and given a fresh lease of life. Pleasant service
and bedrooms, comfortable lounge, and excellent food (Gault Millau toque).
Large garden with small swimming pool. 61 rooms, all with bath and shower,
Dinner, B&B double 590–740 frs. Recent nomination. More reports please.*

GEVREY-CHAMBERTIN 21220 Côte d'Or   Map 10

Hôtel Les Grands Crus   *Tel* 80.34.34.15
Route des Grands Crus   *Fax* 80.51.89.07

In one of the great Burgundy wine villages, an attractive and well-named
new entry this year: "A newish hotel built in the old style, with window-
boxes full of geraniums. It has two special advantages. First, it is on the
Route des Grands Crus, a tiny road running through the vineyards,
connecting the famous wine villages. Secondly, it has no restaurant! So,
without a flicker of conscience, you can walk to one or other of the two
Michelin one-star restaurants in Gevrey: we prefer *Les Millesimes*, with
superior food stylishly presented. The hotel's rooms are good, standard
modern but roomy: get a front one, so that you can look up the vineyards
to the château. Breakfast can be taken in the *jardin fleuri*, which was
splendid when we were there." *(Warren Bagust, C and A Daintree)*

Open 1 Mar–30 Nov.
Rooms 20 double, 4 single – all with bath, shower, telephone.
Facilities Salon. Garden.
Location By church. Private carpark.
Restriction Not suitable for &.
Credit card Visa.
Terms Rooms: single 250–280 frs, double 285–360 frs. Breakfast 32 frs. Children
under 7 free of charge. (No restaurant.)

GIEN 45500 Loiret   Map 10

Hôtel du Rivage   *Tel* 38.67.20.53
1 quai de Nice   *Fax* 38.38.10.21

"A splendid old Loire-side town with floodlit castle and church. A
friendly welcome, open fire, dining room filled with local people, food
superb and service delightful. Beds comfortable but bath rather small."
"Very smoothly run, if rather impersonal. Excellent food, served at a table
overlooking the Loire." So run two of the nine endorsements this year

and last, for this very spruce modern hotel just off the main road, close to the river. *Michelin* awards the food a rosette, and *Gault Millau* a *toque*. Our readers praise dishes such as champagne sorbet and tuna steak in a cream sauce, and also the service and comfort: one visitor had "a charming room overlooking the Loire". All rooms now have double-glazing, so that even front ones facing the road are fairly quiet. (*Roydon Jenkins, HC Robbins Landon, Martin Gilbert, George Atkinson, and others*)

Open All year. Restaurant closed mid-Feb–mid-Mar.
Rooms 5 suites, 15 double, 2 single – all with bath, shower, telephone, TV.
Facilities Salon, piano bar, dining room. Terrace.
Location On road to Nevers, on banks of the Loire (double-glazing). Parking.
Restriction Not suitable for &.
Credit cards All major cards accepted.
Terms Rooms: single occupancy 260 frs, double 310 frs, suite 620 frs. Breakfast 38 frs. Set lunch/dinner 150, 195 and 300 frs; full alc 350 frs. Reduced rates and special meals for children.

GIGONDAS 84190 Vaucluse   Map 11

Les Florets   *Tel* 90.65.85.01
Route des Dentelles

The toothy limestone crags of the Dentelles des Montmirail overlook this pleasant little country hotel outside Gigondas, near to some of the best Côtes du Rhône vineyards (one belongs to the hotel's owners). "It consists of a smallish main house and an annexe on the hill behind, all gravel yard, blossom and sunshine. The service is pleasant, the food a bit boring, but the glory of the place is the deliciously tree-dappled, fountain-rilled, Pernod-supplied, chaise-longued terrace, which looks over vine-yards and mountains, and is absolutely silent except for the clinking of ice in glasses." An endorsement this year: "The shady terrace is lovely. The food was good, sometimes very good, but lacked choice. Our room was adequate, though with rather uncomfortable beds." (*Marilyn Frampton, Peter L Aston, AG Catchpole*) One reader has told us of a "diabolical" shower.

Open All year except 2 Jan–1 Mar. Closed Wed, also Tue evening in low season.
Rooms 13 double, 2 single – 13 with bath and/or shower, all with telephone.
4 bungalows 50 metres from hotel.
Facilities Salon/bar, restaurant, TV room; terrace. Garden.
Location 1.5 km E of Gigondas, which is 18 km E of Orange.
Restriction Not suitable for &.
Credit cards All major cards accepted.
Terms [1990 rates] Rooms 300 frs. Breakfast 35 frs. Dinner, B&B 255–275 frs per person. Set meals 120–170 frs. Reduced rates and special meals for children.

GIVRY 71640 Saône-et-Loire   Map 10

Hôtel de la Halle   **BUDGET**   *Tel* 85.44.32.45
Place de la Halle

A modest but friendly family-run *Logis de France*, well suited for an overnight stop, in a pleasant Burgundy village west of Chalon; it is a venerable building with a fine spiral staircase, facing the former market hall, and offers "excellent old-fashioned Burgundian food". Bedrooms though simple are clean and comfortable (front ones can be noisy) and offer great value for money. "A pleasant place to stay, with excellent food in a pretty dining room" is a typical comment this year. "We had a warm reception from the Renards. It was a pleasure to sit in their good restaurant watching the locals come and go, most of them close friends of the family, judging by all the kissing going on." There are local wine tastings just opposite. (*K and J Cross, PA Catling, Christopher and Angela Davies, and others*) Most visitors find owner-chef Christian Renard a friendly and helpful man – "a live-wire with an infectious laugh and a sense of humour". Curiously, one reader this year found him in unpleasantly aggressive mood: we trust this was an isolated incident.

Open All year except 21–27 Aug, 13–26 Nov.
Rooms 8 double, 1 triple, 1 for 4 people – 6 with bath, 1 with shower, all with telephone.
Facilities Lounge, restaurant. Garden.
Location Givry is 9 km W of Chalon-sur-Saône on D69. Hotel is central. Parking.
Restriction Not suitable for &.
Credit cards All major cards accepted.
Terms [1990 rates] Rooms 145–165 frs. Breakfast 25 frs. Set lunch/dinner 55–175 frs; full alc 295 frs. Special meals for children.

Aux Troix Saisons   *Tel* 85.44.41.58
Le Prémoy   *Fax* (Paris) (1) 40.26.34.33
Dracy-le-Fort

The quintessence of rural Burgundy; this mellow creeper-covered manor, its tower dating from 1622, is the home of Morton Sobel and Dierk Volckers, who have just converted it into a very personal five-room hotel. "A delightful haven, amid a pretty garden and orchard," writes our nominator. "Each of the large bedrooms has been decorated with perfect taste, with fresh flowers to match the decor, pretty sheets and soft pillows. A marvellous welcome, with scones and strawberries from the garden for tea, and an excellent fixed-menu dinner." (*Mrs Alan Hopkins*) Dr Sobel writes that guests are invited to enjoy the library and park, and walks along his trout stream. He also lays on hot-air balloon trips and says he serves a "proper" breakfast. More reports welcome.

Open 1 Apr–31 Oct.
Rooms 5 double – all with bath, shower, radio; TV on request. 1 ground-floor room equipped for &.
Facilities Lounge, library, dining room. 4-acre grounds with trout stream.
Location 5 km W of Chalon-sur-Saône.
Credit cards Access, Visa.
Restriction Not suitable for children under 13.
Terms Rooms: single 375 frs, double 425 frs. Breakfast 35 frs. Set dinner 130 frs (including wine).

GOSNAY 62199 Pas-de-Calais   **Map 9**

La Chartreuse du Val St-Esprit   *Tel* 21.62.80.00
1 rue de Fouquières   *Telex* 134418

This useful stop-over hotel near Calais has an unusual history – it's a former monastery where Princess Isabel of Portugal died in 1471, later rebuilt in classic château style and recently turned into a rather elegant hotel. It lies slap amid the now defunct Pas-de-Calais coal mines – not the most lyrical of settings, but the Béthune motorway exit is conveniently close. "Large room, simply furnished, good dinner," says a reader this year. Others have also praised the comfort, food and friendly staff, though one felt that the place had too "new" a feel and lacked atmosphere. "Great pleasure to walk up the attractive staircase in its classic château style. Our room was of imposing elegance, but breakfast was disappointing." (*C and M Hédoin, GB and Dr CH, P Gill, and others*) One reader this year found the owner/chef's manners uncouth.

Open All year except Christmas Eve.
Rooms 19 double, 4 single – all with bath, shower, telephone, TV, baby-listening. Some ground-floor rooms suitable for &.
Facilities Lounge, bar, breakfast room, 3 restaurants; conference/functions rooms. Garden with 2 tennis courts.
Location 5 km SW of Béthune. Leave A26 at Béthune exit and make for Bruay-en-Artois.
Credit cards Access, Amex, Visa.
Terms [1990 rates] Rooms: single occupancy 300 frs, double 420 frs. Breakfast 40 frs. Set lunch 110 frs, dinner 330 frs; full alc 420 frs. Reduced rates for children sharing parents' room; special meals.

GOUMOIS 25470 Doubs   Map 10

Hôtel Taillard   *Tel* 81.44.20.75
                                                         Fax 81.44.26.15

A spacious and gracious chalet, much reputed for its cooking (*Michelin* rosette), secluded on the slopes of a wooded valley near the Swiss border south of Belfort. It has a large terrace, lovely for summer; many bedrooms, too, have a balcony with views, but some at the back are small and cramped, and upkeep is not always perfect. For 100 years the hotel has been run by the Taillard family, and it has long been popular with Guide readers (admittedly for not *quite* so long). But old Mme Taillard has now handed over to her nephew, and there are some signs that standards may be slipping: two readers this year felt that the cooking was not up to rosette standards, and *Gault Millau* in 1990 withdrew its *toque*. But others this year have much enjoyed the feuilleté de morilles and other dishes such as local trout and salmon. A swimming pool has just been added. (*EH Whitaker, Dr and Mrs PM Rooze, AF Thomas*) More reports needed.

Open 1 Mar–15 Nov. Closed Wed in Mar, Oct, Nov.
Rooms 4 suites, 12 double – all with bath or shower, telephone, TV.
Facilities Salon, bar, 2 dining rooms; terrace. Garden with swimming pool. River nearby with trout fishing and canoeing.
Location 50 km SE of Montbéliard, 18 km E of Maiche on D437A and D437B. Leave *autoroute* A36 at Montbéliard Sud exit. Hotel is near church. Parking.
Restriction Not suitable for &.
Credit cards All major cards accepted.
Terms [1990 rates] Rooms: double 245–265 frs, suite 310–380 frs. Breakfast 34 frs. Dinner, B&B 295–330 frs per person. Set lunch/dinner 125–290 frs; full alc 300 frs. Special meals for children.

If you have kept brochures and tariffs for Continental hotels, do please enclose them with your reports.

GRENOBLE 38000 Isère   Map 10

Park Hôtel   *Tel 76.87.29.11*
10 place Paul-Mistral   *Fax 76.46.49.88*
                                                              Telex 320767

*The best hotel in downtown Grenoble, facing a big park, with mountain views
from some rooms. Panelled bedrooms, some with le Minitel, France's videotex
computer gimmick; deft service, good breakfasts. Closed 28 July–19 Aug,
22 Dec–2 Jan. 56 rooms, 610–995 frs. Meals alc 105–190 frs [1990]. No recent
reports. More welcome.*

GRIMAUD 83310 Var   Map 11

Hostellerie du Coteau Fleuri   *Tel 94.43.20.17*
Place des Pénitents

Grimaud is a fashionable hill-village behind St-Tropez, its ancient stone
houses neatly converted into summer homes for the Parisian intelli-
gentsia. The *Coteau Fleuri*, on the outskirts, is an old building modernised
as a neo-Provençal auberge with tiled floors, and it is as flower-decked as
its name implies. The main drawback: most bedrooms are very small.
But apart from this, we've heard nothing but praise, this year and last:
"Dining on the terrace is magical indeed." "A very friendly atmosphere
and delicious cooking, e.g. gigot de lotte aux lentilles." "Meals on the
terrace, with a marvellous view, are of high quality – exquisite langoustines. The maids are efficient, the bedrooms small but comfortable."
A piano for guests to use, a log fire for chilly days, a spacious lounge and
rambling garden slope, plus superb views over the wooded Maures hills.
(*Jean-Michel and Monique Pictet, and others; endorsed this year by DH
Bennett*)

Open All year except Jan. Restaurant closed Tue except July and Aug.
Rooms 14 double – 9 with bath, 5 with shower, all with telephone.
Facilities Salon, bar, restaurant. Terrace.
Location 10 km from St-Tropez. On edge of village. Parking.
Restriction Not suitable for &.
Credit cards All major cards accepted.
Terms B&B double 390–540 frs. Set lunch 130 frs, dinner 185 frs; full alc 300 frs.
Special meals for children.

GUÉTHARY 64210 Pyrénées-Atlantiques   Map 10

Hôtel Pereria   **BUDGET**   *Tel 59.26.51.68*
Rue de l'Église

An old Basque house in a big, slightly unkempt garden: it has views of the
hills and sea, and you can watch the sunset from the outdoor dining
terrace. Recent visitors have liked the place, "run by youngish, friendly
owners, with an attractive staff". "An uncomplicated holiday hotel
catering mainly for French families. Tasty meals, outstanding value." The
annexe, across a busy road, is possibly more comfortable than the hotel
itself, and bedrooms in both are large. Readers have enjoyed the friendly

efficiency and the good meals (e.g. ttoro, a Basque fish soup). (*Helen and Charles Priday; JAG Stonehouse*)

Open 1 Mar–12 Nov.
Rooms 26 double, 2 single – 26 with bath and shower, all with telephone. 11 in annexe across road.
Facilities 2 salons, 2 restaurants, TV room; terrace where meals are served. Garden with *boules* and swings.
Location On the coast between Biarritz and St-Jean-de-Luz.
Restriction Not suitable for &.
Credit cards Access, Visa.
Terms Dinner, B&B 170–220 frs. Set lunch/dinner 70, 115 and 150 frs; full alc 130 frs. Reduced rates and special meals for children.

HAUT-DE-CAGNES 06800 Alpes-Maritimes   Map 11

Le Cagnard   *Tel* 93.20.73.21
Rue Pontis-Long   *Fax* 93.22.06.39
                                                               Telex 462223

The sizeable town of Cagnes-sur-Mer is divided, like Caesar's Gaul, into three parts: the ugly sprawling resort of Cros-de-Cagnes; just inland, Cagnes-Ville, unremarkable save for the inspiring Renoir museum on its outskirts; and, higher up, Haut-de-Cagnes, one of the region's most sophisticated hill-villages (fascinating museum in the château). Here *Le Cagnard*, a well-known and very smart hotel – "delightful and distinguished", "very romantic", according to readers – has been artfully converted out of some 13th-century houses by the ramparts and virtually clings to the side of a cliff. "Most personal, friendly and warm service," says a reporter this year. "The conversion has been done with imagination. Excellent but expensive food in the restaurant whose beautiful new hand-painted ceiling slides away on command to reveal the sky." This newly extended terrace offers fine views; you can also eat in a graceful candle-lit room, former guardroom of the château, where sometimes there is guitar music. The "delicious" food wins a *Michelin* rosette and two *Gault Millau toques* for adaptations of local dishes, and portions are large. The set menu is expensive, but they do not mind if you take a light snack from the *carte*.

"Our room was the whole floor of a medieval house, with superb antique furniture and a picture window." Rooms, however, vary in size and comfort, and one reader found the beds too soft. It is worth asking for a room with a view of the coast (but these may be the costlier ones). Parking is a nightmare; it is best to park in the new carpark just below the village, or else leave parking to the hotel. (*P Gill, Pat and Jeremy Temple, Dr John Cliffe*) Six new suites have been added this year.

Open All year. Restaurant closed 1 Oct–15 Dec, and Thu midday.
Rooms 10 suites, 14 double, 2 single – 25 with bath and shower, 1 with shower, all with telephone, TV, baby-listening; air-conditioning. Suites in annexe.
Facilities Lift. Salon, bar, 2 restaurants; banqueting room. Terrace.
Location On the ramparts, 2 minutes from château. Parking.
Restriction Not suitable for &.
Credit cards All major cards accepted.
Terms Rooms: single occupancy 300–400 frs, double 460–720 frs, suite 760–1,300 frs. Breakfast 60 frs. Set lunch/dinner 350 and 490 frs; full alc 500 frs. Reduced rates and special meals for children.

HENNEBONT 56700 Morbihan — Map 8

Château de Locguénolé
Route de Port-Louis

Tel 97.76.29.04
Fax 97.76.39.47
Telex 950636

A stately home in south Brittany, family seat of the de la Sablières since 1200, and still owned and run by the countess; set by an estuary in 250 acres of wooded parkland, recently hurricane-damaged. Great comfort, plus antiques; ambience a bit formal but not pretentious. Food highly reputed (two Michelin rosettes, three red Gault Millau toques). Large garden with small swimming pool, tennis. Closed 2 Jan–10 Feb, Mon in winter. 19 rooms, all with bath and shower, 460–1,160 frs. Breakfast 52 frs. Set meals 190–460 frs [1990]. Previously in Guide, dropped for lack of feedback. Re-nominated this year. More reports please.

HESDIN-L'ABBÉ 62360 Pas-de-Calais — Map 9

Hôtel Cléry

Tel 21.83.19.83
Telex 135349

This recently opened country house hotel, a *Relais de Silence*, stands just south of Boulogne, ideal for ferry-goers: "Set in five acres of parkland and approached by a tree-lined avenue, this 18th-century château has a splendid facade, and the entrance hall is appealing with a lovely curving Louis XV wrought-iron staircase. The Osselands, who bought the house recently, are helpful and friendly. Our room had prettily painted modern furniture, and decor in soft pastel shades. Reception rooms are well furnished and homely. Good breakfasts." "The owners treated us well," says an endorsing reader this year. (*Alan Ashley*) The restaurant has closed since last year. And we apologise to readers who were misled by our faulty siting of the hotel on last year's map. More reports welcome.

Open All year except 15 Dec–15 Jan.
Rooms 19 – all with bath and/or shower, telephone, TV.
Facilities Lounges, bar; conference room. Park with tennis court.
Location 9 km SE of Boulogne, off N1.
Credit cards Access, Amex, Visa.
Terms [1990 rates] Rooms 280–480 frs. Breakfast 55 frs. (No restaurant.)

LES HOUCHES 74310 Haute-Savoie — Map 10

Auberge le Beau Site `BUDGET`

Tel 50.55.51.16
Fax 50.54.53.11

A trim pink chalet with a pretty garden, in a small ski-resort at the foot of Mont-Blanc. Fine views, comfortable modern rooms, good service, and food above-average for a ski-hotel (Michelin red "R"). Open Christmas–15 Apr, 1–27 May, 15 June–end Sep. 18 rooms, all with bath or shower. Dinner, B&B 266–312 frs plus tax [1990]. New nomination. More reports please.

> Many hotels put up their prices in the spring. Tariffs quoted in the text may be more accurate before April/May 1991 than after.

IGÉ 71960 Saône-et-Loire   Map 10

Château d'Igé   *Tel* 85.33.33.99
                                                     Fax 85.33.41.41
                                                     Telex 351915

This former hunting lodge of the Dukes of Mâcon, "a beautiful little medieval castle", is now a luxurious hotel beside a stream on the edge of the Mâcon hills, outside a Burgundy village. It has rounded turrets, ivy-covered walls, and stone-flagged floors and stairways, plus a new light conservatory facing the garden that is pleasant for drinks or breakfast. "The building is charming," say returning regulars this year. "Bedrooms have space and character, with modern bathrooms. The food was plentiful and the service helpful and quite informal, but neither quite match up to the grandeur of the medieval dining room." "A good-size garden. Bath towels were rough but better than sandpaper. My main course was only just warm. In the night I heard a nightingale." Visitors have enjoyed breakfast on the terrace, and "the sense of *noblesse* enhanced by Vivaldi". Food is non-fancy and fairly good; service is friendly but slow. And the steep steps up to some rooms are not for the old or infirm. (*Kate and Steve Murray-Sykes, RCJ Gordon, PJ Guy, and others*)

Open All year except 1 Dec–1 Mar. Restaurant closed only 20 Dec–20 Jan.
Rooms 6 suites, 6 double – all with bath, shower, telephone, TV.
Facilities Salon, dining room, conservatory, terrace and garden.
Location 6.5 km N of N79, 14 km NW of Mâcon, 11 km SE of Cluny.
Restriction Not suitable for &.
Credit cards All major cards accepted.
Terms [1990 rates] B&B double 420–550 frs. Set lunch/dinner 180–350 frs. Special meals for children.

LA JAILLE-YVON 49220 Maine-et-Loire   Map 8

Château du Plessis   *Tel* 41.95.12.75
                                                          Fax 41.95.14.41
                                                     Telex 720943 ATTN P Benoist

North of Angers, another new entry this year for those (and this may not be everyone) who like being treated as personal friends by French châteaux-owners: "Not a grand castle, more like a large and mellowed English vicarage, in a fairly modest garden beside woods. It will appeal most to those who appreciate its un-hotel-like ambience, more like that of a private house: one is treated almost as a private guest of the charming owners, M and Mme Benoist. The house pre-dates the Revolution and was in fact sacked by the mob: but antiques and family portraits abound. A circular staircase leads to the bright, comfortable bedrooms. The sitting rooms are stylishly furnished. In the beautiful old dining room, guests who wish to have dinner with their hosts (cooked by Mme Benoist herself) sit round an elegantly appointed, candle-lit table. Breakfast is taken communally in the kitchen." More reports please.

Open 1 Mar–31 Oct.
Rooms 6 double – all with bath, shower; baby-listening on request.
Facilities Sitting room, TV room, bar, dining room. Large park with tennis, jogging, clay-pigeon shooting, fishing.
Location Just S of La Jaille-Yvon village, 35 km N of Angers.

Restriction Not suitable for &.
Credit cards All major cards accepted.
Terms Rooms: single 350–600 frs, double 450–700 frs. Breakfast 40 frs. Set menu
230 frs. Reduced rates for children sharing parents' room; special meals on
request.

JOIGNY 89300 Yonne **Map 9**

Résidence Côte Saint-Jacques	*Tel* 86.62.09.70
14 faubourg de Paris	*Fax* 86.91.49.70
	Telex 801458

A much-admired old coaching inn beside the river Yonne, where
patron/chef Michel Lorain and his son Jean-Michel win the top ratings of
four red *Michelin* gables and three rosettes, and four red *Gault Millau*
toques, for their fine cooking in luxury surroundings, with prices to match.
They have created some opulent rooms from old houses facing the river,
across the noisy N6, and to provide access they have made a paved
tunnel under this road, decorated with Roman remains from the
excavation. A recent visitor's amazement: "This is a very sexy place, as
only the French can do it. The luxurious new bedrooms are sexy, and the
whole set-up slightly outrageous. The dining rooms have gaudy flower
arrangements, paintings of scantily dressed girls, candle-light, and very
sensuous food. It all works, because it is totally professional – and fun.
The entire Lorain family greeted us for dinner, and absurd smiles of
ecstasy were on our faces as we ate terrine of marinated sardines and
tapenade, quail's egg in truffle juice, exquisitely delicate skate in a lemon
sauce, grilled lobster in a Sauternes sauce, and more. Our only complaint:
in one room the tables are set too closely together – nasty if your
neighbours smoke. Our bedroom had a combination of antique and
contemporary furnishings, with dark beams, Berber carpets over plank
floors, a huge marble bathroom. I have never been so conscious of being
surrounded by beauty, peace and comfort." This was no Xanadu-like
dream that flees on waking, for others have echoed the praise in more
down-to-earth terms: "Delicious light cooking, very good breakfast,
faultless service, fittings of the highest quality." A sharper comment this
year: "Our modern, spacious room was rather like a goldfish bowl; the
kitsch taste in decor of upmarket French chefs has long ceased to surprise
one. The food was delicious and exquisitely presented." (*D Barr, Sharon
Gutman*)

Open All year except Jan.
Rooms 4 suites, 25 double – all with bath, shower, telephone, radio, TV, baby-
listening; 15 with air-conditioning. All in annexe linked to main building by
tunnel.
Facilities 2 salons, bar, 3 restaurants; conference facilities. Indoor heated
swimming pool. Garden.
Location 27 km NW of Auxerre on N6; leave at Sens exit.
Restriction Not suitable for &.
Credit cards All major cards accepted.
Terms Rooms 600–1,800 frs, suite 1,550–2,450 frs. Breakfast 80 frs. Set
lunch/dinner 300–560 frs; full alc 500–600 frs. Special meals for children.

Italicised entries are for hotels on which we need more feedback –
either because we are short of reports or because we have had
ambivalent or critical reports.

JOUÉ-LÈS-TOURS 37300 Indre-et-Loire   Map 8

Hôtel du Château de Beaulieu   *Tel* 47.53.20.26
1 rue de l'Épend   *Fax* 47.53.84.20

This modernised 18th-century manor, on the south-west outskirts of
Tours, has an impressively large stone staircase and panelled restaurant,
and is run with style and care by owner/chef Jean-Pierre Lozay. "The
rooms were gorgeous, the colours pretty, the bathrooms big and
modern," says one enthusiast. Another plaudit this year: "The staff were
all kind and friendly, and the foie gras in honey and raspberry sauce was
unforgettable." Others too commend the cuisine, which "draws a smart
and demanding clientele from miles around". But service can be slow,
especially at breakfast. "Our mansarded first-floor bedroom was vast and
a bit stark, despite flowery wallpaper, but was comfortable, clean and
spacious." Others have appreciated mussel soup with puff pastry, as well
as the river views. (*Mary Hanson, Gillian and Michael Hill*) A reader
informed us recently that the hotel's *jardins à la française* had been sold to
make municipal tennis courts, but the hotel now assures us that this is not
true: the gardens remain.

Open All year except Christmas Eve.
Rooms 19 double – 18 with bath, 1 with shower, all with telephone, TV, mini-bar.
10 in pavilion.
Facilities Salon, TV room, bar, 2 restaurants; conference facilities. Large garden.
Location 4 km SW of Tours, by D86 and D207.
Restriction Not suitable for &.
Credit cards All major cards accepted.
Terms Double room 360–650 frs. Breakfast 42 frs. Dinner, B&B double (3 days
min) 700–1,000 frs; full board 920–1,250 frs. Set lunch/dinner 180–380 frs; full alc
250–300 frs. Reduced rates and special meals for children on request. Half board
obligatory (lunch or dinner) Apr–Oct.

LA JOUVENTE 35730 Ille-et-Vilaine   Map 8

Manoir de la Rance   *Tel* 99.88.53.76

*Beautifully set above the boat-filled Rance estuary, 7 km SE of Dinard, a
converted manor with clean rooms, excellent breakfasts, obliging owners, and
decor and furnishings in a mixture of styles, some more sympathetic than others.
Closed Jan, Feb. 8 rooms, most with bath and/or shower, 300–600 frs. Breakfast
35 frs [1990]. No restaurant. Recent nomination. More reports please.*

KAYSERSBERG 68240 Haut-Rhin   Map 9

Hôtel Résidence Chambard   *Tel* 89.47.10.17
13 rue de Général de Gaulle   *Fax* 89.47.35.03
                                                          Telex 880272

Albert Schweitzer was born in this picturesque Alsatian wine village, and
in its main street is a small museum devoted to him. Down the road is
patron/chef Pierre Irrmann's smartish restaurant-with-rooms (*Michelin*
rosette, *Gault Millau toque*), converted from two old buildings with pretty
facades. Approving verdicts this year and last. "Dinner was costly but

excellent; room was comfortable with good view of vineyards." Such dishes as marinated raw salmon and garlicky ragout of lamb have been admired, and the desserts are superb. The Alsatian wines are reasonably priced. (*Mrs RB Richards, CK Belair*) But an inspector thought that the bedroom annexe lacked the personality of a hotel; and the cellar breakfast room is not admired. It might be worth paying extra to secure the special room with a big canopied bed and a quaint round salon in a 15th-century tower. (*Mrs RB Richards, CK Belair*)

Open All year except 1–21 Mar and 22 Dec–4 Jan. Closed Mon and Tue midday except public holidays.
Rooms 2 suites, 18 double – all with bath, telephone, radio, TV. Ground-floor rooms.
Facilities Lift. Lounge/bar, restaurant; cellar for conference/functions.
Location 11 km NW of Colmar. Central, but quiet. Parking.
Credit cards All major cards accepted.
Terms: Rooms 450–500 frs. suite 650–700 frs. Breakfast 55 frs. Set lunch/dinner 220–380 frs; full alc 500 frs. Special meals for children.

LACAVE 46200 Dordogne   Map 10

Le Pont de l'Ouysse   *Tel* 65.37.87.04
                                                 Fax 65.32.77.41

Inventive variations on local dishes, such as salmon with girolles and duck's liver, are on offer at Daniel Chambon's chic restaurant-with-rooms (two red *Gault Millau toques*). Not far from Rocamadour, it is in a fine setting by a river, with a château looming above and a tree-shaded dining terrace for fine weather. "It's charming, and the rooms are delightful with a light, elegant garden look," commented a reader recently. Other comments: "A gem. Quiet, friendly and beautifully furnished, with tasteful bedrooms and bathrooms. The service is helpful and the food 'exquisite' but rather too rich for a long stay." "Rooms utterly chic. Food very urban and *nouvelle*-ish, not cheap and portions not large." The dog, Sacha, likes to go on walks with guests: "He came with us to Rocamadour and back and seemed to know the ropes – I should think he does this every day in season." (Endorsed this year by *Dr John Lunn*)

Open 1 Mar–11 Nov. Closed Mon in low season.
Rooms 1 suite, 12 double – all with bath, shower, telephone, radio, TV. 5 in annexe.
Facilities Lounge, dining room. Terrace; garden with swimming pool.
Location 10 km NW of Rocamadour.
Restriction Not suitable for &.
Credit cards All major cards accepted.
Terms [1990 rates] Rooms: double 350–500 frs. Breakfast 45 frs. Dinner, B&B 400 frs per person. Set lunch/dinner 150–350 frs.

LAMASTRE 07270 Ardèche   Map 10

Hôtel du Midi/Restaurant   *Tel* 75.06.41.50
    Barattéro
Place Seignobos

Returning regulars, who had "an outstanding dinner", remain well pleased this year with owner/chef Bernard Perrier's serious, well-run

hotel/restaurant, in the market square of an attractive little town west of
Valence. "An excellent family-run place, with Madame Perrier much in
evidence. The food fully justifies its *Michelin* rosette and *Gault Millau*
toque, and the menus are a splendid mixture of old and new – including
old favourites such as poularde de Bresse en vessie. The wine list is good
on local Rhône wines, weak if you want to look further afield" (the accent
is on quality, with few cheap bottles). The hotel is in two parts, its well-
cared-for garden and most bedrooms being 30 metres away from the
restaurant. The exterior of this annexe has been criticised in the past but it
has now been improved, and it is "beautiful inside, with large, quiet
rooms and excellent bathrooms. Rooms in the main building are less
special, though OK." Breakfasts are well liked. (*Dr J Cliffe, Anne Stott, GG
Thomas*)

Open 1 Mar–15 Dec. Closed Sun evening and Mon except July, Aug, and public
holidays.
Rooms 13 double – 12 with bath and shower, 1 with shower, all with telephone;
7 with TV. 1 ground-floor room.
Facilities 2 salons, 3 restaurants. Garden.
Location Central. Parking.
Credit cards All major cards accepted.
Terms Rooms: single 250 frs, double 300 frs. Breakfast 42 frs. Dinner, B&B 340–
360 frs per person. Reduced rates and special meals for children.

Château d'Urbilhac   *Tel* 75.06.42.11
Route de Vernoux

Totally different from the *Midi* (above), here is a finely converted 19th-
century château in Renaissance style, complete with pepperpot tower, set
high on a hillside in its own 150-acre wooded park just outside the town.
It might be best for a short stay, as the menu changes little. But three
recent reports have used the words "delightful" and "magnificent",
notably this one: "After our fourth visit, this has become one of two
favourite hotels in France. The food used to be dull, but Madame now has
a new chef and it's lovely, though the wine list is disappointing.
Breakfasts are copious. Rooms, some with antique furniture, are all
comfortable. And the pool is the best you'll find anywhere, superbly
situated amid classic scenery, with modern sun-loungers." "A charming
châtelaine." (*PA Catling, Brenda Gape, FM and CN Grist*)

Open 28 Apr–8 Oct. Restaurant closed Thu for lunch.
Rooms 11 double, 3 single – all with bath or shower, telephone. 2 in pavilion.
1 ground-floor room.
Facilities Bar, salon, 2 dining rooms; terrace. Garden, heated swimming pool,
tennis.
Location 2 km S of Lamastre on D2 to Vernoux.
Credit cards All major cards accepted.
Terms [1990 rates] B&B double 550 frs; dinner, B&B 400–475 frs per person. Set
lunch/dinner 160–250 frs.

Always let a hotel know if you have to cancel a booking, whether
you have paid a deposit or not. Hotels lose thousands of pounds and
dollars from "no-shows".

LANGEAIS 37130 Indre-et-Loire   Map 8

Hôtel Hosten et Restaurant   *Tel* 47.96.82.12
  Le Langeais   *Fax* 47.96.56.72
2 rue Gambetta

Patron/chef Jean-Jacques Hosten's attractively traditional but pricey
hostelry stands in a small Loire-side town with a fine 15th-century
château, west of Tours. "The food richly deserves its *Michelin* rosette
(and *Gault Millau toque*) and service is obliging. Our bedroom, though
overlooking the main road, was comfortable." "The best hotel we found
during three weeks in France. Restaurant outstanding, especially fish
dishes. Breakfast hard to beat, with six different types of brioche,
croissant, etc." (*Janet and Dennis Allom, and others*)

Open All year except 10 Jan–10 Feb, and 20 June–10 July. Closed Mon evening
and Tue.
Rooms 1 suite, 11 double – all with bath, telephone, T V.
Facilities Bar, 2 dining rooms.
Location Central, parking. Langeais is 25 km W of Tours.
Restriction Not suitable for &.
Credit cards All major cards accepted.
Terms Rooms: single 240 frs, double 360 frs, suite 550 frs. Breakfast 42 frs. Full
alc 200–300 frs.

LANGRES 52200 Haute-Marne   Map 9

Grand Hôtel de l'Europe   `BUDGET`   *Tel* 25.87.10.88
23–25 rue Diderot

The "superb" cathedral and ancient ramparts add to the interest of
Langres, a fine old hilltop town north of Dijon. Near its centre is this
traditional stone-fronted hostelry, down to earth and inexpensive, liked
again in 1989/90 by several readers for its simple comforts and good fare
– "friendly, and excellent value". Rooms vary in size and amenities: rear
ones are quietest. "The restaurant was busy, more like a *relais routier* than
an elegant place: many of the portions were enormous, as were the
diners. Parking one's car in the tight space provided was an entertainment in itself, as enthralled onlookers watched the harassed drivers trying
to obey the arm-waving instructions of the receptionist." (*Stefan and
Cosima Sethe, Moira and John Cole, Jean and Tony French, and others*) A
dissenter this year reported traffic noise in front, mediocre food and a
booking not honoured.

Open All year except 2 weeks Apr and 3 weeks Oct. Closed Sun evening.
Restaurant closed Mon midday in season, all day Mon in low season.
Rooms 2 suites, 25 double, 1 single – 8 with bath, 18 with shower, all with
telephone; 22 with T V. 8 in annexe.
Facilities Salon, bar, 2 restaurants.
Location Between Chaumont (35 km) and Dijon (66 km). Hotel is central (rooms
overlooking garden are quietest). Garage facilities for 20 cars.
Restriction Not suitable for &.
Credit cards All major cards accepted.
Terms Rooms: single 100–200 frs, double 130–230 frs, suite 230–270 frs. Breakfast
25 frs. Set lunch/dinner 60, 90 and 150; full alc 210 frs.

LANSLEVILLARD 73480 Savoie   Map 1(

Hôtel Club **BUDGET**   *Tel 79.05.93.5:*
  Résidence Les Prais   *Fax 79.05.97.6(*
                                                             Telex 30998:

In a high ski-resort just below Mont-Cenis, a typical chalet-style ski-hotel ami(
meadows beside the ski-lifts, liked for its good and plentiful food and friendl
staff. Most rooms have mountain views, some have balcony. Swimming pool
Piano bar for après-ski. Open 10 June–17 Sep, 20 Dec–20 Apr. 30 rooms
renovated this year, all with bath or shower. Also annexe with apartments
B&B: single 252 frs, double 302–347 frs. Set menus 78–180 frs. Recen
nomination. More reports welcome.

LAPOUTROIE 68650 Haut-Rhin   Map *

Hôtel-Restaurant Les Alisiers **BUDGET**   *Tel 89.47.52.8:*

This modestly priced *Logis de France* is a farmhouse with beamed ceilings
high up in a secluded valley in the Vosges, but only 19 km from Colmar
There were some criticisms last year, but this year nothing but praise
"Very friendly welcome from Ella and Jacques Degouy, food varied and
interesting, very professionally presented. Stupendous views from the
restaurant. Excellent value." "We had a small typically French room with
hessian wallpaper. Beautiful service, excellent meal, good self-service
breakfast. The owners and guests all seemed to get on like one large
family." All agree on the food, ambience and cleanliness. But it's a simple
place and some rooms are very small. (*John Moseley, Moira and John Cole,
Ian Ziar*)

Open 1 Jan–15 Nov.
Rooms 12 double, 1 single – all with bath and/or shower, telephone.
Facilities Salon, bar, TV room, restaurant. Garden.
Location 19 km NW of Colmar, off N415 to St-Dié. Hotel is 3 km from centre of
Lapoutroie; from church follow signs marked Auster.
Restriction Not suitable for &.
Credit card Visa.
Terms B&B double 260 frs. Dinner, B&B 250 frs per person. Set lunch/dinner 110,
160 and 195 frs; full alc 170 frs. Reduced rates and special meals for children.

LECTOURE 32700 Gers   Map 10

Hotel de Bastard **BUDGET**   *Tel 62.68.82.44*
Rue Lagrange

In a small town in the Armagnac country, a stately 18th-century stone
mansion, well converted. Its name, odd to English speakers, is *bâtard* in
French, so it raises no snigger locally, any more than does the nearby
town of Condom. New to the Guide this year: "Hard to find down a
narrow lane below Lectoure cathedral, but a splendid setting and most
agreeable ambience. Bedroom small but adequate. Evening meal on the
terrace admirably served in all respects (*Gault Millau toque*). The four set-
price menus had varied items: terrine de poisson was enjoyable and the
desserts were excellent (e.g. strawberry soup with mint), but the lamb

steak was fatty. A splendid view across the rooftops, and entertainment provided by the other diners and by manager/chef Jean-Luc Arnaud's three-year-old pyjama'd daughter." (*Joy and Michael Rubinstein*)

Open Mar–Dec.
Rooms 29 double – all with bath or shower, telephone; TV available (20 frs). 5 in annexe.
Facilities Lounge, 2 restaurants; 2 conference rooms. Terrace. Garden with heated swimming pool.
Location Central, parking. Lectoure is 23 km E of Condom.
Restriction Not suitable for &.
Credit cards All major cards accepted.
Terms [1990 rates] Rooms: single 160–215 frs, double 190–270 frs. Breakfast 25 frs. Dinner, B&B 215–250 frs per person. Full alc 280 frs. Reduced rates and special meals for children.

LESTELLE-BÉTHARRAM 64800 Pyrénées-Atlantiques   Map 10

Le Vieux Logis   `BUDGET`   *Tel* 59.71.94.87
Route des Grottes

This simple flower-girt country auberge between Lourdes and Pau has again delighted readers this year, with its peaceful setting, good food, unassuming comforts, and friendly and caring staff and owners: "Nowhere have I been made to feel more welcome." "The Gaye family," runs another report, "have created a charming place, with a park where you can sit under the trees listening to the tinkle of cowbells. There's a huge courtyard where peacocks strut and two creaky old Pyrenean dogs bound up to welcome you, and a sunny terrace with parasols for drinks, but no salon. The cuisine is exceptional (*Michelin* red 'R') – very good trout from the river, and the lightest crêpe I've ever eaten – endorsed by the many locals who come to eat here. The five attractive wooden chalets were full, so we had a huge room in the house, with Pyrenean blue-and-white blankets." (*Eileen Broadbent; Molly and John Burt, Eileen Lister, and others*)

Open 1 Mar–15 Nov. Restaurant open 1 Mar–10 Jan.
Rooms 12 double – all with shower, telephone, TV. 5 chalets in the park.
Facilities Restaurant; 4 functions rooms. Garden; terrace.
Location 12 km W of Lourdes and 3 km E of Lestelle-Bétharram, on N637.
Restriction Not suitable for &.
Credit cards Access, Amex, Visa.
Terms Double room 250 frs; dinner, B&B 400 frs; full board 550 frs. Set lunch/dinner 90, 130 and 180 frs; full alc 210 frs.

LEVERNOIS 21200 Beaune, Côte d'Or   Map 10

Hostellerie de Levernois,   *Tel* 80.24.73.58
   Restaurant Jean Crotet   *Fax* 80.22.78.00
Route de Verdun-sur-le-Doubs   *Telex* 351468

Jean Crotet, one of Burgundy's finest chefs, used to own a much-lauded restaurant at Nuits-St-Georges. Now he has moved to far better premises on the edge of a village near Beaune, bringing with him his two *Michelin* rosettes and earning the new bonus of red print for beauty and tranquillity. Our two 1990 nominators feel that justice has been done: "A lovely house in huge grounds, with a comfortable new bedroom annexe. Friendly service and superb food: the wine list has to be seen to be believed." "A wonderfully hedonistic experience! A peaceful setting near a golf course. You drive in through a big park with magnificent trees. The annexe bedrooms are elegant and spacious – polished wood floors, attractive rugs, double doors on to the terrace. The 350-franc menu was excellent, notably the snails in a cream sauce under light pastry. There was live music in the large green and white dining room: this seemed to be an experiment. Breakfast extensive." (*Tom and Rosemary Rose, Kate and Steve Murray-Sykes*)

Open All year. Closed Christmas.
Rooms 12 double – all with bath (11 also have shower), telephone, TV. 1 ground-floor room suitable for &. All rooms in garden annexe.
Facilities Bar, restaurant, functions room; terrace. Garden with tennis court. Swimming pool planned for 1991.
Location On edge of village, 5 km SE of Beaune.
Credit cards All major cards accepted.
Terms [1990 rates] Rooms 700–800 frs. Breakfast 70 frs. Dinner, B&B 800 frs per person. Set menus 200–420 frs; full alc 350 frs. Extra bed 100 frs. 1-night B&B-only bookings sometimes refused in high season. Special meals for children on request.

LEZOUX 63190 Puy-de-Dôme   **Map 10**

Château de Codignat   *Tel* 73.68.43.03
Bort-l'Étang   *Fax* 73.80.78.81
                                                         Telex 990606

This small town east of Clermont-Ferrand was a major ceramics centre in Roman and Gallo-Roman days, as the local museum bears witness. At Bort-l'Étang, to its south-east, on a wooded hill above a valley, stands this handsome 15th-century château, "delightfully run by a lady and her son". Rather fancifully converted (suits of armour, four-poster beds, etc), it has bedrooms with antiques or genuine replicas; some are in the towers, reached by winding stairways. "Our suite, named Barbe Bleue, was decorated in red and black velvet, with a huge bed, and the bathroom had a jacuzzi," says a visitor this year. "For dinner we sat in a circular room, with all the diners facing one another. Food and wine were excellent." An earlier visitor was also intrigued: "A riot. The castle was bought in a state of collapse by the present owners, who did it up in rather camp baroque: even the walls are carpeted. But it's also a gem, very clean and peaceful, with real chic. Found proprietors scrubbing out the lavatories – always a sign that standards are high." There are large gardens, and a swimming pool also with jacuzzi. (*Amy Irwin*) One reader this year found the *accueil* poor.

Open 20 Mar–4 Nov. Restaurant closed Tue and Thu midday except holidays.
Rooms 3 suites, 11 double – all with bath and/or shower (suites also have jacuzzi), telephone, TV. 1 ground-floor room.
Facilities Salon, 3 restaurants, banqueting room. Large grounds with swimming pool; health and beauty centre, putting green.
Location At Bort-l'Étang, 8 km SE of Ledoux which is 27 km E of Clermont-Ferrand.
Credit cards All major cards accepted.

Terms [1990 rates] Rooms 780–980 frs, suite 1,500. frs. Breakfast 60 frs. Dinner, B&B 715–900 frs per person. Set lunch/dinner 245–295 frs. Special meals for children on request.

LIVERDUN 54460 Meurthe-et-Moselle   **Map 9**

Hostellerie Les Vannes   *Tel* 83.24.46.01
6 rue Porte Haute

Returned to the Guide this year after a change of ownership, this stylish restaurant-with-rooms offers panoramic views over the curving Moselle. There's a new chef, too, and readers this year extol his "mouth-watering cuisine", as does *Michelin* (rosette). One reader had a bedroom "of the usual tatty elegance that we expect of France"; others too have found the furnishings stylish though a bit neglected. (*Paul Tyler, J and M Seymour, and others*) More reports, please, on whether the new owners are refurbishing.

Open All year except Feb. Restaurant closed Mon except holidays, also Sun in Dec and Jan.
Rooms 2 suites, 9 double – all with bath, shower, telephone. 6 in garden annexe. 2 ground-floor rooms.
Facilities Salon/bar, TV room, 2 dining rooms; banqueting room.
Location On river bank on edge of town which is 16 km NW of Nancy.
Credit cards All major cards accepted.
Terms Rooms: double 275–500 frs, suite 500 frs. Breakfast 50 frs. Set lunch/dinner 170, 270 and 370 frs; full alc 300 frs. Reduced rates and special meals for children.

LUNÉVILLE 54300 Meurthe-et-Moselle   **Map 9**

Hôtel-Restaurant   **BUDGET**   *Tel* 83.74.07.09
   Le Voltaire
8 avenue Voltaire

That all can be for the best in the worst of all possible Lorraine towns is candidly demonstrated by our 1990 nominator of this restaurant-with-rooms: "I know of no French town more visually depressing than Lunéville, near Nancy, where Monty took the German surrender. The external appearance of the *Voltaire* does nothing to suggest that a traveller should do anything but keep on travelling, but to do so would mean passing a restaurant with gourmet pretensions and a *menu dégustation* [also a 95-franc menu signalled in red for good value by *Gault Millau*]. Simple but satisfactory rooms. My wife's request for a cup of afternoon tea resulted in a tray with a choice of six teas, and this was again offered at breakfast." Interesting dishes such as filet of pigeon with chicory, and roast monkfish with bacon. (*Ian Ziar*) More reports please.

Open All year except Jan.
Rooms 10 double – all with bath or shower, telephone; some with TV. Ground-floor rooms.
Facilities Restaurant. Garden.
Location On Strasbourg side of town, which is 35 km E of Nancy.
Credit cards All major cards accepted.
Terms B&B: single 200 frs, double 250 frs. Set lunch/dinner 95–250 frs; full alc 350 frs. Reduced rates and special meals for children.

LYON   Map 10

La Cour des Loges   *Tel* 78.42.75.75
6 rue du Boeuf   *Fax* 72.40.93.61
Lyon 69005   *Telex* 330831

*Down an alleyway of Vieux-Lyon, four adjacent Renaissance mansions have
been imaginatively restored to form a striking and unusual luxury hotel. Lofty
foyer, festooned with foliage and silk drapes; small heated jacuzzi/swimming
pool; bedrooms with too many high-tech gimmicks; exemplary service. Superior
snack restaurant,* Tapas des Loges. *Car access possible but difficult. 63 rooms,
all with bath and/or shower, 950–1,400 frs. Breakfast 85 frs. Set meals 90–
160 frs [1990]. Few recent reports. More welcome.*

MAILLY-LE-CHÂTEAU 89660 Yonne   Map 10

Le Castel   **BUDGET**   *Tel* 86.40.43.06
Place de l'Église

This *Relais du Silence* between Auxerre and Avallon, "a rather run-down
19th-century house in a very quiet village", has again been recommended
for a short visit: "Good, rich food, and a comfortable, pleasantly old-
fashioned dining room." (*R Barratt*) Readers have praised such dishes as
snails in garlic butter with chopped hazelnuts, and calf's liver in a cream
sauce. The countryside is lovely, and drinks can be taken under the trees
in the garden. Decor is attractive, but bedrooms vary greatly in size (some
are said to be suitable for elves) and the service can be slow.

Open 15 Mar–15 Nov. Restaurant closed Wed.
Rooms 2 suites, 8 double, 2 single – all with bath and/or shower, telephone.
2 ground-floor rooms.
Facilities Lounge, 2 dining rooms. Garden; terrace where breakfast and drinks are
served.
Location 30 km S of Auxerre, 30 km NW of Avallon. Turn off N6 at either of
these towns or at Nitry. Hotel is in centre of quiet village. Parking.
Credit cards Access, Visa.
Terms Rooms: single 150 frs, double 260 frs, suite 330 frs. Breakfast 30 frs. Set
lunch/dinner 70, 140 and 165 frs. Special meals for children on request.

MALATAVERNE 26780 Drôme   Map 10

Domaine du Colombier   *Tel* 75.51.65.86
Route de Donzère   *Fax* 75.51.79.40
                                                                    Telex 345126

*South of Montélimar (the nougat-making town), just off the N7 and A6, a nicely
converted Provençal bastide in a big garden. Flowery decor, comfortable rooms
with rural views. Excellent nouvelle-ish cooking, Michelin-rosetted, e.g.
bouillabaisse of chicken, hare stuffed with liver. Swimming pool. Closed Feb,
restaurant closed Sun dinner, Mon lunch. 24 rooms, all with bath or shower.
Half board 410–530 frs. New nomination. More reports welcome.*

> In your own interest, always check latest tariffs with hotels when
> you make your bookings.

LA MALÈNE 48210 Lozère   Map 10

Manoir de Montesquiou   *Tel* 66.48.51.12

This 15th-century turreted stone manor house, once a home of the aristocratic Montesquiou family, stands somewhat incongruously inside a village beside the main road along the Tarn gorge, with the cliff looming above (tourist traffic on this road ceases after dark, so nights are quiet). The house has been most gracefully preserved and converted: its old-world charm includes four-poster beds and spiral stairways, but comforts are modern. "The bedrooms were thoughtfully equipped and well cared for," says a visitor this year, "and a good dinner was graciously served on the attractive terrace." Others have commended the regional cooking and courteous staff. Further reports welcome.

Open Apr–Oct.
Rooms 2 suites, 10 double – all with bath or shower, telephone; some with TV.
Facilities Hall, bar, TV room, 2 dining rooms. Garden.
Location La Malène, in the Tarn gorge, is 41 km SW of Mende.
Restriction Not suitable for &.
Credit cards Access, Diners, Visa.
Terms Rooms 290–540 frs. Breakfast 40 frs. Dinner, B&B (min 2 nights) 350–475 frs per person. Set lunch/dinner 135–205 frs. Special meals for children.

MARLENHEIM 67520 Bas-Rhin   Map 9

Le Cerf   *Tel* 88.87.73.73
30 rue du Général de Gaulle   *Fax* 88.87.68.08

A former posthouse at the northern end of the Alsatian Wine Road, now a distinguished restaurant-with-rooms (two Michelin rosettes, two red Gault Millau toques), owned and run by the charming Husser family. Elegant variations on Alsatian dishes. Bedrooms not grand but comfortable. Closed 1 week Feb, Tue, Wed. 17 rooms, most with bath or shower, 330–420 frs. Set meals 210–450 frs. Warm new nomination. More reports welcome.

MARQUAY 24620 Dordogne   Map 10

Hôtel-Restaurant des Bories   `BUDGET`   *Tel* 53.29.67.02
                                                                  Telex 550689

In the heart of the Périgord Noir, between Les Eyzies and Sarlat, this unpretentious rural *Logis de France* has beamed ceilings, a big pool, and views over open country. It is nominated this year: "A marvellous place, outstanding value. The setting was glorious, justifying its red *Michelin* rocking-chair. Our roomy bedroom had fine views; drinks could be taken on the pretty terrace or by the pool. The welcome was warm and the service caring (usually by Madame's three daughters). The food was both serious and unselfconscious – excellent soups, salads, local cheeses, also rabbit, duck of course, all on the *demi-pension* menus, while the dearer ones (authentic Périgord cuisine) were delicious. Excellent house wine for only 35 frs." (*JE Fisher*) More reports welcome.

Open 31 Mar–end-Nov, Christmas and New Year. Restaurant closed Mon midday.

Rooms 3 suites, 27 double – all with bath and/or shower, 28 with telephone.
19 in garden annexe. Ground-floor rooms.
Facilities Salons, bar, TV room, restaurant; conference facilities. Terrace. Garden
with swimming pool. Sailing, windsurfing nearby. Indoor pool, sauna and gym
planned for 1991.
Location 12 km W of Sarlat.
Credit cards Access, Visa.
Terms [1990 rates] Rooms 160–200 frs, suites 315–350 frs. Breakfast 27 frs.
Dinner, B&B 205–290 frs per person; full board 265–350 frs. Reduced rates and
special meals for children.

MARSEILLE Bouches-du-Rhône   Map 11

Hôtel Pullman Beauvau   *Tel* 91.54.91.00
4 rue Beauvau, Marseille 13001   *Fax* 91.54.15.76
                                                              Telex 401778

*Beside the Vieux Port, a famous old hostelry where George Sand, Cocteau and
Mistinguette stayed (and opera stars do so today). Newly restored, it has real
warmth and elegance: period-style bedrooms, double-glazed and air-conditioned; good service, dark-panelled bar, excellent buffet breakfast. 71 rooms, all
with bath and shower, 650–705 frs. No restaurant: hordes nearby. No recent
reports. More needed, please.*

MARTIN-ÉGLISE 76370 Seine-Maritime   Map 9

Auberge du Clos Normand   **BUDGET**   *Tel* 35.82.71.01
22 rue Henri IV

Just inland from Dieppe, on the edge of a forest, this former 16th-century
relais de poste, now a restaurant-with-rooms, is as redolent of Normandy
as its name implies. The bedrooms are in a separate vine-covered
building, once stables or a hayloft, with a romantic garden which has a
pavilion for eating out in summer, and a stream; it's very quiet except for
farmyard noises. Bedrooms used to be decrepit, but have recently been
modernised. Readers in 1989/90 have again written warmly of the
auberge. "What a transformation! The beds are now firm, the bedroom
furniture tasteful, the wallpaper is quite like Laura Ashley. There was
even a bathrobe. The auberge has lost nothing in its modernisation. The
lounge still looked as awful and smelled as musty as ever, but that is part
of its charm." There are still some hints of rotting balconies and other
signs of running-down in public areas, but most visitors find this
acceptable. The farmyard odours, too, are all part of the deal.
    The warmest praise is again for the generous Norman cooking and its
mise-en-scène. "The well-heated restaurant is genuine Norman country
style. One is greeted by Madame and a sleepy old dog. Monsieur, smiling
broadly, prepares all meals in full view, exuding pleasure as he cooks.
The whole staff's teamwork was a joy to see. The meals were delicious
especially poached brill, chicken with cream and calvados, apple and
calvados sorbet. The place has no frills, but the ambience is warm and
friendly." "Food was delicious, and we liked Madame's leisurely persona
service" – but some have found her reserved. Above all, the setting
delights: "We woke to look out on a charming lush garden and stream"

and "a selection of cats, a stick-retrieving dog and the river abounding in young frogs". (*AM Appleby, Eileen Lister, Mrs RB Richards, RM Flaherty, and others*)

Open All year except 15 Dec–15 Jan. Closed Mon evening and Tue.
Rooms 1 family, 8 double – all with bath and/or shower, telephone. All in separate building in garden.
Facilities Lounge with TV, restaurant; functions room. Garden with large lawn and stream; pavilion for outdoor summer meals.
Location 5 km from Dieppe; off D1 to Neufchâtel.
Restriction Not suitable for &.
Credit cards All major cards accepted.
Terms [1990 rates] Dinner, B&B 340 frs. Alc meals 180–200 frs. Guests are expected to dine in the restaurant.

MAUSSANE-LES-ALPILLES 13520 Bouches-du-Rhône   Map 11

Hostellerie l'Oustaloun   `BUDGET`   *Tel* 90.54.32.19
Place de l'Église

"Unusual and charming: it's a converted 16th-century chapel, in the small main square of an untouristy Provençal village just south of ultra-touristy Les Baux. Owned and run by an affable Bolognese, Robert Bartoli, and his shy French artist wife, Emma, whose pictures adorn the main rooms. The ambience is personal, intimate, cosy, but quite sophisticated – and the clientele likewise. Yet prices are most reasonable. Small, pretty bedrooms with period furniture. Three small, attractive dining rooms with unusual decor, and a short *carte* of mostly regional dishes, quite good. The help-yourself buffet that opens the 135-franc [1990] set menu includes the best tapenade and anchoiade I've ever tasted." (*JA*)

Open All year. Restaurant open 15 Mar–2 Jan. Closed Wed.
Rooms 5 double, 4 single – 3 with bath, 6 with shower.
Facilities Lounge with TV, 3 dining rooms.
Location Central, parking. Maussane is 19 km E of Arles.
Restriction Not suitable for &.
Credit cards All major cards accepted.
Terms [1990 rates] Rooms 230–330 frs. Breakfast 27 frs. Set lunch/dinner 135 frs. Special meals for children.

Le Pré des Baux   *Tel* 90.54.40.40

Down a side road near the village square, and quiet. New to the Guide this year: "If you want a bed-and-breakfast hotel with a swimming pool, this is it. It has just been built by a doctor and his wife, who run it, and is very clean, with a charming atmosphere. Drinks and coffee are served cheerfully round the large pool, which has excellent loungers. Each room has a bit of a patio and screen. Breakfasts are particularly good." Rooms are close together round the pool. (*Gerald Campion*)

Open All year except Feb.
Rooms 10 – all with bath and/or shower, telephone, TV.
Facilities Salon, bars. Terrace, garden with swimming pool.
Location Central, protected parking. Maussane is 19 km E of Arles.
Credit cards Access, Visa.
Terms [1990 rates] Rooms 400–480 frs. Breakfast 40 frs. (No restaurant.)

MEGÈVE 74120 Haute-Savoie   Map 10

Hôtel Le Fer à Cheval   *Tel* 50.21.30.39
36 route du Crêt d'Arbois   *Fax* 50.93.07.60

On the edge of one of France's largest Alpine ski resorts, a modern hotel
in traditional chalet style, with elegant but heavy furnishings (lots of dark
wood). This is its Guide debut: "Our room was not large, but downstairs
there's a whole range of lounges, one with a roaring log fire. The dining
room, also with a log fire, was full of woodsy ambience; the food was
superb, and beautiful to look at. The owners were much in evidence, and
the clientele was international." (*Leah Leneman*)

Open 20 Dec–Easter and 1 July–15 Sep.
Rooms 18 suites, 23 double, 4 single – all with bath, shower, telephone, TV.
Ground-floor rooms.
Facilities Lift. 7 salons, 2 bars, restaurant; billiard room; sauna and jacuzzi.
Outdoor swimming pool; terrace.
Location 500 metres from town centre, on side road.
Credit cards Access, Visa.
Terms [1990 rates] Dinner, B&B: single 740 frs, double 1,020–1,490 frs. Set dinner
170 frs; full alc 250 frs. Special meals for children.

MERCUREY 71640 Saône-et-Loire   Map 10

Hôtellerie du Val d'Or `BUDGET`   *Tel* 85.45.13.70
Grande Rue   *Telex* 800660

"Just as good as ever," says a visitor this year to this very traditional and
quietly elegant hostelry, on the busy main street of a village that produces
one of Burgundy's great wines (there are several *caveaux de dégustation*
close by). The "courteous and efficient" Cogny family provides locals as
well as tourists with generous helpings of Burgundian cuisine (*Michelin*
rosette, *Gault Millau toque*, for such dishes as fillet of rabbit and parsleyed
ham) and expensive Mercurey wines. One reader enjoyed the middle-
priced menu and had a small but pretty room with a balcony over the
garden. Others, too, have found the rooms comfortable and charmingly
decorated, if a little cramped. Light and colour in the garden, armchairs in
the salon, and sociable chatter in the attractive restaurant with its stone-
tiled floor, flowers and lamps, and log fire in winter. (Endorsed this year
by *George Atkinson*)

Open 16 Jan–25 Aug and 2 Sep–15 Dec; closed Mon, and Tue midday.
Rooms 10 double, 1 single – all with bath and/or shower, telephone, TV.
Facilities Salon, bar, 2 restaurants. Garden, swings.
Location 13 km from Chalon-sur-Saône. Leave *autoroute* at Chalon Nord, take
D978 Autun–Nevers, turn right to Mercurey. Parking.
Restriction Not suitable for &.
Credit cards Access, Visa.
Terms Rooms: single occupancy 140 frs, double 290 frs. Breakfast 35 frs. Set
lunch/dinner 140, 200, 250 and 320 frs; full alc 295 frs. Reduced rates and special
meals for children.

> We don't lack *Michelin*-rosetted hotels in France but we would be
> glad of more nominations at the budget end of the price scale.

MEYRUEIS 48150 Lozère   **Map 10**

Château d'Ayres   *Tel* 66.45.60.10
                                                        Fax 66.45.62.26

A 12th-century monastery, rebuilt as a château, set alone in open country
outside Meyrueis on the edge of the limestone *causses* and the Cévennes
National Park, close to the Jonte and Tarn gorges. Large bedrooms
overlook a park of giant sequoias, chestnuts and cedars. A regular admirer
this year confirms his earlier accounts: "The owners, the Comte and
Comtesse de Montjou, make you feel like family friends. The staff, too,
are all smiles and courtesy. Huge, comfortable rooms, beautiful breakfasts, more than adequate cuisine, and an air of peace and elegance. It is
in the evening that the hotel's charm best manifests itself: small tables
and chairs are set under the sequoias in the park, with candles on each
table, and subtle floodlighting tints the château's facade and the trees
beneath the hillside, creating perfect reflections in the ornamental pool."
"The friendliest hotel" say visitors this year. "The cooking is mainly
Cévenol and we rate it highly. The *pension* menus are limited, but the
other menus and the *carte* were not exorbitant." (*Colin Pilkington, AJ
Collins*) One 1990 visitor was highly critical of room maintenance and
housekeeping.

Open 1 Apr–7 Nov.
Rooms 3 suites, 21 double – all with bath and/or shower, telephone, TV.
Facilities 3 salons (1 with TV), 2 dining rooms. Garden with tennis.
Location 1½ km SE of Meyrueis.
Restriction Not suitable for &.
Credit cards All major cards accepted.
Terms Double room: B&B 380–690 frs; dinner, B&B 590–900 frs. Set lunch/dinner
122, 230 and 280 frs; full alc 240 frs. Reduced rates and special meals for children.

MIMIZAN 40200 Landes   **Map 10**

Au Bon Coin   *Tel* 58.09.01.55
34 avenue du Lac

The long flat Atlantic coast south-west of Bordeaux has splendid sandy
beaches, lined by a number of popular resorts. Just inland are freshwater
lakes amid the Landes forest, also with resort facilities, and here is *Au Bon
Coin*. This year again readers have relished its cuisine (*Michelin* rosette,
two *Gault Millau toques*) and other features too: "A picturesque and pretty
hotel, beautifully furnished; an oasis of peace." An earlier account: "It is
edged by well-kept public gardens, with woods and beaches beyond, and
it has rowing boats for hire (free to residents). Our bedroom was
luxurious, with repro antique furniture, lace bedspread, huge bathroom.
Dinner was a delightful affair, served with panache and humour by
efficient young waiters; even the cheapest menu was delicious. Gorgeous
china, impeccable napery, silver candlesticks. Blissful peace at night in
the flowery lakeside gardens, and then a good breakfast." Rooms in the
annexe are equally luxurious. (*Prof and Mrs JF Woodward, EH, PW Arnold*)

Open All year except Feb. Restaurant closed Sun evening, and Mon in low
season.

Rooms 3 suites, 5 double – all with bath (5 also have shower), telephone, TV, mini-bar. Suites, with kitchenette, in annexe 100 metres from hotel. Some ground-floor rooms.
Facilities Lounges, bar, dining room; functions rooms; terrace. Garden. Lake with fishing, rowing boats. Sea 4 km.
Location 1 km N of Mimizan, which is 111 km SW of Bordeaux.
Credit cards Amex, Visa.
Terms [1990 rates] Rooms 460–560 frs. Breakfast 60 frs. Dinner, B&B 460–580 frs per person. Set lunch 120 frs, dinner 320 frs. Special meals for children.

MIONNAY 01390 Ain   Map 10

Alain Chapel   *Tel* 78.91.82.02
                                                           Fax 78.91.82.37
                                                           Telex 305605

The French guides continue to give their top ratings to Alain Chapel, in his elegant restaurant-with-rooms just north of Lyon: he is sometimes regarded as the greatest of all the great modern French chefs. And again this year our readers tend to concur ("superb, exciting, innovative food"). He is a serious, rather austere man, not at all a flamboyant showman like his rival Paul Bocuse down the road; a perfectionist and a tireless innovator, he changes his menu with the season and the market, creating superb new tastes from simple high-quality products, in the light modern manner. Of course his prices are very high. Travellers this year have also praised the friendly staff (almost *too* attentive) and luxurious bedrooms, bright and cheerful. An earlier inspector's report: "It's an old rural auberge, much extended and now very grand and spacious, with stone-flagged halls and patios and a floodlit garden. Chapel tries to keep the rural touch, but he does cheat: one dining annexe with ancient beams looks like a medieval barn but was built in 1987! You eat in a series of small discreet flower-filled rooms, where tables are well spaced and the ambience is quiet and dignified (save for the tourists taking snapshots of their meal). We especially liked the écrevisses in a spicy dark-green coriander sauce, the pigeon à la presse and the very ripe cheeses. Quaint loos (the ladies' has a piano)." (*M and D Chambers, N D'Emden and H Osman, P and J T*)
  As we go to press we learn with deep regret of Alain Chapel's death.

Open All year except Jan and Mon. Restaurant closed Mon and Tue midday except public holidays.
Rooms 13 double – all with bath, telephone, TV.
Facilities 3 lounges, bar, restaurant. Small garden where meals are served in fine weather.
Location 17 km N of Lyons, on N83. Coming from Paris on A6, take first exit after Villefranche, then D51 to Neuville, then Montanay. Parking.
Credit cards All major cards accepted.
Terms Rooms 675–800 frs. Breakfast 75 frs. Set lunch/dinner 500–700 frs; full alc 500 frs. Reduced rates and special meals for children.

Do you know of a good hotel or country inn in the United States or Canada? Nominations please to our sibling publication, America's Wonderful Little Hotels and Inns, PO Box 150, Riverside Avenue, Riverside, Conn. 06878, USA.

MOËLAN-SUR-MER 29350 Finistère — Map 8

Les Moulins du Duc
Tel 98.39.60.73
Fax 98.39.75.56
Telex 940080

In south Brittany near Quimperlé, an idyllic 16th-century millhouse beside the quiet river Belon, of oyster-breeding fame. Luxurious conversion, but unpretentious and family-run. Genuine Breton furnishings such as copper cauldrons. Great comfort, good cooking. Ducks charming, but garrulous at night. Closed 15 Jan–end Feb. 22 rooms, all with bath and shower, 420–730 frs. Half board 515–665. Set meals 175–350 frs [1990 prices]. Enticing new nomination. More reports please.

MOLINES-EN-QUEYRAS 05350 Hautes-Alpes — Map 10

Hôtel l'Équipe [BUDGET]
Route de St-Véran
Tel 92.45.83.20

"Modest, but a treasure", "fantastic value", "managed with charm and discretion by the Catalin family" – recent praise for this trim and simple chalet-hotel in a beautiful Alpine setting. It stands in a broad high valley south-east of Briançon, with ski-slopes and wooded hills all round. Nearby is the 13th-century fortress of Château-Queyras, and the isolated village of St-Véran, which at 2,040 metres claims to be the highest in Europe. "The owners were warm and helpful, the meal delicious." "We had a comfortable bedroom with a balcony giving magnificent views." "There's no nightlife around here, but interesting 'happenings' in season, such as folk-singing, and firework displays on the hills. Monsieur leads excursions into the mountains." Sometimes the Catalins throw the guests together for a fondue party. (Endorsed by *Pat and Brian Lloyd*) A new chef this year. Up-to-date reports welcome.

Open 22 Dec–12 May.
Rooms 22 – all with bath (3 also have shower), telephone. 11 with 2–4 beds in annexe.
Facilities Salon, TV room, bar, restaurant. Terrace; garden on river, fishing. Winter sports (ski-lifts 50 metres).
Location 1 km from Molines on road to St-Véran.
Restriction Not suitable for &.
Credit cards All major cards accepted.
Terms B&B double 256–266 frs; dinner, B&B 223–230 frs per person; full board 274–283 frs. Set lunch/dinner 59, 90, 134 frs; full alc 160 frs. Reduced rates and special meals for children.

MONTAIGU-DE-QUERCY 82150 Tarn-et-Garonne — Map 10

Au Vieux Relais [BUDGET]
Place de la Mairie
Tel 63.94.46.63

Off the beaten track, between the Lot and Garonne rivers, and new to the Guide: "A 15th-century *relais de poste* on the main square in the old high village, which has kept its ancient charm and is quiet. Just three bedrooms: ours with a huge bed was as pleasant as any we have found in

France at a hostelry of this unpretentious kind. The daughter of the house, a young woman of energy and charm, cooked our dinners, and the 110-franc [1990] menus gave us pleasure. A gem of a place." (*Joy and Michael Rubinstein*)

Open All year except 5 Jan–1 Mar. Restaurant closed Sun evening and Mon except 15 July–15 Sep.
Rooms 3 – all with shower.
Facilities Lounge, dining room.
Location Montaigu is 30 km SE of Villeneuve-sur-Lot.
Credit cards Access, Visa.
Terms [1990 rates] Rooms 185 frs. Breakfast 25 frs. Set lunch/dinner 115–210 frs.

MONTFORT-EN-CHALOSSE 40380 Landes   Map 10

Aux Touzins   `BUDGET`   *Tel* 58.98.60.22

A mile outside the village of Montfort on the southern fringe of the Landes forest, in pleasant rolling Gascony countryside, is this unpretentious white-walled auberge. Comfortable modern bedrooms, nicely decorated, some with balcony and view; smiling staff; good regional cooking, popular with locals. Garden with new swimming pool. All excellent value. Closed 15 Jan–15 Feb, Mon except July and Aug. 20 rooms, 16 with bath or shower. B&B double 154–224 frs. Set menus 90–150 frs [1990]. Recent nomination. More reports welcome.

MONTPELLIER 34000 Hérault   Map 10

Hôtel Le Guilhem   *Tel* 67.52.90.90
18 rue J-J Rousseau

"Montpellier used to be a sleepy place, but now it's the fastest-growing boom-town in France, an upstart rival to Toulouse and Grenoble, with some monumental new architecture by Ricardo Bofill. None of this has spoilt the charm of the *vieille ville*, to my mind as lovely as Aix or Arles and here in a narrow street is this brand-new B&B hotel, converted from an old building by a former Parisian accountant and his wife, the Charpentiers, both friendly. Rooms are inevitably small, but very well equipped (hair-drier, good reading lights); breakfast comes copiously with flowers, eggs, newspaper, etc. A lovely terrace for summer, amid greenery. Parking is hard." (*JA*, endorsed this year by *Edith A Wheless*) No restaurant, but you can eat well nearby at the *Louvre*.

Open All year.
Rooms 22 double, 2 single – all with bath and/or shower, telephone, TV.
Facilities Lift. Breakfast room, salon. Terrace. Baby-sitting available.
Location Central, in pedestrian zone; follow signs for *centre historique*. Public parking 600 metres.
Restriction Not suitable for &.
Credit cards All major cards accepted.
Terms (Excluding tax) Rooms 270–500 frs. Breakfast 45 frs. (No restaurant.) Children sharing parents' room free of charge.

Before making a long detour to a small hotel, do check that it is open. Some are known to close on impulse.

MONTPINCHON 50210 Manche   Map 8

Château de la Salle   *Tel* 33.46.95.19
                                                                Fax 33.46.44.25

Within an hour's drive of Cherbourg, between St-Lô with its national stud
and Coutances with its sublime cathedral, a handsome 18th-century
stone mansion is now a most elegant country hotel in a peaceful setting.
Its pleasures include elegant furniture, some four-poster beds, a huge
roaring fire in winter, a lovely garden where you can take breakfast in
summer – and "superb" food, a mixture of *nouvelle* and *ancienne* (*Michelin*
rosette, red *Gault Millau toque*). A 1990 report: "The interior is charmingly
rustic, with tiled floors. Our large, comfortable room had a canopied bed,
large antique armoire, white-washed walls and a little nook. But the
bathroom wallpaper was atrocious. The food, mostly delicious, was
presented in the *nouvelle* fashion, very artistic. Smoked duck and foie
gras, salmon in a light tomato sauce and rabbit in a strong mushroom
sauce were all exquisite. Dinner was served in the old kitchen, not elegant
but comfortable. Most guests were American and English." (*J Gazdak*)

Open 20 Mar–5 Nov.
Rooms 1 suite, 9 double, 1 single – all with bath and/or shower, telephone, TV.
Facilities Lounge, 3 dining rooms. Garden.
Location Montpinchon is 12 km E of Coutances, by D7 and D73.
Restriction Not suitable for &.
Credit cards Access, Diners, Visa.
Terms B&B: single 528 frs, double 676–726 frs, suite 846 frs; dinner, B&B: single
828 frs, double 1,076–1,126 frs, suite 1,246 frs. Set lunch/dinner 100, 155 and
230 frs; full alc 350 frs. Reduced rates and special meals for children by
arrangement.

MORLAIX 29210 Finistère   Map 8

Hôtel de l'Europe   BUDGET   *Tel* 98.62.11.99
rue d'Aiguillon   *Telex* 941676

In the centre of this North Breton market town, a classic and dignified hostelry
with fairly simple, modestly priced rooms, many of them spacious and
overlooking a quiet courtyard. Excellent, innovative cooking in a Second Empire
style brasserie (there is also a restaurant under separate management).
57 rooms, most with bath and shower, 120–360 frs. Breakfast 27 frs. Set menus
65–225 frs; in brasserie 60–70 frs. Recent nomination. More reports welcome.

MOYE 74150 Haute-Savoie   Map 10

Relais du Clergeon   BUDGET   *Tel* 50.01.23.80
Moye-Rumilly

This unpretentious *Logis de France*, small, quiet and very friendly, lies
amid the green hills of Savoy, in a hamlet near the town of Rumilly,
south-west of Annecy. It has long been liked for its lovely views, good
food, and the friendly charm of the owners, the Chal family. Some
criticisms of rooms and service caused it to lose its place in recent
editions. But it could appeal to those with unjaded rustic tastes, such as

this year's re-nominators: "Rooms pleasant, service friendly and hard
working, food exciting" (e.g. local dishes such as sauté'd kid, pigeon de
Bresse). Panoramic dining terrace. (*N D'Emden and H Osman*). More
reports welcome.

Open All year except Jan, 1 week Feb and 1 week Oct. Closed Mon.
Rooms 18 double – 12 with bath and shower, 3 with bath, all with telephone;
3 with TV. Ground-floor rooms.
Facilities Lounge, TV room, bar, reading room, restaurant. Garden with children's
play area.
Location 3 km from Rumilly which is 17 km SW of Annecy.
Credit cards Access, Diners, Visa.
Terms Rooms: single 120–260 frs, double 140–300 frs. Breakfast 25 frs. Dinner,
B&B 180–310 frs per person. Set lunch/dinner 65–250 frs. Reduced rates for
children sharing parents' room; special meals.

MUZILLAC 56190 Morbihan   Map

Domaine du Château de   *Tel* 97.41.69.2?
Rochevilaine   *Fax* 97.41.44.8?
Pointe de Pen Lan   *Telex* 95057?

A poetic experience for our reporters, this old manor on the south coast of
Brittany, set on a rocky headland just above the sea. "Its many
outbuildings, ranging from the medieval to the modern, are scattered in
well-tended gardens dotted with ancient Breton sculptures and crosses
these pavilions, each with a private lounge, can be taken by a whole
family. Our room was palatial, and all the hotel's furniture is ancient
Breton and superb: the huge chest, creaky carved wardrobe and writing
desk in our room were of the kind one drools over in antique shops
Bedroom service is impeccable and the breakfast copious. Dinner in the
cavernous dining room under its ancient beams can be somewhat noisy
but the view of the sun setting on the sea takes your breath away
Cooking is *soigné*, exploiting the catch of the day, and the table d'hôte
offers good value (*Michelin* rosette, two red *Gault Millau toques*). You can
take lunch in the modern courtyard. There's a small outdoor swimming
pool above the rocks, also sandy beaches nearby; and the hotel is about to
build a thalassotherapy centre. At high tide, the sea rose right up to our
bedroom on the rocks: here, leaving windows and curtains open, we
woke bathed in the beams of the rising sun at dawn, to the purr of fishing
vessels sailing out. At night, the magical darkness, dotted with distant
lights, was undisturbed save for the gentle swish of the waves below.
was the most striking memory of our trip – that amazing room at the edge
of the world, with nothing beyond but the sea and the stars." (*Francine
and Ian Walsh*)

Open All year except 8 Jan–25 Feb.
Rooms 27 – all with bath and/or shower, telephone, TV. Rooms in pavilions in
garden.
Facilities Lounge, restaurant; conference facilities. Courtyard where meals are
served. Garden with swimming pool.
Location At Pointe de Pen Lan, 4.5 km S of Muzillac which is 25 km SE of
Vannes.
Credit cards All major cards accepted.
Terms [1990 rates] Rooms 400–950 frs. Breakfast 50 frs. Dinner, B&B 495–770 frs
per person. Set lunch/dinner 220–350 frs. Special meals for children.

NAJAC 12270 Aveyron   Map 10

Hôtel Miquel: l'Oustal del Barry   *Tel* 65.29.74.32
Place du Bourg   *Fax* 65.29.75.32

In this remote but scenic part of the Massif Central, Najac is a beautiful
medieval village above the Aveyron gorges, with an old castle high on a
hill above the river. The *Miquel* is on the village square, yet also has a
private garden for sunbathing, with a children's playground. Some rooms
have a balcony, and there are wonderful views. A visitor this year
thought the hotel splendid: "Charming *patronne*, pretty public rooms,
fabulous food" (*Michelin red "R"*). A visitor last year had an "amazingly
generous" lunch with "really good provincial cooking, not *nouvelle*-ish,
served very professionally but with enthusiasm". Rooms vary in size and
quality as the hotel has been converted from several different old houses.
(*M and L Piper, HR, John Gray*) Two veteran reporters this year dissented
from the general praise: they found their room and shower poor, the
service very slow and the food mediocre. More reports please.

Open Early Apr–end Oct. Closed Mon Apr and Oct except holidays.
Rooms 4 suites, 13 double, 4 single – 9 with bath, 9 with shower, all with
telephone, TV. 7 in annexe. Some ground-floor rooms.
Facilities Lift. Salons, bar, 2 restaurants (1 non-smoking); 2 terraces. Large garden
with play area for children.
Location From Villefranche de Rouergue or Cordes on D122 hotel is on right at
entrance of village. Parking.
Credit cards Access, Amex, Visa.
Terms [1990 rates] Rooms: single 185 frs, double 220–235 frs, suite 255–340 frs.
Breakfast 35 frs. Dinner, B&B 233–270 frs per person; full board 277–320 frs. Set
lunch/dinner 105, 185 and 240 frs; full alc 250–280 frs. Reduced rates and special
meals for children.

NARBONNE 11100 Aude   Map 10

Hôtel la Résidence   *Tel* 68.32.19.41
6 rue du Premier Mai   *Fax* 68.41.56.46
                                                               Telex 500441

In a quiet street close to Narbonne's great fortified cathedral, this unusual
but sympathetic B&B hotel is in Victorian boudoir style: Louis XV
furniture, gilt mirrors, silk flowers in vases. "Run by friendly and jovial
local people; it is slightly quaint and theatrical, with decor verging on the
kitschy. In the corridors were old chests, velvet drapes and red candles on
silver sticks. Some of the rooms are in this style too, but ours had plainer
decor. It was comfortable and cosy. Adequate breakfast, taken in one of
the spruce and elegant salons." "Breakfast served on pretty china, with an
accompanying rose-bud that opened and lasted 11 days."

Open All year except 3 Jan–3 Feb.
Rooms 1 suite, 23 double, 3 single – all with bath, shower, telephone, TV, air-
conditioning. 4 ground-floor rooms.
Facilities Lift, 2 salons, TV room.
Location Central, near cathedral and canal. Parking.
Restriction Not suitable for &.
Credit cards Access, Visa.
Terms Rooms: single occupancy 265 frs, double 340–395 frs. Breakfast 40 frs. (No
restaurant.)

NICE 06300 Alpes-Maritimes   Map 1

Hôtel La Pérouse   *Tel* 93.62.34.6:
11 quai Rauba-Capeu   *Fax* 93.62.59.4:
                                                        Telex 46141:

Of Nice's 350 hotels, this is perhaps the most attractive in the upper
medium range, thanks above all to its setting: it is perched halfway up the
castle rock at the east end of the promenade, with "breathtaking" view
of the bay. It has white marble corridors, bedrooms with cool white deco
and marble bathrooms, a beautiful bar, and a log fire for winter. There's
small swimming pool below high rocks, and a terrace with lemon tree
where breakfasts and light lunches are served (no restaurant as such)
This year, we've had a mixed bag of reports. "One of our favourite hotels
we could find no fault," says one reader. "The staff were courteous an
helpful, the beds soporifically comfy, breakfasts excellent and the silenc
incredible, even on Christmas Eve when the general racket down belov
defied description" (high on its rock, the hotel escapes the city din). "A
large, sunny room, and a large roof-terrace with magnificent view. But th
pool area is cramped and the hotel we found a little impersonal." Room
vary in price, but even the cheaper ones without sea views are wel
furnished and comfortable. (*Paul Palmer, David and Kate Wooff, Lise Chase
and others*) One complaint of a muddle over booking and a leaky roof, an
another which began with a booking problem and continued with
variety of irritating weaknesses in the service and room maintenance.

Open All year.
Rooms 2 suites, 60 double, 3 single – all with bath, shower, telephone, radio, TV
Facilities Lifts. Bar/lounge, terrace, conference facilities. Sauna. Garden with
patio; 2 swimming pools. Beach across road.
Location At E end of Promenade des Anglais, by château. Paid parking nearby.
Credit cards All major cards accepted.
Terms Rooms 310–1,050 frs. suite 1,100–1,800 frs. Breakfast 45–50 frs. Reduced
rates for children. (No restaurant but light snacks and room service.)

NIEUIL 16270 Charente   Map 1

Château de Nieuil   *Tel* 45.71.36.3
                                                        Fax 45.71.46.4
                                                        Telex 79123

Originally used as a hunting lodge by François I, this moated Renaissanc
château stands in its own huge wooded park north-east of Angoulême.
has lovely gardens, fine antiques and an imposing marble staircas
Visitors continue to appreciate its beauty and comfort, as well as th
kindliness of M Bodinaud (the owner), and Mme Bodinaud's cookin
(*Michelin* rosette, *Gault Millau toque*). A reader this year had "a lovel
room in a tower overlooking the formal garden, moat and sheep grazir
beyond". This backs up an earlier view: "The château bears the stamp o
several generations of French nobility. Yet the atmosphere is no
pretentious. It is both friendly and sophisticated. Dinner in the panelle
dining room was a mixture of trad and modern, with generous helping
imaginative salads, and a choice of 15 different fruit tarts." The wel
trained waitresses are attentive – "almost too much so". And n
everyone likes M Bodinaud's gimmick of putting the flag of th

appropriate nation on each guest's table – "We duly got our Union Jack. Maybe he'll adapt to a Euro-flag in 1992." M Bodinaud is also an art buff, and in the former stables he exhibits and sells expensive prints, modern paintings and sculptures. (*Lynne M Allen, Dr PEM Curtis*)

Open Late Apr–early Nov.
Rooms 3 suites, 11 double – all with bath and/or shower, telephone, TV; baby-listening on request; some with air-conditioning. 1 in tower 40 metres from main building. 2 ground-floor rooms suitable for &.
Facilities Salon/bar with TV, restaurant; conference facilities. 350-acre wooded park with swimming pool, tennis court, fishing in pond, art gallery.
Location Off D739, between Nieuil and Fontagie; 42 km NE of Angoulême.
Credit cards All major cards accepted.
Terms [1990 rates] Rooms: single 425–740 frs, double 560–820 frs, suite 1,000–1,470 frs. Breakfast 60 frs. Dinner, B&B double 1,200–2,040 frs. Set lunch/dinner 200–260 frs, full alc 350 frs. Special meals for children on request.

NÎMES 30900 Gard   Map 10

Hôtel Imperator Concorde   *Tel* 66.21.90.30
Place A Briand   *Fax* 66.67.70.25
                                                                              Telex 490635

An imperially classic turn-of-the-century hotel, newly and attractively renovated, in a good position between the Maison Carrée and Jardin de la Fontaine. Courteous service, pleasant walled garden; nouvelle cuisine only average. 65 rooms, all with private facilities, 335–780 frs. Breakfast 50 frs. Set menus 195–350 frs [1990]. Recent nomination. More reports welcome.

NOVES 13550 Bouches-du-Rhône   Map 11

Auberge de Noves   *Tel* 90.94.19.21
                                                                              Fax 90.94.47.76
                                                                              Telex 431312

A 19th-century manor amid pleasant open country south-east of Avignon, owned and run by André Lalleman as a stylish and luxurious hotel, long reputed for its food. It has a lovely shaded terrace, gently lit up at night, and bedrooms of sybaritic splendour, some with balcony offering a pastoral view. Plenty of new praise in 1989/90: "Dinners on the terrace were delectable, breakfasts were sumptuous." "Our favourite hotel in France, with a genuine personal welcome." "Lovely room, dinner a delight, the pool a joy." Earlier views: "To listen to M Lalleman discuss in French, English or German the ordering of the meal is an education and entertainment in itself." "M Lalleman proved an amusing and intelligent host. Excellent antiques in the bedroom, elegant pink-marble bathroom." (*Vicki Turner, Joy and Raymond Goldman, MS Thornton, and others*) Not all rooms are air-conditioned. A new chef arrived last year, who has not impressed *Gault Millau*, though the *Michelin* rosette stays; we'd be glad of your views.

Open All year except 2 Jan–20 Feb. Restaurant closed Wed for lunch.
Rooms 4 suites, 19 double – all with bath, shower, telephone, TV; 16 with air-conditioning; some with balcony; baby-listening on request. Ground-floor rooms.

Facilities Lift. Salon, TV room, restaurant; conference facilities. 9-acre park with garden with restaurant; swimming pool, tennis court; helipad.
Location Off D28, 2 km NW of Noves, which is 13 km SE of Avignon.
Credit cards All major cards accepted.
Terms [1990 rates] Rooms 950 frs, suite 1,400 frs. Breakfast 75 frs. Dinner, B&B 920–1,045 frs per person. Set lunch/dinner 270–420 frs; full alc 500 frs. Reduced rates and special meals for children.

ONET-LE-CHÂTEAU 12850 Aveyron   Map 10

Hostellerie de Fontanges   *Tel* 65.42.20.28
Route de Marcillac   *Telex* 521142

Just north of Aveyron's capital, Rodez, with its pink hilltop cathedral: a handsome stone manor with a fountain in its courtyard, a terrace with views, and a garden with swimming pool. Friendly welcome, good bedrooms, cosy bar, restaurant with vaulted ceiling. Excellent food (Gault Millau toque). *Closed 1–15 Jan. 40 rooms, all with private facilities, 320 frs. Set meals 90–250 frs [1990]. New nomination. More reports please.*

PAIMPONT 35380 Ile-et-Vilaine   Map 8

Le Relais de Brocéliande   **BUDGET**   *Tel* 99.07.81.07

An inspector's appealing discovery this year, in a Breton village west of Rennes: "The forest of Brocéliande is supposedly enchanted, part of the Arthurian legend. Certainly it's badly signposted – but desperately pretty, with aged trees, sunlit paths, dozens of ponds. Beside one of the largest of these stands Paimpont village with its 12th-century abbey. The *Relais* is obviously its social centre, with locals dropping in for a drink and a chat – it all feels like the France of 30 years ago, an old-fashioned inn with a welcoming and hardworking family firmly in charge, bustling and generous. An eccentric touch is the obsession with live and stuffed birds and animals, including a parrot, eagles, owls, and a curious little striped African pig. The dining room is elegant, despite the wildlife, with lovely flowers on each table. Bargain menus, old-fashioned portions, but not especially talented cooking – good scallops and sandre, boring chicken and lamb with tinned veg, excellent cheeses. Our bedroom was mammoth, with dark red curtains, comfortable bed. There's a vast sprawling garden that children would adore. I can hardly wait to return!"

Open All year except 24–26 December.
Rooms 6 for 4 people, 16 double, 3 single – 16 with bath and/or shower (12 also have WC), all with telephone, TV. 15 in annexe. Ground-floor rooms.
Facilities 2 salons, bar, 2 dining rooms; banqueting room. Terrace, garden. Lake opposite; fishing 3 km.
Location Central, parking. Paimpont is 40 km W of Rennes.
Credit cards All major cards accepted.
Terms [1990 rates] Rooms: single 120–180 frs, double 120–250 frs. Breakfast 25 frs. Dinner, B&B 160–200 frs per person, full board 190–250 frs. Set lunch/dinner 58–230 frs; full alc 167 frs. Reduced rates and special meals for children.

Give the Guide positive support. Don't just leave feedback to others.

PARIS   Map 9

Hôtel de l'Abbaye St-Germain   *Tel* (1) 45.44.38.11
10 rue Cassette, 75006

This former monastery, restored with simple elegance, is on a busy street near St-Sulpice, but even front rooms are quiet (it's a *Relais du Silence*). Windows open on to a flagged courtyard with palms, pot-plants and flowers, where breakfast or refreshments can be taken. For these qualities, the *Abbaye* continues to be admired – "beautiful" and "excellent" are among recent epithets. (*Phillip Gill, FM and CN Grist*) However, some rooms are very small, and more than one recent visitor has complained of imperfect housekeeping and maintenance.

Open All year.
Rooms 4 suites, 44 double – all with bath and telephone, 8 with TV; suites have terrace.
Facilities Lift. 2 salons, TV room, bar. Interior courtyard/garden.
Location Central, near St-Sulpice church. (Métro St-Sulpice.)
Restriction Not suitable for &.
Credit cards None accepted.
Terms B&B: double 690–1,200 frs, suite 1,500–1,800 frs. (No restaurant.)

Hôtel de l'Angleterre   *Tel* (1) 42.60.34.72
44 rue Jacob, 75006   *Fax* (1) 42.60.16.93

This characterful St-Germain-des-Prés hotel was long ago the British Embassy (hence its name); more recently, Hemingway lived in room 14. And it lives up to these august credentials, as visitors found this year: "A grand old house built round a courtyard, with an ageing French bourgeois feel of faded decadence, and a lobby that seems more like the hall of a house. We were squeezed into the tiny upholstered lift with the portly porter, but preferred to use the elegant but crumbling staircase. Our room overlooking the rue Jacob was sumptuous, with exposed-beam ceiling, and curtains and chairs draped in a heavy cream fabric. Breakfast average. Very comfortable." "Lots of charm. I like the trompe l'œil wallpaper in the hall." Quietest rooms face the courtyard. (*M and SR, Cynthia D Miller*)

Open All year.
Rooms 29 – all with bath and/or shower, telephone, TV.
Facilities Lift. Hall, breakfast room; courtyard.
Location At St-Germain-des-Prés (Métro St-Germain-des-Prés).
Restriction Not suitable for &.
Credit cards Amex, Diners, Visa.
Terms [1990 rates] Rooms 450–1,000 frs. Breakfast 35 frs. (No restaurant.)

Hôtel de Banville   *Tel* (1) 42.67.70.16
166 boulevard Berthier, 75017   *Fax* (1) 44.40.42.77
                                        Telex 643025

Liked again this year, the family-run *Banville* is one of the most pleasant three-star hotels in Paris, with a friendly staff and warm inviting atmosphere. It fills up with regular clients, mostly French provincials, so needs to be booked well in advance. Bedrooms are quite cosy, and so is the large and handsome foyer, with lots of flowers and pretty fabrics. One snag is the location, on a broad boulevard in the unglamorous *17e*, with few good restaurants nearby. The Métro is quite close, however. (*Linda Gumm*)

Open All year.
Rooms 40 double – all with bath and/or shower, telephone, radio, TV.
Facilities Lift. 2 lounges, bar, breakfast room.
Location 2 mins' walk from Porte de Champerret, 10 mins from Étoile. Underground parking nearby. (Métro Porte de Champerret and Pereire.)
Restriction Not suitable for &.
Credit cards Access, Amex, Visa.
Terms Rooms 500–520 frs. Breakfast 35 frs. (No restaurant.)

Hôtel Châtillon   **BUDGET**
11 square de Châtillon, 75014

Tel (1) 45.42.31.17
Fax (1) 45.42.72.09

This cheap and mildly eccentric small hotel is about four kilometres south of central Paris, in the untouristy Alésia district, and useful for access to the motorways. Several readers this year have commented on the good breakfasts, good value for money, quiet location, and "extremely friendly" owners (not always a feature of small Paris hotels). One returning devotee finds these owners, Monique and Daniel Lamouret, "so sweet, so charming, so willing to do all that can make one's stay enjoyable. They are genuinely keen to greet the English (which must singularise them in this city); Monsieur even took himself off to a crash course at Ramsgate." Earlier he had reported: "The whole place reeks of Frenchness. The rooms are spacious with wonderful views of the neighbours – we cannot believe what people wear to go to bed. A charming and quiet place where we awoke to birdsong in the trees. The floorboards creak, the furniture is nothing special, but the beds are comfy." (*Paul Palmer; also J Fides, HC Hart, Pauline Spence*)

Open All year.
Rooms 2 for 4, 29 double – 30 with bath or shower, telephone, TV. 1 ground-floor room.
Facilities Lift. Salon, bar, breakfast room.
Location Near Porte de Châtillon and Porte d'Orléans. Underground parking nearby. (Métro Alésia.)
Credit card Access, Visa.
Terms Rooms 250–290 frs, suite (for 4) 360 frs. Breakfast 22 frs. (No restaurant.)

Hôtel Duc de Saint-Simon
14 rue de Saint-Simon, 75007

Tel (1) 45.48.35.66
Fax (1) 45.48.68.25
Telex 203277

One of the most stylish and sophisticated of the city's smaller hotels, and liked again this year for being "discreetly charming, efficient and welcoming". Centrally but quietly located down a side street just off the boulevard St-Germain, it is usually fully booked months ahead. "The tiny cobbled forecourt, with its shrubs and trellis-work, gives it a somewhat rural air. Converted from a 17th-century mansion, it is now owned and run by a civilised Swedish couple who have filled it with the antiques they love collecting. Tiled walls, old beams and rough stone walls add to the effect, and there's a small and pretty rear garden for breakfast and drinks in summer. My room was small and unremarkable, but many others are larger and better. Clients tend to be reasonably well-off

travellers who prefer Left Bank old-world charm to a luxury palace."
(Endorsed by *Michael Thierens, David Lodge*)

Open All year.
Rooms 5 suites, 29 double – 33 with bath and shower, 1 with shower, all with
telephone; TV on request. 5 in nearby annexe.
Facilities Lift. 2 lounges, bar.
Location Central. (Métro Rue du Bac.)
Restriction Not suitable for &.
Credit cards None accepted.
Terms Rooms: single/double 950 frs, suites 1,500 frs. Breakfast 50 frs. (No
restaurant.)

Hotel Eber *Tel* (1) 46.22.60.70
18 rue Léon Jost, 75017 *Fax* (1) 47.63.01.01
  Telex 649949

*In a side street near the Parc Monceau, a small, newly renovated B&B hotel
used by* les gens de la mode *(fashion models etc). Spruce decor; cheerful,
smallish rooms, many facing an inner courtyard, very quiet. 18 rooms, all with
bath and/or shower, 550–600 frs. Breakfast 40 frs. New nomination. More
reports welcome.*

Hôtel des Grands Hommes *Tel* (1) 46.34.19.60
17 place du Panthéon, 75005 *Fax* (1) 43.26.67.32
  Telex 200185

André Breton and other Surrealist painters and writers are "great men"
who used to stay at this little hotel of character, though the hotel is also
named for the even greater men (Voltaire, Victor Hugo, Rousseau et al.)
entombed in the Panthéon across the street. Its claim to be the place
where Surrealism was created has been formally recognised by the city
with a marble plaque. The hotel has been commended again this year for
its comfort and friendly staff (but would the "pervasive radio in all public
rooms" have appealed to Surrealists?). Breakfast is taken in a charming
vaulted cellar, and rooms are furnished in period style. "Ours had a
stylish canopy bed, and its view of the lighted dome of the Panthéon was
the most beautiful night-light we've ever had." (*Gary and Lorelei Hill,
Marilyn Frampton*)

Open All year.
Rooms 32 double (also let as singles) – all with bath, telephone, radio, TV.
1 ground-floor room.
Facilities Lounge with bar, breakfast room. Small garden.
Location Opposite Panthéon. Underground paying carpark 100 metres. (Métro
Luxembourg.)
Restriction Not suitable for &.
Credit cards All major cards accepted.
Terms Rooms: single 450–570 frs, double 600 frs. Breakfast 30 frs. Extra bed
100 frs. Reduced rates in low season. (No restaurant.)

Deadlines: nominations for the 1992 edition should reach us not
later than 1 June 1991. Latest date for comments on existing entries:
10 June 1991.

Hôtel du Jeu de Paume
54 rue St-Louis-en-l'Ile, 75004

Tel (1) 43.26.14.18
Fax (1) 43.26.14.18 ext 152
Telex 205160

On the lovely Ile-St-Louis, a former royal tennis court (jeu de paume) *of the 17th century, cleverly converted into an elegantly unusual hotel, combining antique grace with modern high-tech. Public rooms and some bedrooms are beamed. Friendly welcome, all comforts. Patio garden. 32 double rooms, all with bath and shower, 700–1,000 frs. Breakfast 65 frs. No restaurant. New nomination. More reports please.*

Hôtel Lancaster
7 rue de Berri, 75008

Tel (1) 43.59.90.43
Fax (1) 42.89.22.71
Telex 640991

Luxurious and exclusive, but quite small and personal, this famous hotel off the Champs-Élysées is owned by the Savoy group, also owners of the somewhat similar *Connaught* in London (q.v.). Its furnishings and decor are Parisian: but it wears something of an upper-class English air, maybe because some senior staff are British. It was dropped from last year's Guide after reports of bad room service and of many bedrooms needing refurbishment – as undoubtedly they do. But a visitor this year fared better: "Extremely friendly staff, impeccable service, and our suite, recently renovated, was as elegant as one could wish in a grand hotel style. A generous breakfast. The courtyard garden must be lovely in summer." Others this year have enjoyed that courtyard and admired the staff. (*HR, Peter Jowitt, GN Levy*) The restaurant, little used, serves food described either as "very competent" or "unexceptional". And there are some renewed criticisms of bedroom upkeep. More reports please.

Open All year.
Rooms 9 suites, 52 double, 14 single – all with bath, shower, telephone, radio, TV; 33 with air-conditioning.
Facilities Lift. Salon, bar, restaurant. Garden patio.
Location Central. (Métro Georges V.) Private garage.
Restriction Not suitable for &.
Credit cards All major cards accepted.
Terms Rooms: single 1,495–1,690 frs, double 1,955–2,300 frs, suite 3,300–6,900 frs. Breakfast 100 frs. Set menu 210 frs; full alc 350 frs. Extra bed 350 frs. Special meals for children on request.

Hôtel La Louisiane **BUDGET**
60 rue de Seine, 75006

Tel (1) 43.29.59.30
Fax (1) 46.34.23.87

Our Continental Editor's regular Paris pad is a simple utility place of no visual grace, but its literary pedigree is extraordinary. Hemingway, Connolly and others used to stay here (it's mentioned in *The Unquiet Grave*); Sartre here wrote *L'Être et le Néant* during the war, when Simone de Beauvoir was staying here too (in a separate bedroom); Juliette Greco lived here in the days of her early fame. Today the plumbing may be better and the geniuses, alas, far fewer, but basically it's unchanged, full of "sort of artistic bohemian" visitors, and it continues to appeal to readers in search of blissful Rive Gaucherie at low cost: "I felt I was really in Paris, far more than I would in some luxury hotel." This is because it gives straight on to the colourful Buci street-market (but there's double-glazing, and back rooms are very quiet). The foyer is cramped and bedrooms plain: but they are clean and modernised, new paint abounds, and the front desk is friendly. (*Rev Michael Bourdeaux, NJW Bell, JA, and others*) But not everyone likes the soda bread for breakfast, in a very dreary room.

Open All year.
Rooms 1 suite, 73 double, 3 single – 74 with bath, 3 with shower, all with telephone.
Facilities Lift. Lounge, breakfast room.
Location Near St-Germain-des-Prés. Underground parking nearby. (Métro St-Germain-des-Prés, Odéon.)
Credit cards Access, Diners, Visa.
Terms B&B: single 300–350 frs, double 500 frs, suite 600 frs. (No restaurant.)

Hôtel des Marronniers   *Tel* (1) 43.25.30.60
21 rue Jacob, 75006

Near the heart of hectic St-Germain-des-Prés, but quiet, for it lies at the back of a courtyard; most rooms, well modernised, face this or the tiny garden where you can breakfast on fine days. Some period furniture; staff friendly. But bathrooms are small and walls can be thin. 37 rooms, all with bath, 505–560 frs [1990]. Breakfast 36 frs. No restaurant. Recently re-nominated. More reports welcome.

Pavillon de la Reine   *Tel* (1) 42.77.96.40
28 place des Vosges, 75003   *Fax* (1) 42.77.63.06
                                                           Telex 216160

An elegant old building on one of Paris's most beautiful squares, sympathetically converted into a charming luxury hotel, with white marble bathrooms. The quietest rooms overlook a flower-filled patio. 53 rooms (including 23 suites), all with bath and shower. Single room 1,050 frs, double 1,300–2,500 frs. Breakfast 70 frs. No restaurant. Endorsed this year, but fuller reports welcome.

Hôtel Relais Christine   *Tel* (1) 43.26.71.80
3 rue Christine, 75006   *Fax* (1) 43.26.89.38
                                                           Telex 202606

Converted from a 16th-century abbey, a small, highly priced luxury hotel in a narrow street near the Seine. Bedrooms finely furnished but some very small; those round the lovely courtyard are quietest. Breakfasts and service admired; no restaurant, but light meals served in rooms. Basement garage. 16 suites, 35 double rooms, all with bath and shower; single 1,100 frs, double 1,100–1,450 frs. Breakfast 70 frs. Re-nominated by two readers this year. Further reports welcome.

Sterling and dollar equivalents of foreign currencies at the date of going to press will be found at the back of the Guide.

Hotel Solférino `BUDGET`   *Tel* (1) 47.05.85.54
91 rue de Lille, 75007   *Fax* (1) 45.55.51.16
                                                       Telex 203865

Near the Seine and the Musée d'Orsay, an attractively furnished hotel with a
comfortable lounge and cheerful breakfast room. Welcoming atmosphere. Even
front rooms are quiet; some have balcony. Closed Christmas. 33 rooms, all with
bath and/or shower, 220–402 frs. Breakfast 30 frs. No restaurant, plenty nearby.
New nomination. More reports welcome.

Hôtel de l'Université   *Tel* (1) 42.61.09.39
22 rue Université, 75007   *Telex* 260717 OREM 310

This converted 17th-century townhouse near the Seine, intimate and
stylish, has again proved popular in 1989/90. "Breakfast was nicely
served in a little room overlooking a pretty courtyard. The bedrooms were
comfortable and quite pretty." "Staff unfailingly pleasant. Our room large
but a bit shabby." "Small, refined and quiet, with an electronic safe in
each room for storing valuables." The public rooms are decorated with
antiques and tapestries; the cellar bar is in a 14th-century crypt of a
commanderie of the Templars. Back rooms are quietest. (*Prof Sir Alan*
Cook, Dr Suzanne Martin, Mrs Ann H Kearton, and others)

Open All year.
Rooms 1 suite, 17 double, 10 single – all with bath or shower, telephone, TV;
baby-sitters available.
Facilities Lift. Lounge, bar.
Location 5 mins from St-Germain-des-Prés. Underground parking nearby. (Métro
Rue du Bac.)
Restriction Not suitable for &.
Credit cards None accepted.
Terms [1990 rates] Rooms: single 480 frs, double 800 frs. Breakfast 40 frs. 1-night
bookings refused in high season. Reduced rates for children sharing parents'
room. (No restaurant, but snacks served in bar.)

Hôtel de Varenne   *Tel* (1) 45.51.45.55
44 rue de Bourgogne, 75007   *Fax* (1) 45.51.86.63
                                                       Telex 205329

Near the Invalides, a converted mansion with a pretty courtyard,
redecorated this year and again well liked – notably by a Californian who
has recently paid four two-week visits: "I have always enjoyed my stay
here." "Very comfortable and attractive room, fairly priced." One
complaint of late-night disco din, but a reader this year says, "Noise from
adjoining courtyards was confined to briefly unhappy children." (*Wallace*
L Sommers, Marian Peglar, Seymour Sachs) You can take breakfast in the
courtyard or lounge, though one visitor this year was told he must have it
in his room. He was also critical of *accueil*; the desk clerks are said to
"vary in personality from brisk and efficient to loquaciously engrossed in
personal phone conversations".

Open All year.
Rooms 24 double – all with bath and/or shower, telephone, TV.
Facilities Lift. Lounge, patio.

Location Within walking distance of the Champs-Élysées and St-Germain-des-Prés. Parking in quiet street, 5 mins' walk away. (Métro Varenne.)
Restriction Not suitable for &.
Credit cards Access, Amex, Visa.
Terms Rooms 430–580 frs. Breakfast 35 frs. (No restaurant.)

Hôtel La Villa   *Tel* (1) 43.26.60.00
29 rue Jacob, 75006   *Fax* (1) 46.34.63.63
                                                  Telex 202437

A new and very fashionable four-star B&B hotel at St-Germain-des-Prés, glossily brittle, and new to the Guide this year: "Entirely devised in high-tech style by one trendy young designer, Marie-Christine Dorner. She says she wanted the rooms to be 'like home but not too cosy' – and cosy they are not. They vary greatly in size from basic cabins to large suites. We had a basic one, which was cunningly devised to provide all necessary life-support systems – unusual lighting, hair-drier etc. Fresh flowers, but no pictures. Furniture designerish rather than ergonomic. Not really our scene, but would appeal to those who like *Blakes* (q.v.) in London." All rooms are sound-proofed and air-conditioned. (*HR*)

Open All year.
Rooms 4 suites, 28 double – all with bath and/or shower, telephone, radio, TV, baby-listening, air-conditioning.
Facilities Lobby, bar, basement night club.
Location Central. (Métro St-Germain-des-Prés.)
Restriction Not suitable for &.
Credit cards Access, Amex, Visa.
Terms Rooms: double 750–1,400 frs, suite 1,800–2,800 frs. Breakfast 60 frs. Extra bed 300 frs. (No restaurant.)

PASSENANS 39230 Jura   **Map 10**

Auberge du Rostaing   **BUDGET**   *Tel* 84.85.23.70

More favourable reports have arrived in 1989/90 on this modest but charming rural auberge, now a firm Guide favourite. Readers stress the excellent value for money, the good, simple meals, and the friendliness of the Franco-Swiss owners (she cooks, he hosts). The hotel is tucked away in unspoilt countryside, "good for walking", on the outskirts of a sleepy village between the Jura hills to the east and the rich farmlands of Bresse to the west: yet it is not hard to reach, for major tourist routes are nearby. An account this year: "The courtyard where meals are served in summer is idyllic, and the food is good and plentiful. Our bedroom was small but prettily decorated." The white 18th-century main building contains a spacious dining room with open fireplace, large peasant cupboards and modern art, and a 'parlour' upstairs with a piano, records, books and games. Some of the rooms are in an attractive vine-balustraded building with an outside staircase. Swiss dishes such as fondue and raclette are sometimes offered; "And the Swissness of the place shows up with the long list of admonitions to guests. We liked the one urging visitors to take their showers on sunny days in view of the solar heating." One recent visitor thought the food "delicious", with good salads and cheeses: but another thought he detected too much use of the microwave. (*Lynne M Allen, Ivana Copelli, E Newall, and others*)

Open 1 Feb–30 Nov. Closed Mon and Tue except school holidays.
Rooms 1 suite, 9 double – 8 with shower (4 also have WC); baby-listening.
Facilities Lounge, restaurant; courtyard.
Location Off N83, 11 km S of Poligny, which is where the Dijon–Geneva road crosses the Lyon–Besançon road.
Restriction Not suitable for &.
Credit cards Access, Diners, Visa.
Terms Rooms: single 80–145 frs, double 90–170 frs, suite 190–245 frs. Breakfast 20 frs. Dinner, B&B 100–205 frs per person. Set lunch/dinner 56, 82, 100 and 140 frs. 1-night bookings sometimes refused. Reduced rates for children; special meals on request.

PEILLON 06440 Alpes-Maritimes   Map 11

Auberge de la Madone   *Tel* 93.79.91.17

Only 18 kilometres from Nice, yet remote in the high hills, the Millo family's attractive auberge stands on the edge of one of the most striking *villages perchés* of the area. Many rooms have a balcony overlooking the valley, as well as tiled floors and country furniture; there's also a garden, and a pretty terrace for meals and drinks – but no lounge. Reports this year: "A charming hotel, with a delightful exuberant proprietress. Evening meals were delicious." "Clean and efficient. Food was served with enthusiasm, coffee and croissants were great." Others have commented on the warm family ambience, and have enjoyed such locally based dishes as boeuf en daube and quails in a rich sauce. (*C Turner, John and Joan Wyatt, EA Sturmer, Amanda Garrett*) But one reader this year found the food repetitive and uneven in quality, and felt that standards might be slipping. Mosquitoes can be a hazard. Most recent report tells of a helipad in preparation: "Hurry before prices sky-rocket."

Open All year except 5 Nov–20 Dec and 7–24 Jan. Restaurant closed Wed.
Rooms 3 suites, 16 double – all with bath and/or shower, telephone; 4 with TV.
Facilities TV room, bar, 2 dining rooms. Large garden with tennis and table-tennis.
Location 18 km NE of Nice on D21.
Restriction Not suitable for &.
Credit cards None accepted.
Terms Rooms 360 frs, suite 550 frs. Breakfast 42 frs. Set lunch/dinner 130–280 frs; full alc 280–320 frs. Reduced rates for children.

LA PEINIÈRE 35220 Ille-et-Vilaine   Map 8

Hôtel Pen'Roc   `BUDGET`   *Tel* 99.00.33.02
                                                          Fax 99.62.30.89
                                                          Telex 741457

Renewed praise for the "marvellous hospitality" and "delicious fish dishes" at the attractive, modern *Pen'Roc*: built in local Breton style, it lies quietly amid meadows, beside a little romanesque church, just off the main road from Rennes to Vitré. "The staff showed warmth and kindness." "The cuisine is refined and imaginative (notably the fisherman's choucroute), the setting is beautiful and the staff charming." An earlier impression: "It's used during the day for business gatherings, but in the evening we found it delightfully peaceful. Family-run by the Frocs. Madame is tall and as elegant (even at 8 am) as the dishes her husband produces." Another Froc speciality is "méli-mélo de la mer à la badiane". (*Robyn Morton, Jack B Ainslie, G Buckland*) A fire destroyed the upper-floor bedrooms in 1989, but they have since been rebuilt and new ones added; we'd welcome reports on them.

Open All year except 1 week Feb. Closed Sun evening in low season.
Rooms 1 suite, 29 double, 3 single – all with bath or shower, telephone, TV. 2 ground-floor rooms.
Facilities Lift. Lounge, bar, 3 dining rooms; conference facilities. Garden with children's play area.
Location 6 km E of Châteaubourg. Turn off D857 at St-Jean-sur-Vilaine, towards St-Didier, then right to La Peinière.
Credit cards All major cards accepted.
Terms Rooms: single 202–230 frs, double 255–290 frs, suite 450 frs. Breakfast 35 frs. Half board 255–353 frs per person. Set lunch 125 frs; full alc 280 frs. Reduced rates and special meals for children.

PÉROUGES 01800 Ain   **Map 10**

Hostellerie du Vieux Pérouges   *Tel* 74.61.00.88
Place du Tilleul   *Telex* 306898

In the main square of an ultra-picturesque medieval village north-east of Lyon, some 13th-century buildings have been converted to form a hotel whose studied folksiness may not suit all tastes. Some rooms have "medieval" furnishings, or are reached via a winding stone tower. A wood fire in the dining room, where costumed waitresses present the menu on large rolls of parchment; but the food is very good, e.g. duck with green pepper and the famous local griddle-cake with raspberries. The plumbing is modern. Closed Wed in winter. 28 rooms, all with bath. B&B double 560–910 frs. Set meals 150–320 frs. No recent reports. More needed, please.

LA PETITE PIERRE 67290 Bas-Rhin   **Map 9**

Lion d'Or ▮BUDGET▮   *Tel* 88.70.45.06
15 rue Principale   *Fax* 88.70.45.56

This Guide newcomer makes a useful alternative to the *Trois Roses* (see below) and is fairly similar: "An old shuttered window-boxed auberge, recently modernised, with a serious dining room (excellent food) and wonderful views. Language and cuisine, typically in Alsace, have a frallemagne feel, but the welcome is warm if extremely correct; service sometimes a little hectic. Good breakfasts, and bracing forest walks all round. There's even an indoor pool with sauna, and a tennis court shielded by fir trees at the foot of the steep garden." (*Tim Heald*)

Open 9 Feb–4 Jan. Restaurant closed Wed evening and Thu for non-residents.
Rooms 33 double, 2 single – 24 with bath and shower, 8 with shower, all with telephone, TV; 7 with radio. 1 on ground floor.
Facilities Lift. 2 salons, bar, breakfast room, TV room, restaurant. Indoor swimming pool, sauna, whirlpool. Garden with tennis court.
Location 60 km NW of Strasbourg; hotel is central.
Credit cards Access, Amex, Visa.
Terms B&B: single 225–250 frs, double 350–440 frs. Dinner, B&B: single 300–320 frs, double 500–600 frs. Set lunch/dinner 100–250 frs; full alc 185 frs. Reduced rates and special meals for children.

Aux Trois Roses   *Tel* 88.70.45.02
                                                             Fax 88.70.41.28
                                                             Telex 871150

A fine 18th-century auberge, white-walled, flower-bedecked, all cosy
inside, and mostly admired again in 1989/90. It is in the main street of an
ancient hilltop Alsatian village, with remains of ramparts, and hilly
forests all around; the dining room has a fine view of the castle, romantic
on summer evenings when it is floodlit. Run hectically by the Geyer
family and a bevy of other Alsatians, it is a sympathetically informal and
lively place, less in the French than in the Central European tradition –
several comfy salons, and a big *Stüberl* where snacks and cakes are served
all day. Some bedrooms in the old building are a bit cramped and shabby
(and front ones can be noisy), but a modern wing has been built down the
hillside, and this is preferred by readers (*Michelin*, too, gives it three
gables, while the rest of the hotel gets two). The dining room has also
been extended, and there is a new outdoor patio. Most readers this year
have enjoyed the cooking with its generous helpings (e.g. help-yourself
hors d'oeuvre and trout in riesling), and the German-style buffet
breakfast. "A hotel of high quality, a private balcony facing sun and
scenery." (*Neville and Kay Varley, Jean and Malcolm Seymour, K Cowherd,
and others*) One visitor had a "suite" in the main house that was
minuscule. Another found the food and welcome poor, and felt that the
hotel had suffered from its recent expansion and acceptance of coach
parties.

Open All year except 1 Jan–8 Feb. Restaurant closed Sun evening and Mon.
Rooms 16 suites, 21 double, 9 single – all with bath and/or shower, telephone,
TV; 16 with radio. Some in annexe.
Facilities 2 lifts. 3 lounges (2 with TV), bar, 5 dining rooms; conference facilities.
Indoor swimming pool. Terrace; garden with tennis court and children's play area.
Location 60 km NW of Strasbourg; hotel is central. Parking.
Credit cards Access, Visa.
Terms [1990 rates] Rooms 230–445 frs. Breakfast 52 frs. Set lunch 65 frs, dinner
240 frs (including wine). Reductions for children under 8; special meals on
request.

PLANCOËT 22130 Côtes-du-Nord   **Map 8**

L'Ecrin (Chez Crouzil)   *Tel* 96.84.10.24
20 Les Quais   *Fax* 96.84.01.93

In a small town near Dinan, just inland from the rocky North Brittany
coast, owner-chef Jean-Pierre Crouzil runs one of the best fish restaurants
of the region (*Michelin* rosette, two red *Gault Millau toques* for, e.g., tartare
of scallops with caviar). The studied elegance of everything extends to the
five bedrooms, as our nominator reports: "Totally renovated to a very
high standard. Marble entrance hall. The bedrooms are each named after
a precious stone (Emeraude, etc) and superbly furnished. Bathrooms
magnificent. Breakfast included boiled egg, pâté, etc" (and even oysters).
Main road close by, but double-glazing keeps out noise. (*ML Dodd*) More
reports needed.

Open All year except 10–24 June and 11–25 Nov.
Rooms 6 suites, 1 double – all with bath, shower, telephone, TV, baby-listening.

Facilities Lounges, restaurant; sauna, solarium. Terraces. Garden with tennis court.
Location Central. Plancoët is 17 km NW of Dinan.
Restriction Not suitable for &.
Credit cards Access, Visa.
Terms [1990 rates] Rooms 480–520 frs. Breakfast 48 frs. Set lunch/dinner 110–420 frs; full alc 350 frs. Reduced rates and special meals for children.

PLÉHÉDEL 22290 Côtes-du-Nord   Map 8

Château Hôtel de Coatguélen   *Tel* 96.22.31.24
                                                   Telex 741300

Not far from some good north Brittany beaches, this elegant 19th-century château stands in its own 170-acre park of woods, lakes and meadows – not to mention a nine-hole golf course. One recent visitor found it "superb", another was more restrained: "We were quite pleased. It's still owned by the Marquis de Boisgelin, but run by the friendly Le Roys: Louis has written books on modern cookery (his own *cuisine* deserves its two red *toques* in *Gault Millau*), and his wife Nicole, front of house, is not only charming, stylish and vivacious but arranges remarkable art exhibitions. Bedrooms have been attractively decorated (ours overlooked the golf course) and there's much old furniture: the drawing room contains lovely antiques, a gorgeous grand piano and spectacular pictures. The dining room has windows overlooking the lake and the food is interesting – baked oysters, lobster steamed in seaweed en vessie, excellent sauces. The service was willing, but sometimes inexperienced. There was a down-at-heel character in reception every evening. Was he a gardener or odd-jobman? My guess is that it was the Marquis in mufti, keeping an eye on the place." (*Francine and Ian Walsh; Helmut Schoen*)

Open All year except 10 Jan–15 Mar. Closed Tue, and Wed midday.
Rooms 2 suites, 14 double – all with bath and/or shower, telephone and TV.
Facilities Salon with TV, bar, restaurant; conference rooms; children's playroom. Large park with unheated swimming pool, tennis, children's play area, horses, ponies, trout fishing, 9-hole golf course. Beach 7 km.
Location 11 km S of Paimpol, on D7 to Lanvollon. Parking.
Credit cards All major cards accepted.
Terms [1990 rates] Rooms 450–1,300 frs. Breakfast 55 frs. Dinner, B&B 580–850 frs per person. Set lunch 170 frs, dinner 380 frs. Special meals for children.

LE POËT-LAVAL 26160 Drôme   Map 10

Les Hospitaliers   *Tel* 75.46.22.32

"This delectable place." "Our little piece of heaven on earth." More raptures again this year from devotees of one of the Guide's favourite French hotels. It stands on a hilltop in a medieval village, above fine wooded countryside where the foothills of the Alps descend to the Rhône valley, on the borders of Dauphiné and Provence. Here the owner Yvon Morin has sensitively restored an old building, with a ruined 12th-century chapel towering above, and a swimming pool facing the glorious panorama. "Food fantastic, pool great." "We dined on an enchanting terrace with tables around a magnificent tree and a superb view over the valley. The owners were most friendly and dinner extremely good" (*Michelin* rosette, two red *Gault Millau toques*). "We had a huge room with balcony overlooking the ruined chapel. The lounge is magnificent – vaulted, beamed, a roaring fire (in March), interesting paintings and M Morin's personal collection of sculptures. Food was excellent." "M Morin is a marvellous host, hardworking and courteous. Delightful pantomime of tasting each bottle of wine." "The best service I have seen anywhere." The foie gras, carré d'agneau, potage of wild mushrooms and the grilled goat's cheese are much praised. (*Barbara A Barratt, Lynne and David Allen, Tom and Rosemary Rose, PA Catling, and others*) Only quibbles: an unchanging set menu, pool furniture a bit worn and one report of a geriatric bed.

Open 1 Mar–15 Nov.
Rooms 23 double – all with bath and/or shower, telephone. 3 annexes adjacent to main building.
Facilities Salon, TV room, bar, 2 restaurants; conference facilities. Garden with terraces and swimming pool.
Location On D540, E of La Bégude-de-Mazenc; Montélimar 25 km.
Restriction Not suitable for &.
Credit cards All major cards accepted.
Terms [1990 rates] Rooms: single 440 frs, double 480–770 frs. Breakfast 75 frs. Set lunch/dinner 200–450 frs; full alc 300 frs. Special meals for children on request.

POLIGNY 39800 Jura   Map 10

Hostellerie des Monts de Vaux   *Tel* 84.37.12.50
Monts de Vaux   *Fax* 84.37.09.07
                                                     Telex 361493

On the N5 from Dijon to Geneva, in a hamlet just south-east of Poligny, here's a smart coaching inn, dating from 1793 but with modern extensions. The site, on the edge of a cliff above Poligny, is lovely. Charming owners (the Carrion family), comfortable rooms, excellent food, sophisticated ambience, splendid wine list – "A rare gem." Garden with tennis court. Closed end Oct–end Dec and Wed evening in low season. 10 rooms, all with bath. Dinner, B&B: single 650 frs, double 900–1,400 frs. Alc (excluding wine) 200–300 frs. Endorsed this year. Fuller reports welcome.

PONS 17800 Charente-Maritime   Map 10

Auberge Pontoise   *Tel* 46.94.00.99
23 avenue Gambetta

This medieval town above the river Seugne, near the *autoroute* down to Bordeaux, has a castle with a vast keep and a hospice once used by pilgrims Compostela-bound. Our own voyagers mostly admire the *Pontoise*, described recently as "modest, clean and comfortable, with a helpful front desk and superbly executed cuisine". "Lovely cream stone courtyard, entrance hall beautiful with Persian rugs on stone floors, much well-polished brass. Chic petite Madame smiles a welcome. Bedroom gently old-fashioned. Dining room full of locals, with black-and-white tiled floor, gleaming glasses and silver. Dinner was magic – home-cured smoked salmon, delicious fish soup, langoustines with pasta." (*WG Frick, Minda Alexander*) However, another recent visitor, while finding the room comfortable, strongly criticised the decor, "pretentious" food, and glum

service. And the *Michelin* rosette has this year been withdrawn. More
reports needed.

Open 29 Jan–20 Dec. Closed Sun evening and Mon 15 Sep–1 July.
Rooms 1 suite, 21 double – all with bath and/or shower, telephone, TV.
1 ground-floor room.
Facilities Lounge, bar, 2 dining rooms.
Location Central. Parking. Pons is 96 km N of Bordeaux.
Restriction Not suitable for &.
Credit cards Access, Visa.
Terms Rooms 220–380 frs, suite 580–620 frs. Breakfast 45 frs. Set lunch/dinner
100, 150 and 300 frs; full alc 350 frs. Reduced rates for children.

PONT-AUDEMER 27500 Eure   Map 8

Auberge du Vieux Puits   *Tel* 32.41.01.48
6 rue Notre-Dame du Pré

Three 17th-century timbered houses around a courtyard make up this
picturesque restaurant-with-rooms, which has again been liked this year:
"The food was superb, the hospitality genuine and warm – and the rooms
plain and small, but so what?" Earlier views: "Beautiful buildings,
delicious cooking, friendly service." "We were warmly welcomed by
Madame Foltz and shown to a comfortable room in the new wing. The
inn is beautifully maintained with fresh flowers in the rooms, and the
courtyard has a pretty garden where people gather for aperitifs on fine
evenings." The eight older bedrooms by the courtyard are charming but
small, and not very well insulated. The six newer rooms have more
comfort but less character. There's good choice on the *carte*, though the
main "menu tradition" of local dishes does not change – "But," says one
happy customer, "if I can eat truite Bovary and canard aux griottes there
once a year, I don't complain." (*RM Flaherty, Mrs RB Richards, E Newall*)

Open 18 Jan–1 July, 11 July–17 Dec. Closed Mon evening and Tue.
Rooms 12 double – 6 with bath and shower, 5 with shower, all with telephone;
6 with TV. 2 ground-floor rooms, accessible for &.
Facilities 2 small salons, 2 restaurants. Small garden.
Location 300 metres from town centre (hotel is signposted), but quiet. Parking.
Credit cards Access, Visa.
Terms Rooms 150–350 frs. Breakfast 33 frs. Set lunch 160 frs, dinner 250 frs; full
alc 240–290 frs. Guests expected to dine at the hotel.

PONT-DE-BRIQUES 62360 Pas-de-Calais   Map 9

Hostellerie de la Rivière   *Tel* 21.32.22.81
17 rue de la Gare

Set in the suburbs just south of Boulogne, near the N1 to Paris,
owner/chef Jean Martin's restaurant-with-rooms could make a good
choice for the notable first or last meal of a French holiday. Outwardly it
looks dull, but inside all is inviting, in a formal way, and there's a pretty
garden at the back. A railway line is 100 metres away but, we're told,
"not with very noisy trains". The bedrooms have just been renovated and
upgraded. "The expensive menus are excellent value," wrote an earlier
visitor, endorsed in 1990: "*Nouvelle cuisine* de luxe – glamorous and

delicious." (*Antony Fletcher*) *Michelin* rosette. *Gault Millau's* toque is in black for "traditional" cuisine, rather than red for "inventive".

Open All year except 16 Aug–12 Sep and 12 days in Feb. Closed Sun evening and Mon.
Rooms 8 – all with bath and/or shower, telephone, TV.
Facilities Bar, restaurant; small garden.
Location 5 km S of Boulogne, close to N1.
Credit cards Access, Visa.
Terms Rooms 250–300 frs. Breakfast 30 frs. Set lunch/dinner 130, 195 and 270 frs; full alc 300 frs. Special meals for children.

PONT-DE-L'ISÈRE 26600 Drôme   Map 10

Michel Chabran   *Tel* 75.84.60.09
Avenue du 45e-Parallèle   *Fax* 75.84.59.65
                                                          Telex 346333

On the N7 just north of Valence, Michel Chabran's restaurant-with-rooms looks dull from the outside but is full of comforts and distinguished cooking (Michelin rosette, three red Gault Millau toques). Graceful welcome, modern bedrooms, copious breakfasts – and how the old French breakfast is changing and expanding, once you move upmarket! Closed Sun night, Mon from Nov–Mar. 12 rooms, all with bath and/or shower, 350–660 frs. Breakfast 60 frs. Set meals 210–430 frs. New nomination. More reports welcome.

PONT-DE-VAUX 01190 Ain   Map 10

Hôtel-Restaurant Le Raisin   `BUDGET`   *Tel* 85.30.30.97
2 place Michel-Poisat

A pleasant little town just east of the Saône, between Tournus and Mâcon; here Gilles Chazot's warmly decorated restaurant-with-rooms offers excellent traditional Bressane cooking at very fair prices (Michelin rosette, Gault Millau toque). Above-average breakfasts, and simple but comfortable rooms. Closed Jan, Sun evening and Mon, except holidays. 8 rooms, all with bath and/or shower. B&B double 232 frs. Set menus 80–250 frs. Recent nomination. Endorsed this year with slight reservations about the basic nature of furnishings. More reports please.

PORQUEROLLES 83540 Var   Map 11

Mas du Langoustier   *Tel* 94.58.30.09
                                                          Fax 94.58.36.02

A most seductive recommendation, secluded in its own 75-acre pine-wooded park beside the sea, at the eastern and virtually uninhabited end of a very lovely island which is mostly a national park (no cars, no smoking outside the village, bike trails with virtually no tarmac, sandy beaches, wooded cliffs). It's a handsome old yellow-walled manor, converted and modernised with some sophistication: "An outstanding hotel. Meals are served on a large terrace: the food is of the highest quality (two red *Gault Millau toques*), the service excellent and the bedrooms well appointed. A new wing of 21 bedrooms blends superbly into the old style of this lovely building. There are new tennis courts, and two sandy beaches three minutes' walk away. Free buses go to the village and port of Porquerolles every hour. Eighty per cent of the clients are French." Full board terms only. (*Sally and Curtis Wilmot-Allistone*) More reports please.

Open 1 May–1 Nov.
Rooms 4 suites, 59 double – all with bath and/or shower, telephone, TV. Ground-floor rooms.
Facilities 2 lounges, bar, restaurant; conference facilities; terrace. Park with tennis, boules; sandy beach, sailing, windsurfing.
Location 3.5 km E of port of Porquerolles which is 15 mins by boat from La Tour Fondue (frequent services). No cars allowed on island. Free bus service from port to hotel.
Credit cards All major cards accepted.
Terms [1990 rates] Full board 630–1,300 frs. Set lunch/dinner 260–450 frs. Special meals for children.

LE PORT-BOULET 37140 Indre-et-Loire   Map 10

Château des Réaux   *Tel 47.95.14.40*
Le Port-Boulet, Bourgueil

Set on a tiny island in the Loire east of Saumur, a small 15th-century castle belonging to Château Accueil *group. Some train noises. Elegant salon and dining room, small but nicely furnished bedrooms; annexe rooms, not on the island and nearer the railway, are simpler and cheaper. "Individual and civilised; excellent food, welcoming hosts." 12 double rooms, 400–600 frs; 4 suites, 600–900 frs [1990]. Recent nomination. More reports please.*

PORTICCIO 2A Corse-du-Sud, Corsica   Map 11

Le Maquis   *Tel 95.25.05.55*
Porticcio 20166   *Fax 95.25.11.70*
     Telex 460597

Widely regarded as one of Corsica's two or three best hotels, the small but sophisticated *Maquis* stands right by the sea in a quiet cove, facing across the bay to Ajaccio; white walls, black beams and red-tiled floors lend style to the interior. A visitor writes this year: "Ketty Salini, a local lady, began it after the war as a beachside café and has built it into a truly glamorous hotel, intimate and cosy despite its glossy clientele. The lovely outdoor restaurant with adjacent *piscine* is the kind of idyllic location that attracts fashion photographers: you'd think you were on the Côte d'Azur. The food is superb, with a Corsican touch and not too *nouvelle*: especially good fish dishes, thick Corsican soup and lavish lunchtime buffet. Efficient and affable local staff. Bedrooms excellent, some right by the beach (this is public, as are all French beaches, and it could be cleaner). La Salini, much in evidence, a real grande dame, has filled the lounge and foyer with an odd collection of owls and shotguns." "One of our happiest memories will be eating lunch on the terrace – pink table-cloths, umbrellas, silver, fine china and glass, the bright blue sky and sea, wonderful fresh seafood, and delicious Corsican wines." (*JA and KA; also Imogen Mottram*)

Open All year.
Rooms 3 suites, 26 double, 1 single – 27 with bath, 3 with shower, all with telephone, TV, video, mini-bar, air-conditioning. Some ground-floor rooms.
Facilities Lift. 2 salons, bar, TV room, dining room; terrace for al fresco meals. Indoor swimming pool. Garden with tennis court, heated swimming pool, and children's play area. On beach with safe bathing.
Location On the coast 15 km SE of Ajaccio, on the D55. 12 km from airport.
Credit cards All major cards accepted.
Terms [1990 rates] B&B (low season only): single 330–600 frs, double 470–600 frs; dinner, B&B: single 980–1,950 frs, double 1,300–2,200 frs. Set meals 220–250 frs. Reduced rates and special meals for children.

PORTICCIOLO 2B Haute-Corse, Corsica   **Map 11**

Hôtel Le Caribou   *Tel 95.35.02.33*
Porticciolo 20228   *Fax 91.33.23.94*

The Catoni family's eccentric but delightful hotel, with its "house-party atmosphere" and "cornucopia of food", lies on the road north from Bastia to Cap Corse, in a small flowery garden just across the road from the sea. It is rambling and a bit ramshackle, and might not suit the staid or elderly, but most visitors remain entranced by the exuberant ambience, the "outstanding" food, and the warm informality of the Catonis who come from Marseille (Madame has been known to present the bill in her nightdress). Fine old trees have been interlaced with vines to make a shady patio for drinks, a swimming pool has been set into the garden, and a gym and a "dancing room for hotel guests only" have been added this year. Bedrooms are old-fashioned and plainly furnished (one reader called his "poky"), but comfortable and cheerfully decorated. All the decor has a lovely and unusual sense of colour; one typical idiosyncrasy is the foyer decorated to look like a Canadian log-cabin. "The place glows with atmosphere and we made many friends, fellow-guests and staff alike. Guests are an interesting mixture of old regulars and young families with children who mingle with the Catonis' grandchildren. For the main dish, you choose from Monsieur's recited selection, but first you have to resist plate after plate of hors d'oeuvre: pâtés, melon and water melon, local smoked ham, langoustines, mussels, home-made pasta . . ." Built into the rocks by the water's edge are several simple suites, each with a small sun-terrace. Rock bathing is fine: but the public sandy beach 600 metres away is poor. (*JNG Buckeridge, JA and KA*)

Open 10 June–25 Sep.
Rooms 1 suite, 29 double – all with bath and/or shower, telephone; 6 with TV. Also bungalows with kitchen for 2–6 people, let by the week. 2 ground-floor rooms.
Facilities Lounge, bar, TV room, restaurant; terraces. Sauna, fitness room, gym; dance room. Outdoor swimming pool, 2 tennis courts. Private harbour, fine sandy beach with bathing and water sports.
Location 25 km N of Bastia.
Credit cards All major cards accepted.
Terms Rooms double 400–700 frs. Dinner, B&B double 1,200–1,500 frs. Set meals 280 frs; full alc 300 frs. Reduced rates and special meals for children.

PORTO-VECCHIO 2A Corse-du-Sud, Corsica　　　**Map 11**

Grand Hôtel de Cala Rossa　　　*Tel* 95.71.61.51
Cala Rossa　　　*Fax* 95.71.60.11
Porto-Vecchio 20137　　　*Telex* 460394

This old harbour town, now a fast-growing summer resort, lies amid cork
forests in a deep bay. Ten kilometres to its north-east, the *Cala Rossa*
stands alone by the sea in its own huge park, amid a landscape of pines,
big rocks and distant hills; its beach with parasols, crowded in summer, is
in a pretty cove. "An idyllic spot," says an inspector this year, restoring it
to the Guide. "The hotel is modern and stylish, with marble floors,
spacious open-plan lounge and dining room, comfortable rooms. We
enjoyed the *nouvelle*-ish *cuisine* – langoustine soup, lamb en croûte, and a
pungent local goat's cheese. In season they serve Corsican dishes such as
wild boar with chestnuts." Another reader found the staff friendly and
the food good, save that main-dish portions were small. He thought the
hotel's sophistication verged on the pretentious. A big buffet lunch is
served by the beach. Front rooms face the lush garden; back ones are
smaller and face the road.

Open Mid-Apr–10 Nov.
Rooms 3 suites, 58 double – all with bath and/or shower, telephone, air-
conditioning.
Facilities Salon, TV room, bar, dining room; conference facilities. Large garden;
direct access to sandy beach.
Location On peninsula 10 km NE of Porto-Vecchio, by N198, D568, D468.
Restriction Not suitable for &.
Credit cards Amex, Diners, Visa.
Terms [1990 rates] Dinner, B&B: single 610–1,700 frs, double 950–2,200 frs.
Special meals for children.

Hôtel San Giovanni　　　*Tel* 95.70.22.25
Route d'Arca　　　*Fax* 95.70.20.11
Porto-Vecchio 20137

Dropped from last year's Guide for lack of reports, and restored by two
this year: "A mile or so inland from the town, in a quiet and pleasant rural
setting, amid the strange boulders that bestrew this area: they look like
menhirs, but are natural. It's a very cheerful, unpretentious family-run
auberge, whose youngish owner, M Vidoni, has none of the gruffness of
so many Corsicans but is truly welcoming. A flower-filled garden, fair-
sized swimming pool, terrace for drinks, lit up at night. The bedrooms, in
bungalow style, might be too basic for some tastes: we found them
adequate. Decent *pension* meals, not exciting, with some Corsican
dishes." "Very pretty garden, enjoyable food but with no choice. The
family work hard." (*JA and KA, D Carswell*)

Open 1 Apr–31 Oct.
Rooms 29 – all with bath and/or shower, telephone. Ground-floor rooms.
Facilities Salon, bar, TV room, restaurant. Garden with swimming pool, sauna,
tennis court.
Location 1.5 km W of town. Parking.
Credit cards Access, Diners, Visa.
Terms B&B: single 263–335 frs, double 315–430 frs. Set lunch/dinner 125 frs.
Reduced rates and special meals for children.

PULIGNY-MONTRACHET 21190 Côte d'Or   Map 10

Le Montrachet   *Tel* 80.21.30.06
                                                          Fax 80.21.39.06

A big traditional stone building in the pretty main square of one of the classic Burgundy wine villages. The food is the thing here (*Michelin* rosette, *Gault Millau toque*) and this year readers have admired it a lot (although criticisms in 1988 led it to lose its place in the 1990 Guide). The hotel is owned and run by Suzanne and Thierry Gazagnes, who moved here from Canada several years ago, assisted by other members of their family. "Charming, comfortable, consistently high standards and good value – especially the two cheaper menus." "Curious mixture of splendid old house with excellent restaurant and basic though newly fitted top-floor rooms. There's no lounge, and the village is dead at night. Good value, so long as you don't mind going to bed early." "Pleasant staff, very good dinner, but wines expensive." (*Kate and Stephan Murray-Sykes, Angela and David Stewart, Mr and Mrs GG Thomas, Bridget Thomson*) Ten rooms, including one adapted for the disabled, are in a new annexe adjacent to the main building. More reports please.

Open All year except Dec–10 Jan. Restaurant closed Wed.
Rooms 1 suite, 31 double – all with bath and/or shower, telephone, baby-listening; TV on request. 10 in adjacent annexe. 1 on ground-floor suitable for &.
Facilities Restaurant, bar, wine cellar; meeting room. Small garden.
Location Village is 10 km S of Beaune.
Credit cards All major cards accepted.
Terms Rooms 335–450 frs, suite 800 frs. Breakfast 42 frs. Set lunch/dinner 140, 210 and 330 frs; full alc 350 frs. Special meals for children.

QUENZA 2A Corse-du-Sud, Corsica   Map 11

Auberge Sole e Monti   *Tel* 95.78.62.53
Quenza 20122

"Good hotels in the wild Corsican hinterland are very, very few," writes an inspector in 1990, "but this one, back in the Guide after a long absence, will just about do. In a mountain village facing the Dolomite-like Bavella peaks, it's a newish creeper-hung building, a bit down-at-heel but friendly and unassuming. Bedrooms adequate; service somewhat vague in the usual Corsican manner. But *patron*/chef Félicien Balesi is quite a character, quirkily charming, and he provides delicious local fare – roast sucking pig, truite meunière, etc. He told us: 'In 1977, Margaret Thatcher spent a week here on her own. She was solemn, silent, not very friendly. Then, by chance, Denis Healey came the same summer, with his wife. He was the life and soul of the party, jolly and exuberant, singing us songs in Italian after dinner.'" More reports please.

Open 15 Mar–30 Sep.
Rooms 20 double – all with bath and/or shower, telephone.
Facilities Lounge, bar, restaurant. Disco on Sat in summer. Terrace.
Location 44 km NE of Sarténe, 47 km NW of Porto-Vecchio.
Restriction Not suitable for &.
Credit cards Amex, Diners, Visa.

Terms Dinner, B&B: single 400–550 frs, double 550–700 frs per person. Set lunch/dinner 120 frs; full alc 200 frs. Reduced rates for children under 5; special meals on request.

QUESTEMBERT 56230 Morbihan   Map 8

Hôtel de Bretagne   *Tel* 97.26.11.12
Rue St-Michel   *Telex* 951801

Located in a small town east of Vannes, here is Brittany's most distinguished restaurant (*patron*/chef Georges Paineau wins two *Michelin* rosettes, three red *Gault Millau toques*), with just six bedrooms. It is described with awe by two of our keenest sleuths: "The ivy-clad exterior is pretty standard, but within the archway surprise followed surprise – not least the spacious garden with lovingly chosen shrubs, populated by a large number of lean oriental cats. Bedrooms are smart and very comfortable. Our huge double bed was vaguely exotic, with palmed net curtains, imitation bamboo tables, adorable wooden Japanese dolls. The bathroom was amazing, giving the feel of a South Sea island, in vivid rainbow hues, with cotton kimonos provided. "This wild exuberance is reflected throughout the hotel. The Paineaus have travelled widely, buying what took their fancy, and installing these objects side-by-side with Breton antiques regardless of the dictums of so-called 'good taste'. And it works. Of the two dining rooms, one is a beautifully panelled expanse of golden wood lit by antique lamps, the other a large glass conservatory straight out of the *1001 Nights*, with a colourful screen painted in 'naive' style by the *patron* himself. The sitting room is dark and dramatic. And the same bravura is evident in Georges Paineau's forceful style of cooking: sauces are deceptively simple but a delight, presentation is superb, with each dish appearing on an appropriate plate of rare porcelain. We enjoyed hot oysters in cream, melting terrine de foie gras, fantastic pigeon cooked in a shell of rock salt. Service is swift and impeccable. Breakfast included hot brioche slices with apple, and superlative coffee. M Paineau is a fine figure of a man with a splendidly bushy moustache, adept at charming compliments; his wife Michèle is also flamboyant, like an explosive orchid." (*Ian and Francine Walsh*; endorsed this year – "close to perfection" – by *ML Dodd*) Prices are remarkably reasonable, save for the wines.

Open 15 Feb–3 Jan. Closed Sun evening and Mon except July, Aug and public holidays.
Rooms 6 double – all with bath, shower, telephone, radio, TV.
Facilities Salon, 2 restaurants. Garden.
Location 27 km E of Vannes. Central, parking.
Restriction Not suitable for &.
Credit cards Access, Diners, Visa.
Terms B&B: single 450 frs, double 680–880 frs; dinner, B&B 780–980 frs per person. Set lunch/dinner 150–450 frs; full alc 380 frs. Reduced rates and special meals for children.

Important reminder: terms printed must be regarded as a rough guide only to the size of the bill to be expected at the end of your stay. For latest tariffs, check when booking.

RABASTENS 81800 Tarn   Map 10

Hostellerie du Pré Vert   `BUDGET`   *Tel* 63.33.70.51
54 promenade des Lices

In the centre of a small town between Toulouse and Albi, a handsome old
creeper-covered 18th-century house with a big shady garden. Recent
reports: "Rabastens is a sleepy old town, time-warped, unspoilt by
tourism (don't miss the 12th-century church of Notre-Dame-du-Bourg),
and the hotel is likewise – not at all smart, but welcoming, and the staff
are friendly in a non-professional way. Satisfactory meals are served in
the summer on a shady garden terrace and in winter in a delightful wood-
panelled dining room, recently refurbished. Bedrooms too are good value,
though front ones can be noisy." "Helpful owners; large rooms furnished
in a solid, old-fashioned way." (*HR, Diana Holmes, John Edington*)
Plumbing criticised this year.

Open All year except Dec. Closed Sun evening and Mon midday in low season.
Rooms 12 double, 1 single – 4 with bath and shower, 8 with shower, all with
telephone, 4 with TV.
Facilities Bar, TV room, 2 dining rooms. Terrace where meals are served. Garden.
Location Central, parking. Rabastens is 37 km NE of Toulouse.
Restriction Not suitable for &.
Credit card Visa.
Terms Rooms: single 145 frs, double 160–220 frs. Breakfast 23 frs. Set
lunch/dinner 62–110 frs; full alc 140 frs. Reduced rates and special meals for
children.

RAGUENÈS-PLAGE 29139 Finistère   Map 8

Hôtel Chez Pierre   `BUDGET`   *Tel* 98.06.81.06

Admired again this year ("comfortable, very friendly, wonderful seafood"), this most sympathetic family hotel stands right next to good
sandy beaches and is within easy reach of Concarneau and Pont-Aven
(where Gauguin painted). Xavier Guillou's cooking (*Michelin* red "R" for
good value) is the strongest feature: "Very good classical fish dishes with
often quite rich sauces. The five-course half-board menu is outstanding
value. And if you want to splurge one night, the lobster with tarragon is
delicious. As M Guillou does all the fish dishes and sauces himself, some
long waits are inevitable." "A spacious room in the annexe and a cordial
reception. Mme Guillou was charm itself, making sure our needs were
met." "Garden a bit run-down, in a pleasant, informal way." Attractive
courtyard, bar and lounge. The plain rooms in the modern annexe are
better than the older ones. Service can be erratic, especially during the
August crush. And this is not a place for those who want to avoid their
fellow-Britons on holiday. (*Martin Adams, Prof and Mrs JF Woodward, and
others*)

Open 6 Apr–26 Sep. Restaurant closed Wed 20 June–5 Sep.
Rooms 29 – 23 with bath and/or shower, all with telephone. 8 in annexe.
1 ground-floor room.
Facilities Salon, bar, TV room, 2 dining rooms. Garden. Sea 250 m.
Location 12 km SW of Pont-Aven. Private parking.
Credit cards Access, Visa.

Terms [1990 rates] Rooms: single 135–155 frs, double 160–345 frs. Breakfast
25 frs. Dinner, B&B 192–282 frs per person. Set meals 90–220 frs. Reduced rates
and special meals for children.

RECQUES-SUR-HEM 62890 Pas-de-Calais   Map 9

Château de Cocove
              Tel 21.82.68.29
              Fax 21.82.72.59
              Telex 810985

Usefully located near the autoroute *south-east of Calais, a grey-fronted 18th-*
century château in a large park, newly opened as a fairly smart hotel.
"Bedrooms light and airy, simply but comfortably furnished." The stone-
walled restaurant serves food which some guests (but not all) have called
"impeccable". Closed Christmas. 24 rooms, all with bath and/or shower.
Rooms 320–595 frs. Breakfast 35 frs. Set meals 99–270 frs. Recent nomination.
More reports welcome.

REIMS Marne   Map 9

L'Assiette Champenoise
40 avenue Paul Vaillant-Couturier
Tinqueux, Reims 51430
              Tel 26.04.15.56
              Fax 26.04.15.69
              Telex 830267

Jean-Pierre and Colette Lallement previously owned a much-laureated
restaurant of this same name in a village near Reims: now they have
moved to this larger 1920s mansion in the western suburb of Tinqueux –
and with them comes their *Michelin* rosette. As they now have bedrooms,
they qualify for our Guide, too. Returning visitors in 1990 endorse their
1989 view: "It's a dull area, but the large park-like grounds mean that you
hardly notice. Despite the relative grandeur of the main building and the
'interior designed' look of the public rooms, there's a homely family feel –
Madame was working as receptionist, and her young son carried our
suitcases. Our room was prettily decorated and furnished. Breakfast was
above average, and dinner was of a high standard, with a strong
emphasis on fish. Service was good, with a human touch." Other readers
this year agree, save that one thought the bedrooms lacked character,
while another found the food good but overpriced. (*Kate and Stephan*
Murray-Sykes; Letitia Sinker, Alison Patey)

Open All year.
Rooms 2 suites, 28 double – all with bath, shower, telephone, TV. 1 ground-floor
room.
Facilities Lounge with TV, bar, restaurant; conference facilities. Garden; terrace.
Indoor swimming pool planned for 1991.
Location 3 km W of centre of Reims; well signposted. Parking.
Credit cards All major cards accepted.
Terms [1990 rates] Rooms 460–500 frs. Breakfast 48 frs. Dinner, B&B 580–780 frs
per person. Set lunch/dinner 250–380 frs. Special meals for children.

> Hotels are dropped if we lack positive feedback. If you can endorse
> an entry, we urge you to do so.

Boyer "Les Crayères"   *Tel* 26.82.80.80
64 boulevard Henri-Vasnier   *Fax* 26.82.65.52
Reims 51100   *Telex* 830959

Still winning three *Michelin* rosettes and four red *Gault Millau toques*,
Gérard Boyer's awesomely superior hotel is much patronised by the
magnates of the leading Reims champagne houses, who use it to wine,
dine and lodge their more important guests and clients. One reader this
year thought that it "emanated corporate hospitality – just *too* many
glossy brochures", and another, on a return visit, felt the standard of
cooking and service had deteriorated – "we wouldn't rush back", but
others have again found the cuisine "wonderful" and bedrooms the
height of luxury (a suite with *two* loos). It is an elegant cream-coloured
château in Reims's south-east suburbs, approached through massive
wrought-iron gates, its proportions blending with the mature trees and
sweeping lawns of its park. The imposing foyer and staircase are in pale
beige marble, and hung with tapestries. The palatial bedrooms have huge
windows facing the park. But there is no salon in which to mingle with
fellow-guests before and after dinner – just a small, dark green bar which
gets crowded when the restaurant is busy. (*Mrs Elaine Cole-Shear, Helen
and Charles Priday*)

Open All year except 22 Dec–19 Jan. Restaurant closed Mon, and Tue midday.
Rooms 3 suites, 16 double – 10 with bath (9 also have shower), telephone, radio,
TV, baby-listening, air-conditioning. 3 in annexe.
Facilities Lift. Hall, bar, restaurant; private dining room. Park with gardens,
tennis, helipad.
Location Leave motorway at St-Rémy exit. Travel towards Luxembourg for ½ km,
then towards Châlons-sur-Marne on N44. Hotel is 3 km from town centre.
Parking.
Credit cards All major cards accepted.
Terms Rooms 980–1,590 frs. Breakfast 76 frs. Full alc 580–680 frs. Special meals
for children.

RIBEAUVILLÉ 68150 Haut-Rhin   Map 9

Le Clos Saint-Vincent   *Tel* 89.73.67.65
Route de Bergheim   *Fax* 89.73.32.20
                                                     Telex 871377

The "delicious" breakfast and fine views have been singled out for praise
by a recent visitor to this sophisticated chalet-style restaurant-with-
rooms, superbly set among Riesling vineyards, and backed by three
ruined castles. Other comments: "Expensive, but an idyllic place to stay,
with management and staff constantly attentive." "Wonderful rooms,
superb meals, though the wines are very dear and the menus stay
unchanged too long." The hotel's interior is spacious and elegant, with
decor in soft muted golds and browns. "Our room was large and airy,
with french windows opening on to a small terrace and attractive
gardens, with views of the gently rolling countryside and the lights of
Colmar in the distance." (*Bettye Chambers*)

Open 15 Mar–15 Nov. Restaurant closed Tue and Wed.
Rooms 3 suites, 12 double – all with bath, shower, telephone, TV; many with
terrace or balcony. 2 ground-floor suites.
Facilities Lift. Salon, bar, restaurant. Indoor swimming pool. Garden.

Location In NE outskirts of town, which is 15 km N of Colmar. Parking.
Credit cards Access, Visa.
Terms B&B: single 540 frs, double 770 frs, suite 880 frs. Set lunch/dinner 250 frs; full alc 300 frs.

RIGNY 70100 Haute-Saône   Map 10

Château de Rigny   Tel 84.65.25.01
                                                        Fax 84.65.44.45
                                                        Telex 362926

Set quietly in its own grounds outside Gray (a small town north-east of Dijon), a select country house hotel (parts date from 1286), newly modernised, but with a baronial salon, old-style furniture and "exotic" bedrooms. Pleasant hosts, above-average food, good swimming pool; tennis. Some criticism of decor and a geriatric bed. Closed Christmas. 24 rooms, all with bath, 290–480 frs. Breakfast 40 frs. Set meals 180–270 frs. Renominated this year. Fuller reports please.

LA ROCHE-BERNARD 56130 Morbihan   Map 8

Auberge des Deux Magots   `BUDGET`   Tel 99.90.60.75
Place du Bouffay

In a village just off the Nantes–Vannes highway, a charming and very soignée family-run auberge, with clean, neat bedrooms, and a pretty panelled dining room where good local dishes (notably fish) are served at moderate prices. Closed 15 Dec–15 Jan, Sun evening and Mon out of season; restaurant closed Mon. 15 rooms, some with bath. B&B: single 308 frs, double 392 frs. Set menus 80–320 frs [1990]. Recent nomination. More reports please.

ROCHEGUDE 26790 Drôme   Map 11

Château de Rochegude   Tel 75.04.81.88
                                                        Fax 75.04.89.87
                                                        Telex 345661

A gracefully restored stone château, dating in part from the 12th century, set in its own park on a rocky bluff above the vineyards of the Rhône plain north of Orange. It is now a smart and expensive hotel, again admired recently: "Friendly staff, faultless cuisine, lovely grounds for strolling, a spacious room with four-poster and sympathetic lighting – but in September the pool was unheated." Earlier views: "Our room, furnished with antiques, overlooked the vast plain. A large pool at which one could have a light but lingering lunch. Breakfast served out in a small courtyard was delicious – Madame was even weeding the garden while we were eating." "Service impeccable, like being in a private house. They make their own wine and olive oil. Food was the best I've had in France" (*Michelin* rosette, two *Gault Millau toques*). (*Caroline and Gary Smith*)

Open 3 Mar–1 Jan.
Rooms 4 suites, 23 double, 2 single – all with bath, shower, telephone, TV, air-conditioning. Some ground-floor rooms.

Facilities Lift, ramps. 2 salons, TV lounge, bar, restaurant; conference facilities. Large grounds with heated swimming pool and tennis court.
Location 14 km N of Orange. From N leave A7 motorway at Bollène and go towards Carpentras. From S leave at Orange and go towards Gap on N7.
Credit cards All major cards accepted.
Terms B&B: single 550–650 frs, double 650–1,500 frs, suite 1,800–2,500 frs. Set lunch 200 frs, dinner 350–400 frs; full alc 400–450 frs. Special meals for children on request.

LA ROCHE-L'ABEILLE 87800 Haute-Vienne Map 10

Au Moulin de la Gorce
La Roche-l'Abeille, St-Yrieix-la-Perche

Tel 55.00.70.66

Jean Bertranet's enchanting millhouse, still one of the Guide's favourite spots in rural France, stands in a hamlet in pleasant hilly Limousin country between the two porcelain centres of Limoges (large and ugly) and St-Yrieix-la-Perche (small and lovely). The *Moulin*, also small and lovely, is the kind of place that warmly appeals to lovers of French rural simplicity plus gastronomic complexity (two *Michelin* rosettes and two red *Gault Millau toques*). Quiet and off the beaten track, it consists of two old buildings; six of the nine bedrooms are in the old mill, beside a small lake with waterfall. The bedrooms have antiques; in one is a fine four-poster bed.

One rave this year: "A haven of peace and quiet. Food very good, e.g. pigeon stuffed with truffles. Breakfast, on the little terrace facing the lake, was fresh and delicious. Our smallish room was charming, if eccentrically decorated – everything neat and cottagey save for three distinctly post-modern doors. Service ultra-courteous and warm. A lovely place with only one drawback – too many English guests." Some of *their* comments: "An enchanting setting, especially if you can watch the sun rise over the lake. Breakfast was expensive but wonderful. Food magnificent." "A lovely place, kind and skilful staff, delectable food." (*Dr and Mrs A Winterbourne; Dr DA and Juliet R Smith*)

Note The hotel expects guests to be on half board.

Open All year except 2–31 Jan. Closed Sun night and Mon 15 Sep–1 May.
Rooms 9 double – all with bath, shower, telephone, TV. 6 in annexe. 2 ground-floor rooms.
Facilities Salon, dining room. Garden with stream; fishing.
Location 12 km NE of St-Yrieix, off the D704. 2 km S of La Roche off D17. Parking.
Restriction Not suitable for &.
Credit cards All major cards accepted.
Terms Dinner, B&B: single 850 frs, double 1,200 frs. Reduced rates and special meals for children.

LA ROCHELLE 17000 Charente-Maritime Map 10

Hôtel les Brises
Chemin Digue Richelieu

Tel 46.43.89.37
Telex 790821

Again much liked this year, this efficient and stylish modern hotel enjoys a prime position right by the sea, just outside the harbour: it overlooks the islands and estuary, and is a ten-minute walk from the heart of La

Rochelle, one of the loveliest old towns in France ("a kind of maritime Bruges"). The range of fresh breads and pastries at breakfast is especially admired. Latest verdicts: "Very friendly service, beautiful view." "Comfort and quiet; polite and very helpful staff; best breakfast I've had in France for years." "A vast terrace on which one can sun oneself over a drink, and two luxurious lounges." It is best to ask for a room with a sea view. And be warned that a nearby foghorn and revolving foglight might disturb sleep on foggy nights. No restaurant: readers this year commend the *Quatre Sergeants* and *Toque Blanche*, both medium price. (*ML Porter, Michael and Julie Potter, Elizabeth Nines*)

Open All year.
Rooms 2 suites, 43 double, 3 single – 38 with bath, 8 with shower, all with telephone; TV on request.
Facilities Lift. TV lounge, reading room, bar; terrace with direct access to sea and rocky beach.
Location On seafront 1½ km from town centre. Underground garage and carpark.
Restriction Not suitable for &.
Credit cards Access, Visa.
Terms Rooms: single 260 frs, double 360–570 frs, suite 750 frs. Breakfast 40 frs. (No restaurant.)

---

33 rue Thiers   *Tel* 46.41.62.23
33 rue Thiers   *Fax* 46.41.64.87

This remarkable new "find" is in an 18th-century townhouse in the heart of this lovely old town. "Maybelle Iribe and her *33 rue Thiers* are wonderful. She is welcoming and helpful (she even lent us her and her son's bikes). She has created a sensational bed-and-breakfast out of this old mansion: six huge guest rooms all with wonderful bathrooms, all decorated differently. Ours, overlooking the tiny interior garden, was decorated with Maybelle's collection of Mexican folk art. The rooms are furnished with pieces from the local auction house. Everywhere you look there is style, character, whimsy and love. Breakfast included delicious scrambled eggs with hot herbs (Maybelle has written several cookbooks)." "Cocktails and canapés are served in the garden or the library, and picnic baskets are on offer in summer." (*L and DA*)

Open All year.
Rooms 1 suite, 5 double – all with bath and/or shower, 3 with radio; all with baby-listening.
Facilities Lounge, library, TV room. Courtyard garden.
Location Central. Parking.
Credit cards None accepted.
Terms B&B: single 380 frs, double 450 frs, suite 500 frs. Set lunch 80 frs, dinner 100 frs.

LES ROCHES-DE-CONDRIEU 38370 Isère   **Map 10**

Hôtel Bellevue ▮BUDGET▮   *Tel* 74.56.41.42

Run by a friendly couple in their sixties, this pleasant modern creeper-covered hotel stands in a village beside the majestically curving Rhône south of Lyon; vine-clad hills rise behind. The restaurant, with its picture-windows facing the river, is popular locally. Again this year, readers agree that the food and wines are pretty good, the bedrooms simple and somewhat run-down, but adequate for a night or two; best are those with a balcony facing the river. "A friendly welcome, excellent food, spectacular views, classical music playing." "Morilles and filet de St-Pierre excellent, poulet tough as old boots. Staff friendly." "Home-made soup and lots of it." (*Christine Lawrie and Dr John Coker, JCA Little, Peter Hallgarten, and others*)

Open All year except 4–14 Aug and 4–27 Feb. Closed Mon, Tue midday Apr–Sep and Sun evening 1 Oct–31 Mar.
Rooms 18 – 9 with bath, 9 with shower, all with telephone. 3 in annexe.
1 ground-floor room.
Facilities Salon, restaurant; conference facilities.
Location 12 km SW of Vienne.
Credit cards All major cards accepted.
Terms [1990 rates] Rooms 165–270 frs. Breakfast 28 frs. Set lunch 100 frs, dinner 270 frs.

LA-ROCHE-SUR-YON 85000 Vendée   Map 10

Logis de la Couperie   *Tel* 51.37.21.19

La-Roche-sur-Yon, with its severe grid of streets, was built by Napoleon as a military town after the crushing of the Vendée Royalist uprising. However, there's nothing military about this rural property just east of the town, described locally as *"une guest house à l'anglaise"*, and new to the Guide this year: "Here we had one of our most pleasant nights in France. A wing of this large 19th-century country house, set in its own extensive grounds, has been *most* graciously and elegantly furnished, with beautiful antique furniture. Even the signs are tastefully hand-painted. There are books on the staircase, and a large sitting room for visitors. The owners are discreet but welcoming, and you feel you are really in your own house. Breakfast is taken in the kitchen." (*Felicity Capey*) No restaurant: try the *Gallet* in town.

Open All year.
Rooms 9 double – all with bath and/or shower, telephone.
Facilities 2 salons (1 with TV). Garden with croquet, boules.
Location 5 km E of La-Roche, which is 67 km S of Nantes.
Restriction Not suitable for &.
Credit cards Access, Visa.
Terms [1990 rates] B&B: single 200 frs, double 259–415 frs. (No restaurant.)

ROLLEBOISE 78270 Yvelines   Map 9

Château de la Corniche   *Tel* 30.93.21.24
5 route de la Corniche   *Telex* 695544

This village on the Seine, between Paris and Rouen, is only 12 kilometres from the splendid Monet museum and garden at Giverny. The *Château de la Corniche*, built by Leopold II of Belgium, stands splendidly in its large gardens above a bend in the river (front bedrooms have fine views of countryside and river). "It retains much of the style and grandeur it must have had as a regal country house," says a visitor this year. "We were made very welcome by a young, stylish and enthusiastic staff. Dinner was well presented and delicious. We liked the furnishings in the public rooms, but those in our bedroom were insubstantial. The view was superb." Each bedroom is different. The restaurant is elegant and the food, awarded a red *toque* by *Gault Millau*, "includes artfully arranged salads and superlative desserts". (*Jeremy and Anthea Larken, Bill Williams*) The swimming pool is liked. But: "The hotel caters much for groups of business people."

Open All year except Christmas week. Closed Sun evening and Mon in low season.
Rooms 1 suite, 37 double – all with bath and/or shower, telephone, TV, mini-bar. 17 in 2 separate buildings in grounds.
Facilities Lift. Salons, bar, TV room, 2 restaurants; conference facilities; terrace. 5-acre grounds with swimming pool and tennis court.
Location Just W of Rolleboise, overlooking the Seine. Leave A13 to Rouen at Bonnières exit.
Restriction Not suitable for &.
Credit cards All major cards accepted.
Terms [1990 rates] Rooms 350–650 frs, suite 1,200 frs. Set lunch/dinner 220 and 350 frs; full alc 400–500 frs.

ROMANÈCHE-THORINS 71570 Saône-et-Loire   Map 10

Les Maritonnes
Tel 85.35.51.70
Fax 85.35.58.14
Telex 351060

More praise in 1989/90 for this fairly sophisticated hotel at the foot of the vine-clad slopes of the Beaujolais, between Fleurie and the N6. Owner/chef Guy Fauvin's Burgundian cooking (e.g. sauté'd frog's legs, salmon braised in Fleurie) wins a *Michelin* rosette; in the flowery garden, parasols and lilos surround the heated pool. "My room was small but pretty and comfortable. Dinner very good though a little over-rich." "Madame Fauvin's influence was evident from the clean, professional and smooth running of the hotel. Excellent local wines." (*Gillian van Gelder, MD Abrahams*) Some rooms are on the small side, and light sleepers may be upset by the nearby railway.

Open 25 Jan–15 Dec. Closed Sun evenings and Mon 15 Oct–Easter; and Mon and midday Tues Easter–15 Oct.
Rooms 20 double – all with bath or shower, telephone, TV.
Facilities Lounge, bar, restaurant. Garden with heated swimming pool.
Location Near station. Parking.
Restriction Not suitable for &.
Credit cards All major cards accepted.
Terms B&B: single 400–430 frs, double 490–550 frs. Set lunch/dinner 190, 240, 290 and 340 frs; full alc 380 frs.

LES ROSIERS 49350 Maine-et-Loire   Map 10

Auberge Jeanne de Laval   *Tel* 41.51.80.17
Route Nationale

A handsome creeper-covered restaurant-with-rooms in a pretty garden by the Loire: the restaurant is much reputed for *patron*/chef Michel Augereau's beurre blanc fish dishes (*Michelin* rosette and two *Gault Millau toques*). Reports this year and last: "Dining room very plush. Food excellent, especially the rillettes and local fish." "A very pretty house, beautifully decorated. Our bedroom, coloured navy-blue and white, had a plush carpet and antique-like furniture. Food very good." Simpler, more rustic bedrooms are in a nearby annexe, the *Ducs d'Anjou*, a converted manor: views on its comfort vary, but it has been called "a pretty house in a big walled garden, with attractively decorated rooms. Breakfast, with good home-made jam, was taken by an open window facing the garden." (*Richard and Wilma Bowden*)

Open All year except 7 Jan–15 Feb. Closed Mon except public holidays.
Rooms 12 double – some with bath or shower, all with telephone. 8 in annexe, *Ducs d'Anjou*, nearby.
Facilities Restaurant; functions facilities. Garden.
Location 15 km NW of Saumur, on banks of the Loire.
Credit cards All major cards accepted.
Terms [1990 rates] Rooms 380–550 frs. Breakfast 45 frs. Dinner, B&B 460–560 frs per person. Set meals 270–330 frs. Special meals for children.

ROUEN 76000 Seine-Maritime   Map 9

Hôtel de la Cathédrale   **BUDGET**   *Tel* 35.71.57.95
12 rue St-Romain   *Telex* 180224

A slightly shabby but efficient and friendly hotel of some character, centrally situated on a pedestrian walkway near the cathedral. Visitors in 1989/90 have found the owners friendly and the rooms warm and clean, if a bit run-down. An earlier view: "From the moment you go through the heavy wooden doorway and into the courtyard with its geranium pots, busy Lizzies and bits of statuary, you feel the delicious Frenchness of it all. Our room with flowered wallpaper overlooked the courtyard with a view of the cathedral spire; comfortable beds and very quiet at night. No restaurant, but we had a good, fairly priced meal at the popular *Petite Auberge* nearby." (*Hilary Coffmann and David Hill*)

Open All year.
Rooms 24 double – 9 with bath and shower, 4 with shower, all with telephone.
Facilities Entrance hall, salon. Courtyard.
Location Central. Public carpark nearby.
Credit cards Access, Visa.
Terms B&B: single 195 frs, double 360 frs. (No restaurant.)

RUFFIEUX 73310 Savoie   Map 10

Château de Collonges   *Tel* 79.54.27.38
                                                    Telex 319144

A converted château not far from Aix or Annecy: "It glows in the memory, not only for outstanding food but also for heart-warming views across the valley to the mountains beyond. The château, with circular stone staircase, is sumptuously furnished with antiques and spotlessly clean. Small but ample swimming pool overlooking the valley below, and a beautiful garden where chickens strut (and serve as an alarm call in the morning) and where the owner relaxed. He was anxious for us to admire the magnificent sunset over the mountains from the terrace where meals are served in summer. In cool weather dinner is served in the comfortably furnished dining room in the cellars." "Excellent food, faultless service, an atmosphere of calm and charm. Cool stone interior, large and beautiful bedroom, breakfast with real orange juice. Expensive, but worth every penny." (*Brian MacArthur, Anthony Hinds*)

Open All year except Jan and Feb. Closed Mon and Tue midday in low season.
Rooms 2 suites, 17 rooms – all with bath, telephone, TV.
Facilities Salon, dining room, terrace. Park with swimming pool. Golf, water sports, winter sports nearby.
Location 21 km N of Aix-les-Bains.
Restriction Not suitable for &.
Credit cards Access, Diners, Visa.
Terms Rooms 450–650 frs. Breakfast 45 frs. Dinner, B&B 440–650 frs per person. Set meals 175, 265 and 400 frs; full alc 260 frs. Special meals for children.

SABRES 40630 Landes   Map 10

Auberge des Pins   `BUDGET`   *Tel* 58.07.50.47
Route de la Piscine

An attractive half-timbered chalet, built in local style with a low sloping roof, in a village in the heart of the vast Landes pine forests, near Mauriac country. In the hands of the Lesclauze family it has won first prize for the best flower-decked hotel in Aquitaine. Again in 1989/90 visitors found it friendly and good value, with simple but pleasant bedrooms, and a bar and big raftered restaurant eagerly patronised by locals. "Good local food. Specialities include woodpigeon cassoulet, and all parts of a duck's anatomy – liver, heart, whole, etc" (not forgetting warm foie gras with grapes in Sauternes sauce). Plenty for children in the big rough garden – sandpit, swings, ping-pong – and a mini-rail takes you to the local outdoor ecology museum. (*Elizabeth Jones, warmly endorsed by JA and Mr and Mrs PC Rose*)

Open All year except Jan. Restaurant closed Sun evening and Mon.
Rooms 26 double – 24 with bath and/or shower, all with telephone, TV. 16 in annexe. Ground-floor rooms.
Facilities Lounge with TV, bar, restaurant; conference facilities. Garden.
Location 35 km NW of Mont-de-Marsan.
Credit card Visa.
Terms Rooms 220–290 frs. Breakfast 30 frs. Set lunch/dinner 80 and 140 frs; full alc 180–220 frs. Reduced rates and special meals for children.

SAILLAGOUSE 66800 Pyrénées-Orientales   Map 10

Auberge Atalaya   *Tel* 68.04.70.04
Llo   *Fax* 68.04.01.29

The Cerdagne, an upland plain of meadows and pine forests, backed by the snowy Pyrenees, is a most appealing corner of France – about two hours' drive from Perpignan. It is surprisingly lush and pastoral for such an altitude (1,066 metres) and has France's highest sunshine level. There's much of interest – the fortress of Mont-Louis, the big ski-resort of Font-Romeu, and the strange black Romanesque Madonna at l'Hermitage. The *Atalaya*, run by Hubert Toussaint, London born and bred, is a converted stone farmhouse in the hamlet of Llo, just outside the resort of Saillagousse. "Quite a sophisticated place, in a quiet and enchanting setting," say returning visitors this year. "Bedrooms have balconies looking over the village. The waitresses were delightful, and the food perfectly adequate, accompanied by taped Mozart." Others had a "charming" bedroom and enjoyed "superb" jugged hare and duck with sour cherries in the "beautifully furnished dining room". Bedrooms are light and spacious. "The Toussaints have a civilised attitude to their guests. A quiet and relaxing place to stay – out of season at least." (*Mr and Mrs RB Tait, and others*) The hotel now has an outdoor swimming pool.

Open All year except 5 Nov–20 Dec. Restaurant closed Mon.
Rooms 1 suite, 12 double – all with bath or shower, telephone, TV.
Facilities Lounge, bar, restaurant. Garden with swimming pool; solarium.
Location In Llo, on D33 2 km E of Saillagouse, which is 91 km W of Perpignan.
Restriction Not suitable for &.
Credit cards Access, Visa.
Terms Double rooms 400–520 frs. Breakfast 42 frs. Dinner, B&B double 750–880 frs. Set lunch/dinner 138 and 170 frs; full alc 250 frs. Reduced rates for children sharing parents' room.

ST-BEAUZEIL 82150 Tarn-et-Garonne   Map 10

Château de l'Hoste   ▉BUDGET▉   *Tel* 63.95.25.61

In deep country between the Lot and Garonne valleys, a yellowish 18th-century *gentilhommière* amid trees and gardens has been converted by its *patron*/chef Christian Naulet into "a lovely comfortable hotel with a nice atmosphere", according to its nominator this year. "M Naulet is very friendly, with an excellent sense of humour, and he is also an exceptional cook. All bedrooms are nicely furnished. Attractive terrace, and lovely but cold swimming pool." *Gault Millau toque* for classic dishes such as saumon frais en papillote, and local ones such as papitou. (*Imogen Mottram*) More reports please.

Open All year. Closed Mon in winter.
Rooms 3 studios, 32 double – all with bath, shower, telephone, TV. 1 on ground floor.
Facilities Salon, bar, TV room, restaurant. Garden with swimming pool.
Location Outside hamlet of St-Beauzeil which is 11 km S of Tournon, 10 km W of Montaigu-de-Quercy, and just off the D656 to Agen.
Credit cards Access, Visa.
Terms Rooms: single 170 frs, double 220 frs. Set lunch/dinner 110 and 240 frs. Special meals for children.

ST-CHARTIER 36400 Indre   Map 10

Château de la Vallée Bleue   ▉BUDGET▉   *Tel* 54.31.01.91
Route de Verneuil

Here you are in the heart of George Sand country. St-Chartier with its high-walled romantic castle is where she set *Les Maîtres sonneurs* and the wedding in *La Mare au Diable*, and just to the south is her family château at Nohant where she lies buried under a yew tree. Her dining room table is set with places for such as Flaubert, Turgenev and Liszt (people she entertained here). So it is appropriate that the bedrooms in the nearby *Château de la Vallée Bleue* should be likewise named – "Our room was called Flaubert," says our reporter who "really loved" this family-run *Logis de France*. "Set quietly in a large park, it's a fine 18th-century house, full of light and sunshine, run by the charming Gasquets. Our bedroom had style – two antique chairs, blissfully comfy beds, pale-green watered silk bedheads, marvellous reading lights. Charming lounge where a log fire was lit. Lots of polished wood – obviously first-rate housekeeping. Lots of lovely flowers. The cooking is tilted towards the *nouvelle*, but not over the top – delicious lapin en sauce courte à l'estragon." (*Eileen Broadbent*) Notable wine list.

Open All year except Feb and Christmas Eve. Closed Sun night and Mon Oct–Easter.
Rooms 12 double, 2 single – all with bath and/or shower, telephone, radio, TV. 3 in rustic-style annexe. 6 on ground floor.
Facilities Lounge, 2 dining rooms; terrace. Garden with children's playground. Bicycles for hire.
Location 9 km N of La Châtre on D918, then D69. Parking.
Credit cards Access, Amex, Visa.
Terms B&B: single 180–210 frs, double 300–430 frs; dinner, B&B 260–325 frs per person. Set lunch/dinner 110, 175, 250 and 300 frs; full alc 250 frs. Reduced rates and special meals for children.

ST-CIRQ-LAPOPIE 46330 Lot — Map 10

Hôtel de la Pélissaria — *Tel 65.31.25.14*

St-Cirq is a famous *village perché*, set dramatically on a cliff high above the river Lot. One of its old houses is now this tiny hotel, lovingly restored by its charming owners, the Matuchet family, and much liked by our readers – "a perfect place", "paradise indeed". It is on such a steep slope that the entrance is at the top and bedrooms are on the floor below. These, cool and spacious, have tiled floors, white walls, old beams, pine doors, rough-woven white curtains and bedspreads, and they look out on to the old church, the apple orchards and the river Lot beyond. "M Matuchet is the perfect front man, welcoming and obliging," says one report this year, "and his wife produces delicious food. The bedrooms and bathrooms are beautiful, and the views over the Lot are dreamy." Trout soufflé and brochette of beef in pepper sauce have been singled out. (*L and D Allen, Dr Anthony Winterbourne, Mr and Mrs J Alan Thornton, and others*) Several recent visitors, however, have thought the food nothing special.

Open 15 Apr–15 Nov. Restaurant closed Thu.
Rooms 1 suite, 5 double, 2 single – all with bath or shower, telephone. Suite, 1 double, with private terrace, in garden.
Facilities Salon, dining room. Music and poetry evenings. Garden.
Location Central. Parking at some distance from hotel. Village 30 km E of Cahors.
Restriction Not suitable for &.
Credit cards Access, Visa.
Terms Rooms: single 255 frs, double 305 frs, suite 425 frs. Breakfast 30 frs. Set meals 125 frs; full alc 200 frs. Special meals for children.

ST-EMILION 33330 Gironde — Map 10

Hostellerie Plaisance — *Tel 57.24.72.32*
Place du Clocher — *Telex 573032*

A former monastery, now a graceful hostelry, built of warm local stone, well befitting medieval St-Emilion and its famous wines. The site is most curious, atop a sandstone cliff that contains a troglodytic church dating from the 9th century and a mass of other caves. The hotel's bedrooms have been recently modernised, and its terrace provides a fine view over the town, the castle and the vineyards. A report this year: "A lovely bedroom with superb bathroom (jacuzzi); excellent meal and, as one might expect, a very good wine (but not cheap)." *Gault Millau toque* for such dishes as darne de saumon, served in an elegant setting. Very crowded during wine festivals. (*John Moseley; endorsed by SW Bickford-Smith, Ralph Dubery*)

Open All year except 2–31 Jan.
Rooms 11 – all with bath and/or shower, telephone.
Facilities Salon, bar, restaurant; functions room. Garden.
Location Central, near Syndicat d'Initiative. Open parking.
Restriction Not suitable for &.
Credit cards All major cards accepted.
Terms [1990 rates] Rooms 440–680 frs. Breakfast 42 frs. Set lunch 110 frs, dinner 235 frs. Special meals for children.

Le Logis des Remparts
Rue Guadet

Tel 57.24.70.43

An old building in the village, newly renovated and prettily decorated, backing on to vineyards. Garden, private parking. No restaurant, but the nearby Francis Goullée is admired. Closed 21 Dec–7 Jan. 15 rooms, all with bath and shower. B&B double 330–480 frs. Endorsed this year, but fuller reports welcome.

ST-ETIENNE-DE-BAIGORRY 64430 Pyrénées-Atlantiques   Map 10

Hôtel Arcé

Tel 59.37.40.14

This charming and archetypal Basque village, up a tiny remote valley near the Spanish border, has a Roman bridge and a fine old church – as well, of course, as a *fronton* for *pelota* and an old smuggling tradition, now on the wane. The riverside *Arcé*, backed by green hills, has been in the hands of the same family for five generations and *its* fine traditions are by no means waning, as we learned again this year: "The food is regionally based, like pipérade with sausages (*Michelin* rosette). I can think of no nicer place to eat lunch on a hot day." An earlier view: "A modest hotel of quiet charm: vulgarisation has passed it by, though modern comforts are not lacking. Set beside the fast-flowing river Nive, its firm-bedded rooms have small terraces from which the beauty of the valley can be savoured. The hotel is a booklover's delight, with a multilingual library. There is a heated swimming pool across the river, and an air of unassuming professionalism at every level."

Open Mid-Mar–mid-Nov.
Rooms 5 suites, 19 double, 1 single – all with bath and/or shower, telephone; TV on request. 3 in annexe by river. 1 ground-floor room.
Facilities Lounge, library, billiard room, 2 restaurants. Gardens and terrace; outdoor swimming pool and tennis court. River fishing.
Location 11 km W of St-Jean-Pied-de-Port; hotel is near church. Garage; parking.
Credit cards Access, Visa.

Terms [1990 rates] Rooms 430–500 frs, suite 900 frs. Breakfast 40 frs. Dinner, B&B 300–450 frs per person. Set meals 100–200 frs. Reduced rates and special meals for children.

ST-FLORENTIN 89600 Yonne   Map 9

Les Tilleuls BUDGET   *Tel 86.35.09.09*
3 rue Decourtive

A pleasant Logis de France, making a useful, inexpensive base in this small Burgundy town. Warm welcome, charming service, excellent value on the cheaper menus (Michelin red "R"). Near centre but not noisy. Small garden. 10 rooms, all with bath or shower; single 210 frs, double 300 frs. Set menus 100–200 frs. Recent nomination. More reports welcome.

ST-GERMAIN-EN-LAYE 78100 Yvelines   Map 9

Cazaudehore et La Forestière   *Tel 34.51.93.80*
1 avenue du Président Kennedy   *Fax 39.73.73.88*
                                                       Telex 696055

Just west of Paris, in the heart of the forest of St-Germain (handy for Charles de Gaulle airport), the Cazaudehore family runs a fashionable restaurant that bears their name and, next door, in a wooded garden, a stylish little hotel that this year and last has delighted readers. It has tasteful modern rooms and suites, elegantly decorated with antiques and prints. Tiled bathrooms, friendly service, and a pleasant outlook on to the oak and beech forest. The restaurant has fresh flowers, gleaming silverware, an interesting menu, and draws a sophisticated clientele – especially at weekends when you need to book, even if you have a room reserved. (*Pat Leer; DJ Harden*) There's a new chef this year, and we'd be glad of more reports on the cuisine (*Gault Millau toque*).

Open All year. Restaurant closed Mon except public holidays (light meals available for hotel guests).
Rooms 6 suites, 24 double – all with bath, shower, telephone, radio, TV, mini-bar.
Facilities Lift. 2 salons, bar, restaurant; conference facilities. Garden.
Location 1.5 km NW of St-Germain, by N284 and route des Mares.
Restriction Not suitable for &.
Credit cards Access, Visa.
Terms [1990 rates] Rooms: single 575 frs, double 680 frs, suite 820–850 frs. Breakfast 50 frs. Alc (excluding wine) 270–360 frs. Weekly half- and full-board rates. Reduced rates for children under 8; special meals.

ST-GIRONS 09200 Ariège   Map 10

Hôtel Eychenne   *Tel 61.66.20.55*
8 avenue Paul Laffont   *Telex 521273*

A heated swimming pool in the garden, with parasol-shaded loungers, has this year proved a welcome addition to this very spruce and attractive hostelry, white-walled, creeper-festooned, and owned and run by the Bordeau family for six generations. It lies down a side street in a small town in the Pyrenean foothills. Latest reports also extol the warm, friendly ambience, solicitous proprietor and excellent regional cooking (*Michelin* rosette, *Gault Millau toque*), nicely served in a large red-walled dining room well patronised by locals. "Fish first-class, good local wines, and a pleasant room with balcony overlooking courtyard and garden." Rooms by the courtyard are quieter than those on the street. (*Brian and Rosalind Keen, Dr JEM Whitehead*)

Open All year except 22 Dec–31 Jan.
Rooms 2 suites, 42 double, 4 single – 22 with bath, 20 with shower, all with telephone and TV; some with balcony.
Facilities Lounge with TV, bar, restaurant; conference facilities. Garden with heated swimming pool.
Location Central; parking. St-Girons is 99 km S of Toulouse.
Restriction Not suitable for &.
Credit cards All major cards accepted.
Terms B&B: single: 260–270 frs, double 480–535 frs; dinner, B&B 350–380 frs per person. Set lunch/dinner 110, 170 and 277 frs; full alc 230 frs. Children sharing parents' room free; special meals on request.

ST-JEAN-DU-BRUEL 12230 Aveyron   **Map 10**

Hôtel du Midi   `BUDGET`   *Tel* 65.62.26.04

"Warmly endorsed, food superb", "irresistible" – the Papillon family's unpretentious *Logis de France* in the western Cévennes remains one of our most popular French rural entries. It is in an old village on the river Dourbie between Millau and Le Vigan, a good centre for visiting the Gorges du Tarn. Recent tributes: "The Papillons' charm, and the remarkable value they offer, make this the best French hotel of its kind that we know. How do they do it at the price (red 'R' in *Michelin*)? Part of the answer lies in M Papillon's skill with unusual ingredients – tripe, gizzards and sheep's feet, for example; his feuilletée aux gésiers is delicious. The combination of scenery and hotel is irresistible." Service is swift and personal. The no-choice but varied menu for residents is far better than what guests *en pension* are normally given in France – excellent soup ad lib, home-made charcuterie, main courses that may include quail, civet de chevreuil, cassoulet, confit de canard aux lentilles. "The whole place is warmed by the Papillon family." "Madame was an elegant bundle of energy." "Our plain but adequate room was in an adjacent building with a fine stone turret stair." Some rooms are modern and pretty; some are a bit cramped and less comfortable; and the church clock chimes the hours. British and German guests are much in evidence. "This is splendid walking country, best in spring when regulars come for the display of wild flowers covering the *causses*. In the evenings, the polyglot conversation between dinner tables is full of botanical Latin." (*Gillian Van Gelder, JP Berryman, AG Catchpole, and others*)

Open 23 Mar–11 Nov.
Rooms 17 double, 2 single – all with bath and/or shower, telephone. 2 pairs of communicating rooms in annexe.
Facilities Salon, TV room, bar, restaurant; terrace. On banks of river Dourbie; bathing, fishing.
Location 40 km SE of Millau on D991; 20 km E of N9. Garage and open parking.
Restriction Only restaurant suitable for &.
Credit cards Access, Visa.
Terms B&B: single 89 frs, double 125–212 frs; half board: single 168–178 frs, double 282–390 frs; full board: single 197–207 frs, double 340–446 frs. Set

lunch/dinner 63–173 frs; full alc 139 frs. Reduced rates for children under 6; special meals.

ST-JEAN-DU-DOIGT 29228 Finistère   Map 8

Le Ty-Pont   **BUDGET**   *Tel* 98.67.34.06

This seaside hotel in northern Brittany is not for those who dislike the basic and down-to-earth, but it does offer remarkable value. And again this year readers have enjoyed the pleasant family welcome and the five-course *en pension* meals (especially lunch, the main meal of the day, and the local fish). The nearby beach is "lovely" and the coastline "stunningly beautiful". A family of regular devotees has written lyrically: "The food was staggering, with the freshest possible ingredients. Lunch might start with crab claws and slices of melon, then a fish in a delicate sauce, then a meat course (perhaps guinea-fowl), then cheese, fromage blanc or yoghurt, then ice-cream (home-made) or a good selection of fresh fruit or crème caramel. The scene in the dining room was astonishing – working-class French families, a baby drinking potage out of its bottle, a two-year-old being spoon-fed fromage blanc. It was very noisy, but the young waitresses were never flustered. Bedrooms were adequate. There is a garden by a stream, where you can sit in the sun and recover from *la bouffe*." There are good amenities for children. (*BW Ribbons, RM Flaherty, RW Collins*) But again this year a minority of readers have found the hotel *too* basic (though clean) and the service in August very slow.

Open 1 Mar–15 Oct. Closed Sun evening and Mon, except 1 June–30 Sep.
Rooms 4 suites, 26 double – 18 with bath and/or shower, 17 with telephone.
Facilities Salon, bar, TV room, 2 restaurants. Garden with children's playground. Sandy beach 700 metres.
Location 17 km NE of Morlaix, 1.5 km E of Plougasnou village.
Restriction Not suitable for &.
Credit cards Access, Visa.
Terms [1990 rates] Dinner, B&B 138–173 frs per person; full board 168–203 frs. Set lunch/dinner 52–195 frs. Reduced rates for children; special meals on request.

ST-JEAN-PIED-DE-PORT 64220 Pyrénées-Atlantiques   Map 10

Hôtel des Pyrénées   *Tel* 59.37.01.01
Place du Général de Gaulle   *Fax* 59.37.18.97
                                                        Telex 570619

St-Jean, at the foot of the Roncesvalles pass into Spain, is one of the most picturesque of Basque towns (15th-century ramparts, hilltop citadel) and a centre of Basque folklore (summer festival and *pelota* championships). It used to be a major resting-place for Santiago-bound pilgrims about to cross the Pyrenees. And today many of our readers choose to halt there, at this gastronomically famous auberge which has been owned and run by the Arrambide family for four generations. Their special distinction is to have developed and refined traditional regional dishes into a Basque *haute cuisine*. Again this year it is judged to be fully deserving of its two stars in *Michelin* and three red *Gault Millau toques*: "Foie gras, poivrons farcis à la morue and lapin farci all fine, also the wines." Others have singled out the whole grilled local salmon, stuffed hare and chocolate desserts – "when the bill came I marvelled at its reasonableness". "The

cooking is rumbustious and copious, no *cuisine minceur* here. And we
loved the Arrambides, warm friendly people with the simple charm of the
working French. Their traditional hostelry has no pretension to elegance,
and evokes the *cossu bourgeois* of the 1950s rather than 1980s flair and
panache." Rooms have recently been remodelled; there are some luxury
suites with lavish bathrooms on the first floor, much enjoyed this year;
back rooms are quietest, but lack a view. (*Dr PEM Curtis, Roger Bennett,
and others*)

Open All year except 5–28 Jan, 15 Nov–22 Dec. Closed Mon evening Nov–Mar,
Tue except holidays and 1 July–15 Sep.
Rooms 2 suites, 18 double – all with bath/shower, telephone, TV.
Facilities Lift. 2 salons, 2 dining rooms; conference rooms; terrace. Garden with
heated swimming pool.
Location 54 km SE of Bayonne on D933. Parking.
Credit cards Access, Amex, Visa.
Terms Rooms 450–700 frs, suite 850 frs. Breakfast 45 frs. Dinner, B&B 500–600 frs
per person. Set lunch/dinner 180–400 frs. Reduced rates for children sharing
parents' room; special meals on request.

ST-LATTIER 38840 Isère   **Map 10**

Le Lièvre Amoureux   *Tel 76.64.50.67*
                                                            Fax 76.64.06.79
                                                             Telex 308534

This "amorous hare" is a pleasant old creeper-covered auberge in the
Isère valley between Valence and Grenoble, and both *Michelin* and *Gault
Millau* give it their red print for attractiveness. The much-admired
cooking is regional, served outside in summer on a candle-lit terrace
under lime-trees, or indoors in a panelled room where a fire blazes in
winter. A reader this year enjoyed an "absolutely luxurious room" in the
new annexe. Earlier views: "An excellent hotel with comfortable rooms
tastefully furnished and a very good swimming pool. Madame Hannelore
Breda, the *patronne*, conducted the service of dinner like a stage director,
and the food and wine were superb." "Breakfasts included optional
orange juice, yoghurt and eggs at no extra charge. The staff were
competent and friendly." Rooms in the old building are smaller and
simpler but have pretty views through the trees to the Vercors mountains.
Those in the new annexe by the open-air heated pool have sliding
"patio" windows; here one reader found the plumbing noisy. There is a
railway nearby, but trains are few and not too noisy. (*Liz King and Bridget
Schenk*) More reports welcome.

Open All year except 17 Dec–17 Jan. Closed Sun evening and Mon in low season.
Rooms 1 suite, 13 double – 12 with bath and shower, all with telephone; 5 with
TV. 5 in annexe. 2 on ground floor.
Facilities Salon, 2 restaurants; terrace. Garden with swimming pool.
Location Halfway between St-Marcellin and Romans on N92.
Credit cards All major cards accepted.
Terms Rooms: single 180 frs, double 320–420 frs. Breakfast 45 frs. Dinner, B&B:
single 350 frs, double 750 frs. Set meals 195 frs; full alc 250 frs. Reduced rates and
special meals for children.

We depend on detailed fresh reports to keep our entries up to date.

ST-MALO 35400 Ille-et-Vilaine   Map 8

La Korrigane   *Tel 99.81.65.85*
39 rue Le Pomellec   *Telex 740802*

A 19th-century mansion in the suburb of St-Servan, gracefully converted
into a superior B&B hotel, full of antiques, and restored to the Guide this
year. "Wonderful," says a reader who stayed for a whole month, while
another enjoyed the "beautifully decorated" bedroom, the quiet, and the
garden with chairs on the lawn. (*Pat Leer, T Nash*) However, the very
special atmosphere may not suit all tastes, and an inspector was less
lyrical: "*La Korrigane* is a stage set, and the leading actor is the voluble
proprietrix's mother. The place is certainly elegant, full of sculptures and
chinoiserie, but not especially comfortable. Bedrooms have dress-
designer names: we were in Chanel. It had stunning furniture and a huge
terracotta sculpture, but was rather cramped and the beds too soft.
Bathroom posh. No breakfast before 8 am, a nuisance for early ferry-
takers." More reports clearly needed.

Open 15 Mar–15 Nov.
Rooms 9 double, 1 single – all with bath or shower, telephone, TV.
Facilities 2 lounges. Small garden. Sea nearby.
Location In centre of St-Servan, 2 km S of old St-Malo.
Restrictions Not suitable for &. No children under 10.
Credit cards Access, Diners, Visa.
Terms Rooms: single 300–350 frs, double 400–550 frs. Breakfast 50 frs. (No
restaurant.)

Le Valmarin   *Tel 99.81.94.76*
7 rue Jean XXIII

*An elegant 18th-century house in the suburb of St-Servan, now modernised as a
clean, friendly and civilised B&B hotel. Attractive garden, finely decorated
rooms, but a lack of easy chairs. Open 1 Mar–24 Dec. 10 rooms, all with bath
and shower. B&B double 480 frs. Some recent criticisms: more reports please.*

ST-MARTIN-DU-FAULT 87510 Haute-Vienne   Map 10

La Chapelle-St-Martin   *Tel 55.75.80.17*
                                                   Fax 55.75.89.50

This pretty mansion in a lovely park, elegantly refurbished as a smart
country hotel, lies in the countryside north-west of Limoges. Dropped
from the 1990 Guide for lack of feedback, it is restored by two reports this
year: "A beautiful house with noble furniture." "A good-sized room, a
gorgeous meal and good breakfast – a super place." *Michelin* rosette,
Gault Millau toque, for such dishes as fresh sardines with caviar.
(*G Villeneuve, Karen Sharp and Steve Wilson*) More reports please.

Open 1 Mar–1 Jan. Restaurant closed Mon.
Rooms 3 suites, 10 double – all with bath, telephone, TV. 2 ground-floor rooms.
Facilities 4 salons, restaurant; conference facilities. Garden with tennis court.
Indoor swimming pool.
Location 12 km NE of Limoges, by N147 and D35; near Nieuil.
Credit cards Access, Visa.

Terms Rooms: single 550 frs, double 890 frs, suite 1,200 frs. Breakfast 70 frs. Set lunch 190 frs, dinner 360 frs; full alc 350–400 frs.

ST-MARTIN-VALMEROUX 15140 Cantal   Map 10

Hostellerie de la Maronne   `BUDGET`   *Tel* 71.69.20.33
Le Theil   *Fax* 71.69.28.22

The good food, the swimming pool, and the rooms in the cottage annexe have all been enjoyed at this rural hostelry in a lovely setting outside the Auvergne hamlet of Le Theil. A *Relais du Silence* with few noises but cowbells at dawn, it stands in its own informal garden in the lush upper valley of the Maronne, quite close to the lovely Renaissance hill-village of Salers. The "engaging but slightly eccentric" Alain de Cock and his Malagasy wife provide "immaculate" comfort and a choiceless evening meal (e.g. rêve d'escargots and tripoux flambés au cognac, but some dishes have been judged more "prosaic" than these). Note that dinner is not served after 8 pm. (*Diana Holmes, John and Rita Newnham*)

Open 7 Apr–5 Nov. Restaurant closed for lunch.
Rooms 25 – all with bath, shower, telephone, mini-bar. 8 in annexe. Some ground-floor rooms.
Facilities Salon, games room, dining room. Garden with heated swimming pool, tennis.
Location 3 km E of St-Martin-Valmeroux on D37 to Fontanges.
Credit cards Access, Visa.
Terms [1990 rates] Rooms 255–360 frs. Breakfast 35 frs. Half board 270–350 frs per person. Set dinner 120 frs.

ST-PAUL-DE-VENCE 06570 Alpes-Maritimes   Map 11

Hôtel Le Hameau   *Tel* 93.32.80.24
528 route de La Colle   *Telex* 970846

This lovely 18th-century farmhouse on a hillside, delightfully converted, represents an oasis of unspoilt rusticity amid the trendy tourist buzz of the St-Paul area – and we are sorry, and surprised, to have had no reports on it since this 1988 rave: "Its low white buildings are on several levels, with doors opening on to terraces. We enjoyed breakfast amid flower-beds, trellised arbours and citrus trees, and were invited to pick oranges, tangerines and grapefruit whenever we wished. The main building holds a spacious lounge with big stone fireplace; there are tables for playing games, and lots of books in English and French. The white-walled bedrooms are attractively furnished in country style, with many antiques. Rooms vary in size and shape, some being a bit low-ceilinged and dark. Staff were all helpful and friendly. Some traffic noise (a main road is nearby)." *Le Hameau* now has a swimming pool. No restaurant, but there are lots in St-Paul. Please, more reports!

Open 15 Feb–16 Nov and 22 Dec–8 Jan.
Rooms 2 suites, 13 double, 1 single – all with bath and/or shower, telephone, mini-bar.
Facilities Lounge with TV, breakfast room. Terraces and garden. Outdoor swimming pool.
Location 1 km SW of St-Paul on road to La Colle.
Restriction Not suitable for &.

Credit cards Access, Amex, Visa.
Terms Rooms: single 260 frs, double 325–440 frs, suite 550 frs. Breakfast 35 frs.
(No restaurant.)

ST-PIERRE-DU-VAUVRAY 27430 Eure   Map 8

Hostellerie Saint-Pierre   *Tel* 32.59.93.29
2 chemin des Amoureux

Five of its *amoureux* have this year taken the *chemin* to this over-timbered
mock-Tudor-style mansion by the Seine south of Rouen, thus restoring it
to the Guide. "Yes, it does look phoney from outside, but our large
bedroom was fine, with a balcony and superb views over the Seine. A
pleasant garden runs down to the river. Food is excellent." "Wonderful to
sit in the gardens. Service very slow, but food excellent when it comes."
"A pleasant welcome and a superlative dinner, notably the seafood,
soups and sorbets." Bedrooms are in various styles, some Empire, some
beamed with four-poster beds. (*GE Samson, Angela Stancer, Catherine
Neville-Rolfe, and others*)

Open All year except 10 Jan–28 Feb. Restaurant closed Tue, and Wed midday.
Rooms 3 suites, 11 double – all with bath, shower, telephone, TV.
Facilities Lift. Salon, restaurant. Garden.
Location Leave A13 motorway at Louviers if coming from Rouen, and Louviers
Sud if coming from Paris: follow signs to St-Pierre-du-Vauvray.
Credit cards Access, Visa.
Terms [1990 rates] Rooms 370–560 frs. Breakfast 40 frs. Dinner, B&B 450–530 frs
per person. Set lunch/dinner 145–315 frs.

ST-PONS-DE-THOMIÈRES 34220 Hérault   Map 10

Château de Ponderach   *Tel* 67.97.02.57
Route de Narbonne

This fine 17th-century manor stands in its own 400-acre wooded park,
just outside the pleasant old town of St-Pons (12th-century cathedral). It
is on the edge of the heavily forested hills of the Haut-Languedoc nature
reserve. And the aristocratic family of the present *patronne*, Mme
Counotte, have owned it for the past 300 years. A recent view: "The fact
that it's run by a woman shows in many small points – a pot of detergent
in our bathroom, flowers in unlikely places. Madame Counotte is an
accomplished pianist and her daughter plays professionally: any music in
the dining room is always good. The food is decent and plentiful, and the
wines reasonably priced. Bedrooms have balconies overlooking the park:
some English people staying longer than us were enchanted with the
quiet beauty of the hotel. And it's the cheapest of the château-type that
I've seen." (*Alan F Thomas*)

Open Apr–Oct.
Rooms 9 – all with bath and/or shower, telephone.
Facilities Salon with TV, bar, restaurant; conference facilities. Large garden where
meals are served in good weather.
Location 1.2 km S of town on Narbonne road.
Credit cards All major cards accepted.
Terms [1990 rates] Rooms 360–430 frs. Breakfast 65 frs. Dinner, B&B 620–660 frs
per person. Set lunch/dinner 160–350 frs. Special meals for children.

ST-QUENTIN 02100 Aisne   Map 9

Grand Hôtel et Restaurant   *Tel* 23.62.69.77
Le Président   *Fax* 23.62.53.52
6 rue Dachery   *Telex* 140225

Picardy's second largest town is worth visiting for the Quentin de la Tour portraits in the Lécuyer museum. And it has other surprises in store – as recent visitors have found: "The town centre and the *Grand* were a revelation – the former for its super reconstructed buildings, the latter for an inspired re-creation. From the outside, despite the floodlighting, it looks like just another turn-of-the-century facade in a dull street near the station: but the interior has been gutted and replaced by a central atrium with a glass roof, glassed-in balconies and a glass lift, all very modern and tasteful. In the modern marble foyer, a receptionist sat at a Louis XV repro table. Our large and pleasant bedroom had a marble bathroom *en suite*. To cap it all, *Le Président* restaurant, very popular locally, fully deserves its *Michelin* rosette." (*David and Angela Stewart*) A new young chef with a high reputation, Jean-Marc Le Guennec, arrived in 1990 and we'd welcome reports on his work. Rooms are said to be noisy despite the double-glazing.

Open All year. Restaurant closed 29 July–26 Aug and 23 Dec–2 Jan.
Rooms 6 suites, 18 double – all with bath, shower, telephone, radio, TV. 1 room suitable for &.
Facilities Lift. Lounge, bar, breakfast room, restaurant; conference room.
Location Central. Parking.
Credit cards All major cards accepted.
Terms B&B: single 445 frs, double 600 frs, suite 680 frs. Set lunch/dinner 195 and 330 frs; alc 380 frs. Children under 12 sharing parents' room free of charge; special meals on request.

ST-RÉMY-DE-PROVENCE 13210 Bouches-du-Rhône   Map 11

Hôtel Château des Alpilles   *Tel* 90.92.03.33
Route Départementale 31   *Fax* 90.92.45.17
                                                 Telex 431487

Lamartine and Chateaubriand were among the celebrities who once stayed at this graceful 19th-century manor (just out of town on the Tarascon road) in the days when it belonged to a leading local family. It is now a well-modernised hotel, in large shady grounds. Dropped from recent Guides partly for lack of feedback, it is now brought back by a report from a recent visitor: "One of the prettiest properties we've seen in a long time – charming, friendly and good value. We liked the casual atmosphere. Bedrooms are high-ceilinged with tall windows and antique armoires. The annexe, a recently converted barn, has bedrooms with old beams. There's an attractive outdoor dining area, shaded by great trees, where the local elegant crowd come for Sunday lunch: no real dining room, but light meals are served (in summer). One jarring note: the intense racket caused by an army of bullfrogs at night." (*Sharon Gutman*) We know these bullfrogs of yore – they helped the hotel to be left out of the Guide in 1987. . . .

Open 20 Dec–4 Jan and 20 Mar–12 Nov.
Rooms 3 suites, 16 double – all with bath, shower, telephone, radio, TV, baby-listening. 3 in annexe. 1 ground-floor room.
Facilities Lift. Bar, lounge with TV, small dining room. Garden with swimming pool, sauna, 2 tennis courts.
Location 2 km W of town, on D31.
Credit cards All major cards accepted.
Terms B&B: double 990–1,030 frs, suite 1,120–1,420 frs. Reduced rates and special meals for children. (No restaurant; grills by the pool (evenings only) in summer 150–200 frs.)

Hôtel Les Antiques   *Tel* 90.92.03.02
15 avenue Pasteur   *Telex* 431146

In the southern suburbs of this typical small Provençal town is the mental home of St-Paul-de-Mausole where Van Gogh spent a year as a patient after cutting off his ear in Arles; nearby are the curious Roman remains of Glanum, known also as Les Antiques. Hence the name of this hotel near the town centre, a gracefully converted 19th-century mansion, with attractive grounds and pool. You can stay in the main building, or in a *pavillon* with its own terrace. Recent reports have focused on the "delightful atmosphere, great welcome", and charming owners. "Beauti-ful gardens, and a grand entrance with marble floors, tapestries, Italian painted ceiling." (*Mrs RB Richards, Ellen and John Buchanan*) No restaurant, but the *France* and the *Arts* in town are both good value. A September visitor found "carnival noises non-stop, bulls running through the streets and bicycle races, and a fun-fair just opposite" – to her, a nightmare, but maybe to others a good reason for visiting joyous Provence.

Open 23 Mar–20 Oct.
Rooms 26 double, 1 single – all with bath and telephone. 10 in building in park. 2 ground-floor rooms with ramp.
Facilities 3 salons, TV room, breakfast veranda. Large grounds with unheated swimming pool.
Location In town centre. Parking.
Credit cards All major cards accepted.
Terms (Excluding tax) B&B: single 365–445 frs, double 410–490 frs. (No restaurant.)

Le Mas des Carassins   *Tel* 90.92.15.48
1 chemin Gaulois

Quietly secluded at the foot of the rocky Alpilles, about 1½ km SW of the town centre, an attractively converted mas *in a big rough garden. Rustic sitting room with log fire; reading room; quaint and cosy bedrooms; good breakfasts; light suppers on request, or try* Les Arts *in town. Open 15 Mar–15 Nov. 10 rooms, all with bath. B&B: single 330–430 frs, double 410–560 frs. New nomination. More reports please.*

Château de Roussan   *Tel* 90.92.11.63
Route de Tarascon   *Fax* 90.49.01.79
                                                        Telex 431169

Long a Guide favourite ("pure magic" is a 1990 view), this stately pink 18th-century château stands secluded in its own big park, just west of St-

Rémy. For over a century it was the country home of the Roussel family, who to make ends meet then accepted paying guests; and this year they have handed over the daily management to "a young francophile Irish/ English woman", Catherine McHugo, who also runs the *Valmouriane* (see below). Bedrooms are modernised, but some have antiques, and the public rooms are in period style. Readers have mostly been ecstatic: "Breakfast with the peacocks and doves is a treat under the huge plane trees with the sound of the small fountains." "You can set your table and chair in a far corner of the park and be disturbed only by the house dogs who take a well-behaved interest when picnic lunchtime has arrived." In the grounds is a 16th-century farmhouse where Nostradamus once lived. Under its new regime, the château now serves meals, and a 1990 visitor enjoyed "a very adequate and reasonably priced dinner". (*Peter JR Jowitt, Mrs Sarah Reid*) However, one report in June 1990 was a stinker: substandard rooms, and complaints treated with discourtesy.

Open 15 Mar–15 Nov.
Rooms 20 double – 16 with bath, 4 with shower, all with telephone, babylistening. 2 ground-floor rooms.
Facilities Lounge, TV room, library, dining room. Large park. Guests have access to the swimming pool at the *Domaine de Valmouriane.*
Location 2 km W of centre of St-Rémy, off Tarascon road. Parking.
Credit cards Access, Amex, Visa.
Terms [1990 rates] Rooms: single 285–900 frs, double 360–1,000 frs. Breakfast 55 frs. Set lunch/dinner 150 frs; full alc 220 frs. Reduced rates and special meals for children.

Domaine de Valmouriane   *Tel* 90.92.44.62
Petite route des Baux   *Fax* 90.49.01.79
                                                     Telex 431169

Just south of town, in the foothills of the rocky Alpilles, here's an old stone *mas* exquisitely converted into a small luxury hotel. It is owned by an Irish/Englishwoman, Catherine McHugo, and run by her in association with Jean-Claude Aubertin who was chef at the *Auberge* at Noves (q.v.) and at *Ma Cuisine* in Chelsea. Little surprise, therefore, that it has two red *toques* in *Gault Millau*. Cool white walls, tiled floors, a sense of space and grace, much admired by our nominators: "Lovely bedrooms and bathrooms, ours was very stylish. A large sitting room with open fireplace and a small panelled bar. In the pleasant restaurant with its huge windows, opening on to the terrace, the food was excellent" – and highly inventive in its posh way, such as foie gras with peaches and ginger, and fricassée of lamb's foot with truffles. (*Pat and Jeremy Temple*, endorsed in 1990 by *Dorset and Victoria White*)

Open All year.
Rooms 13 – 12 with bath and/or shower, telephone, TV, air-conditioning. 3 in annexe. 1 ground-floor room suitable for &.
Facilities Lounge, reading room, bar, restaurant; terrace where meals are served. Garden with heated swimming pool, tennis, putting, bowls.
Location 4.5 km S of St-Rémy, by D27 (petite route des Baux). Parking.
Credit cards Access, Amex, Visa.
Terms [1990 rates] Rooms: single 500–1,100 frs, double 700–1,250 frs. Breakfast 55 frs. Dinner, B&B 275 frs per person added to room rate; full board 465 frs added.

ST-SERNIN-SUR-RANCE 12380 Aveyron   Map 10

Hotel-Restaurant Carayon |BUDGET| *Tel* 65.99.60.26
Place du Fort   *Fax* 65.99.69.26

"A real find," says the nominator of this country hotel in a rural area well off the main north–south tourist routes: it's in a village on the Albi–Millau road, just south of the lovely valley of the Tarn. "Pierre Carayon, ebullient and enthusiastic, spent some years at the *Dorchester* and *Savoy* in London, and is now transforming the family hotel/restaurant into a larger enterprise. There's a garden with diversions for children. Our small but neat room in the old part of the hotel had a splendid view across the valley. The food (*Michelin* red 'R') was fantastic value – our 82-franc [1990] dinner included two terrines, a whole trout, quail flamed in brandy and home-made sorbet. Very much a family affair, with *grandpère* and two small boys all in evidence, and elegant Madame supervising the dining room." The 15 modern rooms newly built on the hillside have been approved this year. (*Diana Holmes*, warmly endorsed by *Alan and Olive Bell*, especially the regional *menu Rouergat*)

Open All year. Closed Sun evening and Mon in low season.
Rooms 5 suites, 34 double, 1 single – all with bath and/or shower, telephone, TV. 2 rooms suitable for &.
Facilities Lifts. 2 salons, bar, 3 dining rooms, disco; terrace. Garden with children's playground and table-tennis; on river with fishing.
Location St-Sernin is 50 km E of Albi on D999. Hotel is central; parking.
Credit cards All major cards accepted.
Terms Rooms 119–309 frs. Breakfast 27 frs. Dinner, B&B 159–279 frs per person. Set meals 62–250 frs; full alc 220 frs. Reduced rates and special meals for children.

ST-SYMPHORIEN-LE-CHÂTEAU 28700 Eure-et-Loir   Map 8

Château d'Esclimont   *Tel* 37.31.15.15
St-Symphorien-le-Château   *Fax* 37.31.57.91
                                                Telex 780560

"*C'est mon plaisir*" is the motto of La Rochefoucauld on the facade of this stately moated Renaissance château, standing in a 150-acre wooded park between Chartres and Rambouillet. A recent American visitor found the pleasure hers, too: "Fairy tale vintage, with its period moats, crenellated towers, stone sculptures. I was charmed by our two-storeyed room, and found the *nouvelle cuisine* good, but expensive; lunch or drinks can be taken on the terrace, overlooking a garden and lovely lake with swans." (*Victoria P Turner*) An earlier view, "Truly glorious, luxuriously appointed. Even on a bitter winter's day everywhere was deliciously warm. The views are amazing, over park, river and woods; the food is delicious and served in generous portions from an inspired menu" (two red *Gault Millau toques*). Two visitors have found the welcome and ambience cool. We'd be glad of more reports.

Open All year.
Rooms 6 suites, 48 double – all with bath, shower, telephone, TV. 24 in 3 separate buildings.
Facilities Salon, bar, 4 dining rooms; conference facilities. Wooded park with small lake, river, tennis court, heated swimming pool, helipad.
Location 6 km NW of Ablis. Leave A11 or N10 at Ablis; go towards Prunay; turn left on D101.

Restriction Not suitable for &.
Credit card Visa.
Terms Rooms: single occupancy 545 frs, double 860–1,350 frs, suite 1,570–2,400 frs. Breakfast 75 frs. Set lunch/dinner 290–460 frs. Reduced rates for children.

ST-THIBÉRY 34630 Hérault   Map 10

Château de Nadalhan   *Tel 67.77.87.93*
Route de Valros

An elegant Italianate mansion in its own big park, set on the vine-clad Languedoc plain halfway between the lovely Renaissance town of Pézenas, where Molière often performed, and the huge new bathing resort of Agde. Run by a friendly young couple, the Théronds, it is commended again this year for its "spacious 18th-century rooms" and good regional cooking (e.g. foie gras chaud aux raisins). An earlier view: "Our spotless room had hand-hemmed linen sheets, two tall arched windows, and a good bathroom. Food well and imaginatively cooked, though the set menu offered limited choice. Piped music during the meal, but we managed to get the cassettes changed to suit our taste. Service cheerful and personal." (*C and M Hédoin*)

Open All year except Jan.
Rooms 1 for 4, 4 double – all with bath; telephone on request.
Facilities Salon, 3 dining rooms. Park. Sea 10 km.
Location On D125 between St-Thibéry and Valros, 7 km SW of Pézenas.
Credit cards Access, Visa.
Terms B&B: single 245–275 frs, double 310–360 frs; dinner, B&B: single 340–370 frs, double 510–560 frs. Set lunch/dinner 95, 150 and 195 frs; full alc 220 frs. Special meals for children.

ST-TROPEZ 83990 Var   Map 11

Les Palmiers   `BUDGET`   *Tel 94.97.01.61*
26 boulevard Vasserot   *Fax 94.97.10.02*
                                    Telex 970941

Centrally located, five minutes' stroll from the harbour, and facing the place des Lices with its trendy-bohemian bar-bistrots, the Café des Arts *and* Bistrot des Lices. *A simple family-run B&B hotel, newly given a face-lift. Patio garden, decent rooms, good value for a town that Michael Frayn has called St-Trop (the saint of excess). 23 rooms, most with bath and/or shower, 250–420 frs. Breakfast 28 frs [1990]. No restaurant. Recent nomination. More reports welcome.*

STE-ANNE-LA-PALUD 29127 Finistère   Map 8

Hôtel de la Plage   *Tel 98.92.50.12*
Plomodiern   *Telex 941377*

Not far from the lovely old village of Locronan, the beachside chapel of Ste-Anne is the venue of one of the largest and most colourful of Breton *pardons,* held on the last Sunday of August. Near this chapel is the *Plage,* not an ordinary seaside hotel as its *Hulot*-ish name might imply, but stylish and expensive – and strongly admired again in 1989/90 especially for its cuisine (*Michelin* rosette, two *Gault Millau toques*): "A lovely place, oozing atmosphere, with its paintings of seascapes and waitresses in Breton costume. The *demi-pension* menu includes oysters, grilled salmon, and char-grilled lobster which you eat with a special pinny draped tenderly round you by a maternal waitress. A picturesque thatched cottage houses a bar. Bedrooms comfortable and tasteful." "A well-run hotel on a beautiful sandy beach, long and uncrowded. Good and friendly service. At dinner, predominance of fish, always fresh and large portions. Classic puddings, incredibly sweet; cheeses fresh and local; a wonderful platter of fruits de mer at lunch; and delicious croissants, brioches and home-made jams for breakfast." "A good tennis court, and a stunning situation, especially with the light of the setting sun reflected on the wet low-tide sands." (*Francine and Ian Walsh; Pamela M Zargarani, Philip Carter; endorsed in 1990 by Mrs Ann Thornton*) A few shortcomings: some front rooms can be noisy; although the beach is on the doorstep the sea is often a long way away because of the tides; the hotel does not have many facilities for small children. One reader reported a booking not honoured, despite confirming and paying a deposit, and the hotel inadequately apologetic.

Open 2 Apr–12 Oct.
Rooms 4 suites, 26 double – all with bath and/or shower, telephone, TV. 2 ground-floor rooms.
Facilities 2 lifts. Salons, bar, TV room, restaurant; conference facilities. Garden with tennis court and swimming pool. Safe, sandy beach.
Location On coast, 16 km NE of Douarnenez.
Credit cards All major cards accepted.
Terms [1990 rates] Rooms 520–800 frs, suite 1,100 frs. Breakfast 50 frs. Half board 550–720 frs per person. Set lunch/dinner 180–340 frs.

SAINTES 17100 Charente-Maritime   Map 10

Relais du Bois St-Georges   *Tel* 46.93.50.99
Rue de Royan   *Fax* 46.93.50.99

Saintes, with its ruined Roman amphitheatre and fine Romanesque churches, is one of the most attractive and historic towns of south-west France. The *Bois St-Georges*, well placed in its own big garden in the western outskirts, is by contrast very modern – in an unusual, elegant way, as recent visitors report. "The indoor heated swimming pool has a grand piano, statuary, and large windows overlooking the lawns." "An excellent hotel with a superb pool. My room was very individual, being on several floors with its own staircase and a good supply of French books. Food and service are excellent. The garden with its lake and fountains is an example of the care and enthusiasm lavished by the owner, who is very much in evidence and clearly proud of his achievement." (*DJ Harden, Victoria P Turner, and others*) There is some traffic noise from the *autoroute*.

Open All year.
Rooms 3 suites, 27 double – all with bath, shower, telephone, TV. Some with balcony. 6 ground-floor rooms specially adapted for &.
Facilities Lounge, 2 bars, TV room, restaurant; indoor swimming pool; terrace where meals are served in season. 14-acre grounds with lake. Tennis nearby.
Location On W outskirts – 1.5 km from exit 25 of *autoroute* A10. Garage parking.
Credit cards Access, Visa.

Terms Rooms: single occupancy 290–430 frs, double 390–570 frs, suite 760–880 frs. Breakfast 60 frs. Set lunch/dinner 135 frs; full alc 190–280 frs. Special meals for children.

LES STES-MARIES-DE-LA-MER 13460 Bouches-du-Rhône   Map 10

L'Étrier Camarguais   *Tel* 90.97.81.14
Chemin bas des Launes   *Telex* 403144

On the edge of the Camargue, just north of Les Saintes-Maries, the *Étrier* ("stirrup") is one of several modern ranch-like holiday hotels here that cater mainly for riders: it has its own herd of white Camarguais horses which it hires to guests by the hour (not cheap). It is a spacious, breezy and youthfully informal place, slightly shabby, with log-cabin decor; the simple bedrooms, in chalets in the garden, have patios where you can breakfast in privacy. A recent letter from a family: "The swimming pool and gardens were attractive, the staff were friendly, and we enjoyed the horse rides. The dinners were mostly good – on one evening there was a magnificent buffet with smoked and fresh salmon, crab, all sorts of shellfish, an array of delicious salads and other delights. Pity that lunch was a full three-course affair, with no chance of just snacks round the pool. Breakfast was adequate." (*JA, and others*) The nearby disco (just out of earshot) is not cheap. Les Saintes-Maries' famous Gypsy festival, every 23–27 May, is well worth seeing.

Open Easter–15 Nov.
Rooms 27 double – all with bath, telephone, TV. 6 on ground floor.
Facilities Bar, restaurant, disco; conference facilities. Terrace, garden with swimming pool and tennis court. Sandy beach 2 km.
Location 3 km N of the town, just off N570 to Arles.
Credit cards All major cards accepted.
Terms [1990 rates] Dinner, B&B: single 630 frs, double 830 frs; full board: single 730–790 frs, double 1,150 frs. Set lunch/dinner 160 frs; full alc 300 frs. Special meals for children on request.

SALON-DE-PROVENCE 13300 Bouches-du-Rhône   Map 11

Abbaye de Sainte-Croix   *Tel* 90.56.24.55
Route du Val de Cuech   *Fax* 90.56.31.12
                                                           Telex 401247

A venerable 12th-century abbey on a hillside north-east of Salon, expensively restored as a luxury hotel. It has a wooded park, and a dining room giving on to a terrace with a fine view across the plain; at night it is candle-lit. An inspector writes this year: "Full marks for its site, its very pleasant staff, its Provençal atmosphere and beautiful public rooms. Food, though limited in scope, is enjoyable. But bedrooms could do with a review: our tiny suite was decorated in spartan rustic style, with terracotta floor tiles, Provençal rugs and fabrics, all very pleasant, but storage space was minimal and the lighting too dim." Others have enjoyed the antique furniture, discreet service and "delicious" food. The outdoor pool is well maintained. If many bedrooms are small, it is because they are former monks' cells; but some have a balcony. (*David and Kate Wooff, SF Riddell, MD Abrahams*)

Open 1 Mar–1 Nov. Restaurant closed Mon midday.
Rooms 5 suites, 19 double – all with bath and/or shower, telephone; radio on request.
Facilities Bar, TV room, restaurant; functions facilities. Garden with swimming pool. Tennis 200 metres.
Location 5 km NE of Salon, off D16.
Credit cards All major cards accepted.
Terms [1990 rates] Rooms 530–870 frs; suite 1,540 frs. Breakfast 65 frs. Dinner, B&B 570–730 frs per person. Set lunch/dinner 180–430 frs. Special meals for children.

SARLAT-LA-CANÉDA 24200 Dordogne   Map 10

La Hoirie   *Tel* 53.59.05.62

An endorsement this year: "An old hunting lodge of the de Vienne family in whose hands it remains. It is far enough outside the congested horrors of Sarlat to be a well-deserved *Relais du Silence*. Rooms are in three buildings around a pretty courtyard. They vary in size and lightness, but all are full of character – beams, thick stone walls, etc. Food, though not cheap, is excellent, with several dishes that feature on the *carte* having won regional gastronomic awards. The waitress was an enthusiast who entered fully into the pleasures of ordering food and wine. Delightful and good-sized outdoor swimming pool." (*Colin Pilkington*)

Open 15 Mar–14 Nov.
Rooms 15 – all with bath and/or shower, telephone.
Facilities Salon, bar, restaurant; garden with swimming pool.
Location 3 km S of Sarlat, off D704.
Credit cards All major cards accepted.
Terms [1990 rates] Rooms: single 300 frs, double 300–500 frs. Breakfast 45 frs. Dinner, B&B 345–445 frs per person. Set lunch/dinner 170–280 frs. Special meals for children.

Hostellerie de Meysset   *Tel* 53.59.08.29
Route des Eyzies

Périgourdine *douceur de vivre* suffuses this pleasant rural hotel, built in local style and set on a hill outside the town, in its own park: from its terrace there are wide views over two valleys. A recent report: "Comfortable, and efficiently run. Madame Brottier is bandbox smart, Monsieur is friendly and likes a joke. Our ground-floor room had french windows opening on to a tiny private lawn. In the well-appointed dining room the atmosphere was relaxing and the five-course *menu pension* was varied: excellent soups." Meals are served on the terrace when fine; the furniture is suitably rustic in style. (*Ann Webber*) A new chef has arrived since that report, and he does not impress *Gault Millau*: your views, please.

Open 28 Apr–6 Oct. Restaurant closed Wed midday.
Rooms 4 suites, 22 double – all with bath or shower, telephone.
Facilities Lounge, restaurant. Large terrace. Garden.
Location 3 km NW of town, off Les Eyzies road (D67). Parking.
Credit cards All major cards accepted.
Terms [1990 rates] Rooms 330–395 frs, suite 610 frs. Breakfast 43 frs. Dinner, B&B 345–395 frs per person. Set lunch/dinner 160–230 frs.

SAULIEU 21210 Côte d'Or   Map 10

Hôtel de La Côte d'Or   *Tel* 80.64.07.66
2 rue d'Argentine   *Fax* 80.64.08.92
                                                       Telex 350778

A noble old coaching inn, with a large walled garden, on the main street
of a dullish small Burgundy town on the old Paris–Lyons highway (N6).
It was long famous, for its former owner Alexandre Dumaine was one of
the great French chefs of his day (three rosettes in *Michelin*). Then it fell
into eclipse, with Dumaine's death and the coming of the *autoroute* which
stole most of the through traffic. Today it is again in form under
patron/chef Bernard Loiseau, who has brought it up to the standard
where it wins two *Michelin* rosettes and *Gault Millau*'s top rating of 19.5
points. The cooking, modern and light, is based on old Burgundy dishes.
And again this year our readers have been enthusiastic. "In the exquisite
candle-lit dining room," says one, "we took their special seven-course
vegetarian menu which was beautifully presented and totally delicious.
The comfortable rooms had the feel of a well-kept country house. *And* our
boots and shoes were cleaned!" Others have extolled "the 'cleanness' and
intensity of flavour which is characteristic of M Loiseau's *cuisine à l'eau*"
and "the masses of fresh flowers and well-polished antique furniture".
The wine list, mostly expensive, contains some house wines at reasonable
prices. Room furnishings are a little heavy, but the lavish new suites are
said to be excellent. (*PG Dwyer, Rosamund V Hebdon, T and R Rose, and
others*)

Open All year.
Rooms 7 suites, 15 double, 1 single – all with bath and/or shower, telephone,
baby-listening; 7 with radio, 17 with TV. Ground-floor rooms.
Facilities Ramps. 2 lounges, 2 dining rooms. Garden.
Location Central. Garage parking.
Credit cards All major cards accepted.
Terms Rooms 260–950 frs, suites 1,500–1,800 frs. Breakfast 70 frs. Set lunch
350 frs. Full alc 550 frs. Reduced rates and special meals for children.

SAUTERNES 33210 Gironde   Map 10

Château de Commarque   `BUDGET`   *Tel* 56.63.65.94

Few names are sweeter than Sauternes – and in 1989/90 visitors were
again enthusiastic about this handsome English-owned wine-producing
château amid the vineyards, 40 kilometres south-east of Bordeaux. Nigel
and Georgea Reay-Jones recently bought it to restore the neglected
vineyards, and they have now planted eight acres with young vines. They
have also converted the outbuildings into self-contained studio apartments with exposed beams, each with an independent entrance opening
on to a courtyard. Meals are served in the barn-like former *chai*, probably
17th century. "The courtyard retains its rustic appearance, with old trees
and ivy-covered walls. Georgea Reay-Jones turns out delicious food, and
the range of wines is amazing. Nigel is terribly enthusiastic and nice." "A
laid-back welcome – there's little to spoil the impression that one is
arriving at a private house. The restaurant is welcoming, with a fire on
cool days." "The Reay-Jones welcome children, and have five well-
behaved ones of their own. There's no high luxury, but the basic

amenities are there, including a swimming pool." Local wine tours can be arranged. And the literary-minded might care to know that this is also the Mauriac country: his family home, Malagar, is just across the Garonne at Vergelais, north of Langon, and his boyhood summer home at St-Symphorien, south-west of Sauternes, was the setting for *Thérèse Desqueyroux* and *Le Mystère Frontenac*. (*Stuart Cole, Allan Gillon, Stephen and Samantha Pollock-Hill*)

Open All year except Feb. Restaurant closed to non-residents Wed in low season.
Rooms 1 suite with 2 bedrooms, 6 double – all with shower. 1 ground-floor room.
Facilities Restaurant. 30-acre grounds; garden with swimming pool; vineyard.
Location 40 km SE of Bordeaux. Leave A62 at Langon. Follow road to Sauternes; château is signposted.
Credit cards Access, Visa.
Terms Rooms: double 180 frs, suite 250–275 frs. Breakfast 25 frs. Set lunch/dinner 75, 125 and 180 frs; full alc 160 frs. 50 frs added for use of sofa bed in sitting rooms. Special meals for children.

SAUVETERRE-DE-COMMINGES 31510 Haute-Garonne   Map 10

Hostellerie des Sept Molles   *Tel* 61.88.30.87
Gesset   *Fax* 61.88.36.42
    Telex 533359

Secluded in a lush wooded valley of the Pyrenean foothills, this large white villa, quite smart and most gracefully furnished, is run by a friendly young couple and makes a most appealing hotel. *Molle* is a local word for *moulin*, as the brochure lyrically explains: "On the slopes of the hills overlooking the valley, seven joyous watermills used to cling to the meanderings of the capricious stream flowing from the plateaux. The locals came down on Sundays to fetch sacks full of white flour and drink their fill of mirth. Sadly, times have changed . . . but the seven mills were retrieved by the management and now adorn our gardens." Several recent visitors have drunk their fill of mirth at the Ferran family's hostelry: "Innovative high-class food and memorable breakfasts." "We took two of their cheapest rooms, which proved to be comfortable and nicely decorated. The only sound was of cowbells. Service and public rooms were as you would expect from *Relais et Châteaux*, but informal. A swimming pool and tennis court in the lawned garden; table-tennis in the gazebo; and children are entertained by the proprietors' small daughter. Nice touches like poached quail's eggs as an appetiser and baskets of fruit in the bedrooms. Menus, using local ingredients (rabbit and pigeon), were imaginative and *nouvelle* in presentation" (red *Gault Millau toque*). (*Helen and Charles Priday, Paul A Hoffstein*) Newer reports requested.

Open Mid-Mar–end Oct and mid-Dec–5 Jan.
Rooms 2 suites, 17 double – all with bath, shower, telephone, TV; some with balcony.
Facilities Lift. Salon, bar, 2 restaurants. Garden with swimming pool and tennis court.
Location At Gesset, 2 km SE of Sauverre, 13 km SW of St-Gaudens.
Credit cards All major cards accepted.
Terms Rooms: single 410 frs, double 490 frs, suite 890 frs. Breakfast 55 frs. Dinner, B&B 490 frs per person. Set lunch/dinner 155 and 255 frs; full alc 290 frs. Reduced rates and special meals for children.

SÉES 61500 Orne Map 8

L'Ile de Sées `BUDGET` *Tel* 33.27.98.65
Macé *Telex* 179000

Between Argentan and Alençon, set peacefully amid the lush pastures of southern Normandy, 5 km from Sées; an attractive creeper-covered manor house turned unpretentious hotel, run by very friendly people. Comfortable rooms and excellent food popular with local diners. Closed 16 Jan–14 Feb; restaurant closed Sun dinner, Mon. 16 rooms, all with bath and shower. B&B: single 238 frs, double 306 frs. Set meals 78–154 frs. New nomination. More reports welcome.

SÉGOS 32400 Gers Map 10

Domaine de Bassibé *Tel* 62.09.46.71
Fax 62.08.40.15

An elegant rural newcomer for the Guide, on the edge of Gascony, north of Pau: "It is down a country lane off the main N134, in a quiet, pretty setting with distant views. There's a gravelled courtyard, and a swimming pool under large oak trees. The place is very stylish, relying on subtle colours in the decor, carefully placed antiques, pianos, french doors leading to the garden; the furniture is smart and modern. All is sunny and light, with crisp white paint. Our suite, with white painted rafters, was a total delight. You can dine in a pretty room with a glowing fire, or under the trees with candle-light and stars. Jean-Pierre Capelle, the *patron*/chef, wins a *Michelin* rosette and *Gault Millau toque*: we much enjoyed his soupe en croûte aux cèpes (Yorkshire pudding raised to a new level), boeuf à la ficelle, marinated raw lamb. Breakfasts were delightful and all the staff friendly. So was the dog, a gorgeous white Saluki." (*Susan Gillotti*)

Open 8 Apr–30 Nov. Restaurant closed Sun evening and Mon in Nov.
Rooms 3 suites, 6 double – all with bath, shower, telephone; suites have TV.
Facilities 2 salons, restaurant; conference room. Terrace; garden with outdoor swimming pool.
Location 40 km N of Pau, just east of N134.
Restriction Not suitable for &.
Credit cards All major cards accepted.
Terms [1990 rates] Rooms 580–620 frs, suite 850 frs. Breakfast 65 frs. Dinner, B&B 640–740 frs per person. Special meals for children.

SÉGURET 84110 Vaucluse Map 11

La Table du Comtat *Tel* 90.46.91.49

This picturesque old village, on a hillside above the Rhône vineyards, is within easy reach of Orange and Roman Vaison, and has fine views of the startling jagged peaks of the Dentelles de Montmirail; it's also a centre of Provençal folk culture, with a Christmas church pageant and craftsmen making *santons*. Here this fine old 15th-century house, now a sophisticated restaurant-with-rooms (*Michelin* rosette and *Gault Millau toque*), is splendidly situated just above the village. A recent inspector's report:

"The view's the thing so it's best to eat by daylight, taking advantage of the big windows of the dining room; it's a bit dull and formal after dark. Service is outstandingly stylish and courteous, and Madame Gomez is friendly though reserved (her husband cooks). The cuisine is superbly done in its more-or-less *nouvelle* way: an amuse-gueule of salmon mousse with oyster, superb lamb and lotte au pistou, good cheeses – they are strong on chèvres – and a fine local white Séguret, better than the Gigondas red, also local. Smart international clientele, classical piped music. Rooms comfortable and well equipped; many with views. The small *piscine*, floodlit at night below its high rock, is a stunner." "Food and wines excellent, staff friendly", is an endorsement this year. (*Roydon Jenkins*)

Open Early Mar–22 Nov, 8 Dec–end Jan. Closed Tue evening and Wed except in summer, Christmas and Easter.
Rooms 8 double – all with bath, shower, telephone.
Facilities Salon, 2 dining rooms; terrace. Small garden with unheated swimming pool.
Location 8 km S of Vaison-la-Romaine off the D23; at entrance to Séguret; hotel is signposted. Parking.
Restriction Not suitable for ♿.
Credit cards All major cards accepted.
Terms Rooms: single 400 frs, double 500–600 frs. Breakfast 60 frs. Set lunch/dinner 210, 270 and 420 frs; full alc 350–400 frs. Reduced rates and special meals for children.

SEPT-SAULX 51400 Marne   **Map 9**

Hôtel Restaurant le Cheval   *Tel* 26.03.90.27
   Blanc   *Fax* 26.03.97.09
2 rue du Moulin   *Telex* 830885

A pleasant old creeper-covered coaching inn, run by the Robert family for five generations. It is liked especially for its food (*Michelin* rosette, *Gault Millau toque*), and for its pastoral setting beside a big garden and a stream (it straddles the main road of a village south-east of Reims). Reports this year and last: "Food and service excellent; our bedroom was large and tastefully decorated." "The garden is pretty and quiet, the grounds charming. Food was very good, especially seafood en papillote, and breakfast the best of our holiday, with large bowls of delicious home-made jam." "We relaxed in garden hammocks and rocking chairs amid trees and murmuring streams." Others have spoken of Madame Robert's charm and the warm attentiveness of her staff. Poulet de bresse, and coquilles St-Jacques with melon and bacon are other dishes praised. (*R and W Bowden, Mrs J Thomas, Mrs CC Roxburgh, and others*) But service can be slow. And some bedroom party walls are thin, while rooms on the road side, where lorries lumber by, hardly justify the hotel's rating as a *Relais du Silence*.

Open All year except mid-Jan–mid-Feb.
Rooms 3 suites, 18 double – all with bath and/or shower, telephone, TV. Ground-floor rooms.
Facilities Hall, salon/bar, restaurant, breakfast room; functions room. Terrace. Large park bordered by river Vesle; fishing. Tennis and mini-golf.
Location On D37 off N44 in direction of Châlons.
Credit cards All major cards accepted.

Terms Rooms: single 300–450 frs, double 340–500 frs, suite 450–500 frs. Breakfast 40 frs. Set lunch/dinner 170, 270 and 370 frs; full alc 400 frs.

SERRES 05700 Hautes-Alpes   Map 10

Hôtel Fifi Moulin   `BUDGET`   *Tel* 92.67.00.01
Route de Nyons

Solidly down-to-earth despite its coy name (who indeed was Fifi?), this hostelry on the main Grenoble–Provence road remains popular with readers, especially for its restaurant (*Michelin* red "R" and *Gault Millau toque*) which is strongly patronised by locals. "Delightful, inexpensive meals, dynamic and charming host, excellent rooms with mountain views." "Pleasing fabrics, remodelled bathrooms, pretty dining room and good food, especially the cheeses." So run two recent reports. The hotel is on several levels, with kitchens next to guest bedrooms: for this reason, some rooms may be a little noisy in late evening. Terrace and back bedrooms on upper levels have views over the town and mountains. The new annexe rooms down the slope are commended this year for their quiet. (*D and J Smith*)

Open 15 Mar–30 Nov. Closed Wed except in season.
Rooms 25 double – all with bath or shower and telephone; some with TV. 12 in annexe.
Facilities Bar, restaurant; terrace. Large garden with swimming pool.
Location 107 km S of Grenoble, 64 km from Nyons on N75.
Credit cards All major cards accepted.
Terms Rooms 230–250 frs. Breakfast 28 frs. Dinner, B&B 240–340 frs per person.

SEURRE 21250 Côte d'Or   Map 10

Le Castel   `BUDGET`   *Tel* 80.20.45.07
20 avenue de la Gare

A cheerful modern *Logis de France* in a small town on the Beaune–Dole road. Its *patron*/chef Lucien Deschamps worked for 13 years in England, and this year he is praised by readers for his friendliness as well as for his excellent local cooking served in a big, bright dining room; portions are large. No lounge, but a flowery terrace; modern bathrooms. (*Sonia and Harold Cohen, JA Dyson, C and M Hédoin*). While some readers find the hotel quiet (it's down a cul-de-sac), others warn of train noises.

Open All year except 2 Jan–5 Feb. Closed Mon 6 Feb–15 Mar, 1 Nov–15 Dec and Christmas.
Rooms 20 – 13 with bath and shower, 3 with shower, all with telephone.
Facilities Salon with TV, bar, 2 dining rooms; terrace.
Location Central, parking. Seurre is 26 km E of Beaune.
Restriction Not suitable for &.
Credit card Visa
Terms Rooms: single 195 frs, double 225 frs. Breakfast 25 frs. Set lunch/dinner 95–260 frs.

If you have difficulty in finding hotels because our location details are inadequate, please help us to improve directions next year.

SOUSCEYRAC 46190 Lot   Map 10

Au Déjeuner de Sousceyrac   `BUDGET`   *Tel* 65.33.00.56

A rustic auberge in a remote village south of the upper Dordogne: under
its previous owners, the Espinadel family, it so much delighted one
académicien, Pierre Benoit, that he wrote a book about it, *Au déjeuner de
Sousceyrac*, and the inn then took that name. Some of our own readers in
the mid-1980s were equally thrilled: but then Pierre Espinadel retired.
Now it has been bought by Richard Piganiol, Paris-trained but a local
man, and he's won a *Michelin* red "R" and *Gault Millau* red *toque* for
dishes such as paupiette de pigeon au foie gras. A recent comment on his
regime: "Our bedroom was cramped but adequate. The dining room
decor was freshly done, about right for this simple hotel, and the cuisine
is excellent, with more than a touch of the *nouvelle*. Some French fellow-
guests praised it highly and clearly they knew what they were talking
about." (*Jack B Ainslie*) If you do too, please give us further news.

Open All year except 15 Nov–6 Dec and 1–20 Feb.
Rooms 10 double – 7 with bath, 3 with shower.
Facilities Salon, TV room, restaurant; terrace.
Location In centre of village, which is between St-Cère and Aurillac, on D673 and
D653. Parking.
Credit card Access, Visa.
Terms B&B: single 150 frs, double 190 frs. Set lunch/dinner 90, 130 and 190 frs;
full alc 280 frs. Reduced rates and special meals for children.

STRASBOURG 67000 Bas-Rhin   Map 9

Nouvel Hôtel Maison Rouge   *Tel* 88.32.08.60
4 rue des Francs-Bourgeois   *Fax* 88.22.43.73
                                                       Telex 880130

Very central, just off the main square, the Place Kléber, this friendly hotel
is fairly priced by expensive Strasbourg standards, and has been
renovated in "modern 1930s" style. Readers continue to commend it,
notably for its spacious, comfortable rooms and generous buffet breakfasts ("mouth-watering croissants"). The hotel caters heavily for groups
but retains its character – even down to the grand piano, for guests' use,
on one upper landing. "Our high room at the back was quiet and
overlooked the rooftops of old Strasbourg." The staff are mostly liked, but
some reports say they are too impersonal. No restaurant, but you can eat
very well all over Strasbourg – for example, expensively at the *Crocodile*,
reasonably at *l'Ancien Horloge* and cheaply at *l'Ancienne Douane*. (*Lynne
and David Allen, C Bagshawe, and others*)

Open All year.
Rooms 2 suites, 137 double, 3 single – all with bath and/or shower, telephone,
radio, TV.
Facilities Lift. Lounge, bar, breakfast room; conference facilities.
Location In town centre (hotel is sound-proofed). Underground parking in Place
Kléber nearby.
Credit cards All major cards accepted.
Terms Rooms: single 350–460 frs, double 390–510 frs, suite 800–950 frs. Breakfast
45 frs. (No restaurant.)

Hôtel Régent-Contades
8 avenue de la Liberté

Tel 88.36.26.26
Fax 88.37.13.70
Telex 890641

A recently converted townhouse facing a canal, 600 metres east of cathedral. Classically furnished bedrooms, quiet (double-glazing); elegant breakfast room (good buffet); attentive service. No restaurant: light dishes served in rooms. Closed 23 Dec–2 Jan. 32 rooms, 650–1,000 frs. Breakfast 55 frs [1990]. New nomination. More reports please.

Hôtel des Rohan
17 rue Maroquin

Tel 88.32.85.11
Fax 88.75.65.37
Telex 870047

In the cobbled pedestrian area beside the cathedral, a small family-run hotel in discreet traditional style, with modern comforts. Readers judge it friendly, efficient and quiet (apart from some cathedral chimes). It has repro furniture in the current French taste and is warm and comfortable. "I was greeted warmly, and my room was prettily decorated; very helpful staff," runs a 1990 report. They will send a bell-boy to bring your bags from the nearby public parking. The Sunday breakfast with Kugelhopf cakes is commended. (*Dr Suzanne Martin*)

Open All year.
Rooms 36 double – all with bath and/or shower, telephone, radio, TV; baby-sitter on request.
Facilities Lift. Salon with TV, 2 breakfast rooms.
Location Central, near cathedral. Public parking nearby.
Credit cards Access, Visa.
Terms Rooms: single occupancy 280–525 frs, double 300–570 frs. Breakfast 45 frs (60 frs on Sun). (No restaurant.)

TALLOIRES 74290 Haute-Savoie   Map 10

Hôtel Beau-Site   *Tel* 50.60.71.04

Set serenely by the shores of the lovely lake of Annecy, with glorious views, this pleasant and unpretentious hotel offers an alternative to the high prices of the famous *Père Bise* and *Abbaye* (both now dropped from the Guide). Owned and run by Louis Conan, whose relatives own the *Prés du Lac* (see below), it has been much modernised this year, with new furniture and a new lift – and it remains liked by readers for its "excellent food and friendly service". Others had "a most enjoyable stay, in a large comfortable room" and found M Conan "an attentive and pleasant host". Smooth management seems to have returned, after what may have been a difficult period. (*J Swarsbrick; Charles P Cords, GE Samson, GB Hart*)

Open May–Oct.
Rooms 1 suite, 27 double, 1 single – all with bath and/or shower, telephone; 18 with radio, TV. 11 in annexe in garden. Ground-floor rooms.
Facilities Lift. Salons, TV room, dining room; terrace. Garden with private beach on lake; fishing, sailing, etc; tennis court.
Location Central, on Lake Annecy. Parking.
Credit cards All major cards accepted.

Terms B&B: single 295 frs, double 405–710 frs, suite 840 frs. Dinner, B&B 340–600 frs per person; full board 390–650 frs. Set lunch/dinner 135–180 frs. Reduced rates for children; special meals on request.

Hôtel Les Prés du Lac   *Tel* 50.60.76.11
Clos Beau-Site   *Fax* 50.60.73.42
                                                        Telex 309288

A select and expensive villa of ultra-modern design, cool and bright, with lawns in front that stretch to its beach. Pleasant welcome, good views; rooms have patios and terraces; new annexes just opened. Open 8 Feb–11 Nov. 15 rooms, all with bath and shower. B&B double 650–1,100 frs [1990]. No restaurant, but meals can be taken at Beau-Site *(above), owned by same family. Endorsed this year but fuller reports requested.*

TAMNIÈS 24620 Dordogne   **Map 10**

Laborderie   `BUDGET`   *Tel* 53.29.68.59

Renewed praise this year for this modern hotel in a rural setting, on the edge of a tiny hilltop village between Les Eyzies and Sarlat, facing out over rolling wooded country. The facade is of yellowish stone; inside are beamed ceilings and a log fire in winter. "The Laborderie family are marvellous, especially the host, and dinner was excellent." "So quiet at night. The food beautifully cooked, generous and well served, the staff helpful and friendly." The "good rustic Périgourdin food" comes in large helpings, especially on the four-course *demi-pension* menu (but one reader thought there was too much Périgourdin emphasis on duck and goose). Rooms are comfortable: some prefer those in the annexe, but one reader this year thought them a bit small and noisy. The "lovely swimming pool" and "attractive terrace" are also admired, and the owners are said to be good with children. (*Cora Diamond, Patricia and Albert Grant, Jo and Mick Feat, and others*)

Open 23 Apr–3 Nov.
Rooms 31 double – all with bath or shower, telephone. 16 in garden annexe.
Facilities Bar, salon, TV room, 2 dining rooms; functions rooms; terrace. Garden with swimming pool. Lake nearby with swimming, fishing, windsurfing, sandy beach.
Location In centre of Tamniès which is 14 km NE of Les Eyzies. Parking.
Restriction Not suitable for ⅚.
Credit cards Access, Visa.
Terms Rooms 160–350 frs. Breakfast 25 frs. Half board 210–485 frs per person; full board 260–535 frs. Set lunch/dinner 100, 115, 160 and 250 frs; full alc 150 frs. Reduced rates for children.

TARDETS-SORHOLUS 64470 Pyrénées-Atlantiques   **Map 10**

Hôtel du Pont d'Abense   `BUDGET`   *Tel* 59.28.54.60
Abense-de-Haut

The old Basque medieval charades (*pastorales* and *mascarades*), with their richly costumed characters, are still sometimes performed in this village south-west of Pau. Here this clean, quiet and modest family-run hotel, friendly and efficient, has again been liked this year: "Delightful, and very popular with the French. Our room was basic but comfortable. The *pension* evening menus offer little choice but the food varies nightly and is of high standard, notably the puddings. A herd of cows with bells went past the window one evening. The hotel's Siamese cat presses her attentions persistently." Small shady garden, where you can eat out in summer. (*Brian and Rosalind Keen, DGA Thomas, BA Wood*)

Open 10 Jan–15 Nov. Closed Thu out of season.
Rooms 12 – 4 with bath and shower, 2 with shower, all with telephone.
Facilities Lounge, bar, TV room, restaurant. Garden; terrace.
Location On edge of village, which is 60 km SW of Pau.
Restriction Not suitable for &.
Credit cards Access, Visa.
Terms Rooms: single 180–220 frs, double 220–240 frs. Breakfast 25 frs. Dinner, B&B 180–200 frs per person. Set lunch/dinner 90 frs; full alc 150 frs. Reduced rates and special meals for children.

TARGET 03140 Chantelle, Allier   Map 10

Château de Boussac   *Tel 70.40.63.20*

Staying with hoteliers who have turned their own gracious home into a guest house, and who treat their paying guests like personal friends, can be a risk for both sides. And whether it works can be a matter of taste. At this 17th-century château, in the Bourbonnais country north-west of Vichy, it does seem to work well – according to its nominator this year: "*Boussac* belongs to the Marquis and Marquise de Longueil, whose family was connected with the Norman Conquest. They have a working farm here but, as farming does not pay well at the moment, they have opened their house to guests and have spent much effort on restoring and redecorating the château. It's a fairy tale sort of square fortified castle, with a round tower at each corner, surrounded by a moat and beautiful gardens which merge with the placid undulating farm landscape beyond. The bedrooms are of modest size but furnished in exquisite taste with matching fabrics, antiques and family treasures; fresh flowers and books complete the picture. The de Longueils are a charming couple, good company, and the way that he copes bilingually with the dinner conversation is a *social tour de force*. Mme de Longueil's cooking is delicious, and her serving of it from a heated trolley, without having to rise from the table, combines elegance and practicality. Breakfast is good, too. The de Longueils welcome their guests into the bosom of the family. But of course this approach relies on the tact and discretion of guests." (*A Liddell*) Let's hear more – noblesse oblige.

Open 1 Apr–30 Oct.
Rooms 2 suites, 3 double – all with bath.
Facilities 2 salons, restaurant. Garden.
Location The hamlet of Target is 10 km SE of Montmarault, south of the D46 Montluçon–St-Pourçain.
Restriction Not suitable for &.
Credit card Visa.
Terms Rooms 525 frs, suite 750 frs. Breakfast 45 frs. Set lunch/dinner 260 frs.

If you have kept brochures and tariffs for Continental hotels, do please enclose them with your reports.

THIONVILLE 57100 Moselle   Map 9

L'Horizon   *Tel* 82.88.53.65
50 route du Crève-Coeur   *Fax* 82.34.55.84
                                                         Telex 860870

This ivy-covered hostelry, smart and appealing, is an "unlikely find" on
the edge of an ugly industrial town amid the decaying Lorraine steel
mills, beside the Luxembourg border. But *Michelin* gives it red print for
pleasantness, and our readers agree: "It is in a quiet position up on a
hillside above the town, with wide views over the countryside as well as
industry. We entered through wrought-iron gates, past well-kept gardens
ablaze with flowers. The house is very attractive, with an elegant paved
terrace at the back where you can have tea or drinks. The light and
spacious hall had fresh flowers, plus a ceiling looking like something out
of the *Arabian Nights*, very pretty when lit up at night. Our large bedroom
had French windows with wide views and excellent lighting, but some of
the fittings were a little worn. The attractive dining room had velvet
drapes and a tapestry. The set menu was mostly excellent, including an
unusual apple sorbet between meat courses. Though quite expensive, the
place has the feeling of a family-run hotel and all the staff were pleasant."
Endorsed by *G Berneck, C Herxheimer*, but we'd welcome more reports.

Open All year except Jan. Restaurant closed Sat midday.
Rooms 8 double, 2 single – all with bath, shower, telephone, TV. 3 in annexe.
Facilities Salon, bar, TV room, breakfast room, restaurant; conference facilities;
terrace. Garden.
Location 2 km NW of Thionville: follow signs to Bel-Air or Crève-Coeur.
Garages.
Restriction Not suitable for &.
Credit cards All major cards accepted.
Terms Rooms 360–380 frs. Breakfast 40 frs. Dinner, B&B: single 540 frs, double
880 frs. Set lunch/dinner 195 frs; full alc 340 frs. Special meals for children.

TOULOUSE 31000 Haute-Garonne   Map 10

Hotel de Diane   *Tel* 61.07.59.52
3 route de St-Simon   *Fax* 61.86.38.94
                                                         Telex 530518

On the western outskirts of France's sprawling, fourth-largest city, a 19th-
century manor in a big garden, converted into a bright modern hotel, with
bedrooms in a new annexe, and plenty to amuse *les sportifs*. This is its
Guide debut: "A useful alternative to staying in the crowded city.
Buildings are set around the pool and tennis courts: our room had a patio
and lawn. There are lots of places for children to run off their energy. The
staff were helpful. The chef had worked on cruise ships, which showed in
the extensive buffet of appetisers spread out to start our excellent meal."
A big outdoor dining terrace for summer, an open fire for winter.
(*CA Hahn*)

Open All year. Restaurant closed Sat midday, Sun, 25 Dec and 1 Jan.
Rooms 1 suite, 34 double – all with bath, telephone, TV. 13 bungalows with
terrace in the garden.
Facilities Salon with TV, bar, restaurant; conference facilities. Terrace; garden
with swimming pool, 5 tennis courts (3 covered), mini-golf.
Location 8 km SW of Toulouse, near Le Mirail. Parking.

Credit cards All major cards accepted.
Terms Rooms 355–475 frs. Breakfast 40 frs. Set lunch/dinner 117 and 155 frs; full alc 200 frs. Weekly rates. Children under 12 sharing parents' room free; special meals 55 frs.

Grand Hôtel de l'Opéra   *Tel* 61.21.82.66
1 place du Capitole   *Fax* 61.23.41.04
       Telex 521998

Our only down-town entry for this capital of the European aviation and aerospace industries. Its medieval rose-pink kernel is the 18th-century place du Capitole, and here stands this visually beautiful hotel, with its superb restaurant. Recently converted from a 17th-century convent and furnished in period style, it is set back in a leafy courtyard – a haven of peace in this hectic town. "Most bedrooms are inviting and cosy. The restaurant well deserves its high ratings (two *Michelin* rosettes, three red *Gault Millau toques*): its chef and co-owner, Dominique Toulousy, local boy made good, serves delicious regional-based cuisine that is inventive without being chi-chi (pigeon with crayfish, ravioli with truffles, and an unusual cassoulet). His wife is a charming host. On fine days you eat under awnings in the flowery patio, beside an ornamental pool that is also the hotel's tiny swimming pool (bathers are forbidden at mealtimes, as they would splash the diners)." "The restaurant has several small rooms, some of whose walls are mirrors: one has all four walls made of mirrors – a narcissist's paradise." Others have concurred; but an inspector felt that his expensive room lacked character, and he disliked the breakfast, even more so the loud muzak served with it. More reports please.

Open All year. Restaurant closed 2 weeks in Aug.
Rooms 15 suites, 39 double, 9 single – all with bath, shower, telephone, radio, TV, air-conditioning; most with 24-hour room service. Some on ground floor.
Facilities Lift. Lobbies, salon, bar, restaurant, brasserie; conference facilities; sports centre with sauna, whirlpool etc. Garden with terrace, restaurant and swimming pool.
Location Central (windows double-glazed). Underground carpark in square.
Credit cards All major cards accepted.
Terms [1990 rates] Rooms: single 650 frs, double 700–1,050 frs, suite 1,300 frs. Breakfast 65 frs. Set meals 180–400 frs. Reduced rates for children sharing parents' room; special meals.

TOURNUS 71700 Saône-et-Loire   **Map 10**

Hôtel de la Paix   **BUDGET**   *Tel* 85.51.01.85
9 rue Jean-Jaurès

In the centre of a beautiful old town with a fine ancient abbey, near the Saône, an unassuming Swiss-owned hotel, very well run, with comfortable carpeted rooms and good food. Closed 14 Jan–4 Feb, 20–30 Apr, 19–29 Oct, Tue except July, Aug. 23 rooms, 22 with bath and shower. Rooms 214–290 frs. Breakfast 24 frs. Set menus 72–154 frs [1990]. Recent nomination. More reports welcome.

Report forms (Freepost in UK) will be found at the end of the Guide.

Le Rempart   *Tel* 85.51.10.56
2 avenue Gambetta   *Fax* 85.40.77.22
                                                        Telex 351019

On the main street of the town, here is a modernised hotel with striking decor
(marble-pillared bar), bright, comfortable, air-conditioned rooms (triple-glazing
keeps out the noise) and affable service. Pretentious-looking menu, but excellent
regional cooking (frog's legs in garlic, etc.), deserving its rosette and two
toques. Open all year. 37 rooms, all with bath. B&B: single 320 frs, double
500 frs. Set menus 155–370 frs. Endorsed this year, but further reports welcome.

TOURS 37000 Indre-et-Loire   **Map 8**

Hôtel de Groison   *Tel* 47.41.94.40
10 rue Groison   *Fax* 47.51.50.28

Set quietly in its own garden near the north bank of the Loire, an 18th-century
mansion, now a delightful hotel newly furnished in Empire style. Many rooms
are large, with marble bathrooms. Distinguished Jardin du Castel *restaurant*
(two Gault Millau *toques); excellent breakfasts. Restaurant closed 15–30 Nov,*
1–15 Mar, Sat lunch, Wed. 10 rooms, 350–710 frs. Breakfast 60 frs. Set meals
195–390 frs. New nomination. More reports please.

Jean Bardet   *Tel* 47.41.41.11
57 rue Groison   *Fax* 47.51.68.72
                                                        Telex 752463

With four red *toques* in *Gault Millau,* two rosettes and plenty of red print
in *Michelin,* Jean Bardet is pretty well in the same class as Boyer at Reims,
Lorain at Joigny or Blanc at Vonnas (qq.v.) as owner/chef of one of
France's most elegantly luxurious and gastronomically formidable small
hotels. It is a white colonnaded, early 19th-century villa in a glorious
landscaped park, set behind high walls in the Tours suburbs. "Dinner was
outstanding," says its 1990 nominator, "but the really memorable meal
was breakfast, a three-course feast. The garden and swimming pool are
lovely, the service friendly in a slightly chic way." Glamorous bedrooms,
equally glamorous innovative dishes such as lobster stew in Vouvray,
spiced with lemon and ginger. (*Paul Cheshire*) Consult your bank
manager, then send us more reports please.

Open All year. Restaurant closed Mon lunch; 1 Nov–31 Mar closed Sun evening
and all day Monday.
Rooms 6 suites, 9 double – all with bath and/or shower, telephone, TV.
Facilities 2 salons, smoking room, restaurant. Large park with terrace; garden,
swimming pool.
Location 2 km N of centre of Tours, in St-Symphorien. Garage.
Restriction Not suitable for &.
Credit cards All major cards accepted.
Terms B&B: single 745–945 frs, double 840–1,040 frs, suite 1,390–1,790 frs. Set
lunch/dinner 250, 470 and 620 frs; full alc 550 frs. Special meals for children.

Hôtel Royal `BUDGET`   *Tel* **47.64.71.78**
65 avenue de Grammont   *Fax* **47.05.84.62**

On a main street close to the centre of Tours, but quiet: a useful modernised hotel with Louis XV and XVI repro furnishings, good bathrooms and breakfasts, friendly service, and garage. No restaurant, but lots nearby. 50 rooms, all with bath and shower, 279–321 frs. Breakfast 31 frs. Recent nomination. More reports welcome.

TOURTOUR 83690 Var   **Map 11**

La Bastide de Tourtour   *Tel* 94.70.57.30
                                              Fax 94.70.54.90
                                              Telex 970827

The medieval hill-village of Tourtour is today a fashionable residential centre and a showpiece: its lovely facades of golden-brown stone have been scoured clean. There are wide vistas on all sides, and the Gorges du Verdon are quite close. *La Bastide*, smart and expensive, was custom-built in the 1960s in mock-château style, and stands in its own wooded garden on the edge of the village. A returning devotee this year found it better than ever: "Delicious cuisine (*Michelin* rosette), service almost instantaneous, glorious swimming pool, excellent tennis court, and a calm relaxing atmosphere among the fragrant pines." An earlier view: "I had a large and cheery room with cloth-covered walls and matching bed-covers. The food was superb, especially the ravioli stuffed with goat's cheese and the sweetbreads in a wine sauce. The dining room is intimate and romantic, with doors open to the terrace. Etienne and Francine Laurent, the owners, work hard to give their guests a perfect stay." They also enjoy showing their rare collection of 200 peasant bonnets and hats. (*M and D Chambers, Tom and Rosemary Rose*) Second-floor rooms are quieter than lower ones, and have the better view. One visitor this year, while liking the food, found the service erratic, the decor vulgar, and room upkeep poor: your comments, please.

Open Early Mar–end Oct. Restaurant closed Mon, and Tue lunch (also Mon in low season).
Rooms 23 double, 2 single – all with bath, shower, telephone, TV.
Facilities Lift. Lounge, bar, restaurant; exercise room and jacuzzi. Garden with heated swimming pool and tennis court.
Location 500 metres SE of Tourtour on road to Draguignan (20 km). Parking.
Credit cards All major cards accepted.
Terms Rooms: single 350–450 frs, double 420–1,100 frs. Breakfast 65 frs. Dinner, B&B 510–850 frs per person. Set lunch/dinner 150–350 frs; full alc 400 frs. Special meals for children.

TRÉBEURDEN 22560 Côtes-du-Nord   **Map 8**

Hôtel Ti al Lannec   *Tel* 96.23.57.26
Allée de Mézo Guen   *Fax* 96.23.62.14
                                              Telex 740656

Few other seaside hotels in France remain more warmly liked by readers than this handsome grey-and-white mansion set high above the sea in its quiet garden on the edge of a pleasant family bathing resort; it's on an especially delightful stretch of the North Breton coast, where rocks in strange shapes alternate with sandy coves. One eulogy this year: "Superbly situated, excellent staff, lovely rooms (ours had a spacious balcony), and marvellous if expensive food: the seafood platter at 215 frs [1989] is a must. And there's never a glimmer of disapproval if you persistently order the cheapest wine. The Jouanny family owners are always around; Madame has impeccable taste." Another couple, with a baby daughter, appreciate the hotel's welcome to children, and a bonus – "a docile and omnipresent St Bernard. The *Ti al Lannec* combines all the essential features of a seaside hotel, in particular a relatively sophisticated restaurant for parents to relax in after a day on the beach." That echoes earlier praise. Many of the beautifully furnished rooms have big balconies with sea views, and some have four-poster beds. A big light sea-facing dining room; snug, elegant lounge with period decor; white tables and chairs under parasols and trees on the lawn. Rare for a summer seaside hotel, the cooking (seafood especially) wins a red *Gault Millau toque*. (*S Parsons, Helen and Charles Priday, also FPA Wood, and others*) Eight bedrooms have just been added. And the gardens are being renovated, "which will probably make them even more splendid," says a reader.

Open 15 Mar–15 Nov.
Rooms 10 suites, 18 double, 2 single – all with bath, shower, telephone, TV, baby-listening.
Facilities Lift, ramps. Salon, billiard room with TV, bar, restaurant; conference facilities. Garden with outdoor chess, table-tennis, boules; path down to sandy beach, safe bathing, fishing. Sauna, jacuzzi and fitness room due for 1990.
Location In centre of village. Signposted from Lannion (10 km).
Credit cards All major cards accepted.
Terms [1990 rates] B&B: single 296–371 frs, double 496–706 frs, suite 718–904 frs. Dinner, B&B 420–515 frs per person. Set lunch/dinner 105–300 frs; full alc 290 frs. Reduced rates and special meals for children.

TRÉGUIER 22220 Côtes-du-Nord   Map 8

Kastell Dinec'h   `BUDGET`   *Tel* 96.92.49.39

Tréguier is an old grey Breton town with a fine cathedral, not far from the beaches of Perros-Guirec and Trébeurden. Just outside it, daubed in red print by the French guides, is this "absolutely splendid" hotel, set quietly down a country lane. "It's an old farmhouse in a pretty garden (with small swimming pool); the comfortable rooms, nicely decorated in Laura Ashley-ish prints, are in the main house and a converted stable block. The food deserves its *Michelin* red 'R': we enjoyed salmon with sorrel sauce, a cassolette of lobster tails, chicken with morels, scallops in Pernod sauce. Good breakfasts, too, and friendly service. Not the place to avoid fellow Brits." (But where is, in northern France these days?) (*Mrs J Thomas*, endorsed in 1990 by *Stephen R Holman*)

Open 15 Mar–10 Oct, 27 Oct–31 Dec. Closed Tue evening and Wed in low season. Restaurant closed for lunch.
Rooms 15 – all with bath and/or shower, telephone.
Facilities Lounge, restaurant. Garden with small swimming pool.
Location 2 km SW of Tréguier, off the Lannion road.
Credit cards Access, Visa.
Terms [1990 rates] Rooms 230–350 frs. Breakfast 38 frs. Dinner, B&B 250–350 frs per person. Set dinner 92–250 frs.

TRÉMOLAT 24510 Dordogne   Map 10

Hôtel Panoramic `BUDGET`   *Tel* 53.22.80.42
Route du Cingle de Trémolat   *Fax* 53.22.80.51

In a superb position overlooking a great loop in the Dordogne river, just outside
Trémolat village (where Chabrol set and filmed Le Boucher), *this old stone*
mansion is now an unpretentious hotel where the welcome is warm, the rooms
plain but pleasant, and the food excellent, including breakfast. Terrace for
drinks and meals, with that fine view. Closed Jan. 24 rooms, 16 with bath and
shower, 160–260 frs. Breakfast 30 frs. Set menus 75–165 frs. Recent nomination.
More reports welcome.

TRIGANCE 83840 Var   Map 11

Château de Trigance   *Tel* 94.76.91.18
                                                       Fax 94.47.58.99

We've had a mixed bag of recent reports on this "most idiosyncratic
hotel" – a boldly battlemented medieval pile on a hilltop above the
Provençal village of Trigance, near the dramatic Gorges du Verdon.
Access, by a steep rocky path and stone stairs, is not easy but you are
rewarded by wide views over the encircling rocky hills where one reader
"felt a great sense of pastoral peace" as he watched a flock of sheep being
herded. The castle is owned by Jean-Claude Thomas, a Paris ex-
businessman. "The physical setting is dramatic and M Thomas is a superb
and entertaining host." "Very imposing from a distance. Warm personal
welcome – it's worth staying just to converse with the owner. Rooms are
severe and dark, but reasonably priced. Dining room and bar charming;
food average. A unique place full of heart." "The only noises to disrupt us
were the sheep bells and the cuckoos. But the food was pretentious and
disappointing." Some readers have enjoyed the "romantic vaulted
restaurant", but one has disliked its "medieval chamber music"; some
have warmed to the "lovely canopied beds", but others have found the
rooms a bit oppressive. Those of infirm step can now reach the hotel by
road. But the able-bodied are still expected to climb up on foot ("The
access is part of the charm," says a reader). At least your luggage is
brought up by winch.

Open 16 Mar–11 Nov. Restaurant closed Wed midday in Mar, Apr, Oct, Nov.
Rooms 2 suites, 8 double – all with bath, shower, telephone, TV.
Facilities Salon, dining room, large terrace.
Location 20 km SW of Castellane, 12 km NW of Comps-sur-Artuby.
Restriction Not suitable for &.
Credit cards All major cards accepted.
Terms B&B: double 500–700 frs, suite 800 frs. Set lunch/dinner 165, 200 and
250 frs. Reduced rates for children; special meals on request.

USTARITZ 64480 Pyrénées-Atlantiques   Map 10

La Patoula `BUDGET`   *Tel* 59.93.00.56

Not far from Bayonne and St-Jean-de-Luz, a restaurant-with-rooms on
the banks of the river Nive, in the centre of a big Basque village. This is its

Guide debut: "A quiet and charming setting, a pleasant terrace by the river, some antiques, friendly owners, and extremely good food, light and inventive (two red *Gault Millau toques*), e.g. morue fraîche au sel de mer. Comfortable room. Only drawback: a slightly outdated bathroom." (*Susan Gillotti*)

Open All year except 15 Jan–25 Feb. Closed Sun evening and Mon except July/Aug.
Rooms 9 – all with bath and/or shower, telephone. 1 on ground floor.
Facilities Lounge, restaurant, TV room; terrace.
Location Central, by church. Ustaritz is 12 km S of Bayonne.
Credit card Visa.
Terms [1990 rates] Rooms 280–420 frs. Breakfast 45 frs. Dinner, B&B 280–360 frs per person. Set lunch/dinner 130–230 frs. Special meals for children.

UZÈS 30700 Gard
Map 10

Hôtel d'Entraigues Tel 66.22.32.68
Place Éveché

Uzès, in the rolling *garrigue* country north of Nimes, is an enchanting old town of narrow streets and lofty towers: the tallest belongs to the massive turreted ducal castle. Secluded in one of the alleys below is the *Entraigues*, a 16th-century mansion once the home of a general. It has been aesthetically converted into a select hotel, with soft-hued stone and dim-lit low-vaulted ceilings. A visitor in January 1990 found it warmly heated, and adds: "Reception friendly. The restaurant is spacious, with discreet classical music. There's a terrace for summer eating. Breakfast was unimpressive." "Comfortable and good value", was a report last year. The *Château* at Arpaillargues (q.v.) is under the same ownership. Uzès has a pig fair in February and a garlic fair in June.

Open All year. Restaurant closed Tue, and Wed midday in low season.
Rooms 12 suites, 18 double – all with bath and/or shower, telephone; some with TV. Some in annexe.
Facilities Salons, TV room, bar, restaurant.
Location Central, opposite cathedral, but quietly situated. Uzès is 25 km N of Nimes. Parking.
Restriction Not suitable for &.
Credit cards All major cards accepted.
Terms [1990 rates] Rooms 245–365 frs, suite 400–650 frs. Breakfast 32 frs. Dinner, B&B 275–325 frs per person. Set lunch/dinner 150 frs.

VALENCE 26000 Drôme
Map 10

Restaurant Pic Tel 75.44.15.32
285 avenue Victor-Hugo

In a tree-lined street on the edge of dusty Valence, in the Rhône valley, Jacques Pic and his charming wife run one of France's most renowned restaurants: he earns three *Michelin* rosettes, as his father did here in the 1930s. As well as a shady garden and just four pretty bedrooms, they offer *nouvelle cuisine* at its least affected, fully worth the high prices. "A generous-spirited place", "high quality and total comfort without ostentation" are two comments this year that endorse this earlier view: "Incredible (but simple) comfort in the bedrooms and total luxury in the dining room. The whole place is so undaunting, the atmosphere is charming and there's no snootiness by anyone, in contrast to what happens at many other prestigious places. Breakfast a dream of warm fresh lemon brioche." "Meals are served to about 120 people at a time, so this is a big festive operation, yet all one feels is intimacy. Food superb, such as stuffed sea bass in black butter sauce, topped by great slices of truffles." "A marvellous room with oriental rugs and marble bathroom." (*Sharon Gutman, P Gill, and others*)

Open All year except Aug and 1 week in Feb. Closed Wed, and Sun evening.
Rooms 2 suites, 2 double – all with bath, shower, telephone, TV, air-conditioning.
Facilities Sitting room, dining room. Courtyard and garden.
Location 1 km S of town centre. Take *autoroute* exit for Valence Sud, follow sign for avenue Victor-Hugo. Parking.
Restriction Not suitable for &.
Credit cards All major cards accepted.
Terms Rooms: double 450–480 frs, suite 600–800 frs. Breakfast 80 frs. Set lunch/dinner 300–550 frs.

VANNES 56000 Morbihan   Map 8

Le Roo   *Tel* 97.63.47.47
Presqu'île de Conleau   *Telex* 951843

Recently enlarged, this spruce modern white-walled hotel has a fine waterside setting on the Gulf of Morbihan, just south of Vannes; its outdoor dining terrace faces the bay. A 1990 visitor sheds oblique light on its odd English name: "We hugely enjoyed our stay. Half the rooms overlook a magnificent vista of maritime activity, and we spent much time gazing from our balcony. The building is like a good American motel: rooms were plain and smallish but warm and clean, with all mod cons. The food was delicious. The maître d' had worked in Houston, Texas and adopted the breezy way of that experience: we were amused, but a pair of upper-class Brits were outraged. The desk staff were tremendously helpful. *Le Roof* was awash with Americans and English." (*S Holman*)

Open All year.
Rooms 42 – all with bath and/or shower, telephone, TV.
Facilities Restaurant; conference facilities. Terrace; garden.
Location At Conleau, 4.5 km SW of Vannes.
Credit cards All major cards accepted.
Terms [1990 rates] Rooms: single 350 frs, double 620 frs. Breakfast 35 frs. Dinner, B&B 330–485 frs per person. Set lunch/dinner 140–320 frs. Special meals for children.

VENCE 06140 Alpes-Maritimes   Map 11

Relais Cantemerle   *Tel* 93.58.08.18
258 chemin Cantemerle   *Fax* 93.58.32.89

In a peaceful setting on the southern outskirts of much-visited Vence, this smart, modern hotel in local Provençal style, lyrically attractive, consists of a sequence of self-contained split-level apartments, set around a swimming pool and garden, beautifully landscaped, with lawns well manicured. Breezy modern decor with traditional touches. "An enormous room with a lovely antique bureau, very good dinner (perfect noisettes d'agneau), well-groomed staff (maybe a bit too laid-back). A peaceful, friendly ambience and fantastic value for money." (*K Jardine-Young*; endorsed this year by *Charles P Cords*)

Open 15 Mar–end Oct. Restaurant closed Wed except July and Aug.
Rooms 19 suites, 1 single – all with bath, shower, telephone, TV, mini-bar, terrace.
Facilities Lounge, bar, restaurant. Garden with unheated swimming pool; terrace, where meals are served.
Location 1 km S of Vence. Parking.
Restriction Not suitable for &.
Credit cards All major cards accepted.
Terms [1990 rates] Rooms 550–830 frs. Breakfast 60 frs. Dinner, B&B 250 frs added per person. Set dinner 200 frs. Extra bed 150 frs.

Hôtel Diana   *Tel* 93.58.28.56
Avenue des Poilus   *Fax* 93.24.64.06

Regulars continue to enjoy this well-run modern hotel near the centre of a busy Provençal town. Bowls of flowers, helpful staff – just one gripe about inadequate dusting of rooms. Not all rooms are spacious, but they are nicely designed and furnished, with well-equipped *cuisinettes* (washing up is part of the hotel's service). The underground garage is not easy to operate: take advice. Breakfasts are variously described as "generous" or "adequate". The hotel has no restaurant, but it will prepare snacks such as omelettes, while nearby the inexpensive *Farigoule* is commended. Do not miss Matisse's lovely Chapel of the Rosary in Vence itself (open Tuesdays and Thursdays only), nor the mountain drive to the north, the *circuit des clues*. (Endorsed this year by *KF Waynforth*)

Open All year.
Rooms 25 double – all with bath, telephone, TV; baby-listening on request. 15 with kitchenette.
Facilities Lift. 3 salons, bar, library, 2 breakfast rooms. Terrace; solarium.
Location 100 metres from town centre. Garage.
Restriction Not suitable for &.
Credit cards All major cards accepted.
Terms Rooms 300–340 frs. Breakfast 35 frs. (No restaurant.)

VERVINS 02140 Aisne   **Map 9**

La Tour du Roy `BUDGET`   *Tel* 23.98.00.11
45 rue du Général Leclerc   *Telex* 155445

A converted manor house, built on the ramparts of a small town near the Belgian border, in an area of orchards and streams. It is run with warmth and skill by Annie Desvignes, who is also chef: but again this year bedrooms have been admired less than the food (*Michelin* rosette). "Annie's robust and enthusiastic presence was obvious, and Monsieur, too, was full of bonhomie, while the staff were cheerful and attentive, especially with children. We have memories of a delicious light monkfish mousseline with prawn sauce, mixed fish with ginger sauce, and a cheese trolley that sent you to bed dreaming." That admirer returned later last year to find the service slow but the food "as supreme as ever, presented and overseen by a charming petite bustling lady who so enjoyed it all".

Others, who have also liked the food, have found some rooms "a bit basic" and poorly maintained. Not all, however, are basic: "When we asked for a 'nice' room, Madame said, 'We will put you in the Tower,' and opening our front door we found ourselves in an enormous circular bathroom with large near-circular bath, and a toilet which was literally a throne, made of decorative porcelain, with chair back and arm rests. We then climbed the spiral staircase to another circular room with a high-domed ceiling, a small decorative sink, and our bed. It was kitschy but comfortable." The hotel is exceptionally kind to children, and it has a pretty garden. (*Diana Cooper; M Wells*) Front rooms can be noisy.

Open All year except 15 Jan–15 Feb.
Rooms 1 triple, 13 double, 1 single – all with bath, shower, telephone, radio, TV, mini-bar, baby-listening. 2 ground-floor rooms in bungalow annexe.
Facilities Salon, bar, TV room, restaurant; functions room. Garden.
Location Vervins is off N2, 71 km N of Reims. Hotel is central. Parking.
Credit cards All major cards accepted.
Terms Rooms: single 200 frs, double 220–380 frs. Breakfast 40 frs. Dinner, B&B: single 390 frs, double 600–760 frs. Set lunch/dinner 150, 250 and 350 frs; full alc 350 frs. Reduced rates and special meals for children.

VÉZAC 24220 Dordogne   Map 10

Manoir de Rochecourbe   **BUDGET**   *Tel* 53.29.50.79

A small manor house amid lush meadows and gentle wooded hills, in the lovely Dordogne valley between Beynac and Domme. "We were delighted with this charming old house," says a recent letter. "We had a large, comfortable room and liked the beautifully furnished salon – such comfortable antiques are rare in French hotels. Service friendly and attentive." Others have spoken of the charm of the owners, the Rogers – "so nice and cheerful". "The old house has been restored with great care. Our spacious room looked out on three castles. Breakfasts are excellent." A spiral staircase in the tower leads from the garden (reclining chairs for drinks) up to the bedrooms. This quiet rural setting is only slightly marred by a nearby road and railway. No restaurant, but Madame will serve residents with light meals to order: "Excellent cooking, especially the warm salads of smoked duck breast, crisp skinned trout and luscious puddings." (*M and J Vella, Mrs JW Makinson, David Lees*)

Open 15 May–15 Oct.
Rooms 1 suite, 5 double – all with bath, shower, telephone.
Facilities Salon with TV, breakfast room. Garden.
Location 8 km SW of Sarlat on D57.
Credit cards Access, Visa.
Terms Rooms 300–400 frs. Breakfast 29 frs. 1-night bookings sometimes refused in high season. (No restaurant but light meals available.)

VÉZELAY 89450 Yonne   Map 10

L'Espérance   *Tel* 86.33.20.45
St-Père   *Fax* 86.33.26.15
                                                     Telex 800005

Just as the hilltop Romanesque basilica of Vézelay, in northern Burgundy, is one of France's 20 finest buildings, so Marc Meneau's *Espérance* is one of its 20 finest restaurants (three *Michelin* rosettes, four red *Gault Millau toques*). Small and very chic, it lies in a valley just east of the little town, on the Avallon road. Antique furniture, strikingly pretty bedrooms; a garden with a rose arbour and a stream lit up at night. Many bedrooms are in the nearby converted mill. "A warm greeting, and superb breakfast," says a reader this year. Recent applause (with some caveats): "Very expensive, but value for money; as near perfect a French hotel/restaurant as I know. Our suite in the mill displayed impeccable taste and luxury, the bathroom being the ultimate for any sybarite (it included a huge cactus). An immense basket of fruit was delivered. Service and reception are very welcoming and friendly, the food needless to say is superb, and breakfast (with scrambled eggs, etc) is the best we have had in France." "An attractive suite in the mill, with expensive if rather heavy rustic-style decor. In the dining room, looking on to the attractive garden, we enjoyed oysters in watercress aspic and brilliant salmon in apple sauce, but the puddings are lack-lustre." The restaurant is in three big glass pavilions full of house plants. "Sipping drinks on the terrace or in the glass-domed cocktail bar to the sound of a grand piano is a delight. Marc Meneau greets diners with a modest charm." (*Vicki Turner, Phillip Gill, Helen and Charles Priday, and others*) One couple felt that the hotel was becoming too commercial – tour coaches and a gift shop.

Open All year except early Jan–early Feb. Restaurant closed Tue, and Wed midday.
Rooms 4 suites, 17 double – all with bath, shower, telephone, radio, TV; baby-sitter on request. Air-conditioning. 8 rooms in annexe.
Facilities Lounge, bar, restaurant. Garden.
Location 3 km E of Vézelay on D957.
Credit cards Amex, Diners, Visa.
Terms [1990 rates] Rooms 600–1,100 frs. Breakfast 90 frs. Set lunch 280 frs, dinner 520 frs. Special meals for children.

Résidence Hôtel Le Pontot
Place du Pontot

Tel 86.33.24.40

This fine 15th-century stone house, with 18th-century additions, stands near the town centre with superb views over the rooftops and the rolling countryside below. It has long been the home of Charles Thum, an American architect, who has converted it into a select and charming bed-and-breakfast hotel, managed by Christian Abadie. "Attentive and erudite hosts, superb bedroom and breakfast." "We were treated with great courtesy. You enter through an arched doorway into a delightful walled garden; a stone-flagged spiral stairway leads up to the bedrooms which share a small, pleasant lounge. Our suite of two rooms and bathroom, ideal for a couple with children, was furnished with a mixture of antiques and simple modern pieces. Breakfast, beautifully presented with blue and gold Limoges china, can be taken in the garden or in a blue-panelled Louis XV salon; coffee and croissants were excellent." More reports requested.

Open 1 Apr–1 Nov.
Rooms 3 suites, 6 double, 1 single – all with bath and/or shower, telephone, radio. 1 suite in separate wing.

Facilities Entrance hall with boutique, lounge, bar, breakfast room. Walled garden with breakfast and bar service in fine weather. Canal trips, hot-air ballooning by prearrangement.
Location Central. Public parking.
Restriction Not suitable for &.
Credit cards All major cards accepted.
Terms Rooms: single 300 frs, double 500 frs, suite 700–850 frs. Breakfast 50 frs. Extra bed 100 frs for child sharing parents' room. (No restaurant.)

VIEILLE-TOULOUSE 31320 Haute-Garonne   Map 10

Hôtel de la Flânerie   *Tel* 61.73.39.12
Route de Lacroix-Falgarde CD4   *Fax* 61.73.18.56

An unusual hotel 10 km south of Toulouse along D4, on a hillside with a splendid view over the curving Garonne just below. The cosy bedrooms are got up in kitschy boudoir style, with a nicely naughty flavour. Period furnishings, affable and very helpful owners, sleek lounge, and a lovely terrace above the river where drinks and the (very good) breakfasts can be served. Swimming pool new this year. 12 rooms, all with bath and/or shower. B&B: single 235–345 frs, double 390–570 frs. No restaurant (but TV suppers served). Recent nomination. More reports welcome.

VILLEFRANCHE-SUR-MER 06230 Alpes-Maritimes   Map 11

Hôtel Welcome et Restaurant   *Tel* 93.76.76.93
  Le St-Pierre   *Fax* 93.01.88.81
1 quai Courbet   *Telex* 470281

Villefranche is a lively and colourful old fishing port on a deep bay – remarkably unspoilt, seeing that Nice and Monte Carlo are both so close. The *Welcome*, a classic and dignified hotel recently modernised, stands on the harbour opposite the tiny fishermen's chapel decorated by Cocteau. The top floor rooms, with bath and shower, resemble cabins, with copper, mahogany, etc. Recent visitors found the staff "charming" – and the food excellent. "Rooms reasonable, with harbourside balconies; the smaller ones at the top, though without bath, are the most quiet and pleasant." "A few faults, such as broken lamp-bulbs, but the food at the delightful ground-floor *St-Pierre* restaurant was exceptional, especially fish in a variety of ways." If you want a cheaper alternative for a meal, try *Ste-Germaine* down the quay, says a reader. (*Peter Wade, Brian MacArthur*) More reports please.

Open All year except 21 Nov–19 Dec.
Rooms 29 double, 3 single – all with bath and/or shower, telephone, mini-bar, air-conditioning; 20 with TV, baby-listening on request.
Facilities Lift, ramps. Breakfast room, bar with TV, restaurant. Terrace. 600 metres from beach; windsurfing, scuba diving etc.
Location Central, on quai. Parking nearby.
Credit cards All major cards accepted.
Terms B&B: single 300–710 frs, double 400–890 frs. Dinner, B&B 350–570 frs per person; full board 500–720 frs. Set lunch/dinner 150–248 frs; full alc 320 frs. Reduced rates for children; special meals on request.

VILLENEUVE-DE-RIVIÈRE 31800 Haute-Garonne   Map 10

Hostellerie des Cèdres   *Tel 61.89.36.00*

In a village just west of St-Gaudens, near the Pyrenean foothills, a stylishly converted 17th-century manor with cedars and palms in its wide courtyard. Garden with swimming pool. Large, pretty rooms. Good regional cooking (Gault Millau toque). *18 rooms, all with bath or shower, single 300–340 frs, double 370 frs. Set menus 135–390 frs. Recent nomination. More reports welcome.*

VILLENEUVE-LEZ-AVIGNON 30400 Gard   Map 11

Hostellerie le Prieuré   *Tel 90.25.18.20*
7 place du Chapitre   *Fax 90.25.45.39*
                                                        Telex 431042

The town of Villeneuve contains almost as much of interest as Avignon itself, directly across the Rhône. Relics of the great age when the popes held sway in their palace include the gigantic Chartreuse, the Fort St-André, the municipal museum (superb painting by Enguerrand Charenton) and the church of Notre-Dame with its remarkable carved ivory statuette of the Virgin. Next to this church is the 14th-century priory, well converted and run with panache by the Mille family as an elegant and sophisticated hotel. It looks out over fields and an ugly school building.

"I judge this to be the nearly perfect hotel," says a returning admirer. "It is larger and grander than when I knew it in the old days, but the Milles have managed to keep an air of informality, and service is excellent. The garden is pleasant and the big shady terrace delightful. The food is not of the highest flight but good and reliable." (*Jacquetta Priestley*) Others have written: "A superb place, expensive but not unfairly so. We had lovely rooms in a new block, with balconies facing the pool. Dinner by candle-light on the lawn under the plane trees is most romantic." "Food, mainly *nouvelle*, served with a theatrical flourish." (*SF Riddell, Vicki Turner, and others*) You can choose between a "characterful" bedroom in the old building (antiques, but modern bathrooms) or a larger, more expensive one in a new annexe (wide balcony, big sofas). Noise from a nearby railway has irritated some readers.

Open 10 Mar–10 Nov. Restaurant closed 1 May.
Rooms 10 suites, 19 double, 7 single – all with bath (16 also have shower), telephone, radio, TV, air-conditioning. Some with access for &.
Facilities Lift. 2 salons, bridge room, library, bar, breakfast room, dining room, dining patio. Large garden with 2 tennis courts, swimming pool.
Location 3 km N of Avignon. In village centre, behind the church. Carpark.
Credit cards All major cards accepted.
Terms B&B: single 555 frs, double 630–1,150 frs, suite 1,750 frs; dinner, B&B: single 804 frs, double 1,455–1,645 frs, suite 2,215 frs. Set lunch/dinner 240–390 frs; full alc 400 frs. Special meals for children on request.

We asked hotels to estimate their 1991 tariffs. About a quarter of the hotels on the Continent failed to reply, so the prices we quote should not be relied upon.

VONNAS 01540 Ain   Map 10

Hôtel-Restaurant Georges Blanc   *Tel* 74.50.00.10
                                                      Fax 74.50.08.80
                                                      Telex 380776

"As always, our welcome was warm and the food superlative. The sheer
hard work and professionalism of all concerned never cease to amaze us"
– a comment this year from seasoned travellers, revisiting M Blanc's
famous and sophisticated hotel/restaurant (three *Michelin* rosettes, four
red *Gault Millau toques*). Half-timbered and pink-bricked, it stands in
pretty countryside beside a river on the edge of a quiet *village fleuri* east of
Mâcon. Another 1990 report: "The *dégustation menu* was ambrosial,
service impeccable and the ambience delightful – unspoilt and natural
despite the *grand luxe*. Only the bedroom, with its heavy furniture and
nowhere to put the breakfast tray, disappointed." Rooms vary in
grandeur, and one reader reports noisy plumbing; most overlook the
pretty river. An 11-room annexe was added last year, as the stunningly
successful M Blanc expands steadily – and one reader, while still finding it
"a marvellous experience", is nostalgic for the days when this was just a
simple local place with marvellous cuisine: "Now it is much more
international." But what excellence! Frog's legs in warm chervil cream
and pancake with salmon and caviar have been singled out this year.
"Georges Blanc *is* Vonnas, with two shops in the village selling his
provisions and souvenirs. But there's a refreshing candour about his
enterprise. His chefs can be seen at work as you walk through the kitchen
to the large elegant dining room with its beamed ceiling, antiques and
tapestries." A "winter garden" – a bar/lounge area, which can become a
riverside terrace in summer, but with a roaring log fire in winter – has
recently been added. (*Pat and Jeremy Temple, M and D Chambers, Mrs Ann
Thornton*)

Open All year except 2 Jan–8 Feb.
Rooms 5 suites, 22 double, 3 single – all with bath or shower, telephone, TV,
mini-bar, air-conditioning. 11 in annexe. 10 more in new annexe planned for
1990.
Facilities Lift. 2 lounges, breakfast room, bar, dining room; conference room;
winter garden, terrace on river Veyle. 2½-acre grounds with tennis court, putting-
green, swimming pool and helipad.
Location 20 km E of Mâcon. From N leave *autoroute* at Mâcon Nord; from S at
Villefranche, then direction Châtillon-sur-Chalaronne, Neuville-les-Dames and
Vonnas.
Credit cards All major cards accepted.
Terms Rooms 450–1,300 frs, suite 1,500–2,700 frs. Breakfast 70 frs. Set meals
350–540 frs. Special meals for children.

WIERRE-EFFROY 62720 Pas-de-Calais   Map 9

Ferme-Auberge du Vert   BUDGET   *Tel* 21.92.82.10

Just off the Calais–Boulogne main road, in a truly rural setting, this
charming *Logis de France* is a converted farm, with a farmyard still full of
ducks and geese – so it provides visitors with an opportunity to move
straight from the hassle of hovercraft and ferries into the bosom of French
country life. Again in 1989/90 readers have been delighted: "A warm
welcome from the Bernard family. Rooms simple but clean, dinner simple

but delicious." "Our huge room was wonderful. It overlooked the
chicken-yard and orchard. The din of roosters woke us up in the morning
– that was our favourite part. The breakfast room was charming, full of
kittens and a dog." "M Bernard is a genial host." The pine-clad rooms
fashioned from converted barns are fairly small and a bit basic, but they
are very clean and good value. One reader loved sleeping in a
modernised hayloft. Breakfasts are admired, too. The restaurant is
separately managed (but the Bernards' son is chef): it gets very crowded
with local French at weekends and in high summer, when service can be
slow and muddled, but the food is still approved by readers as sound and
unpretentious, not aiming at high gastronomy. (*S Gates, Jessica Golden, MA
Godfrey, and many others*)

Open All year except Jan, Christmas, New Year. Restaurant closed Sun evening
and Mon.
Rooms 3 suites, 13 double – all with bath and/or shower, telephone; 2 with TV.
4 ground-floor rooms.
Facilities Salon with TV, bar, restaurant, breakfast room; banqueting room.
Garden with golf practice. Bicycle hire.
Location Off N1 between Calais (N) and Boulogne (S); SE of Marquise. Follow
signs for Ferme-Auberge from Marquise and from Hypermarket Auchan.
Credit cards Access, Visa.
Terms Rooms 260–400 frs, suite 450–500 frs. Breakfast 32 frs. Full alc 160 frs.
Reduced rates and special meals for children.

***

****

Traveller's tale *We arrived by night at a splendid modern resthouse in
this far corner of Cappadocia. We negotiated dinner without difficulty
from the voluble maître d' who had worked for some years in a Wimpy bar
in South London. Getting a room proved more difficult; it depended how
the owner felt, and making him feel good proved to be our evening's
chore. We were alone in the restaurant listening to Turkish music when
the owner came out of his office, somewhat drunk, and sat hunched over
a raki. The maître d' whispered that we might get a room if we acted jolly
and suggested that we danced. So we got up and did a Turkish dance
suitably instructed and led by the maître d'. Then we had to take
photographs of the depressed owner and even kiss him on the cheeks.
Only sheer exhaustion and the prospect of a night sleeping in the car
prompted us to do this, but we managed. Finally, the maître d' whispered
that we had the room. No palace this: thin mattress, few blankets, lumpy
pillows, and the bathroom (the staff washroom it transpired) stank. We
stayed two days. The area was magical – a piece of the Garden of Eden –
the resthouse was in its way restful, if bizarrely managed, the food was
good, and the owner's manic depression did not dampen the maître d's
antics.*

****

Germany

Pension Hotel Sassenhof

Unlike in the UK and US, chain hotels are not at all numerous in Germany. At the upper end of the market, the principal German chains are Steigenberger and Maritim, followed by Scandia Crown; some foreign chains are also represented, such as Crest, Holiday Inn and Mercure. Hotels of this kind are generally efficient, but impersonal, and very large. None of them features in this Guide.

In fact nearly all German hotels, including the smaller hotels of character that we prefer, are individually owned and run. Some of these, as in France, group together for joint promotion and marketing. Probably the best is *Romantik Hotels*, an association of mostly upper–medium price hotels, nearly all in old buildings with some character and atmosphere. Many are extremely attractive, and they are seldom formal or pretentious. *Gast im Schloss*, another good association, consists of well-converted castles, some still run by their family owners; several of these, too, feature in this book. The large *Ring Hotel* association is quite diverse; it includes some dullish city hotels for businessfolk, and also very attractive ones, such as the wonderful old *Zum Roten Bären* in Freiburg (q.v.). The *Silencehotels*, part of the French *Relais du Silence* group, are quiet hotels, often in secluded settings. The German *Michelin* guide may give such a place a red rocking-chair; and as in France it will bestow red print on a hotel whose looks or atmosphere it finds especially pleasant.

Standards of service and cleanliness tend to be very high in Germany, even in the cheapest hotels. There are some peculiarities, however, that may puzzle a first-time visitor. As in most of Central Europe, duvets (*Federbetten* or down-comforters) are universally used in place of top sheets and blankets. German beds tend to be rather hard, with small, thin pillows, for this is considered healthy. Most double rooms have twin beds, often placed close together to form one bed. In many hotels, a chocolate or sweet will be left on the bed as a tiny goodnight gift. Soap and shampoo are not usually provided in guest houses. Breakfast is generally a buffet, included in the room price. Service is always included in the bill; you need not leave anything extra for room service, though in a restaurant it is customary to give a tip of about 2–3 percent direct to the waiter or waitress when paying the bill.

As in France, we make a point of indicating when a hotel has won an award from *Michelin* for its cuisine. The top rating of three rosettes is given to only three restaurants in all Germany (compared with 19 in France); even one rosette indicates food of high quality. We also indicate when a hotel wins a red "Menu", the equivalent of the coveted red "R" in France for "good food at moderate prices".

ALFDORF 7077 Baden-Württemberg   Map 13

Haghof Hotel-Restaurant   *Tel* (07182) 5 45
                                               Telex 7246712

In pleasant Swabian countryside east of Stuttgart, near Schwäbisch Gmünd, a modern purpose-built hotel whose spacious rooms have balconies and local-style wooden furniture; good Swabian cooking and buffet breakfast. Swimming pool; golf course next door. 50 rooms, all with bath. B&B double 125–145 DM. Alc meals (excluding wine) 42–70 DM [1990]. Recent nomination. More reports welcome.

ALT-DUVENSTEDT 2371 Schleswig-Holstein   Map 13

Hotel Töpferhaus   *Tel* (04338) 3 33
Am Bistensee

Go north across the pastoral Schleswig plain from the pleasant old town of Rendsburg (16th-century *Rathaus*), and you'll find this handsome rural hotel: reached down a drive through woods, it is an attractive white-painted building with thatched roof, on a bluff above a lake. Inside, there are Persian rugs on the floor, a comfortable lounge, and sizeable bedrooms. A reader this year had "a charming room and good meal"; others last year wrote of "excellent" food and a "kindly proprietor". Local specialities include labskaus, the traditional sailor's dish of North Germany – a hash of pickled meat, herring and potato with fried eggs, tasting a bit like a pickled shepherd's pie. (*C and M Hédoin, Russell W Field Jnr, TH Monteith*)

Open All year. Restaurant closed Mon.
Rooms 10 double, 11 single – all with bath, shower, telephone, radio, TV.
Facilities Hall, lounge, breakfast room, 2 restaurants. Garden with terrace, tennis. Sauna, solarium. On lake with swimming and sailing.
Location 12 km N of Rendsburg; leave *Autobahn* at Rendsburg-Nord if coming from S, at Owschlag if coming from N. Hotel is at S end of Bistensee. Do *not* go towards town of Bistensee on N side of lake.
Credit cards None accepted.
Terms Rooms: single 70–95 DM, double 120–140 DM. Breakfast 15 DM. Dinner, B&B: single 120–145 DM, double 185–205 DM. Set lunch 30 DM, dinner 60 DM; full alc 60 DM. Reduced rates and special meals for children.

ASPERG 7144 Baden-Württemberg   Map 13

Hotel Adler Ottenbacher   *Tel* (07141) 6 30 01
Stuttgarter Strasse 2   *Fax* (07141) 6 30 06
                    Telex 7264603

In a small town near Ludwigsburg, a half-timbered old hostelry with modern extensions, family run. Friendly, cheerful staff; very good food (snail soup and other Swabian delicacies). Heated indoor pool. 64 rooms, all with bath and/or shower. B&B: single 143 DM, double 190 DM. Set meals 50–60 DM. Re-nominated this year. More reports please.

AUERBACH 8572 Bayern   Map 13

Romantik Hotel Goldener Löwe   *Tel* (09643) 17 65
Unterer Markt 9   *Fax* (09643) 46 70
                    Telex 631404

"This ordinary little North Bavarian town used to be an iron-mining centre, and the theme is studiously reflected in the decor of this pleasant traditional inn: an old black mining cart stands in the foyer, and one part of the restaurant has been done up to look like a mine-shaft, with mining lamps hanging from the ceiling and the back wall made of rough iron-ore. A gimmick, if you like, but a true reflection of local tradition. It's claimed that an inn has stood on this spot since 1144 – almost since the Iron Age! – but today this Golden Lion is nicely modernised, with comfortable rooms, and heavy furnishings in the Bavarian style. The friendly Ruder family have owned the place since 1847. Service is smilingly willing, if not always expert; the local cuisine is good, if hardly sophisticated – Schweinebraten with dumplings, etc." (JA)

Open All year except Christmas and 6–20 Jan.
Rooms 2 suites, 16 double, 5 single – all with bath, shower, telephone, radio, TV, mini-bar.
Facilities Lift. Bar, 3 dining rooms; conference facilities.
Location Central. Parking. Auerbach is 42 km SE of Bayreuth.
Restriction Not suitable for &.
Credit cards All major cards accepted.
Terms B&B: single 110 DM, double 170 DM, suite 338 DM; dinner, B&B 30 DM added per person. Set lunch/dinner 23–48 DM; full alc 35–110 DM. Reduced rates and special meals for children.

AYING 8011 Bayern　　　　　　　　　　　　　　　Map 13

Brauereigasthof Hotel Aying　　　　　　　　　*Tel* (08095) 7 05
Zornedinger Strasse 2　　　　　　　　　　　　　　*Fax* (08095) 88 50

A big creeper-covered pub, very traditional, right next to a famous brewery in a picturesque flower-decked village SE of Munich, where commuters and dairy farmers rub shoulders. Large airy bedrooms with Biedermeier furniture; walloping great breakfasts, served with beer if you wish. Good food served indoors or in the courtyard: some delicate dishes, as well as the usual hefty pork-based Bavarian ones. And beer, beer, beer ... Closed 14 Jan–1 Feb. 18 rooms (more due in 1991), all with bath or shower. B&B double 170–190 DM. Meals 30–80 DM. Recent nomination. More reports welcome.

BAD BERGZABERN 6748 Rheinland-Pfalz　　　　　　Map 13

Hotel-Pension Pfälzer Wald　　　　　　　　　　*Tel* (06343) 10 56
Kurtalstrasse 77

Renaissance buildings and a modern spa centre are features of this small, neat town at the southern end of the Pfalz *Weinstrasse*, just east of the strange red crags of the Wasgau and the ruined clifftop castles of Altdahn. This traditional family hotel stands beside a lake, with green hills behind, and is liked for its warm welcome and "good fish, salads and sweet pancakes". "A good base for a comfortable holiday, and excellent value. Our room was spacious and clean, the cooking was plain but good, buffet breakfasts were copious." (*Ronald S McNeill, Mary Clark*) Some rooms are small and a bit basic, and not all are quiet: the hotel is on a busy main road.

Open All year. Restaurant closed Jan–23 Feb.
Rooms 10 double, 16 single – all with shower, telephone, TV.
Facilities Lounge, TV room, wine bar, dining room, restaurant; functions room; terrace. Large garden by lake.
Location About 1 km W of town centre; 38 km NW of Karlsruhe. Parking.
Restriction Not suitable for &.
Credit cards Access, Visa.
Terms [1990 rates] B&B 45–60 DM; half board 63–78 DM. Alc meals (excluding wine) 21.50–43 DM. Reduced rates and special meals for children.

BAD HERRENALB 7506 Baden-Württemberg　　　　　　Map 13

Mönch's Posthotel　　　　　　　　　　　　　*Tel* (07083) 74 40
Doblerstrasse 2　　　　　　　　　　　　　　　　*Fax* (07083) 7 44 22
　　　　　　　　　　　　　　　　　　　　　　　Telex 7245123

The first hotel that our Continental Editor and his wife ever visited together remains happily unchanged, as they found on a recent visit. Nor are they its only admirers. "Expensive but worth the cost, with a superb restaurant." "Elegant, yet intimate and cosy." So run the latest reports on the Mönch family's smart and stylish old, half-timbered, flower-decked *Posthotel*, at a crossroads in the centre of a Black Forest spa town. The setting is less urban than this may suggest, for the hotel also has an outdoor swimming pool and large and graceful gardens leading to a river

Bedrooms are large and well equipped. The lovely dining room has beamed ceilings, wood panelling and several discreet alcoves. The food, beautifully prepared and presented, tends towards *nouvelle cuisine* and is judged worthy of its *Michelin* rosette. Service was affable. The breakfast buffet was "the most lavish we have found in Germany – and that's saying something. All in all, a romantic place – despite the prevalence of rich businessmen." (*William A Grant; JA and KA*) But front rooms facing the noisy road should be avoided, and service can be slow.

Open All year.
Rooms 2 suites, 23 double, 14 single – all with bath and/or shower, telephone, radio, T V, baby-listening.
Facilities Lift. Salon, T V room, bar, restaurant, breakfast terrace; conference facilities; beauty parlour. Garden with heated swimming pool.
Location Central. (Road-facing rooms can be noisy.) Parking.
Restriction Not suitable for &.
Credit cards All major cards accepted.
Terms B&B: single 95–160 DM, double 150–240 DM, suite 300–400 DM. Breakfast 18 DM. Set lunch 40 DM, dinner 80–130 DM; full alc 80 DM.

BAD HERSFELD 6430 Hessen   Map 13

Romantik Hotel Zum Stern   *Tel* (06621) 18 90
Linggplatz 11   *Fax* (06621) 6 55 52

This sizeable spa town close to the Kassel–Würzburg *Autobahn* contains the ruins of a Benedictine monastery; the *Zum Stern*, now in the spa's pedestrian zone, was once the part of that monastery used to house its secular guests. A recent view: "A hotel of real class, its neat flowery window-boxes overlooking the market square. Our room was in the old building, with antique furniture; the modern extension includes the covered swimming pool. Welcome slightly impersonal, but the meals were excellent, especially salmon soup with caviare and côte d'agneau en croûte. A feast of a breakfast served in a warren of tiny rooms." (*Rev Michael Bourdeaux*)

Open All year except 1–19 Jan. Restaurant closed Fri midday, Christmas and New Year.
Rooms 2 suites, 25 double, 5 single – all with bath and/or shower, telephone, radio, T V; baby-listening on request.
Facilities Lift. Lounge with T V, 2 restaurants; conference facilities. Indoor swimming pool.
Location Central, in pedestrian area. Parking. Bad Hersfeld is 69 km S of Kassel.
Credit cards All major cards accepted.
Terms B&B: single 75–95 DM, double 158–210 DM, suite 185–210 DM; dinner, B&B 30 DM added per person. Set lunch/dinner 22–65 DM. Reduced rates and special meals for children.

BAD MERGENTHEIM 6990 Baden-Württemberg   Map 13

Haus Bundschu   *Tel* (07931) 30 43
Cronbergstrasse 15   *Fax* (07931) 30 46

Bad Mergentheim, on the Romantic Road south-west of Würzburg, in the Tauber valley, has a 16th-century castle of the Teutonic Order and is also a thriving spa centre. "The delightful *Bundschu* naturally has its share of the *Kurgäste* who go in their millions to popular spa resorts such as this:

the Germans are the world's most assiduous spa-cure addicts. But we found it far removed from the usual image of a spa hotel: it's cosy, inviting, informal, run very cheerfully by the kindly Bundschu family, Swabians all, and in summer it gets lots of ordinary tourists too. It's a *Relais du Silence*, set in the outskirts of the town beside fields and woods. A spacious, rambling modern building – no beauty – but the rooms are very comfortable (with unusual brass bed-lamps, resembling old gas-lamps), and the big rustic-style dining room is pretty. Good Maultaschen soup and other Swabian dishes (a red *'Menu'* in *Michelin* for good value, equivalent of its 'R' in France) and a sumptuous buffet breakfast. The hotel has its own spa facilities, such as fango.'' (*JA and KA*)

Open 15 Feb–15 Jan. Restaurant closed Mon.
Rooms 5 suites, 20 double, 40 single – all with bath, shower, telephone, radio, TV. Some ground-floor rooms.
Facilities Lift. Bar, restaurant, TV room; functions room. Garden. Spa cure facilities.
Location In outskirts, parking. Town is 53 km SW of Würzburg.
Credit cards All major cards accepted.
Terms B&B single 75–85 DM, double 120–130 DM, suite 150–160 DM; half board 30 DM added. Set lunch/dinner 28–50 DM; full alc 50 DM. Reduced rates and special meals for children.

BADEN-BADEN 7570 Baden-Württemberg　　　　　　　Map 13

Hotel "Der Kleine Prinz"	*Tel* (07221) 34 64
Lichtentaler Strasse 36	*Fax* (07221) 3 82 64
(entrance Du-Russel Strasse)	*Telex* 781433

A Victorian building in the town centre, now possibly the most elegant and appealing of Baden-Baden's many small hotels: it is owned and run by a charming and sophisticated couple, Norbert and Edeltraud Rademacher, who spent 22 years in the US (he was catering director of the *New York Hilton* and *Waldorf Astoria*), and today many guests are cultivated Americans travelling individually. Several recent customers were very satisfied. ''We adored this lovely hotel, whose owners truly care about their guests. Dinner was outstanding.'' ''Our supper party went superbly, and the pillows were the most comfortable we slept on in Europe.'' ''Intimate and classical, with pleasant modern touches, such as the charming motif of the carrot-mopped, blue-cloaked *Kleine Prinz* that appears in every room – but the hotel has *no* connection with St-Exupéry; its name was chosen at random by the Rademachers. Elegant decor in the salon and restaurant, where food and service are both stylish. We had a lovely suite, with bathroom in grey marble and the thickest bath-foam I've ever seen, covering us so that we emerged from the bath looking like Alps!'' (*David Pritchard, A and D Stewart, and others*) A new tunnel under the town now diverts through-traffic: back rooms are quietest.

Open All year.
Rooms 10 suites, 17 double, 6 single – all with bath and/or shower, telephone, radio, TV; some with air-conditioning. Ground-floor rooms.
Facilities Lift. Lobby/bar, library, restaurant.
Location Central. Parking.
Credit cards All major cards accepted.
Terms B&B: single 150–200 DM, double 200–300 DM, suite 300–350 DM. Set lunch/dinner 65 DM; full alc 75 DM. Children under 16 sharing parents' room free of charge; special meals.

BAMBERG 8600 Bayern	Map 13

Böttingerhaus and	*Tel* (0951) 5 40 74
Gästehaus Steinmühle	*Fax* (0951) 5 20 80
Judenstrasse 14	*Telex* 662946

A baroque mansion (1713) in the heart of old Bamberg, converted into an ambitious restaurant and cultural centre, run by its resident Franco-German owners. Bedrooms are in two nearby annexes on the river, one a converted millhouse (quietest rooms are those not facing the roaring millstream). A third annexe due to open in 1991. Much admired in 1988/89 for its food, ambience and furnishings; this year, breakfasts judged meagre, cooking variable, some bedrooms ordinary – but staff delightful. 23 rooms (35 from April 1991). B&B: single 110–140 DM, double 180–200 DM. Set meals 55–95 DM. Criticisms in 1990. More reports welcome.

Hotel Sankt Nepomuk	*Tel* (0951) 2 51 83
Obere Mühlbrücke 9	

This picturesque and appealing hotel in the old town stands on stilts on the river Regnitz between the rushing millraces. It belongs to an affluent Catholic foundation which has managed the conversion with fastidious taste, notably the big restaurant on two floors with its curving stone stairway and picture-windows facing the river. Readers this year have again admired the "marvellous situation, relaxed atmosphere and food well above average". A previous account: "We enjoyed fresh tomato soup with mushrooms and gin (sic), roast leg of lamb with herbs, and excellent vegetables. The cooking remains ambitious but not pretentious, with generous helpings, and is delightfully and skilfully served by young people. Try Bamberg's curious 'smoky beer' made from smoked malt. The special glass of our bathroom window gave out a dazzling prismatic light effect; glow-worms darted and shone above the river; and we were lulled to sleep by the therapeutic roar of the millrace – to awaken next day to a sumptuous buffet breakfast, served in a lovely room with cheerful modern murals of local scenes." (*Ralph B Robertson, William Rodgers*) Bedrooms, varying in size, some a touch spartan, are in modern Scandinavian style. But not all windows have prismatic dazzle and the glow-worms are often off-duty. One visitor this year was critical of upkeep, design and management.

Open All year.
Rooms 10 double, 2 single – all with bath, shower, telephone, radio, TV, mini-bar.
Facilities Lift. Bar, café, 2 restaurants; conference facilities.
Location Central. Do *not* try to drive car up to hotel (narrow streets); leave it in public carpark in Geyerswörthstrasse just across river.
Credit cards Access, Diners, Visa.
Terms B&B: single occupancy 90–110 DM, double 140–160 DM. Set lunch/dinner 65–80 DM; full alc 60 DM. Reduced rates and special meals for children.

We asked hotels to estimate their 1991 tariffs some time before publication so the rates given are often guesswork. Please always check terms with hotels when making bookings.

BAYREUTH 8580 Bayern   Map 13

Bayerischer Hof   *Tel* (0921) 2 20 81
Bahnhofstrasse 14   *Fax* (0921) 2 20 85
                                                               Telex 642737

A post-war building near the station, outwardly dull-looking but
probably the best of Bayreuth's hotels, owned by the Seuss family since
1918. Rooms are large, quiet and well furnished; the rooftop restaurant
has an outdoor terrace for summer, and serves local dishes. The heated
indoor pool and rooftop bar are also liked. Endorsements this year: "A
friendly welcome, excellent service, food very good." "Super breakfasts."
(*William J and Rosemary B Dircks, JD Eagles*)

Open All year. Restaurant closed for lunch 2–21 Jan and all Sun.
Rooms 2 suites, 34 double, 19 single – all with bath, shower, telephone, TV.
Facilities Lift. Lounge, TV room, 2 restaurants, roof-garden terrace; conference
room. Indoor swimming pool and sauna.
Location Central, opposite station. Garage.
Restriction Not suitable for &.
Credit cards Access, Diners, Visa.
Terms B&B: single 90–150 DM, double 165–250 DM. Full alc 50 DM.

BAYREUTH-SEULBITZ 8580 Bayern   Map 13

Waldhotel Stein   *Tel* (0921) 90 01
                                                               Fax (0921) 9 47 25

Seulbitz is an attractive village just east of Bayreuth (you can see the
floodlit *Festspielhaus* from your window). Here Frau Stein's peaceful
modern family hotel continues to be commended for its "above average"
cooking (most of the ingredients are organically produced locally) and
"beautifully appointed, scrupulously clean", spacious rooms – some are
bedsitters with balcony, some are in bungalows in the large garden.
Swimming pool; very efficient service. A new bungalow with a luxurious
bridal penthouse and eight other suites has just been built. (*Philip A True,
C and M Hédoin, Bill and Marty Jewell*)

Open All year except 20 Dec–10 Jan.
Rooms 10 suites, 30 double, 6 single, 2 penthouses – all with bath and/or shower,
telephone, radio, TV. Ground-floor rooms.
Facilities Lounge, breakfast room, 2 restaurants; conference facilities. Indoor
heated swimming pool, sauna, solarium, massage. Large grounds.
Location 6 km E of Bayreuth, near Seulbitz village; follow signs for Eremitage.
Parking.
Credit cards All major cards accepted.
Terms B&B: single 58–120 DM, double 96–196 DM, suite 240 DM, penthouse
500 DM. (Prices increase hugely during opera festival period.) Set lunch/dinner
28.50–45 DM. Reduced rates and special meals for children.

BAYRISCHZELL 8163 Bayern   Map 13

Romantik Hotel Die Meindelei   *Tel* (08023) 3 18
Michael-Meindl Strasse 13

Bayrischzell is a pleasant hiking and skiing resort in the Bavarian Alps, at
the foot of the rocky Wendelstein peak (go up it by cable-car for roof-of-

the-world views). The *Meindelei*, in a quiet location backed by pinewoods, is named after a local writer, the late Michael Meindl: "It is run by his perfectionist, fiercely hardworking daughter and her quieter husband. The heavily rustic Bavarian decor might not suit all tastes (lots of painted cupboards, china stoves, folk objects, bowls of plastic fruit in the dining room) but it's comfortable, spruce and well run. First-class, sophisticated cooking by the Swabian son-in-law of the owners (paprika soup with cream, delicious mixed salad with pine nuts, rare roast venison), all daintily presented but not too *nouvelle*. Some rooms are in the main buildings, others in bungalows in the big tree-filled garden. A small heated pool is free to guests, and there's a bigger public pool next door." (*JA and KA*) Visitors in 1990 liked the cooking, but disliked the menu's lack of choice and the slow service, and thought that refurbishing was needed.

Open All year except 2 weeks after Easter and 15 Oct–20 Dec. Restaurant closed for lunch and Tue.
Rooms 17 – all with bath and/or shower, telephone. 5 bungalows in garden.
Facilities Lounge, bar, restaurant. Indoor swimming pool, sauna. Garden; terrace for meals.
Location Fairly central; parking. Bayrischzell is 77 km SE of Munich.
Credit cards All major cards accepted.
Terms [1990 rates] B&B: single 85–95 DM, double 135–175 DM; dinner, B&B 98–113 DM per person. Set dinner 30–68 DM.

BEILSTEIN 5591 Rheinland-Pfalz   **Map 13**

Hotel Haus Lipmann   BUDGET   *Tel* (02673) 15 73

Metternich was the last overlord of this picturesque village in the Mosel valley, and his castle stands on the hill above. To the south is the wooded plateau of the Hunsrück where Edgar Reitz set and filmed his 16-hour masterpiece *Heimat*. Admired again this year, the "characterful and atmospheric" *Lipmann* is an unpretentious family-run half-timbered *Gasthof* in the tiny village square. "Our rooms were quaint, but comfortable, and our window opened on to a view of the river." Some rooms are in a modern annexe amid trees; others, newly renovated but smaller, are in the charming old *Alte Zollhaus* annexe (both annexes are now under separate management, but within the same family). Interesting dishes such as smoked Mosel eel with scrambled eggs are served generously in a baronial hall: "Food good if not inspired," said a reader this year. Opposite is the hotel's lovely old vaulted pub where you can drink wine with locals; or you can drink on a terrace facing the river. (*Dr CH Clark, GY Craig, Mrs AJ Goodwin*)

Open 15 Mar–15 Nov.
Rooms 5 double – all with shower, TV. (20 others in annexes, see text above.)
Facilities Restaurant; conference/functions facilities; wine cellar (wine tastings held); terrace on Mosel.
Location Central, near market place. Parking.
Credit cards None accepted.
Terms [1990 rates] B&B: single 65 DM, double 85 DM; dinner B&B 15 DM per person added; full board 22 DM added. Full alc 47 DM. Special meals for children on request.

Please make a habit of sending a report if you stay at a Guide hotel.

BERCHTESGADEN 8240 Bayern   Map 13

Hotel Krone   `BUDGET`   *Tel* (08652) 6 20 51
Am Rad 5

Few German resorts are more teemingly popular than Berchtesgaden.
Hitler's eyrie has been rased to the ground and only its ghosts remain; but
the mountains and alpine lakes are gorgeous, and a guided tour of the
extraordinary salt-mines is not to be missed. This unpretentious hotel,
attractively white-walled and blue-shuttered, and furnished in local rustic
style, stands on a hill just outside the town, aloof from the madding
throng. "In a town where all other hotels seem large and package-tour
orientated, here's just the kind of small, idiosyncratic but wholly
delightful place that should appeal to readers. All its good rooms away
from the road open on to communal balconies facing the valley and hills.
Ours was fairly small, but snug and wood-panelled, and the house is full
of Bavarian hand-painted furniture. The Grafe family gave us a warm
welcome, and they provide good home cooking. Frau Grafe dresses quite
naturally in Bavarian costume as she serves in the dining room." (*Angela
and David Stewart*)

Open All year except 29 Oct–20 Dec. Closed Mon from noon.
Rooms 2 suites, 6 double, 16 single – 3 with bath, 21 with shower, all with
telephone, TV.
Facilities Lounge, restaurant; terrace.
Location 1 km N of town centre, off Salzburg road. Parking.
Credit cards None accepted.
Terms B&B: single 65–75 DM, double 120–150 DM. Half board 12 DM per person
added; full alc 30 DM.

BERLIN 1000   Map 13

Hotel Belvedere   *Tel* (030) 826 10 77
Seebergsteig 4, Grunewald
Berlin 33

"Not the place to stay if you want the nightlife of the Ku'damm", but four
kilometres to its west, in a quiet and leafy side street of the smart and
aptly named suburb of Grunewald (it is next to a forest that leads to the
big Havel lake). This turn-of-the-century villa has been liked again in
1990: "Not luxurious but pleasantly attractive. Lovely garden, nice
breakfast and management." Others have mentioned the thickness of the
feather duvets and the welcome to small children. "Stylish bedrooms
with antique cane and wood furniture. Public rooms have the air of a
bourgeois private house. Peaceful, relaxed, unpretentious." But while
some rooms are large and sunny, basement ones may be gloomy. (*Bill and
Mary Jewell, EW Smallwood, Stephanie and Bryan Lorge*) One American
visitor reported an ambivalent reception. No restaurant, but there are
some nearby such as the lakeside *Chalet Corniche*. Or bus 19, five minutes'
walk, will take you to the city centre. Visit the fabulous Dahlem
museums, nearby.

Open All year.
Rooms 12 double, 7 single – 10 with bath, 2 with shower, all with telephone,
radio, TV; baby-sitter on request.
Facilities Salon with TV, breakfast room. Garden. Sauna, solarium.
Location In Grunewald, 4 km SW of city centre.

Restriction Not suitable for &.
Credit cards Access, Diners, Visa.
Terms [1990 rates] Rooms: single 73–98 DM, double 106–146 DM. Breakfast
8 DM. Reduced rates for children. (No restaurant.)

Schlosshotel Gehrhus   *Tel* (030) 826 20 81
Brahmsstrasse 4–10
Berlin 33

Also set in suburban Grunewald (see above), this unusual hotel evokes a
Berlin long vanished. It was built as a private palace in 1910 by a rich
society lawyer and art-collector who was the Kaiser's personal attorney,
and it became a rendezvous of high society. Its ornate public rooms,
though today a bit run-down, remain striking – the huge hall in Italian
renaissance style, the picture gallery, the lovely library with its hand-
painted ceiling. Ambience and upkeep were so strongly criticised that it
lost its place in the 1990 Guide. This year, however, four out of five
reports have been favourable. "Quite a weird hotel, full of eccentricities,
but clean, friendly and efficient." "Lovely rooms with antique furnishings, a beautiful breakfast, and courteous staff." "Breakfast an ample
buffet. My room very small but comfortable." (*Amanda Garrett, Cathryn
Bryck, Carol Callahan, JD Eagles*) Meals can be taken in the garden, where
an inspector thought the food dull; he also found the ambience chilly and
stilted. The place is used for society parties and weddings, and the salons
are full of photos of its glamorous past. Some readers feel it is still living
in that past. More reports please.

Open All year.
Rooms 5 suites, 14 double, 16 single – 27 with bath and shower, all with
telephone; some with radio, TV.
Facilities Lift. Salons, bar, restaurant; conference facilities. Garden; terrace.
Location 4 km SW of city centre. Garage, parking.
Credit cards Amex, Diners, Visa.
Terms [1990 rates] B&B: single 90–135 DM, double 120–205 DM. Dinner, B&B
25 DM per person added; full board 50 DM added.

Hecker's Hotel   *Tel* (030) 8 89 00
Grolmanstrasse 35   *Fax* (030) 8 89 02 60
Berlin 12   *Telex* 184954

*A friendly, well-run modern hotel (with garage) just off the Ku'damm, very
central. Good traditional German dishes at modest prices (with a Westphalian
accent) served in the big lamp-lit Stube-style restaurant, Hecker's Deele,
popular with Berliners. 52 rooms, all with bath and shower, some with
kitchenette. B&B: single 195–235 DM, double 260–320 DM. Set meals 25–
35 DM. New nomination. More reports welcome.*

Hotel Seehof   *Tel* (030) 32 00 20
Lietzenseeufer 11, Charlottenburg   *Fax* (030) 32 00 22 51
Berlin 19   *Telex* 182943

*A useful new nomination for the world's most mesmerising and talked-about
city of 1989/90 (warning: most of its hotels are booked out months ahead).*

Pleasantly set beside a small lake north of the Ku'damm, here's a fairly smart and formal hotel, not bursting with charm but well run and well staffed, with good conventional food. All rooms face the lake; indoor pool, sauna. 78 rooms, 74 with bath and/or shower. B&B: single 105–235 DM, double 260–290 DM. Set meals 32–45 DM. New nomination: more reports welcome.

BONN 5300 Nordrhein-Westfalen   Map 13

Schlosshotel Kommende   *Tel* (0228) 44 07 34
  Ramersdorf   *Fax* (0228) 44 44 00
Oberkasseler Strasse 10
Bonn 3-Beuel

Just across the Rhine from Bonn, some three kilometres from the city centre, this massive ancient *Schloss* stands incongruously in the middle of a motorway network (but the traffic is not audible). Parts date from 1220, but most is 19th-century neo-Gothic. "A delight. Our large room was furnished with antiques, and a plentiful breakfast was served in a charming room." "We arrived at 10.30 pm but were cosseted with a cold meal. Very good service. Cheap by German standards." Part of the *Schloss* is a museum of furniture, paintings, etc, and some items are for sale. (*Claire W Enders, J Thérèse Simon*) The cooking is Italian: reports on it would be welcome.

Open All year. Restaurant closed in July.
Rooms 10 double, 8 single – all with bath and/or shower, telephone, radio, TV.
Facilities Bar, TV room, breakfast room, restaurant; terrace-café. 2 function rooms. Courtyard and garden.
Location Take A59 motorway towards Königswinter, leave at Niederholtorf exit; turn left; after 300 metres left again.
Restriction Not suitable for &.
Credit cards All major cards accepted.
Terms B&B: single 85 DM, double 150 DM. Set lunch 30 DM, dinner 50–60 DM; full alc 55–88 DM. Reduced rates and special meals for children.

BOPPARD 5407 Rheinland-Pfalz   Map 13

Klostergut Jakobsberg   *Tel* (06742) 30 61
Im Tal der Loreley   *Fax* (06742) 30 69
                          Telex 426323

"All in all, my favourite hotel in Germany" – one of three 1989/90 endorsements for this stylishly converted monastery, set high on the hills above Boppard, overlooking a sublime stretch of the great curving Rhine. Founded by Frederick Barbarossa in 1157, it became a school for French children during the Revolution, and has recently been converted into a large and smart hotel, with new extensions including a fine indoor sports centre. "The courtyard at dusk with its fountain and scores of sculptured glass lanterns is impressive. Reception rooms are vast and comfortable, decked out with modern bronze sculptures, antique wooden statues, stained-glass windows. All bedrooms are individual, with paintings, modern wooden furniture. Some have a sun balcony; ours overlooked a rocky wooded escarpment. It was very cosy, and the bathroom had a ceiling-to-floor mosaic. There are two bars (one in the old wine cellars) and two restaurants, one with views over the trees to the Rhine. Food was interestingly presented (excellent quails, lobster tails, veal in cream) and many ingredients came fresh from the adjacent home farm. Breakfast was superb and lavish, and service quick and pleasant. At the weekend the hotel was full of families with children; during the week, of businessmen and conference guests." Visitors this year have especially enjoyed the swimming pool, the views, the friendly staff and the "superb" food. (TH Nash, Ian Harris, M Firth)

Open All year.
Rooms 110 – all with bath and/or shower, telephone, TV.
Facilities Lift. Lounge, 2 bars, 2 restaurants; conference facilities. Large garden with children's playground. Indoor swimming pool, sauna and solarium. Indoor and outdoor tennis, squash and bowling alley. Rifle range. Chapel for weddings.
Location 12 km N of Boppard. Turn off B9 Rhineside main road at Spay, take Rheingoldstrasse turning.
Credit cards All major cards accepted.
Terms [1990 rates] B&B: single 110–180 DM, double 160–280 DM, suite 450–580 DM; half board 120–220 DM per person. Alc meals (excluding wine) 48–84 DM.

BREITNAU 7821 Baden-Württemberg   Map 13

Hotel Kaiser's Tanne-Wirtshus
Am Wirbstein 27

Tel (07652) 15 51
Fax (07652) 15 07

Set in rolling pastoral country a few miles away from the big resort of Hinterzarten, and thus secluded from the main tourist crowds, here is a welcoming chalet-style Black Forest hotel, all gables and flowery balconies outside, all folksy *Gemütlichkeit* within. "Beautifully decorated, very ornate, full of antiques, pictures and homely touches. Very friendly staff. Bedroom and bathroom clean and airy. Excellent dinner and buffet breakfast; tea a real treat." Many bedrooms have a balcony with peaceful rural views which include cows to-ing and fro-ing. Indoor swimming pool and attractive garden. (*John Moseley, and others*)

Open All year. Restaurant closed Mon.
Rooms 4 suites, 23 double, 6 single – all with bath, shower, telephone, radio, TV.
Facilities Lift. Lounge, bar, 2 restaurants, indoor heated swimming pool and sauna; terrace. Garden, playground for children.
Location Just SW of Breitnau, which is 30 km E of Freiburg, off route 500.
Credit cards None accepted.
Terms B&B: single 75–80 DM, double 130–200 DM, suite 280 DM; dinner, B&B 110–140 DM per person. Set lunch 32–45 DM, dinner 46–66 DM; full alc 45 DM. Reduced rates and special meals for children.

BREMEN 2800   Map 13

Landhaus Louisenthal
Leher Heerstrasse 105, Bremen 30

Tel (0421) 23 20 76
Telex 246925

Hanseatic Bremen has a splendid breezy, quirky atmosphere: do not miss the lovely Renaissance *Rathaus*, or the stylish boutiques of the Böttcherstrasse, a highly original traffic-free alley. The *Louisenthal*, in the northeast suburb of Horn, near the *Autobahn* (but quiet), is an 18th-century cream-coloured Italianate mansion in a garden, now a stylish family-run hotel. After losing its place through lack of reports, it is this year restored by an American reader: "Attractive setting, delightful rooms, friendly staff." (*JK Deuel*) Others have enjoyed the comfort, and the meals served on a terrace by the garden, but the cooking is fairly basic.

Open All year.
Rooms 31 double, 29 single – all with bath or shower, telephone, TV. 20 in annexe. Some ground-floor rooms.
Facilities Salon with TV, 3 dining rooms; conference facilities. Garden with terrace. Bowling alley. Sauna.
Location In Horn-Lehe suburb, 6 km NE of Bremen centre, just off E71/A27 *Autobahn*. Bus and tram services pass the door.
Credit cards All major cards accepted.
Terms B&B: single 78 DM, double 85 DM. Full alc 65 DM.

CELLE 3100 Niedersachsen   Map 13

Fürstenhof Celle – Restaurant   *Tel* (05141) 20 10
   Endtenfang   *Fax* (05141) 20 11 20
Hannoversche Strasse 55   *Telex* 925293

This 17th-century pink-fronted mansion, now a stylish and rather formal hotel, stands near the centre of an historic old city where the Guelph princes ruled (imposing baroque *Schloss*, lovely *Altstadt* of ancient timbered houses). Devotees paying their fifth visit, in 1990, confirm earlier praise: "All the rooms we've tried have been pleasant, with a balcony overlooking the garden where drinks are served. This separates the older part of the hotel from the new bedroom wing. Service is impeccable, the breakfast buffet is good, and excellent duck is served in the hotel's *Endtenfang* restaurant (*Michelin* rosette). The comfortable lounge is in baroque style." (*Stephan and Kate Murray-Sykes*)

Open All year. *Kutscherstube* closed for lunch and on Sun.
Rooms 5 suites, 75 double or single – all with bath, shower, telephone, radio, TV, baby-listening.
Facilities Lift. Lounge, bar, beer cellar, 2 restaurants; conference and functions facilities; indoor swimming pool, solarium, sauna. Garden and terrace.
Location Central, near *Schloss*. Parking.
Credit cards Access, Amex, Diners.
Terms [1990 rates] B&B: single 105–200 DM, double 185–350 DM, suite 300–400 DM. Alc meals (excluding wine): *Kutscherstube* 35–58 DM; *Endtenfang* 68–103 DM.

COCHEM 5590 Rheinland-Pfalz   Map 13

Hotel Alte Thorschenke   *Tel* (02671) 70 59
Brückenstrasse 3   *Fax* (02671) 42 02

Cochem, with its painted houses and neat gardens along the river and its high-pinnacled hilltop feudal castle, is the most picturesque town on the Mosel – and this enticing hotel, in a gabled house dating from 1332, is worthy of it. "The entrance opens on to an ancient carved circular wooden staircase, leading to rooms in the old building. Behind is a post-war bedroom extension, fitted out with splendid antique pictures and furniture. Here we slept deliciously well in a vast family heirloom of a bed, all massive carved oak. The welcome was warm yet professional, and dinner in a superb baronial dining room included the best game we've ever had." (*Angela and David Stewart*)

Open 15 Mar–5 Jan. Restaurant closed on Wed 15 Nov–5 Jan.
Rooms 38 double, 6 single – all with bath and/or shower, 22 with telephone, 34 with radio; TV on request. 4 in nearby annexe.
Facilities Lift. Hall, restaurant, *Weinstube*. Terrace.
Location Central, parking. Cochem is 51 km SW of Koblenz.
Credit cards All major cards accepted.
Terms B&B: single 55–115 DM, double 75–185 DM; half board 28–35 DM per person added; full board 46–55 DM added. Full alc 50–60 DM. Reduced rates and special meals for children on request.

COLOGNE 5000 Nordrhein-Westfalen   Map 13

Hotel Spiegel　`BUDGET`   *Tel* (02203) 6 10 46
Hermann-Löns-Strasse 122
Porz-Grengel

The Guide's search for good hotels in Cologne has lacked success in the past, so this recent find is welcome: a small family-run Gasthof in the south-eastern outer suburb of Porz-Grengel, conveniently near the airport, but set peacefully by a forest. Good food, and a personal touch. 19 rooms, all with bath or shower. B&B double 130–180 DM. Alc meals 53.50 DM. Endorsed this year, but fuller reports welcome.

DAHLEM-KRONENBURG 5377 Nordrhein-Westfalen   Map 13

Eifelhaus　`BUDGET`   *Tel* (06557) 2 95
Burgbering 12

In a hilltop village SW of Dahlem, in the lovely but little-known Eifel massif, quite near the Belgian border, a white-walled old building has been converted into a modest but appealing hotel; vaulted dining room, terraced garden, helpful owners, clean, simple rooms and good food. Amazingly low prices. Lake and castle nearby. Closed 6 Jan–early Feb. 19 rooms, all with bath and/or shower. B&B 30–40 DM. Alc meals 24–43 DM [1990].

DAUN 5568 Rheinland-Pfalz   Map 13

Schloss-Hotel Kurfürstliches   *Tel* (06592) 30 31
　Amtshaus   *Fax* (06592) 49 42
Auf dem Burgberg   *Telex* 4729310

Daun is a resort in the lovely rolling volcanic hills of the Eifel, west of Koblenz. On a hill in the village centre, this handsome yellow-walled 18th-century *Schloss* has been converted into a stylish and fairly expensive hotel, much admired recently. Public rooms and most bedrooms have bracing views of the surrounding woods, hills and ski-slopes. The decor and furnishings are somewhat baronial, with heavy oak chests, etc. "Most of the decor is what we call 'pseudo-Germanic semi-kitsch', though others might call it '*altdeutsch*'. But the main restaurant is inviting and intimate and here we had a wonderful meal, with sophisticated haute cuisine (tomato mousse with smoked breast of goose, fried quail with quince sauce) and excellent service. The high-quality table accessories included fresh roses in December. Our comfortable room had a view of an old chapel and fir trees. Rich buffet breakfast with lots of unusual extras." Another report: "The heated swimming pool is almost as hot as a sauna, for its water comes from the local volcanic springs; it has red and green alcoves and is chiselled out of the volcanic rock. The garden terrace contains barbecue facilities. Bedrooms are smallish but pleasant. One of the splendid suites, the Fürstensuite, contains a famous bed acquired from the Government's hotel at the Petersberg in Bonn, where it was slept in by such as Brezhnev, and the Shah of Iran. It is now covered in fancy orange drapes and an orange silk canopy, and the bath *en suite* is triangular." (*GB and Dr CH, Mrs CM Hunter*)

Open All year except 2–17 Jan.
Rooms 1 suite, 24 double, 17 single – 8 with bath, 34 with shower, all with telephone, radio, TV, baby-listening.
Facilities Lift. Lounge, bar, 2 restaurants, conference facilities. Garden; terrace. Indoor swimming pool, sauna.
Location Central, parking. Daun is 70 km W of Koblenz.
Credit cards All major cards accepted.
Terms B&B: single 95–125 DM, double 170–250 DM, suite 250–350 DM. Dinner, B&B 42 DM per person added. Set lunch 42 DM, dinner 65 DM; full alc 90 DM. Reduced rates and special meals for children. 2 nights minimum stay at weekends.

DEIDESHEIM 6705 Rheinland-Pfalz   Map 13

Romantik Hotel Deidesheimer   *Tel* (06326) 18 11
  Hof   *Telex* 454657
Am Marktplatz

Run by the Hahn family, leading local winegrowers, this stylish and well-known hostelry stands on the main street of a pretty wine town along the Pfalz *Weinstrasse*. The wood-panelled *Weinstube*, full of Germanic warmth and prettiness, is much admired. A recent report: "A real joy! Cheerful, helpful staff, exceptional food. Despite the crowds in the food rooms and front terrace, the back bedrooms are quiet – and beautifully decked out" (rooms do vary). (*SR Holman, JA and KA*) Helmut Kohl and Margaret Thatcher held a summit in the hotel in April 1989. More reports welcome.

Open All year except 1–6 Jan.
Rooms 27 – all with bath and/or shower, telephone, TV.
Facilities Restaurant; conference facilities. Terrace.
Location Central, parking. Deidesheim is 23 km SW of Mannheim.
Credit cards All major cards accepted.
Terms [1990 rates] B&B: single 70–125 DM, double 88–185 DM; dinner, B&B 72–173 DM per person. Alc meals (excluding wine) 42–73 DM.

Most hotels have reduced rates out of season and for children, and some British hotels offer "mini-break" rates throughout the year. If you are staying more than one night, it is always worth asking about special terms.

DÜSSELDORF 4000   Map 13

Hotel Schnellenburg   *Tel* (0211) 43 41 33
Rotterdamerstrasse 120   *Fax* (0211) 437 09 76
Düsseldorf 30   *Telex* 8581828

In a big commercial city full of dull hotels, this one at least has character:
a low white building with iron grilles on the windows, it looks more
Spanish than German. It also has a fine position by the Rhine, in the
northern outskirts near the exhibition ground. A recent verdict: "A light
bedroom where it was easy to work, a first-class breakfast, and smiling
service." (*THN*) The restaurant, newly renovated with lots of brass and
marble, has a good view of the river.

Open All year except Christmas/New Year.
Rooms 3 suites, 35 double, 11 single – all with bath, shower, telephone, radio, TV.
Facilities Lounge, residents' bar, restaurant (under separate management). Small
garden.
Restriction Not suitable for &.
Location 4 km N of city centre, opposite Nord Park, on the Rhine. Parking.
Credit cards All major cards accepted.
Terms B&B: single 140–220 DM, double 180–280 DM, suite 220–420 DM. Full alc
40 DM. Reduced rates and special meals for children.

ESPENAU-SCHÄFERBERG 3501 Hessen   Map 13

Waldhotel Schäferberg   *Tel* (05673) 79 51
Wilhelmsthaler Str 14   *Fax* (05673) 79 73
                                                Telex 991814

A new entry this year: "Ugly industrial Kassel is worth a visit for its art
museums, its extravagantly romantic Wilhelmshöhe park, and the rococo
Schloss Wilhelmsthal just to the north. Close to this, in a rural-suburban
setting, we found this pleasant modern hotel. Affable owner, excellent
Hessen cooking, rustic *Stube*, garden and sauna. The decor of the spacious
rooms is inspired by the fairy tales of the Grimm brothers, who lived in
Kassel." (*JA and KA*)

Open All year.
Rooms 6 suites, 74 double, 15 single – 15 with bath, 80 with shower, all with
telephone, TV; 90 with radio.
Facilities Lift. Bar, 2 dining rooms; conference facilities. Sauna, solarium, fitness
room. Bowling alley, table-tennis, billiards. Garden; terrace; children's
playground.
Location Espenau-Schäferberg is 10 km NW of Kassel, off B68 to Paderborn.
Credit cards All major cards accepted.
Terms B&B: single 95–120 DM, double 140–180 DM, suite 240 DM. Set
lunch/dinner 20–48 DM; full alc 35–50 DM. Reduced rates and special meals for
children.

Do you know of a good hotel or country inn in the United States or
Canada? Nominations please to our sibling publication, America's
Wonderful Little Hotels and Inns, PO Box 150, Riverside Avenue,
Riverside, Conn. 06878, USA.

FASSBERG-MÜDEN 3105 Niedersachsen Map 13

Niemeyer's Posthotel *Tel* (05053) 10 77
Hauptstrasse 7, Müden *Fax* (05053) 2 48

Belying the notion that North Germany has little attractive scenery, the vast Lüneberg Heath is quietly lovely in all seasons, and especially in early autumn when the heather is in bloom. The villages are pleasant too, with their low barn-like half-timbered buildings – and such a one is this hotel, making its Guide debut: "A real find – very comfortable, of high standard, with big bathrooms. The dining room was busy with locals, the atmosphere *gemütlich*, and the menu with its wide choice (plenty of game and fish) left us satisfied. Breakfast's superb buffet included home-made black puddings and thick local heather honey." (*David and Patricia Hawkins*)

Open All year.
Rooms 3 suites, 22 double, 11 single – all with bath and/or shower, telephone, T V. 5 in annexe, Gasthof Lührnhof.
Facilities Lounge, bar, restaurant; conference facilities; whirlpool, sauna. Garden; terrace.
Location In hamlet of Müden, 4 km SW of Fassberg which is 39 km N of Celle. Parking.
Restriction Not suitable for &.
Credit cards Access, Visa.
Terms B&B: single 85–96 DM, double 120–150 DM, suite 170 DM. Set lunch 20 DM, dinner 25 DM; full alc 35 DM. Reduced rates and special meals for children on request.

FEUCHTWANGEN 8805 Bayern Map 13

Romantik Hotel Greifen-Post *Tel* (09852) 20 04
Marktplatz 8 *Fax* (09852) 48 41
 Telex 61137

In the main square of a pleasant old town on the Romantic Road, a solid and spacious old coaching inn, owned and run with a friendly personal touch by the Lorentz family. Good Frankish dishes served in a beamed dining room, antiques everywhere, attractive pool in the style of Roman baths. Rooms in annexe are quietest. Restaurant closed Jan. 44 rooms, all with bath and shower. B&B: single 85–105 DM, double 125–198 DM. Set menus 49–89 DM [1990]. No recent reports: new ones, please.

FRANKFURT-AM-MAIN 6000 Hessen Map 13

Hotel Westend *Tel* (069) 74 67 02 and 74 50 02
Westendstrasse 15, Frankfurt 1

"An old-fashioned German ambience, friendly service, excellent breakfasts, interesting antiques," runs a 1990 report on this small and select hotel of charm and character, most unexpected in downtown Frankfurt. It is in a quiet residential district that has somehow survived the metallic frenzy of post-war rebuilding, yet it is very central, only five minutes' walk from the Fair centre, the *Hauptbahnhof* and the banking district.

Several readers have enjoyed the serenity and efficiency, confirming this earlier view: "The late 20th century has been carefully excluded from the *Westend*, which is tastefully furnished throughout with antiques and old pictures. There is gracious old-world service by discreet middle-aged men in black suits who address lady guests as 'Gnädige Frau' ('esteemed Madame'). Very comfortable rooms; lavish German breakfasts; light evening meals on request; a leafy garden for summer; prices reasonable for central Frankfurt." Several bedrooms have just been modernised; many now have private bath or shower. (*Harvey Herrmann*)

Open All year except Christmas and New Year. Restaurant closed Easter.
Rooms 9 double, 11 single – 9 with bath, 2 with shower, all with telephone, 10 with TV.
Facilities Lift. 3 lounges (1 with TV). Garden and terrace where light meals and drinks are served.
Location Central; 5 mins' walk from station. By car approach from Westkreuz. Private parking.
Credit cards All major cards accepted.
Terms Rooms: single 80–160 DM, double 150–230 DM, triple 280 DM. Breakfast 14 DM. (No restaurant, but light evening meals served on request.)

FREIBURG IM BREISGAU 7800 Baden-Württemberg   Map 13

Hotel Oberkirchs Weinstuben   *Tel* (0761) 3 10 11
Münsterplatz 22

Venerable family-run wine tavern/hotel opposite the soaring cathedral (bells can be noisy). Good food, and wines from the owners' own local vineyards, in the cosy panelled dining room. Main building (no lift) has bedrooms with antiques; duller rooms in annexe with lift. Closed 22 Dec–21 Jan. 27 rooms, 21 with bath and shower. B&B: single 90–130 DM, double 170–200 DM. Alc meals 35 DM. Enthusiastic new nomination. More reports please.

Zum Roten Bären   *Tel* (0761) 3 69 13
Oberlinden 12   *Fax* (0761) 3 69 16
    Telex 7721574

Blue-and-pink diamond-shaped designs adorn the painted facade of this famous and very *gemütlich* old inn, dating back 600 years, and set near the centre of this lovely old university city on the edge of the Black Forest. It has also been comfortably modernised, its newer parts skilfully integrated into the old ones; old prints line the walls, fresh flowers are everywhere. "The best hotel I have stayed at in Germany, and the best German restaurant food I have eaten," writes a much-travelled correspondent. "Very helpful reception staff, unusually friendly waiters, a large and very good buffet breakfast, and a general sense of comfort and relaxation. Our large room faced the courtyard, so was quiet." An earlier view: "Good traditional cooking, e.g. tafelspitz (boiled beef). Staff wear local Baden *Tracht*, including – incongruously – our deft Pakistani waiter. It's a hotel that breathes confident well-being, nicely supervised by its jolly and expansive *Wirtin*, Monika Hansen." (*William Rodgers; Dr RH Freeman, Isabel and John Brasier, John Grammer*) A lounge and a sauna have just been added.

Open All year.
Rooms 3 suites, 17 double, 5 single – all with bath or shower, telephone, TV; some with air-conditioning.
Facilities Lift. Hall/lounge, 3 restaurants; 3 conference rooms. Garden terrace. Courtyards and boulevard café.
Location Central, at SE corner of old part of city. Small private garage; street parking difficult.
Credit cards All major cards accepted.
Terms B&B: single 145–155 DM, double 190–210 DM, suite 280–300 DM; dinner, B&B 35 DM per person added. Set lunch 35 DM, dinner 48 DM; full alc from 55 DM. Special meals for children on request.

FREUDENSTADT 7290 Baden-Württemberg   Map 13

Gut Lauterbad   `BUDGET`   *Tel* (07441) 74 96
Dietrichstrasse 5, Lauterbad   *Fax* (07441) 8 21 88

Freudenstadt, a big Black Forest resort amid fine hiking and skiing country, lies on a pine-clad plateau astride the old hill-road from Stuttgart to Strasbourg. After destruction in 1945, it was completely rebuilt in its former 17th-century style: note its curious church, with the aisles set at right-angles. The *Gut Lauterbad*, a modern building in local style, stands just outside the town, amid meadows, woods and streams; it has a garden terrace beside a trout pond. It has long been admired: "Excellent value," says a visitor this year. "Beautiful setting, friendly owners, lovely breakfasts, generous evening meals in an attractive dining room." (*C Turner*)

Open All year except 15 Nov–15 Dec. Restaurant closed Wed.
Rooms 16 double, 4 single – all with bath, shower, telephone, radio, TV, 1 with baby-listening. 4 in annexe.
Facilities Lounge, bar, TV room, restaurant; conference room; indoor heated swimming pool. Garden with children's playground, small lake and stream; trout fishing.
Location 3 km SE (B294) of centre; follow directions to Freiburg then to Dietersweiler/Lauterbad. Hotel is at end of road on left. Garage and parking.
Restriction Not suitable for &.
Credit cards All major cards accepted.
Terms B&B: single 48–58 DM, double 80–112 DM, suite 150 DM; dinner, B&B 21.50 DM per person added. Set lunch/dinner 22.50–48 DM; full alc 32.50 DM. Children under 2 free; under 12, 50% reduction; special meals.

FULDA 6400 Hessen   Map 13

Hotel Zum Kurfürsten   *Tel* (0661) 7 00 01
Schloss Strasse 2

The old Hesse city of Fulda has fine baroque buildings; also a cathedral where St Boniface, an 8th-century English missionary to Germany, lies buried, having anointed Pippin the Short as King and then himself been murdered. The life of the Zum Kurfürsten has also been eventful; it was built in 1737 as a palace of the Prince Bishop; later Queen Victoria, Bismarck, et al., stayed in it. It is now a sleek, well-run hotel in the classic style, with good food. 69 rooms, 40 with bath or shower. B&B: single 49–95 DM, double 90–170 DM. Alc meals (excluding wine) 38–59 DM [1990]. Recent nomination. More reports please.

FÜSSEN 8958 Bayern   Map 13

Hotel Hirsch
Schulhausstrasse 2–4

Tel (08362) 50 80
Fax (08362) 50 81 13
Telex 541308

In a well-known sub-alpine resort, a solidly traditional hotel, friendly and cosy, with painted wooden Bavarian furniture and scrubbed wooden floors. Good hearty Bavarian food, and a jolly bar full of locals. Closed Jan. 47 rooms, all with bath and shower. B&B: single 97.50–105.50 DM, double 125–180 DM. Set meals 25–28 DM. New nomination. More reports please.

FÜSSEN-WEISSENSEE 8958 Bayern   Map 13

Seegasthof Weissensee   *Tel* (08362) 70 95

In a lakeside village just west of the old town of Füssen, and quite near the Royal Castles, this pleasant Gasthof *has fine mountain views. Two modern buildings with alpine decor (lots of stripped pine); spacious bedrooms, cordial staff, lavish breakfasts, average main meals (good for fish). Closed 11 Jan– 11 Feb, 16 Nov–19 Dec. 22 rooms, all with bath and shower. B&B double 102– 138 DM. Set meals 25–45 DM [1990]. Endorsed this year, but some criticisms of service and housekeeping; fuller reports welcome.*

GEISLINGEN AN DER STEIGE 7340 Baden-Württemberg   Map 13

Burghotel   *Tel* (07331) 4 10 51
Burggasse 41
Weiler ob Helfenstein

An attractive modern building in superior motel style, set amid the rolling hills of the Schwäbische Alb, north-west of Ulm (in the area, don't miss Ulm cathedral, the ruined hilltop fortress of Reussenstein, or at Holzmaden the extraordinary Hauff museum of ichthyosaur skeletons, a mere 170 million years old). "Excellent", "friendly and caring", are readers' comments this year on the *Burghotel*, which has nice rooms with balconies, copious breakfasts, indoor pool plus jacuzzis, and a large garden. No restaurant, but the *Burgstüberl* close by is commended. (*Ralph B Robertson, R and D Voxbrunner*)

Open All year except 3 weeks in July/Aug (check with hotel). Closed Christmas.
Rooms 10 double, 13 single – all with bath and/or shower, telephone, radio, TV, baby-listening.
Facilities Lounge, bar, TV room, breakfast room; indoor swimming pool, sauna. Large garden with terrace.
Location 3 km E of Geislingen: turn at station towards Helfenstein castle. Garage.
Restriction Not suitable for &.
Credit cards None accepted.
Terms Rooms: single 65–100 DM, double 100–150 DM. Breakfast 8–20 DM. (No restaurant.)

GRAINAU 8104 Bayern   Map 13

Hotel Alpenhof   *Tel* (08821) 80 71
Alpspitzstrasse 22

Grainau, just west of Garmisch, is a popular resort village at the foot of the high Alps. Down a quiet side road is this big modern chalet in typical local style. Many rooms have a flower-decked balcony looking on to the craggy Zugspitze massif. The hotel has a pleasant garden and sun-terrace with yellow parasols, and a good indoor swimming pool. Reports this year and last have been mainly enthusiastic, stressing the tasteful decor, good breakfast buffet, friendly staff. "A delightful hotel in a lovely setting. Good honest German food very well presented; our room large and comfortable." "The meals were wonderful." (*Mrs K Plowden, Dr RH Freeman, Diane and Joel Morris*) One 1990 visitor thought the rooms comfortable but food mediocre.

Open All year, except 2 weeks in Apr/May and mid-Nov–mid-Dec.
Rooms 29 double, 7 single – all with bath, shower, telephone, radio, TV; some with balcony.
Facilities Lift. Salon with open fireplace, TV room, restaurant; banqueting room. Indoor heated swimming pool and sauna. Garden and terrace.
Location 6 km SW of Garmisch–Partenkirchen. Hotel 1 km from village centre.
Credit cards All major cards accepted.
Terms [1990 rates] B&B: single 70–125 DM, double 160–225 DM. Alc meals (excluding wine) 40–67 DM. Children under 6 free of charge.

HAGNAU 7759 Baden-Württemberg   Map 13

Erbguth's Landhaus   *Tel* (07532) 62 02
Neugartenstrasse 39   *Fax* (07532) 69 97
                        Telex 733811

Lake Constance (Bodensee) is a busy holiday area. Wisely, the Germans have put the accent here on smallish hotels of character rather than big lakeside palaces, and this *Landhaus* (country house) is typical – a converted private house, newly renovated, on the edge of a pretty lakeside village. It is a hotel of much personality, run with flair by a young couple, the Erbguths (he cooks, she hosts). Two plaudits this year back up these earlier accounts: "The elegant white marble hall leads to an equally elegant restaurant, newly decorated in soothing blue tones. Our comfortable bedroom had a small terrace and solid wooden furniture – more the feeling of a guest house than a luxury hotel. The welcome was warm. We much enjoyed the 8-course menu – excellent salad with sweetbreads. Good buffet breakfast." "You dine by candle-light, amid flowers and modern 'antiques'. Much of the food was smoked and preserved in their own kitchens – e.g. superb home-smoked caviar. Frau Erbguth has panache and artistry. Not a cheap place, but the quality is superb." (Endorsed by *Charles P Cords, Jan A Sarsten*)

Open All year except 4 Jan–1 Mar. Restaurant closed Tue.
Rooms 17 double, 4 single – all with bath and/or shower, telephone, radio, TV. 6 in lakeside annexe 5 mins away. Some ground-floor rooms.
Facilities Lounge, TV room, bar, 2 restaurants; fitness room with sauna and solarium. Gardens and terraces. Private beach on lake.
Location On Lake Constance (Bodensee), just E of Meersburg. Parking.
Credit cards All major cards accepted.

Terms B&B: single 80–200 DM, double 130–320 DM; half board 45 DM per person added; full board 58 DM added. Set lunch 40–60 DM, dinner 90–120 DM; full alc 80 DM. Reduced rates and special meals for children.

HAMBURG 2000	Map 13

Hotel Hanseatic	*Tel* (040) 48 57 72
Sierichstrasse 150	*Fax* (040) 48 57 73
Hamburg 60	

Opera, theatre and film people, visiting Hamburg, often prefer to stay at this select 13-room hotel rather than at one of the big luxury ones. It is a pink-fronted patrician villa in a quiet area north of the big Alster lake, and has a very personal atmosphere created by owner/manager Wolfgang Schüler. But you need to book well ahead. Reports in 1990 have again verged on the ecstatic: "I could live for a year at the marvellous *Hanseatic*! Everything is carefully thought out, reading lamps are for reading, Wolfgang organises dry cleaning, etc, with that wonderful German precision. Breakfasts are healthy and delicious, served with charm and hospitality. We had the wonderful suite, which looks out on to a huge green space at the back. But bathrooms do vary." Earlier views: "Herr Schüler's dedication and courtesy make this small hotel a rare jewel." "He takes great pride in his intimate hotel and should receive the 'Host of the Year' award. Fresh flowers in our room and a plate of fresh fruit on beautiful old Rosenthal china, plus big white towelling bathrobes. Breakfast was wonderful, served in a beautiful room hung with old oil paintings." "He makes his own breads and marmalades, and serves his superb breakfasts personally, in a high style verging on the camp." (*Tatiana Maxwell, H Langenberg, Jeremy and Anthea Larken*)

Open All year.
Rooms 1 suite, 2 studios, 10 double – all with bath, shower, telephone, radio, TV; baby-sitting on request. Ground-floor rooms.
Facilities Lounge/bar, breakfast room; fitness room and sauna. Small garden. Alster lake and city park both 2 blocks away.
Location In Winterhude, 4 km N of city centre. Parking in street, but difficult.
Credit cards Access, Amex, Diners.
Terms Rooms: single occupancy 160 DM, double 200 DM, suite 370 DM. Breakfast 22 DM. Children under 12 sharing parents' room free. (No restaurant.)

Hotel Wedina **BUDGET**	*Tel* (040) 24 30 11
Gurlittstrasse 23,	*Fax* (040) 280 39 94
Hamburg 1	

Modestly priced for Hamburg but quite central (in a quiet side street near the southern end of the Alster lake). Family-run and helpful; spacious bedrooms and good German breakfasts, plus the bonus of a small garden, with outdoor heated pool and sauna. Street parking. Open 10 Feb–18 Dec. 23 rooms, most with bath and shower. B&B: single 65–95 DM, double 95–135 DM. No restaurant. Recent nomination, newly endorsed, but we'd be glad of fuller reports.

If you have had recent experience of a good hotel that ought to be in the Guide, please write to us at once. Report forms are to be found at the back of the book. Procrastination is the thief of the next edition.

HEIDELBERG 6900 Baden-Württemberg   Map 13

Hotel Alt Heidelberg   *Tel* (06221) 91 50
Rohrbacher Strasse 29   *Fax* (06221) 16 42 72
                                                      Telex 461897

Fifteen minutes' walk from the heart of the *alt* part of town (the university
library, former students' prison, and Friedrich-Ebert museum are all
worth a visit), this neat, well-modernised hotel stands on a main street,
but is quiet. Its *Graimberg* restaurant serves some of the best food in town
– "a French chef doing wonders with German dishes" (e.g. venison with
spätzle, warm röte grütze). "Charming, cosy and friendly," says a regular.
But another recent visitor found service erratic. Some rooms are spacious
and modern; others smaller, with antiques. (*Reginald B Vaughan, Eileen
Spencer, JA and KA*) Live jazz on Fridays in the basement bar; but it's more
fun to visit one of the uproarious old student pubs in the old town, such
as *Scnookeloch*, or *Seppl* where you sit round big tables and beer is drunk
communally out of giant glass boots or horns.

Open All year.
Rooms 3 suites, 55 double, 24 single – all with bath or shower, telephone, radio,
TV; baby-listening on request. 24 in annexe.
Facilities Lift. Hall, restaurant, bar; conference facilities. Sauna.
Location Central. Parking.
Credit cards All major cards accepted.
Terms B&B: single 145–165 DM, double 195–210 DM. Alc meals 35–60 DM.

HELLENTHAL 5374 Nordrhein-Westfalen   Map 13

Hotel-Restaurant Haus [BUDGET]   *Tel* (02482) 6 14
  Lichtenhardt

*In the northern part of the Eifel massif, not far from the enchanting old town of
Monschau and the open-air museum of rural life at Kommern, this unpretentious modern hotel is in a quiet hilly setting outside the village. Comfortable
rooms, friendly and personal service. Indoor pool and sauna. Closed 17–27 Dec.
18 rooms, 13 with bath or shower. B&B double 60–86 DM. Set menus 20 DM.
Recent nomination, endorsed this year, but more reports welcome.*

HINTERZARTEN 7824 Baden-Württemberg   Map 13

Hotel Garni Sassenhof   *Tel* (07652) 15 15
Adlerweg 17

"This very spruce and select *pension* is just what you might expect to find
in one of the smartest of Black Forest resorts, popular alike with skiers
and walkers. It's a modern gabled building, flower-decked, facing the
wide village green, with views of the hills. Elegant public rooms, and a
big indoor swimming pool with picture windows facing the lake and
woods." "Fabulous! We had a romantic garret room, with delicious and
copious breakfast; proprietors charming." Warmly endorsed this year,
though one reader found the service cool. (*J and R Williamson, JA and KA,
Bettye Chambers*)

Open All year except 11 Nov–17 Dec.
Rooms 6 suites, 7 double, 10 single – all with bath and/or shower, telephone, radio, TV, tea-making facilities.
Facilities Lift. Hall, lounges, TV room, breakfast room. Indoor swimming pool, sauna, solarium. Terrace; garden.
Location. Central, parking. Hinterzarten is 26 km E of Freiburg.
Restriction No children under 3.
Credit cards All major cards accepted.
Terms B&B: single 50–90 DM, double 60–80 DM. (No restaurant.)

HOFGEISMAR 3520 Hessen   Map 13

Dornröschenschloss	Tel (05678) 10 52
Sababurg	*from 1991* (05671) 80 80
Hofgeismar-Sababurg	*Fax* (05678) 10 32
	from 1991 (05671) 80 82 00

An inspector's discovery on the rolling wooded plateau west of the Weser valley: "A self-consciously romantic old 14th-century *Schloss*, whose twin green cupolas tower up through the oakwoods. It was long a country home of the princes of Hessen: the brothers Grimm were invited here for hunting parties, and it is said to have been the model for the castle in *Dornröschen* (*The Sleeping Beauty*). Today it capitalises on these fairy-tale associations: statuettes of Puss in Boots and Cinderella stand by the entrance, and the garden shop (separately owned) sells some rather grim Grimm kitsch. But the hotel itself is delightful, a stylish conversion, very well run by its cultivated owner, Karl Koseck. Lovely rooms in the tower with canopied beds; lovely views, too, from rooms and restaurant; good food, especially the pheasant and venison in season. Sometimes, Grimm tales are read aloud during meals; in summer, there are concerts and fairy-tale plays in the medieval courtyard. It is very popular for functions (five wedding parties were in progress on the day of our visit). For further good measure, the 120-hectare zoo on the Sababurg estate is Germany's oldest (1571). It has buffaloes, bears, penguins, even Exmoor ponies – but no Frog Prince."

Open 1 Mar–15 Jan. Closed Christmas 1990, open Christmas 1991.
Rooms 18 double – all with bath or shower, telephone, radio; 10 with TV.
Facilities Salon, 5 dining rooms; conference/functions facilities; museum. Courtyard. Garden. Zoo adjacent.
Location 14 km NE of Hofgeismar, 30 km N of Kassel.
Restriction Not suitable for &.
Credit cards All major cards accepted.
Terms Double room: B&B 188 DM; dinner, B&B 288 DM. Set lunch 35 DM, dinner 68 DM; full alc 50 DM. 1-night bookings refused at weekends. Reduced rates and special meals for children.

HOPFEN AM SEE 8959 Bayern   Map 13

Hotel Alpenblick BUDGET	Tel (08362) 5 05 70
Uferstrasse 10	*Fax* (08362) 50 57 73
	Telex 541343

As its name indicates, there are views of the Allgaü Alps (and of the lake) from the front-room balconies of this spruce flower-decked chalet-style hotel, modern but in traditional style, set beside a lake in a pleasant Bavarian resort north of Füssen. Large airy rooms, friendly staff, better-than-average food. 46 rooms, all with bath or shower. Half board 102–134 DM [1990]. Recent nomination. More reports welcome.

HORBRUCH IM HUNSRÜCK 6541 Rheinland-Pflaz   Map 13

Historische Bergmühle   *Tel* (06543) 40 41
                                                          Fax (06543) 31 78

Horbruch is on the Hunsrück plateau where Edgar Reitz set and filmed *Heimat*, his masterly study of German rural tradition (he was born at nearby Morbach). At the bewitching *Bergmühle*, that tradition lives on, in an ornately recherché style of its own – as its nominator ecstatically relates: "We cannot understate the charm and originality of this place: it is not to be dismissed as *gemütlich* or twee. Tucked away by a little stream, the beflowered 1640 building offers an enchanting sight: you are transported to the realm of the Grimm brothers, where everything acquires magical proportions. Beautiful hand-made clothes, enchanting dolls and fantasy jewellery jostle for space in the reception area. Bedrooms are small but cosy, with folksy antiques but modern facilities (e.g. a skilfully disguised mini-bar). The restaurant has cosy nooks, a balcony, views of the waterwheel (the hotel is a converted mill). Old cast-iron wheels mix easily with unorthodox sculptures. Locals pack in to partake of a simple meal or a gastronomic feast – delicate sorrel soup, raw wafer-thin beef, home-roast chicken with wholemeal noodles, walnut sabayon, all excellent, and a selection of over 100 German wines. There's a lounge with lovely books in many languages, and two live parrots that speak only parrot. The garden is full of artistic stoneware, and kittens. Frau Liller and her daughters are charming, and the young maids wear the dresses that she makes in her spare time; service is attentive and swift. Breakfast, served in a small quaint room, is a buffet of magnitude, variety and originality – ten different breads, ten jars of muesli ingredients, eight kinds of tea including Russian, fresh eggs from their own hens; and a lit candle." (*Ian and Francine Walsh*) More reports, quick, ere the dream fades!

Open All year. Restaurant closed Mon.
Rooms 1 suite, 9 double – all with bath, shower, telephone, radio; some with TV.
Facilities Lounge, restaurant; functions room. Terrace. Garden with children's playground.
Location Horbruch is 12 km E of Bernkastel on the Mosel.
Restriction Not suitable for ふ.
Credit cards Access, Diners, Visa.
Terms B&B: double 155–198 DM, suite 250 DM. Set lunch 39 DM, dinner 68–120 DM; full alc 75 DM. Reduced rates and special meals for children.

HÖRSTEL-RIESENBECK 4446 Nordrhein-Westfalen   Map 13

Schlosshotel Surenberg   *Tel* (05454) 70 92
Surenberg 13   *Fax* (05454) 72 51
                                                          Telex 94586

This appealing *Relais du Silence* lies in a little-known part of Germany – the opulent farming country of northern Westphalia, flat but pleasantly pastoral, not unlike Norfolk: "It's *not* a converted *Schloss* but a modern, sporty ranch-hotel on the estate of a moated castle, the home of the influential president of the German farmers' union. He owns this lovely, spacious hotel; it is run for him with jovial efficiency by Klaus Trottier, a Huguenot, who also cooks. In his big open-plan restaurant, popular locally, we especially enjoyed the foie gras salad and braised vegetables. Service was stylishly courteous. Our large bedroom was rather bare in decor, but well equipped, with french windows opening on to a flowery balcony and the wide grounds. The hotel is much used for sporty weekends: as well as a heated indoor pool and various games, it has large riding stables. The restaurant's panoramic windows give straight on to the main indoor riding hall, so that you can watch the riders and horses while you eat. We've never seen this in a hotel before." (*JA and KA*)

Open All year. Restaurant closed Sun for dinner Nov–Mar.
Rooms 23 – all with bath and/or shower, telephone, TV; many with balcony.
Facilities Restaurant; conference facilities. Indoor swimming pool, sauna, fitness centre. Large grounds with stables; children's playground, minigolf; bicycles for hire.
Location 6 km SW of Hörstel which is 44 km N of Münster.
Credit cards Access, Amex, Diners.
Terms [1990 rates] B&B: single 83–94 DM, double 139–160 DM. Alc meals (excluding wine) 33–59 DM.

ISMANING 8045 Bayern   Map 13

Hotel Fischerwirt `BUDGET`   *Tel* (089) 96 48 53
Schlosstrasse 17   *Fax* (089) 96 35 83

In an attractive commuter town on the northern edge of Munich, set back in a quiet courtyard, this typical modern German inn is clean, cheerful and efficient. Nice lounge, small garden; lavish breakfasts. Closed 22 Dec–6 Jan. 44 rooms, most with bath or shower. B&B double 78–165 DM. No restaurant: several nearby. Endorsed this year as excellent value for an overnight stop.

KETTWIG 4300 Nordrhein-Westfalen   Map 13

Hotel Schloss Hugenpoet   *Tel* (02054) 12 040
August-Thyssen-Strasse 51   *Fax* (02054) 12 04 50
                                                 Telex 8579180

The winding valley of the river Ruhr is not an industrial blackspot but quite rural and idyllic (the big mines and steelworks are a few miles to the north); and here on its banks, within the borders of the Essen residential suburb of Kettwig, is this grey moated 16th-century castle, now a luxurious hotel. Its newly renovated bedrooms, stately furnishings, *Michelin*-rosetted cuisine and "warm and welcoming" ambience continue to be admired. One reader had a large room with a curtained-off sleeping area, and a large marble-tiled bathroom. "A fine black marble staircase with red carpet in the foyer, reception staff very thoughtful, wonderful afternoon tea, and interesting French cooking." The hotel and restaurant cater for functions, but these are not usually obtrusive. (*D and A Lambert*) The grandiose Krupp family mansion in Kettwig, Villa Hügel, now a museum, is worth visiting; and do not miss the Folkwang museum of local history in Essen. Both provide poignant insights into the splendours and horrors of the Ruhr's mighty past.

Open All year except 24 Dec.
Rooms 1 suite, 13 double, 5 single – all with bath (suite also has shower), telephone, radio, TV, air-conditioning.
Facilities Lift. Large hall, salon, wine cellar, restaurant; conference facilities; chapel for weddings and christenings; terrace. Large grounds; garden, tennis.
Location 11 km SW of Essen off A52, near A2 and A3 motorways. Parking.
Credit cards All major cards accepted.
Terms [1990 rates] B&B: single 190–265 DM, double 245–365 DM, suite 590 DM. Half board (min 3 nights) 60 DM per person added. Reduced rates for children sharing parents' room; special meals on request.

KOBLENZ 5400 Rheinland-Pfalz   Map 13

Zum Schwarzen Bären `BUDGET`   *Tel* (0261) 4 40 74
Koblenzer Strasse 35,
Koblenz-Moselweiss

The Rhine and Mosel meet at Koblenz, a city largely rebuilt since wartime bombing: it has few buildings of note save the massive Ehrenbreitstein citadel, but is a good base for exploring these two rivers. The "Black Bears", a small modern winehouse-with-rooms in the western suburb of Moselweiss, has been in the same family since 1810. Rooms are comfortable, but rather basically furnished, with poor lighting, few mirrors or easy chairs, and all but one of the bathrooms have shower, not bath. However, "the hotel's real strength lies in the warmth of the welcome provided by the Kölsch family and Peter Kölsch's superlative cuisine – such as stuffed breast of chicken poached in white wine, pigeon with truffles in a whisper of pastry, apple pancakes with cinnamon ice-cream. He cooks with love, and tells you where you're going wrong when choosing your meal." Endorsed by *NR Measey*: further reports welcome.

Open All year except 1 week in Feb and 3 weeks in July/Aug. Restaurant closed Sun evening and Mon.
Rooms 12 double, 1 single – 1 with bath and shower, 12 with shower; all with telephone, 8 with radio, 5 with TV. 8 in annexe. Some ground-floor rooms.
Facilities Lounge, *Bierstube*, TV room; conference facilities; terrace.
Location 1.5 km W of Koblenz. Parking.
Credit cards All major cards accepted.
Terms B&B: single 70 DM, double 110 DM; dinner, B&B 32 DM per person added. Set lunch 28 DM, dinner 50 DM; full alc 40 DM. Reduced rates and special meals for children.

KÖNIGSTEIN IM TAUNUS 6240 Hessen   Map 13

Hotel Sonnenhof   *Tel* (06174) 2 90 80
Falkensteinerstrasse 9   *Fax* (06174) 29 08 75
                                                        Telex 410636

A ruined feudal fortress looms above this small resort in the Taunus foothills, and here the *Sonnenhof*, formerly owned by Baron Rothschild, stands on a hill in its own large park with giant trees – a big gabled hunting-lodge, spacious and gracious, rather grand in a traditional way. Frankfurt is only 20 minutes' drive away (more at rush-hour) and business visitors with a car might well find it a useful alternative to the downtown hotels, few of them pleasant. It dropped out of last year's Guide, but is now restored by two reports: "Private and peaceful, very good food." "The best hotel that we stayed in. Our room and bathroom were huge, the menu good, and the maître d' most personable." (*Rosemary Dircks, Judge Ralph B Robertson*) Rooms in the modern annexe may be smaller, but have pleasant views.

Open All year.
Rooms 20 double, 25 single – 30 with bath and shower, 15 with TV; all with baby-listening. Ground-floor rooms.
Facilities Hall, salon, bar, restaurant; functions room. Heated indoor swimming pool, sauna, solarium; sun terrrace. Large garden with tennis court.
Location On edge of town, which is 23 km NW of Frankfurt.
Credit cards All major cards accepted.
Terms B&B: single 105–142 DM, double 148–240 DM; dinner, B&B: single 140–177 DM, double 218–310 DM. Set lunch 30 DM, dinner 65–88 DM; full alc 80 DM. Reduced rates and special meals for children.

KRONBERG IM TAUNUS 6242 Hessen   Map 13

Schlosshotel Kronberg   *Tel* (06173) 70 01 01
Hainstrasse 25   *Fax* (06173) 70 12 67
                                             Telex 415424

This vast, grey, towered and gabled *Schloss*, eminently Victorian, was built for Queen Victoria's eldest daughter after the death of her husband, Kaiser Friedrich III. It is now a classy hotel (still sometimes used privately by visiting royalty) but is no more expensive than the leading hotels in central Frankfurt, 17 kilometres away. Recently returning devotees found that standards had if anything improved under a new management; they enjoyed the exotic fruit salad at the lavish breakfast. "For comfort and style, still our favourite hotel in the Frankfurt area," is their view. "Our bedroom overlooking the beautiful grounds was lovely. The public rooms are imposing, with wood panelling and huge tapestries. Staff are polite, the dining rooms attractive and the food good." (*Stephan and Kate Murray-Sykes*) Male guests must wear jacket and tie for dinner.

Open All year.
Rooms 7 suites, 25 double, 25 single – all with bath and/or shower, telephone, radio, TV.
Facilities Lift. Lobby, lounge, bar, restaurant; functions facilities. Park with 18-hole golf course.
Location 15 mins' walk from centre of Kronberg. Open parking.
Restriction Not suitable for &.
Credit cards All major cards accepted.
Terms Rooms: single 274–374 DM, double 413–618 DM, suite 728–1,598 DM. Breakfast 24 DM. Set lunch 60 DM, dinner 135 DM; full alc 110 DM. Special meals for children on request.

LENZKIRCH 7825 Baden-Württemberg   Map 13

Hotel Ursee   *Tel* (07653) 68 80
Grabenstrasse 18

Set amid rolling wooded country just outside the popular resort of Lenzkirch, in the southern Black Forest near Titisee: a big modern chalet, mixing the smart and cosy in true local style. Spacious rooms (with clashing decor), excellent food

including buffet breakfast. Closed early Nov–mid-Dec. Restaurant closed Mon.
49 rooms, most with bath and/or shower. B&B double 106–148 DM. Full alc 33–
60 DM [1990]. Recent nomination. More reports please.

LIMBURG AN DER LAHN 6250 Hessen   Map 13

Romantik Hotel Zimmermann   *Tel* (06431) 46 11
Blumenröderstrasse 1   *Fax* (06431) 4 13 14

Only a short walk from Limburg's picturesque old quarter and Gothic hilltop
cathedral, this modern hotel near the station is dull-looking from outside but
inside is richly furnished with antiques. Triple glazing ensures quiet. Prices
moderate, owner friendly, service thoughtful; dinner for residents only. Closed
Christmas, New Year. 30 rooms, all with bath and/or shower. B&B: single 95–
140 DM, double 125–205 DM. Endorsed recently, but further reports welcome.

LÜBECK 2400 Schleswig-Holstein   Map 13

Hotel Kaiserhof   *Tel* (0451) 79 10 11
Kronsforder Allee 13   *Fax* (0451) 79 50 83
                                                      Telex 26603

It is a token of how seldom Anglo-Americans go on holiday in North
Germany that this should be our first ever entry for one of Europe's most
distinguished cities, the former leader of the Hanseatic League and
birthplace of Thomas Mann, where he set his masterpiece *Buddenbrooks*.
Lübeck lies right on the old GDR border, so has just regained its
hinterland. It has several fine hotels, and readers in 1990 have unearthed
one of the best – a smart conversion of two adjacent patrician houses, just
across the Trave from the historic town centre. "Very friendly welcome,
staff young and attentive. Two elegant lounges, a good buffet breakfast in
a cheerful room. Our bedroom was quiet and comfortable but very
small." "A delightful hotel, where one senses the permeating influence of
the proprietress. No evening meal as such, but the 'snack' was more than
ample, freshly prepared to order. Rooms are double-glazed, and most
face away from the main road. The swimming pool and health club were
invitingly open till 10 pm." (*Gabriele Berneck and Christine Herxheimer,
William N Greenwood*)

Open All year. Restaurant closed Sat and Sun.
Rooms 6 suites, 54 double, 12 single – 32 with bath, 40 shower, all with
telephone, TV. 22 in 3 nearby annexes
Facilities Lift. Lounge, bar; conference facilities. Garden terrace. Indoor
swimming pool, sauna, solarium, fitness centre.
Location 1.5 km S of city centre. Garages and parking.
Credit cards All major cards accepted.
Terms B&B: single 110–155 DM, double 145–195 DM, suite 260–330 DM. (No
restaurant but light evening meal available.)

Don't keep your favourite hotel to yourself. The Guide supports: it
doesn't spoil.

MARKTHEIDENFELD 8772 Bayern   Map 13

Hotel Anker   *Tel* (09391) 40 41
Obertorstrasse 6–8   *Fax* (09391) 15 63
                                                             Telex 689608

In a small wine-growing town on the Main, west of Würzburg, this smart
modern white building is stylishly furnished in good taste (red print in
Michelin) and is owned by the Deppisch family who also have the elegant
Weinhaus Anker restaurant just opposite. "A delightful family-run place.
Much care and pride has been lavished on the rooms. Herr Deppisch
owns extensive vineyards round the hotel, and you can buy his excellent
Franconian wines. The *Weinhaus* well deserves its *Michelin* rosette: all
food, including butter and cheese, comes from their local farm. The
perfect combination of a hotel and restaurant run by people who really
care for their guests." (*Judy and Gordon Smith*) Most rooms overlook a
courtyard and are quiet.

Open All year. Restaurant closed Mon and Tue midday.
Rooms 3 suites, 22 double, 13 single – 30 with bath and shower, 8 with shower,
all with telephone, radio, T V; baby-sitting on request. Ground-floor rooms
suitable for &.
Facilities 2 lifts, ramps. Lounge, T V room, breakfast room, restaurant, cellar (wine
tastings); conference facilities. Courtyard where meals are served.
Location Central, next to church. Garage (8 DM). Town is 29 km W of Würzburg
on B8.
Credit cards Access, Amex, Diners (restaurant only).
Terms B&B: single 90–100 DM, double 140–180 DM, suite 260 DM. Set lunch
40 DM, dinner 50 DM; full alc 90 DM. Reduced rates and special meals for
children.

MEERSBURG 7758 Baden-Württemberg   Map 13

Hotel-Gasthof zum Bären   **BUDGET**   *Tel* (07532) 60 44
Marktplatz 11

Germany's greatest woman poet, Annette von Droste-Hülshoff, died of
consumption and a broken heart, in 1848, gazing out across Lake
Constance from her room (now open to visitors) in the awesome old
fortress at Meersburg, the prettiest town on the lake. Here in the tiny
market square is this stunning old building with flower-pots and carvings
on its quaint corner-tower, an inn since the 17th century, now owned and
run by the charming Gilowsky family. Recent visitors have again liked
this "unpretentious guest house with its creaking wooden floors" and its
warm family welcome. Others have enjoyed the beamed ceilings, Baden
furniture and cheerful rooms, and dishes such as baked perch from the
lake in the "delightful" and informal restaurant: "A spacious, comfortable
room facing the square, with a charming sitting-alcove in the old tower."
(*Dr FP Woodford*) Be warned that the stairs are fairly steep and there is no
lift; also the quieter back rooms lack a view.

Open 20 Mar–15 Nov. Restaurant closed Mon.
Rooms 13 double, 3 single – all with shower.
Facilities 2 restaurants.
Location Central (back rooms quietest). 15 garages.
Restriction Not suitable for &.
Credit cards None accepted.

Terms B&B: single 55 DM, double 105–115 DM. Set lunch/dinner 22–34 DM; full alc 50 DM. Special meals for children.

Hotel Weinstube Löwen
Marktplatz 2

Tel (07532) 60 13
Fax (07541) 7 13 57

Just opposite the *Bären* (see above), and strongly recommended this year as an alternative, especially for its food: "A most picturesque old building (1742), swathed in a wistaria vine, its window-boxes fitted with red geraniums. The interior is furnished with a hodgepodge of antiques, family hand-me-downs, and a forest of potted plants. Bedrooms have sofas and easy chairs. Breakfast was a bountiful buffet. The three-room restaurant is both lovely and cosy, and here we had two outstanding dinners, including shrimp in mustard sauce, fresh Bodensee trout, veal in white wine sauce." (*Dorothy Eggers, also KA*)

Open All year except mid-Nov–mid-Dec. Restaurant closed Wed Nov–May.
Rooms 17 double, 4 single – all with bath and/or shower, telephone, TV.
Facilities 3 dining rooms.
Location Central. Parking nearby.
Restriction Not suitable for &.
Credit cards All major cards accepted.
Terms B&B: single 80–95 DM, double 115–155 DM. Full alc 39 DM. Children under 6 free of charge.

MUNICH 8000 Bayern   Map 13

Acanthus-Hotel
Blumenstrasse 40
Munich 2

Tel (089) 23 18 80
Fax (089) 2 60 73 64

The former Hotel am Sendlinger Tor, *now under new management, with a new name, and newly redecorated. Very central, on Inner Ring. Friendly owners, good service, attractive rooms with antiques. Breakfast only (a "superb" buffet). Indoor garage. Bar open 24 hours. 36 rooms, all with bath and/or shower. B&B: single 120–190 DM, double 160–230 DM. More reports welcome.*

Hotel Marienbad
Barerstrasse 11, Munich 2

Tel (089) 59 55 85
Fax (089) 59 82 38

Centrally and quietly located near the Alte Pinakothek, a small B&B hotel with few frills or graces but friendly and serviceable. Many rooms large and well equipped. 27 rooms, most with shower. B&B: single 65–120 DM, double 160–180 DM. No credit cards accepted. Few recent reports. More welcome.

Hotel an der Oper
Falkenturmstrasse 10
Munich 2

Tel (089) 29 00 27 0
Fax (089) 29 00 27 29
Telex 522588

Down a small side street off the fashionable Maximilianstrasse, this bed-and-breakfast hotel is much frequented by visitors to the nearby Opera – as its name implies. "Friendly atmosphere, good breakfast, and quiet enough", is a 1990 verdict. Earlier an inspector wrote: "The white-walled bedrooms are plain (apart from the ubiquitous chandeliers) but comfortable, with modern bathrooms. A comfortable lobby, too, where newspapers on wooden handles are available in the best Mitteleuropa tradition. Service was helpful and personal. The elegant, intimate and expensive *Bouillabaisse* restaurant is in the same building: its French cooking did not greatly impress us, but there are many cheaper and better places nearby" (e.g. the huge, bustling *Franziskaner*). (*David and Edith Holt, Dale Idiens*)

Open All year.
Rooms 55 – all with bath and/or shower, telephone.
Facilities Lift. Lounge, TV room, breakfast room.
Location Central, near Opera House.
Restriction Not suitable for &.
Credit cards Access, Amex, Diners.
Terms [1990 rates] B&B: single 120–130 DM, double 178–195 DM. (No restaurant.)

Trustee Parkhotel
Parkstrasse 31, Munich 2

Tel (089) 51 99 50
Fax (089) 51 99 54 20
Telex 5218296

This stylish modern hotel, very well equipped, lies west of the city centre and close to the main station, exhibition centre and Theresien park (where the *Oktoberfest* is held). "The bedrooms are enormous, the service friendly and efficient." "First-class welcome, good food, and every facility for the business traveller." The hotel is quiet, built around its own courtyard; all rooms have a balcony. (*G and JC*)

Open All year except 23 Dec–1 Jan.
Rooms 7 suites, 29 double – all with bath, shower, telephone, radio, TV, balcony. Ground-floor rooms.
Facilities Lift. Lounge, piano bar, restaurant; conference facilities. Garden.
Location 1 km SW of central station. Parking.
Credit cards All major cards accepted.
Terms Rooms: single 175–260 DM, double 220–300 DM, suite 290–390 DM. Breakfast 19 DM. Set lunch 35 DM; full alc 60 DM. Children under 12 free of charge; special meals.

MÜNSTER 4400 Nordrhein-Westfalen   **Map 13**

Hotel Schloss Wilkinghege   *Tel* (0251) 21 30 45
Steinfurter Strasse 374

The area around Westphalia's historic capital is well known for its numerous *Wasserburgen* – old castles girt by broad moats or even by lakes. These watery surrounds were originally defensive, but are now ornamental. Some of the castles are still lived in by descendants of the original owners in this very aristocratic part of Germany; others are now colleges, or museums. This one in the city's north-west outskirts, dating from the 16th century, is a fairly smart hotel: "A lovely peaceful setting. Ducks, geese, peacocks, etc, strut in the courtyard within the moat. We stayed in a modern room in the annexe, converted from the stables. The food was excellent and the young staff were pleasant." "We got a friendly welcome and a huge family suite. There's an atmospheric *Schlosskeller*, but we dined out on the terrace – a relaxed ambience, thoughtful service and the best food we had in Germany (but not cheap). The very pretty chapel is open to guests.'' (*Dr Carolyn A Cooper, Mary Hanson*)

Open All year except over Christmas.
Rooms 5 suites, 26 double, 7 single – all with bath or shower, telephone, radio, TV. 18 in annexe.
Facilities Lounge, 3 restaurants, conference and banqueting facilities; terrace. Park with tennis courts and golf course.
Location 2 km NW of city centre, just off B54. Parking.
Credit cards All major cards accepted.
Terms B&B: single 130–165 DM, double 185–210 DM, suite 260–390 DM. Set menus 59–105 DM; full alc 82 DM. Reduced rates for children; special meals on request.

MÜNSTERTAL 7816 Baden-Württemberg   Map 13

Romantik Hotel Spielweg   *Tel* (07636) 70 90
Spielweg 61, Obermünstertal   *Fax* (07636) 7 09 66

Amid beautiful Black Forest meadowland south of Freiburg, an elegant and charming old inn run by the Fuchs family for five generations. Serious nouvelle-*ish cooking* (Michelin *rosette*), *with traditional dishes too, all excellent; cosy comforts, without the folksiness so common in this region. Restaurant closed Mon, Tue lunch. 42 rooms, all with bath or shower. B&B double 160–300 DM. Set meals 45–95 DM. New nomination. More reports please.*

NECKARGEMÜND 6903 Baden-Württemberg   Map 13

Hotel zum Ritter   *Tel* (06223) 70 35
Neckarstrasse 40   *Fax* (06223) 7 33 39
                                            Telex 461837

In a pretty part of the Neckar valley, just east of Heidelberg, here's an old hunting lodge dating from 1579, well modernised but with period touches such as suits of armour. Rooms with riverside views; good breakfasts. 39 rooms, all with shower, 3 also with bath. B&B double from 98 DM. Set meals 50–60 DM. Recent nomination. More reports please, especially on the food.

NECKARZIMMERN 6951 Baden-Württemberg   Map 13

Burg Hornberg   *Tel* (06261) 40 64
                                            Fax (06261) 1 88 64
                                            Telex 466169

The Neckar valley upstream from Heidelberg is festooned with hilltop castles, such as this half-ruined medieval stronghold set amid vines – and new to these pages: "Built in the former stables, the restaurant is the major attraction here: it overlooks the valley, a spectacular sight at dusk especially. The food is good and interesting – salmon in remarkable gratin sauce, duck liver with chanterelles, generous venison ragout with dumplings. The house wine from their own vineyards is excellent. Most bedrooms are in a purpose-built chalet in the old barn foundations: they are pleasant enough but some are noisy. New rooms are to be converted in the 17th-century part of the building (it houses a museum). The three best rooms, light and spacious, are up in the woods above the private flat of the baroness, a Grace Kelly lookalike, who owns the castle. She welcomed us warmly, and gave us a bottle of their own bubbly to apologise for a muddle they had made over booking. The buffet breakfast is substantial." (*Ian and Francine Walsh*)

Open 1 Mar–1 Dec.
Rooms 2 suites, 19 double, 3 single – all with bath, shower, telephone, radio, TV, baby-listening; most with air-conditioning.
Facilities Lounge, TV room, 2 restaurants; conference facilities. Garden.
Location 25 km N of Heilbronn.
Restriction Not suitable for &.
Credit cards Access, Visa.
Terms [1990 rates] B&B: single 100–120 DM, double 150–180 DM, suite 250–279 DM. Half board 40 DM per person added. Full alc 70 DM.

OBERAMMERGAU 8103 Bayern   Map 13

Gasthof Zur Rose   BUDGET   *Tel* (08822) 47 06
Dedlerstrasse 9

Even outside Passion Play Year (once a decade, next one in 2000 AD), Oberammergau remains an unashamedly touristy place, with every other shop a *Holzschnitzerei* selling wood carvings, mostly religious but trashy (best are those in the Pilatushaus cooperative). In any year it is also a good centre for hiking or cross-country skiing. The modest *Zur Rose*, admired again this year as "excellent value", has been called "the quintessence of the *gemütlich* – a fine example of a friendly Alpine inn. The Stückl family innkeepers are warmly hospitable. The rooms, well heated, are simple but not spartan. In the big attractive dining room, meals are substantial meaty affairs; public rooms are full of fine furniture and old paintings (family heirlooms)." (*Stephen Ruell, Esler Crawford*)

Open All year except 1 Nov–15 Dec, Christmas, New Year. Closed Mon.
Rooms 21 double, 2 single – all with shower. 10 self-catering units for 2–6 people with telephone and TV.
Facilities Salon, dining room. Garden.
Location In town centre. Parking. Oberammergau is 19 km N of Garmisch.
Credit cards Access, Visa.
Terms B&B 35–40 DM; dinner, B&B 25 DM per person added. Full alc 30 DM. Reduced rates and special meals for children.

OBERKIRCH 7602 Baden-Württemberg   Map 13

Romantik Hotel zur Oberen   *Tel* (07802) 80 20
  Linde   *Fax* (07802) 30 30
Hauptstrasse 25   *Telex* 752640

An archetypal half-timbered hostelry in a busy town on the western fringe of the Black Forest, not far from Strasbourg. Its nominator this year found that its folksiness was not the enemy of true quality: "Lorries rumble by its windows, but guests are mostly put up in a newer half-timbered building at the back, overlooking well-tended gardens where you can take lunch or tea. Here we had a room with beautifully carved furniture, a four-poster bed and a flower-decked balcony. The long corridors are adorned with knick-knacks – costumed dolls, witches on broomsticks, etc. There's a children's play area with rocking horses and battered teddies. The restaurant has two rooms, each with a very different atmosphere – one rustic style, the other sophisticated. Service was variable, but the food was delightful: goose liver with chanterelles, fresh river crayfish, venison in red fruit sauce. And breakfast was superb, including carrot juice and a large variety of muesli. In sum, a good place with a friendly staff and warm atmosphere." (*Ian and Francine Walsh*)

Open All year.
Rooms 1 suite, 32 double, 4 single – all with bath, shower, telephone; some with radio, TV. 20 in annexe.
Facilities Lift. TV lounge, 2 restaurants, *Weinstube*; conference facilities. Terrace; garden with tennis court and children's playground.
Location Central, parking. Town is 30 km E of Strasbourg.
Restriction Not suitable for &.
Credit cards All major cards accepted.
Terms B&B: single 100–145 DM, double 160–210 DM, suite 240 DM. Dinner, B&B 35 DM per person added; full board 58 DM added. Full alc 60 DM. Reduced rates and special meals for children.

OBERWESEL 6532 Rheinland-Pfalz   Map 13

Burghotel-Restaurant Auf   *Tel* (06744) 70 27
   Schönburg   *Fax* (06744) 16 13
Oberwesel   *Telex* 42321

Recent visitors were mightily impressed: "Upstream from Koblenz, towering high above the west bank of the Rhine, the massive medieval stronghold of the Dukes of Schönburg is three fortresses in one, each with its own keep. One is now used as a Catholic holiday and social centre, and the others have been tastefully converted into as delightful a hotel as any that we have visited recently in Germany. It is owned and run by a friendly and civilised young couple, the Hüttls. While the *Burg*'s outward aspect is severe, inside all is intimate and cosy – small beamed courtyards and dining rooms, a handsome library, slightly twee bedrooms with four-posters (best are those with balconies in the old tower). It's the kind of obviously super-romantic place that foreign tourists would adore, yet is no phoney tourist-trap, for it's all done with taste and unaffected grace. Of course the view over the river is superb. The Hüttls have painted one of the outer walls bright red, because that's how it was in the 16th century, when painted walls were a sign of wealth." "Attractively furnished with antiques; beautiful restaurant with a sense of intimacy, excellent food and service." (*ECM Begg, and others*)

Open 1 Mar–30 Nov. Restaurant closed Mon.
Rooms 2 suites, 17 double, 3 single – 13 with bath and shower, 8 with shower, all with telephone, radio, TV; baby-listening on request.
Facilities Lift. Sitting room with open fire, small library, conference room, 3 dining rooms; courtyard where meals are served in fine weather.
Location 2 km S of Oberwesel, which is 42 km S of Koblenz.
Restriction Not suitable for &.
Credit cards All major cards accepted.

Terms B&B: single 85–95 DM, double 135–220 DM, suite 260–320 DM. Set menus: vegetarian 40 DM, regional 50 DM, gourmet 92 DM; full alc 60 DM. Reduced rates and special meals for children.

OFFENBURG 7600 Baden-Württemberg   Map 13

Hotel Sonne   `BUDGET`   *Tel* (0781) 7 10 39
Hauptstrasse 94

Conveniently close to Strasbourg, the Black Forest and the Frankfurt–Basel *Autobahn*, Offenburg is an industrial town with a pleasant traffic-free old quarter – and here stands this venerable family-run coaching-inn. A hostelry is thought to have stood here since about 1350; and though much rebuilt in the 19th century, the hotel still has many earlier antiques. Napoleon stayed here, and you are shown the pewter tureen he used. But despite this weight of history, the *Sonne* is quite unpretentious – no foyer, the front door leads straight into the big beamed *Stube*, which today is very much a social centre for local worthies. The sound Baden cooking goes well with the local wine from the owners' own vineyards. Reports this year and last: "Amazing building; service marvellous, breakfasts excellent, menu meals not exciting but good value." "Wholesome, unsophisticated cooking." Rooms vary, some being old and full of charm but unmodernised, others newer but duller. (*WP and BJ Barry*)

Open All year.
Rooms 2 suites, 14 double, 21 single – 20 with bath, shower, telephone; 16 rooms in annexe.
Facilities TV room, 2 dining rooms, functions room.
Location Central; in pedestrian zone in old part of town. Parking.
Restriction Only restaurant suitable for &.
Credit cards Access, Amex, Visa.
Terms B&B: single 48–67 DM, double 70–90 DM, suite 145–160 DM. Set lunch/dinner 20–28 DM. Special meals for children on request.

PASSAU 8390 Bayern   Map 13

Hotel Wilder Mann, Restaurant   *Tel* (0851) 3 50 71
** Kaiserin Sissi**   *Fax* (0851) 3 17 12
Am Rathausplatz

In a beautiful old city on the Danube, by the Austrian border, a tactfully converted old merchant's house, with period furnishings. Comfortable rooms with views. Tiny indoor swimming pool. Excellent food in separately managed restaurant. 49 rooms, most with bath or shower. B&B: single 60–130 DM, double 100–240 DM. Alc meals (excluding wine) 58–90 DM [1990]. New nomination. More reports welcome.

We should like to offer entries for hotels of genuine character in Eastern Europe. They may be hard to find, but if you know of any that meet our criteria, please let us know.

PEGNITZ 8570 Bayern   Map 13

Pflaum's Posthotel Pegnitz   *Tel* (09241) 72 50
Nürnberger Strasse 12–16   *Fax* (09241) 4 04
                                                        Telex 642433

The Pflaum family's characterful old posthouse in a small Franconian
town is now a stylish and "very civilised" hotel, patronised by famous
musicians visiting nearby Bayreuth, and again this year it has drawn
eulogies from readers. "In the atmospheric restaurant, service was
brilliant, food and wine superb (*Michelin* rosette). My room was of nostalgic elegance. Public areas a bit over-decorated, too many souvenirs."
"Charming welcome, attentive service, food and drink as good as we
have had anywhere in Germany. Beautiful breakfast. Bedrooms comfortable, but decor a bit 'fifties'." A devotee wrote earlier: "All Pflaums
hospitable as ever. One brother is the charming manager, another is
considered one of Germany's best chefs. They gave us a delicious room
full of colour. Breakfast is pure theatre – five round tables laid out with
everything. The staff look slinky and *moderne* in pretty blouses and skirts.
If you like a country house-style hotel with an international and musical
flavour, this one is very much worth a detour. Drinks by the fire in
winter, with pretty little curved sofas to sit on; in summer, coffee out in
the sunshine with the fountains playing, or strawberry cake for tea." (*A
and C Herxheimer and Gabriele Berneck, D Barr and others*) The Pflaums also
offer Bayreuth Wagner operas on a large screen.

Open All year.
Rooms 25 suites, 25 double – all with bath, shower, telephone, radio, TV.
1 ground-floor suite.
Facilities Lift. Lounge, bar, 2 restaurants; conference facilities. Health club,
swimming pool, sauna. Garden with terrace for dining.
Location 1 km SW of Pegnitz, 33 km N of Nuremberg.
Credit cards All major cards accepted.
Terms Rooms: single 135–258 DM, double 168–490 DM, suite 295–1,150 DM.
Buffet breakfast 18 DM. Set lunch 35 DM, dinner 140 DM; full alc 110 DM.
Reduced rates and special meals for children.

RAVENSBURG 7980 Baden-Württemberg   Map 13

Romantik Hotel Waldhorn   *Tel* (0751) 1 60 21
Marienplatz 15   *Fax* (0751) 1 75 32
                                                        Telex 732311

*In an attractive old Swabian town, a family-run hotel of some character, in an
old building with panelled public rooms. Pleasant bedrooms, excellent local
dishes (Michelin rosette), good buffet breakfasts in a cosy room. 35 rooms, all
with bath and shower. B&B: single 90–135 DM, double 135–200 DM. Set menu
44 DM. Endorsed this year, but fuller reports welcome.*

The length of an entry need not reflect the merit of a hotel. The more
interesting the report or the more unusual or controversial the hotel,
the longer the entry.

REGENSBURG 8400 Bayern   Map 13

Bischofshof am Dom   *Tel* (0941) 5 90 86
Krauterermarkt 3

Our first entry for one of Bavaria's loveliest medieval cities, nominated
this year: "A former bishop's residence, sprucely converted, it stands next
to the splendid soaring cathedral, in a quiet patio (beer garden in summer)
with one of those comic fountains that the Germans adore. This one is of
a goose-luring fox disguised as a priest: once a year it flows beer, not
water. Cosy bedrooms and good classic food such as sucking pig and
tafelspitz: the owner/chef, Herr Schmalhofer, was for 13 years the private
chef of Germany's richest man, the Fürst von Thurn und Taxis, whose
Schloss is down the road. Considering this, prices are pretty reasonable."
"An outstanding and enjoyable place to stay." (*JA, Ido Pittman Jnr*)

Open All year.
Rooms 60 – all with bath and/or shower, telephone, TV.
Facilities Lift. Lounge, restaurant, patio; conference facilities.
Location Central.
Restriction Not suitable for &.
Credit cards All major cards accepted.
Terms [1990 rates] B&B: single 90–185 DM, double 125–280 DM. Alc meals
(excluding wine) 22–75 DM.

REICHENAU (Insel) 7752 Baden-Württemberg   Map 13

Romantik Hotel Seeschau   *Tel* (07534) 2 57
Schiffslände 8   *Fax* (07534) 78 94

Reichenau is a flat island in the western part of the Bodensee (Lake
Constance), linked to the mainland by a causeway. In the Middle Ages it
was a major monastic centre, and two glories survive from that time: the
late 9th-century Carolingian church of St-George (amazing wall paintings
of around AD 1000), and the Romanesque abbey at Mittelzell. Today the
island is given over to market gardening and tourism, and its best hotel
is the *Seeschau*, a gabled building by the water's edge, run by the
Winkelmann-Roser family for 60 years. A recent report: "Charming and
friendly, quite spruce and smart – panelled walls, old framed prints,
uniformed waitresses. Bedrooms a bit small, but most have lake views.
Good local fish, prepared by Horst Winkelmann in a *nouvelle*-ish style,
just about deserving its *Michelin* rosette. Lovely setting by the little
landing-stage, but very trippery in summer." (*JA and KA*) More reports
please.

Open Feb–mid-Oct. Restaurant closed Sun and Mon.
Rooms 4 suites, 11 double – all with bath or shower, telephone, TV.
Facilities Salon, 2 restaurants; conference facilities. Garden, terrace.
Location 10 km W of Konstanz. Reached by ferry or causeway. Parking.
Restriction Not suitable for &.
Credit cards All major cards accepted.
Terms [1990 rates] B&B: single 70–130 DM, double 140–180 DM, suite 200 DM.
Set lunch/dinner 60 DM; alc meals (excluding wine) 38–75 DM. Special meals for
children.

ROTHENBURG OB DER TAUBER 8803 Bayern   Map 13

Hotel-Gasthof Glocke   *Tel* (09861) 30 25
Am Plönlein 1   *Fax* (09861) 8 67 11
                                                    Telex 61318

Our only surviving entry for this much-visited medieval ramparted town
on the Romantiker Strasse. It is quite central but just away from the main
tourist concourse, down a side street, and has been commended by four
reports this year. "Cosy, friendly and *gemütlich*, with different levels and
staircases. Our room, very quiet and comfortable, had a balcony looking
over a little wild garden full of roses. Staff were young and pleasant,
but dinner was ordinary." "Big, clean rooms and a good restaurant."
"Cooking is Bavarian, and comes with good red wine from the owners'
vineyards. The garage is useful." (*Mrs RB Richards, Mrs K Plowden, Mr and
Mrs Marioni*)

Open 14 Jan–23 Dec.
Rooms 28 – all with bath, 12 with shower, telephone.
Facilities Lift. Restaurant, TV room, wine bar with wine tasting, children's games
room; conference facilities.
Location Central. Parking.
Restriction Not suitable for &.
Credit cards All major cards accepted.
Terms B&B: single 89–105 DM, double 140–162 DM. Set lunch 36 DM; dinner
22–48 DM. Reduced rates and special meals for children.

ROTTACH-EGERN 8183 Bayern   Map 13

Seehotel Überfahrt   *Tel* (08022) 66 90
7 Überfahrtstrasse   *Fax* (08022) 6 58 35
                                                    Telex 526935

Rottach, "the Sylt of the South", is Bavaria's trendiest lakeside resort, full
of boutiques and Munich *Schickeria* (but that does not prevent herds of
cows from parading serenely down its main street, Bavarian-style). Egern
is its quieter residential bit, and here right by the lovely crystal-green
Tegernsee is this Guide newcomer, large and smart but family-owned,
patronised by Bavarian government VIPs. "Public rooms are spacious,
partly elegant with velvet armchairs and oriental rugs, partly rustic with
painted peasant cupboards. Friendly atmosphere, attentive service,
delicious food and wine, generous buffet breakfast including smoked
salmon and roast beef. Nice head waitress in local costume. Cosy
bedrooms (some of the pseudo-Bavarian decor not to our taste)." (*Gabriele
Berneck and Christine Herxheimer; JA and KA*)

Open All year.
Rooms 25 suites, 115 double and single – all with bath and/or shower, telephone,
TV; some with balcony or terrace.
Facilities Lift. Lounges, restaurant; conference facilities. Indoor swimming pool,
sauna, massage. Terrace.
Location 56 km S of Munich, 1 km from centre of Rottach. Parking.
Credit cards Access, Amex, Diners.
Terms [1990 rates] B&B: single 150–220 DM, double 220–280 DM, suite 320–
360 DM. Alc meals (excluding wine) 48–75 DM.

RÜDESHEIM-ASSMANNSHAUSEN 6220 Hessen   Map 13

Hotel Krone   *Tel* (06722) 20 36
Rheinuferstrasse 10   *Fax* (06722) 30 49

Hoffmann von Fallersleben composed *Deutschland über Alles* in 1841 at
this famous old Rhineside inn which dates from 1541 and has long been a
haunt of writers and musicians. It is now a fairly big and grand hotel in
two buildings: many bedrooms have a balcony overlooking the gardens
and river. Many reports have reached us recently, nearly all favourable.
"Wonderful. We were given a sumptuous room, close to the secluded,
beautiful swimming pool, surrounded by climbing roses. The view of the
Rhine from the creeper-covered dining terrace is unforgettable, and the
food is masterly – start your meal with the local red Sekt and you will be
at peace with the world." The rooms in the main annexe are heavily
furnished in pompous Victorian style (stag's antlers a bit off-putting) but
comfortable, clean and well plumbed. "We had a room with circular
turret and elegant marble bathroom" (as of 1990, all rooms have marble
bathrooms). "Super classical food as always." (*Dr RP Woodford, Angela and
David Stewart, and others*) A reader this year had a spacious suite facing
the river, but thought the food to be lacking distinction and the service
lacking warmth. Be warned of some night noise from the railway.

Open 1 Mar–1 Jan.
Rooms 11 suites, 41 double, 11 single – 56 with bath and shower, 7 with shower,
5 with jacuzzi, all with telephone, radio, TV; many with balcony. Most rooms in
annexe. Some on ground floor.
Facilities Lift. Salon, TV room, bar, restaurant; riverside terrace/restaurant;
conference facilities. Garden with lawn and swimming pool.
Location On the Rhine; parking. Assmannshausen is 5 km W of Rüdesheim,
36 km W of Wiesbaden.
Restriction Not suitable for &.
Credit cards Access, Diners, Visa.
Terms Rooms: single 120–240 DM, double 190–320 DM, suite 340–680 DM.
Breakfast 18 DM. Set lunch 45 DM, dinner 80–115 DM. Special meals for children.

ST GOAR 5401 Rheinland-Pfalz   Map 13

Hotel Landsknecht   `BUDGET`   *Tel* (06741) 20 11
An der Rheinufer   *Fax* (06741) 74 99

*A traditional gabled inn, on a picturesquely castle-strewn stretch of the Rhine,
near the Lorelei. Well-equipped bedrooms, many with good river views.
Friendly staff, pleasant dining room and outdoor river-terrace; food so-so. 15
rooms, all with bath and shower. B&B: single 65–95 DM, double 110–170 DM.
Set meals 20–30 DM. Attractive new nomination. More reports please.*

****
Traveller's tale *The plates for the steak were cold. On being told this,
the waitress (one of the owners) said: "Chefs simply won't heat plates
these days."*
****

SCHARBEUTZ 2409 Schleswig-Holstein Map 13

Kurhotel Martensen – Die Barke
Strandallee 123

Tel (04503) 71 17
Fax (04503) 7 35 40
Telex 261445

Just north of elegant Travemünde (the Deauville of the Baltic, where Thomas Mann used to stay and set parts of *Buddenbrooks*), Scharbeutz is a less prestigious but lively family bathing resort; and the *Martensen*, white-walled and red-roofed, is the best of its many holiday hotels along the beach. Bedrooms, some in the older building, some in a new annexe, are nearly all spacious, and some have big sea-facing balconies. Renewed praise this year. "Friendly, with good food." "Old-fashioned but a delight, and excellent value. Our room was bright and airy. The fish dishes were especially good." The "superb" indoor heated pool, and the buffet breakfast with local dishes, have also been commended. (*William A Grant, David and Patricia Hawkins*)

Open 1 Mar–15 Nov.
Rooms 3 suites, 20 double, 15 single – all with bath or shower, telephone, radio, TV; many with balcony.
Facilities Lift. Lounge, TV room, 2 restaurants. Indoor swimming pool, sauna, massage. Garden.
Location On seafront. Parking. Scharbeutz is 26 km N of Lübeck.
Restriction Not suitable for &.
Credit cards Access, Diners, Visa.
Terms B&B: single 75–125 DM, double 150–250 DM. Dinner, B&B 20 DM added per person; full board 32 DM added. Set lunch/dinner 25–35 DM; full alc 50–55 DM. Reduced rates and special meals for children.

SCHLESWIG 2380 Schleswig-Holstein Map 13

Strandhalle Ringhotel **BUDGET**
  Schleswig
Strandweg 2 (am Jachthafen)

Tel (04621) 2 20 21
Fax (04621) 2 89 33
Telex 221327

This ancient city looks on the map as if it is well inland, but in fact it is linked to the Baltic by a long inlet, the Schlei. The museum at lovely Gottorf Castle contains not only the remarkable 4th-century Nydam boat, but skeletons of people who 2,000 years ago were trussed up and put out on the marshes to die slowly, as a punishment. No such harm will befall you at the attractive *Strandhalle*, a modern hotel whose pleasant café-terrace faces a marina on the Schlei. "Comfortable and charming, with an excellent quiet swimming pool," says a reader this year. "My balcony gave lovely views over the Schlei. Half-board dinners were of good quality (e.g. lobster bisque and ragoût of tongue) but there was no choice." Others have enjoyed the friendly atmosphere, and the unusual nautical decor and knick-knacks. (*Adrian J Lyons*)

Open All year.
Rooms 18 double, 6 single – all with bath and/or shower, telephone, radio, TV, mini-bar.
Facilities Salons, restaurant; conference facilities. Café-terrace and garden. Indoor swimming pool, solarium, sauna.
Location Central; by yacht harbour. Parking.
Credit cards All major cards accepted.
Terms B&B: single 75 DM, double 120–160 DM. Set meals 20–40 DM.

SCHÖNWALD 7741 Baden-Württemberg   Map 13

Hotel Zum Ochsen   *Tel* (07722) 10 45
Ludwig-Uhland Strasse 18   *Fax* (07722) 30 18
                                                   Telex 792606

"Elegant rustic" is how readers describe this typical chalet-style Black
Forest hotel, set amid rolling woods and meadows just outside the resort-
village of Schönwald, south of Triberg. Owned by the Martin family for
generations, it has recently been rebuilt in a style at once smart and
folksy, with lots of light new wood and pale carpets. The ambience too is
informal yet sophisticated, appealing to "the classier kind of hiker" – you
could arrive in an old jersey with a rucksack or dressed by Lagerfeld and
feel equally at ease. Good Baden-cum-Alsatian cooking (soupe aux
escargots, foie gras maison, etc) served by waitresses in Baden costume,
on the patio in summer, by a log fire in winter. Musical evenings and
excursions are organised. Pleasant indoor hexagonal pool. "Good food,
and Frau Martin a welcoming hostess," says a recent visitor. (*JA and KA,
Mr and Mrs RW Beacroft*)

Open All year.
Rooms 4 suites, 34 double, 5 single – all with bath and/or shower, telephone, TV.
Facilities Lounge, 3 restaurants; terrace. Indoor heated swimming pool, sauna
and solarium. Large grounds with tennis court and lake with fishing. Bicycles.
Location 8 km S of Triberg. Just outside village. Parking.
Restriction Not suitable for &.
Credit cards All major cards accepted.
Terms B&B: single 53–101 DM, double 96–176 DM, suite 202 DM; dinner, B&B
74–127 DM per person; full board 86–139 DM. Set lunch/dinner 30 DM; full alc
45 DM. Reduced rates and special meals for children.

SCHWANGAU 8959 Bayern   Map 13

Schlosshotel Lisl und Jägerhaus   *Tel* (08362) 8 10 06
Neuschwansteinstrasse 1–3   *Fax* (08362) 8 11 07
Hohenschwangau   *Telex* 541332

The Bavarian royal castles in their glorious mountain setting – mad
Ludwig's high-pinnacled fairy-tale Neuschwanstein, and Hohenschwangau – are both close to this "unusual hotel". The dining room's big
windows have Hohenschwangau in full floodlit view, and many of the
bedrooms share this panorama – "What a romantic spot to spend the
night!" Two visitors this year thought the hotel "elegant but eccentric"
(velvet carpeting may cover walls as well as floor), and a third explained
more fully: "An excellent stop-over. Our room in the attractive Jägerhaus
annexe was immense and had every comfort, but the restaurant was of
varying standard. Our waiter, somewhere between Fawlty's Manuel and
Charlie Chaplin, rated high in entertainment value but was a non-starter
otherwise." Others, however, have found the staff "efficient and
courteous" and have enjoyed the food. (*Lon Bailey, Mrs JA Powell, Dale
Idiens*) It seems that a heavy influx of package groups can affect service,
though tour groups are put in separate dining rooms. Dinner is served
early – 6.30–8 pm.

Open All year except 4 Jan–15 Mar.

Rooms 45 double, 11 single – 45 with bath, 19 with shower, 49 with telephone, 29 with radio, 4 with TV. 20 in annexe.
Facilities Lift. Lounge, TV room, 5 dining rooms. Swimming in Alpssee nearby.
Location 6 km SE of Füssen.
Restriction Not suitable for &.
Credit cards All major cards accepted.
Terms B&B: single 70–100 DM, double 100–243.60 DM. Full alc 47 DM. Reduced rates and special meals for children.

SCHWARZWALD-HOCHSTRASSE 7580 Baden-Württemberg   Map 13

Höhen-Hotel Unterstmatt   *Tel* (07226) 2 04
Bühl 13

The Black Forest High Road winds along the hillcrest south from Baden-Baden, with fine views over the Rhine plain below. Here, circled by meadows and deep pine-forests, stands "this lovely hotel" (to quote from one report this year). Friendly and informal, it has been owned and run since 1905 by the Reymanns, and caters for families who come to ski in winter or hike in summer. "Very well run," says another recent visitor, "I had a superb meal in the more formal restaurant, clad in collar and tie, but also enjoyed eating in the cosy cellar *Stube* wearing my walking gear, and I felt at home in both." Returning inspectors have also been delighted: "Quite unchanged. The lively *Stube* has harmonica music and singing, and attracts locals. Superb local smoked ham, served with kirsch and crispy country bread by dirndl'd waitresses. Bedrooms are simple, in rustic style, with bright colours; some have four-posters and Baden painted cupboards. The hotel's own ski-slope (for beginners) rises from its back terrace: this is floodlit for night-skiing and has a snow machine using up to 100,000 litres of water a day." (*CWH Vandermeer, Trevor Lockwood, and others*)

Open All year except 5 Nov–15 Dec. Restaurant closed Mon evening and Tue.
Rooms 1 suite, 11 double, 6 single – 6 with bath, 9 with shower, all with telephone; radio and TV on request.
Facilities Hall, bar, restaurant, cellar tavern. Beer garden; sun terrace, where meals are served. 4 ski-lifts.
Location 15 km S of Baden-Baden.
Credit cards All major cards accepted.
Terms [1990 rates] B&B 55–60 DM; dinner, B&B 25 DM per person added; full board 45 DM added. Full alc 75 DM. Reduced rates and special meals for children.

SEEBRUCK 8221 Bayern   Map 13

Hotel Restaurant Malerwinkel   *Tel* (08667) 4 88
Lambach 23

In a small resort on the north shore of Bavaria's largest lake, the quiet Chiemsee (do not fail to visit the enchanting Fraueninsel with its Benedictine convent), a friendly and unpretentiously elegant modern hotel with a lovely lakeside setting. Very good food and service. 20 rooms, all with shower. B&B: single 65–110 DM, double 140–150 DM. Alc meals 50 DM. New nomination. More reports welcome.

SEEG 8959 Bayern   Map 13

Pension Heim   **BUDGET**   *Tel* (08364) 2 58
Aufmberg 8

This quiet and appealing family-run *pension* is a modern building in white-washed, flower-decked Bavarian style, set on a low hill north of Füssen and the royal castles; it has views of Alps, lakes and forests, and south-facing rooms have balconies. A recent verdict: "A luxurious version of the homely style, with solid carved furniture, both in the room and on the balcony, and a ravishing view of the Alps beyond nearby lush meadows. The single-choice evening meal can be hampering, especially if you don't like pork, but they cooked us a huge omelette on request." (*Dr FP Woodford*) Others, too, have found the cooking a little plain – but you can eat out in the village if you prefer, or in the nearby town of Hopfen. Apart from this one drawback, readers stress the comfort of the rooms, the "superb" breakfasts, the idyllic rural setting. "Charming host and hostess, sparkling cleanliness." There is a pleasant lounge; some of the carved furniture is Herr Heim's own work. (Endorsed in 1990 by *Jennifer M Dougan*)

Open 20 Dec–1 Nov. Restaurant closed for lunch.
Rooms 14 double, 4 single – all with bath or shower, telephone; some with balcony; TV on request.
Facilities Hall, restaurant, *Allgäuer Stube*, TV room; sauna. Terrace.
Location On hilltop outside Seeg, which is 15 km NW of Füssen.
Restriction Not suitable for &.
Credit cards None accepted.
Terms B&B: single 55–60 DM, double 100–110 DM. Half board 12 DM per person added. Reduced rates for children sharing parents' room.

STUTTGART 7000 Baden-Württemberg   Map 13

Gaststätte zum Muckenstüble   **BUDGET**   *Tel* (0711) 86 51 22
Solitudestrasse 25
Stuttgart 31–Weilimdorf

A bare ten kilometres from the city centre, yet on the edge of deep country, just below the hilltop Schloss Solitude that an 18th-century Duke of Württemberg built for one of his mistresses. An inspector has again enjoyed the "excellent Swabian cuisine" (e.g. Stuttgartertopf, and roast sucking-pig with spätzle) which is served at modest prices on a garden terrace or in the rustic-style *Stube* at this unpretentious family-run inn, a modern building in traditional half-timbered style. Bedrooms are plain and fairly small, but newly modernised; there's a garden with kids' playground. "We were so close to the big industrial city, yet seemed to be in the heart of rural Swabia. If you have a car, it's an ideal alternative to the soulless downtown hotels."

Open All year except 3 weeks in July. Restaurant closed Tue.
Rooms 25 – all with bath, telephone; many with balcony.
Facilities Lift. TV room, restaurant. Garden with terrace and children's play area.
Location In suburb of Weilimdorf. 10 km W of city centre. Parking.
Credit cards None accepted.
Terms [1990 rates] B&B: single 62 DM, double 104 DM. Set meals 20–30 DM; full alc 45 DM. Special meals for children.

TIEFENBRONN 7533 Baden-Württemberg   Map 13

Ochsen Post   *Tel* (07234) 80 30
Franz-Josef-Gall-Strasse 13   *Fax* (07234) 55 54
                                                   Telex 783485

Tiefenbronn, near the jewellery-making town of Pforzheim, is a big
village with an ancient Gothic church. Here the Weis family's *Ochsen Post*
is suitably lavish and ornate – an old 17th-century inn, black-beamed and
flower-girt outside, opulently folksy inside in the south German manner,
and with modern comforts. Visitors in 1990 much enjoyed a meal in the
light and summery conservatory (*Michelin* rosette): "Tables are well
spaced and the low piped music is not obtrusive. Mushrooms with
noodles in a cream sauce, duck breast in madeira sauce, and lobster and
sweetbreads with different sauces were all excellent – and the portions
much larger than at similar *nouvelle cuisine* restaurants in France or
Britain. Our room was furnished in local style with lots of natural wood
and painted wooden furniture – slightly heavy and dark, but reasonable
value." Tables are set for dinner with silver platters edged with gold,
silver cutlery and crystal glass. On warm evenings you can sit in the
courtyard with a cool beer. (*Kate and Stephan Murray-Sykes*)

Open All year except 2 weeks in Jan and Christmas. Restaurant closed Sun
evening, Mon and Tue midday.
Rooms 14 double, 5 single – 7 with bath, 11 with shower, all with telephone and
radio; some with TV.
Facilities Lounge, bistro/bar, restaurant, winter garden.
Location Leave A8 (E52) at Heimsheim exit. Continue to Heimsheim; turn right at
Tiefenbronn sign. Hotel is central; parking.
Restriction Not suitable for &.
Credit cards All major cards accepted.
Terms B&B: single 75–98 DM, double 98–138 DM. Set menus 69–145 DM; full alc
89 DM. Special meals for children.

TRIBERG IM SCHWARZWALD 7740 Baden-Württemberg   Map 13

Parkhotel Wehrle   *Tel* (07722) 8 60 20
Gartenstrasse 24   *Fax* (07722) 86 02 90

Triberg is a leading Black Forest resort known for its high terraced
waterfall, its cuckoo clock-making and its local costumes (the folk
museum is fascinating). Here this fairly luxurious old hostelry has been
owned and run by the Wehrle/Blum family since 1707, and has been
admired again this year and last for its sumptuous furnishings, warm
ambience and excellent cuisine (*Michelin* rosette). This is *nouvelle*-ish, but
helpings are not stinted; trout is a speciality, prepared in 20 ways. Some
rooms are in the old building, where party walls are thin; others are in
two more modern buildings beside a garden. "Claus Blum is a civilised
host and imparts a cultivated atmosphere; service is skilled and stylish.
Delightful outdoor and indoor swimming pools. Many rather grand
people, such as groups of Arab sheikhs or Stuttgart tycoons, come here
for special occasions." "Scrupulously managed in old-fashioned style but
with plenty of space-age plumbing facilities." (*Angela and David Stewart,
WG Francis, Dr Ian Anderson*)

Open All year.

Rooms 2 suites, 42 double, 12 single – all with bath and/or shower, telephone, radio, TV. 20 in garden annexe.
Facilities 2 lounges, bar, 4 dining rooms; conference room. Indoor and outdoor heated swimming pools; sauna, solarium, massage. Large garden.
Location Central, near market place (quietest rooms overlook garden). Parking.
Restriction Only dining rooms suitable for &.
Credit cards All major cards accepted.
Terms B&B: single 89–157 DM, double 159–254 DM. Half board 35 DM per person added. Set lunch 38 DM, dinner 49–75 DM; full alc 65 DM. Reduced rates and special meals for children.

TRIER 5500 Rheinland-Pfalz **Map 13**

Petrisberg Hotel *Tel* (0651) 4 11 81
Sickingenstrasse 11–13

Trier is not only the centre of the Mosel wine trade and the town where Karl Marx was born (his house is a museum), but under the Emperors Diocletian and Constantine it was a major Roman capital. This past grandeur is today evoked by the Porta Nigra, finest Roman relic in Germany, and by other imperial buildings. One merit of the *Petrisberg*, a modern family-run bed-and-breakfast hotel, is that it stands in a splendid position amid vineyards, high on a hill above the city with a view of those Roman ruins – and rooms facing the city have a balcony. Again in 1989/90 it has been much liked – for the personal service by its "gracious" owner, Herr Pantenburg, its "bountiful" breakfasts (sometimes including bacon and egg), and the fine views and spacious rooms. "The hotel is full of plants, statues, pictures, antiques. Watching the sun rise over the city was memorable." "The best Mosel we tasted in the region" comes from the hotel's vineyards, leased to the Bishop of Trier. (*Norma Kessler, JD Eagles, Capt JW Behle and others*) One 1989 dissenter found a lack of human and physical warmth.

Open All year.
Rooms 3 suites, 26 double, 2 single – 3 with bath, 28 with shower, all with telephone; many with balcony. 12 in annexe. 2 ground-floor rooms.
Facilities Salon, TV room, breakfast room, wine bar. Garden and terraces.
Location 20 mins' walk from town centre (near Roman amphitheatre). Parking area and garages (5 DM).
Restriction Not suitable for &.
Credit cards None accepted.
Terms B&B: single 80 DM, double 125 DM, suite 180 DM. Reduced rates for children sharing parents' room. (No restaurant, but light evening meals available.)

Hotel Villa Hügel *Tel* (0651) 3 30 66
Bernhardstrasse 14

An attractive alternative to the Petrisberg: *a white chalet-like Jugendstil villa, on a hillside with good views of the city. Helpful hosts, tasteful furnishings, large rooms, simple but well-prepared food. 26 rooms, all with bath or shower. B&B double 100–145 DM. Full alc 25–45 DM. Recent nomination. More reports please.*

Give the Guide positive support. Don't just leave feedback to others.

WANGEN IM ALLGÄU 7988 Baden-Württemberg   Map 13

Romantik Hotel Alte Post   *Tel* (07522) 40 14
Postplatz 2   *Fax* (07522) 26 04
                                                Telex 732774

An inspector's recent report: "Wangen, quite near the Bodensee and the
Allgäu Alps, is a picturesque old Swabian town of painted facades; it also
has some quirky modern sculptures in its main streets – we especially
liked the scattered bronze piglets in the Marktplatz. The centrally situated
Alte Post, a coaching inn dating from 1409, is well run by the Veile family;
the bedrooms, full of character, are reasonably priced. Ours had a four-
poster canopied Himmelbett, sofas, hair-drier, chintzy curtains, and a
rafter inscribed 1610. The dining room is elegant in a restrained way,
entirely lacking the heavy kitsch you find across the Bavarian border. We
were nicely served by a polite young man in *Tracht*. The à la carte dishes
we thought too bland and dull, but the Swabian ones were fine, including
beef braised in cider, accompanied by a version of spätzle known as
Buabenspitzle which literally means little boys' penises. That's just what
it looks like, too."

Open All year except 6–20 Jan. Restaurant closed Mon.
Rooms 3 suites, 16 double, 8 single – all with bath, shower, telephone, radio, TV.
8 rooms in annexe.
Facilities Lounge, TV room, 2 restaurants. Garden.
Location Central, parking. Wangen is 20 km NE of Lindau.
Restriction Not suitable for &.
Credit cards All major cards accepted.
Terms B&B: single 80–98 DM, double 140–175 DM, suite 195–280 DM. Dinner,
B&B double 210–245 DM; full board double 254–279 DM. Set lunch/dinner 18–
38 DM; full alc 65 DM. Reduced rates and special meals for children.

WEIKERSHEIM 6992 Baden-Württemberg   Map 13

Laurentius   *Tel* (07934) 70 07
Marktplatz 5   *Fax* (07934) 70 77

This attractive small town on the Romantic Road, 42 kilometres south of
Würzburg, is built round a 17th-century Hohenlohe castle beside the
Tauber, worth seeing for its splendid Knights' Hall (it also hosts an
international music school). Here the *Laurentius* is a recently opened hotel
in an old building where Goethe's ancestors lived. It overlooks the pretty
market square, where this year an American visitor watched a harvest
festival parade from her window: "The little girls had garlands in their
hair and it was all very sweet." She adds that the charm extends to the
hotel itself: "It is very pretty, and our room was lovely, with an exquisite
marquetry desk. The sheets were heavenly, they felt like silk. Dinner was
a feast, nicely served in the vaulted cellar." Others have found the
management helpful and friendly, and agree that the food is excellent.
You can take drinks and breakfast on a flowery patio. (*Norma Kessler,
Ralph B Robertson*)

Open All year. Restaurant closed Feb and Tue.
Rooms 10 double, 1 single – all with bath and/or shower, telephone, TV; 6 with
radio.
Facilities Lift. Lounge, restaurant, breakfast room, café; conference room; terrace.

Location Central. Parking.
Credit cards Access, Diners, Visa.
Terms B&B: single 65–80 DM, double 100–130 DM; dinner, B&B 95 DM per
person. Set lunch 30–46 DM, dinner 30–80 DM; full alc 42 DM. Reduced rates and
special meals for children.

WEITENBURG 7245 Baden-Württemberg   Map 13

Hotel-Restaurant Schloss   *Tel* (07457) 80 51
  Weitenburg   *Fax* (07457) 80 54

A large 16th-century hilltop castle with striking views over the Neckar
valley between Horb and Tübingen. Owned since 1720 by the Barons of
Rassler, it is one of a number of *Schlösser* in the area that have been
turned into hotels by their baronial owners as the best way of keeping the
family estates together. It is run by a manager, but the baron still lives
there and is much in evidence, a charming and cultivated man and a great
hunter. He has sensibly kept the hotel in its original style, modernising
only those aspects that need it (e.g. bathrooms). Recent visitors have
enjoyed the indoor swimming pool, the food (with a few reservations)
and the large bedrooms furnished with antiques (but some rooms could
do with a spot of paint). The grounds are extensive, with a riding school.
A 1990 report: "Be sure to take a room with a view, unless vertigo is a
problem. Food good, wine list uninspired." (*TH Nash*) Another reader
liked the service but criticised upkeep.

Open All year except over Christmas.
Rooms 1 suite, 19 double, 15 single – 31 with bath or shower, all with telephone,
radio, TV.
Facilities Lift. Hall, 4 lounges, TV room, dining room; chapel for weddings and
christenings; conference facilities; large balcony for drinks and meals. Park with
riding school, golf, heated covered swimming pool, sauna and solarium.
Location 7 km N of Starzach; from A81 motorway take Rottenburg exit, drive 5–
10 mins towards Ergenzingan then follow signposts to Weitenburg.
Credit cards Access, Diners, Visa.
Terms B&B: single 69–100 DM, double 130–176 DM, suite 240 DM. Set
lunch/dinner 26–100 DM; full alc 40-110 DM. Special meals for children.

****

* **Traveller's tale** *Roast chicken with assistant chef's stuffing was a*
* *gastronomic disaster; the assistant chef turned out to be the 12-year-old*
* *local lad who polished guests' cars during the day. Gaffes included the*
* *hostess/barmaid/waitress/proprietress sampling a guest's drink before*
* *handing it to him, and gossiping about two guests who had not yet*
* *arrived, hinting that they were obviously on a dirty weekend.*

****

Greece

Villa Argentikon, Chios

ATHENS Map 17

Clare's House BUDGET *Tel* (01) 922.2288
24 Sorvolou Street
Mets, 116 36

Much liked again in 1989/90, this simple and friendly B&B inhabits a
fairly modern house on a quiet hill south-west of the Akropolis, near the
Temple of Zeus. "The entrance has a cool marble floor with some good
modern furniture. My white-walled bedroom was simply but well
furnished with nice lamps and varnished wood, and an efficient modern
bathroom. The balcony overlooked the small garden and had a grape-
vine trailing from top to bottom – I was told I was welcome to pick the
grapes. I cannot praise enough the staff who helped me when I had
problems with a delayed flight. Manos Anglias, the owner, speaks perfect
English; he is a mine of information on the Greek islands and has a
wonderful collection of up-to-date guides." Rooms are very simple, but
clean; some have a private shower, some adjoining ones share a shower
and can be let as a family suite. "Only minus is dismal quality of breakfast

tea and coffee, but delicious bread is fresh every day", and you can make your own tea and coffee ad lib any time. "Manos is delightful. Super value." "Staff's crisis-solving abilities are often audibly used in communal rooms, thus giving glimpses into other lives." (*Peter Dickinson, JS Jenkinson, Anne-Marie Sutcliffe*) Mr Anglias writes: "We know people by their names. If the opportunity arises I invite them for a drink in my flat or go out to dinner with them."

Open All year.
Rooms 20 double (also let as single) – 6 with bath and shower, all with telephone.
Facilities Lounge with TV.
Location 1 km from Syntagma Square. Garage for 3 cars.
Restriction Not suitable for &.
Credit cards None accepted.
Terms B&B: single 4,500–4,800 drs, double 5,500–10,000 drs. Reduced rates for children. (No restaurant.)

Herodion Hotel   *Tel* (01) 923.6832
Rovertou Galli Street 4   *Fax* (01) 923.5851
Makriyanni, 117 42   *Telex* 219423

The cradle-city of Western civilisation hardly distinguishes itself by its hotels; but the *Herodion*, an unbeautiful modern cube in a quiet street quite near the Akropolis, is at least better than most. It has a patio garden where drinks are served beneath the trees, and a roof terrace with views of the Akropolis. And it has been well liked recently: "Cool, comfortable and clean, with quite pleasant rooms and willing and friendly staff. The inclusive breakfast was standard international, but adequate. We didn't try the restaurant since the lively Plaka is so close, and about the best place in Athens for good medium-priced eating, the *Dionysius*, is just up the road." (*Elizabeth Stanton*)

Open All year.
Rooms 4 suites, 77 double, 9 single – all with bath and/or shower, telephone, radio, TV.
Facilities Lounge, bar, restaurant. Patio, rooftop terrace.
Location Central; near Plaka and Akropolis.
Restriction Not suitable for &.
Credit cards All major cards accepted.
Terms B&B: single 8,000–12,000 drs, double 10,700–15,500 drs. Set lunch/dinner 2,000 drs; full alc 4,000 drs.

St George Lykabettus Hotel   *Tel* (01) 729.0711
Kleomenous 2   *Fax* (01) 729.0439
Platia Dexamenis, 106 75   *Telex* 214253

A modern hotel, luxury class but not too expensive by British standards, in the fashionable Kolonaki district, on the foothills of Lykabettus hill and ten minutes on foot from Constitution Square. It is used by some tour groups, "but not taken over by them". Recent epistles: "Views from the bedrooms vary from good to sensational. It has recently been refurbished and the air-conditioning now works well. Staff are helpful and efficient. There's a rooftop restaurant, and another pleasant open-air one serving light meals." "The location is magnificent: from the bedroom balconies you look across to the Parthenon. The rooms are comfortable rather than opulent, but they have good bathrooms. The rooftop swimming pool is a rarity in Athens, and the roof-level restaurant serves excellent food and also has a view of the Akropolis." (*Sir William Goodhart, FR*) Some rooms, however, have been judged too small, or imperfect in upkeep, and front ones may suffer from traffic noise.

Open All year.
Rooms 4 suites, 124 double, 21 single – all with bath, shower, telephone, radio, TV, air-conditioning. Some ground-floor rooms.
Facilities Lift. Lounge, TV room, bar, snack bar, restaurant, roof garden and swimming pool; nightly entertainment in restaurant; dancing on roof.
Location At foot of Lykabettus hill. Large garage.
Credit cards All major cards accepted.
Terms B&B: single 13,930–16,880 drs, double 16,410–19,600 drs, suite 32,400–39,070 drs; dinner, B&B 2,100 drs added per person.

CHANIA 73100 Crete   Map 17

Hotel Contessa   `BUDGET`   *Tel* (0821) 57437
Theofanous 15, Palio Limani

With its mix of Turkish and Venetian architecture, Chania is probably Crete's most attractive town. Here, in a maze of pretty streets by the harbour, an old family house has been carefully converted into a tiny bed-and-breakfast hotel, enjoyed for its "hospitality and atmosphere", though it can be a bit noisy. "Breakfast was really good and elegantly served. I'd advise asking for a front room with a view (one has a lovely painted ceiling), for ours at the back was rather airless. Tasteful decor and a courteous owner. It may be hard to persuade taxi-drivers to enter the old town with its narrow streets, but we phoned the hotelier and he helped us solve the problem." (*Col TCH Macafee*) More reports welcome.

Open 1 Apr–end Oct.
Rooms 2 triple, 4 double – all with bath, shower, telephone, radio. All in annexe.
Facilities Breakfast room. Swimming pool at *Xenia* hotel nearby. 15 mins' walk to beach.
Location Overlooking old Venetian harbour; 1 km from town centre. Public parking 100 metres.
Restriction Not suitable for &.
Credit card Diners.
Terms B&B: single 5,600 drs, double 7,630 drs, triple 8,960 drs. (No restaurant.)

CHIOS 82100 Aegean Islands   Map 17

Villa Argentikon   *Tel* (271) 31599 and 31465
                                                              Telex 294135

"Run more like an English country home than a hotel", this very sophisticated venture lies on the plain of Campos in the southern part of the island of Chios, whose former Genoese rulers have left a legacy of fine buildings. One is the *Villa Argentikon* which the Argenti family from Genoa built in the 16th century and still own today. Together with two adjacent mansions of the same period, all in patterned marble, they have turned it into an elegant hotel. There are only four suites, whose sitting rooms can be used as bedrooms when required. There are flowered colonnades, beautiful gardens, bedrooms gracefully furnished in period style, with marble bathrooms. You can dine by candle-light in the floodlit gardens, where good food, expensive by Greek standards, is elegantly presented. Superb breakfasts; efficient, caring staff. More reports welcome.

Open 1 June–15 Sep.
Rooms 4 suites – all with bath, shower, and terrace or patio.
Facilities Reading room, restaurant. Large grounds with terrace, garden.
Location About 5 km S of town of Chios.
Terms [1990 rates] B&B: single occupancy £77–£121, double £112–£171, for 3 £148–£212, for 4 £170–£248. Set dinner £25. Reduced rates for children under 10.

DELPHI 33054 Central Greece   Map 17

Hotel Pan   BUDGET   *Tel (0265) 82294*
53 Vassileos Pavlou

Peacefully located at the quieter end of town, an unassuming and hospitable family-run B&B hotel, with glorious views from the balconies of rooms facing the valley. Clean, simple bedrooms; cheerful breakfast room. 30 rooms, all with bath and shower. B&B double 4,400–5,500 drs [1990]. Recent nomination. More reports please.

FIRA 84700 Santorini, Cyclades   Map 17

Atlantis Hotel   *Tel (0286) 22232*
                          Fax (0286) 22821
                          Telex 293113

The white town of Fira is perched high on the spectacular cliffs of the volcanic island of Santorini (you can go up by mule or cable-car). Just above Fira is this bright, comfortable hotel, its white arched facade visible from afar. Helpful staff, airy lounge and spacious rooms, many with balcony giving views of sea and volcano. No restaurant: some in town. Open 1 Apr–31 Oct. 26 rooms, all with bath or shower. B&B: single 12,600–15,000 drs, double 18,000–21,250 drs [1990]. Lack of recent reports. More please.

GALAXIDION 33052 Central Greece   Map 17

Hotel Ganimede   BUDGET   *Tel (0265) 41328*
Euthumiou Blamis 6

"Quiet, relaxed, informal, all-round idyllic, the sort of place one dreams of finding in Greece but never does," said one reader of this idiosyncratic Italian-owned *pensione* in a tiny ancient town on the Gulf of Corinth, near Delphi. It is formed by two houses back-to-back, one a 19th-century captain's house, the other a modern facsimile, with a large garden-cum-patio in between – trees, flowers, comfortable chairs. "It's in a quiet part of town, almost suburban, though in itself it is nearly louche. The house has been beautifully kept and furnished, and has a marble tiled hall and fine woodwork. The ambience is somewhat precious. We were warmly welcomed. You can take drinks in the garden with its central fountain. The two best bedrooms are on the first floor front; they have tall panelled doors, coffered ceilings and lovely old wooden furniture. The breakfast room is also pretty, but covered with ikons, pictures, home-made preserves for sale, and postcards from patrons saying how lovely their stay had been. Breakfast is very generous (for Greece), and includes good fig jam, and eggs poached, scrambled and even 'mumbled', whatever that might be." An earlier visitor has written: "If Bruno Perocco, the owner, does not like the look of you, you will not get a room. In winter he runs courses on making ikons. The British and American embassies have found the place, but he is careful to spread the nationalities." Others have considered the rooms "comfortable, dark and cool". No restaurant, but *To Steki* and *To Galaxidi* are good harbourside tavernas. (*DM*)

Open 1 Mar–31 Oct.
Rooms 6 double, 1 single – 2 with shower, air-conditioning. Ground-floor rooms.
Facilities Lounge/bar, garden terrace. 10 mins' walk to sea.
Location Central; Galaxidion is 33 km SW of Delphi, via Itea and the coast road. Parking.
Restriction Children under 10 by special arrangement only.
Credit cards None accepted.
Terms [1990 rates] B&B: single 4,659 drs, double 7,934 drs. (No restaurant.)

HERMOUPOLIS Cyclades   Map 17

Hotel Vourlis `BUDGET`   *Tel* (0281) 28440 and 23750
Mavrogordatou 5   *Telex* 293206
Hermoupolis, Syros

The capital of the Cycladean island of Syros is a picturesque town of predominantly neo-classical architecture, with houses that rise in tiers on the slopes of two hills. A 19th-century mansion in this neo-classical style has been transformed into this gracious private hotel, beautifully furnished. It is owned by Alexandra Mavrogordatou Petritzh, a well-known Greek artist, and recent visitors have endorsed this earlier praise: "A real oasis and sheer luxury. We were warmly welcomed and given two very elegant rooms in pink and blue, with lots of space and beautiful pictures. The bathroom was big, and we found chocolates and Metaxa brandy by the bed. Service was excellent and breakfast superb, including fruit salad and scrambled eggs." No restaurant, but snacks available, and plenty of tavernas nearby. More reports please.

Open All year.
Rooms 1 suite, 5 double, 1 single – all with bath and/or shower, telephone. 3 ground-floor rooms.
Facilities Hall, lounge/breakfast room, bar. Small front garden and patio. 100 metres from shingle beach with safe bathing and fishing. Windsurfing, water-skiing, sailing, tennis and mini-golf nearby.
Location Daily boats to Syros from Piraeus and Rafina. Hotel is central. Parking.
Credit cards All major cards accepted.
Terms On application.

We asked hotels to estimate their 1991 tariffs some time before publication so the rates given are often guesswork. Please always check terms with hotels when making bookings.

HYDRA 18040 Saronic Gulf   Map 17

Hotel Miranda   *Tel* (0298) 52230
Hydra Town

*Hydra town, on the island of Hydra, has a beautiful harbour where the houses
rise in tiers. Up one of these steep narrow streets is this finely converted 18th-
century mansion with hand-painted ceilings and parquet floors; now a most
select hotel, it is furnished with genuine local antiques and run in a somewhat
lordly way. Its own regular clientele (smart Athenians) keep it often full. No
restaurant: good tavernas nearby. Closed Nov–Feb. 14 rooms, all with shower.
B&B single 7,000–7,637 drs, double 10,000–14,174 drs [1990]. Endorsed this
year but fuller reports welcome.*

KASTRON ILIAS 27050 Peleponnesus   Map 17

Hotel Chryssi Avgi   **BUDGET**   *Tel* (0623) 95224 and 95380
9 Loutropoleos

Near the western tip of the Peloponnese, an hour's drive from Patras, a
simple hotel run by a Greek and his French wife, both anglophone.
Dropped from last year's Guide for lack of reports, it is borne back this
year: "Quite excellent, Madame Lepidas is delightful." "A model of
friendly efficiency." A shady garden for breakfast and drinks. Kastron
is an attractive village dominated by a medieval Frankish castle. The nearest
sandy beach is "filthy and overrun", but there's a good one further away.
"Ninety percent of our guests become our friends," write the Lepidases.
(*Mr and Mrs PH Miles, Dr RJ Brown*)

Open 1 May–10 Oct.
Rooms 10 double – 1 with bath and shower, 9 with shower, all with telephone.
Facilities Bar, lounge, restaurant, cafeteria; terrace. Garden. Sandy beaches 2 km.
Location 60 km SW of Patras towards Pyrgos; turn west to Kyllini at Lechina. On
road; back rooms quietest.
Restriction Not suitable for &.
Credit card Access.
Terms Rooms: single 4,100 drs, double 5,200 drs. Breakfast 500 drs. Full alc
2,000 drs. Special meals for children on request.

KORONI 24010 Peloponnesus   Map 17

Logga Beach Hotel   **BUDGET**   *Tel* (0725) 31583 and 31165
Paliokabos
Logga, Messinia

*Just north of Koroni, a town with a Venetian castle at the south tip of the
Messinian peninsula: a small modern family-run hotel by the sea, friendly and
cheap. Good, simple cooking; private beach. Open 1 Apr–end Oct. 15 rooms, all
with shower. B&B double 4,500–6,000 drs. Alc dinner (excluding wine) about
1,500 drs. Re-nominated this year. More reports please.*

Hotels are dropped if we lack positive feedback. If you can endorse
an entry, we urge you to do so.

METSOVO 44200 Epirus   Map 17

Hotel Egnatia   `BUDGET`   *Tel* (0656) 41263
L. Tossitsa

An appealing discovery in a small town on the main road over the
mountains from Kalambaka (Meteora) to Ioannina: "The drive to
Metsovo takes one up the spine of the Pindus range, over what not long
ago must have been a road of hair-raising difficulty and which still affords
spectacular views. Metsovo is a small, prosperous town hidden in a
mountain valley; it is being developed as a ski resort, but still retains its
tradition and integrity, and has a rich heritage of handicrafts (needlework,
copperwork, wood-carving). Many of the older women still wear the
traditional costume on a daily basis. The *Egnatia*, on the main road in the
town centre, has a somewhat alpine exterior (flower-pots and balconies),
but the interior is traditional Greek. The public rooms have warm wooden
panelling, coffered wooden ceilings that are beautifully carved, and
lovely old brass lamps. The lobby is lined in the old style with benches
covered with rich red weavings and intricately designed cushions; above
the fireplace is a wild boar's head. The bedrooms are simple but
comfortable, and their balconies afford delightful views of the town and
hills. We met a warm and genuine welcome." (*Dr SL Martin*) The hotel's
restaurant serves simple dishes.

Open All year.
Rooms 2 suites, 24 double, 8 single – all with bath and shower; many with
balcony.
Facilities Lounge, TV room, bar, restaurant. Garden. Winter sports 2 km.
Location Central. Metsovo is 50 km E of Ioannina.
Credit cards All major cards accepted.
Terms B&B: single 3,450–4,574 drs, double 4,500–5,850 drs, suite 7,500–9,974 drs.
Set meals 1,500 drs.

Hotel Victoria   `BUDGET`   *Tel* (0656) 41771 and 41761

Our other Metsovo entry, slightly more expensive, is on the town's
outskirts overlooking the deep valley, and was nominated by a reader
who was also struck by local craft traditions: "The hand-carved ceiling of
the spacious dining room, the hand-carved chairs, hand-woven cushions
and wall decorations make a stay at this hotel a visit to a living museum.
It is family-run, and the multilingual staff are friendly and helpful. The
meals included local dishes not normally available in restaurants, such as
mountain sausage and a kind of feta soup. Good local red wine. A highly
recommended hotel." (*Patricia Peterson*) Metsovo also has a museum of
local arts and crafts, and an interesting monastery.

Open All year.
Rooms 34 double, 3 single – all with bath and/or shower, telephone.
Facilities Lounge, bar, restaurant. Night club.
Location On W outskirts. Parking.
Credit cards Access, Visa.
Terms [1990 rates] B&B: single 4,725–6,000 drs, double 5,500–7,500 drs. Set
lunch/dinner 1,550 drs.

We are particularly keen to have reports on italicised entries.

MONEMVASSIA Peloponnesus   Map 17

Hotel Malvasia   *Tel* (0732) 61323 and 61435

In an ancient town with a 6th-century castle in the south-east of the Peloponnese, several old houses with barrel-vaulted ceilings have been attractively converted into a hotel of character, with a sense of history. Spacious rooms, nicely furnished in modern style. Lounge, bar and café; plenty of restaurants close by. Very quiet (town is closed to car traffic), but not midge-free. 12 rooms, all with shower. B&B double 6,000 drs. Meals 500–2,000 drs [1990]. Endorsed this year, but fuller reports welcome.

MYRINA 81400 Aegean Islands   Map 17

Hotel Akti Myrina   *Tel* (0254) 22681
Myrina Beach, Lemnos   *Fax* (0254) 22352

Athens office: *Tel* (01) 4138001
107 Vas. Pavlou Kastella   *Fax* (01) 4137639
Piraeus, Athens 18533

"Must be a strong candidate for the Mediterranean's most attractive hotel" – this is among the many continuing plaudits for this large, fairly luxurious and unusual holiday venture, set above a bay just outside Myrina, tiny capital of the lovely island of Lemnos. Spread over the hillside, in a garden of flowering shrubs, are 125 bungalows with fine facilities – air-conditioning, room service, etc – each hidden by greenery from its neighbours. Most have a little patio/garden with a view, "idyllic for one's breakfast or evening drink". The central services (pool, beach) are all within two minutes' walk. "If you are lucky enough to be in the front row of the bungalows your garden looks straight over roses and grapes down to the sea. You can have delicious Greek yoghurt with honey and wholemeal toast for breakfast. For dinner you can choose between buffet-type restaurants and one serving a more conventional five-course meal. For lunch you can eat in a small taverna or at another restaurant serving a great variety of salads and hot dishes. The sea is shallow for a long way out and the beach is very clean. Service is efficient and courteous." "Captain Yannis, skipper of the hotel yacht, teaches everyone to dance on Thursday evenings." Others have praised the poolside bars for snacks and drinks, and the beach sports and caïque excursions. (*Conrad and Marilyn Dehn, MD Janson, JS Rutter, and others*) One criticism this year of restaurant service, but generally there's admiration for the "clockwork efficiency" (the hotel is German-owned, with a Greek staff).

Open May–Oct.
Rooms 15 suites, 110 double – all with bath and/or shower, telephone, refrigerator, baby-listening, air-conditioning, veranda, small garden. All in bungalows.
Facilities Lounge, TV lounge, coffee shop, restaurants, taverna; hairdresser, boutique; disco. 25-acre grounds with 3 tennis courts, swimming pool, children's pool, mini-golf, table-tennis, private sandy beach with restaurant; fishing, bathing, water sports.

Location 2 km (about 15 mins' walk) from Myrina Town. Lemnos is reached by direct flight from Athens, or by boat from Piraeus.
Restriction Not suitable for &.
Credit cards All major cards accepted.
Terms [1990 rates] Rooms: single 7,222–18,958 drs, double 9,930–39,722 drs, suite 16,250–46,041 drs. Breakfast 1,348–1,797 drs. Set lunch/dinner 3,145–4,492 drs. Reduced rates and special meals for children.

NAFPLION 21100 Peloponnesus   Map 17

Hotel Leto ▐ BUDGET ▌   *Tel (0752) 28093*
28 Zygomala Street

Up on the hill with good views of the old town, but only 600 metres from the front, a simple but clean and friendly hotel; good breakfasts served on a floral terrace. Upstairs rooms with balconies are best. Open Mar–Oct. 11 rooms, most with bath. B&B double 4,000 drs without bath, 5,200 drs with. No restaurant. Renominated this year. More reports please.

PALEA EPIDAVROS Peloponnesus   Map 17

Paola Beach Hotel ▐ BUDGET ▌   *Tel (0753) 41397*

On the edge of an unattractive fishing village 12 km from the classical theatre at Epidaurus, a modern hotel set quietly by a sandy beach; clean and comfortable, with plumbing that actually works. Open 1 Apr–30 Oct. 27 rooms, all with bath, shower and balcony facing sea or farmland. B&B double 3,500–5,500 drs. No restaurant: tavernas in village. Endorsed recently, but fuller reports welcome.

SKOPELOS Sporades   Map 17

Prince Stafylos Hotel   *Tel (0424) 22775*
Skopelos   *Telex 282229*

Skopelos is the second largest of the Sporades islands, and just outside its main town, also called Skopelos, is this pleasant modern hotel, long, low and white, built in local style. Clean, well-kept swimming pool amid lawns and flowers; light, attractive bedrooms. Decent, uninspiring food. Open 1 May–25 Oct. 49 rooms, most with bath or shower. More planned for 1991. B&B double 6,000–14,000 drs. Set menus 1,300–1,800 drs [1990]. Endorsed this year. Further reports welcome.

SPETSES Saronic Gulf   Map 17

Hotel Possidonion ▐ BUDGET ▌   *Tel (0298) 72208 and 72308*
Spetses

This island off the Argolid coast is where John Fowles set *The Magus*, having taught here in the 1950s at a well-known boarding school that was founded as a copy of an English public school. Today the English connection continues, in a different manner, for Spetses is given over to the UK package-tour trade. But it also remains a haunt of wealthy Athenians, who have built summer homes along the coast: so, if you wander off into the pinewoods, you might always – who knows? – stumble into the enchanted clutches of some latter-day Conchis. Failing that, you can certainly be beguiled by the 1920s' ghosts that haunt the *Possidonion*. It was built in 1914 by Sotiros Anagyros, a Spetsian who emigrated to the US, became a rich tobacco baron, then returned to found the boarding school and the hotel. He built it in the grand European manner, with terrace, esplanade and attendant casino, scene of great society parties in the inter-war years. Today it is somewhat down-at-heel, but it remains characterful. It keeps away from the package-tour trade. "Decaying grandeur at its best: not luxurious, but lovely," says a 1990 visitor. More reports, please, on mundane matters such as food and bedrooms.

Open Apr–Oct.
Rooms 55 – most with bath and/or shower.
Facilities Lounge, restaurant. Beach 300 metres.
Location In Spetses town, 30 mins by boat from the mainland.
Terms B&B double 10,000–12,500 drs.

TOLO 21056 Peloponnesus   **Map 17**

Hotel Minoa `BUDGET`   *Tel* (0752) 59207
56 Aktis Street   *Fax* (0752) 59707
                                                   Telex 298157

Run by a large family of Cretans, this is one of many modern hotels along the sandy beach of this popular resort, once a simple fishing village. It has a strong British following, including group bookings as well as many faithful individual returnees. Readers continue to appreciate the "charming, intelligent and helpful" Yannis Georgidakis and his brother, the pleasant staff and the "enchanting *pieds-dans-l'eau* position – you even drive your car on to the sandy beach in front to unload. Apart from the boats putting out for night fishing, it's very peaceful." It is essential to ask for a room at the front with a balcony (the moon on the sea at night is beautiful); back ones overlook a sprawl of houses. Bedrooms are spacious and well maintained. The dining room has full-length windows overlooking the beach. There's a set menu changing every day, with "better than average Greek fare. Excellent breakfasts." "The waiters had time to be pleasant, everyone speaks English, and there's a comfortable lounge." (*JS Jenkinson, Patricia Peterson, John Bush, Anne-Marie Sutcliffe, and others*)

Open 18 Mar–5 Nov.
Rooms 75 double, 7 single – 28 with bath, 47 with shower, all with telephone; some with radio. 18 in annexe *Knossos*, 20 in annexe *Phaistos*.
Facilities Lift. Lounge, bar, restaurant. Garden. *Phaistos* has swimming pool and tennis court.
Location Near old port; parking. Tolo is 12 km SE of Nafplion.
Restriction Not suitable for &.
Credit cards All major cards accepted.
Terms [1990 rates] B&B: single 4,085–4,580 drs, double 5,020–6,000 drs; dinner, B&B: single 5,020–5,920 drs, double 7,600–8,650 drs. Set lunch 800–1,000 drs, dinner 1,200–1,500 drs; full alc 1,400–1,600 drs. Reduced rates and special meals for children.

ATHIA 23071 Lakonia   **Map 17**

raditional Settlement [BUDGET]   *Tel (0733) 54244*
  of Vathia

*lot a hotel but a "traditional settlement" owned by the National Tourist
)rganisation of Greece, but locally run. Not far from Areopoli, by the sea near
he tip of the wild and gorgeous Mani peninsula in the southern Peloponnese, a
onversion of eight 17th-century grey towers: well-modernised and nicely
urnished bedrooms, cafeteria, large restaurant, terraces, lovely views, friendly
nultilingual staff. No TV, no nightlife. 47 rooms, most with private facilities,
ome with kitchen. B&B: single 5,804–6,392 drs, double 7,580–8,313 drs. Set
neals 1,500 drs [1990]. Recent nomination. More reports please.*

****
Reader's complaint *It irritates us when people describe visits to hotels
as "like staying with friends". You stay with your friends to enjoy their
company – you expect to help with the washing up and to make your own
bed. In a hotel we do not expect to have to fraternise with strangers
(who may or may not be delightful). We expect to be looked after
professionally. And we all know that guests, like fish, stink after three
days!*
****

****
Traveller's tale *The best of the house rules was the one pinned up in the
bathroom. To avoid unnecessary noise – remember that "unnecessary"
noise" – we were instructed to fill the bath slowly and – wait for it –
finish filling the bath using the shower-head, not the taps! Have you ever
tried to do this? Do you know how long it takes? The explanation for this
piece of high comedy was that the "architectural constraints" on the
building made the plumbing rather noisy. The plumbing was noisy; it
wasn't nightingales that kept us awake, but the sound of loos flushing,
and basins swishing. Breakfast is syncopated by a relay of flushing
lavatories.*
****

Italy

Il Bottaccio, Montignoso

ACQUAVIVA PICENA 63030 Ascoli Piceno   **Map 16**

Hotel O'Viv   `BUDGET`   *Tel* (0735) 764649
Via Marziale 43   *Fax* (0735) 83697

This medieval stone building, once the residence of the local archbishop,
stands in a newly renovated hill-village just inland from the coast
between Pescara and Ancona. It is now an oddly named small hotel,
delightfully run by its young Anglo-Italian owners. Bedrooms are large
and characterful, though furnished simply. Readers this year enjoyed the
peaceful, relaxed ambience, and meals in the panoramic restaurant with
views across vine-clad hills to the sea. Local Italian dishes are cooked by
the English half of the partnership. Good local wines. (*Joanna Bregosz*)

Open All year.
Rooms 1 suite, 11 double – all with shower, telephone, TV; baby-listening on
request.
Facilities Lounge, bar, TV room, breakfast room, 2 restaurants (1 outdoor);
terrace.

Location Central, parking. Village is 8 km W of San Benedetto del Tronto, which
is on coast S of Ascona.
Restriction Not suitable for &.
Credit cards Access, Amex, Visa.
Terms [1990 rates] Rooms: single 33,000–40,000 L, double 55,000–65,000 L.
Breakfast 9,000 L. Dinner, B&B 44,000–68,000 L per person. Set lunch 30,000 L,
dinner 35,000 L; full alc 40,000 L. Reduced rates for children sharing parents'
room; special meals on request.

ALPE FAGGETTO 52033 Arezzo   Map 16

Fonte della Galletta `BUDGET`   *Tel* (0575) 793925
Caprese Michelangelo

Secluded amid woodlands in the wild Apennines near Michelangelo's birth-
place, 50 km NE of Arezzo: an idiosyncratic restaurant-with-rooms, more of a
"typical Italian experience" than a conventionally dependable hotel. Superb
robust cooking, with the accent on local mushrooms, by the jovial and energetic
patron/chef or members of his family (his grandson speaks good English).
Vigorous service, boisterous local guests, lovely local walks; bedrooms adequate.
Closed Wed Oct–May. 18 rooms, all with bath and shower. B&B: single
42,000 L, double 69,000 L. Set meals 20,000–35,000 L. Few recent reports, but
warmly endorsed as we go to press.

AMALFI 84011 Salerno   Map 16

Hotel Luna Convento   *Tel* (089) 871002
Via P Comite 19   *Fax* (089) 871333

St Francis of Assisi is said to have lived in this cool, white-walled
Byzantine monastery, where Goethe and Ibsen once stayed, too. It is
superbly situated on the dramatically beautiful Amalfi coast, with fine
views over town and sea. "The *Luna* is a calming place, and its staff have
that grave, serious sweetness that charms and reassures. There's a lift
down to the old tower and private bathing rocks and pool, an old cloister
for breakfast outside, and comfortable though simple accommodation. No
air-conditioning, but prompt and friendly room service, and good, simple,
varied meals (excellent fish). There was a large wedding party going on in
the hotel, yet we were not neglected but treated as a welcome audience to
a fine free spectacle. A friendly, cheerful hotel with personal attention.
And one would never tire of sitting on that balcony." Endorsed by an
inspector who points out that some road-traffic is audible.

Open All year.
Rooms 5 suites, 40 double – all with bath and shower, telephone, TV.
Facilities Lift. Lounge, bar, 2 restaurants; banqueting facilities; discothèque.
Garden with cloisters, terrace, sea-water swimming pool.
Location 300 metres from centre. Garage and private parking.
Credit cards All major cards accepted.
Terms B&B: single 120,000–130,000 L, double 150,000–180,000 L; dinner, B&B
115,000–150,000 L per person. Set meals 50,000 L. Reduced rates and special
meals for children.

RGEGNO 22010 Como Map 16

Hotel Belvedere BUDGET *Tel (031) 821116*

In a village 20 km north of Como, a solid 18th-century lakeside villa converted into a modest but attractive hotel, owned and run by an Italo-Scottish couple. Large lakeside terrace, pleasant rooms with lake views, very good food. Open Mar–Oct. 18 rooms, 11 with bath or shower. B&B: single 35,000–40,000 L, double 65,000–79,000 L. Set meals 35,000 L. New nomination. More reports welcome.

ASOLO 31011 Treviso Map 16

Hotel Villa Cipriani *Tel (0423) 55444*
Via Canova 298 *Fax (0423) 52095*
Telex 411060

In an old town of arcaded streets, a Venetian villa that was once the home of Robert Browning: now it is a luxury hotel, part of the big CIGA chain. Quiet garden, beautiful views of valley and mountains, ornate rooms (those in main building, not annexe, are best). Food good but expensive. 31 rooms, all with bath and shower, 251,000–327,000 L. Breakfast 20,000 L. Alc meals (excluding wine) 58,000–100,000 L [1990]. Management and service much criticised this year. More reports welcome.

ASSISI 06081 Perugia Map 16

Hotel Country House BUDGET *Tel (075) 816363*
San Pietro Campagna 178 *Fax (075) 8042903*

A *pensione* with a garden, about a mile outside the city walls. "An old house with a big chaise-longuey patio, fine views over the valley and pleasant walks around. The place doubles up as an antique shop, so if you take a fancy to any of the excellent furniture in your bedroom, you can make an offer for it." This shop is called the "3 Esse" (three Ss) because "it's kept by three women all of whose names begin with S: I met only one of them, a lady of equal charm and volubility" (probably Silvana Ciammarughi, the owner). (*Jan Morris*) A reader this year, while enjoying the hotel, felt that its pastoral idyll was tinged with commercialism ("Signora Silvana, clad in a bright red designer suit and jangling Gucci jewellery, was a bit of a culture shock when we were expecting rusticity") and warns that room bookings may not be honoured if you arrive even ten minutes later than stated.

Open All year.
Rooms 1 apartment with kitchen and private balcony, 13 double, 2 single – 6 with bath, 9 with shower. 2 ground-floor rooms. 2 rooms in annexe.
Facilities Lounge with TV, bar. Garden and terraces.
Location 1½ km from Assisi towards Perugia. Parking.
Credit cards Amex, Visa.
Terms [1990 rates] B&B 40,000 L. Reduced rates for children. (No restaurant.)

Hotel Umbra   *Tel* (075) 81224
Via degli Archi 6

A reasonably priced family-run hotel down an alley off the main square
It has a touch of Italian elegance about the public rooms, and a pleasan
patio at the back where you can eat out under the trees. The food is wha
counts here, far more than the bedrooms, described as clean bu
somewhat basic (a report this year speaks of poor lighting, lukewarm bat
water). "My room was institutional, suitable for earnest young YMC/
pilgrims. By contrast, dinner was superb, served in a strikingly beautifu
high-ceilinged room: I was given the sweetest prosciutto crudo I've eve
tasted, and enough of it to paper my room." "A delicious veal en croût
with madeira sauce and wild mushrooms." (*PA Bispham, Philippa Herber*
ME Emson) Most readers find the management friendly and helpful, bu
two this year reported surly staff: more reports welcome.

Open 15 Mar–15 Jan.
Rooms 4 suites, 18 double, 5 single – 18 with bath, 7 with shower, all with
telephone; 8 with TV. Some ground-floor rooms.
Facilities 3 lounges, TV lounge, bar, 2 restaurants. Garden with terraces for meal
in fine weather.
Location In town centre, near main square.
Credit cards All major cards accepted.
Terms B&B: single 65,000–70,000 L, double 100,000–105,000 L, suite 140,000–
147,000 L. Full alc 35,000–45,000 L.

BELLAGIO 22021 Como   **Map 1**

Grand Hotel Villa Serbelloni   *Tel* (031) 95021
Via Roma 1   *Fax* (031) 95152
                                                     Telex 38033

This sumptuous villa beside Lake Como enjoys the lake vistas tha
Stendhal once called "sublime" and is backed by a large park famous fo
its display of magnolias, camellias and pomegranates. Inside, the palatia
public rooms are hung with gold chandeliers and decorated with origina
frescos; the staircase is flanked by gilt *putti* on giant candelabra, and th
spacious bedrooms have wonderful views over lake or gardens. There is
heated swimming pool and a private beach. Of course prices are high, bu
do they buy you perfection? Maybe not. In recent years, both manage
ment and cuisine have come in for criticism; this year, readers found th
staff courteous and helpful and the buffet breakfast excellent (they di
not try a main meal), but like others in the past they warn that room
facing the road can be noisy. (*Wendy Whelan*) The swagger *Serbelloni* stil
risks eviction from our pages: your views are much needed, please.

Open Mid-Apr–mid-Oct.
Rooms 5 suites, 75 double, 15 single – all with bath, many with shower, all with
telephone, baby-listening; some with radio, 65 with TV, 13 with air-conditioning.
Some ground-floor rooms.
Facilities Lifts. Lounge, TV room, writing room, games room, bar, breakfast room
restaurant; banqueting and conference facilities; hairdressing salon, boutique;
terrace (also for meals), evening orchestra with dancing. Gardens with tennis
courts, heated swimming pool with snack bar; private beach with boating,
windsurfing, water-skiing, boating excursions.
Location Central. Private garage and large parking place.
Credit cards Access, Diners, Visa.

Terms [1990 rates] B&B: single 230,000 L, double 330,000 L, suite 640,000 L; dinner, B&B: single 270,000 L, double 410,000 L, suite 720,000 L. Set lunch/dinner 65,000 L; full alc 60,000 L. Reduced rates and special meals for children.

BOLOGNA 40123   Map 16

Hotel Roma   *Tel* (051) 226322
Via Massimo d'Azeglio 9   *Fax* (051) 239909
Bologna   *Telex* 583270

"The best medium-priced hotel in Bologna, and we've tried quite a few", is a recent comment on the biggish *Roma*, centrally located in a narrow street just off the magnificent Piazza Maggiore, heart of the historic part of medieval Bologna. Admired again this year, it is fairly quiet, save for a few clock chimes, and even has a roof-garden. The air-conditioning is appreciated; however, one visitor in July found it turned off from 2 to 8.30 am ("a police regulation", she was told), making her room very hot. The food is "acceptable" though expensive: but there are masses of good cheap places all around in the world capital of good pasta. (*W Ian Stewart, Brian MacArthur*)

Open All year. Restaurant closed 1–23 Aug.
Rooms 84 – most with bath or shower, telephone, TV, air-conditioning (12,000 L).
Facilities Lift. Restaurant; roof-garden.
Location Central: by car, go to the back entrance which is not in pedestrian zone. Garage.
Credit cards All major cards accepted.
Terms [1990 rates] Rooms: single 88,000 L, double 129,000 L. Breakfast 15,000 L. Set lunch/dinner 35,000 L.

BORDIGHERA 18012 Imperia   Map 16

Hotel Villa Elisa   *Tel* (0184) 261313
Via Romana 70   *Telex* 272540

This handsome white Victorian-style villa with a pretty garden, owned by the Oggero family for over 100 years, stands quietly on an elegant avenue ten minutes' walk above the seafront of a busy Riviera resort. Many rooms have a big south-facing balcony, but only top-floor rooms get a sea view. Earlier praise is endorsed by a full report this year: "A perfect holiday. The public rooms are furnished and decorated with beautiful antiques, all is immaculately clean and tidy, and an air of calm and luxury pervades. The grounds are lovely, with orange and lemon trees: you can sit and eat the fruit straight from the tree. Our room was large and comfortable: front rooms get some noise from the road, but we were too relaxed to be troubled by it, even the noise of celebrating football fans didn't worry us. Meals are very good if unadventurous: outstanding pasta starters, but the rest is 'Euro-grub' to suit the clientele – and beware the German 'fruit-cake' at breakfast. Dining room service is excellent: our waiter served in style, bursting through the swing-doors with tray held aloft, like an Italian opera singer making a grand entry." (*Dr J Coker and Christine Lawrie, C and S Wright, and others*) Only one gripe: "The management's tight rein on the hotel does verge on penny-pinching, e.g., toiletries in the bathroom were not replaced during our stay."

Open 20 Dec–15 Nov.
Rooms 30 double, 2 single – 19 with bath, 13 with shower, all with telephone, TV.
Facilities Lift. 2 salons, TV room, bar, restaurant; terrace. Garden with swimming pool.
Location Central, 1 km from sea. Garage, parking. Town is 12 km west of San Remo.
Credit cards Access, Amex, Visa.
Terms B&B: single 60,000–70,000 L, double 100,000–110,000 L; dinner, B&B 75,000–110,000 L per person. Full board 80,000–115,000 L. Set lunch/dinner 35,000 L; full alc 50,000 L. In Aug half or full board only. Reduced rates and special meals for children.

BORGO PRETALE 53018 Siena   Map 16

Albergo Torre Pretale   *Tel* (0577) 345401
Sovicille   *Fax* (0577) 345625

Experienced italophiles have this year unearthed this enticing and newly opened hotel, high on a forested hill south-west of Siena: "It has been created by converting a tower dating from 1100 and the surrounding hamlet of Borgo Pretale into a soigné small hotel of character. The rooms in the tower, one a suite with a huge panoramic sitting room, are beautifully furnished and equipped, with smart modern bathrooms. In the neat and pretty dining room, our lunch was simple but well handled, based on local farm produce; service was exemplary, a little formal but benevolent. Large, well-equipped swimming pool. The hotel's isolation might seem to some a drawback, to others an asset." (*David and Kate Wooff*) More reports welcome.

Open Mar–Nov.
Rooms 2 suites, 26 double, 1 single – 8 with bath, 19 with shower, all with telephone; TV on request.
Facilities Lounge with TV, bar, restaurant; banqueting room. Large grounds with swimming pool and tennis court.
Location Borgo Pretale hamlet is 7 km SW of Sovicille, a small town 10 km SW of Siena.
Restriction Not suitable for &.
Credit cards All major cards accepted.
Terms B&B 115,000–380,000 L; dinner, B&B 150,000–460,000 L. Set lunch/dinner 50,000–60,000 L.

BRESSANONE 39042 Bolzano   Map 16

Hotel Dominik   *Tel* (0472) 30144
Via Terzo di Sotto 13   *Fax* (0472) 36554
                                                     Telex 401524

A bright and breezy modern hotel, all orange and yellow, set close to the Rienz river on the edge of this busy resort, a good centre for exploring the Dolomites and Tyrol. "Wonderful, and good value," says a recent visitor. "Staff friendly and professional, food excellent – and the indoor swimming pool is marvellous." The gardens are pretty too. (*Martin L Dodd*)

Open Easter–Nov. Restaurant closed Tue except July, Aug, Sep.
Rooms 19 double, 10 single – all with bath, shower, telephone, radio; 15 with TV.

Facilities Lounge, bar, TV room, restaurants. Indoor swimming pool. Garden and terrace.
Location Central, parking. Bressanone is 41 km NE of Bolzano.
Restriction Not suitable for ♿.
Credit cards Access, Amex, Visa.
Terms [1990 rates] B&B 75,000–125,000 L per person; dinner, B&B 100,000–145,000 L. Set lunch/dinner 30,000–40,000 L; full alc 35,000–45,000 L. Reduced rates for children; special meals on request.

Hotel Elefante
Via Rio Bianco 4

Tel (0472) 32750
Fax (0472) 36579
Telex 400491

"There can't be many old-world grand hotels like this left," says a visitor this year to this 16th-century building near the town centre, lavishly furnished with antiques, old paintings and tapestries, "acres of parquet flooring, marble staircases, chests, tallboys, and flowers everywhere. In our room, a bowl of apples, peaches, apricots and strawberries. We found the meals unexciting, but the buffet breakfast was splendid, and the staff were all delightful, with old-fashioned ideas of service: shoes were taken to be cleaned, etc. There's a huge garden, some of it pretty, and a lovely pool." "The food is outstanding, and it's nice to have your luggage carried by porters in green baize aprons." Rooms are comfortable, but front ones are dark and "face a leafy, innocent-looking road that is a race-track into town for motorbikes and buzzy little cars": those at the back are quieter and lighter. (*Mrs RB Richards, Rev Michael Napier*)

Open 2 Mar–7 Jan. Restaurant closed Mon to non-residents.
Rooms 44 – all with bath and/or shower, telephone, TV.
Facilities Lounge, bar, 3 restaurants, conference facilities. Garden with heated swimming pool.
Location Central. Garage.
Restriction Not suitable for ♿.
Credit card Visa.
Terms B&B 92,000 L; dinner, B&B 145,000 L; full board 156,000 L. Full alc 40,000 L. Reduced rates for children; special meals on request.

CANNERO RIVIERA 28051 Novara   **Map 16**

Hotel Cannero
Lunga Lago 2

Tel (0323) 788046
Fax (0323) 788048
Telex 200285

A family hotel standing right by the shore of Lake Maggiore, beside the landing stage of this small unspoilt resort. It lost its place in last year's Guide after some criticisms, but all five reports this year have spoken warmly of the good food, friendly service, and especially the charm and warmth of the owner, Mariacarla Gallinotto, always in evidence. "The hotel has every comfort, a pleasantly varied menu and good wines." "Looking out over the lake is a joy. You can take drinks on the hotel's terrace by the water's edge. Very clean swimming pool." "Dinner was excellent, beautifully served. Many guests dressed for dinner, in the large, rather formal dining room." "The hotel is impeccably kept," says a visitor this year, whereas last year upkeep was criticised. Many room balconies face the lake, but as the hotel faces east they get sun only in the morning.

And Italians at the landing stage can be noisy at night. (*AR Salliss, DJ Milner, Stephen Rose and others*) One reader this year, who otherwise liked the hotel a lot, was bitten by its dog in the foyer, and found the management startlingly unapologetic.

Open 15 Mar–7 Nov.
Rooms 30 double, 6 single – all with bath and/or shower, telephone; 8 with TV. Ground-floor rooms.
Facilities Lift. Lounges, TV room, bar, restaurant. Garden with tennis, swimming pool; lakeside terrace; bathing, water sports.
Location Central, on Lake Maggiore. Garage and parking.
Credit cards All major cards accepted.
Terms B&B 40,000–50,000 L; dinner, B&B 65,000–80,000 L; full board 75,000–85,000 L. Set lunch 25,000 L, dinner 30,000 L. Reduced rates and special meals for children.

CAPRI 80073 Naples   Map 16

Hotel Flora   *Tel* (081) 8370211
Via F Serena 26   *Fax* (081) 8378949

A friendly, modern bed-and-breakfast pensione *near the main square of Capri town. Antiques and tiled floors; rooms clean and spacious, front ones with fine views; balconies with bougainvillea; no lounge, but a sun-terrace where a good breakfast is served; excellent service. Open Apr–Oct. 24 rooms, most with bath and shower. B&B double 240,000 L [1990]. Renominated this year. More reports please.*

CASTELLINA IN CHIANTI 53011 Siena   Map 16

Pensione Salivolpi   `BUDGET`   *Tel* (0577) 740484
Via Fiorentina   *Fax* (0577) 741034

A converted Tuscan farmhouse with beamed ceilings, set on a hill with broad views towards Siena and Volterra; it consists of three buildings in a pretty garden with a sizeable swimming pool. Recent visitors have called it friendly, modest and agreeable: "Comfortable, very clean, with lovely typical Tuscan rooms; manageress efficient but a bit aloof. Breakfast boring." Others have mentioned elegant bathrooms and a family ambience. No restaurant, and the trattoria in the village is not rated highly: but there are others a bit further afield. (*Simon Small, John RL Cook, Michael and Margaret Crick, Richard Osborne*)

Open All year.
Rooms 18 double, 1 single – all with bath or shower. 7 rooms in 2 annexes.
Facilities Lounge with bar and TV, breakfast room. Garden with swimming pool.
Location 1 km NW of Castellina towards San Donato.
Restriction Not suitable for &.
Credit cards Access, Visa.
Terms [1990 rates] Double rooms 75,000 L. Breakfast 7,000 L. (No restaurant.)

Tenuta di Ricavo   *Tel* (0577) 740221
                                        Fax (0577) 741014

Here we are in the heart of "Chiantishire", where so many Britons have
bought up old houses. This one has escaped their grasp: a fine Tuscan
manor, it belongs to the Swiss family Scotoni, who have converted it into
a delightfully informal hotel with "a Quattrocento atmosphere". It is
admired again this year for its "peace and tranquillity" and for comfort,
good wines from the owners' own vineyards, and pleasant if not very
varied cooking. "The central manor contains the dining room, lounges
and libraries, plus a few guest rooms; outbuildings around the 'village
square' of the old hamlet have been converted into studio rooms and
apartments, plus good bathrooms, with Tuscan furniture and Mara
Scotoni's luscious flower paintings. The terraces face beautiful views of
the hills, with oak woods, vineyards and distant towns. The food is *alla
casalinga*, simple Italian." "The nice Scotoni family speak all languages.
Lunch can be taken under trees in the garden, near the two swimming
pools. Our room was charming and comfortable." "Beautiful, remote,
peaceful and wonderful." (*Dr Alec and Elizabeth Frank, SO Quin*) Some
have found the ambience more international than Italian. Guests are
expected to dine in the hotel.

Open Easter–Oct.
Rooms 9 suites, 13 double, 2 single – all with bath/shower, telephone. Ground-
floor rooms. Some in annexe.
Facilities 3 lounges, TV room, bar, dining room. Garden with 2 swimming pools;
table-tennis.
Location 22 km NW of Siena, 34 km S of Florence. Leave Siena *superstrada* at San
Donato exit.
Restrictions Not suitable for severely &. No smoking in dining room.
Credit cards None accepted.
Terms Dinner, B&B 150,000–210,000 L. Alc lunch (summer only) 30,000–
40,000 L. 1-night bookings sometimes refused. Reduced rates for children sharing
parents' room; special meals on request.

Villa Casalecchi   *Tel* (0577) 740240
                                        Fax (0577) 741111

*A handsome villa in its own large grounds, overlooking vineyards and olive
groves. Friendly staff, good Tuscan cooking, luxurious furnishing with antiques,
several lounges. Terrace and swimming pool; tennis. Open 28 Mar–Oct. 19
rooms, all with bath and shower. Half board 180,000 L. Renomination. More
reports please.*

CASTIGLIONCELLO 57012 Livorno   **Map 16**

Hotel Villa Godilonda   *Tel* (0586) 752032
Via Biagi 12   *Fax* (0586) 753286

This pleasant seaside hotel stands on a rocky promontory with small
sandy beaches on either side, in a family bathing resort south of Livorno.
"All rooms have a sea view. Ours, decorated in glass and plastic, Italian
style, was clean and pleasant. The excellent public rooms are modern,
clean, comfortable, expensively done, with marble floors and chromium.

Service impeccable, lots of staff; breakfast room charming with excellent breakfasts – good coffee, etc. The attractive swimming pool is not crowded, and has plenty of places to sit and sunbathe." Endorsed in 1990 by *Gerald Campion*, author of that report last year, who recommends the rock pool bathing, and the fairly expensive *Scacciapensieri* restaurant at Cecina, 20 kilometres away.

Open All year.
Rooms 23 – all with shower, telephone, radio, TV, baby-listening.
Facilities 2 lounges, TV room, bar. Indoor and outdoor swimming pools; direct access to private beach.
Location On edge of village 20 km S of Livorno. Parking.
Credit card Access.
Terms B&B double 150,000–295,000 L. (No restaurant.)

CAVALESE 38033 Trento   Map 16

Mas del Saügo   *Tel* (0462) 30788
Masi

A 17th-century farmhouse, secluded in a forest at the western end of the Dolomites, newly converted with exquisite taste into a fine restaurant with just four guest rooms. It is owned and run by a young couple, Lorenzo Bernardini and Donatella Zampoli: he is an architect (as well as artist and oenophile). "Absolutely unique: a beautiful building in an idyllic location, a superb five-course dinner, complemented by fine Italian wines." That report this year backs up an earlier panegyric by the British hotelier who discovered the place: "Lorenzo has renovated with great style – stripped wood floors and beams, modern pictures (mostly his own work), bright colours in carpets and fabrics. Window frames and fittings are in bright red which sounds ghastly but looks great. In fact everything delights the eye. They use Ginori china embossed with their own logo. There is a small study with family photographs where they serve breakfast. We spent three and a half hours over the seven-course set menu that Donatella had composed and cooked. Everything close to perfect: carpaccio, white truffles, freshly gathered porcini, really good gnocchi, fillet of beef in an intense red wine sauce. Lorenzo is a most professional *sommelier*." "We thoroughly agree. Like visiting a friend's home. Dinner and wines delicious. Even breakfast was way above Italian standard." (*Esler Crawford, Anne and Martin Smith, William and Anita Taylor, Paul Henderson*)

Open All year. Restaurant closed Thu.
Rooms 1 suite, 2 double, 1 single – all with shower.
Facilities 2 lounges, bar, restaurant. Large grounds.
Location At Masi, 4 km SW of Cavalese which is 42 km SE of Bolzano.
Restriction No children under 8.
Credit card Visa.
Terms B&B 90,000–120,000 L. Set lunch/dinner 90,000–120,000 L.

Hotels often book you into their most expensive rooms or suites unless you specify otherwise. Even if all room prices are the same, hotels may give you a less good room in the hope of selling their better rooms to late customers. It always pays to discuss accommodation in detail when making a reservation.

CAVASAGRA DI VEDELAGO 31050 Treviso   Map 16

Villa Cornèr della Regina   *Tel* (0423) 481481
   Country Hotel   *Fax* (0423) 451100
Via Corriva 10   *Telex* 433391

"Everyone's idea of a Palladian villa" – built in c. 1500, then rebuilt in c.
1700 by one of Palladio's pupils, it stands in its own formal park, amid
vineyards that provide it with red, white and sparkling wine. Venice is a
bare hour's drive away. Two recent, lyrical accounts: "Never before have
I come across a hotel of this quality. It has no lifts: but who wants a lift if
one can walk up a lovely staircase lined with old prints, to a bedroom the
size of a ballroom, decorated in 18th-century Venetian style, with
breathtaking views across the Veneto countryside? Beautifully restored in
keeping with its illustrious history, the villa has courteous and attentive
staff and an excellent restaurant. On our visit, guests were mainly Italian:
the hotel doesn't seem to have been much discovered yet by tourists."
And this, written *in situ*: "The interior is elegant, more through clever
modern design than the use of antiques, though a few of these are
sprinkled around. The huge central hall on the *piano nobile* has been
decorated in a tent style with pink and white stripes, irresistibly
reminiscent of Leander during Henley regatta. In my suite, the luxurious
bathroom is housed in a kind of pagoda. The dining room (in what was
once the orangerie and keeps that character) aims high, but does not quite
get there: my meal last night was mediocre, but tonight's was delicious.
The adjacent farm and stable buildings are now an annexe." Large heated
swimming pool; bedrooms all different and superbly elegant. (*Robert
Ribeiro, ATW Liddell*)

Open All year.
Rooms 7 suites, 16 double – all with bath and/or shower, telephone. 12 doubles
in annexe.
Facilities Lounges, bar, 2 restaurants; conference facilities. Park with tennis courts
and swimming pool, sauna.
Location 18 km W of Treviso, near Albaredo.
Credit cards All major cards accepted.
Terms [1990 rates] B&B 110,000–170,000 L per person. Meals alc.

CHIAVERANO D'IVREA 10010 Torino   Map 16

Hotel Castello San Giuseppe   *Tel* (0125) 424370
                                                   Fax (0125) 422574

Eight kilometres north-east of industrial Ivrea, where Olivetti produces its
computer-age wizardry, here in utter contrast is an ancient hilltop
mansion, once a monastery, then turned into a fortress by Bonaparte, and
now an unusual but charming hotel with large garden and terrace,
reached along a narrow winding hill road. "Quite an experience, and it
can be an eerie one if you come upon the tower and castle walls in the
dark," say readers this year. "One almost expects to be met by Count
Dracula. The black-gowned Signora rose from the desk at the end of a
passage when we finally found the hotel entrance. What, we wondered,
lay behind the massive doors of our rooms (we had taken two singles, all
that remained for the night)? They were former monastic cells, but were
provided with all mod cons and attractively furnished, though one

spectacular room had a bed on a sort of tiled plinth, presenting traps for the unwary. Dinner, with good wine, was excellent, and cheerfully served at 10 pm. In the morning our surroundings seemed entirely enchanting and delightful; it was quite an effort to tear ourselves away. There was a pleasant and helpful receptionist who telephoned to our next hotel to book a room. Not cheap, but it deserves inclusion in the Guide for sheer oddity and the picturesque setting – but it's not for those who can't cope with steps." Others have enjoyed home-cooking served by candle-light. (*J and J Wyatt*) Only criticism: poor breakfast.

Open All year. Restaurant closed Fri.
Rooms 1 suite, 12 double, 4 single – 6 with bath and shower, 10 with shower, all with telephone, TV. Ground-floor rooms.
Facilities Lounge with TV, bar, restaurant, breakfast room; conference room. Terrace; large garden. Swimming pool under construction in 1990.
Location 8 km NE of Ivrea, along hairpin bends.
Restriction Not suitable for &.
Credit cards Amex, Diners, Visa.
Terms [1990 rates] B&B: single 90,000 L, double 130,000 L. Set lunch/dinner 35,000–55,000 L; full alc 35,000–40,000 L. Reduced rates for children under 10; special meals on request.

CIOCCARO DI PENANGO 14030 Asti   Map 16

Locanda del Sant'Uffizio   *Tel* (0141) 91271
                                                      Fax (0141) 916068

The "superb" and gargantuan seven-course set menu (*Michelin* rosette) is a special attraction of this small hotel converted from a 16th-century monastery, in a tiny village amid the quiet hills of the wine area northeast of Asti. The owner, Beppe Firato, and his family occupy the larger monastery building, while the cloister buildings are now the guest rooms, elegantly furnished in rural style, each with a small terrace overlooking a garden which leads down to a swimming pool. The *Locanda* has views over the hills and vineyards. Breakfast, taken in the open beside the pool, is a self-service buffet with cheese, meats etc; a buffet lunch is served there too. Plaudits this year and last: "The nicest hotel I can remember staying in. The food was excellent but helpings ridiculously large." "A fantastic place, luxurious and comfortable, with charming rooms." "The charming owner carried our cases to our room, which had a sitting area and a bed up a spiral staircase. Dinner, with no written menus, consisted of course after course, beautifully cooked and presented, including the local speciality white truffles. Not cheap, but worth it, and their local wines are included in the price." "A relaxing, informal, casual place." (*C and M Hédoin, David C Craig, Betsy C Maestro, and others*) The hedonistic blow-out, "totally inappropriate for children", is more or less obligatory, for you must take half- or full-board terms. A reader this year who wanted just bed-and-breakfast was treated angrily by Signor Firato.

Open All year except Jan and Christmas. Restaurant closed Tue.
Rooms 3 suites, 26 double, 2 single – all with bath and/or shower, telephone, TV, balcony or terrace, air-conditioning. 7 ground-floor rooms.
Facilities 2 salons, bar, restaurant; billiard room, games room, small gym; conference facilities. Large grounds with unheated swimming pool, tennis; bicycles available.
Location Village is 20 km NE of Asti, 5 km SE of Moncalvo.
Credit cards All major cards accepted.

Terms Dinner, B&B 200,000–250,000 L; full board 260,000–310,000 L. Set lunch 70,000 L, dinner 90,000 L. Reduced rates and special meals for children.

COGNE 11012 Aosta   Map 16

Hôtel Bellevue   *Tel* (0165) 74825
Rue Grand Paradis 20   *Fax* (0165) 749192

Continued praise for this solid traditional hotel – a big square block of a building – just outside a skiing and hiking resort in a mountain valley south of Aosta, facing the Gran Paradiso massif: "The location is superb, with the elegant dining room seeming to float out over the view. Food and comfort are excellent, and the service is warm and welcoming, maybe because the place has been in the same family for 50 years or more, and many of the staff are old-timers. It has the human qualities of a family place." Others have written in similar vein – "Good traditional local food." (*Peter Dingley, Lon Bailey*)

Open Christmas–Easter; 1 June–30 Sep.
Rooms 4 chalets, 39 double, 6 single – 21 with bath and shower, 18 with bath, all with telephone, radio, TV. Chalets have cooking facilities.
Facilities Lift. 3 lounges, 2 bars, 2 dining rooms; conference room. Indoor swimming pool, whirlpool, sauna, solarium and gymnasium. Garden.
Location 27 km S of Aosta. Hotel is central; parking.
Credit cards Access, Visa.
Terms [1990 rates] B&B: single 92,000–112,000 L, double 129,000 L, chalet 154,000 L; dinner, B&B 80,000–144,000 L per person. Set lunch/dinner 35,000 L; full alc 50,000 L. Reduced rates and special meals for children.

CORTONA 52044 Arezzo   Map 16

Albergo San Michele   *Tel* (0575) 604348
Via Guelfa 15   *Fax* (0575) 630147

In a small Tuscan town, an elegantly modernised Renaissance palazzo with beamed ceilings and tiled floors. Comfort and quiet; friendly family service. Good value. Open Mar–Dec. 32 rooms, all with bath and shower. No restaurant. B&B single 58,000 L, double 86,000 L. Last year's nomination, endorsed, but with reservations about breakfast: "A rather morbid affair; better to go to one of the bars in the square." More reports please.

ERICE 91016 Sicily   Map 16

Elimo Hotel   *Tel* (0923) 869377
Via Vittorio Emanuele 75   *Fax* (0923) 869252

An old stone building, fastidiously converted in a whole series of styles, some a bit bizarre, and newly opened as a smart hotel. Charming owner, helpful staff, nice bedrooms, good pension menu. Roof-terraces. 21 rooms, all with bath. B&B double 100,000 L, set menus 35,000–40,000 L. Recent nomination. More reports please.

We need feedback on all entries. Often people fail to report on the best-known hotels, assuming that "someone else is sure to".

Hotel Moderno   *Tel* (0923) 869300
Via Vittorio Emanuele 63   *Fax* (0923) 869139

Beautiful but tourist-filled Erice has been described as "an atmospheric
sun-bleached town at the tip of a high pinnacle of rock, with views of the
sea. The medieval atmosphere is stronger than virtually anywhere we've
seen." This hotel, however, is as up to date as its name implies, and its
bedrooms look out over Trapani, not the sea. But it is family-run, with the
friendly English-speaking owner chatting with his guests in the evening.
It is furnished with style and originality, and has been liked again this
year as "attractive and welcoming, with pleasant rooms and good
restaurant". Earlier accounts: "Lots of stairs and odd-shaped corridors,
but warm, clean and welcoming. The food is very good (rare in Sicily),
and a large family are all involved in reception, cooking, waiting, and
eating with the guests." "A wonderful oasis of luxury in parched Sicily."
Driving through the narrow one-way streets is difficult: it is best to park
in the square just inside the town gate. (*NR Walton, Jane Dorrell, Kate
Schofield*)

Open All year.
Rooms 6 suites, 28 double, 6 single – all with bath and/or shower, telephone, TV.
Some ground-floor rooms. TV room.
Facilities Lift. Lounge, bar, dining room; terrace.
Location Central. Parking.
Credit cards All major cards accepted.
Terms [1990 rates] B&B: single 60,000–65,000 L, double 100,000–110,000 L;
dinner, B&B 70,000–100,000 L per person. Set lunch/dinner 40,000 L. Reduced
rates and special meals for children.

FASANO DEL GARDA 25083 Brescia   Map 16

Grand Hotel Fasano   *Tel* (0365) 21051
Corso Zanardelli 160   *Fax* (0365) 21054

*A fairly smart and sizeable holiday hotel in traditional style, with a fine lakeside
setting outside the busy resort of Gardone Riviera; many rooms have lake view.
Comfortable lounges, some antique furniture; lovely swimming pool amid
flowers and lawns, with parasols and loungers; ping-pong and tennis. Service
and food mostly approved, notably the help-yourself salads (but one hostile
view this year). Open May–Sep/Oct. 75 rooms, all with bath and/or shower.
Half board 81,000–130,000 L plus tax [1990]. Some recent criticisms. More
reports welcome.*

Hotel Villa del Sogno   *Tel* (0365) 20228
Via Zanardelli 107   *Fax* (0365) 21145
Fasano del Garda

Perched high above Lake Garda, amid finely landscaped gardens, this big
yellowish 1920s villa is a fairly grand but not-too-daunting hotel, whose
wide flowery terrace has lovely views of the lake. "Gardens and view
superb," writes a reader this year, "staff courteous, full of character, and
good *demi-pension* meals with hardly a course repeated in 14 days."
Others have judged the food copious but unremarkable. A 1990 visitor

had "a lovely big room overlooking the lake" and found the staff friendly. (*Col and Mrs AJW Harvey, Mr and Mrs Martin Roberts*) A fitness centre has just been added, with sauna, massage, etc.

Open Apr–Oct.
Rooms 4 suites, 28 double, 2 single – all with bath and/or shower, telephone, TV; 9 also have radio and air-conditioning. 7 ground-floor rooms.
Facilities Lift, ramp. 2 salons, bar, 2 dining rooms; conference room. Large terrace. Fitness centre. Garden with swimming pool and tennis court.
Location 3 km N of Gardone Riviera, above the lake.
Credit cards All major cards accepted.
Terms B&B: single 130,000–150,000 L, double 220,000–260,000 L, suite 260,000–310,000 L; dinner, B&B: double 240,000–370,000 L. Set lunch/dinner 50,000 L; full alc 50,000 L. Reduced rates and special meals for children.

FLORENCE   Map 16

Pensione Annalena   *Tel* (055) 222402
Via Romana 34   *Fax* (055) 222402
Florence 50125

Built as an aristocratic mansion, then successively a convent, a school for young ladies, a home for the poor and a gambling house, this building on the quieter south side of Arno has housed a family *pensione* on its upper floors since 1919. Readers have again enjoyed it in 1990: "The exterior aspects are discouraging – a heavy door, opening on to an empty, dim-lit passage leading to a cold stone staircase. But three floors up is a beautiful reception area, where a hospitable man showed me to a charming bedroom with high ceilings, nice old furniture, interesting paintings. It evoked the spirit of the Renaissance – but the bed was comfortable and the bathroom modern. It also overlooked the courtyard in which a romantic murder had taken place in the 15th century." "Efficient modern plumbing and quiet." (*Dr Suzanne Martin, JS and F Waters*)

Open All year.
Rooms 16 double, 4 single – all with bath and/or shower.
Facilities Lounge, bar.
Location South of Arno, near Boboli gardens.
Credit cards All major cards accepted.
Terms B&B: single 87,0000 L, double 136,000 L. (No restaurant.)

Hotel Calzaiuoli   *Tel* (055) 212456
Via Calzaiuoli 6   *Fax* (055) 268310
Florence 50122   *Telex* 580589

Centrally situated on a pedestrian street leading from the Duomo to the Palazzo Vecchio, a clean and well-run hotel, recently modernised, with air-conditioning and a friendly staff. Back rooms are largest and quietest, front ones may be noisy. Some upper rooms have views of the Duomo. Street parking difficult; garage nearby, but expensive. 49 rooms, all with bath and shower: single 95,000 L, double 130,000 L. Breakfast 11,000 L [1990]. No restaurant. Endorsed recently, but fuller reports welcome.

> Don't let old favourites down. Entries are dropped when there is no endorsement.

Hotel Loggiato dei Serviti   *Tel* (055) 219165
Piazza SS. Annunziata 3   *Fax* (055) 289595
Florence 50122   *Telex* 575808

Popular with visiting English art lecturers, this lovely building in the
heart of Florence was built in 1527 for a religious order, the Serviti, and
has been newly and sympathetically restored. It is admired again this
year: "small, intimate and subtly elegant"; "very good value, with
prompt and friendly service; rooms clean, bright and cool" (and air-
conditioned). Last year a visitor had "a light and spacious two-level room
with gorgeous beamed ceiling". "It combines the best of old (Renaissance
building, antique furnishings) and new (including the plumbing). The
lovely piazza has been mercifully rescued from its undignified role as a
parking lot (but the hotel will park your car for you)." (*Wende West, Dr DM
Keyzer and others*) One dissenter thought the hotel overrated and the staff
harassed.

Open All year.
Rooms 4 suites, 19 double, 6 single – all with bath, shower, telephone, radio, TV,
air-conditioning.
Facilities Lift. Lounges, TV room, bar, breakfast room.
Location Central, 200 metres from cathedral in pedestrian zone. Garage service.
Restriction Not suitable for &.
Credit cards All major cards accepted.
Terms [1990 rates] B&B: single 110,000 L, double 160,000 L, suite 450,000 L. (No
restaurant.)

Hotel Morandi alla Crocetta   *Tel* (055) 2344747
Via Laura 50   *Fax* (055) 2480954
Florence 50121

*Owned and run by an English woman and her two adult children, a small and
graceful B&B hotel in a former 16th-century convent, central but quiet, close to
the Academy of Fine Arts. Has been in the same ownership since 1915. Large
rooms, friendly ambience. Open all year. 9 rooms, all with private facilities. No
restaurant. B&B: single 78,000 L, double 129,000 L. New nomination. More
reports please.*

Hotel Tornabuoni Beacci   *Tel* (055) 268377 and 212645
Via Tornabuoni 3   *Telex* 570215
Florence 50123

Centrally situated near the Palazzo Strozzi, this admirable hotel is in a
14th-century palace – and it's on the top floor, so it suffers very little from
street noise. "Indeed most pleasant," says a recent visitor. "Every room is
different and all are large and beautifully decorated. The restaurant is
nice, the roof-terrace is a lovely oasis after a day in Florence, and the
ambience is homey, helped along by the smiling, willing staff and the
ever-present whirlwind of Signora Beacci." Others have called the food
"satisfactory", and have enjoyed taking breakfast on the roof-garden,
amid trees and shrubs, or sitting in the comfortable lounge amid
tapestries, plants, bookcases and fine old furniture. (*Roberta Garza de
Elizondo*) More reports please.

Open All year.
Rooms 31 double – all with bath and telephone; TV on request. 5 in annexe.
Facilities Lift. Salon, bar, restaurant; roof-terrace.
Location Central, close to Palazzo Strozzi. Parking.
Credit cards Amex, Diners, Visa.
Terms Dinner, B&B: single 125,000 L, double 200,000 L.

Hotel Villa Belvedere   *Tel* (055) 222501
Via Benedetto Castelli 3   *Fax* (055) 223163
Florence 50124   *Telex* 575648

This "delightful small hotel" (one of two plaudits this year) stands
peacefully on Poggio Imperiale hill, and has a very clean, small
swimming pool set in a flowery garden. It is modern, friendly and family-
run. "We had a large well-furnished room with a huge terrace
overlooking the garden and the city below." An earlier rhapsodic view: "I
drove down through a tunnel of trees to the delightful villa, where only
the cicadas disturbed the silence. Inside were cool, shiny marble floors,
and simply but elegantly furnished rooms. Breakfast is served in a glass-
walled veranda which looks down on to the Duomo, the roofs of Florence
and the hills beyond. At night you can sip coffee or drinks in the garden,
the perfume from the roses scenting the air and the lights of Florence
twinkling below." No restaurant: but the bar serves snacks and simple
dishes such as pasta and omelettes. Some rooms are quite small, and it
might be worth asking for one of the larger (and more expensive) upper
rooms with a big terrace. (*Arnold Horwell, E and PH Simon*)

Open 1 Mar–30 Nov.
Rooms 2 suites, 22 double, 3 single – 25 with bath and shower, 2 with shower, all
with telephone, TV, air-conditioning. Some ground-floor rooms.
Facilities Lift. Lounges, TV room, bar with veranda. Garden with swimming pool,
tennis, children's play area.
Location 2.5 km S of centre; leave Florence by Porta Romana, turn E off Via
Senese.
Credit cards All major cards accepted.
Terms B&B: single 130,000–150,000 L, double 200,000–220,000 L, suite 250,000–
260,000 L. Reduced rates for children sharing parents' room. (No restaurant, but
light meals available.)

FORTE DEI MARMI 55042 Lucca   **Map 16**

Hotel Tirreno   *Tel* (0584) 83333
Viale Morin 7

Very Italian in atmosphere, Forte dei Marmi is a traditional Ligurian
seaside resort, with villas and shady gardens, a wide traffic-free
promenade, a pier and a long golden beach. Here the family-run *Tirreno*
with its "lovely peaceful garden" has been specially commended this year
for its "marvellous but expensive food, notably the antipasto, an
unlimited choice of fresh vegetables and seafood". An earlier view:
"Warm and homey; generous rooms with balconies, a staff who work
hard to please." Another reader had a pink marble bathroom "as big as a
bedroom in some hotels". Most guests receive a complimentary bottle of
Italian champagne with dinner on the night before their departure.

(*Dorothy Eggers, Diane and Joel Morris*) The beach close by is said to be uncrowded and clean.

Open Easter–end Sep.
Rooms 49 double, 10 single – 12 with bath, 47 with shower, all with telephone; 20 have balcony with sea views. 21 in villa in garden.
Facilities Lounge, TV room, games room, bar, dining room; dancing. Garden. 50 metres from fine, safe beach with bathing and boat rental.
Location Central; parking. Town is 35 km NW of Pisa.
Restriction Not suitable for ᵫ.
Credit cards Amex, Diners, Visa.
Terms [1990 rates] B&B: single 71,500 L, double 113,000 L; dinner, B&B 98,000 L per person; full board 108,000–143,000 L. Reduced rates for children sharing parents' room; special meals.

GARDONE RIVIERA 25083 Brescia   Map 16

Villa Fiordaliso   *Tel* (0365) 20158
Via Zanardelli 132   *Fax* (030) 919012
                                                      Telex 301088

The brochure of this exquisitely beautiful villa on Lake Garda does not balk at reminding its public that this was a favourite residence of Claretta Petacci, Mussolini's consort. But that's past history. And today's Guide readers love the place: "Now a restaurant with seven bedrooms, it's been carefully restored to its former (pre-Petacci) glory – marble, alabaster, tapestries and paintings, blended with modern lighting and high, black lacquer and leather chairs in the dining rooms, to produce a relaxing and attractive atmosphere. The situation is superb – lovely views, its own small pier, waterside gardens and outdoor dining terrace. Our room was lovely, with traditional furniture, and the bathroom was a delight. The excellent cooking is in modern style, but based on traditional and local recipes, with a changing daily menu related to the market; service, a little unsure, was by local women. Front, lake-view rooms are best: back ones could be noisy, for the main road passes there." (*Pat and Jeremy Temple*)

Open 15 Mar–30 Oct.
Rooms 1 suite, 6 double – all with bath and/or shower, telephone, radio, TV, mini-bar.
Facilities Hall, piano bar, TV room, 4 dining rooms. Terrace where meals are served. Garden, private beach.
Location 500 metres from centre of Gardone which is 34 km NE of Brescia. Parking.
Restrictions Not suitable for ᵫ or for small children.
Credit cards All major cards accepted.
Terms [1990 rates] B&B double 129,500 L; dinner, B&B 261,500 L, full board 393,500 L. Full alc 70,000 L.

GARGONZA 52048 Arezzo   Map 16

Castello di Gargonza   *Tel* (0575) 847021
Monte San Savino   *Fax* (0575) 847054
                                                      Telex 571466

"Ah, the Gargonza, what a sylvan setting!" says a visitor this year to this much-loved and unusual paradise which is not exactly a hotel. On a hilltop in the Tuscan woodlands above the Chiana valley, it is an intact

13th-century walled village which Count Roberto Guicciardini's family have owned for centuries and which he has converted into a partly self-catering hotel-cum-conference centre and rural community. Below the *Castello* itself with its tall turreted tower are a score of red-roofed cottages that cluster round it for ramparted protection. The count has turned these village homes into bedrooms and suites which can be hired either for a week or more on a self-catering basis, or else per night as hotel rooms. He and his wife have done the conversion most elegantly, with true Italian flair – clean stone walls, beamed ceilings, pretty rustic decor, neatly cobbled alleys.

A recent description: "You enter the village through its single great portal, surmounted by a plaque commemorating Dante's stay here in 1302 at the start of his exile from Florence. The count has aimed at recreating a living community (there are concerts, exhibitions, study groups, etc). The cottages are furnished in individual style, and there are always flowers when you arrive. Inside the village are two small gardens, one shady under pines, the other an enclosed hanging garden embellished with lemon trees and grapevines. At the foot of the old mule-track down from the village is the restaurant, whose pleasures are country ones. Calf's liver, brains, fillet of beef with green peppercorns, spatchcocked bantam and other meats grilled over charcoal are delicious. In winter you eat indoors with a blazing log fire and the wrought-iron candelabra lit; on warm summer evenings you can sit in the open on the long roofed terrace above the wooded valley, with bats flitting through the rafters." (*Lynne M Allen, Adrian Wright and John Lay*) Those booking just for a night or two should be warned that hotel service as such hardly exists. And cars can enter the village only for loading or unloading baggage. A reader this year warns that some of the central ground-floor *case* can be noisy.

Open All year except 7 Jan–4 Feb. Restaurant closed Mon.
Rooms 37 double – all with bath and/or shower, telephone; TV on request. 30 in 18 cottages with self-catering facilities, 7 in guest house.
Facilities Lounge, TV room, restaurant; auditorium, meeting halls, conference rooms. Large grounds with garden, children's play area, woods and farm.
Location 8 km W of Monte San Savino on SS73 towards Siena (35 km). From *autostrada* A1, exit 27, Monte San Savino is 10 km.
Restriction Not suitable for &.
Credit card Amex.
Terms [1990 rates] B&B 65,000–90,000 L; dinner, B&B 93,000–118,000 L; full board 121,000–146,000 L. Full alc 28,000–35,000 L. 10% discount for children under 10.

GIARDINI NAXOS 98035 Messina, Sicily　　　　　　　　**Map 16**

Hotel Arathena Rocks　　　　　　　　　　　　　*Tel* (0942) 51348
Via Calcide Eubea 55

This is for those who seek peace and flowery prettiness, and don't mind if the food is dull. Situated in a busy seaside resort just below Taormina, it's a traditional family-run hotel in a quiet location down a private road, and has antique furniture, doors painted with local scenes, and rooms bright with fresh flowers from the large garden. The swimming pool hewn out of the lava rocks is a special feature: or you can swim in the clear sea close by. A report this year: "A light lounge with views of the sea and an airy summery feel. A large patio with comfortable chairs for sunbathing, and a lovely walled vegetable garden with lemon trees. Large balcony to our room. Friendly welcome, waiters young and helpful. But food unimaginative." The food has been criticised before, apart from the pasta. (*Fred Mawer, also David Gadsby*)

Open 1 Apr–31 Oct.
Rooms 2 suites, 40 double, 10 single – 42 with bath, 10 with shower, all with telephone; 2 with air-conditioning. 3 in annexe.
Facilities Lift. Lounge, TV room, 2 bars, restaurant. Gardens with sea-water swimming pool and tennis court.
Location In Naxos, 5 km S of Taormina. Hotel has minibus to take guests to Taormina.
Credit cards Access, Visa.
Terms Dinner, B&B: single 85,000–90,000 L, double 160,000–170,000 L, suite 200,000–220,000 L. Set lunch/dinner 30,000 L. Reduced rates and special meals for children.

LECCE 73100   **Map 16**

Hotel Risorgimento   *Tel* (0832) 42125
Via Augusto Imperatore 19   *Telex* 860144

The second city of Apulia (Italy's heel) has some glorious Baroque architecture: one of the fine old buildings in its centre is this old-fashioned, slightly shabby but comfortable three-star albergo. Rooms air-conditioned, good baths and plumbing, excellent food, friendly staff. 57 rooms, most with bath or shower, 54,000–99,000 L. Breakfast 11,500 L. Set meals 25,000 L [1990]. Endorsed in 1990. Fuller reports needed.

LUCCA 55050   **Map 16**

Villa La Principessa   *Tel* (0583) 370038
                                                     Fax (0583) 379019
                                                     Telex 590068

Set just south of Lucca on the Pisa road, this stately home in its lovely park was in the 14th century the home and court of the Duke of Lucca, and later belonged to Napoleon's sister Pauline. Since 1973 a luxurious and strikingly elegant hotel, it is nominated in two reports this year: "Everything is on a grand scale – the house, the giant trees that shield it from the road, and many of the other guests by the large swimming pool set in a beautiful garden at the foot of a wooded mountain. The vast hall has a ceiling the height of two floors, an immense fireplace, chandeliers and gloomy old pictures. Other rooms experiment with bold, vibrant colours: our bedroom, overlooking lawn and woods, was very ritzy with lots of glass – quite out of keeping with the age of the house, but brilliantly successful. One could be nowhere else but Italy. The serious bustling restaurant serves creditable food, with some interesting local specialities (e.g. Luccan stew of salt cod) and nods towards modern cooking too. Breakfast, a huge buffet, was the best we had in Italy. The hotel is a little impersonal, and the receptionists should be trained to look more cheerful and interested." Another visitor thought the service excellent, and found the air-conditioning a boon. (*David and Kate Wooff, Marie and Dominic Chambers*)

Open All year except 7 Jan–18 Feb. Restaurant closed Wed.
Rooms 8 suites, 36 double – all with bath, shower, telephone, T V, air-conditioning.
Facilities Lift. Lounge, bar, restaurant; conference facilities. Park with swimming pool.
Location 4 km S of Lucca, along SS 12r towards Pisa.
Restriction Not suitable for &.
Credit cards All major cards accepted.
Terms [1990 rates] Rooms 200,000–360,000 L, suite 450,000–530,000 L. Breakfast 18,000 L. Dinner, B&B 220,000–280,000 L per person.

MALEO 20076 Milano   Map 16

Albergo del Sole   *Tel* (0377) 58142
Via Trabattoni 22   *Fax* (0377) 458058

In a village between Cremona and Piacenza, an old hostelry dating from the 15th century has been converted by Franco and Silvana Colombani into a stylish restaurant-with-rooms. Here they lovingly practice regional cuisine (*Michelin* rosette), in a family atmosphere, as nominators report this year: "The main dining room comprises a large wooden table at which you are allocated your places, and a huge fireplace with roasting-spit. Local or traditional dishes include minestrone, polenta, stracotto, sabbiosa with mascarpone sabayon. Ask to see Franco's balsamic vinegar: the loft contains barrel after barrel, each of some different aromatic wood, where his pride and joy is made and aged. The Colombanis felt like friends after a couple of days, and their pride in the region shines throughout. The bedrooms, mostly converted stables, are across a courtyard: they are really small suites, sparsely but elegantly furnished, with the T V boxed into a cupboard – Italian T V programmes must surely have been devised as part of Dante's Purgatory." "Very good cooking; friendly and rustic hotel." There are some individual dining tables too, and meals are served outdoors in summer, amid vines, bird's nests, and the sound of church bells. (*Shaun Hill, and others*)

Open All year except Jan and Aug. Closed Sun evening and Mon.
Rooms 1 suite, 5 double, 1 single – all with bath and/or shower, telephone, T V, baby-listening. 2 ground-floor rooms.
Facilities Bar, T V room, restaurant. Garden.
Location 20 km W of Cremona. Parking.
Credit cards Access, Amex, Visa.
Terms [1990 rates] B&B: single 165,000 L, double 230,000 L, suite 260,000 L. Full alc 80,000 L. Reduced rates and special meals for children.

MANTUA 46100   Map 16

Albergo San Lorenzo   *Tel* (0376) 220500
Piazza Concordia 14   *Fax* (0376) 327194

There is a sombre quality to the flat Mantuan countryside, which may explain the melancholy of Virgil, who was born in a village nearby. Mantua itself, however, is a beautiful city, and has a grand and colourful ducal palace. The *San Lorenzo*, one of its two best hotels, is a modern building with elegant period furnishings and a well-kept roof-terrace. Recent visitors have found it comfortable, cool and very friendly: "Our room with its terracotta floor tiles was a bit austere but well decorated. The quality of the cotton sheets is amazing." "Good breakfast with first-rate coffee." Many rooms have a view of the Piazza delle Erbe and the lovely rotunda church of San Lorenzo. The hotel is quiet (if you don't count the ringing of church bells as noise). (Endorsed by *Mary Ann Meanwell*) More reports please.

Open All year.
Rooms 3 suites, 28 double, 10 single – all with bath or shower, telephone, radio, TV, air-conditioning.
Facilities Lift. Lounges, bar, TV room, meeting room. Roof-terrace.
Location Central, near Piazza delle Erbe, in pedestrian precinct. Garage 100 metres.
Credit cards All major cards accepted.
Terms [1990 rates] Rooms: single 122,500 L, double 183,000 L. Breakfast 15,000 L. (No restaurant.)

MELE 16010 Genova   Map 16

Hotel Fado '78   BUDGET   *Tel* (010) 631802
Via Fado 82

Gianni Canepa and his English wife Christine run a much-liked hotel on the road going inland from the Riviera at Voltri, west of Genoa. It's a gracious old building with bedrooms in a modern extension, all with fine views across the valley. The warm welcome, the food and the "large, clean, airy rooms" were again liked this year. Recent reports: "Worth a detour to enjoy Italian regional cooking at its best. Excellent dinner, comfortable beds, fresh mountain air and pleasant views." "My room was high and airy, with a marble floor. A first-class dinner of crêpes and rabbit casserole with garden herbs. Lovely secluded garden." (*Peter Saynor, Lesley Lee, Stuart W Holland*) Traffic noise is only slight.

Open All year.
Rooms 6 double, 2 single – all with bath and/or shower, telephone; some with TV.
Facilities Lounge, bar, 2 dining rooms. Garden, terrace.
Location 7 km N of Voltri on SS456 to Ovada. Leave A26 motorway at Masone or Voltri.
Restriction Not suitable for &.
Credit cards None accepted.
Terms Rooms: single 40,000 L, double 65,000 L. Breakfast 8,000 L. Full alc lunch/dinner 28,000–30,000 L. Reduced rates for children sharing parents' room; special meals.

MENAGGIO 22017 Como   Map 16

Grand Hotel Menaggio   *Tel* (0344) 32640
Via IV Novembre 69   *Fax* (0344) 32350
                                                 Telex 328471

Right on the shore of Lake Como, in a "picturesque but overgrown village", this fairly elegant four-star holiday hotel, "old-fashioned but recently refurbished", makes its Guide debut this year: "Remarkably pleasant, and catering for locals as well as package tours. Bedrooms are well appointed, with ridiculously romantic views over the lake, and the lakeside garden and swimming pool are a haven of peace. Public rooms are spacious and gracious. Service was old-fashioned but un-snooty. Meals, though not gourmet, kept up a good standard: but wine mark-ups were excessive. Breakfast was an impressive spread, including lots of fruit. Some nuisance caused by a nearby nightspot, *Pam-Pam*, frequented by youth, so we had to sleep with the windows closed; but fortunately there is good air-conditioning." (*J and J Wyatt*) More reports welcome.

Open All year.
Rooms 3 suites, 45 double, 1 single – all with bath, shower, telephone, radio, TV, baby-listening.
Facilities 2 lounges, bar, restaurant; conference facilities. Garden, terrace. Swimming pool. Water sports.
Location Menaggio is 35 km N of Como. Parking.
Restriction Not suitable for &.
Credit cards Access, Visa.
Terms [1990 rates] B&B: single 123,000 L, double 203,000 L, suite 304,000 L; dinner, B&B 150,000–225,000 L per person. Full alc 60,000 L. Reduced rates and special meals for children.

MERANO 39012 Bolzano   **Map 16**

Hotel Villa Mozart   *Tel* (0473) 30630
Via San Marco 26

Black and white is a dominant theme of Emmy and Andreas Hellrigl's much-admired small hotel: it extends to the china and candles on the tables, the chequered marble floors, even the towels and the brochure. The hotel is about ten minutes' walk from the town centre, approached through big iron gates that open electronically to bona fide guests. "We had a lovely room and a memorable dinner in this gem of a hotel," says a visitor this year. Others have written: "Dinner, served at 8 pm to hotel guests only, with printed dated menu cards, offered no choice (even the wines are chosen for you), but all was exquisite. Breakfast on the terrace was also excellent, the indoor pool was refreshing and the staff pleasant and polite." "The building, outside as well as in, is immaculately designed and furnished in the style of the Viennese Secession. This includes everything – carpets, curtains, door fittings, cutlery, crockery, glasses and even the waitresses' uniforms! For architects and interior designers the hotel is worth a detour." Red print and a rosette from *Michelin*, needless to say. (*Marie and Dominic Chambers, Dan and Michlyne Thal*) The Hellrigls' "unsurpassed personal attention to detail" has been praised, also the "light and innovative" cooking of their chef Raimund Frötscher. He closed the restaurant one night, in the owners' absence, to the bitter disappointment of readers who had come specially to experience it.

Open Easter–Nov.
Rooms 8 double, 2 single – 8 with bath, 2 with shower, all with telephone, radio, TV.
Facilities Lift. Lounges, library, bar, restaurant. Large grounds with sun-terrace, covered heated swimming pool, sauna, solarium.
Location Coming on main road from Bolzano, via Rome, take third street on right. Private parking.
Restriction Not suitable for &.
Credit card Access, Amex, Diners.
Terms [1990 rates] Dinner, B&B 189,000 L. Set dinner 98,000 L.

MILAN   Map 1

Hotel Gran Duca di York   *Tel* (02) 874863 and 87494:
Via Moneta 1/a   *Fax* (02) 869034
Milan 20123

"A gem," says a recent lodger at this medium-range hotel near the
Duomo, neither grand nor ducal apart from its suits of armour outside the
lift. "The atmosphere was calm, quiet and elegant, the staff were
competent, the quiet lounge had a lovely desk on which to write. My
room was small, but clean and well decorated." Others have had large
rooms and big bathrooms, and have praised the breakfast coffee, served
in a nondescript room. (*GB Brook, Bettye Chambers*) No restaurant, but the
fairly cheap *Al Mercanti* (super fresh fish) is five minutes' walk away
Parking in the area is tricky, and the one-way system makes car access
difficult.

Open All year except Aug.
Rooms 33 – some with bath or shower, all with telephone, TV.
Facilities Lift. Lounge, breakfast room.
Location Central; 500 metres W of Duomo. No private parking.
Credit cards None accepted.
Terms B&B: single 120,000 L, double 133,000 L. (No restaurant.)

Hotel Manzoni   *Tel* (02) 7600570(
Via Santo Spirito 20   *Fax* (02) 78421:
Milan 20121

*A modern hotel, well run and fairly cheap by Milan standards, in a small side
street near the Via Manzoni which leads to the Piazza della Scala and the
cathedral. Difficult to reach by car, and back rooms can be noisy. Staff
courteous, rooms pleasant, breakfast fair. 52 rooms, most with bath and/or
shower, single 97,000 L, double 137,400 L. Breakfast 14,000 L [1990]. No
restaurant. Endorsed again this year, but further reports welcome.*

Hotel Pierre Milano   *Tel* (02) 7200058
Via Edmondo de Amicis 32   *Fax* (02) 8052157
Milan 20123   *Telex* 33330:

*Fairly central, about 1 km W of the Duomo, a newly opened luxury hotel with
striking decor, a mix of ancient and modern. Relaxed ambience, good cooking
and buffet breakfasts. Most rooms overlook a quiet street or inner courtyard
47 rooms, all with bath and shower. B&B double 640,000–950,000 L. Set meals
68,000–75,000 L [1990]. Recent nomination. More reports welcome.*

> Set dinner refers to a fixed price meal (which may have ample,
> limited or no choice on the menu). Full alc is the hotel's own
> estimated price per person of a three-course meal taken à la carte,
> with a half-bottle of house wine.

MONTEFOLLONICO 53040 Siena   Map 16

La Chiusa   *Tel* (0577) 669668
                                                      Fax (0577) 669593

An elegant restaurant-with-rooms in the hills south-east of Siena, serving some of the best food in Tuscany (*Michelin* rosette) and new to the Guide this year: "It is an ancient farmhouse in a small medieval hill town, renovated with taste by Umberto and Dania Lucharini: she cooks, he runs the stylish restaurant. Rooms are comfortable and rustic, and have dramatic private bathrooms. We were given a wonderful reception. There is a six-course menu of their specialities, and other dishes à la carte. All are good, notably the risotto, duck with wild fennel, pigeon with sage. Breakfast can be taken in a vine-covered courtyard." "Outstanding cooking. Four of the six bedrooms have a great view of Montepulciano, the neighbouring hill town." (*Shaun Hill, AN Other*)

Open All year except 6 Jan–15 Mar and 5 Nov–5 Dec. Closed lunchtime in July/Aug.
Rooms 1 suite, 7 double – all with bath/shower, telephone.
Facilities Restaurant. Courtyard, garden.
Location 60 km SE of Siena, just N of Montepulciano.
Restriction Not suitable for &.
Credit cards All major cards accepted.
Terms [1990 rates] Double room 210,000 L. Breakfast 15,000 L. Alc meals (excluding wine) 70,000–90,000 L.

MONTIGNOSO 54038 Massa-Carrara   Map 16

Ristorante-Relais Il Bottaccio   *Tel* (0585) 340031
                                                     Fax (0585) 340103
                                                     Telex 500283

"Tucked away under a ruined castle", between Carrara and Viareggio, here's a most startling place: "A beautiful 18th-century olive-oil mill, converted with Italian style and panache into a charming, sophisticated restaurant with just five incredible rooms. The spectacular restaurant is beside a cascading fountain with pools: our ten-course *menu degustazione* was fantastic, fully deserving its *Michelin* rosette. Service was by the owners. The delicious breakfast was equally impressive. And so too was our vast room, containing an original mill wheel and a Roman-style sunken bath. The tiled floor had exotic rugs and on the walls were pictures that looked as if they should have been in a museum. Our large modern black steel-framed four-poster had a silk embroidered bedspread; on an antique Arabian chest stood bottles of cognac, grappa, etc. It was all an amazingly successful blending of ancient and modern. The bathroom, covered with tiny mosaic tiles and hand-painted antique tiles, was also fantastic. There's a Roman pavement in the garden, and a beautiful terrace. It was the most expensive night we have ever had anywhere: but worth it." (*Pat and Jeremy Temple*)

Open All year.
Rooms 5 suites – all with bath, shower, telephone, radio, TV.
Facilities Lounges, restaurant. Terrace with bar.
Location Montignoso is 5 km SE of Massa: leave Genova–Livorno *autostrada* at exit 12.

Credit cards All major cards accepted.
Terms [1990 rates] Suites 420,000–450,000 L. Breakfast 30,000 L. Set lunch
100,000 L, dinner 120,000 L.

ORTA SAN GUILIO 28016 Novara   Map 1●

La Bussola `BUDGET`   *Tel* (0322) 9019●

A comfortable hotel on a low hill, with views of lovely Lake Orta, in an ol●
village on a peninsula by the lake. Flowery garden, swimming pool. Pleasan●
owners. Goodish food, poor breakfasts. Closed Nov–3 Jan. 16 rooms, all wit●
bath or shower. Dinner, B&B 70,000–80,000 L [1990]. Renominated this year
More reports please.

ORVIETO 05018 Terni   Map 1●

Hotel Virgilio   *Tel* (0763) 41882
Piazza del Duomo 5–6

Described as "marvellous value", this small hotel faces the side of the●
gloriously decorated Duomo. It is designed and furnished in good moder●
Italian style – gleaming chrome, white and pink marble. In the receptio●
area, a large piece of Roman sculpture is flanked by good contemporar●
original drawings; a beautiful old tapestry is hung alongside delightfu●
puppets. Bedrooms are not large but attractively furnished, with goo●
bathrooms. Breakfasts are poor, and one reader this year thought the●
decor out of character. Staff are pleasant. No restaurant, but the nearb●
Maurizio is recommended.

Open All year except 20 days in Jan.
Rooms 14 double, 2 single – all with bath, shower, telephone. 2 doubles in
annexe 20 metres away. Some ground-floor rooms.
Facilities Lift. Bar, TV room.
Location Central, near Duomo. Parking.
Credit cards None accepted.
Terms Rooms: single 65,000 L, double 90,000 L. Breakfast 15,000 L. (No
restaurant.)

PALESTRINA 00036 Rome   Map 1●

Albergo Ristorante Stella `BUDGET`   *Tel* (06) 9558172
Piazzale della Liberazione 3   *Fax* (06) 957336●

The 16th-century composer Palestrina was born in this ancient town tha●
bears his name, set in the lovely hills east of Rome: it contains the ruins o●
a classical Roman temple dedicated to Fortune. A visitor returnin●
recently to the modern and unpretentious *Stella* found the food a●
excellent as before: ". . . antipasto a meal in itself, Easter lamb roast t●
perfection." Earlier he had written: "There in the tiny piazza is thi●
delightful hotel, its restaurant very popular with locals. We loved the●
place. Our room was large and clean, the bathroom modern, and only the●
church clock disturbed the peace." (*Paul Palmer*) More reports welcome

Open All year.

Rooms 1 suite, 14 double – all with bath and/or shower, telephone.
Facilities Lift. Lounges, bar, restaurant. Next to public garden.
Location Central. Town is 38 km E of Rome, off S6 to Frosinone. Public parking.
Credit cards Amex, Diners, Visa.
Terms Rooms: single 30,000 L, double 55,000 L, suite 105,000 L. Breakfast 5,000 L. Dinner, B&B 48,000 L; full board 68,000 L. Full alc 23,000–32,000 L. Reduced rates for children.

PANZANO IN CHIANTI 50020 Florence   Map 16

Villa Le Barone
Via San Leolino 19

Tel (055) 852215
Fax (055) 852277

A former home of the famous Della Robbia family, this graceful villa stands high on a hilltop between Florence and Siena. It has a swimming pool, and spread out below it is the hilly Tuscan landscape of vineyards, olive groves and cypresses. The Duchessa Visconti is the present owner of what is now a sophisticated *pensione*, retaining the atmosphere of a cared-for private home. Most rooms are elegantly furnished with good antiques, carefully arranged flowers and fine linen sheets. Two latest reports describe the *Villa* as "delightful" and praise the food highly, whereas some earlier visitors had found it too "bland and international" (to suit the mainly Anglo-American and German clientele?). But all agree that the public rooms are charming and the staff discreetly helpful. The "honour system" with the evening drinks is also admired. (*RA, JH*)

Open 1 Apr–1 Nov.
Rooms 26 double, 1 single – 21 with bath, 6 with shower; 5 with air-conditioning. 17 in 3 garden annexes. Some ground-floor rooms.
Facilities 4 sitting rooms (1 with TV), bar, breakfast room, dining room. 5-acre grounds with swimming pool and table-tennis.
Location Off SS222 to Siena, 31 km S of Florence. Hotel is SE of Panzano.
Credit card Amex.
Terms Dinner, B&B 140,000–160,000 L; full board 180,000–200,000 L. Reduced rates and special meals for children.

Hotel Villa Sangiovese
Piazza Bucciarelli 5

Tel (055) 852461
Fax (055) 852463

Uri and Anna Maria Bleuler, from Switzerland, were till recently managers of the much-admired *Tenuta di Ricavo* in nearby Castellina (q.v.); now they have opened their own hotel in this little town south of Florence. "The villa lies on the edge of the town, surrounded by the beautiful steep Tuscan hills where cypresses, olives and vines grow. It is an old stone house, remodelled and restored, with terraces offering fine views of countryside, which comes right up to the edge of the hotel's grounds. The Bleulers' welcome could not have been kinder, and it is clear that they are aiming to create a homely atmosphere combined with Swiss efficiency. The comfortable public rooms are decorated mainly in soft yellows and fawns to give a cool, cheerful atmosphere. You can dine on the terrace when it's fine. Our bedroom, not large, was simply furnished with meticulous attention to detail – excellent bedside lamps. A Florentine cook produces a limited à la carte menu: the dishes change nightly and all were good. Breakfast with excellent Swiss-style coffee is served in an attractive small room." Other praise this year and last: "Most delightful: a cordial welcome and excellent dinner." "Beautiful rooms, food simple and excellent, staff friendly." An outdoor swimming pool was being built in 1990. (*Margaret and Charles Baker, Wendy Geiringer, Dr NB Finter*)

Open All year except Jan/Feb. Restaurant closed Wed.
Rooms 3 suites, 15 double, 1 single – all with bath and/or shower, telephone; TV on request.
Facilities 2 lounges, bar, restaurant; terrace. Garden with swimming pool; bicycles.
Location Central, on square; back rooms quietest. Parking.
Restriction Not suitable for &.
Credit card Access.
Terms [1990 rates] B&B: single 80,000–100,000 L, double 100,000–160,000 L, suite 160,000–210,000 L. Alc meals 30,000–35,000 L. Reduced rates and special meals for children.

PERUGIA 06100   Map 16

Hotel La Rosetta   *Tel* (075) 20841
Piazza Italia 19   *Fax* (075) 20841
                                                       Telex 563271

A reader who recently spent all August here thought the staff friendly and the food excellent, and especially enjoyed eating in the attractive shady courtyard. Others this year have also spoken well of the comfort, cooking and efficiency. "We had a quiet and cool room over the dining courtyard." "The decor is not always alluring – our bathroom in shiny bronze was a bit much – but the bedrooms were large." The hotel enjoys a prime situation at the top of the main street, Corso Vanucci, but this is where Perugia's nightly *passeggiata* takes place – and one reader warns that "this non-stop cocktail party" makes sleep in the front rooms difficult – "Bring earplugs, or ask for rooms at the back, which are less attractive." (*NM Williamson*)

Open All year. Restaurant closed Mon.
Rooms 4 suites, 60 double, 32 single – all with bath and/or shower, telephone, radio, TV, baby-listening. Some ground-floor rooms.
Facilities Lift. Salons, bar, games room, reading room, restaurant; conference/banqueting facilities. Courtyard where meals are served in fine weather.
Location Central; some traffic noise. Parking and 2 garages (extra charge).
Credit cards All major cards accepted.
Terms [1990 rates] Rooms: single 70,000 L, double 120,000 L. Breakfast 10,000 L. Half board 100,000–110,000 L per person. Reduced rates and special meals for children.

PETTENASCO 28028 Novara   Map 16

Hotel Giardinetto   `BUDGET`   *Tel* (0323) 89118
Via Provinciale 1, Lago d'Orta   *Fax* (0323) 89219

A sizeable modern white-walled hotel, family-run, in a superb position on the shore of Lake Orta, a busy summer resort. "Our room faced the lake, and we sat on its terrace watching the sunset. Meals were exceptional." "Friendly informal service, and a fantastic Thursday dinner buffet." "Hardworking staff with a sense of humour; outstanding food."

These and other reports this year and last back up earlier praise for the seafood buffet, the swimming pool, and the watchfulness of the owners, Oreste and Caterina Primatesta. The Thursday buffet is followed by live entertainment, which might be a touring string quartet; some windsurfing, pedalo and tennis facilities are free to guests. Rooms facing the road are rather dark and noisy, lake-facing ones are quieter and have a better view, notably those in a new wing with balconies. (*David Pinfield, Brian Farmer, Brian MacArthur, and others*)

Open Easter–end Oct.
Rooms 2 suites, 45 double, 7 single – all with bath and/or shower (2 with jacuzzi), telephone, baby-listening; air-conditioning; TV on request.
Facilities Lift, ramps. Lounge, 2 bars, TV room, restaurant, coffee shop; conference room; gala evening with dancing Thu in summer. Garden with heated swimming pool, children's play area.
Location 4 km S of Orta San Giulio. Hotel is 500 metres from town centre, on lake shore. Private parking.
Credit cards All major cards accepted.
Terms [1990 rates] Dinner, B&B 60,000–85,000 L. Set lunch/dinner 35,000 L; full alc 38,000 L. Reduced rates and special meals for children.

POMPONESCO 46030 Mantova   Map 16

Trattoria Il Leone   `BUDGET`   *Tel* (0375) 86077
Piazza IV Martiri 2

A recent view of this stylish trattoria-with-rooms beside the river Po, between Parma and Mantua: "In a distinctly uncharming village of the Po valley we found this hotel of idiosyncratic charm, with excellent food. It fronts on to the street, giving no outward clue to its inner delights – antiques and bric-à-brac everywhere, chaotically organised, and at the back a tiled courtyard with swimming pool and white garden furniture. In the ornately decorated dining room (strange blue-tinted frieze of classical scenes just below the beamed 16th-century ceiling), we were served by members of the family, charmingly concerned that we should enjoy our meal. And we did – delicious fish salad with salmon, trout and octopus; a rich ravioli; wild duck with fruit, marvellously tender; and a tempting sweet trolley. Oddly, there were no prices on the menu (we were told this was their custom); but we found them to be very fair. The weak spot of the place is the bedrooms, a bit basic, but with modern bathrooms and comfortable enough for a night stop." (*Philippa and Peter Herbert*) New and better rooms in a garden annexe are promised for autumn 1991.

Open All year except Jan and Christmas.
Rooms 5 double, 3 single – all with shower, telephone, baby-listening; TV on request.
Facilities Lounges, bar, restaurant, TV room; conference room. Garden with swimming pool.
Location In village, 32 km from Parma, 38 km from Mantova, off S 420. Parking.
Credit cards All major cards accepted.
Terms [1990 rates] B&B: single 41,000 L, double 67,000 L; dinner, B&B 65,000 L per person. Full alc 40,000 L. Reduced rates for children.

If you have difficulty in finding hotels because our location details are inadequate, please help us to improve directions next year.

PORTO ERCOLE 58018 Grosseto   Map 16

Hotel Il Pellicano   *Tel* (0564) 833801
Cala dei Santi   *Fax* (0564) 833418
                                              Telex 500131

"An escapist dream of a Mediterranean paradise," writes a devotee
returning this year to this stylish and very expensive hotel on a lovely
stretch of rocky coast. "Small, peaceful and relaxed, it's the best-
maintained hotel we know. Its young owners, Nadia and Ennio Emili,
bring an Italian warmth to their personal style of management, and we
regard them as old friends. Everyone likes the barbecues; smoked fish,
shellfish and pastas all first-class, antipasti superb and generous with
robust gutsy flavours, but main courses less successful." This reader had a
room with a vast terrace that "looked out across the gardens to the
mountain on one side, over tiled roofs to the pool and sea on the other."
Another paean this year: "As perfect as they come. The hotel has been
built into the mountainside; everything is harmonious and beautiful.
Down the stone steps through the pine trees is the salt-water pool,
shaded by trees, overlooking the magnificent Argentario coast. Lunch is
served under the trees on the terrace. The Sunday barbecue has on
display everything that Italy has to offer, including grilled lobsters. Down
the steps are boats for water-skiing and sailing. The helpful and efficient
staff checked the rooms about three times a day: when my mother asked
for an apple, a massive fruit bowl arrived." Bedrooms are "furnished with
lots of glamour": the cheaper ones above the garden are less nice than
sea-facing ones. (*David and Kate Wooff, Andrena Woodhams*) Some judge the
prices too high. And note that it's 90 steps down to the sea.

Open Easter–3 Nov.
Rooms 4 suites, 30 double – all with bath, shower, telephone; TV and radio on
request. 9 in annexe, 7 in cottages.
Facilities Lounge, TV room, bar, restaurant; conference facilities; terrace; dinner-
dance Fri July and Aug. Large grounds with restaurant, heated swimming pool
with bar and barbecue, tennis, rocky beach with safe bathing, water-skiing.
Location 4.5 km S of Porto Ercole on Monte Argentario coast. Parking.
Restrictions Not suitable for &. No children under 12.
Credit cards All major cards accepted.
Terms B&B: double 225,000–571,000 L, suite 520,000–1,025,000 L. Dinner, B&B
205,000–605,000 L per person; full board 285,000–685,000 L. Set lunch/dinner
90,000 L.

POSITANO 84017 Salerno   Map 16

Hotel Casa Albertina   *Tel* (089) 875143
Via della Tavolozza 3   *Fax* (089) 811540
                                              Telex 720519

"The fabulous view of Positano that you have from every room" is just
one of the qualities that draw readers back to Michele Cinque's medium-
priced hotel in a justly renowned but expensive resort. The lobby and
lounges have cool white walls and vaulted ceilings, while the rooms and
dining room are decorated in pastels. "Our favourite hotel, run by
gracious people; rooms with their balconies were wonderful," runs one
1990 report. "Style, intimacy, friendliness, great quality and good value.
Grandmother cooks – 'you eat what we eat' – and it is perfect Italian

cuisine paysanne. Quiet, the murmur of the sea, spotless tiled bedrooms, clean sheets every other day – and cheap, by Positano prices." (*Dr SK Wolfson, Tex and Hella Sessoms*) Some, however, have been less impressed by the food, and drink charges are high. The best rooms are on the first floor, but the quietest are the smaller top-floor ones.

Open All year.
Rooms 3 suites, 17 double, 1 single – all with bath and/or shower, telephone; baby-listening on request. Air-conditioning.
Facilities Lift. Sitting room, TV room, bar, dining room, open-air restaurant; terraces. 10 mins' walk to beach.
Location Central, but quietly situated. Parking 300 metres.
Credit cards All major cards accepted.
Terms Dinner, B&B 90,000–150,000 L. Set lunch 40,000 L, dinner 50,000 L.

PRAIANO 84010 Salerno   **Map 16**

Hotel Tramonto d'Oro   `BUDGET`   *Tel* (089) 874008
Via Gennaro Capriglione 119   *Telex* 720397

In a small resort on the glorious coast between Amalfi and Positano, here's a spruce modern hotel in a splendid setting high above the sea. Most rooms have a balcony with sea views. Swimming pool on roof; bus service down to the beach. Friendly staff. 50 rooms, all with bath and shower. B&B double 80,000 L. Set menu 20,000 L [1990]. Recent nomination. More reports please.

RANCO 21020 Varese   **Map 16**

Albergo-Ristorante Del Sole   *Tel* (0331) 976507
Piazza Venezia 5   *Fax* (0331) 976620

In a village at the south-east end of Lake Maggiore, the Brovelli family runs a well-known stylish restaurant (two *Michelin* rosettes) with six smart modern bedrooms. "One of North Italy's best restaurants. It is charmingly situated by the lake's edge, with views over the harbour and across to the shore opposite. The restaurant is most attractive, with a huge chandelier and fresh flowers; there's a large terrace, too, for summer eating. The food is superb: a small menu with specialities that change daily (including fish from the lake), and an excellent wine list. Breakfast is also very good, served on the terrace in summer. Service was charming and friendly. The bedrooms are split-level, cleverly designed to obtain maximum space, and with good modern furniture." (*Pat and Jeremy Temple*) Warmly endorsed in 1990 for its "very good cooking; rooms with good lake views".

Open All year except 1 Jan–9 Feb and Christmas. Closed Mon evening and Tue except public holidays.
Rooms 7 suites, 1 double, 1 single – 6 with bath, 3 with shower, all with telephone, TV, baby-listening, air-conditioning.
Facilities Lounge, bar, restaurant; functions room. Terrace where meals are served, garden.
Location 67 km NW of Milan. Parking.
Restriction Not suitable for &.
Credit cards All major cards accepted.

Terms [1990 rates] Rooms: double 155,000–160,000 L, suite 200,000 L. Breakfast 12,500 L; dinner, B&B 170,000 L per person. Set lunch/dinner 75,000–95,000 L; full alc 95,000–110,000 L. Special meals for children on request.

RAVELLO 84010 Salerno   Map 16

Hotel Marmorata   *Tel* (089) 877777
Strada Statale 163   *Telex* 720667

This former papermill, redesigned as a hotel in nautical style, is four miles from Ravello itself, nestled in the cliff face beneath the coastal road to Amalfi. "Clean, well managed and quiet", "excellent in every way", are reports this year and last. Earlier views: "The cool, restful interiors, the seafront terraces and the friendly, helpful service are simply superb." "My cabin-like room had a simple stylishness that combined superbly with its fine view of the sea." (*Jane Gibbs, PA Bispham, Mrs MP Richards*) One recent visitor found the staff and the Signora most helpful, but adds, "It's on the English package-tour circuit, which means they play very safe with the food." Others agree that the food, though well cooked and presented, is plain. It is essential to ask for a room with a sea view: others have no view at all. And the steep steps and slopes make the hotel unsuitable for the infirm.

Open All year. Restaurant closed 30 Oct–30 Apr.
Rooms 5 suites, 36 double, 3 single – 3 with bath, 36 with shower, all with telephone, radio, TV, mini-bar, air-conditioning.
Facilities Hall, lounge, 2 bars, restaurant. Small grounds with terraces down to sea, sea-water swimming pool, private rocky beach with safe bathing and fishing.
Location 1 km W of Minori, 3 km E of Amalfi, 300 metres off the road to Ravello. Parking.
Restriction Not suitable for &.
Credit cards All major cards accepted.
Terms [1990 rates] B&B: single 103,000–139,000 L, double 165,000–231,000 L. Set lunch/dinner 45,000 L; full alc 55,000 L. Reduced rates and special meals for children.

Hotel Palumbo   *Tel* (089) 857244
Via S Giovanni del Toro 28   *Fax* (089) 857347
                                                      Telex 770101

Pasquale Vuilleumier's strikingly beautiful hotel, which with exquisite taste he converted from a 12th-century *palazzo*, has again left readers swooning this year: "Cool marble, high white ceilings, rich foliage, tasteful furniture, and the stunning views to the sea way below. Our room, a delightful eyrie at the top reached by outside steps, had its own patio facing that magnetic view. Food good in a lovely frescoed romantic restaurant; staff pleasant, especially the waiter from Bolton, Lancs." "Would be a great place for a honeymoon if you could afford it." The lemon-tree-shaded lounge terrace, the bedrooms with blue and white tiles, and the "above average" food have also been admired.

What's more, the hotel has a strange past. In the mid-19th century, Signor Vuilleumier's Swiss grandfather bought a 12th-century episcopal palace up the road and on the advice of Wagner (who was writing bits of *Parsifal* in a nearby villa) turned it into a hotel. Over the years his guests there included Longfellow, Grieg, DH Lawrence (he worked on *Lady*

Chatterley in one of the rooms), Garbo, Bogart and the Kennedys. But about eight years ago the Signor transferred the hotel to his own residence, the Palazzo Confalone, leaving the original *Palumbo* deserted save for its illustrious ghosts. Now in his seventies and still much in evidence, this grand old man is said to be "very amiable but regretting the grandeur of the past". (*M and M Lawson, Gary Hirsch*)

Open All year.
Rooms 3 suites, 18 double – all with bath, shower, telephone, TV, baby-listening, air-conditioning. 7 in annexe.
Facilities Salon, bar, TV lounge, restaurant. Garden with restaurant; solarium. Beaches 10–15 mins by car.
Location Above the Amalfi Drive, overlooking Ravello. Parking.
Restriction Not suitable for ⅃.
Credit cards All major cards accepted.
Terms [1990 rates] Dinner, B&B 219,000–257,000 L; full board 235,000–290,000 L. Set lunch/dinner 55,000 L; full alc 70,000 L. Reduced rates and special meals for children.

RIVA DI SOLTO 24060 Bergamo   Map 16

Albergo-Ristorante Miranda   **BUDGET**   *Tel* (035) 986021
"da Oreste"
Via Cornello 8

The little-known Lake Iseo lies amid hills and olive groves to the east of Bergamo. High up on its western shore, with glorious views, is this charming white modern villa, much enjoyed in 1989/90 for the Polini family's warm hospitality and their "wonderful food" (*Michelin* red *Pas* for good value). "Unbeatable value: a quiet, relaxed and friendly atmosphere, with good food. Signor Polini's description of the meals of the day makes your mouth water." "The ravioli and fresh lake fish would wake up even the most jaded palate." "Bedrooms are clean, well lit, with spacious wardrobes, and many have a balcony. Pleasant swimming pool down a steep path in the garden." (*Vincent Connor, Darrell Lund, Lynne M Allen*)

Open All year except 15 Jan–15 Feb. Restaurant closed to non-residents Tue in winter.
Rooms 3 suites, 20 double, 2 single – 7 with bath and shower, 15 with shower, all with telephone. Suites in annexe.
Facilities Lounge with TV, restaurant. Terrace, garden with swimming pool.
Location In centre of village 40 km E of Bergamo.
Credit cards None accepted.
Terms Rooms: single 32,000 L, double 43,500 L. Breakfast 6,000 L. Half board 38,000 L per person, full board 45,000 L. Set lunch 35,000 L, dinner 40,000 L; full alc 35,000–40,000 L. Reduced rates for children; special meals on request.

ROME   Map 16

Hotel Canada   *Tel* (06) 4957385
Via Vicenza 58   *Fax* (06) 4450749
Rome 00185   *Telex* 613037

In a quietish street six blocks from the main station. Very helpful staff, lavish buffet breakfast, rooms plain but serviceable, small bar/lounge, lift. 62 rooms, all with bath and/or shower. B&B: single 90,000–105,000 L, double 128,000–156,000 L [1990]. No restaurant. New nomination. More reports please.

Hotel Cesàri						*Tel* (06) 6792386
Via di Pietra 89a						*Fax* (06) 6790882
Rome 00186

Off the strident via del Corso but down a cul-de-sac, therefore quiet, this former palace has been a hotel since the 18th century (Stendhal and Garibaldi were among its guests). It remains old-fashioned, simple and modestly priced, with pleasant staff but poor breakfasts. 50 rooms, most with bath and/or shower: single 55,000–100,000 L, double 93,000–122,000 L. Breakfast 15,000 L. No restaurant. Rooms this year judged too simple. More reports please.

Hotel Forum						*Tel* (06) 6792446
Via Tor de' Conti 25–30					*Fax* (06) 6786479
Rome 00184						*Telex* 622549

Down a side street near the Foro Romano, and fairly quiet by ear-splitting Roman standards, a pleasant but pricey classic hotel with modern amenities. Period furniture, smallish but comfortable rooms, air-conditioning. Service obliging, food average (panoramic restaurant); roof-garden. 79 rooms, all with bath or shower: single 150,000–285,000 L, double 250,000–420,000 L. Set menu 75,000 L [1990]. Some recent criticisms: more reports welcome.

Hotel Gregoriana					*Tel* (06) 6794269
Via Gregoriana 18					*Fax* (06) 6784258
Rome 00187

More praise this year for the friendly and efficient service, and general good value for money, at this spruce hotel, a converted convent, near the top of the Spanish steps. Despite its location it is fairly quiet, especially rooms at the back (there is some street noise in front). A few upper rooms look out over roof-gardens and orange and lemon trees. There is no lounge, and bedrooms are quite small, but they are bright and pretty, and the hotel's decor is amusingly unusual, e.g. a landing with black satin walls and leopard-skin cushions. One reader had a comfortable room "in a mixture of Erté and American Chinese, with a big, sunny bathroom in blues and mauves". Book well ahead. (*Dr DM Keyzer, I Zetterström*)

Open All year.
Rooms 16 double, 3 single – all with bath/shower, telephone, TV, air-conditioning. 4 ground-floor rooms.
Facilities Lift. Hall.
Location Central, above Spanish steps. Parking.
Credit cards None accepted.
Terms [1990 rates] B&B: single 120,000 L, double 185,000 L. Reduced rates for children. (No restaurant.)

Hotel Lord Byron
Via G de Notaris 5
Rome 00197

Tel (06) 3220404
Fax (06) 3220405
Telex 611217

The expensive and sophisticated *Lord Byron*, set in a quiet district near the Villa Borghese, is notable for its *Relais le Jardin* restaurant, one of Rome's best (two rosettes and four red *couverts* in *Michelin*). This unfortunately was closed in August when this year's two nominators visited, but they admired the hotel itself: "Quiet, and luxuriously furnished, with very obliging service." "Newly renovated, its decor is striking, with no expense spared. Marble bathrooms, very good lighting, furnishings of the highest quality. Congenial staff." (*Shaun Hill, and others*) Reports on that restaurant most welcome.

Open All year. Restaurant closed 2nd half of Aug.
Rooms 8 suites, 42 double – all with bath, shower, telephone, radio, TV, air-conditioning. 1 suite in garden.
Facilities 2 lounges, bar, restaurant; banqueting facilities. Small garden.
Location Just NW of Borghese gardens in Parioli district. Garage.
Restriction Not suitable for &.
Credit cards All major cards accepted.
Terms [1990 rates] B&B: single 260,000–415,000 L, double 350,000–520,000 L. Full alc 120,000 L. Special meals for children on request.

Hotel La Residenza
Via Emilia 22
Rome 00187

Tel (06) 460789
Fax (06) 485721
Telex 410423 attn LA RESIDENZA

"A delightful hotel" and "excellent value" are 1989/90 reports on this small but quite luxurious hotel, nicely located around the corner from the Via Veneto and near the Villa Borghese. Everyone speaks well of the friendly staff, the breakfast buffet, the comfortable rooms and pleasing decor. Some rooms, however, are quite small, and reading lights are poor. Moreover the hotel faces a night club and a busy road which can be noisy; rooms at the back are preferable. No restaurant; but there are good ones in the area, such as the *Piccolo Mondo* and the small family-run *Tempio di Bacco*, via Lombardia. (*Arnold H Wolfe, CR, L Abeles, Michael Owens*)

Open All year.
Rooms 7 suites, 17 double, 3 single – 24 with bath, 3 with shower, all with telephone, radio, TV, mini-bar.
Facilities 2 lounges, bar, breakfast room; terrace and patio.
Location Central, near the Via Veneto and American Embassy (back rooms quietest). Parking.
Restriction Not suitable for &.
Credit cards None accepted.
Terms B&B: single 115,000 L, double 190,000 L, suite 210,000 L. (No restaurant.)

SAN GIMIGNANO 53037 Siena   **Map 16**

Bel Soggiorno   **BUDGET**
Via S Giovanni 91

Tel (0577) 940375
Fax (0577) 940375

A lovely 13th-century building, offering superb views of the Tuscan hills and olive groves from its wide windows. It stands just inside the ramparts of this stunning medieval Tuscan town, famous for its 14 slender towers

rising above the rooftops. Nearly every *soggiorno* reported to us recently
has been *bello*, with service, food and fair prices all commended. The top
floor of the hotel is to be avoided if possible: hot, and noisy with
plumbing. The remaining rooms, though small, are adequate, some with
terraces and most with fine views. There is a TV salon but no garden. On
the unchanging but "excellent" menu, readers especially admire "a
delicious first course called trittico" and "pollo al diavolo which comes
aflame". (*Richard Osborne, and others*) Hot water supply can be erratic.

Open All year. Restaurant closed Mon.
Rooms 2 suites, 22 double – all with bath, shower, telephone.
Facilities Lift. Salon with TV, bar, restaurant. Terrace.
Location 30 km from Siena; cars allowed in for loading and unloading only.
Carpark nearby (10,000 L per day).
Restrictions Not suitable for &. No children under 8.
Credit cards All major cards accepted.
Terms B&B double 89,000 L. Half board 70,000 L per person, full board
105,000 L. Full alc 32,000 L.

Hotel La Cisterna   *Tel* (0577) 940328
Piazza della Cisterna 24   *Fax* (0577) 942080
                                                        Telex 575152

Contented travellers ("splendid value for money") have again in 1989/90
visited this 14th-century ivy-clad *palazzo*, which fronts the animated main
piazza. Many rooms have a balcony facing either this scene or the wide
Tuscan landscape: "Waking up to look down into the square was a real
treat." Rooms are quite large, some simple, some (notably Nos. 58, 59
and 60) more interesting with painted furniture. There's a splendid
church-like lounge, and a beamed restaurant with stunning panoramic
views: here a new chef provides reliable cooking. "Manager a bit bad-
tempered, but not with us", and his staff are judged friendly. (*Gerald
Campion, DM Livesley, Jack Digby and others*) One dissident gives the
Cisterna a comprehensive thumbs down, having known it in earlier days
when it was still a "discovery"; he found the service now lacked courtesy,
and the coach trade oppressive. More views badly needed.

Open Mar–Nov. Restaurant closed Tue and Wed midday.
Rooms 43 double, 7 single – 20 with bath, 30 with shower, all with telephone.
Ground-floor rooms.
Facilities Lift. Hall, 2 lounges, TV room, bar, restaurant.
Location Central. Cars allowed in for loading and unloading only. Private carpark
250 metres.
Credit cards All major cards accepted.
Terms [1990 rates] B&B: single 56,000 L, double 99,000 L; dinner, B&B 79,500–
86,000 L per person; full board 107,500–114,000 L. Set lunch/dinner 28,000 L;
full alc 50,000 L.

Le Renaie   **BUDGET**   *Tel* (0577) 955044
Pancole   *Fax* (0577) 955044

A quiet and unpretentious rural hotel with lovely views over the Tuscan
hills, outside the hamlet of Pancole, just north of San Gimignano. "We
enjoyed drinking Chianti on the pretty veranda, while the children
played in the well-lit play park just opposite," says a reader this year. A
view last year: "The decor is light and gay, our bedroom was spacious

and comfortable. We dined out on the terrace by candle-light: the food was honest Tuscan, very good value, e.g. wild boar casserole and pork tenderloin in herbs and Chianti." Many rooms have a balcony, and there's a cool lounge in modern design, also a swimming pool. (*Linda Alleyne, Sarah Milward; Philippa and Peter Herbert*) The staff are said to be rather impersonal, and the plumbing can be noisy.

Open All year. Restaurant closed Tue.
Rooms 24 double, 2 single – all with bath or shower, telephone, TV.
Facilities Lounge with TV, bar, restaurant. Terrace, garden with swimming pool.
Location 5 km N of San Gimignano towards Certaldo. Parking.
Restriction Not suitable for &.
Credit cards All major cards accepted.
Terms B&B: single 57,000 L, double 89,000 L; dinner, B&B 69,000–86,000 L per person. Set lunch/dinner 28,000–35,000 L. Reduced rates and special meals for children.

SAN GREGORIO 06081 Perugia   Map 16

Castel San Gregorio   **BUDGET**   *Tel* (075) 8038009

"Man enters into this magic place with his soul" proclaims the brochure of this offbeat hotel – and also, we suggest, with his sense of humour and conviviality. It's a creeper-covered crenellated neo-Gothic castle, set amid vines and parkland between Assisi and Perugia, overlooking the plain. "Fairly eccentric, but delightfully so. It's a peaceful, rambling place with varied, well-furnished bedrooms. The dining room has one big table where you all dine together, chatting to your neighbours; food ranges from the very good to the pedestrian, and is washed down by good local cheap wine. We thought the *Castel* bliss and can't wait to get back." Endorsed this year: "Rooms comfortable; second helpings offered." "Dinner at one big table very congenial." (*Ian Stewart, Ian Harris, Ray Everett*) Some rooms have antique beds, others have four-posters with medieval-style linen drapes; the bathrooms in the towers are circular. Beamed ceilings, spiral stairways, fancy atmospheric lighting all add to the ambience. Rooms above kitchen can be noisy.

Open All year except 15–30 Jan.
Rooms 12 – all with bath and/or shower, telephone.
Facilities Reading room, dining room. Small garden.
Location 13 km NW of Assisi.
Restriction Not suitable for &.
Credit cards Access, Visa.
Terms [1990 rates] Half board 81,000 L, full board 104,000 L.

SAN MAMETE 22010 Como   Map 16

Hotel Stella d'Italia   *Tel* (0344) 68139
Piazza Roma 1   *Fax* (0344) 68729
(postal address: PO Box 46
San Mamete, Valsolda
6976 Castagnola, Switzerland)

Popular again in 1989/90, this "gem of a place" stands right on Lake Lugano by the Swiss border. Its English-speaking owners, the Ortellis, have been running it for decades, and their "warmth and professionalism" (a verdict this year) have won them a loyal clientele, partly English. The bedrooms, each with its own balcony on which you can breakfast, have views across the lake to the green slopes and mountains in the distance. There is a garden leading down to a lido for swimming or sunbathing. In good weather, dinner is served on the pretty trellised terrace, with the water at one's feet, but the dining room also has fine views.

"A warm welcome from our gracious and helpful hosts, and a clean, comfortable room with a view of the sparkling blue lake that was like fairyland," says one reader this year. "The un-Italian aura is more than compensated for by the fat delights of the beautiful veranda restaurant, the attentive service, the tranquil lido by the lake and a library which must have the largest collection of Warwick Deeping in north Italy." (*Norma Kessler, Sally Burt, and others*) Some judge the food excellent, others have found the *en pension* cooking too plain and "un-Italian".

Open Apr–Oct.
Rooms 31 double, 5 single – 23 with bath, 13 with shower, all with telephone and balcony.
Facilities 2 lounges, bar, restaurant. Garden with restaurant. Beach, lake bathing, fishing, surfing, boating.
Location 10 km NE of Lugano on Lake Lugano between Gandria and Menaggio. Garage for 14 cars.
Restriction Not suitable for &.
Credit cards All major cards accepted.
Terms B&B: single 59,000 L, double 93,500 L. Set lunch/dinner 28,000–29,000 L; full alc 30,000–40,000 L. Reduced rates for children.

SAN PAOLO APPIANO 39050 Bolzano   Map 16

Hotel Schloss Korb   *Tel* (0471) 633222
Missiano   *Fax* (0471) 633333

West of Bolzano, in a marvellous open setting amid terraced vineyards and fortress-crowned rocky hills, a medieval castle very stylishly converted – beamed ceilings, rough stone walls, strange statuary. Quaint and pretty bedrooms, those in the tower specially recommended. Hearty Tyrolean food. Indoor and outdoor swimming pools, sauna, sun-terrace, floodlit tennis courts. Open 1 Apr–5 Nov. 60 rooms, all with bath and shower. Half board from 105,000 L. Enticing recent nomination. More reports eagerly requested.

SANTA MARGHERITA LIGURE 16038 Genova   Map 16

Grand Hotel Miramare   *Tel* (185) 287013
Via Milite Ignoto 30   *Fax* (185) 284651
                                                 Telex 270437

Nominated this year by a visitor to this big, busy Riviera resort: "The *Miramare* is a palace hotel of the old-fashioned type, looking bigger than its 83 rooms, not the kind of place we normally go for. But despite its size it doesn't seem impersonal, staff are pleasant and efficient, housekeeping is excellent. We liked our room: large, high-ceilinged, with solid old-style furniture and a small balcony facing the sea (spectacular views across the gulf to the mountains). Rooms do vary in size, and some have no balcony. Breakfast, served out on the terrace when fine, is a generous buffet; we didn't try the main meals, but the poolside lunch buffet looked tempting. There's a large swimming pool and private beach." (*David Wooff*) More reports welcome.

Open All year.
Rooms 9 suites, 61 double, 13 single – all with bath, telephone, radio, TV, air-conditioning. Some with balcony.
Facilities Lift. Salon, reading room, TV room, bar, restaurant; conference facilities. Terrace and large grounds; swimming pool with bar/restaurant. Private beach.
Location By sea; central. Town is 31 km E of Genoa.
Credit cards Access, Amex, Visa.
Terms [1990 rates] B&B: single 155,000–185,000 L, double 260,000–320,000 L, suite 370,000–530,000 L; dinner, B&B 160,000–325,000 L per person. Set lunch/dinner 80,000 L. Reduced rates and special meals for children.

SELVA DI VAL GARDENA 39048 Bolzano   Map 16

Hotel Dorfer   *Tel* (0471) 795204
Via Cir 5   *Fax* (0471) 795068

Selva, between Bolzano and Cortina, is a Ladinisch and German-speaking village in the upper Val Gardena, now a popular skiing and summer resort. This is one of its simpler hotels, but homely and comfortable, run with great warmth by Frau Dorfer, and quietly insulated from Selva's noisy bustle. "Friendly, with good professional service," says a reader this year. "The view from the front rooms is magnificent, but the back ones are to be avoided. The restaurant manager, a Humphrey Bogart look-alike, is witty and solicitous, breakfast is extensive, and the set dinner menu is good." The skiing, too, is good. (*Esler Crawford, and others*)

Open 15 Dec–15 Apr, 10 June–31 Sep.
Rooms 21 double, 9 single – all with bath or shower, telephone, radio, TV, air-conditioning; many with balcony.
Facilities Bar, TV room, restaurant; gym, whirlpool, sauna, solarium. Garden with terrace for al fresco meals and table-tennis.
Location 42 km E of Bolzano.
Restriction Not suitable for &.
Credit cards None accepted.
Terms [1990 rates] Dinner, B&B 60,000–103,000 L. Set lunch 18,000 L, dinner 25,000 L; full alc 35,000 L. Reduced rates and special meals for children.

SIENA 53100   Map 16

Villa Scacciapensieri   *Tel* (0577) 41441
Via di Scacciapensieri 10   *Fax* (0577) 270854
     Telex 573390

A Tuscan villa on a hillside, surrounded by vineyards and olive trees (but industrial suburbia is close). Despite some criticisms, it has long been liked for its lovely garden, quiet atmosphere and friendly owners, the Nardi family, and reports this year and last have all been favourable. "The Nardis are always friendly, and the food good. Pool, garden and terrace are inviting and cool in summer. Bedrooms prettily furnished and well maintained." "We had an excellent large bedroom facing Siena. The service was exemplary, the food first-class, and the grounds are lovely. The weak spots are the bar and lounge." "Many dishes quite superb. Service both professional and warm-hearted." (*Sally Burt, VN Wright, and others*)

Open All year except Feb. Restaurant closed Wed.
Rooms 2 suites, 22 double, 4 single – all with bath and/or shower, telephone, TV. 10 in annexe with air-conditioning.
Facilities Lift. Lounge, TV room, bar, restaurant; terrace. Garden with swimming pool and tennis.
Location 3 km N of Siena. Regular bus service.
Credit cards All major cards accepted.
Terms [1990 rates] B&B: single 162,500 L, double 250,000 L, suite 310,000 L; dinner, B&B: single 195,000 L, double 320,000 L, suite 380,000 L. Set lunch 42,000 L, dinner 50,000 L; full alc 60,000 L. Reduced rates for children under 6.

SIRMIONE 25019 Brescia   Map 16

Hotel Golf et Suisse   *Tel* (030) 916176
Via Condominio   *in winter* (030) 919108
                                                  Telex 300395

Catullus's *venusta Sirmio* is now a delightful medieval walled townlet on a small peninsula at the south end of Lake Garda. A mile or so from its centre, and set back from the road, is this clean, modern, family-run hotel, judged "friendly, efficient and comfortable" by visitors this year. It has a small garden with chairs, a good swimming pool, and its own nearby jetty and private beach for lake bathing. "The owner was charming, and our large rooms had balconies." A buffet breakfast is served until noon. No restaurant, but lots in town. (*Gillian Casey, Wende West*) Seven new suites have been added this year.

Open 1 Mar–31 Oct.
Rooms 21 suites in annexe opposite hotel, 30 double – all with bath and/or shower, telephone, radio, TV; suites have air-conditioning. Ground-floor rooms.
Facilities Lift. Lounge with TV, bar; terrace. Garden with swimming pool. Private beach.
Location 1 km from Sirmione which is 35 km W of Verona. Traffic noise in some rooms.
Credit cards Access, Amex, Visa.
Terms B&B: single 70,000–100,000 L, double 90,000–140,000 L, suite 130,000–230,000 L. Reduced rates for children sharing parents' room. (No restaurant.)

SORAGNA 43019 Parma   Map 16

Locanda del Lupo   *Tel* (0524) 690444
Via Garibaldi 64   *Telex* 533283

In a small town between Parma and Cremona, an 18th-century mansion of the Princes Meli Lupi has been converted into a spacious and gracious inn, with antique furnishings, large courtyard. Friendly welcome, good food, poor breakfast. Closed 27 July–24 Aug. 46 rooms, all with bath and/or shower. B&B: single 98,000 L, double 156,000 L. Set meals 40,000 L [1990]. New nomination: more reports please.

SORISO 28018 Novara   Map 16

Al Sorriso   *Tel* (0322) 983228
Via Roma 18   *Fax* (0322) 983328

Down a winding lane, in a village, amid lovely scenery near Lake Orta, a stylish and expensive restaurant-with-rooms whose owner Angelo Valazza speaks English with a Huddersfield accent (he lived and worked there); his wife Luisa's superb cooking, strictly non-Huddersfield, wins two Michelin *rosettes. Bedrooms adequate. Closed 10–31 Jan, 13–24 Aug; restaurant closed midday Mon and Tue. 8 rooms, with private facilities, 65,000–90,000 L. Breakfast 10,000 L. Alc meals (excluding wine) 80,000–124,000 L. New nomination. More reports please.*

TAORMINA 98039 Messina, Sicily   Map 16

Ipanema Hotel   *Tel* (0942) 24720
Via Nazionale 242   *Fax* (0942) 625821
                                                      Telex 980169

Two miles from the centre of town, an attractive modern hotel above the beach, well run by the affable Bruno Valastro. Flowers around the terraces and swimming pool area, many rooms with sea-facing balcony, cheerful hardworking staff and good food, including breakfast buffet. 50 rooms, all with bath and/or shower. B&B: single 74,600 L, double 143,200 L. Set meals 25,000 L. Renominated this year. More reports please.

San Domenico Palace Hotel   *Tel* (0942) 23701
Piazza San Domenico 5   *Fax* (0942) 625506
                                                      Telex 980013

This famous and palatial hotel on its high promontory began life as a monastery. In 1943 Kesselring used it as his headquarters and much of the original 15th-century building, apart from the cloister, was destroyed by Allied bombs. Today it is rebuilt, and in many ways is very beautiful. The view from its balcony, of Etna and the coast, is sensational; below stretch the palm-studded gardens, ablaze with colour. But there have been tales of dull food, and a sharp-eyed British hotelier has given this view: "Lovely cloister and courtyards to which has been added an ill-proportioned, gloomy and ill-furnished Edwardian block. We much preferred the old section, though the rooms lack the large balconies of the Edwardian part. Garden beautifully kept – unusual for Sicily. Housekeeping poor. Would be a wonderful place if properly managed. As it is, passable." And a visitor this year adds: "Front desk rude and unhelpful, but a magic place and we'd return." So you know what to expect. But a leading playwright regards these critical noises as "off": "All these comments are ridiculously unfair. It turned out to be the most delightful hotel we've ever stayed at anywhere in the world." (*Michael Frayn, JR Hall*)

Open All year.

Rooms 10 suites, 80 double, 28 single – all with bath, telephone, radio, TV, air-conditioning.
Facilities Lift. Hall, 4 lounges, bar, TV room, games room, dining room; conference facilities; courtyard terrace. Garden with heated swimming pool and snack bar. Private beach (car service).
Location On promontory on W side of town, but close to centre.
Restriction Not suitable for &.
Credit cards All major cards accepted.
Terms [1990 rates] Dinner, B&B 295,000–335,000 L. Set lunch/dinner 100,000 L. Reduced rates for children sharing parents' room.

Hotel Villa Belvedere   *Tel* (0942) 23791
Via Bagnoli Croci 79   *Fax* (0942) 625830

"Run with a sense of caring efficiency" (a verdict this year) by a cultivated Franco-Italian family, this pleasant B&B hotel has a fine location overlooking the bay, and an exuberant tree-filled garden and swimming pool "with a palm growing up through the middle". The bar by this pool serves good snacks. This earlier report has never been bettered: "One of the two prettiest places to stay in Taormina. The sea is 800 feet below, palm trees sway and creak, Mount Etna smoulders moodily, the lights of Naxos twinkle in the dark. My room was unique. It was cool and shaded, with a little garden of its own; the bathroom was cramped but functioning, though prone to ant invasions. The garden rambles as much as steep terracing will allow, with little hidden places for a quiet read. The pool is not for Olympic swimmers, nor for those muscular Germans who tense their pectorals and breasts at each other; it is a pool for a quick cooling dip. Beside it one can have a tolerable and cheapish lunch." (*NR Walton, Christina Bewley*) Top-floor rooms have balconies; those facing the street can be noisy. There are new, quiet ones this year which overlook the garden.

Open 15 Mar–31 Oct.
Rooms 41 double, 3 single – all with bath and/or shower, telephone, air-conditioning. Ground-floor rooms.
Facilities Lift. Lounge, 2 sitting rooms (1 with TV), bar, breakfast room; terrace. Garden with swimming pool and snack bar. Sea 3 km away.
Location Central, near public gardens and tennis court. Parking.
Credit cards Access, Visa.
Terms [1990 rates] B&B: single from 73,000 L, double from 136,000 L. Reduced rates for children. (No restaurant.)

Villa Fiorita   `BUDGET`   *Tel* (0942) 24122
Via L Pirandello 39

A villa that clings to the hillside, amid paved patios filled with flowers and foliage, right next to the cable car station that takes you down to the beach. Recent honeymooners much enjoyed their private terrace and fine views over the coast. Others have written: "It's on the busiest stretch of the approach road to Taormina yet manages to be cool and quiet. Our room was large and comfortable with french windows opening on to a large terrace, where breakfast amid the flowers was the high spot of our stay. But the lounges are somewhat gloomy." "For those who want solitude and quiet this place is excellent; and the staff are charming." No restaurant: lots in town. (*Andrew Meyn, Philippa Herbert, Angela and David Stewart, and others*)

Open All year.
Rooms 2 suites, 22 double – all with bath and/or shower, telephone, radio, TV, mini-bar, air-conditioning; some have terrace or balcony.
Facilities Hall, 2 lounges, bar, restaurant (for breakfast and snacks), games room. Large garden with terraces and swimming pool. 50 metres to sandy beach (cable car down).
Location Central, near Greek theatre, but quiet. Garage (8,000 L).
Restrictions Not suitable for &. No children under 10.
Credit cards All major cards accepted.
Terms [1990 rates] Rooms 76,000 L, suite 99,000 L. Breakfast 7,000 L. (No restaurant.)

TELLARO DI LERICI 19030 La Spezia   Map 16

Albergo Il Nido   *Tel* (0187) 967426
Via Fiascherino 75   *Fax* (0187) 964225

This bright and airy modern hotel is splendidly located above a cove in a village near Lerici, on the lovely Gulf of Spezia (where Shelley drowned). It has fine views over beach, rocks and pine trees from many bedroom balconies and from the "cool, white and spacious" dining room. "Charming, friendly and well run," say returning devotees this year. "The breakfasts have improved, but there's now less of their delicious shellfish on the menu: apparently pollution is the problem." "The staff are wonderfully friendly, and the waiters hysterically amusing; but it's a pity the dining room windows aren't washed more often" is another view this year. Others have enjoyed the self-service salad and breakfast buffets, and "our room with balcony overlooking the bay where waves crashed thrillingly day and night over the rocks below". (*Harriet and Tony Jones, Lynne M Allen, Lon Bailey*) But rooms in the annexe have much less of a view; and there are 140 steps down to the small private beach which is crowded in high summer.

Open Mar–Nov and Christmas and New Year.
Rooms 1 suite, 34 double, 4 single – 2 with bath, 35 with shower, all with telephone, TV, air-conditioning; some with balcony. 22 in annexe across road.
Facilities TV room, bar, 2 dining rooms; terraces. Garden. Small private beach.
Location 2 km SE of Lerici; follow signs for Lerici and Tellaro. Parking.
Restriction Not suitable for &.
Credit cards All major cards accepted.
Terms B&B: single 74,000–78,000 L, double 126,800–131,200 L; dinner, B&B 88,000–121,000 L per person. Set lunch/dinner 41,800 L; full alc 50,000 L. Reduced rates for children; special meals.

TORGIANO 06089 Perugia   Map 16

Le Tre Vaselle   *Tel* (075) 982447
Via Garibaldi 48   *Fax* (075) 985214
                                                     Telex 564028

This "elegant country residence" is set quietly in a side street of a charming Umbrian village south of Perugia; it is owned by the ambitious Lungarotti wine firm, which also runs a wine museum in Torgiano. A reader this year praised the restaurant highly for its "local cuisine" and

found the hotel "discreet and classy but relaxing". Last year's view: "We
enjoyed the undeniable style, the refined yet honest food, the attentive
and friendly staff. The interior has thick white walls, archways, wooden
beams, terracotta tiles, comfortable sofas. Rooms are tranquil and simple,
in very good Italian pared-down style (but bathrooms are small: heaven
help the obese). Cooking is regional, gently modernised, using first-rate
local ingredients, and flavours are fresh and uncluttered – try insalata di
rucola (rocket with sliced mushrooms and cheese), home-made papar-
delle with truffles. Breakfast is buffet-style, with fruit, ham, sausages. The
admirable Lungarotti firm, much concerned with self-promotion, runs
wine courses locally, and their hotel gets much custom from groups."
(*David Wooff; Robert Ribeiro, A Liddell*) Back rooms are quietest.

Open All year.
Rooms 1 suite, 47 double – all with bath and/or shower, telephone, air-
conditioning.
Facilities Lift. Reading room, piano bar, TV room, breakfast room, restaurant;
conference facilities. Terrace where meals are served.
Location 15 km S of Perugia, just E of *autostrada*.
Restriction Not suitable for &.
Credit cards All major cards accepted.
Terms B&B: single 190,000 L, double 280,000 L, suite 390,000 L. Full alc 65,000 L.
Children under 8 free of charge; special meals on request.

TORNO 22020 Como   Map 16

Villa Flora   **BUDGET**   *Tel* (031) 419222

A big pink villa superbly located on a stone platform sticking out into
Lake Como. It is now a good and lively restaurant, very popular locally
with some rather basic bedrooms attached. A report this year caught its
eccentricity well: "Like some attractive people, if you take each feature
separately you can find fault, but when they are all viewed together, it is
appealing and beguiling. The bedrooms are like a study at a spartan
British public school, but this hardly seemed important, as our room led
on to a large balcony facing the lake. The views are splendid, and the
hotel seems to run a perpetual wedding party, like the one at the
beginning of *The Godfather*. The food was above average, the service
interesting if erratic. I can thoroughly recommend this place, even if it is
like some seedy stage set for a 1960s melodrama." Others have made the
same points less graphically. When that Mario Puzo activity is in full
spate, service to residents suffers acutely. (*MJ Hutton; Stefan and Cosima
Sethe, Anne and Breck Hitz, Bridget Thomson, and others*)

Open Mar–Oct. Restaurant closed Tue.
Rooms 20 double – all with shower, telephone.
Facilities Lounge with TV, bar, restaurant; conference facilities; terrace, where
meals are served. Garden with private beach on lake, bathing.
Location 6 km N of Como. Take road to Bellagio: hotel is down road on left just
past centre of Torno. Private parking.
Restriction Not suitable for &.
Credit cards Access, Visa.
Terms [1990 rates] Rooms: single 45,000 L, double 70,000 L. Breakfast 8,000 L.
Dinner, B&B 48,000 L per person. Full alc 27,000–48,000 L. Children sharing
parents' room free of charge; special meals.

TRICESIMO 33019 Udine   Map 16

Hotel Ristorante Boschetti   *Tel* (0432) 851230
Piazza Mazzini 10   *Fax* (0432) 851216

In a small town just north of delightful Udine, this old inn has been much
enlarged and modernised, with a new wing, and is now a smart hotel well
known for its food (*Michelin* rosette). It is family-owned and run, and well
kept. A devotee returning this year confirms his earlier view: "The staff
were kind and thoughtful, my room was comfortable, and the food and
wine were fantastic, a combination of regional and traditional recipes
with a modern approach." This reader found the place much quieter, now
that a newly opened motorway is diverting much heavy traffic, but
another visitor still found the rooms noisy (as well as small).

Open All year except 5–20 Aug.
Rooms 18 double, 14 single – all with bath or shower, telephone, TV.
Facilities Lift. 3 salons, bar, restaurant.
Location 12 km N of Udine.
Credit cards All major cards accepted.
Terms Rooms: single 80,000 L, double 110,000 L. Breakfast 13,000 L. Set
lunch/dinner 65,000–75,000 L; full alc 65,000–75,000 L.

TRIESTE 34014   Map 16

Hotel Riviera e Maximilian   *Tel* (040) 224396
Strada Costiera 22   *Fax* (040) 224300
                                              Telex 460297

Our only entry for the Trieste area lies on an attractive stretch of the coast
road running north-west from Trieste along a wooded hillside, with fine
views of the sea. "It is in two buildings on either side of the road, close to
the castle of Miramare in its romantic park and the busy little fishing and
pleasure port of Grignano. A lift goes down to its seaside bar and bathing
places. The rooms are furnished differently in the two buildings: ours was
in the *Riviera*, and had elegant comfortable modern furnishings and a
good bathroom. The outstanding experience is to dine on the flowery
terrace as the sun sets over the sea and the lights come up around the bay.
Early in 1990 the hotel changed hands. Two visitors in the new regime
report favourably: slightly pretentious but good and imaginative cooking
("it could be called *nouvelle Triestini*"), excellent house wines, helpful
staff, striking modern pictures in bedrooms and public areas. Only
complaint: inadequate heating in a cold April. But we'd welcome more
reports.

Open All year.
Rooms 7 suites, 44 double, 2 single – all with bath and/or shower, telephone, TV.
Rooms in 2 separate buildings.
Facilities Lift. Bar (piano on Fri/Sat evenings), 2 restaurants; conference facilities;
terrace. Garden with swimming pool. Lift to seaside bar and bathing.
Location NW of Trieste on coastal road S14.
Credit cards All major cards accepted.
Terms B&B: single 73,000 L, double 114,000 L, suite 155,000 L. Set lunch/dinner
30,000 L; full alc 55,000 L.

TRINITÀ D'AGULTU 07038 Sassari, Sardinia   Map 16

Albergo Corallo ▮BUDGET▮   *Tel* (079) 694055
Isola Rossa

Outside a fishing village on the north coast of Sardinia, a modern family-run hotel, not beautiful to look at but commended for its good Sardinian cooking (seafood, roast sucking pig) and clean, pleasant rooms: some are bungalows with their own little gardens. Breakfasts poor. Good beaches nearby. Closed Nov. 37 rooms, all with bath and shower. B&B: single 31,000–46,000 L, double 52,000–71,000 L. Set meals 20,000–23,500 L [1990]. New nomination. More reports welcome.

TURIN 10128   Map 16

Hotel Conte Biancamano   *Tel* (011) 546058 and 513281
73 Corso Vittorio Emanuele II   *Fax* (011) 531027

In an arcaded corso near the 17th-century Piazza San Carlo, a small family-owned B&B hotel with the feel of a private residence and a touch of faded grandeur, typically Torinese. Elegant sitting room, comfortable rooms (front ones noisy), cheerful breakfast room; literary and artistic clientele. Closed Aug, Christmas. 27 rooms, all with bath and shower. B&B: single 96,000–110,000 L, double 134,000–158,000 L [1990]. No recent reports. More welcome.

VAGGIO-REGGELLO 50066 Firenze   Map 16

Villa Rigacci   *Tel* (055) 8656718
                                                     Fax (055) 8656537

In the lovely Tuscan hills not far from Florence, a graceful 15th-century villa-farmhouse, full of antiques and of "warmth and character", run by an affable French-Italian family, the Pierazzi. Our thanks to those readers who sent us new feedback this year: "The rooms were superb and the food fantastic; there's an honour system for late-night drinks." "We were warmly welcomed, and a large log fire was lit each evening in April." "A charming spot, with courteous service, rose-garden, swimming pool, meadows all around." A library, beautiful country furniture, and Tuscan/French food that some have judged expensive but is fairly priced for the area. (*A and B Hitz, Mrs JA Patterson, WS Pazoz*)

Open All year. Restaurant closed to non-residents Tue.
Rooms 2 junior suites, 14 double, 2 single – all with bath and/or shower, telephone, radio, TV, mini-bar. 4 with air-conditioning.
Facilities Bar/lounge, library, 4 salons, 2 dining rooms. Garden with swimming pool. Riding, tennis nearby.
Location 1 km N of Vaggio which is 30 km SE of Florence. Take exit Incisa off Autostrada del Sole.
Restriction Not suitable for &.
Credit cards All major cards accepted.
Terms B&B: single 98,000–105,000 L, double 155,000–185,000 L, suite 220,000–242,000 L; dinner, B&B 128,000–185,000 L per person. Set lunch 45,000 L, dinner 65,000 L; full alc 80,000 L. Half board compulsory in season. Reduced rates for children under 12.

VARENNA 22050 Como   Map 16

Hotel du Lac   *Tel* (0341) 830238
Via del Prestino 4   *Fax* (0341) 831081

*Set charmingly by the water's edge in an unspoilt fishing village on the east side
of Lake Como, a clean and pleasant holiday hotel with good food, helpful
Signora and fine views. Some rooms are small. Open 1 Mar–31 Oct. 19 rooms,
all with bath and/or shower. B&B double 143,000 L. Set menu 38,000 L.
Recently renominated. More reports please.*

VENICE   Map 16

Pensione Accademia   *Tel* (041) 5237846
Fondamenta Maravegie   *Fax* (041) 5239152
Dorsoduro 1058–1060
Venice 30123

Plenty more praise has arrived in 1989/90 for this bed-and-breakfast
pensione: it is housed in a charming 17th-century villa facing a side canal
(sometimes a bit noisy) only a few metres from the Grand Canal at the
Accademia bridge. In its patio garden you can take breakfast, tea or
drinks, or even bring your own snacks and picnics for which they will
supply plates and cutlery at no charge. "Staff were cheerful and helpful
and breakfast was delightful, with a different selection of cakes each
day." Public rooms are attractively furnished, but bedrooms vary in size,
some being fairly small. The housekeeping seems to have improved, after
what may have been a bad patch. (*Ennio Troili, Isabel and John Brasier,
David Walker, Ido Pittman*)

Open All year.
Rooms 20 double, 6 single – 8 with bath, 13 with shower, all with telephone.
Facilities 2 lounges, TV room, breakfast room; terrace. Garden.
Location Central, near Grand Canal.
Restriction Not suitable for &.
Credit cards All major cards accepted.
Terms [1990 rates] B&B: single 47,000–91,000 L, double 90,000–160,000 L.
Reduced rates for children. (No restaurant.)

Hotel Flora   *Tel* (041) 5205844
Calle larga 22 Marzo 2283/a   *Fax* (041) 5228217
Venice 30124   *Telex* 410401

A friendly bed-and-breakfast hotel just west of St Mark's, "full of baroque
mahogany and blue velvet". Its great assets are the good service and the
quiet walled garden, "beautifully landscaped with vines and flowers",
and these have again won praise this year. But bedrooms vary
considerably in size and quality: some are "large and lovely, with
baroque decor, overlooking the garden, blissfully quiet", or "nicely
decorated with antiques and Venetian glass", but others are "rather small
and dark" (front ones, not facing the garden, can be noisy too). Room
maintenance was also sharply criticised by one 1990 visitor. The Art
Buchwald of regular Guide correspondents gives his slant on this debate:
"The beds are the sort that Habitat sold for £39.95 before it owned

Mothercare, but they are comfortable and do not squeak. The bathroom
proves that Italian plumbing has long defied the laws of physics, but is
beautifully appointed. In sum, a delightful place, where the laughing
smiling desk staff are a scream. The rolls are fresh and the coffee divine.
(*Philip Harrison, Mrs M Roberts, Paul Palmer*) More reports clearly needed

Open 1 Feb–20 Nov.
Rooms 38 double, 6 single – all with bath or shower, telephone, air-conditioning.
2 ground-floor rooms.
Facilities Lift. Lounge, T V room, bar, small breakfast room. Courtyard/garden
where breakfast and drinks are served.
Location Central, near St Mark's Square.
Credit cards All major cards accepted.
Terms B&B: single 138,000 L, double 190,000 L. (No restaurant.)

Hotel Monaco and Grand Canal   *Tel* (041) 520021
Calle Vallaresso 1325   *Fax* (041) 520050
San Marco   *Telex* 41045(
Venice 30124

Commended again in 1989/90 for its pleasant staff and good food, this
elegant and expensive hotel on the Grand Canal near San Marco has a
leafy courtyard and impeccably kept public rooms. "A thrilling restaurant
on the waterfront, with almost *too* much bustle and activity," says a
visitor who thought the food "average": but another spoke of "the best
food we had in Venice, with some local dishes". Breakfasts are so-so, as
so often in Italy. "Our favourite Venice hotel, with a superb view," says a
reader this year, who nonetheless could have done with an apology when
the hot-water system broke down. (*Mr and Mrs B Dunstan, Adrian EB Scott,
Diane and Keith Moss*)

Open All year.
Rooms 3 suites, 53 double, 19 single – all with bath, shower, telephone, radio.
Facilities Lift. Lounges, piano bar, restaurant; conference room; terrace. Garden.
Location Central, near Piazza San Marco. Quietest rooms overlook garden.
Credit cards Access, Amex, Visa.
Terms [1990 rates] Dinner, B&B 220,000–260,000 L. Reduced rates and special
meals for children on request.

Hotel Saturnia e International   *Tel* (041) 520837
Calle larga 22 Marzo 2398   *Fax* (041) 520713
Venice 30124   *Telex* 41035

This "cool haven after hot sightseeing" is a comfortable and unpretentious 14th-century *palazzo*-cum-hotel about three minutes' walk from S
Mark's. The impressive reception area is a Gothic patio with an elaborate
inlaid ceiling. Recent views: "We had a huge room with huge bed an
attractive carved and gilded ceiling. Staff helpful and courteous." "W
liked the ambience, the friendly staff and, in particular, our room – on
back canal with two large windows and a huge Venetian glass
chandelier." "The bathroom's modern decor was a bit alarming at first."
The hotel has two restaurants: the *Michelin*-rosetted *Caravella*, recently
described as "excellent" though sometimes criticised in the past, and the
slightly cheaper, but still expensive, *Cortile* (much liked by readers) where

ou can eat outdoors in summer. (*David and Patricia Hawkins*) Further
•ports welcome.

pen All year. Restaurants closed Wed in winter.
ooms 79 double, 16 single – all with bath and/or shower, telephone, TV; baby-
•tening on request.
acilities 2 lounges, bar, TV room, 2 restaurants; conference facilities.
ocation Central, W of Piazza San Marco.
estriction Not suitable for ♿.
redit cards All major cards accepted.
erms B&B: single 170,000–240,000 L, double 260,000–380,000 L; dinner, B&B
),000 L per person added.

---

ensione Seguso   *Tel* (041) 5222340
)orsoduro, Zattere 779
'enice 30123

he superb view of the Giudecca canal from front-facing windows is one
ttraction of this modest and amiable *pensione* on the Zattere; side rooms
verlook a small canal. It's a refined, old-fashioned establishment,
omewhat shabby, with fine old Venetian furniture, and embroidered silk
⁄all-coverings in the dining room. "It's the imperfections of the place
⁀at make it so charming. Our room was clean and peaceful. The decor is
⍺uietly elegant and the dining room has a relaxed, refined air. But meals
re served at rigidly set times, and the food is no more than adequate,
⁄ith poor breakfasts." Others have relished "Madame's gracious wel-
ome"; one said of the place, "Comfortable and quaint, full of character
nd of characters. I enjoyed the quiet, and the Venetian windows and
⁀handeliers." (*Francis Durham*) More reports please.

)pen 1 Mar–30 Nov. Restaurant closed Wed.
:ooms 31 double, 5 single – 9 with bath, 9 with shower, all with telephone.
acilities Lift. Lounge, restaurant; breakfast terrace.
.ocation 15 mins from the centre, overlooking the Giudecca canal.
:redit cards Access, Amex, Visa.
'erms [1990 rates] Dinner, B&B: single 116,000 L, double 183,000 L. Half board
nly.

/ERONA 37121   **Map 16**

Iotel Colomba d'Oro   *Tel* (045) 595300
⁄ia Cattaneo 10   *Fax* (045) 594974

'ery central, on a traffic-free side street near the Arena. A dignified hostelry
ⱼith a club-like atmosphere. Pleasant staff; rooms comfortable, of varying size.
.9 rooms, all with bath or shower. B&B: single 135,000 L, double 187,000 L. No
estaurant. No recent reports. More welcome.

Iotel Torcolo   *Tel* (045) 8007512
'icolo Listone 3

n a side street near the Arena, a small B&B hotel, fairly quiet, with air-
onditioned rooms, some large and furnished with antiques, some more modern,
ome a little basic. Good breakfast, charming Signora and staff, but room

*bookings not always honoured. Closed 10 days Jan. 19 rooms, all with bath and
shower. No restaurant. B&B: single 55,000–72,000 L, double 81,000–102,000 L.
Some criticisms. More reports welcome.*

VICENZA 36100   **Map 1**

Hotel Campo Marzio   *Tel* (0444) 545700
Viale Roma 21   *Fax* (0444) 32049?
                                                          Telex 341138

*A good practical modern hotel, very spruce, and usefully situated between the
station and the wonderful centre of this old city, beside a canal and facing a
park. Small but comfortable modern-style, air-conditioned rooms with excellent
bathrooms. Good service and quite good food; for a superb meal, try the Cinzia e
Valerio. 35 rooms, all with bath and/or shower. B&B double 175,000 L. Full alc
29,000–45,000 L [1990]. Re-endorsed this year, but further reports welcome.*

ZERMAN 31020 Treviso   **Map 1**

Hotel Villa Condulmer   *Tel* (041) 457100
Zerman, Mogliano Veneto   *Fax* (041) 45713

A sumptuously elegant 18th-century Venetian villa in a pastoral setting
on the misty plain between Venice and Treviso. Ronald and Nancy
Reagan chose to stay here during the 1987 Venice summit; their
autographed photo is displayed in the foyer. The hotel has been much
approved recently, especially for its palatial public rooms in rococo style.
"A lovely old building, with a dining terrace overlooking the attractive
grounds where comfortable loungers surround the swimming pool. We
had a delightful large room in the new wing, which has been skilfully
integrated into the old part. The restaurant nicely presents good food at
fair prices." "Food a bit on the *nouvelle* side in portions. All staff helpful
save the receptionist." The rooms in the old part are not yet air
conditioned: but the newer ones are, and have been called "the only truly
cool and comfortable rooms we found in all Italy". (*Betsy C Maestro*)

Open All year except 9 Jan–14 Feb. Restaurant closed Mon.
Rooms 5 suites, 35 double, 5 single – 37 with bath, 8 with shower, all with
telephone; 20 with air-conditioning. 33 in annexe. Some ground-floor rooms.
Facilities Salon, reading room, TV room, bar (with piano and singer),
3 restaurants; conference room. Park with unheated swimming pool, tennis, 18-
hole golf course, riding.
Location Outside village; 4 km NE of Mogliano Veneto and 22 km N of Venice.
Credit cards All major cards accepted.
Terms B&B: single 97,000 L, double 184,000 L, suite 234,000 L; dinner, B&B
160,000–180,000 L per person. Full alc lunch from 50,000 L, dinner from 60,000 L.
Special meals for children on request.

There are many expensive hotels in the Guide. We are keen to
increase our coverage at the other end of the scale. If you know of a
simple place giving simple satisfaction, please write and tell us.

Luxembourg

Hôtel Simmer, Ehnen

Hôtel Bel-Air   *Tel* 729383
route de Berdorf   *Fax* 728694
      Telex 2640

A rather grand country house hotel, recently renovated, on the edge of the attractive resort town of Echternach, in the wooded and hilly "Luxembourg Suisse" near the German frontier. It is a palatial kind of place, with extensive and imposing gardens full of pools, flowering shrubs and Doric columns; pity that the facade by the gardens is such an ugly jumble of styles. Most of the bedrooms are in the modern part, each with a balcony where you can take breakfast: here readers enjoyed their spacious room and also liked the food in the panoramic dining room (*Michelin* rosette for such dishes as loup de mer en croûte). "Very comfortable and peaceful, rather formal atmosphere", runs a report this year. (IW Lloyd, Geo F Outland)

Open 15 Feb–13 Nov, 25 Nov–3 Jan.
Rooms 8 suites, 23 double, 2 single – all with bath, shower, telephone, radio, TV.

Facilities 2 salons, TV room, bar, 2 dining rooms; conference facilities. 1½-acre grounds with tennis court and children's playground.
Location On W side of Echternach, off Diekirch road; follow river Sure to Berdorf turn-off. Parking.
Credit cards All major cards accepted.
Terms B&B: single 2,500–3,500 Lfrs, double 3,600–5,000 Lfrs, suite 5,500–6,000 Lfrs; dinner, B&B 2,800–4,500 Lfrs per person; full board 3,200–4,900 Lfrs. Set lunch 1,400 Lfrs, dinner 1,500 Lfrs; full alc 3,200 Lfrs. Reduced rates and special meals for children.

EHNEN 5416 Map 9

Bamberg's Hôtel *Tel 76022*
131 route du Vin

This neat modern hostelry lies across a busy road from the Moselle river. Hospitable family owners, comfortable rooms (some with balcony), and excellent food in the restaurant with its river views. Some traffic noise. Closed 1 Dec–mid-Jan and Tue. 15 rooms, all with bath and shower. B&B double 2,600–2,700 Lfrs. Set meals 1,400–1,900 Lfrs. More reports needed.

Hôtel Simmer *Tel 76030*
117 route du Vin *Fax 76306*

A confident, family-run hotel facing the river; its 15th-century dining room, with soft lighting and discreet recorded music, attracts many a Eurocrat from nearby Luxembourg city. A report this year: "Good friendly welcome, courteous staff, super views of the Moselle from many rooms (but these tend to suffer from traffic noise: rear ones are quieter). The gourmet-style food (*Michelin* rosette) is first-class, but expensive unless you stay a minimum of three nights and can benefit from *demi-pension* terms." Others have commended the "wonderfully fresh fish", "homely atmosphere" and "very quiet back rooms". (*Ian Harris, Diana Cooper, Stephen Ruell*)

Open 12 Mar–6 Jan. Closed Tue in low season.
Rooms 19 double, 4 single – all with bath and/or shower, telephone.
Facilities Salon, TV room, bar, dining room, banqueting facilities; terrace. Garden.
Location 10 km N of Remich. Central (some traffic noise), parking.
Restriction Not suitable for &.
Credit cards Access, Amex, Visa.
Terms B&B: single 1,800 Lfrs, double 2,300 Lfrs; dinner, B&B 2,300–2,650 Lfrs per person; full board 2,500–2,850 Lfrs. Set menus 1,450, 1,680 and 2,100 Lfrs; full alc 1,300–2,800 Lfrs. Reduced rates and special meals for children.

ETTELBRÜCK 9010 Map 9

Hôtel Central et Restaurant *Tel 82116*
 Taste-Vin *Fax 82138*
25 rue de Bastogne

In a small town where two rivers meet, the Central is no beauty from the outside but has inner virtues, such as pleasant owners, faultless service, large

German-style breakfasts, and an elegant dining room with nouvelle-*ish cuisine worthy of its* Michelin *rosette. Comfortable rooms: upper ones have the best views and are quietest (some noise on the street side). Closed 31 July–31 Aug, 24 Dec–4 Jan. 16 rooms, all with bath or shower. B&B double 1,900–2,700 Lfrs. Set menus 950–2,000 Lfrs. Briefly endorsed this year, but fuller reports requested.*

LUXEMBOURG 1611   **Map 9**

Arcotel   *Tel* 494041
Avenue de la Gare 43   *Telex* 3776

Near the station, a pleasant small hotel with tasteful furnishings and large, bright rooms (the mini-bars contain food as well as drink). Helpful staff, ample breakfasts. 30 rooms, all with private facilities, 2,900–3,500 Lfrs, breakfast included. No restaurant. New nomination. More reports please.

****
Traveller's tale *Roast chicken with assistant chef's stuffing was a gastronomic disaster; the assistant chef turned out to be the 12-year-old local lad who polished guests' cars during the day. Gaffes included the hostess/barmaid/waitress/proprietress sampling a guest's drink before handing it to him, and gossiping about two guests who had not yet arrived, hinting that they were obviously on a dirty weekend.*
****

Malta

Hotel Ta' Cenc, Sannat

MARSALFORN BAY Gozo Map 16

Atlantis Hotel `BUDGET` *Tel* 55.46.85
Qolla Street *Fax* 55.56.61

Small, modern, family-run hotel with large swimming pool in quiet new residential area, not far from seafront. Warmly recommended for "kind, friendly and efficient" hosts, Godfrey and Frances Farrugia, "very good home-cooked dinners and breakfasts – including Granny's excellent marmalade"; service thoughtful and attentive; bedrooms comfortable "apart from slippery (possibly nylon) duvets". 25 rooms, all with bathroom, most with balcony or patio. Dinner, B&B LM5.25–12 [1990]. Our first new nomination for the archipelago in many years. More reports please.

SANNAT Gozo   Map 16

Hotel Ta' Cenc   *Tel* 55.68.19
                                                Fax 55.81.99

This single-storey building, in local honey-coloured limestone, is beautifully located on a high promontory on a little island off the north-east
coast of Malta, cunningly terraced to blend into the hillside. Some rooms
are bungalows, most with their own small patio, ranged round a central
pool, amid oleanders, fig trees and cacti. There are lovely views of the sea
and Malta beyond. In recent years there have been criticisms of the hotel,
but it is now fully air-conditioned and bedrooms and public areas have
been refurbished. Reports on the food are mixed, ranging from "good and
plentiful, if not outstanding" to "second-rate, served by half-trained,
inadequately supervised waiters", and some visitors have found reception
unhelpful. More reports please.

Open All year except possibly Jan and Feb.
Rooms 12 suites, 38 double – all with bath, shower, telephone, radio, TV, air-
conditioning, patio or garden. All on ground floor.
Facilities Lounge, bar, snack bar, games room, restaurant; disco; live music in
season. 3-acre grounds with swimming pool, bar, tennis; rock beach with bar 2½
km (free transport by hotel bus), water-skiing, boats for hire.
Location 5 mins' walk from village (hotel provides free transport), on southern
part of island, near Ta' Cenc cliffs.
Credit cards All major cards accepted.
Terms [1990 rates] Dinner, B&B LM17–40; full board LM20–44. Reduced rates
and special meals for children.

XAGHRA Gozo   Map 16

Cornucopia Hotel   **BUDGET**   *Tel* 55.64.86
10 Gnien Imrik Street   *Fax* 55.29.10
                                                Telex 1467

This cheerful family-run hotel, two miles inland, is a converted
farmhouse with modern extensions in white stone, set attractively beside
its swimming pool. The new modern bedrooms, well equipped and
maintained, either overlook this pool or have a splendid view of the
valley; again this year, readers have much preferred them to the rooms in
the old building. "Children are well looked after, not just tolerated, staff
are very friendly, and food is well cooked." A view last year: "Relaxed
and informal, with plentiful and imaginative food (poolside barbecues
most enjoyable). Well run, without being regimented." (*Susan K Williams,
Fiona Mutch*) There's a new honeymoon suite with jacuzzi.

Open All year.
Rooms 6 suites, 47 double – all with bath, shower, telephone, radio, TV; baby-
listening on request. 2, with self-catering facilities, in annexe. Some on ground
floor.
Facilities Lounges, bar, TV room, games room, restaurant. Garden; terraces.
2 swimming pools, children's pool, whirlpool. Hairdresser, boutique.
Location Outside village of Xaghra: follow signs to Xerri's Grotto.
Credit cards All major cards accepted.
Terms [1990 rates] B&B LM6.50–12; dinner, B&B LM7.75–14; full board LM9.25–
15.50. Set lunch/dinner LM3; full alc LM5.25. Reduced rates and special meals
for children.

Morocco

Hôtel Tichka, Marrakech

EL JADIDA   **Map 19**

Hôtel de Provence `BUDGET`   *Tel* (34) 23.47
42 avenue Fkih Rafy

A very simple, inexpensive hotel previously on our shortlist, now gets a
full entry: ''El Jadida is a charming seaside town, relatively undiscovered
by foreign tourists. It has a fine beach and café-lined promenade, delicate
Moorish municipal architecture, colourful *souks* and a splendid old
Portuguese walled 'city' where it is worth paying the guardian 10 Dirhams
(80p) to see the dramatically vaulted water cistern and to walk round the
ramparts. In February the sun shone every day in a blue sky and the
temperature was between 60° and 70°F. It gets hotter, and more crowded
with Moroccan holiday-makers from Casablanca, in summer. The hotel is
only a few minutes' walk from the sea and old town. It is owned by a
friendly, retired British solicitor, Geoffrey Hurdidge, and managed by an
equally pleasant Moroccan, Mohamed Koraimi. The staff are all courteous
and efficient. My bedroom had a tiled floor, shuttered balcony windows,
comfortable bed, two chairs, curtained-off washbasin, shower and WC –

all for about £5! The three-course menu, with a choice of three French or Moroccan-style dishes for each course, was equally good value – under £4, or one could eat à la carte. There are more expensive restaurants in town, but none where the food tasted better. The dining room is cheerfully decorated with Moorish rugs and paintings of Moroccan scenes and fresh flowers. In summer one can eat in the trellised garden courtyard. There is a comfortable lounge with TV, much patronised in the evening by Moroccan guests." (*Tim Brierly*)

Open All year except Ramadan (approx 6 Mar–6 Apr).
Rooms 16 double – all with bath and/or shower.
Facilities Lounge with TV, bar, restaurant. Courtyard, garden with restaurant. Sandy beach nearby.
Location In town centre. Parking.
Credit cards Access, Visa.
Terms B&B: single 86 Dhs, double 138 Dhs. Set meals 60 Dhs; full alc 100 Dhs. 1-night bookings sometimes refused in summer.

FES	Map 19

Hôtel Palais Jamai   *Tel* (6) 343.31
Bab El Guissa   *Telex* 71974

The spiritual capital of Morocco, founded in 808, lies in a bowl north of the Middle Atlas; in summer the lower part of the city is oppressively hot. Its grandest buildings are in Fes el-Jedid (new Fes), above Fes el-Bali (old Fes); one of these is the *Palais Jamai*, built in the 18th century by Sidi Mohamed Ben Arib El Jami, Grand Vizier to the Sultan. It is now a large and luxurious hotel, "beautifully and conveniently sited, most attractively furnished", in a magnificent Andalusian garden with panoramic views of the city. The bedrooms are decorated in traditional Moroccan style; the most luxurious are in the old building, while those in the new wing have breathtaking views of the old town. It is "efficiently run, but a little cold and impersonal", with an international restaurant and a traditional Moroccan one. "The food is entirely satisfactory, but not memorable – the Moroccan restaurant is worth visiting for the decor, but the food and atmosphere in similar restaurants in the old town are to be preferred." Breakfasts, with fresh orange juice, have been praised. "It is a treat to stay in a hotel that has capitalised on Moroccan architecture and history; very helpful concierge." (*PR Glazebrook, Carol Hahn*) A 1990 visitor adds: "As a grand old lady it was a little worn down." More reports please.

Open All year.
Rooms 136 rooms – most with bath, telephone, radio, TV, air-conditioning. Some on ground floor.
Facilities Lift, bar, 2 restaurants, night club. Garden with swimming pool and tennis court.
Location N of Fes el-Bali.
Credit cards All major cards accepted.
Terms [1990 rates] Rooms: single 650–800 Dhs, double 900–1,500 Dhs. Set meals 210 Dhs.

Important reminder: terms printed must be regarded as a rough guide only to the size of the bill to be expected at the end of your stay. For latest tariffs, check when booking.

Hôtel Es-Saadi   *Tel* (4) 488.11
Avenue Quadissia   *Fax* (4) 476.44
                                                          Telex 72042

This old-established, privately owned hotel, built in the 1960s, is set in
attractive gardens with good views to the Atlas mountains and is less
than ten minutes' walk from the old town. It has pleased most recent
visitors. Bedrooms have all the facilities you would expect of a five-star
hotel; all, except the cabanas by the pool, have a small balcony, and are to
be preferred to the cheaper poolside rooms. There is a beautiful large
swimming pool with a small island; lunch by the pool offers a choice of
simple and more elaborate dishes. The decor is international bland rather
than Moroccan. "We could find no fault; extremely well run, with very
friendly staff. Food is quite simple, but beautifully cooked and presented." (*B Ollendorff, PR Glazebrook*) One reader took an opposite view:
"Rooms and staff in considerable need of rejuvenation; lobby always full
of package tours. Poor breakfasts." More reports please.

Open All year.
Rooms 15 suites, 132 double – all with bath and/or shower, telephone, radio, TV,
balcony, air-conditioning. 8 cabanas by pool. 8 ground-floor rooms.
Facilities Lifts. Salon, bar, restaurant; boutique, hairdresser; sauna. Large grounds
with terrace, outdoor restaurant, garden, tennis, swimming pool with snack bar.
Casino with restaurant in park.
Location ½ m from centre.
Credit cards All major cards accepted.
Terms [1990 rates] (Excluding tax) Rooms: single 500–660 Dhs, double 600–
760 Dhs, suite 1,250 Dhs. Breakfast 50 Dhs. Set lunch/dinner 225 Dhs; full alc
300–350 Dhs. Extra bed for child under 4 years 80 Dhs.

La Mamounia   *Tel* (4) 498.81
Avenue Bab Jdid   *Fax* (4) 446.60
                                                          Telex 72018

Winston Churchill's favourite, once a pasha's palace, now the most lavish
hotel in Marrakech – "very expensive, even by European standards" – is
upgraded from a place on the shortlist to a full entry: "Really the only
place to stay in Marrakech if you like refinement and luxury and don't
mind more than an element of snobbery with it. Unable to book in
advance, we were challenged by the doorman each time we tried to go
into the hotel *before* we had secured a reservation, despite being smartly
dressed. But we were admitted in the scruffiest of clothes with a pleasant
smile and greeting once we had booked a room. The hotel cultivates a
feeling of being a very exclusive club – which is what it is really, owing to
the outrageous prices. Staying at *La Mamounia* is an experience not to be
missed. The lobby area is vast, with lots of fresh flowers, pot-pourri,
luxurious deep-pile carpets and striking art-deco type furniture. A side
courtyard of marble with a fountain reminds you that you are in Africa, as
do the impeccably maintained gardens with their views towards the
snow-capped Atlas mountains. The rooms were all redesigned and
renovated in 1986; the style is 1920s, lots of glass, chrome and richly
coloured fabrics. Room service is faultless, although there was a
surprising parsimony about the bread and croissants at breakfast. Lunch

by the pool is a buffet of monumental proportions. Despite the quantity, one felt that quality had in no way been sacrificed. At dinner in the most formal of the five restaurants, whose furnishings reflect understated luxury rather than opulence, the emphasis was on *nouvelle cuisine*. La *Mamounia* lays on its own guides, excursions, etc – a good idea in a city where most of the population lives off its ability to extort money from tourists. It's a hotel as close to paradise as can be found in Africa. But be prepared to be part of a rather arrogant and self-satisfied fraternity – and to spend a *lot* of money." (*David Barnes*)

Open All year.
Rooms 3 3-bedroomed villas, 57 suites (2 2-bedroomed), 171 rooms – all with bath, shower, telephone, radio, TV, mini-bar, air-conditioning.
Facilities Lounges, 6 bars, 6 restaurants, banqueting hall, conference hall, night club, casino, art gallery, boutiques, beauty salon, hammam, sauna. Large grounds with tennis, swimming pool (heated in winter), squash; riding; golf nearby.
Location Between Medina and new city. Free open parking.
Credit cards All major cards accepted.
Terms [1990 rates] (Excluding tax) Rooms: single 1,400–3,000 Dhs, double 1,700–3,200 Dhs, suite 2,700–13,500 Dhs. Villas 20,000 Dhs. Breakfast 105 Dhs, buffet lunch 350 Dhs. Dinner alc. Extra bed for child under 12, 300 Dhs.

Hôtel Tichka   *Tel* (4) 487.10
Route de Casablanca,   *Fax* (4) 486.90
Semlalia BP 894   *Telex* 74855

Less expensive than the above two hotels, the *Tichka*'s chief drawback is that it is in the new city, a mile or two from the Medina, in an area full of look-alike multi-storey package hotels. The *Tichka* itself eschews group tourism, and is an architectural and designer's treat. Dusky-rose from the outside, like most buildings in the city, its windows and balconies are chocolate-brown and turquoise; and the interior decor is equally striking in its colour contrasts, as well as in the quality of the materials. The rooms are a pleasure to behold, besides being as comfortable as one could wish – no sign of cheese-paring anywhere. There is a large pool surrounded by palms, willows and orange trees and a well-kept substantial garden. Best rooms are those with a pool view. Breakfast, lunches and evening drinks are taken poolside; there's a Moroccan restaurant, "very good by Marrakech standards". In early 1990 the hotel went through a bad patch when there was no manager, but all now seems to be under control. More reports please.

Open All year.
Rooms 138 double – all with bath, shower, telephone, radio, TV, air-conditioning.
Facilities Lounges, bar, restaurant; night club; health club; sauna. Garden with swimming pool.
Location In new part of city, 3 km from Medina.
Credit cards All major cards accepted.
Terms On application.

Always let a hotel know if you have to cancel a booking, whether you have paid a deposit or not. Hotels lose thousands of pounds and dollars from "no-shows".

OUIRGANE   Map 19

Résidence La Roseraie   *Tel* (via Marrakech) (4) 320.94
Val d'Ouirgane   *Fax* (4) 320.95
BP 769 Marrakech   *Telex* 74022

A charming small hotel in a singularly beautiful setting outside a very
simple mountain village. Bedrooms are in rustic-style bungalows, each
with an individual patio, set in a fragrant rose garden, with the High Atlas
Mountains as a backdrop and a rushing river in the valley below. It is just
over an hour's drive from Marrakech, and there is not a great deal of
sightseeing in the immediate surroundings, but *La Roseraie* has two
immaculately maintained tennis courts, a large swimming pool (alas
unheated in winter), and an equestrian centre where you can ride by the
hour or from which you can go on treks of several days into the
mountains, staying with Berber families. There are lovely walks in the
grounds and surrounding mountains. Coach parties may stop for lunch,
but are generally accommodated out of ear and eyeshot of the residents.
Staff are friendly, the atmosphere is relaxed and peaceful. Breakfast and
lunch are al fresco when the weather is fine; the former is not particularly
good, and the lunch and dinner menu does not vary much, but there are
good salads and grills and Moroccan dishes. For a change you can eat at
the *Auberge au Sanglier Qui Fume* in the village. If you go in winter pack an
anorak as well as a sun hat, and ask for a central-heated room; although
the sun is bright by day, the nights can be cold. (*CR, JNG Buckeridge, JR
Lloyd*) A few niggles: housekeeping can be somewhat erratic; changing
money is not easy here; the telephone line has been known to go down
for days at a time; nocturnal silence can be shattered by the barking of the
hotel's watch-dogs.

Open All year.
Rooms 13 suites, 7 double – all with bath and/or shower, telephone, patio. All in
bungalows.
Facilities 4 salons, TV room, 2 bars, restaurant. Terraces. 25-acre grounds with
garden, swimming pool, 2 tennis courts, riding centre. Health club planned for
1990.
Location 10 mins' walk from village which is 60 km S of Marrakech.
Credit cards Access, Amex, Visa.
Terms [1990 rates] B&B: single 310 Dhs, double 420 Dhs, suite 560–760 Dhs. Set
meals 140–150 Dhs. Reduced rates for children 5–10 sharing parents' room.

TANGIER   Map 19

Hôtel El Minzah   *Tel* (9) 358.85
85 rue de la Liberté   *Fax* (9) 345.46
                                                            Telex 33775

"One of the best hotels in Morocco." "Thoroughly well run. Staff have a
flair for service which they render with obvious pleasure and dignity."
"A high standard of cleanliness, comfort, peace and quiet. Atmosphere in
the piano bar very romantic." Three satisfied visitors in 1989/90 to a
long-established and luxurious hotel, built by the Marquess of Bute in the
centre of the cosmopolitan port, and set in exotic gardens with extensive
views of the harbour and the Straits of Gibraltar. Other readers have
admired the "splendid Moorish decor: international standard of fittings

combined with genuine local style". Last year there were some criticisms
of the cooking, but recent visitors are positive: food in the Moroccan
restaurant is found "excellent"; in the pleasant main European one it is
"carefully served and very edible". Others have liked the small
bar/restaurant best. (*Dr I Anderson, JP Marland, Mr and Mrs FPA Wood*) The
management tells us that traffic past the hotel has been re-routed and
rooms on the road are now much less noisy; and they are double-glazed
and air-conditioned.

Open All year.
Rooms 8 suites, 83 doubles – all with bath, shower, telephone, radio, TV, mini-bar, air-conditioning.
Facilities 4 lounges, 2 bars, 2 restaurants, snack bar, tearoom. Courtyard. Large
garden with swimming pool. Beach 10 mins' walk.
Location Central, near French consulate. Roadside rooms double-glazed. Parking.
Credit cards All major cards accepted.
Terms [1990 rates] (Excluding tax) Rooms: single 460–575 Dhs, double 600–
750 Dhs, suite 1,100–2,400 Dhs. Supplement for balcony 140 Dhs. Breakfast
70 Dhs. Set lunch/dinner 220 Dhs. Reduced rates for children sharing parents'
room; special meals on request.

TAROUDANT   Map 19

La Gazelle d'Or   *Tel* (85) 20.39
BP 260 Taroudant   *Fax* (85) 27.37
                                                       Telex 81902

Two kilometres from Taroudant, and an hour by a fast road from Agadir,
La Gazelle d'Or was once the home of a French baron, who built
bungalows in the grounds for his guests. There are now 30 small villas
scattered round a large garden, with the High Atlas Mountains framing
the horizon. They have a fireplace with a log fire, and a private terrace
where you breakfast. The newer units are said to be "particularly
comfortable and tastefully decorated". There are tennis courts and riding
stables; a buffet lunch is served round the large swimming pool, dinner is
in an elegant tented dining room. Rooms are often booked months ahead,
and a high proportion of the clientele is English-speaking, many of them
regulars. Service is "wonderful, without being fussy". "Top of the bill in
all respects." (*Ann Flinn, C de Koning*) But there is little sight-seeing in the
area, particularly if the weather is poor, though Taroudant has a good
souk. The *Gazelle d'Or*'s most satisfied customers are those who want to
get away from it all in sybaritic comfort – and don't mind paying its
prices. For several visitors in 1989/90 the hotel has been altogether too
remote, the pool inadequately heated in winter, and the food and the
restaurant service not up to the prices charged.

Open All year except August.
Rooms 2 suites, 28 double, all with bath (2 also have shower), telephone, TV,
baby-listening, terrace. All in cottages.
Facilities 3 lounges, TV room, bar, 2 restaurants; conference facilities. Gardens
with heated swimming pool with grill, tennis, hammam and stables.
Location 2 km from Taroudant.
Restriction "Preferably no children."
Credit cards All major cards accepted.
Terms Half board rates only: single 1,500 Dhs, double 2,050 Dhs, suite 3,900 Dhs.
Buffet lunch 250 Dhs.

Hôtel Palais Salam   *Tel* (85) 25.01

A romantic palace built into the impressive red-earth walls of the ancient city, with rooms scattered higgledy-piggledy around the premises. "It has been transformed into a charming hotel with excellent accommodation around courtyards with fountains, mosaic floors and heavy, elaborately carved wooden 'doors. There are two swimming pools, one on the ground floor, surrounded by palms and flowering shrubs; the other (for residents only) is on the first floor next to the atmospheric Moroccan bar with wall-to-wall rugs and silken cushions on the floor." Readers have particularly enjoyed the recently built split-level rooms on an old courtyard, "with a sort of minstrels' gallery, nice bathroom and sitting room below". Others are in the original palace facing banana groves, largely used for the in-and-out coach parties. There are two restaurants, one serving inter-national fare, often crowded with tourists, and another (reservations necessary) in Moroccan style serving national specialities – "very good food and lovely pâtisserie; excellent and witty head waiter". The hotel is a popular lunch or drinks stop for coach parties, but the coaching crowds are kept to the public rooms and swimming pool on the ground floor. Upstairs, the hotel "is a peaceful and sympathetic haven". (*Lesley Goodden, Kate Currie, also Claire Enders*)

Open All year.
Rooms 38 suites, 95 double – all with bath and/or shower, telephone.
Facilities Lounge, 2 bars, TV room, 2 restaurants; conference facilities; health club. Garden with 2 swimming pools; tennis nearby; bicycles available.
Location In town centre, within the old walls. Parking.
Credit cards All major cards accepted.
Terms [1990 rates] (Excluding tax) Dinner, B&B: single 438 Dhs, double 670 Dhs.

ZAGORA   Map 19

La Fibule du Drâa   `BUDGET`   *Tel* Zagora 118
BP 11

1 km outside the town, by Pont Oued Drâa, next to oasis, in an "enchanting" garden with reclining seats and swimming pool – a simple, inexpensive hotel, privately owned. Rooms in three buildings, casbah style. Liked for genuinely traditional design and laid-back air, "staff and restaurant first-rate". Camel trekking arranged. 26 double rooms, 20 with bath, 120–150 Dhs. Breakfast 15 Dhs. Set meals 60–100 Dhs. New nomination. More reports please.

This short list is generously contributed by Annie Austin of Creative Leisure Management in London. We should be glad to get feedback from readers who have visited any of these hotels recently, or who can add fresh deserving names.

CASABLANCA **Hôtel Riad Salam Meridien** (5-star) *Tel* 363535 and 367922 *Telex* 24692. On beachside corniche of Casablanca. 100 rooms, 12 suites and 50 bungalows. Also an excellent and unique (to Morocco) Health Institute of Seawater Therapy.

EL JADIDA **Club Salam des Doukkala** (4-star B) Avenue El Jamaiaa Al Arabia. *Tel* (34) 3622 and 2575 *Telex* 78014. Well-equipped club hotel with many sporting facilities and 82 rooms. Right on beach; about ten minutes' walk from centre of town. Ideal in summer for those who want a social sporting holiday on the beach in an unspoilt Moroccan town.

ESSAOUIRA **Hôtel des Iles** (4-star A) *Tel* (47) 2329 *Telex* 31907. Essaouira is a charming unspoilt fishing village. The *Hôtel des Iles*, with 77 rooms, belongs to the ONCF chain. Well run; popular with British tourists.

IMMOUZER, Nr Agadir **Hôtel des Cascades** (3-star B) *Tel* 14. A lovely small (14-room) hotel recently refurbished. Next to the eponymous cascades and with superb views – a perfect place for a break. An hour's picturesque drive up from Agadir.

LAYOUNE **Hôtel Parador** *Tel* 2245 and 2200 *Telex* 28800. A beautifully decorated 31-room modern hotel in the far south run by Club Mediterranée. New on the Morocco tourist map. Superior cuisine.

MARRAKECH **Hôtel Imilchil** (3-star) Avenue Echouhada. *Tel* (4) 476.53 *Telex* 72018. A relatively small hotel – 86 rooms – with Moroccan decor but no bar serving alcohol. Swimming pool reinstated this year. Good value.

MARRAKECH **Hôtel Semiramis Meridien** (5-star) Route de Casablanca *Tel* (4) 313.77 *Telex* 72906. Well-run modern hotel in the new part of town. 186 rooms and a splendid swimming pool set in spacious gardens.

MARRAKECH **Hôtel Tafilalet** (4-star) Route de Casablanca. *Tel* (4) 345.18 *Telex* 72955. Immaculately run hotel with 84 rooms personally supervised by its owner, Madame Lamon.

MIDELT **Hôtel Ayachi** (3-star A) Route d'Agadir. *Tel* 21.61. 28-room *pension* hotel, owned and run by resident family, useful as a stop-over.

MIDELT **Dayet Aoua** (2-star) Route de Fes, Ifrane. *Tel* 0. A simple small hotel with 26 rooms but one of the best French restaurants in Morocco. Set on a lovely lake with good fishing and shooting. Hotel has boats for hire.

OUALIDIA **Hôtel Hippocamp** (2-star A) *Tel* 111. On road from El Jadida to Safi overlooking the lagoon. A simple establishment, with 20 rooms. Excellent fish meals at reasonable cost.

OURZAZATE **Hôtel Riad Salam** (4-star A) Rue Mohamed Diouri. *Tel* 22.06. *Telex* 74049. Built prettily as a modern casbah round a swimming pool with two good clay tennis courts outside the walls. 70 double bedrooms, well maintained, with tiled floors. Cool desert sun, cooler nights. Good French restaurant, better Moroccan one. Convenient posting point for desert and oasis drives.

RABAT **La Tour Hassan** (5-star) *Tel* (7) 21401 and 33814 *Telex* 31914. First opened its doors to guests in 1914 and can be considered one of the best traditional hotels in Morocco. 150 bedrooms, decorated in the latest modern pastel shades. Facilities include an excellent Moroccan restaurant. Centrally situated and built around a pretty Andalusian garden. No swimming pool.

TAFRAOUT **Hôtel Les Amandiers** (4-star B) *Tel* 8. A rather run-down 60-room hotel (the pool has not been filled for years), but friendly and a good base for anyone wishing to visit this spectacularly picturesque area.

ZAGORA **Hôtel Tinsouline** (4-star A) *Tel* 22 An unpretentious 90-room hotel at the edge of the desert in exotic, rugged surroundings. Plain but comfortable rooms and a swimming pool. Very French – many French tourists including children – and interesting food in restaurant.

****
* **Traveller's tale** *The bathroom wall sloped. It was impossible to stand* *
* *under the shower; the only way was to kneel.* *
****

The Netherlands

Kasteel Wittem, Wittem

ALMEN Gelderland   **Map 9**

De Hoofdige Boer `BUDGET`   *Tel* (05751) 1744
Dorpsstraat 38   *Fax* (05751) 1567
Almen 7218 AH

Almen is a village in eastern Holland, close to the charming old town of
Zutphen and not far from Arnhem and the Kröller-Müller museum
(splendid Van Goghs). Here readers have again commended the rural
setting, good food, and "friendly informality" at this old-established
hotel. It has a comfortable lounge and unusual beamed decor, and a tea-
garden giving on to open fields. "An excellent place. The bedrooms are
quite modern in decor, spacious and well lit, with lots of attention to
homey detail – in our room, sewing and shoe-shine kit, and fresh fruit.
The food is good substantial Dutch fare, and the ever-present staff are full
of good cheer." (*Lynne and David Allen; John W Behle*)

Open All year except New Year's Day.
Rooms 18 double, 2 single – all with bath and/or shower, telephone, TV, baby-
listening. 2 ground-floor rooms.

Facilities Bar, lounge, TV room, restaurants; functions room; table-tennis. Garden with tea-garden and dinner terrace. 5 mins' walk to heated swimming pool.
Location Central, near the church. Parking.
Credit cards Access, Amex, Diners.
Terms [1990 rates] B&B: single 75 glds, double 120–150 glds; dinner, B&B 85–110 glds per person. Full alc 59 glds. Reduced rates for children sharing parents' room; special meals.

AMSTERDAM Noord-Holland   Map 9

Hotel Ambassade	*Tel* (020) 262333
Herengracht 341	*Fax* (020) 245321
Amsterdam 1016 AZ	*Telex* 10158

"The best small hotel in Amsterdam" (bed-and-breakfast only) has again been warmly admired in 1989/90. Part of its quality depends on the building and its location: seven adjoining 17th-century patrician houses on the Herengracht, the city's grandest canal. But the secret of its popularity lies with Mr van der Velden, the owner, "always there, courteous, friendly, running the whole show without effort or tension", and with his team – "The most charming and polite hotel staff I've ever come across." Rooms, varying in size according to their altitude in these tall buildings, are furnished in period or modern Dutch style: "Ours, high-ceilinged, had a crystal chandelier, beautiful antique desk, two large velvet easy chairs, and a balcony facing the canal," says a reader this year. The public rooms have many items from the owner's personal collection of antiques – old china, clocks, paintings. Room service is amazing: "No charge for baby-sitting – one night the bell-boy rocked our son back to sleep." The steps to upper floors are steep (normal in these old Amsterdam houses), and the spiral staircases are "hard to climb if you've been knocking back the Heineken". But a lift in a newly acquired house connects with two of the others; and there are seven ground-floor rooms. Breakfast, taken in "a splendid room overlooking the canal", is "typical sturdy Dutch", but its cooked dishes cost extra. (*Norma Kessler, D Cooper, Roger Diamond, Neil and Jacqueline Britton, and others*)

Open All year.
Rooms 5 suites, 39 double, 3 single – all with bath (17 also have shower), telephone, TV; baby-sitters available. 15 in annexe. 7 on ground floor.
Facilities Lift. 2 lounges, breakfast room.
Location Central, but quietly situated on Herengracht canal. Meter parking; public garage 5 mins' walk.
Credit cards All major cards accepted.
Terms B&B: single 180 glds, double 220 glds, suite 280 glds. Reduced rates for children sharing parents' room. (No restaurant, but drinks and light refreshments and 24-hour room service.)

Hotel Asterisk	*Tel* (020) 262396
Den Texstraat 14–16	*Fax* (020) 382790
Amsterdam 1017 ZA	

In a quiet street 2 km S of the centre, near the Weteringplein and Rijksmuseum, a comfortable family-run B&B hotel. Helpful staff, copious buffet breakfasts; usual steep Dutch staircases. 26 rooms, most with private facilities, 8 in annexe.

Kitchenette available for long stays. B&B: single 55–70 glds, double 70–139 glds. New nomination. More reports welcome.

Het Canal House   *Tel* (020) 225182
Keizersgracht 148   *Fax* (020) 241317
Amsterdam 1015 CX   *Telex* 10611

Owned by Americans, Jane and Len Irwin, this graceful 17th-century merchant's house stands quietly on a canal close to the Anne Frank House and quite near to the city centre; some of the friendly staff are young Irishwomen in period costume. It has an attractive enclosed garden, illuminated at night. Visitors this year and last have enjoyed the cosy bar and the "large, bright and airy" rooms, some furnished with antiques, some more ordinary (such as the small single attic rooms). Some big rooms overlook the canal, and one of these retains the wooden wheels and axle that were formerly used with a hook attached to raise and lower items. Renovation in the past two years has not disturbed these classic features. "The hall opens on to a high-ceilinged breakfast room with huge mirrors, a grand piano and white lilies everywhere." Stairs are steep, as in most canal houses of this type, but there is now a lift. (*John and Suzanne Price, Dr Madeleine Montefiore, GB Kay, and others*) When the Irwins are absent, standards may fall; and breakfasts have again been criticised this year.

Open All year.
Rooms 22 double, 4 single – all with bath and/or shower, telephone.
Facilities Lift. Lounge, bar, breakfast room. Garden.
Location Central. Street parking.
Restrictions Not suitable for &. No children under 12.
Credit cards All major cards accepted.
Terms B&B: single 135–150 glds, double 165–210 glds. (No restaurant.)

Hotel de l'Europe   *Tel* (020) 234836
Nieuwe Doelenstraat 2–8   *Fax* (020) 242962
Amsterdam 1012 CP   *Telex* 12081

Built on the Amstel in 1895, this is one of the city's grander hotels. It has beautiful rooms and pleasant service, and has been much liked by returning visitors who endorse their earlier account: "Our room was not so spacious, but prettily decorated in cream and blue. All the public rooms are attractive, but the continental breakfast is very basic." However, an inspector enjoyed a New Year's brunch that was anything but basic: "A huge variety of spectacular seafoods, and many delicious desserts. This was served in a restaurant of the highest elegance, overlooking the Amstel. The whole place had an air of ineffable grand-hotel superiority without being disdainful or snobbish." Bedrooms at the back, facing the river, are quietest. (*K and S M-S*)

Open All year.
Rooms 19 suites, 66 double, 16 single – all with bath, shower, telephone, radio, TV, air-conditioning; baby-listening on request.
Facilities Lift, ramp. Lounge, bar, 2 restaurants; banqueting and conference facilities; indoor heated swimming pool, sauna, solarium; terrace overlooking Amstel where meals and drinks are served in summer.

Location Central, opposite the Mint Tower and Flower Market (rooms double-glazed: quietest ones at back). Parking, public garage nearby.
Credit cards All major cards accepted.
Terms Rooms: single 400–450 glds, double 425–475 glds, suite 995 glds. Breakfast 26 glds. Set lunch from 52.50 glds, dinner from 65 glds; full alc 100 glds. Reduced rates for children; special meals on request.

Hotel Pulitzer   *Tel* (020) 5235237
Prinsengracht 323   *Fax* (020) 276753
Amsterdam 1016 GZ   *Telex* 16508

This large and sophisticated hotel facing the Prinsengracht, an imaginative conversion of nine 17th-century houses linked by a pretty garden, has been liked again in 1990: "Rooms retain beamed ceilings, but furniture, lighting and pictures are fiercely modern. Ours was attractive but it felt bland, like a chain hotel room. Breakfast was a good buffet, including bacon and scrambled eggs. The hotel does a busy trade in groups and packages. But staff are helpful beyond the call of duty." An earlier and different slant: "Despite its size, it feels intimate and friendly rather than impersonal. The rooms are a decent blend of old and new – original beams, exposed brickwork, slightly rustic furnishings. There is a pleasant glass-covered walkway through the gardens, with modern pictures on its walls and sculptures in the courtyards." Garden-facing rooms are quieter; the others enjoy the prospect over the canal. (*David Wooff, Arnold Howell, A Farrow*) We should welcome comments on the restaurant, which serves French food and is reasonably priced for Amsterdam.

Open All year. Restaurant closed 8 July–6 Aug and Sat, Sun for lunch.
Rooms 7 suites, 178 double, 44 single – all with bath, shower, telephone, radio, TV, mini-bar, air-conditioning; baby-listening arranged. 25 ground-floor rooms.
Facilities Lifts. 2 lounges, bar, 2 restaurants; conference facilities; art gallery; gift shop; terrace for light meals, drinks, concerts in summer. Large garden. Private landing stage and canal boat.
Location Central, near Wester Church; garden rooms best for light sleepers. Garage 8 mins' walk; valet parking.
Credit cards All major cards accepted.
Terms [1990 rates] Rooms: single 290 glds, double 390 glds. Breakfast 29 glds. Alc meals (excluding wine) 69–103 glds. Reduced rates for children; special meals on request.

BLOKZIJL Overijssel   **Map 9**

Kaatje bij de Sluis   *Tel* (05272) 1833
Brouwerstraat 20   *Fax* (05272) 1836
Overijssel 8356 DV

Blokzijl used to be a prosperous Hanseatic port on the Zuiderzee and has many fine 17th-century houses; today it's an attractive yachting centre. This restaurant-with-rooms, "Katie by the canal lock", is named after a local 17th-century heroine who became an expert cook – and today the cooking is still stylish enough to earn a *Michelin* rosette, as our reporter attests: "The food is exceptional, far removed from the deservedly stodgy image that Dutch food has. The style is French-influenced, but Dutch ingredients are used intelligently, and the dishes are beautifully presented. The staff are helpful and attentive. The bedrooms, created more recently, are in a building across the drawbridge: our large double room was elegantly furnished and had a profusion of potted plants, typically Dutch. Breakfast – also typically Dutch, with five types of bread – is served on the terrace or in the garden room, with a good view of the small but pretty garden and the boating manoeuvres." (*Diana Cooper*)

Open All year except Feb. Closed Mon and Tue.
Rooms 8 double – all with bath, shower, telephone, radio, TV. All in separate building from restaurant.
Facilities Lounge, restaurant, breakfast room. Garden, 2 terraces.
Location Blokzijl is 33 km N of Zwolle. Hotel is central (rooms double-glazed). Parking.
Credit cards All major cards accepted.
Terms [1990 rates] B&B: single 160 glds, double 225 glds; dinner, B&B: single 235 glds, double 425 glds. Set lunch 75 glds, dinner 100 glds; full alc 100 glds. Special meals for children.

BREUKELEN Utrecht   **Map 9**

Hofstede Slangevegt   *Tel* (03462) 61525
Straatweg 40
Breukelen 3621 BN

Set in pretty country just south of Amsterdam, amid stately homes, old farms and villages, windmills and drawbridges, this converted merchant's house is an excellent and charming restaurant whose five guest bedrooms are simple – too simple for some tastes, so it lost its place in recent Guides. But two reports this year claim that this was a wrong decision: "What you get is a comfortable homey room with funky furnishings and adequate bathroom. The de Bruins, young, hardworking and very gracious, have chosen to spend their money on the dining room and food – and the latter, cooked by a Dutch chef, is delicious, better than most in France. Decorated with treasures from the de Bruins' Indonesian days, the dining room opens on to a terrace right by the canal. Ask for one of the two quiet rooms at the back, with canal views. There's a road at the front, and a resident peacock." "Friendly service, food of very high quality – red mullet with samphire, minty chocolate terrine. Excellent Dutch breakfast." (*Lynne and David Allen, Dr M Burke*)

Open All year except first two weeks Feb.
Rooms 4 double, 1 single – all with shower, radio.
Facilities Bar, restaurant, winter garden; terrace. Garden.
Location 29 km S of Amsterdam, 2 km S of Breukelen.
Restriction Not suitable for &.
Credit cards All major cards accepted.
Terms B&B: single 80 glds, double 100 glds; dinner, B&B: single 130 glds, double 200 glds. Set lunch 45 glds, dinner 60–80 glds; full alc 65 glds. Reduced rates and special meals for children.

Hotels often book you into their most expensive rooms or suites unless you specify otherwise. Even if all room prices are the same, hotels may give you a less good room in the hope of selling their better rooms to late customers. It always pays to discuss accommodation in detail when making a reservation.

DELFT Zuid-Holland   Map 9

Hotel Leeuwenbrug   *Tel* (015) 147741
Koornmarkt 16   *Fax* (015) 159759
Delft 2611 EE

A recent visitor found the buffet breakfast "sumptuous" and enjoyed his front room facing the canal, at this friendly B&B hotel in one of the best parts of Delft. Opposite, across the canal, are a picturesque footbridge and gabled houses – "The loveliest view from a hotel bedroom that I've ever had" (and at least one room has a flower-decked balcony). Some rooms are small. Only limited space in the lounge but a pleasant bar. (*Geo F Outland*, endorsed this year by *R and S Turner*)

Open 1 Jan–25 Dec.
Rooms 7 suites, 26 double, 4 single – all with bath, shower, telephone, radio, TV. 6 ground-floor rooms.
Facilities Lift. Lounge/bar, TV room, conference facilities.
Location Take Delft Zuid turning off Rotterdam–Amsterdam highway, and follow signs to Centre West. Paid parking next to hotel.
Credit cards All major cards accepted.
Terms [1990 rates] B&B: single 110–150 glds, double 135–175 glds, suite 150–175 glds. (No restaurant.)

THE HAGUE (DEN HAAG) Zuid-Holland   Map 9

Hotel des Indes   *Tel* (070) 3632932
Lange Voorhout 54–56   *Fax* (070) 3451721
Den Haag 2514 EG   *Telex* 31196

Built in 1856 as a baron's residence, this expensive and elegant hotel stands opposite the Lange Voorhout Palace in the city centre, facing a large tree-lined square. "An excellent place where old-fashioned values of courtesy and good service are allied with efficiency and good food (presented prettily in the modern manner)." "The more sumptuous ground- and first-floor bedrooms are better than the smaller ones higher up. But all are well equipped, with extras such as potions and fluffy bathrobes. Twin beds were narrow. Impressive flower-filled public rooms and pretty furniture. Service willing, but sometimes slow. Excellent breakfast, wonderful afternoon tea." (Endorsed by *Kate and Stephan Murray-Sykes*)

Open All year.
Rooms 7 suites, 15 double, 55 single – most with bath and shower, all with telephone, radio, TV. 24-hour room service. Ground-floor rooms.
Facilities Lift. Lounge, bar, restaurant; conference facilities. Park opposite.
Location Central, near palace. Private parking.
Credit cards All major cards accepted.
Terms B&B: single 387.50 glds, double 515 glds, suite 627.50–1,277.50 glds. Dinner, B&B: single 433.50 glds, double 625 glds, suite 682.50–1,332.50 glds. Set lunch/dinner 55–89 glds; full alc 75 glds. Reduced rates and special meals for children.

We asked hotels to quote 1991 prices. Not all were able to predict them in the late spring of 1990. Some of our terms will be inaccurate. Do check latest tariffs at the time of booking.

Parkhotel den Haag	*Tel* (070) 3624371
Molenstraat 53	*Fax* (070) 3614525
Den Haag 2513 BJ	*Telex* 33005

Large, sedate, centrally located, and nominated in 1990: "Set in a quiet street backing on to the royal park, it has been formed from several buildings, and floors are at different levels. Our palatial room, with a big window looking over the park, had matching fabrics, Japanese prints, a sofa, spotless bathroom. Breakfast is generous, including excellent ham and sumptuous ginger and raisin bread. No restaurant: of the six in the street, we recommend *Turners.*" (*F and I Walsh*)

Open All year.
Rooms 77 double, 37 single – all with bath and/or shower, telephone, radio, TV.
Facilities Lounge, bar, breakfast room; conference facilities.
Location Central, by Palace gardens. Garage, parking.
Restriction Not suitable for &.
Credit cards All major cards accepted.
Terms B&B: single 130–151 glds, double 190–217 glds. (No restaurant.)

HEEZE Noord-Brabant   **Map 9**

Hostellerie du Château	*Tel* (04907) 3515
Kapelstraat 48	*Fax* (04907) 3876
Heeze 5591 HE	

This ambitious restaurant-with-rooms (one rosette in *Michelin*) is in a pretty town with an impressive castle in pleasant wooded country to the south-east of the big, ugly industrial town of Eindhoven, headquarters of Philips. It is an attractive, long, two-storey yellow building with a Mediterranean touch: dark green shutters, flower-boxes, and lots of tables for outside eating and drinking. Two recent visitors have liked the bedrooms as much as the food: "Our large room had a sitting area divided from the sleeping area by fitted wardrobes. Its yellow and pale green colour scheme was pastel and soothing; lots of windows added to the light spacious impression. The staff were helpful and unpretentious, and our 'menu royale' included an outstanding fish souflé." "Furnishings excellent, service and housekeeping perfect. Dinner superb – *nouvelle* but with a local touch. Suite in attic well worth the extra money." (*Kate and Stephan Murray-Sykes, Cyril and Joyce Baily*) A warning: "The steep stairs to the bedrooms make them inaccessible to anyone with a walking problem."

Open All year except New Year. Restaurant closed Sat midday.
Rooms 4 suites, 8 double, 2 single – all with bath, shower, telephone, radio, TV, mini-bar, baby-listening.
Facilities Lounge, bar, 2 restaurants; conference/functions facilities; covered terrace. Large garden. Golf, tennis, riding, walking and cycling nearby.
Location 10 km SE of Eindhoven, between E34 and E25 motorways.
Restriction Not suitable for &.
Credit cards All major cards accepted.
Terms [1990 rates] B&B: single 160–190 glds, double 210–240 glds, suite 280 glds. Set meals 52.50–115 glds; full alc 75 glds. Reduced rates and special meals for children.

HILVERSUM Noord-Holland
Map 9

Hotel Lapershoek
Utrechtseweg 16
Postbus 609
Hilversum 1200 AP

Tel (035) 231341
Fax (035) 284360
Telex 73068

Near the Amsterdam–Utrecht motorway, on the edge of a city that houses the main Dutch TV and radio stations, a newly opened modern hotel, quite smart, with attentive and enthusiastic staff. Rooms vary in size but all are well furnished; some have water-beds. Very good nouvelle-ish food. 39 rooms, all with bath and shower; 30 more to be added in 1991. B&B double 195 glds. Full alc meals 45–65 glds. Recent nomination. More reports please.

LAGE VUURSCHE Utrecht
Map 9

De Kastanjehof
Kloosterlaan 1
Lage Vuursche 3749 AG

Tel (02156) 248
Fax (02156) 444

In a village north-east of Utrecht, near Baarn, a white-walled restaurant-with-rooms in a large garden beside a stream, amid wooded countryside. "We found it lovely," say readers this year, "all spic and span, attractively decorated. Our room had a balcony facing the garden. Wonderful Dutch breakfast served on a silver tray. The chef/owner, Wulf Engel, is personally rather cool, and restaurant service is not perfect, but the cooking is very good." *Michelin* rosette for sophisticated dishes such as biscuit d'avocats et de homard. (*John and Connie Partridge*)

Open All year except 31 Dec–5 Jan.
Rooms 10 – all with bath and/or shower, telephone, TV.
Facilities Restaurant, functions room. Garden; terrace.
Location 7 km SW of Baarn.
Credit cards All major cards accepted.
Terms [1990 rates] B&B double 155 glds. Alc meals (excluding wine) 87–107 glds.

LEEUWARDEN Friesland
Map 9

Oranje Hotel
Stationsweg 4
Leeuwarden 8911 AG

Tel (058) 126241
Fax (058) 121441
Telex 46528

Northern Holland's second largest city is an attractive place of canals and gabled houses. Here the *Oranje* is a sizeable and very spruce modern hotel, across a busy road from the station: rooms, however, are quiet as well as spacious. "Ours was clean, modern and lovely," says a 1990 visitor, "and the food in their beautiful restaurant was superb, notably the local fish." An earlier view: "Benign owner, friendly and relaxed atmosphere, an outstanding restaurant with *nouvelle*-ish dishes, and breakfast the best I've had in Holland." (*Diana Antonsen; Imogen Cooper*)

Open All year except Christmas.
Rooms 2 suites, 57 double, 19 single – all with bath, shower, telephone, radio, TV, baby-listening. 1 room suitable for &.
Facilities Lift. Lounge, bar, coffee shop, restaurant; conference facilities.

Location Opposite central station. Parking.
Credit cards All major cards accepted.
Terms B&B: single 140–180 glds, double 180–220 glds, suite 295 glds. Set lunch/dinner 35–79.50 glds; full alc 61.50 glds. Reduced rates for children sharing parents' room; special meals.

LEUSDEN Utrecht   Map 9

Hotel Huize den Treek   *Tel* (03498) 1425
Treekerweg 23   *Fax* (03498) 3007
Leusden 3832 RS

A 17th-century mansion in a quiet wooded lakeside setting near Amersfoort, a good base for cyclists. Public rooms – "an antique enthusiast's delight" – of faded elegance; some bedrooms modern, functional, and in need of refurbishment; others with antiques and gold brocade bedspreads, facing the lake. Excellent French cuisine. Service can be patchy. Closed 23 Dec–1 Jan. 18 rooms, all with bath and/or shower. Dinner, B&B 96 glds [1990]. Endorsed this year, but further reports welcome.

OISTERWIJK Noord-Brabant   Map 9

Hotel-Restaurant De Swaen   *Tel* (04242) 19006
De Lind 47   *Fax* (04242) 85860
Oisterwijk 5061 HT   *Telex* 52617

"A lovely hotel with excellent staff and beautiful food," says a 1990 visitor to this elegant and sophisticated hostelry on the tree-lined main street of the pleasant shady town of Oisterwijk. Others have called the food "wonderful" and "exquisite" (in *Michelin* this is one of the three restaurants in the whole country with as many as two rosettes). Other delights include a terrace in the front and a beautiful formal garden at the back; bedrooms are modern and comfortable, each with a small balcony. One reader, on her sixth visit, praised especially the breakfasts and the maid service, and the availability of free bicycles. "From the outside it looks like many other pleasant Dutch provincial hotels. But inside it's a veritable Aladdin's cave." (*Robert Bonner; also Mrs V Walker-Dendle, and others*)

Open All year except 2 or 3 weeks in July.
Rooms 18 double – all with bath, shower, telephone, radio, TV, air-conditioning.
Facilities Lift. Bar, lounge, restaurant; 2 conference rooms. Garden, terrace.
Location Central. Oisterwijk is 10 km NE of Tilberg. Parking.
Credit cards All major cards accepted.
Terms B&B: single 225 glds, double 275–345 glds. Set lunch 85 glds, dinner 110–165 glds. Weekend rates. Reduced rates for children; special meals on request.

Set dinner refers to a fixed price meal (which may have ample, limited or no choice on the menu). Full alc is the hotel's own estimated price per person of a three-course meal taken à la carte, with a half-bottle of house wine.

OOTMARSUM Overijssel   Map 9

De Wiemsel   *Tel* (05419) 2155
Winhofflaan 2   *Fax* (05419) 3295
Ootmarsum 7631 HX   *Telex* 44667

A spacious and sophisticated ranch-style hotel, set quietly in its own grounds, in gentle pastoral country near the German border just east of the pretty town of Ootmarsum. It consists of a number of low bungalow-style apartments attached to the main block which houses the restaurant; the modern decor is light and attractive. "Superbly luxurious, with excellent food and impeccable service" is a recent comment. Earlier ones: "Our room was lovely with a view over fields, and its bathroom was luxurious." (*Dr GM Chapman*) One correspondent considers the food to be even better at *De Wanne* which is down in the town and under the same management. The hotel has a stable of horses for guests' use, as well as a floodlit tennis court and a big indoor pool. It is 20 minutes' drive to the German casino across the border at Bad Bentheim.

Open All year.
Rooms 42 suites, 5 double (all also let as single) – all with bath, shower, telephone, radio, TV, baby-listening; many with terrace. 2 in villa, 50 metres from main building. 39 ground-floor rooms, some equipped for &.
Facilities Hall, lounge, bar, restaurant; conference facilities; indoor heated swimming pool, sauna, solarium, billiard room. Large garden with terrace, tennis, stables. Bicycles for hire.
Location 1 km E of Ootmarsum, which is 28 km N of Enschede.
Credit cards All major cards accepted.
Terms Rooms: single 130 glds, double 190 glds, suite 235–290 glds. Breakfast 23 glds. Set lunch 55 glds, dinner 80 glds. Reduced rates and special meals for children.

ROOSTEREN Limburg   Map 9

Hotel De Roosterhoeve   *Tel* (04499) 3131
Hoekstraat 29   *Fax* (04499) 4400
Roosteren 6116 AW

On the edge of a quiet village beside the Belgian border, north of Maastricht, a nicely converted farmhouse with plenty of rustic touches (beamed ceilings, log fire, painted furniture) but large modern bedrooms. Indoor and outdoor swimming pools, sauna; garden, patio; friendly staff, quite good, simple food. 45 rooms (10 in annexe), most with bath or shower. B&B double 120–140 glds. Alc meals 55 glds. Recent nomination. More reports welcome.

VALKENBURG Limburg   Map 9

Hotel Prinses Juliana   *Tel* (04406) 12244
Broekhem 11   *Fax* (04406) 14405
Valkenburg 6301 HV

Set in pretty countryside east of Maastricht, the historic and charming old town of Valkenburg has a ruined castle, Roman catacombs and many grottoes, and is now a flourishing summer resort. Its best hotel, though

t its largest, is the very superior *Prinses Juliana*, with cool modern decor.
has a garden, and a delightful shady terrace for summer eating; the
od, mainly traditional, wins a rosette in *Michelin*. "Dinner was superb,
rved slowly, but that's the way they like to run things," writes a 1990
sitor. "Service and welcome are friendly, and our large bedroom was
stefully furnished." The spacious restaurant has silver candelabra; here
ie *menu gastronomique* might include smoked duck with foie gras and
mb with spinach and truffles. The hotel is decorated in soft colours,
ith subdued lighting, and there's an open fire in the lounge. Bedrooms
e provided with trouser-press and hair-drier. Annexe rooms, previously
iticised, have just been refurbished. (*Stephen and Patricia Hawkey*)

pen All year. Restaurant closed Sat midday.
ooms 6 suites, 17 double, 2 single – all with bath and/or shower, telephone,
dio, TV. 8 in annexe across road.
icilities Lounge, bar, restaurant; conference facilities. Garden with summer
staurant.
ocation Central. Garage and open parking.
estriction Not suitable for &.
redit cards All major cards accepted.
erms Rooms: single 180 glds, double 225 glds, suite 300–340 glds. Breakfast
glds. Dinner, B&B 175–215 glds per person. Set lunch 55 glds, dinner 80 glds;
ll alc 115 glds. Special meals for children.

ASSENAAR Zuid-Holland   Map 9

uberge De Kieviet   *Tel* (01751) 19232
toeplaan 27   *Fax* (01751) 10969
Vassenaar 2243 CX

*NE outer suburbs of the Hague, a sophisticated, elegant and expensive
restaurant-with-rooms (Michelin rosette), much frequented by top diplomats
nd politicians. Great comfort, delicate modern colour schemes, flowery garden
rrace, very good food. 24 rooms, all with bath and shower, 250–395 glds.
reakfast 23 glds. Alc meals (excluding wine) 87–138 glds [1990]. Change of
vnership, renominated this year. More reports please.*

ELLERLOOI Limburg   Map 9

ostellerie de Hamert   *Tel* (04703) 1260
Vellerlooi 5856 CL   *Fax* (04703) 2503

his fairly expensive restaurant-with-rooms stands pleasantly amid lawns
nd tall trees by the banks of the wide Meuse (Maas), near the German
ontier in northern Limburg. A main road goes close by, but bedrooms
ice away from it. "The people of this little-known part of the
letherlands are more voluble and convivial than most Dutch, and
erhaps this contributes to the dining room's relaxed and pleasant
tmosphere and its excellent service from owner and staff. On a fine day
ou can dine on the terrace and watch the river flow past. The food is
ery rich, good but not exceptional – lots of high-quality expense-account
ngredients such as salmon, quail and the local asparagus. The cooking is
ld-fashioned, with lots of creamy vague-tasting sauces. None of your
puvelle plating in the kitchen, but carving at table. The place does not

have the feel or amenities of a hotel (no lounge) and is deserted in th
morning: breakfast was poor and its service brusque. The bedrooms a
comfortable, clean and neat, with some nice furniture, but have an air c
faded gentility." More reports welcome.

Open All year, but closed Tue and Wed 1 Nov–31 Mar.
Rooms 4 double – 2 with bath, all with radio.
Facilities Restaurant; 2 conference/functions rooms; 2 terraces (meals served
outdoors in fine weather). Garden leading to river.
Location 15 km N of Venlo on road to Nijmegen. Parking.
Credit cards All major cards accepted.
Terms [1990 rates] B&B: single 80 glds, double 130 glds. Set lunch/dinner 80–
95 glds. Alc meals 83–120 glds.

DE WIJK Drenthe   Map

Havesathe de Havixhorst   *Tel* (05224) 148
Schiphorsterweg 34–36   *Fax* (05224) 148
De Wijk 7957 NV

In a little-known part of the Netherlands, De Wijk is a village north-ea
of Zwolle, just off the motorway to Groningen – and here a reader ha
discovered this small 18th-century moated castle: "The red carpet leadir
to the front door gives way to marble inside. High ceilings, large windov
– pity about the muzak. Our room was clean and comfortable but nc
remarkable: the rooms are due to be refurbished very soon. The staff a
young, friendly and very professional. We opted for no-meat meals an
enjoyed fried quail egg, red pepper soup, herb soufflé, amid much else: a
was thoughtfully conceived, and breakfast was the usual robust Dutc
affair. I would recommend *Havesathe* for the food and welcome." (*Dian
Cooper*)

Open All year.
Rooms 8 double, 1 single – all with bath and/or shower, telephone, radio, monc
TV.
Facilities Lounge, 2 bars, restaurant; conference/functions facilities. Garden;
terrace.
Location 6 km SE of Meppel and 25 km NE of Zwolle. Parking.
Restriction Not suitable for &.
Credit cards All major cards accepted.
Terms [1990 rates] B&B: single 90 glds, double 140 glds; dinner, B&B 110–
127.50 glds per person. Reduced rates and special meals for children.

WITTEM Limburg   Map

Kasteel Wittem   *Tel* (04450) 120
Wittemerallee 3   *Fax* (04450) 126
Wittem 6286 AA   *Telex* 5628

"Europe's best breakfast", backed up by warm, personal service and onl
slightly let down by imperfectly kept rooms – that, again this year, is th
general verdict on this grey-walled 15th-century castle east of Maastrich
Renovated in neo-Gothic style, it is now an elegant restaurant-with
rooms (*Michelin* rosette), surrounded by a flower garden, ancient tree
and a pond with black swans. Reports in 1989/90: "Friendly and graciou
service (the staff immediately reached for our bags), breakfast a venerabl

feast, a large room with a lovely view, but it needed refurbishing."
"A lived-in family atmosphere: the slightly old-fashioned decor and the
personal attention of the Ritzen family give it warmth and cosiness. We
enjoyed the food very much." "The food is better than ever. But pity
about the restaurant's cigar and cigarette smoke – does *every* Dutchman
smoke? Breakfast super: it's a serious meal in Holland so allow an hour!"
This breakfast "comes with strawberries, cherries, pumpernickel, three
fruit breads, eggs, tomatoes – 'A real castle breakfast,' said my daughter",
while main meals could include ravioli filled with scallops, duck with
honey, grilled goat's cheese with quince sauce – mmmm! A royal red
carpet leads to the rooms. One reader took the turret suite, with window-
seats overlooking the moat, and found the sitting room and the grounds
all "gorgeous". (*Cathryn Bryck, K and S Murray-Sykes, P and J Temple, Diana
Cooper, and others*) Pity about the dripping tap and plastic shelf with
cigarette burns.

Open All year.
Rooms 12 double – all with bath, shower, telephone, radio, TV.
Facilities Lounge, bar, breakfast room, restaurant; conference/banqueting
facilities; terrace. Park with garden, river.
Location Between Maastricht (17 km) and Aachen (15 km). 2 km SW of Gulpen
on Maastricht road.
Restriction Not suitable for &.
Credit cards All major cards accepted.
Terms B&B double 190–250 glds. Set lunch 55 glds, dinner 80 glds; full alc
115 glds. Reduced rates and special meals for children.

****
Traveller's tale *For my main course I chose roast best end of Welsh
lamb in garlic and rosemary. When it arrived on one plate I sat and
stared at it. It was artistically arranged; it needed to be. There were five
tiny pieces of lamb, nine mange touts, four pieces of carrot, lozenge
shaped but approximately 3 × 1 × 1 cms, and a slab of mashed potato
approximately 6 × 5 × 1 cms. The latter had a beautiful pattern on top
but it still constituted only two mouthfuls. It is the first time I have felt
like measuring my food. Heaven help a hungry adolescent!*
****

****
Traveller's tale *Clearly the place had some pretensions to style. Well-
warmed plates for our main course were deftly placed, held between
spoon and fork with a "no touch" technique that would have done credit
to an operating theatre. There appeared to be only one set of serving
implements and I was wondering how the waiter was proposing to serve
my wife's poached salmon after my steak. However, more thought had
gone into the operation than I had imagined, as he dived into his trouser
pocket and triumphantly brought forth another spoon and fork.*
****

Norway

Ulvik Fjord Pensjonat, Ulvikl

ASKIM 1800   **Map 7**

Granheim Hotell   *Tel (09) 88.15.30*
Vammaveien 6

Useful as a stop-over, a small inn recently renovated with a new bedroom wing, in a town 50 km east of Oslo on road to Stockholm. Comfortable bedrooms with modern decor, relaxing atmosphere, good à la carte meals. Gentle hills, meadows, forests and inland lakes nearby; good cycling country. 31 rooms, all with shower. B&B: single 400–610 Nkr, double 580–730 Nkr. Recent nomination. More reports please.

BERGEN   **Map 7**

Augustin Hotel   *Tel (05) 23.00.25*
C Sundtsgt 24   *Fax (05) 23.31.30*
5004 Bergen   *Telex 40923*

A dapper small hotel centrally located near the harbour in a busy fjord-girt city. "The bedrooms are small but clean and neat. The large parlour and TV room, and delightfully decorated breakfast room and adjoining restaurant, make the hotel feel spacious. The staff are pleasant and helpful. The central location made it easy to explore the city on foot." (*JT Simon; also Lizbeth and Craig Anderson*)

Open All year except Christmas.
Rooms 28 double, 10 single – all with shower, telephone, radio, TV. 2 suitable for ᕦ.
Facilities Lounge, TV room, breakfast room, restaurant.
Location Central, near harbour. Public parking.
Credit cards All major cards accepted.
Terms [1990 rates] B&B: single 515 Nkr, double 750 Nkr. Set lunch/dinner 100 Nkr. Reduced rates for children under 12; special meals.

Myklebust Pensjonat   `BUDGET`   *Tel* (05) 31.13.28
Rosenbergsgt 19
5015 Bergen

Run by the friendly and efficient Wiig family, who speak good English, this unpretentious hotel occupies the upper floor of a block of flats, in a quiet but steep street fairly near the city centre. "Mrs Wiig, who weaves in the winter on looms on the ground floor, is charming, and so is her son," runs a letter this year. "Her interest in weaving can be seen throughout the house. Rooms are of high standard, and breakfast included eggs, sausage and cheese. Excellent value for money." Others have found the rooms "large, airy and clean". (*Ann and Sidney Carpenter*)

Open All year except Christmas, New Year and Easter.
Rooms 1 family, 3 double, 2 single – 3 with bath, shower; all with radio, TV.
Facilities Reception, breakfast room.
Location Central. Street parking.
Restriction Not suitable for ᕦ.
Credit cards None accepted.
Terms B&B: single 250 Nkr, double 350 Nkr, family room 480–680 Nkr. (No restaurant.)

Hotell Neptun   *Tel* (05) 90.10.00
Walckendorffsgt 8   *Fax* (05) 23.32.02
5001 Bergen   *Telex* 40040

Modern, well equipped and centrally situated, overlooking harbour and old market, but quiet at night. Soothing bedrooms, elegant restaurant with "delicious" food; generous buffet breakfasts. 120 rooms, all with bath and/or shower. B&B: single 995–1,195 Nkr, double 1,250–1,435 Nkr. Full alc 450 Nkr [1990]. Weekend reductions May–Sep. Endorsed but fuller reports welcome.

Hotel Park Pension   *Tel* (05) 32.09.60
Harald Hårfagresgt 35   *Fax* (05) 31.03.34
5007 Bergen   *Telex* 40365

This unpretentious family-run B&B hotel comprises two old houses two minutes' walk apart, in a quiet residential district near the university and an attractive park: it is 15 minutes' walk *down* to the city centre, but rather

1ore to climb the steep hill back. Public rooms are slightly fussily
urnished, but with some pleasant antiques. Our inspector's bedroom on
he top floor was small but comfortable; lower rooms are more spacious.
.eception was friendly and helpful. Breakfast was the customary
Jorwegian self-help cold buffet, with good coffee. More reports please.

Open All year except Easter and Christmas.
Rooms 16 double, 6 single – all with shower, telephone, radio, TV.
Facilities Breakfast room, meeting room.
Location 10–15 mins' walk from station. Parking.
Restrictions Not suitable for &. No smoking in breakfast room.
Credit cards Amex, Visa.
Terms B&B: single 550 Nkr, double 650 Nkr. Reduced rates for children. (No
estaurant.)

Hotel Victoria
Long Oscarsgt 29
1017 Bergen

Tel (05) 31.50.30
Fax (05) 32.81.78
Telex 42190

*Attractive white bow-windowed building, central and extremely comfortable.
Much modern art on display. Well-equipped bedrooms, with duvets or sheets
and blankets, as desired. "Splendid buffet breakfast. Friendly, helpful staff with
excellent English." 43 rooms, all with bath/shower. B&B: 940–990 Nkr. Set
meals 150 Nkr. Recent nomination. More reports please.*

IDFJORD 5783 | **Map 7**

'øringfoss Hotel **BUDGET**

Tel (054) 65.184
Fax (054) 65.297

*omfortable and welcoming white-washed hotel in lovely position at water's
1ge, in small village at head of Eidfjord, a branch of the great Hardangerfjord.
Jell situated for exploring Hardangervidda national park. Warm welcome from
wner. Pleasant sitting room and bar, with old photographs, interesting
ictures. Bedrooms in modern block at rear. Pretty, well-appointed dining room
verlooking water; evening meals available until 10 pm (unlike many Norwe-
ian hotels, which serve promptly at 7). Recommended for a brief visit, with
eservations about the food. 41 rooms, most with bath and shower. B&B: single
90 Nkr, double 550 Nkr [1990]. Recent nomination. More reports welcome.*

FJÆRLAND 5855 | **Map 7**

Hotel Mundal

Tel (056) 93.101
Fax (056) 93.179

Fjærland lies amid spectacular scenery at the head of a stretch of the
Sognefjord, Norway's longest and deepest. The trim white clapboard-
fronted *Mundal* sits here by the water, in the shadow of Norway's largest
lacier, the Jostedalsbreen. It has been run by the same family since it was
built in 1891, and the present owner's wife is English. "One of the best
otels of its type that we've stayed in," says one visitor this year. "The

owners have succeeded admirably in matching a modern hotel with th
looks of a typical Norwegian rural hotel. They take an interest in the
guests, and provide hot waffles, strawberries and cream at tea. The room
were excellent." Returning regulars have noted continual improvement
and have found the owners as kind and charming as ever. "The bedroom
are all different and all Norwegian in atmosphere. There is a library wi
English books, a billiard room and a music room with a piano. The food
plentiful and very good – for example fjord trout with butter sauce an
cucumber salad – and served punctually at 7 pm. There are antiques an
beautiful furnishings made by past members of the family. Even the sta
carpet is hand-woven." Olav Orheim, a grandson of the hotel's found
and a glaciologist who has led three Norwegian expeditions to Antarctic
will take guests to visit the glacier at some 1,500 metres. (*ME Oversb
Elizabeth Sandham*) Service, though kindly, can be slow, and a reporter th
year did not find the bedrooms very attractive.

Open 1 Apr–mid-Nov.
Rooms 2 suites, 24 double, 11 single – all with bath and/or shower, telephone.
Facilities Lounge, music room, library/billiard room, bar, 2 restaurants. Garden
on fjord; rowing boat free of charge; fishing; swimming for the hardy.
Location 180 km NE of Bergen. Reached by express boat service, ferry and bus.
Restriction Not suitable for &.
Credit cards None accepted.
Terms B&B 320–550 Nkr; dinner, B&B 490–720 Nkr. Set dinner 190 Nkr. Reduc
rates for children sharing parents' room; special meals on request.

GEIRANGER 6216   **Map**

Union Turisthotel   *Tel* (071) 63.0(
                                                              Fax (071) 63.1(
                                                              Telex 423:

An elegant family-run hotel in a small resort on the lovely mountain-back
Geirangerfjord, between Bergen and Trondheim. Simple but large rooms wi
fine views of the fjord, excellent indoor swimming pool, two large lounges, ve
good help-yourself smorgasbord. Closed Jan, Feb. 160 rooms, all with ba
and/or shower. B&B double 820–900 Nkr. Set meals 120–190 Nkr [1990]. Ne
nomination. More reports please.

LOM 2686   **Map**

Røisheim Hotell   *Tel* (062) 12.0:
Bøverdalen

High above sea-level on the ancient Sognefjell road, a group of picturesque tu
roofed 18th-century farm buildings, forming a hotel since 1858. Some bedroor
have painted wooden walls, but sparse furniture. Recommended for warmt
comfort, charming decor, good food, attractive public rooms, welcoming hos
Open 1 Apr–15 Oct. 25 rooms, 12 with bath or shower. B&B double 60(
750 Nkr. Set dinner 200 Nkr. Recent nomination. More reports please.

We need feedback on all entries. Often people fail to report on the
best-known hotels, assuming that "someone else is sure to".

NORDFJORDEID 6770   Map 7

Nordfjord Hotell   *Tel (057) 60.433*
POB 144   *Fax (057) 60.680*

Near a fjord and not far from the west coast and mountains, well placed for tours of the region. Modern Scandinavian in style with spruce furnishings; open-plan sitting rooms, spacious dining room; discos, billiards, sauna, large garden with tennis; fishing, excellent walks nearby. Recommended for friendly staff, well-equipped bedrooms, high standard of cooking. Closed 23 Dec–3 Jan. 55 rooms, all with shower. B&B: single 400–710 Nkr, double 590–1,000 Nkr. Set meals 90–190 Nkr. Recent nomination. More reports please.

OSLO   Map 7

Hotel Continental   *Tel (02) 41.90.60*
Stortingsgaten 24–26   *Fax (02) 42.96.89*
0161 Oslo 1   *Telex 71012*

This "venerable hotel" opposite the National Theatre, dating from 1900, has been in the same family for four generations and epitomises a certain traditional Oslo atmosphere. "It offers solid comfort as well as elegance," says a 1990 visitor, "even the small bedrooms have sofas. Edvard Munch liked it so much that he gave it nine drawings, which hang round the small brown bar. The hotel boasts Norway's most famous chef, Willy Wyssebach, who rules all its restaurants. Of them, the place to go is the downstairs *Theatercaféen*, where I ate tender reindeer fillet and a delicious cloudberry ice. It's called the last Viennese café in Norway, with strings playing in the afternoon, and is so popular that guests are expected to indicate an approximate leaving time when booking." This huge room has mirrors and a stuccoed ceiling supported by tall white columns. Another view: "The *Continental* retains a grave dignity, courtesy and friendly warmth. I could wax even more lyrical over the breakfast's cold table." The main dining room is classically formal, with chandeliers and serious waiters. Bedrooms are triple-glazed against street noise. (*Pepita Aris*)

Open All year except Easter.
Rooms 12 suites, 124 double, 43 single – all with bath, shower, telephone, radio, TV with video.
Facilities 2 lifts. Lounge, bar, restaurant, grill, café; conference/banqueting facilities; discothèque daily except Sun and Mon; terrace.
Location Central, between Royal Palace and National Theatre. Underground carpark.
Restriction Not suitable for &.
Credit cards All major cards accepted.
Terms B&B weekdays: single 1,285–1,470 Nkr, double 1,405–1,650 Nkr; weekends: single 545 Nkr, double 880 Nkr. Extra bed 100 Nkr (cots free).

> Always let a hotel know if you have to cancel a booking, whether you have paid a deposit or not. Hotels lose thousands of pounds and dollars from "no-shows".

Gabelshus Hotel
Gabelsgt 16
0272 Oslo 2

Tel (02) 55.22.6(
Fax (02) 44.27.3(
Telex 7407.

A friendly and moderately priced hotel on a tree-lined residential stree
not far from the centre of Oslo, with the city's excellent public transpor
only three minutes' walk away. "Fine and quiet," says a visitor this yea
"Meals were quite good, and breakfast kept us going for the whole day."
The lobby, decorated in dark wood, is like a rural hunting lodge
Bedrooms are clean and comfortable with an "understated and ver
restful decor. We had an early train to catch so the staff prepared
continental breakfast for us at 6.30 am." Meals are reasonably priced
good but not gourmet. (*Arnold and Joan Wolfe, Lizbeth and Craig Anderson*

Open All year except 7–17 Apr.
Rooms 32 double, 14 single – all with bath, shower, telephone, radio, T V.
Facilities Lift. Lounge, T V room, bar, dining room; conference facilities. Garden.
Location Between Bygdøy alle and Drammensv. 15 mins' walk from city centre;
bus and tram nearby. Parking.
Restriction Not suitable for &.
Credit cards All major cards accepted.
Terms [1990 rates] B&B: single 720 Nkr, double 950 Nkr.

Holmenkollen Park Hotel Rica
Kongeveien 26, Oslo 3

Tel (02) 14.60.9(
Fax (02) 14.61.9.
Telex 7209(

Set on a hillside outside Oslo, this Guide debutant is a large and unusua
ski-hotel, with a glittering modern extension tacked on to what looks lik
a red Chinese pagoda: "In the lee of the world's first ski-jump, nov
extended to a vertiginous height, here's a peaceful escape (out of the sk
season) from the centre of Oslo, with breathtaking views of the fjords o
two sides. The original hotel is a fine 19th-century wooden structur
painted red and blue, with a dragon neck on each rising gable: this was
Viking talisman. Modern blocks contain the bedrooms, each of which ha
a view over the fjord. In the old hotel, the dining room has a fin
marquetry ceiling. A buffet lunch of Victorian proportions included col
salmon raw, *gravad* or poached, and hot rolled shoulder of reindeer."
(*Pepita Aris*) More reports welcome.

Open All year except 21 Dec–2 Jan.
Rooms 8 suites, 79 double, 104 single – all with bath and/or shower, telephone,
radio, T V, air-conditioning. 2 suitable for &.
Facilities Lounges, bar, night club, restaurants; extensive conference facilities.
Indoor swimming pool, sauna, solarium. Skiing, good walks on Holmenkollen
hill.
Location NW of Oslo, 20 minutes by car from city centre or airport. Courtesy
coach into town.
Credit cards All major cards accepted.
Terms [1990 rates] B&B: single 595–1,195 Nkr, double 695–1,350 Nkr, suite
1,895 NKr. Set lunch/dinner 160, 180 and 195 Nkr, full alc 350–500 Nkr.
Weekend rates. Reduced rates for children sharing parents' room.

Please make a habit of sending in a report as soon as possible after a
visit when details are still fresh in your mind.

SKJOLDEN 5833   Map 7

Skjolden Hotel   *Tel* (056) 86.606
                                                          Fax (056) 86.720

Recommended for its lovely situation and good value, this square flat-roofed hotel (outwardly no beauty) stands at the end of the Lusterfjord, a branch of the long Sognefjord. It is popular as a base for hiking, fishing and other sports. Owned by the Galde family for 75 years, the hotel offers large sitting rooms furnished in a modern style, an open terrace, a fairly big garden, and a "very large and light restaurant serving plain, well-cooked food in substantial portions". Bedrooms are simply but comfortably furnished with light wood furniture and feathered duvets, though with poor insulation.

Open May–Sep.
Rooms 39 double, 16 single – all with bath, shower, telephone. Ground-floor rooms.
Facilities Lift. Lounges, bar, TV room, restaurant; terrace. Large garden. Fjord 20 metres, free rowing boats.
Location In the western fjords NE of Bergen, 75 km from Sogndal airport.
Credit cards Visa.
Terms B&B 300–400 Nkr. Set meals 140 Nkr.

STEINSLAND 5395   Map 7

Marsteinen Fjordhotell   *Tel* (05) 33.87.40
Sotra   *Fax* (05) 33.87.58

This Guide newcomer is a modern hotel in a lovely setting on an island west of Bergen, linked to it by bridge: "Very comfortable. Fish dishes are a speciality, and at the weekend you choose your fish from its pool. The menu was very good. There were some wild parties while we were there, including teachers singing action songs and Bergen shopkeepers whooping it up in a most un-Norwegian way. But we managed to sleep through it. Breakfast was a good buffet: lots of choice of fish. We enjoyed our stay. The rocks are magnificent." Modern decor; a log fire in the lounge. (*Theresa and John Stewart*)

Open All year.
Rooms 76 – all with bath and/or shower, telephone, TV.
Facilities Lounge, bar, restaurant, conference facilities. Gymnasium. Boats for hire.
Location West of Bergen, about 40 mins by car.
Credit cards Probably most accepted.
Terms [1990 rates] B&B: single 375 Nkr, double 550 Nkr. Set lunch 110 Nkr, dinner 120 Nkr.

TRONDHEIM 7011   Map 7

Grand Hotel Olav   *Tel* (07) 53.53.10
Kjøpmannsgt 48   *Fax* (07) 53.57.20
                                                          Telex 65035

"Is this the best breakfast in Norway?" asks its nominator. "I counted six sorts of marinaded herring, eggs cooked four ways, cold and hot meats.

Abdul Bastit, managing director, is also a skilled Pakistani chef. His hotel has three restaurants. It occupies one corner of a glassed-in shopping centre, sealed against the Norwegian winter. The bedrooms, each with a sofa in a separate sitting area, have a pleasant cosiness, and all the fabrics are of first-class modern design. In the all-marble bathroom, the underfloor heating was much appreciated. Rooms with double beds look into the courtyard; twin-bedded ones have an outside window. The hotel caters for business people rather than tourists, and is much less expensive at weekends." (*Pepita Aris*)

Open All year.
Rooms 106 – all with bath and/or shower.
Facilities Lounges, bar, 3 restaurants.
Location Central.
Credit cards Probably some accepted.
Terms [1990 rates] B&B: single 975–1,290 Nkr, double 1,155–1,470 Nkr. Set lunch 140 Nkr, dinner 198 Nkr.

Neptun Hotel and Bistro
Ths Angellsgt 12b

Tel (07) 51.21.33

A modern, newly renovated hotel in the centre of the historic cathedral city. "Our spacious bedroom, with four windows facing the street, was remarkable. The double bed, with a comfortable mattress in a creaking old bedframe, was in a curtained alcove. The furniture had been rescued from a Norwegian cruise ship built in 1908. More modern facilities included telephone and mini-bar. Most of the double rooms look over the street which was noisy; singles face the rear. The reception area was part of the bistro/restaurant and there was a lounge. We did not dine in the hotel but the à la carte meals seemed to be reasonably priced and adequate. The breakfast buffet offered a good choice including fresh fruit." (*Susan and John Aglionby*)

Open All year. Bistro/restaurant closed Sun evening.
Rooms 36 – all with bath/shower, telephone, radio, mini-bar.
Facilities Lounge, bistro/restaurant; banqueting room.
Location Central.
Credit cards Probably some accepted.
Terms [1990 rates] B&B: single 375–665 Nkr, double 590–790 Nkr. Dinner 70 Nkr Summer reductions.

ULVIK 5730   Map 7

Ulvik Fjord Pensjonat   BUDGET

Tel (05) 52.61.70
Fax (05) 52.61.60

A small guest house on the edge of an attractive village, now a popular resort, in western Norway on an arm of the Hardangerfjord, sheltered on three sides by impressive mountains. Run by Lilly and Odd Hammer, who speak excellent English, it has a white weatherboarded exterior and is separated from the road by a small garden. Pleasantly furnished lounges, spacious dining room: dinner, announced by a bell, is served punctually at 7 pm – "beautifully cooked by Odd Hammer, and served by Lilly and her assistant in a friendly, unhurried manner. No choice, but it included fresh sea trout, and second helpings were offered. Breakfast was the usual generous self-help buffet. Our bedroom was small but adequate, though lighting, except for the bedside lights, was rather poor. The private shower/loo was really too small, but the baths for general use were excellent. All the other guests were British; it is well situated for walking holidays." (*Francis and Susan Aglionby*)

Open 1 May–1 Oct.
Rooms 18 double, 2 single – 17 with shower. 7, with balcony, in separate wing.
Facilities 3 lounges (1 with TV), dining room. Garden.
Location 500 metres from centre. 44 km E of Voss.
Restriction Not suitable for &.
Credit card Visa.
Terms B&B 225–375 Nkr; dinner, B&B 290–440 Nkr. Set dinner 135 Nkr.

UTNE 5797   **Map 7**

Utne Hotel   *Tel* (054) 66.983
Hardanger   *Fax* (054) 66.950

Adored yet again this year ("by far the loveliest hotel we have ever stayed in"), the charming little *Utne* is Norway's oldest hotel (founded 1722) and has been run by the same family since 1787. Situated east of Bergen, on the Hardangerfjord, it is a white clapboard building, lovingly maintained, with flowers in all the public rooms, embroidered cushions, lace curtains, and lots of old painted Norwegian furniture. "Its setting is splendid, at the foot of a steep promontory where the Hardanger branches into two small fjords: high blue mountains across the water, sheer cliffs above it, a waterfall plunging down the cliff face and rushing through the village, apple orchards on each side. There are fine walks along the fjord in both directions or you can climb paths to the high pastures. The village is small and tranquil; the *Utne* stands in its centre opposite the boat landing. Behind it, on the hillside, is a small modern annexe. Fru Aga Blokhus and her staff, wearing the Hardanger costume, look after you with grace and enthusiasm." "We were made to feel as house guests in a gracious and charming country house." An inspector recently had "a comfortable, charmingly furnished room" and delicious, copious food. Meals are taken communally, which "brings back the art of conversation", according to one reader, while another has called it "enforced conviviality, not to my taste". (*Arnold and Joan Wolfe, Elizabeth Sandham*)

Open All year except Christmas and New Year.
Rooms 21 double, 3 single – 3 with bath, 15 with shower. 1 ground-floor room. 7 in annexe.
Facilities 3 sitting rooms, basement café, dining room; some off-season conference facilities; games room, badminton. Garden and terrace; sailing, fishing, boating, cycling and good walks.
Location At tip of Folgefonn Peninsula; at Odda cross bridge on to peninsula, or take ferry from Kvanndal or Kinsarvik.
Restriction Not suitable for &.
Credit cards All major cards accepted.
Terms B&B 275–460 Nkr; dinner, B&B (min 3 nights) 355–540 Nkr. Set lunch 125 Nkr, dinner 170 Nkr. Reduced rates for children; special meals on request.

> Don't let old favourites down. Entries are dropped when there is no endorsement.

VOSS 5700   **Map 7**

Park Hotell Voss   *Tel* (05) 51.13.22
Boks 190   *Fax* (05) 51.00.39
                                                       Telex 42587

*Voss is a well-known resort at the east end of Vangsvatn, in the heart of
beautiful fjord country – Sognefjord to the north, Hardangerfjord to the south –
a region of orchards, waterfalls, glaciers, winter sports. The* Park *is central; well
run, with attractive public rooms and bedrooms, "magnificent" buffet dinner
including four hot dishes, good breakfasts. Coffee bar always open. Bedrooms
"nice but small". 63 rooms. B&B double 900–1,250 Nkr. Set meals 150–225 Nkr.
Recent nomination. More reports please.*

****
* **Traveller's tale** *The best of the house rules was the one pinned up in the* *
* *bathroom. To avoid unnecessary noise – remember that "unnecessary* *
* *noise" – we were instructed to fill the bath slowly and – wait for it –* *
* *finish filling the bath using the shower-head, not the taps! Have you ever* *
* *tried to do this? Do you know how long it takes? The explanation for this* *
* *piece of high comedy was that the "architectural constraints" on the* *
* *building made the plumbing rather noisy. The plumbing was noisy; it* *
* *wasn't nightingales that kept us awake, but the sound of loos flushing,* *
* *and basins swishing. Breakfast is syncopated by a relay of flushing* *
* *lavatories.* *
****

****
* **Traveller's tale** *The rooms have barely enough room for two normally* *
* *sized adults with luggage. We had to pass around the bed to the window* *
* *and back to the wardrobe and bathroom in shifts.* *
****

Portugal

Casa do Barreiro, São Tiago da Cemieira

In a country where in remote spots one may be happy just to find somewhere to lay one's head, some general guidance on accommodation may be useful. A number of the better-known international hotel chains are represented in Portugal – Sheraton, Best Western and Trust House Forte, for example – mainly in larger urban and seaside areas. Sadly, as elsewhere, most lack the character or individuality that would earn them a place in these pages.

It is no accident that many entries in the Guide are hotels in the government-sponsored *pousada* chain, since, as with the *paradores* in Spain, they have often been created out of castles, monasteries and similar ancient monuments whose atmosphere or romantic situation is generally preferred by users of the Guide. There are also others, purpose-built, largely in a rural style, which are designed to cater for tourists in areas which lack other accommodation. Except for the deluxe *pousadas*, their amenities are rarely better than serviceable. It is also advisable to book as far ahead as possible; *pousadas* are becoming much used by coach tours and, in towns, by businessfolk.

However, two other forms of accommodation are well worth experimenting with – *estalagems* and *Turismo de Habitação*. The former are country inns not offering a full range of hotel services (though often falling not far short). Some are modern and featureless, but those in older buildings often amply compensate for their more basic appointments with their charm. Like the *pousadas*, the *estalagems* have individual tourist signs for guidance at the entrance to towns and villages.

Turismo de Habitação, a sort of upmarket bed-and-breakfast, is the Portuguese equivalent of the French *Château Accueil* except that it offers a more numerous and varied selection, ranging from manor houses (mainly in the north) to rather humbler dwellings. Some are small private hotels run in old family homes. Unfortunately *Turismo de Habitação* is not as efficiently organised as it should be. The descriptive literature (obtainable from Rua Alexandre Herculano, 51–30, PO Box 1329, 1200 Lisbon, Portugal) is sometimes out of date. To prevent disappointment you should stress that your booking is conditional upon the accommodation described being available. Check prices carefully: one user of this Guide, making a booking after his arrival in Portugal, was invited to pay in sterling at prices fixed the previous year which took no account of a subsequent 20% appreciation of the pound against the escudo! If you survive these hazards you could find yourself most hospitably received in an elegant *palacete* or *solar*.

AMARANTE 4600 Porto　　　　　　　　　　　　　　　　　　**Map 12**

Pousada de São Gonçalo　　**BUDGET**　　　　　　　*Tel* (055) 46.11.13
Serra do Marão　　　　　　　　　　　　　　　　　　　　*Telex* 26321

New to the Guide this year, a *pousada* midway between Amarante and Vila Real, "with breathtaking views from the bar, restaurant and front bedrooms", approached by a road "which winds steeply up an unforgiving mountainside bereft of life except for the occasional small home and a few trees. Clinging to the top of the mountain, the *pousada* has superb views towards the west. Inside it is warm and cosy with a comfortable sitting area, roaring fireplace and windows overlooking beautiful sunsets." "Comfortable lounge and bar, good restaurant with some notable Portuguese red wines on offer and a friendly and attentive staff – they came stalwartly to our rescue when we discovered a puncture on the morning of our departure. Simple but very adequate bedrooms (no TV etc)." "A good base from which to explore this area. Good food: unpretentious and sustaining. Amarante is charming and just outside Vila Real is Mateus, home of the rosé wine, an 18th-century country house in Italian style." (*Suzanne Carmichael, SW Bickford-Smith, AJE Brennan*)

Open All year.
Rooms 15 – all with bath, telephone.
Facilities Salon, dining room.
Location 19.5 km SE of Amarante on N15.
Credit cards All major cards accepted.
Terms [1990 rates] B&B double 5,750–9,000 esc. Set meals 1,950 esc.

We get less feedback from smaller and more remote hotels. But we need feedback on all hotels: big and small, far and near, famous and first-timers.

Zé da Calçada   `BUDGET`   *Tel* (055) 42.20.23
Rue 31 da Janeiro

Just by the old bridge, in the centre of a picturesque small town well
known for its pastries and vinho verde, a rustic restaurant-with-rooms
new to the Guide last year. The town has many 16th-, 17th- and 18th-
century houses with wooden balconies and wrought-iron grilles built in
tiers up a hillside overlooking the river Tâmega. "You eat well and
prettily on the riverside terrace. The restaurant has a house across the
narrow cobbled street containing seven bedrooms; all are refurbished,
with a touch of the Laura Ashleys. The topmost room, reached up four
flights of gleaming wooden steps, has a tiny terrace and three-star view of
the Italianate front of the church of San Gonçalo, the patron of conjugal
love – on his day the town celebrates by baking properly priapic
pastries." Sadly, a reader this year found the accommodation noisy and
was disappointed in the food: "The suckling pig was served cold from the
fridge." More reports please.

Open All year.
Rooms 7 double – all with bath, 1 with kitchen. All in building opposite
restaurant.
Facilities Restaurant; terrace.
Location In centre of town 64 km E of Oporto.
Credit cards All major cards accepted.
Terms [1990 rates] B&B double 6,150 esc. Alc meals 4,500 esc.

AZEITÃO 2925 Setúbal   Map 12

Estalagem Quinta das Torres   `BUDGET`   *Tel* (065) 208.00.01

Azeitão, on the old Lisbon–Setúbal road, consists of two small adjacent
villages set amid vineyards and olive orchards. It is a good base for
touring the Arrabida peninsula with its beautiful coastline and fine
beaches. The *Quinta das Torres* – "a poetic retreat" – is approached up a
long overgrown drive between flowering shrubs. It is a beautiful, rather
shabby old house, in its own grounds with a small ornamental lake, and
finely furnished with family antiques, portraits and prints including, a
visitor tells us this year, some of Portugal's finest 16th-century painted
tiles and "a curious and faded set of engravings of Scottish scenes".
Readers enjoy its "old-world charm" and the high-ceilinged bedrooms.
One is in a tower wing overlooking the courtyard with its Renaissance
fountain and orange trees, and has a four-poster bed "worthy of
Catherine of Braganza". "Dinner was excellent and exquisitely served;
breakfast is taken in the bedroom." "I stay again and again. It is still a
delightful experience; one of the most atmospheric places to stay in
Portugal." (*Alex Liddell*)

Open All year.
Rooms 2 suites, 6 double, 2 single – all with bath and shower. 2 bungalows in
grounds with kitchenette, lounge. Some ground-floor rooms.
Facilities Lounge, bar/TV room, restaurant; terrace. 30-acre grounds. Sandy
beaches 15 km.
Location 27 km W of Setúbal off N10; in village centre. Parking.
Restriction Not suitable for &.
Credit cards Access, Visa.

Terms B&B single: 6,000–7,000 esc, double 8,000–9,000 esc, suite 11,000–12,000 esc. Alc meals 2,500–3,500 esc. Reduced rates and special meals for children.

BATALHA 2440 Leiria | Map 12

Quinta do Fidalgo BUDGET | *Tel (044) 961.14*
Batalha

Charming bed-and-breakfast in white-washed, red-tiled house (the name means Squire's Farm), next to glorious 14th-century monastery. Recommended for "warm welcome from kind and helpful owners, 'old world' atmosphere, characterful bedroom, spotlessly clean, nice breakfast, unbelievable location – a most enjoyable place to stay". 1 suite, 4 double rooms – all with bath and/or shower. B&B: double 5,500–9,500 esc, suite 8,000–11,000 esc. (No restaurant.) New nomination. More reports please.

CALDAS DE RAINHA Leiria | Map 12

Pensão Portugal BUDGET | *Tel (062) 342.80*
Rua Almirante Candido dos Reis 30

A new nomination in a small town known for its thermal baths, off the main tourist track, just north of Óbidos: "A three-star residence with helpful and welcoming owners and staff, offering simple but comfortable accommodation and very good value for money. We had a well-kept room with solid furniture, comfortable double bed, and a light, airy bathroom with plenty of towels, changed daily. Breakfast was straightforward. The restaurant is run separately and here again value is good – it offers decent family cooking in a conventional setting, with well-spaced tables. Service is correct and friendly. There is a printed menu plus a daily offering of about six dishes including regional specialities and fresh fish. The hotel is a few yards from the main square in a pedestrian street. You can park in the square long enough to unload your luggage and there is a large free carpark three minutes' walk away." (*Mrs Sheilagh Jones*) More reports please.

Open All year except Nov and Tue.
Rooms 30 – most with bath or shower, all with telephone.
Facilities Lounge with TV, dining room. Sea 10 mins' drive.
Location Central.
Credit cards All major cards accepted.
Terms [1990 rates] B&B double 2,800–4,300 esc. Set meals 1,750 esc.

CANIÇADA 4850 Braga | Map 12

Pousada de São Bento BUDGET | *Tel (053) 64.71.90*
Caniçada, Vieira do Minho | *Telex 32339*

At SW end of Peneda-Gerês national park, with stupendous view of river valley and mountains, small welcoming pousada built in style of alpine chalet. Recommended for fabulous views, excellent food, smiling staff, and above-average room comfort. Extensive enlargement in progress, pool being restored.

Comparatively cheap as pousadas *go. 18 double rooms (as we go to press), with breakfast 7,000–12,900 esc. Set meals 2,900 esc [1990]. Re-nomination. More reports please.*

CASCAIS 2750 Lisbon	Map 12

Hotel Albatroz
Rua Frederico Arouca 100

Tel (01) 28.28.21
Fax 284.48.27
Telex 16052

A trim classical villa, built for the Portuguese royal family in the mid-19th century, now a hotel with a modern wing, and "highly recommended for understated luxury". "An ideal location for exploring Cascais on foot or Lisbon by train, yet right by the sea. It couldn't be better." The *Albatroz* is set on a rocky headland in this relatively unspoiled fishing port west of Lisbon; most rooms have panoramic views over the Bay of Cascais and the adjacent coastline. Recent reports have praised the locally popular restaurant, "very good if expensive", the immaculate linen and towels, and the comfortable beds. But there have been criticisms too – of snooty and inefficient service. Rooms on the street side are said to be noisy. More reports please.

Open All year.
Rooms 3 suites, 35 double, 2 single – all with bath, shower, telephone, radio, TV; most with air-conditioning and balcony. 2 ground-floor rooms.
Facilities Lift. Salon, bar, TV room, dining room; conference facilities; terrace. Music evenings. Unheated salt-water swimming pool.
Location On bay, near station. Parking.
Restriction Not suitable for &.
Credit cards All major cards accepted.
Terms B&B (continental in room, full in restaurant): single 15,500–32,500 esc, double 18,000–37,500 esc, suite 30,000–53,000 esc. Full alc 5,000 esc. Extra bed 6,500–11,500 esc.

FUNCHAL 9000 Madeira	Map 12

Quinta Penha de França   `BUDGET`
Rua da Penha de França 2

Tel (091) 290.87

A small hotel of real character, not far from the centre of busy Funchal, and one of only two in Madeira to enjoy a red *Michelin* entry (the other is *Reid's*, below). It is exceptional in Madeira's sadly overdeveloped capital, now crammed with many large and impersonal hotels. An old building, it has a charming garden; readers praise the peace and comfort, the friendly, hard-working staff, the leisurely, elegant breakfasts on the terrace, and the nicely furnished bedrooms, particularly the studios in the grounds and the rooms in the handsome new annexe. "The sea-water swimming pool is spotless; there are several restaurants within walking distance, but if you are unambitious you can survive pleasantly on the simple but tasty and well-presented meals – soups, salads, omelettes, dish of the day and fruit – served on the terrace." Last year our postbag was full of reports, this year there are none. May we have more, please?

Open All year.

Rooms 39 double – all with bath and/or shower, telephone. Some in annexe, some in garden studios.
Facilities Lounge, snack bar, terrace. Large garden with sea-water swimming pool; near sea and rock beach.
Location Central.
Restriction Not suitable for &.
Credit cards All major cards accepted.
Terms [1990 rates] B&B double 8,200–12,600 esc. (No restaurant, but light meals served.)

Reid's Hotel   *Tel* (091) 230.01
Estrada Monumental 139   *Fax* (091) 304.99
                                                   Telex 72139

Celebrating its centenary in 1991, *Reid's* is a large, grand and famous resort hotel on the outskirts of Madeira's capital. Set gracefully on a cliff above Funchal Bay, with magnificent semi-tropical gardens, it was built as a civilised warm weather retreat for European and British visitors, and was popular with Britons travelling throughout the Empire. Its visitor's book lists royalty and celebrities, but the hotel also welcomes the not-so-famous, including many packaged bookings. *Reid's* has numerous impressive and high-ceilinged public rooms, including a "superb pre-war style billiard room". There are two swimming pools on the level of the hotel, where a buffet lunch is served, and you can walk down through the gardens to swim in the sea or in a rock pool. All the sea-facing rooms have a balcony. The hotel keeps up the old traditions such as afternoon tea on a terrace and formal dress at dinner, where there is a pianist who plays "the tunes of yesteryear". It has many devotees who return year after year. Sadly, in this centenary year, our reports have been a mixed bunch. The high mark-up on wines and the charges for laundry and other extras elicited raised eyebrows; slow service, poor breakfasts and mean portions were other causes for complaint. Not everyone gave the thumbs down. A visitor this year was greeted by name at the airport, helped to a waiting taxi, and welcomed at reception "in a very friendly way, even though it was only our second trip". Where there were slips of service (none serious), she found the staff "racing to make things right". We'll hope for more happy returnees next year.

Open All year.
Rooms 15 suites, 130 double, 21 single – all with bath, shower, telephone, radio, baby-listening, air-conditioning. Suites have TV. 24-hour room service.
Facilities Lifts. 3 lounges, 2 bars, TV room, card room, 4 restaurants, billiard room; tea terrace. Large garden with 2 heated swimming pools, 2 tennis courts; lift and 3 flights of stairs down to sea with swimming pool, changing rooms and bathing platform; windsurfing, sailing, fishing etc.
Location 1 km from town centre.
Restriction Not suitable for severely &.
Credit cards All major cards accepted.
Terms B&B: single 22,500–31,100 esc, double 32,200–44,100 esc, suite terms on request. Half board 6,750 esc added to room rate; full board 10,150 esc added. 1-night bookings refused New Year. Reduced rates and special meals for children.

There are many expensive hotels in the Guide. We are keen to increase our coverage at the other end of the scale. If you know of a simple place giving simple satisfaction, please write and tell us.

GUIMARÃES 4800 Braga   **Map 12**

Pousada de Santa Maria **BUDGET**   *Tel* (053) 41.21.57
de Oliveira   *Telex* 32875
Largo de Oliveira

This ancient town at the foot of the mountains north-east of Oporto was
the birthplace in 1109 of Portugal's first king, Alfonso Henriques, and is
now a prosperous commercial city. It has two *pousadas*, the older of
which, in the centre of the old town and reached through a maze of
squares and narrow streets, was dropped last year for lack of feedback,
and is now brought back by two recent visitors: "I don't think its big new
sister [see below] should be allowed to eclipse it. It's more modest, but
just as good as ever." "Difficult to find as it is indicated by only the
smallest of signs, but the nicest hotel of our holiday. Our bedroom was
spacious, with a large tiled bathroom. Service was friendly." Furnishings
are elegant and comfortable; there are hand-made beds, embroidered
spreads and fine local linen. Good and plentiful regional cooking is
served in the dining room overlooking the market place. (*Alex Liddell,
Josie Mayers*)

Open All year.
Rooms 14 double or suites, 2 single – all with bath, shower, telephone, radio, air-
conditioning.
Facilities Lift. 2 salons, TV room, 2 bars, dining room; terrace.
Location Central, near church of Santa Maria de Oliveira. Private parking.
Credit cards All major cards accepted.
Terms [1990 rates] B&B: single 6,100–12,700 esc, double 7,700–14,200 esc. Set
meals from 2,500 esc. Reduced rates for children sharing parents' room.

Pousada de Santa Marinha   *Tel* (053) 51.44.53
Estrada da Penha   *Telex* 32686

This recently opened *pousada* entered the Guide last year, offering, as one
reader put it, "discreet luxury in an authentic and romantic setting". It is a
former monastery with beautiful cloisters and formal gardens, set above
Guimarães, overlooking the surrounding hills. Some comments: "One of
the most spacious, well-furnished *pousadas* we visited. It has enormous
reception rooms filled with antiques, oil paintings, luxurious carpets,
hand-painted wall tiles." "The atmosphere is rather formal but the public
rooms are a delight." "Some bedrooms are in a lower wing, modern,
luxurious, but impersonal; the most attractive ones are in the former cells,
comfortably furnished, each with private bath; ours had an unusual small
double window with a prayer stool. They look over the garden or the
town (we recommend the town view)." "The dining room is a somewhat
cavernous refectory with high ceilings and many archways. Food
typically *pousada*, i.e. acceptable but not noteworthy." "Service efficient
and unobtrusive, room quiet, gardens and woods to wander in. Peace and
tranquillity." (*Mr and Mrs RB Tait, and others*) One complaint: of long
delays as the kitchens were unable to cope with an ambitious à la carte
menu.

Open All year.
Rooms 2 suites, 48 double – all with bath, shower, telephone, radio, air-
conditioning.

Facilities Lift. Salons, bar, 3 dining rooms; conference facilities; courtyard, terrace, garden. 22 acres of garden and forest.
Location 2.5 km E of Guimarães on road to Penha.
Credit cards All major cards accepted.
Terms B&B: single 9,200–17,000 esc, double 12,000–20,000 esc, suite 22,200–33,000 esc. Set meals 3,000–4,100 esc; full alc 5,000 esc. Reduced rates for children under 8.

LAMEGO 5100 Vale do Douro   Map 12

Villa Hostilina   `BUDGET`

Tel (054) 623.94
Fax (054) 637.58
Telex 27731

A former farmhouse on a hill overlooking the old town of Lamego, in a wine-growing area near the Douro Valley. Readers for many years have enjoyed the gracious hospitality of the Santos family and the comfortable, up-to-date accommodation; there is a swimming pool, and a health centre (Instituto Kosmos) with a gym. Readers continue to praise the cheerful service, the charming hosts, and the breakfasts, "the best we had in Portugal, especially the caramelised plums and freshly made pineapple cake". There is no restaurant, but there are places to eat nearby, and guests may find themselves invited to eat with the Senhor in his private dining room – "a superb five-course dinner". "Our host was delightful, but conversation (in my laborious pidgin Portuguese and English) was a bit of a strain." Others have found communication easiest in French. (*John and Madeleine Westlake, Malcolm Seymour, and others*) Sadly, we have had reports of a five-storey apartment block being built right beside the *Villa Hostilina*, overlooking the grounds and villa. The pool has been opened to locals at certain times. More reports welcome.

Open All year.
Rooms 7 double – all with bath or shower, telephone, radio, TV.
Facilities Lounge, TV room, bar, dining room; health centre with gymnasium, massage, sauna etc. Garden with swimming pool (unheated) and tennis courts.
Location 1,000 metres from war memorial; private parking.
Restriction Not suitable for &.
Credit cards None accepted.
Terms B&B: single 6,000 esc, double 9,000 esc. Meals by arrangement 3,500 esc. (No restaurant.)

LISBON   Map 12

Hotel Príncipe Real
Rua da Alegria 53
Lisbon 1200

Tel (01) 346.01.16
Fax (01) 52.34.92
Telex 44571

Clean and comfortable, centrally located near Botanical Gardens, Avenida da Liberdade and the Bairro Alto, known for its restaurants and casas de fado. Top-floor restaurant with panoramic views. Rooms vary: all have TV, direct-dial telephone, air-conditioning; some have balcony; some are said to be small and dull. "The biggest surprise was a tray of tea and cake each day at 5 pm – and on the house!" English-speaking, friendly staff. 24 rooms, all with private facilities. B&B double 13,000–16,500 esc. Set meals 2,000 esc. July 1990 visitors warmly endorse but would be glad of more feedback.

Albergaria da Senhora do Monte　　　　　*Tel* (01) 86.28.46
Calçada do Monte 39　　　　　　　　　　　　　*Fax* (01) 87.77.83
Lisbon 1100

In residential area with colourful tile-faced houses, small shops and cafés, few
tourists. Slightly awkward to find, the exterior is more like a house than a hotel.
Inexpensive, simple accommodation – clean, comfortable bedrooms with modern
bathrooms; some, on ground floor, have terrace, others have marvellous views
over Lisbon. "We felt someone had placed the city at our feet – definitely the
place we'll stay next time." Basement bar, continental breakfasts, no restaurant.
28 rooms, all with bath and shower. B&B: single 7,500–9,000 esc, double 9,000–
12,000 esc, suite 11,000–15,000 esc. Recent nomination, now endorsed but more
reports welcome.

Hotel Tivoli Jardim　　　　　　　　　　　*Tel* (01) 53.99.71
Rua Júlio César Machado 7　　　　　　　　　*Fax* (01) 55.65.66
Lisbon 1200　　　　　　　　　　　　　　　　*Telex* 12172

A useful modern establishment, centrally located just off the city's main
avenue, and catering for the business and package trade as well as the
individual traveller. Readers enjoy the comfort, quiet location down a side
street, and general value for money. A correspondent this year praised
the tennis and swimming pool, but preferred dining at the *Tivoli Lisboa*
terrace restaurant at its more expensive sister hotel next door (with which
the *Jardim* should not be confused). "Nothing fancy, but adequate
facilities, friendly staff and pleasant atmosphere." (*GA McKenzie, and*
others)

Open All year.
Rooms 69 double, 50 single – all with bath, shower, telephone, radio, TV, air-
conditioning, mini-bar; baby-listening on request.
Facilities Lift. Hall, bar, restaurant. Gardens with Tivoli club, heated swimming
pool, tennis.
Location 10 mins from town centre, off Avenida da Liberdade, NE of Botanical
Gardens. Garage and carpark.
Credit cards All major cards accepted.
Terms B&B: single 13,500 esc, double 16,500 esc. Alc meals. Reduced rates for
children under 8; special meals.

York House (Residencia Inglesia)　　　　*Tel* (01) 66.24.35
Rua das Janelas Verdes 32　　　　　　　　　*Telex* 16791
Lisbon 1200

Converted 17th-century convent with annexe across the street (the latter
decorated in contemporary style). Its great attraction is its shady courtyard for
drinks and snacks – "an oasis of calm". Poor location 2 km from city centre, but
convenient for National Art Museum, embassies, and Tower of Belem. Front
rooms overlooking a tram route, are noisy; courtyard ones are quieter. Staff
friendly. 48 rooms, all with bath or shower. B&B double 17,000 esc. Set meals
2,200–3,500 esc. Complaints about food recur. More reports badly needed.

We are particularly keen to have reports on italicised entries.

MANTEIGAS 6260 Guarda   Map 12

Pousada de São Lourenço   *Tel* (075) 981.50
                                                          Telex 53992

Well placed for exploring the Serra da Estrela in the highest part of
Portugal, a welcoming *pousada* with splendid views. The location is
peaceful; the weather can be extreme (hot in the summer, nine feet of
snow in the winter). Formerly readers have enjoyed the charming, family
feel of the hotel, with cooking to match. "The locally costumed restaurant
staff could not have been nicer. After finishing a gargantuan dinner (we
had forgotten that the fish and meat courses would both come with
substantial vegetable accompaniment), we were presented with *pousada*
port on the house. The breakfast included fruit juice, fresh fruit, local
mountain cheese, ham, rolls, toast, madeira cake, butter, jams and good
coffee and tea." Rooms are pleasantly furnished, and there's a terrace
where guests can sit to enjoy the view over the valley. The local lake, near
Penhas Douadas, has a small beach surrounded by wooded slopes, with
clear water for swimming. Spring 1990 visitors had less happy experiences: poor food, overworked staff, some rooms too hot, others too cold,
we hope just a bad patch. . .

Open All year.
Rooms 23 double – all with bath, shower, telephone; some with balcony.
7 ground-floor rooms.
Facilities Bar, TV room, restaurant. Garden. Lake with beach and safe bathing
4 km.
Location 13 km N of Manteigas on estrada de Gouveia. An alternate route, less
steep, is 65 km.
Credit cards All major cards accepted.
Terms [1990 rates] B&B double 10,600 esc. Set lunch/dinner 2,250–2,400 esc.
Reduced rates for children sharing parents' room.

MARVÃO 7330 Portalegre   Map 12

Pousada de Santa Maria   *Tel* (045) 932.01
                                                          Telex 42360

Just six kilometres north of the main Lisbon–Madrid road, thus useful for
a stop-over, this *pousada* has been recommended by readers for many
years. It is simple, small and charming, built of stone with tile floors, in an
equally small and charming village on a rocky escarpment near the
Spanish border. The white houses and narrow cobbled streets are entirely
inside the walls of a castle over which the keep stands guard. You can
walk round the ramparts, looking within at the roofs, gardens, chicken
runs, kitchens and television sets, or without over the Sierra de Torrico in
Spain and the valleys below in Portugal. In the older part of the *pousada*
one reader had a small but pretty room with a balcony from which you
could see the hills, farms and Spain; others have liked the newer rooms,
with air-conditioning. This year, we are told, there will be more rooms
added in a building across the small street.

Open All year.
Rooms 1 suite, 12 double – all with bath, telephone, 5 with air-conditioning.
Some ground-floor rooms.
Facilities Lounge, TV room, bar, restaurant. Garden.

Location 27 km N of Portalegre on N521.
Credit cards All major cards accepted.
Terms B&B: single 6,100–12,700 esc, double 7,700–14,200 esc. Set lunch/dinner from 2,500 esc. Reduced rates for children under 12 sharing parents' room; special meals on request.

MONCHIQUE 8550 Faro   Map 12

Estalagem Abrigo da Montanha   **BUDGET**   *Tel* (082) 921.31
Corte Pereira/Estrada de Fóia

"The warmth of welcome was most endearing, they are all so anxious to please," wrote a visitor last year to this small family-owned restaurant-with-rooms, a pretty building in a flower-filled garden. The surrounding forests of cork, chestnut and eucalyptus trees are lovely, and the inn, which is halfway between the Algarve hill town of Monchique and the peak of Fóia, has fine views over green hills, lush valleys and the coastline. There is a main building and, at the other end of a pretty garden, a tier of apartments which readers have approved. "Breakfasts are memorable, with freshly squeezed orange juice and local honey; given notice they are willing to arrange any requested dish for dinner." "Try tamboril, which is 'frog fish', or chicken piri-piri, charcoal-grilled in a chilli spice." "Even in January, the flowers are in bloom. Saw 52 species of bird including a blue rock thrush. The owls sit on the roof each night and communicate with a clear night sky." The peacefulness of the surroundings is only slightly marred by a rock quarry down the hillside. Prices are very modest. (*Wm A Howard*) Warnings: It can be cold and wet in Monchique even when blazing on the coast, and the peace can be shattered when coach parties arrive for lunch.

Open All year.
Rooms 3 suites, 5 double – all with bath, shower, telephone. 2 suites in annexe with sitting rooms and fireplace.
Facilities Bar, restaurant, terrace. Garden.
Location About 25 km inland from Portimão. Hotel is 2 km from Monchique on road to Fóia.
Restriction Not suitable for &.
Credit cards All major cards accepted.
Terms B&B: single 8,000 esc, double 12,000 esc, suite 14,000 esc. Set meals 2,000 esc, alc meals 4,500 esc.

MONSARAZ 7200 Évora   Map 12

Estalagem de Monsaraz   **BUDGET**   *Tel* (066) 551.12
Largo de S Bartolomeu

Modest inn, charming in a simple, rural way, in old fortified town on a hilltop near the Guadiana Valley on the border with Spain, much visited by tours by day, but totally quiet at night. Overhanging beams, tiny stairs, rooms and bathrooms at different levels. Tiny dining room serving acceptable fare, handkerchief-size garden with mini swimming pool. 10 rooms, 7 with bath and shower. B&B double 3,700–4,200 esc. Alc meals (excluding wine) 1,500 esc. Recent nomination. More reports please.

ÓBIDOS 2510 Leiria   Map 12

Pousada do Castelo   *Tel* (062) 951.05
Paço Real   *Telex* 15540

A 15th-century castle, now a small, fairly expensive pousada, in the walls of picturesque medieval hilltop town, rather spoiled by tourism, near coast north of Lisbon. Well restored, "maintaining the ambience of an old castle without too many of the discomforts", but little in the way of public rooms. Most bedrooms overlook the delightful courtyard, not the view. Good regional cooking, staff pleasant and helpful. 3 suites, 6 double rooms, all with bath, shower, air-conditioning. Dinner, B&B double 14,050–20,800 esc [1990]. Advance reservations essential. Recently endorsed, but more reports welcome.

Estalagem do Convento   *Tel* (062) 952.16
Rua Dom João de Ornelas   *Fax* (062) 959.159
                                                Telex 44906

"Friendly hotel, good restaurant, good service, good value" begins a report this year on this part ancient, part modern white hotel just outside the walls of a showplace medieval hilltop town full of cobbled alleys and flower-girt piazzas. Readers have enjoyed rooms in the new annexe, which are "beautifully designed to blend with the older existing house. We had a very pretty room with balcony overlooking the countryside and city walls. Nice staff, and the best hotel food we had in Portugal." The rooms are comfortable (if somewhat tiny), the decor stylish, and the building has a lot of character. Writes another: "I'd be surprised if anyone failed to be enchanted." (*GA McKenzie, and others*) The only complaint: a monotonous menu that "began to pall after 2–3 days. Ideal for a short stay."

Open All year.
Rooms 4 suites, 26 double – all with bath, shower, telephone, radio; suites have TV.
Facilities 2 lounges, 2 bars, TV room, dining room.
Location In town centre. Parking.
Restriction Not suitable for &.
Credit cards All major cards accepted.
Terms B&B: single 5,500–8,000 esc, double 7,000–9,500 esc, suite 11,500–15,000 esc. Set lunch, dinner 2,200–3,100 esc, full alc 5,600 esc. Reduced rates for children; special meals.

OPORTO 4000   Map 12

Hotel Infante de Sagres   *Tel* (02) 200.81.01
Praça D Filipa de Lencastre 62   *Fax* (02) 31.49.37
                                                Telex 26880

"A splendid old-style Anglo-Portuguese hotel", the grandest in town, "where the British connection is still appreciated, and where you can find superb ports and the best vinho verde outside the Tras es Montes". Many visitors confirm this previous verdict. "We endorse all praise for this most serious of hotels. Service is extraordinarily attentive, both indoors and out; and you can forget all parking problems (how Oporto has them!)

once the doorman has taken over your car keys. The rooms, public and private, are luxuriously furnished in keeping with another era." "Bustling outside, but inside, quiet, and with a luxury that is hard to find now." "The patio and first-floor terrace were a boon in the middle of a hot city." (*Malcolm Seymour, Mr and Mrs RB Tait, and others*) The hotel was originally built by a textile magnate to accommodate his clients. The restaurant specialises in French and "good traditional" Portuguese dishes, but also grilled salmon and roast beef "English style".

Open All year.
Rooms 4 suites, 60 double, 16 single – all with bath, shower, telephone, radio, TV, air-conditioning.
Facilities Lift. Lounges, bar, restaurant. Garden. Sandy beach with safe bathing 15 km.
Location In city centre, near Avenida dos Aliados. Parking arranged.
Credit cards All major cards accepted.
Terms B&B: single 19,000–21,000 esc, double 22,000–25,000 esc, suite 50,000–90,000 esc. Set lunch/dinner 4,000 esc; full alc 9,000 esc. 50% reduction for children under 8 sharing parents' room; special meals.

PALMELA 2950 Setúbal   Map 12

Pousada de Palmela   *Tel* (01) 235.13.95 and 235.04.10
                                                           Telex 42290

This small and pretty white-walled town stands in tiers on the northern slopes of a hillside, 43 kilometres south of Lisbon. Here a convent, built in 1423, has been transformed into a state-run *pousada*, liked by readers especially for its setting and its location. "High above the beautiful town with its houses cascading down the slopes, surrounded by the plains and olive groves, and in the distance the coastline in clear view. Our room afforded splendid views over the plains towards Évora. The swimming pool, open during the summer months, is in a delightful location, in a low-walled courtyard. The cloisters are wonderful, full of the most exotic and vivid array of plants." "Beautifully maintained, unbelievable view! Excellent food (all eight of our meals very tasty), helpful and friendly waiter, large elegant room (we had four people in ours). A wonderful experience." Another reader warmly praised the breakfasts but was rather less enthusiastic about dinners: "Not the hotel's strong point, but it is worth its entry for the position alone." Another correspondent this year recommends a walk around the castle "where there are artist's studios and a medieval chapel". (*CA Hahn, and others*)

Open All year.
Rooms 28 double – all with bath, shower, telephone, radio, TV, air-conditioning, mini-bar. Some ground-floor rooms.
Facilities Lift. Lounge, bar, TV room, dining room; conference room; art gallery. Large grounds with unheated swimming pool and children's play area. Sandy beaches with fishing, safe bathing and life-guard nearby.
Location 7 km from Setúbal in centre of village; signposted. Parking for 40 cars.
Credit cards All major cards accepted.
Terms B&B: single 8,300–15,500 esc, double 10,800–17,500 esc. Set lunch/dinner 2,650–3,600 esc; full alc 4,200 esc. Reduced rates for children; special meals.

Hotels are dropped if we lack positive feedback. If you can endorse an entry, we urge you to do so.

PONTA DELGADA 9500 Azores   Map 12

Hotel de São Pedro   *Tel* (096) 22223
Largo Almirante Dunn   *Telex* 82602
Ponta Delgada, São Miguel

Our only hotel in the Azores, the former townhouse of a wealthy orange importer, on the beautiful island of São Miguel. "The countryside is like a lush, giant garden, with rows of hydrangeas separating the fields, blue-green lakes dotting the volcanic landscape, and pineapple and tea plantations. The pavements of Ponta Delgada are made from squares of white marble and black lava arranged in artistic patterns. The hotel, a 19th-century building with green shutters and awnings, has white and black volcanic stones decorating its windows and doors. Inside, there are handsome antiques and comfortable chairs; the floors are polished wood and the tones are warm. The bedrooms are simply and handsomely furnished; some have views towards the quay. The dining room, with white-clothed tables and fresh bird of paradise centre-pieces, serves fair food, but service was excellent, and the fresh pineapple for dessert exquisite." (*Suzanne Carmichael*) A combination of French and English works as a *lingua franca*. More reports please.

Open All year.
Rooms 6 suites, 17 double, 3 single – all with bath and/or shower, telephone, TV. Some on ground floor.
Facilities Lift. Lounge, bar, 2 restaurants. Garden. Beach 10 mins by car.
Location 5 mins from centre, opposite inner harbour. Parking.
Credit cards All major cards accepted.
Terms B&B: single 8,300 esc, double 9,700 esc, suite 18,200 esc. Set lunch/dinner 1,800–2,100 esc. No charge for children under 3; special meals.

SAGRES 8650 Faro   Map 12

Pousada do Infante   *Tel* (082) 642.22
                    Telex 57491

On the most south-western tip of all Europe, a starting point for the great Portuguese navigators in the 15th century, a modern purpose-built *pousada* ideal for rest and relaxation. "For us the high point was sitting outside our room having tea as we looked at the waves crash on the adjacent cliff. There is striking scenery visible both from the hotel and from the cliffs within a drive of just a mile or two." Readers have praised the meals – "not at all bad, and served to perfection" – and the staff. Sagres is a good base from which to explore the Algarve, though the early or late season can be chilly with strong Atlantic winds. Fish is landed daily at the port, and there are good seafood restaurants nearby. (*CA Hahn, and others*) Plumbing fixtures are said to be due for honourable retirement.

Open All year.
Rooms 2 suites, 21 double – all with bath, shower, telephone, radio, TV, air-conditioning, balcony.
Facilities Lounge, bar, restaurant. Garden with terrace, swimming pool, tennis court. Sandy beach 100 metres; safe bathing and fishing.
Location 35 km W of Lagos. Follow *pousada* signs in Sagres.
Credit cards All major cards accepted.

Terms [1990 rates] B&B: single 8,300–15,500 esc, double 10,800–17,500 esc, suite 13,500–23,000 esc. Set lunch/dinner 3,000 esc; full alc 4,800 esc. Reduced rates for children; special meals by arrangement.

SÃO BRÁS DE ALPORTEL 8150 Faro — Map 12

Pousada de São Brás `BUDGET` *Tel* (089) 423.05
Telex 56945

In a small town of Moorish origin, high on a hill with beautiful views towards Faro and the sea, a *pousada* that has pleased readers in the past for its comfort, reasonable prices, good service and smiling, friendly staff. It has also won praise for its simple food done in the regional style, with particularly good local fish. Some rooms are large, with a balcony; others are small but adequate: "Ours had recently been decorated most tastefully – but had no view as it was at ground level." There is a cosy bar and a swimming pool, and the location is quiet.

Open All year.
Rooms 23 – most with bath/shower, telephone.
Facilities Salon, restaurant. Garden with swimming pool.
Location 19 km N of Faro, 2 km N of São Brás de Alportel on the Lisbon road.
Credit cards All major cards accepted.
Terms [1990 rates] B&B: single 5,500–11,500 esc, double 7,000–12,900 esc. Set lunch/dinner from 2,150 esc.

SÃO TIAGO DA GEMIEIRA 4990 Ponte de Lima — Map 12

Casa do Barreiro `BUDGET` *Tel* (058) 94.19.37

"A guest house on a gentle slope, looking down over its own vineyards to the Lima valley, one of the *Turismo de Habitação* group (see introduction to this section). The *Casa* is rectangular, with a central court. There are many painted tiles, including a tiled description of its history going back to 1643, erected when the building was restored in 1928. Furnishings are rustic and antique and the house has a delightfully rural character with a very agreeable swimming pool next to the hen-run. The front rooms overlooking the vines are the nicest, though they have basins and loos but not bath or shower – but there is a large and well-equipped bathroom serving them; they also overlook the road, but it is not busy. The back rooms are self-catering duplexes, which might be a godsend for a young family, but to my mind are lacking in atmosphere. No restaurant, but snacks are available." (*AWT Liddell*) More reports please.

Open All year.
Rooms 1 suite, 6 double, 2 single – 6 with bath and shower. 2 with wc.
Facilities Salon, TV room, bar, games room. Garden with unheated swimming pool.
Location 4.5 km from Ponte de Lima.
Credit cards None accepted.
Terms [1990 rates] B&B: single 6,100 esc, double 7,200 esc. (No restaurant.)

> If you have difficulty in finding hotels because our location details are inadequate, please help us to improve directions next year.

SINTRA 2710 Lisbon   Map 12

Quinta da Capela   *Tel* (01) 929.01.70
Monserrate

Immortalised by Byron in *Childe Harold*, this famous hill town is set
dramatically against the north face of the serra. This manor house, four
kilometres up the old road to Colares, was rebuilt after the 1755
earthquake, and is now an inviting country inn, tastefully restored. "It is
lovely – light and airy public rooms, very clean, pretty pink breakfast
room, smallish bedrooms (but not poky), and fantail doves in a garden
with a pond and orange grove. Friendly staff." "Superlative, and good
value. On the edge of a wooded hill, with lovely views. Magical peace:
breakfast from 8 am up to noon, and it's the only hotel I've ever been in
without a single admonitory notice. A big and beautiful garden and the
absence of formality make one feel one is staying in a friendly Cotswold
manor house." "The decor is a judicious mixture of ancient and modern.
There is no restaurant, but omelettes and sandwiches are readily
produced. Impeccably clean and civilised; I would rather stay here than at
the *Palácio de Seteais* (q.v.) at twice the price." One reader this year
encountered plumbing problems and "only just hot enough water", and
didn't like the music in the lounge. "The garden *is* impressive," she
wrote, "the best feature."

Open 1 Mar–15 Nov.
Rooms 3 suites, 10 double – all with bath and/or shower (not all *en suite*) and
telephone. 3 self-catering cottages in the garden. Some ground-floor rooms.
Facilities 2 lounges, dining room, bar; gym and sauna. Large garden with very
small unheated swimming pool; sandy beaches, fishing nearby.
Location 4 km W of Sintra on old Colares road (follow signs to *Palácio de Seteais*
through Sintra), past Palace of Monserrate.
Credit cards All major cards accepted.
Terms B&B: single 13,500 esc, double 16,500 esc, suite 18,500 esc. Reduced rates
for children sharing parents' room. (No restaurant.)

Quinta São Thiago   *Tel* (01) 923.29.23
Estrada de Monserrate

A 16th-century manor house down a long rough private road, the *São
Thiago* is owned and run by Teresa Braddell – Portuguese, Spanish and
American by birth and English by marriage. "Mildly eccentric" to some,
"a bit over the top" to others, the *quinta* offers bedrooms individually
furnished with antiques and bathrooms decorated with hand-painted
tiles. "The bedrooms are charming, though some are fairly small. Family
collections of porcelain and silver and photographs are displayed
throughout the house." Once or twice a week Mrs Braddell organises a
home-cooked dinner: "She is a splendid cook and we especially enjoyed
the best fish from the market, superbly presented, and some lovely
puddings." "Evening meals are like successful dinner parties, eaten at a
huge refectory table loaded with candles and flowers. Music figures
largely." At other times, guests are advised on restaurants in the area.
Nearby are lovely walks with plenty of birdlife and wild flowers – "We
had some trouble convincing Mrs Braddell that we actually wanted to
relax in the sunshine in her beautiful garden." (*Frances Roxburgh, and
others*) No recent reports. More welcome.

Open All year except Christmas, Jan and Feb.
Rooms 1 suite, 8 double – 8 with bath, 1 with shower. 1 ground-floor room.
Facilities Drawing rooms, library, TV room, music room with dancing, bar. Patio, garden with swimming pool and tennis court.
Location 4 km W of Sintra, off road to Colares. After *Hotel Seteais*, first turning right, then down 300 metres.
Credit cards None accepted.
Terms [1990 rates] B&B: single 12,000 esc, double 13,000 esc, suite 18,000 esc. Light meals 1,000–3,000 esc, 5-course meal 3,500–4,000 esc. Low season 10% reduction. Special meals for children.

Hotel Palácio de Seteais   *Tel* (01) 923.32.00
Rua Barbosa do Bocage 8   *Fax* (01) 923.42.77
                                                                Telex 14410

About a mile away on the Colares road there sits a regal hotel, built a year before Byron's birth (he who later immortalised the town). It is one of the few deluxe country houses in Portugal – "A beautifully proportioned classical mansion with an elegant formal garden on one side and a series of terraces, lemon groves and wilder gardens spilling down the hillside on the other. Everything is spotless. The staff are friendly and considerate, yet discreet. The salons have fine tapestries and exceptional murals and, like the bedrooms, are carefully furnished with antiques." A recent report praised the well-equipped bedrooms ("big bowls of fresh fruit, towelling gowns, even a safe") and the food – international hotel fare, but with "particularly good soups, a traditional Portuguese dish in each course, delicious Portuguese white wine, and excellent pastries". The swimming pool is heated all year and there are fine walks to the Monserrate gardens and in the hills around. Views from the front of the hotel up to the Pena Palace, "floodlit at night, very romantic"; and from the back, down over farmland and little hamlets to the (indistinct) sea. (*CA Hahn, and others*)

Open All year.
Rooms 1 suite, 17 double – all with bath, shower, telephone; TV, baby-listening on request. Some ground-floor rooms.
Facilities Lift. Salons, bar, TV room, restaurant (piano and harp music); terrace. Garden. Heated swimming pool, tennis courts and riding centre. Beach 10 km.
Location 1 km W of Sintra on Colares road. Parking.
Credit cards Probably all major cards accepted.
Terms B&B: single 23,500 esc, double 25,000–30,000 esc, suite 35,000 esc. Set meals 4,600 esc. Reduced rates for children, special meals on request.

Villa das Rosas   *Tel* (01) 923.42.16
Rua António Cunha, 2–4

Attractive and architecturally interesting 19th-century guest house a kilometre from centre on road to Ericeira. Recommended for beautifully furnished bedrooms – "period furniture yet modern as well" – and "excellent, friendly service". Pleasant garden, tennis court. Breakfasts served in communal dining room. Owners enjoy helping guests plan visits to nearby beaches, villages, restaurants, and will serve dinner given one day's notice. 7 rooms, all with bath or shower, 3 in garden cottage with kitchen. B&B: single 6,000–11,000 esc, double 7,000–12,000 esc. Set meals 4,000 esc [1990]. Recent nomination. More reports please.

VALENÇA DO MINHO 4930 Viana do Castelo   Map 12

Pousada de São Teotónio   *Tel* (051) 222.42
                                                     Telex 32837

*On 17th-century ramparts of Vaubanesque frontier fortress, with views of river
Minho border with Spain and Spanish cathedral of Tuy, pleasant welcoming
pousada with airy lounge and restaurant. "Clean and comfortable public
rooms, great views." Readers have enjoyed river salmon and broa, the local
bread made with cornmeal. Valença gets many tourists, but the Minho valley
offers gentle classical landscapes; it's well placed for a stop near the main road
into Portugal from the north. 16 rooms – all with bath and shower. B&B double
7,000–12,900 esc. Set meals from 1,900 esc. In italics for lack of recent feedback.
More reports needed.*

VIANA DO CASTELO 4900 Viana do Castelo   Map 12

Hotel de Santa Luzia   *Tel* (058) 828889
Santa Luzia   *Telex* 32420

"One of the most beautifully sited hotels in Europe." Five kilometres
from one of the showplace towns of northern Portugal, with sweeping
views of the river, valley and Atlantic coast, this hotel, recently
refurbished in art deco style, returns to the Guide after an absence of
some years. It is recommended for the "warm welcome, rooms with huge
balconies, good service, generous breakfast and excellent value". It has a
garden, tennis court, and outdoor pool; the beach is eight kilometres
away. "Not imaginatively run, but the hotel has a sort of 'period
nostalgia' and is the best in the area. Many readers would be enchanted."
(PC Cheshire, A Liddell)

Open All year.
Rooms 3 suites, 52 doubles, all with bath and/or shower, telephone, radio; some
with TV.
Facilities 2 lounges, card room, TV room, bar, restaurant. Outdoor swimming
pool. Large garden with swimming pool, tennis court.
Location 5 km from town (small train). Parking.
Restriction Not suitable for &.
Credit cards None accepted.
Terms B&B: single 5,500–14,000 esc, double 7,100–15,700 esc, suite 11,500–
22,000 esc. Set lunch/dinner 2,500 esc (2 courses), 3,500 esc (3 courses). Reduced
rates for children sharing parents' bedroom.

VILA NOVA DE CERVEIRA 4920 Viana do Castelo   Map 12

Pousada de Dom Diniz   *Tel* (051) 954.01
Praça da Liberdade   *Telex* 32821

This unusually atmospheric *pousada*, like a village within a village, was
brought to the Guide by an enthusiastic recommendation from an
American travel writer who was there in December: "This quiet town
centred on a small square is at the foot of a mountain on the bank of the
Rio Minho which divides Portugal from Spain, and not far from the sea.
To reach the hotel we walked up a cobbled path through a double walled

gate to the interior of the walled city which, except for the church, is entirely owned by the *pousada*. Our bedroom was part of a series of rooms built directly out from the ancient fortress wall. It was large, with a bathroom, separate sitting room, well-stocked refrigerator and private courtyard. The dining area was in a large modern building with views of the river, the sea, and Spain; other public rooms are in a converted old building. We were served dinner by a waiter and waitress who were charming and friendly, and the food was grand." A reader this year endorses the recommendation but warns that the modern dining room, built mainly of glass, suffers in summer from an almost constant beating down of the sun. Venetian blinds obscure the view one has come for. "Perhaps air-conditioning will eventually solve the problem. In the summer it's an extremely uncomfortable sauna."

Open All year.
Rooms 3 suites, 26 double – all with bath/shower, telephone, TV.
Facilities Lounge, 2 bars, library, dining room, banqueting room; terraces, patios.
Location In town centre. Hotel registry in small office facing square.
Credit cards All major cards accepted.
Terms [1990 rates] B&B double 10,800–17,500 esc. Set meals from 2,300 esc.

****
* **Reader's complaint** *It irritates us when people describe visits to hotels* *
* *as "like staying with friends". You stay with your friends to enjoy their* *
* *company – you expect to help with the washing up and to make your own* *
* *bed. In a hotel we do not expect to have to fraternise with strangers* *
* *(who may or may not be delightful). We expect to be looked after* *
* *professionally. And we all know that guests, like fish, stink after three* *
* *days!* *
****

Spain

Hotel Ses Rotges, Cala Ratjada

The splendour of many of the buildings is the big lure of the *paradores*, Spain's state tourist hotels. There were 88 of them at the last count, criss-crossing the country. Almost all are housed in historic buildings of considerable diversity: castles as different as those at Olite and Bayona, grandiose former monasteries like León or Santiago de Compostela and pleasant rural houses like that at Argomaniz. Here you are sure of a safe haven – air-conditioned, comfortable, spacious – and lunch until about five in the afternoon and dinner until at least ten at night. Like every other eating place in Spain, they offer a set meal of three courses with wine, which is good value, and an à la carte menu. But when Señor Emilio Gomez Calcerrado was put in charge of *parador* restaurants a few years ago, he encouraged them to serve regional wines and food and use local recipes, and you will find these set out on the right-hand side of the menus. Prices compare so well with luxury lodgings elsewhere that it is tempting never to stray outside this comfortable circle. Many visitors to Spain stay nowhere else. In the end one tires of them because they are cocooned away from Spanish people and life outside. It is also possible to travel for a third of the price.

If sleeping cheaply but eating well is your policy then, in town, two-star *hostals*, many of which are "sleeping only" hotels, may suit you. These hotels can be quite spacious and comfortable, with *en suite* bathrooms. Some but not all have a breakfast room. Breakfasting in a bar is a Spanish habit anyway. In any event, it is hardly ever worth booking half board at hotels which do have restaurants – financially or otherwise.

In the countryside many weary miles can pass while you look for accommodation at the end of the day. Here your best bet may be the large *mesón*. These restaurants offer a reasonable selection of country dishes and often have half a dozen rooms, with loos and hot showers *en suite*.

Simpler still, and more romantic, are the *hospederias* attached to monasteries. They are usually in remote places of considerable beauty, such as mountain foothills, and Navarra in particular has been developing the ones in their region. Built for pilgrims and people on retreat, they are very cheap and also quite jolly. Most are open only in summer, and some are so simple that they have no telephone. However, at Montserrat, inspiration for Wagner's *Parsifal*, it is advisable to book in advance.

LA ALBERCA 37264 Salamanca   Map 12

Hotel Las Batuecas   `BUDGET`   *Tel (923) 43.70.09*
Carretera Las Batuecas s/n

Comfortable two-star hotel in fairly rural situation 76 km SW of Salamanca on edge of national monument village in lovely mountain country. Garden and private parking. Recommended for well maintained, roomy bedrooms and "unusually good public rooms". Food well and freshly cooked, if unexciting, and good value, but bar and restaurant service somewhat uneven. 24 rooms, all with bath or shower, double 4,100–5,000 pts. Breakfast 350 pts. Set meals 1,200 pts [1990]. New nomination. More reports please.

ALMAGRO 13270 Ciudad Real   Map 12

Parador de Almagro   *Tel (926) 86.01.00*
Ronda de San Francisco   *Fax (926) 86.01.50*

A converted 16th-century convent in a small town on the open plain of *La Mancha*, 190 kilometres south of Madrid – a short detour off the main road south to Granada, and an important milestone on the route taken by Don Quixote in Cervantes's epic. The town has many fine 16th-century buildings with heraldic facades and gutter pipes shaped like serpents, and a splendid main square. The *parador* is "a delightful calm oasis, beautifully furnished in the public areas with handsome dark chests and tables, lots of attractive pottery, and pleasing pictures and tapestries on the walls. Our bedroom was large, extremely comfortable and well equipped." "Nothing elaborately decorated or modern. In spite of its austere look my room, a former cell, had everything I needed. Meals are taken in the refectory which still has the pulpit where a Sister would read while others ate." "Top of our ten *paradors* – good regional food, attentive and courteous service." Breakfast is an "excellent buffet". (*Mrs KE Rawes; Mrs EH Prodgers, WK Reid*)

Open All year.
Rooms 55 rooms – all with bath and/or shower, telephone; some with air-conditioning. 5 on ground floor.
Facilities Bar, salon with TV, 2 restaurants; conference rooms. Garden with swimming pool.
Location Central (*parador* is signposted). Parking.
Credit cards All major cards accepted.
Terms [1990 rates] (Excluding tax) Rooms: single 5,600–6,800 pts, double 7,000–8,500 pts. Breakfast 800 pts. Set lunch/dinner 2,500 pts.

ANTEQUERA 29200 Málaga   Map 12

Parador de Antequera   *Tel* (952) 84.02.61
Paseo Garcia del Olmo   *Fax* (952) 84.13.12

Little more than an hour by car from Málaga airport, a useful stop on the way to Seville, this modern *parador* is on the outskirts of an old white-walled town – "a living, noisy place, but genuine Andalusia" – up in the hills behind Málaga and useful for exploring the Andalusian countryside away from the frenzy of the coast. It is designed rather in Swedish style with split-level reception areas and first-class furnishings. The bedrooms are large, and the interior courtyards and public rooms have decent modern furniture and antiques. It is liked again in 1989/90 for the food, which is mainly Spanish traditional, the dining room with well-spaced tables, the "beautifully displayed" breakfast buffet, the large swimming pool, and the helpful and friendly staff. (*Diana Sumner, Juliet and David Sebag-Montefiore*) Only niggle: some dishes a bit greasy.

Open All year.
Rooms 55 double – all with bath, shower, telephone, air-conditioning.
Facilities 3 lounges, TV room, bar, dining room; conference room. Garden with swimming pool.
Location Off N342 between Granada and Jerez de la Frontera. Hotel is on the outskirts of town. Parking.
Credit cards All major cards accepted.
Terms [1990 rates] (Excluding tax) Double room 6,500–8,500 pts. Breakfast 900 pts, set lunch/dinner 2,700 pts.

BAGUR 17255 Gerona   Map 12

Hotel Aigua Blava   *Tel* (972) 62.20.58
Playa de Fornells, Aigua Blava   *Fax* (972) 62.21.12
                                                 Telex 56000

Built in the style of a typical Catalan village round a small fishing beach and harbour, *Aigua Blava* (the name means blue water in Catalan) has been a Guide favourite since its first entry in 1979. It has an exceptional return rate; many couples and families make an annual pilgrimage. There is a particularly strong British following. Its charm is due partly to its setting, amid trees and rocks, on various levels, on a specially lovely stretch of coast, far from our stereotyped image of the Costa Brava. It has "literally grown from a fisherman's hut, extended in such a way that you never see the whole place at one go – and everything is in excellent taste. Nothing kitsch – all fresh, spotless and loved." And the "lovely large pool, attractive public rooms, well-maintained tennis court" and "friendly and helpful" staff also play a big role in its success story. Children are warmly welcomed. For many, the highpoint is "the really lively nightlife that starts at midnight at the pool bar and continues with dancing and singing till the wee hours". Xiquet (pronounced Chickee) Sabater, the youthful septuagenarian owner, is "a great charmer, around the place all the time exuding warmth and setting the tone for his staff". (*HR, A and C Raphael, Sally Kibble, and others*) When the hotel is full, there are two sittings at dinner (8.30 and 10), with an à la carte menu in the Grill Room. Service can sometimes be hurried, and the menus are on the bland side, international rather than regional. The hot-water system sometimes fails in the evening rush-hour.

Open Apr–Oct.
Rooms 14 suites, 67 double, 8 single – all with bath and/or shower, telephone; 17 with air-conditioning, 4 with T V, some with balcony. All in 5 different buildings.
Facilities 4 lounges, 2 bars, 4 restaurants, T V room; conference and banquet rooms; boutique, hairdresser. Gardens with tennis (floodlit after dark), volleyball, paddling pool, swimming pool (disco by pool every night in season); children's play area. Sand and rock beaches with safe bathing and water sports. Golf 7 km.
Location 4 km SE of Bagur, 8 km E of Palafrugell. Garage and parking.
Restriction Not suitable for &.
Credit cards Access, Amex, Visa.
Terms (Excluding tax) B&B: single 5,400–6,750 pts, double 7,700–11,600 pts, suite 12,000–15,800 pts; half board: single 6,450–8,100 pts, double 11,200–16,600 pts, suite 16,600–20,900 pts. Set lunch/dinner 2,600 pts; full alc 4,200 pts. Reduced rates for children under 7; special meals.

BAÑALBUFAR 07191 Mallorca Map 12

Hotel Mar I Vent BUDGET *Tel* (971) 61.80.00
Calle Major 47–49

A small, inexpensive hotel in a fishing village on the rugged west coast of Mallorca, popular with readers since our first edition. There are fine views of the sea from the hotel and its swimming pool. You can also bathe from a tiny cove about 15 minutes' stroll away by taking the winding paths through the terraced tomato fields; the hills behind the hotel offer exhilarating walking, too. Run by a brother and sister, Tony and Juanita Vives, it has been in the same family for four generations. It still retains some older features, in spite of considerable modernisation. There is antique furniture; the comfortable lounges have English books (the Viveses speak excellent English) and many of the guests are British. Bedrooms are furnished in local style: some are small, but all are bright and airy. "The balconies are delightful and the bathing cove uncrowded and beautiful." "Don't expect luxury – but the hospitality is great and the ambience enchanting." "Dinner was a pleasant experience with good wine and straightforward home-cooking." (*J Shapland, and others*) Warning: there is a house rule of up-to-bed by 11.30 – and sometimes earlier. Lunch is served only on Sunday, and the restaurant is closed on Sunday night; lunch is available at a café down the road.

Open 1 Feb–25 Nov. Restaurant closed for lunch except Sun, for dinner Sun.
Rooms 16 double, 3 single – all with bath, telephone, balcony. 8 in adjoining annexe. Some on ground floor.
Facilities 2 salons (1 with T V), bar/restaurant. Terrace with swimming pool. Sea bathing.

Location 24 km NW of Palma, at entrance to village. Parking.
Restriction Not really suitable for &.
Credit cards None accepted.
Terms B&B: single 4,215 pts, double 5,685 pts; dinner, B&B: single 5,915 pts, double 9,085 pts. Set lunch/dinner 1,700 pts. 10–20% reduction for children sharing parents' room; special meals.

BAYONA 36300 Pontevedra — Map 12

Parador Conde de Gondomar
Carretera de Bayona

Tel (986) 35.50.00
Fax (986) 35.50.76
Telex 83424

Famous as the Atlantic port that first received news of Columbus's discovery of America, Bayona lies 21 kilometres south of Vigo. This white-walled "absolutely beautiful" *parador* is splendidly set high above the sea, a mock *pazo* in the public grounds of the old Monte Real fortress and governor's palace; the old walls and tower remain, but the hotel itself is thoroughly modern. It is large, on two floors only – be prepared for long walks through corridors. Huge tapestries and suits of armour adorn the main staircase. The bedrooms have traditional furnishings, good lighting, comfortable beds, and well-equipped bathrooms. It is worth asking for a sea view, preferably overlooking the bay. "A lovely place to break your touring holiday. Peaceful, but only five minutes' walk from town. You can digest your breakfast with a three-kilometre circuit of the ramparts." Another reader warns that tourists also enjoy the ramparts, and out of curiosity visit the pool ("which in the event was closed – and stagnant – a great disappointment"). The food is judged "good", but some prefer eating in the bar rather than the more formal dining room, or visiting some of the seafood restaurants in town. (*SC Jones-Parry, and others*) The plumbing is said to be archaic.

Open All year.
Rooms 2 suites, 110 double, 12 single – all with bath, shower, telephone, radio; 20 with TV. Some ground-floor rooms.
Facilities Salons, TV room, bar, 3 restaurants; conference facilities. Park with swimming pool, tennis court and children's play area. Beach nearby with bathing and fishing.
Location On coast, 21 km SW of Vigo by C550. Garage and parking.
Credit cards All major cards accepted.
Terms [1990 rates] (Excluding tax) Rooms: single 5,500–7,300 pts, double 9,000–12,000 pts, suite 14,500–19,250 pts. Breakfast 900 pts, set lunch/dinner 2,900 pts. Full alc 3,500 pts. Reduced rates and special meals for children.

BENAOJÁN 29370 Málaga — Map 12

Molino del Santo
Bda Estación s/n

Tel (952) 16.71.51
Fax (952) 87.43.78
In UK (071) 283 0878

A British couple, Andy Chapell and Pauline Elkin, own and manage this small hotel high in the Andalusian mountains in the national park of Grazalema, and two hours from the coast. It entered the guide in italics last year; warm endorsements now earn it a full entry. It is a sympathetically converted old watermill about ten minutes' walk below the village, in flower-filled gardens beside a stream. The setting is "spectacular mountain country, great if you want somewhere quiet and secluded; walking, bird watching, mountain biking or just lounging, with occasional dips in the pool, are all easy. There's an above-average selection of books. Group excursions are run on alternate days. Some rooms have sun-trap terraces, worth asking for, though you pay a bit extra. Don't be misled by the informal, almost amateurish style: it's an extremely well-run hotel. Food is good, sensibly not too ambitious. Breakfast and afternoon tea are British style." "Friendly informality combined with efficiency. House party atmosphere; guests generally dine at two large tables, but you can opt for separate seating. Cooking is peasant style, with a choice of a meat, a fish and a vegetarian dish; there is also an à la carte menu. Bedrooms are simply furnished, but the beds are comfortable." "We liked the fact that you didn't need a car; Benaoján's station is only three minutes' walk away. Staff are friendly, helpful and patient, children are welcome." (*Robert Jones, Ann Webber, Laura Mason; also Sheilagh Jones*) Not a place to avoid the British, however, and some minor gripes: "I'd have liked a few more salads or imaginative vegetables; the swimming pool is smaller than it looks in the brochure."

Open Mid-Mar–mid-Nov.
Rooms 9 double or family, 1 single – all with shower.
Facilities Lounge, bar, library, terrace, indoor and outdoor dining areas, garden with swimming pool.
Location On edge of village 15 mins' drive SW of Ronda.
Restriction Not suitable for &.
Credit cards Access, Visa.
Terms B&B: single 3,500–7,000 pts, double 5,500–10,000 pts. Set dinner 1,980 pts; full alc 2,200 pts. Reduced rates and special meals for children.

CALA RATJADA 07500 Mallorca   **Map 12**

Hotel Ses Rotges   *Tel* (971) 56.31.08
Calle Rafael Blanes 21   *Fax* (971) 56.42.53

A newcomer to the Guide in 1989, and warmly endorsed since, this hotel is in a small fishing resort on the north-east coast of Mallorca, near the mighty Artá caves and adjoining clean sandy beaches. It is an old stone mansion of some character, gracefully converted. The decor is inviting; fabrics and pictures have been chosen with care. The *patron*, Gérard Tétard, is French and his food has earned a *Michelin* rosette. "It is undoubtedly the best in this part of the island." "We can truthfully say that we could find no fault. Arriving at 1 am, we found the tone was set by Madame Tétard's being there to greet us and a cold meal being served in our room. The bedroom was spacious and furnished in the Spanish style; the bathroom was well equipped and the heating/air-conditioning unit a welcome addition on cool April evenings. The food, as expected, was of the highest standard. In the summer one eats out in a lovely courtyard. A highly efficient small hotel run by a hardworking, dedicated and delightful young couple." Mme Tétard does not allow casual dress in the restaurant, "so she has ended up with clients who come for the best food in beautiful surroundings". (*B Carr, also Ann and Sydney Carpenter, and others*)

Open End Mar–end Oct. Restaurant closed Wed morning in Oct.
Rooms 2 suites, 20 double, 2 single – all with bath, shower, telephone, air-conditioning.

acilities 2 salons (1 with TV), bar, restaurant. Terrace for summer meals. Sea
00 metres; sandy beach nearby.
ocation Fourth street to the right after sign Cala Ratjada.
Restriction Not suitable for &.
Credit cards All major cards accepted.
Terms B&B: single 6,045 pts, double 7,540 pts, suite 10,515 pts; dinner, B&B:
ingle 7,850 pts, double 11,150 pts, suite 14,125 pts. Set menu 2,095 pts. Full alc
,500–5,500 pts.

CARMONA 41410 Seville   **Map 12**

Parador Alcázar del Rey   *Tel* (954) 414.10.10
Don Pedro   *Fax* (954) 14.17.12
                                                     Telex 72992

Carmona is 33 kilometres east of Seville, and a useful base from which to
visit that lovely city where driving is difficult – there is a good bus service.
The *parador* is built inside the massive walls of the ancient Moorish *alcázar*
on the top of a hill, with marvellous views over the wide green plain of
the Guadalquivir valley, with mountains on the horizon. Moorish
influences prevail in the decor – pierced wooden shutters and doors in the
public rooms, a patio with a fountain in the middle. The interior walls,
white-washed or of honey-coloured brick, are complemented by black or
brown wood-and-leather furniture. The swimming pool is "a model of
good taste, with natural brick and grass surrounds, arcades to protect you
from the sun, white-painted garden furniture and colourful flowers".
Dinner, served in the baronial dining hall, generally receives good
reports; the buffet breakfast is praised, and so is the service. But only the
top-floor rooms have a balcony with views; there is some traffic noise if
windows are opened; insulation between rooms and between floors can
be poor and some visitors have thought the bedroom furnishings not up
to the standard of other *paradores*. And one reader this year is strongly
critical of the *parador*'s system of charging – since he was given no chits to
sign there was no way he could check his final bill.

Open All year.
Rooms 51 double, 8 single – all with bath and/or shower, telephone; 25 with
adio, TV; some with balcony. 6 ground-floor rooms.
acilities Lifts. Hall, sitting room with TV, bar, dining room; room for functions
nd banquets; air-conditioning. Patio and garden with swimming pool.
ocation In town centre (hotel is signposted). Parking.
Credit cards All major cards accepted.
Terms [1990 rates] (Excluding tax) Rooms: single 8,475–9,200 pts, double 10,500–
1,500 pts. Breakfast 900 pts, set lunch/dinner 2,900 pts.

CAZORLA 23470 Jaén   **Map 12**

Parador El Adelantado   *Tel* (953) 72.13.03
                                                     Fax (953) 72.10.75

A *parador* built 26 years ago, 27 kilometres from the pretty village of
Cazorla (shady squares, winding narrow streets, balconies cascading with
flowers, towering mountains all around). It was new to the Guide last
year. "The distance seems much more because the road through the
glorious national park winds up and up, and the *parador* is sited at around
4,000 feet with mountains still climbing up behind it. It has a rather

austere monastic feel about it. There is a large lounge with a huge wood fire and a pleasant dining room serving excellent soups and traditional main courses. Our bedroom was spacious and adequate, but a little dark. It is worth asking for one with a view. The place would be heaven for the serious walker – wild goats with huge curly horns reputed to be nearby." More reports please.

Open All year except 24 Jan–end Feb.
Rooms 33 double – all with bath, shower, telephone, TV.
12 in annexe. 4 on ground floor.
Facilities Bar, lounge with TV, restaurant. Garden, outdoor swimming pool, children's play area.
Location 27 km from Cazorla, in the mountains. Follow sign Carretera de la Sierra.
Credit cards All major cards accepted.
Terms [1990 rates] (Excluding tax) Rooms 7,500–9,000 pts. Breakfast 900 pts. Set lunch/dinner 2,700 pts; full alc 3,000 pts. No charge for child in cot.

CHINCHÓN 28370 Madrid   Map 12

Parador de Chinchón   *Tel* (91) 894.08.36
Avenida Generalisimo 1   *Fax* (91) 894.09.08

Dropped from our 1990 edition, this converted monastery is brought back to the Guide following an impassioned plea from a reader *in situ*: "Pray restore it forthwith! Of all the *paradores* we know it remains a firm favourite. The building is delightful, a typical restoration of *parador* type which means that without too much attempt at 'authenticity' the architects have conserved the style and feel of the building. Perhaps the furnishings in the bedrooms are a bit too authentic in that they are painted to look old and slightly grubby which may put some people off. The atmosphere is peaceful, the staff smile and are helpful, the food is of the best *parador* standard and the house wine is local. The gardens in spring and summer are a delight to sit in, the pool is large and shady, the bedrooms are comfortable and well appointed. And it stands bang in the middle of a lively and as yet unspoiled small town, just off one of the nicest Plaza Mayors in Spain." Other visitors in 1990 write in much the same vein, praising the "very friendly" reception, the food, the colonnaded swimming pool, and appreciating the secure lock-up garage. (*P Harryman; also Dr and Mrs A Robson, E Ring, C and P Manning*)

Open All year.
Rooms 2 suites, 36 double – all with bath, shower, telephone, radio, TV. Some on ground floor.
Facilities 2 bars, salon, TV room, restaurant. Garden with swimming pool.
Location Central. Chinchón is 52 km SE of Madrid.
Credit cards All major cards accepted.
Terms [1990 rates] (Excluding tax) Rooms: single 8,000–9,800 pts, double 10,000–11,000 pts. Breakfast 900 pts. Set lunch/dinner 2,900 pts.

The success of this guide in North America has led to sister publications on American and Canadian hotels based on the same principles. Readers with recent experience of good hotels in North America are urged to send their nominations to Sandra W Soule, America's Wonderful Little Hotels and Inns, PO Box 150, Riverside Avenue, Riverside, Conn. 06878, USA.

CORDOBA 14003 Map 12

Marisa **BUDGET** *Tel* (957) 47.41.44
Cardenal Herrero 6

A picturesque bed-and-breakfast hotel in the old district of the Juderia, dropped last year after criticism of poky rooms and poor plumbing. But it boasts a marvellous situation, across a narrow street from the Mezquita itself. Now re-recommended for friendly and helpful staff, "simple but exquisitely clean rooms, extra pillows; all with smiles. No restaurant, but one eats well in a shaded courtyard with splashing fountain at *Mesón Bandolero*, a two-minute walk away." From another reader: "Superb location and value for money. But air-conditioning in bedrooms inadequate in high summer. Able to book by telephone in French; Berlitz Spanish not understood." (*Dr FP Woodford, Chris Chapman*)

Open All year.
Rooms 23 double, 5 single – all with bath, shower, telephone, air-conditioning. Ground-floor rooms.
Facilities Salon, bar.
Location Central, by Mezquita. Parking arranged.
Credit cards Access, Diners, Visa.
Terms B&B: single from 3,500 pts, double from 5,100 pts. (No restaurant.)

COSGAYA 39539 Cantabria Map 12

Hotel el Oso Pardo *Tel* (942) 73.04.18

In the Picos de Europa National Park in northern Spain, an area renowned for winter sports, mountaineering, horseback riding, trout and salmon fishing. Handsome stone hotel in spectacular setting, with inviting public rooms, lovely swimming pool, good tennis court, spotlessly clean modern bedrooms (some with balcony). Helpful and attentive staff. Recommended "for lovers of mountain scenery, bird watching, and comfort in out-of-the-way places". Closed 1 month (Jan/Feb). 36 rooms, all with bath and shower. B&B: single 4,100–5,200 pts, double 6,000–7,100 pts [1990]. (Excluding tax.) Alc lunch/ dinner approx 3,000 pts. Recent nomination. More reports please.

DEYÁ 07179 Mallorca Map 12

Hotel Es Molí *Tel* (971) 63.90.00
Carretera de Valldemossa *Fax* (971) 63.93.33
Telex 69007

This village, at the foot of the Teix mountains on the rugged coast of north-west Mallorca, has one of the loveliest settings in the Mediterranean, not far from a beautiful coastline, with sunny valleys of oranges and lemons. And it is this setting above all that draws many readers back again and again to the *Es Molí*. "Luxurious. The gardens, dazzling with blossom and fruit, fragrant with scents galore, alive with huge colourful butterflies and cheerful gossipy frogs shouting across the lily ponds. Stunning views to the sea and a marvellous meandering walk through olive, orange and lemon groves down to the rocky cove of Port Deyá."

Meals in summer are served on the terrace overlooking the gardens. The swimming pool is "bedazzling in its beauty"; the hotel also provides a minibus to its small private beach at Muleta, 20 minutes' drive away, for deep-water bathing from a rocky platform rather than sunbathing. (There is no nearby sandy beach.) "The area is superb for walking"; Pepe, a reception, is an expert on walks and leads small parties on Mondays. The hotel is scrupulously well maintained; the lighter, more modern rooms in the annexe "have the highest and therefore the best view of the sea". The cooking, a weak point in the past, is said to have greatly improved. "Meal times are fixed to suit Anglo-German customs, but this isn't allowed to detract from the general standard of the place, which is well run and friendly." Mr Peters, the manager, has retired this year; Mrs Peters is continuing with the new manager, Sr A Fernandez. (*D and P Hawkins, Max and Ruby Milner, N and H Drucker, and others*)

Open Mid-Apr–end Oct.
Rooms 3 suites, 69 double, 9 single – all with bath, shower, telephone, radio, air-conditioning; most with terrace (small supplement). Annexe with 15 rooms, 50 metres from main buildings.
Facilities 3 lounges, T V room, 2 bars, 2 restaurants, card and writing room; dining terrace, dancing weekly in summer. Large gardens with swimming pool, tennis court, pétanque. Free minibus to rock beach with bar.
Location ½ km from Deyá; Palma 29 km.
Restriction Not suitable for &.
Credit cards All major cards accepted.
Terms B&B 7,700–16,500 pts; dinner, B&B 9,200–18,000 pts. Set lunch/dinner 3,000 pts; full alc 4,500 pts. 1-night bookings sometimes refused. Reduced rates for children sharing parents' room.

La Residencia

Tel (971) 63.90.11
Fax (971) 63.93.70
Telex 69570

Smaller, more exclusive, and pricier than the *Es Molí* above, *La Residencia* also causes its admirers to reach for their superlatives: "Absolute magic - just what we needed. Peace, tranquillity, and beautiful surroundings." "Without a doubt the best hotel on the island." "A perfect place to relax." Two adjacent manor houses in the heart of the village have been converted most elegantly, and the setting plus the "welcoming staff" and "surprisingly good restaurant" have again pleased visitors to this visually stunning hotel. "It is in the style of a Spanish grandee's house, cool, spacious and a bit dark, the swimming pool lined with elegant cypresses and silver birches, against a magnificent backdrop of mountains and forests, and in grounds of orange and lemon trees, lawns and bright flowers. Our room was a charming mixture of elegance and austerity, with antique furniture including a four-poster bed, and original modern paintings. A superb breakfast was brought punctually by smiling waiters; luxurious towels and bed-linen were changed daily. The restaurant was a beautiful evocation of a stately banqueting hall, with its minstrel's galleries and intimate alcoves, lit by white candles in silver and wrought-iron sticks and candelabra. The *nouvelle cuisine* was delicious." (*Lisa Morley, Dr JR Backhurst, and others*) A few criticisms: newspapers in German, none in English; a single high-chair for children, and no food available between 3 pm and 8 pm. "Some guests clearly felt this was not a place for small children; the staff, however, were very eager to help."

Open Mar–early Jan.
Rooms 15 suites, 24 double, 10 single – all with bath and/or shower, telephone, air-conditioning; baby-listening, T V on request. 15 in extension by pool.
Facilities 5 salons, 3 bars, 2 restaurants (1 by pool), T V room; conference room; concerts, poetry readings, fashion shows etc in summer. 32-acre grounds with gardens, tennis court, 32-metre swimming pool. 20 mins from sea – tiny rocky private beach, snack bar.
Location On edge of village, on road to Sóller.
Restriction Not suitable for &.
Credit cards None accepted.
Terms [1990 rates] (Excluding tax) B&B: single 11,000–13,000 pts, double 19,500–23,000 pts, suite 25,000–30,000 pts. Set lunch 3,000 pts, dinner 4,500 pts; full alc 6,000 pts. Reduced rates for children; special meals on request.

FORMENTOR 07470 Mallorca   **Map 12**

Hotel Formentor   *Tel* (971) 53.13.00
Playa de Formentor   *Fax* (971) 53.11.55
                                                                        Telex 68523

"A dream spot. Swimming first-class – about the best on the island – and so also the service and food. More expensive than the Es Molí, *(q.v.), but there is no comparison."* In splendid setting amid pine trees and flowers, grand five-star hotel with loyal international clientele. Air-conditioned public rooms and bedrooms, two restaurants (terrace and beach), heated swimming pool, children's pool and play area, tennis, riding and miniature golf. 127 rooms and suites, all with bath – single 15,500 pts, double 24,000 pts. Breakfast 1,650 pts. Set meals 5,400 pts [1990]. (Excluding tax.) Recent nomination. More reports please.

FUENTERRABIA 20280 Guipuzcoa   **Map 12**

Parador El Emperador   *Tel* (943) 64.21.40
Plaza de Armas del Castillo   *Fax* (943) 64.21.53

Dropped from earlier editions for lack of feedback, this once near-impregnable grey stone fortress played a major role in the 17th-century wars with the French. Fuenterrabia (Hondarribia on Basque road signs) is now a popular seaside resort, perched high above the border river with France, about halfway between St-Jean-de-Luz and San Sebastian. The town is full of steep narrow streets and old mansions (though the modern town itself is ugly). "With only 16 rooms, the hotel occupies part of the former palace of Charles V, only partly restored to give guests the feel of what the building was like before restoration began. The effect is somewhat sombre but it is a fascinating place to stay, giving a good insight into what life in a medieval castle must have been like. Our rooms were small but adequate and the staff were extremely helpful, directing us to a restaurant down the street where we had an excellent meal amid a crowd of local people, with not another tourist in sight." (*C and P Manning*) Bed-and-breakfast only.

Open All year.
Rooms 14 double, 2 single – all with bath, shower, telephone.
Facilities Salon, bar, T V room, dining room. Small garden. Sea 5 mins; sandy beaches.

Location 23 km E of San Sebastian; in centre. Parking in square.
Credit cards All major cards accepted.
Terms [1990 rates] (Excluding tax) Double rooms 7,500–9,500 pts. Breakfast
900 pts. (No restaurant.)

GIBRALTAR   Map 12

The Rock Hotel   *Tel* (956) 73.000
3 Europa Road   *Fax* (956) 73.513
                                                            Telex 2238

Our only entry for Gibraltar, nominated last year, is a large, old-fashioned
British hotel in terraced gardens with fine views across the bay to
Algeciras. It reminded a correspondent of a Trust House hotel of ten years
ago – a mixture of English custom and a Spanish setting, familiar yet
strange. Bedrooms were refurbished in 1989. The public rooms, where
many locals meet, are "very nice". The dining room serves traditional
British food now rarely found in the UK. *The Rock* is recommended as a
useful stop between the Costa del Sol and Cadiz, now that the frontier
with Spain is open. (*Yolande Jewson, and others*) Caution: "Anyone with a
heart problem will find Gibraltar and *The Rock* hard work. The hotel is up
a sharp incline to the front door. There are steps to the entrance, then
further steps to the lift. It is in a beautiful position overlooking the
harbour and town, but the carpark and the sea-water pool are on the level
below."

Open All year.
Rooms 8 suites, 120 double, 32 single – all with bath, shower, telephone.
Facilities Lounge, restaurant, terrace. Garden, swimming pool.
Location In centre, on hill overlooking harbour, near Alameda Gardens.
Credit cards All major cards accepted.
Terms [1990 rates] Rooms from 15,000 pts. Breakfast 1,200 pts. Set meals
3,000 pts.

GOMERA 38800 Canary Islands   Map 12

Parador Conde de la Gomera   *Tel* (922) 87.11.00
Cerro de la Horca   *Fax* (922) 87.11.16
San Sebastián de la Gomera

"If you have come this far," urges a reader, "go just a bit further, an hour
and a half by ferry, to Gomera." This tiny island, neglected by the tourist
hordes, is a far cry from its extrovert sister, Tenerife. It has a mountain,
valleys and forests, and hidden beaches along the coast. In the capital
port of San Sebastián, Christopher Columbus prepared his ships to sail
for the New World (arrival nowadays is by roll-on roll-off ferry). On a
cliff above the town sits this aristocratic *parador*, a long, low-built stone-
and-tile mansion surrounded by a garden of date palms. "A splendid
situation overlooking the harbour with attractive scented gardens." "Our
main memory is of abundant birdsong and tropical trees." "It's hard to
believe it's a new building. Utterly timeless and harmonious, with cool
leafy courtyards and lots of lovely places to sit indoors and in the garden.
The staff, especially the receptionists, are pleasant and helpful."
"Bedrooms are beautifully appointed and furnished (even the reading
lamps are good) and the public rooms are magnificent." "The bathroom

ad two large wash-basins and good plumbing." In the past readers have
dmired the "delicious Spanish cooking" and the "buffet breakfast where
ou can have delicacies like gofio, miel de palma, chorizo and local dates
nd figs". Others have mentioned tinned tuna, tinned sweetcorn, tinned
sparagus and "greasy and stodgy *parador* food". Could we have more
eports, please?

Open All year.
Rooms 38 double, 4 single – all with bath, shower, telephone, TV. Some in
nnexe.
Facilities 3 salons (1 with TV), 2 bars, restaurant (air-conditioned). Large garden
ith unheated swimming pool, bar. Black sand beach 15 mins' walk, safe bathing.
Location 600 metres from centre of San Sebastián, overlooking the port. Parking.
Restriction Not suitable for &.
Credit cards All major cards accepted.
Terms (Excluding tax) Rooms: single 9,600 pts, double 12,000 pts. Breakfast
00 pts. Half board: single 13,400 pts, double 19,600 pts. Reduced rates for
hildren; special meals.

GRANADA 18009   **Map 12**

Hostal América   `BUDGET`   *Tel* (958) 22.74.71
Real de la Alhambra 53

An oasis of peace and calm." "Enchanting." "A lovely situation." "Such
ind people." Once again there's much praise for this civilised small hotel
n the Alhambra hill, with its colourful architecture and flower-bedecked
windows and doors. The rooms are on the small side, but comfortable,
imply furnished with Moorish curtains and bedspreads and lemon-
cented sheets; some have views of the Sierra Nevada. In summer meals
re served under a canopy in a charming patio to the strains of piped
Vivaldi and Mozart. The hotel insists on half-board terms; the food, plain
ut good, is limited in choice, but if there is a real objection to the main
ish, they will readily cook an omelette or, sometimes, fish. The wines are
airly priced. (For lunch, a reader recommends *Las Mimbres*, an open-air
estaurant just outside the walls of the Alhambra.) It is advisable to book
n advance, and be prepared to speak Spanish. (*Dr FP Woodford, P and M
Horswell, Sara A Price, PD Scott, and others*)

Open Mar–early Nov.
Rooms 1 suite, 8 double, 4 single – all with bath and/or shower, telephone.
Facilities Lounge, dining room. Patio.
Location On Alhambra hill. Parking, guarded by day.
Restriction Not suitable for &.
Credit cards None accepted.
Terms [1990 rates] (Excluding tax) Rooms: single 4,100 pts, double 6,500 pts.
reakfast 500 pts, set dinner 1,400 pts.

Parador de San Francisco   *Tel* (958) 22.14.40
Alhambra   *Fax* (958) 22.22.64
                                                    Telex 78792

Often regarded as a flagship among *paradores*, and certainly one of the
most expensive, the *San Francisco* is splendidly situated on the Alhambra
hill. "As I walked through the various courtyards I had to pinch myself
nd say it was really a hotel." It has modern extensions, and has been

much renovated, but its core is an old Franciscan monastery. "Such a marvellous setting," wrote an inspector. "The delights of sitting in the lovely patio, and walking round the garden and exquisite Moorish courtyard, outweigh most failings." Other comments: "The gardens are out of this world." "Our welcome was cordial and our car was safely parked." "Reception courteous and helpful." "Service in the bar and restaurant, even when busy, was good." Bedrooms are comfortable and well furnished, with good lights. The rooms to go for are in the 200s and 300s (the 400s are downstairs and lack a view). (*Mrs S Dumner, Mrs EH Prodgers, Nancy Raphael, and others*)

Open All year.
Rooms 35 double, 4 single – all with bath, shower, telephone, TV, air-conditioning. Ground-floor rooms.
Facilities Salon, bar, breakfast room, restaurant; patio, garden.
Location On Alhambra hill. Parking.
Credit cards All major cards accepted.
Terms [1990 rates] (Excluding tax) Rooms: single 10,450 pts, double 16,000 pts. Breakfast 900 pts, set lunch/dinner 2,900 pts.

GRAZALEMA 11610 Cádiz   Map 12

Hostal Grazalema   BUDGET   *Tel* (956) 14.11.36
Carretera Comarcal 344

Across a narrow valley from a delightful mountain village, modern white-washed hotel with red tile floors, vaulted ceilings, ample lounge space, log fire in winter, dining terrace, outdoor pool. Bedrooms with terrace or balcony overlooking town, good private bathrooms. Recommended for welcoming atmosphere and friendly service. "An ideal place to take a break from the cultural riches of nearby Granada and Seville. Food only fair, but other restaurants in town." 24 rooms, all with bath/shower. B&B double 5,300-5,905 pts. Set meals 1,900 pts [1990]. (Excluding tax.) New nomination. More reports please.

GUADALUPE 10140 Cáceres   Map 12

Hospederia del Real   BUDGET   *Tel* (927) 36.70.00
Monasterio   *Fax* (927) 36.71.77
Plaza Juan Carlos I

A welcome return to the Guide after having been dropped for lack of recent reports, the *Real Monasterio* is praised by readers for its location, history and good value. "The monastery simply reeks of history and is well worth a visit. Part of the ancient building has been restored and is now a comfortable hotel. The remainder of the monastery has paintings and gold treasures that are fabulous." Guadalupe is a small town about 2,000 feet up in the mountains roughly halfway between Toledo and Mérida or Cáceres. The approach from the east over the *sierras* is especially beautiful. During the Middle Ages, this was a pilgrimage centre: there is a cult still of the Virgin of Guadalupe whose image is kept within the church. Readers remark on the value for money: "It is as good as any *parador* we have stayed at. It lacks a swimming pool, and doesn't have an elaborate breakfast, but it is so much less expensive. Dinner was very good indeed." *(JA Matheson; Mr and Mrs Peter C Rose, E Ring)*

Open Open all year except 15 Jan–15 Feb.
Rooms 1 suite with TV, air-conditioning; 37 double, 2 single – all with bath, shower, telephone.
Facilities Lift. Hall, 2 salons, TV room, bar, 2 restaurants.
Location Central. Parking.
Credit cards Access, Visa.
Terms [1990 rates] (Excluding tax) B&B: single 3,700 pts, double 5,650 pts, suite 15,300 pts. Set lunch/dinner 1,750 pts; full alc 2,500 pts. Special meals for children.

GUALCHOS 18614 Granada　　　　　　　　　　　　　　**Map 12**

La Posada　**BUDGET**　　　　　　　　　　　　*Tel* (958) 64.60.34
Plaza Constitución 9　　　　　　　　*Reservations in UK* (0223) 323618

"Wonderful food. Lovely place in the most unlovely part of Spain. An enchanting village to return to." Gualchos is a still unexploited inland village in the foothills of the Sierra de Lujar, just out of reach of the crowds on the Costa del Sol. In the main square, two 18th-century houses have been restored to create a *posada* (inn). Readers continue to write glowingly of the food and the charming rooms: "The high point of three months' travel through Europe. Sr Gonzalez is a kind and helpful host (he speaks fluent English), full of valuable advice about places off the beaten track. And his cooking! An intriguing and absolutely successful mix of Spanish, English and *nouvelle*-ish (but huge portions), e.g., country pâté with a delicious onion marmalade, a salad made from avocados, oranges and smoked anchovies, a delicately poached salmon with saffron sauce. Rooms are furnished with English and Spanish antiques without a hint of pretentiousness. The restaurant and two cosy lounges have fireplaces, and there's a self-service 'honour bar'." *(Anthony and Laurel Gilbert, also Sara A Price, John Guest, Richard Nott, Sally C Lloyd, Mrs FM Harrison, Mrs JE Lyes, and others)* A few relatively minor criticisms: service is informal and not always available, dinner may not be served on time, breakfast can disappoint. One room is said to be "airless and dark".

Open 1 Mar–30 Nov. Closed 28 Sep–1 Oct. Restaurant closed Mon.
Rooms 7 double, 2 single – all with bath, shower.
Facilities Lounge, bar, restaurant; patio. Small garden with pergola, tiny swimming pool. Pebble beach 20 mins' drive.
Location 9 km inland from coast, via very steep road, at Castell de Ferro which is E of Motril. Hotel is in village centre; leave your car at edge of village and walk; hotel will collect and park it.
Restrictions Not suitable for &. No children under 12.
Credit card Visa.
Terms [1990 rates] B&B (Mon only) £25; dinner, B&B £38. Meals 2,650–3,700 pts.

The success of this guide in North America has led to sister publications on American and Canadian hotels based on the same principles. Readers with recent experience of good hotels in North America are urged to send their nominations to Sandra W Soule, America's Wonderful Little Hotels and Inns, PO Box 150, Riverside Avenue, Riverside, Conn. 06878, USA.

JAÉN 23000   Map 12

Parador Castillo de Santa Catalina   *Tel* (953) 26.44.11
Carretera del Castillo   *Fax* (953) 26.44.11

Some call this the best *parador* in Spain. It is in a spectacular position,
perched on a crag above the town of Jaén, with magnificent views on
every side. The architect and builders worked hard to blend old and new.
"The interior is impressive, with many examples of Spanish art." Only
south-facing rooms have a balcony, but all have remarkable vistas. The
ante-room to the dining room has an arch springing from each of the four
corners to meet 60 or 70 feet above, and is worthy of a cathedral. The
dining room itself, with its priceless tapestries, is only slightly less grand.
From a report this year: "The bedroom was large, cool and pleasantly
furnished with a triptych painting between the twin beds. The swimming
pool was large and impeccably clean. At dinner the fish soup was
delicious. Breakfast was ample, and efficiently presented." "Outstanding
pastries and cakes," writes another. "What singles this *parador* out is the
extremely friendly, *smiling* staff who could not have been nicer – porter,
reception, barmen, waiters, and swimming pool attendants." (*WK Reid,
Mrs D Sumner, Dr FP Woodford, and others*)

Open All year.
Rooms 45 rooms – all with bath, shower, telephone; some with balcony. 11
ground-floor rooms.
Facilities Lift. 2 lounges, chess and card room, TV room, bar, 2 restaurants; air-
conditioning. Large garden with trees; swimming pool (seasonal).
Location 3 km SW of Jaén.
Credit cards All major cards accepted.
Terms [1990 rates] (Excluding tax) Rooms: single 7,200–8,000 pts, double 9,000–
10,000 pts. Breakfast 900 pts, set lunch/dinner 2,700 pts.

LAGUARDIA 01300 Álava   Map 12

Hotel Marixa   `BUDGET`   *Tel* (945) 10.01.65
Sancho Abarca 8

*High on a hill, overlooking Riojan plain, restaurant with "truly breathtaking
views" and bedrooms "well furnished with lots of wardrobe space and nice
bathrooms". Bar, terrace. Recommended for good food and friendly staff.
Welcoming to families. Riding can be arranged. Open 1 Feb–24 Dec. 10 rooms,
with bath and shower. B&B 3,000–4,250 pts. Set meals 1,700 pts [1990].
(Excluding tax.) Recent nomination. More reports please.*

LEÓN 24001   Map 12

Hotel de San Marcos   *Tel* (987) 23.73.00
7 plaza de San Marcos   *Fax* (987) 23.34.58
                                                   Telex 89809

A very grand hotel, with five red *Michelin* gables, in a city renowned for
its huge Gothic cathedral, one of Europe's finest. The *San Marcos* is a
parador, and one of the most admired; it is a former 16th-century

monastery and has a splendid Renaissance facade. Inside, there are three-quarters of a mile of carpeted corridors, lined on both sides with exquisite reproductions of Spanish furniture through the ages. Large paintings and tapestries soften the cool stone walls; the furnishings are understated and elegant – many rooms on the first two floors were redecorated this year. Stone staircases are carpeted; but there are also fast, efficient lifts. Some bedrooms are in a modern extension, still on the grand scale. All are well equipped, with big towels in the bathrooms. The restaurant, more modern in style, gives on to a summer terrace, with the river beyond: "The entrance provides guests with reassuring glimpses of chefs at work in a sparklingly clean kitchen." The cuisine is said to be not *haute* and not very Spanish, but better than average *parador* fare. One 1990 visitor appreciated having her scruffy small car parked without a sneer or expectation of tip and was suitably wowed by the "lovely lovely building". (*Anne-Marie Sutcliffe*)

Open All year.
Rooms 15 suites, 243 double – all with bath, shower, telephone, radio, TV, baby-listening.
Facilities Lift. Salons, TV room, bar, restaurant, breakfast room; conference facilities; hairdresser, beauty parlour. Garden.
Location On river. Parking.
Credit cards All major cards accepted.
Terms [1990 rates] (Excluding tax) B&B: single 9,700–11,300 pts, double 12,800–14,800 pts. Set lunch/dinner 2,900 pts.

LOJA 18300 Granada   **Map 12**

Hotel La Bobadilla   *Tel* (958) 32.18.61
Finca la Bobadilla, Apartado 52   *Fax* (958) 32.18.10
                                                                      Telex 78732

A modern, Swiss-owned "hotel village" of striking originality and character. Set in the heart of Andalusia, surrounded by rolling hills, forests of oak, olive groves and almond tree orchards, it offers every kind of outdoor pleasure, as well as luxurious comfort. "We were enchanted. It is not so much a building as an assembly of 35 suites, brilliantly designed; the building style is *cortijo* – that of an old country house. Once past a foyer of breathtaking beauty, you enter a quiet, almost austere world: the finest traditional materials have been used, and it is hard to believe it is all new. There is much carved wood and tile, and small patios where fountains bubble. The five-star luxury here is very subtle. Sherry greets you at lunchtime, and champagne before dinner, where the food in the charming *La Finca* restaurant is memorable (*Michelin* rosette e.g. for duck with truffles). A reader this year writes: "The staff are very kind, though little English is spoken. The whole establishment is relaxed and untainted by the hysteria of modern tourism. You can shoot rabbits and pigeons or ride from their own stables, or just walk for ten miles every afternoon. There's a swimming pool/lake with arctic water or a charming indoor pool with jacuzzi." It is possible to have a room, but "the suites cost only 30 percent more, and not to have one is to escape the special flavour and atmosphere of the hotel" – including "an open fire which was lit every evening". (*MD Janson, and others*)

Open All year.

Rooms 7 suites, 24 double, 4 single – all with bath, shower, telephone, T V.
Facilities Salons, T V room, bar, breakfast room, 2 restaurants; weekend concerts;
extensive conference facilities. Indoor swimming pool, sauna, fitness centre. Large
grounds with outdoor swimming pool, tennis, riding, clay-pigeon and bow
shooting.
Location 20 km from Loja. At km 502 marker on N342 Granada–Málaga road,
turn off towards Rute. Hotel, down 3 km drive, is signposted.
Restriction Not suitable for &.
Credit cards All major cards accepted.
Terms (Excluding tax) B&B: single 23,600–25,700 pts, double 31,600–40,700 pts,
suite 45,600–57,700 pts. Set lunch/dinner 6,600 pts. Reduced rates for children;
special meals on request.

MÁLAGA 29016   Map 12

Parador de Gibralfaro   *Tel* (952) 22.19.03
Apartado de Correos 274   *Fax* (952) 22.19.02

"The situation, in its own woodland, is spectacular. There are beautiful
views over the city, which turns bright pink at sunrise." "The views are
amazing – of Málaga, the docks and the sea." "Even the hideous high-rise
modern blocks acquire a certain grandeur at this distance." The *parador*,
3 kilometres above the city, with stone arcades and terraces, is popular
with locals and is often fully booked. The bedrooms, all with balcony and
view, are in Spanish style, with tiled floors, heavy carved furniture and
large bathrooms; a recent visitor noted "plain linen curtains, prints of
Málaga mixed with some modern pictures, local metal lampshades and
lamps". "Breakfast was in a delightful room looking out over the
mountains. Self-service, good madeleines, undercooked croissants, tasteless buns and orange juice *not* fresh." Of the food, a reader warns: "Much
of the menu is edible, but only aficionados will want to essay the squid
casseroled in its own ink."

Open All year.
Rooms 12 double – all with bath and/or shower, telephone.
Facilities Lounge, bar with T V, restaurant. Terrace.
Location In large park, 3 km E of town centre, towards Almería; after bull ring
follow signs to left, uphill, towards Granada.
Credit cards All major cards accepted.
Terms [1990 rates] (Excluding tax) Double room 8,500–9,500 pts. Breakfast
900 pts. Set lunch/dinner 2,700 pts.

MÉRIDA 06800 Badajoz   Map 12

Parador Via de la Plata   *Tel* (924) 31.38.00
Plaza de la Constitución 3   *Fax* (924) 31.92.08

Convenient for visiting nearby Roman ruins and magnificent new Roman
museum, cloistered former convent (also once a prison) offering quiet rooms,
pretty surroundings. "A beautiful example of how to combine the best of old and
new: domed chapel now a lounge, luxurious modern bathrooms. Small garden
and underground carpark. Staff helpful and informed, dinner excellent." But
another reader tells of an insolent receptionist. Hotel has been in the Guide
before, but dropped because of a similar incident. 82 rooms. B&B double
13,500 pts. Set meals 3,000 pts. (Excluding tax.) More reports please.

MOJÁCAR 04638 Almería   Map 12

Parador Reyes Católicos   *Tel* (951) 47.82.50
Playa de Mojácar   *Fax* (951) 47.81.83

Above the coast on a rocky hill, with views of the sea, a striking modern white-walled *parador*, just outside a small ancient town between Almería and Murcia. From the road it looks a little like a sanatorium, but inside it proves a peaceful haven from the once lovely, but now increasingly garish and touristy Mojácar. The reception area is spacious, and there are many lounges with soft leather sofas, lovely pottery, and good modern prints on the walls. Everything is built for coolness – corridors to the bedrooms are open to the sky and the bedrooms are large, 40 feet from the door to the terrace. Below are terraces on different levels, and a good-sized pool with palm trees. Breakfast is a generous buffet. Room service is quick and efficient. Recommended as a good place for a complete rest, or for touring the interesting small villages nearby. But we badly need more reports.

Open All year.
Rooms 89 double, 9 single – all with bath, shower, telephone, TV; some with balcony. Some ground-floor rooms.
Facilities 2 salons, bar, TV room, restaurant; terrace. Garden with swimming pool. Beach nearby.
Location 2.5 km SE of Mojácar on N340 coastal road. Parking.
Credit cards All major cards accepted.
Terms [1990 rates] (Excluding tax) Rooms: single 7,600 pts, double 9,500–12,825 pts. Breakfast 900 pts. Set meals 2,700 pts.

MONZÓN DE CAMPOS 34410 Palencia   Map 12

Hotel Castillo de Monzón **BUDGET**   *Tel* (988) 80.80.75

On road to Santander, restaurant-with-rooms in quiet setting, a good overnight stop en route to ferry. Comfortable and modern; inside restored 10th-century castle, medieval, but light in feeling. Bedrooms are basic; some beds said to be geriatric; hot-water system antiquated too. Acceptable food. 10 rooms, all with bath and shower, double 7,000–8,000 pts. Breakfast 500 pts, set meals 2,000 pts [1990]. (Excluding tax.) Original nomination endorsed but we'd welcome more reports.

MORELLA 12300 Castellón   Map 12

Hotel Cardenal Ram **BUDGET**   *Tel* (964) 16.00.00
Cuesta Suñer 1

In northernmost province of Valencia, in the interior, a "cut-price parador" in famous Templar town perched on hill, surmounted by castle. "Lovingly restored and very clean. Spartan bedrooms, excellent advice about local excursions, well worth the drive from the coastal motorway even for one night. Above-average regional food. A taste of the overworked description, 'the real Spain'." 19 rooms; double 5,000 pts. Breakfast 300 pts, set meals 1,200 pts [1990]. (Excluding tax.) New nomination. More reports please.

> When telephoning the Republic of Ireland from abroad, omit the 0 at the beginning of the dialling code.

NERJA 29780 Málaga   Map 12

Parador de Nerja   *Tel* (952) 52.00.50
El Tablazo s/n   *Fax* (952) 52.19.97

Civilised modern parador *splendidly situated high on cliff above beach at the eastern edge of one of largest resorts on Costa del Sol. Large well-furnished bedrooms with good bathroom and large balcony with sea or mountain view. Attractive swimming pool in shady garden with good bar snacks. Restaurant average, but plenty to choose from in town. Staff exceptionally helpful and friendly. 73 rooms, all with bath and shower. Single 9,600 pts, double 12,000 pts. Breakfast 900 pts, set meals 2,900 pts [1990].* (Excluding tax.) *Recently endorsed but more reports welcome.*

NUÉVALOS 50210 Zaragoza   Map 12

Hotel Monasterio de Piedra   *Tel* (976) 84.90.11
     Fax (976) 84.90.54

This "unique" hotel between Madrid and Zaragoza began life in the 12th century as a Cistercian monastery; part of it is open to the public as an ancient monument, the other part is a hotel. Surrounding the monastery are "magnificent gardens full of waterfalls – some very dramatic, and all amazing considering the miles of arid countryside around". The hotel is also impressive – the vestibule has a beautiful romanesque ceiling with paintings and gilded rib-vaulting. "There are large grand hallways and staircases and an enormous dining room, but the general atmosphere is relatively informal rather than luxurious." Bedrooms vary – "the best are roomy with a sitting room and balcony"; others are in the former monks' cells, "most with balcony, but the rooms themselves are fairly small and plain". An à la carte dinner was "very fresh, well prepared and enormous". Readers are cautioned that the park is a major tourist attraction; while the hotel itself remains tranquil, there are full parking lots, souvenir stands and cafés nearby. More reports please.

Open All year.
Rooms 45 double or family, 9 single – all with bath, shower, telephone. Ground-floor rooms.
Facilities 2 lounges with TV, 2 cafeterias, 2 restaurants. Large park with gardens, swimming pool, tennis court. Fishing and shooting nearby.
Location Turn off main Zaragoza–Madrid road at Catalayud; hotel is 28 km S.
Credit cards All major cards accepted.
Terms [1990 rates] (Excluding tax) Rooms: single 4,000–5,000 pts, double 5,000–7,200 pts. Breakfast 425 pts. Set lunch/dinner 1,900 pts; full alc 2,900 pts.

OJEN 29610 Málaga   Map 12

Refugio de Juanar   *Tel* (952) 88.10.00
Sierra Blanca   *Fax* (952) 88.10.01

In a state nature reserve in the foothills of the Sierra Blanca, just inland from Marbella, up a narrow twisting road, this attractive small white-walled hotel is a converted hunting lodge. "It is where the Spanish come. When it's busy, you can stay only two nights. Our bedroom was small but adequate, with a large bathroom. Comfortable public areas with sofas and a log fire. You can find yourself legless over the generous gins in the bar. Specialities are the superb game casseroles – we watched wild deer on the lawn eating chestnuts." Another reader wrote: "The atmosphere is relaxing and friendly; the staff are local people whose lack of skill is made up for by their charm. The food is uncomplicated but freshly cooked and hot. The surroundings are pine forests, away from the cosmopolitan coastline. The bedrooms are rustic, but with all amenities; everything works, very cosy." "Walk up to the viewpoint for sunsets over Marbella."

Open All year.
Rooms 6 suites, 18 double, 1 single – all with bath, shower, telephone, TV, baby-listening. Ground-floor rooms.
Facilities 3 salons, 2 bars, TV room, restaurant; functions room. Garden with swimming pool. Horse-riding weekends. 18 km sea.
Location 20 km N of Marbella, 10 km W of Ojen. Hotel is signposted.
Credit cards All major cards accepted.
Terms (Excluding tax) Rooms: single 5,300 pts, double 6,600 pts, suite from 8,600 pts. Breakfast 600 pts. Set lunch/dinner 2,100 pts; full alc 3,800 pts. Reduced rates for stays of 3 or more nights.

ORIENT 07110 Mallorca   Map 12

Hotel L'Hermitage   *Tel* (971) 61.33.00
Carretera de Sollerich

In a beautiful valley of orchards hemmed in by mountains, up in the wooded hills near the rugged north-west coast of Mallorca, a converted 17th-century country mansion whose former guests include King Farouk of Egypt and the King of Bulgaria. The present clientele is roughly half English-speaking, half German. There is a swimming pool among pine trees, and two tennis courts. A reader this year described the atmosphere as "blissfully quiet, relaxed, informal and friendly". In the main house there is a reading room and games room, a small bar with interesting Mallorcan watercolours, and large bowls of splendid fresh flowers. The dining room, in the old olive-mill, has an olive-press as its focal point, and the grinding-stone is now used as a table where a lavish breakfast buffet is laid out, including the island's delicious speciality, ensaimadas. Bedrooms are mostly comfortable, four in the older building, the rest in a chalet-like block, though there have been complaints about poor lighting and an unattractive sitting area. Readers have praised the adventurous food: "Fresh, and soundly cooked." "Consistently the best hotel food we experienced anywhere in Spain." Guests seeking beaches should be warned that any coastline with sea swimming will be at least an hour's drive. There is no public transport in Orient, so a car is essential: "The scenic, climbing, shorter route to Palma is 28 kilometres; the faster, 35 kilometres, is via Alaró and Consell." (*Mrs D Gladstone, and others*) There are reports of expansion this year, raising some concern among regulars that the peaceful atmosphere may change. More reports please.

Open All year. Closed Nov–15 Dec.
Rooms 20 double – all with bath, telephone, TV, terrace.
Facilities Lounge, salons, bar, TV room, games room, restaurant. Garden with 2 tennis courts, swimming pool, sauna.
Location 1.3 km NE of village of Orient, 25 km N of Palma.

Credit cards Access, Diners, Visa.
Terms [1990 rates] (Excluding tax) Double room 10,200–16,500 pts. Full board
13,000–15,200 pts per person. Set meals 2,225–3,100 pts.

PALAFRUGELL 17200 Gerona   Map 12

Hotel Tamariu `BUDGET`   *Tel* (972) 30.01.08
Playa de Tamariu

*Brightly decorated simple small hotel on beachfront in unspoiled fishing village
4 km E of Palafrugell. Ask for outside room with sea view (others have a central
well). Furnishings spartan; plumbing adequate but primitive. Spotlessly clean,
flowers everywhere. The multilingual owners, present 7 am to midnight, and
their staff, "smile, are helpful, and enjoy meeting people. Best food in village
(succulent steaks, fish just off the boat); imaginative wine list. The whole set-up
(owners, staff, hotel, restaurant, village) is a joy to behold – mass tourism has
passed it by. Extremely good value." Open 15 May–30 Sep. 25 rooms, all with
bath or shower. B&B: single 2,775–3,060 pts, double 5,100–5,680 pts. Set meals
1,500 pts [1990]. New nomination. More reports please.*

PORT MAHÓN 07700 Menorca   Map 12

Hotel Port Mahón   *Tel* (971) 36.26.00
Avenida Fort de l'Eau 12   *Fax* (971) 36.43.62
                                                         Telex 69473

*Our only entry for the smaller, less touristy Balearic island of Menorca: "A
comfortable, old-fashioned, four-star hotel in best position in Mahón, near
harbour. Bedrooms overlooking water recommended for view; breakfast served
on balconies. Excellent service from maids and waiters (staff in reception and
bar less welcoming). Average food, well cooked, with good buffet of desserts.
Swimming pool and terrace. Close to harbour walk, where there are lots of little
cafés." 74 double rooms – all with bath or shower, 5,000–10,500 pts. Breakfast
800 pts, set meals 2,450 pts [1990]. (Excluding tax.) Recent nomination. More
reports please.*

RIBADEO 27700 Lugo   Map 12

Parador de Ribadeo   *Tel* (982) 11.08.25
                                                         Fax (982) 11.03.46

"A lovely place to start a holiday in Galicia . . . miles of empty beaches,
lots of ancient churches, very friendly people." The *parador*, relatively
modern, overlooks a magnificent deep inlet on the Galician coast, just
outside Ribadeo, a town of once notable elegance. There's an unusual
feature: you go down by lift from the ground floor to the bedrooms below
– the most expensive, and quietest, have fine views over the estuary.
From the outside the hotel seems small and unimpressive, though with
obvious charm and a pretty garden. Inside all is clean and comfortable.
Readers have praised the good food, large and airy bedrooms, "even
bigger" bathrooms, and very helpful staff. More reports please.

Open All year.
Rooms 42 double, 5 single – all with bath, shower, telephone, TV.
Facilities Lift. Salon, restaurant, bar, terrace. Beaches nearby.
Location On outskirts of town. Parking.
Credit cards All major cards accepted.
Terms [1990 rates] (Excluding tax) B&B: single 5,140–8,100 pts, double 8,800–10,800 pts. Set lunch/dinner 2,700–3,500 pts.

RONDA 29400 Málaga	Map 12

Hotel Reina Victoria   *Tel* (952) 87.12.40
Calle Dr Fleming 25

In one of Spain's oldest cities, steeped in Roman and Arab history, 700 metres up in the heart of the mountains, the *Reina Victoria* is an old-fashioned hotel with 88 bedrooms and pleasant terraces and gardens, perched on the lip of the gorge, with dramatic views. Public rooms are somewhat tatty. "Ideal for a restful reading holiday. I had a delightful room, small but well furnished and spotlessly clean, a small modern bathroom, and a large terrace with magnificent views. The elderly chambermaids were charming, the receptionists kind and helpful. There is no piped or live *musica continuosa* to disturb conversation. The food is quite good, better than average *parador* (though the waiter service could be much better, and the barman should be avoided). Guests are mostly elderly English and Americans, and a few Germans. Ronda is an attractive, quiet town with many small restaurants, parks and public gardens." (*CA Brunton*)

Open All year.
Rooms 2 suites, 71 double, 15 single – all with bath, shower, telephone, air-conditioning.
Facilities 2 lounges, TV room, bar, restaurant. Large gardens, with swimming pool; barbecues in summer.
Location 5 mins' walk from centre. Parking.
Restriction Not suitable for &.
Credit cards All major cards accepted.
Terms (Excluding tax) B&B: single 6,000–6,600 pts, double 9,500–10,800 pts, suite 16,200–17,700 pts. Alc meals approx 3,300 pts. Reduced rates for children; special meals.

SANTIAGO DE COMPOSTELA La Coruña	Map 12

Hotel de los Reyes Católicos   *Tel* (981) 58.22.00 and 58.23.00
Plaza de España 1   *Fax* (981) 56.30.94
Santiago de Compostela 15705   *Telex* 86004

Built by Ferdinand and Isabella in the 15th century as a hostel for pilgrims ("A cross between Hampton Court and All Souls," wrote one reader), this *very* large, grand and famous hotel stands in the heart of medieval Santiago, forming one side of the plaza on which the cathedral sits. It merits five red gables in *Michelin*, and has many splendid furnishings. Bedrooms are reached through a series of small, cloistered courtyards with fountains, flower-beds, and miniature topiary. "Staying here was certainly an experience," wrote a recent visitor, "though I don't think I'll take my mother – she would never manage the half-mile walk from bedroom to dining room!" "Expensive but worth it" has been the theme of most correspondents – though taking a room with a shower, not a bath, and eating in the elegant cafeteria can reduce the cost. (*M and R Milne-Day, and others*) The dining room is an enormous, gracefully vaulted crypt, but the food gets mixed notices. "For a knock-out hotel experience (honeymoon or something), you really couldn't do much better in Spain," concluded a visitor last year. "Not *our* choice for a honeymoon," responds a 1990 visitor. "Magnificent, yes, but in a cold, austere way. The building is spectacular but precludes the modern comforts we have come to expect."

Open All year.
Rooms 3 suites, 114 double, 13 single – all with bath and/or shower, telephone, radio, TV, baby-listening. Some ground-floor rooms.
Facilities Lifts. Reception hall, salons, TV room, bars, dining room, cafeteria; conference facilities; hairdressing salon, boutiques; Chapel Royal with occasional concerts. Gardens.
Location In town centre, by cathedral. Garage parking nearby. Special bus to station.
Credit cards All major cards accepted.
Terms [1990 rates] (Excluding tax) Rooms: single 9,600–13,600 pts, double 12,000–17,000 pts. Breakfast 900 pts. Set meals 2,900 pts. Reduced rates and special meals for children.

Hostal Windsor   `BUDGET`   *Tel* (981) 59.29.39
República de El Salvador 16
Santiago de Compostela 15701

Useful for short stay; less than half the price of Reyes Católicos, *above. B&B in newer part of town, 5 mins' walk from historic quarter; a variety of restaurants nearby. Built in 1982, and attractively decorated in traditional Spanish style using wood, glass and brasswork to great effect. Most bedrooms comfortable (avoid those giving on to staircase well), beds good, electricity reliable, but some bathrooms minute and plumbing noisy. No restaurant, but* San Clemente *recommended. 50 rooms, all with bath and/or shower, 4,075–5,175 pts. Breakfast 385 pts. (Excluding tax.) More reports please.*

SEGOVIA 40003   **Map 1**

Parador de Segovia   *Tel* (911) 43.04.6
Carretera de Valladolid   *Fax* (911) 43.73.6.
                                                          Telex 4791

An elegant, modern hotel perched on a hill above the town, with fine views of the golden cathedral and the romantic *alcázar*. It earns praise once again: "Well worth the slight detour off the main road south through Spain. Brilliantly built, with views from every room." "With its two pool and grassy lawn, this is a great place to relax in. The lobby is vast with glass from floor to ceiling." "It should be ugly since it is only concrete beams and brick walls. But lines in every direction give pleasure to the eye, and the place is full of small gardens." "Bedrooms are ultra-modern and have refrigerators and balconies." (*Mrs EH Prodgers, JW Clarke*) Reports on the food have been varied, but recently are more encouraging there are also good restaurants in the town. A new wing with 30 more bedrooms is planned for the end of 1990.

Open All year.
Rooms 5 suites, 70 double, 5 single – all with bath, shower, telephone, radio, T V, air-conditioning. Some ground-floor rooms.
Facilities Salons, library, T V room, bar, restaurant; conference facilities; indoor swimming pool, sauna. Garden with swimming pool.
Location 2 km N of Segovia on N601.
Credit cards All major cards accepted.
Terms [1990 rates] (Excluding tax) Rooms: single 7,600–8,800 pts, double 9,500–11,000 pts, suite 12,820–14,850 pts. Breakfast 900 pts. Set lunch/dinner 2,900 pts; full alc 3,500–4,000 pts. Special meals for children.

LA SEU D'URGELL 25700 Lerida   **Map 12**

Hotel El Castell   *Tel* (973) 35.07.04
Route de Lerida, Km 129   *Fax* (973) 35.15.74
                                                         Telex 93610

Nestled into the side of a hill, below the ruins of a pale stone castle, with sweeping views over trees and gently sloping grounds, *El Castell* is a handsome modern luxury hotel with an excellent, *Michelin*-rosetted restaurant. It lies in the Urgellet valley, 10 kilometres south of Andorra, well situated for exploring the Pyrenees, with fishing, river canoeing and golf nearby. A recent report: "There is an attractive swimming pool, surrounded by a rose garden. All the bedrooms are off a long corridor, well appointed with private bathrooms, small fridge and T V. Balconies have pleasant views. The dining room is restful, and the owners (or managers), very much in evidence, speak excellent English. Food superb as one might expect from the *Michelin* rosette. I had a perfectly cooked roast kid and my wife had an equally perfect duck. Hot puff-pastry sweets – which I can still taste! Presentation modern without being excessively *nouvelle*." More reports welcome.

Open All year, except 15 Jan–15 Feb. Restaurant closed Christmas.
Rooms 2 suites, 38 double – all with bath, shower, telephone, T V, mini-bar, baby-listening by arrangement. Ground-floor rooms.
Facilities Salon, T V room, reading room, bar, dining room; conference/functions rooms. Garden with unheated swimming pool. Fishing (permits arranged); Nordic and Alpine skiing nearby.
Location On edge of village, 1 km from centre, on Lerida road.
Credit cards All major cards accepted.
Terms [1990 rates] (Excluding tax) Room: single 8,500 pts, double 11,000 pts, suite 22,000 pts. Breakfast 1,250 pts. Full alc lunch/dinner 5,500 pts. Special meals for children by arrangement.

Parador de la Seu d'Urgell   *Tel* (973) 35.20.00
Santo Domingo   *Fax* (973) 35.23.09

Alternative to El Castell, *above, recently opened modern* parador *on site of ancient church and convent, with cloister preserved and indoor swimming pool ("a treat"), in most beautiful part of Spanish Pyrenees. "Exterior rather unattractive, but modern, well-appointed bedrooms, pristine and comfortable. Friendly and helpful reception." The restaurant specialises in Catalan cooking. 79 rooms, all with bathroom. B&B 4,700–8,150 pts. Set meals 2,900 pts. (Excluding tax.) New nomination. More reports please.*

SEVILLE 41000   Map 1

Hotel Alfonso XIII   *Tel* (954) 22.28.5(
San Fernando 2   *Fax* (954) 21.60.3:
                                                            Telex 7272!

In the historic heart of Seville, near the cathedral, Giralda, Alcazár and
river, a famous grand hotel. High-ceilinged vast public rooms, Moorish in
style, comfortable large bedrooms, considerable if slightly faded glamour.
"The level of service was impeccable, cheerful and ungrudging. The
welcome was genuine and relaxed. The dining room is a vast Italianate
hall with a painted and gilded ceiling and imitation intaglio walls.
Predictably, it serves rather pretentious dishes from an international
'grand hotel' à la carte menu, with a somewhat restricted table d'hôte. It
turned out to be hit and miss: when good, it was very good, when not, it
was very ordinary. Is it affordable? Not by everyone, but part of the low
season is actually during July and August when, no doubt, the pool is at
its best. Anyone wanting to feel cosseted and enjoy the charm of one of
the old-fashioned 'palace' hotels would not go far wrong booking into the
Alfonso XIII for a few days." (*Alex Liddell*)

Open All year.
Rooms 19 suites, 112 double, 18 single – all with bath, shower, telephone, TV,
mini-bar, air-conditioning.
Facilities Lift, reception hall, salons, bar, restaurant; meeting rooms, boutiques,
hairdressers. Gardens with patio, swimming pool.
Location In centre. Parking, underground garage.
Credit cards All major cards accepted.
Terms [1990 rates] Rooms: single 14,000–21,000 pts, double 17,500–28,600 pts,
suite 55,000–75,000 pts. Breakfast 1,750 pts, set lunch/dinner 4,750 pts.

Hotel Doña Maria   *Tel* (954) 22.49.9(
Don Remondo 19   *Fax* (954) 22.97.6!

*In small side street off square behind cathedral, away from the noise of traffic.
B&B hotel with stylish interior decoration, "extremely unusual in a hotel of this
relatively modest type". Comfortable bedrooms with bathroom, plumbing and
lighting of high standard. Rooftop swimming pool offers exceptional view of
Giralda. Last in Guide in 1984, renominated by a regular visitor to the city, who
prefers it to the grander Alfonso XIII, above. 61 rooms, single 5,500–11,000 pts,
double 8,900–18,000 pts. Breakfast 650 pts [1990]. (Excluding tax.) More reports
please.*

SIGÜENZA 19250 Guadalajara   Map 12

Parador Castillo de Sigüenza   *Tel* (911) 39.01.0(
Plaza del Castillo   *Fax* (911) 39.13.64
                                                            Telex 22517

Built in steep tiers on a hillside, and dominated by its bishop's castle,
Sigüenza is a small historic town 129 kilometres north-east of Madrid. It
also has a fine cathedral. The *parador* is set in a medieval fortress, with
splendid views from the ramparts. "Well worth a journey just for the
opulence of the setting." Inside, the furnishings are "usual-*parador*" -

suits of armour guarding the TV – plus well-furnished bedrooms and
warm central heating in the winter. No recent reports; more welcome.

Open All year.
Rooms 2 suites, 62 double, 5 single – all with bath, shower, telephone, TV.
Facilities Lifts. Restaurant, bar, TV room. Small gardens.
Location 200 metres from town.
Credit cards All major cards accepted.
Terms [1990 rates] (Excluding tax) Rooms 6,800–9,500 pts. Breakfast 900 pts, set
lunch/dinner 3,000 pts.

SOLDEU Andorra   Map 12

Hostal Sant Pere   *Tel* (9738) 510.87
El Tarter-Canillo   *Telex* 234

Our only entry for the principality of Andorra, this restaurant-with-rooms
on the main road from the capital to the French border was nominated
recently by a distinguished British restaurateur, now retired: "In my
experience it is by far the best hotel and restaurant in Andorra, where
nearly all the others are either cheap for skiers or overdone Pyrenean
style." The decor has a light and pleasing feeling to it: rough hewn stone
walls and beamed ceilings contrast with crisp white table-cloths in the
dining room; sitting areas have comfortable leather sofas and chairs.
Another reader writes: "Location – excellent! At the foot of a ski trail,
10 miles from very noisy downtown Andorra. Room very nice, appropriately alpine, but not rustic. A wonderful shower room. Only the skiers
were noisy and awoke before I did – sound-proofing was sparse. Food –
excellent! Catalan-inspired and very expertly presented. Service was
equal to the food." Other supporters of this entry have been less
enthusiastic about the food.

Open All year.
Rooms 6 double – all with shower, telephone. 11 studio apartments nearby.
Facilities 4 salons, 2 restaurants; terrace.
Location 3 km W of Soldeu on main road to Andorra la Vieja. Parking.
Restriction Not suitable for &.
Credit cards All major cards accepted.
Terms B&B double 9,000 pts. Full alc meals 4,000–5,000 pts. Special menus for
children.

TOLEDO   Map 12

Hostal del Cardenal   *Tel* (925) 22.49.00
Paseo de Recaredo 24   *Fax* (925) 22.29.91
Toledo 45004

This "true Toledan palace", home of the local archbishop in the 18th
century, adjoins the city walls. It is well known for its excellent
restaurant, and offers good hotel accommodation as well; some of its
rooms overlook the terraced garden which extends to the city gates. "The
hotel is elegant, spacious and quiet, and tastefully furnished in period
style. Service professional, English spoken. Dinner for two – partridge
and suckling pig – was very good." "A complete contrast to food at the
average *parador*: far better and cheaper." At night, from the restaurant,
there's a view of floodlit city gates. "The walk through the gardens and

along the inner walls is a delight – a haven from the crowded streets
outside." "Memorable. Proof that excellence doesn't have to cost a
fortune." (*Cyril Aydon, Yorick Wilks, E Ring, and others*) Minor grievance:
"Why, in a palace with so many spectacular rooms, must breakfast be
offered in a cramped and sunless chamber?"

Open All year.
Rooms 2 suites, 22 double, 3 single – all with bath, shower, telephone; many with
air-conditioning.
Facilities Lounge, TV room, dining room. Garden, patios and courtyards.
Location 10–15 mins' walk from centre; by the old walls at Puerta de Bisagra.
Parking.
Restriction Not suitable for &.
Credit cards All major cards accepted.
Terms (Excluding tax) Rooms: single 4,500 pts, double 7,500 pts, suite 10,800 pts.
Breakfast 450 pts. Set meals 2,000 pts; full alc 3,500 pts.

Parador Conde de Orgaz   *Tel* (925) 22.18.50
Paseo de los Cigarrales   *Fax* (925) 22.51.66
Toledo 45002   *Telex* 47998

On the site where El Greco executed his famous painting of Toledo, high
on a hill to the north, a showpiece *parador* overlooking the historic city.
"For the view alone it is the place to stay," wrote a reader recently. The
parador is often full, with coach parties as well as locals who come to the
restaurant, so the atmosphere is lively. At first glance it reminds one of
16th-century Spain at its most baronial – coats of arms, shields and
antique weapons forged from Toledo steel in the halls and corridors, and
banners and portraits of grave-faced bearded grandees. In fact it was built
in 1968, and the rooms, although furnished in the old style, have every
modern amenity including a fridge. A room with a view of the city is well
worth the extra money for the stupendous sight of the floodlit cathedral at
night. "Splendid furnishings – heavily fringed woollen curtains and bed-
covers to match. Plentiful lighting. Pretty rugs on the tiled floor: 45 feet
from the door to the balcony." Last year readers complained of poor food,
indifferent service, unhelpful staff. This year's news is better: receptionists who spoke good English, "quite good food and waitress service". (*JW
Clarke, and others*)

Open All year.
Rooms 71 double, 6 single – all with bath, shower, telephone, radio, TV.
Facilities Lift. 3 salons, TV room, bar, restaurant – all with air-conditioning.
Extensive landscaped grounds with terraces and unheated swimming pool.
Hunting and fishing nearby.
Location 3 km S of town centre; well signposted.
Restriction Not suitable for &.
Credit cards All major cards accepted.
Terms [1990 rates] (Excluding tax) Rooms: single 8,800–9,600 pts, double 11,000–
12,000 pts. Breakfast 900 pts; set lunch/dinner 2,900 pts.

Hotel Maria Cristina   `BUDGET`   *Tel* (925) 21.32.02
Marqués de Mendigorria 1   *Telex* 42827
Toledo 45000

*Just outside city walls 100 metres from Puerta de Bisagra, modern hotel with
traditional Spanish interior. Spacious cool dining room with blue painted*

ceiling, red tiled floors, soft muslin curtains. Recommended for well-appointed bedrooms, comfortable beds, spotless bathrooms, friendly staff. "Service in dining room impeccable – though food not spectacular." Air-conditioned. Used by tour groups, it has extensive business and conference facilities. 65 rooms, all with bath and shower. Single 4,125–4,450 pts, double 6,250–6,750 pts. Breakfast 495 pts, set lunch/dinner 1,950 pts [1990]. (Excluding tax.) Recent nomination based on suitability for independent travellers as well. More reports needed.

TORTOSA 43500 Tarragona   **Map 12**

Parador Castillo de la Zuda   *Tel* (977) 44.44.50
                                                   Fax (977) 44.44.58

A much-restored massive castle, dating from Moorish times, which sits on a hilltop dominating the town; there are splendid views, from all sides, of the river Ebro, mountains, rooftops, the cathedral and the old town. Readers recommend wandering round the perimeter walls and looking out from each vantage point. The public rooms are well kept and attractive (except the bar). Bedrooms are pleasantly furnished in traditional Spanish style – terracotta tiled floors with patterned cotton rugs, dark wooden furniture, iron lamps, heavy wooden doors, shutters. All have a balcony, making the best of the views. The restaurant is a baronial hall, with a tiled ceiling between wooden beams; it serves simple authentic local food. Outside there is a swimming pool of unusual shape, using the contours of the old castle walls, but one disappointed reader found the water not clean. We have mixed reports on the food. Last year the breakfasts were considered "excellent"; this year a reader writes: "About the worst we have encountered." More reports welcome.

Open All year.
Rooms 3 suites, 70 double, 9 single – all with bath, shower, telephone, TV.
Facilities Lift. Salon, bar, restaurant. Garden with swimming pool.
Location 500 metres from centre, signposted. Sea 15 km.
Restriction Not suitable for &.
Credit cards All major cards accepted.
Terms [1990 rates] (Excluding tax) Rooms: single 6,000–7,200 pts, double 7,500–9,000 pts, suite 9,400–11,200 pts. Breakfast 900 pts, set lunch/dinner 2,700 pts; full alc 3,275 pts.

TRUJILLO 10200 Cáceres   **Map 12**

Parador de Trujillo   *Tel* (927) 32.13.50
Plaza de Santa Clara   *Fax* (927) 32.13.66

A relatively new *parador* (opened in 1985) in the birthplace of Pizarro, whose magnificent statue stands in the town square. Originally the convent of Santa Clara, it is on a hilltop in the ancient citadel, and has been skilfully modernised. The old building is rambling, with courtyards; there is also a modern annexe. Recent visitors have praised the tranquil atmosphere (quiet even during fiesta days with fireworks and bands). There is a well-maintained swimming pool and a bar that provides good service. Readers also like the food: "Superb." "Interesting, and most

attractively presented, with a wide choice also available at breakfast."
The staff are helpful and friendly. No recent reports. More please.

Open All year.
Rooms 1 suite, 45 double – all with bath, telephone, mini-bar. Some in annexe.
Facilities TV room, bar, dining room; conference facilities. Garden with
swimming pool.
Location 47 km E of Cáceres. Hotel is central. Garage.
Restriction Not suitable for &.
Credit cards All major cards accepted.
Terms [1990 rates] (Excluding tax) Rooms: single 6,800–7,600 pts, double 8,500–
9,600 pts. Breakfast 900 pts, set lunch/dinner 2,700 pts.

UBEDA 23400 Jaén   **Map 12**

Parador Condestable Dávalos   *Tel* (953) 75.03.45
Plaza Vázquez de Molina 1   *Fax* (953) 75.12.59

Ubeda, in north-eastern Andalusia, is an exceptionally beautiful old town
with some fine churches (notably San Pablo and El Salvador), and many
Renaissance buildings. In its historic main square is this "lovely 16th-
century stone palace with a wonderful internal patio, surrounded by tiled
corridors leading to cool rooms; the best ones look on to the square or
small courtyards". "Antiques add to a sense of nobility, though our room
was not entirely in keeping with this style, having bright and modern
furnishings. It was, however, spacious, and had a cavernous bathroom."
Readers continue to praise the food, especially the tapas, and "the most
delicious olives – Ubeda is surrounded by miles of olive groves". Service
is "helpful and friendly", by "rather taciturn ladies, attired in national
costume". Welcome improvements this year: "Small lounge area now to
be found at the end of the bar, and evening meals served from 8.30
onwards." (*Diane Sumner, and others*)

Open All year.
Rooms 1 suite, 30 double – all with bath, shower, telephone, TV, air-conditioning.
5 ground-floor rooms.
Facilities Bar, TV room, restaurant. Garden.
Location Central. Ubeda is 57 km NE of Jaén.
Credit cards All major cards accepted.
Terms [1990 rates] (Excluding tax) Rooms: single 8,800 pts, double 11,000 pts,
suite 12,980 pts. Breakfast 900 pts. Set lunch/dinner 2,700 pts; full alc 3,200 pts.
Special meals for children.

VALENCIA DE DON JUAN 24200 León   **Map 12**

Hotel Villegas `BUDGET`   *Tel* (987) 75.01.61
Calle Palacio 10

Modest hotel in small market town 38 km south of León, "quiet, cheap,
unpretentious, agreeably managed, comfortable and charmingly decorated".
Attractive outdoor dining, regional menu, garden and, in season, swimming
pool. The rather simpler 24-roomed Villegas nearby is under the same
management. 5 rooms, all with bath, 4,000–9,000 pts. Breakfast 250 pts; set
lunch/dinner 1,250 pts (excluding tax). Recent nomination. More reports
please.

ERÍN 32600 Orense   Map 12

arador de Monterrey   *Tel* (988) 41.00.75
                                                  Fax (988) 41.20.17

า the style of an old Spanish manor house, with a pear-shaped
wimming pool surrounded by lawn and trees, a modern, two-storey
arador with well-appointed bedrooms. It lies just a few kilometres north
f the Portuguese border, in a well-preserved medieval town with narrow
treets and old houses. It is clean and light outside, cool and dark inside,
/ith long corridors. Readers have enjoyed the food, but been divided on
าe service and the casual system of charging. There are fine views of the
_astilian countryside and a writer last year called it "the most perfect site
วr a hotel we have ever seen". More reports welcome.

)pen All year.
.ooms 1 suite, 22 double – all with bath, telephone. 8 in annexe.
acilities Lounge with TV, bar, dining room. Garden with swimming pool.
ocation 71 km SE of Orense on N525. 4 km NW of Verín.
.estriction Not suitable for &.
redit cards All major cards accepted.
erms [1990 rates] (Excluding tax) Rooms: single 4,800–6,400 pts, double 6,000–
.000 pts. Breakfast 900 pts, set lunch/dinner 2,700 pts.

ICH 08500 Barcelona   Map 12

arador de Vich   *Tel* (93) 888.72.11
                                                  Fax (93) 888.73.11

•plendidly sited above a lake, with far-reaching views of the Pyrenees, an
ustere stone Catalan *parador* recommended for its peaceful surroundings.
\ recent report conveys it well: "As in other *paradores*, the room was large
nd clean, the beds large, and comfortable, the furniture large and ornate,
าe bathroom large and the management nicely assumes that you will
เeed at least ten towels. The water was abundant and always hot. The bar
/as large and well stocked. There are plenty of public rooms laid out for
illiards, cards, television or just conversation. Dinner was acceptable and
ery reasonably priced: artichokes stuffed with cod, and quail and bean
asseroles followed by lamb cutlets. After dinner came the first highlight
we drank wine on the balcony until about midnight. It was peaceful and
•ur conversation was accompanied by the croaking of what sounded like
housands of frogs, calling and answering back and forth down the
alley. In the morning we saw our view – we overlooked the swimming
•ool, which in turn overlooked the lake. We ate breakfast on the balcony
ccompanied by our second highlight – our first cuckoos of the year, not
ıst one or two, but maybe ten or twenty calling down the valley in the
ame manner as the frogs the night before. This *parador* was not the
•rettiest we have stayed in, but it was certainly in an extremely attractive
etting."

)pen All year.
:ooms 1 suite, 31 double, 4 single – all with bath, shower, telephone, TV, air-
onditioning.
acilities Lift. 3 lounges, bar, TV salon, restaurant. Garden with swimming pool.
.rtificial lake nearby.
ocation 14 km NE of Vich, on Roda de Ter road, signposted.

Credit cards All major cards accepted.
Terms [1990 rates] (Excluding tax) B&B: single 6,900–8,500 pts, double 9,300–11,300 pts. Set meals 2,700 pts. Special meals for children by prior arrangement.

VILLAFRANCA DEL BIERZO León Map 12

Parador de Villafranca *Tel* (987) 54.01.75
 del Bierzo *Fax* (987) 54.00.10
Avenida Calvo Sotelo

In the north-west of Spain, surrounded by lovely and interesting country, a white-walled modern parador, traditionally furnished. Recommended for good beds and lighting, friendly and helpful staff, spotless housekeeping. "It was cosy and relaxed, the waitresses encouraged you to enjoy what you were having. Fair choice of wines, including half-bottles. No pressure to spend, all good value. The other outstanding feature is the fascinating town, neither neglected nor over-restored." 40 rooms, single 4,800–5,700 pts, double 6,000–7,000 pts. Break fast 900 pts, set lunch/dinner 2,700 pts [1990]. (Excluding tax.) New nomination. More reports please.

VILLALBA 27800 Lugo Map 1

Parador Condes de Villalba *Tel* (982) 51.00.11
Valeriano Valdesuso *Fax* (982) 51.00.90

A former medieval bastion, with enormously thick walls, this small *parador* is a useful stopping place between Gijon and Santiago, on the Galician plain. It has a drawbridge and an octagonal tower: "A delight and quite astonishing," a reader wrote last year. "We had a huge room with magnificent antique furniture, a vast bathroom, and a curtained alcove with loopholes for shooting at pedestrians below." Traditional high-quality furnishings, comfortable beds, "service nice, but amateur" No recent reports. More please.

Open All year.
Rooms 6 double – all with bath, shower, telephone, TV.
Facilities Lift. Salon with TV, cafeteria, dining room. Garden.
Location 36 km N of Lugo. Central; parking.
Restriction Not suitable for &.
Credit cards All major cards accepted.
Terms [1990 rates] (Excluding tax) Rooms 8,000–10,000 pts. Breakfast 900 pts, set lunch/dinner 2,700 pts.

VITORIA-GASTEIZ 01192 Álava Map 12

Parador de Argomániz *Tel* (945) 28.22.00
Carratera Nacional Madrid-Irún *Fax* (945) 28.22.00

"It's very good – an excellent stop-over for a night, but there's really nothing to do if you stay longer. Efficient, friendly service and the food better than most *paradores*. Good-sized, well-appointed bedroom and bathroom." This 1990 endorsement is of a converted 18th-century country mansion in a peaceful setting amid the Navarre hills of the Basque country, just off the Pamplona–Vitoria road. Vitoria, capital of the largest of the Basque provinces, lies 12 kilometres to the west. It has attractive public rooms – ancient stone floors, modern wooden floors – and readers have especially liked the raftered, barn-like restaurant, where "good wine and *very* good food" are served. (*Ralph Dubery, and others*)

Open All year.
Rooms 54 double – all with bath, shower, telephone.
Facilities Lift. Salon, TV room, bar, restaurant. Garden.
Location 12 km E of Vitoria by N1 to Irun.
Restriction Not suitable for &.
Credit cards All major cards accepted.
Terms [1990 rates] (Excluding tax) Double rooms 6,000–7,500 pts. Breakfast 900 pts, set lunch/dinner 2,700 pts.

ZAFRA 06300 Badajoz   Map 12

Parador Hernán Cortés   *Tel* (924) 55.02.00
Plaza Corazón María 7   *Fax* (924) 55.10.18

Well-converted castle, massive and austere from the outside, cool and inviting inside. It lies just off the Badajoz–Seville road, in a small town. A regular correspondent told us last year: "It's the only *parador* I have encountered that I think is splendid. Distinguished architecture, a humane and well-furnished interior, exceptionally well-furnished bedroom and the best-appointed bathroom I have found in Spain." But we also have reports that the insulation between rooms is poor, and that rooms facing the square may be noisy. The food is rated "average". More reports please.

Open All year.
Rooms 22 double, 6 single – most with bath or shower, all with telephone.
Facilities Salon, bar, dining room. Garden with swimming pool.
Location Central; parking. Town is 76 km SE of Badajoz.
Credit cards All major cards accepted.
Terms [1990 rates] (Excluding tax) Rooms: single 5,200–6,400 pts, double 6,500–8,000 pts. Breakfast 800 pts, set lunch/dinner 2,500 pts.

ZAMORA 49001   Map 12

Parador Condes de Alba y Aliste   *Tel* (988) 51.44.97
Plaza Viriato 5   *Fax* (988) 53.00.63

A carefully restored 15th-century palace on the banks of the upper Duero, in the heart of old Zamora – "a heavenly town". Some *paradores*, in the words of a reader this year, "are more like museums than hotels, and offer few facilities. This one, 62 kilometres from Salamanca, has solved the problem and is a delightful place to stay: a beautiful old palace with antiques, etc, but with a swimming pool and bar/café much used by locals. There's a terrace for tea and drinks and outdoor dining in the summer (unusual for a *parador*); local weddings take place in the central courtyard (the music stops at midnight). A very good place to see and enjoy the real Spain." Other readers have praised the large bedrooms, modern well-lit bathrooms, and fine view. Reports on the food have been mixed: "Average," said one; "The best we have had – *cuisine bourgeoise* with a strong regional accent," said another. (*I Anderson, and others*)

Open All year.
Rooms 27 rooms – all with bath, TV, air-conditioning.
Facilities 3 salons, bar, dining room, courtyard. Garden with swimming pool.
Location Central, near Plaza Mayor. Parking.
Credit cards All major cards accepted.
Terms [1990 rates] (Excluding tax) Rooms 8,000–10,000 pts. Breakfast 900 pts, se
lunch/dinner 2,700 pts.

Sweden

Tidbloms Hotel, Göteborg

ARILD 260 43 Skåne   **Map 7**

Hotel Rusthållargården   *Tel* (042) 462.75
PO Box 5   *Fax* (042) 34.67.93

This handsome 17th-century stone building, well modernised, stands just outside the fishing village of Arild on Sweden's west coast, with good views of the bay; nearby are sandy beaches and a national park, excellent for walking. The hotel is said to be cosy and unpretentious, with a strong individuality and solid traditional furniture. Each bedroom has its own name, e.g. Poet's Room, Major's Room. One dining room is blue, the other green; the "careful cooking" has been generally liked. The Malgren family have been the owners for four generations, and they and their staff are friendly. The hotel lost its place in last year's Guide for lack of feedback: this year it is tentatively restored by a reader who liked the cosy rooms, affable service and "excellent" breakfasts, but thought the cooking suffered from "the *nouvelle cuisine* which seems to have swamped Scandinavia in the past year. I had very good local fish spoilt by a sauce that failed to say anything." Reports that are not like that sauce would be welcome.

Open All year.
Rooms 5 suites, 33 double, 18 single – all with bath, shower, telephone, radio, TV. Some in garden annexes.
Facilities Lift. Lounges, TV room, bar, library, restaurant; terrace. Garden with tennis.
Location On coast, about 30 km NW of Helsingborg. Parking.
Restriction Not suitable for &.
Credit cards All major cards accepted.
Terms B&B: single 570–740 Skr, double 720–900 Skr, suite 1,200–1,500 Skr. Set meals 100 Skr; full alc 350–550 Skr. Reduced rates and special meals for children.

BORGHOLM 387 00 Öland   Map 2

Hotell Guntorps Herrgård   *Tel* (0485) 130.00
Guntorpsgatan   *Fax* (0485) 133.19

A four-mile bridge, Europe's longest, links the mainland to Öland, Sweden's second largest island. It is a breeding ground for many kinds of birds, and has an abundance of protected wild flowers (30 species of orchid, 15 of violet); there are also Viking rune-stones and prehistoric burial chambers. *Guntorps Herrgård* is a picturesque manor house, converted from a family home six years ago, with self-contained suites in one wing, ten minutes' walk from the village centre. "Sheer paradise; wonderfully peaceful; we spent a whole vacation here. We chose one of the suites, furnished in warm light pinks and creams with typically Scandinavian furniture. Breakfast was pure delight. The owner and manager treated us like family rather than guests." (*Capt Richard M Seitz*) Only breakfast is served, but the hotel has an arrangement with restaurants in the area and will sometimes provide transport for guests. We'd be glad of more reports, on this hotel and on another in Borgholm, *Halltorps Gästgiveri*, recently dropped from the Guide for lack of feedback.

Open All year.
Rooms 14 suites, 6 double, 1 single – all with shower, telephone, radio, TV. Suites, with fridge and kitchenette, are on ground floor in a separate wing.
Facilities Ramps. Salon, breakfast room; conference room. Garden with heated swimming pool, children's pool, croquet. Sandy beaches 1 km.
Location 800 metres from centre; 50 metres N of traffic lights.
Credit cards All major cards accepted.
Terms [1990 rates] B&B: single 540–635 Skr, double 635 Skr, suite 745 Skr. Reduced rates for children. (No restaurant but snacks available.)

GÖTEBORG 400 60   Map 7

Tidbloms Hotel   *Tel* (031) 19.20.70
Olskroksgatan 23   *Fax* (031) 19.78.35
                                                     Telex 27369

Göteborg is an attractive walled city with a lively waterfront and "a fabulous new amusement park, Liseborg, which our children enjoyed." *Tidbloms*, in a turn-of-the-century, turreted redbrick house near the centre, has again been liked this year: "We had a lovely big room at a decent rate. The stone-walled dining room is attractive: breakfasts were

nple, and lunch had a good, fairly priced set menu, but dinner is very
;pensive." Others have found the rooms both comfortable and pretty,
n lovely soft colours". "We were charmed by the very helpful staff in
oth the hotel and the restaurant. The place felt Swedish rather than
iternational, but they made us feel at home." The restaurant and bar,
dark and cosy", are built into the rocky hillside and have a cavernous
el, softened by hand-woven rugs, real oil lamps and rustic furniture.
he food includes a good selection of Swedish specialities (including
now goose and reindeer fillet) with carefully prepared sauces. (*Mary
'anson, Miriam D Ross*) Service can sometimes be haphazard.

pen All year except 23 Dec–2 Jan.
ooms 28 double, 14 single – all with bath, shower, telephone, radio, TV. Some
aitable for &.
acilities Lift. Bar, reading room, restaurant; conference facilities. Sauna. Rock
nd sand beach 20 mins.
ocation In E part of Göteborg, within a pedestrian housing area (take small
:cess road behind filling station). Parking.
redit cards All major cards accepted.
erms [1990 rates] B&B: single 390–820 Skr, double 540–960 Skr. Extra bed
25 Skr. Dinner, B&B 530–910 Skr per person.

UND 22104 Skåne   **Map 7**

lotel Lundia   *Tel* (046) 12.41.40
nut den Stores Gata 2   *Fax* (046) 14.19.95
     Telex 32761

*omfortable modern hotel in centre of an old university town 20 km north of
lalmö. Attractive, well-equipped, well-lit bedrooms. Excellent Swedish buffet
reakfast and popular, reasonably priced self-service lunch. Closed 24–26 Dec.
7 rooms, all with bath/shower. B&B double 1,100 Skr [1990]. An alternative is
ie Lundia's older sister hotel, the aptly named Grand. Recent nomination.
lore reports please.*

IMRISHAMN 272 31 Skåne   **Map 7**

lotell Svea   *Tel* (0414) 117.20
trandv 3   *Fax* (0414) 143.41
     Telex 33473

, quiet seaside town east of Malmö, in an area of gently rolling
ountryside with sandy beaches and wooded dunes. "Built in 1936, and
verlooking the Baltic Sea, the *Svea* has the charm of an old hotel, but has
:cently been completely renovated. Every inch is new, fresh and very
wedish – contemporary, but not stark. Nice prints on draperies and
edspreads. Spotless hardwood floors, lots of white and lots of light. The
ining room was large, comfortable and restful; wonderful meals and
ood breakfasts. Staff extremely friendly and helpful." (*Lizbeth and Craig
nderson*)

pen All year.
ooms 37 double, 23 single – all with bath and/or shower, TV. Some suitable
r &.
acilities Lounge, bar, dining room; functions room. Sauna. Garden.

Location On seafront.
Credit cards All major cards accepted.
Terms B&B: single 500 Skr, double 620 Skr. Set meals 100–200 Skr.

STOCKHOLM   Map 7

Värdhuset Clas på Hörnet   *Tel* (08) 16.51.30
Surbrunnsgatan 20   *Fax* (08) 33.53.15
Stockholm 113 48   *Telex* 14619

*Fifteen minutes' walk from the city centre, this elegant restaurant-with-rooms
was first opened as an inn in 1731, then became successively a smart ballroom,
hospital, apartment block and garage, but has now reverted to its original
vocation. Excellent restaurant, well known locally; lovely bedrooms, 18th-
century furnishings. Closed Christmas, New Year, midsummer. 10 rooms, all
with shower. B&B double 750–1,560 Skr. Set meals 185–350 Skr [1990]. Recent
nomination. More reports please.*

Hotell Diplomat   *Tel* (08) 663.58.00
Strandvägen 7C   *Fax* (08) 783.66.34
Postal address PO Box 14059   *Telex* 17119
Stockholm 104 40

"The most pleasant Stockholm hotel we have yet stayed in. Comfortable
rooms, helpful staff, excellent breakfast room." So runs a very recent
report on the fashionable *Diplomat*, which enjoys a fine central position
by the waterfront. Its attractive ground-floor tea house, with potted
plants, white chairs and check table-cloths, is a smart local rendezvous, as
well as serving lavish buffet breakfasts. Bedrooms vary in price; the better
ones face the harbour, while front ones can be noisy in warm weather
(*John Woolsey*) More reports please.

Open All year except 3 days over Christmas.
Rooms 7 suites, 72 double, 51 single – all with bath and/or shower, telephone,
radio, TV.
Facilities 2 lounges, TV room, bar, tearoom, restaurant, open-air café, sauna;
conference facilities.
Location 5 mins' walk from centre. Parking.
Credit cards All major cards accepted.
Terms [1990 rates] B&B: single 1,050–1,630 Skr, double 1,630–1,890 Skr, suite
2,600–4,890 Skr. Full alc 280 Skr. Children under 12 half price.

Lady Hamilton Hotel   *Tel* (08) 23.46.80
Storkyrkobrinken 5   *Fax* (08) 11.11.48
Stockholm 111 28   *Telex* 1043

Lord Nelson Hotel   *Tel* (08) 23.23.90
Västerlånggatan 22   *Fax* (08) 10.10.89
Stockholm 111 29   *Telex* 1043

These twin B&B hotels in the old-town area have long been enjoyed b
readers: "Excellent housekeeping, friendly helpful staff, simple but mor
than adequate Swedish breakfast", is a recent comment. Each hote

portrays its historical theme: there are models of ships, nautical pictures and items taken from boats, such as figureheads and brass rails. And the basement plunge pool at the *Lady Hamilton* was a well in the 15th century. The *Lord Nelson* is in a fascinating area of cobbled pedestrian streets that are full of animation, but can be noisy late at night; it also has "an open-air rooftop for a drink while viewing the city skyline". Bedrooms are modern and attractive but small, some of them *very* small ("it helps if you think of them as cabins"). (*Mrs A Rooker*) One reader this year found various imperfections in the furnishings.

Lady Hamilton Hotel
Open All year.
Rooms 3 triple, 18 double, 13 single – all with bath and/or shower, telephone, radio, TV. Some suitable for &.
Facilities Bar/breakfast room/tearoom; conference facilities; sauna, plunge pool.
Location Central, in pedestrian zone, near Palace. (Front rooms might be noisy.) Street parking.
Credit cards All major cards accepted.
Terms [1990 rates] B&B: single 1,050–1,150 Skr, double 1,150–1,480 Skr. (No restaurant, but light meals available.)

Lord Nelson Hotel
Open All year.
Rooms 9 double, 22 single – all with shower, telephone, radio, TV.
Facilities Small lift. Bar, breakfast room; functions room. Sauna.
Location Central, in pedestrian zone, near Palace. Street parking.
Credit cards All major cards accepted.
Terms [1990 rates] B&B: single 795–870 Skr, double 1,020–1,150 Skr. (No restaurant, but light meals available.)

Hotel and Restaurant   *Tel* (08) 24.36.00
  Mälardrottningen   *Fax* (08) 24.36.76
Riddarholmen   *Telex* 15864
Stockholm 111 28

A converted 140-ft yacht once owned by Barbara Hutton, tied to a pier on Riddarholmen, a tiny island opposite Stockholm's old town. Rooms small but pleasant, helpful staff, excellent main meals and buffet breakfast; good value for expensive Stockholm. Closed Christmas, New Year. 59 rooms, all with shower. B&B single 550–895 Skr, double 650–995 Skr [1990]. New nomination. More reports please.

TÄLLBERG 793 03 Dalarna   **Map 7**

Hotell Åkerblads   *Tel* (0247) 508.00
     Fax (0247) 506.52

Praised for years by readers, this "remarkable place for a rural holiday" stands halfway between Leksand and Rättvik on Lake Siljan. The oldest part is a 17th-century farmhouse, but all is comfortable and spacious in the old style. Bedrooms are pleasantly furnished, hardly any two alike. "Delightful: a friendly welcome, and a pretty room in annexe," says a reader this year. Earlier views: "Classically Swedish in style, warmth and comfort. Our suite had views over the beautiful lake and forests. Staff friendly and efficient." "We had a delightful bedroom with verandas

painted in different shades of green and orange. The atmosphere in the
hotel is easy and informal. We loved the meals too. Lunch seemed to be
the main one – often with several kinds of fish and potatoes with dill. It
always ended with cake and excellent coffee in the upper hall. Local
parties coming for meals often included men and women in national
costume." Christina and Arne Åkerblad, the owners, and their sons are
the 19th and 20th generations of the founders – among the oldest hotel
families in Europe. (*C and M Hédoin*)

Open All year except Christmas.
Rooms 15 suites, 30 double, 14 single – 51 with bath and/or shower, all with
telephone, radio, TV. 39 in 3 annexes in garden. Ground-floor rooms with ramps.
Facilities 2 lounges, 2 TV rooms, bar, coffee/dancing room, restaurant; functions
facilities; sauna, whirlpool. Large garden with tennis, badminton, table-tennis,
skating rink. Lake with beach, bathing, fishing, boating nearby.
Location 12 km from Leksand; on road between Leksand and Rättvik. Parking.
Credit cards All major cards accepted.
Terms [1990 rates] B&B: single 540 Skr, double 430 Skr per person, suite 590 Skr.
Dinner, B&B 580–760 Skr; full board (min 3 nights) 630–1,000 Skr. Set lunch 150–
165 Skr, dinner 165–190 Skr; full alc 315 Skr. 1-night bookings sometimes
refused. Reduced weekend rates in low season. Reduced rates for children
under 12; special meals.

Switzerland

Hotel Chesa sur l'En, St-Moritz

APPENZELL 9050   **Map 14**

Romantik Hotel Säntis   *Tel* (071) 87.87.22
Landsgemeindeplatz   *Fax* (071) 87.48.42
                                 Telex 883733

In an attractive small mountain town south of Lake Constance, not far
from Austria, here is a highly traditional chalet-style inn, family-run, with
painted facade and antique wood furnishings. Recently renovated, the
light and airy rooms are a blend of the old and the high-tech new, with
lots of mirrors. A 1990 report: "We had a gorgeous suite, looking out on
to the Alpine foothills, with lots of cows and barns; the rooms were a little
noisy from a busy street. Breakfast was a huge buffet, with plenty of good
Swiss cheeses. The staff were very friendly." (*La Juana West*)

Open All year except 10 Jan–1 Mar.
Rooms 1 suite, 28 double, 4 single – all with bath and/or shower,
telephone, radio, TV.
Facilities 3 restaurants; functions room. Terrace; garden.
Location Central. Appenzell is 18 km S of St-Gallen.

Credit cards All major cards accepted.
Terms B&B: single 95–120 Sfrs, double 150–220 Sfrs, suite 220–300 Sfrs. Set lunch/dinner 30–50 Sfrs; full alc 45–55 Sfrs. Reduced rates and special meals for children.

AROSA 7050 Graubünden	Map 14

Hotel Hof Maran	*Tel* (081) 31.01.85
	Fax (081) 31.45.28
	Telex 851629

"Superb hospitality," say devotees revisiting this fairly large and very well-equipped modern hotel that has been grafted on to an old chalet: it has a fine mountain setting, high above Arosa, beside the golf/cross-country-ski course. Its bedrooms are well sound-proofed, furnished in honey-gold wood. Regular fans have again admired the food, both in the main restaurant and in the atmospheric *Stübl*. "Half board is almost inevitable because it is a long way down to the town. Dinner at 7 pm – ushered in and out with Swiss efficiency – did mean rather a long evening, but on some nights the lounge fairly rocked with music and dancing. Surprisingly, the only thing missing was a swimming pool." But at least a fitness centre has been installed this year.

Open Mid-June–mid-Oct, mid-Dec–mid-Apr.
Rooms 44 double, 15 single – all with bath or shower, telephone, radio, TV, baby-listening.
Facilities Lift. Lounge, TV room, bar (dancing), 3 restaurants; conference room; games room with table-tennis; sun-terrace on roof. Large grounds with 2 tennis courts, children's play area; skating rink in winter, 4 curling rinks. Sauna, solarium, fitness room. Ski-lift and ski school behind hotel; 9-hole golf course nearby.
Location 1 km from Arosa near Maran golf course. Bus service every 20 mins. Parking.
Restriction Not suitable for &.
Credit cards All major cards accepted.
Terms B&B: single 55–165 Sfrs, double 110–350 Sfrs; dinner, B&B: single 80–190 Sfrs, double 160–400 Sfrs; full board: single 100–210 Sfrs, double 200–440 Sfrs. Reduced rates and special meals for children. (Lower prices are for summer.)

ASCONA 6612 Ticino	Map 14

Hotel Casa Berno	*Tel* (093) 35.32.32
	Fax (093) 36.11.14
	Telex 846167

This modern four-star hotel stands on a hillside above Lago Maggiore, between Monte Verità and Ronco: it's about 30 minutes' walk up a steep winding road from the centre of smart, animated Ascona, so a car is an asset. The views from its terraces and heated swimming pool are stunning; all rooms face south over the lake and have a balcony. "Excellent and good value," say readers again this year. "A very well-run hotel, full of courtesy, with breathtaking vistas of the lake from the beautiful rooms. The food is excellent. But we cared less for the hotel's utter formality – guests dress for dinner." Another reader, too, has found the style "rather tired 1960s". But others continue to speak well of the charming managers, the Goetschis, and their staff, also the bedrooms, breakfast buffet, and "delicious" Franco–Helvetico–Ticinese cuisine, including the pension meals. (*Arnold Horwell, Mrs Don Simecheck, Jan A Sarsten*)

Open Mar–Oct inclusive.
Rooms 11 suites, 43 double, 7 single – all with telephone, radio, TV, balcony/terrace.
Facilities Lift. Lounges (1 with TV), bar on roof-garden, grill room, restaurant with terrace; sauna, massage, solarium, fitness room, ladies' hairdresser. Garden with heated swimming pool. Golf, tennis nearby.
Location Between Monte Verità and Ronco; 20–30 minutes' walk from Ascona. Parking.
Credit cards Access, Amex, Visa.
Terms B&B 132–182 Sfrs; half board 152–192 Sfrs; full board 172–202 Sfrs.
Reduced rates for children sharing parents' room; special meals. Weekly package in spring.

BASLE 4001　　　　　　　　　　　　　　　　　　　**Map 14**

Hotel Drei Könige　　　　　　　　　　　*Tel* (061) 25.52.52
Blumenrain 8　　　　　　　　　　　　　　　*Fax* (061) 25.21.53
　　　　　　　　　　　　　　　　　　　　　Telex 962937

Basle's grandest hotel, and one of Europe's oldest (royalty have stayed often). A bit old-fashioned, but comfortable, with a fine service and a great Rhineside position: some room balconies face the river, as does the dining room terrace (food is good). 90 rooms, all with bath and shower. Double room 280–400 Sfrs. Breakfast 18 Sfrs. Set meals 53–95 Sfrs.

BERN 3001　　　　　　　　　　　　　　　　　　　**Map 14**

Hotel Bären　　　　　　　　　　　　　*Tel* (031) 22.33.67
Schauplatzgasse 4　　　　　　　　　　　　*Fax* (031) 22.69.83
　　　　　　　　　　　　　　　　　　　　　Telex 912951

Named after the city's mascot, and full of emblems of the black teddy rampant; but the service, happily, is more bullish than Bär-ish. A four-star and usefully central hotel, near the station and main square; but also quiet (rooms are double-glazed, most face the inner courtyard). A modern interior, plenty of modern facilities and comforts. Excellent but expensive Swiss–French food in a stylish restaurant. 45 rooms, all with bath and shower. B&B double 155– 195 Sfrs. Set meals 20–45 Sfrs [1990]. Again endorsed this year. Fuller reports welcome.

CHÂTEAU-D'OEX 1837 Vaud　　　　　　　　　　**Map 14**

Hostellerie Bon Accueil　　　　　　　　*Tel* (029) 4.63.20
　　　　　　　　　　　　　　　　　　　　　Fax (029) 4.51.26

This big green-shuttered chalet, dating in parts from the 18th century, stands just inside French-speaking territory, up a steep road from the sunny Alpine village of Château-d'Oex. With plenty of polished wood

and leather chairs, it breathes spacious comfort and good management.
Bedrooms are wood-panelled, with fine views over meadows and snowy
peaks. Regular visitors have enjoyed taking drinks in the garden and
eating dinner by a log fire, and report that New Year's Eve can be "like a
private house party". (*K and S M-S*)

Open 20 Dec–15 Oct.
Rooms 1 suite, 17 double, 2 single – 17 with bath, 3 with shower, all with
telephone, 8 with TV. 8 in annexe.
Facilities 2 lounges, cellar bar, dining room. Garden.
Location 1 km from centre of village which is 15 km SW of Gstaad.
Credit cards All major cards accepted.
Terms B&B: single 80–100 Sfrs, double 120–190 Sfrs; half board 30 Sfrs added per
person. Set dinner 35 Sfrs; full alc 50–70 Sfrs. Reduced rates and special meals for
children.

DAVOS 7270 Graubünden   Map 14

Hotel Flüela   *Tel* (081) 47.12.21
Bahnhofstrasse 5   *Fax* (081) 46.44.01
                                                    Telex 853100

A sizeable ski-hotel, owned and managed by the Gredig family for over a
century, and now much modernised. Open only in winter, it is close to
the Parsenn Bahn, the largest ski-lift in this big resort. The service has
always been extolled, and never so much as in 1990 by a couple who
brought their 11-month baby: "In advance we were nervous, after three
bad experiences with our baby in British hotels. But our fears were
unfounded. The service of Michael's meals was wonderful. Each day we
told the head waiter what he should eat, and at six we took him to the
main dining room; the sight of the little chap being served in a grand
manner by uniformed waiters was unforgettable. We did not need a baby-
sitter, as the chambermaid on our floor was on duty all evening. And the
head porter even offered to lend us his own baby's sledge. The rooms
were superb, and all the staff genuinely friendly." The babyless will be
glad to hear that the feeding of adults is also admired: "Five- or six-course
meals, a mixture of traditional and *nouvelle*, with second helpings
encouraged." "Super lounges, with pianist every evening, open log fire,
indoor swimming pool, sauna, solarium; and quite outstanding breakfast
and dinner." (*Dr and Mrs TJ David; AJ Ormerod*)

Open 24 Nov–15 Apr.
Rooms 10 suites, 60 double, 19 single – all with bath and/or shower, telephone,
radio, TV.
Facilities Bar lounge (with pianist), sitting rooms, restaurants; functions rooms;
games room. Indoor swimming pool, sauna, solarium, massage, fitness room; ski
boutique, barber, hairdresser; bank.
Location In town centre. A few roadside rooms may be noisy. Parking.
Restriction Not suitable for &.
Credit cards All major cards accepted.
Terms B&B 130–315 Sfrs. Set lunch 35 Sfrs, dinner 50–70 Sfrs; full alc 70–
100 Sfrs. Reduced rates and special meals for children.

Do you know of a good hotel or country inn in the United States or
Canada? Nominations please to our sibling publication, America's
Wonderful Little Hotels and Inns, PO Box 150, Riverside Avenue,
Riverside, Conn. 06878, USA.

Hotel National
Obere Strasse 31

Tel (081) 43.60.46
Fax (081) 43.16.50
Telex 853103

On the edge of Davos Platz, the lower part of this straggling resort, this great white modern cube of a hotel might not be to every taste, but a recent visitor was well pleased: "Isolated from all but the noise of church bells, it has rooms with balconies that look along the valley, while others look back along the town. The staff all seemed enthusiastic and interested. Over ten days we had the best half-board evening food I've ever encountered, generally in the *minceur* style, invariably interesting and attractively served. Wines are moderately priced. Occasionally a piano player entertained – preferable to the Swiss night when a poor accordionist did his worst and an alpen-horn blasted nearby. Breakfast was the usual spread. A small games room with table-tennis, and a lounge with a fire. Warmly recommended." (*TH Nash*)

Open 1 Dec–7 Apr, 1 June–29 Sep.
Rooms 4 suites, 40 double, 24 single – all with bath and/or shower, telephone, radio, TV.
Facilities Lift. Lounge, TV room, 2 bars, 2 restaurants; pianist, dancing, entertainment. 2 games rooms for children. Garden.
Location 400 metres from town centre.
Credit cards All major cards accepted.
Terms B&B 62–142 Sfrs; dinner, B&B 70–150 Sfrs. Set lunch 15–30 Sfrs, dinner 25–45 Sfrs; full alc 35 Sfrs. Reduced rates for children; special meals on request.

LES DIABLERETS 1865 Vaud   Map 14

Hôtel Les Lilas `BUDGET`   *Tel* (025) 53.11.34

"Our children were sure that Heidi must live somewhere in the village and would appear at any minute" – that report sets the tone for this "charming and homely" chalet-like roadside hotel, run by the Matti family, in an unspoilt village between Aigle and Gstaad. Some rooms are large and pine-panelled, others smaller; many have a balcony with mountain views. "The food was not exciting but it was adequate, and the *patron* was delightful and helpful", is one report this year. Others have enjoyed "excellent" dishes such as chicken with beer and beef with morilles; the main candle-lit restaurant is lovely, but *pension* meals are served in a duller one. (*Dr NB Finter, R Maxwell-Gumbleton, and others*) A dissenter this year reports a very poor welcome, a shabby ill-kept room and only average food: more reports please.

Open All year.
Rooms 8 double, 7 single – 8 with bath and shower.
Facilities Bar, TV room, 2 restaurants; terrace. Garden.
Location In village 20 km E of Aigle on road to Gstaad.
Credit cards Access, Amex, Visa.
Terms B&B: single 50–60 Sfrs, double 90–110 Sfrs; dinner, B&B: single 80–90 Sfrs, double 150–170 Sfrs. Set lunch 15 Sfrs, dinner 30 Sfrs; full alc 50–80 Sfrs. Reduced rates and special meals for children.

Our italicised entries indicate hotels which are worth considering, but which, for various reasons – inadequate information, lack of feedback, ambivalent reports – do not at the moment warrant a full entry. We should particularly welcome comments on these hotels.

ENGELBERG 6390 Unterwalden Map 14

Hotel-Restaurant Eden
Tel (041) 94.32.94
Fax (041) 94.39.47

Newly modernised and improved, this spruce and friendly *Restaurant-mit-Zimmer* stands in a well-known resort high up in a lovely isolated mountain valley south of Lucerne. "Our lasting memory is of the superb food and warm hospitality provided by Sybille and Thomas Reinhardt-Waser", according to a recent report. Others this year have agreed, stressing the good level of comfort and furnishing (but one reader found the food disappointing). "The homely gentle ambience created by Sybille in the restaurant is so fitting for the food that Thomas prepares. Both find time to spend talking with their guests." "Yes, a real Eden, this *Eden* – delightful public rooms, atmosphere, rocking-chairs, a nursery which would keep any child quiet on a wet day." Some rooms, but not all, have balcony with mountain views. (*Kevin G Lee, Dr NB Finter*)

Open Mid-Dec–Oct.
Rooms 3 suites, 7 double, 2 single – all with bath or shower, telephone, radio, TV; some with balcony.
Facilities Lift, bar, TV room, library, bistro, restaurant, conference room, children's games room, sauna, solarium. Garden, terrace for meals in summer.
Location Central, near station. Garage and outdoor parking.
Restriction Not suitable for &.
Credit cards All major cards accepted.
Terms B&B: single 80–100 Sfrs, double 130–180 Sfrs, suite 170–210 Sfrs; dinner, B&B: single 110–130 Sfrs, double 190–270 Sfrs, suite 230–270 Sfrs. Set lunch 17–20 Sfrs, dinner 39–68 Sfrs; full alc 45–70 Sfrs. Reduced rates and special meals for children.

FLIMS-WALDHAUS 7018 Graubünden Map 14

Hotel Adula
Tel (081) 39.01.61
Fax (081) 39.43.15
Telex 851960

In a popular summer and winter resort in the Grisons, west of Chur, amid fine alpine hiking and walking country: a large chalet-style hotel, somewhat staid, best suited for older people (but there's a children's playroom). Good food and service, friendly owners; indoor pool, sauna, piano bar, tennis, barbecues, etc. Closed mid-Oct–mid-Dec. 99 rooms, most with bath and/or shower. B&B: single 85–185 Sfrs, double 160–320 Sfrs. Set meals 25–55 Sfrs. Lack of recent news from Adula-*tors: more welcome.*

GENEVA 1204 Map 14

Hôtel L'Arbalète
3 rue de la Tour Maîtresse
Tel (022) 28.41.55
Fax (022) 21.96.60
Telex 427293

Well located near the lake, museums and best shops, a small deluxe hotel (arbalète means crossbow) that continues to be liked. "Reception charming and helpful, food and service very good. A spacious, comfortable room, but decor a bit heavy." "The staff were marvellous, serving us a special breakfast when we overslept." "A homely feel, and quiet, because windows are double-glazed; good food." "Nice touches like an umbrella in the bedroom to help with Geneva rain." The ground-floor brasserie is cheaper than the main first-floor restaurant. (*NPD and J Levine, Fiona Sausman*) Some rooms could do with a facelift, one 1990 visitor suggests.

Open All year.
Rooms 20 double, 12 single – all with bath, shower, telephone, radio, TV, minibar, baby-listening, air-conditioning.
Facilities Lift. Hall, 2 bars, pub with pianist, 3 restaurants. Lake Geneva 2 mins' walk, with sandy beach, safe bathing, fishing.
Location Central; near Mont-Blanc bridge. Windows double-glazed. Garage and parking.
Credit cards All major cards accepted.
Terms [1990 rates] B&B: single 215–255 Sfrs, double 280–320 Sfrs. Set lunch/dinner 20–50 Sfrs. Reduced rates for children sharing parents' room; special meals on request.

Hôtel Les Armures   *Tel* (022) 28.91.72
1 rue du Puits St-Pierre   *Fax* (022) 28.98.46
                                                   Telex 421129

In a small square near the cathedral, up in the old town, this elegant small hotel makes a pleasant contrast to the grand, impersonal places down by the lake; but like them it is not cheap – in Geneva, what is? It is an old stone building dating mainly from the 17th century when it was extended to accommodate Huguenots fleeing from France. One report this year: "Our room was large and lovely, the restaurant atmospheric (good raclette), the lounge cosy – but the welcome could have been warmer." The quietest rooms are on the interior court, where a reader had one "beautifully furnished, with a small roof-garden outside its window". (*Mary E Hanson*) Charges for breakfast extras are high.

Open All year. Restaurant closed Easter, Christmas and New Year.
Rooms 4 suites, 20 double, 4 single – all with bath, shower, telephone, radio, TV, baby-listening, air-conditioning.
Facilities Lift. Lobby, salon, breakfast room, bar, lounge, restaurant, *Stübl*.
Location Central, near St-Pierre cathedral. No special parking facilities.
Restriction Not suitable for &.
Credit cards All major cards accepted.
Terms [1990 rates] B&B: single 205–245 Sfrs, double 320 Sfrs, suite 410 Sfrs. Full alc 50–60 Sfrs. Special meals for children.

GRUYÈRES 1663 Fribourg   Map 14

Hôtel Fleur-de-Lys   *Tel* (029) 6.21.08
                                                   Fax (029) 6.10.67

Between Fribourg and Vevey, in a medieval ramparted village famous for its cheeses (it has a fine old castle too), a traditional but nicely modernised hostelry with spacious bedrooms and beamed ceilings. Good food including cheese fondue; service slowish but cheerful. Closed Feb. 8 rooms, all with bath, single

90 Sfrs, double 130 Sfrs. Set meals 26–95 Sfrs [1990]. New nomination. More reports please.

GSTAAD 3780 Bern   **Map 14**

Hotel Christiania   *Tel* (030) 4.51.21
Hauptstrasse   *Fax* (030) 4.71.09
                                                          Telex 922250

In the main street of fashionable Gstaad, a small, spruce hotel with a four-star rating. Recent accounts: "A warm greeting, wonderful breakfasts, and good food in their cosy restaurant. Our bedroom had a balcony, writing desk, easy chairs. Very quiet." "The public rooms are small and cosy, and have a lived-in feel. In the rustic-style restaurant we had a good lunch. Many bedrooms overlook a pleasant garden." The owner's daughter is chef and her son-in-law head waiter – a true family affair. (*Ellen and John Buchanan, Kate and Stephan Murray-Sykes*)

Open All year.
Rooms 3 suites for 4–6 people with bath, shower, salon, dining room; 9 double, 6 single – 11 with bath, all with telephone, radio, TV; most with balcony.
Facilities Lift. Salon with TV, bar, restaurant (pianist in high season). Garden with restaurant.
Location Central, near station; street-facing rooms can be noisy. Garage (16 Sfrs).
Credit cards Diners, Visa.
Terms [1990 rates] B&B: single 70–230 Sfrs, double 220–370 Sfrs, suite 600–1,800 Sfrs; dinner, B&B 46 Sfrs per person added. Set lunch/dinner 50 Sfrs. Special meals for children.

HERTENSTEIN 6352 Lucerne   **Map 14**

Hotel Hertenstein   *Tel* (041) 93.14.44
                                                         Fax (041) 93.27.66
                                                          Telex 862984

Right by the lovely lake of Lucerne, alone on a peninsula 3 km outside Weggis, a spacious modern hotel in huge lakeside grounds. Comfortable rooms, some with lake-facing balcony; good heated swimming pool; adjacent steamer landing stage. Good buffet breakfast, but main meals ordinary. Closed 21 Oct–31 Mar. 50 rooms, all with bath and shower. B&B double 136–234 Sfrs. New nomination. More reports please.

ISELTWALD 3807 Bern   **Map 14**

Hotel Bellevue   *Tel* (036) 45.11.10
                                                         Fax (036) 45.12.77

Iseltwald is a picturesque hamlet and summer resort on a peninsula beside the lake of Brienz, east of Interlaken. You can sail or water-ski, or go for mountain walks or climbs; the beautiful Giessback falls are worth a visit. The quite pricey chalet-style *Bellevue* has a good position close to the lake, with two terraced gardens for drinks and light meals; but woods rise steeply just behind and some visitors have found this setting sombre, especially if you have a back room (front ones with a balcony are best). The hotel's design is "typically Swiss", with much use of wood and folkweave fabrics. The food served in its two restaurants is its strongest feature, especially local fish, again hugely admired this year: charcoal-grilled trout or pike with fresh herbs, lake fish with light fresh sauces, salmon trout in pernod, washed down with good Swiss wines. The breakfast buffet is lavish; the service much improved. (*Joanie Daily, Eileen Broadbent, Padi and John Howard, and others*)

Open 15 Feb–31 Dec. Restaurant closed Tue.
Rooms 9 double, 2 single – all with bath and/or shower, telephone, radio, TV, baby-listening; many with balcony.
Facilities Salon, bar, 2 restaurants. 2 terraces; garden. On lake shore with beach and sailing.
Location On S shore of Lake Brienz, 10 km E of Interlaken.
Restriction Not suitable for &.
Credit cards All major cards accepted.
Terms B&B: single 45–60 Sfrs, double 90–130 Sfrs. Half board 22 Sfrs per person added. Set lunch 30–45 Sfrs, dinner 55–75 Sfrs; full alc 64 Sfrs. Reduced rates and special meals for children.

Hotel Chalet du Lac   *Tel* (036) 45.11.12

An authentic lakeside chalet remodelled as a small hotel, family owned and well run, with modern wood furnishings. Some rooms face the mountain, others have a balcony above the lake. Meals can be taken on a lakeside terrace when fine. "Excellent and beautifully furnished," says a visitor this year. "The *demi-pension* meals were simple but good value, with very good lake fish and salads. But portions were not large, and desserts lacked imagination. Good breakfast buffet." Others, too, have commended the food and informal service. (*Daphne and Ed Borton*) There is a large family suite suitable for self-catering.

Open All year except Nov. Restaurant closed Mon (in winter also Tue).
Rooms 1 family suite, 11 double – all with bath and/or shower, telephone, TV.
Facilities Restaurant; functions room. Terrace
Location On S shore of Lake Brienz, 10 km E of Interlaken.
Credit cards All major cards accepted.
Terms [1990 rates] B&B double 84–138 Sfrs. Dinner, B&B 22 Sfrs per person added. Special meals for children.

KANDERSTEG 3718 Bern   **Map 14**

Hotel Ermitage   **BUDGET**   *Tel* (033) 75.15.12

Run by the friendly Hirschi family, the *Ermitage* stands amid meadows and trees on the edge of this big resort, near a chair-lift and a carpark. Again this year visitors have liked the cheerful service, relaxed atmosphere, newly installed lounge, and the very good food: the *pension* meals allow no choice, but vary daily. "The evening meal was a delight, but it took a long time because each dish is specially prepared." "The food was delicious, astonishingly sophisticated, but with rather too much cream." "Good buffet breakfast." Rooms vary: those at the front have a balcony, and some have a kitchenette, but rear ones can be cramped. "If you love the sound of rushing water to go to sleep by, several waterfalls and a steep brook provide that. Lovely garden restaurant." (*WP and BJ Barry, Mrs EA Rudd, Richard Pinner*)

Open 22 Dec–2 Apr, 19 May–26 Oct. Restaurant closed Mon in low season.
Rooms 2 suites, 11 double – all with bath and/or shower, telephone, radio, TV; 6 with baby-listening; many with balcony.
Facilities Lounge with TV, restaurant, bar with occasional folk music/disco, breakfast room; sun-terrace. Garden with children's play area.
Location Turn left off road from Spiez and Thun, near the Oeschinensee chair-lift. Hotel is quietly situated. Parking.
Restriction Not suitable for &.
Credit cards Access, Diners, Visa.
Terms B&B 60–90 Sfrs; dinner, B&B 80–110 Sfrs. Set lunch 12–30 Sfrs, dinner 20–43 Sfrs; full alc 40–45 Sfrs. Reduced rates and special meals for children.

KLOSTERS 7250 Graubünden Map 14

Hotel Chesa Grischuna *Tel* (081) 69.22.22
Bahnhofstrasse 12 *Fax* (081) 69.22.25

Flowery balconies, panelled walls, bright rugs and waitresses in local dress, all help to intensify the *gemütlichkeit* at this lovely characterful hotel (but well modernised too) in the heart of a busy resort. "Friendly staff, food and service excellent" is the latest endorsement of previous panegyrics: "Lots of antiques, pretty dining room (excellent fresh vegetables). We had a nice large room with balcony in the chalet-annexe." "An ancient timber door unlatches into a bright interior, modernised with honey-coloured wood set off with furnishings in the traditional Swiss green, white and scarlet. The bright reception area is new, but the rest of the hotel is delightfully old and mellow, made of wood dark with age. Our room on the fourth floor of the main building (no lift) was not large, but had bright rugs on the polished floor and hand-woven bedspreads. The food is good and pleasantly served. The cellar bar is where the young locals and the après-skiers meet: wonderful lively friendly atmosphere." (*David Thibodeau*)

Open June–Easter. Bar open in winter only.
Rooms 16 double, 10 single – 13 with bath, 4 with shower, all with telephone, radio; TV on request. 11 in annexe opposite.
Facilities Lounge with TV, restaurant; cellar bar with pianist in high season; bowling. Sun-terrace, small garden.
Location In centre of Klosters Platz, near the station.
Restriction Not suitable for &.
Credit cards All major cards accepted.
Terms Dinner, B&B: single 120–195 Sfrs, double 220–380 Sfrs; full board 25 Sfrs per person added. Set lunch 15–28 Sfrs, dinner 45–61 Sfrs; full alc 91 Sfrs. Reduced rates for children; special meals on request.

MEGGEN 6045 Lucerne Map 14

Hotel Sonnegg *Tel* (041) 37.14.00
Hauptstrasse 37

A popular family hotel just east of Lucerne, up a hill above its lovely lake. "Simple, unpretentious and comfortable, with meticulous house-keeping," says a recent visitor. "The seafood restaurant is superlative, with a friendly, informal ambience." Others agree that the fish and seafood dishes are excellent, if expensive (but there's also a cheaper coffee shop, serving pizzas, etc). "Good service and modern comfort combined with Swiss rustic touches. The helpful staff will baby-listen and even supervised our teenage sons. There is a small park on the lake's edge." "The bar, popular with locals, has a good atmosphere," says a reader this year. (*Carol Martin, Anne Rapley, H and B Shames*) Most rooms look towards the lake and are quiet; some others can be noisy. There is a useful local train to Lucerne from a nearby station.

Open All year. Restaurant closed Sun, and Mon lunch.
Rooms 18 double – 9 with bath, shower; all with TV.
Facilities Lift. Bar, restaurant.
Location On lake Lucerne, 5 km E of Lucerne towards Rigi, Gotthard on old road.
Credit cards All major cards accepted.
Terms [1990 rates] B&B: single 55–60 Sfrs, double 85–90 Sfrs; half board 30 Sfrs per person added.

MONTREUX 1820 Vaud   Map 14

Hôtel Eden au Lac   *Tel* (021) 963.55.51
11 rue du Théâtre   *Fax* (021) 963.18.13
                                                   Telex 453151

"Perfectly run, beautifully furnished, supremely comfortable, with splendid views across the lake" is this year's endorsement of earlier praise for this large, classic hotel, recently restored to its Edwardian glory. It stands right by the lake in this sprucely plush resort. "The glorious pink-and-white first-floor dining room, looking out on the lake, makes a romantic setting for dinner. The food is excellent (you can eat in the garden in the summer) and breakfasts are buffet affairs with wonderful muesli. Service combines style with friendliness. Bedrooms well equipped, bathrooms large but old-fashioned." A reader this year preferred the expensive à la carte restaurant to the "average food" of the cheaper one. All lake-facing rooms have a balcony with awning. (*DJ Milner, DW Tate*)

Open Feb–mid-Dec.
Rooms 10 suites, 77 double, 18 single – all with bath, shower, telephone, radio, TV, baby-listening.
Facilities Hall, 2 salons, TV room, bar, 2 restaurants; 3 conference rooms. Garden; terrace for meals.
Location Central, on lake. Parking.
Credit cards All major cards accepted.
Terms [1990 rates] B&B: single 100–180 Sfrs, double 160–260 Sfrs; dinner, B&B 35 Sfrs per person added. Set lunch/dinner 30–73 Sfrs.

NEUHAUSEN 8212 Schaffhausen   Map 14

Hotel Bellevue   *Tel* (053) 22.21.21
Bad Bahnhofstrasse 17   *Fax* (053) 22.83.50

Just two kilometres from the attractive medieval town of Schaffhausen are the Rhine Falls, not the highest waterfalls in Europe but the most powerful, and 150 metres wide. Here the aptly named *Bellevue*, outwardly dull-looking, has a glorious setting: most bedrooms, and some bathrooms, overlook the falls. "From my bed, in my splendid double room, I had a fine view of the falls," says a recent visitor, "and the food was excellent, especially the game (huge helpings), and the service was *svelte*." Another reader had "an interesting room with the structural beams appearing out of the floor". The spectacular views extend also to the "splendid lofty dining room" where there is plenty of choice and breakfast includes cooked dishes. Service is pleasant. (*Margret Wells*) One reader this year found the bedroom decor rather too 1960s.

Open Feb–Dec.
Rooms 24 double, 3 single – 13 with bath, 7 with shower, all with telephone, radio, TV.
Facilities Lift. Lounge, restaurant; functions room. Large garden with terrace.
Location By the Rhine on outskirts of Neuhausen. 2 km SW of Schaffhausen. Parking.
Credit cards All major cards accepted.
Terms B&B: single 45–100 Sfrs, double 85–170 Sfrs.

PONTRESINA 7504 Graubünden   Map 14

Hotel Garni Chesa Mulin   *Tel* (082) 6.75.75
Via Mulin   *Fax* (082) 6.70.40

This resort is smaller and quieter than its flashy neighbour, St-Moritz, and the modern white-walled *Chesa Mulin* is not untypical of its better family-run B&B hotels. Visitors in 1990 endorsed these earlier accounts: "A warm personal welcome from the Schmid family, who work hard. Rooms are attractively furnished, and the excellent and varied buffet breakfast is served in a bright Alpine-style room." "Bedrooms have comfortable beds and good reading lights. There is a lovely garden with a fine view. Led by Mr and Mrs Schmid, the staff are most polite and helpful." In summer there are walks in woods and across meadows and glaciers. There is a snack bar, and good restaurants nearby. (*Alan J Pike, RP*)

Open Dec–Apr, June–Oct.
Rooms 23 double, 4 single – 24 with bath and shower, 3 with shower, all with telephone, radio, mini-bar, TV. 1 specially designed for &.
Facilities Lift. Lounge, snack bar, breakfast room. Sauna, solarium. Garden; terrace.
Location Central; turn off main road towards station. Garage and parking.
Credit cards All major cards accepted.
Terms B&B: single 75–100 Sfrs, double 130–180 Sfrs. 1-week bookings (Sat–Sat) preferred in winter; ski packages in winter low season. Reduced rates for children sharing parents' room; special meals on request. (No restaurant, but snacks available.)

RIGI-KALTBAD 6356 Lucerne   Map 14

Hotel Bergsonne   BUDGET   *Tel* (041) 83.11.47

"From the bedroom windows, what a stupendous panorama! The position of this hotel is one of the most magnificent in Switzerland," says its nominator this year. It stands just outside a hamlet three-quarters of the way up the famous Rigi, a mountain on the north side of Lake Lucerne, and can be reached by rack or cable railway from Vitznau or Weggis. "It's a three-star hotel, a little old-fashioned, with bedroom furniture and plumbing much as in many other hotels of this grade. The large restaurant, again with the wonderful view, offers well-cooked tasty food; Willy and Dorly Camps, the owners, work hard and are very friendly. And that wonderful silence, except for the bells of cows!" (*Richard Pinner*)

Open June–Nov and Dec–Apr.
Rooms 20 double – all with bath or shower, radio; telephone, TV on request.
Facilities Lounges, restaurant; terrace.
Location 3 km NE of Weggis, by cable railway (no access by car).
Restriction Not suitable for &.
Credit cards All major cards accepted.
Terms [1990 rates] B&B: single 55–75 Sfrs, double 100–140 Sfrs; dinner, B&B 20 Sfrs per person added; full board 35 Sfrs added. Reduced rates and special meals for children.

RINGGENBERG 3852 Bernese Oberland   Map 14

Hotel Seeburg   `BUDGET`   *Tel* (036) 22.29.61

An unpretentious hotel, owned and run by the Michel family, in a peaceful and idyllic position on the Brienzersee just outside Interlaken. The lakeside gardens are attractive, with tables and chairs for drinks and al fresco meals. After some years' absence, it is restored to the Guide this year by its original nominator, making a return visit: "The Michels made a great fuss of us all and their staff were friendly too. Rooms are basic but adequate, bathrooms tiny but well thought out. We had some good meals, including lake fish, superb venison with noodles, and rösti. The dining room has been newly decorated." (*Padi Howard*)

Open Apr–Oct.
Rooms 30 – most with bath or shower. Ground-floor rooms.
Facilities Lift. Salon, dining room; terrace. Garden; on lake with facilities for water sports, sailing, fishing.
Location 3 km NE of Interlaken, on Brienzersee. Parking.
Credit card Visa.
Terms [1990 rates] B&B: single 32–66 Sfrs, double 52–110 Sfrs. Dinner, B&B 15 Sfrs per person added; full board 28 Sfrs added.

ROUGEMONT 1838 Vaud   Map 14

Hôtel Valrose   `BUDGET`   *Tel* (029) 4.81.46
                                                 Fax (029) 4.88.54

Set on the edge of a pretty village west of Gstaad, here is a simple modern chalet-style hotel without frills or graces: but it is clean and welcoming, and offers good value to those on a budget holiday in an expensive country. "The owner is pleasant and humorous, the food is plentiful, and nearly every room has a view of the mountains. The railway station is close by, but Swiss trains are quiet, and after 10 pm the only sound was the tinkling of cowbells." (*Esler Crawford; Kate and Stephan Murray-Sykes*)

Open All year except Nov. Restaurant closed Tue.
Rooms 12 double, 3 single – 7 with shower, all with mini-bar; TV on request.
Facilities Salon with TV, bar/café, 2 dining rooms. Terrace, garden.
Location Rougemont is 4 km W of Saanen. Parking.
Restriction Not suitable for &.
Credit cards All major cards accepted.

Terms [1990 rates] B&B 34–48 Sfrs; dinner, B&B 17 Sfrs per person added; full board 30 Sfrs added. Set lunch/dinner 18–22 Sfrs; full alc 45–50 Sfrs. Reduced rates for children; special meals on request.

SAANENMÖSER 3777 Bern   Map 14

Hotel Hornberg   *Tel* (030) 4.44.40
                                                               Fax (030) 4.62.79

The von Siebenthals' chalet-style holiday hotel stands alone at the foot of the Hornberg, looking out over the valley near Gstaad. This year and last, readers have commended its lovely situation and good cooking, and the genuine warmth of the owners and staff, who welcome children and provide for them well. An earlier view: "The bedrooms are comfortable and well equipped. The food is imaginative, artistically presented and *hausgemacht*, and the breakfast buffet is the best I've ever seen. The owners run excursions at no extra charge: the trip may be to the family cheese-making hut high up in the mountains, or some remote local beauty spot." (Confirmed by *K and S M-S*)

Open June–Oct, Dec–Apr.
Rooms 7 suites, 18 double, 8 single – most with bath and/or shower; all with telephone, radio; TV on request. Some with balcony.
Facilities Lounge, salon, bar, TV room, children's playroom, restaurant; terrace. Large garden, indoor and outdoor swimming pool, sauna. Winter sports. Trips, barbecues, picnics organised for guests.
Location 20 km N of Gstaad.
Restriction Not suitable for &.
Credit cards Access, Diners, Visa (restaurant only).
Terms B&B: single 80–110 Sfrs, double 160–220 Sfrs, suite 280–320 Sfrs. Half board 100–140 Sfrs per person. Set lunch 15–27 Sfrs, dinner 40–65 Sfrs; full alc 45 Sfrs. Reduced rates and special meals for children.

ST-LUC 3961 Valais   Map 14

Hotel Bella Tola et St-Luc   *Tel* (027) 65.14.44
                                                               Fax (027) 61.01.24
                                                               Telex 472094

This venerable old hostelry stands in a mountain village high up on the slopes of a sunny valley west of Zermatt; it dates from 1859 when it could be reached only by mule-track, and for four generations it has been owned and run by the Pont family – currently by young Olivier Pont and his Thai wife, Sulinda. It lost its place in recent Guides, but has two admirers this year: "For 40 years on and off our family has been visiting this delightful, simple, comfortable hotel, where the food is good, the service friendly, and the garden and bedrooms have a view of the Matterhorn. Sulinda cooks a delicious Thai dinner every Thursday." "The food has greatly improved, the service is charming." Others have spoken of "beautifully furnished cottage-style rooms" and "the view of sunrise over the Matterhorn while breakfasting in bed". (*Lady Elizabeth Brunner, Lady Shirley Anglesey*)

Open June–Oct and Dec–Apr.
Rooms 28 double, 14 single – 21 with bath and/or shower.

Facilities Lift, 3 salons (1 with TV), bar, restaurant, children's playroom; functions room. Sauna. Garden; terrace.
Location St-Luc is 15 km SE of Sierre.
Restriction Not suitable for ⅃.
Credit cards Amex, Visa.
Terms [1990 rates] B&B: single 50–95 Sfrs, double 92–150 Sfrs. Dinner, B&B 30 Sfrs per person added.

ST-MORITZ 7500 Graubünden   Map 14

Hotel Chesa sur l'En   *Tel* (082) 3.31.44
                                           Fax (082) 3.64.74

A romantic and unusual hotel, probably not to all tastes, and very different from most others in swanky St-Moritz. It is a huge 19th-century chalet, set amid pines on a hillside just outside the town, and its old-style decor is lavish: the massive front door opens on to a richly panelled and ornately carved main hall. The warm personal touch of the ever-present owners, the Schwarzenbachs, is admired: but the rooms are defiantly old-fashioned (few have private baths), and this has often led to criticisms. Yet the *Chesa* has many devotees who return affectionately year after year – such as the American couple who sent this recent report: "A jewel of Swiss *belle époque* architecture, with an enveloping ambience – a wonderful experience. The Schwarzenbachs have been running the inn for 30 years. Eliane is in front organising glühwein parties and making little favours for the ladies; Dieter is preparing delicious four-course meals. This is not a place for those who want mod cons. Many of the rooms would be ruined if *en suite* bathrooms were installed. In fact, with a little imagination one can picture oneself back in the 1880s: to get a bath you ring a bell, soon there's a soft knock on the door and clean towels are presented. But it's a very dreary bathroom." Upper rooms have fine views over the mountains. Four rooms *do* now have baths *en suite*. (*Lynne and David Allen*)

Open 15 Dec–30 Apr, 14 July–5 Nov. Dining room closed for lunch.
Rooms 12 double, 2 single – 4 with bath and shower, 3 with shower; 5 with radio, 7 with TV.
Facilities Hall, salon with TV, dining room, functions room. Garden, sun terrace.
Location In St Moritz Bad, 5 mins by bus from St-Moritz. Parking.
Restriction Not suitable for ⅃.
Credit cards All major cards accepted.
Terms B&B 35–108 Sfrs; dinner, B&B 58–132 Sfrs. Set dinner 34 Sfrs. 50% reduction for children sharing parents' room.

SCHAFFHAUSEN 8200   Map 14

Rheinhotel Fischerzunft   *Tel* (053) 25.32.81
Rheinquai 8   *Fax* (053) 24.32.85
                                           Telex 897162

A picturesque medieval town on the upper Rhine, close to Europe's most powerful waterfall, the Rhine Falls – that is the suitable setting for this former fishermen's guild house, now a brilliant and stylish restaurant (three red *Gault Millau toques*), with glorious bedrooms and bathrooms to match. The owner/chef André Jaeger met his Chinese wife Doreen in Hong Kong, and reports this year endorse this earlier praise: "Cooking with a decidedly oriental accent, served with great style by the glamorous Doreen and her team in a beautiful dining room; she runs her busy restaurant with discipline *and* style. The food is served on clear glass plates which are placed on black lacquer trays decorated with flower petals. My favourite dishes were sauté'd foie gras coated with sesame, and crisply fried duck breast with shitake mushrooms in oyster sauce. There are large spectacular flower arrangements in the restaurant and in the bedrooms. Our room had every mod con imaginable, including beds which adjust so that either your head or your feet can be elevated." A reader this year took one of the cheapest rooms and found it very small but cosy and well fitted. She then relished her meal: "Interesting juxtaposition of textures and flavours. Not cheap, but money well spent as you learn something with every mouthful" – from such dishes as tempura of poulet de Bresse and "cheese in the form of a tiny terrine with the essence of white truffles". Reports also comment on the Closomat machines attached to the loos, with "a warm water jet if you press one lever, a warm air jet if you press another". (*Padi Howard, Minda Alexander*) One dissenter this year was disappointed by the food.

Open All year, except last week Jan, first 2 weeks Feb, 23/24 Dec.
Rooms 4 suites, 6 double – all with bath and/or shower, telephone, radio, TV, mini-bar.
Facilities 2 lounges, card room, restaurant; conference facilities. Terrace for al fresco dining in summer.
Location On banks of Rhine, 5 mins' walk from centre (all windows triple-glazed). Parking.
Restriction Not suitable for &.
Credit cards All major cards accepted.
Terms [1990 rates] B&B: single occupancy 150–260 Sfrs, double 160–230 Sfrs, suite 290 Sfrs. Set lunch/dinner 100–140 Sfrs; full alc 110 Sfrs. Children under 6 sharing parents' room free; special meals on request.

SCHÖNRIED-GSTAAD 3778 Bern   Map 14

Hotel Ermitage-Golf   *Tel* (030) 4.27.27
                                                      Fax (030) 4.71.95
                                                      Telex 922213

Surrounded by pinewoods and upland meadows, smooth with snow in winter, the village of Schönried stands 180 metres higher than Gstaad and is now an established resort with superb skiing facilities. This is the smartest and largest of its hotels, again admired by devotees this year. It consists of two big connecting chalets, magnificently equipped, recently refurbished and enlarged. "The young staff are pleasant and attentive, and the food is interesting, varied and plentiful, much of it buffet style. The breakfast buffet is enormous, and can be taken out on the terrace facing the pretty garden." There are two French restaurants, also a charcoal grill and an intimate *Stübl* for simpler dishes. In the basement is a disco, and a sauna park with steam baths and bio-sauna. The garden provides beautiful views. A prime attraction is the *Solbad*, a large indoor swimming pool fitted with briny water heated to 35°C. This indoor pool opens to an outdoor one heated similarly: "It was a sensational experience in December to swim outside, the body most comfortably warmed, but the head in the nippy night air of −10°C, the steam of the water rising to reveal the surrounding high banks of snow." (*Arnold Horwell*)

Open 21 Dec–7 Apr. 8 May–20 Oct.
Rooms 28 suites, 28 double, 15 single – all with bath and/or shower, telephone, radio, T V.
Facilities Lift. Hall, salon, 2 bars (one with live jazz), 2 restaurants, café, terrace restaurant; conference facilities. Billiards, table-tennis, squash, indoor and outdoor swimming pool, sauna, fitness room. Garden with tennis. Ski-lifts, cable-cars opposite hotel.
Location On N11, 8 km E of Gstaad. Underground parking (5–12 Sfrs).
Credit cards All major cards accepted.
Terms [1990 rates] Dinner, B&B 95–280 Sfrs. Full board 20 Sfrs added per person. Reduced rates for children sharing parents' room; special meals on request.

SCHWANDEN 3657 Bern   Map 14

Gasthof-Restaurant Rothorn
Tel (033) 51.11.86
Fax (033) 51.33.86

A big brown chalet, amid meadows backed by pinewoods, in a village high above Gunten with views of the Bernese Alps. Several recent visitors have spoken favourably of the rooms, the good and copious food, the superb views, the professionalism and the "friendly and gracious hospitality" of the owners, the Amstutz-Rentsches – and even of the yodelling in the bar. "The place is a social centre for the village – pensioners sit smoking, gossiping and playing cards, and spontaneous singing comes and goes." "The food was wholesome, plentiful, local in style: fresh wild fruit (bilberries, etc) were often the basis of delicious puddings." Rooms are described as "simple but tasteful and spacious". Those at the back look out on to the hillside and are very quiet; those at the front are larger and have balconies, but suffer from some noise from traffic and from the bar around midnight. (*David and Hanna Rampton, AD and JE Stokes, Ellen Buchanan, R Barratt*) After so much praise, it was odd to get a long report in 1989 from out-of-season visitors who complained of poor room and bathroom maintenance, indifferent food, and noises in the night: more reports please.

Open All year except Nov. Restaurant closed Mon.
Rooms 13 double – 2 with bath and shower, 8 with shower; some with balcony. 3 in chalet annexe.
Facilities Lounge, T V room, dining room, restaurant; occasional folk music.
Location 30 mins' drive NW of Interlaken, 15 mins NE of Thun.
Credit cards None accepted.
Terms B&B: single 40–52 Sfrs, double 70–100 Sfrs; dinner, B&B: single 58–70 Sfrs, double 106–136 Sfrs. Set lunch/dinner 13–27 Sfrs. Reduced rates for children sharing parents' room.

SOGLIO 7610 Graubünden   Map 14

Pension La Soglina   `BUDGET`   *Tel* (082) 4.16.08

Formerly known as *Stüa Granda*, this is an unpretentious, appealing and very well-run hotel, in a high mountain village above the main valley road from St-Moritz to Chiavenna in Italy. "A perfect, inexpensive, away-from-it-all stop-over en route to the Italian lakes." "A very warm welcome, magnificent views, comfortable beds, tasty evening meal,

breakfast with delicious local bread." These 1990 reports back up earlier
praise: "The courteous owner, Roland Nass, took us to a lovely room with
a balcony and fine view down the valley. The food was delicious, and
though the set menus offered little choice, they varied daily. Staff were
efficient." "Chestnut trees surround the village and the air is crisp. The
sunny terrace restaurant is a favourite meeting place for hikers and the
fare is hearty and fresh. Guest rooms (some small) have high-beamed
ceilings and lace curtains. The aroma of fresh bread and local specialities
such as bundner gerstensuppe fill the air. A romantic hotel in a beautiful
setting." (*John Beddoe and Dr Ann Pitcher, J Bruner, Dr R Wise, Mrs Don
Simecheck*)

Open All year except Nov.
Rooms 31 double – all with bath, shower, telephone, radio; some with balcony.
Ground-floor rooms.
Facilities 2 sitting rooms, restaurant. Garden terrace. Sauna, turkish bath,
whirlpool, solarium and fitness room.
Location On edge of village, just N of route N3 between Chiavenna (to W) and
Maloja pass (to E). Nearby parking.
Credit cards None accepted.
Terms [1990 rates] B&B 43–50 Sfrs; dinner, B&B 68–75 Sfrs. Special meals for
children on request.

VADUZ 9490 Liechtenstein   **Map 14**

Park-Hotel Sonnenhof   *Tel* (075) 2.11.92
Mareestrasse 29   *Fax* (075) 2.00.53
                                                       Telex 889329

*In a glorious mountain-backed parkland setting just outside Liechtenstein's tiny
capital, a luxurious and elegant villa-style hotel, run by the warmly welcoming
Real family. Large, well-fitted bedrooms, spacious gardens and lounges, indoor
heated pool, excellent food. Closed 15 Jan–28 Feb, 23–26 Dec. 29 rooms, all with
bath and shower. B&B double 240–350 Sfrs. Set menu 45 Sfrs [1990].*

VEVEY 1800 Vaud   **Map 14**

Les Trois Couronnes   *Tel* (021) 921.30.05
49 rue d'Italie   *Fax* (021) 922.72.80
                                                       Telex 451148

A five-star late 19-century hotel in the grand tradition, right on the
lakeside promenade in one of the smartest of Lac Léman resorts, well
known for its exclusive girl's finishing schools. "A peaceful old-world
hotel with first-rate service and atmosphere, good food, superb local
wines," says a visitor this year. Others have praised the lake views from
bedroom balconies, the embroidered bed-linens, the courteous service,
and the food served in the beautiful Louis XV-style dining room or on the
terrace facing the lake. Public rooms have an abundance of carved, gilded
and marbled decor, with much fine furniture. There are fountains and
flowers on the terrace. (*Sally Burt*)

Open All year.
Rooms 8 suites, 41 double, 26 single – all with bath, shower, telephone, radio; TV;
baby listening on request. Some ground-floor rooms.

Facilities Lift. Salons, TV room, piano bar (nightly entertainment), restaurant; conference facilities; large terrace with restaurant.
Location Central, but quietly situated. Parking in courtyard.
Credit cards All major cards accepted.
Terms B&B: single 170–210 Sfrs, double 260–390 Sfrs, suite 550–1,100 Sfrs; dinner, B&B 45 Sfrs per person added. Set lunch 58 Sfrs, dinner 62 Sfrs; full alc 90 Sfrs. Reduced rates and special meals for children.

VILLARS 1884 Vaud   Map 14

Hôtel Alpe-Fleurie   *Tel* (025) 35.34.64
Rue Centrale

This Guide newcomer is an unpretentious chalet-style hotel in the centre of a Rhône Valley resort: "Villars has been developed at a great rate and has lost some of its bucolic Swiss charm. But the *Alpe Fleurie* remains what it was in my boarding-school days – a pleasant, comfortable, traditional hotel, decked with flower-boxes and serving as a centre of local village life (such as it is). It is just across from the station, but my room was quiet enough. The dining room, terrace and half the rooms look out on to the Rhône valley, Dents du Midi and Mont Blanc – a spectacular view. The *demi-pension* meals were very tasty and nicely served, and the owner and all the staff were hospitable." (*Dr Suzanne Martin*)

Open All year except 10 June–10 July and 24 Nov–7 Dec. Restaurant closed Wed.
Rooms 12 double, 7 single – all with bath, shower, telephone, radio, TV.
Facilities Café, bar, restaurant. Large terrace.
Location Central. Villars is 27 km SE of Montreux.
Restriction Not suitable for &.
Credit cards All major cards accepted.
Terms B&B: single 70–120 Sfrs, double 130–180 Sfrs; dinner, B&B 95–150 Sfrs per person. Set lunch/dinner 20–65 Sfrs; full alc 25–100 Sfrs. Reduced rates and special meals for children.

VITZNAU 6354 Lucerne   Map 14

Hotel Floralpina   `BUDGET`   *Tel* (041) 83.13.86
PO Box 62   *Fax* (041) 83.10.54

One of the more elegant resorts on Lake Lucerne and, just outside it, in a glorious lakeside setting backed by steep wooded hills, this handsome modern hotel, which is liked again this year for its fine views and large, comfortable double bedrooms. It has huge grounds, direct access to swimming in the lake (private beach), and is called "a children's paradise – right on the edge of the forest, with farm animals, a playground and table-tennis". "Our host was friendly and gracious." (*Norma Kessler, WP Jaspert, Lon Bailey, and others*) The dining terrace has fine views, but the food does not live up to this setting: it is plentiful but very simple, and some judge it too plain and utilitarian. The breakfast buffet is also "large and basic". One reader felt the hotel was too closely geared to package holidays and conferences.

Open 20 Apr–19 Oct.
Rooms 6 suites, 49 double, 9 single – all with bath, shower, telephone, radio, TV. 1 ground-floor room.
Facilities Lift, ramps. Lounge, TV room, bar, restaurant; whirlpool, sauna, solarium. Terrace, park with children's playground, private beach.

Location 2 km S of Vitznau on Brunnen road.
Credit cards All major cards accepted.
Terms B&B 50–66 Sfrs. Set lunch/dinner 17 Sfrs; full alc 30 Sfrs. Reduced rates
and special meals for children.

WEGGIS 6353 Lucerne   Map 14

Hôtel Beau Rivage   *Tel* (041) 93.14.22
                                                  Fax (041) 93.19.81
                                                     Telex 862982

Weggis is a delightful resort some 30 minutes by road or 45 by steamer
from Lucerne; other lake pleasures are easily accessible, as are the heights
of Rigi, served by Weggis's funicular. This "excellent" hotel has a choice
position right by the water, a few minutes' walk from the quay, with its
own garden and swimming pool. And it has been as well liked as ever
this year, for its "lovely" rooms with lake views, its "beautiful" dining
room, friendly service, and the "charm and hardworking efficiency" of
the Geering family owners. The food is "good but not extraordinary". (*RS
McNeill, Dr IHD Johnston, D and J Smith*) One or two cavils: poor bedroom
lighting, and a noisy church clock. Some package tours, out of season
only.

Open Early Apr–mid-Oct.
Rooms 4 suites, 31 double, 9 single – all with bath and/or shower, telephone,
radio, TV.
Facilities Lift. Hall, lounges, TV room, bar, garden room, restaurant; lakeside
terrace; band twice a week. Garden with heated swimming pool, beach, fishing.
Location 20 km E of Lucerne; on lake, near quay. Garages and parking.
Credit cards All major cards accepted.
Terms B&B: single 85–130 Sfrs, double 140–240 Sfrs, suite 250–280 Sfrs; half
board 40 Sfrs per person added; full board 70 Sfrs added. Set lunch/dinner 40–
48 Sfrs; full alc 70 Sfrs. Reduced rates for children sharing parents' room; special
meals.

WENGEN 3823 Bern   Map 14

Hotel Alpenrose   *Tel* (036) 55.32.16
                                                  Fax (036) 55.15.18
                                                     Telex 923293

*An old, family-run but much modernised hotel, facing across to the Jungfrau in
this high-altitude Bernese Oberland resort. Efficient and peaceful; good food
(some Swiss dishes); bedrooms not smart but comfortable. Large garden. Guests
mainly British. Closed Oct, Nov. 50 rooms, all with bath and shower. Half board
70–140 Sfrs. Set meals 30–55 Sfrs. New nomination. More reports please.*

Hotel Eiger   *Tel* (036) 55.11.31
                                                  Fax (036) 55.10.30
                                                     Telex 923296

A ski-hotel run by the Fuchs family for generations, but rebuilt in 1980 in
traditional style (neat balconies, masses of stripped pine). Two recent
plaudits: "Very comfortable. The rooms are large, and the beds, duvets,

etc, are pushed away each morning to create a sitting room, reinstated as a bedroom at 7 pm. The well-designed balconies look on to a marvellous view of the Jungfrau. Breakfast buffets were excellent (muesli with blackcurrants and bilberries); dinner was not so good, but adequate." "Warm and welcoming. Next door to station, so convenient for skiers. The charming staff join in the fun of your being on holiday. The small Eiger bar is the focal point of Wengen *après-ski*." (*M Scott Russell, and others*)

Open All year except 29 Apr–17 June. Grill room closed Mon.
Rooms 9 suites, 20 double, 4 single – all with bath or shower, telephone, radio; TV on request.
Facilities Lift. Lounge, TV room, 2 restaurants, terrace bar.
Location Central. No cars in Wengen. Park in Lauterbrunnen and take train.
Credit cards All major cards accepted.
Terms [1990 rates] Dinner, B&B: single 75–138 Sfrs, double 150–276 Sfrs. Full board 15 Sfrs per person added. Reduced rates and special meals for children.

WORB 3076 Bern   Map 14

Romantik Hotel Löwen   *Tel* (031) 83.23.03
Enggisteinstrasse 3   *Fax* (031) 83.58.77

In a village east of Bern, this small traditional hotel of character has been run by the same family for over 300 years, and has a solid local reputation for its good food. "A fine, elegant hostelry whose staff are courteous beyond courtesy, helpful to a fault. The rooms are spacious: ours had an armoire whose door hinges and locks were sensuously magnificent. Dinner was beautifully served and the atmosphere was relaxed." (*H and B Shames*)

Open All year. Restaurant closed Sat/Sun and mid-July–mid-Aug.
Rooms 6 double, 8 single – all with bath and/or shower, telephone, radio, TV.
Facilities Lounge, bar, TV room, restaurant, functions room. Garden restaurant, children's playground, bowling alleys.
Location Central, by church; parking. Worb is 10 km E of Bern on Lucerne road.
Restriction Not suitable for &.
Credit cards All major cards accepted.
Terms [1990 rates] B&B: single 70–85 Sfrs, double 135–150 Sfrs. Set lunch/dinner 15–30 Sfrs; full alc 55 Sfrs. Reduced rates for children sharing parents' room; special meals.

ZERMATT 3920 Valais   Map 14

Hôtel Garni Metropol   *Tel* (028) 67.32.31
                                                  Fax (028) 67.23.42

"An outstanding hotel, the Taugwalder family are wonderful hosts." This was the verdict of one 1990 report on this unpretentious hotel beside a river in the town centre. The views of the Matterhorn, from the bedrooms with a balcony on the south side, are a star feature: "The sight of this peak from your window each morning, so close you could almost touch it, is exhilarating." Among much other recent praise is this: "Good and clean as ever, and everyone so friendly. Frau Taugwalder's cooking is good and the helpings enormous, while the buffet breakfast seems to improve each year." One devotee earlier wrote: "Zermatt with its 107 hotels has developed in such an ugly way that almost every bit of green is replaced by grey concrete. But the Taugwalders bought a meadow in front of their hotel, so you have a clear view to the south. The rooms have sensible beds, spacious cupboards and well-equipped bathrooms. The constant rush of the river is soothing at night." There is no full-scale restaurant, but snacks are available in the evening, and more substantial dishes can be ordered specially in advance. (*Ido Pittman, Karen and David Bashkin, Richard Pinner, and others*)

Open 1 Dec–10 May, 10 June–20 Oct.
Rooms 20 double, 4 single – 16 with bath and shower, 4 with shower, all with telephone, radio, baby-listening; TV on request. Ground-floor rooms.
Facilities Lift. Bar, TV room, dining room. Garden and terrace.
Location Central; near station. Hotel porter will fetch you (no cars in Zermatt).
Credit cards All major cards accepted.
Terms B&B: single 55–97 Sfrs, double 105–194 Sfrs. Reduced rates for children.

ZUOZ 7524 Graubünden Map 14

Posthotel Engadina *Tel* (082) 7.10.21
Fax (082) 7.33.03

This summer resort in the Inn valley, north-east of St-Moritz, is a typically picturesque Engadin village (the houses, some of which have painted facades, have built-in barns). Here the five-storey pink-fronted *Engadina*, over 100 years old, is outwardly sedate-looking but less formal within, and is brought back to the Guide by visitors in 1990: "An elegant building in a superb location, with sumptuous public rooms, magnificent bedrooms, beautiful views, polite and attentive staff. Food good, though for my taste it leans too much towards the *nouvelle* and portions can be stingy." Others have spoken of "a friendly house-party ambience among the guests". (*Esler Crawford, JM Clayton*)

Open Dec–Apr and June–Oct.
Rooms 1 suite, 30 double, 9 single – all with bath and/or shower, telephone, radio, TV.
Facilities Lift. Lounge, 2 bars, 2 restaurants, banqueting room. Heated outdoor swimming pool, sauna, solarium. Tennis and winter sports nearby.
Location 10 km NE of St-Moritz. Hotel is central; parking.
Credit cards All major cards accepted.
Terms B&B: single 89–125 Sfrs, double 138–228 Sfrs, suite 206–244 Sfrs. Dinner, B&B double 190–296 Sfrs. Set lunch 20–30 Sfrs, dinner 25–35 Sfrs; full alc 45–50 Sfrs. Reduced rates and special meals for children.

ZÜRICH Map 14

Hotel Florhof *Tel* (01) 261.44.70
Florhofgasse 4 *Fax* (01) 261.46.11
Zurich 8001 *Telex* 817364

A converted 16th-century patrician house with a small garden, in a residential street near the Kunsthaus and university, and next to the music conservatoire. Readers' recent accolades focus on the friendly staff, good food and beautiful public rooms (but two reports this year thought the bedrooms, though comfortable, somewhat characterless). "If you don't turn up by the time breakfast ends, you get a call asking if they may ring it up to you (free of charge). Most hotels don't care a bit whether you have had your breakfast. We also had an outstandingly good lunch in the garden." The restaurant is closed at weekends. (*H Langenberg, Dr TJ David, K and S M-S, and others*)

Open All year. Restaurant closed Sat and Sun.
Rooms 23 double, 10 single – all with bath and/or shower, telephone, radio, TV, mini-bar.
Facilities Lift. Salon, restaurant. Garden with restaurant.
Location Near Kunsthaus and university. Parking.
Restriction Not suitable for &.
Credit cards All major cards accepted.
Terms B&B: single 125–165 Sfrs, double 180–230 Sfrs. Set lunch 25–35 Sfrs, dinner 30–50 Sfrs. Reduced rates and special meals for children.

Hotel Tiefenau	*Tel* (01) 251.24.09
Steinwiesstrasse 8–10	*Fax* (01) 251.24.76
Zürich 8032	*Telex* 816395

A comfortable, well-located, family-run hotel, gracefully furnished in Louis-XV style, with friendly service. "Cosy without being Swiss-stuffy. It's in a tiny quiet street very close to the Kunsthaus (with its wonderful Munchs, Impressionist and post-Impressionist collections). There's a terrace where you can eat or drink under huge shady trees and the food is quite good. You can walk to any number of good restaurants, including the *Kronenhalle*, James Joyce's favourite." This year, a different slant: Hyper-Swiss, with a family feeling. In the bedroom, a bowl of fruit and personalised book-matches, in the bathroom a mini-bar offering gold-plated toothbrushes. Patriotic Klee prints illuminate an attractive dining room where the cuisine is light and imaginative. Generous buffet breakfast. Bedrooms have a commanding view of the mouths of the dentist's patients in the surgery opposite." (*Nadine Gordimer, Stephen Wright*)

Open 7 Jan–19 Dec.
Rooms 5 suites, 8 double, 17 single – all with bath, shower, telephone, radio, TV/video.
Facilities Lift. Salon, bar, restaurant; conference facilities. Garden; terrace.
Location Fairly central, by Schauspielhaus. Free parking.
Credit cards All major cards accepted.
Terms B&B: single 150–230 Sfrs, double 210–320 Sfrs, suite 310–420 Sfrs. Set lunch/dinner 17.90–26.50 Sfrs; full alc 50 Sfrs. Reduced rates and special meals for children.

Turkey

Kanuni Kervansaray Oteli, Çeşme

Turban Adalya Oteli   *Tel* (31) 11.80.66
Kaleiçi Yat Limani   *Fax* (31) 12.36.79
                                                              Telex 56241

Antalya's famous harbour has been much restored and is now a
showplace resort. "Sleek yachts," we are told, "are moored alongside
beautifully preserved Turkish houses with their dark wooden balconies
and colourful tiled roofs. The *Turban Adalya*, originally a bank and then a
warehouse, has been converted into a most individual small luxury hotel.
The sound of running water from the fountains in the atrium-patio greets
you as you walk into its welcome coolness; the charmingly decorated
bedrooms lead off from upstairs galleries. There is an excellent restaurant
on the top floor." One recent visitor had a spacious, clean and quiet room
with efficient air-conditioning, and found breakfast "a feast". Others
agree that the rooms are charming, but point out that they have no view;
there are two bars, but no lounge. A "presidential suite" has just been

opened in an old house nearby, with all modern facilities, balconies and harbour views. (*Mr and Mrs SC Jones-Parry*)

Open All year.
Rooms 3 suites, 26 double – all with shower (1 also with bath), telephone, radio, TV, air-conditioning, mini-bar. 1 suite in building 15 metres away.
Facilities Lift. 2 bars, restaurant; terrace. Garden. Swimming pool 150 metres away.
Location Central, near harbour; parking.
Credit cards All major cards accepted.
Restriction Not suitable for &.
Terms [1990 rates] B&B: single US$54–74, double US$71–96, suite US$100–135. Set lunch/dinner US$9. Reduced rates for children; special meals on request.

ARTVIN   Map 18

Hotel Karahan   `BUDGET`   *Tel* (0581) 1800
İnönü Caddesi 16   *Fax* (0581) 2420
                                                 Telex 83393

Artvin is a town in the far north-east of Turkey, inland from the coast near the Soviet Georgian frontier, and set amid grandiose mountain scenery near Mount Ararat. Our nominator's ark came to rest this year at the modern, unbeautiful but useful *Karahan*: "A jewel. It is the top three floors of a block in the busy main street. The terrace restaurant, and the adequately comfortable rooms, have staggering views down to the Coruh river. The management are delightful and the Turkish food is superb. Possible drawback: the nearby mosque will summon you early to prayer. Some traffic noise, too." (*Lord Dervaird*) More reports please. The hotel tells us that the surrounding countryside is "particularly rich in flora and fauna, butterflies and migrating birds".

Open All year.
Rooms 48 double, 9 single – 8 with bath, 49 with shower, all with telephone.
Facilities Lift. Lounge/bar, TV room, restaurant; terrace.
Location Central. Parking. Artvin is about 150 km E of Trabzon.
Credit card Visa.
Terms B&B: single US$18–21.30, double US$25–29.40. Dinner, B&B: single US$22–25.30, double US$33–37.40. Full board: single US$26–29.30, double US$41–45.40. Set lunch/dinner US$4; full alc US$7.

ÇEŞME İzmīr   Map 18

Kanuni Kervansaray Oteli   *Tel* (549) 26490
Çeşme Kalesi Yani   *Telex* 53868

This attractively converted caravanserai (inn for travellers), with a massive arcaded courtyard and rooms of real Turkish character, is in a small town on the coast west of Izmīr: "Çeşme is destined to be a major Turkish resort and big hotels are shooting up outside it: but as yet it retains a quiet village ambience. This atmospheric hotel looks up to the superb 15th-century walled castle, lit up at night. The garden courtyard itself is a wonderful place to sit of an evening. Rooms are fair sized with good bathrooms, and cool because of the thickness of the walls. The staff are charming and attentive. Food is twice the price of a Turkish restaurant but nicely prepared and less bland and 'international' than in many hotels: we enjoyed our meals by the beautiful old fountain in the courtyard. There's no pool, but guests can go three kilometres to the pool and beach of the *Golden Dolphin*, part of the same chain. Nearby beaches are sandy and pleasant." (*C and N Brooks-Matthew*)

Open Apr–Oct.
Rooms 2 suites, 30 double – 30 with bath, 2 with shower, all with telephone, radio. 9 on ground floor.
Facilities Lounge, TV room, bar, restaurant. Garden, courtyard. Swimming pool 3 km.
Location Central, parking. Çeşme is 70 km W of İzmir.
Credit cards All major cards accepted.
Terms On application.

DATÇA Muğla   Map 18

Perīlī Köşk   *Tel* (081) 44027
PO Box 46   *Fax* Istanbul (1) 345.36.25
                                                          Telex 29279

This beguilingly idiosyncratic Fairy Chalet (literal translation) lies on the coast opposite Rhodes, and is reached from Marmaris along a tortuous road through the mountains. "Finally a lovely tiled roof and chimneys come into view, peering over cascades of oleander and bougainvillea. The hotel faces a beautiful crescent bay with no other building in sight (Datça village is 18 kilometres away). The design is impressive – a wealth of lovely natural pine, with balconies and latticed windows, and the rooms have stunning traditional framed and panelled ceilings. We had a good-sized room – some are cramped, but all have a bathroom." That nominator's report has since been qualified: "The *Köşk* is the fantasy of a rich Turk (seldom there) who regards it as his toy, which he delights to embellish. Tiled terraces at different levels, a blue-tiled fountained courtyard, a wrought-iron gateway leading to the beach, and a white wrought-iron pavilion like a Victorian bandstand. The interior is even more Turkish, its core being a windowless mosque-like dome. My husband thought it all a bit over the top, but I swallowed it delightedly, partly because it's the only hotel in Turkey outside Istanbul that we found to have any personal eccentricity. However, there are drawbacks. While most rooms have a balcony, those at the rear must be dark (though cool). It's a summer place, and in mid-October it was all a bit *triste*." Since that report reached us, the hotel has acquired a new manager, and has added 17 bedrooms in pavilions in the grounds, almost doubling its size. Summer 1990 reports suggest that the hotel has lost a little of its wayward charm but, "despite all this the hotel is still a delight." (*Paul Thackray*)

Open 1 Apr–11 Oct.
Rooms 38 double – all with shower. Ground-floor rooms.
Facilities Lounge with TV, bar, dining room; terrace. Garden with swimming pool. Direct access to beach.
Location 18 km E of Datça towards Marmaris.
Restriction Not suitable for &.
Credit card Visa.
Terms [1990 rates] Rooms: single occupancy US$33–41, double US$45–55. Breakfast US$6. Set lunch/dinner US$10. Extra bed US$10.

> We are keen to develop our Yugoslav section. More nominations would be especially welcome.

FATSA Ordu   Map 18

Dolunay Motel `BUDGET`   *Tel* (3721) 1528 and 1633
PO Box 7   *Fax* (3721) 1633

On the Black Sea coast between Samsun and Ordu, in an area where good hotels are rare: a motel with spacious reading and TV rooms, private beach, helpful English-speaking staff, excellent well-served food. 15 rooms all with shower. B&B: single US$32.5–38, double US$40–45. New nomination. More reports please.

ISTANBUL   Map 18

Ayasofya Pansiyonlari   *Tel* (1) 513.36.60
Soğukçeşme Sokaği   *Fax* (1) 513.36.69
Sultanahmet   *Telex* 23841

As at the *Hīdīv Kasrī* and *Yeşil Ev* (see below), Mr Çelik Gülersoy and the Touring Club of Turkey have done a notable work of restoration. It is a terrace of eleven historic houses, with attractive pastel-coloured wooden exteriors, down a narrow lane between Topkapi Palace and Hagia Sophia. Two houses have ground-floor breakfast and tea rooms, one has been converted into a library, strong on books about Old Constantinople. The old Roman cistern in the same road has recently been converted into a good restaurant, whose food, service and atmosphere are much admired. One of the gardens has a café; in another breakfast is served. A 1990 visitor reports: "It provides an essential for anyone visiting Istanbul – a quiet retreat; the street is now out of bounds to traffic. It exudes a well-cared-for air. The rooms are immaculate, the street outside regularly swept. Our al fresco breakfast included some of the best yoghurt imaginable. Staff were helpful, if sometimes forgetful." Some earlier comments: "Try to get front rooms with the view of Hagia Sophia, for back ones face a wall. The omnipresent muzak of a good sort (such as Chopin) seems to symbolise the yearning to make westerners feel at home." "The buildings are modernised yet have kept the charm of the period; their decor is lovely, with Turkish rugs on every floor." "Rooms comfortable, but plumbing could be better." (*Diana Cooper, and others*)

Open All year.
Rooms 6 triple, 5 suites, 36 double, 14 single – all with bath and/or shower, telephone, radio. 2 on ground floor.
Facilities 2 lounges, library, 2 bars, 3 restaurants. 2 gardens, 1 with café, 1 where breakfast is served.
Location Central, near Hagia Sophia.
Credit cards Access, Amex, Visa.
Terms [1990 rates] B&B: single US$60–75, double US$80–100, suite US$170.

Hīdīv Kasrī   *Tel* (1) 331.26.51
Çubuklu, Beykoz   *Fax* (1) 322.34.34
                                                      Telex 23346

The old summer palace of the last Viceroy of Egypt, another conversion by the Touring Club of Turkey, was introduced to the Guide by the late *Jeremy Round*, expert on Turkey, before his early death in 1989: "Set on a ooded hill on the Asian side of the Bosphorus, built and originally rnished in a fabulous mixture of styles, from Middle-Eastern opulent to lgian *Art Nouveau*. The restoration has kept many of the old fittings, cluding regal mahogany loos. There's also a vast marble fountain in the ntral hall, a salon hung with a riot of crystal and gilt chandeliers. A ano trio plays in the banana-shaped dining room. Most rooms have perb views, over the Bosphorus or a rose field framed by cypresses. In der not to destroy the room plan of the palace, bathrooms and loos ve not been knocked into the bedrooms – they are shared between two three bedrooms so have the advantage of retaining their original pressive proportions. The grounds are popular with day trippers." A 90 visitor adds: "The place is wonderful, and like Mr Gülersoy's other ations, eccentric. Upstairs it is slightly shabby country house style. nfirming our booking the hotel wrote: 'Toilet and shower is in the rridor', and this was almost literally true. Both were magnificent amples of Edwardian workmanship (by George Jennings of Lambeth) their mahogany and marble splendour. But there were no locks on the ors. Presumably the Viceroy had no need of them. The bathroom was ge and only for the intrepid. I managed only a scalding shower or a ld plunge. The plumbing is pure Turkish. Breakfast was on a balcony ge enough to accommodate the entire Royal Family. But the hotel is for laxation, not a base for exploring Istanbul, two hours away by boat (the st one leaves at 8.40 am) or 40 minutes to the Asian part of the city by tremely crowded bus. But it is only a short taxi-ride from Atatürk rport." (*David Gladwell*)

en All year.
oms About 30 including 2 suites – all with telephone, radio.
cilities 3 restaurants, tearoom; tavern, beer garden, terrace. Wooded grounds.
cation On Asian shore of the Bosphorus, 2 hours by boat from city centre (40 nutes by ferry and land transport).
edit cards Probably some accepted.
rms On application.

---

alyon Hotel	*Tel* (1) 511.44.00
hil Yolu	*Fax* (1) 526.62.51
ltanahmet	*Telex* 23364

cently much enlarged, this modern hotel stands on the edge of the sphorus, away from the crowds yet only ten minutes' walk from the ue Mosque, Hagia Sophia and Topkapi Palace. "Our room looked out er the hotel lawn, past the fishermen who sit by the water to the nstant, silent fascinating stream of ships moving through the Bosorus: I was enchanted by the combination of the hotel's peaceful tting and the swirl of activity in the crowded, ancient streets just hind. Our rooms were clean and nice, the staff were pleasant, and we joyed our Turkish buffet breakfasts (with yoghurt, honey, fresh fruit, rb-scented breads, etc), taken facing the water." (*Dr Suzanne L Martin*) thers have reported that rooms at the back can be small; front ones are rger, with sea views, but lower floors would hear traffic noise.

pen All year.
oms 8 suites, 100 double, 2 single – all with bath, shower, telephone, radio, TV, ni-bar, air-conditioning. Many with balcony.
cilities Lift. Lounges, bar, restaurant, cafeteria; conference/functions rooms.

Location Central; on the waterfront; near Blue Mosque. Parking.
Terms [1990 rates] B&B: single US$69–85, double US$92–112, suite US$138–1
Set lunch US$17, dinner US$20; full alc US$25. Reduced rates and special mea
for children.

Hotel Sokullu Paşa   *Tel* (1) 512.37.
Ishakpaşa Mah. Mehmetpaąsa
Sokak 10
Sultanahmet

*Another splendid Ottoman conversion of a wooden house in the Old City, j
round the corner from the superb Sokullu Paşa mosque. Attractively decorate
small lobby with fountain; Turkish bath; quiet garden at back. Staff very help
and friendly. But some bedrooms very small, with awkwardly instal
plumbing, and buffet breakfast, though generous, criticised for too ma
packaged items. 35 rooms, all with private facilities. Prices on applicati
Recent nomination. More reports please.*

Yeşil Ev Oteli   *Tel* (1) 511.11.
Kabasakal Caddesi 5   *Fax* (1) 519.49.
Sultanahmet   *Telex* 304

Located high up in the oldest part of the Old City, in an area of carp
shops between Hagia Sophia and the Blue Mosque, this charming hotel
character is a large wooden Ottoman mansion, painted a fresh apr
green and white. Till recently it was derelict, but the Touring Club
Turkey has restored it lovingly. The late *Jeremy Round* gave us this vie
"The interiors are now in highest 19th-century Victorian–Ottoman tas
with velveteen chaises-longues, loving-bird table lamps, heavy flo
drapes, ornate wooden pelmets and the like. The wooden floors crea
the light bulb wattage is low; a pianist at an upright accompani
afternoon tea in the cramped lobby; out back is a sheltered courtya
with marble fountain – the idea is that one should feel like a guest
an Ottoman household. It all worked perfectly for me, but I cou
understand some finding it precious and vulgar. The food is unimagin
tive, clumsy attempts at Turkish international. The dining rooms a
small and low-ceilinged (the back one is best)." Another view: "O
ground-floor•bedroom was almost more bed than room: the huge a
well-sprung bed left just enough room to squeeze past an armchair,
polished mahogany wardrobe and a chest of drawers. The room was hi
and had tall sash windows hung with lace and brocade curtains, a
fitted with latticed shutters giving what were basically light rooms
pleasantly secretive, Ottoman feeling. Communication with the outsi
world – and the present century – was via a brass 'candlestick' telepho
made in Coventry in 1930. The walled, paved garden is the hote
happiest asset. Water splashes down from a porphyry fountain; fig a
plane trees are edged with pansies and stocks, wallflowers and marigolc
roses and vines climb the walls. On one side stands a pelargonium-fill
conservatory, for cool evenings. The food is good, typically Turkish, wi
enough variety for a week's stay. And where better than here to take t
last Turkish coffee of the day, turning one's gaze from the great dome
Hagia Sophia to the six slender minarets of the Blue Mosque?" But

repared also for the muezzin at 5 am. Another reader enjoyed the food
nd comfort, but found the Turkish ambience spoilt by the large numbers
f tourists. (*Claire Enders;* endorsed this year by *Margaret B McGregor*)

pen All year.
ooms 1 triple, 1 suite, 18 double – all with shower, telephone, radio; suite has
v and Turkish bath. 2 ground-floor rooms.
acilities Salon, coffee shop, bars, restaurant. Garden with restaurant.
ocation In Old City, midway between Hagia Sophia and Blue Mosque.
redit cards Access, Amex, Visa.
erms B&B: single US$90, double US$120, suite US$180. Children under 6 free
f charge.

ALKAN Antalya   **Map 18**

alkan Han Hotel   `BUDGET`   *Tel* (3215) 1151
                                                             Telex 56524

alkan is a fishing village in a deep bay backed by mountains, on
urkey's south-west coast. "This old merchant's house, sympathetically
onverted, is the nicest place to stay in Kalkan," says a visitor in 1990.
White tiles and marble everywhere, very clean. Manager, the perfect
ost, quietly looks after every detail. Roof-terrace stunning at night:
lassical music as background to dinner served on a terrace. Food plain
ut prepared with loving care. Delightful! Rooms simple and adequate:
econd-floor front ones are best, with small balcony and sea view. Plenty
f beaches reachable by taxi. Quiet." (*Gillian Phillips*) But another reader
ound the bar adjoining the hotel very noisy.

pen 1 May–31 Oct. Restaurant closed for lunch.
ooms 16 double – all with shower.
acilities Lobby, roof-terrace where meals are served, bar. Rock beach 5 mins'
valk.
ocation Central. Kalkan is 210 km W of Antalya.
estrictions Not suitable for &. Children discouraged.
redit cards None accepted.
erms B&B: single US$29–36, double US$39–49. Set dinner US$12; full alc
JS$16.

KÖYCEĞIZ Muğla   **Map 18**

Iotel Özay   *Tel* (6114) 1300 and 1361
ordon Boyu 11   *Fax* (6114) 2000
                                                       Telex 50024

n small town on N side of Köyceğiz lake, just off the İzmir–Antalya main road,
n area of great natural beauty, a family-run 2-star lakeside hotel on the
romenade, with efficient plumbing, clean and airy bedrooms, all with balcony
nd fine views. Pleasant staff, garden with nice swimming pool, goodish food. 32
ooms, all with shower. B&B double US$12–20. Alc meals US$4–6 [1990].
ndorsed this year, but fuller reports needed.

We should like to offer entries for hotels of genuine character in
Eastern Europe. They may be hard to find, but if you know of any
that meet our criteria, please let us know.

OF Trabzon   Map 1

Hotel-Restaurant Çaykent   *Tel (0441) 2424 and 123*
Cumhuriyet Cad.

In town E of Trabzon on Black Sea coast, at mouth of a lovely valley wit
luxuriant vegetation and curious covered footbridges, a modern concrete hote
no beauty, but clean, comfortable and efficient, with good plumbing and se
views; excellent if expensive restaurant, best for fish. 27 rooms, all with showe
Double room £20 [1990]. Recent nomination. More reports please.

SUNGURLU Çorum   Map 1

Hitit Motel `BUDGET`   *Tel (4557) 1042 and 140*
Ankara-Samsun Yolu   *Fax (4557) 387*

In small town 100 km E of Ankara on Samsun road, a good base for visitin
Hittite sites, a motel set round an inner garden with swimming pool. Fair
spacious rooms; restaurant with terrace. 23 rooms, all with shower, singl
US$16.50, double US$24.20. New nomination. More reports please.

VAN Van   Map 1

Hotel Akdamar   *Tel (0611) 810*
Kâzimkarabekir Cad. 56   *Telex 7316*

In far east of Turkey, on main street of town near shores of beautiful mountain
girt Lake Van. Outwardly characterless three-star hotel with somewha
cheerless "East European" ambience and decor, but clean and quite comfortabl
with plumbing that works. Good Turkish cooking, helpful staff. Back rooms ar
quietest. 75 rooms, all with bath, double 82,500 Tl. Breakfast 10,000 Tl. Recer
nomination. More reports please.

Yugoslavia

Hotel Vila Bled, Bled

Grand Hotel Toplice   *Tel* (064) 77.222
Telex 34588

Set beside Yugoslavia's loveliest lake, in its smartest inland resort, this traditional "grand hotel" was built soon after 1918 but has now been brought up to date, and is well run by a charming and efficient management who speak good English. "It has kept its old-world charm, good food and friendly service," says a report this year, backing up last year's: "We had a beautiful room facing the lake. The breakfasts were huge and sumptuous." "Old-fashioned rooms with curtained sleeping alcoves. The classic 'grand hotel' atmosphere is barely affected by the large number of English group tours." "Our quiet room on the third floor had excellent beds, comfortable furniture upholstered in gold velvet (with curtains to match) and a terrace with a splendid view. The chef creates magnificent things à la carte (e.g. roast sucking pig, rašniči, good soups). Staff were always smiling and anxious to please." Back rooms mostly lack

views and can be small. (*John P Brooke, S and E Holman, H and B Shames*)
The covered colonnaded swimming pool has its own thermal spring.

Open All year.
Rooms 10 suites, 121 double or single – all with bath, telephone, balcony. Also 194 beds in 3 annexes.
Facilities Lift. Salon, reading room, TV room, bar, restaurant; conference facilities, reading room. Indoor swimming pool, sauna, solarium, fitness room. Lakeside terrace and bathing beach; boats, fishing available.
Location Central. Bled is 55 km NW of Ljubljana.
Credit cards Access, Amex, Diners.
Terms [1990 rates] Dinner, B&B 102–135 DM.

Hotel Vila Bled   *Tel* (064) 77.436
Cesta Svobode 26   *Fax* (064) 77.320
                                                       Telex 34515

This white palace above Lake Bled, Yugoslavia's most sumptuous hotel, was remodelled by President Tito after World War II and was used as his official summer residence: here he entertained Eden, Nehru, Brandt, and many other world leaders. The government in 1984 turned it into a luxury hotel, which stands in its own 13-acre park, overlooking Yugoslavia's leading inland resort: views of the lake and the Alps are spectacular. Prices for so much pampered splendour are low by western standards, but quality is not skimped, as a recent visitor discovered: "A wonderful display of flowers just inside the big gates. Our taxi deposited us on the red carpet. The receptionist rushes to meet you, then you are handed over lovingly to undermanager, then to cocktail-lounge waiter. There's an awful lot of marble, white and black, and lots of chandeliers – all very 1930s. A pianist tinkles. The dining room has wonderful white linen, good modern prints, good silver and candles – everything glistens. Large menu, too large (most of it must be frozen): but dinner was good. The bedrooms are well modernised, with bathrooms of gleaming white marble. The rooms don't really have a lake view, I suppose for security reasons. On the top floor is a small concert hall, which Tito used for receptions." This year and last, other readers have been equally impressed by the gardens, the views and the general splendour. Most admired the bedrooms, food and service too, including "real local Slovene dishes". "Refined taste, efficient staff, best dinner we had in Yugoslavia." (*RLA Gollin, AJ Ormerod and others*) But some have criticised the food and service. Readers visiting out of season saw no red carpet, no rushing receptionist, no flowers; service was haphazard, the rooms with the lake view were closed for the winter, and the mattress was acutely uncomfortable.

Open All year except 10 Jan–15 Mar.
Rooms 10 suites, 21 double – all with bath or shower, telephone, radio; 21 with TV.
Facilities 3 lifts. Lounge, TV lounge, bar with piano music, 2 breakfast rooms, restaurant; concert hall, conference facilities; terrace. Garden with tennis, private beach on lake with café in summer, rowing boats. Golf, riding, hunting, fishing, gliding nearby.
Location 1 mile along the lake from Bled, towards Bohinj.
Restriction Not suitable for &.
Credit cards All major cards accepted.

Terms B&B: single US$86–116, double US$112–142, suite US$142–302. Dinner, B&B US$20 per person added; full board US$36–40 added. Set lunch/dinner US$20; full alc US$35. Special meals for children on request.

DUBROVNIK 50000 Croatia   Map 17

Villa Dubrovnik   *Tel* (050) 22.933
                                                      Telex 27503

Of the three smart hotels on the south side of Dubrovnik, this is the smallest and perhaps the best. It is a modern building, terraced into a cliff, with lovely views of the old walled town and harbour, and the island of Lokrum opposite. Pine trees, flowers and blue awnings give a Riviera flavour. The bar and dining room both have superb views, and you can eat outdoors in fine weather. Most bedrooms face the front with a small balcony, and are well furnished; it's worth paying extra for a sea-facing room. The hotel has its own concrete "beach" with rock bathing in unpolluted water. A recent account: "A beautifully run hotel, with neat, clean rooms: ours had a lovely view from its balcony. The food was ordinary, but the staff are courteous and helpful." Others agree that the food is only average – but very cheap. "Our room was beautifully quiet save for the lapping of the waves below." A few minor gripes, such as bed-lights too dim, furnishings not perfect. There is no nightlife on the spot, but you can wander down to the city in about 20 minutes or take the hotel's own motor-boat. A hotel not recommended for the elderly or infirm, as there are 66 steep steps up from the hotel to the road above. (*H and B Shames, Joe van der Sneppen*)

Open All year.
Rooms 54 – most with bath or shower, all with telephone; many with sea-facing balcony.
Facilities Lifts. Lounge, bar, restaurant. Sub-tropical gardens.
Location On S side of Dubrovnik. Garage parking.
Restriction Not suitable for &.
Credit card Amex.
Terms [1990 rates] Dinner, B&B US$41–112.

HVAR 58450 Croatia   Map 17

Palace Hotel   `BUDGET`   *Tel* (058) 74.966
                                                      Fax (058) 74.169
                                                      Telex 26235

About an hour by hydrofoil from Split, this charming port on Hvar island has a gentle winter climate, and is backed by pines, olives and vines. You can visit the remains of a Greek colony and a neolithic cave. The *Palace*, a classic white-fronted hotel, centrally located just above the busy quay, has drawn more enthusiasm this year: "Paradise! Our room, sparkling clean, had a beautiful view and a constant breeze. Service was cordial. Beautiful coves where you can swim and lunch alone." "Hvar's best hotel. The food was excellent and service efficient, while the weekly cocktail party was enjoyed by everyone. Entertainment was provided on several evenings." Front rooms are more attractive and have a view; back ones are duller but quieter. Best avoid high summer and its package tours. (*Margaret B McGregor, Noreen Redfern*)

Open All year.
Rooms 4 suites, 65 double, 7 single – all with bath and/or shower, telephone.
Facilities Lift. Lounge, salon, TV room, bar, restaurant; heated indoor swimming pool. Sun-terrace overlooking harbour with music and dancing every night during summer.
Location Central.
Credit cards All major cards accepted.
Terms [1990 rates] Dinner, B&B: single 34–90 DM, double 58–150 DM. Reduced rates for children.

LOVRAN 51415 Croatia   Map 17

Hotel Beograd   *Tel* (051) 731.022
                                                          Telex 24578

A large *fin-de-siècle* hotel "with a calm 1920s flavour", in a quiet Istrian seaside resort just west of Opatija. "The rooms with bath and balcony are clean and spacious," says a recent visitor, "and some have superb views of the bay. The large restaurant resembled a typical package-tour eaterie and we did not try it, but we ate well at the small *Hotel Belvedere* next door." Endorsed this year: "A lovely spot, wonderful staff." An expert's view: "It was built in about 1900 for the Austrian aristocracy and still has a strong Hapsburg flavour (the Grand Duchess Stephanie did a lot along this coast). Friends who went recently said it was 'like staying in Buckingham Palace'. Our rooms were furnished in rich Venetian style, with gold velvet upholstery. Set in a pleasant garden facing the sea, the hotel has discreet creeper-covered booths where you can sit in the evenings listening to live music. There's no beach, but to swim you go down an iron ladder into a roped-off bit of sea, full of fish and very clear. The food was as good as any we have eaten in Yugoslavia, with the names of various Austrian royals used for puddings. The day we left, the other packagers had to vacate their rooms by noon, but our chambermaid let us remain until we had to leave for the airport at five. Could it have been because of my Christian name?" (*Stephanie Sowerby; also Bill and Marty Jewell*)

Open 1 May–31 Oct.
Rooms 102 – all with bath and/or shower; many with balcony. Some on ground floor.
Facilities Lounge, restaurant; terrace. Garden with tables and chairs. Sea bathing.
Location Lovran is 16 km W of Rijeka. Parking.
Credit cards None accepted.
Terms [1990 rates] Dinner, B&B 22–77 DM. Reduced rates for children sharing parents' room.

PLITVIČKA JEZERA 48231 Croatia   Map 17

Hotel Jezero   **BUDGET**   *Tel* (048) 76.526
                                                          Fax (048) 76.310
                                                          Telex 23817

The Plitvice national park, in the wooded hills of western Croatia, is a place of "serene beauty", and its focal point is this huge and unusual holiday complex, much liked for its pleasant staff, good food, comfort, and "wonderful ambience". An earlier account set the scene: "Sixteen lakes, linked by streams and waterfalls, are surrounded by lovely maple trees, firs and beeches. A few boats commute to hamlets on the largest lake: there is no machinery and no pollution. Here the *Jezero* is a huge, well-planned, wooden chalet-type hotel, and no one looking at it would guess that it held 247 bedrooms, a big lounge with snug bar area, an attractive restaurant, an indoor swimming pool, ladies' hairdresser and souvenir shop. Plus a night bar with dancing during the high season, and facilities for many sports. The hotel is mainly concealed by the forest, but there are glimpses of lakes from some bedrooms. Staff are efficient; food is good, with lake trout among the specialities. Prices are moderate and cleanliness ideal." "Rooms are clean, quiet and spartan." (*H and B Shames*) More reports please.

Open All year except 1 Feb–9 Mar.
Rooms 7 suites, 240 double or triple – all with bath, shower, telephone, radio; many with balcony. Some on ground floor.
Facilities Large lounge with bar (dancing in high season), 2 bars, 3 restaurants; cinema and conference hall; heated indoor swimming pool, sauna, ladies' hairdresser. Adjoins sports and recreation centre with automatic 4-lane bowling alley. Near lake with safe bathing.
Location In national park, 140 km SW of Zagreb.
Credit cards Access, Diners, Visa.
Terms [1990 rates] Dinner, B&B 85–107 DM.

SVETI STEFAN 85315 Montenegro   **Map 16**

Hotel Miločer   *Tel (all hotels)* (086) 41.333
Hotel Maestral   *Telex* 61188
Vila Miločer

This is not one hotel but four (one not included in the Guide), all state-run and close together on the lovely Montenegrin coast just south of the old walled city of Budva. The large *Maestral* takes a lot of package groups, but is considered by a devotee to be much the best of the four, and she was again delighted this year: "Relaxing on the beautiful, flower-decked spacious terrace is one of my favourite things. The head waiter reserved us a good table by the window, away from the English groups. The four-course menu is amazing for Yugoslavia, and the food as good as I've had anywhere in Europe, including superb escalope de veau and national dishes such as ražnići; the wine list is comprehensive and the breakfast amazing (eggs done any way you like). Bedrooms are spacious and comfortable, equipped with mini-bars, etc; ours was cool, with a large balcony bright with petunias. They have done their best to cover up the hotel's horrid concrete and red brick exterior, built that way to withstand earthquakes, as it did admirably in 1979." (*Stephanie Sowerby*) Earlier she had written: "Though outwardly hideous, the hotel inside is beautifully furnished, with cool marble floors, a good private beach with water-skiing school, and a superb swimming pool." As for the small *Miločer*, it was built as a summer palace by Alexander I for his wife, and still retains an air of opulence. Its central block has a handsome vine-shaded terrace where meals are served; most of the rooms are in annexes in the grounds. Readers enjoy its privacy, its big gardens, and its fine, if pebbly, beach. A recent verdict: "Food good by Yugoslav standards. Breakfast under the vines, with toast, toast and more toast, and anything cooked that you want. Bedroom like a suite, with damask linen, fresh flowers, a fireplace." However, Mrs Sowerby this year considers food and service to be well below *Maestral* levels – and the same, she suggests, is true of the *Vila Miločer*, more recently opened, with its own beach. The fourth and much the most expensive hotel in the complex, *Sveti Stefan*, is on a small island joined to the mainland by a causeway. It has been liked in the past, but food and service have recently been sharply criticised, and we have dropped it from the Guide. ("It's fit only for oil kings and ageing film stars," says a reader.)

Hotel Miločer
Open May–end Oct.
Rooms 27 – most with bath or shower. Also cottages in grounds.
Facilities Bar, large terrace for meals. Large secluded wooded grounds and gardens; private beach; tennis.
Terms [1990 rates] Rooms: single 110–157 DM, double 180–280 DM.

Hotel Maestral
Open May–end Oct.
Rooms 156 – all with bath or shower, telephone, TV, mini-bar, most with terrace.
Facilities Lift. Bar, café, restaurant; indoor swimming pool, sauna. Grounds with swimming pool, tennis, private beach.
Terms [1990 rates] Dinner, B&B 97–149 DM.

Vila Miločer
Open May–end Oct.
Rooms 4 villas, 55 double rooms – most with bath or shower, telephone.
Facilities Café, restaurant. Indoor swimming pool, sauna. Private beach.
Terms [1990 rates] Dinner, B&B 93–143 DM.

Alphabetical list of hotels

England

Wales

Scotland

Channel Islands

Northern Ireland

Republic of Ireland

Germany

Greece

Italy

Spain

Maps

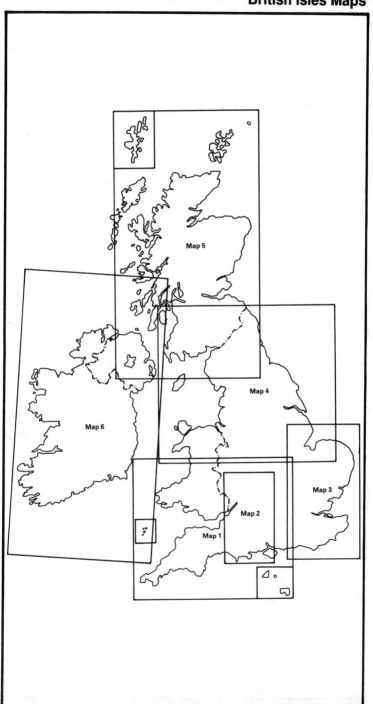

Map 5

Map 4

Map 6

Map 3

Map 2

Map 1

Map 1 South-West England and South Wales

Isles of Scilly

St Martin's
Bryher
Tresco
St Mary's

kms
0   5   10   15
0   5   10
miles

Welshpool
Machynlleth
A470
Montgomery
A483
Eglwysfach
Aberystwyth A44
A470
Cwmystwyth
Llandrindod Wells
A44
W A L E S
Builth Wells
Llangammarch Wells
Hay-on-Wye
Cardigan
Newport
Llandovery
A40
A487
Llyswen
A470
Three Cocks
Fishguard
St David's
A40
Carmarthen
Brecon
Haverfordwest
A40
Crickhowell
Milford Haven
A477 A40
Pembroke
Tenby
M4 A465
Swansea
Merthyr Tydfil
Port Talbot
A470
Bridgend
Cardiff Barry
Porthkerry

Lynmouth
Heddon's Mouth **Middlecombe** **Holford**
Ilfracombe Minehead **Kilve**
Croyde **Simonsbath** **Williton** **West Bagborough**
Barnstaple **East Buckland** **Hawkridge**
Bishops Tawton **Dulverton** **Langley Marsh**
South Molton **Huntsham**
Chittlehamholt **Waterrow**
Bude **Poughill**
M5
Spreyton **Whimple**
Okehampton **Sandy Park**
Trebarwith Strand **Sourton** **Drewsteignton** **Branscombe**
Lifton **Chagford** Exeter
Lewdown Exmouth
Constantine Bay **Postbridge** **Haytor**
Teignmouth
Newquay A38 A390 **Calstock** Torquay
Crantock **St Blazey** Plymouth
Mithian **St Keyne** **North Huish**
St Ives **St Austell** **Talland-by-Looe**
Truro **Fowey**
Penzance **Veryan** **Soar Mill Cove**
Falmouth **Portloe** **Salcombe**
Budock Vean **Mawnan Smith**
Mullion **Gillan**

A39
A30
A386
A377
A39
A30

0   15   30   45   60 kms
0   10   20   30 miles

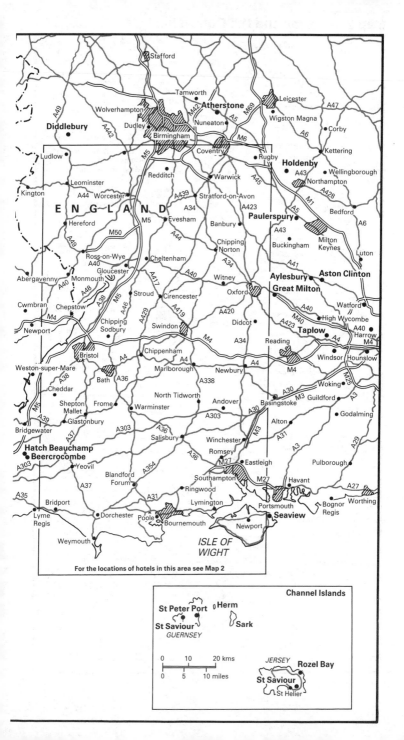

For the locations of hotels in this area see Map 2

Map 2 Wessex and the Cotswolds

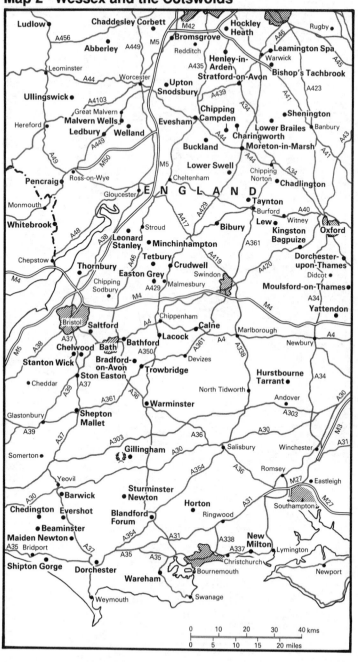

Map 3 South-East England

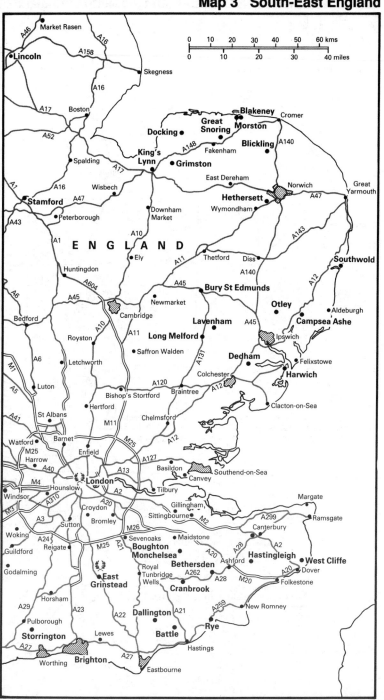

Map 4 North Wales, the Midlands and the North of England

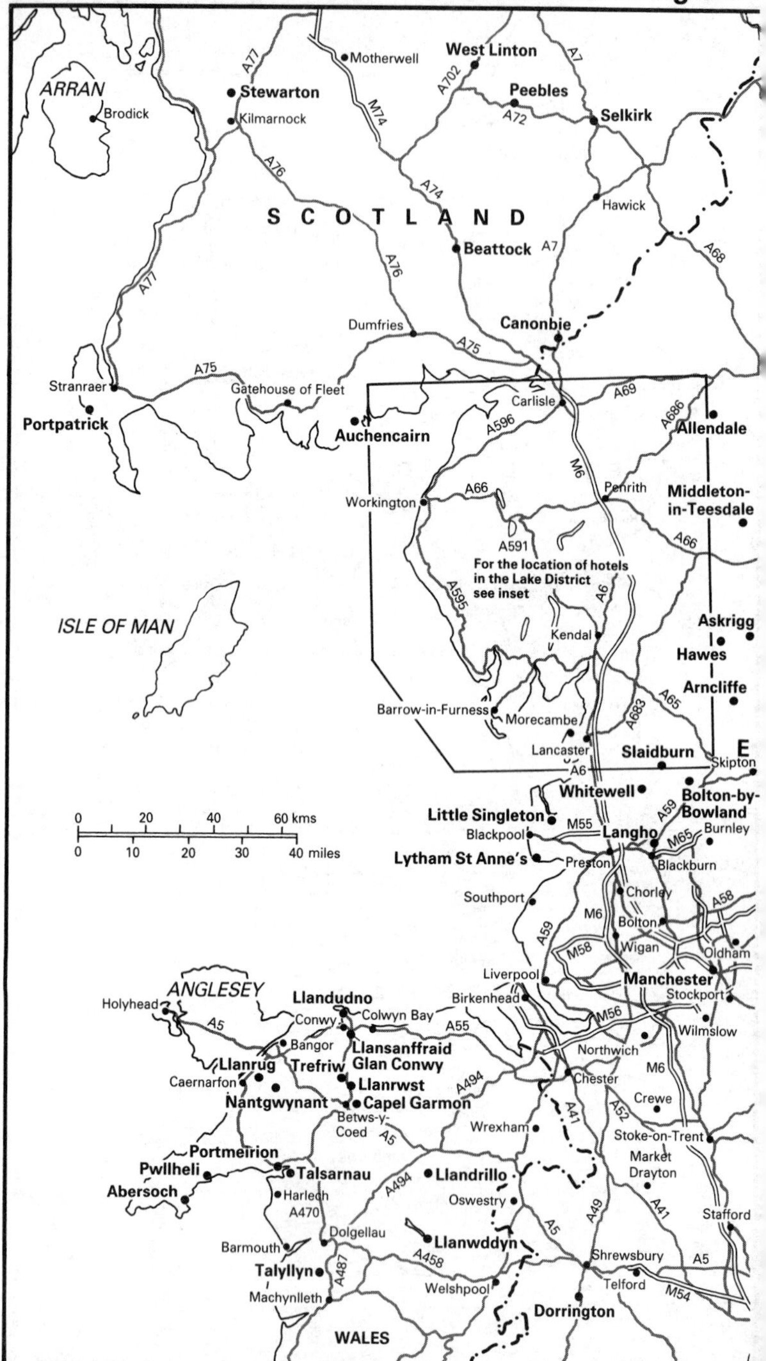

ARRAN
Brodick
Motherwell
West Linton
Stewarton
Kilmarnock
Peebles
Selkirk
A702
A72
A7
M74
A74
A76
SCOTLAND
Hawick
Beattock
A7
A76
Dumfries
Canonbie
A75
A75
Stranraer
Gatehouse of Fleet
Carlisle
A69
A686
Allendale
Portpatrick
Auchencairn
A596
Penrith
Middleton-in-Teesdale
A66
M6
Workington
A66
A591
A66
For the location of hotels
in the Lake District
see inset
A6
Askrigg
A595
Kendal
Hawes
ISLE OF MAN
Arncliffe
Barrow-in-Furness
Morecambe
A683
A65
Lancaster
Slaidburn
E
A6
Skipton
Whitewell
Bolton-by-Bowland
Little Singleton
M55
Langho
A59
Blackpool
Burnley
Lytham St Anne's
Preston
Blackburn
M65
Southport
Chorley
A58
M6
Bolton
A59
M58
Wigan
Oldham
Liverpool
Manchester
ANGLESEY
Llandudno
Birkenhead
Stockport
Holyhead
Conwy
Colwyn Bay
Wilmslow
A5
A55
Bangor
Llansanffraid
Northwich
M56
Llanrug
Trefriw
Glan Conwy
M6
Caernarfon
Llanrwst
Chester
Crewe
Nantgwynant
Capel Garmon
A494
Betws-y-Coed
A5
Wrexham
Stoke-on-Trent
Portmeirion
Market
Drayton
Pwllheli
Talsarnau
Llandrillo
A41
Abersoch
Harlech
A494
Oswestry
A5
Stafford
A470
Dolgellau
Llanwddyn
A49
Barmouth
Shrewsbury
A5
Talyllyn
A458
Welshpool
Telford
M54
A487
Machynlleth
Dorrington
WALES

0   20   40   60 kms
0   10   20   30   40 miles

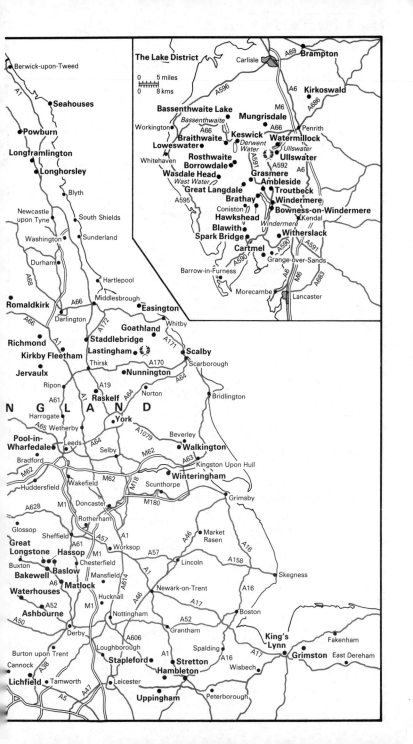

Map 5 Scotland

Map 6 Ireland

SCOTLAND

Coleraine
A2
A26
Londonderry
Larne
NORTHERN
IRELAND
A8
Belfast
N15
A29
M1
Donegal
Omagh
Downpatrick
Rossnowlagh
A1
Newry
Newcastle
N16
A3
Annalong
Sligo
N54
Ballymote
Riverstown
Dundalk
Ballina
N17
Castlebaldwin
N1
Castlehill
N59
Cavan
N5
N4
Drogheda
Castlebar
N55
N3
N2
R E P U B L I C
Moyard
Letterfrack
Athlone
N4
Dublin
Cashel Bay
N59
Oughterard
Rosemount
Prosperous
Naas
Blessington
Galway
O F
N7
Dunlavin
Rathnew
Ballyvaughan
Aglish
Mountrath
Ballinderry
N9
I R E L A N D
Ennis
Gorey
N18
N11
Limerick
N8
Kilkenny
Adare
N24
Cashel
Wexford
N21
N8
N24
Rosslare
Tralee
N20
Waterford
Kanturk
Mallow
Killarney
N25
Kenmare
N71
N22
Cork
Ballylickey
Shanagarry
Bantry
Clonakilty
N71

0   50   100 kms
0   30   60 miles

Europe Maps

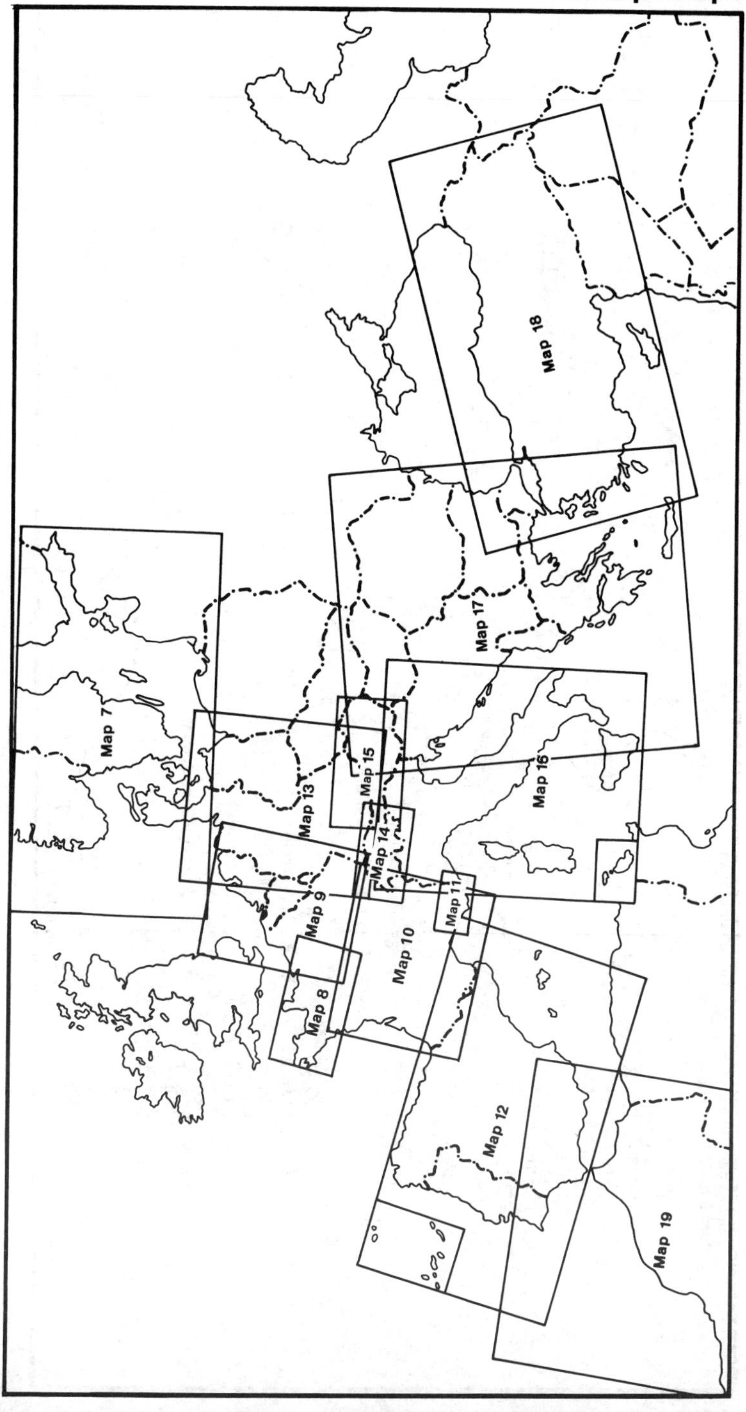

Map 7
Map 8
Map 9
Map 10
Map 11
Map 12
Map 13
Map 14
Map 15
Map 16
Map 17
Map 18
Map 19

Map 7 Southern Scandinavia

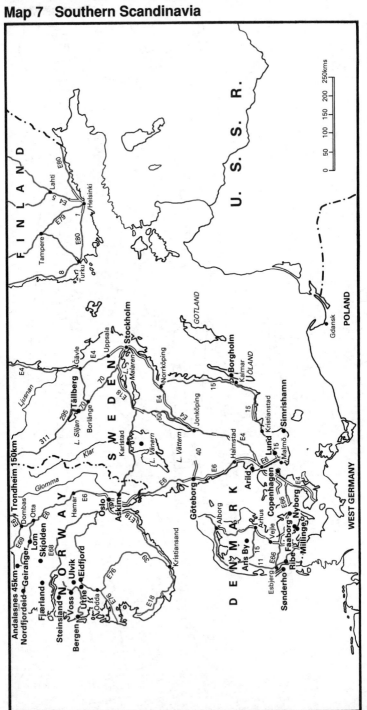

Map 8 North-West France

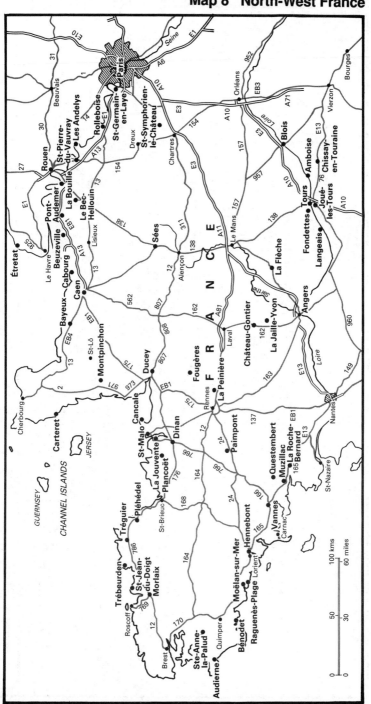

Map 9 Benelux and North-East France

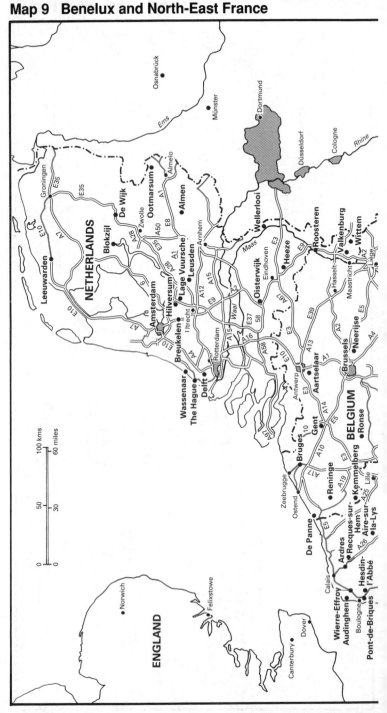

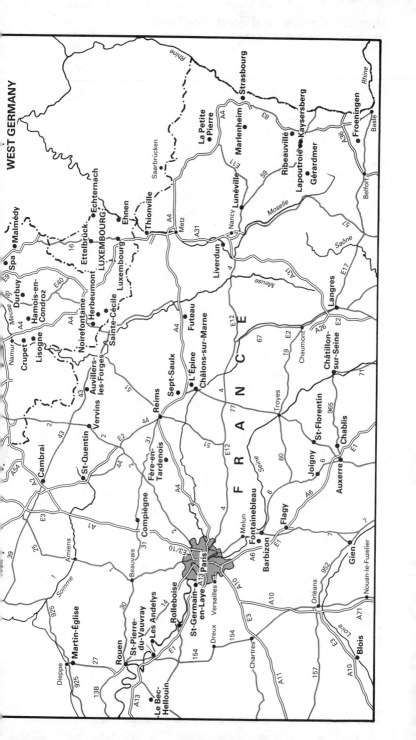

Map 10 Central and Southern France

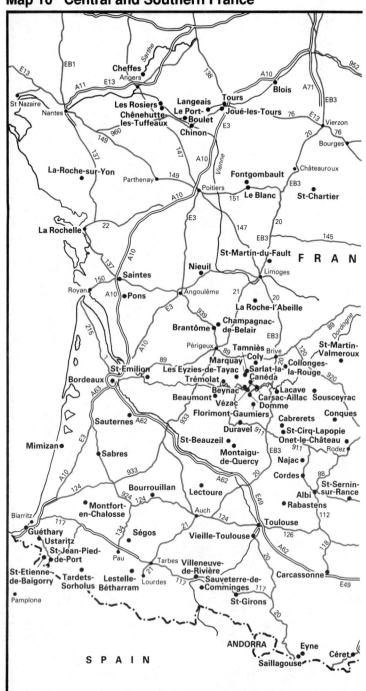

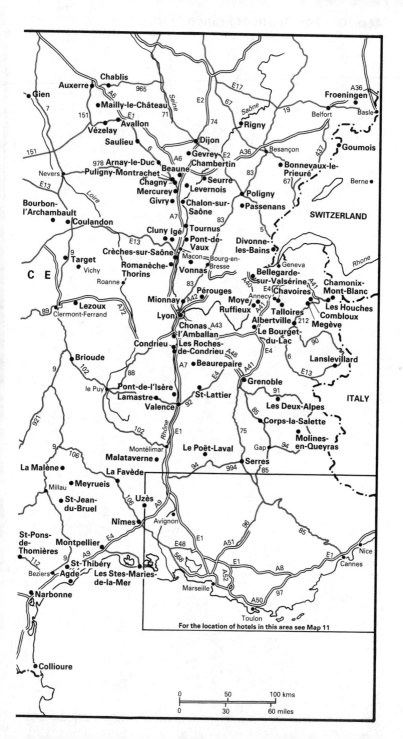

For the location of hotels in this area see Map 11

Map 11   The South of France

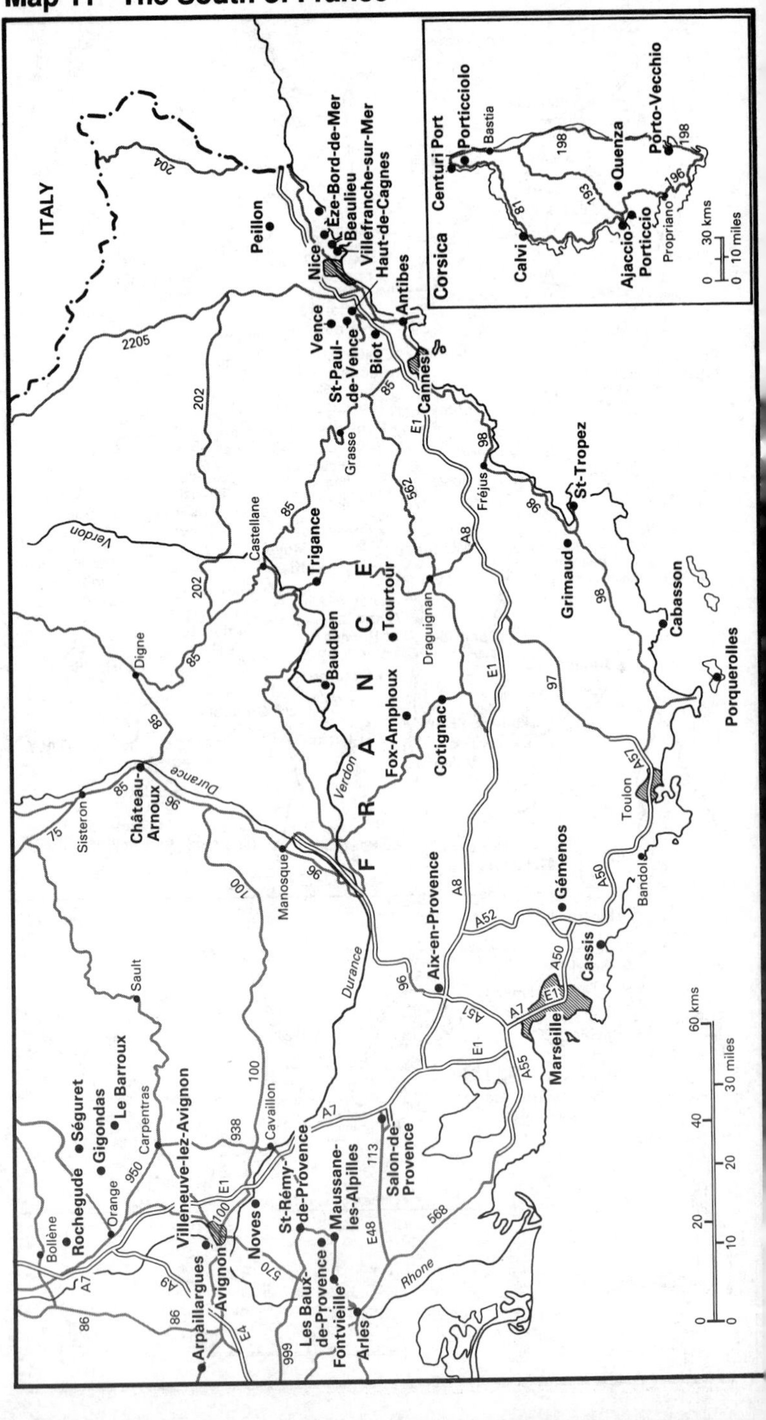

ITALY

Inset (top right):

Corsica

Centuri Port
Porticciolo
Bastia
198
Quenza
Porto-Vecchio
198
Calvi
81
193
196
Ajaccio
Porticcio
Propriano
196

0   30 kms
0   10 miles

Main map labels:

Peillon

Éze-Bord-de-Mer
Beaulieu
Villefranche-sur-Mer
Haut-de-Cagnes
Nice
Antibes
St-Paul-de-Vence
Vence
Biot
Cannes
Grasse
Fréjus
St-Tropez

2205
202
2205
85
562
E1
98
96

Castellane
Verdon
202
85
Digne
85
Trigance
Bauduen
Tourtour
Draguignan
Grimaud
Cabasson

88
96
75
Sisteron
Château-Arnoux
Durance
Fox-Amphoux
Cotignac
E1
97
Porquerolles

FRANCE

100
Sault
Manosque
96
Verdon
A8
A52
A50
Toulon
A57
Bandol

Digne
96
Aix-en-Provence
Gémenos
Cassis
A51
A7
E1
A50
Marseille
A55

Bollène
Séguret
Gigondas
Le Barroux
Rochegude
Carpentras
Orange
960
938
Villeneuve-lez-Avignon
Cavaillon
A7
100
113
Salon-de-Provence
568

86
A7
A9
E1
100
570
Avignon
St-Rémy-de-Provence
Maussane-les-Alpilles
Noves

Arpaillargues
E4
999
Les Baux-de-Provence
Fontvieille
Arles
E48
Rhône

60 kms
30 miles

0   10   20   30   40

Durance

Map 12   Spain and Portugal

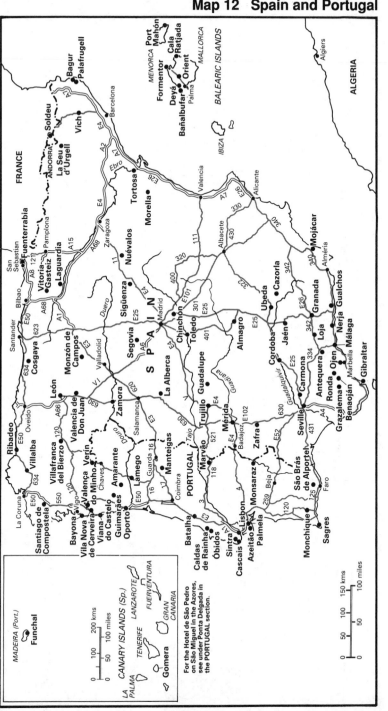

Map 13 Germany

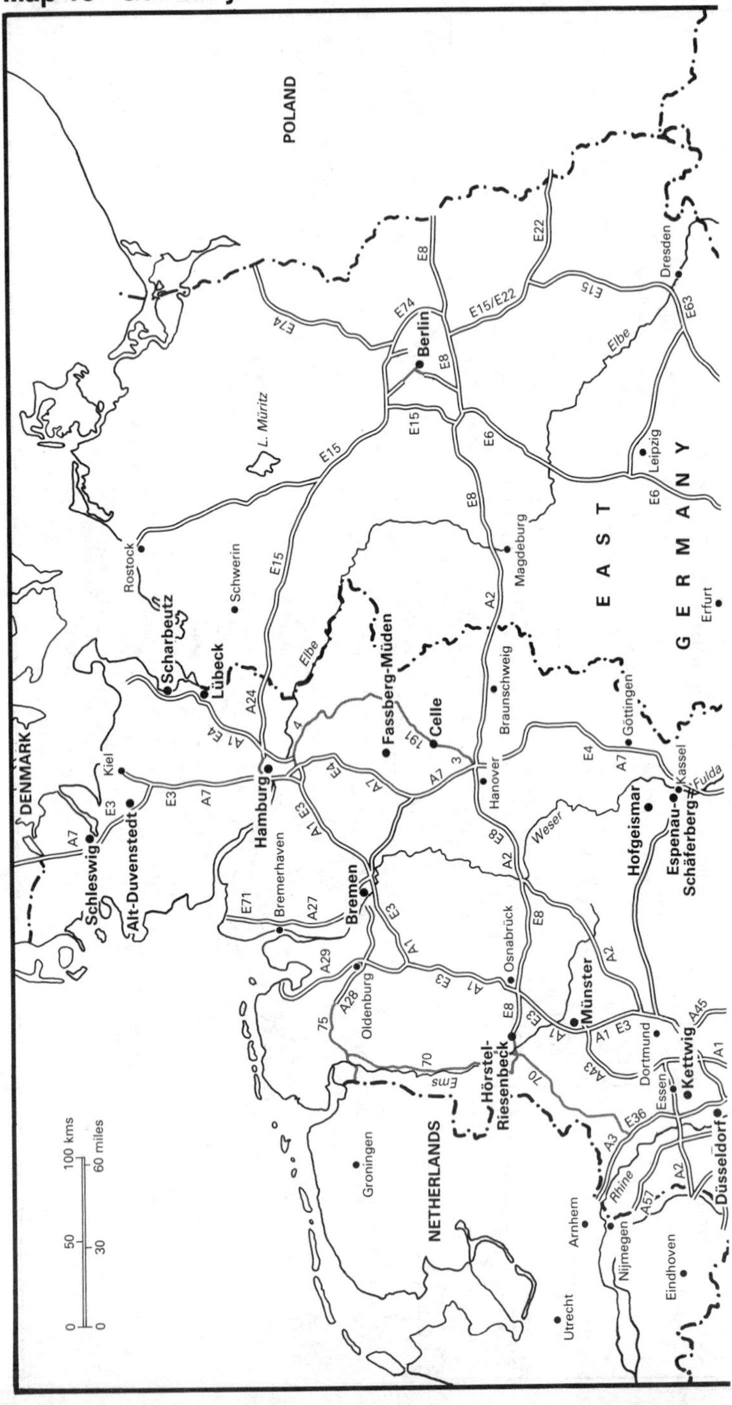

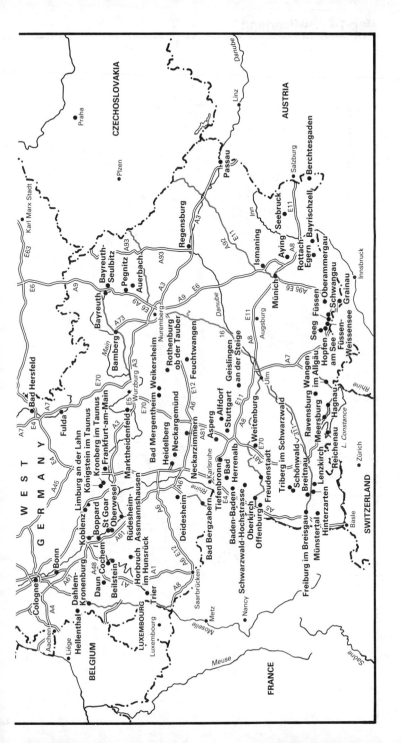

Map 14 Switzerland

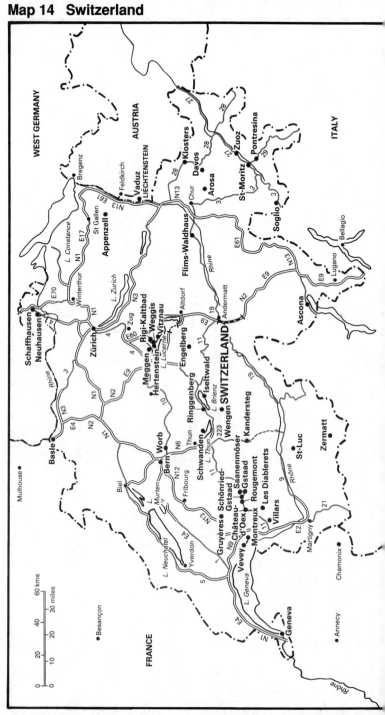

Map 15 Austria

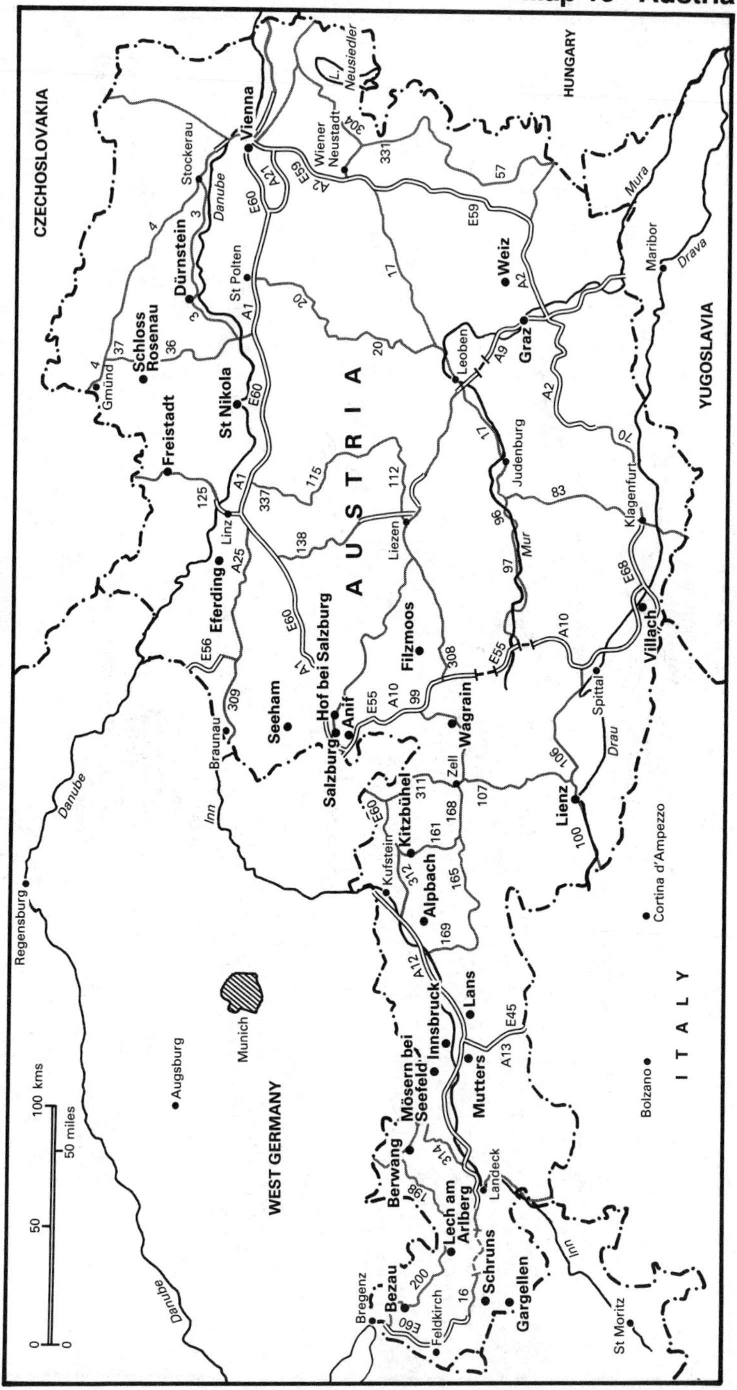

Map 16   Italy and Malta

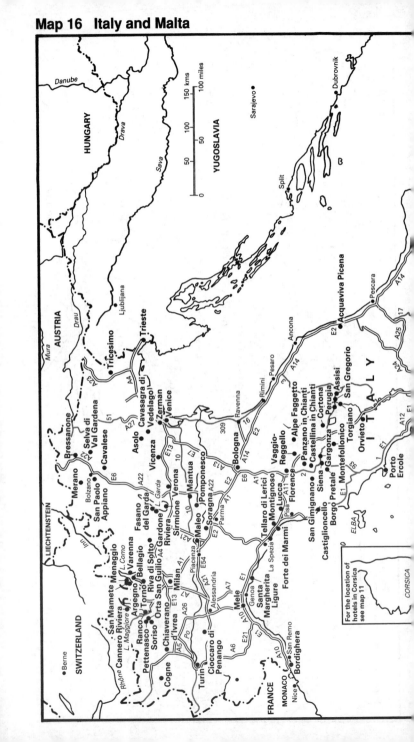

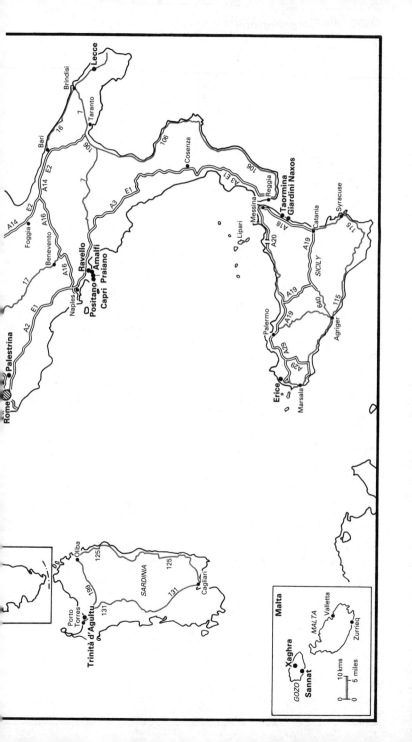

Map 17   Greece and Yugoslavia

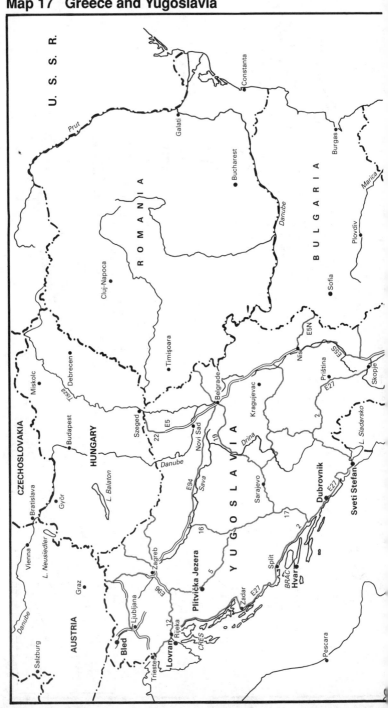

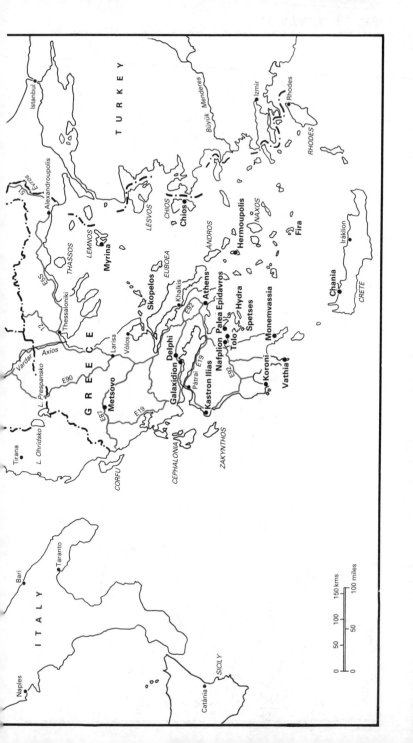

Map 18 Turkey

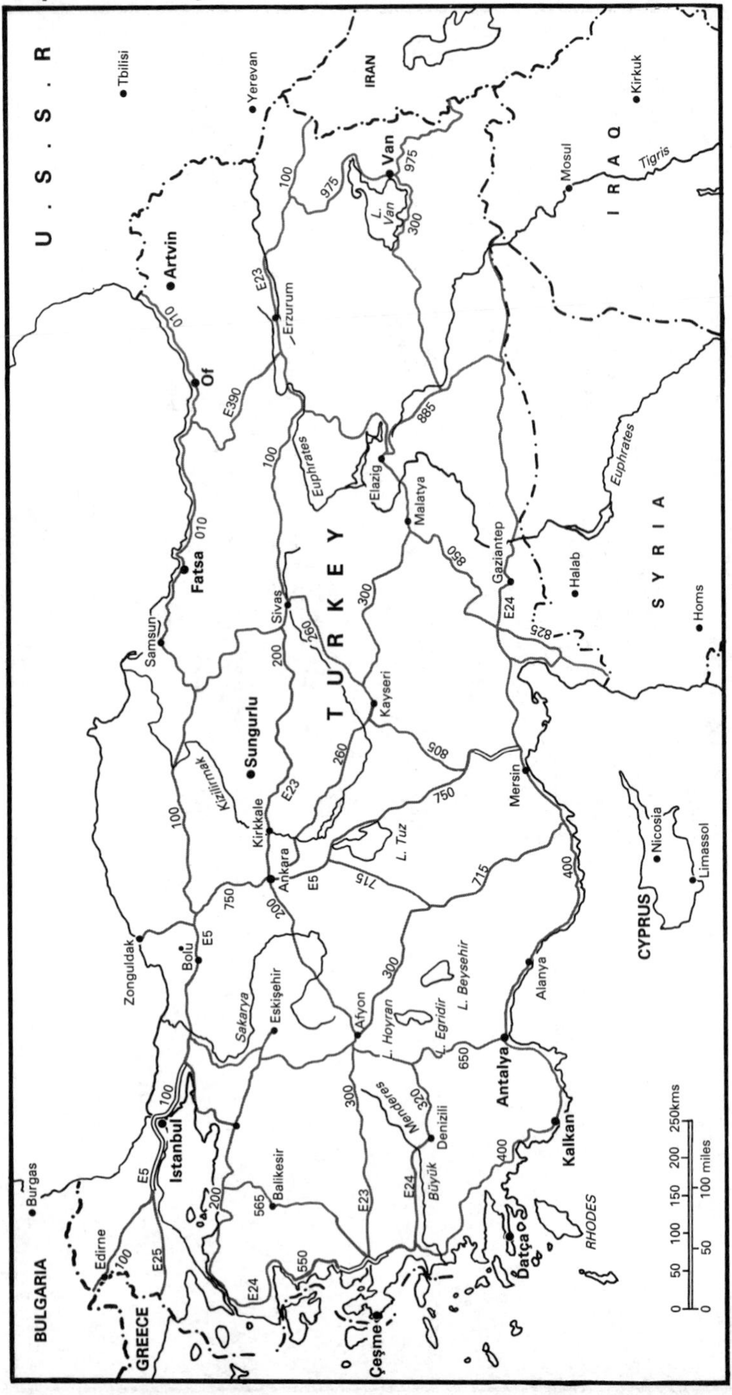

Map 19   Morocco

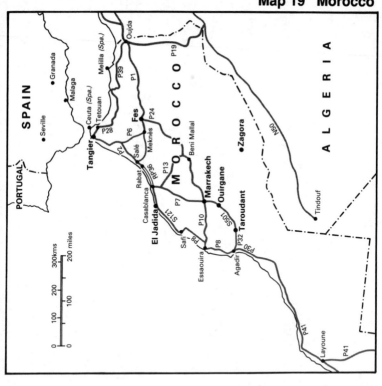

Dr Alan Lucas

Room at the inn – but not for children

We have a most idiosyncratic attitude towards children in Britain. This is reflected in the extraordinary statistic that Hilary Rubinstein has brought to public attention: compared with continental hotels in this Guide, those in Britain were nearly fifty times more likely to exclude children or to make them unwelcome. That we are so dramatically out of line with the rest of Europe on this issue is surely not a matter for national pride.

My general concern on this issue has been reinforced by personal experience. *Chewton Glen*, one of Britain's top country house hotels, recently refused to accept a booking for my wife and me with our breast-fed baby. The manager was keen to point out that he was a good father and loved young children – he just did not want them in his hotel. He saw his premises as a place where people could escape (indeed were obliged to escape) from their families. This quintessentially British view perfectly illustrates our ambivalence towards children.

I protested to the hotel, pointing out that we had offered to bring our own cot and have a babysitter in the room at mealtimes – and one can hardly leave a tiny breast-fed baby at home (though we had agreed to leave our six-year-old – also below their seven year limit). The manager maintained that it was an expression of the hotel's individuality that it excluded babies and small children, and that in any case the hotel had carefully taken into account the wishes of the majority of its customers. I was astonished that so many guests from just one hotel would regard the presence of a baby as offensive. Or is it that hoteliers in Britain are unduly sensitive?

Proprietors readily risk admitting adults who are unruly, socially unpleasant, noisy, drunk or frankly bellicose – yet display a deep-rooted fear of the child (naturally it is reasonable to expect unruly adults and children to be controlled, though I suspect the latter are often more difficult to contain). Hoteliers who accept children in this country commonly do so with the pained tolerance of the archetypal British butler. The child may then be banned from using the hotel's recreational facilities. We should be giving children a chance to learn how to take part in hotel and restaurant life, but the conventional hostility to their presence is so strongly felt that the most suboptimal learning conditions are created. As a paediatrician I am heartened that, at least in the rest of Europe, restaurants and hotels welcome children with genuine warmth and pleasure.

Paedophobia, of the type I am describing, is a very British condition. Those who exhibit it usually fail to recognise it as a problem. (Doubtless it will be my apparent eccentricity that is lampooned when this article is printed.)

Nevertheless, there is now an accelerating change in the way we view children in Britain. More and more people wish to see children integrated into British social life. It is sad, and perhaps a serious error of judgement, that the hotel trade has not responded to this change in its market.

It is now very common for professional or re-married people to have children relatively late in their life at a stage when they may be more able to afford and are more interested in fine food and accommodation. Yet many parents either cannot or do not wish to abandon their babies or small children at home. All the same, I guess that if babies and young children were integrated into the life of hotels in Britain, any customers who left on their account would be more than compensated for by a new clientele of visitors from abroad and people at home who feel as I do.

The acceptance of children in hotels is one problem – actually looking after them is another. I can hardly think of a hotel in England that provides on the one hand first-rate accommodation and food and on the other sophisticated entertainment and care for children. It is, of course, normal for parents to seek some freedom from the responsibility of child care while taking a break. Some of the larger top hotels outside Britain staff their hotels so that children can, if their parents wish, go off together during a part of the day for exciting activities under full and expert supervision; and a children's sitting for dinner is an appealing concept as an alternative to the child eating solo in the bedroom while parents are dressing for a late meal.

My family and I stay in such a hotel in the USA where both children and adults are cared for to the same high standard. We should dearly like to see such hotels in Britain – at present providing entertainment for children is generally a feature of holiday camps or exclusively child-orientated hotels rather than of fine hotels in the mainstream. I am sure that business opportunities are being missed in Britain – indeed the manager of a child-friendly yet five-star hotel in the USA confided to me: "It is good business to look after children; they are our best sales force for regular custom."

There is another facet to this problem. In paediatric practice, sadly, I have been faced with reminding people that as parents they do not have comprehensive rights – for instance they have no right to mistreat their child. It is also important to define limits on the rights that society (or indeed the hotelier) has in dealing with children. In parts of Europe, it is regarded, in law, as an infringement of the rights of children to refuse them admission – in the same way that it would be unacceptable to turn away someone because they belonged to a racial minority group. As we learn to respect children more in Britain, I believe that this attitude will be adopted. Hoteliers who are slow to change their *idées fixes* may soon find it difficult to reverse an unfavourable public image.

Miles Kington

A room with a superfluity

I wonder if any reader can tell me immediately what the following list is all about, or, as we say these days, what its subtext is:

1 solitary chocolate wrapped in gold paper.
1 set stationery, including envelopes, writing paper and cards.
2 cakes of soap in plastic boxes.
1 mini-canister shampoo.
1 very small bowl of fruit.
1 mini-canister bath/shower gel.
1 ditto aftershave.
1 box tissues.
1 courtesy shower cap.
1 regulation helping of shoe-cleaning paper.

If you should exclaim immediately: "Yes, I recognise this list!", it's a fair bet that you have recently been staying in a hotel with more stars than good sense. I was forced to spend a night in one such last week, and when I couldn't get to sleep and hadn't brought a book and found that the television set was showing only TV programmes, I started, on a whim, to make an inventory of all the things that hotels now provide free. And I had never realised before just how well a hotel tips its guests.

The thing is, I have previously only noticed free hotel gifts one at a time. When I have needed the shampoo I have gratefully uncorked it (or hysterically attacked the sachet with my bare teeth). When I needed to shine my shoes, I reached for the shoe-cleaning paper (which, interestingly, tends to make shoes slightly dirtier). But before the other night I had never added them all together and found what a mighty list they make.

Here are some more items:

1 manicure kit, containing four lengths of rigid sandpaper.
1 large bag marked For Your Laundry.
1 courtesy flannel.
1 bag for disposal of sanitary towels.
1 spare blanket.
1 hanger inscribed with name of quite different hotel.
1 spare roll of lavatory paper.
1 local telephone directory.
1 Gideon Bible.

1 list of hotels belonging to same chain in New York, Barbados, Paris and the wilds of Scotland.

1 other box of tissues I hadn't noticed first time round, in container screwed to bathroom wall.

Now, not all these things are designed to be taken away with you. Being provided free is not the same as being given away free, and although the hotel management would be quite delighted if you removed the small boxes of soap (with the hotel's name in curly illegible writing), they wouldn't be quite so delighted if everyone took the spare rolls of lavatory paper. If people started unscrewing the tissue box holders on the bathroom wall, they would get distinctly shirty.

That people do take these things away is, unfortunately, proved by the precautions hotels take against it – those hangers which won't work in your own wardrobe, for instance. But in a sense hotels have brought this upon themselves; they provide so much free, with a smile, that they encourage the visitor to think of everything as free.

Anyway, here's some more of my list.

1 hotel group magazine.

1 courtesy miniature of nearly nice sherry.

1 telephone message pad.

1 book of matches.

1 video film guide.

1 piece of card with hole in the middle to hang on doorknob to signify desires for breakfast.

1 plastic key for door.

1 private bar tariff.

1 remote-control panel for TV.

1 sewing/mending kit containing thread, needles and safety pin.

In this particular hotel bedroom there was no electric kettle, crockery, tray of instant drinks sachets, trouser press, etc, which was presumably because room service will do it for you (or because these things had been taken by the previous guest), but there might well have been. What worries me is that when you add all these things together, they cost a lot of money. Those things are not provided "free" by the hotel for if they were, they would go out of business tomorrow. You and I pay for them. That is why the room rate is as high as it is.

The next time I have to stay in a hotel, I shall write in advance with a list of things I shall be bringing with me from shampoo to hangers, private whiskey to my own writing paper. I shall give a written undertaking that I do not intend to use any of their free samples and miniature offers, which they can remove from the room if they wish. I shall then ask for a healthy discount on the room rate. I'll let you know how I get on.

Independent, 23/10/89

Exchange rates

These rates for buying currency are correct at time of printing but in some cases may be wildly awry at the time of publication. It is essential to check with banks or newspapers for up-to-date pound and dollar equivalents.

	£1 sterling	$1 US
Austria (Schillings)	19.90	11.75
Belgium (Belgian francs)	58.25	34.35
Denmark (Danish kroner)	10.78	6.36
France (French francs)	9.54	5.63
Germany (Deutschmarks)	2.83	1.67
Greece (drachmae)	275	164
Ireland (punts)	1.05	0.63
Italy (lire)	2,078	1,230
Luxembourg (Luxembourg francs)	58.30	34.40
Malta (liri)	0.55	0.33
Morocco (Dirhams)	15	8.88
The Netherlands (guilders)	3.18	1.88
Norway (Norwegian kroner)	10.90	6.44
Portugal, Madeira (escudos)	248	147
Spain, Andorra, Balearics, Canaries (pesetas)	176	103
Sweden (Swedish kronor)	10.26	6.06
Switzerland (Swiss francs)	2.38	1.4
Turkey (lira)	4,500	2,662
Yugoslavia (dinars)	20	11.84

Hotel reports

The report forms on the following pages may be used to endorse or criticise an existing entry or to nominate a hotel that you feel deserves inclusion in next year's Guide. Either way, there is no need to use our forms or, if you do, to restrict yourself to the space available. All nominations (each on a separate piece of paper, please) should include your name and address, the name and location of the hotel, when you stayed there and for how long. Please nominate only hotels you have visited in the past 12 months unless you are sure from friends that standards have not fallen off since your stay. And please be as specific as possible, and critical where appropriate, about the character of the building, the public rooms and the bedrooms, the meals, the service, the nightlife, the grounds. We should be glad if you would give some impression of the location as well as of the hotel itself, particularly in less familiar regions. And any comments about worthwhile places to visit in the neighbourhood and – in the case of bed-and-breakfast hotels – recommendable restaurants, would also be much appreciated.

You should not feel embarrassed about writing at length. More than anything else, we want the Guide to convey the special flavour of its hotels; so the more time and trouble you can take in providing those small details which will help to make a description come alive, the more valuable to others will be the final published result. Many nominations just don't tell us enough. We mind having to pass up a potentially attractive hotel because the report is inadequate. There is no need to bother with prices or with routine information about number of rooms and facilities. We obtain such details direct from the hotels selected. What we are anxious to get from readers is information that is not accessible elsewhere. And we should be extremely grateful, in the case of foreign hotels and new nominations, to be sent brochures if you have them available. Nominations for the 1992 edition, which will be published in the autumn of 1991, should reach us not later than 1 June 1991. The latest date for comments on existing entries is 10 June 1991.

We would ask you please never to let on to a hotel your intention to file a report. Anonymity is essential to objectivity. We would not have thought it necessary to say this, but we have heard that some readers have made a habit of telling hotel managers or owners that they would be reporting to us.

Please let us know if you would like more report forms. Our address is The Good Hotel Guide, Freepost, London W11 4BR, for

UK correspondents (no stamp needed). Reports sent from outside the UK should be addressed to The Good Hotel Guide, 61 Clarendon Road, London W11 4JE, stamped normally.

These report forms may also be used, if you wish, to recommend good hotels in North America to our equivalent publication in the States, America's Wonderful Little Hotels and Inns. They should be sent adequately stamped (no Freepost to the United States), not to The Good Hotel Guide, but to America's Wonderful Little Hotels and Inns, PO Box 150, Riverside, Conn. 06878, USA.

Champagne winners

As usual we have awarded a dozen bottles of champagne for the best reports of the year, and a bottle apiece will go to the following generous and eloquent readers: Marcia and Dominic Chambers of Broadway, Worcestershire; Dr John Coker and Christine Lawrie of London; Professor Sir Alan Cook of Cambridge; Martin L Dodd of St Helier, Jersey; Carolyne and Michel Hédoin of Lindfield, Sussex; Stephen Holman of San Rafael, California; Eileen Lister of London; Dr Suzanne Martin of Walla Walla, Washington; Don and Maureen Montague of Long Crendon, Buckinghamshire, Oxfordshire; Hugh Pitt of Sherborne, Dorset; Stephen and Christine Wright of Shipton-on-Stour, Warwickshire; Ian Ziar of Penzance, Cornwall.

A further case will be on offer for 1992. No special entry form is required; everything we receive in the course of the year will qualify. A winner may be someone who nominates a new hotel or comments on an existing one. We award champagne to those whose reports are consistently useful as well as to individually brilliant examples of the art of hotel criticism.

To: *The Good Hotel Guide,* Freepost, London W11 4BR

NOTE: No stamps needed in UK, but letters posted outside the UK should be addressed to 61 Clarendon Road, London W11 4JE and stamped normally. Unless asked not to, we shall assume that we may publish your name if you are recommending a new hotel or supporting an existing entry. If you would like more report forms please tick ☐

Name of Hotel _____

Address _____

_____

Date of most recent visit   Duration of visit
☐ New recommendation   ☐ Comment on existing entry

Report:

I am not connected directly or indirectly with the management or proprietors

Signed _____

Name and address (capitals please) _____

_____

To: *The Good Hotel Guide,* Freepost, London W11 4BR

NOTE: No stamps needed in UK, but letters posted outside the UK should be addressed to 61 Clarendon Road, London W11 4JE and stamped normally. Unless asked not to, we shall assume that we may publish your name if you are recommending a new hotel or supporting an existing entry. If you would like more report forms please tick ☐

Name of Hotel _____

Address _____

_____

Date of most recent visit Duration of visit
☐ New recommendation ☐ Comment on existing entry
Report:

Please continue overleaf

I am not connected directly or indirectly with the management or proprietors

Signed _____

Name and address (capitals please) _____

_____

To: *The Good Hotel Guide*, Freepost, London W11 4BR

NOTE: No stamps needed in UK, but letters posted outside the UK should be addressed to 61 Clarendon Road, London W11 4JE and stamped normally. Unless asked not to, we shall assume that we may publish your name if you are recommending a new hotel or supporting an existing entry. If you would like more report forms please tick ☐

Name of Hotel _____

Address _____

_____

Date of most recent visit   Duration of visit
☐ New recommendation   ☐ Comment on existing entry
Report:

Please continue overleaf

I am not connected directly or indirectly with the management or proprietors

Signed _____

Name and address (capitals please) _____

_____

To: *The Good Hotel Guide,* Freepost, London W11 4BR

NOTE: No stamps needed in UK, but letters posted outside the UK should be addressed to 61 Clarendon Road, London W11 4JE and stamped normally. Unless asked not to, we shall assume that we may publish your name if you are recommending a new hotel or supporting an existing entry. If you would like more report forms please tick ☐

Name of Hotel ⎯⎯⎯⎯⎯⎯⎯⎯⎯⎯⎯⎯⎯⎯⎯⎯⎯⎯⎯⎯⎯⎯

Address ⎯⎯⎯⎯⎯⎯⎯⎯⎯⎯⎯⎯⎯⎯⎯⎯⎯⎯⎯⎯⎯⎯⎯⎯⎯

⎯⎯⎯⎯⎯⎯⎯⎯⎯⎯⎯⎯⎯⎯⎯⎯⎯⎯⎯⎯⎯⎯⎯⎯⎯⎯⎯⎯⎯⎯

Date of most recent visit   Duration of visit
☐ New recommendation   ☐ Comment on existing entry

Report:

Please continue overleaf

I am not connected directly or indirectly with the management or proprietors

Signed _____

Name and address (capitals please) _____

_____

To: *The Good Hotel Guide,* Freepost, London W11 4BR

NOTE: No stamps needed in UK, but letters posted outside the UK should be addressed to 61 Clarendon Road, London W11 4JE and stamped normally. Unless asked not to, we shall assume that we may publish your name if you are recommending a new hotel or supporting an existing entry. If you would like more report forms please tick ☐

Name of Hotel _____

Address _____

_____

Date of most recent visit   Duration of visit
☐ New recommendation   ☐ Comment on existing entry

Report:

Please continue overleaf

I am not connected directly or indirectly with the management or proprietors

Signed _____

Name and address (capitals please) _____

_____

To: *The Good Hotel Guide*, Freepost, London W11 4BR

NOTE: No stamps needed in UK, but letters posted outside the UK should be addressed to 61 Clarendon Road, London W11 4JE and stamped normally. Unless asked not to, we shall assume that we may publish your name if you are recommending a new hotel or supporting an existing entry. If you would like more report forms please tick ☐

Name of Hotel _____

Address _____

_____

Date of most recent visit   Duration of visit
☐ New recommendation   ☐ Comment on existing entry

Report:

Please continue overleaf

I am not connected directly or indirectly with the management or proprietors

Signed _____

Name and address (capitals please) _____

_____